CASH
FOR COLLEGE™

REVISED EDITION

CASH FOR COLLEGE™

REVISED EDITION

Cynthia Ruiz McKee

and

Phillip C. McKee, Jr.

QUILL / WILLIAM MORROW

New York

Library of Congress Cataloging-in-Publication Data

McKee, Cynthia Ruiz.
    Cash for college / Cynthia Ruiz McKee and Philip C. McKee, Jr.
—Rev. ed.
    p. cm.
  Includes index.
  ISBN 0-688-16190-1 (alk. paper)
  1. Student aid—United States—Handbooks, manuals, etc. 2.
Student aid—United States—Directories. 3. Scholarships—United
States—Handbooks, manuals, etc. 4. Scholarships—United
States—Directories. 5. Universities and colleges—United
States—Admission. I. McKee, Phillip C. II. Title.
  LB2337.4 .M285 1999
  378.3'0973—dc21
                                      98-41995
                                          CIP

Printed in the United States of America

First Edition

1 2 3 4 5 6 7 8 9 10

BOOK DESIGN BY MM DESIGN 2000, INC.

www.williammorrow.com

We dedicate this book to our son, Phillip C. McKee III. He dared to dream and reached for the stars, causing us to do our best for him. Without him this book would never have been written.

This edition is also dedicated to all the students and parents who have enriched our lives and those yet to come.

ACKNOWLEDGMENTS

We wish to acknowledge and thank those people who provided assistance and support to us, especiallly when we first began our efforts to help students and parents. Bonnie Risley, Linda Lyssy, James Racanelli, Toby Summers, and the Coca-Cola Enterprises of the Southwest provided unending support in helping us get this information to students and parents.

This book is a compilation of facts, addresses, scholarship listings, charts, forms, timetables, and advice. In the fifteen years since we began guiding our son through high school, and in the eleven years since we began sharing this information with others, we've met thousands of people who have helped us with this book. Along the way, we met students, parents, grandparents, teachers, administrators, college admissions officers, financial aid officers, and concerned individuals who provided wisdom, wit, and winning ideas.

This edition couldn't have been completed without the assistance, moral support, encouragement, and input from many people. The first person on the list is Eileen Fallon, our agent, who has always believed in us and in the information we have to share with students. At William Morrow, there's Lisa Wolff, who copyedited the revised edition, Katharine Cluverius, Associate Editor, but most of all Toni Sciarra, Senior Editor. Toni not only helped us through the arduous task of revising this book, but always did it with insight and friendship.

We give heartfelt thanks to all of you.

CONTENTS

PLEASE READ THIS PAGE BEFORE USING THIS BOOK.

Every effort has been made to ensure that the information provided in this book is up-to-date and correct. Scholarship foundations, companies, and other organizations create and discontinue scholarships continually, change the criteria, relocate, or go out of business without warning. We have no control over these occurrences. Please notify us of any listings that need to be updated, so that we can locate current information to provide to you and anyone else who contacts us.

Some discrepancies are unavoidable because of the lengthy lead time in producing a book of this type. Our database currently contains almost 400,000 listings. Even though we are constantly updating the listings, with your help we can continue to provide quality information to all of our students. If you hear of any new scholarships, we would be glad to add them to our database.

With this book, we have provided you with the most comprehensive, step-by-step guide available for searching out scholarship opportunities. Your success will depend on your qualifications and your perseverance in applying to as many scholarships and contests as possible. We can't guarantee results, because we have no control over the student or scholarship committee. Anyone who does guarantee that you will win scholarships is probably a scam artist. Thank you for purchasing our book, and we hope to hear from you soon.

Contact us at: College Resource Materials
1633 Babcock Road, PMB 425
San Antonio, TX 78229-4725
(210) 614-5919 Phone
(210) 614-5937 Fax
mckee@cashforcollege.com
www.cashforcollege.com

PART I

CHAPTER 1

HOW TO USE THIS BOOK

Would you like to attend college almost for free? Then you're in luck. You're about to embark on a journey on the College Scholarship Expressway. We're providing the map you'll need to avoid potholes, detours, and dead ends.

Blue-chip or Ivy League college costs start at $16,000 or more! Average tuition, room, and board at an Ivy League college for the 1990–1991 school year was $20,000; for 1991–1992 it was $23,000; and for 1992–1993, $25,000. In 1997–1998 it was $32,000. As you can see, college costs are increasing by 6 to 15 percent or more each year. We won't even hazard to guess what it will cost in another twenty years.

In order to be prepared to become tomorrow's leaders, today's students must be nurtured and guided so that they are ready to meet the challenges of a college education. Unfortunately, not all parents are certain how to do this. Not all families have had someone who has attended college. Not all students are academic stars, yet they deserve as much of a chance to attend college as anyone else.

We believe a student shouldn't have to select a college solely on a financial basis. Unfortunately, the reality of today's economy makes the cost of tuition a major factor in deciding which college to attend and even whether to attend college at all.

Applying to college and financing it shouldn't be a frustrating experience for students and their parents. It distresses us to read articles written by financial planners suggesting that parents set aside $125–$240 per month per child in order to save for their college education. To be able to save that kind of money would require most families to do without something basic, such as food. It's for these reasons that we formed College Resource Materials and wrote this book.

While he was still in middle school, our son, Phillip, decided that he wanted to attend an Ivy League college when he graduated from high school. Since he was an excellent student, we knew that he stood a good chance of attending whichever school he chose. We also knew that tuition costs were steadily rising, but we felt that he was bright enough to be offered scholarships from private sources. Besides, high school graduation and college seemed so far away. We thought we had plenty of time before we had to look into scholarships.

In the spring of 1989, when our son was a junior in high school, we began researching college scholarships, thinking we were getting a head start on the process. Much to our dismay, we found there were many scholarship opportunities that Phillip had missed. In fact, students can begin obtaining money for college as early as kindergarten!

During the next six months, we spent more than a hundred hours reading every reference we could find to locate possible scholarships. While we spent days sifting through information at libraries, we saw many students and parents come in, take a book or two off the shelves, turn the pages looking as if the book were written in hieroglyphics, and then leave within an hour or two. There was no way these people could have found more than a handful of scholarships. Researching scholarships takes time even if you're skilled at doing it.

We also found that although our son was attending an excellent science magnet school, he wasn't well rounded enough to qualify for some scholarship programs. For example, the Coca-Cola Scholars Program, which awards fifty scholarships of $20,000 ($5,000 per year for four years), seeks students with good grades and good SAT/ACT scores who are involved in sports, extracurricular activities, and volunteer work. Phillip had a long list of school-related extracurricular activities and community involvement, but he didn't participate in any sports. In fact, his high school didn't offer phys ed until his senior year, when the school gymnasium was completed. Had we known that sports activities would strengthen his student profile, we would have insisted that our son continue to take the private karate classes he had begun several years earlier.

Nonetheless, by the time our son graduated from high school, he had been accepted by all the colleges to which he applied, approached by four other universities offering full scholarships, and offered over $342,000 in scholarships. Although our son was an extraordinary student, he wasn't the class valedictorian or salutatorian. Still, he was offered more scholarship money than any other student in his class.

We're sharing our story to demonstrate that students don't have to have straight A's or a 4.0 grade point average (GPA) to win scholarships. Honors and Advanced Placement classes are a big plus for a student, but even an average student with a solid B average, or a student who raised his or her grades during high school, can win scholarships. The nontraditional student, who postponed starting or returning to college, has an equally strong chance of winning scholarships.

When our friends found out how much time we had spent seeking scholarships, they began to ask us how to do it. Our friends told their friends, and so on. We soon realized that many people could benefit from learning our methods, so we formed College Resource Materials (CRM) in August 1989.

College Resource Materials is a family-owned and -operated company that knows how difficult and expensive it is to send a student to college. We realize that not every parent or student knows how to research scholarships, knows how to stay organized while applying for scholarships (in order not to miss a scholarship application deadline), or has the time and/or the inclination to do either.

Cynthia assumed the task of organizing all the information we had found. The result of her efforts was the Organizer Kit. The Organizer Kit provided advice on how, when, and where to apply for schol-

arships. It included the forms listed in the appendices, as well as sheet protectors and ready-made postcards. There was an Organizer Kit for high school, college, nontraditional, graduate, and professional (medical, dental, veterinary, or law) students. Although each Organizer Kit included a list of scholarships, the lists weren't very long, since the cost of printing a long list would have increased the cost of the Organizer Kits. In order to bring a comprehensive version to the public, Cynthia decided to write a book designed to help as many students and parents as possible. This book offers a great deal of advice on how to apply for college money and provides the largest scholarship listing of any book. Each scholarship is listed only once, with the indices providing cross-references to make it easier for students and parents to find scholarships to which to apply.

We've heard many parents and students say that most books on the subject of scholarships are hard to use, difficult to understand, and simply not enough help when it comes to knowing what to do, how to do it, and when to start. Well, not anymore. Having spent the past decade helping thousands of people obtain college scholarships, and having gone through the process ourselves, we're able to give you the shortcuts and warn you about possible pitfalls.

This book is straightforward, organized, and simple. We want you to be able to read it and come away feeling confident about applying for scholarships. That's why this book doesn't just offer information on where to look for scholarships. There's more to obtaining scholarships than just knowing where to look. Early chapters lead you through the application process while teaching you organizational skills that will help you stay on track. A missed deadline is money lost. Being neat, orderly, and prompt are traits not all students have mastered, yet they are essential in giving the best impression possible to a scholarship committee. If you have only one shot, make it your best one! We'll help you do just that.

HOW WE OBTAINED OUR INFORMATION

Information about the scholarships offered by organizations, foundations, clubs, or businesses was

obtained either by direct contact or by scholarship information printed in a magazine or newspaper.

In some instances, we contacted scholarship committees by letter or by phone to get an accurate description of the scholarship and eligibility requirements, the address, and (when available) the phone number.

Information about scholarships offered by colleges or universities was obtained by public-domain information sources, by direct contact with the institution, by information printed in magazines or newspapers, or on the Internet.

We update our addresses each summer or when we're contacted by an organization, foundation, club, business, college, or university about a change in eligibility requirements or address. The fact that some addresses change is a reality we all must face. Even after we update the addresses, a company or organization may relocate (because of a rent increase, for example). When there is a change, we update our computer listing, but you might find out about the change before we do. We invite you to notify us of any such changes so we can include them in future editions.

For the same reason, if you know of a scholarship not listed (whether it's offered by a foundation, organization, business, college, or university), please let us know!

A TASTE OF WHAT'S TO COME

The chapters that follow are organized according to the step-by-step process of researching and applying for money. Parents will learn how to prepare students for high school and college ("Ten Steps to Painless Planning"). This book is also an excellent resource for families who have never had anyone attend college or for adults who are choosing to attend college later in life. We provide tips for these nontraditional students ("It's Never Too Late to Go Back!") that will save them valuable time. We give you information on requesting applications ("Requesting Applications and Information") and what you should list on a résumé ("Creative Résumés"). You'll also learn what you should be doing to save time ("Organization Made Easy"), which tests you should be anticipating ("Take Those Tests!"), and special scholarship categories to be aware of ("Outstanding Qualities Count"). This new edition includes chapters for home-schooled students, athletes, and military-related opportunities. Subsequent chapters provide the nuts and bolts of requesting recommendation letters, interviews, and writing essays ("Writing Persuasive Essays"). Chapter 15 helps you understand federal and state financial aid information.

The Glossary provides explanations of terms students and parents may encounter during the application procedure. Not only does it explain what FAFSA, CSS, SAT, and ACT mean, but it also points out the differences among scholarships, grants and loans, and the various types of grants and loans.

Although the At-a-Glance Scholarship Index is a fast way to look for scholarships offered by organizations, foundations, clubs, and businesses, we strongly suggest that you take the time to read through all the scholarship listings. There might be a scholarship you qualify for that you never even considered.

Not all of the scholarship awards in the listings go toward college tuition. Some go directly to the students, to use at their discretion. In addition, many writing competitions are listed that do not evaluate academic achievement or extracurricular activities. The winners are chosen solely on the merit of what they've written. The awards for these competitions go directly to the students. By winning enough of these, students can easily pay for books they'll need to purchase or for other incidental college expenses.

Colleges and universities also offer a variety of scholarships. Scholarships offered by colleges and universities are listed by state, in alphabetical order, in Part II. We've listed those schools that responded to requests for scholarship information.

HOW CONCERNED OTHERS CAN HELP

When searching for scholarships for high school students, we strongly suggest that at least one parent or other concerned individual get actively involved in the process. As a first step, you can keep track of all scholarship opportunities you find. You also can help send out request letters or postcards and even type applications. As much work as it may be for you, remember that the student will be inundated by going to school, doing homework, writing essays for scholarships and college applications, and pursuing extracurricular activities.

Senior year is a particularly busy and important year in a high school student's life. Not only is the student a year away from college, which will bring many challenges and changes, but lots of memories are being made. There are football games, homecoming dances, proms, and club activities. These may seem trivial to adults confronted by the financial demands of college, but to high school seniors these events mark the end of a familiar way of life before entry into the unknown territory of college. Any help you can provide will be appreciated in the long run. Think of it as an investment in your student's future.

OUR ADVICE TO YOU

Read all the chapters; then go back and reread "Organization Made Easy." Then, start working. If you follow our suggestions, send out as many inquiries as possible to scholarships for which you qualify, and stay on track in your application process, you will significantly improve your chances of getting scholarships. Good luck, and best wishes as you build toward your future and realize your dreams!

If there's anything you don't understand in this book, write us a letter. Our address is: College Resource Materials, 1633 Babcock Rd., PMB 425, San Antonio, TX 78229. Don't think any question is stupid or silly. If you've never applied for a scholarship or to college, you can't be expected to know all the answers. Remember, we're here for you.

UNDERSTANDING THE SCHOLARSHIP LISTINGS

As you use the scholarship listings in this book, you may find it helpful to keep these guidelines in mind:

Deadlines

Whenever possible, we have included an application deadline at the end of a scholarship listing. These are several exceptions, however:

- If a listing reads "Deadline: none," you can apply at any time.
- If a listing reads "Deadline: varies," you should inquire about the deadline when you request a scholarship application.
- If *no* deadline is mentioned, the scholarship committee did not supply it to us. Be sure to inquire about the deadline when you request a scholarship application.

Tuition Scholarship

- When the term *tuition scholarship* is used, full tuition (excluding room and board) is offered by that scholarship.
- When the term *up to tuition* is used, the scholarship may offer partial tuition as well as full tuition.

A Word About College Scholarships

- In the section titled "From Selected Colleges," we have offered a selected listing because not all colleges responded to our requests for information about their scholarship programs. Nearly all colleges offer some kind of need-based financial assistance, and they may offer types of scholarships as well. If a college you're interested in isn't listed, contact that college's Financial Aid Office or the department of your projected major to inquire about available scholarships.

A Word About Changes

- Although we tried to include the latest scholarship information in this book, it's always possible that the address or phone number of a scholarship source will change. You might want to check out our website. One section offers information on address changes. If the scholarship address you need isn't listed, please contact us. If you cannot locate a particular source, contact us at the address below and we'll do our best to provide you with updated information.

College Resource Materials
1633 Babcock Road, PMB 425
San Antonio, TX 78229
(210) 614-5919 Phone
(210) 614-5937 Fax
mckee@cashforcollege.com
http://www.cashforcollege.com

CHAPTER 2

TEN STEPS TO
PAINLESS PLANNING

A parent asked us recently if middle school was too early for a student to start thinking about college. We can assure you it isn't.

We can't stress enough how important it is to start as early as possible to investigate scholarship opportunities. There are many scholarships available even as early as kindergarten, much less middle school. There are writing competitions that give cash awards to students in the seventh and eighth grades and even as early as third grade! These cash awards can help pay for PSAT, SAT, ACT, Advanced Placement, or Achievement tests.

Perhaps you won't win an $18,000 scholarship while you're still a freshman, but you'll be gaining valuable experience in the application procedure, and you could conceivably win a sizeable scholarship. Anything you do more than once, you get better at doing. Particularly if you enter art, writing, or speech competitions more than once, you will increase your chances of winning money.

The competition for admission into college and for winning scholarships is stiff. You can gain an early edge in middle school by working to become a well-rounded student, which is the type of applicant scholarship and college admissions committees are seeking.

It's also helpful to spend some time becoming aware of your areas of achievement, your abilities, your interests, and your ambitions. Your initiative in developing these aspects of your personality will influence your success.

Even if you don't begin this process in middle school, however, the ten steps below will help you go after college money with a much greater chance of success.

1. LEARN TO STUDY!

It's important to learn how to study to retain information. Cramming for a test means that you retain the information only long enough to pass the test. That isn't true learning.

Bill Cosby, as his fictional Cliff Huxtable character on *The Cosby Show*, once compared studying to flying an airplane. If an airplane went up then down, up then down, all the way to its destination, it would take an enormous amount of energy to make a trip. It does take a great deal of energy to get the plane into the air, but once there it isn't hard to stay there. If you study regularly, it won't take as much energy on the night before a test to study as it does to cram. If you learn how to study in middle school, high school and college will be that much easier.

Making good grades is extremely important. Straight A's are great, but don't get discouraged if you're an A–B or B–C student. Always do your best. Most students and parents don't think grades made in middle school will matter, but they do. If you learn how to do your very best in middle school, you'll continue to do the same in high school.

We've helped high school seniors who were

B-average students find sources of college money. These students' combined SAT scores were between 800 and 900, which many (but not all) colleges view as low scores. Nonetheless, these students won several thousand dollars in scholarships to attend the colleges of their choice because they followed our tips and aggressively sought out all the scholarships for which they were qualified to apply.

2. ASK ABOUT TAKING FRESHMAN-LEVEL COURSES IN MIDDLE SCHOOL

If you take Algebra I or the first year of a foreign language in the eighth grade, sometimes even seventh grade, these courses might be included on your high school transcript and could exert a positive influence on your class rank in your senior year. Some colleges will accept a student with a low SAT or ACT score if the student's class rank is high—the reasoning being that some good students simply don't do well on standardized tests.

Ask your counselor or school district what the regulations are concerning taking freshman classes in middle school. Some school districts require that the grades students earn in Algebra I or a foreign language taken in middle school follow the student into high school. The classes won't be listed among the classes taken in high school, but they *will* be used when determining class rank, since the majority of high school students take these classes as freshmen in high school.

3. PURSUE HOBBIES AND NONACADEMIC INTERESTS

Academics are important, but don't close your eyes to other areas of interest. Develop hobbies and participate in school events (talent shows, clubs, student government, etc.). Become involved in a community project and in church activities. Don't get so wrapped up in making good grades that you don't have time to do other things.

Having different types of activities on your high school résumé in which you've participated looks good to college and scholarship selection committees because this portrays you as a well-rounded person. Try not to participate only in academic competitions. Audition for the school play, or join the debate team or the bowling club.

Be a volunteer. Donate your services to a nursing home, local hospital, library, city animal control facility, or veterinary clinic, or other pursuits that appeal to you. If none of these ideas suits you, call your local United Way. That organization can usually provide an impressive list of volunteer positions for you to choose from.

Volunteer work can be used to "try on" activities that may interest you as careers. If there's a profession in which you're interested and you want to see if you'll like it—volunteer! If you think you'd like to work with animals, volunteer to work at the zoo. Interested in engineering or architecture? Call local engineering or architecture firms and offer to volunteer during the summer. Most businesses welcome someone working without pay. Most professionals enjoy showing others what their profession is about.

If you live in a small town that doesn't have a branch office of United Way, ask the local newspaper if you can write a story about volunteer jobs. Request input from residents, businesses, and organizations about what's needed within your community. There are lots of things that need to be done by volunteers. You just need to know how to find out about them. Maybe your talent is organizing and managing. If that's the case, perhaps you can start a volunteer network for your community. If you do, your achievement will be impressive on a résumé because it shows that you are a self-starter: You saw something that needed to be done, and you did it.

4. START THINKING ABOUT YOUR GOALS

Even as early as middle school, you can begin to inquire about occupations and professions. Find out everything you can about many different careers and professions, not just the glamorous, high-paying ones that quickly come to mind. Talk to people who work in professions that interest you. Ask such questions as:

1. How long did it take to get the necessary education and training?

2. How available are jobs once you finish college?

3. How much room is there for advancement?

You might ask your school counselor if your school could sponsor a Career Night. On a Career Night, various professionals in the community are asked to come to a school and talk about their work. Career Nights provide an excellent place to start your career research. If your school doesn't routinely sponsor such an event, try to organize one yourself, or suggest the idea to a school club, the student government, or an outside organization (such as 4-H, Boy or Girl Scouts, or a church group). Volunteer your services to help get one started. You'd be surprised to discover how many people will volunteer to talk to students about themselves!

Any decision you make about a future career won't be written in granite. No one will hold it against you if you change your major, or even your college. Even if you change interests in midstream, you can still benefit from your work.

Our son attended a magnet high school called Health Careers High School in San Antonio, Texas, because when he was in middle school he was considering a career as a physician. Thus, he took the courses necessary for someone who was considering science as a college major. By the time he was a high school junior, however, he changed his mind. He took his first economics course and decided that he wanted to be an economics professor. Despite his change in interests, he didn't change high schools. In fact, he continued entering local, regional, and state science fairs. None of his efforts were wasted. Even though he no longer wanted to major in science, many colleges sought him out because of his strong performance in the science fairs. At one of the college recruiting parties he attended, the college representative even knew the titles of his science projects! That's how impressed they were with the work he'd done. They knew he would be able to do good work in any area he chose to study. As it turned out, once in college, he declared a major in history, with an emphasis on economics.

People change, and as you change, so might your goals in life. It's always important to examine your life and seek goals, but even if you're undecided or if you change your mind, you can still get colleges interested in you by your good efforts.

5. START PLANNING FOR COLLEGE COSTS

It's never too early for students and their parents to begin planning for college costs. If you haven't started a college savings account, you should consider it now. Even if you were to be offered a full scholarship to the school of your choice, there are still other expenses to think about. You'll need books, school supplies, clothes, and traveling expenses; perhaps you'll need luggage. If you live at home, you'll still need gas money or bus money to get to school.

The moment you enter high school, or maybe the summer before high school, begin looking for competitions to enter that will result in scholarship money. A good way to start is by ordering a copy of *The National Advisory List of Contests and Activities* for the current year from the National Association of Secondary School Principals. Write to: 1904 Association Drive, Reston, VA 22091. There is a charge and the price of the publication may increase from year to year, but it's a small price to pay for the possibility of significant amounts of scholarship money.

Once you start high school, ask your history, English, or science teachers if they know of any competitions that you can enter for scholarship money. If you're serious about winning scholar-ship money, you have to start early, be creative, and be aggressive.

Another good source of information is your high school or college counselor, but remember that counselors are responsible for more than just one student. Ultimately, you will be the one who must do the searching.

6. CONSIDER OTHER ALTERNATIVES

You needn't limit your financial planning to seeking out scholarships and saving money. Parents can in-quire about many cooperative programs and prepay-ment or loan plans that can freeze the cost of college tuition. Prepayment programs allow the parent or stu-dent to pay four years' worth of tuition at the current cost. Even if tuition is later increased, you aren't billed, because your tuition is already paid. In a loan pro-gram, the parent takes out a loan for the cost of four years, pays the college or university, and then repays the loan without fear of having to pay tuition increases during a student's undergraduate years.

Approximately a thousand colleges and univer-sities offer cooperative educational plans. These pro-grams allow a student to attend college classes for twelve weeks, then work for twelve weeks with a company involved in the program. Programs differ from school to school. Some programs pay the stu-dent and the student then handles living expenses, tuition, and room and board for the next twelve-week class session. Other programs will provide money for tuition and room and board directly to the college, which also dispenses a stipend to the student. Some schools offer co-op plans as optional programs; some offer them only in certain majors or programs of study, or a co-op plan can be part of an honors program. Students should contact the college or university in which they are interested and ask if that institution offers any cooperative pro-grams.

7. START SHOPPING AROUND FOR A COLLEGE

After you've selected a possible major or career, you should begin selecting several colleges or universities or vocational or technical schools you might want to attend and which offer strong programs of study in the areas that interest you.

You can usually find college catalogs at city or school libraries. If none are available, ask the librar-ian to order some. Better yet, volunteer to help the library begin a college catalog file. You can also write to college or university admissions offices and re-quest that catalogs be sent to you. Once you have the catalogs, which will list college costs, look at the department in which you have an interest. Each de-partment will list not only the courses a student must take while in college but also which courses the student should have taken in high school in or-der to be prepared for college courses.

Ask a financial aid officer of the college or uni-versity if there are any scholarships available that are targeted toward your career goal. Contact the de-partment that teaches the major you're interested in and inquire about the outlook for future employ-ment in your career of choice.

You should try to plan your high school courses of study with college and career plans in mind. If you're interested in science, engineering, or computers, you're going to need as many sci-ence, math, and computer courses as you can take. If you're interested in fine arts, take music, drama, or art. Keep in mind, however, that certain courses outside your field of interest may be required for entrance to some colleges and universities. For ex-ample, some colleges require you to have had three years of a foreign language or to have taken specific computer courses in order to be eligible for admission.

Every year in September/October, *Time*, *Newsweek*, *U.S. News & World Report*, and *Money* magazine publish guides on colleges. These magazines can be purchased at most bookstores, even in the magazine section of many grocery stores, or Wal-Mart (which is where we bought ours). They list the best value per dollar in colleges. They also list facts such as student-teacher ratio, tuition and room and board costs, average financial aid awards, and much more. They are another great place to start your college search. But beware. For example, the University of North Carolina is a great school, is consistently ranked in the top ten, and it's located in a beautiful part of the country; but if you're interested in engineering, you're out of luck: UNC doesn't offer an engineering program. So shop around and read carefully. These magazines are excellent resources to use in researching colleges. They list many four-year colleges in the U.S., along with information about tuition, financial aid, and admission requirements, and they include the address and phone number of each college.

As you do your reading, be wary of advertisements for a private computer search for college scholarships. Some companies will search for scholarships and colleges for a student. If you choose to use a private service, ask a lot of questions. Some companies guarantee to find you at least six and possibly up to twenty-five scholarships or grants that provide free money opportunities. Some of what they send you—such as information about grants and loans—can be found at most libraries or through your high school counselor. Similarly, some companies offer a college matching service, whereby you provide information about the type of college you want to attend (including preferred location) and the company supplies college profiles. Bear in mind that you can get all the details needed about colleges by writing to them or by going to a school or city library instead of paying a fee for someone to do it for you.

Through College Resource Materials, we offer private services, but we don't do anything you couldn't do. We just save you time. When you need butter, do you spend hours churning it, or do you go to the grocery or convenience store to buy it? When you need a car, do you purchase it from a dealer or individual, or do you buy a kit and build one? If you value your time, you might want to consider using some of our products or services.

This book offers more scholarship listings than other books, and we own one of the premiere scholarship databases in the country. Many companies boast that they have information no other company has. We can assure you that the CIA is not trying to access this "private" information. The information in scholarship databases is public domain. Anyone with patience, persistence, time, and money can track down the information. Just be ready to spend years doing it. Many companies boast that they own the largest database. This is debatable. Companies and individuals owning scholarship databases don't gather once a year to compare databases. Individuals and companies have approached us wanting to lease our database. We always turn down their offers. No one but our private clients have access to our scholarship database. We've helped thousands of students receive millions of dollars in scholarships to attend college.

If you're interested in any of our products or services, they are listed in the back of the book, along with an order form. We also have a website you might want to access: http://www.cashforcollege.com

This book offers many strategies for seeking money for college, as well as more than six thousand different scholarship opportunities. If you follow our suggestions, you won't need to pay a private company to do your work.

8. ATTEND COLLEGE NIGHTS

Each year, most high schools conduct a College Night, where parents and students can go from booth to booth talking to representatives from different campuses and from some lending institutions. College Nights aren't just for seniors. While we wouldn't suggest that middle-school students attend College Night and take every catalog or pamphlet available (because juniors and seniors need the information much more than younger students do), any student or parent can attend these functions and find out about many schools. This way a student can begin to gather facts, weigh preferences, and make a more informed and educated decision when the time comes to decide on a college. Call your local high school or school district to find out if and when it sponsors a College Night.

If for some reason you can't attend a College Night, don't despair. Your school library should have college catalogs on microfiche. If for some reason your school library doesn't carry them, try your city library or write to the college in question and ask for some information about college admissions procedures, financial aid, and even information from a department in which you have an interest. Or better yet, volunteer to help start a College Night at your school or in your community. We held a workshop in a small town that had never conducted one. By the end of the session, the 4-H Club was enthusiastic about conducting a College Night in the County Fairground's enclosed building. Don't think that just because you live in a small community, you can't have a College Night.

If you do go to a College Night, learn about the process of college acceptances. Some questions you might ask: How many openings are there in each entering class? How many students usually apply? How many students receive financial aid? Armed with this valuable information, you'll be better prepared to figure out the logistics of applying to and paying for college.

9. CHOOSING THE BEST COLLEGE FOR YOU

Selecting and analyzing colleges and universities is a great deal like buying a car. Let's say you're in the market to buy a car. Would you check the phone directory, call a dealer and say, "Hello. I'd like to buy a car. I don't care if it's new or used. I don't care what year it is. I don't care about the model or color. No, I won't be test driving it. I won't even go by to kick the tires. As for options, surprise me. You tell me when I can pick it up. How much will it cost, so I can have the check ready?"? Doesn't sound probable, does it?

You might laugh at the absurdity of this scenario, yet that is exactly how many students and parents select a college or university. Thought and planning are needed when selecting which colleges or universities to apply to and when deciding which ones to attend. Yet students and parents don't always ask enough questions or evaluate enough schools. How many schools should you consider?

- Middle schoolers can look at a hundred or more schools. They have time on their side.

- High school freshmen—forty schools or fewer.

- High school sophomores—thirty schools or fewer.

- High school juniors—twenty schools or fewer.

- High school seniors—ten schools or fewer.

Don't apply to just one school. Remember, you might not be accepted. What will you do then? You need to apply to at least three schools, and to no more than ten. If you can't narrow down the list to fewer than ten, you haven't taken the time to know yourself. We suggest you fill out a Cash for College™ College Checklist for each school you're considering. The checklist is at the end of this chapter.

Whether you choose to apply to three schools or ten, one school should be your dream school—the one you would love to attend if you could get in and could get the money. You also should select a backup school—a school you know will admit you and that you can afford to attend. Then select one to eight in-between schools.

On any given college campus, chances are low that two students will have identical financial aid packages. If you apply only to one school, you don't have any negotiating room when it comes to your financial aid packages. (We discuss financial aid packages in Chapter 15.)

You also should apply to comparable schools. If you are from Texas and are considering applying to the University of Texas at Austin, you should also apply to Texas A&M University. These are comparable schools. If you are considering applying to an Ivy League school, you should apply to at least two Ivy League schools and then to a comparable school, such as Stanford University, Rice University, or Duke University.

Students tend to spend more time getting ready for their proms than they do selecting and applying to college. They will spend days looking for the right dress or tuxedo and shoes. On the day of the prom, students spend hours in the bathroom primping. All this time spent for an event that is over in a matter of hours. Yet they don't take the time to carefully select schools, plan campus visits, or analyze the best college to attend. This decision will affect the rest of your life. Take the time to do a good job. Parents, make sure your students keep their priorities straight. College selection *is* more important than prom night.

10. PREPARE FOR SCHOLARSHIPS AND COLLEGE APPLICATIONS

Prepare for scholarships and admission applications early. Keep records of the kinds of clubs to which you belong, your community involvement, and awards and honors you've won during each year of high school and college. The better your records, the better you'll be able to present yourself.

Scholarships open to high school students who will be entering college during the fall after graduation depend mostly on the activities students participated in while they were in high school. Some people think that everything students accomplish during middle school is wasted, but this isn't true. If a student learns how to study, develops extracurricular interests, and begins to enjoy the benefits of working as a volunteer while in middle school, he or she will keep at it in high school. Middle school is a time to learn about yourself and to prepare for what lies ahead.

NONTRADITIONAL STUDENTS

The nontraditional student needs to prepare records or résumés in a slightly different manner. This information is covered in greater depth in Chapter 4, "It's Never Too Late to Go Back!"

It's never too early to start thinking about college, but the summer after your senior year in high school is pushing it. Whenever you have a question, be persistent in getting an answer. If the first person can't give you an answer, ask who can. Ask questions today. Be prepared for tomorrow.

Cash for College™ College Checklist

Fill out a checklist for every college in which you are interested and which you are considering attending.

School's Name: _____

School's Address: _____

_____

School's Phone: (____) _____ **Fax: (____)** _____ **E-mail:** _____

Catalog Requested: ☐ Yes ☐ No

Toured Campus: ☐ Yes ☐ No ☐ scheduled

Interview: ☐ not requested ☐ requested ☐ scheduled

Distance from home: _____

Will be able to visit home: ☐ once/week ☐ once/month
☐ once/semester ☐ once/year

Size: ☐ large, 20,000 or more students ☐ medium, 5,001 to 19,999 students
☐ small, 2,001 to 5,000 students ☐ smaller, 2,000 or less students

Location: ☐ big city ☐ suburbs ☐ small town
☐ rural environment ☐ in-state ☐ out-of-state ☐ out of the country

Major: What will be your intended major(s)? _____

Does the college you're considering offer that major? ☐ Yes ☐ No

Housing: ☐ Entering freshmen must live on campus ☐ Most students live on campus
☐ Campus housing is offered on a first-come, first-serve basis

☐ Campus housing is offered on a lottery system ☐ Majority of students live off campus

Student Body: ☐ Single sex campus ☐ Coed campus **Male/Female Ratio:** _____

Climate: _____

Type: ☐ Public, state-supported college/university ☐ Private college/university
☐ Private, religion-affiliated college/university

Academic standing: Most students accepted are in the top:
☐ 10% ☐ 25% ☐ 50% of their class

Cost/year: _____

Financial Aid Information: ☐ Requested ☐ Am applying

School Scholarship Information: ☐ Requested ☐ Am applying

Type of forms needed: ☐ FAFSA ☐ School Forms ☐ PROFILE Registration Form

Have contacted: ☐ School's Financial Aid Office ☐ School's Scholarship Office

Why do I want to attend this school? _____

_____

_____

_____

_____

CHAPTER 3

A PRIVATE MATTER: HOME-SCHOOLING

When our country was young and a family's nearest neighbor was miles away, it was common for a family to home-school their children. As we grew, education took a turn toward teaching students in public and private school settings. Now, more than two hundred years after our nation was established, education has taken another turn. As communities and schools have grown, they have suffered growing pains. It's not uncommon nowadays for high schools in large cities to have from five hundred to one thousand students in one class, and for multiple high schools to exist within a single community. Even elementary schools are being pushed to their limit, with classes being conducted in portable buildings. Our schools, at all levels, are seeing an increase in crime, drugs, violence, and a myriad of other harmful activities. This new environment may not be what you want your children exposed to every day of the week. Thus, more and more families are opting for home-schooling.

Whatever your reason for home-schooling, your avenues for finding financial assistance for a college education shouldn't be fewer, and in fact they aren't. The only factor that might limit a home-schooled student when it comes to attracting free money is the student's or family's failure to create extracurricular activities. After all, home-schooling is nothing more than an ultra-private school. For the most part, scholarships are generally open to students in public and private schools. Unless a scholarship specifically states that it isn't available to home-schooled students, then the student is eligible to apply. The statistics already show that SAT scores for home-schooled students are not only competitive with those of public-schooled students, but in some areas of the country, a home-schooled student's SAT scores are higher than those of public-schooled students.

The scholarship application process for a home-schooled student is just slightly different from that for a student in a public or private school. Our first bit of advice for home-schooled students and their parents is to join a local or regional home-schooler's association (if you don't already belong to one). If there isn't a home-schooler's association close enough to where you live, form one. It will be the best thing you can do to help yourself as a student or as a parent.

We've talked to local, state, and national organizations and foundations, and all of them are eager and willing to consider home-schooled students for scholarships. The only drawback is that many home-schooled students don't have the necessary activities on their résumés to make them competitive.

Once you've succeeded in forming a home-schooler's association, your opportunities will be limited only by your own creativity and level of involvement. You decided to home-school your child for a reason. You wanted to be able to have more input in what and how he or she learns. A home-schooler's association will only enhance your student's chances of winning scholarships to attend the college or university you feel will be best for your student.

To form an association, you might want to start small and approach friends or church members whom you know home-school their children. Find a meeting place and a convenient time for students and parents to gather. Ask your local newspaper to run an article about your association. You might also want to put fliers in store windows.

If you're already a member of an association or just starting one, make sure that it provides all types of opportunities for students. Students and parents (as sponsors) should create a service club, an academic club, and special interest clubs. It doesn't matter if a club has only four members; those four members need to have that activity or accomplishment on their résumés. We've included a sample résumé in the appendices for a home-schooled student. Leadership positions, volunteer activities, memberships, sports, and honors and awards all can be enjoyed by home-schooled students.

If you're already a senior, you have no time to lose. Get these activities going. It won't matter that you didn't participate in an activity in the preceding three high school years (or however long it took to complete high school). If you create an ac-

tivity or opportunity when you're a senior, an organization can't expect you to have been a member any earlier. You might want to investigate community projects that might not take as much of your time, for example, serving at a Thanksgiving dinner for the elderly, starting a toy drive to help children of the homeless, or even hosting a Halloween party to keep kids off the streets and safe.

You're not at a disadvantage just because you're home-schooled, any more than if you lived in a small, rural community. You just have to create opportunities, or take advantage of opportunities that arise. You might want to obtain a copy of our Cash for College™ Audio or Video Tape for Home-Schoolers, which contains additional information. Be sure to read the chapter on résumés, which will give you additional hints for possible volunteer projects.

STATE HOME-SCHOOL ORGANIZATIONS

If you are currently home-schooling your children and are interested in joining a state organization, you might want to get in touch with the nearest state organization for home-schoolers.

Alabama

Christian Home Education Fellowship of Alabama
Box 563
Alabaster, AL 35007
(205) 664-2232

Alaska

Alaska Private & Home Educators Association
Box 141764
Anchorage, AK 99541
(907) 696-0641

Arizona

Arizona Families for Home Education
Box 4661
Scottsdale, AZ 85261
(602) 941-3938

Arkansas

Arkansas Christian Home Education Association
Box 4410
North Little Rock, AR 72116
(501) 758-9099

California

Christian Home Educators Association
Box 2009
Norwalk, CA 90651
(800) 564-2432

Colorado

Christian Home Educators of Colorado
1015 S. Gaylord, #226
Denver, CO 80209
(303) 777-1022
(303) 388-1888

Connecticut

The Education Association of Christian Homeschoolers
25 Field Stone Run
Farmington, CT 06032

(800) 205-7844
(203) 677-4538 (out-of-state)

Delaware

Delaware Home Education Association
Box 1003
Dover, DE 19903
(302) 653-6878

Florida

Florida at Home
4644 Adanson
Orlando, FL 32804
(407) 740-8877

Home Educational Resources & Information
711 St. John's Bluff Road
Jacksonville, FL 3225
(904) 565-9121

Georgia

Georgia Home Education Association
245 Buckeye Lane
Fayetteville, GA 30214
(404) 461-3657

Hawaii

Christian Homeschoolers of Hawaii
91-824 Oama Street
Ewa Beach, HI 96706
(808) 689-6398

Idaho

Idaho Home Educators
Box 1324
Meridian, ID 83680
(208) 482-7336

Illinois

Christian Home Educators
Box 261
Zion, IL 60099
(708) 662-1909

Indiana

Indiana Association of Home Educators
1000 North Madison, Suite S-2
Greenwood, IN 46142
(317) 638-9633, ext. 7000

Iowa

Network of Iowa Christian Home Educators
Box 158
Dexter, IA 50070
(800) 723-0438
(515) 830-1614 (out-of-state)

Kansas

Teaching Parents Association
Box 3968
Wichita, KS 67201
(316) 755-2159

Christian Home Educators Confederation of Kansas
Box 3564
Shawnee Mission, KS 66203
(316) 755-2159

Kentucky

Christian Home Educators of Kentucky
691 Howardstown Road
Hodgenville, KY 42748
(502) 358-9270

Louisiana

Christian Home Educators Fellowship of Louisiana
Box 74292
Baton Rouge, LA 70874
(504) 766-5545

Maine

Homeschoolers of Maine
HC 62, Box 24
Hope, ME 04847
(207) 763-4251

Maryland

Maryland Association of Christian Home
  Educators
Box 3964
Frederick, MD 21701
(301) 663-3999

Christian Home Educators Network
Box 2010
Ellicott City, MD 21043
(410) 444-5465

Massachusetts

Massachusetts Home Schooling Organization of
  Parent Educators
15 Ohio Street
Wilmington, MA 01887
(508) 658-8970

Michigan

Information Network for Christian Homes
4934 Cannonsburg Road
Belmont, MI 49306
(616) 874-5656

Minnesota

Minnesota Association of Christian Home
  Educators
Box 188
Anoka, MN 55303
(612) 753-2370

Mississippi

Mississippi Home Educators Association
Route 9, Box 350
Laurel, MS 39440
(610) 649-6432

Missouri

Missouri Association of Teaching Christian Homes
307 East Ash Street, #146
Columbia, MO 65201
(314) 443-8217

Montana

Montana Coalition of Home Educators
Box 43
Gallatin Gateway, MT 59730
(406) 587-6163

Nebraska

Nebraska Christian Home Educators Association
Box 57041
Lincoln, NE 68505
(402) 423-4297

Nevada

Home Education and Righteous Training
Box 42264
Las Vegas, NV 89116
(702) 593-4927

New Hampshire

Christian Home Educators of New Hampshire
Box 961
Manchester, NH 03105
(603) 898-8314

New Jersey

Education Network of Christian Home-Schoolers
65 Middlesex Road
Matawan, NJ 07747
(908) 583-7128

New Mexico

New Mexico Christian Home Educators
5749 Paradise Boulevard, N.W.
Albuquerque, NM 87114
(505) 897-1772

New York

Loving Education at Home
Box 332
Syracuse, NY 13205
(315) 468-2225

North Carolina

North Carolinians for Home Education
419 North Boylan Avenue
Raleigh, NC 27603
(919) 834-6243

North Dakota

North Dakota Home School Association
4007 North State Street
Bismarck, ND 58501
(701) 223-4080

Ohio

Christian Home Educators of Ohio
Box 262
Columbus, OH 43216
(800) 274-2436

Christian Home Educators of Cincinnati
9810 Sparrow Place
Mason, OH 45040
(513) 398-5795

Oklahoma

Coalition of Christian Home Educators of
    Oklahoma
Box 741032
Tulsa, OK 74147

Oklahoma Central Home Educators Consociation
Box 270601
Oklahoma City, OK 73137
(405) 521-8439

Oregon

Oregon Christian Home Education Association
    Network
2515 N.E. 37th
Portland, OR 97212
(503) 288-1285

Pennsylvania

Christian Home School Association of
    Pennsylvania
Box 3603

York, PA 17402
(717) 661-2185

Rhode Island

Rhode Island Guild of Home Teachers
Box 11
Hope, RI 02831
(401) 821-1546

South Carolina

South Carolina Home Educators Association
Box 612
Lexington, SC 29071
(803) 951-8960

South Dakota

Western Dakota Christian Home Schools
Box 528
Black Hawk, SD 57718
(605) 787-4153

Tennessee

Tennessee Home Education Association
3677 Richbriar Court
Nashville, TN 37211
(615) 834-3529

Middle Tennessee Home Education Association
Box 1181
Brentwood, TN 37027
(615) 834-3529

Texas

Texas Home School Coalition
P.O. Box 6982
Lubbock, TX 79493
(806) 797-4927

Big Country Home Educators
Box 6861
Abilene, TX 79608
(915) 676-2749

Christian Home Education Association of Central
  Texas
P.O. Box 141998
Austin, TX 78714
(512) 450-0070

Family Educators Alliance of South Texas (FEAST)
4719 Blanco Road
San Antonio, TX 78212
(210) 342-4674

Hearth & Home Ministries
P.O. Box 835105
Richardson, TX 75083
(214) 231-9838
(972) 231-6841 Fax

Home-Oriented Private Education for Texas
Box 59876
Dallas, TX 75229
(214) 358-2221

Southeast Texas Home School Association
Box 692075
Houston, TX 77269
(713) 370-8787

Utah

Utah Christian Homeschoolers
Box 3942
Salt Lake City, UT 84110
(801) 394-4156

Vermont

Christian Home Educators of Vermont
2 Webster Avenue
Barre, VT 05641
(801) 394-4156

Virginia

Home Educators Association of Virginia
Box 1810
Front Royal, VA 22630
(703) 635-9322
(703) 635-3811 Fax

Washington

Washington Association of Teaching Christian
  Homes
554 Pletke Road
Tieton, WA 98947
(509) 678-5440

West Virginia

Christian Home Educators of West Virginia
Box 8770
South Charleston, WV 25303
(304) 776-4664

Wisconsin

Wisconsin Christian Home Educators
2307 Carmel Avenue
Racine, WI 53405
(414) 637-5127

Wyoming

Homeschoolers of Wyoming
Box 926
Evansville, WY 82636
(307) 237-4383

The Home School Legal Defense Association is a
nonprofit advocacy organization that was established to assist in defending the legal rights of parents
to educate their children at home. With six attorneys
and a staff of fifty-five, this group has a membership
of more than 60,000 families. If you'd like more information, or want to keep up with current legislation surrounding home-schooling, contact the
HSLDA by mail, phone, or the Internet.

Home School Legal Defense Association

P.O. Box 3000
Purcellville, VA 20134
(540) 338-5600
http://www.hslda.org

CHAPTER 4

IT'S NEVER TOO LATE
TO GO BACK!

Who are nontraditional students? In order to start to answer that question, let's define the traditional student. Traditional students go straight from being high school seniors to being college freshmen and continue their education until they acquire their bachelor's degree. Traditional students are between sixteen and eighteen years old when starting college. Everyone else is a nontraditional student.

A nontraditional student might be a student who attended college for one to three years and didn't obtain a bachelor's degree for whatever reason and now wants to return; a student who chose to go to work immediately after high school before attending college; a student who is anywhere from nineteen to ninety years of age; a student who obtained a GED (Anyone who didn't complete high school may take the tests required to receive a General Education Development diploma. Many school districts or communities offer day and/or night classes on GED preparation.); or a person with a college degree who wants to change careers or update skills.

According to the National Center for Educational Statistics (NCES), students over the age of twenty-five comprised thirty percent of college students in 1970 and had risen to forty-five percent in 1987. From 1988 until 1996 there was an increase of twenty percent. The NCES projects a decrease of .2 percent by the year 2008. In 1988, there were 5.2 million students over the age of twenty-five. In 1996, there were approximately 6.24 million students over the age of twenty-five. By the year 2008, the NCES expects the number to decline to approximately 6.23 million students over the age of twenty-five, which will account for approximately thirty-six percent of

all students enrolled in college. Given this rising enrollment, and with college costs always increasing, nontraditional students must be creative in searching for financial assistance to afford their ambitions.

Like a traditional student, a nontraditional student must still apply to college, compile a résumé, write application essays, obtain recommendation letters, and even look for financial aid. He or she just does it differently. A nontraditional student usually has been working, for at least a semester if not for years. The nontraditional student might have a spouse and, perhaps, children. A single parent who is returning to or starting college has a great deal of responsibility and little time. These factors can actually enhance a scholarship application. You just need to know how to present them in the most attractive light.

Nontraditional students don't always have time to belong to clubs or fraternities or sororities, or to do volunteer work within the community. Although scholarship committees want to see that applicants are involved in school-related extracurricular activities and volunteer their time to community service, committees do realize that nontraditional students have other responsibilities.

Fortunately, work is considered an outside activity. Having a family may involve going to baseball games, Brownie meetings, or PTA meetings, all of which are volunteer community activities. So don't think you don't do anything just because you don't belong to organizations!

Does that mean that a nontraditional student has less of a chance of getting a scholarship than a traditional one? Are there scholarships that specifically target the nontraditional student? Can they apply for scholarships that are open to traditional students? No, yes, and yes.

Whether a nontraditional student is twenty-two or 102 doesn't matter. One of the 1991 recipients of Orville Redenbacher's Second Start Scholarship was a fifty-eight-year-old who wanted to make a difference. When Arlene Shealer returned to college after forty-one years of marriage, she majored in criminal justice. Arlene insists that she felt no age barriers in dealing with her college classmates.

Unfortunately, this scholarship is no longer available.

Being a parent or a spouse or being employed doesn't detract from a student's chances of getting a scholarship. On the contrary, nontraditional students are just as accomplished as, if not more accomplished than, traditional students by virtue of having had more and varied life experiences. Nontraditional students just have to know how to present their overall picture differently than traditional students.

RÉSUMÉS FOR THE NONTRADITIONAL STUDENT

When compiling a résumé (which a nontraditional student will need), nontraditional students must learn how to phrase what they do in a way that sounds most impressive. If you're a room mother for your child's class, for example, you might say you're the coordinator for recreational activities for the fourth-grade class. If you routinely drive children to their soccer games, you could be the transportation coordinator for a soccer team. Get a thesaurus and think creatively! A word of warning: You don't want to invent an activity or stretch the truth. Your résumé should truthfully reflect your busy life and should list your activities concisely.

If you're an older student returning to college, you may have been selected employee of the month or year, or you may have been commended for your sales or other performance. If you work for the government or serve on certain committees in your company, you might have received commendations or awards for belonging to those committees. Men-

tion all such honors. They show that you're involved and responsible and have leadership abilities.

If you don't have time to join organizations because you work and/or have a family, don't worry. You just have to be creative in how you explain the activities you participate in. Most applications have a section in which a student may explain unusual circumstances, such as the need to work double shifts or two jobs to support a family, or other circumstances that limit your time and money.

All students should start looking for scholarships and colleges at least a year before they want to start college and should follow all leads for obtaining financial assistance. If you're awarded more money than you need for a semester's costs, the money often can be used to defray living expenses or may be kept in your account at a college or university to be used at a later time. That is a much better situation to be in than to be looking for financial assistance on registration day!

SELECTING SCHOLARSHIPS

Nontraditional students can't apply for scholarships targeted specifically toward high school seniors, but they *can* apply for undergraduate scholarships. As long as a scholarship doesn't require a student to be eighteen and a college freshman or nineteen and a college sophomore, for example, an older student is eligible for it. For instance, the Rotary clubs offer scholarships to unmarried undergraduates who are between the ages of eighteen and twenty-four to study in a foreign country. Another example is the

Tylenol Scholarship, which offers five hundred scholarships of $1,000 and ten scholarships of $10,000 each year. High school seniors can apply, but so can any student who is in a vocational or technical school or a two- or four-year college or university and working on the first undergraduate degree. Therefore, you can be an undergraduate college student of any age and still be eligible for the Tylenol Scholarship.

Some foundations assist nontraditional students

specifically. Generally, there are many more scholarships for older (twenty-five years or older) female students than there are for male students. Perhaps this is because women earn much less than men on average, especially women without a college degree, so may be less able to afford higher education.

— RECOMMENDATION LETTERS AND OTHER ESSENTIALS —

Like any other student, the nontraditional student will need recommendation letters. If you're applying to college for the first time, recommendation letters could come from employers, supervisors, pastors, priests, doctors, or friends. If you have recently taken some college-level classes, recommendation letters should come from professors, especially if the professor teaches in your field of interest. Ideally, this professor would be one who "mentored" you, guiding you in which courses to take to reach your educational goals.

Recommendation letters from recent college professors or teachers are usually preferable because these professionals will be able to comment on your most current academic performance. The second most preferred recommendations are from employers in the career for which you are preparing. They can comment best on your potential for success in that field. A recommendation from an employer who works outside your career field of interest is acceptable, but he or she will be able to comment only on things like responsibility, honesty, and work ethic.

As a nontraditional student, you can use the postcard system (outlined in Chapter 6, "Requesting Applications and Information") to obtain applications and information. You also must inquire at the financial aid office of the college or university you wish to attend to learn whether you must fill out special forms. *Be sure to do this!* Not doing it might result in your losing out on money! You also should check with the department of your chosen major to inquire about scholarships.

We recommend that you read our chapter on writing essays (Chapter 14, "Writing Persuasive Essays") because you will be writing at least one essay per scholarship application. The tips in that chapter will be helpful in refreshing your skills. The most likely topics for a college or scholarship essay are either your professional goals or the importance of a college education.

Some scholarship awards won by nontraditional students are paid directly to the college or university. Since scholarship awards sometimes can be used to cover living expenses, some colleges will deduct tuition costs from this amount, then turn over any leftover money to you each semester to defray living expenses. Because most nontraditional students already have established family budgets, however, some organizations and foundations will send the full scholarship awards directly to you. You may then use the money at your own discretion, to pay for tuition, fees, books, and whatever else you decide.

For example, one client of ours won so many renewable scholarships that once he'd paid tuition and fees, he still had $2,500 left over each semester. That money could then be used to pay rent, books, costs for traveling to the school, meals eaten at school, clothes, etc. Scholarships gave this student the luxury of not having to work, so he's able to concentrate fully on his studies.

For this reason, nontraditional students should always look for scholarship and/or writing competitions that present cash awards directly to the student. Look for writing competitions advertised in your local newspaper. So what if you've never written a story or a poem in your life? You don't know if you can do something until you try. Besides, maybe everyone who entered the competition has never entered a writing competition. If you win, the money is yours to do with as you wish.

INDEPENDENT STATUS

Students may request that colleges or universities accept them as financially independent of their parents for financial aid purposes. Most colleges and universities don't allow independent status unless the student is over twenty-four years of age, is an orphan or a ward of the court, has a bad family situation, is a veteran of the U.S. Armed Forces, is married, has a child, or is a graduate or a professional-school student.

A student who is classified as being independent usually cannot apply for scholarships awarded on the basis of a parent's employment, career, or activities. Some exceptions include children of members of the Daughters of the American Revolution, students who are descendants of a signer of the Declaration of Independence, lineal descendants of a Confederate soldier or sailor, or lineal descendants of a Union veteran of the Civil War. A student applying for any of these scholarships may be a dependent or independent student.

A friend of ours once commented that she wanted to go to medical school but wasn't sure if she should, since she would be forty years old by the time she finished. We looked at her and asked, "How old will you be in four years if you *don't* go to medical school?"

Age is no more relevant than gender, ethnicity, or physical limitations if you want to get a college education. The only thing that's really important is to be committed to improving yourself.

There are many scholarship opportunities available for nontraditional students. You just have to be alert to opportunities and willing to spend some time figuring out how your unique background and experience fit the needs of the various scholarships. Don't give up!

CHAPTER 5

ATTEN–HUT!
MILITARY OPTIONS

Hup, two, three, four. The military may just pay
more.
Five, six, seven, eight. You'd better hurry and not
be late.

That's right, the military. Maybe you've thought
about going to college but you don't have the
slightest idea of how you'll ever pay for it. This book
covers many, many possible options, but the topic
we're about to discuss is one that goes vastly overlooked. The military offers many benefits, a great salary, medical benefits and hospitalization, housing,
leadership, and management training. Perhaps best
of all, it can help pay for your education.

There are several ways in which the military
could help you fulfill your education aspirations.
You could choose to participate in the Reserve Officers' Training Corps (ROTC), you might attend a
military academy, you could consider enrolling in a
special program, or you could enlist in the military
and take part in either "in-service" or "after-service"
education.

Although there are wonderful perks that come
with military duty, the military isn't for everyone.
The educational benefits offered by the military
weren't enough of an incentive to lure my son! On
the other hand, my nephew, Izaak, is currently participating in Navy Junior ROTC. Nothing would
make him happier than attending the United States
Naval Academy and then pursuing a career as a
Naval officer. Although both Phillip and Izaak are
academically strong, they're quite different in personality. Of course, none of the Armed Forces requires that you make a career of the military. In
return for your education, you commit to only four
or five years of active duty.

There are many issues to be considered when deciding if the military will provide what you need.
Cash for College deals with obtaining the financial assistance needed to attend college, so we won't be
going into much detail on whether or not the military may be right for you. Our book highlights the
various possibilities the military can offer in return
for an education.

RESERVE OFFICERS' TRAINING CORPS (ROTC)

This is how most students utilize the military to obtain their education. Approximately 13,000 officers
are trained through ROTC each year. Military academies yield only about three thousand officers. The
Air Force, Army, and Navy offer ROTC programs,
while the Marines utilize Navy ROTC programs. Although there are Coast Guard and Merchant Marine
Academies, they don't offer ROTC programs.

Not all campuses offer ROTC programs. The
Navy has sixty-nine ROTC units; the Air Force has
150 ROTC units. The Army has the most, with 315
units or detachments. If the campus you will be or
are attending doesn't have an ROTC detachment,
you might be able to join one through a college or
university that participates in cross-enrollment. This
is an excellent opportunity to put your time man-

agement skills to use by coordinating with classroom and drill instructors so that you don't miss any sessions due to commuting. Students who are in ROTC must take a class in military science, as well as drill sessions that concentrate on physical fitness, military formations, and field exercises.

There are four ways to utilize ROTC opportunities:

- Four-year (sometimes three-year) scholarships awarded to high school seniors.
- Two- or three-year scholarships for ROTC members who didn't initially receive a scholarship.
- Two-year scholarships to undergraduate students who weren't members of an ROTC unit.
- Membership in ROTC, though without a scholarship.

If you're considering any of these ROTC opportunities, you must meet eligibility criteria. You must:

- Be a U.S. citizen.
- Have graduated from high school, but not yet be enrolled in college.
- Be at least seventeen years of age, but not more than twenty-one (age limit may be extended for veterans).
- Be accepted by a college with an ROTC unit on campus
- Plan to pursue a specific course of study.
- Be of good moral character, with no personal convictions prohibiting service.

In addition, you must meet the following requirements:

- Have a combined score of at least 850 on SAT or 17 on ACT for Army ROTC; 430 SAT verbal, 520 SAT math, 18 ACT English, and 24 ACT math for Navy ROTC; 1000 SAT or 22 ACT for Marine Corps; and 1000 SAT or 23 ACT for Air Force ROTC.
- Meet academic minimums (there are no minimums for Army, Navy, or Marine Corps, but the Air Force requires at least a 2.5 GPA on a 4.0 scale, and also requires that students be in the top 25 percent of their class).

- Have been involved in extracurricular activities, leadership roles, and athletics.
- Provide three or more recommendation letters from high school teachers, counselors, or other administrators.

Finalists must:

- Be interviewed by an officer or panel of officers.
- Pass a medical exam (specific requirements vary with branch of service).
- Pass a physical fitness test.

If you're already in college and wish to join an ROTC unit, you must meet the same criteria as for four-year students, with the exception of already being enrolled in college.

There are some definite perks to a four-year ROTC scholarship. Students receive:

- $7,000 or 80% of tuition costs (whichever is higher).
- Required fees.
- Book allowance.
- $100 per month for ten months.
- A travel allowance from home to college beginning your first year.
- $400 per month salary during summer training.
- Free flights on military passenger aircraft (space permitting).

There are certain majors that are preferred, obligations you incur, and summer training in which you must participate. There are also special one- or two-year scholarships for students majoring in a health profession, science, engineering, law, meteorology, and nursing.

For more information, contact:

U.S. Air Force

HQ AFROTC/RROO
551 East Maxwell Boulevard
Maxwell AFB, AL 36112-6106
(800) 423-USAF

U.S. Army

U.S. Army ROTC
Gold QUEST Center
P.O. Box 3279
Warminster, PA 18974-9872
(800) USA-ROTC

U.S. Marines

Command General
Marine Corps Recruiting Command

Code ON
2 Navy Annex
Washington, DC 20380-1775
(800) MARINES

U.S. Navy

Navy Opportunity Information Center
P.O. Box 9406
Gaithersburg, MD 20898-9979
(800) USA-NAVY

SERVICE ACADEMIES

Service academies provide another way for students to obtain a college education, with all college costs paid for by the federal government. Bear in mind that admission into a service academy is just as competitive as entry into an Ivy League school, or top engineering schools.

If you attend an academy, you are a full-time member of the military. Unlike ROTC, where you wear your uniform only on specified dates, students at military academies must always wear their uniform and follow military rules and regulations. Service academies are regimented and disciplined, but if you're considering the military as a career, there's no time like college to begin your training.

Students at academies pursue a bachelor of science degree. Generally, students seek to major in science, math, or engineering, though there are some exceptions when students select a major in the humanities. If you're interested in a career in the liberal arts or the performing arts, however, skip this section and try another avenue for funding your college education.

APPLICATION PROCESS

Annapolis, West Point, and the Air Force Academy

Just as for ROTC, students must:

- Be a U.S. citizen.

- Be unmarried (throughout time at the academy).

- Be between seventeen and twenty-two years of age.

- Register as an applicant by submitting a two-page questionnaire during high school junior year.

- Obtain a nomination from a congressperson (the military service can nominate a son or daughter of an active or retired Armed Forces member, Medal of Honor recipient, or deceased or disabled veterans. These students are given "Presidential" appointments.)

Once nominated, a variety of criteria are evaluated for admission. Among the criteria are:

- SAT or ACT score,

- academic record,

- recommendation letters,

- physical fitness, and

- a medical exam.

Once you are admitted, tuition, room, and board costs are paid by the federal government. Cadets (in the Air Force or at West Point) or midshipmen (Navy and Coast Guard) receive a monthly allotment of approximately $500 per month. The academy deducts the cost of books, uniforms, and laundry from that allotment. During freshmen year, after costs are deducted, students receive about $60 per month for personal use. During subsequent years, students receive more of the allotment, since the cost of uniforms is deducted during their first year. Though the government is covering most of the costs, students must be aware that they are required to make a deposit ranging from $1,000 to $2,000 to meet initial expenses until their allotments are received.

Coast Guard Academy

Admission to the Coast Guard Academy is much like admission to any other college or university. While the application process to West Point, Annapolis, or the Air Force Academy should begin in the Spring semester of a student's high school junior year, a student applying to the Coast Guard Academy begins the process in his or her senior year. Students need not obtain congressional nominations. Unlike the other academies, during times of peace, the Coast Guard falls under the jurisdiction of the Department of Transportation. During wartime, the Coast Guard becomes part of the Navy.

Students applying to the Coast Guard Academy must:

- Take three years of high school math (four years are recommended, not required).

- Take three years of high school English.

- Take high school American history.

- Take one year of a high school laboratory science.

- Take one year of a high school foreign language.

- Be a U.S. citizen.

- Be unmarried throughout time at Academy.

- Be between seventeen and twenty-two years of age.

- Be of good moral character.

Just as when applying to other colleges and universities, a student is judged on:

- SAT or ACT score.

- Academic record.

- Leadership abilities as demonstrated through extracurricular activities, sports, and community involvement.

- Recommendations.

- Career goals—wanting to be a Coast Guard officer.

Merchant Marine Academy

The Merchant Marine is a civilian service, though it transports strategic materials for our defense and delivers military supplies overseas. The federal government covers tuition, room, and board costs. Students must pay $850 annually to cover other expenses. Students don't receive an allotment while attending the academy, but do receive pay (approximately $500 per month) while they undertake the shipboard portion of their training.

Students applying to the Merchant Marine Academy should:

- Take three years of high school math (four years are recommended, not required).

- Take three years of high school English.

- Take one year of a high school laboratory science; chemistry and physics are preferred.

- Take one year of a high school mechanical drawing course (recommended).

- Take one machine shop course (recommended).

- Be a U.S. citizen.

- Be single or, if married, must live on campus.

- Be between seventeen and twenty-five years of age.

- Be of good moral character.

They also must:

- Be in the top 40 percent of their high school graduating class.

- Have at least a 1050 combined SAT or 21 English and 25 Math ACT score.

- Submit recommendation letters from teachers or administrators.

- Obtain a nomination from a congressperson.

Upon completion of their degree, students are required to be an employee of the Merchant Marine and are commissioned in the U.S. Naval Reserve. Reservists may choose two types of duty: selected and ready reserve. Both types of duties are incurred for eight years. Selected reservists participate in monthly drills and serve two weeks of active duty each year for the eight years. Ready reservists participate only in the two weeks of active duty each year for the eight years. Selected reservists receive pay for their monthly drills and their two weeks of active duty, while ready reservists receive compensation only for their two weeks of active duty.

For more information, contact:

U.S. Air Force

Director of Admissions
HQ USAFA/RRS
2304 Cadet Drive, Suite 300
USAF Academy, CO 80840-5025
(800) 433-9266
www.usafa.af.mil

U.S. Army

Director of Admissions
U.S. Military Academy
606 Thayer Road
West Point, NY 10996-1797
(800) 822-USMA
www.usma.edu
admissions@www.usma.edu

U.S. Coast Guard

Director of Admissions
U.S. Coast Guard Academy
31 Mohegan Avenue
New London, CT 06320-8103
(800) 424-8883
www.cga.edu/

U.S. Merchant Marine

Admissions Office
U.S. Merchant Marine Academy
Kings Point, NY 11024
(561) 773-5391
(561) 773-5390 Fax
www.usmma.edu
admissions@usmma.edu

U.S. Navy/Marines

U.S. Naval Academy
ATTN: Candidate Guidance Office
121 Blake Road
Annapolis, MD 21402-5000
(410) 293-1000
www.nadn.edu

SUMMER ACTIVITIES AT THE ACADEMIES

If you're not sure whether you'd like to attend an academy, you might want to participate in one of its summer programs. Depending on the program, students from eighth grade through twelfth grade can participate. Here is a brief description of five summer programs and how to obtain more information.

Invitational Academic Workshop

The United States Military Academy provides four hundred openings in a week-long summer program open to students who are about to finish the eleventh grade and who scored at least 65 math and 67 verbal on PSAT. The program costs $175 plus travel expenses. Students work in mathematics, engineering, natural sciences, social sciences, humanities, and computer science. Students live in the dorms. Deadline: April 30. Contact:

United States Military Academy Invitational Academic Workshop

Admissions Office
606 Thayer Road
West Point, NY 10996-1797
(914) 938-4041

Summer Eighth Grade Science Workshop

The United States Military Academy also conducts a Summer Science Workshop, which is open to eighth-grade students. For information on cost, availability, duration, and registration, contact:

United States Military Academy Summer Eighth Grade Science Workshop

Science Department
606 Thayer Road
West Point, NY 10996-1797
(914) 938-2100

Falcon Summer Sports Camp

The United States Air Force Academy conducts three one-week sessions in June (last session is for commuters only) for students ages eight through eighteen. There are approximately eighteen sports to choose from, with 150 students enrolled per sport. Registration for the program is conducted on a first-come, first-serve basis. The camp is conducted at the Air Force Academy in Colorado. Deadline: mid-May. For information about the program, call (800) 666-8723 or visit their home page at: http://www.usafa.af.mil/ah/sportscamp/ahcamp. htm

Summer Foreign Language Camp

The United States Air Force Academy conducts a Foreign Language Camp for students ages thirteen through nineteen. One camp, ranging from fifteen to seventeen days, is held in June. Registration is on a first-come, first-serve basis, with possible enrollment ranging from eighty to one hundred students. Instruction is provided in Chinese, French, German, Japanese, Russian, or Spanish (languages may vary each summer). The camp is conducted at the Air Force Academy in Colorado. Deadline: mid-May. Contact:

United States Air Force Academy

Department of Foreign Language
2354 Fairchild Hall, Suite 4 K 12
Colorado Springs, CO 80840
(719) 333-3202

Summer Scientific Seminar

The United States Air Force Academy provides two one-week sessions in June, with three hundred openings per session to students who have finished their junior year and are rising seniors. Students work in math, science, and engineering. Students live in dorms on the Colorado Springs campus. Deadline: January 31. For more information, contact: (800) 443-3864 (Option 2/Plans and Program) or visit their home page at: http://www.usafa.af.mil/rr/pubs/sss/sss.htm

SPECIAL PROGRAMS

None of the programs we've discussed requires that you participate in military duties or activities during the academic year. The officer training takes place during the summer or upon completion of your degree.

Here is a quick sketch of each program:

- **Air Force College Senior Engineering Program** is open to undergraduate juniors or seniors who are engineering majors. While in college, you receive a monthly salary. Upon graduation you attend Officer Training School for three months, are commissioned as a second lieutenant in the Air Force, and incur a four-year service commitment. Contact: Air Force Recruiter.

- **Navy Civil Engineering Corps Collegiate Program** is open to undergraduate juniors or seniors who are engineering or architecture majors. While in college, you receive a monthly salary. Upon graduation you attend Officer Candidate School; you are then commissioned as an ensign in the Navy and incur a four-year service commitment. Contact: a Navy Recruiting Station.

- **Navy Nuclear Propulsion Officer Candidate Program** is open to undergraduate sophomores or juniors who are engineering, math, physics, or chemistry majors. While in college, you receive a signing bonus plus a monthly salary. Upon graduation you attend Navy Officer Candidate School for four months, are commissioned, and incur a five-year service commitment. You must also attend a six-month nuclear power school and either a submarine or surface warfare school. Contact: a Navy Recruiting Station.

- **Armed Forces Health Professions Scholarship Program** is open to students who will be attending an accredited medical school in the United States or Puerto Rico. You apply during undergraduate senior year. Recipients receive tuition, fees, and a monthly stipend. When you enter medical school, you are commissioned a second lieutenant or ensign. You must participate in basic officer training during your first summer break. Every summer break thereafter, you are on active duty for forty-five days. You incur as many years of service in any of the Armed Forces as you received scholarship assistance, usually four. Contact: Medical Officer Recruiting Office for the service in which you're interested, or Office of the Assistant Secretary of Defense (Health Affairs), The Pentagon, Washington, DC 20301, or:

U.S. Air Force
Health Professions Recruiting
HQ-USAF Recruiting
Randolph AFB, TX 76150
(800) 423-USAF

U.S. Army
U.S. Army Recruiting Command
1307 Third Avenue
ATTN: National AMEDD Augmentation
  Detachment
Ft. Knox, KY 40121-2726
(800) USA-ARMY

U.S. Coast Guard
Health Professions Recruiter/G-KOM
USCG Headquarters
2100 2nd Street, S.W.
Washington, DC 20593-0001
(202) 493-9458
(202) 267-4338 Fax

U.S. Navy/Marines
Medical Command
U.S. Navy
BUMED-512
Washington, DC 20372-5120
(202) 762-1756

- **Uniformed Services University of the Health Sciences** (USUHS) is basically the same as the Armed Forces Health Professions Scholarship Program, except that you attend the Uniformed Services University of the Health Sciences, a military medical school. You apply to it just as you would any medical school. There is no tuition, because USUHS is subsidized by the federal government. You receive a salary while attending school. Most students have graduated from ROTC, an academy, or Officer Candidate School. You can be a civilian and then receive officer training. Graduates of USUHS incur a seven-year military commitment. Contact: Director of Admissions, Uniformed Services University of the Health Services, National Naval Medical Center, 4301 Jones Bridge Road, Bethesda, MD 20014, (301) 295-3101.

- **Navy Baccalaureate Degree Complete Program** is open to undergraduate students in any major. While in college, you receive a monthly salary. Upon graduation you attend Officer Candidate School and incur a four-year service commitment. Contact: a Navy Recruiting Station.

- **Marine Corps Platoon Leaders Class** is open to undergraduate freshmen, sophomores, or juniors in any major. While in college, you receive a monthly salary. If you're a freshman or sophomore, you must participate in two six-week training sessions in Quantico, Virginia. Juniors go through one ten-week session. Your commission and military commitment are based on when you enter this program. After receiving your commission, you go through Basic School, then either enter the Fleet Marine Force or flight training (if you're selected for aviation). There is a special PLC program if you're pursuing a law degree. Contact: a Marine Corps Officer Selection Office.

MILITARY "IN-SERVICE" AND "AFTER-SERVICE" EDUCATION

- **"In-Service" education** means that you earn college credit for the training you receive while in the military, for on-the-job training, and for college courses taken with a 75 percent reduction in tuition.

- **"After–Service" education** is available to enlisted personnel as part of the New G.I. Bill that went into effect after July 1, 1985. The New G.I. Bill commits the military to contributing $8 for every $1 you contribute.

WHERE ELSE CAN YOU LOOK?

- If you have questions on any aspect concerning the military, contact the appropriate recruiter, program, or Academy.

- *Need a Lift?* is available through The American Legion National Emblem Sales, P.O. Box 1050, Indianapolis, IN 46206. Stock # 75207, $3 (plus shipping & handling).

- An excellent book on how to finance an education through the military is *How the MILITARY Will Help You Pay for College*, by Don M. Betterton, Peterson's Guides. ISBN 0-87866-996-5, $9.95.

We hope that this chapter has given you an idea of what military options are available and where to obtain more information. We didn't specify salaries received while incurring active military duty because salary benefits vary. If you have specific questions, contact the program of interest, the specific recruiter, or us.

My (Cynthia's) father had a thirty-year Navy career. He was primarily onboard ships, but we did travel to some of his home ports. My younger brother, Steve Martinez, also made the Navy his career and is a Lieutenant Commander. My older brother is a major in the U.S. Air Force Reserves. Had it not been for the Navy, I wouldn't have met Phil. So, what can I say? I think a military career, especially in the Navy, is great. Though such a career wasn't for Phil or Phillip, our son, it seems that my nephew, Izaak Martinez, is headed that way. Perhaps the military will play a role in your education and life.

If you think you'd like to defend your country against enemies, foreign and domestic, you might want to consider taking advantage of all the military has to offer. Whatever your final choice, we wish you luck.

CHAPTER 6

REQUESTING APPLICATIONS AND INFORMATION

You wouldn't think requesting applications would be difficult, and it really isn't. But there are certain things you should keep in mind when requesting an application from a scholarship or college. These easily done details may lead to some much-needed money.

Query letters are an important part of the application process. Query letters give scholarship and college admission committees their first glimpse of you. When you write a query letter to an organization, foundation, college, or university, don't think that you have to tell your life history. The committee members are not going to care that Grandma Jones, your mother, and Aunt Harriet all went to Rahrah College. The only time it might be worthwhile to mention a detail such as this is if the college library is named after your grandfather. But chances are if

the library is named after your grandfather, you probably don't need financial assistance anyway!

Scholarship committees will need to know your name, the grade you are presently in (if you are in high school or college), and the year in which you will graduate from or graduated from high school or college. Avoid starting the letter by saying, "My name is...."; they'll know who wrote it by the name at the bottom of the letter. We've included three different query letters in the Appendices to give you some examples of what you might include in your letter.

An organization or foundation scholarship committee receives thousands of letters each year. The more you write, the more they have to read. So say what you need to say, but be concise. They'll appreciate your brevity.

ITEMS TO INCLUDE IN A QUERY LETTER
GPA (GRADE POINT AVERAGE)

If the scholarship you seek is for academic achievers only, you should let them know what your current GPA is. If you're in your first semester of college when you're applying for a scholarship, you might not have received any grades yet. If that's the case, include your high school GPA, if you were in high school within two to three years ago. If you've been out of high school more than three years and haven't taken any college courses, state that. If you took some college courses many years ago, you may choose whether to mention it or not. If you attended

college fresh out of high school and weren't quite serious enough, this may be reflected in your grades. If this is the case, don't mention your grades in your cover letter.

TEST SCORES

If you're in high school, you need to include PSAT, SAT, or ACT scores as well as Advanced Placement or Achievement Test scores. If a scholarship clearly states that you must have scored an 1100 on your

SAT and you didn't, don't request an application. You're wasting your time and you're causing the organization or foundation to waste theirs by sending you an application for a scholarship for which you are not qualified.

ELIGIBILITY INFORMATION

If, however, there is any question in your mind about whether you qualify for a given scholarship, write and ask. State in your letter the reason why you think you may qualify. Perhaps it's been a few years since you graduated from high school, but you did belong to 4-H or Future Farmers of America (FFA) and a scholarship is available to undergraduates who were members during high school. You might want to write, "I was a member of 4-H during my high school junior and senior years..." or, "I was

a member of FFA for my four high school years...." The committee can then decide whether you qualify and will send you an application if you do.

FINANCIAL NEED

If a scholarship is based on financial need and you aren't sure you qualify, *briefly* explain your financial situation in the letter. Perhaps your family has had to pay unexpected, costly medical bills due to a family member's illness. Perhaps, by the time you go to college, two other children in the family or one or both of your parents will be in college as well. Tell this to the committee, because having even one student in college can be expensive, depending on your family's income and on the cost of the college involved.

TYPES OF QUERY LETTERS

Four different types of request letters are included in Appendix G. The first one is written with a high-schooler in mind, the second one is for a home-schooled student, the next one is for a student already in college, and the last one is for a student who wants to return to college after an absence or who wishes to start college later in life.

ALTERNATIVES TO QUERY LETTERS

Now that we've explained how to write query letters, we'd like to tell you about an easier way to request applications and information: postcards! They cost less to mail and they're easier to write. You can make it even easier if you photocopy the master copy included in the Appendices onto a ream (250 sheets) of 8½" × 11" cover stock (available at most office-supply stores that carry paper. A ream of cover stock usually costs from $7 to $9.). Here's how:

Purchase cover stock (basis 110 white or other conservative shade). Don't get hot pink or fluorescent green, thinking you'll make an impression (you'll make the wrong kind)!

Once you've bought the cover stock, take the ream to any photocopy center. We suggest you make a copy (on regular 20-lb.-bond photocopy paper) of the master copy in the book and keep it in a folder. That way you'll always have a good copy in

a safe place. If the store has self-service machines, you might try making one copy using a sheet of cover stock to see if the machine will handle heavy paper. If the image comes out distorted, have someone from the center run the copy. If they hesitate because this book is copyrighted, show them this page. We created these postcards, and you have our permission to reproduce the postcard master copy for your own use, not for resale (see copyright page for full explanation).

On the other hand, you might want to make your own postcard master. You can write a brief description of your situation (much as you would in a query letter, but shorter), your level in school, GPA, intended major, the college you want to attend, and, if applicable, the cost of one year's tuition, room, board, and additional costs at the college of your choice. You might also mention that you and your family will have financial need. Include whether you're a member of the organization offering the scholarship, if appropriate. Be sure to make four copies of your postcard to place on one master copy.

If you're a freshman in high school, one ream of cover stock will probably provide enough postcards to last through all four years of high school. If you don't want or need a thousand postcards, that's understandable. You needn't photocopy the entire ream. Make only as many photocopies as you need. You might want to find two or more friends who also want postcards and share the cost of the ream.

If you want to create one postcard at a time, you can purchase blank postcards at any U.S. post office. If you've brought a ream of paper for yourself or for you and a group of friends, you can make postcards one at a time, but it does take much more time this way.

NOTE: Some scholarship committees want to see a student take the time to write an individual letter.

Do whatever it takes to apply for free scholarship money. Look at it as an investment in YOUR future. (The listings in this book will state if this is a requirement. Follow this guideline if necessary.)

Whether you decide to reproduce the master postcard sheet in Appendix H or make your own, both ways will be inexpensive. Making photocopies can range in price from 4¢ to 10¢ for an 8½" × 11" sheet. A ream of 8½" × 11" cover stock costs approximately $9. Photocopying an entire ream of postcards ranges in cost from $10 to $25, which comes to 10¢ to 14¢ per sheet, or 2½¢ to 3½¢ per postcard.

In order to make an educated choice about the colleges you want to apply to, you need to request catalogs and information about admission and financial aid from a broad range of colleges. The same holds true for scholarship applications. Whether you use postcards or letters, requesting information, catalogs, and applications doesn't have to be a chore. All it takes is a little preparation and persistence.

CHAPTER 7

CREATIVE RÉSUMÉS

The day you start middle school, start keeping a résumé. If you're already a high school junior or senior, begin today. If you can't remember what you did during your freshman year in high school, sit down with a copy of your high school annual and page through it to jog your memory. If you don't know what a résumé looks like, check the samples in Appendix E.

Keep a record of every membership in a school-related club, organization, honor society, committee, play, band, or athletic activity (as a player, trainer, or manager). Keep an accurate list of every leadership position you have held in clubs, organizations, or student government. Dates are important because some scholarship committees ask that you be specific about when you participated in the activities you're telling them about. Leadership positions are especially important because they show you have initiative and can take responsibility. Don't be shy. Try for those positions. If you don't want to be president, vice-president, secretary, or treasurer of a club, remember that there are some positions that aren't so high-profile but are still important, such as historian and parliamentarian (the student who ensures that Robert's Rules of Order for parliamentary procedure are followed).

At one of our workshops, a parent gave us an excellent suggestion. If you take part in activities for which there is a printed program listing your name and role, keep copies of the programs. (These are typically printed for musical or theater events.) This way you have an exact record of when the activity took place and your involvement in it. You can keep this type of information in the same notebook where you keep other college and scholarship information, or you might want to keep a scrapbook. Either way, you've got the information you need.

Remember your out-of-school activities, too.

Keep a record of any community work you may do, whether as an unpaid volunteer or a paid employee. If you read to children at your local library on Saturday mornings, put it on your résumé. If you're active in your church (singing in the choir, teaching Sunday School), keep a record of it. (And don't overlook activities like baby-sitting or mowing lawns, either. After all, you're self-employed. You're an entrepreneur!) Self-employment shows that you have the confidence, responsibility, and maturity to find yourself a job.

Volunteer work is important. One school district in San Antonio, Texas, is considering making volunteer work part of its graduation requirements. Volunteer work not only looks good on a résumé, but students often become more compassionate as a result of doing volunteer work. If you're not sure what type of volunteer work you would want to do, call the local branch of United Way to get a list of possible volunteer positions. It will include a wide variety of volunteer positions needed within a community. If you live in a small community without a branch of United Way, why not ask the local newspaper to run a story about various community groups in need of volunteers? Maybe you can take the initiative to start a volunteer network. Businesses, organizations, hospitals, or individuals could contact you with volunteer positions for other students. You could conduct the network out of your home and still be serving a needed volunteer task.

When our son started high school, we insisted that he begin volunteering one hour per weekend at a local nursing home. As we drove him to the first visit, he complained endlessly. At the end of the hour, the change in our son was unbelievable. He realized that these people needed to talk to someone and to have someone talk to them. Some of the residents received few, if any, visitors. Our son's visits made a difference in their lives, and they certainly made a difference in his. He continued the visits throughout his high school years, and whenever he's home from college, he returns to visit the residents. He sends them cards and letters. One of the residents even introduces him as her grandson! Any student can have a wonderful experience like our son's if they do volunteer work.

Be sure to keep track of how much time you spent on each activity. Maybe the German Club met for only thirty minutes every other week. But perhaps you spent thirty minutes twice a week as Student Council representative. Student Council therefore demands more of your time, which shows that you are dedicated to it. Scholarship committees should know this about you.

Almost everything you do twenty-four hours a day, seven days a week, fifty-two weeks a year during the four years you are keeping a résumé is important. If you take dance classes or karate classes or help coach a Little League team, let it be known. In the long run, the special things you did will distinguish you from the next person and could possibly mean the difference in who wins scholarship money and who doesn't. They could also determine whether or not you get into the college of your choice.

Some other things to keep in mind:

- Save all certificates of achievement you might receive while in high school. A few scholarship committees allow you to send photocopies of awards.

- Most applications have a section where a student can explain unusual circumstances. Use this space if obligations, such as having to work to support your family, have cut down on the amount of time you were able to spend on extracurricular activities.

- If in doubt about whether something qualifies as an extracurricular or volunteer activity, list it on your résumé. The college or scholarship committee can decide whether it wants to acknowledge the activity. One thing is certain: If you don't list it, a committee won't know about it at all.

- Be sure to update your résumé each year. By the time you're ready to apply for college admission and for scholarships, you'll be much better prepared than those students who haven't been as organized.

In Chapter 17, "Additional Sources of Information," we've included the names of some good books that show a wide variety of ways to construct a résumé. Also, in Appendix E, we've included examples of four résumés—one for a high school student one for a home-schooled student, one for a nontraditional student, and one for a student in college. These are just suggestions of what a résumé can look like. Use these references to help you create your own résumé. Just don't leave any important information off it! Pay close attention to the "Top Ten Tips for Creating Sparkling Résumés" in Chapter 19.

Think of your detailed résumé as a travelogue about your life. It should provide all the information scholarship committees need to know about the roads you chose to take in your life to date and how those choices reflect your goals, ideals, and ambitions for the future.

CHAPTER 8

GOING FOR THE GOLD! ATHLETES AND ATHLETIC RECRUITMENT

Most people know that sports scholarships in football, baseball, basketball, soccer, swimming, and other types of athletics are available for male students, but few realize that there are also sports scholarships for females.

Athletic scholarships can be offered for the usual basketball and football, as well as alpine skiing, archery, badminton, baseball, bowling, crew, cross country, cross-country skiing, diving, equestrian, fencing, field hockey, golf, gymnastics, ice hockey, indoor track, lacrosse, martial arts, racquetball, riflery, rodeo, rugby, soccer, softball, squash, swimming, swimming and diving, synchronized swimming, tennis, and our favorite, ultimate Frisbee. There are even scholarships for students who have been golf caddies.

ATTRACTING ATHLETIC SCHOLARSHIPS

In the first edition of our book, we didn't include an entire chapter for athletes because our son wasn't an athlete. When our son was in high school, his idea of an athletic sport was bowling, because you played it in an air-conditioned bowling alley. If you're a quarterback or basketball center, you probably chuckled just now, but there are scholarships for student bowlers.

In the first edition, athletes were addressed as part of the chapter entitled, Outstanding Qualities Count. In this edition, we've increased the information that is pertinent to athletes and their families by providing an entire chapter dedicated to athletes and their needs. In the appendices, you'll find a Sample Recruitment Profile for a male and a female. Just as there is a Common Application in applying for college admission, we hope that our sample will become the Common Recruitment Profile form. We want to make the application process as easy as possible and attracting money from all sources a simple, no-nonsense method of compiling information.

Don't wait until a student's high school senior year to begin actively contacting college coaches. In today's tough game of attracting athletic scholarship money, the stakes are high. That's why it's important to begin looking at and comparing colleges in middle school. By freshman year, an athlete should have narrowed down his or her list of colleges to fifty or fewer. By junior year, the list should be down to twenty or fewer, and by senior year, a maximum of ten.

ATHLETIC RECRUITMENT

We've seen students hire individuals to produce slick brochures, videos, and letters to gain the attention of college athletic recruiters. You don't have to spend a great deal of money in hopes of attracting athletic scholarships. If you're approached by an athletic placement service, you might want to think twice before agreeing to use it.

It isn't difficult to put together your own recruitment package, though you need to be sure your package contains certain items: a résumé, an athletic profile, a current school profile, a videotape, article clippings, a coach recommendation letter, and a cover letter. You shouldn't wait until junior year, much less senior year, to put together your package. Start compiling your data in freshman year. If you're active in athletic activities in middle school, you should be doing the same things as high school-

ers to prepare for college admission; you just won't be sending the recruitment package to college coaches yet.

The single most important aspect of a recruitment package is that it should reflect only one sport. Though there are those exceptional athletes who excel in more than one sport, such athletes are rare. Don't be so dazzled by your talents that you can't be objective.

If you're active and accomplished in more than one sport, you may want to compile an appropriate package for each sport. Submit only the additional package(s) if requested by a college coach.

RÉSUMÉ

Your package should include the same type of résumé we discuss in Chapter 7, Creative Résumés. The resume should include information about what

you've been doing for four years (the current year and three previous years). There are sample résumés in the Appendices.

ATHLETIC PROFILE

Your athletic profile will include your name and address, just as in the résumé, but it will also list your height, weight, age, and information about your school's athletic program. We've included sample athletic profiles in the Appendices. The sample profiles will give you an idea of the vital information

that must be included. Your athletic profile may contain slightly different information, depending on the sport in which you participate. You also may want to include any sports camps in which you have participated or will be participating.

SCHOOL'S ACADEMIC PROFILE/DESCRIPTION

You might want to get a copy of your school's transcript cover letter to include with your package. Most schools' transcript letters have one or two pages or more explaining the standard courses, grade scale, honors, advance placement courses, and dual credit courses available at the school. The school's description will be invaluable to coaches. It's

important that coaches know the academic strengths and weaknesses of potential student athletes. Coaches must know if students will be able to succeed in their transition from high school to college and be able to participate in sports while maintaining satisfactory academic progress.

VIDEOTAPE

Begin keeping a video library of every game, match, meet, or competition in which the student participates. All the games or meets won't be used, but parents need to make it a habit to videotape the games.

The videos need to show the entire game, yet must follow the student's every move. Jerky camera movements make watching the video difficult. Don't move the camera from one side of the playing field to another in a quick motion. Fast camera movement will cause the viewer to feel nauseous. Always try to keep the best angle on your student. You don't have to zoom in on the student, because coaches have plenty of practice watching game films. They know how to follow a student through an athletic event.

The videos shouldn't look like they were professionally done with computer graphics and narration. The only thing a professional video will show is how much the student can afford, not the quality of the athlete. Coaches know this. One thing you must never do is offend a coach. When putting together a recruitment package, use the KISS method: Keep It Simple, Stupid!

When you send a video, make sure you include the name of the opponent (or school), the date of the event, and the score. Make sure each tape is accurately marked. If you don't include game information on the tape, include a sheet of paper with it and mark the tape appropriately. If you want to include it on the video, you don't have to have expensive video editing equipment. You can use a computer (if you don't have one, use one at your high school or library) to type a one-page introduction, point the camera at the page, and *voilà!* You have an introduction on the videotape.

A tape of a full game, match, meet, or whatever is appropriate may be followed by various highlights, or you may submit a second tape containing only highlights. Never submit just a tape of highlights; always submit a copy of a full game. As one coach put it, "Everyone looks good in highlights."

CLIPPINGS

From the moment the first article is written about your athletic ability, you should begin a scrapbook or file containing all the articles. Over time, you'll be able to tell the difference between a clipping that says nothing about your ability and those that could only have been better if you or your parents had written them.

- If you play more than one sport, keep the clippings in separate files.

- Make sure the clippings highlight you, not another player or just the team.

- Though you might begin maintaining your clippings in middle school, those should be separate from those you obtain while you're in high school. A college coach isn't going to be impressed with articles dating from your years in middle school.

- Be sure to include clippings that do not comment on a particular game, but rather on any awards you receive.

When you begin keeping your files, always make photocopies of newspaper articles. Newsprint yellows with age. If an article includes a color picture, make a color photocopy. If you decide to highlight your name, don't use orange, blue, or green. Those colors are hard to look at. Use a yellow highlighter. Remember to highlight the photocopy, not the original article. Highlighted text in a newspaper article will photocopy in gray, which isn't easy to read.

When you submit your clippings with a recruitment package, send only four or five. Take time to be objective about which articles to select. If you're not sure, ask your parents or your coach. Though you don't want to appear arrogant or vain, you also don't want to be humble. You need to let a coach know your strengths and that you're interested.

ATHLETIC RECOMMENDATION LETTERS

Athletic recommendation letters are different from those you use in college or other scholarship applications. These recommendation letters shouldn't be written by core teachers. The letters should be objective and written by people with credentials to back their opinions. Just as with other recommendation letters, never submit one written by a relative—especially a parent. Let's face it, they love you (at least we hope so) and their recommendation will not impress a coach.

Just as the average recommendation letter should mention positive characteristics of the student, an athletic recommendation letter should mention your determination, skills, leadership abilities, staying power, and ability to always put the good of the team ahead of your desire to be center stage. If you're on any special teams (district, regional, or state, etc.) or participate in a workshop or camp, you might want to ask one or more of the coaches to write one. Make sure you ask for an open recommendation letter. This will allow you to read the letters and select the one that puts you in the best light. Some people are better at writing than others, and some coaches may have more experience in writing these letters.

COVER LETTER

A cover letter is different from a recommendation letter. A cover letter introduces you to the coach whom you want to notice you. This letter can be written by your high school coach, or you can write it. Who writes it doesn't matter as much as what it says. If you write the letter, make sure you mention any camps, clinics, or programs you will be attending before you arrive on a college campus. You also want to mention the school's academic program and how it fits in with your career goals and planned major. If you choose to have a coach write the letter, make sure it's the coach in the principal sport in which you're interested. You certainly wouldn't want your swim coach to write a letter to send with a recruitment package centering on basketball.

The letter really shouldn't be more than one page in length. It need not restate anything that is covered in other parts of the recruitment package, though you or the coach can mention one or two items (pick the items carefully). Of course, the letter should be typed and neat in appearance, but so should all of the items in your package. If you don't have a typewriter or computer, use one at your school or public library.

CAMPUS VISITS

When you visit a campus, don't just visit the sports facility and schedule a meeting with the coach or coaches. See if you can talk to some of the student athletes, especially those in the sport in which you have an interest.

Some of the questions you might ask the players are:

1. Did you get to play much your freshman year?

2. How much playing time do the coaches give lower classmen?

3. Is there a curfew? If so, are coaches strict on enforcing the curfew?

4. How many professional athletes have come from this school and who were they?

5. Was the current coach instrumental in helping those athletes make the transition to professional athletics?

EVALUATING ATHLETIC SCHOLARSHIPS

If you're offered an athletic scholarship, you need to evaluate all your options. In making your decision, bear in mind the following:

- Some schools might offer you more money than others. Don't necessarily jump at the first offer.

- Some nonathletic scholarships prohibit you from using their money if you receive an athletic scholarship. If this is the case, the award letter will state that you can't accept an athletic scholarship along with it. If the letter doesn't mention this, then you can use both scholarships.

- Which college is best for you (size, location, weather, academics, etc.)?

- At which college will you have more opportunity to use your athletic talents? You certainly don't want to sit on the bench because the college has so many good athletes that you won't get a chance to hone your skills in actual play.

- Ask your coach what he or she knows about the college's athletic department and how its athletes are treated.

We wouldn't recommend that any student accept an athletic scholarship just because it offers a lot of money if the college doesn't offer the classes, major, or academic support he or she wants and needs. This is an important time in your life. Don't just jump at the thought of playing on an elite, high-profile team if you're not sure you can succeed academically. You don't want to be the subject of a story coaches tell their high school students of a player who couldn't cut it academically. You want to be a role model for students in your school and community. So keep your sights focused on your goal: to play on an athletic team, possibly obtain and then keep an athletic scholarship, and, most important, get your college degree.

NCAA CLEARINGHOUSE

Students need to register with the National Collegiate Athletic Association (NCAA) Clearinghouse before graduating from high school, or they will be unable to accept scholarships to Division I or Division II schools. If a student fails to register, he or she can either attend a Division I or II school and not receive an athletic scholarship or attend a Division III school with an athletic scholarship and transfer at the end of two years. Unfortunately, not all Division III schools have athletic teams.

In San Antonio, there are four community colleges: San Antonio College, Palo Alto Community College, St. Phillip's Community College, and Northwest Vista Community College. Not one of the four schools offers athletic scholarships. If a San Antonio student didn't register with the NCAA Clearinghouse, he or she wouldn't be able to receive athletic monies to attend a local community college. That student would have to go out of town to attend a com-

munity college. This would defeat the purpose of a community college—to allow students access to an inexpensive education in their community while living at home.

To register with the NCAA Clearinghouse, students must meet certain criteria: (1) have at least a 2.0 GPA on a 4.0 scale, (2) score at least 700 on SAT or 17 on ACT, and (3) pay a registration fee. Fee waivers are available. To obtain a fee waiver, talk to your high school coach or counselor. To contact the NCAA: NCAA Clearinghouse, 2510 North Dodge, P.O. Box 4043, Iowa City, IA 52244-4043, (800) 638-3731 or (319) 339-3003.

Be aware that registering with the Clearinghouse doesn't guarantee that you'll attract, much less win, an athletic scholarship. Every year, there are approximately one million high school football players and 500,000 basketball players. Of all those students who want to become professional athletes, few actually achieve their dreams. Of those one million high school football players, only about 150 get drafted to NFL teams. Of the 500,000 high school basketball players, about 50 reach NBA status. Students need to realize that only 0.01 percent of student athletes go on to become professional athletes.

The most important aspect of attracting an athletic scholarship is that it will enable you to finance a college education. Even if you reach the professional athlete level, you will one day have to stop being an athlete and depend on your degree. This should be the primary reason why you're striving to attend college.

WHERE ELSE DO YOU LOOK?

To find out more about NCAA guidelines—and there are lots of conditions, exceptions, and standards—you might want to get a copy of the *NCAA Guide to Financial Aid*. The guide costs $5. Contact: NCAA, 6201 College Boulevard, Overland Park, KS 66211-2422, (913) 339-1906. You might also want to ask them to include a copy of the free *NCAA Guide for the College-Bound Student-Athlete*.

Female athletes may want to consider obtaining a copy of the "Women's Sports Foundation College Athletic Scholarship Guide." The guide lists most two- and four-year colleges and universities, each sport for which a scholarship is offered, how many scholarships are offered in each sport, and whether they are partial or full. Contact: Eisenhower Park, East Meadow, NY 11554, (516) 542-4700. The guide currently costs $3 (price may change from year to

year), which is minimal if you're interested in athletic scholarships.

Another good book that presents an honest, insightful view of athletic competition is *College Admissions for the High School Athlete*, by Jack DiSalvo and Theresa Foy DiGeronimo. The book is published by Facts on File.

In Part II, we've listed athletic scholarships by colleges and universities. If you're interested in a specific school and want to see if it offers a scholarship for the sport in which you participate, look in the alphabetical listing of colleges and universities in Part II. Just remember that we have not listed all schools and that some athletic departments change from year to year. If a college or university didn't respond to our inquiries, we didn't list it. Also, we were unable to list every program offered by every school.

CHAPTER 9

ORGANIZATION MADE EASY

One of the most important things to remember when applying for scholarships is to stay ORGAN-IZED! To help you do that, we've listed ten tips to help you stay on track and on time.

THE IMPORTANCE OF AN ORGANIZATIONAL SYSTEM

It's important to stay as organized as possible. The type of organizational system you use will be entirely up to you. Recently, we developed our own Cash for College™ Organizer. The Organizer is a fast and easy way to get a jump on the application process. It consists of a portable file box with handle, including: twelve files labeled by months for scholarships, and college applications, one file labeled for awards and certificates, one file labeled for recommendation letters and résumés, one file labeled for tracking charts and forms, one file labeled for financial aid forms, one file labeled for essays, one file labeled for miscellaneous items, one Cash for College™ Academic Year Calendar, one Cash for College™ Resource Kit, and six highlighters. To order any of our products, see the order form at the back of this book.

Whether you choose to use a file cabinet, crate files, a notebook, or just an old box, be sure it will help you stay organized. If there is more than one student in your family, set up a system for each student. Developing a system helps keep all scholarship and college information in one convenient place. You are less likely to lose an important application, address, or information if it's all in one place. Place the photocopied College Resource Materials Scholarship List Form (the master copy is in the Appendices) in the front of your notebook, to keep track of all scholarships you've requested or want to request. If you fill up one notebook, get another. You might want to keep your scholarship and college information and applications in separate notebooks or sections.

DIVIDERS/HANGING FOLDERS HELP YOU STICK TO DEADLINES

Use dividers, with or without pockets, or hanging file folders to keep your applications organized. We advise students to label twelve dividers/folders, one for each month of the year. If the due date for a completed application is December 1, place the application in the November section. If it's due March 15, put it in the February section. Obvi-ously, it's better to be a week early than to miss a deadline.

If you miss a deadline, there are NO second chances.

When our son was a high school senior, we became so involved with applications and essays that a writing competition slipped past us! He had an excellent essay that I'm sure could have won something, but we missed the opportunity. As you can see, we learned the hard way—deadlines are important!

As you receive scholarship information, note in a calendar (any calendar will do, as long as you have room to write on it) the date when the application is due and place the application in a sheet protector, large envelope, or hanging folder. Sheet protectors can be purchased at most school- or office-supplies stores. Or you can even use an old 9" × 12" (or larger) envelope.

NEATNESS COUNTS

It is important that you keep your materials all in one place and that you protect them from getting torn, dirty, or lost. Why? Because you have only one opportunity to make a good first impression. In some cases, it is the only impression. What do you think a selection committee will think about you if you don't take the time and effort to turn in a neat, clean application? The selection committee members will award money to students who they think can complete a task and do it to the best of their ability. Don't give them the opportunity to think you didn't care enough to try to make a good impression. Don't jeopardize your chances of obtaining scholarship money or being accepted into the college of your choice. Do the best job possible. It's not hard or expensive to be careful.

During our son's senior year in high school, we filled up three three-inch notebooks with scholarship applications and information. The first notebook contained pamphlets and booklets we had requested by mail. The second notebook contained all his scholarship applications. The third notebook was dedicated to the five colleges he was applying to. Our effort paid off: By the end of his senior year, we needed a one-inch notebook to hold all the acceptance and scholarship-award letters.

USE THE LISTS IN THIS BOOK TO STAY AHEAD OF THE GAME

Students who are high school seniors or above need to start looking for scholarships one year before they're going to need them. Students in kindergarten through the eleventh grade can start at any time. As you send for information from different sources (scholarships, foundations, companies, or colleges), fill in the CRM Scholarship List Form (Appendix B). This form helps you keep track of what you've done or still need to do, as well as when information was received. Make several copies of the CRM form for each year you will be applying for scholarships. Use this form only for tracking your requests for information. Use the College and Scholarship Application Form (in the Appendices) to keep track of the actual application process.

After using the At-a-Glance Scholarship Index to locate the scholarships you wish to apply to, write all the addresses on the CRM List Form (found in Appendix B). Also add any scholarships you may find elsewhere (newspapers, magazines, etc.). Send out either request letters or the easy-to-use Information Request Postcards we discussed in Chapter 6, and note this on your list, too.

It's especially important to note exactly when you sent a postcard or letter requesting information. If six weeks go by and you haven't heard a response from a scholarship, write to the committee again. Many times a scholarship committee or foundation may not be able to send out applications before a certain date, or sometimes your request is lost or misplaced. After all, committee members are only human. You might want to call, but if a scholarship listing in this book doesn't show a phone number or if the listing specifies that written inquiries are desired, don't call. But don't give up: write again instead.

KNOW YOUR ACCOMPLISHMENTS

Once all the request postcards and letters have been sent out, start your résumé (for résumé tips, see Chapter 7, "Creative Résumés"). If there are some writing or scholarship competitions you might want to enter that have deadlines coming up, you can't put them aside. You have to start learning how to balance more than one task at a time. Now is as good a time as any to start. Stay calm and keep reading!

Once you're in college, keep a copy of your high school résumé on hand. Some scholarships ask students to list the activities they've participated in for the last four years regardless of whether the student is in high school or college (the Tylenol Scholarship is one example). Being able to cite examples from the last four years is a definite plus, because usually students aren't as active in extracurricular activities during their college freshman year. So students can use their activities from high school to show their involvement in school or community.

If you're an older student returning to college, you'll still need a résumé. Chapter 4, "It's Never Too Late to Go Back!" will help you to create a résumé suited to your circumstances.

DON'T LOSE THOSE AWARDS AND CERTIFICATES!

Save all certificates of achievement you might receive while in high school. A few scholarship committees allow you to send photocopies of awards (perfect-attendance certificates don't usually carry much weight, however).

If you don't have time to join organizations because you work or because you have to take care of younger brothers and sisters in the afternoon, don't worry. Most applications have a section for students to explain unusual circumstances that prevent them from participating in extracurricular activities.

RELY ON TIMETABLES AND CALENDARS

Make a photocopy of the appropriate Timetable provided in Appendix A and keep it handy. You might want to keep a copy in a notebook pocket, taped to the inside cover of your notebook, or wherever you can refer to it easily. Check the timetable at least once a month, though once a week would be better.

In addition, get a calendar to help keep you on track. A month-at-a-glance calendar is even better. Don't think you have to go out and buy an expensive calendar, however. If your bank, insurance company, or school gives out calendars, get one of those and use it. Just make sure it has enough space for you to write on.

We now produce a Cash for College™ Academic Year Calendar. The calendar was designed to help students in middle school (6th, 7th, or 8th grades), high school, or even college (undergraduates). Each month has new information and some common areas. The monthly calendar has major application request and due dates marked. Some dates are for all students, while others might be specifically for students in high school, or just for high school seniors to stay on track and on time. We included vocabulary words and math problems in some months, to help middle school and high school students prepare for PSAT, SAT, and ACT tests. We also included suggested times to start volunteer and service projects. To order a calendar, refer to the order form at the back of this book.

Note the due dates for scholarship applications, college applications, financial aid information, and other important dates (College Night, Career Night, or when college representatives will be at your school, for example) on the calendar. Look at the calendar once a week. Remember, some colleges and most scholarship committees will not accept applications past their due dates. Even if you were able to get an extension (your chances are slim), it still wouldn't put you in the best light with the committee.

USE POSTCARDS AND A CHECKLIST TO KEEP TRACK OF INFORMATION

As you mail applications, transcripts, or recommendation letters, include a self-addressed, stamped return-receipt postcard with your mailing. A return-receipt postcard is a postcard that is mailed to you after an item is received by a scholarship or college admissions committee. If, a week or two before the application deadline, you still haven't received the postcard, start asking questions. If it was included in something you mailed, call the scholarship or college admissions committee and ask if they've received it and perhaps overlooked mailing it back. If the return-receipt postcard was included in a recommendation form, you can send that person a thank-you card (as we discuss in Chapter 12) as a way to give him or her a gentle reminder to complete and send the recommendation letter.

Keep each returned postcard with the relevant scholarship or college information. We've provided a master copy of return-receipt postcards in Appendix H. These can be made the same way we described in Chapter 6 for making Information Request Postcards. Once again, we created this master copy, and you have our permission to copy it for your personal use only (not for resale).

When you send an application or give a recommendation letter form to the person writing your letter of recommendation, fill in the date on the College and Scholarship Applications Tracking Chart provided in Appendix C. This lets you know at a glance what materials still remain to be sent for each scholarship or college application.

If you're applying to colleges during your high school senior year, you may need to send mid-year school reports. It's best if you hold on to the midyear school report forms until midterm. Take the forms to the registrar (if your high school has one), counselor's office, or principal's office, and have them send the updated information to the college.

Once you've been accepted to the college of your choice, you might also have to send an end-of-the-year report. This is just to let the college know how you did during the last semester of high school. Try hard not to get "senioritis"—don't let your grades slip just because you're nearing the end of high school. If you've been a consistent student, a small slip in grades probably won't matter. However, if your grades drop dramatically or if you had to work hard to get the grades needed for college acceptance and they slip back down, the college could change your status to "conditional" or "provisional," which might require your starting school in the summer or making a certain grade point average (GPA) during your first term in order to continue. Don't take that chance. You've worked too hard to blow it now!

KEEP COPIES

We strongly suggest that you photocopy all applications or any information you mail to scholarship foundations or colleges. If you can't afford to do this, then copy your answers onto another piece of paper and label it (by college, scholarship, financial aid packet, application, etc.). It isn't unheard of for an application to be lost or never received. If you have an exact duplicate of the application, it won't be difficult for you to photocopy it and send it again quickly. It's amazing how often the one application you don't have a copy of is the one that gets lost. Be sure to have copies of them all.

FILLING OUT APPLICATIONS

When you begin to fill out applications, first make a rough draft on scrap paper. This allows you to revise an answer until you get it just the way you want it. If you're not sure whether your answers are grammatically correct, ask someone to help you. If your English teacher doesn't have time, find an English tutor. If you think this suggestion is excessive or entails a lot or work, just remember that scholarship or college applications are some of the most important applications you will ever fill out. It's worth a little extra effort.

Try to type the information on the applications. If you don't know how to type, ask a friend to help you. If you don't have a typewriter, ask if there's one at your school you can use before or after school. Whatever you do, never type an application using a poor ribbon; no one likes to read print that is barely legible. Make it easy for them to read about you!

If you're unable to type your application, print the information in ink, using your best penmanship, and use Liquid Paper to correct any mistakes.

Persistence is your best tool in your search for scholarships. Take the time to inquire about any grant, foundation, or scholarship for which you might be eligible. You only have a postage stamp to lose and scholarship money to gain.

Just because you can't afford college tuition doesn't mean you can't get a college education. You just have to be more tenacious, more inventive, and more adventurous in finding a way to do so. You have to try. You have to be prepared.

You have to dream.

CHAPTER 10

TAKE THOSE TESTS!

Check with the colleges or universities to which you are considering applying to determine whether their preference is the Scholastic Assessment Test (SAT), former known as the Scholastic Aptitude Test, or the American College Test (ACT). Both tests are college-admissions tests, but they're not always interchangeable.

The SAT is scored on 1600 points. The ACT is scored on 36 points. There are comparable scores: a 950 SAT score equals a 20 ACT score; an 1110 SAT score equals a 24 ACT score; a 1220 SAT score equals a 27 ACT score; and a 1300 SAT score equals a 29 ACT score. One thing to keep in mind is that the SAT is half math, while the ACT is one-fourth math. So, if you're strong in math, you might score a bit higher on the SAT than on the ACT, and vice versa.

PRELIMINARY SAT (PSAT)

A student should take the PSAT during the junior year. If your high school allows it, you can take a practice PSAT as a sophomore. Doing this helps you be better prepared in knowing what type of information will be asked when you take the PSAT in your junior year. PSAT scores are used to determine which students will be invited to apply for schol- arships offered in the National Merit competition. If you're selected as a National Merit Semifinalist after taking the PSAT during the junior year, you will re- ceive an application during September of your se- nior year, which will then be used to determine Finalist standing.

SAT

If you can take the SAT while in middle school, do it. If you make a certain score or above, you may be eligible to apply to a summer-study program con- ducted by Duke University.* Regardless of whether

*Duke University Talent Identification Program
P.O. Box 40077
Durham, NC 27706-0077
(919) 684-3847
A three-week summer residential program on the Duke University campus. The program is open to students from 7th to 10th grade (with emphasis on 7th grade). Students who were selected to take the SAT early (in 7th to 10th grade) and who score above a certain score are eligible to participate. Students are able to take college-level classes in art, computer science, a foreign language, mathematics, natural sci- ences, and social studies. The cost of the program ranges from $1,350

you decide to take part or not, you will begin to receive information from colleges and universities, and it's excellent experience to have taken the SAT this early. It is a good idea to take the SAT as a high school junior, too. Regardless of how many times you take the SAT, only the highest scores count. Within that general rule, however, each college or university may choose how it assembles and eval- uates your SAT score. For example, a college may look at the highest combined score from *one* test, or

to $1,570, with limited to full scholarships available. Admission opens in December. Deadline: early May.

it may choose the highest math and highest verbal from *separate* tests.

The top 1 percent of all students who take the SAT are designated National Merit Finalists. Those students who are awarded National Merit scholarships (usually less than half of those chosen as Finalists) are designated National Merit Scholars. National Merit Finalists and Scholars are chosen based on a student's application, recommendations from the high school, grade point average, and their highest combined math and verbal SAT score from *one* test. Finalists and Scholars are announced in the spring of a student's senior year. All colleges and universities want to have National Merit Finalists and Scholars attend their schools. That's why it's important to do as well as possible on the SAT and, especially, the PSAT. If you're selected as a Finalist or a Scholar, colleges and universities may seek you out, asking that you apply.

TEST PREPARATION

Once in high school, you can take a practice SAT or ACT during your freshman and sophomore years.

You need to take another SAT or ACT at the end of your junior year (April, May, or June). This will enable you to evaluate whether or not you have a strong chance for admission to your first choice school. If you score isn't within an acceptable range, you can utilize the summer to prepare for the fall test dates. If you're dissatisfied with your SAT or ACT test scores, there are several ways to try to improve your scores. You might want to check with your high school or city library and see if any books or videos are available on preparing for the SAT or ACT. You also can purchase SAT or ACT prep books (usually available at local bookstores). Some bookstores and computer stores also offer computer programs that coach students on how to take these tests. Many schools and school districts offer modestly priced SAT or ACT test-prep courses, and there are some services that do this as well.

AP AND CLEP TESTS

During your junior and senior years of high school, ask your counselor about advance standing or academic credit to students who do well on the College Board's Advanced Placement (AP) tests. You can take AP courses in various subjects while in high school. These courses are geared to teach you more than you would learn in a regular high-school-level class. You can then take an AP test that may allow you to skip freshman, and even sophomore, college classes in those areas. Alternately, College-Level Examination Program (CLEP) exams can be taken when you enter college to see if you can "test out" of introductory-level classes. You might not have to go to college for as many years as you thought, which in turn can save you a lot of time and money.

ACHIEVEMENT TESTS

Some colleges and universities might also want you to take some Achievement Tests for college admission or for placement within a subject once you're accepted for admission. These tests are administered by the College Board, the same corporation that administers the PSATs and SATs. You can obtain the appropriate forms from your high school counselor to sign up for these tests.

CHAPTER 11

OUTSTANDING QUALITIES COUNT

Outstanding qualities count when applying for scholarships, whether you're going to attend a two- or four-year college or university or a vocational or technical school. Take time now to evaluate yourself and your parents to see if you might be overlooking a possible source of FREE MONEY!

COMPANIES

If one of your parents works for a large company, have them find out whether the company offers scholarships to children of employees. The company's human resource department (personnel) should have this information.

UNIONS

Many unions offer scholarships to members' children. A free booklet is available to dependents of AFL-CIO union members (see Chapter 17, "Additional Sources of Information").

MEMBERSHIPS

Many organizations offer scholarships to students who are or have been members. Some of these include American Legion, Boy Scouts, Distributive Education Clubs of America (DECA), 4-H, Future Farmers of America (FFA), and the YMCA.

RELIGIOUS AFFILIATION

Various religious groups offer scholarships to members. Baptist Life Association, Aid Association for Lutherans, Council of Jewish Federations, Fellowship of United Methodists, Knights of Columbus, and the Presbyterian church are a few that do.

DISABLED STUDENTS

Handicapped students can also receive assistance. For example, students who are blind can contact the National Federation of the Blind to apply for the various scholarships offered by the federation to legally blind students. Gallaudet University offers financial aid to students who are hearing impaired. Physically challenged students can contact their state's rehabilitation commission. At the rehab commission, students are assigned counselors who work with them to find the career, education, training, and financial assistance they may need to further their education within their physical limits. The Gore Family Memorial Foundation and the Foundation for Exceptional Students both offer scholarships to handicapped students. Check to see if any local disability groups sponsor scholarships.

STATE AGENCIES

Contact the educational agencies in your state (addresses are listed in Chapter 18, "Where to Go for State and Federal Help") to inquire about special state-sponsored programs. Often, financial aid programs exist for children of disabled firefighters and police and children of POWs and MIAs. There are also programs for students who are deaf or blind; for the highest-ranking high school graduate; for children of Armed Forces members who were killed in action or who died while in service; for children of members of the National Guard who were killed since January 1, 1946, while on active duty; and to state-resident veterans whose Veterans Administration benefits have been exhausted, among others.

ETHNIC BACKGROUND

Other organizations provide financial help to students having a particular ethnic ancestry. The United Negro College Fund, the Roy Wilkins Educational Scholarship Program, and the Jackie Robinson Foundation all offer African American students a variety of scholarships, some of them valued up to $5,000 per year for four years. The Commission for Racial Justice offers a scholarship opportunity open to any minority high school senior and undergraduate students, as does the National Urban League.

Hispanic American high school seniors can contact the League of United Latin American Citizens (LULAC) or inquire at local McDonald's restaurants about the HACER Scholarship program. Hispanic American students who already have at least fifteen hours of college credit can contact the National Hispanic Scholarship Fund.

Special programs also exist for students who are Japanese American, Native Alaskans, or Native Americans. These programs vary for students seeking degrees in accounting, business administration, education, engineering, geosciences, journalism, law, psychology, nursing, pharmacy, and other health professions.

WOMEN

Many scholarship opportunities are available to women of all ages. The Business and Professional Women's Foundation helps women through a variety of programs. The American Association of University Women (AAUW) provides assistance to women completing graduate and professional degrees. The AAUW also sponsors PROJECT RE-NEW, which helps women whose last degree was obtained over five years prior to returning to college and who wish to update their education and skills or change careers. From AT&T Bell Laboratories to Zonta International, there are programs that assist women in undergraduate programs in science and engineering fields; these programs are all described in the scholarship listings in this book.

To see which special categories you belong to, flip to the index in Part II of this book. It lists many different categories that might apply to you and tells which scholarship opportunities are available in those categories. There are thousands of scholarships available in special categories. You just have to know what to ask, when to ask it, and where to write for information.

CHAPTER 12

RECOMMENDATION LETTERS

There are two types of recommendation letters—confidential and open. A confidential letter either must be sent directly to the scholarship or college admissions committee by the person writing it or it must be in a sealed envelope with the person's signature written across the sealed flap to show that the envelope hasn't been opened or tampered with. In contrast, an open letter is one the student may view, and can be sent by the student along with the rest of the application material. Most scholarship applications don't specify the type of recommendation letter that is required, which means that an open letter is acceptable. If recommendation letters must be confidential, the application will plainly state this.

Some people would rather not write a recommendation letter if there's a chance that the student might see it. If the person you ask tells you that he or she will write the letter only if it's kept confidential, then you must decide if you want to give up the right to read it. If you're comfortable in your relationship with that person, chances are you have nothing to fear. If you had disagreements with the person in the past or if you're less than comfortable in your relationship, then thank him or her politely and ask someone else.

WHAT IS A GOOD RECOMMENDATION LETTER?

A good recommendation letter is typed on one side only, is grammatically correct, and gives some insight into the student's potential, academic ability, leadership ability, motivation, responsibility, integrity, honesty, diligence, perseverance, cooperativeness, emotional stability, judgment, and common sense.

WHOM TO ASK

For the most part, scholarships and colleges require two recommendation letters. Sometimes they ask for letters from specific teachers, such as a science teacher and an English teacher. If a third, fourth, or fifth recommendation letter is requested, it can usually come from a teacher of a favorite class, a counselor, principal, employer, or close family friend.

If you're in high school, the letters must be from individuals who knew you while you were in high school. If you're in your first semester of college and have not completed a college course, you can ask high school teachers to write your recommendation letters. Once you've completed one semester of college, you need to ask college professors to write your recommendation letters.

Whether you're submitting two or more letters, one letter should be from a teacher or professor who taught you in a core subject (English, science, math, or history). The second and subsequent letters can be written by anyone. But if you're going to be an art major, you'd want your art teacher to write one; a music major would want a band or choir director to write the letter, etc.

You might want to ask a past employer, a person

who was your supervisor in a volunteer activity, a pastor, priest, or Sunday School teacher, or even a neighbor. The neighbor might know that you've supervised neighborhood children during the summer or after school or may know that you've done volunteer work of some type. Whoever you ask, remember that they must know you very well. Never ask a relative, guardian, or godparent, however, even if you work for your uncle, aunt, father, or mother. Relatives aren't considered objective sources. Find someone who isn't related to you to write the recommendation letter. A recommendation letter should not be written by another student.

This may sound obvious, but it's worth repeating: Never ask for a recommendation from someone who you're not certain will write a positive one. We know of students who asked their current science, English, or computer teacher for recommendations only to have the teacher relate in a confidential letter incidents that hurt the students' chances of obtaining scholarships. Just because an application asks for a recommendation letter from a specific type of teacher doesn't mean that you have to ask for one from your *current* teacher. If you're a senior, it's better to ask your freshman, sophomore, or junior year teacher in that subject than to risk a bad recommendation.

If a scholarship asks for a third, fourth, or fifth optional recommendation letter, the choice of whom to ask is up to you. Someone who is a prominent figure in the area where you live (mayor, senator, member of Congress, or prominent businessperson) would be a good choice. But if you don't know the mayor, don't worry. An employer, pastor, teacher, or anyone of that sort who knows you well can give a recommendation, too.

When you ask people to write a recommendation letter, ask them if they have time to write one. Be sure they truly want to write the letter and that they will have time to do a thorough job. After all, you are the person who stands to lose if a recommendation letter is written in haste, so you should do everything you can to make sure your recommendations are excellent.

RECOMMENDATION LETTER FORMS

Sometimes, scholarship committees don't supply forms on which people should write the letters of recommendation. We have supplied a copy of a sample Recommendation Letter Form in Appendix I. This form can be photocopied and used in the event that a scholarship or college application doesn't include its own form.

Some organizations like to receive a letter that shows it was written especially for them. Therefore, after you make copies of the form, type the title of the scholarship application over the heading "Letter of Recommendation Form." Whoever is writing the recommendation will then be able to refer to the name of the scholarship in the letter.

If the people writing your recommendations prefer to use school or business letterhead rather than a copy of the recommendation letter form supplied in this book, let them. Just remember to have the letter writer mention your full name, the name of the scholarship or college to which the letter will be submitted, and, possibly, your Social Security number on each page of the letter. Your Social Security number might not be needed if you have a unique full name and/or if you're applying for a local scholarship or to a small college. On the other hand, if you're a David, Elizabeth, George, Juan, Mary, Pat, Richard, or Tony, and your last name is something like Adams, Garcia, Jones, Sanchez, Smith, Thompson, or Washington, you might be in trouble. There may be more than one applicant with that name, which could lead to confusion. It's especially important to include your Social Security number if you are applying to a large college or university.

Whether you use a form supplied by the scholarship committee or college or the one in this book, fill in the information at the top of the form that pertains to you before you give it to the person writing the recommendation. Type your part of the information, if possible. Most people will also type the recommendation letter, but it is acceptable for it to be handwritten. Recommendation letters should be written on one side of the page only, with additional sheets added if necessary (this requirement is usually written on the form).

MAKE IT EASY FOR THEM

Once people have agreed to write recommendation letters, make it as easy as possible for them to write the letters. This is especially true if they're teachers, counselors, principals, or other community leaders, since these people are probably writing a number of recommendation letters for other students as well. When you give them the recommendation form, always provide an envelope in which to mail it. The envelope should be addressed and stamped with sufficient postage. During our son's search for college money, we always supplied 9" × 12" envelopes so the letters would arrive flat, without a crease, but standard business-size envelopes will do.

You might also want to consider giving the people writing your recommendation letters a copy of your résumé. They'll then know exactly what you have accomplished and when you've participated in certain activities or won awards. They will appreciate this kind of assistance, and it also may impress a selection committee that your participation in various activities is so consistently noted and praised by the teachers, counselors, principals, or employers writing your letters of recommendation. This little extra effort might make the difference in your getting a scholarship.

Let whoever is writing the letter know that you will need more than one letter. This will alert them to keep a photocopy of the letter. Sometimes this is impossible, since you may not know what scholarship you'll discover in March when it's only October. If you know you're applying to five colleges and for at least five scholarships and you are asking your favorite science teacher for a letter of recommendation, then you know you'll need at least ten copies of the same recommendation letter.

Each letter, even if it's a photocopy, needs to have an original signature and current date. Have the people writing the recommendation letters sign their names in blue ink. Then it's obvious that the signature is an original.

Don't wait until the day before a deadline to ask for a recommendation letter. Chances are, the people you ask are busy and need ample advance notice. You want to allow them enough time to write a well thought out, complimentary letter, not a dashed-off note that says nothing. After all, it is your future in the balance.

HOW TO SEND RECOMMENDATION LETTERS

Some scholarships require you to send all the information (application, transcripts, recommendation letters, and essays) at one time. If recommendation letters must be confidential and sent with your application, have the teachers put the recommendation letter in a sealed envelope and have them sign it across the sealed flap. This will assure the committee receiving the information that you never saw the letter. Some scholarship committees require you to send all the information (application, letters, copies of certificates of merit, résumés, and other information) flat, open, and either stapled together or spiral-bound in a convenient package. If you choose to spiral-bind the application package, most photocopy centers will do this for a small fee. Spiral-binding is an attractive and convenient way to put an application package together.

RETURN-RECEIPT POSTCARDS

Whenever our son asked someone for a recommendation letter, we would enclose (in the self-addressed, stamped envelope—SASE—we provided) a stamped return-receipt postcard, addressed to our son. When the recommendation letter arrived at the college, university, or scholarship committee, whoever opened the letter would date and sign the postcard. This way, we were able to keep track of what had been sent or not sent, received or not received. We received every return-receipt postcard we included with recommendation letters, applications, and financial aid information.

Sometimes, when the applications were sent to colleges, the person who placed the postcard in the mail would include a small note, saying something like, "Hope to see you next year." That was always nice. Senior year is tough. Students are putting their egos on the line and facing rejection from colleges. Even a small note can brighten up their day.

Information on how to make return-receipt postcards is covered in Chapter 9.

HOW TO GIVE GENTLE REMINDERS

Helen Huffman, a Fredericksburg, Texas, high school counselor, gave us an excellent suggestion on how to remind a person about writing a recommendation letter. She suggested you write thank-you cards to everyone you've asked to write a recommendation letter for you. Then a week or two before the letter is due at the scholarship or college admissions committee, take the card to the person. This is a gentle way of nudging people who might be so busy that they've forgotten to write your recommendation letter.

WHAT NOT TO DO

Never use for one scholarship opportunity, internship, or college a recommendation letter written for *another* scholarship opportunity, internship, or college. Some students, in an effort to save time, will photocopy a recommendation letter that referred to a different scholarship in the body of the letter. When this happens, a scholarship committee can only assume one thing: that it was the student who sent the copy, not the person who wrote the letter. Scholarship committees want to see that a student has taken time to obtain required material. Also, a scholarship committee has no way of knowing if you asked permission of the letter writer to send copies to several different committees. Even with the letter writer's permission, don't submit a recommendation letter to one scholarship that was written for another.

When a committee requests a recommendation letter, a student cannot substitute a copy of an academic report, a copy of a nomination letter (for a noncash award, not a scholarship), or a list of people the scholarship or college admissions committee members can call to talk to for a recommendation. We can assure you that committee members don't have time to chase down people by telephone to get an oral recommendation. Scholarship and college application instructions are usually simple, reasonable, and straightforward. Not following the directions doesn't make a good impression on the selection committee. How can a committee believe you'll complete college when you can't complete the application requirements?

A recommendation letter should never be written on a piece of scratch paper, on colored paper, or on notebook paper. You also don't want a recommendation letter to look as if it was written in a hurry. That's why it's important for the person to have ample time to write a recommendation letter.

SOMETHING TO REMEMBER

We've started a foundation that presently administers scholarships funded by private organizations or businesses. This service allows businesses and organizations offering scholarships to be able to assure students that no favoritism will be used in selecting the winners. This year we administered several scholarships and saw a wide variety of recommendation letters. Although we took into account that a student shouldn't be penalized because the person who wrote the recommendation letter did a poor job of writing it, not all committees are as lenient.

This is the only opportunity a scholarship or college acceptance committee has to hear someone else's opinion of you. Take your time in deciding whom to ask. Make it your best choice!

CHAPTER 13

IMPRESSIVE INTERVIEWS

You've just been notified that you've been granted an interview by either a scholarship or college representative or committee. What do you do? Don't panic. There aren't many dos and don'ts about interviews.

DON'T BE LATE

Be as punctual as possible. If you must rely on public transportation to get to the interview, allow enough time. It's better to wait in a lobby or spend a few minutes browsing in a nearby shop than to show up late.

TAKE A COPY OF YOUR RÉSUMÉ WITH YOU

The person or persons conducting the interview may not have a copy of your application. A résumé will give them something on which to base their questions. Even if the interviewer does have a copy of your application, bringing an extra copy of your résumé shows that you prepared for the interview well.

BE PREPARED

Before you go to the interview, take some time to think about why you need a particular scholarship or want to attend a particular college. You may be asked to discuss this in the interview. The rest of the interview may deal with your academic record, your extracurricular activities, or any community work you've done.

You need to let the interviewer know you're the best candidate for a scholarship or admission to a college, without just stating that fact. You must explain why you're the best candidate. Have a story ready that makes a good impression. You might want to consider relating an academic experience, a volunteer experience, or an important instance where you learned something. Don't be defensive or abrasive or make grand claims. Don't tell the interviewer that you know you'll be making the Dean's List when you never made the Honor Roll while in high school.

In Chapter 19, we've included the Top Ten Interviewing Tips. Review them and keep them in mind before and during the interview. The more prepared you are for an interview, the better you'll come across.

BE READY TO ANSWER AND ASK QUESTIONS

We've included some sample interview questions to consider. Think about how you would answer them. The last thing you want to do is answer with, "Uh...." You also want to think of some questions to ask the interviewer. This could give you extra points for enthusiasm.

Listen carefully during the interview. Don't let your mind wander. If you don't understand a question, say so. Think about a question for a second or two, but not more. Don't just blurt out the first thought that comes to mind. Answer the question once. Don't repeat yourself. Always be prepared to answer the follow-up question, "Why?"

If an admissions committee asks you about the other colleges or universities you're considering, don't denigrate the schools or other interviews you've been granted. If you're being interviewed for a scholarship and are asked about a school you're *not* considering, don't make negative comments about the school. For all you know, the interviewer may have attended that school. You won't earn any points for being tacky.

DRESS APPROPRIATELY

If you can afford to buy new clothes and want to do it, fine, but it isn't necessary. The important thing is to be clean, neat, and well groomed. You want to give the best impression possible. You should dress conservatively. This isn't the time to wear a hot pink short skirt or dress that requires that you keep tugging on it while sitting. Some good colors are (any shade) blue, green, black, brown, gray or charcoal, and maroon. Women shouldn't wear a great big bow at the collar. Men don't have to wear a tie, but if you do, wear a bright color—not gaudy. If you're being interviewed by a college admissions committee, don't wear a school tie. It will look like you're trying to impress the interviewers.

Shoes should also be conservative. Don't wear a spiky, four-inch heel or an open-toed shoe. Shoes to avoid include sandals, tennis shoes, mountain boots, clogs, and any shoe that will slap back on your heels when you walk.

Keep jewelry to a minimum. This goes for both men and women. Don't wear long, dangly earrings. These distract the interviewer. Don't wear a lot of clangy bracelets. They make too much noise and will only emphasize that you move your hands a lot.

Keep perfume and cologne to a minimum. Don't take a bath in it, no matter how much you like the way it smells. The interviewer could be allergic or sensitive to odors. Wash your hands after applying perfume and cologne. This way you won't pass on the scent when you shake hands. Before you leave home, ask someone if you have too much perfume or cologne on.

BODY LANGUAGE

When you walk into the interview room, don't run, drag your feet, or lumber. Make eye contact, but don't appear aggressive. You don't want to alarm the interviewer. When you reach the interviewer, extend your hand. Don't shake the interviewer's hand in a death grip or so weakly that the interviewer will wonder if you have bones in your hand. State your name in a clear, distinct tone. You want the interviewer to hear you and know what to call you, especially if you prefer a nickname, and you want the interviewer to know how to pronounce a unique name.

How you sit during an interview tells the interviewer a great deal about you. When you sit down, don't sit on the edge of the chair; it will appear as though you're ready to bolt at the interviewer or out the door. It could make you appear overly aggressive. You want to sit back in the chair, but not slouch.

If you generally cross your legs when you sit, do so. But if you tend to jiggle your foot, then keep your feet firmly planted on the floor. If you cross your legs so that one foot is on your knee, don't grab at your foot—especially the bottom of your shoe. Remember, you should shake the interviewer's hand when you leave.

Some hand movement is acceptable. If you look like you're swatting flies, however, you should consider clasping your hands in your lap. This will keep them still.

If your hair has a tendency to fall in your face, either cut it or pin it back. It doesn't look appropriate for you to continually reach up to push it out of the way. Don't play with your hair if you get nervous. DO NOT under any circumstances put your hair in your mouth. This may sound foolish, but when you're nervous you may not even think about what you're doing.

When the interviewer stands or says, "Thank you for coming," the interview is over. Don't keep talking or try to lengthen the interview. The interviewer probably has another appointment and a schedule to keep. Shake the interviewer's hand and thank the interviewer for taking the time to see you.

RELAX

Being granted an interview means that your application impressed the scholarship committee or college admissions committee and that they want to know more about you. Try to remain relaxed and enjoy the time to get to know the people interviewing you. If the interviewer is a college representative and has attended your first-choice college, take this opportunity to ask him or her some questions about the college. Your curiosity and interest will reflect well on you.

The people interviewing you simply want to get to know you. Remember, no one knows you better than you. Enjoy yourself!

One last bit of advice to keep in mind comes from an old and familiar deodorant commercial: "Never let them see you sweat!"

POSSIBLE INTERVIEW QUESTIONS
Goals

1. Have you set any goals that you have already accomplished?

2. What would you like to be doing by your twenty-five-year high school reunion?

3. Many students say they want to be successful. What does being successful or a success in your field mean to you?

4. Why do you want to succeed?

5. What are your long-term goals?

College

1. Why do you want to attend college?

2. Why do you want to attend this college?

3. What if you don't gain admission to any college? What will you do?

4. How will you make your final choice on which college to attend?

5. What worries you most about college?

6. Why do you think you and this college are a good match?

Strengths and Weaknesses

1. What would you say is your best quality?

2. What would you say is your worst quality?

3. What are you doing to improve that quality?

4. If you were evaluating this interview, what would you say?

5. Select one adjective you, an adult, and your best friend would use to describe you?

Academic Issues

1. What subject do you most enjoy in high school? Why?

2. What subject do you enjoy least? Why?

3. Which book or books have you read for enjoyment and not an assignment, that have made a lasting impression on you? Describe the impression.

4. Describe the perfect teacher and explain why.

5. If you know what you would like to major in, how did you choose it? If you don't know your possible major, how will you select it?

Extracurricular Interests and Activities

1. What contribution have you made to your school or community of which you are proudest?

2. What school extracurricular activity or membership has been the most important to you and why?

3. If you could start high school again, what would you do differently?

4. What are your hobbies?

5. How would either your favorite teacher or supervisor in a volunteer activity describe you?

Personal Odds and Ends

1. What moral value is most important to you at this point in your life?

2. How have you changed in the last four years?

3. Why should we select you?

4. Describe a high school memory that has special meaning for you.

5. What have you done during your high school summers? Why?

Others

1. What do you want me to know that I haven't asked you?

2. Who has helped you most in your college selection and why?

3. Imagine that earlier today you met Ben Franklin or Leonardo da Vinci. Describe in detail your first twenty minutes together.

4. As a teenager in today's society, what are some of the problems you face, and how would you solve them?

5. Who is the most important person in your life and why?

Trap Questions to Avoid

1. Describe the ideal college.

2. How many other colleges are you considering?

3. To which colleges are you applying?

4. Which college is your number-one choice?

5. Is there anything you should explain?

Ways to Avoid Trap Questions

1. You might want to answer, "The ideal college will be one where I can flourish and energize others while energizing myself, and that will prepare me for my future."

2. Mention that you are considering several other colleges. If you want to deflect the question, ask the interviewer how many he or she considered when applying to college.

3. Name two or three other colleges.

4. Don't say that the interviewing college is your first choice if it isn't. It will only look like you're kissing up to the interviewer.

5. If there is something in your academic record, extracurricular activities, or family situation that should be explained, do so, but don't whine. You need to take responsibility for your actions and not blame others.

CHAPTER 14

WRITING PERSUASIVE ESSAYS

In a college or scholarship essay, your goal is to inform the reader why you should be selected over someone else. Unless you are asked to appear at an interview, the essays are the only chance you have to tell the committee your thoughts and dreams, to express in your own words those things that make you a unique individual.

Writing essays shouldn't be an agonizing or frustrating experience. That's why we included a variety of essays in this chapter for you to use as examples. These essays were written for either college or scholarship applications. Please note that they are meant only to be examples: Your essay must be 100 percent *you*—written *by* you *about* you.

The essay is one of the most important parts of your application and is as crucial as an interview. Be sure to write it thoughtfully.

It goes without saying that no one but you should write your essay. It must be your work. If you try to pass off someone else's work as your own, you will come to regret it. First of all, it is cheating. Also, if you were granted a college interview, you could be questioned about the essay you submitted in your application. It would be horrifying to be unable to discuss it because you didn't write it. Besides, an essay is supposed to reveal the type of person you are. If someone else writes it, it can't reveal anything about you.

It is acceptable, however, to ask a teacher, counselor, librarian, or your parents to *proofread* an essay. It's sometimes easier for someone else to catch a mistake than it is for you. When others read your essay, bear in mind that they can tell you what they like or don't like, but they can't rewrite it. You still have the final say!

The essays in this chapter are actual essays written by our son, who was admitted to five prestigious U.S. universities and was actively recruited by many universities. Use these essays as examples to help you write your own. They are copyright-protected and can't be copied. Submitting someone else's written work as your own is plagiarism.

When you're writing your essay, make sure you're not under time pressure. Don't wait until the night before you have to mail it to write it. Above all, the most important thing to remember is to be yourself.

If you're not sure whether your essays are grammatically correct, ask someone to help you. If your English teacher doesn't have time to do this, find an English tutor. If you think this suggestion seems excessive, think twice. Scholarship and college applications are some of the most important applications you will ever fill out, and good grammar is a very important component.

If you know a professional writer or editor, have him/her proofread your essay and give you pointers, but be wary of companies that promise to write your essay for you. These companies just want your money; they don't care one way or the other about how good the essay is or whether it says anything about you. Again, doing something like this is just plain dishonest.

Try to type the essay, as well as the rest of the application. If you don't know how to type, ask a friend. If you don't have a typewriter, ask if you can use one in your school before or after school. If you're still unable to have it typed, print the information in ink in your best penmanship. If you are asked to write the essay on a separate sheet of paper, use white 20-lb. bond. Don't use erasable paper (it smears on handling) or colored paper (it's hard to read). You want to make it as easy as possible for the committee members to read your essay.

If you are asked to write your essay directly on the application, consider photocopying the blank application. When you have drafted your final essay, practice typing it on the photocopy. If your essay is within the required word count but is too long to fit in the space provided, try using a smaller-size type. Pica type has ten characters per inch, while elite has twelve characters per inch. You might be able to make your essay fit just by using smaller type.

If an essay must be under a specific number of words and your essay is too long, reread it. Can you take out excess words? If a sentence says the same thing with fewer words, it's probably a better sentence anyway.

If you weren't given a word count but must fit an essay into a given space, you might want to consider typing it on another piece of paper and reducing it on a copy machine, then gluing it in place. Don't reduce it too small. It's better to cut words than to strain someone's eyesight.

If at any time you're in doubt about the meaning of a question, ask your parents, high school counselor, a favorite teacher, or the organization offering the scholarship, or (if there's time) write to us (our address is on page 7 of Chapter 1). Don't jeopardize your chances to get a scholarship by failing to understand the question.

Make sure you keep a copy of every essay you write. This way, if you find another scholarship you want to apply for later, you might be able to reuse an essay or modify one you've already written. Recycling an essay saves you time. Reusing your own work isn't plagiarism. Perhaps all you have to do is update it a bit, reslant it more toward the question you're answering, or cut or add some words. Our son, who applied to scholarships each year, used the first essay he wrote for a scholarship during his high school senior year for subsequent years. Each year he just updated the information, and he avoided having to write an entirely new essay from scratch.

After having seen many scholarship and college applications, we were able to make a list of some of the most commonly asked questions or topics covered. Read through this list and consider how you might answer these points.

- Describe your short-term and long-term goals.

- Describe an experience that has deeply influenced your development.

- How have your background and upbringing influenced your personal development and outlook?

- Describe what you're like, using information about your most significant accomplishments.

- Name one to three persons you admire and respect and why. They don't have to be prominent or national personalities.

- Choose a book (or books) you have read on your own (not as a school assignment) that has affected you deeply, and explain why.

- Make up a question that is personally relevant to you and answer it.

- Describe how you have demonstrated leadership ability both in and out of school.

Although an essay should express your beliefs, ideas, and personality, there are some topics you should consider avoiding when writing an essay, because you jeopardize your chances if your reader strongly disagrees with your opinion. Avoid discussing:

- relationships (boyfriend or girlfriend)

- religious beliefs

- political beliefs

- views on or about drugs and/or alcohol

- opinions about sex or other moral beliefs

- views on current events (from abortion to disarmament)

College and scholarship committees essentially evaluate five things in an essay: grammar, spelling, syntax and word usage, content, and creativity. Of these, creativity is probably the most important. This is where you can show a committee your distinctiveness. You might try using humor or actual dialogue. However you use your creativity, be sure to remember the topic and sustain the tone of the essay. If the essay is lighthearted, it can be so throughout, but if you've just related a somber incident that influenced your life, you don't want to ruin the moment with inappropriate humor.

Avoid repeating information that appears elsewhere on the application, unless the essay allows you to expand on an activity or a leadership position. Most applications will have a section where you list your activities, or you'll be asked to include a résumé. If you choose to discuss some of your activities as a way to make a point in an essay, by all means do so.

Don't generalize in your essay. Don't assume that "everybody" thinks or does something. Cite specific examples when you can.

If you've been given the opportunity to write about any topic, choose something you care deeply about. It might be an event that changed your life, a teacher who introduced you to a new, interesting subject area, or an activity that revealed a side of yourself you didn't know about. If you are asked to discuss your favorite academic interest, don't just say that you like science and geography. That type of answer says nothing about you. Go into why science and geography are your favorite classes. Explain how your teachers make those classes come alive. Be specific.

College and scholarship committees read hundreds, even thousands, of essays every year. Your first sentence should hook them. Your essay must not only tell them about yourself but must also hold the reader's attention. We wouldn't recommend telling jokes, but try to be lively and upbeat. The idea is to have them remember you.

All writers know that their work should answer the questions of who, what, when, and where. What you must also answer is how and why. Tell committees as much as possible as excitingly as you can. If you're not sure you've done this, ask someone else to read it and provide feedback.

We strongly recommend *The Elements of Style*, by William Strunk, Jr., and E. B. White. This little book is full of explanations of important rules all writers should remember, as well as a list of commonly misused words. It's entertaining, too. The book costs about $5, but you can probably find it in most libraries, too.

As mentioned earlier, the essays that follow were written by our son and are intended only as examples. We hope they'll provide you with some insights on how to write an essay. When you've finished reading them, sit back and consider: What have you learned about the student? What do you want selection committees to know about *you*?

Briefly describe your short-term and long-term goals.

Goals are one of the most important parts of a person's life, and yet as a teenager they're the last thing you want to think about. So when I came across this essay question, I found myself thinking about what was deep inside me. "What are my short- and long-range goals?" I asked myself. Here is the answer I found.

In the short term, my goals are simple. I want to get into a good college and get a bachelor's degree in economics. Then I want to continue on and get my master's and my doctorate. Of course, somehow I have to pay for this, so another short-range goal is to get adequate financial aid. All of these are stepping stones to higher things.

For long-range goals, I have several choices. One is that I would like to receive a position in the private sector as an economist or I'd like to become a professor of economics at a university. In the end, I hope to become a well-known authority and advise heads of state on economic policy or even run for office myself. All the while I hope for the usual things such as a wife, children, house, etc....To some, these goals may seem odd and simplistic, but that is what I wish for from deep inside me.

Pick the one experience that has most influenced your development, and briefly describe how it has done so.

The activity that has most influenced my development has been my volunteer work at a nursing home. When I'm there, my primary duty is to walk with an elderly woman who requires exercise but who has osteoporosis and dizzy spells. I also visit with the other residents and listen to their stories. It creates immense personal satisfaction for me when I see their eyes light up at my approach. They know that I'm someone who will listen to their stories, and they enjoy talking. It makes me feel good to know that I've made their last years just that much more pleasant. This experience has made me a more compassionate individual. I value the time at the nursing home because of this.

Write a short note telling your future college roommate what to expect from you in the coming year.

Dear Future Roommate,

When it comes to housekeeping I'm a bit of a slob, so expect a little mess. I don't play music very loud, although you may not like my taste in music. I mostly listen to classical or big band music, but I do listen to a few modern groups. When I'm working, I don't like to be interrupted at all. I'm usually drinking a nonalcoholic beverage. I'm a nonsmoker. I'm an evening person who stays up late to work on things, but I also sleep late. The good thing is that I'm very flexible about things. Well, that's essentially me.

In 250 words or less, choose a book or books that have affected you deeply, and explain why.

Recently, I reread two books and in them I found meaning which I had missed the first time. Those books were *1984* and *Brave New World*. When I first read them they had been nothing but stories. When I read them again, they were more than stories; they were biting social commentaries. The books told of two societies with totalitarian governments.

One, *1984*, showed a government that controlled through terror and violence, yet the regime enjoyed wide popular support. Many of its inhabitants didn't know what was going on and were happy to have their lives controlled. Others believed it was all for the best and that the government was doing good. Only a few were against the government, and these were dealt with promptly. This situation has already existed, most notably in Nazi Germany.

The other, *Brave New World*, depicted a society which had rigid genetic classes but which controlled society by making life so enjoyable that hardly anyone wanted to rebel. However, it was just as repressive as the society in *1984*.

That was what scared me about both novels. It would be so easy for modern Americans to become members of societies such as those. These books taught me to appreciate every single right protected by our Constitution. They taught me to be wary of those advocating the limiting of a right for the good of society. They taught me how to be a good citizen.

In 250 words or less, discuss one or two activities that have meant the most to you during your secondary school years.

During my high school years there have been two activities which have meant a great deal to me. One was the Student Council presidency and the other was my volunteer work at a local nursing home.

The Student Council presidency is a wonderful learning experience. I have always assumed the leadership role in classroom group activities, but these roles don't entail true leadership. As Student Council president, I am the leader who sets the agenda, who can make binding policy decisions, and who affects the voting of the council by the simplest variations in speech. The powers that our Student Council constitution gave me brought great responsibility. From this post I learned the value of hard work and of setting a good example.

My volunteer work also helped develop my character. My primary duty at the nursing home is to walk with an elderly woman who requires exercise. While there, I also visit with the residents. It warms my heart to see their eyes light up at my approach. They enjoy my visits because I have time to just sit and listen to their stories. In my own little way I make their last years that much more enjoyable. This volunteer work has made me a compassionate individual who is more attuned to the needs of others.

When both experiences are combined, they join to make me a better person; a person more capable of compassion and of handling responsibility.

What is the most stimulating book or article (other than those you have read for school assignments) that you have read in the last six months? Why do you think it was stimulating?

The most stimulating article I have read in the past six months was "Japanese Tract Rankles Americans" in the November 20 edition of *Insight*. This article dealt with the contents of a book called *The Japan that Can Say 'No,'* written by Akio Morita, founder of the Sony Corporation, and Shintary Ishihara, an ultra-nationalist politician; and the subsequent reactions when a pirated version surfaced in the United States.

The book, according to the article, boiled down to the idea that Japan holds complete economic and technological supremacy in the world and could therefore say no to the United States and world demands. The article also stated that Sony Corporation never intended that the book be read outside of Japan. To say the least, there were some violent reactions in the United States. The article, quite frankly, outraged me. It also made me more interested in our economic relations with Japan and has prompted me to read more on the topic.

Discuss one or two academic interests or out-of-class activities that have meant the most to you.

One interest of mine that has transcended the boundary between academic and out-of-class activities is my violin. I originally began taking private violin lessons at the age of seven. At that age it was a task which had to be done, not enjoyed. I quit after several years of lessons and didn't resume lessons until this year. I found that I had room in my schedule for one more class, and Orchestra was offered that period. I returned to the violin, and now it holds meaning. Every note is a shade of emotion, every piece of music a creation of feelings. I am able to see a beauty to which I was blind before. I now appreciate art and music much more, and I enjoy playing my violin.

Describe what you are like, using information about your most significant accomplishments. Include extracurricular and community activities, awards, hobbies, primary interest, volunteer work, and employment, as well as future plans and goals.

My major extracurricular activity has been to participate annually in regional science fairs and in Junior Academy of Science competitions. I was able to participate in these competitions because for the last three summers I have interned at a medical research laboratory. My projects have not only expanded my knowledge and that of others in that area of medical research, but they have also allowed me to participate at the State Science Fair and at State Junior Academy competitions.

In my sophomore year I was class parliamentarian and a Student Council representative. In my junior year, I was Student Council treasurer, and I am Student Council president this year. Under my guidance, the council has attempted to create institutions, such as a student store, which will help to increase student involvement.

Throughout my high school years, I have organized and supported projects which have encouraged school spirit; such as being co-founder and editor of the school newspaper, which has evolved into a journalism class, and I have also founded and am Vice-President of the school's Bowling Club, which has expanded into a district-wide league. These activities, and my exposure to economics class, have led me to pursue a career in what I perceive to be one of the driving forces of our society: economics.

I have always been interested in the great events of history, especially in the mass movements which have changed the fate of nations and molded our political view. I wish to understand the forces that shape our daily lives, as well as the ones which mold the destinies of our nation's industries and those of the entire world. I wish to understand all of this, not only in its present state but also in its historical context. This will probably require study in areas outside of economics alongside the traditional studies and unrelated courses, but this extra work is welcome and anticipated because of my hunger for knowledge.

To relax after work and school, I have several hobbies. My favorite is to exercise my imagination with creative writing. It invigorates me to create a person from scratch and to define his personality by his words and actions. I also enjoy paper modeling. Paper modeling is just like other types of modeling except that instead of wood or plaster, you're cutting, folding and pasting together paper. I can make planes, boats, buildings and even birds with paper. Finally, if I just don't feel like moving, it's nice just to sit back and read a good book while I listen to classical music. I prefer science-fiction, fantasy, and mystery in my books.

I also find the time to spend a few hours, every weekend, at a local nursing home. I visit with the residents, take some on walks and try to brighten the lives of a few elderly people.

My short-term goals are simple. I want to get into a good college and get a bachelor's degree in economics. Then I want to continue on and get my master's and my doctorate.

For long-range goals I have several choices. I would like to hold a position in the private sector as an economist, or I'd like to become a professor of economics at a university. In the end, I hope to become a well-known authority and advise heads of state on economic policy or even run for office myself. All the while I hope for the usual things such as a wife, children, house, etc. . . . To some, these goals may seem odd and simplistic, but that is what I wish for from deep inside me.

This essay may have made me sound almost angelic, but let me set the record straight. Even I enjoy going out with my friends and often I make minor sacrifices in other areas, such as house cleaning duties, so that I can. That, in brief, is a summary of my major activities. I hope it has been informative, or at least entertaining!

We live in a complex and ever-changing society, yet our family heritage and tradition allow certain values to be maintained. How has your background influenced your personal development and outlook? Is there something special about you as a person you would like the committee to know? Support your statement with experiences you have had.

When I was a small child, the part of my Hispanic background which influenced me most was the concept of the extended family and family loyalty. Most children are lucky if they know their uncles and aunts. Because of my Hispanic tradition, I not only know my aunts and uncles, but also my great-aunts, second and third cousins, and many more. Whenever trouble surfaced, there were many arms to fall back on for support. This family loyalty and the continuity between generations has helped me adjust to changes in my environment due to my mother's increasing physical disability and due to the death of my grandfather. The loyalty I've found in my family has spread into my friendships and made those friendships much closer. I value my heritage and what it has contributed to my life and my personality.

Even though only my mother is Hispanic, I know that I have a heritage rich with legends, such as Don Pedrito Jaramillo and La Llorona; a culture based on a civilization hundreds of years old; and a language whose words carry feelings that can't possibly be conveyed in translation.

Being Hispanic is as much a part of me as being a male, or being an American. That heritage will always be part of my conscious and unconscious mind. That heritage will follow me as I move on to college and grow into adulthood. It will always be a part of me that no one can take away.

Make up a question that is personally relevant to you, state it clearly, and answer it. Feel free to use your imagination.

What is success? Success is such an abstract term, yet so many of us strive for it with a single-minded determination. We fight for success so hard that it drives many to their graves, or, even worse, to living nightmares of substance abuse. It is the driving force in our lives, yet we don't know exactly what it is.

How should we define success? For any normal animal or plant species, it would be survival, but for man it is different. We are thinking animals living in a highly developed, materialistic society. In that context, even survival takes on an ambiguous meaning. Survival could mean breaking even financially or making a meager profit. Survival could also take on its literal meaning of staying alive, or it could mean maintaining one's lifestyle. The definition of survival is different for each and every one of us because we are all individuals.

It is the same with success. Because we are all individuals with different personalities, success means a different thing to each of us. In a society where yearly income is so important, it is reassuring and comforting to a teenager to discover that success is a unique phenomenon for everyone. Here we are trying to set out our life-time goals and adults keep reminding us of the average yearly income of various professions. This just confuses us about the meaning of success. When we discover that success is individual and is measured by our personal satisfaction with our life, then we can truly set realistic goals. The meaning of success is therefore unique for each and every one of us. We, as individuals, are the only ones who must find satisfaction in our own success. We are our own best judges for the meaning of success.

Describe how you have demonstrated leadership ability both in and out of school.

During my high school years there have been two activities which have meant a great deal to me and which serve as examples of my leadership ability. One was the Student Council presidency and the other was my volunteer work at a local nursing home. They have both contributed significantly to my development.

The Student Council presidency is a wonderful learning experience. I have always assumed the leadership role in classroom group activities, but these roles don't entail true leadership. As Student Council president, I am the leader who sets the agenda, who can make binding policy decisions, and who affects the voting of the council by the simplest variations in speech. The powers that our Student Council constitution gave me brought great responsibility. From this post I learned the value of hard work and of setting a good example.

My volunteer work also helped develop my character. My primary duty at the nursing home is to walk with an elderly woman who requires exercise. While there, I also visit with the other residents. Having been influenced by the Hispanic tradition of respecting and revering my elders, it warms my heart to see their eyes light up at my approach. They enjoy my visits because I have time to just sit and listen to their stories. In my own little way, I make their last years that much more enjoyable. This volunteer work has made me a compassionate individual who is more attuned to the needs of others.

When both experiences are combined, they join to make me a better person; a person more capable of compassion and handling responsibility.

We hope you'll use your essay to help us understand your thoughts and feelings about what's important to you. Name three persons whom you admire and respect or who changed your view of life in a deep and significant way.

Three people whom I admire and respect would be my maternal grandfather, my mother, and a former middle school teacher.

I admired my grandfather for many reasons. The first was respectability. He not only deserved respect, he earned and commanded respect from all people.

The second reason was loyalty. He was loyal to his country by serving it in the Navy for thirty years. He was loyal to his family and friends as well.

When I was 11 years old, my grandfather died. It started out like any other day. Grandpa drove me to school and I told him I had remembered the coupons. The day before we had planned to get hamburgers after school, but I had forgotten the coupons. I had remembered them that day and we were going to go out to eat together. Little did I know that when I hugged him and told him goodbye that morning, it would be the last time I would see him alive.

My day at school was going by fast. I couldn't wait to go get hamburgers with Grandpa. Then, a little before noon, my parents came to pick me up. I thought they were taking me out to lunch. Once I was in the car they told me Grandpa had died. He'd gotten home and had a heart attack. I couldn't believe what they were telling me. I kept thinking he would show up and it would all be fine. He never showed up. Grandpa had always told me not to cry at his funeral, so when the time came, I sat there holding in my emotions. I didn't cry for him until months later when I finally accepted that he was dead.

I had never really faced death until that moment. Death had always come to obscure relatives who I didn't know. Now death had taken my Grandpa, who had raised me, who loved me and cherished me. I can't fully describe the emotions that flowed through me. It finally dawned on me that our life on earth is a finite span of time. Grandpa had accomplished much in his lifetime and I saw then that in the short stretch of years I was destined to live through, I needed to accomplish much as well. I finally became motivated to succeed. Even now when I do something, I want to succeed not only for myself, but for my Grandpa. He taught me many things during his life and in death he taught me how to work.

When my mother was three months old, she caught polio. That disease has handicapped her all of her life. Despite it, she struggled and got a college education. Her physical handicap hasn't stopped her from getting involved in numerous groups, such as the Polio Survivors Support Group, and three local and one national writers groups, or from being a City Council appointed member of the Animal Control Advisory Board.

She currently is working part-time as a Research Associate in a medical school. This part-time endeavor will soon cease, as her doctors have strongly advised her to stop working. As an alternative, she has turned to writing. She has published many non-fiction articles and is working on a novel.

Now she is suffering from post-polio muscle syndrome, which means she is facing further neuromuscular deterioration. Everyday tasks are becoming tiresome or impossible and with these restrictions come frustrations.

It is hard to see one you love slowly getting worse. Especially when they refuse your help. I understand she wants to be independent, but it hurts to see her tire from trying. From her struggle I am drawing strength. She has shown me the value of trying. She has shown me that one must never quit, because the more the obstacles, the sweeter the victory. She has implanted within me a drive to succeed that is so powerful it can knock down walls. My mother has become a role model for me.

My mother is a very special woman, no matter what the circumstances. I know that if I ever have a problem, I can come to her and she will force me to rise to the occasion. She has done so much to shape my life. This is why I respect and admire my mother.

Finally, I admire my middle school history teacher. He took me under his wing and taught me the importance of history and the humanities. He never accepted second-best from anyone and was always willing to help his students become more efficient. Never once did he tolerate dishonesty or a lack of integrity in anyone, and he stood up for his ideals no matter what the consequences.

He had an indomitable fighting spirit which especially manifested itself in the end. In my sophomore year, he was diagnosed as having leukemia. He never stopped fighting, but after fighting the Nazis, the North Koreans, and years of unruly students, he finally found an adversary he couldn't beat. He taught me the value of spirit, honesty, integrity and efficiency. I admire the way he lived.

I admire all of these people because they are or were true to themselves, each one epitomizing virtuous characteristics or qualities. I try to emulate them in my everyday life so I might be a better person.

Did these essays give you a better idea of what an essay should say about you?

If you have worries on your mind while you're writing your essays, it's probably best to stop writing for a while and try again when you're feeling more focused. You don't want to sound wishy-washy or indecisive. You want a reader to realize that you know what you want and how to get it. Also, don't worry that your essays sound as if you're giving yourself a pat on the back. They should honestly reflect your talents and achievements. Don't be afraid to mention accomplishments of which you are proud.

Remember to take your time, check your spelling, watch your grammar, and, most important, be yourself. Show a committee that you're a sensitive, humorous, one-of-a-kind type of person, and they'll remember you.

Writing isn't hard; it just takes practice. The first essay you write might seem laborious. By the time you've written four or five essays, however, you'll find that it gets easier and easier. You might even find yourself enjoying it!

CHAPTER 15

UNDERSTANDING FINANCIAL AID

About $30 billion is available annually in the form of grants, loans, and scholarships from colleges, the states, and the federal government. Most Ivy League schools maintain that if students are accepted to their school, there shouldn't be any reason why they can't afford to go. The financial aid officers at these schools work hard to put together attractive financial aid packages. Sounds good, doesn't it? But students and parents must be aware that they both may have to contribute financially to a student's education, and it sometimes happens that students must decline acceptance into their first-choice schools because the school doesn't offer them sufficient financial aid.

Most colleges and universities don't accept students based on whether the student can afford the tuition costs. Many schools use "blind admissions policies," whereby a student is accepted on academic merits alone, and only after acceptance is the financial situation considered.

Though it would be great to know how much financial aid you will qualify for *before* you apply to a given school, it doesn't work that way. Colleges and universities have enough work to do processing financial aid packages for students who are already attending the school without having to determine what every applicant (who may not be accepted) would be eligible to receive.

HOW MUCH FINANCIAL ASSISTANCE WILL YOU NEED?

Not knowing how much you or your parents will have to contribute doesn't mean that you must blindly pick and choose a college or university. Postsecondary institutions ascertain financial need by calculating how much a family can afford to spend on college costs, which is also known as "expected family contribution" (EFC).

In Appendix D you'll find a simplified worksheet you can fill out in order to estimate your expected family contribution. Other similar questionnaires are also available in *Applying for Financial Aid*, a free brochure available from ACT Financial Aid Services, Educational Services Division-11, P.O. Box 168, Iowa City, IA 52243. Ask your guidance counselor if any of these are available at your high school.

BASIS FOR FINANCIAL AID

The lower a family's income, the better its chances of eligibility for financial aid. But that doesn't mean that a family with an income of $50,000 or higher can't receive aid.

Many factors are considered:

- How much was paid in taxes in the previous year?

- What are your family's income and assets?

- How many dependents are in the family?

- How many children in your family are in college?

- Are there special circumstances (change in family/ student income, medical expenses, private primary and/or secondary school tuition)?

- What is the age of the older parent?

HOW IS A FAMILY'S EXPECTED CONTRIBUTION DETERMINED?

In order to determine your expected family contribution, all colleges require that you fill out a Free Application for Federal Student Aid (FAFSA) and either a PROFILE™ Registration Form, the school's financial aid form, or both. If you are a high school senior, you or your parents should ask each college or university you are applying to which forms the institution prefers you to use. If you're already in college, go to the financial aid office and request the financial aid form you're required to use. The information on these forms will be analyzed to determine the type of financial assistance (federal and state grants) you will be qualified to receive.

Whichever form you use—and whether you are a high school senior, a college student, or returning to college—you must submit some type of financial aid form as soon as possible after January 1 prior to the fall semester in which you will need the financial assistance. If you're a high school senior, you can obtain the FAFSA and PROFILE™ Registration Form from your high school counselor. If you're in college or want to return to college, obtain the forms from the financial aid office of the college you are attending or wish to attend. Any student needing financial aid to attend college (during any year in college) must fill out a new form each year.

EXPECTED FAMILY CONTRIBUTION

A family's expected contribution (EFC) stays the same, regardless of the varying costs of tuition and room and board from one college to another. Therefore, if Family 1 is expected to contribute $6,000, and college costs (tuition, room, and board) for one year are $12,000, that family's financial need is $6,000. On the other hand, if the student from Family 1 is applying to a state-supported school

whose cost for one year is $5,000, then Family 1 wouldn't need any extra financial assistance. In contrast, a student from Family 2 whose expected family contribution is $2,000 will need financial assistance at either the $12,000 or the $5,000 school. That student's need varies from $3,000 (for the $5,000 school) to $10,000 (for the $12,000 school).

	Private College		State-Supported College	
	Family 1	Family 2	Family 1	Family 2
College Cost	$12,000	$12,000	$5,000	$5,000
Expected Family Contribution	$ 6,000	$ 2,000	$6,000	$2,000
Financial Need	$ 6,000	$10,000	$0	$3,000

IMPROVING YOUR FINANCIAL AID PACKAGE

Financial aid packages for entering college freshmen are based on the family's financial situation during the student's high school junior year. Therefore, if you'd like to improve your financial aid package, you need to assess your situation during the student's high school sophomore year and implement the changes during the student's high school junior year. There are many ways that families can change their financial aid situation in order to be eligible for more aid, such as:

- Keeping any income from bonuses, capital gains, and other sources as low as possible. If you plan to sell stocks to pay for tuition, sell them before January 1 of the student's junior year.

- Reassessing the value of your assets.

- If you own or work for a small company, converting income money into a business asset by purchasing equipment, or setting up a pension plan.

- Making sure to account for all college expenses—including transportation.

If you think you might not be eligible for aid, some planners suggest you shift assets into your child's name. Though you'll reduce how much you pay in taxes, this move can come back to haunt you. Keep in mind that the government requires that 6 percent of a parent's assets be used toward college costs, while 35 percent of a student's assets must be used.

The higher a family's income, the more strongly we recommend that the family seek a reputable financial planner, as early as possible. If you will need financial assistance in your college freshman year, you and your family should start looking for ways to qualify for more financial aid in the fall of your high school junior year at the latest, because your college financial need will be based on your family's tax information from that year.

College financial planning is a highly effective and specialized method of income and asset management that allows families to benefit from the billions of dollars in financial aid funds available each year. If you're interested in utilizing a financial planner, contact the Certified Financial Planner Board of Standards for a list of reputable financial planners in your area. Or call the Board at (888) 237-6275. You can also drop us a note and a self-addressed, stamped envelope, and we will send you the list of the top tips on how to choose a financial planner.

HOW OUTSIDE SCHOLARSHIPS CAN CHANGE YOUR FINANCIAL NEED

Outside scholarships are scholarships that provide money from clubs, businesses, organizations, and foundations not affiliated with a college or university. How much scholarships can help you reduce you or your family's expected contribution depends on the college or university you are attending.

Some schools deduct the first $500 in outside scholarships from the amount of the student's expected contribution (not the parents' expected contribution). Each subsequent dollar amount provided by an outside scholarship is then split either 50-50 or 60-40, and deducted from what you (not your parents) must contribute and from in-college scholarships. Some colleges will deduct all outside scholarship money won from your expected contribution, which means your hard work in applying for and winning scholarships will pay off!

Outside scholarships won't change parents' expected contribution unless certain conditions are met. If you've been awarded enough outside scholarships to cover full college costs for a year or enough outside scholarship money to cover all the amount of money offered by the college and all of your expected contribution, then your family's expected contribution consists of only your traveling costs and other incidental expenses.

College financial aid officers will appreciate your saving them money. Generally financial aid packages for a student's second and subsequent years may have more loan than the first year. If you save a school money, you might be able to get more free money in your financial aid package during your remaining college years.

BECOMING A SOUGHT-AFTER STUDENT

Being sought after means that you are being wooed to attend a particular college or university. Sought-after status is something you should strive for. The better your grades, class rank, and SAT or ACT scores, the better the chances of getting more gift money (which you don't repay) from a school.

All colleges and universities want to attract National Merit Scholars. Of the million high school seniors who graduate each year, only about 14,000 or less are chosen as National Merit Finalists. They are the students who scored in the top 1 percent on the PSAT. Not all National Merit Finalists receive money from the National Merit Corporation (making the students National Merit Scholars), but since all schools want to claim that they have a certain number of National Merit Finalists in their freshman class, these students are often offered substantial financial aid packages.

Even National Merit Commended students can receive fully paid four-year scholarships from some colleges and universities.

INDEPENDENT STUDENT STATUS

Parents are sometimes under the impression that if they keep their student off their taxes for two or more years, the student is considered an independent student. In fact, parents could have kept their student off their taxes since the student was born and the student would still be a dependent! Parents just aren't getting to use the deduction.

Students are independent if they can answer yes to one of the following government guidelines:

- Are you an orphan or a ward of the court (or were you a ward of the court until age eighteen)?

- Are you married?

- Do you have a legal dependent other than a spouse?

- Are you twenty-four years of age or older?

- Are you enrolled in a graduate or professional school program (beyond a bachelor's degree)?

- Are you a veteran of the U.S. Armed Forces (including students who attended a U.S. military academy but who were released under a condition other than dishonorable)?

If you answered yes to at least one of the six questions, then you are an independent student. If not then you are a dependent student. We all know you can't argue with the federal government. If you are truly independent, there is one alternative. You can appeal to the financial aid officers at each college or university to which you are applying.

Financial aid officers have some leeway and can use their own discretion in determining independent status.

FINANCIAL AID FORMS

The procedures for applying for financial aid recently have been changed. The federal government now requires that students needing financial aid fill out a Free Application for Federal Student Aid (FAFSA) in order to be considered for federal assistance. All graduating high school seniors and undergraduate college students who need financial assistance the following year must file a FAFSA. The information you provide on the FAFSA will be evaluated to determine what your family's expected contribution will be and how much federal assistance you qualify to receive. There is no cost in filing a FAFSA.

Students also must contact the financial aid office of the college or university they are interested in attending and inquire whether they must fill out the PROFILE™ Registration Form, the school's financial aid form, or both.

The PROFILE™ Registration Form is a supplemental form that will indicate a loss in income, as well as other financial indicators. This form is used to determine how much state and/or institutional money, and in some instances how much private scholarship money, the student will receive. There is a charge for filing the form, which is determined by how many schools you request receive the evaluation.

Some colleges don't require the PROFILE™ Registration Form. Whether it will some day become obsolete is unknown at present, so keep in touch with the financial aid office of the college or university you want to attend.

Either alone or with your parents, you should complete all necessary financial forms and send them to the appropriate agencies.

FILING FINANCIAL AID FORMS

You can obtain the FAFSA from your high school counselor, from a college or university, by calling (800) 433-3242 and requesting it from the Department of Education, or by downloading the form from the Department of Education's website at http://www.ed.gov. There are two ways in which to file the FAFSA: You can fill out the form and mail it via the U.S. Post Office, or you can file it on floppy disk via modem.

If you mail the actual FAFSA form, it will take four to six weeks to evaluate the data. If you file it on disk or by modem, it takes three to seven days to

evaluate the data. The latter method is called the FAFSA Express. If you don't have Internet access, you can call (800) 801-0576 and request the FAFSA Express program. If you have Internet access, you can download it from their website. One bit of advice: You might want to log on to the site at night. The Department of Education website is accessed up to 40,000 times a day. This causes the program to download slowly. If you log on at night, it should take a matter of two to five minutes to download the information.

STUDENT AID REPORT (SAR)

After you've submitted the FAFSA, you will receive a Student Aid Report (SAR) within six weeks, or within two weeks if you file the FAFSA Express. The SAR contains the information you reported on the FAFSA and the Expected Family Contribution (EFC).

The SAR will inform you whether or not you qualify for financial assistance from the federal government. It will not tell you how much you can receive because it depends on the cost of education. You might qualify for more aid at a private school with higher tuition costs than at a state-sponsored school. The EFC should be in the upper right corner of the SAR; the letters EFC are followed by a number. Though it doesn't show a dollar sign, that number is how much the family is expected to contribute. The number is in dollars, no cents. The EFC number will be used to determine the type of aid you will receive from the federal government (Pell Grant, Supplemental Educational Opportunity Grant, Work-Study, Subsidized Stafford Loans, or Perkins Loans). For more information on any of these programs, see Chapter 16, "Glossary of Terms."

WHICH COLLEGES SHOULD RECEIVE THE INFORMATION

There is a section in both the FAFSA and the PROFILE™ for you to list which colleges are to receive the evaluations. If, after you've completed the FAFSA and returned the SAR, you decide to apply to other colleges, you must get in touch with the Federal Student Aid Programs and ask to be sent an Additional College Request (ACR) form. If you want more schools to receive the PROFILE™ evaluations, there will be an additional fee.

Once colleges receive your SAR, each college determines how much in federal and state grant money, institutional scholarships, federal student loans, and federal work-study you are eligible to receive. There may be times when colleges will ask for copies of parents' income-tax returns. If this happens, send the information directly to the individual schools requesting the returns, not to the Federal Student Aid Programs.

COLLEGE FINANCIAL AID FORMS

In addition to filling out the FAFSA or PROFILE™, you might also have to fill out financial aid applications at each school you are applying to. When requesting college applications, contact the financial aid offices of the colleges or universities and ask if there are any other forms that need to be filed. You will not be eligible for financial aid until all necessary forms are completed. If you neglect to complete them all, you or your parents may have to take care of the entire cost of tuition for that year without any aid.

SOURCES OF FINANCIAL AID

The money needed to fulfill a student's "financial need" can be obtained from a variety of sources, including federal grants (Pell and SEOG); federal guaranteed loans; federal unsubsidized loans; state grants; grants, scholarships, and loans from within a college; federal work-study jobs; and outside scholarships. Remember, loans are considered financial assistance.

FEDERAL PELL GRANTS

Named after a Rhode Island senator who developed the idea for a grant of this type, the Pell Grant is the most common federal grant for an undergraduate student. The sum of money, which you don't pay back, can vary from $200 to $3,000 or 60 percent of college costs (whichever is lower). The cost of education minus your family's contribution determines the amount of Pell Grant money you are eligible to receive. The difference is your financial need. Since a family's income may vary from year to year, the amount of federal aid you are eligible to receive may also vary.

A student must be enrolled at least half-time (at least twelve semester hours per year, not per semester) and maintain a minimum 2.0 grade point average (GPA) in order to be eligible for the Pell Grant. The Pell Grant is an entitlement grant, which means that if you qualify for a Pell Grant, you are guaranteed to receive that money. If the school has allocated all the Pell Grant money it has received, it requests more money from the federal government in order to meet the needs of its students until all money allocated for Pell Grants is disbursed by the federal government. In order to be considered for state or institutional grants and scholarships, you must apply for a Pell Grant. Schools must be notified as to whether or not you qualify for federal aid before considering you for other types of aid. You must file a FAFSA to receive any other type of financial aid.

The eligibility requirements for a Pell Grant have been loosened by the federal government. Unfortunately, more money wasn't allotted for Pell Grants. Therefore, there are more people qualifying for Pell Grants, but there is no additional money to give. Once all the money has been disbursed by colleges and universities, there is no more Pell Grant money. So apply early or you might lose out!

You must file the FAFSA as early as possible after January before the fall semester in which the funds will be used. Each school knows which students will receive Pell Grant money and how much. Therefore, you may not have to pay the amount of tuition money the Pell Grant will cover. You may file the FAFSA up to June 30 of the academic year in which you will be needing the assistance. If you wait to file your FAFSA until you are registered and attending college classes, you will be reimbursed the amount provided by the Pell Grant, but *only if there is Pell Grant money available at the time.*

Pell Grant money is credited to your account and can either be used to pay on your account or (if all costs have been met) you will receive a refund check from your school.

FEDERAL SUPPLEMENTAL EDUCATIONAL OPPORTUNITY GRANTS (FSEOG)

The amount of SEOG you are awarded can vary from year to year, depending on your family's income. This grant is available only to undergraduate students who have exceptional need. If you received a Pell Grant and you still have unmet need, you will be given priority over other applicants. An SEOG, like the Pell Grant, doesn't have to be paid back. You may receive up to $4,000 per year, depending on your financial need, the amount of other aid you will be receiving, and the availability of FSEOG money at your school. However, unlike the Pell Grant, SEOG money isn't guaranteed. Once a school runs out of the SEOG money allotted to it, students who are eligible won't be able to receive any SEOG money.

FOR MORE FEDERAL GRANT INFORMATION

To find out more about federal grants, send for *The Student Guide.* This free booklet can be requested from: U.S. Department of Education, U.S. Government Printing Office, Washington, D.C. 20402. If you still have questions about student aid, call the Federal Student Aid Information Center at its toll-free number: 1-800-4 FED AID. The office hours are Monday through Friday, from 9:00 A.M. until 5:30 P.M. (Eastern Time).

OTHER SOURCES OF FINANCIAL AID

Ask the colleges where you're applying if they know of any other scholarships available from outside sources (such as clubs, foundations, and private companies). Take the time to write to the department in which you're interested (engineering, journalism, music, agriculture, etc.) and ask if it offers scholarships in its specific area. Many departments do.

While waiting for acceptance letters, or after acceptance, check with banks about special low-

interest loan programs for students or parents who wish to save or borrow for college expenses. Some low-interest and no-interest loan programs are provided in the list of scholarship opportunities in this book.

Federal loans can be obtained directly through some colleges and universities, with some deferment of loans through National Service. A student can work off part of the loan through specific jobs targeted through the National Service Program, which has many such programs currently available. Some colleges and universities still utilize banks, credit unions, and savings and loans in providing student loans.

FEDERAL STAFFORD LOANS

There are now two types of Stafford loans: Direct Stafford Loans and Federal Family Education Loans (FFEL). Direct Stafford Loan funds are lent to you directly by the U.S. government. FFEL Stafford Loan funds are lent to you through banks, credit unions, or other lenders that participate in the FFEL Program.

Direct and FFEL Stafford Loans are either subsidized or unsubsidized. A subsidized loan is based on your financial need. The interest the loan accrues while you are in college or during a deferment period is subsidized by the government. An unsubsidized loan is not based on financial need. You will be responsible for the interest while you are in school and this will increase the amount of money you owe. You can choose to repay the loan interest while you are in college, which means that what you actually pay will be lower. With the Unsubsidized Stafford Loan, *there is no qualifying by income.* Any student may apply for an Unsubsidized Stafford Loan, regardless of the student's or parents' income.

If you are a first-year college or vocational/technical school student, you can borrow up to $2,625 per year in total Stafford Loans. If you have been approved for only $1,000 from the Subsidized Stafford Loan program, then you may also borrow $1,625 from the Unsubsidized Stafford Loan program to increase your total loan to $2,625. If you've been denied a Subsidized Stafford Loan, you may borrow up to $2,625 from the Unsubsidized Stafford Loan program.

Undergraduate sophomores can borrow up to $3,500, juniors and seniors may borrow up to $5,500, and graduate students may borrow up to $8,500. Once again, if you've been granted any amount up to the maximum in a Subsidized Stafford Loan, you can borrow the remainder from the Unsubsidized Stafford Loan program. If you've been denied a Subsidized Federal Stafford Loan, you may borrow up to the maximum from the Unsubsidized Federal Stafford Loan program.

You should begin the application procedure for a Federal Stafford Loan as soon as you've received your acceptance to the college of your choice. Obtain an application from a bank, credit union, savings and loan, your school, or your state guaranty agency. (See Chapter 18, "Where to Go for State and Federal Help.")

FEDERAL PERKINS LOANS

A Perkins Loan is a low-interest loan (through a college or university) available to first-time undergraduate students who have exceptional financial need. Once again, Pell Grant recipients are given priority. Qualified students may borrow up to $3,000 for each undergraduate year (up to $15,000 total) and $5,000 for each year of graduate or professional school study.

You are expected to begin repaying your Federal Perkins Loan after a certain amount of time, or "grace period," has elapsed. If you're attending school at least half-time (twelve semester or eighteen quarter hours per year), you have up to nine months after graduation, after you leave school. If you're attending school less than half-time, the grace period varies. You should contact your financial aid officer for more information. You have up to ten years to repay the loan, but there are cancellation provisions. If a student enters teaching or law enforcement, a portion of the Federal Perkins Loans will be canceled.

FEDERAL PARENT LOANS (PLUS)

Federal Parent Loans for Undergraduate Students (PLUS) allow parents with good credit to borrow money for each child enrolled in college at least half-time. Parents receiving first-time loans on or after July 1, 1993, may borrow up to the amount needed for a child's cost of education minus any other financial aid the student is receiving.

Holders of PLUS loans must begin repaying the principal and interest within sixty days after the loan payment is sent to their parents or to the college. Students may defer payment of the principal until graduation or leaving school. Deferments are sometimes granted to parents, but they are more limited than those granted to students.

DON'T FORGET

Be sure to fill out financial aid applications completely. Some reasons why financial aid is rejected or delayed are as simple as no signature on the form, no Social Security number on the form, or incorrect information. Make sure the forms are completed and mailed by the due date. See Chapter 19 for the Top Ten Financial Aid Mistakes.

FINANCIAL AID PACKAGES

High school seniors usually receive financial aid awards from colleges during March and April. Students who are already in college will receive them later, even as late as the summer.

If you haven't heard from the financial aid office at the college you will be (or are) attending by the end of May, call the college's financial aid office. If the office is still working on the awards, it could be a couple of weeks before the award letters are sent. If you haven't received word by the end of June, call again. If the end of July arrives and you haven't been notified, call every two weeks. It's important for you and your parents to keep on top of your financial aid situation, because once registration starts you and/or your parents might have to resort to taking out a loan in order to cover tuition and other costs.

Once you've received your financial aid package, take the time to fill in the Financial Assistance Analysis Chart in Appendix D. This chart provides an easy way to compare packages from different colleges and universities.

Once the financial aid packages are offered, if you know that you or your parents will be unable to contribute as much tuition as is expected by the college, call the financial aid office. Explain your situation to the financial aid officer and see if your federal grants and/or loans, school grants and/or loans, or student loans can be increased. There are a few things to remember when doing this:

1. Always write down the name of the person with whom you spoke so you can ask for him or her by name the next time you call. This ensures that the person you deal with will know the details of your file. It's not unheard of to talk to ten different people within a financial aid office and receive ten different answers to a question.

2. Students or parents calling the financial aid office should have as much documentation on hand as possible. A student might have to provide details proving that a parent has lost his or her job, that a divorce has occurred and has altered the family finances, that a parent has suffered an injury that has diminished earnings, or that a sibling has suddenly decided to return to college, causing additional financial strains on the family.

3. Keep in mind that although some colleges have some leeway in how much they can change a financial aid package, there isn't much flexibility here. If, however, the student was offered a greater amount of money by a comparable school, then a financial aid officer might match that offer, assuming the student is sought after (see explanation earlier in this chapter).

When evaluating aid packages, be sure to be thorough, but don't take so long that the deadline slips by for accepting the college's offer. Compare your offers carefully so you can start college knowing you've made the best choice.

CHAPTER 16

____ GLOSSARY OF TERMS ____

Academic Year The time in which a full-time student is expected to complete the equivalent of two semesters, two trimesters, or three quarters at a college, university, vocational, or technical school.

Accreditation Type of approval given to schools that have fulfilled certain requirements set by the state, federal government, or a recognized accrediting agency. Students who attend a nonaccredited school will not qualify for federal or state aid and sometimes not even for scholarships.

American College Testing Program (ACT) A company (based in Iowa City, Iowa) that offers national testing. Used primarily in the central and southern United States. This company currently holds the federal contract to evaluate the FAFSA.

Appeal Procedures Procedures that follow the request by a student for the college Financial Aid Officer (FAO) to reevaluate a student's financial aid eligibility or awards. Some of the reasons for an appeal may include: loss of a parent's job, ill health of a parent, death of a parent, a student's or parent's request to change the self-help (the money the student is expected to contribute from savings, summer earnings, student loans, or a work-study job), mix-up in a financial aid package, or any reason the school should reconsider a student's financial aid package because of additional information that wasn't previously available.

Assets Assets may vary from the money in checking and savings accounts or investments (money market funds, certificates of deposit, stocks, bonds, trust funds) to the value of boats and real estate. Homes and family farms or ranches are no longer considered assets when determining financial need. Cars usually aren't considered assets by the federal government or by a college; neither are possessions such as stamp collections, antiques, or musical instruments. Usually, only net assets of no more than 12 percent are considered (in evaluating financial need) after deducting money earmarked for retirement purposes. Some schools may make additional adjustments in their assessment of a family's finances to offset gross income, parental salaries, or other primary income sources. A school may choose not to allow income shelters, tax write-offs, or secondary or passive income sources (second or summer homes, rental property, real estate for sale, alimony, business income, capital gains, pensions, annuities, unemployment, or Social Security) to be deducted from earned income and could possibly consider that income as an asset.

Campus-Based Financial Aid Program Financial aid programs (primarily federally funded programs) administered by postsecondary institutions (colleges and universities). Some examples include Federal Perkins Loans, Federal Supplemental Educational Opportunity Grants (SEOG), and Federal College Work-Study Programs.

Citizen/Eligible Noncitizen In order to be eligible to receive federal aid, a student must be a U.S. citizen, a U.S. national (native of American Samoa or Swain's Island), or a U.S. permanent resident with an Alien Registration Receipt Card. If a student does not fall into one of these categories, he or she must inquire about his or her eligibility for financial assistance from a college or outside scholarship.

College Board   A nonprofit organization (based in Princeton, New Jersey) that administers the SAT and the College Scholarship Service (CSS). A student submits the PROFILE™ Registration Form to the CSS for analysis to determine financial need.

College Scholarship Service (CSS)   A service performed by a subsidiary of the College Board that evaluates a student's financial need based on the information submitted on the PROFILE™ Registration Form by the student or parent.

College Work Study (CWS)   A federal program, open to both undergraduate and graduate students, that provides limited funding to create on- and off-campus jobs for financially disadvantaged students. For a student to be eligible, the amount he or she earns cannot exceed the level of financial need as determined by the financial aid forms. Each school sets its own deadlines for applying for CWS. Undergraduates are paid by the hour; graduates are paid by the hour or may receive a salary. All students are paid at least monthly.

Conditional Awards   Any award (grant, scholarship, or loan) that requires additional documents (such as a tax statement) be provided to the school before the award goes into effect. Conditional awards may be modified or withdrawn if the information on the documentation varies from information previously provided on the PROFILE™ Registration Form.

Congressional Methodology (CM)   A federal guideline, developed by Congress and revised in 1992, used by most colleges and universities to determine how much a student seeking financial aid must contribute toward his or her college education.

Cost of Education   The total amount it will cost a student to go to school (including tuition, room, board, books, transportation, miscellaneous fees, and other expenses).

Default   A student's failure to repay a student loan and to abide by the rules of the loan contract the student must sign. If the loan is a federally funded one, the IRS may withhold the family's or the student's income tax refund until the loan is paid.

Deferment Loan   Repayment of loans often can be deferred by a student until he or she has the financial resources to begin repaying. Most loan payments are deferred until the student is no longer a full-time student, with the payment schedule usually beginning six to nine months after the student has stopped his or her education. Student loans can sometimes be canceled if certain requirements set by the lending institution are met. For information on these requirements, contact your lending institution.

Emergency Loans   Short-term loans available to enrolled students to meet an emergency or unexpected expense, such as high book costs, or purchase of expensive equipment (architectural or drawing supplies, etc.), or for living expenses until a grant, stipend, or scholarship is paid to the school. Can't be used to pay the student's tuition bill. Loans may range from $50 to $500 and are usually interest-free but must be repaid by a certain date. Overdue loans can accrue interest charges.

Enrollment Status   Describes a student's course/credit hour load at a college. A student must have at least half-time enrollment status in order to qualify for student aid. If a full-time student is awarded $1,000, a three-quarter student receives $750, and a half-time student receives $500.

Expected Family Contribution (EFC)   The amount that parents and/or the student can reasonably be expected to pay for a postsecondary education. Determined by an evaluation of the family's financial data by the Free Application for Federal Student Aid (FAFSA).

Federal Parent Loans for Undergraduate Students (FPLUS)   *see* Parent Loans for Undergraduate Students (PLUS).

Federal Pell Grant   *see* Pell Grant.

Federal Perkins Loans   *see* Perkins Loan.

Federal Stafford Loans   *see* Stafford Loans.

Federal Supplemental Education Opportunity Grants (FSEOF) *see* Supplemental Education Opportunity Grants (SEOG).

Federal Work Study *see* College Work Study and Work-Study Job.

Financial Aid Officer (FAO) An individual at an educational institution responsible for preparing and communicating information pertaining to student loans, grants, scholarships, and employment programs, as well as for advising, awarding, reporting, counseling, and performing office functions related to student financial aid.

Financial Aid Package The combination of many types of financial aid commonly put together by most schools. May vary from school to school, but most incorporate student loans, self-help, scholarships, and grants.

Financial Need Each family's unique financial situation, evaluated individually. Based on family income, assets, number of dependents in the family, number of dependents in college, medical expenses, etc. There is no bottom line of family income that must be met in order to ascertain financial need, so it's always worth the effort to apply for federal financial assistance and have your family's circumstances evaluated.

Free Application for Federal Student Aid (FAFSA) The new federal form that all undergraduate students needing financial assistance to attend college must file. This form will evaluate the student's and parents' income and assets and determine whether a student is eligible for federal assistance. There is no cost in filing this form.

Grant A type of federal, state, or school financial aid award that is "free money"—which the student doesn't have to repay. Students must contact the financial aid office of the school they want to attend or their current high school counselor in order to obtain the necessary forms to apply for this money.

Guaranteed Student Loans (GSL) Federally sponsored loans administered by private lending institutions (banks, savings and loans, and credit unions). Insured by the federal government or by a state guarantee agency. Repayment of the loan and interest begins six months after the student leaves school or graduates. The student may have from five to ten years to repay the loan, depending on the amount borrowed. *See also* Stafford Loans.

Independent Student Status Students may request that colleges or universities accept them as financially independent of their parents for financial aid purposes. Some schools don't allow independent status unless the student is an orphan or a ward of the court, is in a bad family situation, is at least twenty-four years old, is a veteran of the U.S. Armed Forces, is married, has a child, or is a graduate or a professional school student.

Loan A type of financial aid award that must be repaid by a student or parent over a specified amount of time, usually after the student has graduated or has left school. Some loans don't start accruing interest until the student graduates or leaves school. A Perkins Loan is borrowed from, and must be repaid to, the university. Stafford and PLUS (Parent Loan for Undergraduate Students) Loans are offered through lending institutions and are repaid to the institution.

Parental Contribution The same as Expected Family Contribution. Using the income of the year prior to the year when financial assistance will be needed (i.e., 1992 if applying for 1993–1994), the Congressional Methodology (CM) determines the available income that can be used by a student or parents for a student's college education based on parents' income and assets. The CM takes the following items into consideration: federal and FICA, estimated state and local taxes; work expenses of both parents (or of one parent, in the case of a single-parent household); medical expenses not covered by insurance; elementary and secondary private school tuition (usually only up to a certain limit); and basic living expenses (rent/mortgage, food, clothing, transportation, insurance, etc.). The allowable basic living expenses are determined using a federally determined guideline and are based on the size of the family and the number of dependents in college. The parental contribution may be appealed (at the college financial aid office) if special circumstances arise (such as loss of a parent's job, a parent's ill health, or death of a parent).

Parental–Leave Deferment The period of time (usually up to six months) that loan payments can be postponed if a borrower is pregnant or is taking care of a newborn or a newly adopted child and cannot be attending school. During this time of deferment, the student (new parent) must be unemployed. To find out about other types of deferments, contact the lending institution from which the money was borrowed.

Parent Loan Plan (PLP) The PLP is a type of loan available to parents whose credit is good enough to qualify for the loan.

Parent Loans for Undergraduate Students (PLUS) PLUS loans are available to parents of undergraduate students. Parents may borrow up to the total amount needed for a child's cost of education minus any other financial aid the student is receiving (taking into account that some degrees take five years to complete), from a bank, a credit union, or a savings-and-loan association. There are no deadlines for applying, but parents should apply well in advance of the semester for which the money will be needed. Interest on PLUS loans disbursed on or after October 1, 1992, is variable but cannot exceed 10 percent. Repayment of a PLUS loan begins within sixty days of the disbursement of funds. The college or university's financial aid officer must certify the student's enrollment and eligibility for a PLUS loan. A lender (bank, credit union, etc.) then makes the loan. The lender and the federal government will collect from parents who default on the loan, typically through the IRS. Limited deferments are available for PLUS loans, but they apply only to the principal, not to the interest, owed. Repayment cancellation is considered only in the case of total permanent disability or death.

Pell Grant A federally funded program for undergraduate students. A student must submit a Free Application for Federal Student Aid (FAFSA) in order to qualify. The amounts range up to a maximum $2,300 per year. Students must apply in the spring before the funds will be needed, though students may apply up until June 30 of the academic year in which funds were needed. A student receives payment by submitting a Student Aid Report (SAR) to the school of his or her choice by the deadline given on the form. When a student is awarded a federal grant, the money is applied to the student's account. If there is a balance owing on the student's tuition bill, the amount is deducted and any remaining funds are given to the student. If the student owes nothing to the school, the grant money is refunded to the student.

Perkins Loan This federal loan program (formally called the National Direct Student Loan) is open to both undergraduate and graduate students. It is a loan from the federal government that must be repaid directly to the school. It has a 5 percent interest rate, and repayment must begin nine months after the student stops being a full-time student. This loan can be deferred for up to three years for military service, Peace Corps work, or other such service work or if the student is still a half-time student. Under certain conditions, loan repayment may be canceled.

PROFILE™ Registration Form The form that some colleges and universities require the student and parent to fill out in addition to the FAFSA. The PROFILE™ form can be obtained from high school counselors or college financial aid offices, and is evaluated by the College Scholarship Service (CSS).

Promissory Note This is the contract you sign when you receive a student loan. The student should carefully read this document and save it, since it contains the conditions under which the money was borrowed.

Satisfactory Academic Progress This term describes a student who is making measurable progress toward the completion of a course of study. Financial aid is revoked if the student is not making satisfactory progress.

Scholarship A type of financial aid that is free money—that is, it is not a loan and need not be repaid. Students may automatically be nominated (as in the case of National Merit Scholars—who are selected by their PSAT and SAT scores) or they may need to request an application. A student doesn't have to repay a scholarship but must fulfill all requirements (academic, extracurricular, athletic, or essay) to be awarded the scholarship. If the scholarship is renewable, the student may have to maintain a certain grade point average (GPA) in order to continue to receive it.

Scholastic Assessment Test (SAT)   Formerly called the Scholastic Aptitude Test, it is a test that students may take as early as middle school but that is used for college acceptance only when the student is either a junior or senior in high school. The SAT contains a verbal section and a math section. In each section the top score is 800, making a combined possible score of 1600.

Self-Help Funds   Funds such as loans and work-study jobs borrowed or earned by a student. These funds must be used to further her or his education.

Stafford Loans   These loans are open to both undergraduate and graduate students. If your loan was disbursed to the school on or after October 1, 1992, and you had no unpaid federal student loans, the interest rate is variable, but cannot be higher than 9 percent. If your loan was before October 1, 1992, check with the lender for the interest rate. Various lenders (banks, credit unions, etc.) may make this loan. There is no deadline for applying, but students should apply as soon as possible after acceptance into a college and after they have received their financial aid package. Students must sign a promissory note, agreeing to repay the loan. The lender or the federal government will collect any unpaid loan balance from students who default by garnishing wages or by taking any federal income tax refunds they are due. Under certain conditions, the loan may be deferred. Loan repayment can be canceled only in the event of a student's total and permanent disability or death.

Student Budget   The amount of money a typical undergraduate student, attending college on a full-time basis, who is unmarried, financially dependent on his or her parents, and has dorm or off-campus living expenses will need each academic year. Actual costs will vary from school to school but will include tuition, room and board, books and supplies, personal expenses, travel allowance, and freshman or transfer orientation fees. The transportation allowance is based on two trips per academic year for United States residents and one trip per year for foreign students and will vary depending on the student's place of permanent residence.

Student Certification   Also called Statement of Educational Purpose and State of Registration Status. A document signed by a student financial aid applicant indicating that all information submitted for aid is true and complete and that he or she has fulfilled registration requirements for the aid program.

Supplemental Education Opportunity Grants (SEOG)   The Federal SEOG is "free money" for undergraduate students with financial need, with priority given to Pell Grant recipients. This grant is funded by the federal government but administered by the school the student attends. A student must apply early because once the funds are exhausted, no more are available for that year. A student can receive from $400 to $4,000 per academic year, depending on financial aid funds available at each school. Schools set the deadlines for applying. Awards are paid either directly to the school or directly to the student.

Transcript   The record kept by a school that lists all classes taken and the grades received by a student. If an official transcript is required by a college or scholarship committee, the transcript must show the school seal on one of its pages and must bear an *original* signature from a school official.

Work-Study Job   Most financial aid recipients can expect to have employment as part of the financial aid package offered by schools. Most financial aid recipients should expect to work anywhere from ten to twenty hours a week, but students are not encouraged to work more than twelve. Most students work on campus in various university departments, offices, cafeterias, or in the school library, but some work off-campus at jobs like waiter or bartender. A work-study job counts toward the self-help requirement.

CHAPTER 17

ADITIONAL SOURCES OF INFORMATION

We suggest that you send for all the free information you would like to receive, then look for the books at your school or public libraries, at nonprofit foundation libraries (contact the foundations listed in this book about these), or at your local bookstore before purchasing other books directly from the organization. Prices are subject to change. Many students and parents will find useful information in these books.

$27.95 Allied Health Education Directory
American Medical Association
P.O. Box 10946
Chicago, IL 60610

$99.75 Annual Register of Grant Support
National Register Publishing Co.
3004 Glenview Road
Wilmette, IL 60091

Free Applying for Financial Aid
College Board
45 Columbus Avenue
New York, NY 10023-6992
(800) 323-7155

$14.95 Arco College Financial Aid Annual
Arco Test Preparation & Career Guides
Macmillan Publishing Co.
201 West 103rd Street
Indianapolis, IN 46290

Free Army College Fund
U.S. Army Department of Defense
620 Central Avenue
Federal Center Building "R"
Alameda, CA 95401

Free Association on Handicapped Student Service Programs in Post-Secondary Education
P.O. Box 21192
Columbus, OH 43221
(614) 488-4972 (Voice/TDD)

$5.95 Bear's Guide to Finding Money for College
Ten Speed Press
P.O. Box 7123
Berkeley, CA 94707
(510) 845-8414 or (800) 841-2665

$21.95 Chronicle Student Aid Annual
Chronicle Guidance Publications, Inc.
P.O. Box 1190
Moravia, NY 13118
(315) 497-6657 or (800) 622-7284

Contact for current price College Blue Book: Scholarships, Fellowships, Grants & Loans
Simon & Schuster Publishing Co.
1230 Avenue of the Americas
New York, NY 10020
(212) 698-7000
http://www.simonandschuster.com

$21.00 College Cost Planner
Capitol Information Publishers
P.O. Box 18623
Washington, DC 20077-2617

Free College Costs Today
New York Life Insurance Company
51 Madison Avenue
New York, NY 10010

$6.00 College Planning/Search Book
American College Testing Program
P.O. Box 168
Iowa City, IA 52243
(319) 337-1410

Free	Compendium of Texas Colleges and Financial Aid Calendar Minnie Stevens Piper Foundation in San Antonio, TX (available only to Bexar County, Texas, students through their high school counselor)	$10.00 for non-members	Fellowships & Grants of Interest to Historians American Historical Association 400 A Street, S.E. Washington, DC 20003
$6.00	Directory for the Arts Center for Arts Information 152 W. 42nd Street New York, NY 10036	$2.50	Financial Aid Association of American Colleges 1818 R Street, N.W. Washington, DC 20009
$84.50 + 10% shipping and handling	Directory of Biomedical and Health Care Grants The Oryx Press 4041 North Central, Suite 700 Phoenix, AZ 85012-3397	Contact for current price	Financial Aid and Disabled Students Newsletter Health Resource Center National Clearinghouse on Post-Secondary Education for Individuals with Disabilities One Dupont Circle, N.W., Suite 670 Washington, DC 20036-1193 (202) 939-9320 (202) 833-4760 Fax health@ace.nche.edu
$17.95 + $2.00 shipping and handling	Directory of College Athletics (Men) Collegiate Directories P.O. Box 450640 Cleveland, OH 44145 (216) 835-1172		
$12.95 + $2.00 shipping and handling	Directory of College Athletics (Women) Collegiate Directories P.O. Box 450640 Cleveland, OH 44145 (216) 835-1172	Free	Financial Aid for Texas Students Texas Higher Education Coordinating Board Division of Student Services P.O. Box 12788, Capitol Station Austin, TX 78711 (check Chapter 18 for each state's address for similar information)
Free	Educational Awards Handbook The Rotary Foundation of Rotary International 1600 Ridge Avenue Evanston, IL 60201	$45.95	Financial Aids Catalog for Higher Education Wm. C. Brown Publishers 2460 Kerper Boulevard Dubuque, IA 52001 (319) 588-1451 or (800) 338-5578
$5.00	Educational Financial Aids American Association of University Women 2401 Virginia Avenue, N.W. Washington, DC 20009	Free	Financial Aid to Education Knights of Columbus 1 Columbus Plaza New Haven, CT 06507
$3.75	Federal Benefits for Veterans and Dependents Superintendent of Documents P.O. Box 371954 Pittsburgh, PA 15250	$1.00	Financial Assistance for Library Education American Library Association Library Education Office for Library Personnel Resources 50 East Huron Street Chicago, IL 60611
Free	Federal Funds to Minority Students Pursuing Science Careers Director, MARC Program NIGMS, Room 9a-18 Westwood Building Bethesda, MD 20205	$26.00	Foundation Grants to Individuals The Foundation Center 79 5th Avenue, 8th Floor New York, NY 10003
$5.00	Fellowships & Grant Opportunities of Interest to Philosophers American Philosophical Association University of Delaware Newark, DE 19716	$6.00	Grants and Awards Available to American Writers PEN American Center 568 Broadway New York, NY 10012

$17.00 | Guide to California Foundations
Northern California Grantmakers
334 Kearny Street
San Francisco, CA 94108

Free | Health Educational Assistance Loan
U.S. Office of Education
U.S. Bureau of Student Financial
Assistance
Washington, DC 20202

Free | Helping Hand
American Medical Association
535 N. Dearborn Street
Chicago, IL 60610

$8.00 | Higher Education Opportunities for
Minorities & Women
Superintendent of Documents
U.S. Government Printing Office
Washington, DC 20402-9325
(request document #065-000-
00252-3)

$4.95 | How to Put Your Children Through
College Without Going Broke
National Institute of Business
Management, Inc.
1328 Broadway
New York, NY 10001
(212) 971-3300

Free | International Brotherhood of Teamsters
Scholarship Fund
25 Louisiana Avenue, N.W.
Washington, DC 20001

$7.00 | Internship Programs for Women
Kathryn L. Mulligan
National Society for Internships &
Experiential Education
3509 Haworth Drive, Suite 207
Raleigh, NC 27609

$3.00 | Journalism Career and Scholarship
Guide
The Newspaper Fund
P.O. Box 300
Princeton, NJ 08543-0300

Free | Minority Fellowship Program Aimed at
Supporting Education Opportunities
in Psychology
American Psychological Association
1200 17th Street, N.W.
Washington, DC 20036

Contact for current price | National Contests and Activities
Advisory List of National Contests &
Activities
National Association of Secondary
School Principals
1904 Association Drive
Reston, VA 22091
(request #210-8788)

$24.95 | National Directory of Grants and Aid to
Individuals in the Arts
Washington International Arts Letter
P.O. Box 12010
Des Moines, IA 50312

Free | National Information Center for
Children and Youth with Disabilities
7926 Jones Branch Drive, Suite 1100
McLean, VA 22102
(800) 999-5599

$3.00 | "Need a Lift?"
The American Legion
National Emblem Sales
P.O. Box 1055
Indianapolis, IN 46206

$7.95 | Pay Your Way Through College (The
Smart Way)
Banbury Book/Putnam Publishing
Group
200 Madison Avenue
New York, NY 10016
(212) 951-8400 or (800) 631-8571

Free | Profiles of Financial Assistance
Programs
Public Health Service
5600 Fishers Lane
Rockville, MD 20857

$14.95 | ROTC Scholarship, Army
74D Harmon Gym
UC Berkeley
Berkeley, CA 94720

$12.50 | Scaling the Ivy Wall, 12 Steps to College
Admission
Little, Brown & Co.
1271 Avenue of the Americas
New York, NY 10020
(212) 522-8068 or (800) 343-9204

Free | Scholarship Pamphlet for USN-USMC-
USCG Dependent Children
Commander, Naval Military Personnel
Command
NMPC-121D
Navy Department
Washington, DC 20370-5121

$10.45	Scholarships and Loans in Nursing Education National League for Nursing 10 Columbus Circle New York, NY 10019 (request publication #41-1964)
$80.00	Scholarships, Fellowships & Loans Bellman Publishing Co. P.O. Box 34937 Bethesda, MD 20817 (301) 897-0033
Contact for current price	Selected Information Resources on Scholarships, Fellowships, Grants and Loans National Referral Center Science and Technology Division 10 First Street, S.E. Washington, DC 20540
Free	Selected List of Fellowship Opportunities and Aids to Advanced Education for US Citizens & Foreign Nationals Publications Office The National Science Foundation 1800 G Street, N.W. Washington, DC 20550
$1.25	Student Financial Aid: Speech-Language Pathology and Audiology American Speech and Hearing Association Attn: Publication Sales 10801 Rockville Pike Rockville, MD 20852
$4.50	The College Financial Aid Emergency Kit Davis, Bob and Kennedy P.O. Box 368-II Cardiff, CA 92007

Free	The National Commission for Cooperative Education 300 Huntington Avenue Boston, MA 02115
$18.95	The Public Ivys Viking Press 375 Hudson Street New York, NY 10014 (212) 366-2000 or (800) 331-4624
$11.55	The Résumé Catalog: 200 Damn Good Examples Yana Parker—author Ten Speed Press P.O. Box 7123 Berkeley, CA 94707 (tax not included) (510) 845-8414 or (800) 841-2665
Free	The Student Guide—Five Federal Financial Aid Programs U.S. Department of Education U.S. Government Printing Office Washington, DC 20402 (call 1 (800) 4 FED AID to request a copy)
$8.20	The Vista College Money Book for Hispanics VISTA Magazine 999 Ponce de Leon Boulevard, Suite #600 Coral Gables, FL 33134
Free	United Negro College Fund, Inc. 500 East 62nd Street New York, NY 10021
Free info about loans	USA Funds Loan Information Services M.C. 5704 P.O. Box 50437 Indianapolis, IN 46209-5096
Free	U.S. Public Health Service 200 Independence Avenue, S.W. Washington, DC 20201

CHAPTER 18

WHERE TO GO FOR STATE AND FEDERAL HELP

These agencies should have information about or have responsibility for most state student aid programs. State agencies generally don't have information about health-profession programs, minority programs, veterans' assistance, or National Guard programs (for information about National Guard programs, write to the State Adjutant General; address is in your local or state capital's telephone directory).

Alabama

Student Assistance Program
Alabama Department of Education
P.O. Box 30201
Montgomery, AL 36130-2101
(334) 242-9700
http://www.alsde.edu/

Alaska

Alaska Commission on Post-Secondary Education
3030 Vintage Boulevard
Juneau, AK 99801-7109
(907) 465-2962
http://www.state.ak.us/acpe

Arizona

Commission on Postsecondary Education
2020 N. Central Avenue, Suite 275
Phoenix, AZ 85004-4503
(602) 229-2591
(602) 229-2599 Fax
http://www.acpe.asu.edu/
toni@www.acpe.asu.edu

Arkansas

Department of Higher Education
1220 West Third Street
Little Rock, AR 72201
(501) 371-1441
(800) 443-6030
(501) 682-1258 Fax
http://www.state.ar.us./kidz/college.html

California

Student Aid Commission
P.O. Box 419026
Rancho Cordova, CA 95741-9027
(916) 526-7590
(916) 526-8002 Fax
http://www.csac.ca.gov/about.html

Colorado

Colorado Commission on Higher Education
1300 Broadway, 2nd Floor
Denver, CO 80203
(303) 866-2723
http://www.state.co.us/cche-dir/hecche.html

Connecticut

Student Financial Assistance Commission
Department of Higher Education
61 Woodland Street
Hartford, CT 06105
(860) 947-1800
(860) 947-1310 Fax
http://ctdhe.commnet.edu/dheweb/default.htm

Delaware

Delaware Postsecondary Education Commission
State Office Building
820 North French Street
Wilmington, DE 19801
(302) 577-3240
(800) 292-7935
(302) 577-6765 Fax
http://www.doe.state.de.us/high-ed/index.htm
mlaffey@state.de.us

District of Columbia

Office of Postsecondary Education
2100 Martin L. King Jr. Avenue, S.E., Suite 401
Washington, DC 20020
(202) 727-3688
http://www.ci.washington.dc.us/

Florida

Student Financial Assistance Commission
255 Collins Building
Tallahassee, FL 32399-0400
(850) 488-4095
(888) 827-2004 Hotline
(850) 488-3612 Fax
http://www.firn.edu/doe

Georgia

Georgia Student Finance Commission
2082 East Exchange, Suite 200
Tucker, GA 30084
(770) 414-3000
(800) 776-6878 (in-state)
http://www.gsfc.org/

Hawaii

Department of Education
P.O. Box 2360
Honolulu, HI 96804
(808) 733-9124
http://www.k12.hi.us/

Idaho

State Board of Education
P.O. Box 83720
Boise, ID 83720-0027
(208) 332-6800
http://www.sde.state.id.us/dept/

Illinois

State Scholarship Commission
4 West Old Capitol Plaza, Room 500
Springfield, IL 62701-1214
(217) 782-2551
(217) 782-8548 Fax
(217) 524-3494 TDD
http://www.isbe.state.il.us/

Indiana

State Student Assistance Commission
150 W. Market Street
Indianapolis, IN 46204
(317) 232-2350
http://www.state.in.us/ssaci/
grants@ssaci.state.in.us

Iowa

College Student Aid Commission
200 10th Street, 4th Floor
Des Moines, IA 50309-2036
(515) 281-3501
(800) 383-4222
http://www.iowaccess.org/
icsac@max.state.ia.us

Kansas

Kansas Department of Education
120 S.E. 10th Avenue
Topeka, KS 66612-1182
(785) 296-3201
http://www.ksbe.state.ks.us/
tlowe@smtpgw.ksbe.state.ks.us

Kentucky

Council on Postsecondary Education
1024 Capital Center Drive, Suite 320
Frankfort, KY 40601
(502) 573-1555
http://www.kheaa.state.ky.us
lindarobinson@mail.state.ky.us

Louisiana

Louisiana Department of Education
626 North 4th Street
P.O. Box 94064
Baton Rouge, LA 70804-9064
(504) 342-4411
http://www.doe.state.la.us/
webteam@mail.doe.state.la.us

Maine

Division of Higher Education Services
Department of Education & Cultural Services
23 State House
Augusta, ME 04333
(207) 289-2183
(207) 623-3263
(800) 228-3734
http://www.state.me.us/education

Maryland

State Scholarship Administration
16 Francis Street
Annapolis, MD 21401-1781
(410) 974-5370
(800) 735-2258 TDD
http://www.msde.state.md.us/
ssamail@mhec.state.md.us

Massachusetts

Board of Higher Education
One Ashburton Place, Room 1401
Boston, MA 02108-1696
(617) 727-7785
(617) 727-6397 Fax
http://www.mass.edu/
bhe@bhe.mass.edu

Massachusetts Office of Student Financial Assistance
330 Stuart Street, Suite 304
Boston, MA 02116
(617) 727-9420
(617) 727-0667 Fax
http://www.osfa.man.edu

Michigan

Michigan Department of Education
Scholarships & Grants
608 West Allegan Street
Lansing, MI 48933
(517) 373-3394
http://www.mde.state.mi.us/money/

Minnesota

Minnesota Higher Education Services Office
1450 Energy Park Drive
Suite 350
Saint Paul, MN 55108-5227
(651) 642-0533
(800) 657-3866
http://www.heso.state.mn.us/
info@heso.state.mn.us

Mississippi

Office of State Student Financial Aid
3825 Ridgewood Road
P.O. Box 2336
Jackson, MS 39211-6453
(601) 982-6663
(800) 327-2980
http://www.state.ms.us/

Missouri

Student Assistance Resource Services
3515 Amazonas Drive
Jefferson City, MO 65109-5717
(573) 751-3940
(800) 473-6757
http://www.mocbhe.gov/mostovs/finmenu.htm

Montana

Commission of Higher Education
2500 Broadway
P.O. Box 203101
Helena, MT 59620-3101
(406) 444-6570
(406) 444-1469 Fax
http://www.montana.edu/wwwoche/

Nebraska

Nebraska Coordinating Commission for
   Postsecondary Education
140 North 8th, Suite 300
P.O. Box 95005
Lincoln, NE 68509-5005
(402) 471-2847
http://nol.org/NEpostsecondaryed/

Nevada

State Board of Education
1850 East Sahara, Suite 200
Las Vegas, NV 89104
(702) 486-6455
http://www.nsn.k12.nv.US/nvdoe/

New Hampshire

New Hampshire Department of Education
101 Pleasant Street
Concord, NH 03301-3860
(603) 271-3494
(603) 271-1953 Fax
http://www.state.nh.us/doe/about.htm

New Jersey

Department of Higher Education
Office of Student Assistance
4 Quakerbridge Plaza CN 540
Trenton, NJ 08625
(609) 984-2709
(800) 792-8670 (in NJ)
http://www.state.nj.us/treasury/osa

New Mexico

Commission on Higher Education
P.O. Box 15910
Santa Fe, NM 87506-5910
(505) 827-7383
(800) 279-9777
http://www.nmche.org/
highered@che.state.nm.us

New York

Bureau of Higher Education Opportunity Programs
Scholarship Unit
Cultural Center, Room 5A 55
Albany, NY 12230
(518) 474-5642
http://www.higher.nysed.gov/
HEOPI1@higher.nysed.gov

North Carolina

State Education Assistance Authority
P.O. Box 2688
Chapel Hill, NC 27515
(919) 549-8614
http://www.dpi.state.nc.us/
ncseaa@ga.unc.edu

North Dakota

North Dakota Department of Public Instruction
600 East Boulevard Avenue
Bismarck, ND 58504-0440
(701) 328-2260
(701) 328-2461 Fax
http://www.state.nd.us/
rdietric@mail.dpi.state.nd.us

Ohio

Ohio Board of Regents
P.O. Box 182452
Columbus, OH 43218-2452
(614) 466-7420
(888) 833-1133
(614) 752-5903 Fax
http://www.bor.ohio.gov/sgs/

Oklahoma

Oklahoma State Regents for Higher Education
500 Education Building, State Capitol Complex
Oklahoma City, OK 73105
(405) 524-9100
(800) 858-1840
(405) 524-9230 Fax
http://www.okhighered.org/
studentinfo@osrhe.edu

Oregon

State Scholarship Commission
1500 Valley River Drive, Suite 100
Eugene, OR 97401-2130
(541) 687-7400
http://www.ossc.state.or.us/

Pennsylvania

PA Higher Education Assistance Agency (PHEAA)
P.O. Box 8114
Harrisburg, PA 17105-8114
(717) 720-3600
(800) 692-7435 (in PA)
http://www.pheaa.org:80/

Rhode Island

Board of Governors for Higher Education
301 Promenade Street
Providence, RI 02908
(401) 222-2088
(401) 222-2545 Fax
http://www.state.uri.edu
ribog@etal.uri.edu

South Carolina

South Carolina Tuition Grants Commission
P.O. Box 12159
1310 Lady Street
Columbia, SC 29211
(803) 734-1200
(803) 734-1426 Fax
http://www.state.sc.us/edu/

South Dakota

Office of the Secretary
Department of Education & Cultural Affairs
700 Governor's Drive
Pierre, SD 57501-2291
(605) 773-3134
(605) 773-6139 Fax
http://www.state.sd.us/deca
janellet@deca.state.sd.us

Tennessee

Tennessee Higher Education Commission
404 James Robertson Parkway
Suite 1900, Parkway Towers
Nashville, TN 37243
(615) 741-3605
(800) 342-1663 (in TN)
http://www.state.tn.us/edu.htm/

Texas

Higher Coordinating Board
P.O. Box 12788, Capitol Station
Austin, TX 78711
(512) 483-6101
(512) 483-6169 Fax
http://www.state.tx.us/agency

Utah

Utah State Office of Education
250 East 500 South
Salt Lake City, UT 84111
(801) 538-7500
(801) 538-7521 Fax
http://www.state.ut.us/html/education.htm

Vermont

Vermont Department of Education
120 State Street
Montpelier, VT 05620-2501
(802) 828-3147
(802) 828-3140 Fax
http://www.state.vt.us/educ/

Virginia

State Council of Higher Education
James Monroe Building, 9th Floor
101 North 14th Street
Richmond, VA 23219
(804) 225-2137
(804) 371-8017 TDD
http://www.schev.edu/wufinaid

Washington

Higher Education Coordinating Board
917 Lake Bridge Way, GV-11
Olympia, WA 98504-3105
(360) 753-5662
(360) 586-5862 Fax
http://www.wa.gov/wtb

West Virginia

West Virginia Department of Education
1018 Kanawha Boulevard East, Suite 700
Charleston, WV 25301
(304) 558-4618
http://www.scusco.wvnet.edu

Wisconsin

Wisconsin Department of Public Instruction
125 South Webster Street
P.O. Box 7841
Madison, WI 53707-7841
(608) 266-3390
(800) 441-4563
http://badger.state.wi.us/education/

Wyoming

Department of Education
2300 Capitol Avenue
Hathaway Building, 2nd Floor
Cheyenne, WY 82002-0050
(307) 777-7674
(307) 777-6234 Fax
http://www.state.wy.us/

Guam

Student Financial Assistance
University of Guam, UOG State
Mangilao, Guam 96923
(671) 734-4469
http://www.doe.edu.gu/

Puerto Rico

Council on Higher Education
P.O. Box F, University of Puerto Rico Station
San Juan, PR 00931
(809) 758-3350

Virgin Islands

Department of Education
No. 44–46 Kongens Gade
Charlotte Amalie, U.S. Virgin Islands 00802
(809) 774-0100
(804) 779-7153 Fax
http://www.gov.vi/html

For federal student aid information call: 1 (800) 4-FED AID (1-800-433-3243). To get information explaining the formula used to get the Expected Family Contribution, write to:
Federal Student Aid Information Center
P.O. Box 84
Washington, DC 20044

CHAPTER 19

CASH FOR COLLEGE'S "TOP TEN LISTS"

David Letterman isn't the only person who can compile Top Ten lists. We chose ten areas that apply to obtaining cash for college. We hope these lists will provide quick and easy points for you to follow to keep yourself on track and on time. The other chapters in this book provide comprehensive information on most of these topics.

Keep in mind that only one thing is guaranteed. If you don't apply, you won't get it. No one can **GUARANTEE** you'll win a scholarship unless they're going to give you the scholarship. If it sounds too good to be true, it probably is. We wish you the best of luck as you build toward your future and realize your dreams.

TOP TEN TIPS FOR WINNING CASH FOR COLLEGE

1. **You must be motivated.** You must make an effort to help yourself. If possible, make applying to scholarships and college a joint effort. A parent or any concerned adult should try to help out in the application process.
2. **You must be aggressive.** Look for scholarships everywhere: newspapers, magazines, radio, television, books, and your high school counselor's office or college financial aid office.
3. **You must be organized.** Whether you use a file cabinet, an old box, or the "Cash for College Organizer System," keep everything in one place. Keep a calender (such as the "Cash for College Academic Year Calendar") in a place where you'll see it every day, or at least once a week, and use it.
4. **Start early.** Don't wait until you're going to register at a college or university to start looking for scholarships. Don't wait until you're accepted by a program to start applying for scholarships. Students can start applying for scholarships in kindergarten and researching colleges in middle school.
5. **Get to know yourself.** Take a long look at yourself and get acquainted with your talents and strong points. There are many scholarship competitions that are based on talents: art, debate, filmmaking, photography, writing, and many more. Ask your employer, your parents' employers, and clubs or organizations to which you or your parents belong if they offer scholarships.
6. **Put together a sparkling résumé.** Start your résumé the moment you enter middle school and maintain it through college. Keep track of everything: memberships, leadership positions, and honors and awards.
7. **Start planning for college costs early.** Students and parents should put money aside, if possible. Even if you get a full scholarship, you'll still need clothes, school supplies, travel

costs, and other incidentals. You want to show admissions and scholarship committees that you're trying to help yourself.

8. **Consider other alternatives.** Cooperative programs allow students to attend classes for a semester or quarter and then work the next semester or quarter to earn money for college tuition as well as obtain valuable experience. Prepayment programs allow parents to lock in tuition costs by paying for them before the student begins college. There are also AP Tests, CLEP Tests, dual-credit courses, and ROTC to consider.

9. **Prepare for recommendation letters.** Most scholarship applications will require two or more letters. Select at least five people to write recommendation letters. If you're in high school, at least one letter for each application should be from a teacher who taught you a core subject in high school. If you're in college, one person should have taught you in college. Give them a copy of your résumé so they can refer to it and write a great recommendation letter.

10. **Be thorough.** *Before* you mail an application, read through the directions. Don't leave any question blank; either write "not applicable" or "NA," or draw a line through the space. Make sure your name and Social Security number are on each page of your application. Appearances count!

TOP TEN TIPS FOR SUCCEEDING IN HIGH SCHOOL

1. **Plan ahead and set goals.** Don't just stumble through high school and hope everything turns out all right. Sit down and plan what you want to accomplish in high school and where you might want to attend college. Don't be afraid to dream.

2. **Take time to make decisions.** The summer before each high school year, decide what clubs you want to join. Decide whether you'd like to try a new activity or membership.

3. **Learn time management.** The best thing you can do is to take responsibility for setting a reasonable time schedule. Set aside time to study, do homework, do volunteer work, get involved in school activities, fulfill household responsibilities, and most important, set aside time to relax. Succeeding isn't only about working, it also involves relaxing and having a good time.

4. **If you have a question about something, ASK SOMEONE FOR HELP.** No one can be expected to know everything all of the time. If you don't know whom to ask, ask a parent, your favorite teacher, a counselor, a school administrator, or pastor or priest, or someone else you trust. If they don't have the answer, they may be able to tell you who would.

5. **Don't be afraid to try something new.** If you have an interest in or just curiosity about a new activity, join a club or volunteer to help get a project started. To learn more about careers that might be of interest, consider summer volunteer activities and internships.

6. **Always do your best.** As long as you know you've done your best, don't worry. Don't push yourself to the point of burnout. It's impossible for everyone to do everything in top form all the time.

7. **Learn how to study effectively.** Studying isn't the same for everyone. Some students need to be alone and in absolute quiet, while others study best in groups with some background music. Some students need to read a chapter only once to remember it, while others need to outline chapters. Do whatever it takes to do your best.

8. **Make new friends.** Don't wait for people to introduce themselves to you—introduce yourself. For all you know, they might be as hesitant as you are about making the first move. The best way to make new friends is to be a friend.

9. **Don't be so afraid of failure that you never try to succeed.** You'll never know whether you can do something until you try.

10. **Don't wait for something to happen.**

Make it happen. Only you can decide whether you'll succeed or fail. You might not always get what you want, but if you don't try, you'll never reach your goals.

TOP TEN TIPS TO AVOID COMMON MISTAKES MADE ON COLLEGE AND SCHOLARSHIP APPLICATIONS

1. **Be sure to sign the application.** Some applications might require a parent or a school administrator to sign verifying that the information is correct or that the student is in good standing. Get all the necessary signatures.

2. **Answer all of the appropriate questions.** If a question doesn't pertain to you, fill in the blank with "Not Applicable." Don't leave it blank.

3. **Submit a complete application.** Double check to be sure that a school transcript was sent. If the transcript is being sent directly from the school, provide a Return Receipt Postcard to send with it. Check to see if all required letters of recommendation were sent. If a recommendation letter is being sent directly by the person writing it, *you* must make sure it arrived. If possible, provide the person with a Return Receipt Postcard to send with the letter. This will help to verify that the recommendation letter was indeed received.

4. **Do not submit a recommendation letter written for another scholarship or school.** Never submit a recommendation letter written on a form required by a different scholarship or college/university.

5. **Do not submit a recommendation letter that's over one year old.** The only exception to this would be for a student who is in the military or is a military dependent. If the student or family moved just prior to applying for a scholarship or college, a recommendation letter from the previous year could be used, though it would be better to ask the letter writer to put a more recent date on the letter.

6. **Do not submit an inappropriate recommendation letter.** Once you've completed one college semester and have received grades, you should never have a high school teacher write a recommendation letter. The letter can be written by a college/ university professor, an employer, a supervisor in a volunteer position, a pastor or priest, or even a family friend.

7. **Don't submit something that wasn't requested**, including letters, pictures, an unsolicited résumé, a portfolio, additional essays, poetry, or short stories, etc.

8. **Follow the directions.** Read the application guidelines before submitting the application. If the directions clearly state that an essay should be on one sheet of paper, don't submit two or more. If the guidelines specify a word count, don't exceed the word count. Answer the question being asked; don't wander off in another direction.

9. **Proofread all parts of the application.** Have someone read your essay before submitting it. If you're not sure about the grammar, ask your English teacher, your college English professor, or an English tutor to check it. Your essay shouldn't have spelling or grammar errors or typos. Make sure you fully answer the topic or question.

10. **Send in a clean application.** Your application represents you. Make sure the condition of the application is neat and not dirty, smudged, or overly wrinkled. You may only have one chance to impress—make it your best effort.

TOP TEN FINANCIAL AID MISTAKES

1. Not filing the Free Application for Federal Student Aid (FAFSA) because you think you won't qualify for assistance.
2. Not filing other required forms (PROFILE, state's financial aid forms, or school's financial aid forms).
3. Not answering all the appropriate questions.
4. Answering a question incorrectly because you didn't understand it.
5. A simple mathematical error. Your information is plugged by the computer into a formula. Your mistakes won't be caught. A mistake also may be made by the processor. Check your SAR.
6. Filing too early. Always file after January 1 of the year you will begin attending a college, university, or vocational/technical school.
7. Filing too late to meet the required deadlines set by the school. Each school has a set amount it can award. There is a cap on the amount of government money allocated for federal assistance. Award money is distributed on a first-come, first-serve basis. Once the money runs out, you're out of luck.
8. Listening to well-intentioned, but inaccurate, information from friends or others not qualified to give advice.
9. Not obtaining current guidelines and information. Each year request a new Student Guide from the Department of Education. Programs and guidelines could change from one year to the next.
10. Not filing next year because you think since you didn't get any aid this year, you won't get any next year.

TOP TEN TIPS ON WRITING WINNING ESSAYS

1. **Choose your words carefully.** What you don't say is as important as what you do say.
2. **Don't repeat yourself.** Don't include information that is provided in a résumé. Don't use up precious word count by repeating the question or introducing yourself.
3. **Use contractions, except for emphasis.** (*Example:* I do not want to do that.) Essays written for scholarship and college applications should be informal. They must sound as if the student is talking to an interviewer or committee member. The use of contractions bridges the gap between an unseen student and an unseen committee member.
4. **Explain yourself fully.** Don't mention an accident without explaining who was involved, when it occurred, or the outcome. Don't mention someone who was ill and never explain whether the person survived or not.
5. **Don't generalize.** *Example:* People judge success by their earning potential. *Change to:* Sometimes people are judged...or, better yet, leave out generalizations.
6. **Progress through your essay logically.** Don't jump around in time. Don't start a story in the present and switch to the past. When discussing your goals, start with current goals, educational goals (college), and long-term goals (professional), and end with a conclusion (why you can accomplish these goals).
7. **Keep your viewpoint consistent.** If you're telling your story about an experience, in the first-person viewpoint, don't include another person's thoughts, and don't warn the reader of what is to come (*Example:* Little did I know that what was about to happen would change my life.).
8. **Use active voice, not passive voice.** (*Example:* I'll choose the college I'll attend. *NOT:* The college I will attend will be chosen by me.)
9. **Maintain sentence variety.** Don't start each sentence with "I plan," "I will," "I hope,"

"I want," or "My goals are…" It is best not to start an essay with "My goals are…." A large percentage of essays start that way, and you'll never stand out when your essay sounds like all the rest.

10. **Be creative.** Don't use clichés. (*Examples:* Hot as the sun, cold as ice, dark as night, straight as an arrow.)

____ TOP TEN TIPS FOR CREATING SPARKLING RÉSUMÉS ____

1. **Keep them short and to the point.** A scholarship and college application résumé should be from one to two pages in length, three pages at the most. Fill three pages only if you're involved in lots of competitions (sports, University Interscholastic League [UIL] science fairs, agricultural competitions, etc.).

2. **Never include a statement of objective.** The objective is understood: to win free scholarship money and get into college. Including an objective could make committee members assume you think they're so dim they don't know why you submitted the résumé.

3. **Never include a section detailing your education.** You don't need a section listing the classes you've taken, are taking, or will take. You don't need to include your grade point average, class rank, test scores, or any other information that is included in your transcript. If a scholarship or college requires a résumé, they'll also require a transcript.

4. **Never list references.** If a scholarship or college application requires recommendations, they'll want them in the form of letters, and these will be requested.

5. **Put your name and Social Security number on all pages.** A header including this information should appear at the top of pages 2 and 3.

6. **Do include information for four academic years.** Include information on what you've done during the current year and for the three previous years, regardless of your age.

7. **Do include three sections: leadership, memberships, and honor/awards.** Besides your name, address, the school you are currently attending, and the school's address, you need to include only these three sections.

8. **Your membership section can contain subheadings.** This section should include school activities: clubs, student council, sports, committees, etc.; community involvement: clubs, organizations, volunteer work, church activities; summer activities: classes, summer programs, internships, travel; and employment: any type of employment, including lawn mowing and baby-sitting.

9. **Never include: a section on hobbies or skills.** Hobbies and skills don't belong in a résumé.

10. **Keep your résumé as up-to-date as possible.** Update your résumé to include each new accomplishment, honor, or membership.

_____ TOP TEN INTERVIEWING TIPS _____

1. **Don't be late.** If you're driving and don't know the way, take a practice drive the day before. If you're depending on public transportation, take possible delays into consideration.

2. **Dress appropriately.** You don't want to

look like you're cleaning the attic or going to the prom.

3. **Be courteous.** When you walk in, shake the interviewer's hand firmly (not like a dead fish or as if you're in a contest to see if you can

bring the interviewer to his/her knees) and state your name clearly.

4. **Relax.** The interviewer(s) won't ask you anything you don't already know. They just want to get to know you better. Remember: "Don't let them see you sweat."

5. **Show your enthusiasm and leadership.** Don't look as though you're about to have your wisdom teeth pulled. Don't give one-word answers. Elaborate. Don't just tell what; tell *why*.

6. **Don't fidget.** Don't jiggle your foot, wave your hands, or shift in your seat. All such movements are distracting.

7. **Look the interviewer(s) in the eye.** You don't want to look evasive, but you don't want to appear threatening, either. When you're asked a question, don't avoid eye contact.

8. **Be prepared.** Take a résumé with you. Have someone ask you practice questions ahead of time. Go in with possible answers.

9. **Be aware of body language.** If the interviewer(s) stands, the interview is over. Don't keep talking. Interviewers have a time schedule to keep and others to interview.

10. **Be gracious.** As you leave, thank the interviewer and shake his or her hand. When you get home, write a thank-you card or note.

TOP TEN TIPS FOR
RECRUITING ATHLETIC SCHOLARSHIPS

1. **Preparation.** Start investigating schools, teams, and coaches at least by freshman year in high school, if not while in middle school. Make a list of dream schools (where you would love to go if you could get in and pay for it), safety schools (those schools where you know you can get accepted and can pay for it), and those in between. Keep in mind that it's better for you if you know you'll be able to play and not be kept on the bench.

2. **Coachability.** You should be able to receive and understand instruction and follow what the coach is trying to teach you. Future coaches want to know that you're not stubborn about taking advice. You don't want to be a prima donna.

3. **Overall attitude.** You need to be a team player. You need to willingly put in the practice it takes to reach your potential. This will show coaches that you will do whatever it takes to reach your goals.

4. **Academic accomplishments.** You need to be able to maintain your grades and succeed academically at the school that may offer you a scholarship.

5. **Look for schools that are top-heavy in upper classmen.** Those athletes will be graduating, which means more opportunities for you to be seen if you're considering becoming a professional athlete.

6. **Keep an up-to-date résumé.** Your résumé needs to include athletic, academic, extracurricular, and volunteer activities. You are more than just an athlete.

7. **Keep a clippings file.** This should include every article that mentions you, not just the team. These articles can come from local newspapers, school newspapers, etc. When you send letters to college coaches, select four or five of the best clips to send along. Keep all the other articles in a neat notebook, each one with a description of where it was published. When you visit a campus or a coach visits you, you can pull out your notebook and share all of the articles.

8. **Keep a video file.** Start your video file during freshman year. If you don't own a camcorder, remember that most coaches videotape athletic events. All you have to do is link two VCRs and tape from one machine to the other.

9. **Have your coach write an introduction letter.** This letter should include specific information about you. Regardless of how well the coach knows you, he or she doesn't remember every award and statistic, as well as

your other accomplishments. When you ask for the introduction letter, give the coach a copy of your résumé. You don't want it to look like a form letter.

10. **Write a cover letter.** The letter should explain that you're interested in a school's particular athletic program. It should include any camps, clinics, or other events that you will be attending. You also want to include a schedule of upcoming games, meets, matches, or other athletic events in which you will participate. This will allow an interested coach the opportunity to see you in action.

—— TOP TEN TIPS FOR CHOOSING A COLLEGE ——

1. **Academics.** Will you be bored, challenged, or in over your head? Though most students have dream schools, you have to be able to stay at your dream school. Getting in isn't the biggest challenge. The biggest challenge will be staying in school. Does the school offer your major? If you don't know exactly what you want to major in, does it offer those areas in which you're interested?

2. **Success rate.** How many of the students who start actually graduate? How many students get jobs upon graduation? How many students go on to graduate or professional school?

3. **Size.** How many students are there: 1,000, 5,000, 10,000, 20,000, or 30,000? Do you want to be a big fish in a little pond or a little fish in a big pond? Would you rather attend a class in a room with 25 other students or 500 other students? Do you want to be taught by a graduate student or by a professor?

4. **Location.** How often will you be able to go home? Right now you may think you'll never go home to visit, but by the time you need to do laundry, home will start looking good. Is the school close enough to go home once a week, once a month, once a semester, or once a year? Will you have a car or will you need to travel by bus, train, or plane? How often can you afford to fly home? Keep in mind that, generally, airline ticket prices go up at about the time you'll need to go home.

5. **Educational facilities.** How large is the library's holdings? Do undergraduates have access to special holdings? Do they have top-of-the-line computers available for student use? Is the school networked? Are the dorms wired for Internet access? Whatever your major, does the school have appropriate facilities: planetarium, science (biology, chemistry, physics, engineering) research equipment, radio station, etc.?

6. **Athletics.** Does the school offer the sport in which you'd like to participate? What are the odds that if you make a team, you'll have playing time? What kind of athletic facilities are available for student use? Do students actively support athletics by attending games?

7. **Social activities.** Will you seek out groups in which you have an interest, or do you need to have someone approach you about joining? Are you interested in joining a fraternity or sorority? Not all schools have access to frats or sororities, so if you're interested, make sure you find out if they're available.

8. **Housing.** Does the school have enough dormitories to enable you to live on campus, or do most students live off campus? Are you required to live on campus? Are dorm rooms assigned by lottery? Do you prefer single-sex or coed dorms?

9. **Cost.** Have you found enough free money to attend the school, or will you and your family have to incur enormous loan debt to attend? What kind of financial aid package were you offered? Remember, generally you may get a great package freshman year, but subsequent financial aid packages may have more loans than free money offered. This may be the last thing, or the first thing, you think about, but we think students should choose a school because it's the best place for them, not because they can afford it.

10. **Why did you choose this school?** Did you choose this school because all your friends are going there? Did you choose this school because your boyfriend/girlfriend is going there? These are the wrong reasons.

Though all of these ten items are important, the most important question to remember is: Is this the best place for you?

NOTE: If after a semester, a couple of months, or a few weeks of being at the school, you find it's not what you thought it would be, don't be afraid or hesitant to transfer to another school. You want to be happy at a school so you can complete your degree. After all, the reason for going to college is to get a degree in order to build toward your future and realize your dreams.

TOP TEN TIPS FOR SUCCEEDING IN COLLEGE

1. **Take time to discover who you are.** Ask yourself serious questions about your talents, interests, likes, and dislikes. What are your preferences? Would you prefer to work alone or with others, for someone else or yourself, indoors or outdoors, with people, computers, or animals? Once you've eliminated what you don't like, you can focus on what you want and how to obtain it.

2. **Be open to new ideas and new opportunities.** When an opportunity to learn more about yourself, a subject, or career presents itself, take advantage to grow as an individual.

3. **Join a club or other organization.** Membership in a club or organization can help you learn more about yourself and a possible career. When you apply to graduate, law, medical, or other professional school, committees will want to know that you're serious about a career. Membership in related clubs or organizations can help establish that.

4. **Inquire about summer internships.** Internships are a great way to find out about careers and possibly make money to help yourself pay for college. Some internships even pay travel and housing expenses.

5. **Focus on what you want to accomplish.** Maybe you'll save money by attending a local school and living at home. Ask yourself, what do I want in the long run—to go away to school, or save money?

6. **Continue good time management.** At times, going out for pizza with friends is great, but not if you're sacrificing studying or completing a paper or project.

7. **Seek out a mentor.** Take the time to get to know your professors. Read papers they've written. Go to their office to discuss any academic questions you may have. Get involved in an organization they may sponsor. A professor may be able to provide you with information about careers, schools, summer programs, and even scholarship and fellowship opportunities. Most professors are receptive to becoming a mentor to students who've demonstrated an interest or talent in their field.

8. **You'll get out of a school what you put into it.** If all you do is go to class, eat, and hang out in your room or apartment, you'll never feel a part of the school you're attending. Whether a school is a top-tier school doesn't matter. What matters is that you get as involved as possible and take the best advantage of all your opportunities.

9. **Allow time to relax.** Don't be so obsessed with being the perfect student that you don't make time to relax. You don't want to burn out and be unable to do a good job. Always try to do your best and have a good time in the process.

10. **Don't wait for something to happen.** Make it happen. Just as in in high school, only you can decide whether you'll succeed or fail. You might not always get what you want, but if you don't try, you'll never reach your goals.

PART II

AT-A-GLANCE SCHOLARSHIP INDEX*

FIELDS OF STUDY

*Listings are by entry number, not page number.

QUALIFYING CHARACTERISTICS OF RECIPIENTS

Academic Merit 61, 206, 208, 213, 222, 223, 225, 228, 229, 232, 257, 266, 282, 574, 600, 606, 618–619, 751, 818, 872, 954, 1119–1120, 1151, 1167, 1200, 1391, 1410, 1432, 1811, 1976–1978, 2574

Amateur Licensed Radio Operator 1242

Athletic 55, 141, 683, 1167, 1200, 1785, 1827, 2017, 2322, 2592, 2627, 2753, 2780

Background 208

Big Brother/Big Sister 595

Child Care 1721

Children of Cranberry Growers 2637

Children with Single Parent 1705

College Campus Activities 1788–1790

Community Service 141, 231, 573, 1268, 1647, 1727, 1786, 2503, 2796

Custodial Students (Wards of the State) *see* Foster Child

Descendant of a Civil War Veteran (Union or Confederate) 696, 1340, 2581

Descendant of a Signer of the Declaration of Independence 1076

Descendant of a Student of the Pullman Free School of Manual Training 1307

Dislocated Rural Workers 1723

Dislocated Worker 2078

Displaced Homemakers 1704, 1723, 2078, 2102

Dog Breeder, Handler, Exhibitor, Judge, or Club Officer 1091

Elementary School Students (K–5th) 1, 1934, 1996–1998

Employed in Footwear, Leather, or Allied Industries 2572

Extracurricular Activities 228

Farm Family/Communities 710, 880, 1579, 1723–1724, 1889, 1905, 1908, 2069

Financial Need 206, 208, 223, 225, 228, 232–233, 239–240, 245, 253, 260, 262, 276, 280, 282, 285, 295, 993, 905, 2078

Foster Children 1858

Gay 684

Gifted 1244

Golf (Women) 2782

Golf Caddies 1174, 1254

Golf-Related 1254, 2234

High School Juniors 1085, 1177, 1348

Internships 6, 10, 14, 15, 28, 77, 121, 165, 178, 194, 212, 457, 520, 550, 571, 575, 586, 592, 596, 628, 644, 646, 661, 664, 681, 713, 746, 749, 752, 758–759, 762–763, 771, 782–783, 790, 817, 826–827, 829, 837, 846, 875, 885, 887, 890–900, 902, 938, 946, 959, 1009, 1014, 1017, 1022, 1050, 1096–1098, 1149, 1189, 1194, 1196, 1240, 1252, 1271–1275, 1279, 1298, 1301, 1335, 1343, 1351–1352, 1383, 1385, 1390, 1399, 1447–1448, 1450, 1457, 1483, 1503, 1535, 1546, 1558, 1575, 1591, 1596, 1607, 1611–1612, 1618, 1621, 1631, 1640, 1661, 1692, 1695, 1699, 1701, 1713, 1773, 1775, 1818, 1821, 1933, 1940, 1941, 1967, 1990, 2022–2023,

2088, 2105–2107, 2113–2114, 2234, 2278, 2279, 2299, 2300, 2306–2307, 2312, 2320, 2322, 2350, 2458–2459, 2461, 2479, 2485, 2492, 2494, 2504, 2557, 2571, 2588, 2591, 2593–2601, 2613, 2627–2628, 2679, 2681, 2685, 2690–2691, 2705, 2714–2716, 2718, 2743–2749, 2752, 2785, 2788, 2795

Leadership 232, 954, 1085, 1151, 1809–1810

Little Brother/Little Sister Program 595

Men & Women Over Age 35 1808, 2585

Migrant Families 1715, 2384

Newspaper Carriers 859, 915, 1260, 2692

Nontraditional Students 463, 839–844, 1519, 1808, 2378 2585

Orphans 2214

Prepayment Plans 60

Prep School 9, 773

Public Housing Residents 2285

SCUBA Diving 2215

Senior Citizens 62, 994

Single Parent 1704

Single Pregnant Woman 1704

Student Government Officer 2629

Valedictorian 75

Volunteer Work 141, 231, 573, 1268, 1647, 1727, 1786, 2503, 2796

Women Over Age 25 463, 839–844

Women Over Age 30 839–844, 2378

Women Over Age 35 1519

NATIVE ANCESTRY/ETHNICITY

African 105, 106, 111, 145, 208, 487, 589, 611, 618, 741, 770, 773, 883, 924, 1019, 1031, 1080, 1084, 1158, 1232, 1441, 1776, 1780–1781, 1783, 1792–1794, 1796–1797, 1800, 1822–1823, 2059, 2334–2335, 2589

Alaskan Native 2270, 2602–2603

Aleuts 2270

Anglo 1688

Armenian 614–617, 1302

Asian 1080, 1108

Canadian 2232

Chinese 202, 928

Colonial 962

Croatian 1020

Cuban 934

Danish 1036–1037

Eskimo 208, 2270

Evrytanian 1175

General Minority 225, 504, 549–550, 661, 739, 924, 965, 977, 984, 1016, 1096–1097, 1160, 1244, 1296, 1300, 1429, 1441, 1448, 1501, 1728, 1737, 1776, 1788, 2022, 2095, 2234, 2268, 2293, 2380, 2405, 2410, 2508, 2514, 2516, 2536, 2539, 2606, 2792, 2794

German 1688

Greek 1039–1042, 1175

Guam 1347

Hawaiian 208

Hispanic 135, 145, 487, 611, 742, 847, 883, 944, 985, 1080, 1227, 1388, 1441, 1609, 1687, 1691, 1781, 1800, 1802, 1936, 2354, 2612, 2630, 2659–2660

Indian (India) 226

Inuit 2232

Italian 1499–1500, 1942–1973, 2456

Japanese 1517

Lebanese 1565

Native American Indian 67, 145, 208, 217–218, 301, 487, 604, 611, 626, 656, 748, 772, 833, 851, 883, 889, 921–922, 1080, 1233, 1405, 1446, 1481, 1637, 1650, 1705, 1718, 1725, 1765, 1781, 1800, 2004, 2013, 2146, 2232, 2270, 2353, 2373, 2602–2603, 2733, 2793

Pacific Islander 1109

Polish 227

Portuguese 1638

Puerto Rican 145, 1781

Samoan 208

Scot 510

Serbian 511, 2376–2377

Swiss 2498

Welsh 2701

CONTESTS

Agriculture 1861–1932

Art 1, 100, 632, 637, 1389, 1435, 1989, 1996, 2657

Beauty/Pageantry 1736, 1760

Citizenship 1268

Computer 2501

Cooking 1007–1008

Dance 633

Design 100, 1471

Drama 636

Fabric Design 100, 637

Filmmaking 12, 637, 770, 1989, 2119

Foreign Language 144, 149

Government/History/Social Studies 99, 367, 443

History 948, 2038, 2386

Math 1685, 2501

Music Composition 123, 533, 635, 709, 825, 1061, 1064, 1477, 1550, 1935, 1989, 2257, 2289

Music Performance (Instrumental) 154, 634–635, 831, 1023, 1033, 1270, 1325, 1778, 2349, 2689

Music Performance (Piano) 1023, 1033, 1270, 1322, 1589, 1613, 1778, 2636, 2689

Music Performance (Vocal) 635, 745, 1033, 1270, 1613, 1620, 1813

Oration, Speeches 352, 354, 356–357, 359–361, 366, 369, 373, 380, 389, 392, 394, 396, 401–403, 406, 415, 417, 422–423, 425, 427, 431,

433, 435, 437–438, 440, 442, 447, 449, 451, 2038, 2185, 2658

Painting, Oil 637, 1389

Painting, Watercolor 637, 1389

Photography 637, 701, 1389, 1985, 1989, 2290, 2622, 2624–2625

Science or Engineering 98, 220, 1561–1562, 1995–1998, 2367, 2501, 2550, 2704

Sculpture 632, 1389

Sewing and Design 637

Soap Box Derby 94

Sports 55, 378

Writing 29, 95, 122, 203, 637, 1114, 1352, 1556, 1989, 2080, 2264–2267, 2290

Writing, Essay 98–101, 122, 261, 290, 365, 460–463, 585, 637, 711–

712, 878, 1153, 1267, 1348, 1378, 1449, 1749, 1791, 1828, 2012, 2080, 2184, 2319, 2371, 2386, 2481, 2614, 2617–2621, 2623

Writing, Fiction Short Story 29, 95, 101, 122, 583, 585, 637, 1109, 1114, 1210, 1241, 1326, 1377–1378, 1407, 1593, 1696, 1749, 2080, 2265, 2267, 2290, 2319, 2333, 2481, 2493, 2786–2787

Writing, Fiction Novel 637, 1109, 1350

Writing, Nonfiction Article 101, 701, 1109, 1378, 2449, 2267, 2290, 2481

Writing, Nonfiction Book 1109

Writing, Play 101, 156, 637, 768, 1015, 1046, 1504, 2258, 2375, 2486, 2635, 2717

Writing, Poetry 95, 101, 122, 583–585, 637, 1114, 1134, 1147, 1241, 1378, 1593, 1623, 1749, 2080, 2259–2261, 2267, 2290, 2317, 2319, 2480, 2482, 2490, 2493, 2721

Writing, Screenplay 11, 13, 14, 101, 102, 156, 158, 637, 2119, 2375, 2635

Writing, Script 101, 637, 2119, 2375, 2635

DISABILITIES

Asthma 683

Disabled 202, 1244, 1373, 1497, 1840, 1870, 2274–2276, 2316, 2363, 2460

Epilepsy 1164

Hearing–Impaired 81–92, 856, 1104

Learning 2303

Mental 1769, 2274–2276

Neurological 856

Physical 855–856, 863, 1769, 1870–1871, 2363

Speech/Language 856

Visually–Impaired Parents 69, 198–205, 2476

Visual Impairment 167, 168, 198–205, 657–658, 778, 856, 932, 1835, 1845–1857, 2135, 2592, 2738

RELIGIOUS AFFILIATION

Baptist 740–743, 904, 1253, 1820, 2125–2126, 2514, 2662

Catholic 1500, 1511, 1584–1586

Christian 2777

Congregational Church 1262

Disciples of Christ 1084

Episcopalian 754

Jewish 978, 1269, 1374, 1523–1532, 1651, 1829

Lutheran 25, 26, 27, 781, 1634–1637, 2777

Methodist 1195, 2584–2587

Presbyterian 1536, 2268–2273, 2499, 2590

Protestant 20, 1540, 2201

Unitarian Universalist Society 2577–2578

United Church of Christ 977

STUDENT, PARENT, OR RELATIVE IN MILITARY SERVICE

Reserve Officer Training Corps (ROTC) 404–405

ROTC Air Force 44, 45, 49, 50

ROTC Army 623–625

ROTC Navy 51, 2043

Reserve Unit of an Armed Forces 1770, 2056

Currently in or retired from:

Navy Supply Corps 2051

Submarine Force 788–789, 1092

Submarine Services 788–789, 1092

U.S. Air Force 42, 43, 46, 49, 50, 452, 1043, 2206

U.S. Armed Forces 453, 1043, 1263, 1770, 2121, 2130, 2190, 2206

U.S. Army 621–625, 1043, 2206, 2408

U.S. Coast Guard 19, 454, 1043, 1075, 1211–1214, 1592, 2206, 2626

U.S. Marine Corps 455, 1043, 1075, 1198, 1211-1214, 1592, 2042, 2045-2048, 2206, 2372, 2616, 2626

U.S. National Guard 49, 50, 1431, 1726, 1756, 2057, 2142, 2170, 2206, 2464, 2477

U.S. Navy 51, 456, 812, 1043, 1075, 1198, 1211-1214, 1592, 2042, 2045-2048, 2206, 2626

STUDENTS WHO ARE CHILDREN OR DEPENDENTS OF VETERANS

Blind Veteran 777
Civil War Veteran Descendant 696, 1340, 2581
Deceased Crewmembers of U.S.S. Iowa 2044
Deceased Crewmembers of U.S.S. Stark 2048
Deceased Crewmembers of U.S.S. Tennessee 2049
Deceased Veteran 51, 66, 232, 234-350, 355, 358, 362-363, 576-581, 723, 852-853, 988, 1057, 1198, 1205, 1248-1250, 1263, 1412-1417, 1419-1420, 1496, 1576, 1622, 1642, 1664, 1681, 1712, 1759, 2034, 2058, 2067, 2087,

2090, 2130, 2141, 2144, 2168, 2224-2226, 2305, 2360, 2362, 2408, 2469, 2507, 2555-2556, 2616, 2663, 2676, 2706, 2734
Disabled Veteran 51, 66, 232, 234-350, 355, 362-363, 576-581, 723, 852-853, 988, 1198, 1250, 1263, 1412-1417, 1419-1420, 1496, 1537, 1576, 1622, 1642, 1664, 1712, 2034, 2090, 2130, 2141, 2144, 2168, 2224-2226, 2360, 2469, 2555-2556, 2616, 2663, 2676, 2734
Jewish War Veteran 1532
Living Veteran 66, 232, 234-350, 355, 362-363, 576-581, 723, 812,

970, 995, 1198, 1248, 1263, 1412-1417, 1496, 1576, 1643, 1770, 2034, 2058, 2077, 2085, 2130, 2144, 2190, 2206, 2360, 2469, 2556, 2626, 2676, 2734
Missing-in-Action 51, 66, 995, 1057, 1411, 1419, 1569, 1576, 1664, 1681, 1733, 1745, 2034, 2058, 2074, 2130, 2143-2144, 2226, 2305, 2362, 2475, 2507, 2663
Prisoner-of-War 51, 66, 995, 1057, 1411, 1419, 1569, 1576, 1664, 1681, 1733, 1745, 2034, 2058, 2074, 2130, 2143-2144, 2226, 2362, 2469, 2475, 2507, 2663

STUDENT OR PARENT PARTICIPATION/MEMBERSHIP IN CLUBS, COMPANIES, FRATERNITIES, ORGANIZATIONS, PROFESSIONS, SORORITIES, OR UNIONS

Abbot Laboratories 7
ABC/Capitol Cities, Inc. 2
AFL-CIO 23, 598, 963, 986, 1073, 1461, 1486-1487, 1538, 2187, 2192, 2223, 2513, 2515
Agriculture Extension Workers 1186
AHEPAN 1041-1042
Aircraft Electronics Association (AEA) 41
Air Force Sergeants Association 46, 47
Airline Pilots Association 48

Alcoa Foundation 79
Alpha Eta Rho 1549
Alpha Kappa Alpha 106
Alpha Mu Gamma 107-110
Alpha Phi 113
Alpha Phi Alpha 111
Alpha Phi Delta 112
Alpha Tau Delta 114, 115
Amalgamated Clothing and Textile Workers Union 117
Amax Consolidated 120
American Association of Airport Executives 126

American Association of Community & Junior Colleges (School Is Member) 2245
American Association of State Troopers, Inc. (AAST) 142, 143
American College of Nurse-Midwives 155
American Congress of Surveying and Mapping 525-528
American Express 182

United Food & Commercial Workers 2583
United Steel Workers of America, District 37 2630–2631

USAA Employees 2638–2640
U.S. Bancorp 2211
Warbirds of America 1549

Westinghouse Electric Corp. 2703
Women Marines Association 2776

STUDENT ATTENDS PARTICULAR HIGH SCHOOL

Agawam High School, MA 1394
Andover High School, MA 726
Bob Hope High School, TX 1102
Borrego Springs High School, CA 785
Bridgehampton High School, NY 1103
Brookline High School, MA 744
Broome County High School, MA 1522
Buckeye Central High School, OH 1545
Bucksport High School, ME 1264
Bucyrus High School, OH 1545
Business Careers High School, TX 2639
Chester High School, CA 103
Chester High School, MA 733–734
Chicopee High School, MA 1394
Chinook High School, MT 1619
Clark County High Schools, KS 1520
Clinton High School, SC 716
Colonel Crawford, OH 1545
Denham High School, MA 729

East Longmeadow High School, MA 1394
East Noble High School, IN 629
Framingham High School, MA 726
Fredericksburg High School, TX 688
Glencoe High School, OR 2200
Harlowton High School, MT 913
Health Careers High School, TX 2639
Hillsboro High School, OR 2200
Homestead High School, WI 1258
Lake County High School, OR 961
Laurens High School, SC 716
Longmeadow High School, MA 1394
Ludlow High School, MA 1394
Meagher County High Schools, MT 913
Merrimack High School, NH 4
Methuen High School, MA 724
Monroe High School, WI 1541
Newport High School, OR 2645

New York City High Schools, NY 2582
San Diego High Schools, CA 1521
Santa Barbara Area High Schools, CA 2351
Sheboygan High Schools, WI 1588
Sheridan County High Schools, WY 769
Springfield High School, MA 1394
Stoughton High School, MA 742
St. Mary's Academy, NY 1145
Union High School, VT 1187
West Springfield High School, MA 1394
Weymouth North High School, MA 730
Weymouth South High School, MA 730
White Sulphur Springs High School, MT 913
Wilbraham High School, MA 1394
Wynford High School, OH 1545

STUDENT RESIDES IN PARTICULAR SCHOOL DISTRICT

Adams–Chesire, MA 16
Center School District, MO 703
Chautauqua School District, NY 919
Cherry Valley School District, NY 939
Chester Massachusetts School System, MA 733

Cooperstown School District, NY 939
Delano School District, MN 942
Edmeson School District, NY 939
Kansas City School District, MO 703
Lake Wales High School District, FL 926

Laurens School District, NY 939
Lodi Unified School District, CA 630
Middletown Ohio School District, OH 1132
Milford School District, NY 939
Newark School District, DE 704

Pasadena Unified School District, CA 705

Portland Public School District #1, OR 2203

Princeton School District, OH 707

Ramapo Central School District, NY 706

Rice Consolidated School District, TX 1045

Richfield Springs School District, NY 939

Scenevus School District, NY 939

Sheridan County High School, WY 769

South District 1, Rensselaer, NY 1115

Springfield School District, NY 939

Union High School District 27, VT 1187

Union Joint School District, PA 1652

Van Horn School District, NY 939

West Winfield School District, NY 939

Worchester School District, NY 939

STUDENT RESIDES OR ATTENDS SCHOOL IN PARTICULAR CITY

Abbeville, SC 1505

Abington, PA 2700

Akron, OH 2757

Aliquippa, PA 511

Alsea, OR 941

Amarillo, TX 119

Amesbury, MA 715

Andover, MA 736

Appleton, WI 1582

Ashfield, MA 1265

Athens, PA 631

Atlanta, GA 1016

Aurora, IL 689

Baltimore, MD 1689

Beaumont, CA 903

Bernardston, MA 1265

Blackwell, OK 1011

Bloomsburg, PA 1505

Boston, MA 1829

Boyertown, PA 1610

Bronx, NY 1761

Brooklyn, NY 1761

Buckland, MA 1265

Buffalo, NY 832

Charlemont, MA 1265

Cheshire, CT 721, 2304

Chester, CA 103

Chester, MA 732

Chicago, IL 778, 780, 924, 1006, 1524, 1689

Chinook, MT 1619

Cincinnati, OH 1021

Clairton, PA 511

Cleveland, OH 944–945

Colorado Springs, OH 1168

Columbus, OH 2758–2759

Concord, MA 78

Conway, MA 1265

Corpus Christi, TX 2221

Crane, OR 941

Daytona Beach, FL 1337

Deerfield, MA 1265

Delano, MN 942

Denver, CO 917

Detroit, MI 1088, 1176, 1404, 1689, 2762, 2764

Duluth, MN 1131

Duxbury, MA 1100

Eagle Lake, TX 1045

Eddyville, OR 941

Elmira, NY 1511

Erie City, NY 832

Eugene, OR 787

Fairfax, MN 1156

Fairhaven, VT 1141

Farmington, NH 908

Farrell/Hermitage, PA 511

Fort Worth, TX 935, 2765

Framingham, MA 804

Gill, MA 1265

Glen Falls, NY 1145

Greenfield, MA 1265

Harrisburg, PA 978

Havana, IL 1694

Hawley, MA 1265

Heath, MA 1265

Helotes (Grey Forest), TX 1345

Hill City, MN 910

Hood River, OR 2205

Houston, TX 928, 2519, 2766

Indianapolis, IN 2767

Jamestown, ND 1365

Janesville, WI 1515

Johnstown, PA 511

Joplin, MO 2366

Juneau, AK 1329

Kansas City, MO 703

Kauauna, WI 1582

Lake Mills, WI 1582

Lake Wales, FL 926

Las Vegas, NV 1970

Leeward–Oahu, HI 1369

Leyden, MA 1265

Long Beach, CA 1573

Los Angeles, CA 494, 905, 1735, 2767–2768

Lyme, CT 1639

Madison, NJ 1641

Manchester, NH 1130

Manhattan, NY 1761

Maxeys, GA 686

McKeesport/Duquesne, PA 511

Melba, ID 1927

Menasha, WI 1582

Meriden, CT 2304

Merrimack, NH 4

Middlefield, CT 2304

Middletown, OH 1132

Midland, PA 511

Minneapolis, MN 1346, 1552

Monroe, MA 1265

Monroeville, PA 511

STUDENT RESIDES OR ATTENDS SCHOOL IN A PARTICULAR COUNTY

STUDENT RESIDES OR ATTENDS SCHOOL IN PARTICULAR STATE

STUDY IN OTHER COUNTRIES

EXCHANGE PROGRAMS

SCHOLARSHIP LISTING

FROM PRIVATE SOURCES

1.
AAA School Traffic Safety Poster Program
Poster Program Manager
American Automobile Association
1000 AAA Drive
Heathrow, FL 32746
(407) 444-7910

U.S. Savings Bonds from $75 to $125 for students in K–11 and up to $650 for high school seniors who are selected winners in the AAA School Traffic Safety Poster Program in two levels of competition: K–6 and 7–12. Apply to local AAA office after September. Deadline: February 1.

2.
ABC/Capital Cities, Inc.
Merit Scholarship Program
Corporate Benefits Department
77 West 66th Street
New York, NY 10023
(212) 456-7777

Scholarships ranging from $500 to $2,000 per year to dependent children of ABC/Capital Cities employees for one year or more. Students must take the PSAT in October of their junior year and have scores sent to ABC/Capital Cities, Inc. Renewable for up to four years. Deadline: none.

3.
ABCI Educational and Scholastic Foundation
Automotive Booster Clubs International, Inc.
1806 Johns Drive
Glenview, IL 60025
(847) 729-2227

Scholarships of $800 to high school seniors, with preference given to students seeking a career in the automotive industry, engineering, business administration, economics, mathematics, or science, and who attend or will attend Northwood Institute in Midland, Michigan, or the University of Colorado in Pueblo, Colorado, only.

4.
Abbie M. Griffin Educational Fund (Scholarships)
c/o Winer & Bennett
111 Concord Street
P.O. Box 488
Nashua, NH 03061-0488
(603) 882-5157

5 to 7 scholarships ranging from $300 to $2,000 to high school seniors who are residents of Merrimack, New Hampshire. Awards may be used at any accredited undergraduate college or university. Contact Merrimack High School counselor for application. Deadline: April 1.

5.
Abbie Sargent Memorial Scholarship, Inc.
RFD #10, P.O. Box 344D
Concord, NH 03301
(603) 224-1934

Scholarships of $200 to undergraduate and graduate students who are residents of New Hampshire and majoring in agriculture, veterinary medicine, or home economics. Based on academic achievement and character. Must be legal U.S. residents. Renewable with reapplication. Deadline: March 15.

6.
Abbott Laboratories
Manager of College Relations
Department 39K, Building AP6D
200 Abbott Park Road
Abbott Park, IL 60064-3500
(847) 937-7000
http://www.abbott.com

150 to 280 twelve-week internships providing from $340 to $600 per week for undergraduates and from $650 to $1,000 per week for graduate students. Includes round-trip travel and housing expenses. Internships are in Lake County,

Illinois. Accepted majors are accounting, business, computer science, finance, marketing, science (biology, biochemistry, chemistry, pharmacology, physiology, etc.), and engineering (chemical, industrial, electrical, and mechanical). Preference given to undergraduate juniors and above. Submit résumés from January 1 through March 1 either by mail or online. Deadline: March 1.

7.
Abbott Laboratories
Clara Abbott Foundation Award Program
Executive Director
200 Abbott Park Road
Abbott Park, IL 60064
(847) 937-3642

Scholarships of up to $1,800 for graduating high school seniors, high school graduates, and undergraduate students who are children of Abbott Laboratories employees. Students must be between ages seventeen and twenty-nine. Award is good for any undergraduate major. Deadline: January–March, varies.

8.
Abe and Annie Seibel Foundation
Trust Director
c/o The United States National Bank
P.O. Box 179
Galveston, TX 77553
(409) 763-1151

Interest-free loans of $2,500 for freshmen and $3,000 for sophomores, juniors, and seniors. Must be Texas residents who have graduated from a Texas high school and are planning to attend or are attending a college/university on a full-time basis. Based on certain academic qualifications. Interview required. Deadline: February 28.

9.
A Better Chance (ABC)
419 Boylston Street
Boston, MA 02116
(617) 421-0950

ABC helps place academically talented and highly motivated minority students in private secondary schools throughout the nation. It provides a variety of support services.

10.
Academy for Advanced and Strategic Studies
Internship Coordinator
1647 Lamont Street, N.W.
Washington, DC 20010-2796
(202) 234-6646
(202) 667-4042 Fax

7 internships providing a stipend ranging from $500 to $1,000, plus free room and board to high school students, high school graduates, undergraduates, recent college graduates, and graduate students. International students are eligible. The Academy is a think tank that focuses on issues that are vital for social and personal progress. It is helpful if applicants have experience in architecture, design, computer programming, engineering, expository writing, productions, project management, publishing, science and statistics, or research. Interns are assigned research counselors and conduct research on one or more projects. Internships last fifteen weeks to one year during the summer, fall, or spring. Deadline: rolling.

11.
Academy Foundation
Nicholl Fellowship in Screenwriting
8949 Wilshire Boulevard
Beverly Hills, CA 90211-1972
(310) 247-3020

5 fellowships of $20,000 to U.S. citizens who are pursuing a career as screenwriter and haven't been paid to write a screenplay or teleplay. Charges $30 entry fee. Deadline: May 1.

12.
Academy of Motion Picture Arts and Sciences
Student Academy Awards
8949 Wilshire Boulevard
Beverly Hills, CA 90211
(310) 247-3000

Awards of $1,000 (Bronze), $1,500 (Silver), and $2,000 (Gold) are available in each of the following categories: animation, documentary, dramatic, and experimental disciplines. Based on resourcefulness, originality, entertainment, and production quality. No entry must be longer than sixty minutes. Send a self-addressed stamped, envelope (55¢ postage). Deadline: April 1.

13.
Academy of Television Arts & Sciences
4605 Lankershim Boulevard, #800
North Hollywood, CA 61601-3109
(818) 754-2830
(818) 761-2827 Fax
http://www.emmys.org
collegeawards@emmys.org

1 first-place award of $2,000, 1 second-place award of $1,000, and 1 third-place award of $500 in each of the following categories: comedy; drama; music; documentary; news, sports, and magazine shows; animation—traditional; and animation—nontraditional (computer-generated). There is no entry fee for the competition. The awards are presented to recipients at a gala attended by industry people, such as Brandon Tartikoff, Garry Marshall, James Earl Jones, Roger Ebert, Jane Alexander, Barney Rosenzweig, and many others. The aim of the competition is to give outstanding students' work exposure to the television and film industry. The College Awards serves as a point of industry contact for students as they pursue their careers. Deadline: December 15.

14.
Academy of Television Arts & Sciences Student Internship Program
5220 Lankershim Boulevard
North Hollywood, CA 91601-3109
(818) 754-2830
(818) 761-2827 Fax
internships@emmys.org

28 eight-week summer internships providing a $1,600 stipend and a $300 disbursement if living outside of Los Angeles. Open to full-time undergraduate or graduate students, and recent graduates, as long as they didn't graduate before March 31 of the prior year. Students must select one of the following categories: agency; animation—traditional; animation—computer-generated; art direction; broadcast advertising and promotion; business affairs; casting; children's programming and development; cinematography; commercials; costume design; development; documentary—reality production; editing; entertainment news; episodic series; movies for television; music; network programming management; production management; public relations and publicity; sound; syndication and distribution; television directing—single camera; television directing—multicamera; television scriptwriting; or video postproduction. Though open to all majors, it is preferred that students have experience in the area of interest. All finalists are required to submit a videotaped interview on ½" VHS (not Beta) responding to questions sent by the Academy. Interns must have a car. Most internships start in late June or early July and last eight weeks. Approximately 75 percent of former interns land jobs in the television industry. Alumni include an Emmy award–winning art director for *The Bold and the Beautiful*, a producer of *Northern Exposure*, a story editor for *Star Trek: The Next Generation*, and an assistant director for *The Simpsons*. Deadline: mid-March.

15.
Accredited Care, Inc.
200 East 82nd Street
New York, NY 10028
(212) 517-8110

Varying numbers of nonsalaried internships that last a varying amount of time open to high school graduates, undergraduate or graduate students, or anyone with a desire to work in the home health care field. Individuals with health care training and basic math skills are preferred. Interns assist with hands-on care by working as a companion, personal care aide, or home health aid, or can work as office staff assisting and scheduling, billing, marketing, recruiting, and filing. Internships may be full- or part-time, with openings available year-round. Interested individuals must submit a letter outlining their interests, and application form, a résumé, references, and a transcript, and must have an interview in person or by phone. Send résumé to the above address. Internship is conducted in Jamestown, NY. Deadline: open.

16.
Adams Scholarship Fund
125 Savoy Road
Adams, MA 01220
(413) 743-8413

14 scholarships ranging from $100 to $300 to students who are residents of Adams-Cheshire, Massachusetts, Regional School District. Contact high school counselor for details and application. Deadline: May 1.

17.
Addison H. Gibson Foundation
Secretary
1 PPG Place, Suite 2230
Pittsburgh, PA 15222
(412) 261-1611

87 loans ranging from $1,000 to $10,000 to male college students who are residents of western Pennsylvania and have completed one year of college study. Deadline: rolling.

18.
ADMA Scholastic Program Aviation/Engineering/Computer Science Scholarships
1900 Arch Street
Philadelphia, PA 19103

2 scholarships of $2,000 to undergraduate students majoring in aviation. Must apply during sophomore year; award is used during junior year of study. Emphasis is given to students interested in pursuing careers in general aviation, flight engineering, airway science, or aircraft systems management. Deadline: April 15.

19.
Admiral Roland Student Loan Program
Commanding Officer
Headquarters Support Command (HSC/A-1)
2100 2nd Street, S.W.
Washington, DC 20593-0001
(202) 267-2085
(202) 267-1683

Loans to members, members' spouses, and dependent children of members who are on active duty or are retired or reserve members of the Coast Guard, active members of the Coast Guard Auxiliary, or civilian employees of the Coast Guard. Deadline: April 1.

20.
Adrian M. Sample Trust No. 2
5311 Burningtree Drive
Orlando, FL 32811
(305) 423-0314

94 scholarships ranging from $200 to $4,500 to students who are residents of St. Lucie or Okeechobee counties, Florida. Applicants must be unmarried and active Protestant church members. Deadline: April 15.

21.
Aeolian Foundation
2625 Concord Pike
P.O. Box 7138
Wilmington, DE 19803
(302) 656-1200

10 scholarships of varying amounts totaling $22,000 to high school seniors and undergraduate students. Must be Delaware residents. Based on academic potential. Write a letter briefly detailing your educational and financial situation. Other restrictions may apply. Deadline: none specified.

22.
Aerospace Education Foundation
Aviation Scholarship Program
Education Office
Oshkosh, WI 54903
(920) 426-4888

Up to 10 scholarships of $200 to graduating high school seniors or undergraduate students majoring and pursuing a career in aviation. Selection based on academic criteria and financial need. Other restrictions may apply. Deadline: April 1.

23.
AFL–CIO Guide to Union Sponsored Scholarships
AFL-CIO Department of Education
815 16th Street, N.W.
Washington, DC 20006

Numerous scholarships of varying amounts totaling approximately $3,000,000. This guide covers scholarship opportunities and readily admits it only scratches the surface. This is an excellent resource for families of union members. It covers scholarship opportunities at the national, state, and local union levels. The guide is free to union members. Members and dependents of union members are encouraged to contact their local union office to ask about local scholarship opportunities.

24.
AFS Intercultural Programs
International Exchange Student Program
310 S.W. 4th Avenue, Suite 630
Portland, OR 97204-2309
(800) AFS-INFO

Scholarships of varying amounts to international-exchange high school students who live with host families and attend local secondary schools. Includes fifty-five countries. Deadline: fall and spring.

25.
Aid Association for Lutherans (AAL)
Attn: Scholarships
4321 North Ballard Road
Appleton, WI 54919-0001
(920) 734-5721

1,700 renewable scholarships ranging from $500 to $2,000 and 500 nonrenewable $500 scholarships to high school seniors. Applicant's parents must hold an AAL certificate of membership and insurance or annuity in their own home. Students with renewable scholarships must maintain satisfactory academic progress. Other restrictions may apply. Deadline: November 30.

26.
Aid Association for Lutherans (AAL)
4321 North Ballard Road
Appleton, WI 54919-0001
(920) 734-5721

1,000 scholarships of $200–$1,000 per year to members of AAL who are attending or planning to attend a Lutheran and/or Bible institute. Deadline: November 30.

27.
Aid Association for Lutherans (AAL)
Vocational/Technical Scholarship Program
4321 North Ballard Road
Appleton, WI 54919-0001
(920) 734-5721

100 renewable awards of $500 to students who hold an AAL certificate in their name before deadline date and who are enrolled in or plan to enroll in a course of study leading to a vocational/technical diploma or a two-year associate's degree. Deadline: January 30.

28.
AIESEC United States
International Association of Students in
  Economic & Business Management
135 West 50th Street, 17th Floor
New York, NY 10020
(212) 757-3774
aiesec@aiesec.org

Up to 5,000 interns participate in internships lasting two to eighteen months. A salary ranging from $175 to $600 per week is provided to undergraduates who are AIESEC student members and recent college graduates (within one year). International students may also apply. Internships take place in fifty-five cities in twenty-nine states and Washington D.C., and in eighty-two countries worldwide. U.S. students work abroad and foreign students work in the U.S. Interns are assigned at one of nearly 200 companies in areas of accounting, economics, finance, human resources, management, marketing, and sales. Deadline: rolling.

29.
Aim Magazine Short Story Contest
7308 S. Eberhart Avenue
Chicago, IL 60619
(773) 874-6184

Contest for unpublished short stories (4,000-word maximum) promoting brotherhood among people and cultures. This is a cash award for the winner to use at his or her discretion and is not a scholarship. Deadline: August 15.

30.
Air–Conditioning & Refrigeration Wholesalers
  Association
ARW Memorial Scholarship Fund
Manager of Education
6360 N.W. 5th Way, Suite 202
Ft. Lauderdale, FL 33309

12 scholarships of up to $750 each to undergraduate juniors who will use the scholarship in their last year of undergraduate study and will be returning for the completion of their HV AC-R or Distribution studies. Minimum 3.0 GPA or better required. Deadline: May 30.

31.
Aircraft Electronics Association (AEA) Educational Foundation
Bud Glover Memorial Scholarship
P.O. Box 1963
Independence, MO 64055
(816) 373-6565

1 scholarship ranging from $1,000 to $2,500 to a high school senior or undergraduate student. Must be planning to attend or attending an accredited school in an avionics or A&P program. Request application in the fall; include a self-addressed, stamped envelope. Pilots and air traffic controllers are not eligible. Deadline: February 2.

32.
Aircraft Electronics Association (AEA) Educational Foundation
Castleberry Instruments Scholarship
P.O. Box 1963
Independence, MO 64055
(816) 373-6565

1 scholarship of $1,000 to a high school senior or undergraduate student. Must be planning to attend or attending an accredited school in an avionics or A&P program. Request application in the fall; include a self-addressed, stamped envelope. Pilots and air traffic controllers are not eligible. Deadline: February 2.

33.
Aircraft Electronics Association (AEA) Educational Foundation
College of Aeronautics Scholarship
P.O. Box 1963
Independence, MO 64055
(816) 373-6565

1 scholarship of $3,000 to a student in a two-year avionics program (associate or occupational). Recipient receives $750 per semester for up to four semesters. Request application in the fall; include a self-addressed, stamped envelope. Pilots and air traffic controllers are not eligible. Other restrictions may apply. Deadline: February 2.

34.
Aircraft Electronics Association (AEA) Educational Foundation
Colorado Aero Tech Scholarship
P.O. Box 1963
Independence, MO 64055
(816) 373-6565

1 full-tuition scholarship of $15,225 to a high school senior. Must be planning to attend Colorado Aero Tech in Broomfield, Colorado. Award is for tuition only, not to purchase books, tools, or living expenses. Request application in the fall; include a self-addressed, stamped envelope. Pilots and air traffic controllers are not eligible. Deadline: February 2.

35.
Aircraft Electronics Association (AEA) Educational Foundation
David Arver Memorial Scholarship
P.O. Box 1963
Independence, MO 64055
(816) 373-6565

1 scholarship of $1,000 to a high school senior. Must be planning to attend an accredited school in an aviation-related program in Illinois, Indiana, Iowa, Kansas, Michigan, Minnesota, Missouri, Nebraska, South or North Dakota, or Wisconsin. Request application in the fall; include a self-addressed, stamped envelope. Pilots and air traffic controllers are not eligible. Deadline: February 2.

36.
Aircraft Electronics Association (AEA) Educational Foundation
Gulf Coast Avionics Scholarship
P.O. Box 1963
Independence, MO 64055
(816) 373-6565

1 scholarship of $1,000 to a high school senior or undergraduate student. Must be planning to attend or attending an accredited school in an avionics program. Request application in the fall; include a self-addressed, stamped envelope. Pilots and air traffic controllers are not eligible. Deadline: February 2.

37.
Aircraft Electronics Association (AEA) Educational Foundation
Leon Harris/Les Nichols Memorial Scholarship
P.O. Box 1963
Independence, MO 64055
(816) 373-6565

1 scholarship of $16,000 to a student pursuing an associate's degree in applied science in aviation electronics (avionics) at the NEC Spartan School of Aeronautics in Tulsa, Oklahoma. The scholarship covers tuition for eight quarters or until recipient completes the degree. Can be used for tuition only. Applicants can't be enrolled at Spartan at the time of application. Request application in the fall; include a self-addressed, stamped envelope. Pilots and air traffic controllers are not eligible. Deadline: February 2.

38.
Aircraft Electronics Association (AEA) Educational Foundation
Lowell Gaylor Memorial Scholarship
P.O. Box 1963
Independence, MO 64055
(816) 373-6565

1 scholarship of $1,000 to a high school senior or undergraduate student. Must be planning to attend or attending an accredited school in an avionics or A&P program. Request application in the fall; include a self-addressed, stamped envelope. Pilots and air traffic controllers are not eligible. Deadline: February 2.

39.
Aircraft Electronics Association (AEA) Educational Foundation
Navair Limited Scholarship
P.O. Box 1963
Independence, MO 64055
(816) 373-6565

1 scholarship of $1,000 to a high school senior or undergraduate student. Must be planning to attend or attending an accredited college or aviation-related program in an accredited vocational/technical program in Canada. Request application in the fall; include a self-addressed, stamped envelope. Pilots and air traffic controllers are not eligible. Deadline: February 2.

40.
Aircraft Electronics Association (AEA) Educational Foundation Scholarships
P.O. Box 1963
Independence, MO 64055
(816) 373-6565

3 scholarships of $1,000 and 1 scholarship of $2,000 to high school seniors or undergraduate students. Must be planning to attend or attending an accredited vocational/technical aviation-related program in Canada. Request applications in the fall, please include a self-addressed, stamped envelope. Pilots and air traffic controllers are not eligible. Deadline: February 2.

41.
Aircraft Electronics Association (AEA) Educational Foundation
Terra Avionics Collegiate Scholarship
P.O. Box 1963
Independence, MO 64055
(816) 373-6565

1 scholarship of $2,500 to a high school senior or undergraduate student who is the child or grandchild of an AEA member. May major in any field of study. Selection is based on an essay. Pilots and air traffic controllers are not eligible. Request an application in the fall. Include a self-addressed, stamped envelope to: Terra Avionics, 3520 Pan American Freeway, Albuquerque, NM 87107. Deadline: February 2.

42.
Air Force Aid Society
General Henry H. Arnold Education Grant
1745 Jefferson Davis Highway, Suite 202
Arlington, VA 22202
(703) 607-3072
(703) 607-3064

Up to 5,000 scholarships of $1,500 to graduating high school seniors or undergraduate students. Must be dependents of an active-duty, retired, or deceased member of the Air Force. Selection based on financial need. Renewable with maintained academic progress. Other restrictions may apply. Deadline: March 20.

43.
Air Force Aid Society
Student Loan Programs
1745 Jefferson Davis Highway, Suite 202
Arlington, VA 22202
(202) 692-9313

Loans to children of Air Force members and to members, their spouses, and widow(er)s. $2,625 loans are for first- and second-year undergraduates; $4,000 for third- and fourth-year students. Graduate and professional-school students may borrow up to $7,500 per academic year. Based on financial need.

44.
Air Force Reserve Officer Training Corps
Air Force ROTC, Recruiting Division
Maxwell Air Force Base, AL 36112-6106
(334) 953-2694

Three- and four-year scholarships providing full tuition, books, fees, and a $150 tax-free monthly allowance during the academic year, plus pay, to high school and college students in various academic areas depending on the current needs of the Air Force. Deadline: December 1 (senior year).

45.
Air Force ROTC Nursing Scholarships
HQ AFROTC Scholarship Actions Section
Maxwell AFB, AL 36112-6106

Varying numbers of scholarships providing financial assistance. High school seniors or high school graduates who are not attending college full-time are eligible for four years of assistance. Undergraduates are eligible for one- to three-year scholarships. Type I scholarships pay full college tuition, most mandatory fees, plus a checkbook allowance. Type II scholarships pay the same benefits, up to $8,000 per year. All Air Force ROTC cadets on scholarship receive a $150 monthly nontaxable allowance during the school year. Upon completion of AFROTC program and degree requirements, the student is commissioned a second lieutenant in the Air Force Nurse Corps and must serve four years of active duty. May be used for both undergraduate and graduate study. Deadline: none

46.
Air Force Sergeants Association (AFSA)
Scholarships
P.O. Box 50
Temple Hills, MD 20748-0050
(800) 638-0594/95 or (301) 899-3500
http://www.afsahq.org

Varying numbers of scholarships of $1,000 to graduating high school seniors or undergraduate students. Must be eligible dependent children of AFSA or AFSA Auxiliary members. Must be attending a two- or four-year college or university. Based on academic ability, character, leadership, writing ability, and potential for success; financial need is not considered. Include a self-addressed, stamped envelope (78¢ postage). Deadline: April 15.

47.

**Air Force Sergeants Association
Trade/Technical Scholarships for Electronic
    Engineering**
P.O. Box 50
Temple Hills, MD 20748-0050
(800) 638-0594/95 or (301) 899-3500
http://www.afsahq.org

Varying numbers of scholarships ranging from $600 to
$1,000 to eligible dependent children of AFSA or AFSA
Auxiliary members. Must be attending a vocational/
technical school. Based on academic ability, character,
leadership, writing ability, and potential for success;
financial need is not considered. Include a self-addressed,
stamped envelope (78¢ postage). Deadline: April 15.

48.

Airline Pilots Association Scholarship
1625 Massachusetts Avenue, N.W.
Washington, DC 20036
(202) 797-4050

1 renewable scholarship of $3,000 per year for four years to
a graduating high school senior or college undergraduate
son or daughter of medically retired or deceased pilot
member of the APA. Based on academic capability and
financial need. Deadline: April 1.

49.

Airmen Memorial Foundation
Scholarship Program
5211 Auth Road
Suitland, MD 20746
(301) 899-3500 or (800) 638-0594
http://www.amf.org

16 scholarships ranging from $1,000 to $3,000 to unmarried
dependent children (under twenty-five years of age) of
enlisted members, current or retired, of the Air Force, Air
National Guard, or Air Force Reserve. Award may be used
at an accredited two- or four-year college or university or
vocational/technical school. Based on academic record,
character, leadership, writing ability, and potential for
success. Financial need is not considered. Request
applications after November 1. Include a self-addressed,
stamped envelope (legal size, with 78¢ postage). Deadline:
April 15.

50.

**Airmen Memorial Foundation
CMSAR Richard D. Kisling Scholarships**
Scholarship Program
5211 Auth Road
Suitland, MD 20746
(301) 899-3500 or (800) 638-0594

8 scholarships ranging from $1,000 to $3,000 to unmarried
dependent children (under twenty-five years of age) of an
enlisted member, current or retired, of the Air Force, Air
National Guard, or Air Force Reserve. Request applications
after November 1. Include a self-addressed, stamped
envelope (legal size, with 78¢ postage). Deadline: April 15.

51.

**Air Test Evaluation Squadron One (VX–1)–
    Officers' Wives Club**
Scholarship Committee
P.O. Box 135
NAS Patuxent River, MD 20670-5479
(301) 737-3228

2 scholarships of $1,000 to dependents (including spouses)
of regular or reserve Navy, Marine Corps, and Coast Guard
members on active duty or retiree-with-pay, disabled,
deceased, or missing-in-action. Applicants or parents must
be residents of St. Mary's, Calvert, or Charles counties,
Maryland. Based on academic record, character, and
financial need. Application forms must be requested from:
Commander, Naval Military Personnel Command, NMPC-
641 D, Washington, DC 20370-5641. Deadline: April 30.

52.

Air Traffic Control Association Scholarships
Gabriel A. Hartl, President
2300 Clarendon Boulevard, Suite 711
Arlington, VA 22201
(703) 522-5717/(703) 527-7251 Fax
http://www.aviation.uiuc.edu/

Numerous scholarships ranging from $1,500 to $2,500 to
undergraduates enrolled in an aviation-related course of
study. Recipients must reapply for renewal. Scholarships of
up to $600 are also available to full-time aviation-industry
career employees. Deadline: May 1.

53.

A. J. DeAndrade Scholarship Fund
Graphic Communications International Union
1900 L Street, N.W.
Washington, DC 20036
(202) 462-1400

10 scholarships of $500 (for four years) to dependents of
union members. 2 scholarships per region in five regions.
Member must have been in good standing for at least two
years. Graduating high school seniors and first-semester
freshmen are eligible to apply. Based on academic record,
SAT/ACT scores, Achievement Test scores, essay, and
recommendations. Applications are available from the local
unions between October 1 and mid-February. Deadline:
February 15.

54.

**Alabama Commission on Higher Education
Appalachian Youth Scholarships**
P.O. Box 30200
Montgomery, AL 36130-2000
(334) 242-1998

Scholarships of up to $1,500 to high school seniors who
will be entering freshmen and undergraduate students who
are living in and attending an undergraduate institution in
the Alabama Appalachian region (northern portion of the
state). Contact high school counselor, school's financial aid
office, or above address. Deadline: August 15.

55.
Alabama Commission on Higher Education Junior and Community College Athletic Scholarships
P.O. Box 302000
Montgomery, AL 36130-2000
(334) 242-1998

Awards not exceeding total tuition and books to full-time students enrolled in a public two-year community college in Alabama. Based on athletic ability, not financial need. Contact school's coach, athletic director, or financial aid officer. Deadline: varies with each institution.

56.
Alabama Commission on Higher Education Junior and Community College Performing Arts Scholarships
P.O. Box 302000
Montgomery, AL 36130-2000
(334) 242-1998

Awards not exceeding total tuition and books to full-time students enrolled in a public two-year community college in Alabama. Based on talent, not financial need. Contact school's financial aid officer. Deadline: varies with each institution.

57.
Alabama Commission on Higher Education National Guard Assistance Program
P.O. Box 302000
Montgomery, AL 36130-2000
(334) 242-1998

Scholarships ranging from $500 to $1,000 to students who are members of the Alabama National Guard and are attending a public institution in Alabama. Obtain applications from unit commander. Deadline: none.

58.
Alabama Commission on Higher Education Nursing Scholarships
P.O. Box 302000
Montgomery, AL 36130-2000
(334) 242-1998

Scholarships and loans of varying amounts to students who are Alabama residents and have been admitted to a nursing program at participating Alabama institutions. Deadline: varies, depending on institution.

59.
Alabama Commission on Higher Education Police Officers' and Firefighters' Survivors Educational Assistance Program
P.O. Box 302000
Montgomery, AL 36130-2000
(334) 242-1998

Numerous scholarships of varying amounts to dependents or spouses of police officers or firefighters killed in the line of duty in Alabama. Students must be enrolled for undergraduate study in a public Alabama institution. Deadline: varies.

60.
Alabama Commission on Higher Education Prepaid Affordable College Tuition Program
State Treasurer's Office
100 N. Union Street, Suite 660
Montgomery, AL 36130-2530
(800) ALA-PACT

A guaranteed tuition payment program that allows prepayment of four undergraduate years of tuition at any public two- or four-year institution in Alabama. Payment may be in a lump sum or periodic. There is a variable age limit for students enrolled in the program. Deadline: none.

61.
Alabama Commission on Higher Education Robert C. Byrd Honors Scholarship
Attn: Dr. Frank Heatherly
Gordon Persons Bldg., Room 339
50 Ripley Street
Montgomery, AL 36104-3833
(334) 242-8082

Numerous one-time scholarships of $1,500 to high school seniors who are Alabama residents who meet two of three requirements: rank in the top 5 percent of their class, have at least a 3.5 GPA, or have at least an 1100 on SAT or 27 on ACT. For use during first year of study. Contact high school counselor for applications. Deadline: May 1.

62.
Alabama Commission on Higher Education Senior Adult Scholarships
Attn: Nataline Holt
Jefferson State Community College
Birmingham, AL 35215-3098
(205) 856-7709

Free tuition is available to Alabama residents who are sixty years of age or older and are attending a public two-year institution in Alabama. Deadline: varies with each institution.

63.
Alabama Commission on Higher Education Student Assistance Program
P.O. Box 302000
Montgomery, AL 36130-2000
(334) 242-1998

Assistance ranging from $300 to $2,700 to undergraduate students pursuing any major. Must be Alabama residents enrolled in a participating undergraduate Alabama college or university. Amount of award depends on financial need as determined by FAFSA. This is a state and federally funded program. Deadline: varies with each school.

64.
Alabama Commission on Higher Education Student Grant Program
P.O. Box 302000
Montgomery, AL 36130-2000
(334) 242-1998

Grants of up to $600 to full-time undergraduate students or up to $300 per year to part-time undergraduate students.

Must be Alabama residents and attending a private Alabama college or university. Renewable annually upon application for as many years as are required to obtain baccalaureate degree. Deadline: September 15 (fall semester); January 15 (winter quarter); February 15 (spring semester); April 15 (spring quarter).

65.
Alabama Commission on Higher Education Two-Year College Academic Scholarships
P.O. Box 302000
Montgomery, AL 36130-2000
(334) 242-1998

Awards not exceeding in-state tuition and books are available to students accepted at public two-year institutions in Alabama. Based on academic merit, not financial need. Renewable. Deadline: varies with each institution.

66.
Alabama Department of Veterans Affairs G.I. and Dependents Educational Benefit Act
P.O. Box 1509
Montgomery, AL 36102
(334) 242-5077

Educational benefits covering full tuition plus fees and cost of books to any child, spouse, or unmarried widow or widower of veterans who meet specific requirements. Applicants must apply prior to twenty-sixth birthday. Deadline: none for spouse or unremarried widow(er).

67.
Alabama Indian Affairs Commission
1 Court Square, Suite 106
Montgomery, AL 36104
(334) 242-2831

Varying numbers of scholarships of varying amounts totaling up to $80,000 to Native American Indian students. Must be Alabama residents wanting to attend an Alabama college, junior college, or trade school. Recipients are nominated while high school seniors, from tribal groups as well as the at-large Indian population of the state. Deadline: March 3.

68.
Alabama State Department of Education Elementary Teachers Scholarships
Assistant State Superintendent of Education
Division of Administration & Financial Services
P.O. Box 302101
Montgomery, AL 36130
(334) 242-8782

250 scholarships of $100 to students majoring in elementary education. Applicants must plan to teach at least three years in the elementary grades of the tax-supported public schools of Alabama and must have financial need.

69.
Alabama State Superintendent of Education Scholarships for Dependents of Blind Parents
Attn: Elaine Kirkpatrick
Division of Administration & Financial Services
P.O. Box 30201
Montgomery, AL 36130
(334) 242-9792

Numerous waivers of all tuition or fees for four academic years in any Alabama college or university. Must attend college within two years after graduating from high school. Must not be over twenty-three years of age. Must be a permanent resident of Alabama for at least five years. Family income is considered. There are various financial limitations. Deadline: none specified.

70.
Alaska Commission on Postsecondary Education Alaska A. W. "Winn" Brindle Memorial Scholarship Loan Program
3030 Vintage Boulevard
Juneau, AK 99801-7109
(907) 465-6740

Scholarship/loans covering tuition, fees, books, supplies, room and board, and transportation for up to two round trips between recipients' home and school each year. Can be used for five years of undergraduate study, five years of graduate study, or a combined maximum of eight years of study. Recipients have up to ten years to repay the loan, with 8 percent interest. Applicants must be residents of Alaska and full-time undergraduate or graduate students at an accredited institution. Deadline: August 31.

71.
Alaska Commission on Postsecondary Education Alaska Family Education Loans
3030 Vintage Road
Juneau, AK 99801-7109
(907) 465-6740

Loans of $5,500 per year to undergraduates for up to five years of study (including Alaska Student or Teacher loans). The loan is guaranteed by the student's parent, guardian, or spouse, which reduces the student's indebtedness by allowing the student's family to share the indebtedness. The student's family must have lived for two years in Alaska and have claimed the student on its income tax return for the year before applying. Repayment begins within thirty days after loan is disbursed and is repaid over a ten-year period. Deadline: August 31.

72.
Alaska Commission on Postsecondary Education State Educational Incentive Grant Program
3030 Vintage Road
Juneau, AK 99801-7109
(907) 465-6740

120 grants ranging from $100 to $1,500 to undergraduate students who have been Alaska residents for at least two years and who are accepted to or enrolled in their first undergraduate degree at an accredited in-state or out-of-state institution. Deadline: May 31.

73.
**Alaska Commission on Postsecondary Education
Student Loan Program**
3030 Vintage Road
Juneau, AK 99801-7109
(907) 465-6740

Open to Alaska residents of at least two years. These low-
interest loans (up to $5,500) support full-time study at any
accredited vocational, undergraduate, or graduate
institution. Renewable. Deadline: August 31.

74.
**Alaska Commission on Postsecondary Education
Teacher Scholarship Loan Program**
3030 Vintage Road
Juneau, AK 99801-7109
(907) 465-6740

Loans of up to $7,500 per year to graduates of Alaska high
schools pursuing a career in teaching. Award may be used
for tuition, room and board, books, supplies, and
transportation costs. After graduation, the loan is forgiven if
the student teaches in a rural elementary or secondary
school in Alaska and meets other program conditions.
Nominated through Rural School Program. Deadline: varies.

75.
**Alaska Programs for High School Students
Highest-Ranking Senior Scholarships**
Financial Aid Office
University of Alaska
P.O. Box 756360
Fairbanks, AK 99775
(907) 474-7256

Scholarships of varying amounts to the highest-ranking
senior in each high school in Alaska. Covers dormitory rent
at the University of Alaska for two years. Must be Alaska
resident. No application process. Must be nominated by a
school official. Deadline: March 1.

76.
**Alaska State Troopers
Michael Murphy Memorial Scholarship Loan
    Fund**
Attn: Lt. Gorder
5700 East Tudor Road
Anchorage, AK 99507
(907) 269-5655

3 to 6 scholarship/loans of up to $1,000 to full-time
undergraduate and graduate students majoring in criminal
justice, criminology, law enforcement, police administration,
social services, or other law-enforcement-related field. Must
be attending an accredited two- or four-year institution
and be a resident of Alaska. 20 percent of the full loan
amount is forgiven for each year employed in law
enforcement. Renewable. Deadline: April 1.

77.
Alaska Student Summer Internship Program
Alaska Department of Natural Resources
Attn: Lee McFarland
Human Resource Section
3601 C Street, Suite 1222
Anchorage, AK 99503
(907) 269-8670

Internship program providing $4.75 to $16.50/hour to high
school or undergraduate students. Must be Alaska residents
at any level of study who are at least sixteen years of age.
Applicants must be enrolled or plan to enroll as a full-time
student at any college, university, or technical program.
Open to most areas of study. Deadline: rolling.

78.
Albert B. and Evelyn H. Black Scholarship Fund
Fleet Investment Management
Attn: Grantmaking Associate
75 State Street
MA BO F07 B
Boston, MA 02109
(617) 346-4000

42 scholarships ranging from $500 to $850 to graduating
high school seniors. Must be attending public schools in
Concord, Massachusetts. Selection based on academic
achievement, transcript, essay, extracurricular activities,
general appearance of the application, and financial need.
IRS forms must be submitted. Request applications from
above address after January 1. Other restrictions may apply.
Deadline: early April.

79.
**Aloca Foundation
Sons & Daughters Scholarship Program**
Program Assistant
425 6th Avenue
Pittsburgh, PA 15219
(412) 553-4786

52 scholarships of $2,000 to high school seniors who are
children of current or retired Alcoa employees. Scholarship
recipients are chosen by local committees. Based on high
school academic standing and promise, personal qualities,
character and leadership ability, and SAT scores. Renewable
based on academic standing. Deadline: October 31.

80.
Alexander Educational Fund
c/o Santa Barbara Scholarship Foundation
P.O. Box 1403
Santa Barbara, CA 93102
(805) 965-7212

110 loans and scholarships ranging from $500 to $2,500 to
students who have been residents of Santa Barbara County,
California, for at least two years. Applicants must not have
resided in Santa Barbara County just to attend college. The
scholarships are administered by the Santa Barbara
Foundation, but funded by the Alexander Educational
Fund. Deadline: January 30.

81.
Alexander Graham Bell Association for the Deaf
A. G. Bell Scholarship for Deaf Adults
3417 Volta Place, N.W.
Washington, DC 20007-2778
(202) 337-5220 Voice or TDD
(written inquiries only)
http://www.agbell.org
agbell2@aol.com

1 scholarship of $1,000 to an oral deaf graduating high school senior or undergraduate student who was born with profound hearing impairment or who lost his/her hearing before acquiring language. Applicants must be able to use speech and residual hearing and/or speech reading as their preferred form of communication. Applicants must be accepted to or enrolled in a college or university. Deadline: April 1.

82.
Alexander Graham Bell Association for the Deaf
David J. Von Hagen Scholarship Awards
3417 Volta Place, N.W.
Washington, DC 20007-2778
(202) 337-5220 (Voice or TDD)
(written inquiries only)
http://www.agbell.org
agbell2@aol.com

2 scholarships of $750 to an oral deaf student who was born with profound hearing impairment or who lost his/her hearing before acquiring language. Must be able to use speech and residual hearing and/or speech reading as preferred form of communication. Must be accepted to or enrolled in a college or university. Preference is given to students majoring in science or engineering. Deadline: April 1.

83.
Alexander Graham Bell Association for the Deaf
Elsie Bell Grosvenor Scholarship Awards
Scholarship Awards Committee
3417 Volta Place, N.W.
Washington, DC 20007-2778
(202) 337-5220 (Voice or TDD)
(written inquiries only)
http://www.agbell.org
agbell2@aol.com

1 scholarship of $500 and 1 scholarship of $1,000 to oral deaf students from the metropolitan Washington, DC, area or those who will be attending college in the DC area. Must have been born with a profound hearing impairment or suffered the loss before acquiring language. Open to students in all areas of study. Deadline: April 1.

84.
Alexander Graham Bell Association for the Deaf
General Scholarship Awards
3417 Volta Place, N.W.
Washington, DC 20007-2778
(202) 337-5220 Voice or TDD
(written inquiries only)
http://www.agbell.org
agbell2@aol.com

Up to 20 scholarships ranging from $500 to $1,000 to oral deaf graduating high school seniors or undergraduate students who were born with profound hearing impairment or who lost their hearing before acquiring language. Applicants must be able to use speech and residual hearing and/or speech reading as their preferred form of communication. Applicants must be accepted to or enrolled in a college or university for hearing students. Deadline: April 1.

85.
Alexander Graham Bell Association for the Deaf
Herbert P. Feibelman (IPO) Award
3417 Volta Place, N.W.
Washington, DC 20007-2778
(202) 337-5220 (Voice or TDD)
(written inquiries only)
http://www.agbell.org
agbell2@aol.com

1 scholarship of $1,000 to an oral deaf student who was born with profound hearing impairment or who lost his/her hearing before acquiring language. Must use speech and residual hearing and/or speech reading as the preferred form of communication. Must be accepted to or enrolled in a college or university and pursuing a degree. Deadline: April 1.

86.
Alexander Graham Bell Association for the Deaf
Lucile A. Abt Awards
3417 Volta Place, N.W.
Washington, DC 20007-2778
(202) 337-5220 (Voice or TDD)
(written inquiries only)
http://www.agbell.org
agbell2@aol.com

5 scholarships of $1,000 to oral deaf students who were born with profound hearing impairment or who lost their hearing before acquiring language. Must use speech and speech reading as preferred form of communication. Must be accepted to or enrolled in a college or university and pursuing a degree. Deadline: April 1.

87.
Alexander Graham Bell Association for the Deaf
Margaret Marsh Memorial Scholarship Awards
3417 Volta Place, N.W.
Washington, DC 20007-2778
(202) 337-5220 (Voice or TDD)
(written inquiries only)
http://www.agbell.org
agbell2@aol.com

2 scholarships of $500 to oral deaf students who were born with profound hearing impairment or who lost their hearing before acquiring language. Must use speech and residual hearing and/or speech reading as the preferred form of communication. Must be accepted to or enrolled in a college or university for hearing students and pursuing a degree. Deadline: April 1.

88.

Alexander Graham Bell Association for the Deaf
Maude Winkler Scholarship Awards

3417 Volta Place, N.W.
Washington, DC 20007-2778
(202) 337-5220 (Voice or TDD)
(written inquiries only)
http://www.agbell.org
agbell2@aol.com

Up to 5 scholarships of $1,000 to oral deaf students who were born with profound hearing impairment or who lost their hearing before acquiring language. Must use speech and speech reading as preferred form of communication. Must be accepted to or enrolled in a college or university and pursuing a degree. Deadline: April 1.

89.

Alexander Graham Bell Association for the Deaf
National Rural Letter Carriers' Association
Ladies' Auxiliary Scholarships

3417 Volta Place, N.W.
Washington, DC 20007-2778
(202) 337-5220 (Voice or TDD)
(written inquiries only)
http://www.agbell.org
agbell2@aol.com

2 scholarships of $500 to oral deaf students who were born with profound hearing impairment or who lost their hearing before acquiring language. Must use speech and residual hearing and/or speech reading as the preferred form of communication. Must be accepted to or enrolled in a college or university for hearing students and pursuing a degree. Deadline: April 1.

90.

Alexander Graham Bell Association for the Deaf
Robert H. Weitbrecht Scholarship Awards

3417 Volta Place, N.W.
Washington, DC 20007-2778
(202) 337-5220 (Voice or TDD)
(written inquiries only)
http://www.agbell.org
agbell2@aol.com

2 scholarships of $750 to oral deaf students who were born with profound hearing impairment or who lost their hearing before acquiring language. Must use speech and residual hearing and/or speech reading as the preferred form of communication. Must be accepted to or enrolled in a college or university and pursuing a degree. Preference is given to students majoring in science or engineering. Deadline: April 1.

91.

Alexander Graham Bell Association for the Deaf
The Oral–Hearing–Impaired Section Scholarship

3417 Volta Place, N.W.
Washington, DC 20007-2778
(202) 337-5220 (Voice or TDD)
(written inquiries only)
http://www.agbell.org
agbell2@aol.com

1 scholarship of $1,000 to an oral deaf student who was born with profound hearing impairment or who lost his/ her hearing before acquiring language. Must use speech and speech reading as preferred form of communication. Must be accepted to or enrolled in a college or university for hearing students and pursuing a degree. Deadline: April 1.

92.

Alexander Graham Bell Association for the Deaf
The Volta Scholarships

3417 Volta Place, N.W.
Washington, DC 20007-2778
(202) 337-5220 (Voice or TDD)
(written inquiries only)
http://www.agbell.org
agbell2@aol.com

2 scholarships of $500 and 1 scholarship of $300 to oral deaf students. Must use speech and speech reading as preferred form of communication. Must be accepted to or enrolled in a college or university for hearing students and pursuing a degree. Deadline: April 1.

93.

Alfred Moore Foundation

Attn: Chairperson
c/o C. L. Page Enterprise, Inc.
P.O. Box 18426
Spartanburg, SC 29318
(864) 573-5298

34 scholarships ranging from $500 to $2,000 to students who are residents of Anderson or Spartanburg Counties, South Carolina. Deadline: March 29.

94.

All–American Soap Box Derby

General Manager
P.O. Box 7225
Akron, OH 44306
(330) 733-8723

3 scholarships—of $2,000, $3,000, and $5,000 each year—to the top three male or female winners of the Senior Division race. Applicants must be between twelve and sixteen years of age for the Senior Division. Applicants between the ages of nine and twelve compete in the Junior Division, with woodworking tools presented to the winners. Deadline: varies.

95.

Allegheny Review Literary Awards

Allegheny Review
Review Editors
P.O. Box 32, Allegheny College
Meadville, PA 16335
(814) 332-3100

A $50 prize, and publication, for best entry in each division (fiction and poetry). This contest for unpublished short fiction and poetry is for college students only. Fiction submissions aren't to exceed fifteen pages, double-spaced. Poetry submissions can be three to five poems. All work must be typed and accompanied by name, address, school name, and class year. If you want your submissions returned, include a self-addressed, stamped envelope. This is a cash award for student to use at his/her discretion. Deadline: January 15.

96.

Allen H. and Nydia Meyers Foundation
4107 N. Adrian Highway
Adrian, MI 49221
(517) 265-1629

25 grants ranging from $350 to $500 to high school seniors
planning on majoring in the physical sciences, engineering,
aviation, or related fields. Must be residents of Lenawee
County, Michigan. Deadline: March 1.

97.

Alliance for Health Reform
1900 L Street, N.W., Suite 512
Washington, DC 20036
(202) 466-5626
(202) 466-6525 Fax

4 internships lasting from three to four months open to
undergraduate juniors, seniors, graduate students, or mid-
career persons. Media interns work locating, cataloging, and
securing reprint permission for articles, update database of
media contacts, and assist with press releases. Policy interns
work with the Executive Director in transcribing and
compiling notes from high-level meetings and draft policy
papers and memorandums. Individuals must have
knowledge of the U.S. governmental process and of health-
care issues. Strong writing skills are essential. Individuals
with experience in policy work, health-care course work, or
media exposure are preferred. Must submit a letter
outlining interests, a résumé, letters of recommendation, a
transcript, and a writing sample. Decisions are made by mid-
March. Deadline: February 1.

98.

Alliance for Young Artists & Writers, Inc.
American Museum of Natural History Young
   Naturalist Awards
c/o Scholastic
555 Broadway, Fourth Floor
New York, NY 10012
(212) 343-6493
(800) 631-1586

12 awards ranging from $500 to $2,500 U.S. Savings Bonds
to students in grades 7 through 12. Students can complete
one of three projects. Competition is between grades 7–8,
grades 9–10, and grades 11–12. Include a copy of the entry
form and submit the $3 entry fee. Deadline: early February.

99.

Alliance for Young Artists & Writers, Inc.
Fulbright Young Essayists Awards
c/o Scholastic
555 Broadway, Fourth Floor
New York, NY 10012
(212) 343-6493
(800) 631-1586

12 scholarship awards to students in grades 7 through 12
(two awards of $500 for 7th graders, two awards of $750
for 8th graders, two awards of $1,000 for 9th graders, two
awards of $1,500 for 10th graders, two awards of $2,000 for
11th graders, and two awards of $2,500 for 12th graders).
Awards are in the form of U.S. Savings Bonds. Students
submit essays exploring international issues and cross-
cultural experiences. They must be attending public or non-
public schools in the United States, a United States territory,
or a United States–sponsored school abroad. Deadline: mid-
January.

100.

Alliance for Young Artists & Writers, Inc.
Scholastic Art/Photography
555 Broadway, Fourth Floor
New York, NY 10012
(212) 343-6493
(800) 631-1586

Students from 7th through 12th grade can enter, with
awards ranging from $50 to $1,000. Enter in Fine Arts:
painting, drawing, mixed media, printmaking, sculpture,
photography, computer graphics, video, film, and animation;
Design: architecture, landscape architecture, interior design,
computer software, and computer web sites, products—
clothing, products—appliances, toys, robots, scientific
instruments, cars, trucks, rv's, furniture; Crafts: ceramics,
jewelry, metalsmithing, textile and fiber design; Portfolios:
art and photography. Enclose a self-addressed, stamped
envelope. There is a fee of $60 per school for students to
enter. Deadline: mid-January (fee form submission) and
early February (for entries).

101.

Alliance for Young Artists & Writers, Inc.
Scholastic Writing Awards
555 Broadway, Fourth Floor
New York, NY 10012
(212) 343-6493
(800) 631-1586

Students from 7th through 12th grade can enter, with
awards ranging from $100 to $1,000. Students compete
within groups: Group I—grades 7, 8, 9; Group II—10, 11,
12. Categories are: Short Story; Short Short Story; Essay/
Nonfiction/Opinion Writing; Dramatic Script; Poetry;
Humor; and Science Fiction/Fantasy. Lengths of entries
vary by group. There is a $3 processing fee for each
submission. Deadline: mid-January.

102.

Alliance of Motion Picture and Television
   Producers & Directors Guild of America
Directors Guild Producer Training Plan
15503 Ventura Boulevard
Encino, CA 91436-3140
(818) 386-2545
http://www.dgptp.org
trainingprogram@dgptp.org

10 to 20 four-hundred-day internships open to
undergraduate seniors, graduate students, or a person with
an associate's degree, a bachelor's degree, or two years paid
employment in film/television production. Interns have on-
the-job training for the position of Second Assistant
Director in motion pictures or television. The internships
are based in Los Angeles County, though some of the work
may be out of town or out of state. Must submit
application form and transcript (or work equivalency
forms). There is a $50 application fee. Request applications
after August 1. Deadline: mid-November.

103.
Almanor Scholarship Fund
c/o Collins Pine Company
P.O. Box 796
Chester, CA 96020
(916) 258-2111

1 scholarship of $1,200 available to Chester, California, resident who graduated from Chester High School. Must have at least a 3.0 GPA. Good for any major and for full-time at any accredited institution. Deadline: August 1.

104.
Alpha Delta Kappa Fine Arts Grant
1615 West 92nd Street
Kansas City, MO 64114
(816) 363-5525

Grants ranging from $2,500 to $5,000. The biennial grant program is designed to assist students in additional study and/or in projects furthering their artistic skills. Specific performing-art and fine-art categories change each biennium. Open to all qualified individuals. Write for complete details. Deadline: April 1 of even-numbered years.

105.
Alpha Kappa Alpha Domestic Travel Tour Grant
5656 South Stony Island Avenue
Chicago, IL 60637
(773) 684-1282

30 Travel Grants of $1,000 to African American female high school juniors and seniors in U.S. with at least a B average. Provides an opportunity for young women to gain knowledge through travel tours to historical sites in the U.S. AKA membership not required. Awarded in odd-numbered years. Based on a 1,000-word essay.

106.
Alpha Kappa Alpha Educational Advancement Foundation
5656 South Stony Island Avenue
Chicago, IL 60637
(773) 684-1282 or (773) 684-1282

Scholarships ranging from $500 to $1,500 and one merit award of $2,000 to undergraduate students who have completed at least one full year of study. Applicants must submit three letters of recommendation and an official transcript. Request applications between December 1 and January 31. Deadline: February 15.

107.
Alpha Mu Gamma (AMG) Scholarships
Los Angeles City College
855 North Vermont Avenue
Los Angeles, CA 90029
(213) 669-4255

1 scholarship of $500 to a bilingual student majoring in language, literature, or linguistics. Must be AMG member. Deadline: February 1.

108.
Alpha Mu Gamma (AMG) Scholarships
Full-Tuition Summer Scholarship
Los Angeles City College
855 North Vermont Avenue
Los Angeles, CA 90029
(213) 669-4255

1 full-tuition scholarship to a student member to study French from July to August at Laval University in Quebec. Deadline: December 31; may vary.

109.
Alpha Mu Gamma (AMG) Scholarships
Merit Scholarship
Los Angeles City College
855 North Vermont Avenue
Los Angeles, CA 90029
(213) 669-4255

1 scholarship providing full tuition for one academic year to an AMG member for study at the Monterey Institute of International Studies. Must be studying Arabic, Chinese, French, German, Greek, Japanese, Portuguese, Russian, or Spanish. Deadline: December 31; may vary.

110.
Alpha Mu Gamma (AMG) Scholarships
National Scholarships
Los Angeles City College
855 North Vermont Avenue
Los Angeles, CA 90029
(213) 666-1018

3 scholarships of $500 to undergraduate or graduate student members for use at any accredited institution. Must be studying a foreign language. Deadline: December 31; may vary.

111.
Alpha Phi Alpha Fraternity
1930 Sherman Avenue
Evanston, IL 60201
(847) 475-0663

Scholarships to members of this African American fraternity. Write to above address to find out which chapters make grants to high school seniors about to enter college.

112.
Alpha Phi Delta
404 Provincetown Drive
Cape May, NJ 08204
(609) 884-7216

Scholarships of $750 to students who are fraternity members. Based on recommendation, academic record, career goals, and financial need. Deadline: June 30.

113.
Alpha Phi Foundation Scholarships
Alpha Phi Foundation, Inc.
Chairperson, Scholarship Committee
1930 Sherman Avenue
Evanston, IL 60201
(847) 475-0663

40 scholarships of $1,000 to undergraduate members. Based on above-average academic achievement and service record to Alpha Phi Fraternity, members' own university, and/or the community. Financial need is considered but not required. Renewable with reapplication. Deadline: March 1.

114.
Alpha Tau Delta (ATD)
Miriam Fay Furlong Grants
National Awards Committee Chairperson
Ferdinand Chong
18805 Leesbury Way
Rowland Heights, CA 91748
(626) 964-4244

Grants of varying amounts to undergraduate juniors or seniors who are pursuing careers in nursing. Must be ATD members. Students accepted in a graduate nursing program may apply to PRN Grant. Request applications from Chapter president at college. Other restrictions may apply. Deadline: April 15.

115.
Alpha Tau Delta (ATD)
Scholarships
Attn: Kerri Kaye
150 Chuickshank Drive
Folsom, CA 95630
(916) 984-9150

Varying numbers of scholarships of $1,000 to undergraduate and graduate students who are members of Alpha Tau Delta. Based on academic achievement, financial need, interest in, and support of organization, recommendations, and professional activities. Must have at least a 2.5 GPA. Deadline: March 1.

116.
Altrusa International Foundation, Inc.
Attn: Josie Lucent
Founders Fund Vocational Aid Committee
332 South Michigan Avenue, Suite 1123
Chicago, IL 60604
(312) 427-4410

Financial assistance to females who have finished high school, as well as to mature women who have never worked outside the home or who are sole supporters of families and to handicapped women for training in X-ray technology, dental hygiene, and other vocational professions. Must have financial need. Deadline: varies.

117.
Amalgamated Clothing and Textile Workers Union
William Duchessi Scholarships
UNITE
1710 Broadway
New York NY 10019
(212) 265-7000

3 scholarships of $2,000 ($1,000 per year for first two years) to high school seniors who are children of Amalgamated Clothing and Textile Workers Union members who have been a member in good standing for two or more years. Renewable for two years. Deadline: June 30.

118.
Amalgamated Transit Union
5025 Wisconsin Avenue, N.W.
Washington, DC 20016
(202) 537-1645

5 nonrenewable scholarships of $2,000 and 1 nonrenewable scholarship of $1,000 to high school graduates who are members or children of an ATU member. Must be entering college or a technical/vocational school for the first time. Deadline: January 31.

119.
Amarillo Area Foundation, Inc.
Executive Director
801 South Fillmore, Suite 700
Amarillo, TX 79101
(806) 376-4521

Numerous scholarships, ranging from $250 to $500 per semester, totaling $25,650, to high school seniors, undergraduate, graduate, professional, or nontraditional students from one of the six most southern counties in the Texas Panhandle (Briscoe, Castro, Childress, Hall, Parmer, and Swisher). Write an introductory letter briefly describing educational and financial situation. Deadline: April 1.

120.
Amax Foundation Scholarships
Amax Foundation, Inc.
Amax Center
Greenwich, CT 06836
(203) 629-7000

Scholarships ranging from $500 to $4,000 to children of current employees of Amax Inc. or any U.S. or overseas Amax Consolidated subsidiary. Based on academic achievement, extracurricular activities, recommendation, SAT scores, and essay. Deadline: November 15.

121.
Amelia Island Plantation
Internship Coordinator
Resort Operations Building
P.O. Box 3000
Amelia Island, FL 32035-1307
(904) 277-5904
(904) 277-5994 Fax

70 internships lasting from twelve to sixteen weeks during the summer, fall, or spring provide $100/week housing

stipend and one free meal per day to undergraduates, recent college graduates, college graduates of any age, and graduate students. International students are eligible. The Amelia Island Plantation is a 1,250-acre luxury resort and residential community situated 29 miles northeast of Jacksonville, Florida. The Plantation offers forty-five holes of golf, twenty-five tennis courts, bicycling, paddleboating, horseback riding, fishing, swimming pools, seven dining facilities, and a health and fitness center. Interns work in flora/horticulture, culinary, promotions, recreation, health and fitness center, special events, and public relations. Submit résumé, cover letter, and recommendations. Deadline: February 15 (summer); May 15 (fall); November 15 (spring).

122.
Amelia Student Awards
Amelia Magazine
329 East Street
Bakersfield, CA 93304
(805) 323-4064

A contest providing numerous awards of varying amounts to previously unpublished poems, nonfiction essays, and short stories written by high school students. These are cash awards that can be used at the students' discretion. Deadline: February 1; February 15; March 1.

123.
American Accordion Musicological Society Contest
Attn: JoAnn Arnold
322 Haddon Avenue
Westmont, NJ 08108-2864

Awards ranging from $100 to $250 to amateur composers who are high school, undergraduate, or graduate students or professional music composers. Must write a serious composition for the accordion at least six minutes in length. This is a cash award and may be used at students' discretion. Deadline: February 28.

124.
American Accounting Association
Arthur H. Carter Scholarships
5517 Bessie Drive
Sarasota, FL 34233
(941) 921-7747
(941) 923-4093 Fax

40 scholarships of $2,500 to undergraduate juniors and seniors and graduate students for study of accounting at any accredited U.S. institution. Must have completed at least two years of undergraduate study and have at least one full year of study remaining. Based on merit, not financial need. Deadline: April 1.

125.
American Advertising Federation
Minority Advertising Internships
1101 Vermont Avenue, N.W., Suite 500
Washington, DC 20005-6306
(800) 999-2231

60 ten-week summer internships to minority undergraduate seniors and graduate students. Internships are conducted throughout the United States. Provides transportation and 60 percent of housing costs, plus a salary of approximately $250 to $300 per week. Interns are responsible for performing duties in account management, art direction, copy writing, research, and media. Applicants should have strong communication and writing skills. Placement assistance and letters of recommendation are provided to interns upon completion of internship. Write an introductory letter briefly stating educational and career goals and financial situation. Deadline: January 15.

126.
American Association of Airport Executives (AAAE)
AAAE Scholarships
Northeast Chapter, NEC/AAAE
Executive Secretary
4212 King Street
Alexandria, VA 22302
(703) 824-0500

Scholarships of $1,000 to undergraduate juniors, seniors, or graduate students in an aviation program. Must be members, spouses of members, or dependent children of members of AAAE. Must have a cumulative GPA of 3.0 on a 4.0 scale or equivalent. Selection based on academic achievement, financial need, and community activities. Must submit transcripts. Applications must be submitted to the AAAE Foundation Scholarship Program; address is provided on the application. Deadline: May 15.

127.
American Association of Airport Executives (AAAE)
Foundation Scholarships
c/o AAAE
4212 King Street
Alexandria, VA 22302
(703) 824-0500, ext. 26

Scholarships of $1,000 to undergraduate juniors, seniors, or graduate students in an aviation program. Applicants must be full-time students enrolled in an aviation program at an accredited college or university. Must have a 3.0 GPA or higher. Selection based on academic achievement, financial need, school and community activities, work experience, and personal statement. Obtain applications from your school's scholarship office. Deadline: March 31.

128.
American Association of Blood Banks (AABB)
Fenwal Scholarships
8108 Glenbrook Road
Bethesda, MD 20814-2749
(301) 215-6539
jeannine@aabb.org

5 scholarships of $1,500 to undergraduate and graduate students enrolled in accredited SBB programs. Must submit original essays to the AABB for review. The three categories are: scientific, analytical, and educational. Awards must be used for educational endeavors. Deadline: April 1.

129.

American Association of Cereal Chemists (AACC) Milling & Baking Division Scholarships
3340 Pilot Knob Road
St. Paul, MN 55121
(612) 454-7250

4 scholarships each of $1,000 and $1,500 to undergraduate student members of AACC who will be entering their senior year of study. Must be majoring in food science and pursuing a career in cereal chemistry, milling and baking, or a related field. Must have at least a 3.0 GPA on a 4.0 scale. Deadline: April 1 (received by).

130.

American Association of Cereal Chemists (AACC) Undergraduate Scholarships and Graduate Fellowships
3340 Pilot Knob Road
St. Paul, MN 55121
(612) 454-7250

Scholarships ranging from $1,000 to $1,500 to undergraduates and from $1,000 to $3,000 to graduate students majoring in or interested in a career in cereal science or technology, including baking or a related area. Based on academic achievement and career goals. AACC membership is helpful but not required. Deadline: April 1 (received by).

131.

American Association of Critical Care Nurses (AACN)
BSN Completion
101 Columbia
Aliso Viejo, CA 92656-1491
(714) 362-2000

Scholarships of $1,500 to undergraduate juniors or seniors who don't have an RN license in order to complete a bachelor of nursing degree. Must be an AACN or NSNA member and enrolled in an NLN-accredited bachelor of nursing degree program. Must have at least a 3.0 GPA or better, be currently working in critical care or have one year's experience in the last three years, and be currently enrolled in an NLN-accredited nursing program. Past recipients may reapply. Students in nontraditional degree programs need to contact AACN for eligibility determination. Selection based on an essay where student describes how his/her nursing practice will change as a result of obtaining a BSN and must describe contributions to acute- or critical-care nursing, which include work, community, and profession-related activities. Request materials by calling (800) 899-2226. Deadline: May 15.

132.

American Association of Critical Care Nurses (AACN)
Clinical Practice Grant
101 Columbia
Aliso Viejo, CA 92656-1491
(714) 362-2000

1 award of up to $6,000 to a student with an RN license who is beginning research, with limited or no research experience, in the area of proposed investigation. Must be a current member of AACN. Award may fund research for an academic degree. The research study must be relevant to critical-care nursing practice. The principal researcher must be a registered nurse. Request materials by calling (800) 899-2226. Deadline: October 1 (grant proposals).

133.

American Association of Critical Care Nurses (AACN)
Generic BSN
101 Columbia
Aliso Viejo, CA 92656-1491
(714) 362-2000

Scholarships of $1,500 to undergraduate sophomore or junior students when applying, to juniors or seniors during time of award and who don't have an RN license, and to nursing students with degrees in other fields. Must be an AACN or NSNA member and enrolled in an NLN-accredited bachelor of nursing degree program. Must have at least a 3.0 GPA and not yet be licensed as an RN, but can be an LVN or LPN. Selection based on academic achievement and demonstrated commitment to nursing through involvement in student organizations and/or school and community activities related to health care. At least 20 percent of the awards are allocated to minority students. Obtain applications from NSNA, 555 West 57th Street, New York, NY 10019, (212) 581-2211. Deadline: February 1.

134.

American Association of Family & Consumer Scientists
Kappa Omicron Phi—Home Economics Grant
Attn: Fellowships and Awards Committee
1555 King Street, 4th Floor
Alexandria, VA 22314
(703) 706-4600
http://www.aafcs.org

1 fellowship of $1,500 to undergraduate, graduate, doctoral, and postdoctoral students in home economics to conduct research on a related topic. Selection based on proposed research. Award may be used at any accredited U.S. institute. Must be an active member or alumnus of Kappa Omicron Phi and a U.S. citizen or permanent resident. Deadline: January 15.

135.

American Association of Hispanic CPAs
P.O. Box 871
Bronx, NY 10465-2455
(626) 965-0643

Numerous scholarships of varying amounts to student members. Encourages advancement in the certified public accounting field. Deadline: varies.

136.

American Association of Housing Educators (AAHE)

Executive Director
College of Architecture
Texas A&M University
College Station, TX 77843-3137
(409) 845-3211

Scholarships of $200 to undergraduates and $300 to graduate students or reasonable travel costs to conference to present a paper at the Annual Conference of the AAHE. Students must write and submit an original paper on research or a position about some aspect or current issue in housing. Papers must not be over fifteen typed pages, including title page, abstract, references, tables, and figures. Submit papers and applications to: Chairperson, AAHE Awards Committee, 6953 Campbell Drive, Salem, VA 24153. Deadline: June 12.

137.

American Association of Medical Assistants Endowment
Maxine Williams Scholarship Fund

20 North Wacker Drive, #1575
Chicago, IL 60606
(312) 899-1500

Approximately five $500 scholarships to high school graduates who submit a written statement expressing interest in a career as a medical assistant. Renewable. Deadline: May 1.

138.

American Association of Nurse Anesthetists (AANA)
AANA Educational Loans

Attn: Finance Director
222 South Prospect Avenue
Park Ridge, IL 60068-4001
(847) 692-7050
http://www.aana.com

Numerous loans from $500 to $2,500 for undergraduate and graduate nursing students who are members of the AANA. Must have completed six months of an anesthesia program and have financial need. Repayment begins sixty days after graduation or withdrawal from program. 7 percent interest begins accruing at time repayment begins. Deadline: none.

139.

American Association of Occupational Health Nurses
Charles J. Turcotte Academic Scholarship Awards

2920 Brandywine Road, Suite 100
Atlanta, GA 30324
(770) 455-7757/(770) 455-7271 Fax
http://www.aaohn.org

Scholarships of $2,000 to undergraduate, graduate, or doctoral students. Must be pursuing nursing degrees with emphasis on occupational health. For additional application criteria, write to above address. Other restrictions may apply. Deadline: none specified.

140.

American Association of Occupational Health Nurses
Otis Clap Award

2920 Brandywine Road, Suite 100
Atlanta, GA 30324
(770) 455-7757
(770) 455-7271 Fax
http://www.aaohn.org

Awards of up to $2,000 for undergraduate or graduate students to conduct research on issues relating to occupational health nursing. For more information on application guidelines, write to above address. Other restrictions may apply. Deadline: none specified.

141.

American Association of Overseas Studies

158 West 81st Street, #112
New York, NY 10024
(800) EDU-BRIT
(212) 724-0804

100 internships lasting at least four weeks during the summer, fall, or spring, providing a stipend of $1,000 plus room and board ranging from $600 to $1,000 per month to high school students, high school graduates, undergraduates, recent college graduates, and graduate students. Internships are tailored to the requirements of the intern and may be arranged in the following areas: architecture; art; banking; business; community service; computer science; economics; engineering; fashion; film; geology; government; journalism; languages; law; marketing; museum; music; physical and life sciences; politics; public relations; publishing; sports; stock market trading; theater; and women's studies. Internship sites include New York, NY; London, England; and Israel. For a list of participating organizations in your field of interest, contact AAOS's Director in London collect (AAOS, 51 Drayton Gardens, London SW10 9RX, England, 44-171-835-2143, Fax 44-171-244-6061). Deadline: rolling.

142.

American Association of State Troopers, Inc. (AAST)
Post–Secondary Education Stipend Benefit

1949 Raymond Diehl Road
Tallahassee, FL 32308
(800) 765-5456

Installment awards of up to $1,000 to members in good standing. The stipend requires a minimum of five years of AAST membership before drawing at $200 per year as reimbursement for classes successfully completed. If the benefit is not used for college-related costs, the remainder may be taken as a retirement gift upon full retirement. Deadline: none.

143.

American Association of State Troopers, Inc. (AAST)
Scholarships to Members' Children

1949 Raymond Diehl Road
Tallahassee, FL 32308
(800) 765-5456

Scholarships of $1,000 to graduating high school seniors who are children (natural birth, adopted, or stepchildren raised as own for at least five years before the application). The parent must have been a member of AAST for the year prior to the application year, or if the parent has died, he or she must have been an active member in good standing. Applicant must have at least a 2.5 GPA. Renewable for an additional scholarship of $1,000 if student maintains a 3.5 GPA. Obtain applications from above from January 1 to June 1. Deadline: June 1.

144.

American Association of Teachers of Italian
College Essay in Italian

c/o Indiana University
Language Department
Bloomington, IN 47401
(812) 337-2508

Awards of $100 and $250 to undergraduate and graduate students at any accredited college or university in North America. Essay topic must relate to literature or literary figures. Must be U.S. citizen. Deadline: June 30.

145.

American Bar Foundation
ABF Summer Research Fellowships in Law and Social Science for Minority Undergraduate Students

750 North Lake Shore Drive, 4th Floor
Chicago, IL 60611
(312) 988-6500
(312) 988-6769 Fax
http://www.abf-sociolegal.com

4 stipends of $3,300 and ten-week summer fellowships to undergraduate students who are Native American, African American, Mexican American, or Puerto Rican. Must have completed at least their undergraduate sophomore year in college, not have received a bachelor's degree, have at least a 3.0 GPA on a 4.0 scale, and be preparing for a social-science career. Based on academic record, recommendations, and essay. Must be U.S. citizens or legal residents. Deadline: March 1.

146.

American Board of Funeral Service Education Scholarships

American Board of Funeral Service Education
14 Crestwood Road
Cumberland, ME 04021
(207) 829-5715

$250 and $500 scholarships to high school graduates who are enrolled or will be enrolling in a funeral service education program. The award is paid directly to the American Board–accredited program or college offering funeral service or mortuary science. Must be U.S. citizen.

Based on academic record, recommendation, extracurricular and community activities, and financial need. Deadline: September 15; March 15.

147.

American Business Women's Association

National Headquarters
P.O. Box 8728
9100 Ward Parkway
Kansas City, MO 64114-0728
(816) 361-6621

Financial assistance of varying amounts to undergraduate and graduate female students to continue their education. Interested students must contact and apply through local chapter. DO NOT contact national association. The national association will not provide information on local chapters. Need not be members of the national association. Deadline: varies by chapter.

148.

American Business Women's Association Scholarships

Severn River Chapter
Ways and Means Chairperson
1891 Poplar Ridge Road
Pasadena, MD 21122
(301) 255-1067

1 to 2 awards ranging from $500 to $1,500 to female residents of Anne Arundel County, Maryland. Must be seeking a business or professional career. Based on academic achievements and the number of applicants. Applicants must reapply every year. Deadline: varies.

149.

American Classical League/National Junior Classical League
National Latin Examination

P.O. Box 95
Mount Vernon, VA 22121

10 scholarships of $1,000, gold and silver medals, and certificates to high school students enrolled in first-, second-, third-, fourth-, or fifth-year Latin study. Award is based on an exam. The advanced-level students must also complete an application, write an essay, and submit recommendation letters. Students wanting to purchase past exams may send a $5 check or money order payable to: ACL, Miami University, Oxford, OH 45056. Application forms are sent in September or early October to teachers who are members of ACL. Nonmembers need to request applications. Deadline: early January (application forms); 2nd week in March (test date).

150.

American College of Medical Practice Executives
Edward J. Gerloff Scholarship

Administrative Director
104 Inverness Terrace East
Englewood, CO 80112-5306
(888) 608-5601, ext. 573
(303) 643-9574
http://www.mgma.com

1 scholarship of $500 to a full-time undergraduate or graduate student majoring in ambulatory care or medical

group management at an accredited institution. Based on academic record, recommendations, and career goals. Deadline: June 30.

151.
American College of Medical Practice Executives Ernest S. Moscatello Scholarship
Administrative Director
104 Inverness Terrace East
Englewood, CO 80112-5306
(888) 608-5601, ext. 573
(303) 643-9574
http://www.mgma.com

1 scholarship of $500 to a full-time undergraduate or graduate student majoring in ambulatory care or medical group management at an accredited institution. Based on academic record, recommendations, and career goals. Preference is given to (but not limited to) practitioners who have returned to academic studies. Deadline: June 30.

152.
American College of Medical Practice Executives Harry J. Harwick Scholarship
Administrative Director
104 Inverness Terrace East
Englewood, CO 80112-5306
(888) 608-5601, ext. 573
(303) 643-9574
http://www.mgma.com

1 scholarship of $2,000 to a full-time undergraduate or graduate student majoring in ambulatory care or medical group management at an accredited institution. Based on academic record, recommendations, and career goals. Preference given to students enrolled in a program accredited by the Accrediting Commission on Education for Health Services Administration. Deadline: June 30.

153.
American College of Medical Practice Executives Richard L. Davis Scholarships
Administrative Director
104 Inverness Terrace East
Englewood, CO 80112-5306
(888) 608-5601, ext. 573
(303) 643-9574
http://www.mgma.com

2 scholarships of $1,000 to undergraduate or graduate students who are enrolled as full-time students and pursuing a career in ambulatory care or medical group management. One scholarship is specifically for a student enrolled at the University of North Carolina at Chapel Hill Graduate School of Business Administration. The other scholarship is open to the pool of applicants. Based on academic record, career goals, and recommendation letters. Deadline: June 30.

154.
American College of Musicians Projects
Piano Guild USA
P.O. Box 1807
Austin, TX 78767
(512) 478-5775

145 scholarships of $100 to graduating high school seniors or graduates (of no more than one year) who are Guild

students of a Guild teacher. Must have entered auditions for ten years in national classification. Must have earned 140 more C's (commendations) than A's (attention to). For further information, write to above address. Deadline: one year after high school graduation.

155.
American College of Nurse–Midwives Foundation (ACNM)
Scholarship Program
818 Connecticut Avenue, N.W., Suite 900
Washington, DC 20006-2702
(202) 728-9865

5 to 10 awards of up to $1,500 to undergraduate students enrolled in an ACNM-accredited certificate or graduate nurse-midwifery program. Must be student members of ACNM and have completed one clinical module or semester. Obtain applications from director of nurse-midwifery program at accredited schools. Deadline: February 15.

156.
American College Theatre Festival
Embassy Communications Playwriting Award
JFK Center for the Performing Arts
Washington, DC 20566
(202) 254-3437

1 award of $10,940 to an undergraduate or graduate student who has written the best comedy play. The student must write a teleplay for one of Embassy Communications Television's series. Deadline: December 20.

157.
American College Theatre Festival
Irene Ryan Acting Scholarships
JFK Center for the Performing Arts
Washington, DC 20566
(202) 254-3437

Numerous scholarships ranging from $250 to $2,500 to student actors. Deadline: December 10.

158.
American College Theatre Festival
Michael Kanin Playwriting Awards Program
JFK Center for the Performing Arts
Washington, DC 20566
(202) 254-3437

10 playwriting awards ranging from $500 to $10,940 to undergraduate and graduate students majoring in theater or drama. Awards go to student writers whose plays (drama, comedy, or musical) are produced as part of the festival. Deadline: December 10.

159.
American Congress of Rehabilitation Medicine
Baruch Essay Contest
122 South Michigan Avenue, Suite 1300
Chicago, IL 60603
(847) 375-4725

Awards ranging from $50 to $200 to undergraduate and graduate students. Cash awards are given for the best essays relating to physical medicine and rehabilitation. Essays must not exceed three thousand words. Deadline: May 1.

160.
American Congress on Surveying and Mapping (ACSM)
American Cartographic Association (ACA) Scholarships
ACSM Awards Director
5410 Grosvenor Lane, Suite 100
Bethesda, MD 20814
(301) 493-0200

Numerous $1,000 scholarships to undergraduate juniors and seniors who are enrolled in a cartography or other mapping sciences program in a four-year institution. Must be nominated by an ACSM member or may nominate himself or herself by submitting the appropriate documentation. Based on academic record, recommendations, and career goals. Deadline: January 1.

161.
American Congress on Surveying and Mapping (ACSM)
Berntsen Scholarship in Surveying
ACSM Awards Director
5410 Grosvenor Lane, Suite 100
Bethesda, MD 20814
(301) 493-0200

1 scholarship of $1,500 to a full-time undergraduate student enrolled in a four-year degree program in surveying. Based on academic record, recommendations, career goals, and financial need. Deadline: January 1.

162.
American Congress on Surveying and Mapping (ACSM)
National Society of Professional Surveyors Scholarship
ACSM Awards Director
5410 Grosvenor Lane, Suite 100
Bethesda, MD 20814
(301) 493-0200

1 scholarship of $1,000 to a full-time undergraduate student enrolled in a two- or four-year institution offering a degree program in surveying. Based on academic record, recommendation, career and educational goals, and financial need. Deadline: January 1.

163.
American Congress on Surveying and Mapping (ACSM)
Schonstedt Scholarship in Surveying
ACSM Awards Director
5410 Grosvenor Lane, Suite 100
Bethesda, MD 20814
(301) 493-0200

1 scholarship of $1,500 to an undergraduate student in a surveying program who has completed at least two years of a four-year degree plan. Based on academic record, career goals, and recommendations. Deadline: January 1.

164.
American Congress on Surveying and Mapping (ACSM)
Wild Lietz Scholarships
ACSM Awards Director
5410 Grosvenor Lane, Suite 100
Bethesda, MD 20814
(301) 493-0200

2 scholarships of $1,000 to undergraduate students at a two- or four-year institution offering a degree in surveying or a related field. Must have completed at least one course in surveying. Open to members of ASCM or ASPRS or to any student sponsored by a member. Based on academic record, recommendations, career goals, and financial need. Deadline: January 1.

165.
American Conservatory Theater
Internship Program
450 Geary Street
San Francisco, CA 94102
(415) 749-2200

9 to 13 eight-month-long internships providing $165 per week, with possible financial assistance to undergraduate students taking a leave of absence from school and recent graduates. Interns are placed in stage management, properties construction, stage technician, scenic design, sound design, lighting design, makeup and wig construction, costume rentals, and costume construction. Previous stage management experience is not essential. Interviews are conducted in person or by phone. Deadline: May 15.

166.
American Consulting Engineers Council
National Scholarships
1015 15th Street, N.W., #802
Washington, D.C. 20005
(202) 347-7474
http://www.acec.org/

15 to 20 scholarships ranging from $1,000 to $5,000 to college juniors and seniors majoring in engineering. Applicants must be U.S. citizens. Based on GPA, work experience, recommendation by engineering professor or consulting engineer, and college activities. Deadline: March 17 (national); between December and February (state).

167.
American Council of the Blind
ACB Scholarships/Vteck Scholarships
1155 15th Street, N.W., Suite 720
Washington, DC 20005
(800) 424-8666 or (202) 467-5081

7 scholarships ranging from $1,000 to $1,500 to students who are legally blind and who are accepted to or enrolled in an accredited institute for vocational/technical, undergraduate, graduate, or professional studies. May be used for any major. Must be U.S. citizens or legal residents. Deadline: March 1.

168.
American Council of the Blind
Floyd Qualls Scholars
1155 15th Street, N.W., Suite 720
Washington, DC 20005
(800) 424-8666 or (202) 467-5081

4 scholarships ranging from $1,000 to $2,000 to legally
blind students who are entering freshmen, undergraduate
sophomores, juniors, and seniors, graduate students, or
students in vocational/technical schools. Based on academic
record, recommendation, and biographical sketch. Must be
U.S. citizen or legal resident. Deadline: March 1.

169.
American Criminal Justice Association
Lambda Alpha Epsilon National Scholarships
P.O. Box 601047
Sacramento, CA 95860-1047
(916) 484-6553

9 scholarships ranging from $100 to $400 to undergraduate
and graduate students majoring in criminal justice,
criminology, legal services, or social sciences. Open to
members and nonmembers. Selection is based on a paper
written on an assigned theme of the upcoming national
conference. Must be enrolled in a two- or four-year
institution. Must submit an application, transcript, essay,
and recommendation letters. Deadline: December 31.

170.
American Culinary Federation (ACF)
10 San Bartolla Road
St. Augustine, FL 32086-3466
(904) 824-4468

Loans of up to $1,500 to undergraduate student members
of ACF in a culinary arts program. Must have completed
one semester and be in good academic standing.
Applications are accepted year-round, with awards being
made in April, August, and December.

171.
American Dental Assistants' Association
Southard Scholarships for Dental Assistant
**   Teacher Education**
203 North LaSalle, Suite 1320
Chicago, IL 60601-1225
(312) 541-1550
http://members.aol.com/adaa/index.htm

Numerous scholarships ranging from $100 to $2,000 to
students who are high school graduates, enrolled in a
dental-assisting teacher education program leading to a
bachelor's degree, a member of the American Dental
Assistants' Association, and have a minimum of one year's
experience in a dental situation. Based on academic
achievement, financial need, ability, and interest in dental
assisting. Deadline is July 15.

172.
American Dental Hygienists' Association (ADHA)
Carol Bauhs Benson Memorial Scholarships
444 North Michigan Avenue, Suite 3400
Chicago, IL 60611
(312) 440-8944
http://www.adha.org

Scholarships of $1,500 are available to undergraduates in
dental hygiene studies with at least a 3.0 GPA (B average)
on a 4.0 scale and working toward a bachelor's degree in
dental hygiene. Based on academic record and financial
need. Must attend a dental hygiene program in ADHA
District VII. Deadline: May 1.

173.
American Dental Hygienists' Association (ADHA)
Certificate Scholarships
444 North Michigan Avenue, Suite 3400
Chicago, IL 60611
(312) 440-8944
http://www.adha.org

Scholarships of $1,500 are available to students in a
certificate or associate degree program leading to a license
in dental hygiene. Students must have at least a 3.0 GPA
(B average) on a 4.0 scale and be working toward a
bachelor's degree in dental hygiene. Based on academic
record and financial need. Deadline: May 1.

174.
American Dental Hygienists' Association (ADHA)
Minority Scholarship Program
444 North Michigan Avenue, Suite 3400
Chicago, IL 60611
(312) 440-8944
http://www.adha.org

Scholarships ranging from $1,000 to $1,500 available to
minority students who have completed one year of dental
hygiene studies with at least a 3.0 GPA (B average) on a 4.0
scale and are working toward a bachelor's degree in dental
hygiene. Deadline: May 1.

175.
American Dental Hygienists' Association (ADHA)
Esther Wilkins/Williams & Wilkins Scholarships
444 North Michigan Avenue, Suite 3400
Chicago, IL 60611
(312) 440-8944

Numerous scholarships of $1,500 to full-time
undergraduate students in dental hygiene in a U.S.
program. Applicants must have at least a 4.0 GPA on a 4.0
scale and be members of ADHA. Based on academic record
and financial need. Deadline: May 1.

176.
American Dental Hygienists' Association (ADHA)
Sigma Phi Alpha Undergraduate Scholarships
444 North Michigan Avenue, Suite 3400
Chicago, IL 60611
(312) 440-8944

Numerous $1,500 scholarships to students who have
completed at least one year of dental hygiene study with at

least a 3.0 GPA (B average) on a 4.0 scale and be members of ADHA. Based on academic record and financial need. Deadline: May 1.

177.
American Dietetic Association Foundation (ADA)
ADA Dietetic Technician Scholarships
Education Department
216 West Jackson Boulevard, Suite 800
Chicago, IL 60606-6995
(312) 899-0040

Numerous scholarships ranging from $500 to $600 available to students in the first year of study in an ADA-approved dietetic technician program. Must be U.S. citizens. Request applications after September 15. Deadline: February 15.

178.
American Dietetic Association Foundation (ADA)
ADA Internships
216 West Jackson Boulevard, Suite 800
Chicago, IL 60606-6995
(312) 899-0040

Unspecified numbers of internships ranging from $500 to $1,000 for students accepted into an ADA-accredited dietetic internship program. Must have financial need and be U.S. citizens. Request applications after September 15. Deadline: February 15.

179.
American Dietetic Association Foundation (ADA)
ADA Undergraduate/Coordinated Undergraduate Scholarships (Category C)
216 West Jackson Boulevard, Suite 800
Chicago, IL 60606-6995
(312) 899-0040

Numerous scholarships ranging from $500 to $1,000 to undergraduates for the study of dietetics and nutrition. Must be entering junior year and have financial need. Must be U.S. citizens. Request applications after September 15. Deadline: February 15.

180.
American Dietetic Association Foundation (ADA)
Scholarships
216 West Jackson Boulevard, Suite 800
Chicago, IL 60606-6995
(312) 899-0040

Up to 200 scholarships and fellowships of varying amounts available to undergraduate juniors and seniors and graduate students who are ADA members or are eligible to become members. Must be U.S. citizens. Awards must be used in the area of dietetics and nutrition. Request applications after September 15. Deadline: February 15.

181.
American Economics Association
2014 Broadway, Suite 305
Nashville, TN 37203
(615) 322-2595

The association sponsors a summer program available to minority students. Undergraduate minority students who

have shown promise in economics and who might be interested in obtaining a Ph.D. degree are recruited. The program lets students test their abilities in graduate-level economics and reveals professional options they may not have considered. Costs plus a $1,000 stipend are paid. The program is held on the campus of Temple University in Philadelphia. Deadline: March 1.

182.
American Express Foundation
Scholarship Program
Employee Services Manager
World Financial Center
American Express Tower
New York, NY 10004
(212) 640-2000

Scholarships of varying amounts available to the children of American Express employees for undergraduate study in any major at any accredited institution. Deadline: none.

183.
American Federation of Musicians (AFM)
Congress of Strings Summer Scholarships Program
1501 Broadway, #600
New York, NY 10036
(212) 869-1330

Summer scholarships of varying amounts available to young string instrumentalists between the ages of sixteen and twenty-three. Applicants do not have to be children of AFM members to compete. Audition required. Audition winners go on to study and perform for six weeks during the summer. Deadline: early February.

184.
American Federation of Musicians Local 451
611 East Sunset Drive
Bellingham, WA 98225

Awards ranging from $50 to $250 available to high school seniors in Whatcom County, Washington. Must be interested in attending Western Washington State University in Bellingham, Washington. Must be able to perform on the guitar or other band instruments. Deadline: April 30; before the auditions, on the first Monday in May, at the Music Building of Western Washington State College.

185.
American Federation of Police & National Association of Chiefs of Police Scholarship Program
3801 Biscayne Boulevard
Miami, FL 33137
(305) 573-0070
http://www.aphf.org/p20_scholarship.html
policeinfo@aphf.org

50 or more scholarships of $1,000 to graduating high school seniors, undergraduates, or graduate or professional school students. Must be family survivors of police officers killed in the line of duty or law enforcement officers who have been injured or disabled, or members of their immediate family. Award may be used for books, tuition, or other school-related expenses at an approved university,

college, or vocational school. Must provide a copy of the letter of acceptance to the institution they will be attending. Obtain applications from above address. Deadline: rolling.

186.
American Federation of State, County, &
Municipal Employees (AFSCME)
AFSCME Family Scholarship Program
Education Department
1625 L Street, N.W.
Washington, DC 20036
(202) 452-4800

Scholarships of $2,000 per year available to high school seniors whose parents are active members of AFSCME. Scholarships are for full-time study at any accredited four-year institution. Must be U.S. citizens or legal residents. Deadline: December 31.

187.
American Federation of Television and Radio
Artists (AFTRA)
Bud Collyer Memorial Scholarships
Memorial Foundation, Inc.
260 Madison Avenue, 7th Floor
New York NY 10016
(212) 532-0800
http://www.aftra.org

Scholarships available to members in good standing for at least five years or their children. To be used for study in the academic and performing-arts fields.

188.
American Federation of Television and Radio
Artists (AFTRA)
Bud Jacoby Memorial Scholarships/Jerry Walter
Fund
Memorial Foundation, Inc.
260 Madison Avenue, 7th Floor
New York, NY 10016
(212) 532-0800
http://www.aftra.org

Scholarships available to members in good standing for at least five years or their children. May be used for any course of study.

189.
American Federation of Television and Radio
Artists (AFTRA)
George Heller Memorial Scholarships
Memorial Foundation, Inc.
260 Madison Avenue, 7th Floor
New York, NY 10016
(212) 532-0800
http://www.aftra.org

Scholarships of varying amounts available to AFTRA members in good standing for at least five years or their children. Intended for college enrollment, general study, study in the performing-arts fields, or study of labor relations.

190.
American Federation of Television and Radio
Artists (AFTRA)
Ken Harvey Scholarship Fund
Memorial Foundation, Inc.
260 Madison Avenue, 7th Floor
New York, NY 10016
(212) 532-0800
http://www.aftra.org

1 scholarship available to members in good standing for at least five years or their children. Offers financial aid for vocal coaching.

191.
American Federation of Television and Radio
Artists (AFTRA)
Travis Johnson Memorial Scholarships
Memorial Foundation, Inc.
260 Madison Avenue, 7th Floor
New York, NY 10016
(212) 532-0800
http://www.aftra.org

Scholarships of varying amounts available to AFTRA members in good standing for at least five years or their children. To be used for the study of any branch of music.

192.
American Foreign Service Association (AFSA)
AFSA Financial Aid Program
Scholarship Programs Administrator
2101 E Street, N.W.
Washington, DC 20037
(202) 338-4045

Scholarships ranging from $500 to $2,500 available to dependents of career American Foreign Service personnel (active, retired with pension, or deceased) who have served or are serving abroad in foreign affairs agencies of the U.S. government. Membership in AFSA isn't required. Must be full-time undergraduate students in an accredited U.S. institution. If more than one family member is applying, total limit is $3,000. Based on financial need. Request applications after October 1. Deadline: February 15.

193.
American Foreign Service Association (AFSA)
AFSA Merit Award Program
Scholarship Programs Administrator
2101 E Street, N.W.
Washington, DC 20037
(202) 338-4045

20 scholarships of $750 and 10 scholarships of $100 to dependents of career American Foreign Service personnel (active, retired with pension, or deceased) who have served or are serving abroad in foreign affairs agencies of the U.S. government. Membership in AFSA isn't required. Must be full-time undergraduate students in an accredited U.S. institution. Based on academic merit. Request applications after October 1. Deadline: February 15.

194.
American Forests
Education Coordinator
P.O. Box 2000
Washington, DC 20013
(202) 667-3300

20 to 25 internships open to undergraduate sophomores, juniors, seniors, graduate students, and recent graduates to work in a national citizens' conservation organization. Students work as either interns or fellows in the areas of advertising and marketing, communications, education, Global ReLeaf International, management, policy, publications, research, and urban forestry. International applicants are eligible. Internships last from three to six months on an ongoing basis in Jacksonville, FL, and Washington, DC. Deadline: rolling.

195.
American Foundation for Aging Research
   Fellowship
AFAR Scholarships
P.O. Box 7622
North Carolina State University
Raleigh, NC 27695-7622
(919) 737-5679

Scholarships of $500 to $1,000 available to undergraduate, graduate, or pre-doctoral students who are involved in research related to aging. Research cannot be sociological or psychological. Based on student's personal qualifications and project proposal. Must have at least a 3.0 GPA. Based on academic record, recommendations, and research proposal. Deadline: none.

196.
American Foundation for AIDS Research
Intern Coordinator
1828 L Street, N.W., Suite 802
Washington, DC 20036
(202) 331-8600

4 ten-week summer internships providing a $2,500 stipend to undergraduate juniors, seniors, and graduate students. Internships are conducted at the D.C. office only. Interns monitor, research, and evaluate HIV/AIDS policy issues at AmFAR, the nation's leading organization supporting AIDS research. Interns work on public policy research and development. Deadline: February 15.

197.
American Foundation for Pharmaceutical
   Education
AASP–AFPE Gateway Scholarships
618 Somerset Street
P.O. Box 7126
North Plainfield, NJ 07060
(908) 561-8077

4 scholarships of $9,250 available to students in the last three years of a bachelor's degree program or Pharm. D. program and planning on seeking a Ph.D. in a pharmacy graduate project. The award is divided: $3,750 for undergraduate research project, $500 to attend AAPS Annual Meeting, and $5,000 to cover graduate school expenses. Must be U.S. citizens or legal residents. Contact:

American Association of Pharmaceutical Scientists, 601 King Street, Alexandria, VA 22314-3105. Deadline: October 1.

198.
American Foundation for the Blind
Delta Gamma Foundation
Florence Margaret Harvey Memorial Scholarship
11 Penn Plaza, Suite 300
New York, NY 10001
(800) 232-5463 or (212) 502-7600
http://www.afb.org/afb/
afbinfo@afb.org

1 scholarship of $1,000 available to a legally blind undergraduate or graduate student majoring in a field in rehabilitation and/or education of visually impaired and blind persons. Based on evidence of legal blindness, academic record, recommendations, and essay. Must be U.S. citizen. Deadline: April 1.

199.
American Foundation for the Blind
Dr. Katherine Michalowski Memorial
   Scholarship Fund
11 Penn Plaza, Suite 300
New York, NY 10001
(800) 232-5463
(212) 502-7600
http://www.afb.org/afb/
afbinfo@afb.org

1 scholarship of $500 available to female California residents who are legally blind and are either undergraduate or graduate students at an accredited institution. Deadline: June 1.

200.
American Foundation for the Blind
Gladys C. Anderson Scholarship Fund
11 Penn Plaza, Suite 300
New York, NY 10001
(800) 232-5463
(212) 502-7600
http://www.afb.org/afb/
afbinfo@afb.org

2 scholarships of $1,000 available to legally blind women enrolled in either religious or classical-music study at a recognized institution. Sample performance tape of voice or instrumental selection is required. Must be U.S. citizens. Based on evidence of legal blindness, academic record, recommendations, talent, and essay. Deadline: June 1.

201.
American Foundation for the Blind
Helen Keller Scholarship Fund for Deaf–Blind
   College Students
11 Penn Plaza, Suite 300
New York, NY 10001
(800) 232-5463
(212) 502-7600
http://www.afb.org/afb/
afbinfo@afb.org

Numerous $1,000 scholarships available to undergraduate students who are legally "blind and deaf." Intended to be used toward the students' reading, tutoring, and/or purchase of equipment. Must be U.S. citizens. Based on evidence of legal blindness and deafness, academic record, recommendation, and essay. Deadline: June 1.

202.
American Foundation for the Blind
National Chinese–American Scholarship Fund
11 Penn Plaza, Suite 300
New York, NY 10001
(800) 232-5463
(212) 502-7600
http://www.afb.org/afb/
afbinfo@afb.org

1 scholarship of $2,000 available to a Chinese-American student who is blind and is either an undergraduate or graduate student at any accredited college or university. May be used for habilitation, rehabilitation, and/or vocational training. Preference given to students ineligible for federal or state assistance. Must be U.S. citizens. Deadline: June 1.

203.
American Foundation for the Blind
R. L. Gillette Scholarship Fund
11 Penn Plaza, Suite 300
New York, NY 10001
(800) 232-5463
(212) 502-7600
http://www.afb.org/afb/
afbinfo@afb.org

2 scholarships of $1,000 available to legally blind women enrolled in creative writing or music performance in a four-year bachelor's degree program at a recognized institution. Writing sample or music-performance tape required. Must be a U.S. citizen. Based on evidence of blindness, academic record, recommendations, talent, and essay. Deadline: June 1.

204.
American Foundation for the Blind
TeleSensory Scholarship
11 Penn Plaza, Suite 300
New York, NY 10001
(800) 232-5463
(212) 502-7600
http://www.afb.org/afb/
afbinfo@afb.org

1 scholarship of $1,000 to a legally blind undergraduate or graduate student majoring in a field related to rehabilitation and/or education of visually impaired and blind persons. Must submit proof of visual impairment in a statement from an optometrist. Based on evidence of blindness, academic record, recommendations, and essay. Deadline: April 1.

205.
American Foundation for the Blind
Vtek Scholarship Fund
11 Penn Plaza, Suite 300
New York, NY 10001
(800) 232-5463
(212) 502-7600
http://www.afb.org/afb/
afbinfo@afb.org

1 scholarship of $1,000 to a legally blind undergraduate or graduate student accepted to or enrolled in an accredited program within the broad areas of rehabilitation and/or education of the blind and visually impaired. Deadline: June 1.

206.
American Fund for Dental Health
Dental Laboratory Technology Scholarships
Director of Programs
410 N. Michigan, Suite 352
Chicago, IL 60611-4211
(312) 787-6270

12 scholarships ranging from $500 to $600 to high school graduates enrolled in or planning to enroll in an accredited dental laboratory technology program. Based on academic achievement, financial need, and letter of acceptance. Renewable. Deadline: June 1.

207.
American Gas Association
Scholarship and Loan Program
Educational Programs
1515 Wilson Boulevard
Arlington, VA 22209
(703) 841-8400

1 $500 grant and 1 $500 interest-free loan to be repaid within three years of graduation. Open to undergraduate juniors and seniors in energy, mechanical, chemical, petroleum, environmental, or geology engineering, physics, or other fields related to the natural-gas industry. Deadline: April 1.

208.
American Geological Institute's Minority
Participation Program
American Geological Institute
4220 King Street
Alexandria, VA 22302-1507
(703) 379-2480
http://www.agiweb.org

30 to 50 renewable scholarships of $500 to $10,000 to undergraduates and graduates. Open to African Americans, Hispanic Americans, and Native Americans (American Indians, Eskimos, Hawaiians, Samoans) who are citizens of the U.S. Must be majoring in geosciences (geology, geochemistry, geophysics, hydrology, meteorology, oceanography, planetary geology, marine sciences, and earth-science education). Based on academic achievement, maturity, background, financial need, and likelihood of becoming a successful geoscientist. Must submit financial profile, résumé, SAT or ACT scores, and three letters of recommendation. Must have at least a 3.0 GPA in science

and mathematics. Award can be used only at a four-year institution. Deadline: February 1.

209.
American Geophysical Union (AGU)
AGU Student Travel Grants
2000 Florida Avenue, N.W.
Washington, DC 20009
(202) 462-6903
http://www.agu.org

Awards up to $250 plus registration fees to student members of AGU presenting papers at the fall or spring meetings. Deadline: 6 to 8 weeks prior to meeting.

210.
American Geophysical Union
June Bacon–Bercey Scholarships
2000 Florida Avenue, N.W.
Washington, DC 20009
(202) 462-6903
http://www.agu.org

Numerous $500 scholarships to women pursuing a career in atmospheric sciences. Deadline: May 1.

211.
American Health Information Management
Association (AHIMA)
Foundation of Record Education (FORE)
919 North Michigan Avenue, Suite 1400
Chicago, IL 60611-1683
(312) 787-2673

5 scholarships ranging from $1,000 to $5,000 to full-time undergraduate students in a program leading to a degree in medical record administration and one in a medical record technology degree program. Must be members of AHIMA, and have at least a 2.5 GPA on a 4.0 scale or 3.5 GPA on a 5.0 scale. Applicants must be citizens of U.S. or one of its territories. Must have three letters of recommendation, a letter of acceptance into the program, and a transcript. Deadline: April 1.

212.
American Heart Association (AHA)
Summer Internships
732 Greenville Avenue
Dallas, TX 75231
(214) 748-7212
http://www.amhrt.org

250 to 300 ten- to twelve-week summer internships providing stipends ranging from $600 to $3,000 to high school students, undergraduates, and graduate and medical students. No research experience is required, though some programs require students to have completed organic chemistry, biology, and physics or calculus. Internships are conducted at state AHA affiliates. Contact the Research division of the AHA state affiliate in which the student wishes to work. Deadline: varies according to state affiliate.

213.
American Heart Association, California Affiliate
Student Research Program
Chairman, Student Research Sub-Committee
805 Burlway Road
Burlingame, CA 94010
(415) 342-5522

Grants of $2,500 to first-time junior or senior undergraduate students who have an interest in cardiovascular or cerebrovascular research. Students are able to work for a ten-week period during the summer in a leading research laboratory in California. Based on academic achievement, interest in research, and recommendations. Must be residents of California. Applications must be requested by December 15. Deadline: January 15.

214.
American Heart Association, Minnesota Affiliate
VFW Heart Scholarships
4701 West 77th Street
Minneapolis, MN 55435
(612) 835-3300

3 scholarships of $1,800 to high school seniors, undergraduate freshmen, or sophomores to conduct a three-month summer research project. Students must submit a paper briefly explaining how this scholarship will assist them in pursuing their career. Must submit an abstract of proposed project, résumé, sponsor's curriculum vitae, and two letters of recommendation. Must be Minnesota residents and attending a Minnesota high school or undergraduate college or university. Deadline: April 1.

215.
American Holistic Nurses Association (AHNA)
Charlotte McGuire Scholarships
4104 Lake Boone Trail, Suite 201
Raleigh, NC 27607
(919) 787-0116

Varying numbers of scholarships of varying amounts to undergraduate or graduate students in an accredited nursing program. Awards may be used for tuition in programs in nursing, holistic health, or holistic nursing and may also be used for AHNA-sponsored conferences. Preference is given to students with experience in holistic health care or alternative health practices. Applicants must be members of AHNA, with nursing prerequisites nearly completed, and have at least a 3.0 GPA on a 4.0 scale. Request applications after January 1. Number of awards and amounts are determined by selection committee. Deadline: 90 days before AHNA annual meeting.

216.
American Hotel & Motel Association (AH&MA)
1201 New York Avenue, N.W., Suite 600
Washington, DC 20005-3931
(202) 289-3100
http://www.ahma.com

Periodically offers scholarships of varying amounts to undergraduate students with a hotel/motel management, hospitality, and/or tourism-related major. Funds are subject to fluctuations in finances. For more information, contact above address. Other restrictions may apply. Deadline: varies.

217.
American Indian Heritage Foundation
National Miss Indian U.S. Scholarships
Pageant Director
6051 Arlington Boulevard
Falls Church, VA 22044
(703) 237-7500
http://www.indians.org

Awards of up to $10,000 are available to female Native American high school graduates between the ages of eighteen and twenty-six, who were never married or pregnant and who never cohabited. Applicants must have a Native American sponsor (tribe, business, or organization). Deadline: September 15.

218.
American Indian Science and Engineering Society
Director, College Programs
1630 30th Street, Suite 301
Boulder, Co 80301-1014
(303) 939-0023
http://www.bioc02.uthscsa.edu/

Scholarships ranging from $1,000 to $2,000 for AISES members who are at least on-quarter Native American (must have proof of tribal affiliation). Applicants may be undergraduate or graduate students majoring in science, engineering, business, math, education, or the health-related fields. May be used at a two- or four-year institution. Based on academic record, financial need, and recommendation. Deadline: June 15.

219.
American Institute of Aeronautics and Astronautics (AIAA)
AIAA/Industry Scholarships
Director of Student Programs
1801 Alexander Bell Drive
Reston, VA 20194-4344
(703) 264-7500
(703) 264-7551 Fax
http://www.aiaa.org

30 scholarships of $2,000 to college sophomores, juniors, or seniors pursuing a science or engineering career in the area of aeronautics or astronautics. Must have completed at least one semester or quarter of full-time college work at an accredited institution. Must maintain a 3.0 GPA on a 4.0 scale and must be U.S. citizens or legal residents. Recipients cannot receive scholarships that when combined with this one would provide more than the cost of tuition and other educational expenses (books, fees, etc.). Deadline: February 1.

220.
American Institute of Aeronautics and Astronautics (AIAA)
Design Competitions
Director of Student Programs
1801 Alexander Bell Drive
Reston, VA 20194-4344
(703) 264-7500/(703) 264-7551 Fax
http://www.aiaa.org

5 undergraduate and 4 graduate design competitions in various disciplines with varying awards. The AIAA Foundation has plans to increase support of the undergraduate competitions by 100 percent, and the graduate competitions by almost 30 percent. In both cases, the enhancements will lead to greater, more relevant competitions and increased rewards for winners. The Student Activities Committee will continue to establish competition guidelines as well as decide on the best uses of available funds.

221.
American Institute of Architects
Minority/Disadvantaged Scholarship Program
1735 New York Avenue, N.W.
Washington, DC 20006-5292
(202) 626-7511
http://www.aiaonline.com/

25 awards ranging from $500 to $2,500 to graduating high school seniors, technical school or junior college students, or undergraduate freshmen pursuing a career in architecture. Must be nominated by an individual who knows the students and their potential to become an architect. Renewable up to three years with satisfactory academic progress and adherence to program requirements. Deadline: mid-December (nomination) and January 15 (application).

222.
American Institute of Architects
RTKL Traveling Fellowship
1735 New York Avenue, N.W.
Washington, DC 20006-5292
(202) 626-7511
http://www.aiaonline.com/

1 award of $2,500 to second-to-last-year undergraduate students in a bachelor's degree program or graduate students in a master's of architecture program. Must be planning to travel outside the United States or accepted in a professional degree program and planning foreign travel that will have a direct relationship to educational goals. Selection based on statement of purpose, relevance of travel plans to educational goals, academic achievement, and letters of recommendation. Deadline: mid-February.

223.
American Institute of Architects
Scholarship Program for First Professional Degree Candidates
1735 New York Avenue, N.W.
Washington, DC 20006-5292
(202) 626-7511
http://www.aiaonline.com/

Scholarships ranging from $500 to $2,500 to third- or fourth-year undergraduate students in a five-year bachelor of architecture degree, fourth- or fifth-year undergraduate students in a six-year degree program resulting in a master of architecture, or second- or third-year graduate students in a three- to four-year program that results in a master's degree and whose undergraduate degree was not in architecture. Selection based on goals, academic achievement, recommendations, a drawing, and financial need. Obtain applications from school's architecture department. Deadline: February 2.

224.
American Institute of Architects
Scholarships for Advanced Degree/Research
Candidates
Director, Scholarship Programs
1735 New York Avenue, N.W.
Washington, DC 20006-5292
(202) 626-7349
http://www.aiaonline.com/

Varying numbers of scholarship grants ranging from $500 to $2,500 to undergraduates in their last two years or graduate students in their final year of study in architecture or related fields. Selection based on proposed research and study. Award is for one full year. Applicants must be enrolled in an accredited U.S. or Canadian institution. Send a self-addressed, stamped envelope for details. Deadline: February 1.

225.
American Institute of Certified Public
Accountants Scholarships
AICPA Scholarships for Minority Undergraduate
Accounting Majors
1211 Avenue of the Americas
New York, NY 10036-8775
(212) 596-6200
http://www.aicpa.org/

700 renewable scholarships ranging from $500 to $2,000 to minority students majoring in accounting who have completed thirty credit hours. Based on financial aid and academic performance. Deadline: July 1.

226.
American Institute of Indian Studies
AIIS 9–Month Language Program
c/o University of Chicago
1130 East 59th Street, Foster Hall #212
Chicago, IL 60637
(312) 702-8638

12 fellowships ($3,000 plus travel) in India to undergraduate or graduate students with a minimum of two years of study (240 classroom hours) in a language of India. Write for details. Deadline: January.

227.
American Institute of Polish Culture, Inc.
Scholarships
Mr. Fred Martin, Chairman, Scholarship Committee
1440 79th Street Causeway, Suite 117
Miami, FL 33141
(305) 864-2349
http://www.ampolinstitute.org
info@ampolinstitute.org

10 scholarships of $1,000 to encourage young undergraduate or graduate American students of Polish

descent to pursue full-time journalism, communications, or public relations study at any accredited U.S. college. Selection is based on achievement, talent, and involvement in public life. Renewable. Send a stamped, self-addressed envelope. Deadline: February 15.

228.
American Junior Quarter Horse Association
AJQHA Scholarships
Director of Youth Activities
1600 Quarter Horse Drive
Amarillo, TX 79104
(806) 376-4811
http://www.aqha.com
aqhamail@aqha.org

Renewable scholarships of $1,000 to students who have been members of the American Junior Quarter Horse Association for at least three years. Must be under twenty-one years of age, have at least a 2.5 GPA, or be in the top 20 percent of the class. Based on academic record, recommendations, extracurricular activities, involvement in AJQHA, and financial need. Deadline: May 15.

229.
American Kinesiotherapy Association
Scholarships
Scholarship and Grant-in-Aid Committee
Tim Warner, RKT
75 Rockefeller Plaza
New York, NY 10019
(212) 484-8000
http://www.orst.edu/instruct/

Scholarships of $500 awarded semiannually to qualified student members. Awards cover tuition, books, and fees. Students must be attending an AKTA-accredited kinesiotherapy program. Must be sponsored by a registered kinesiotherapist. Based on application, recommendation letters, transcript, AKTA membership, and projected graduation date. Deadline: May 1.

230.
American Legion Auxiliary "Eagle Scout of the
Year"
777 North Meridian Street, 3rd Floor
Indianapolis, IN 46204
(317) 635-6291
http://www.legion-aux.org
alahq@legion-aux.org

1 scholarship of $8,000 and 3 scholarships of $2,000 to male high school students who are registered, active members of a Boy Scout Troop, Varsity Scout Team, or Explorer Post sponsored by an American Legion Post or Auxiliary Unit; or registered, active members of a Boy Scout Troop, Varsity Scout Team, or Explorer Post and the son or grandson of an American Legion or Auxiliary member. Award must be used within four years of graduation from an accredited high school. May be used at any accredited institution in the continental U.S. or a U.S. possession. Obtain applications from state's Department Headquarters

of the American Legion or from the National Americanism Commission at above address. Deadline: none specified.

231.
American Legion Auxiliary Girl Scout Achievement Award
National Headquarters
777 North Meridian Street, 3rd Floor
Indianapolis, IN 46204
http://www.legion-aux.org/scholarship.htm
alahq@legion-aux.org

1 scholarship of $1,000 to a female high school student who has received the Gold Award; is an active member of her religious institution and has received the appropriate religious emblem; has demonstrated practical citizenship in church, school, scouting, and community; and is in at least the ninth grade. Obtain applications from local American Legion Auxiliary Unit President, State Department Secretary, or State Department Education Chairperson. Deadline: February 15.

232.
American Legion Auxiliary National President's Scholarships
National Headquarters
777 North Meridian Street, 3rd Floor
Indianapolis, IN 46204
(317) 635-6291
http://www.legion-aux.org
alahq@legion-aux.org

5 scholarships each of $2,000 and $1,500 to graduating high school seniors. Must be children of veterans who served in the Armed Forces during eligibility dates of membership in the American Legion. The eligibility dates are as follows: WWI (April 6, 1917, through November 11, 1918); WWII (December 7, 1941, through December 31, 1946); Korean War (June 25, 1950, through January 31, 1955); Vietnam War (December 22, 1961, through May 7, 1975); Lebanon/ Granada (August 24, 1982); Panama (December 20, 1989, through January 31, 1990); or Persian Gulf (August 2, 1990, through August 12, 1990). Selection is based on character, Americanism, leadership, academic achievement, and financial need. Awarded annually by the National Organization of the American Legion Auxiliary. One of each award is given in each of the five divisions. Obtain applications from: local American Legion Auxiliary Unit President, State Department Secretary, or State Department Education Chairperson. Deadline: March 15.

233.
American Legion Auxiliary Spirit of Youth Scholarships
National Headquarters
777 North Meridian Street, 3rd Floor
Indianapolis, IN 46204
(317) 635-6291
http://www.legion-aux.org
alahq@legion-aux.org

5 scholarships of $1,000 awarded to a member who is a high school senior. Must be a child of veteran who served in WWI, WWII, Korean War, or Vietnam War. Based on character, Americanism, leadership, academic achievement, and financial need. Deadline: mid-March.

234.
American Legion Auxiliary (Alabama) Scholarships
Alabama Department Headquarters
American Legion Auxiliary
120 North Jackson Street
Montgomery, AL 36104
(205) 262-1176

40 scholarships of $850 to children and grandchildren of veterans of WWI, WWII, Korea, or Vietnam, for study at any Alabama college. Must be residents of Alabama. Enclose a stamped, self-addressed envelope. Deadline: May 1.

235.
American Legion Auxiliary (Alaska) Annual Scholarships
235 East 8th Avenue
Anchorage, AK 99522-0887
(907) 283-3222

1 first-place scholarship of $1,000 and 1 second-place scholarship of $250 available for a student who is a child of a veteran. Must be an Alaska resident and between the ages of seventeen and twenty-four. The scholarship can be applied to tuition, registration, and fees. Both awards are nonrenewable. Deadline: March 15.

236.
American Legion Auxiliary (Arizona) Nurses' Scholarship
Executive Secretary
4701 North 19th Avenue, Suite 200
Phoenix, AZ 85015-3727

1 scholarship of $400 per year to a second-year student nurse with one year's residence in Arizona prior to application. Renewable, if grades are satisfactory. Preference given to immediate family members of a veteran.

237.
American Legion Auxiliary (Arizona) Wilma D. Hoyal Memorial Scholarship
Executive Secretary
4701 North 19th Avenue, Suite 200
Phoenix, AZ 85015-3727

1 scholarship of $400 awarded at each state university in Arizona to an undergraduate junior or senior student enrolled full-time in political science. Renewable, if grades are satisfactory. Preference given to immediate family members of a veteran.

238.
American Legion Auxiliary (Arkansas)
P.O. Box 3280
Little Rock, AR 77203
(501) 375-5836

1 scholarship of $1,000 and 1 nurse's scholarship of $500 to a graduating high school senior or a high school graduate who hasn't attended college. Must be dependents of

veterans. Must be residents of Arkansas and attend Arkansas institutions. Other restrictions may apply. Deadline: March 15.

239.
American Legion Auxiliary (California)
Department President's Scholarship
Department of California Headquarters
401 Van Ness #113
San Francisco, CA 94102-4586

1 scholarship of $500 to a graduating high school senior. Must be a dependent of a veteran. Based on financial need. Other restrictions may apply. Deadline: none specified.

240.
American Legion Auxiliary (California)
Department President's Scholarship for Junior Members
Department of California Headquarters
401 Van Ness #113
San Francisco, CA 94102-4586

1 scholarship of $250 to high school seniors. Must be a dependent of a veteran. Based on financial need. Other restrictions may apply.

241.
American Legion Auxiliary (California)
Lucille Ganey Scholarship
Department of California Headquarters
401 Van Ness #113
San Francisco, CA 94102-4586

1 scholarship of $1,000 for undergraduate students majoring in public relations, news media, television, newsprint, or teaching of same. Must be a dependent of a veteran. Award must be used at Stephens College in Missouri. Must be a California resident. Special scholarship applications are available by writing the department office. Other restrictions may apply. Deadline: March 15.

242.
American Legion Auxiliary (California)
National President's Scholarships
Department of California Headquarters
401 Van Ness #113
San Francisco, CA 94102-4586

1 scholarship of $2,000 and 1 scholarship of $1,500 to a graduating high school senior. The State winner competes in Western Division competition. Only one candidate from a Unit; no elimination in the District. Send directly to the Department President. If California's candidate doesn't win, a $500 scholarship will be awarded by Department of California. Special scholarship applications are available by writing the department office. Other restrictions may apply. Deadline: March 15.

243.
American Legion Auxiliary (California)
National President's Scholarships for Junior Members
Department of California Headquarters
401 Van Ness #113
San Francisco, CA 94102-4586

1 scholarship of $1,000 to high school seniors. Must be a Junior member of the American Legion, have had the membership for the past three years, and hold a current Junior member's card. If California's candidate doesn't win, a $250 scholarship is awarded by the Department of California. Special scholarship applications are available by writing the department office. Other restrictions may apply. Deadline: March 15.

244.
American Legion Auxiliary (California)
Past Department President's Scholarships for Junior Members
Department of California Headquarters
401 Van Ness #113
San Francisco, CA 94102-4586

1 scholarship of $1,000 to a high school senior. Must be a Junior member of the American Legion, have had the membership for the past three years, and hold a current Junior member's card. If California's candidate doesn't win, a $250 scholarship is awarded by the Department of California. Special scholarship applications are available by writing the department office. Other restrictions may apply. Deadline: March 15.

245.
American Legion Auxiliary (California)
Scholarships
Department of California Headquarters
401 Van Ness #113
San Francisco, CA 94102-4586

1 scholarship of $2,000 ($500 per year) to a high school senior or a high school graduate who hasn't attended college due to circumstances of finance or illness. Must be the child of a veteran and a California veteran for at least five years. Must be pursuing a career in the medical profession, engineering, law, law enforcement, or business. Must demonstrate financial need. Deadline: March 15.

246.
American Legion Auxiliary (California)
Scholarships
401 Van Ness #113
San Francisco, CA 94102-4586

1 scholarship of $1,000 to a high school senior. Must be a member of the American Legion Auxiliary. Must be attending an accredited high school in the U.S. or its territories, but not have attended a college or university. Special scholarship applications are available by writing the department office. Other restrictions may apply. Deadline: March 15.

247.
American Legion Auxiliary (California)
Scholarships
Department of California Headquarters
401 Van Ness #113
San Francisco, CA 94102-4586

5 scholarships of $500 to graduating high school seniors. Must be children of veterans, California residents, and

planning to attend an accredited institution. Must hold a current Junior member's card. Must demonstrate financial need. Deadline: March 15.

248.
American Legion Auxiliary (California)
Spirit of Youth Scholarship
Department of California Headquarters
401 Van Ness #113
San Francisco, CA 94102-4586

1 scholarship of $1,000 to a high school senior. Must be a member of the American Legion Auxiliary. Must hold a current Junior member's card. Must be attending an accredited high school in California, but not have attended a college or university. Special scholarship applications are available by writing the department office. California residency is required. Other restrictions may apply. Deadline: March 15.

249.
American Legion Auxiliary (Colorado)
Department President's Scholarship
Department Headquarters
3003 Tejon Street
Denver, CO 80211

1 scholarship of $500 and 1 scholarship of $250 to graduating high school seniors or high school graduates who haven't attended college. Must be children of a veteran of WWI, WWII, Korean War, Vietnam War, or Desert Storm. Must be Colorado residents and have been accepted by an accredited Colorado college. Deadline: March 12.

250.
American Legion Auxiliary (Colorado)
Department President's Scholarships for Junior Auxiliary Members
Department Headquarters
3003 Tejon Street
Denver, CO 80211
(303) 492-7322

1 scholarship of $500 to a graduating high school senior or high school graduate who hasn't attended college. Must be the child of a veteran of WWI, WWII, Korean War, Vietnam War, or Desert Storm and a member of Junior Auxiliary of Colorado. Must be a Colorado resident and attend an accredited Colorado institution. Deadline: March 12.

251.
American Legion Auxiliary (Colorado)
Past Presidents' Parley Nurses' Scholarship
Department Headquarters
3003 Tejon Street
Denver, CO 80211

1 scholarship of $300 to a graduating high school senior or high school graduate who hasn't attended college. Must have been accepted to an accredited school of nursing in Colorado. Must be a veteran or the child or spouse of a veteran. Must be a Colorado resident. Other restrictions may apply. Deadline: April 1.

252.
American Legion Auxiliary (Connecticut)
Department Headquarters
P.O. Box 266
Rocky Hill, CT 06067
(860) 721-5945

4 scholarships of $500 for children of veterans who are Connecticut residents and between the ages of sixteen and twenty-three. One award is for a student in a nursing course. Deadline: March 1.

253.
American Legion Auxiliary (Connecticut)
Past Presidents' Parley Nurses' Scholarships
Department Headquarters
P.O. Box 266
Rocky Hill, CT 06067
(860) 721-5945

4 scholarship of $500 for students who are Connecticut residents, need financial assistance, and are between the ages of sixteen and twenty-three. First preference given to children of an ex-servicewoman and second preference given to children of an ex-serviceman. Deadline: March 1.

254.
American Legion Auxiliary (Delaware)
Past Presidents' Parley
Executive Secretary
43 Blades Drive
Dover, DE 19901

1 scholarship of $300 to a son or daughter of a veteran who is a Delaware resident and is going into nursing. Deadline: February 28.

255.
American Legion Auxiliary (Florida) Scholarship
Department Secretary
P.O. Box 547917
Orlando, FL 32854-7917

1 scholarship of $1,000 to a child of an honorably discharged veteran. Must be used at a Florida four-year college or university. 1 scholarship of $500 to a Florida junior-college or technical/vocational-school student. Must be sponsored by an Auxiliary unit and be a Florida resident. Deadline: March 1.

256.
American Legion Auxiliary (Florida) Scholarship
Memorial Scholarships
Department Secretary
P.O. Box 547917
Orlando, FL 32854-7917

1 two-year college scholarship of $500 and 1 four-year university scholarship of $1,000 for members, daughters, or granddaughters of members with three years of continuous membership in Florida Auxiliary Unit prior to application. Must be Florida residents and attending a Florida institution. Deadline: March 1.

257.
American Legion Auxiliary (Georgia)
Department Headquarters
3284 East Main Street
College Park, GA 30337

2 scholarships of $1,000 to outstanding high school seniors who are sons or daughters of veterans. Must be Georgia residents. Preference to children of deceased veterans.

258.
American Legion Auxiliary (Georgia)
Past Presidents' Parley Nurses' Scholarship
Department Headquarters
3284 East Main Street
College Park, GA 30337

1 scholarship of varying amount to an outstanding high school senior who is the daughter of a veteran. Must be a Georgia resident. Preference to daughters of deceased veterans.

259.
American Legion Auxiliary (Idaho)
Nurses' Scholarships
Department Headquarters
901 Warren Street
Boise, ID 83706
(208) 342-7061

Scholarships of $750 to students pursuing a nursing career. Must either be veterans or veteran's children. Must be residents of Idaho for five years prior to application. Deadline: April 1.

260.
American Legion Auxiliary (Illinois)
Ada Muckleston Memorial Scholarships
Department of Illinois
P.O. Box 1426
Bloomington, IL 61702-1426
(309) 663-9366

3 ($800, $1,000, and $1,200) scholarships to daughters or sons of veterans who served during WWI, WWII, Korea, or Vietnam. Veteran parent must be American Legion member. Students must be in their senior year or graduates of an accredited high school who have not yet attended an institution of higher learning. Must have financial need and be a resident of Illinois. Deadline: March 15.

261.
American Legion Auxiliary (Illinois)
Americanism Essay Contest Scholarship Awards
Department of Illinois
P.O. Box 1426
Bloomington, IL 61702-1426
(309) 663-9366

Awards ranging from $50 to $75 to students in grades 8 to 12 based on a 500-word essay on a selected topic. Students must be attending an accredited Illinois school and be Illinois residents. Amount of award depends on grade level. Obtain guidelines from local American Legion Auxiliary. Deadline: February 12.

262.
American Legion Auxiliary (Illinois)
Knoles Opportunity Scholarship
Department of Illinois
P.O. Box 1426
Bloomington, IL 61702-1426

1 scholarship of $800 and 1 scholarship of $1,200 to students who are veterans (WWI, WWII, Korea, Vietnam) or children of veterans who must have financial assistance to continue their education. May be undergraduate or graduate students; must have resided in Illinois for at least three years. Deadline: March 15.

263.
American Legion Auxiliary (Illinois)
Nursing Scholarship
Department of Illinois
P.O. Box 1426
Bloomington, IL 61702-1426
(309) 663-9366

1 scholarship of $1,000 to a graduating high school senior or undergraduate student who is pursuing a degree in nursing. Must be an Illinois resident, attend an accredited Illinois institution, and be sponsored by local Unit. Obtain guidelines from local American Legion Auxiliary. Deadline: March 15.

264.
American Legion Auxiliary (Illinois)
Trade School Scholarship
Department of Illinois
P.O. Box 1426
Bloomington, IL 61702-1426

1 scholarship of $800 to a student entering or enrolled in a trade school. Must be a child of a veteran and a resident of Illinois. Deadline: March 15.

265.
American Legion Auxiliary (Illinois)
Special Education Teaching Scholarships
Department of Illinois
P.O. Box 1426
Bloomington, IL 61702-1426
(309) 663-9366

Scholarships of $1,000 to undergraduate sophomores or juniors who are pursuing careers in education of mentally or physically challenged children. Must be Illinois residents. Must be sponsored by local Unit. Applications may be obtained from local Unit. Deadline: March 15.

266.
American Legion Auxiliary (Indiana)
Edna M. Barcus Memorial Scholarship
Department Secretary
777 North Meridian Street, Room 107
Indianapolis, IN 46204
(317) 630-1390

1 scholarship of $500 to a student who is a child of a veteran. Must be an Indiana resident and planning to

attend an Indiana college or university. Based on academic achievement. Deadline: April 1.

267.
American Legion Auxiliary (Indiana)
Past Presidents' Parley Nurses' Scholarship
Department Secretary
777 North Meridian Street, Room 107
Indianapolis, IN 46204
(317) 630-1390

1 scholarship of $300 to a daughter of an Auxiliary member or deceased member. Must be an Indiana resident and a member of the American Legion Auxiliary. Deadline: April 1.

268.
American Legion Auxiliary (Iowa)
Department Executive Secretary
720 Lyon Street
Des Moines, IA 50309

13 scholarships of $200 to members of the Legion or Auxiliary or to sons or daughters of veterans (WWI, WWII, Korea, or Vietnam). Must be Iowa residents. Deadline: June 1.

269.
American Legion Auxiliary (Iowa)
Harriett Hoffman Memorial Scholarship
Department Executive Secretary
720 Lyon Street
Des Moines, IA 50309

1 scholarship of $400 ($200 for first year, $200 for second year) to Iowa students pursuing a teaching career. May be a son, daughter, grandson, or granddaughter of a deceased or disabled veteran. Deadline: June 1.

270.
American Legion Auxiliary (Iowa)
Mary Virginia Macrea Memorial Nurses
  Scholarship
Department Executive Secretary
720 Lyon Street
Des Moines, IA 50309

1 scholarship of $400 ($200 for first year and $200 for second year) to a student pursuing a nursing career. May be a mother, daughter, wife, widow, granddaughter, son, or grandson of a veteran (WWI, WWII, Korea, or Vietnam). Must be Iowa resident. Deadline: June 1.

271.
American Legion Auxiliary (Kansas)
Education Committee Scholarships
1314 Topeka Boulevard
Topeka, KS 66612-1886
(913) 232-1396

8 scholarships of $250 per year for two years to graduating high school seniors or high school graduates who haven't attended college. Must be children, spouses, or unremarried widows of veterans. Must be Kansas residents and attend accredited Kansas institutions. Renewable the second year with satisfactory academic progress. Deadline: April 1.

272.
American Legion Auxiliary (Kentucky)
Laura Blackburn Memorial Scholarship
Department of Kentucky
P.O. Box 189
Greensburg, KY 42743

1 scholarship of $1,000 to a graduating high school senior. Must be a child, grandchild, or great grandchild of a veteran who served in the Armed Forces during eligibility dates for membership in the American Legion. Must be a Kentucky resident, attending an accredited high school, and planning to attend an accredited Kentucky college/ university. Deadline: March 31.

273.
American Legion Auxiliary (Kentucky)
Mary Barrett Marshall Scholarship
Department of Kentucky
P.O. Box 189
Greensburg, KY 42743

1 scholarship of $500 to a graduating high school senior or high school graduate who hasn't attended college, or an undergraduate student. Must be a daughter, granddaughter, wife, widow, or sister of a veteran who is eligible for membership in the American Legion. Must be a Kentucky resident and attend an accredited Kentucky institution. Award may be used for any area of study. Send a #10 self-addressed, stamped envelope with request for an application. Deadline: April 1.

274.
American Legion Auxiliary (Maine)
Department Secretary
P.O. Box 887
Bucksport, ME 04416

2 scholarships of $300 available to high school seniors who are sons or daughters of a veteran. Must be Maine residents. Based on financial need. Deadline: April 15.

275.
American Legion Auxiliary (Maine)
Past Presidents' Parley Nurses' Scholarship
Department Secretary
P.O. Box 887
Bucksport, ME 04416

1 scholarship of $300 to a high school graduate who is a daughter of a veteran. Must be a Maine resident. Deadline: varies.

276.
American Legion Auxiliary (Maryland)
Past Presidents' Parley Nurses' Scholarship Fund
Department Secretary
5205 East Drive, Suite R-1
Baltimore, MD 21227
(410) 242-9519

1 scholarship of $1,000 to the daughter of an ex-serviceman/ woman. Must be preparing for a career in nursing. Student must be between the ages of sixteen and twenty-two and have been a Maryland resident for at least five years. Based

on financial need and letters of recommendation. Deadline: May 1.

277.
American Legion Auxiliary (Maryland)
Scholarship
Department Secretary
5205 East Drive, Suite R-1
Baltimore, MD 21227
(410) 242-9519

1 scholarship of $2,000 to a high school senior who is a dependent of a veteran. Must plan to pursue a degree in the arts, sciences, business administration, public administration, home economics, or education at a Maryland college or university. Must be a resident of Maryland. Deadline: May 1.

278.
American Legion Auxiliary (Massachusetts)
Department Secretary
546-2 State House
Boston, MA 02133

1 scholarship of $500 and 10 scholarships of $100 to children of deceased veterans. Must be between the ages of sixteen and twenty-two, be Massachusetts residents, and not eligible for state aid. Deadline: April 10.

279.
American Legion Auxiliary (Massachusetts)
Past Presidents' Parley Nurses' Scholarship
Department Secretary
546-2 State House
Boston, MA 02133

1 scholarship of $100 to a child of a deceased veteran. Must be planning on a career in nursing, not eligible for state aid, and a Massachusetts resident. Deadline: April 10.

280.
American Legion Auxiliary (Michigan)
Memorial Scholarships
212 North Verlinden Street
Lansing, MI 48915

Several scholarships of $500 to daughters of honorably discharged or deceased men or women veterans. Students must be between the ages of sixteen and twenty-one, attend an institute in Michigan, and be Michigan residents. Must have financial need. Renewable for second year. Request applications after November 15 and return to address on the application. Deadline: March 15.

281.
American Legion Auxiliary (Michigan)
National President's Scholarships
212 North Verlinden Street
Lansing, MI 48915

5 scholarships each of $2,000 and $1,500 to graduating high school seniors. Must be children of veterans who served in the Armed Forces during eligibility dates for membership in the American Legion. Must request applications after November 15. Must be Michigan residents. Deadline: March 11.

282.
American Legion Auxiliary (Michigan)
Nursing, Physical Therapy or Respiratory
  Therapy Scholarship
212 North Verlinden Street
Lansing, MI 48915

1 scholarship of $500 for first-year training to a daughter, son, wife, or widow of an honorably discharged or deceased veteran of WWI, WWII, Korea, or Vietnam. Must be a Michigan resident and accepted to an accredited school of nursing in Michigan. Based on academic merit and financial need. Request applications after November 15 and return to address on the application. Deadline: March 15.

283.
American Legion Auxiliary (Minnesota)
Department Scholarships
State Veterans Building
St. Paul, MN 55155
(651) 224-7634

7 scholarships of up to $500 to children of veterans. Must be used for vocational training in education. Minnesota residency required. Deadline: March 15.

284.
American Legion Auxiliary (Minnesota)
Past Presidents' Parley Nurses' Scholarship
Department Headquarters
State Veterans Building
Columbus Drive
St. Paul, MN 55155
(651) 224-7634

3 scholarships of $500 to members of the Minnesota American Legion Auxiliary who are preparing for a nursing career. Must be Minnesota residents and attend school in Minnesota. Deadline: March 15.

285.
American Legion Auxiliary (Mississippi)
Department Secretary
P.O. Box 1382
Jackson, MS 39205-1382

1 scholarship of $500 to a son or daughter of a deceased or disabled veteran of WWI, WWII, or Korean War. Must be a graduating senior of an accredited Mississippi high school, have financial need, and Mississippi residency. Deadline: varies.

286.
American Legion Auxiliary (Missouri)
Department Secretary
210 West Dunklin Street
Jefferson City, MO 65101

2 scholarships of $500 to children of veterans of WWI, WWII, Korean War, or Vietnam War. Deadline: March 15.

287.
American Legion Auxiliary (Missouri)
Past Presidents' Parley Nurses' Scholarship
Department Secretary
210 West Dunklin Street
Jefferson City, MO 65101

1 scholarship of $1,000 to a dependent child or grandchild of a veteran. Must be pursuing a career in nursing.

288.
American Legion Auxiliary (Montana)
Department Secretary
5835 Lewis & Clark Road
Wolf Creek, MT 59648
(406) 235-4205

2 scholarships of $500 to children of veterans. Must be high school seniors or graduates (with no college education) and be residents of Montana for at least two years. Children of deceased veterans are given preference. 500-word essay required.

289.
American Legion Auxiliary (Montana)
Aloha Scholarship
Department Secretary
5835 Lewis & Clark Road
Wolf Creek, MT 59648
(406) 235-4205

1 scholarship of $400 to a daughter of an Auxiliary member who has been accepted into a nursing program. Must be a high school senior and a two-year resident of Montana.

290.
American Legion Auxiliary (Montana)
Department Secretary
5835 Lewis & Clark Road
Wolf Creek, MT 59648
(406) 235-4205

2 scholarships of $500 to children of veterans. Must be completing undergraduate sophomore year. Based on qualifications, an essay concerning interest in children and youth leadership, and Montana residency.

291.
American Legion Auxiliary (Nebraska)
Averyl Elaine Keriakedes Memorial Scholarship
Department Secretary
P.O. Box 5227, Station C
Lincoln, NE 68505

1 scholarship of $500 to a female student at the University of Nebraska who plans to teach junior high social studies. Must be related to a veteran Nebraska resident and daughter of a veteran. Deadline: April 10.

292.
American Legion Auxiliary (Nebraska)
Junior Member Scholarship
Department Secretary
P.O. Box 5227, Station C
Lincoln, NE 68505
(402) 464-6338

1 scholarship of $200 for first place, $150 for second place, and $100 for third place to graduating high school seniors or high school graduates who haven't attended college.

293.
American Legion Auxiliary (Nebraska)
Nurse Gift Tuition Scholarship
Department Secretary
P.O. Box 5227, Station C
Lincoln, NE 68505
(402) 466-1808

1 or more scholarships ranging from $400 to $500 (as funds permit) to graduating high school seniors or high school graduates who haven't attended college. Must be veterans or their dependents. Must have been accepted to an accredited Nebraska hospital nursing school. Must have financial need and be Nebraska residents. Deadline: April 10.

294.
American Legion Auxiliary (Nebraska)
Practical Nurse Scholarship
Department Secretary
P.O. Box 5227, Station C
Lincoln, NE 68505

1 scholarship of $400 to a student who is a dependent of a veteran and has been accepted to a Nebraska school of practical nursing. Must be a Nebraska resident. Deadline: April 10.

295.
American Legion Auxiliary (Nebraska)
Presidents' Scholarships
Department Secretary
P.O. Box 5227, Station C
Lincoln, NE 68505
(402) 466-1808

1 award each of $200, $150, and $100 to Nebraskan entrants to the National President's Scholarship who were not winners at the national level. Must be a dependent of a veteran, a Nebraska resident, and have financial need. Deadline: varies.

296.
American Legion Auxiliary (Nebraska)
Roberta Marie Stretch Memorial Scholarship
Department Secretary
P.O. Box 5227, Station C
Lincoln, NE 68505
(402) 466-1808

1 scholarship of $300 to an undergraduate or graduate (master's) student enrolled or accepted into a four-year college or university. Preference is given to former Nebraska Girls State citizens. Must be a Nebraska resident and veteran-connected. Deadline: April 10.

297.
American Legion Auxiliary (Nebraska)
Ruby Paul Campaign Fund Scholarship
Department Secretary
P.O. Box 5227, Station C
Lincoln, NE 68505
(402) 466-1808

1 scholarship of $300 (as funds permit) to a graduating
high school senior or high school graduate who hasn't
attended college. Must have maintained a "B" or better
grade point average during the last two semesters of senior
high school year. Students already enrolled in a school of
nursing are not eligible. Applicant must be the child or
grandchild of an American Legion or American Auxiliary
member who has held NE membership for the past two
years or be a member of the American Legion, American
Legion Auxiliary, or Sons of the American Legion for two
years prior to application. Applicants must be Nebraska
residents for previous three years and have been accepted
by an accredited college or university for the fall term in
the year the scholarship is applied. Deadline: April 10.

298.
American Legion Auxiliary (Nebraska)
Student Aid Grant or Vocational Technical
    Scholarship
Department Secretary
P.O. Box 5227, Station C
Lincoln, NE 68505

1 scholarship ranging from $200 to $300 to a student
attending a college, university, or vocational/technical
school. Open to veterans or dependents of veterans.
Applicant must be a Nebraska resident for at least five
years and have financial need. Other restrictions may apply.
Deadline: varies.

299.
American Legion Auxiliary (Nevada)
Past Presidents' Parley Nurses' Scholarship
Department of Nevada
Attn: Department Secretary
1718 Statz Street
North Las Vegas, NV 89030-7260

1 scholarship of $100 to a student who is a dependent of a
veteran. Must be accepted into a Nevada nursing school, be
a Nevada resident, and have financial need. Deadline:
varies.

300.
American Legion Auxiliary (Nevada)
President's Scholarship
Department of Nevada
Attn: Department Secretary
1718 Statz Street
North Las Vegas, NV 89030-7260

1 scholarship of $200 and 1 scholarship of $100 to the top
Nevada entrants in the National President's Scholarship
Competition who were not winners at the national level.
Must be a high school senior or graduate who is a
dependent of a veteran. Must be a Nevada resident.
Deadline: varies.

301.
American Legion Auxiliary (Nevada)
Silver Eagle Indian Scholarship
Department of Nevada
Attn: Department Secretary
1718 Statz Street
North Las Vegas, NV 89030-7260

1 scholarship of $200 to a graduating high school senior.
Must be a child or grandchild of an American Indian
veteran. Recipient must have been born in Nevada. Must
plan to attend an accredited institution in any field of
study. Deadline: varies.

302.
American Legion Auxiliary (New Hampshire)
Elsie B. Brown Scholarship
Department Secretary
25 Capitol Street
Concord, NH 03301-6312

1 scholarship of $150 to a daughter of a deceased veteran.
Must be a high school graduate who will be attending a
college or university in New Hampshire. Deadline: April 15.

303.
American Legion Auxiliary (New Hampshire)
Grace S. High Memorial Child Welfare
    Scholarships
Department Secretary
25 Capitol Street
Concord, NH 03301-6312

2 scholarships of $300 to high school graduates who are
daughters of Legionnaires or Auxiliary members. Based on
financial need. Deadline: April 15.

304.
American Legion Auxiliary (New Hampshire)
Marion J. Bagley Scholarship
Department Secretary
25 Capitol Street, Room 432
Concord, NH 03301-6312

1 scholarship of $1,000 to a graduating high school senior,
high school graduate who hasn't attended college, GED
recipient, or undergraduate student. Must be a New
Hampshire resident and dependent of a veteran. Deadline:
May 1.

305.
American Legion Auxiliary (New Hampshire)
Past Presidents' Parley Nurses' Scholarship
Department Secretary
25 Capitol Street
Concord, NH 03301-6312

1 scholarship of varying amount to a high school graduate
with financial need. Preference given to the daughter of a
veteran. Deadline: May 10.

306.
American Legion Auxiliary (New Jersey)
Claire Oliphant Memorial Scholarship
Department Secretary
Legion 146
Route 130
Bordertown, NJ 08505-2226
(609) 291-9338

1 scholarship of $1,800 to a daughter or son of an honorably discharged veteran. Must have been a resident of New Jersey for at least two years and have graduated from a New Jersey high school. Deadline: March 15.

307.
American Legion Auxiliary (New Jersey)
Department Scholarships
Department Secretary
Legion 146
Route 130
Bordertown, NJ 08505-2226
(609) 291-9338

7 scholarships of varying amounts to daughters, sons, or grandchildren of honorably discharged veterans. Must have been a resident of New Jersey for at least two years and have graduated from a New Jersey high school. Deadline: varies.

308.
American Legion Auxiliary (New Jersey)
Past Presidents' Parley Nurses' Scholarships
Department Secretary
Legion 146
Route 130
Bordertown, NJ 08505-2226
(609) 291-9338

Scholarships to students who are daughters, sons, or grandchildren of honorably discharged veterans. Must be pursuing a nursing career. Must have been residents of New Jersey for at least two years and have graduated from a New Jersey high school. Deadline: March 15.

309.
American Legion Auxiliary (New Mexico)
Past Presidents' Parley Nurses' Scholarship
Department Secretary
1215 Mountain Road, N.E.
Albuquerque, NM 87102

1 scholarship of $150 to a New Mexico entrant in the national competition who doesn't win at the national level. If student wins at the national level, the award goes to first runner-up. Must be a high school senior or graduate who is a child of a veteran. Deadline: April 1.

310.
American Legion Auxiliary (New York)
Judicial District Scholarships
112 State Street, Suite 409
Albany, NY 12207
(518) 463-2215

1 scholarship of $500 in each of the ten Judicial Districts in New York to graduating high school seniors or high school graduates who have not attended college. Must be daughters of a veteran. Must be pursuing a medical or teaching field, not be older than twenty years of age, and be a New York resident. Deadline: March 25.

311.
American Legion Auxiliary (New York)
Past Presidents' Parley Student Nurses'
   Scholarship
112 State Street, Suite 400
Albany, NY 12207
(518) 463-2215

1 scholarship of $500 to a child or grandchild of a veteran. Must not be over twenty years of age. Must be a high school graduate and have financial need. Must be a resident of New York. Deadline: March 25.

312.
American Legion Auxiliary (New York)
Scholarship
112 State Street, Suite 400
Albany, NY 12207
(518) 463-2215

1 scholarship of $1,000 to a graduating high school senior or high school graduate who hasn't attended college. Must be a child or grandchild of a deceased veteran. Award may be used along with other awards. Must be a New York State resident. Deadline: March 25.

313.
American Legion Auxiliary (North Carolina)
Nannie W. Norfleet Educational Loan Fund
Department Headquarters
P.O. Box 25726
Raleigh, NC 27611
(919) 832-4051

2 loans of $1,500 per year to children of deserving World War I or World War II veterans. Interest accrues only after graduation. Must be North Carolina residents. Deadline: none.

314.
American Legion Auxiliary (North Dakota)
Department Secretary
P.O. Box 250
Beach, ND 58621
(701) 872-3865

4 or more scholarships of $350 (when funds are available) for residents of North Dakota who are already attending a North Dakota college or university. Must be children of veterans. Must have financial need. Deadline: December 15.

315.
American Legion Auxiliary (North Dakota)
Past Presidents' Parley Nurses' Scholarship
Department Secretary
P.O. Box 250
Beach, ND 58621
(701) 872-3865

1 scholarship of $350 to a child, grandchild, or great-grandchild of a Legionnaire or Auxiliary member in good

standing who is a resident of North Dakota. Must attend a North Dakota institution. Deadline: April 25.

316.
American Legion Auxiliary (Ohio)
Department Secretary
1100 Brandywine Boulevard, Building D
P.O. Box 2279
Zanesville, OH 43702-2279

1 scholarship of $1,500 to a daughter, son, or grandchild of a WWI, WWII, Korean War, or Vietnam War veteran. Must be an Ohio resident and high school graduate; must have financial need. Deadline: April 1.

317.
American Legion Auxiliary (Ohio)
Past Presidents' Parley Nurses' Scholarships
Department Secretary
1100 Brandywine Boulevard, Building D
P.O. Box 2279
Zanesville, OH 43702

10 scholarships of $300 and 2 scholarships of $500 to graduating high school seniors, high school graduates, or undergraduate students. Must be child, stepchild, grandchild, or wife of a veteran. Award must be used for nurses' training. Applicants must be sponsored by an Auxiliary unit and be Ohio residents. Deadline: June 1.

318.
American Legion Auxiliary (Oklahoma)
Student Educational Loan Fund
Department Headquarters
P.O. Box 53068, State Capitol Station
Oklahoma City, OK 73152

1 loan of up to $1,000 to assist children, wives, or sisters of veterans. Must be used for educational purposes at a college or vocational school. Must be Oklahoma resident.

319.
American Legion Auxiliary (Oregon)
Department Scholarships
Chairman, Education and Scholarships
P.O. Box 1730
Wilsonville, OR 97070-1730

3 scholarships of $1,000 to graduating high school seniors, high school graduates who haven't attended college, or undergraduate students. 1 of the 3 scholarships must be used for a vocational or business school. Open to children or wives of disabled veterans or widows of veterans. Must be Oregon residents and attend an accredited Oregon institution. Deadline: March 15.

320.
American Legion Auxiliary (Oregon)
National Nurse's Scholarship
Chairman, Education and Scholarships
P.O. Box 1730
Wilsonville, OR 97070-1730

1 scholarship of $1,500 to a graduating high school senior, high school graduate who hasn't attended college, or

undergraduate student. Must have been accepted into an accredited nursing program at a hospital or university in Oregon. Must be an Oregon resident. Deadline: June 1.

321.
American Legion Auxiliary (Oregon)
National President's Scholarships
Chairman, Education and Scholarships
P.O. Box 1730
Wilsonville, OR 97070-1730

2 scholarships each of $2,000 and $1,500 in each AL Auxiliary District to graduating high school seniors. Must be children of veterans who served in Armed Forces during eligibility dates for membership in the American Legion. Must be Oregon residents and attend an Oregon institution. Deadline: March 15.

322.
American Legion Auxiliary (Oregon)
One-Time Grants
Chairman, Education and Scholarships
P.O. Box 1730
Wilsonville, OR 97070-1730

Scholarships of $1,000 to graduating high school seniors, high school graduates who haven't attended college, or undergraduate students. Open to children or wives of disabled veterans or widows of veterans. Must be Oregon residents and attend an accredited two- or four-year college, university, or vocational or business school in Oregon. Deadline: March 15.

323.
American Legion Auxiliary (Pennsylvania)
Department Chairman
Education and Scholarships
P.O. Box 2643
Harrisburg, PA 17105
(717) 763-7545

1 scholarship of $600 to a high school senior who is the son or daughter of a deceased or totally disabled veteran. Must have financial need. Must be a Pennsylvania resident. Renewable for four years. Deadline: March 15.

324.
American Legion Auxiliary (Pennsylvania)
Department Chairman
Education and Scholarships
P.O. Box 2643
Harrisburg, PA 17105
(717) 763-7545

1 scholarship of $600 to a son or daughter of a living veteran. Applicant must be a high school senior and attend a Pennsylvania institute. Must be a Pennsylvania resident. Renewable for four years. Deadline: March 15.

325.
American Legion Auxiliary (Puerto Rico)
Education and Scholarship Chairman
P.O. Box 11424, Caparra Heights
Caparra Heights, PR 00922

2 scholarships of $250/year to high school seniors who will be entering nurses' training at any Puerto Rico Nurses

Training Educational Institution. Renewable for two years. Deadline: March 15.

326.
American Legion Auxiliary (South Carolina)
Floyd Memorial Scholarship Fund
Department Secretary
132 Pickens Street
Columbia, SC 29205
(803) 799-6695

2 interest-free loans of $400 to sons and daughters of World War I or World War II veterans. Must be South Carolina residents. Deadline: none.

327.
American Legion Auxiliary (South Carolina)
Department Secretary
132 Pickens Street
Columbia, SC 29205
(803) 799-6695

1 scholarship of $1,000 to a South Carolina Junior member who has been a member for three consecutive years. Must be a child of a veteran and a resident of South Carolina.

328.
American Legion Auxiliary (South Dakota)
College Scholarships
Department Secretary
P.O. Box 117
Huron, SD 57350
(605) 353-1793

2 scholarships of $300 to sons or daughters of veterans or Auxiliary members. Must be South Dakota residents and between sixteen and twenty-two years of age. Funds must be used at a South Dakota college or university. Deadline: March 1.

329.
American Legion Auxiliary (South Dakota)
Nurses' Scholarships
Department Secretary
P.O. Box 117
Huron, SD 57350
(605) 353-1793

3 scholarships of $200 to sons or daughters of veterans or Auxiliary members. Must be South Dakota residents and between sixteen and twenty-two years of age. Deadline: March 1.

330.
American Legion Auxiliary (South Dakota)
Scholarship for Junior Members of American
** Legion Auxiliary**
Department Secretary
P.O. Box 117
Huron, SD 57350
(605) 353-1793

1 scholarship of $300 to a graduating high school senior or high school graduate who hasn't attended college. Must be a Junior member of the American Legion Auxiliary for the past three years plus the current year. Must be the son or

daughter of a veteran. Must be a South Dakota resident and attend a South Dakota institute. Deadline: March 1.

331.
American Legion Auxiliary (South Dakota)
Scholarship for Senior Members of American
** Legion Auxiliary**
Department Secretary
P.O. Box 117
Huron, SD 57350
(605) 353-1793

1 scholarship of $300 to a Senior member of the American Legion Auxiliary for the past three years plus the current year. Must be a dependent of a veteran. Must be a South Dakota resident and attend a South Dakota institute. Deadline: March 1.

332.
American Legion Auxiliary (Tennessee)
Vara Gray Scholarship Fund
Department Headquarters
1007 Murfreesboro Road, Suite 100
Nashville, TN 37217
(615) 361-8822
(615) 361-8919 Fax

3 scholarships of $500 for students pursuing a nursing major and 3 scholarships of $500 for any scholastic major. Must be a child or dependent of a veteran. Must be Tennessee residents and high school seniors. Deadline: March 1.

333.
American Legion Auxiliary (Texas)
Department of Texas
709 East Tenth Street
Austin, TX 78701
(512) 472-4138

Scholarships of $500 to graduating high school seniors or high school graduates. Must be children of veterans of WWI, WWII, Korea, Vietnam, Lebanon, Granada, Panama, or Persian Gulf. Recipients must be pursuing a nursing career. Based on financial need, career goal, character, citizenship, objective, and war service of father or mother. Must be Texas residents and attend Texas colleges or universities. Applications available after November 1. Deadline: February 1.

334.
American Legion Auxiliary (Texas)
General Education Scholarships
Department of Texas
709 East Tenth Street
Austin, TX 78701
(512) 472-4138

Scholarships of $500 to high school seniors. Must be children of veterans of WWI, WWII, Korean War, or Vietnam War. Based on financial need, career goal, character, citizenship, objective, and war service of father or mother. Must be used at a Texas college or university. Applications available after November 1. Must be Texas residents. Deadline: February 1.

335.
American Legion Auxiliary (Utah)
B61 State Capitol Building
Salt Lake City, UT 84114
(801) 538-1014

1 scholarship of $2,000 and 1 scholarship of $1,500 to graduating high school seniors or high school graduates who haven't attended college. Must be a child of a veteran. Must be a Utah resident and attend a Utah institution. Deadline: varies.

336.
American Legion Auxiliary (Virginia)
Dr. Kate Waller Barrett Grant
Secretary-Treasurer Department
1805 Chantilly Street
Richmond, VA 23230
(804) 355-6410

1 grant of $1,000 to a child of a veteran or Auxiliary member. Must have financial need. Must be a high school senior or a graduate of a Virginia high school. Deadline: March 15.

337.
American Legion Auxiliary (Washington)
Department Headquarters
P.O. Box 5867
Lacey, WA 98509-5867

3 scholarships of $300 to children of deceased or disabled veterans who are residents of Washington State. Deadline: March 15.

338.
American Legion Auxiliary (Washington)
Margarite McAlpine Nurses' Scholarship
Department Headquarters
P.O. Box 3917
Lacey, WA 98503

1 scholarship of $700 to a student who is a Washington State resident. Need not be a veteran's child. Deadline: mid-March.

339.
American Legion Auxiliary (Washington)
Susan Burdett Scholarship
Department Headquarters
P.O. Box 5867
Lacey, WA 98509-5867

1 scholarship of $400 to a student who is a former Evergreen Girls State Citizen. Must be a Washington State resident. Deadline: March 11.

340.
American Legion Auxiliary (Washington)
Florence Lemcke Memorial Scholarship
Department Headquarters
P.O. Box 5867
Lacey, WA 98509-5867

1 scholarship of $500 to a student who is a veteran's child. Must be a Washington State resident. Must be used for study in fine arts. Deadline: April 20.

341.
American Legion Auxiliary (Washington)
Scholarships
Department Headquarters
P.O. Box 3917
Lacey, WA 98503

2 scholarships $1,000 and $1,500 for sons or daughters of living or deceased Washington Legionnaire or Auxiliary members. Must have financial need. Good for college, trade, or vocational schools in Washington State. Deadline: April 1.

342.
American Legion Auxiliary (West Virginia)
Executive Secretary-Treasurer
RR Box 144 A
Proctor, WV 26055-9616
(304) 455-3449

4 scholarships of varying amounts to students who are children of veterans. Must be residents of West Virginia, attend a West Virginia institution, and be under twenty-two years of age. Based on financial need. Deadline: March 1.

343.
American Legion Auxiliary (Wisconsin)
Badger Girls State Scholarships
Department Executive Secretary
812 East State Street, Second Floor
Milwaukee, WI 53202-3493
(414) 271-0124

5 scholarships of $500 to graduating high school seniors or high school graduates who haven't attended college and who were Badger Girls State participants. Must be children of a veteran. Grandchildren and great-grandchildren are eligible if they are members of the American Legion Auxiliary. Must have at least a 3.2 GPA on a 4.0 scale. Must be Wisconsin residents, attend an accredited institution, and have financial need. Scholarships must be used for education past high school. Applications are automatically mailed to eligible students. Deadline: March 15.

344.
American Legion Auxiliary (Wisconsin)
Health Careers Awards
Department Executive Secretary
812 East State Street, Second Floor
Milwaukee, WI 53202-3493
(414) 271-0124

2 scholarships of $750 to graduating high school seniors, high school graduates who haven't attended college, or undergraduate students. Must be children, wives, or widows of veterans. Grandchildren and great-grandchildren are eligible if they are members of the American Legion Auxiliary. Must have at least a 3.2 GPA on a 4.0 scale. Must be Wisconsin residents, attend accredited institutions, and have financial need. Scholarships must be used for education past high school. Must be entering a hospital, university, or technical school and preparing for a health-care career. Deadline: March 15.

345.
American Legion Auxiliary (Wisconsin)
H. S. and Angeline Lewis Scholarships
Department Executive Secretary
812 East State Street, Second Floor
Milwaukee, WI 53202-3493
(414) 271-0124

3 scholarships of $2,500, 2 scholarships of $2,000, and 3 scholarships of $1,000 to graduating high school seniors, high school graduates who haven't attended college, or undergraduate students. Must be children, wives, or widows of veterans. Grandchildren and great-grandchildren are eligible if they are members of the American Legion Auxiliary. Must have at least a 3.2 GPA on a 4.0 scale. Must be Wisconsin residents, attend accredited institutions, and have financial need. Scholarships must be used for education past high school. Deadline: March 15.

346.
American Legion Auxiliary (Wisconsin)
Merit and Memorial Scholarships
Department Executive Secretary
812 East State Street, Second Floor
Milwaukee, WI 53202-3493
(414) 271-0124

10 scholarships of $1,000 to graduating high school seniors, high school graduates who haven't attended college, or undergraduate students. Must be children, wives, or widows of veterans. Grandchildren and great-grandchildren are eligible if they are members of the American Legion Auxiliary. Must have at least a 3.2 GPA on a 4.0 scale. Must be Wisconsin residents, attend accredited institutions, and have financial need. Scholarships must be used for education past high school. Deadline: March 15.

347.
American Legion Auxiliary (Wisconsin)
Registered Nurse Degree Awards
Department Executive Secretary
812 East State Street, Second Floor
Milwaukee, WI 53202-3493
(414) 271-0124

2 scholarships of $750 to graduating high school seniors, high school graduates who haven't attended college, or undergraduate students. Must be children, wives, or widows of veterans. Grandchildren and great-grandchildren are eligible if they are members of the American Legion Auxiliary. Must have at least a 3.2 GPA on a 4.0 scale. Must be Wisconsin residents, attend accredited institutions pursuing a nursing degree, and have financial need. Scholarships must be used for education past high school. Deadline: March 15.

348.
American Legion Auxiliary (Wisconsin)
State Presidents Scholarships
Department Executive Secretary
812 East State Street, Second Floor
Milwaukee, WI 53202-3493
(414) 271-0124

3 scholarships of $1,000 to sons or daughters of veterans or Auxiliary members. Must be used at a college or university in Wisconsin. Mother of applicant or applicant must be Wisconsin resident and Auxiliary member. Deadline: March 15.

349.
American Legion Auxiliary (Wyoming)
Past Presidents' Parley Scholarships
Department Secretary
118 Ridge Road
Torrington, WY 82240

2 scholarships of $300 to students who are in their third quarter of nurses' training. Preference given to children of veterans. Must have at least a 3.0 GPA. Must be Wyoming residents. Deadline: varies.

350.
American Legion Departments (Alabama)
Department Adjutant
P.O. Box 1069
Montgomery, AL 36101-1069
(334) 262-6638

130 scholarships of $850 to sons, daughters, or grandchildren of veterans of WWI, WWII, Korean War, or Vietnam War. Must attend an Alabama college and be Alabama residents. Renewable for four years. Send a 4" × 9½" stamped, self-addressed envelope. Deadline: May 1.

351.
American Legion Departments (Alabama)
State Oratorical Contest
Department Adjutant
P.O. Box 1069
Montgomery, AL 36101-1069
(334) 262-6638

Scholarships of $5,000, $3,000, and $1,000 to high school students under the age of twenty in the State Oratorical Competition. Based on a prepared oration and an extemporaneous discussion. Topic varies from year to year. Scored on presence, poise, logic, personality, knowledge of subject, originality, composition, and effectiveness. Must be an Alabama resident. Contact local or state American Legion in September or October for application and details. State contests are usually held from December to March.

352.
American Legion Departments (Alaska)
State Oratorical Contest
Department Adjutant
519 West 8th Avenue, Suite 208
Anchorage, AK 99501
(907) 278-8598

1 scholarship each of $500 and $1,000 to the winner of the State Oratorical Contest. Open to all Alaska high school students under the age of twenty. Based on a prepared oration and an extemporaneous discussion. Topic varies from year to year. Scored on presence, poise, logic, personality, knowledge of subject, originality, composition, and effectiveness. Contact local or state American Legion in September or October for application and details. State contests are usually held from December to March.

353.
American Legion Departments (Alaska)
Western District Postsecondary Scholarship
1417 Lacey Street
Fairbanks, AK 99701
(907) 456-3183

1 scholarship of $500 to a graduating high school senior in the Western District of Alaska. Must have a 2.5 to 3.7 GPA on a 4.0 scale. Selection based on academic achievement, extracurricular activities, and community service. Must be an Alaska resident. Deadline: February 15.

354.
American Legion Departments (Arizona)
State Oratorical Contest
4701 North 19th Street, Suite 200
Phoenix, AZ 85019

1 scholarship each of $800, $400, and $200 to high school students under the age of twenty. Based on a prepared oration and an extemporaneous discussion. Topic varies from year to year. Scored on presence, poise, logic, personality, knowledge of subject, originality, composition, and effectiveness. Must be Arizona residents. Contact local or state American Legion for application and details in September or October. State contests are usually held from December to March.

355.
American Legion Departments (Arkansas)
Department Adjutant
Box 3280
Little Rock, AR 72203
(501) 375-1104

4 scholarships of $500 to graduating high school seniors. Must be the children, grandchildren, or great-grandchildren of an American Legion member. Must be Arkansas residents and attend an Arkansas institution. Deadline: varies.

356.
American Legion Departments (Arkansas)
State Oratorical Contest
Department Adjutant
P.O. Box 3280
Little Rock, AR 72203
(501) 375-1104

Scholarships of $500, $250, $150, and $100. Open to all Arkansas high school students under the age of twenty. Based on a prepared oration and an extemporaneous discussion. Topic varies from year to year. Scored on presence, poise, logic, personality, knowledge of subject, originality, composition, and effectiveness. Contact local or state American Legion in September or October for application and details. State contests are usually held from December to March.

357.
American Legion Departments (California)
State Oratorical Contest
Department Adjutant
117 Veterans War Memorial Building
San Francisco, CA 94102

Scholarships of $1,200, $1,000, $800, $600, and 2 of $500 to California high school students under the age of twenty. Based on a prepared oration and an extemporaneous discussion. Topic varies from year to year. Scored on presence, poise, logic, personality, knowledge of subject, originality, composition, and effectiveness. Contact local or state American Legion in September or October for application and details. State contests are usually held from December to March.

358.
American Legion Departments (Connecticut)
Second District War Orphan Education Fund
c/o Department of Connecticut, The American Legion
P.O. Box 208
Rocky Hill, CT 06067

Provides financial assistance to a high school senior who is the child of a deceased veteran. Must be a Connecticut resident.

359.
American Legion Departments (District of
   Columbia)
State Oratorical Contest
Department Adjutant
3408 Wisconsin Avenue, N.W., Suite 212
Washington, DC 20016
(202) 362-9151

Savings bonds of varying amounts are awarded to the top four winners of the State Oratorical Contest: $200–first place; $100–second place; $75–third place; and $50–fourth place. Open to all District of Columbia high school students under the age of twenty. Based on a prepared oration and an extemporaneous discussion. Topic varies from year to year. Scored on presence, poise, logic, personality, knowledge of subject, originality, composition, and effectiveness. Contact local or state American Legion in September or October for application and details. State contests are usually held from December to March.

360.
American Legion Departments (Florida)
Oratorical Contest
Department Headquarters
P.O. Box 547936
Orlando, FL 32854-7936
(407) 295-2631
fllegion@orl.mindspring.com

Awards of $2,000 for first place, $1,800 for second place, $1,600 for third place, $1,400 for fourth place, $1,200 for fifth place, and $1,000 for sixth place to top winners in an oratorical competition open to all Florida high school students under the age of twenty. Based on a prepared oration and on an extemporaneous discussion. Topic varies from year to year. Scored on presence, poise, logic, personality, knowledge of subject, originality, composition, and effectiveness. Must be residents of Florida. Contact local or state American Legion for application and details. Deadline: October 1.

361.
American Legion Departments (Hawaii)
State Oratorical Contest
Department Headquarters
612 McCully Street
Honolulu, HI 96826
(808) 946-6383

Awards of $300 first place, $200 second place, $100 third place, and $50 fourth place to top winners of the State Oratorical Contest. Open to all Hawaii high school students under the age of twenty. Based on a prepared oration and an extemporaneous discussion. Topic varies from year to year. Scored on presence, poise, logic, personality, knowledge of subject, originality, composition, and effectiveness. Contact local or state American Legion in September or October for application and details. State contests are usually held from December to March.

362.
American Legion Departments (Idaho)
Department Headquarters
901 Warren
Boise, ID 83706
(208) 342-7061

6 scholarships of varying amounts to children or grandchildren of Idaho Legion or Auxiliary members with at least two consecutive years of membership. Applicants must be Idaho residents and attending or planning to attend an Idaho college or university.

363.
American Legion Departments (Illinois)
The American Legion, Department of Illinois
P.O. Box 2910
Bloomington, IL 61702

As many as 20 scholarships of up to $1,000 to sons and daughters of members of Illinois Legion posts. Based on academic achievement and financial need. Deadline: March 15.

364.
American Legion Departments (Illinois)
The American Legion, Department of Illinois
P.O. Box 2910
Bloomington, IL 61702
(208) 342-7066

1 scholarship of $1,000 and 4 scholarships of $200 awarded to Senior Boy Scouts or Explorers who are Illinois residents and high school seniors. Based on a 500-word essay on Americanism and Boy Scout programs.

365.
American Legion Departments (Illinois)
Americanism Essay Contest
P.O. Box 1426
Bloomington, IL 61702

Awards of $50 and $75 to students in grades 8 to 12 who are attending accredited high schools in Illinois. Must write

a 500-word essay on selected topic. Must be Illinois residents. Deadline: mid-February.

366.
American Legion Departments (Illinois)
State Oratorical Contest
The American Legion, Department of Illinois
P.O. Box 2910
Bloomington, IL 61702
(208) 342-7066

The following awards are given to entrants in State Oratorical Contest: $1,600–first place; $1,300–second place; $1,200–third place; $1,000–fourth place; $1,000–fifth place. 5 awards of $100 to second-place division winners; third–$75; fourth–$50. Open to all Illinois high school students under the age of twenty. Based on a prepared oration and an extemporaneous discussion. Topic varies from year to year. Scored on presence, poise, logic, personality, knowledge of subject, originality, composition, and effectiveness. Contact local or state American Legion in September or October for application and details. State contests are usually held from December to March.

367.
American Legion Departments (Indiana)
Americanism and Government Test
Department Adjutant, Department Headquarters
777 North Meridian Street
Indianapolis, IN 46204
(317) 630-1263

6 awards of $500 are given to one boy and one girl each in grades 10, 11, and 12 who are the first-place winners with the highest score. Must be Indiana residents. Deadline: varies.

368.
American Legion Departments (Indiana)
McHale Memorial Scholarships
Department Adjutant, Department Headquarters
777 North Meridian Street
Indianapolis, IN 46204
(317) 630-1263

3 scholarships of varying amounts to high school juniors selected Hoosier Boy's Staters. Must be Indiana residents. Deadline: varies.

369.
American Legion Departments (Indiana)
State Oratorical Contest
Department Adjutant, Department Headquarters
777 North Meridian Street
Indianapolis, IN 46204
(317) 630-1263

Awards to top winners in The State Oratorical Contest are: $1,000–first place; $400–second place, third place, and fourth place. Open to all Indiana high school students under the age of twenty. Based on a prepared oration and an extemporaneous discussion. Topic varies from year to year. Scored on presence, poise, logic, personality, knowledge of subject, originality, composition, and effectiveness. Contact local or state American Legion in September or October for application and details. State contests are usually held from December to March.

370.
American Legion Departments (Iowa)
Boy Scout of the Year Award
Department Headquarters
729 Lyon Street
Des Moines, IA 50309
(515) 282-5068

1 scholarship each of $2,000, $600, and $400 to a Boy Scout. Based on outstanding services to his church, school, and community. Recipient must be an Eagle Scout and an Iowa resident. Deadline: February 1.

371.
American Legion Departments (Iowa)
"Outstanding Citizen of Boys State" Scholarship
Department Headquarters
729 Lyon Street
Des Moines, IA 50309
(515) 282-5068

1 scholarship of $2,500 to a male student who has attended Boys State and will be attending a college or university in Iowa. Must be a high school senior and Iowa resident. Deadline: varies.

372.
American Legion Departments (Iowa)
"Outstanding Senior Baseball Player"
 Scholarship
Department Headquarters
729 Lyon Street
Des Moines, IA 50309
(515) 282-5068

1 scholarship of $1,000 to a participant in the Iowa American Legion Senior Baseball Tournament. Based on outstanding sportsmanship, team play, and athletic ability. Must be an Iowa resident.

373.
American Legion Departments (Iowa)
State Oratorical Contest
Department Headquarters
729 Lyon Street
Des Moines, IA 50309
(515) 282-5068

The following awards are given to the top winners of the State Oratorical Contest: $2,000–first place; $600–second place; and $400–third place. Open to all Iowa high school students under the age of twenty. Based on a prepared oration and an extemporaneous discussion. Topic varies from year to year. Scored on presence, poise, logic, personality, knowledge of subject, originality, composition, and effectiveness. Contact local or state American Legion in September or October for application and details. State contests are usually held from December to March.

374.
American Legion Departments (Kansas)
Albert M. Lappin Scholarship
1314 S.W. Topeka Boulevard
Topeka, KS 66612-1886
(913) 232-9315

1 scholarship of $1,000 to a graduating high school senior, undergraduate freshman, or sophomore. Must be a child of a Legion or Auxiliary member. Must be a Kansas resident and use award at an approved Kansas college, university, or trade school. Deadline: February 15.

375.
American Legion Departments (Kansas)
Dr. Click Cowger Scholarship
1314 S.W. Topeka Boulevard
Topeka, KS 66612-1886
(913) 232-9315

1 scholarship of $500 to a student who now plays or has played American Legion Baseball in Kansas. Must be a high school senior and Kansas resident and attend an approved Kansas institute. Deadline: July 15.

376.
American Legion Departments (Kansas)
Hugh A. Smith Scholarship
1314 S.W. Topeka Boulevard
Topeka, KS 66612-1886
(913) 232-9315

1 scholarship of $500 to sons and daughters of Legion or Auxiliary members. High school seniors and college freshmen and sophomores are eligible. Must be used at a Kansas college, university, or trade school. Deadline: February 15.

377.
American Legion Departments (Kansas)
John and Geraldine Hobble Licensed Practical
 Nurse Scholarship
1314 S.W. Topeka Boulevard
Topeka, KS 66612-1886
(913) 232-9315

1 scholarship of $250 to a dependent of a veteran. Must be a Kansas resident who is eighteen prior to taking Kansas State Board Examination. Must attend an accredited Kansas institution that awards diplomas for Licensed Practical Nurse (LPN). Deadline: February 15.

378.
American Legion Departments (Kansas)
Paul E. Flaherty Athletic Scholarship
1314 S.W. Topeka Boulevard
Topeka, KS 66612-1886
(913) 232-9315

1 scholarship of $250 to any boy or girl who has participated in any form of high school athletics at a Kansas high school. Must be a Kansas resident and attend an approved Kansas college, university, or trade school. Deadline: July 15.

379.
American Legion Departments (Kansas)
State American Legion Music Scholarship
1314 S.W. Topeka Boulevard
Topeka, KS 66612-1886
(913) 232-9315

1 scholarship of $1,000 to a high school senior in a Kansas Legion-sponsored Color Guard or Drum and Bugle Corps. Must be a Kansas resident. Deadline: February 15.

380.
American Legion Departments (Kansas)
State Oratorical Contest
1314 S.W. Topeka Boulevard
Topeka, KS 66612-1886
(913) 232-9315

Awards of $1,000, $500, $250, and $150 to high school students under age twenty. Selection based on a prepared oration and on an extemporaneous discussion. Topic varies yearly. Scored on presence, poise, logic, personality, knowledge of subject, originality, composition, and effectiveness. Must be Kansas residents. Contact local or state American Legion in September or October for application and details. State contests are usually held from December to March.

381.
American Legion Departments (Kansas)
Ted and Nora Anderson Scholarships
1314 S.W. Topeka Boulevard
Topeka, KS 66612-1886
(913) 232-9315

4 scholarships of $500 to graduating high school seniors, undergraduate freshmen, or sophomores. Must be children of Legion or Auxiliary members. Must be attending a Kansas institution and be Kansas residents. Scholarships must be used at an approved Kansas college, university, or trade school. Deadline: February 15.

382.
American Legion Departments (Maine)
Children and Youth Scholarships
Department Adjutant
American Legion State Headquarters
P.O. Box 900
Waterville, ME 04901
(207) 873-3229

7 scholarships of $300 to seniors who are in the upper 50 percent of their class. Based on character and financial need. Must be residents of Maine, children of a veteran who is a member, or a veteran with financial need. Deadline: May 1.

383.
American Legion Departments (Maine)
Daniel E. Lambert Memorial Scholarships
Department Adjutant
American Legion State Headquarters
P.O. Box 900
Waterville, ME 04901
(207) 873-3229

Varying numbers of scholarships of varying amounts to high school graduates who are children of veterans. Must be Maine residents. Renewable. Applications can be requested after September 1. Deadline: May 1.

384.
American Legion Departments (Maine)
James L. Boyle and Alexander A. LeFleur
Department Adjutant
American Legion State Headquarters
P.O. Box 900
Waterville, ME 04901
(207) 873-3229

2 scholarships of $300 to high school juniors who are attending Boys State. Recipients chosen by Boys State staff. Must be children of veterans and Maine residents. Students cannot apply for this scholarship.

385.
American Legion Departments (Maine)
James V. Day Scholarship
Department Adjutant
American Legion State Headquarters
P.O. Box 900
Waterville, ME 04901
(207) 873-3229

1 scholarship of $300 to a high school senior who is in the upper 50 percent of his or her class. Based on character and financial need. Must be residents of Maine. Deadline: May 1.

386.
American Legion Departments (Maryland)
Adler Science and Math Award
Department Adjutant
War Memorial
Baltimore, MD 21202
(301) 752-3104

1 scholarship of $500 to a student planning on a math or science major. Must be the son or daughter of veteran, a Maryland resident, and between the ages of sixteen and nineteen. Student must not have reached twentieth birthday by January 1 of school year in which he or she is applying. Deadline: March 31.

387.
American Legion Departments (Maryland)
Maryland Boys State Scholarships
Department Adjutant
War Memorial
Baltimore, MD 21202
(301) 752-3104

5 scholarships of $500 are awarded to students who are graduates of Maryland Boys State and are between the ages of sixteen and nineteen. Must be children of veterans and residents of Maryland. Deadline: May 1.

388.
American Legion Departments (Maryland) Scholarships
Department Adjutant
War Memorial
Baltimore, MD 21202
(301) 752-3104

11 scholarships of $500 are awarded, without restrictions on majors. Must be son or daughter of veteran, Maryland resident, and between the ages of sixteen and nineteen. Students must not have reached twentieth birthday by January 1 of school year in which they are applying. Deadline: March 31.

389.
American Legion Departments (Maryland) State Oratorical Contest
Department Adjutant
War Memorial
Baltimore, MD 21202
(301) 752-3104

The following awards are given to the top winners of the State Oratorical Contest: $2,500–first place; $1,000–second place; $500–third place through seventh place. Open to all Maryland high school students under the age of twenty. Based on a prepared oration and an extemporaneous discussion. Topic varies from year to year. Scored on presence, poise, logic, personality, knowledge of subject, originality, composition, and effectiveness. Contact local or state American Legion for application and details. Deadline: October 1.

390.
American Legion Departments (Massachusetts) Nursing Scholarships
Department Adjutant
State House, Room 546-2
Boston, MA 02133

6 scholarships of $1,000 and 10 scholarships of $500 to graduating high school seniors who will be pursuing a nursing career. Must be the children or grandchildren of a member in good standing of the Department of Massachusetts Legion. Must be Massachusetts residents. Deadline: April 1.

391.
American Legion Departments (Massachusetts) Past County Commander's Scholarships
Department Adjutant
State House, Room 546-2
Boston, MA 02133

1 scholarship of $500 and possibly additional scholarships of $250 (if funds allow), to graduating high school seniors. Must be children or grandchildren (including adopted children or others under legal guardianship) of current members of American Legion Post in Hampden County or of deceased member who was a current member at time of death. Must be Massachusetts residents. Contact: any American Legion Post in Hampden County or Chairperson, W.J. Craven, 46 Brickett Street, Springfield, MA 01119. Deadline: April 15.

392.
American Legion Departments (Massachusetts) State Oratorical Contest
Department Adjutant
State House, Room 546-2
Boston, MA 02133

The following awards are given to the top winners of the State Oratorical Contest: $1,000–first place; $600–second place; $500–third place; and $400–fourth place. Open to all Massachusetts high school students under the age of twenty. Based on a prepared oration and an extemporaneous discussion. Topic varies from year to year. Scored on presence, poise, logic, personality, knowledge of subject, originality, composition, and effectiveness. Contact local or state American Legion for application and details. Contact in September or October. Deadline: December 15.

393.
American Legion Departments (Michigan) Guy M. Wilson Scholarships
The American Legion
212 North Verlinden Street
Lansing, MI 48915
(517) 371-4720

20 scholarships of $500 to high school seniors or graduates (who haven't attended college) who are children of living or deceased veterans. Must be Michigan residents. Scholarship must be used at a Michigan college or junior college. Deadline: February 1.

394.
American Legion Departments (Michigan) State Oratorical Contest
The American Legion
212 North Verlinden Street
Lansing, MI 48915
(517) 371-4720

The following awards are given to the top winners of the State Oratorical Contest: $1,000–first place; $800–second place; and $600–third place. Open to all Michigan high school students under the age of twenty. Based on a prepared oration and an extemporaneous discussion. Topic varies from year to year. Scored on presence, poise, logic, personality, knowledge of subject, originality, composition, and effectiveness. Contact local or state American Legion in September or October for application and details. Deadline: February 1.

395.
American Legion Departments (Michigan) William D. Brewer, Jewell W. Brewer Scholarship Trust
The American Legion
212 North Verlinden Street
Lansing, MI 48915
(517) 371-4720

1 scholarship of $500 to a high school senior or graduate (who hasn't attended college) who is the child of living or deceased veteran. Must be a Michigan resident. Deadline: February 1.

396.
American Legion Departments (Minnesota)
Department Oratorical Competition
Education and Scholarship Committee
State Veterans Service Building
St. Paul, MN 55155
(612) 291-1800

Scholarships of $1,200, $900, $700, and $500 to high school students under age twenty. Selection based on a prepared oration and an extemporaneous discussion. Topic varies yearly. Scored on presence, poise, logic, personality, knowledge of subject, originality, composition, and effectiveness. Must be Minnesota residents. Contact local or state American Legion in September for application and details. Deadline: mid-December.

397.
American Legion Departments (Minnesota)
Legionnaire Insurance Trust Scholarships
Education and Scholarship Committee
State Veterans Service Building
St. Paul, MN 55155
(612) 291-1800

3 scholarships of $500 to high school seniors or graduates (who haven't attended college) who are veterans or children of living or deceased veterans. Must be Minnesota residents. Based on academic achievement. Deadline: April 1.

398.
American Legion Departments (Minnesota)
Memorial Scholarships
Education and Scholarship Committee
State Veterans Service Building
St. Paul, MN 55155
(612) 291-1800

6 scholarships of $500 to high school seniors or graduates who are children of a member or Auxiliary member. Based on financial need. Must be Minnesota resident. Deadline: April 1.

399.
American Legion Departments (Missouri)
Lillie Lois Ford Scholarships
Department Adjutant
P.O. Box 179
Jefferson City, MO 65102
(573) 893-2353
(573) 893-2980 Fax

Scholarships of $900 each to one male and one female who have attended a complete session of Missouri's Boys/Girls State or the Cadet Patrol Academy. Must be child of a Missouri veteran, not receiving any other financial assistance, and a Missouri resident.

400.
American Legion Departments (Missouri)
M. D. "Jack" Murphy Scholarship
Department Adjutant
P.O. Box 179
Jefferson City, MO 65102
(573) 893-2353
(573) 893-2980 Fax

1 scholarship of $600 to a high school senior or graduate (who hasn't attended college) who is a child or grandchild of a living or deceased Missouri veteran. Must use the award to finance a nursing degree. Must be eighteen years of age and a Missouri resident.

401.
American Legion Departments (Missouri)
State Oratorical Contest
Department Adjutant
P.O. Box 179
Jefferson City, MO 65102
(573) 893-2353
(573) 893-2980 Fax

The following awards are given to the top winners of the State Oratorical Contest: $2,000–first place; $1,800–second place; $1,600–third place; and $1,400–fourth place. Must be used for educational expenses. Open to all Missouri high school students under the age of twenty. Based on a prepared oration and an extemporaneous discussion. Topic varies from year to year. Scored on presence, poise, logic, personality, knowledge of subject, originality, composition, and effectiveness. Contact local or state American Legion in September or October for application and details. State contests are usually held from December to March.

402.
American Legion Departments (Montana)
State Oratorical Contest
P.O. Box 6075
Helena, MT 59604

Scholarships of $800 and one-year fee waiver for first place, $400 and one-semester fee waiver for second place, $250 and one-half semester fee waiver for third place, and $200 and one-half semester fee waiver for fourth place. Open to all Montana high school students under the age of twenty. Based on a prepared oration and an extemporaneous discussion. Topic varies from year to year. Scored on presence, poise, logic, personality, knowledge of subject, originality, composition, and effectiveness. Contact local or state American Legion in September or October for application and details. State contests are usually held from December to March.

403.
American Legion Departments (Nebraska)
Department Oratorical Contest
Department Adjutant
P.O. Box 5205, Station C
Lincoln, NE 68505
(402) 464-6338

The following savings bonds given to top winners of the State Oratorical Contest: $1,000–first place; $600–second place; $400–third place; $200–fourth place. Also, the top district winner receives $100. Must be used for educational expenses. Open to all Nebraska high school students under the age of twenty. Based on a prepared oration and an extemporaneous discussion. Topic varies from year to year. Scored on presence, poise, logic, personality, knowledge of subject, originality, composition, and effectiveness. Contact local or state American Legion in September or October for application and details. State contests are usually held from December to March.

404.
American Legion Departments (Nebraska)
Edgar J. Borschult Memorial Scholarships
Department Adjutant
P.O. Box 5205, Station C
Lincoln, NE 68505
(402) 464-6338

4 or more scholarships of $200 to students who will attend or are attending the University of Nebraska. Based on academic achievement, high standing in ROTC, and financial need. Must be a veteran or a child of a living or deceased veteran and a Nebraska resident.

405.
American Legion Departments (Nebraska)
Maynard Jensen American Legion Memorial
  Scholarships
Department Adjutant
Box 5205, Station C
Lincoln, NE 68505
(402) 464-6338

6 or more scholarships of $500 to high school seniors, high school graduates who haven't attended college, or current undergraduates. Based on academic achievement, high standing in ROTC, and financial need. Must be children (birth, adopted, or step), grandchildren, or great-grandchildren of members of American Legion, or POW, MIA, KIA, or any deceased veteran. Must be Nebraska residents and attend a Nebraska institution. Deadline: March 1.

406.
American Legion Departments (Nevada)
State Oratorical Contest
Department Adjutant
737 Veterans Memorial Drive
Las Vegas, NV 89010

Awards of U.S. Savings Bonds of $500 for first place, $250 for second place, and $100 for third place. Open to all Nevada high school students under the age of twenty. Based on a prepared oration and an extemporaneous discussion. Topic varies from year to year. Scored on presence, poise, logic, personality, knowledge of subject, originality, composition, and effectiveness. Must be Nevada residents. Contact local or state American Legion in September or October for application and details. State contests are usually held from December to March.

407.
American Legion Departments (New Hampshire)
Albert T. Marcoux Memorial Scholarship
Department Adjutant
State House Annex
25 Capitol Street, Room 431
Concord, NH 03301-6312
(603) 271-2211

1 scholarship of $1,000 to a graduating high school senior or graduate (who hasn't attended college) who is a child of a New Hampshire American Legion or AL Auxiliary member or deceased member. Must have been a New Hampshire resident for at least three years. May be working toward any undergraduate degree. Deadline: May 1.

408.
American Legion Departments (New Hampshire)
Christa McAuliffe Memorial Scholarship
Department Adjutant
State House Annex
25 Capitol Street, Room 431
Concord, NH 03301-6312
(603) 271-2211

1 scholarship of $1,000 to a graduating high school senior or graduate (who hasn't attended college) who is a child of a living or deceased veteran. Must have been a New Hampshire resident for at least three years and be majoring in education. Deadline: May 1.

409.
American Legion Departments (New Hampshire)
Department of New Hampshire Scholarships
Department Adjutant
State House Annex
25 Capitol Street, Room 431
Concord, NH 03301-6312
(603) 271-2211

2 scholarships of $1,000 to graduating high school seniors. Must have been New Hampshire residents for at least three years and be graduating from a New Hampshire high school. Deadline: May 1.

410.
American Legion Departments (New Hampshire)
John A. High Child Welfare Scholarship
  Endowment Fund
Department Adjutant
State House Annex
25 Capitol Street, Room 431
Concord, NH 03301-6312
(603) 271-2211

1 scholarship of $200 to a high school senior who is the son of a veteran. Parent must have been a continuous New Hampshire American Legion member for three years. Must be a New Hampshire resident. Deadline: April 15.

411.
American Legion Departments (New Hampshire)
New Hampshire Boys State Scholarship
   Subscription
Department Adjutant
State House Annex
25 Capitol Street, Room 431
Concord, NH 03301-6312
(603) 271-2211

1 scholarship of varying amount to a male student who has attended Boys State. The award is matched by the department to the nearest $100. Must be a New Hampshire resident and the child of a veteran. Deadline: April 15.

412.
American Legion Departments (New Hampshire)
State Oratorical Contest
Department Adjutant
State House Annex
25 Capitol Street, Room 431
Concord, NH 03301-6312
(603) 271-2211

The following awards are given to the top winners of the State Oratorical Contest: $500–first place; $250–second place; $150–third place; and $100–fourth place. Open to all New Hampshire high school students under the age of twenty. Based on a prepared oration and an extemporaneous discussion. Topic varies from year to year. Scored on presence, poise, logic, personality, knowledge of subject, originality, composition, and effectiveness. Contact local or state American Legion in September or October for application and details. State contests are usually held from December to March.

413.
American Legion Departments (New Hampshire)
Vocational Scholarship
Department Adjutant
State House Annex
25 Capitol Street, Room 431
Concord, NH 03301-6312
(603) 271-2211

1 scholarship of $1,000 to a graduating high school senior or graduate (who hasn't attended college) who is a child of a living or deceased veteran. Must have been a New Hampshire resident for at least three years. Scholarship must be used to finance a vocational degree. Deadline: May 1.

414.
American Legion Departments (New Jersey)
American Legion Press Club of New Jersey
   Scholarships
Department Adjutant
135 West Hanover Street
Trenton, NJ 08618
(609) 695-5418

2 scholarships of $4,000 ($1,000 per year for four years) and 2 scholarships of $2,000 ($500 per year for four years) to graduating high school seniors. Must be children of a veteran who is a member of the New Jersey American

Legion. Must be New Jersey residents. Deadline: February 15 (postmark).

415.
American Legion Departments (New Jersey)
David C. Goodwin Memorial Scholarship
Department Adjutant
135 West Hanover Street
Trenton, NJ 08618
(609) 695-5418

1 scholarship of $4,000 ($1,000 per year for four years) and $2,000 ($500 per year for four years) to a high school junior taking part in the New Jersey American Legion Baseball Program. Applications mailed to players. Deadline: varies.

416.
American Legion Departments (New Jersey)
Lawrence Luterman Memorial Scholarships
Department Adjutant
135 West Hanover Street
Trenton, NJ 08618
(609) 695-5418

2 scholarships of $4,000 ($1,000 per year for four years), 2 scholarships of $2,000, and 2 scholarships of $1,000 to a graduating high school senior. Must be the natural or adopted dependent of a member of the American Legion, Department of New Jersey. Must be a New Jersey resident. Deadline: February 15.

417.
American Legion Departments (New Jersey)
State Oratorical Contest
Department Adjutant
135 West Hanover Street
Trenton, NJ 08618
(609) 695-5418

The following awards are given to the top winners of the State Oratorical Contest: $4,000–first place; $2,000–second place; $1,000–third place; $750–fourth place and fifth place. Open to all New Jersey high school students under the age of twenty. Based on a prepared oration and an extemporaneous discussion. Topic varies from year to year. Scored on presence, poise, logic, personality, knowledge of subject, originality, composition, and effectiveness. Contact local or state American Legion in September or October for application and details. State contests are usually held from December to March.

418.
American Legion Departments (New Jersey)
Stutz Memorial Scholarship
Department Adjutant
135 West Hanover Street
Trenton, NJ 08618
(609) 695-5418

1 scholarship of $4,000 ($1,000 per year for four years) to a graduating high school senior who is the child of a veteran who is a New Jersey American Legion member. Must be a New Jersey resident. Deadline: February 15.

419.
American Legion Departments (New York)
Dr. Hannah K. Vuolo Memorial Scholarship
Department Adjutant
112 State Street, Suite 400
Albany, NY 12207
(518) 463-2215

1 scholarship of $250 to a graduating high school senior
who is a child of a living or deceased member of New
York American Legion. Must be under the age of twenty-
one, an entering freshman at an accredited institution, and
an education major. Preference to New York State resident.
Based on academic achievement and financial need.
Deadline: May 1.

420.
American Legion Departments (New York)
James F. Mulholland Scholarships
Department Adjutant
112 State Street, Suite 400
Albany, NY 12207
(518) 463-2215

2 scholarships of $500 to graduating high school seniors
who are children of New York American Legion members.
Applicants must be residents of New York. Based on
academic achievement and financial need. Deadline: May 1.

421.
American Legion Departments (New York)
New York State Legion Press Association Award
Department Adjutant
112 State Street, Suite 400
Albany, NY 12207
(518) 463-2215

1 scholarship of $1,000 to a graduating high school senior
or undergraduate. Must be a child of a veteran who is an
American Legion or American Legion Auxiliary member, or
student who is a member of American Legion Auxiliary
Juniors, or Boys or Girls State. Must be entering or
attending a four-year institution and a communications
major. Must be a New York resident. Contact: Scholarship
Chairperson, P.O. Box 1239, Syracuse, NY 13201-1239.

422.
American Legion Departments (New York)
State Oratorical Contest
Department Adjutant
112 State Street, Suite 400
Albany, NY 12207
(518) 463-2215

The following awards to the top winners of the State
Oratorical Contest: $6,000–first place; $4,000–second place;
$2,500–third place; $2,000–fourth place and fifth place. Open
to all New York high school students under the age of
twenty. Based on a prepared oration and an extemporaneous discussion. Topic varies from year to year.
Scored on presence, poise, logic, personality, knowledge of
subject, originality, composition, and effectiveness. Contact
local or state American Legion in September or October for
application and details. State contests are usually held from
December to March.

423.
American Legion Departments (North Carolina)
Oratorical Contest
P.O. Box 26657
Raleigh, NC 27611-6657

Scholarships of $1,500 for first place, $500 for second place,
and $250 for third, fourth, and fifth places. Open to high
school students under the age of twenty. Based on a
prepared oration and an extemporaneous discussion. Topic
varies from year to year. Scored on presence, poise, logic,
personality, knowledge of subject, originality, composition,
and effectiveness. Must be North Carolina residents, U.S.
citizens, or legal permanent residents. Contact local or state
American Legion in September or October for application
and details. State contests are usually held from December
to March.

424.
American Legion Departments (North Dakota)
John K. Kennelly Memorial Scholarship
Box 2666
Fargo, ND 58108-2666
(701) 293-3120

1 award of a $100 Savings Bond to a graduating high
school senior who was an enthusiastic participant of North
Dakota Boys State. Based on leadership, cooperation, and
conduct. Must be the child of a veteran and a North
Dakota resident. No application; selection made during
Boys State. Deadline: none specified.

425.
American Legion Departments (North Dakota)
State Oratorical Contest
P.O. Box 2666
Fargo, ND 58108
(701) 293-3120

Awards of $400 for first place, $300 for second place, $200
for third place, and $100 for fourth place; the East and
West Divisional Contest provides $300 for first place and
$200 for second place. Open to all North Dakota high
school students under the age of twenty. Based on a
prepared oration and an extemporaneous discussion. Topic
varies from year to year. Scored on presence, poise, logic,
personality, knowledge of subject, originality, composition,
and effectiveness. Contact local or state American Legion in
September or October for application and details. State
contests are usually held from December to March.

426.
American Legion Departments (Ohio)
Department Scholarship Committee
4060 Indianola Avenue
Columbus, OH 43214
(614) 268-7072
(614) 268-3048 Fax

16 scholarships of $1,500 and 1 scholarship of $2,000 to
graduating high school seniors or high school graduates
who haven't entered college. Must be children or direct

descendants of members in good standing, deceased Legionnaires, or spouse or children of deceased U.S. military personnel who died on active duty or of injuries received on active duty. Students must be entering college freshmen. Applicants must be Ohio residents. Deadline: April 15.

427.
American Legion Departments (Oregon) Department Oratorical Awards
P.O. Box 1730
Wilsonville, OR 97070-1730
(503) 685-5006

Scholarships of $500, $400, $300, and $200 to high school students under age twenty. Based on a prepared oration and an extemporaneous discussion. Topics vary from year to year. Scored on presence, poise, logic, personality, knowledge of subject, originality, composition, and effectiveness. Must be Oregon residents and U.S. citizens. Contact local or state American Legion in September or October for application and details. State contests are usually held from December to March.

428.
American Legion Departments (Pennsylvania) Robert W. Valimont Endowment Fund Scholarship
Department Adjutant
Attn: Scholarship Secretary
P.O. Box 2324
Harrisburg, PA 17105-2324
(717) 730-9100
http://www.pa-legion.com
palegion@redrose.net

1 scholarship of $300 to a student attending a vocational school or institution. Must be a Pennsylvania resident and child of a veteran. Renewable. Deadline: June 1.

429.
American Legion Departments (Pennsylvania) Joseph P. Gavenonis Scholarships
Department Adjutant
Attn: Scholarship Secretary
P.O. Box 2324
Harrisburg, PA 17105-2324
(717) 730-9100
http://www.pa-legion.com
palegion@redrose.net

Scholarships of $1,000 to graduating high school seniors. Must be children of a living member in good standing at a Pennsylvania American Legion Post or children of Pennsylvania American Legion members who are deceased, KIA, or MIA. Must be Pennsylvania residents and attend a Pennsylvania college or university. Preference is given to children of members with the greatest continuous number of years of membership. Renewable up to four years, with continued academic progress at the end of each semester. Deadline: June 1.

430.
American Legion Departments (Pennsylvania) Scholarship Fund
Department Adjutant
Attn: Scholarship Secretary
P.O. Box 2324
Harrisburg, PA 17105-2324
(717) 730-9100
http://www.pa-legion.com
palegion@redrose.net

Numerous scholarships of $800 to children of veterans to attend the Scotland School for Veterans' Children in Scotland, Pennsylvania. Applicant must be Pennsylvania resident. Deadline: June 1.

431.
American Legion Departments (Rhode Island) State Oratorical Contest
83 Park Street, Room 403
Providence, RI 02903-1079
(401) 421-7390

Awards of U.S. Savings Bonds of $500, $250, $100, and $50 to winners at the State Level of the Oratorical Contest. Open to all Rhode Island high school students under the age of twenty. Based on a prepared oration and an extemporaneous discussion. Topics vary from year to year. Scored on presence, poise, logic, personality, knowledge of subject, originality, composition, and effectiveness. Contact local or state American Legion in September or October for application and details. State contests are usually held from December to March.

432.
American Legion Departments (South Carolina) Robert E. David Children's Scholarship
Department Adjutant
P.O. Box 11355
132 Pickens Street
Columbia, SC 29211
(803) 799-1992

1 scholarship of varying amount to a graduating high school senior or high school graduate who hasn't attended college. Must be the child of a War Era veteran and a relative of a South Carolina Legionnaire. Must be a South Carolina resident. Selection based on academic achievement and financial need. Deadline: May 1.

433.
American Legion Departments (South Carolina) State Oratorical Contest
Department Adjutant
P.O. Box 11355
132 Pickens Street
Columbia, SC 29211
(803) 799-1992

The following awards are given to the top winners of the State Oratorical Contest: $400 per year for four years–first place; $250 per year for four years–second place; and $125 per year for four years–third place. Open to all South Carolina high school students under the age of twenty. Based on a prepared oration and an extemporaneous discussion. Topic varies from year to year. Scored on presence, poise, logic, personality, knowledge of subject, originality, composition, and effectiveness. Contact local or state American Legion in September or October for application and details. State contests are usually held from December to March.

434.
American Legion Departments (South Dakota)
Department Adjutant
P.O. Box 67
Watertown, SD 57201

Educational loans of up to $1,000 per year, with a $2,000 maximum to children of living or deceased veterans. Must be a South Dakota resident and attend a South Dakota college or vocational school. Deadline: none.

435.
American Legion Departments (South Dakota)
State Oratorical Contest
Department Adjutant
P.O. Box 67
Watertown, SD 57201-0067
(605) 886-3604

The following awards are given to the top winners of the State Oratorical Contest: $600–first place; $400–second place; $300–third place; and $100–fourth and fifth places. Open to all South Dakota high school students under the age of twenty. Based on a prepared oration and an extemporaneous discussion. Topic varies from year to year. Scored on presence, poise, logic, personality, knowledge of subject, originality, composition, and effectiveness. Must attend a South Dakota institution. Contact local or state American Legion in September or October for application and details. State contests are usually held from December to March.

436.
American Legion Departments (Tennessee)
Eagle Scout of the Year Scholarship
State Headquarters
215 Eighth Avenue
North Nashville, TN 37203
(615) 254-0568

1 scholarship of $1,500 to the Tennessee Eagle Scout of the Year who is submitted to the National Organization. Award may be used at any accredited U.S. postsecondary institution. Must be a Tennessee resident. Deadline: early January.

437.
American Legion Departments (Tennessee)
State Oratorical Contest
State Headquarters
215 Eighth Avenue
North Nashville, TN 37203
(615) 254-0568

Scholarships of varying amounts to be used to cover costs at a college, university, or vocational/technical school. Open to all Tennessee high school students under the age of twenty. Based on a prepared oration and an extemporaneous discussion. Scored on presence, poise, logic, personality, knowledge of subject, originality,

composition, and effectiveness. Contact local or state American Legion in September or October for application and details. Deadline: early January.

438.
American Legion Departments (Texas)
State Oratorical Contest
P.O. Box 789
Austin, TX 78767
(512) 472-4183

Awards: $1,000–first place; $750–second place; $500–third place; and $250–fourth place to winners at the State Level of the Oratorical Contest. Open to all Texas high school students under the age of eighteen. Based on a prepared oration and an extemporaneous discussion. Topics vary from year to year. Scored on presence, poise, logic, personality, knowledge of subject, originality, composition, and effectiveness. Contact local or state American Legion in September or October for application and details. State contests are usually held from December to March.

439.
American Legion Departments (Vermont)
Education and Scholarship Committee
P.O. Box 396
Montpelier, VT 05602-0396
(802) 223-7131

1 scholarship of $250 per year for four years and 4 scholarships providing $250 per year for two years to graduating Vermont high school seniors who are in the upper third of their class. Applicants' parents must be Vermont legal residents. Deadline: varies.

440.
American Legion Departments (Virginia)
State Oratorical Contest
Department Adjutant
1805 Chantilly Street
Richmond, VA 23230
(804) 353-6606

The following awards are given to the top winners of the State Oratorical Contest: $1,100–first place; $600–second place; and $600–third place. Open to all Virginia high school students under the age of twenty. Based on prepared orations and an extemporaneous discussion. Topic varies from year to year. Based on presence, poise, personality, logic, knowledge of subject, originality, content, and effectiveness. Contact local or state American Legion in September or October for application and details. Deadline: December 1.

441.
American Legion Departments (Washington)
P.O. Box 3917
Lacey, WA 98503-3917
(360) 491-4373

1 scholarship of $1,000 and 1 scholarship of $1,500 to high school seniors or graduates (who haven't attended college) who are children of living or deceased American Legion members or American Legion Auxiliary members. Must be Washington residents. Based on financial need. Must be

used at a college, university, or vocational/technical school in Washington. Deadline: April 1.

442.
American Legion Departments (West Virginia)
State Oratorical Contest
Department Adjutant
2016 Kanawha Boulevard East
Charleston, WV 25332
(304) 343-7591

Each of the nine district winners of the Oratorical Contest wins $200, with the state winner being awarded an additional $500, plus a four-year scholarship to any state college under the control of the Board of Regents or West Virginia University (worth about $1,600). Open to all high school students under the age of twenty. Based on prepared orations and an extemporaneous discussion. Topic varies from year to year. Based on presence, poise, personality, logic, knowledge of subject, originality, content, and effectiveness. Contact local or state American Legion in September or October for application and details. State contests are usually held from December to March.

443.
American Legion Departments (Wisconsin)
Americanism & Government Test Program:
    Sixteen Scholarships
Department Headquarters
812 East State Street
Milwaukee, WI 53202
(414) 271-1940

6 scholarships of $500 to high school seniors, 5 scholarships each of $250 to high school juniors and sophomores in this competition. Sponsored by American Legion Department of Wisconsin and local Legion Post. Must be Wisconsin residents. Obtain information from high school principal, teachers, or counselor.

444.
American Legion Departments (Wisconsin)
Baseball Player of the Year Scholarship
Department Headquarters
812 East State Street
Milwaukee, WI 53202
(414) 271-1940

1 scholarship of $500 to the student selected by the Board of Directors for the Baseball Program. Must be a Wisconsin resident.

445.
American Legion Departments (Wisconsin)
Eagle Scout of the Year Scholarship
Department Headquarters
812 East State Street
Milwaukee, WI 53202
(414) 271-1940

1 scholarship of $250 to the student selected the Wisconsin American Legion Eagle Scout of the Year. Student goes on to participate in the National American Legion Eagle Scout of the Year with 1 scholarship of $8,000 ($2,000 per year for four years) and 2 scholarships of $2,000 ($500 per year for four years). Must be a Wisconsin resident.

446.
American Legion Departments (Wisconsin)
Schneider–Emanuel AL Scholarships
Department Headquarters
812 East State Street
Milwaukee, WI 53202
(414) 271-1940

3 scholarships of $500 to sons of Wisconsin members. Applicants must have participated in the State Youth Programs. Must be Wisconsin residents.

447.
American Legion Departments (Wisconsin)
State Oratorical Contest
Department Headquarters
812 East State Street
Milwaukee, WI 53202
(414) 271-1940

The following awards are given to the top winners of the State Oratorical Contest: $1,000–first place; $750–second place; $500–third and fourth places; and $300 to Regional Runner-up. These awards must be used toward tuition at the school of winners' choice. Open to all high school students under the age of twenty. Based on prepared orations and an extemporaneous discussion. Topic varies from year to year. Based on presence, poise, personality, logic, knowledge of subject, originality, content, and effectiveness. Contact local or state American Legion in September or October for application and details. State contests are usually held from December to March.

448.
American Legion Departments (Wyoming)
E. B. Blackmore Memorial Scholarship
Department Adjutant
P.O. Box 545
Cheyenne, WY 82003
(307) 634-3035

1 scholarship of $700 to a Legionnaire member who is a veteran or to the child of a Legionnaire member. Must be Wyoming resident.

449.
American Legion Departments (Wyoming)
State Oratorical Contest
Department Adjutant
P.O. Box 545
Cheyenne, WY 82003
(307) 634-3035

1 award of $500 to the top winner of the State Oratorical Contest. Open to all Wyoming high school students under the age of twenty. Based on prepared orations and an extemporaneous discussion. Topic varies from year to year. Based on presence, poise, personality, logic, knowledge of subject, originality, content, and effectiveness. Contact local or state American Legion in September or October for application and details. State contests are usually held from December to March.

450.

American Legion National 20 & 4
Memorial Scholarships of the Twenty and Four
6000 Lucern Court, #2
Mequo, WI 53092

Numerous $500 scholarships to children, grandchildren, or great-grandchildren of members in good standing of the Twenty and Four or of deceased members who were in good standing at the time of death. Must be between the ages of sixteen and twenty-five. Members may also apply. Based on financial need, academic achievement, and extracurricular activities. Deadline: none.

451.

American Legion Oratorical Contest
Attn: Oratorical Contest Chairman
American Legion Department Adjutant
(in your state)

Open to all high school students under the age of twenty. Annual scholarships ranging from $1,000 to $18,000 awarded at the national competition, based on a prepared oration and an extemporaneous discussion. Topic varies from year to year. Scored on presence, poise, logic, personality, knowledge of subject, originality, composition, and effectiveness. Contact local or state American Legion in September or October for application and details. State contests are usually held from December to March. National contests are held in mid-April.

452.

American Logistics Association
CDR. William S. Stuhr Scholarship Fund—Air
** Force**
Commanding Officer
438 Combat Support Group
McGuire AFB, NJ 08641
Attn: Mr. Robert Bursley, 438 MSSQ/MSE, Education Office

1 scholarship of $500 per semester for eight semesters ($4,000 total) to a student who is a dependent of an active or retired member of the U.S. Air Force. Must live within a 100-mile radius of New York City. This requirement may be waived if the student has moved due to parent being relocated by the service. Must have been in the upper 10 percent of class during junior and senior years and have financial need. Recipient may attend the institution of his or her choice. Request applications up to February 1. Deadline: early April; may vary.

453.

American Logistics Association—New York
** Chapter**
CDR. William S. Stuhr Scholarship Fund–Army
Commanding Officer
U.S. Army
Fort Hamilton, NY 11252
Attn: Howell Hurst, DPCA

1 scholarship of $500 per semester for eight semesters ($4,000 total) to a student who is a dependent of an active or retired member of the U.S. Army. Must live within a 100-mile radius of New York City. This requirement may be waived if the student has moved due to parent being relocated by the service. Must have been in the upper 10

percent of class during junior and senior years and have financial need. Recipient may attend the institution of his or her choice. Request applications up to February 1. Deadline: early April; may vary.

454.

American Logistics Association—New York
** Chapter**
CDR. William S. Stuhr Scholarship Fund—Coast
** Guard**
Commanding Officer
U.S. Coast Guard
Governors Island, NY 10004
Attn: Lt. Edward Equia

1 scholarship of $500 per semester for eight semesters ($4,000 total) to a student who is a dependent of an active or retired member of the U.S. Coast Guard. Must live within a 100-mile radius of New York City. This requirement may be waived if the student has moved due to parent being relocated by the service. Must have been in the upper 10 percent of class during junior and senior years and have financial need. Recipient may attend the institution of his or her choice. Request applications up to February 1. Deadline: early April; may vary.

455.

American Logistics Association—New York
** Chapter**
CDR. William S. Stuhr Scholarship Fund—Marine
** Corps**
Commanding Officer
1st Marine Corps District
605 Steward Avenue
Garden City, NY 11530
Attn: Lt. T. Lyman, PAB

1 scholarship of $500 per semester for eight semesters ($4,000 total) to a student who is a dependent of an active or retired member of the U.S. Marine Corps. Must live within a 100-mile radius of New York City. This requirement may be waived if the student has moved due to parent being relocated by the service. Must have been in the upper 10 percent of class during junior and senior years and have financial need. Recipient may attend the institution of his or her choice. Request applications up to February 1. Deadline: early April; may vary.

456.

American Logistics Association—New York
** Chapter**
CDR. William S. Stuhr Scholarship Fund—Navy
Commanding Officer
Naval Station New York
Department of the Navy
355 Front Street
Staten Island, NY 10304
Attn: Chaplain B. R. Wilson

1 scholarship of $500 per semester for eight semesters ($4,000 total) to a student who is a dependent of an active or retired member of the U.S. Navy. Must live within a 100-mile radius of New York City. This requirement may be waived if the student has moved due to parent being relocated by the service. Must have been in the upper 10 percent of class during junior and senior years and have

financial need. Recipient may attend the institution of his or her choice. Request applications up to February 1. Deadline: early April; may vary.

457.
American Management Association
Internships
Attn: Coordinator
1601 Broadway
New York, NY 10019
(212) 903-8021
(212) 903-8163 Fax

60 twelve-week internships providing $170 per week to high school students, high school graduates, undergraduates, recent college graduates, and graduate students. International students may also apply. The Association provides seminars on management issues, creates videos on subjects such as negotiating skills and communications, and publishes a variety of periodicals covering management subjects. Interns work in training and development, human resources, publishing, general management, marketing, international, market research, and sales and marketing. Applicants must submit a résumé, cover letter, and recommendations (one academic and one employment). Deadline: rolling.

458.
American Management Association
Operation Enterprise—Training Seminars
P.O. Box 88
Hamilton, NY 13346
(315) 824-2000

30 to 35 openings for the eight-day program open to high school students who have finished the 11th or 12th grade. The program is held at a lakeside camp near Syracuse, NY. Students interact with visiting business leaders in round-table discussions, in small workshops, and in one-to-one conversations. Executives share their views on effective management, and teach leadership skills such as setting goals, organizing to meet goals, motivation, and human relations. Students use a business simulation to practice new skills. The program emphasizes personal growth, leadership, and career awareness in business. Program cost: $1,500. There are limited partial to full scholarships available. Acceptance is based on academic achievement, essay, and one recommendation. Deadline: April.

459.
American Medical Technologists
AMT Scholarships
710 Higgins Road
Park Ridge, IL 60068
(847) 823-5169

Numerous $250 awards to high school graduates and seniors planning to enroll in or currently enrolled in an accredited program in medical technology or medical assistant. Deadline: April 1.

460.
American Mensa Education and Research
Foundation
General Scholarships
Attn: National Scholarship Chairperson
American Mensa, Ltd
201 Main Street, Suite 1101
Fort Worth, TX 76102
(817) 332-2600

Numerous awards ranging from $200–$1,000 to high school seniors, undergraduate, graduate, or professional students. Based on a 550-word essay that describes the applicant's career, vocational, or academic goal toward which the scholarship is to provide aid. Need not be a member or qualify to be a member of Mensa to apply. Request and submit only one Mensa application. Applicant will be considered for all scholarships for which he or she qualifies. Write to Scholarship Chairperson, American Mensa, 3437 West 7th Street, Suite 264, Fort Worth, TX 76107. Include a self-addressed, stamped envelope. Request application after October 1. Deadline: varies, generally January 31.

461.
American Mensa Education and Research
Foundation
Mensa Scholar
Attn: National Scholarship Chairperson
American Mensa, Ltd.
201 Main Street, Suite 1101
Fort Worth, TX 76102
(817) 332-2600

1 additional $500 scholarship to one of the first-place regional winners. Based on an essay of 550 words or less that describes the applicant's career, vocational, or academic goal toward which the scholarship is to provide aid. Applicant need not be a member of or qualify to be a member of Mensa to apply. Request and submit only one Mensa application. Applicant will be considered for all scholarships for which he or she qualifies. Write to Scholarship Chairperson, American Mensa, 3437 West 7th Street, Suite 264, Fort Worth, TX 76107. Include a self-addressed, stamped envelope. Request application after October 1. Deadline: January 15; may vary.

462.
American Mensa Education and Research
Foundation
Regional Scholarships
Attn: National Scholarship Chairperson
American Mensa, Ltd.
201 Main Street, Suite 1101
Fort Worth, TX 76102
(817) 332-2600

The American Mensa Ltd. divides the U.S. into nine distinct regions. Each region awards the following scholarships: 1 of $200; 3 of $300; 1 of $500; and 1 of $1,000. Based on a 550-word essay that describes career, vocational, or academic goal toward which the scholarship is to provide aid. Applicant need not be a member of or qualify to be a member of Mensa to apply. Request and submit only one Mensa application. Applicant will be considered for all scholarships for which he or she qualifies. Write to: Scholarship Chairperson, American Mensa, 3437 West 7th Street, Suite 264, Fort Worth, TX 76107. Include a self-addressed, stamped envelope. Request application after October 1. Deadline: January 15; may vary.

463.
American Mensa Education and Research Foundation
Rita Levine Memorial Scholarship
Attn: National Scholarship Chairperson
American Mensa, Ltd.
201 Main Street, Suite 1101
Fort Worth, TX 76102
(817) 332-2600

1 scholarship of $600 to a woman returning to school after an absence of seven or more years. Must be enrolled (for the academic year following the award) in a degree program in an accredited U.S. college or university. Also available to women who are already in college but who had at least seven years between their last time in school and returning to college. Based on a 550-word essay that describes the applicant's career, vocational, or academic goal toward which the scholarship is to provide aid. Need not be a member or qualify to be a member of Mensa to apply. Request and submit only one Mensa application. Applicant will be considered for all scholarships for which she qualifies. Write to: Scholarship Chairperson, American Mensa, 3437 West 7th Street, Suite 264, Fort Worth, TX 76107. Include a self-addressed, stamped envelope. Request application after October 1. Deadline: January 15; may vary.

464.
American Meteorological Society Awards
Father James B. Macelwane Annual Awards
45 Beacon Street
Boston, MA 02108
(617) 227-2425

Awards of $300, $200, and $100 are provided by the Weather Corp. of America to honor the world-renowned geophysicist Father James Macelwane. This is a competition designed to stimulate interest in meteorology. Based on an original paper concerning some aspect of atmospheric science. Open to all college students who are attending college in North, Central, or South America. Deadline: June 15.

465.
American Meteorological Society Awards
Howard H. Hanks Jr. Scholarship in Meteorology
45 Beacon Street
Boston, MA 02108
(617) 227-2425

1 scholarship of $500 to a student of atmospheric science entering final year of study. Must have completed fifty-four semester hours toward a bachelor's degree and must intend to pursue a career in atmospheric science. Based on academic excellence and achievement. Deadline: June 15.

466.
American Meteorological Society Awards
Howard T. Orville Scholarship in Meteorology
45 Beacon Street
Boston, MA 02108
(617) 227-2425

1 scholarship of $1,000 to a student of atmospheric science entering final year of study. Must have completed fifty-four semester hours toward a bachelor's degree and must intend to pursue a career in atmospheric science. Based on academic excellence and achievement. Deadline: June 15.

467.
American Nephrology Nurses' Association
National Office
200 East Holly Avenue
Pitman, NJ 08071-0056
(609) 256-2320

Scholarships and fellowships of varying amounts to students pursuing undergraduate and graduate degree programs in nursing. Applicants must be interested and dedicated to contributing to information advancement in nephrology. Deadline: varies.

468.
American Nuclear Society
ANS Environmental Sciences Division Scholarship
555 North Kensington Avenue
La Grange Park, IL 60526
(708) 352-6611

1 scholarship of $2,500 to an undergraduate student who has completed at least two years in a four-year nuclear-science or engineering program. Must be U.S. citizen or legal resident. Based on academic record. Send a #10 self-addressed, stamped envelope with all application requests. Deadline: March 1.

469.
American Nuclear Society
ANS Fuel Cycle and Waste Management Scholarship
555 North Kensington Avenue
La Grange Park, IL 60526
(708) 352-6611

1 scholarship of $1,000 to an undergraduate student who has completed at least two years in a four-year nuclear-science or engineering program. Must be U.S. citizen or legal resident. Based on academic record. Send a #10 self-addressed, stamped envelope with all application requests. Deadline: March 1.

470.
American Nuclear Society
ANS Power Division Scholarship
555 North Kensington Avenue
La Grange Park, IL 60526
(708) 352-6611

1 scholarship of $2,500 to an undergraduate student who has completed at least two years in a four-year nuclear-

science or engineering program. Must be U.S. citizen or legal resident. Based on academic record. Send a #10 self-addressed, stamped envelope with all application requests. Deadline: March 1.

471.
American Nuclear Society
ANS Reactor Operations Division Scholarship
555 North Kensington Avenue
La Grange Park, IL 60526
(708) 352-6611

1 scholarship of $1,000 to an undergraduate student who has completed at least two years in a four-year nuclear-science or engineering program. Must be U.S. citizen or legal resident. Based on academic record. Send a #10 self-addressed, stamped envelope with all application requests. Deadline: March 1.

472.
American Nuclear Society
ANS Student Design Competition
555 North Kensington Avenue
La Grange Park, IL 60526
(708) 352-6611

A design competition awards certificates and cash awards as well as travel costs to the winter meeting for the competition, to winners. Open to undergraduate and graduate students in nuclear science or engineering. Contact the nuclear-engineering department at your institution for information. Send a #10 self-addressed, stamped envelope with all application requests.

473.
American Nuclear Society
ANS Undergraduate Scholarships
555 North Kensington Avenue
La Grange Park, IL 60526
(708) 352-6611

4 scholarships of $1,000 to undergraduate sophomores, and 11 scholarships of $2,000 to undergraduate students who have completed at least two years in a four-year nuclear-science or engineering program. Must be U.S. citizens or legal residents. Based on academic record. Send a #10 self-addressed, stamped envelope with all application requests. Deadline: March 1.

474.
American Nuclear Society
Chave Scholarship
555 North Kensington Avenue
La Grange Park, IL 60526
(708) 352-6611

1 scholarship of $2,500 to an undergraduate student who has completed at least two years in a four-year nuclear-engineering program. Must be U.S. citizen or legal resident. Based on transcript. Send a #10 self-addressed, stamped envelope with all application requests. Deadline: March 1.

475.
American Nuclear Society
James R. Vogt Scholarship
555 North Kensington Avenue
La Grange Park, IL 60526
(708) 352-6611

1 scholarship of $3,000 to an undergraduate student who is conducting or proposing to conduct research in radioanalytical chemistry or analytical applications of nuclear science. Must be U.S. citizen or legal resident. Based on academic record. Send a #10 self-addressed, stamped envelope with all application requests. Deadline: March 1.

476.
American Nuclear Society
John and Muriel Landis Scholarships
555 North Kensington Avenue
La Grange Park, IL 60526
(708) 352-6611

7 scholarships of $3,000 to high school seniors or undergraduate and graduate students pursuing a career in nuclear engineering or a related field at a U.S. institution. Must have financial need or be disadvantaged (poor high school or undergraduate preparation due to family poverty). Must be U.S. citizen or legal resident. Based on academic record and financial need. Send a #10 self-addressed, stamped envelope with all application requests. Deadline: March 1.

477.
American Nuclear Society
John R. Lamarsh Scholarship
555 North Kensington Avenue
La Grange Park, IL 60526
(708) 352-6611

1 scholarship of $3,000 to an undergraduate student who has completed at least two years in a four-year nuclear-science or engineering program. Must be U.S. citizen or legal resident. Based on academic record. Send a #10 self-addressed, stamped envelope with all application requests. Deadline: March 1.

478.
American Nuclear Society
Joseph R. Dietrich Scholarship
555 North Kensington Avenue
La Grange Park, IL 60526
(708) 352-6611

1 scholarship of $3,000 to an undergraduate student who has completed at least two years in a four-year nuclear-science or engineering program. Must be U.S. citizen or legal resident. Based on academic record. Send a #10 self-addressed, stamped envelope with all application requests. Deadline: March 1.

479.
American Nuclear Society
Paul A. Greebler Scholarship
555 North Kensington Avenue
La Grange Park, IL 60526
(708) 352-6611

1 scholarship of $2,500 to an undergraduate student who has completed at least two years in a four-year nuclear-

science or engineering program. Must be U.S. citizen or legal resident. Based on academic record. Send a #10 self-addressed, stamped envelope with all application requests. Deadline: March 1.

480.
American Nurses Association
Baccalaureate Scholarship Program
Attn: Director
600 Maryland S.W. Avenue
Washington, DC 20005
(202) 651-7055

Fellowships of $2,000 to undergraduate students enrolled in an accredited nursing program. Must be members in good standing of their state Nurse's Association for at least two years. For an application, contact above address or state association. Deadline: varies.

481.
American Occupational Therapy Foundation, Inc.
Carolyn W. Kohn Scholarship Fund
4 Research Place
Rockville, MD 20850
(301) 990-7979

30 scholarships ranging from $150 to $1,500 to full-time undergraduate juniors and seniors and graduate students enrolled in or accepted to an approved occupational therapy program at the professional or assistant level. A student may be eligible for more than one scholarship but can be awarded only one scholarship. Students are also considered for any state scholarships available from state AOTF chapters. Based on financial need and scholastic excellence. Request applications by writing or calling between September 1 and November 30. Deadline: December 15.

482.
American Occupational Therapy Foundation, Inc.
Mary K. Minglin Fund/Kappa Delta Phi
  Scholarship Fund
4 Research Place
Rockville, MD 20850
(301) 990-7979

Numerous $750 scholarships to undergraduate or graduate students who are accepted to or enrolled in an accredited assistant- or professional-level program. Deadline: December 1.

483.
American Occupational Therapy Foundation, Inc.
Scholarships
4 Research Place
Rockville, MD 20850
(301) 990-7979

25 scholarships ranging from $500 to $1,000 to undergraduate (preference given to juniors and seniors) and graduate students majoring in occupational therapy. Based on financial need. Must have at least a 3.2 GPA. Some of these scholarships are sponsored by state associations and have residency restrictions. Deadline: December 15.

484.
American Ornithologists' Union
Student Research Awards
Attn: Research Awards Committee
National Museum of Natural History
Constitution Avenue at 10th N.W. Street
Washington, DC 20090
(202) 357-1300

5 to 15 research awards ranging from $500 to $1,500 to undergraduate students majoring in animal or veterinary science, graduate students, or veterinary students. Award is meant to assist students who have no access to regular funding for research on any aspect of avian biology. Individuals who already have their doctorate degrees are ineligible. Selection based on application and references. Other restrictions may apply. Deadline: May 1.

485.
American Ornithologists' Union
Travel Awards
Attn: Research Awards Committee
National Museum of Natural History
Constitution Avenue at 10th N.W. Street
Washington, DC 20090
(202) 357-1300

1 to 5 travel awards ranging from $500 to $1,000 to undergraduate, graduate, or veterinary students who are majoring in animal science, ornithology, or veterinary science. Awards provided to assist in defraying travel expenses to attend to meeting at which they present a paper in the area of ornithology. Awards are not renewable. Deadline: May 1.

486.
American Paint Horse Association
Youth Development Foundation APHA-YDF
  Scholarships
P.O. Box 961023
Ft. Worth, TX 76161-0023
(817) 439-3400

1 academic scholarship of $1,000 and 1 vocational scholarship of $750 to students who have been members (regular or junior) for at least one year before applying. Must be a high school graduate and have financial need. Applicants for the vocational scholarship must have at least a 2.5 GPA. Applicants for academic scholarship must have at least a 3.0 GPA. Deadline: April 1.

487.
American Physical Society
Corporate Sponsored Scholarships for Minority
  Students in Physics
25 West 45th Street, Suite 1007
New York, NY 10036
(212) 398-6775

Awards of $2,000 for tuition, room, or board to the student and $500 to each college or university physics department that hosts one or more APS minority undergraduate scholars. Open to high school seniors or college freshmen or sophomores who are African American, Hispanic, or Native American. Must be U.S. citizen and majoring in or planning on majoring in physics. Deadline: February 25.

488.
American Physical Therapy Association
Mary McMillan Scholarships
Director, Department of Education
1111 North Fairfax Street
Alexandria, VA 22314
(703) 684-2782

Scholarships of varying amounts to undergraduate students who will be entering their final year of study in a physical therapy program. Faculty members nominate individuals. Other restrictions may apply. Deadline: varies.

489.
American Planning Associates
Charles Abrams Scholarships
1776 Massachusetts Avenue, N.W.
Washington, DC 20090
(202) 872-0611

Scholarships of $1,000 for minority undergraduate second- or third-year students at a planning school. Based on academic record, leadership, recommendation by the college or university, and financial need. Deadline: May 15.

490.
American Pomological Society (APS)
Hendrick Awards
1137 Fifield Hall
University of Florida
Gainsville, FL 32611
(352) 392-1753

A writing competition with prizes of $50 and $150 (plus one-year subscription) to undergraduate and graduate students alone or coauthoring a paper with an adviser. Papers must be acceptable for publication by *Fruit Varieties Journal* and must focus on some aspect of fruit cultivation (deciduous, tropical, or subtropical with relation to climate, soil, experiments, history, etc.). May be a literature review, a thesis paper, or personal experience. Deadline: no later than 60 days before the APS meeting.

491.
American Postal Workers Union
Hallenback Memorial Scholarship Program
1300 L Street, N.W.
Washington, DC 20005
(202) 842-4200

Numerous scholarships of $1,000 to high school seniors who are children of active or deceased members of the American Postal Workers Union. Renewable for up to five years with satisfactory academic progress. Selection based on academic record, SAT/ACT, and financial need. Deadline: varies.

492.
American Production and Inventory Control Society, Inc.
Undergraduate and Graduate Student Awards Program
500 West Annandale Road
Falls Church, VA 22046
(703) 237-8344

Prize for best paper dealing with operations management; production management; industrial management; or business administration. Open to full-time undergraduate or graduate students at U.S. or Canadian colleges or universities. Write for complete details. Deadline: June 1.

493.
American Public Power Association
DEED Scholarships
2301 M Street, N.W.
Washington, DC 20037
(202) 467-2960 or 467-2900

10 scholarships of $3,000 to undergraduate and graduate students in energy-related majors at four-year accredited institutions. For information on qualifying criteria, send a self-addressed, stamped envelope to above address. Deadline: varies; usually in February and August.

494.
American Radio Relay League (ARRL) Foundation
Charles N. Fisher Memorial Scholarship
225 Main Street
Newington, CT 06111
(860) 594-0200

1 scholarship of $1,000 to a student attending a two- or four-year institution or vocational/technical school. Must hold any class of amateur radio license. Preference given to students studying electronics, communications, or related fields who are residents of the Southwestern Division (Arizona, Los Angeles, Orange, San Diego, or Santa Barbara). Deadline: February 1 (applications); February 15 (transcripts).

495.
American Radio Relay League (ARRL) Foundation
Dr. James Lawson Memorial Scholarship
225 Main Street
Newington, CT 06111
(860) 594-0200

1 scholarship of $500 to a student who is a resident of Connecticut, Massachusetts, New Hampshire, Rhode Island, Vermont, or New York; must attend an institution in any of those states. Must hold a general amateur license and be an ARRL member. Must be majoring in electronics or communications. Deadline: February 1 (applications); February 15 (transcripts).

496.
American Radio Relay League (ARRL) Foundation
Edmund A. Metzger Scholarship Fund
225 Main Street
Newington, CT 06111
(860) 594-0200

Numerous scholarships of $500 to ARRL members who are licensed radio amateurs, who are residents of ARRL Midwest Division (Iowa, Kansas, Missouri, Nebraska), who are attending a four-year institution in ARRL Midwest Division, and who are majoring in electrical engineering. Deadline: February 1 (applications); February 15 (transcripts).

497.
**American Radio Relay League (ARRL)
Foundation
Edward D. Jaikins Memorial Scholarship**
225 Main Street
Newington, CT 06111
(860) 594-0200

1 scholarship of $500 to a student who is a resident of the
FCC Eighth Call District in Michigan, Ohio, or West
Virginia. Must be an ARRL member. May attend any
vocational/technical school or a two- or four-year college
or university in that district. Must hold a general amateur
license. Deadline: February 1 (applications); February 15
(transcripts).

498.
**American Radio Relay League (ARRL)
Foundation
L. Phil Wicker Scholarship**
225 Main Street
Newington, CT 06111
(860) 594-0200

1 scholarship of $1,000 to an undergraduate and graduate
student. Preference given to a student studying electronics,
communications, or related fields. Must be a resident of the
Roanoke Division (North Carolina, South Carolina, Virginia,
or West Virginia) and attend an institution in that area.
Must hold a general amateur license and be an ARRL
member. Deadline: February 1 (applications); February 15
(transcripts).

499.
**American Radio Relay League (ARRL)
Foundation
Paul and Helen L. Grauer Scholarship**
225 Main Street
Newington, CT 06111
(860) 594-0200

2 scholarships of $500 to undergraduate and graduate
students who are residents of the ARRL Midwest Division
(Iowa, Kansas, Missouri, or Nebraska). Must be attending
an institution in that area. Must be ARRL members.
Preference given to students majoring in electronics,
communications, or related areas. Deadline: February 1
(applications); February 15 (transcripts).

500.
**American Radio Relay League (ARRL)
Foundation
Perry F. Hadlock Memorial Scholarship Fund**
225 Main Street
Newington, CT 06111
(860) 594-0200

1 scholarship of $5,000 to a student who is a general-class-
licensed radio amateur, promotes amateur radio, and is
enrolled as a full-time undergraduate or graduate student at
an accredited institution and majoring in electrical
engineering. Need not be an ARRL member. Deadline:
February 1 (applications); February 15 (transcripts).

501.
**American Radio Relay League (ARRL)
Foundation
Senator Barry Goldwater (#K7UGA) Scholarship
Fund**
225 Main Street
Newington, CT 06111
(860) 594-0200

1 scholarship of $5,000 to a full-time undergraduate or
graduate student at an accredited institution studying a field
related to communications. Must be a licensed radio
amateur and an ARRL member. Deadline: February 1
(applications); February 15 (transcripts).

502.
**American Radio Relay League (ARRL)
Foundation
"You've Got a Friend in Pennsylvania"
Scholarship Fund**
225 Main Street
Newington, CT 06111
(860) 594-0200

1 scholarship of $500 to a student who is a Pennsylvania
resident. Must be at least a general-class-license radio
amateur and a member of ARRL. Must have an "A"
average (sports and physical education grades are
excluded). No restrictions in field of study. Deadline:
February 1 (applications); February 15 (transcripts).

503.
American Red Cross
Attn: Volunteer Personnel
100 Peartree Lane
P.O. Box 14405
Raleigh, NC 27620
(800) 989-2721
(919) 231-1602

Varying numbers of internships of varying length to
anyone interested in helping prevent, prepare for, and cope
with emergencies. Interns help develop public relations
campaigns for Red Cross service departments, provide crisis
counseling for military families, provide emergency
assistance to disaster victims, assist in planning for response
to disasters, assist with health and safety courses and
programs, assist with all aspects of blood services
department, help with fund-raising, including special events,
and work in the volunteer personnel service department.
No compensation is provided. Open to individuals with
backgrounds in the following areas: advertising, business,
education, English, fund-raising, health, journalism,
marketing, nursing, personnel management, physical
education, psychology, public administration, public policy,
public relations, social services, sociology, or speech
communications. Deadline: open.

504.
**American Respiratory Care Foundation
Jimmy A. Young Memorial Scholarship**
11030 Ables Lane
Dallas, TX 75229
(214) 243-8892

1 scholarship of $1,000 to a minority freshman student
enrolled in an American Medical Association (AMA)-

approved respiratory care training program. Must have at least a 3.0 GPA, write an original reference paper on respiratory care, and submit letters of recommendation from the program director and medical director. Must be U.S. citizen. Deadline: June 1.

505.
American Respiratory Care Foundation
Morton B. Duggan Jr. Memorial Scholarship
11030 Ables Lane
Dallas, TX 75229
(214) 243-8892

1 scholarship of $500 and 1 scholarship of $1,250 to first- or second-year students enrolled in an American Medical Association (AMA)-approved respiratory care training program. Open to students from all states, but preference given to applicants from Georgia or South Carolina. Must have at least a 3.0 GPA, write an original reference paper on respiratory care, and submit letters of recommendation from the program director and medical director. Must be U.S. citizen. Deadline: June 1.

506.
American Respiratory Therapy Foundation
Student Scholarship Programs
11030 Ables Lane
Dallas, TX 75229
(214) 243-8892

Numerous scholarships ranging from $300 to $1,000 to undergraduate students in an American Medical Association (AMA)-approved respiratory therapy program. Must have at least a 3.0 GPA and submit letters of recommendation from the program director and medical director. Must be U.S. citizen. Deadline: June 15.

507.
American Samoa Government
Financial Aid Program
Department of Education
Office of Student Services
Pago Pago, American Samoa 96799
(684) 633-4255

Approximately 50 scholarships of $5,000 to residents of American Samoa to use in any major at undergraduate or graduate levels at an accredited institution. Off-island applicants may also be eligible if their parents are citizens of American Samoa. Renewable. Deadline: April 30.

508.
American School Food Service Association
  (ASFSA)
Professional Growth Scholarship
5600 South Quebec Street, Suite 300-B
Englewood, CO 80111
(800) 877-8822
(303) 761-0061

Numerous $500 scholarships to students who are members of the American School Food Service Association. Must be

updating education for a career in food service (food science technology/nutrition or food service) and have at least a 2.7 GPA. Deadline: April 15.

509.
American Schools of Oriental Research
Jennifer C. Groot Fellowships
711 West 40th Street, Suite 354
Baltimore, MD 21211
(301) 889-1383

2 fellowships of $1,000 to undergraduate or graduate students to assist them in participating in an archaeological excavation or survey in Jordan for one to three months. Must be or become members of ASOR or be attending an institution that is a corporate member. Deadline: February 1.

510.
American Scottish Foundation
Lady Malcolm Douglas–Hamilton Scholarship
P.O. Box 537
Lenox Hill Station
New York, NY 10021
(212) 605-0338

1 scholarship of $5,000 to an undergraduate or graduate student pursuing Scottish studies. Preference given to students of Scottish ancestry. Submit a letter of application with an outline of study plans. Deadline: April 15.

511.
American Serbian Eastern Rite Brothers
Education Committee Chairperson
2524 Sarah Street
Pittsburgh, PA 15203
(412) 741-7298

5 or 6 scholarships of $1,000 to graduating high school seniors. Must be residents of the greater Pittsburgh, Pennsylvania, area (including: Aliquippa, Clairton, Farrell/ Hermitage, Johnstown, McKeesport/Duquesne, Midland, Monroeville, Pittsburgh, Steubenville, Youngstown, and Youngwood). Students must be of Serbian descent and be children of members. Must be planning to attend an accredited two- or four-year college or university in the U.S. Other restrictions may apply. Deadline: May 15.

512.
American Society for Clinical Laboratory Science
AMTF Undergraduate Scholarships
Executive Director
Education & Research Fund
7910 Woodmont Avenue, Suite 1301
Bethesda, MD 20814
(301) 657-2768 ext. 3012

Several scholarships of up to $1,000 to undergraduate students entering last year of study in NAACLS-accredited programs in clinical laboratory science. Recipients must be citizens or permanent residents of the U.S. Applicants only have to submit one application to be considered for all undergraduate scholarships. Deadline: March 15.

513.

**American Society for Clinical Laboratory Science
ASCLS Education & Research Fund
 Undergraduate Scholarships**
Executive Director
Education & Research Fund
7910 Woodmont Avenue, Suite 1301
Bethesda, MD 20814
(301) 657-2768 ext. 3012

Several scholarships of up to $1,000 to undergraduate
students entering last year of study in NAACLS-accredited
programs in clinical laboratory science. Recipients must be
citizens or permanent residents of the U.S. Applicants only
have to submit one application to be considered for all
undergraduate scholarships. Deadline: March 15.

514.

**American Society for Clinical Laboratory Science
Dorothy Morrison Undergraduate Scholarship**
Executive Director
Education & Research Fund
7910 Woodmont Avenue, Suite 1301
Bethesda, MD 20814
(301) 657-2768 ext. 3012

1 scholarship of $1,000 to an undergraduate student
entering last year of study in NAACLS-accredited programs
in clinical laboratory science. Must be a citizen or
permanent resident of the U.S. Applicants only have to
submit one application to be considered for all
undergraduate scholarships. Deadline: March 15.

515.

**American Society for Clinical Laboratory Science
Fisher Scientific Undergraduate Scholarships**
Executive Director
Education & Research Fund
7910 Woodmont Avenue, Suite 1301
Bethesda, MD 20814
(301) 657-2768 ext. 3012

Varying numbers of scholarships of $3,000 to
undergraduates who have completed the first semester of
their sophomore year in an bachelor's degree program in
medical technology. Award is paid in equal installments
during the student's junior and senior years. Students
should also check with their state societies for possible
scholarships for state residents. Deadline: March 1.

516.

**American Society for Clinical Laboratory Science
Harleco Cytopathology Scholarship**
Executive Director
Education & Research Fund
7910 Woodmont Avenue, Suite 1301
Bethesda, MD 20814
(301) 657-2768 ext. 3012

1 scholarship of $500 to an undergraduate and graduate or
advanced specialty study in cytopathology. The award is
open to clinical laboratory practitioners and educators who
have performed clinical laboratory duties for at least one
year. Deadline: March 1.

517.

**American Society for Clinical Laboratory Science
Instrumentation Laboratory Undergraduate
 Scholarship**
Executive Director
Education & Research Fund
7910 Woodmont Avenue, Suite 1301
Bethesda, MD 20814
(301) 657-2768 ext. 3012

1 scholarship of $3,000 to a full-time undergraduate student
who is completing his/her sophomore year and about to
enter junior year in September. Award is paid during the
junior and senior years and pays for travel and
accommodation costs to attend the annual meeting. Must
be permanent resident of the U.S. Deadline: February 1.

518.

**American Society for Clinical Laboratory Science
Ruth M. French Scholarship**
Executive Director
Education & Research Fund
7910 Woodmont Avenue, Suite 1301
Bethesda, MD 20814
(301) 657-2768 ext. 3012

1 scholarship of up to $1,000 to a full-time undergraduate
or graduate student in an approved program in areas
related to clinical laboratory science, including Clinical
Laboratory Education or Management Programs.
Undergraduates must be entering their last year of study.
Graduate students cannot complete their education before
receiving the award. Must be a U.S. citizen or permanent
resident of the U.S. Deadline: March 1.

519.

**American Society for Clinical Laboratory Science
Skonie Undergraduate Scholarship**
Executive Director
Education & Research Fund
7910 Woodmont Avenue, Suite 1301
Bethesda, MD 20814
(301) 657-2768 ext. 3012

1 scholarship of $1,000 for an undergraduate student
enrolled in a med-tech program who will be entering the
senior year within twelve months. Applicants must be U.S.
citizens or permanent residents. Deadline: February 1.

520.

**American Society for Engineering Education
Washington Internships for Students of
 Engineering**
1818 N Street N.W, Suite 600
Washington, DC 20036
(202) 331-3500

A ten-week summer program in Washington, DC, for a
third-year engineering student. Program teaches how
engineers contribute to public-policy decisions on complex
technological matters. 15 internships available. Students
receive $2,400, travel allowance, and five quarter credits
from the University of Washington. Based on academic
achievement. Deadline: December 31.

521.
American Society for Enology and Viticulture Scholarships
Scholarship Committee
P.O. Box 1855
Davis, California 95617
(530) 753-3142

20 scholarships of up to $1,500 to undergraduate and graduate students for the study of enology, viticulture, and related subjects. Renewable. Must submit a written statement of career goals in the area of wine making, grape growing, food science, horticulture, or plant physiology. Deadline: March 1.

522.
American Society for Hospital Food Service Administrators
Dietary Products/Baxter Healthcare Corporation Award
840 North Lake Shore Drive
Chicago, IL 60611
(312) 280-6416

1 scholarship of $500 to a full-time student in a four-year program and 1 scholarship of $500 to a part-time student in a two- or four-year program. Must be enrolled in undergraduate-degree programs in hotel, restaurant, and institutional food service management or administrative dietetics and an active member in ASHFSA. Must be employed as director or assistant director of food service in a health-care institution. Deadline: March 1.

523.
American Society for Hospital Food Service Administrators
Dorothy Killian Scholarship
840 North Lake Shore Drive
Chicago, IL 60611
(312) 280-6416

1 scholarship of $1,000 to a full-time student in a four-year program and 1 scholarship of $500 to a part-time student in a two- or four-year program. Must be enrolled in undergraduate-degree programs in hotel, restaurant, and institutional food service management or administrative dietetics. Deadline: March 1.

524.
American Society for Information Science
ASIS Student Paper Award
8720 Georgia Avenue, Suite 501
Silver Spring, MD 20910
(301) 495-0900

Awards of varying amounts to undergraduate, graduate, or doctoral students who submit papers on work done in the field of information science. Must be enrolled in an accredited institution and pursuing a degree. Papers must follow criteria for publication in the *Journal of the American Society for Information Service.* Doctoral dissertations may not be used. Applicant must be endorsed by a faculty member. Deadline: June 15.

525.
American Society for Photogrammetry and Remote Sensing (ASPRS)
Analytical Surveys Photogrammetric Scholarship
ASPRS Awards Program
5410 Grosvenor Lane, Suite 210
Bethesda, MD 20814-2160
(301) 493-0290
http://www.asprs.org/asprs

1 scholarship of $4,000 to an undergraduate or graduate student who is a member of the ASPRS or the American Congress of Surveying and Mapping. Must have completed at least one course in surveying or photogrammetry. Deadline: December 1.

526.
American Society for Photogrammetry and Remote Sensing (ASPRS)
Cambridge Instruments Photogrammetric and Remote Sensing Award
ASPRS Awards Program
5410 Grosvenor Lane, Suite 210
Bethesda, MD 20814-2160
(301) 493-0290
http://www.asprs.org/asprs

Numerous scholarships of $500 to undergraduate and graduate students at recognized institutions worldwide. The purpose of the award is to enhance a student's interest in photogrammetry and remote sensing. Deadline: December 1.

527.
American Society for Photogrammetry and Remote Sensing (ASPRS)
EOSAT Award
ASPRS Awards Program
5410 Grosvenor Lane, Suite 210
Bethesda, MD 20814-2160
(301) 493-0290
http://www.asprs.org/asprs

1 scholarship of varying amount to an undergraduate or graduate student enrolled full-time in an accredited institution with image-processing facilities. Must submit a proposal for this award. For more information about qualifying criteria, contact above address. Deadline: December 1.

528.
American Society for Photogrammetry and Remote Sensing (ASPRS)
Robert Altenhofen Memorial Scholarship
ASPRS Awards Program
5410 Grosvenor Lane, Suite 210
Bethesda, MD 20814-2160
(301) 493-0290
http://www.asprs.org/asprs

1 scholarship of $500 to an undergraduate or graduate student who is a student member or active member of the ASPRS. Must list the completed courses in theoretical and mathematical photogrammetry and the grades received. For more application criteria, contact above address. Deadline: December 1.

529.
American Society of Civil Engineers (ASCE)
ASCE Construction Engineering Scholarship &
Student Prizes
345 East 47th Street
New York, NY 10017-2398
(212) 705-7496

1 scholarship of $1,000 awarded to a full-time
undergraduate student. Must be member of school's ASCE
student chapter or club. Based on essay. Renewable.
Deadline: February 15.

530.
American Society of Civil Engineers (ASCE)
B. Charles Tiney Memorial Scholarship
345 East 47th Street
New York, NY 10017-2398
(212) 705-7496

1 scholarship of $2,000 is available to an undergraduate
student who is a civil-engineering major and member of
school's ASCE student chapter. Award can be used at any
institution accredited by the Accreditation Board for
Engineering and Technology (ABET). Deadline: February 15.

531.
American Society of Civil Engineers (ASCE)
O. H. Ammann Research Fellowship
345 East 47th Street
New York, NY 10017-2398
(212) 705-7496

1 research fellowship of $5,000 to an undergraduate or
graduate student who is an ASCE member. Submit a
proposal on an original proposed research project in the
area of structural engineering. Deadline: February 1.

532.
American Society of Civil Engineers (ASCE)
Samuel F. Tapman Scholarships
345 East 47th Street
New York, NY 10017-2398
(212) 705-7496

12 scholarships of $1,500 awarded to college freshmen,
sophomores, and juniors. Applicants must belong to a
student chapter of ASCE and be national ASCE members.
Contact: Assistant Manager of Student Services for more
information and application. Deadline: February 15.

533.
American Society of Composers, Authors, and
Publishers Foundations
Music Composition Awards Program
ASCAP Building, 1 Lincoln Plaza
New York, NY 10023
(212) 621-6000

15 awards of $800 to young composers under the age of
thirty as of March 15 of the year of application. Open to
undergraduate or graduate students. Awards help young
composers continue their studies and develop their skills.
Write for complete information. Deadline: March 15.

534.
American Society of Criminology
ASC Gene Carte Student Paper Competition
1314 Kinnear Road, Suite 212
Columbus, OH 43212
(614) 292-9207
http://www.asc41.com/

Awards of $300, $150, and $100 to undergraduate and
graduate students who submit empirical and/or theoretical
papers related to criminology. Send a self-addressed,
stamped envelope for information on how to submit
papers. Deadline: April 15.

535.
American Society of Health System Pharmacists–
Research and Education Foundation
Executive Vice-President
7272 Wisconsin Avenue
Bethesda, MD 20814
(301) 657-3000
http://www.ashp.org

A $500 honorarium award plus a $500 expense allowance
to attend the midyear meeting to undergraduate and
graduate students (B.S., M.S., and Pharm.D.) who submit an
unpublished paper on a subject related to hospital
pharmacy written during the preceding academic year.
Request information after January 1. Deadline: May 15.

536.
American Society of Heating, Refrigeration, & Air
Conditioning Engineers
Alwin B. Newton Scholarship Fund
Staff Liaison, Scholarship Fund Trustees
1791 Tullie Circle, N.E.
Atlanta, GA 30329
(404) 636-8400
http://www.ashrae.org

Scholarships of varying amounts to undergraduate students
majoring in heating, refrigeration, and air-conditioning.
Must have a 3.0 GPA on a 4.0 scale. Awards are good at
any U.S.- or Canadian-accredited institution. Deadline:
February 15.

537.
American Society of Heating, Refrigeration, & Air
Conditioning Engineers
General Scholarships
Staff Liaison, Scholarship Fund Trustees
1791 Tullie Circle, N.E.
Atlanta, GA 30329
(404) 636-8400
http://www.ashrae.org/

Numerous $2,000 scholarships to undergraduate students
majoring in heating, refrigeration, and air-conditioning.
Must have a 3.0 GPA on a 4.0 scale or be on dean's list
(whichever is higher). Awards are good at any U.S.- or
Canadian-accredited institution. Deadline: December 15.

538.

American Society of Heating, Refrigeration, & Air Conditioning Engineers
Grants-in-Aid for Undergraduates
Staff Liaison, Scholarship Fund Trustees
1791 Tullie Circle, N.E.
Atlanta, GA 30329
(404) 636-8400
http://www.ashrae.org/

Scholarships of up to $2,500 to undergraduate students majoring in heating, refrigeration, and air-conditioning. A $500 award is presented to the students' faculty adviser. Awards are good at any U.S.- or Canadian-accredited institution. Deadline: December 15.

539.

American Society of Interior Designers (ASID)
Educational Foundation/Steelcase Contract Design Scholarship
Educational Foundation Scholarships
608 Massachusetts Avenue, N.E.
Washington, DC 20002
(202) 546-3480
http://www.asid.org/

2 awards of $3,000 to students enrolled in three-, four-, or five-year FIDER-accredited design programs offering course work in contract design. Based on academic record, grade point average, creativity, and potential. Request information after December 1. Deadline: March 15.

540.

American Society of Interior Designers
Environmental Design Award
Educational Foundation Scholarships
608 Massachusetts Avenue, N.E.
Washington, DC 20002
(202) 546-3480
http://www.asid.org/

1 award of $4,000 to individuals (undergraduates or graduate students or professional interior designers), organizations, institutions, or project groups. Award encourages the interaction of the design profession using a holistic approach to the design process when solving environmental problems. Design proposal must illustrate the problem-solving process resulting from research as well as design ability. Deadline: February 15.

541.

American Society of Interior Designers
S. Harris Memorial Scholarship
Educational Foundation Scholarships
608 Massachusetts Avenue, N.E.
Washington, DC 20002
(202) 546-3480
http://www.asid.org/

2 scholarships of $1,500 to undergraduate students majoring in interior design who have completed at least one year. Based on academic record, creative accomplishments, and recommendations. Request information after December 1. Deadline: March 14.

542.

American Society of Interior Designers
Yale R. Burge Competition
Educational Foundation Scholarships
608 Massachusetts Avenue, N.E.
Washington, DC 20002
(202) 546-3480
http://www.asid.org/

An award of $500 plus an additional $250 reserve award to students entering their final year of undergraduate study of interior design. Based on portfolios. Judged on professional quality of design solutions, visual communication of solutions, and quality of layout. Deadline: November 10-entry fee ($10) and registration requests; April 1-for entry submissions.

543.

American Society of Magazine Editors Internships
Executive Director
919 Third Avenue
New York, NY 10022
(212) 752-0055
http://www.magazine.org/

ASME provides summer internships at consumer magazines and business publications for college students interested in magazine journalism. The internships begin with a four-day orientation program and run from early June to mid-August. Applicants must have completed their junior year in college in May or June of the internship year and be heading for their senior year the following autumn. Interns receive a minimum of $250 per week (before taxes). Interns in New York City are housed at New York University. Applicants must be nominated by the dean or department head familiar with their journalistic ability and experience. Deadline: September 15.

544.

American Society of Mechanical Engineers (ASME)
ASME International
Marjorie Roy Rothermel Scholarship
3 Park Avenue
New York, NY 10016-5990
(800) THE-ASME
(212) 591-7000
http://www.asme.org
webmaster@asme.org

1 scholarship of $1,500 to an undergraduate senior or a graduate student for graduate study in the area of mechanical engineering. Based on character, academic achievement, and financial need. Contact above address or local ASME faculty advisor. Deadline: February 15.

545.

American Society of Mechanical Engineers (ASME)
ASME International
Student Assistance Loans
ASME Student Section Faculty Advisor/Director
Education Services
3 Park Avenue
New York, NY 10016-5990
(800) THE-ASME
(212) 591-7000
http://www.asme.org
webmaster@asme.org

Loans of up to $2,500 to full-time undergraduate students majoring in mechanical engineering or mechanical technology who are ASME student members. Must be U.S. citizens. Deadline: April 1 and November 1.

546.
American Society of Mechanical Engineers (ASME) Auxiliary, Inc.
ASME International
Sylvia W. Farny Scholarships
Education Services
3 Park Avenue
New York, NY 10016-5990
(800) THE-ASME
(212) 591-7000
http://www.asme.org
webmaster@asme.org

1 or more scholarships of $1,000 to students entering their fourth or fifth year of undergraduate study in a school with an accredited mechanical engineering curriculum. Must be student members of ASME. Based on character, academic achievement, and financial need. Contact above address or local ASME faculty advisor. Deadline: February 15.

547.
American Society of Mechanical Engineers (ASME) National Office
ASME International
Student Assistance Loan Program
United Engineering Center
3 Park Avenue
New York, NY 10016-5990
(800) THE-ASME
(212) 591-7000
http://www.asme.org
webmaster@asme.org

60 loans of up to $2,500 to undergraduate freshmen, sophomores, or juniors who are ASME student members. Must be full-time students in an ABET-accredited U.S. engineering program. Based on character, academic achievement, and financial need. Deadline: none.

548.
American Society of Naval Engineers
Scholarships
Overseer of Scholarships
1452 Duke Street
Alexandria, VA 22314-3403
(703) 836-6727
http://www.jhuapl.edu/ASNE/

16 scholarships of $2,000 awarded to college juniors or seniors or graduate students seeking a degree in engineering with a planned career in naval engineering. Based on interest in naval engineering, academic achievement, competence, and financial need. Renewable if not a graduate student. Must be U.S. citizens. Deadline: February 15.

549.
American Society of Newspaper Editors
Foundation
Minority Journalism Scholarships
Minority Affairs Director, ASNE
P.O. Box 4090
Reston, VA 22090-1700
(703) 648-1144
http://www.asne.org/

60 scholarships of $750 to college-bound minority students. Students must submit a formal application form, two letters of recommendation, and write an essay stating their career interests and journalism-related activities while they were seniors in high school. Must have a 2.5 GPA and sign a statement of intent of pursuing a career in journalism. Deadline: first week of November.

550.
American Society of Newspaper Editors
Project Focus for Minority Freshmen &
Sophomores
Minority Affairs Director
P.O. Box 4090
Reston, VA 22090-1700
(703) 648-1144

Open to minority college freshmen and sophomores at an accredited U.S. college or university. Students receive paid summer internships at their hometown or nearby newspapers and a $250 bonus if they complete program. Deadline: January.

551.
American Society of Safety Engineers
ASSE Student Paper Awards
1800 East Oakton
Des Plaines, IL 60018-2187
(847) 699-2929
http://www.asse.org/

Awards of $500, $750, and $1,000 and publication to full-time undergraduate students majoring in safety, health, or related specialty who submit original, unpublished papers written during the year before the deadline. Based on relevance to important safety issues, persuasiveness, impact, quality of writing, technical accuracy, and feasibility. One entry per student. Need not be ASSE student members. Deadline: January 31.

552.
American Society of Safety Engineers
John E. Anderson Safety Student of the Year
Award
1800 East Oakton
Des Plaines, IL 60018-2187
(847) 699-2929
http://www.asse.org/

1 award of $1,000 and a plaque to a full-time undergraduate student who has completed at least one year of study and is preparing for a career in safety/health or related specialties. Must be ASSE student member attending an accredited institution. Graduate students may apply, but only the activities completed during their undergraduate years in safety and health will be considered. Based on academics, activities, and recommendation by faculty advisor, chapter officer, or other faculty member. Deadline: January 31.

553.
American Society of Safety Engineers
SEDA Scholarships
1800 East Oakton
Des Plaines, IL 60018-2187
(847) 699-2929
http://www.asse.org/

2 scholarships of $2,500 to full-time undergraduate or graduate students majoring in safety/health or a related specialty at an accredited institution. Must be ASSE student members and have at least one semester of study remaining. Must have at least a 2.75 GPA on a 4.0 scale. Based on academic record and recommendations. Deadline: January 31.

554.
American Society of Travel Agents (ASTA)
Air Travel Card Scholarship
1101 King Street
Alexandria, VA 22314
(703) 739-2782
http://www.astanet.com

1 scholarship of $3,000 to an undergraduate student majoring in business travel management at an accredited two- or four-year institution. Must be working toward a degree in travel management or business management, with a minor in tourism or hospitality management. Deadline: June 10.

555.
American Society of Travel Agents (ASTA)
A. J. "Andy" Spielman Scholarships
1101 King Street
Alexandria, VA 22314
(703) 739-2782
http://www.astanet.com

2 scholarships of $1,000 to students entering into or reentering a travel career. Must be attending a travel school or two-year college to obtain a degree in travel and tourism. Must submit an essay on "What Goals I Hope to Achieve in the Travel Industry." Deadline: June 10.

556.
American Society of Travel Agents (ASTA)
Alaska Airlines Scholarships
1101 King Street
Alexandria, VA 22314
(703) 739-2782
http://www.astanet.com

3 scholarships of $1,000 to sophomore, junior, or senior undergraduate students enrolled in travel-and-tourism courses at a recognized college, proprietary travel school, or Certified Travel Counselor (CTC) program. Must have at least a 2.5 GPA on a 4.0 scale. Based on essay, academic record, and recommendation. Deadline: June 10.

557.
American Society of Travel Agents (ASTA)
American Express Travel Scholarships
1101 King Street
Alexandria, VA 22314
(703) 739-2782
http://www.astanet.com

3 scholarships of $1,000 to an undergraduate student enrolled in travel-and-tourism courses at a recognized college, proprietary travel school, or Certified Travel Counselor (CTC) program. Based on essay, academic record, and recommendation. Must have at least a 2.5 GPA on a 4.0 scale. Deadline: June 10.

558.
American Society of Travel Agents (ASTA)
Arizona Chapter Scholarship
1101 King Street
Alexandria, VA 22314
(703) 739-2782
http://www.astanet.com

1 scholarship of $1,000 to an undergraduate student in an accredited travel school in Arizona. Based on an essay, "Why I Want to be in the Travel Industry, and the Rewards I Expect." Must be a U.S. citizen. Deadline: June 10.

559.
American Society of Travel Agents (ASTA)
Avis Rent A Car Scholarship
1101 King Street
Alexandria, VA 22314
(703) 739-2782
http://www.astanet.com

1 scholarship of $1,000 to a student learning automation and communication skills for use in a travel-and-tourism career. Must be a sophomore, junior, or senior undergraduate or a graduate who has worked part-time in a travel career. Deadline: June 10.

560.
American Society of Travel Agents (ASTA)
David Hallissey Memorial Fund
1101 King Street
Alexandria, VA 22314
(703) 739-2782
http://www.astanet.com

1 award of $1,200 to an undergraduate or graduate student to do research in a travel field. Student must be a travel or tour educator at a postsecondary institution or preparatory school. Deadline: June 10.

561.
American Society of Travel Agents (ASTA)
Fernanco R. Ayuso Fund
1101 King Street
Alexandria, VA 22314
(703) 739-2782
http://www.astanet.com

2 scholarships are provided by ASTA and the Ministry of Tourism of Spain. One award is for an American student to travel in Spain for three weeks. The other award is for a Spanish student to travel to the U.S. and attend the ASTA World Congress. American student must be a U.S. citizen between twenty-three and thirty years of age, with an interest in Spanish culture and familiarity with Spanish language. Must have at least two years of college education and two years of employment in a travel-related field. The Spanish student must be a citizen of Spain, be between twenty-three and thirty years of age, have an interest in U.S. culture, and be fluent in English. Must have at least

two years of college education and two years of employment in a travel-related field. Based on essay. Deadline: June 10.

562.
American Society of Travel Agents (ASTA)
George Reinke Scholarships
1101 King Street
Alexandria, VA 22314
(703) 739-2782
http://www.astanet.com

2 scholarships of $1,000 to students in a travel school or two-year college. Based on an essay, "The Value of Travel Experience in One's Life." Award may not exceed 50 percent of annual tuition. Deadline: June 10.

563.
American Society of Travel Agents (ASTA)
Healy Scholarship
1101 King Street
Alexandria, VA 22314
(703) 739-2782
http://www.astanet.com

1 scholarship of $1,200 to a sophomore, junior, or senior undergraduate student who is enrolled in travel-and-tourism courses at a recognized college, proprietary travel school, or Certified Travel Counselor (CTC) program. Must have at least a 2.5 GPA on a 4.0 scale. Based on essay, academic record, and recommendation. Deadline: June 10.

564.
American Society of Travel Agents (ASTA)
Holland–America Line/Westours Inc. Scholarships
1101 King Street
Alexandria, VA 22314
(703) 739-2782
http://www.astanet.com

2 scholarships of $1,000 to students who will be sophomore, junior, or senior undergraduates and who have an interest in travel and tourism. Must have been out of high school for at least five years. Award can't exceed 50 percent of annual tuition. Deadline: June 10.

565.
American Society of Travel Agents (ASTA)
Joseph R. Stone Scholarships
1101 King Street
Alexandria, VA 22314
(703) 739-2782
http://www.astanet.com

2 scholarships of $2,400 to students who have at least one parent in the travel industry. Must be in a travel-and-tourism program, with twenty-one credit hours of travel and tourism. Must have at least a 3.0 GPA on a 4.0 scale. Based on an essay. Deadline: June 10.

566.
American Society of Travel Agents (ASTA)
Orange County Chapter/Harry Jackson
Scholarship
1101 King Street
Alexandria, VA 22314
(703) 739-2782
http://www.astanet.com

1 scholarship of $1,000 to an undergraduate student who is enrolled in travel-and-tourism courses at a recognized college, proprietary travel school, or Certified Travel Counselor (CTC) program in Orange County, California. Must have at least a 2.5 GPA on a 4.0 scale. Based on essay, academic record, and recommendation. Deadline: June 10.

567.
American Society of Travel Agents (ASTA)
Pollard Scholarships
1101 King Street
Alexandria, VA 22314
(703) 739-2782
http://www.astanet.com

2 scholarships of $1,000 to students enrolled in a travel-and-tourism program in a recognized travel school. Award can't exceed 50 percent of annual tuition. Must be U.S. or Canadian citizens and have been out of high school for at least five years. Deadline: June 10.

568.
American Society of Travel Agents (ASTA)
Scholarship Foundation
1101 King Street
Alexandria, VA 22314
(703) 739-2782
http://www.astanet.com

Scholarships ranging from $250 to $3,000 to undergraduate or graduate students majoring in travel and tourism at an accredited proprietary school. Deadline: June 10.

569.
American Society of Travel Agents (ASTA)
Southeast Chapter Scholarships
1101 King Street
Alexandria, VA 22314
(703) 739-2782
http://www.astanet.com

6 scholarships of $250 to SEASTA candidates. Must be members of SEASTA chapter, have an 85 average or higher, and apply within one year of receiving Certified Travel Consultant (CTC) certification. Students must have excelled in obtaining their CTC accreditation from the Institute of Certified Travel Agents (ICTA). Deadline: June 10.

570.
American Welding Society Scholarship Program
550 N.W. Lejeune Road
P.O. Box 351040
Miami, FL 33135
(800) 443-9353
(305) 443-9353
(305) 443-7559 Fax
http://www.amweld.org

Scholarships of varying amounts to undergraduate or graduate students pursuing careers in welding technology and are enrolled in an accredited material joining or similar program. May be used at a two- or four-year college or university. Open to U.S. citizens who reside in the U.S. Deadline: June 1.

571.
American Wind Energy Association
Internship Coordinator
122 C Street, N.W., 4th Floor
Washington, DC 20001
(202) 383-2500
(202) 383-2505 Fax
http://www.lgc.apc.org/awea
windmail@mcimail.com

10 twelve-week internships providing a salary ranging from $240 to $320 per week to undergraduates, graduate students, and recent graduates to work at AWEA to advance the development of wind energy as an economically and technically viable energy alternative. Interns work in administration, finance, legislative, international, membership, and meetings at the Washington, DC office. Internships are conducted during the summer, fall, and spring. Deadline: rolling.

572.
American Women in Radio & Television
Houston Internships/Scholarship Program
P.O. Box 980908
Houston, TX 77098-0908
Written inquiries only

Internships with pay (ranging from $800 to $1,600) for students who are juniors, seniors, or graduate students at greater Houston area colleges and universities. Internships are at companies chosen to suit students' interests. Deadline: March 1.

573.
AmeriCorps ★ NCCC
Office of Recruitment
1201 New York Avenue, N.W., 9th Floor
Washington, DC 20525
(800) 942-2677

Program provides $4,725 a year for up to two years of community service in one of four priority areas: education, human services, the environment, or public safety. Open to anyone of any age interested in earning assistance to cover educational costs by completing community service. Must complete 1,700 hours of service work per year. Work can be completed before or after attending a vocational or trade school, undergraduate college or university, or graduate or professional school. Funds are used to pay current educational expenses or to repay federal student loans. The program provides a living allowance of at least $7,400 per year and, if necessary, health-care and child-care allowances.

574.
AMETEK Foundation
National Merit College Scholarship Program
Station Square
Paoli, PA 19301
(610) 647-2121

Up to 5 scholarships ranging from $500 to $2,000 to graduating high school seniors who are in the top 20 percent of their class. Must receive National Merit designation and be a dependent of a parent who is affiliated with AMETEK.

For information, contact company's benefits office. Renewable. Deadline: December 1.

575.
Amity Institute
Box 118
Del Mar, CA 92014
(619) 755-3582

Provides opportunities for teaching internships for students (who are fluent in English) from other countries to work as teachers and teacher's aides in schools. There are also internships for students from the U.S. who are fluent in Spanish to go to a Latin American country or fluent in French to work in French-speaking countries in the Caribbean. Students must provide travel expenses. Program offers free room and board with a host family, free school lunches, and a small stipend. Internships are for three to nine months in length. Deadline: rotating.

576.
AMVETS National Headquarters
Continuation Scholarships
4647 Forbes Boulevard
Lanham, MD 20706
(301) 459-9600
http://www.amvets.org/

Varying numbers of scholarships of up to $2,000 to undergraduate students who are dependents of an Army veteran. Must apply during sophomore year and use during junior year. Must have at least a 3.0 GPA. Must be U.S. citizens and have exhausted all possible federal aid. Based on application, verification of veteran status, FAFSA, SAT/ACT, and essay. Applications must be requested by January 15. Deadline: February 15.

577.
AMVETS National Headquarters
Four-Year Scholarships
4647 Forbes Boulevard
Lanham, MD 20706
(301) 459-9600
http://www.amvets.org/

15 scholarships of up to $1,000 to graduating high school seniors who are dependents of a veteran. Must have at least a 3.0 GPA. Must be U.S. citizens and have exhausted all possible federal aid. Based on application, verification of veteran status, FAFSA, SAT/ACT, and essay. Applications must be requested by January 15. Deadline: February 15.

578.
AMVETS National Headquarters
Memorial Scholarships
4647 Forbes Boulevard
Lanham, MD 20706
(301) 459-9600
http://www.amvets.org/

15 scholarships of up to $1,000 to graduating high school seniors who are dependents of a veteran. Must have at least a 3.0 GPA. Must be U.S. citizens and have exhausted all possible federal aid. Based on application, verification of veteran status, FAFSA, SAT/ACT, and essay. Applications must be requested by January 15. Deadline: February 15.

579.

AMVETS National Headquarters
National Scholarship Program
4647 Forbes Boulevard
Lanham, MD 20706
(301) 459-9600
http://www.amvets.org/

Varying numbers of scholarships of up to $2,000 to graduating high school seniors who are dependents of a veteran. Must be U.S. citizens and have exhausted all possible federal aid. Based on application, verification of veteran status, FAFSA, SAT/ACT, and essay. Applications must be requested by January 15. Deadline: February 15.

580.

AMVETS National Headquarters
Two-Year Scholarships
4647 Forbes Boulevard
Lanham, MD 20706
(301) 459-9600
http://www.amvets.org/

15 scholarships of up to $2,000 to graduating high school seniors who are dependents of a veteran. Must have at least a 3.0 GPA. Must be U.S. citizens and have exhausted all possible federal aid. Based on application, verification of veteran status, FAFSA, SAT/ACT, and essay. Applications must be requested by January 15. Deadline: February 15.

581.

AMVETS National Scholarships
4647 Forbes Boulevard
Lanham, MD 20706
(301) 459-9600
http://www.amvets.org/

15 scholarships of $1,000 to high school seniors whose fathers, mothers, or grandparents are American veterans or to veterans who have exhausted all possible federal aid. Based on application, verification of veteran status, FAFSA, SAT/ACT, and essay. Renewable. Deadline: February 15.

582.

Ancient Order United Workmen (AOUW)
Memorial Student Loan Fund
Supreme Master Workman
17805 41st Avenue South
Seattle, WA 98188

Loans of $500 for sophomore year of college, $750 for junior year, and $1,000 for senior or graduate years, but no more than $2,000 for the entire period. Loans are only for members of the Ancient Order United Workmen. Based on academic standing, career goals and prospects of success, financial need, and purpose of the loan. Deadline: none.

583.

Annual Fiction and Poetry Contest
Rambunctious Press
1221 West Pratt
Chicago, IL 60626
(312) 338-2439

A writing contest with cash prizes of varying amounts for unpublished short stories and poems. Entry fee: $3 per story or $2 per poem. Send self-addressed, stamped envelope for guidelines. Deadline: varies.

584.

Annual Poetry Contest
National Federation of State Poetry Societies
3520 State Rt. 56
Mechanicsburg, OH 43033
(513) 834-2666

A contest for previously unpublished poetry, with varying cash prizes. There are fifty categories. Send self-addressed, stamped envelope (legal size #10) for guidelines. Charges: entry fees. Deadline: March 15.

585.

Annual Poetry/Fiction/Nonfiction Awards
Sonora Review
Department of English
University of Arizona
Tucson, AZ 85721
(602) 626-8383

A contest for previously unpublished poetry, fiction, and nonfiction, with varying cash awards. Charges: $2 entry fee per entry. Deadline: April 15 (poetry); November 15 (fiction and nonfiction).

586.

The Antarctic Project
Internship Coordinator
P.O. Box 76920
Washington, DC 20013
(202) 544-0236
(202) 544-8483 Fax
antarctica@igc.apc.org

20 internships open to undergraduate juniors and seniors, graduate students, and recent graduates to work from twelve- to fifteen-week internships at the TAP office in Washington, DC. Interns conduct research, write fact sheets, and attend conferences that are geared to protecting the natural resources of Antarctica and the Southern Ocean. No compensation is provided. Internships are conducted during the summer, fall, and spring. Deadline: rolling.

587.

AOPA Air Safety Foundation
Donald Burnside Memorial Scholarship
421 Aviation Way
P.O. Box 865
Frederick, MD 21701
(301) 695-2170

1 scholarship of $1,000 to an undergraduate sophomore who is enrolled in or planning to continue a college curriculum leading to a degree in the field of aviation. Applicants must have an overall grade point average of at least 2.5 on a 4.0 scale, and submit a 250-word (typed, double-spaced) paper on "Why I Wish to Pursue a Career in Aviation." Submit an official transcript with application. Other restrictions may apply. Deadline: March 31.

588.

AOPA Air Safety Foundation
McAllister Scholarships
421 Aviation Way
Frederick, MD 21701
(301) 695-2170
http://www.aopa.org/

2 scholarships of $1,000 to undergraduate sophomores, juniors, and seniors pursuing a degree in aerospace or aeronautical engineering and a career in the field of aviation. Must have an overall grade point average of at least 2.5 on a 4.0 scale, and submit a 250-word (typed, double-spaced) paper on "Why I Wish to Pursue a Career in Aviation." Submit an official transcript with application. Awarded jointly annually by the AOPA Air Safety Foundation and the University Aviation Association. Other restrictions may apply. Deadline: March 31.

589.

Apex Scholarship Fund
c/o Maretta Nelson
911 Sunridge Drive
Sarasota, FL 34234

2 scholarships of $500 to African American students who are residents of Sarasota or Manatee counties, Florida. Can be used at a two- or four-year institution. Based on academic achievement, extracurricular activities, financial need, and an interview. Deadline: April 10.

590.

Appaloosa Horse Club, Inc.—Appaloosa Youth Program
Appaloosa Youth Foundation Scholarship Committee
P.O. Box 8403
Moscow, ID 83843
(208) 882-5578
http://claresholm.net/clubs/appaloosa/docl.htm

8 scholarships of $1,000 for high school seniors or graduates. 1 scholarship awarded to a student from each of the five territories, 2 scholarships at large, and 1 to a past winner. Based on academic record, leadership, sportsmanship, community involvement, and general knowledge and accomplishments in horsemanship. Two applications are provided to each regional club and racing association. Deadline: June 10.

591.

Appaloosa Youth Foundation
Lew and Joann Eklund Educational Scholarship
Attn: Youth Coordinator
P.O. Box 8403
Moscow, ID 83843
(208) 882-5578
http://claresholm.net/clubs/appaloosa/docl.htm

1 scholarship of $2,000 to undergraduate juniors, seniors, or graduate students majoring in animal science, veterinary science, or a field related to the equine industry. Must be a member or a dependent of a member of the Appaloosa Horse Club. Selection based on application, academic achievement, and three recommendation letters. Must submit a picture. Deadline: June 10.

592.

Apple Computers, Inc.
Internship Program
College Relations
20525 Mariani Avenue
MS: 75-2J
Cupertino, CA 95014
(408) 996-1010
http://www.apple.com/

Twelve-week summer internships providing salaries ranging from $600 to $1,100 per week (depending on education and work experience) plus round-trip travel expenses to undergraduate and graduate students. Though the majority of interns are majoring in computer science, electrical engineering, and computer engineering, the program is open to all majors. Students must submit a cover letter describing their academic background and how it applies to their area of interest. Include a résumé. The information is placed into a database that is used by managers of various departments. Candidates are interviewed by phone. Deadline: February 28.

593.

Appraisal Institute Education Trust Scholarships
Romanita Rencher Education Trust
875 North Michigan Avenue
Chicago, IL 60611-1980
(312) 335-4136
(312) 335-4200 Fax
http://www.appraisalinstitute.org/

Scholarships ranging from $2,000 to $3,000 to undergraduate and graduate students majoring in real estate, land economics, real estate appraising, or an allied field (related to real estate) at an accredited four-year institution. Based on academic record, essay, and recommendations. Deadline: March 15.

594.

Apprentice Training
Bureau of Apprenticeship and Training
Employment and Training Administration
U.S. Department of Labor
Washington, DC 20210

An apprenticeship training system for male and female students who are at least sixteen years of age. Some, but not all, occupations require a high school diploma, GED, or a written test. The program assists persons who want on-the-job training in one of over eight hundred occupations. The program offers a student the opportunity to work for an employer, group of employers, or union while at the same time going to school. Apprenticeships in construction, health, manufacturing, services, and many others are available. To obtain the regional or state address for information on this program, contact above address.

595.

Arby's Foundation—Big Brothers/Big Sisters of America
230 North 13th Street
Philadelphia, PA 19107
(215) 567-7000

2 scholarships of $5,000 to students who have been a Little Brother or Little Sister in an affiliated Big Brother/Big Sister

program for at least one year (doesn't have to be current) and have later volunteered their time. Based on academic record, financial need, and recommendations. Renewable. Deadline: varies.

596.
Archive Films
Internship Coordinator
530 West 25th Street
New York, NY 10001
(212) 645-2137 Fax

10 internships lasting from six to twelve weeks and providing a daily transportation stipend are open to high school graduates, undergraduates, recent college graduates, and graduate students. Students work in film and photo research, film sales, marketing, or acquisitions/duplications. Archive Films has a collection dating back to 1890 and includes news footage on virtually every twentieth-century famous event, personalities, documentaries, and over 10,000 films. Deadline: rolling.

597.
Argonne National Laboratory (Student Research Participation Program; Thesis Research)
Division of Educational Programs
9700 South Cass Avenue
Argonne, IL 60439
(312) 972-3365
http://www.anl.gov/

Stipends of $175 to $200 per week for one-semester accredited internship program to provide students majoring in physical sciences, life sciences, earth sciences, mathematics, computer sciences, engineering, fusion, and fission energy an opportunity to work in areas related to energy development. Open to full-time undergraduate juniors and seniors or first-year graduate students. Must be U.S. citizens or legal residents. Thesis research awards open to doctoral candidates working on their dissertation. Deadline: February 1; May 15; October 15.

598.
Arizona Central Labor Councils
Central Arizona Labor Council, AFL-CIO
5818 North 7th Street, #202
Phoenix, AZ 85014

2 scholarships ($500 and $1,000) to graduating high school seniors who are dependents of a union member in good standing with the Central Arizona Labor Council. Based on an essay; proof of acceptance to college, university, or technical school; and high school transcript. Deadline: varies.

599.
Arizona Commission for Post–Secondary Education
2020 North Central Avenue, Suite 275
Phoenix, AZ 85004-4503
(602) 229-2591
(602) 229-2599 Fax
http://www.acpe.asu.edu

Grants of up to $2,500 to students enrolled in Arizona postsecondary institutions. Must be Arizona residents.

Contact the financial-aid office at college of interest. Deadline: varies with each school.

600.
Arizona Commission for Post–Secondary Education
Robert C. Byrd Scholarships
2020 North Central Avenue, Suite 275
Phoenix, AZ 85004-4503
(602) 229-2591
(602) 229-2599 Fax
http://www.acpe.asu
toni@acpe.asu.edu

Numerous scholarships of $1,000 to graduating high school seniors, high school graduates who haven't attended college, or GED recipients. High school seniors or graduates must rank in upper fourth of class (GED recipients must have at least a score of 300), have at least a 1200 on SAT or 27 on ACT, enroll at least half-time in an accredited Arizona college or university, and be Arizona residents. This is a federally funded program. Application for this award varies; some high school counselors nominate students without an application process. High school graduates and GED recipients must contact above address after January 1. Deadline: March 31.

601.
Arizona Communications Workers of America–Local 7019
Joseph P. Hennessy Scholarship Fund
Central Arizona Labor Council, AFL-CIO
5818 North 7th Street, #202
Phoenix, AZ 85014

4 scholarships of $250 to students who are members of this local union and their dependents. Deadline: varies.

602.
Arizona Society of Professional Engineers
24 West Camelback, Suite M
Phoenix, AZ 85013
(602) 264-4871

Scholarships of $1,000 to high school seniors planning to enter into an engineering curriculum. Some scholarships may require attendance at a certain college or university. For Arizona residents only. Deadline: late November; local chapters may vary.

603.
Arizona State Scholarships
Financial Aid Office
Mesa Community College
Mesa, AZ 85202
or
Financial Aid Office
Arizona State University
Tempe, AZ 85287

Each of three state universities and fifteen state community colleges offers the full range of federal-aid programs, as well as the Arizona State Student Incentive Grant Program and private donor scholarships. Contact college's financial aid office. Deadline: varies.

604.
Arizona State Board of Regents
Regents Scholarships
2020 North Central Avenue, Suite 230
Phoenix, AZ 85004
(602) 229-2500
(602) 229-2955 Fax
http://www.acpe.asu.edu
toni@acpe.asu.edu

Scholarships of tuition and fees to Native American graduating high school seniors and undergraduate students. Must be in the top 5 to 10 percent of class. Must be Arizona residents and attend an Arizona public college or university. Awards are renewable with satisfactory academic progress. Contact financial aid office at individual schools. Deadline: varies by school.

605.
Arkansas Department of Higher Education
Governor's Scholars Program
1220 West Third Street
Little Rock, AR 72201
(501) 371-1441
http://www.state.ar.us/kidz/college.html

Scholarships of $2,000 to high school seniors. Must have at least a 3.6 GPA on a 4.0 scale (based on seven semesters) and have scored at least a 26 on ACT. Based on academic achievement, class rank, leadership in high school and community. Must attend a private or public accredited institution in Arkansas and be an Arkansas resident. Deadline: March 1.

606.
Arkansas Department of Higher Education
Robert C. Byrd Scholarships
1220 West Third Street
Little Rock, AR 72201
(800) 443-6030
(501) 371-1441
(501) 682-1258 Fax
http://www.state.ar.us/kidz/college.html

Numerous scholarships of $1,000 to graduating high school seniors, high school graduates who haven't attended college, or GED recipients. High school seniors or graduates must rank in upper fourth of class (GED recipients must have at least a score of 300), have at least a 1200 on SAT or 27 on ACT, enroll at least half-time in an accredited Arkansas college or university, and be Arkansas residents. This is a federally funded program. Application for this award varies; some high school counselors nominate students without an application process. High school graduates and GED recipients must contact above address after January 1. Deadline: March 31.

607.
Arkansas Department of Higher Education
Student Assistance Grant Program
1220 West Third Street
Little Rock, AK 72201
(501) 371-1441
http://www.state.ar.us/kidz/college.html

Grants ranging from $100 to $800 to high school seniors or full-time undergraduate students. Based on academic achievement and financial need. Must be Arkansas residents. Contact high school counselor or school's financial aid office. Deadline: varies.

608.
Arkansas Electronic, Electrical, Salaried, Machine and Furniture Workers, International Union–District 11
Director
8803 Oman Road
Little Rock, AR 72209
(501) 565-3488

3 scholarships of $500 to high school seniors who are dependents of members. Must be Arkansas residents. Write to above address or contact the district union. Deadline: varies.

609.
Arkansas Rural Endowment Fund Loan Program
P.O. Box 750
Little Rock, AR 72203

Loans are granted annually to students from rural areas and smaller towns in Arkansas. Loans may be applied toward a four-year college program or toward professions or trades such as nursing, mechanics, welding, etc. Repayment must begin as soon as the student completes training and is employed; in no case later than six months after graduation. Training must be taken in an Arkansas school, college, or university, if the course is available (typical exceptions are dentistry and veterinary medicine).

610.
Arkansas Society of Professional Engineers
Uerling & Associates
P.O. Box 3290
Fort Smith, AR 72913
(501) 782-0474

Scholarships of $1,000 for high school seniors planning to enter into an engineering curriculum. Some scholarships may require attendance at a certain college or university. For Arkansas residents only. Deadline: late November; local chapters may vary.

611.
Armco Foundation
Armco Scholarships/George M. Verity Memorial Scholarships
300 Interpace Parkway
Parsippany, NJ 07054-0324

1 scholarship of $3,000 (Verity) and varying numbers of $2,000 scholarships to students who are children of eligible employees of Armco or a wholly owned subsidiary. Employee must have been working on a full-time basis for at least one year at the time of the award. Students must be in top 50 percent of class and plan to major in insurance. Two of the $2,000 scholarships are designated for African, Hispanic, or Native American high school seniors. Renewable. Deadline: November 30.

612.

Armed Forces Communications & Electronics Assoc. Educational Foundation
General Emmett Paige Scholarships
Administrator of Scholarships and Awards
4400 Fair Lakes Court
Fairfax, VA 22033-3899
(800) 336-4583, ext. 6149
(703) 631-6149
http://www.afcea.com/

Scholarships of $1,000 to rising undergraduate freshmen and sophomores enrolled in an accredited U.S. four-year college or university. Must be majoring in electrical engineering, electronics, mathematics, physics, photometry, communications engineering or technology, computer science or technology, or information management systems. Based on academic achievement, character, leadership abilities, dedication, and financial need. Deadline: May 1.

613.

Armed Forces Communications & Electronics Assoc. Educational Foundation
General John S. Wickham Scholarships
Administrator of Scholarships and Awards
4400 Fair Lakes Court
Fairfax, VA 22033-3899
(800) 336-4583, ext. 6149
(703) 631-6149
http://www.afcea.com/

Scholarships of $2,000 to rising undergraduate juniors and seniors enrolled in an accredited U.S. four-year college or university. Must be majoring in electrical engineering, electronics, mathematics, physics, photometry, communications engineering or technology, computer science or technology, or information management systems. Based on academic achievement, character, leadership abilities, dedication, and financial need. Deadline: May 1.

614.

Armenian General Benevolent Union Loan Program
Scholarship Committee
585 Saddle River Road
Saddle Brook, NJ 07662
(210) 797-7600

Grants and interest-free loans averaging $1,000 to students of Armenian descent only. Must be enrolled in an accredited U.S. college, university, or trade school. Based on financial need, good character, academic achievement, and involvement in the Armenian community. Request applications between January 1 and March 15. Deadline: April 30.

615.

Armenian Relief Society of North America, Inc.
Scholarship Committee
47 Nichols Avenue
Watertown, MA 02172
(617) 923-2132

Grants ranging from $400 to $1,000 to undergraduates of Armenian descent who are attending an accredited four-year institution. Must submit a high school transcript, college

transcript, and three letters of recommendation. Based on academic merit and financial need. Deadline: April 1.

616.

Armenian Relief Society Scholarships
Regional Executive
Armenian Relief Society of North America, Inc.
47 Nichols Avenue
Watertown, MA 02172
(617) 923-2132

25 scholarships of varying amounts to undergraduate students. Must be U.S. citizens attending an accredited four-year institution, or non-U.S. citizens or permanent-resident undergraduates attending an accredited four-year institution in North America or abroad. Must be of Armenian ancestry. Deadline: April 1.

617.

Armenian Students' Association of America, Inc.
GPO Box 1557
New York, NY 10116
(212) 965-2350

50 scholarships, 10 fellowships, and 20 loans ranging from $500 to $1,500 to undergraduate or graduate students of Armenian descent who have completed at least one year of college. Good for all areas of study. Must have at least a 2.5 GPA. Renewable. Number of awards each year may vary with availability of funds. Deadline: April, July, and December.

618.

Armstrong World Industries, Inc.
Achievement Scholarships
P.O. Box 3001
Lancaster, PA 17694
(717) 397-0611

2 scholarships of $2,000 to African American students who have been selected National Merit Scholars. Renewable up to four years. Based on PSAT and SAT scores. Obtain applications between August 1 and December 1. Deadline: varies.

619.

Armstrong World Industries, Inc.
Merit Scholarships
P.O. Box 3001
Lancaster, PA 17694
(717) 397-0611

10 scholarships of $2,000 to children of present or retired employees. Students must have been selected National Merit Scholars. Based on PSAT and SAT scores. Obtain applications between August 1 and December 1. Deadline: varies.

620.

Army Aviation Association of America (AAAA) Scholarship Foundation, Inc.
AAAA Scholarships
49 Richmondville Avenue
Westport, CT 06880-2000
(203) 226-8184

Numerous scholarships, totaling $100,000, to students who are members of AAAA or spouses, siblings, or dependents of a member. When requesting an application, list the name of the AAAA member. Deadline: May 1.

621.
Army College Fund
Contact local Army Recruiter for latest information.

The Army offers opportunities to earn considerable financial assistance to further your education while on active duty and after you complete your Army service. This option is made available through the Montgomery GI Bill plus the Army College Fund, as well as other in-service tuition assistance programs.

622.
Army Emergency Relief Funds
National Headquarters
Department of Army, Education Department
200 Stovall Street
Alexandria, VA 22332-0600
(202) 325-0184

Limited scholarships, based on Free Application for Federal Student Aid (FAFSA). Offers Guaranteed Student Loans by private lenders of up to $2,625 for first two undergraduate college years and $4,000 for each remaining undergraduate year. Apply after mid-October. Deadline: March 1.

623.
Army ROTC Enrichment Scholarships
College Army ROTC
Gold Quest Center
P.O. Box 1688
Ellicot City, MD 21043-0010

1 scholarship of $7,500 or 80 percent of tuition for graduating high school seniors planning to attend a Historically Black College hosting an Army ROTC Program. Must major in engineering, nursing, or physical science and must complete at least one semester of a major Indo-European or Asian language. Apply after April 1 of junior year. Deadline: October 15.

624.
Army ROTC Nursing Opportunities
Gold Quest Center
P.O. Box 3279
Warminster, PA 18974-0128
(800) USA-ROTC

Varying numbers of scholarships providing financial assistance for four, three, and two years of assistance toward an undergraduate degree at an NLN-accredited school of nursing. Scholarships pay for most tuition cost, required educational fees, book allowance, supplies, equipment, and an allowance of up to $1,000 a year. Students must be at least seventeen years of age before the scholarship is used and under twenty-five years of age when eligible for appointment as an officer. There is a military obligation. Request applications between April 1

and October 15. Contact above address or Chief Nurse, U.S. Army ROTC Cadet Command, Attn: ATCC-N, Fort Monroe, VA 23651-5000, (800) USA-ROTC. Deadline: varies.

625.
Army ROTC Scholarship
U.S. Department of Defense
Washington Headquarters Services
Directorate for Information and Operation
1215 Jefferson Davis Highway, Suite 1204
Arlington, VA 22207-4302

Scholarships of up to $12,000 per year, plus a tax-free monthly stipend of at least $150 for up to ten months for each year the scholarship is in affect. Students may pursue any course of study leading to a bachelor's degree and may engage in any activity that doesn't interfere with ROTC requirements. Army ROTC provides college-trained officers for the Regular Army, Army Research, and Army National Guard and is offered at more than 600 colleges and universities throughout the U.S. To qualify, applicants must be U.S. citizens; be seventeen by October 1 and under twenty-one on June 30 of the application year; must not reach their twenty-fifth birthday by June 30 of the year they graduate from college and receive commission (age extensions may be granted if the student has prior military service); must be high school graduates or have a GED; must not have any moral obligation or personal conviction that will prevent them from supporting and defending the Constitution of the U.S. against all enemies, foreign and domestic, and be able to conscientiously bear arms; must be able to explain any record of arrest and/or civil conviction; and must receive at least an 850 SAT or 19 ACT score. Applicants must agree to serve in the military for at least eight years, accept a commission, and attend the six-week ROTC Advanced Camp, and agree to repay the U.S. government for all financial aid received if they don't fulfill the terms of the contract. There are three- and four-year scholarships available.

626.
Arrow, Inc.
1000 Connecticut Avenue, N.W., Suite 401
Washington, DC 20036

Founded in 1949, Arrow, Inc., is dedicated to the advancement of the American Indian. Limited financial aid available to students who plan to work assisting Native Americans after college graduation. Deadline: varies.

627.
Arthur and Doreen Parrett Scholarship Trust Fund
c/o U.S. Bank of Washington
Trust Department
P.O. Box 720
Seattle, WA 98111
(206) 344-3685

15 scholarships of up to $1,000 to high school seniors or undergraduate students planning a career in engineering, science, medicine, or dentistry. Must be Washington State residents. Awards are good at any U.S. accredited undergraduate college or university. Deadline: July 31.

628.

Arthur Anderson & Co., SC Foundation
Internship Program
69 West Washington Street
Chicago, IL 60602-3002
(312) 580-0069

300 ten- to twelve-week internship programs in the summer and winter providing from $500 to $625 per week open to undergraduate juniors and seniors with at least twelve hours of accounting course work. "Provides the same experiences and situations that a new hire would have during their first year." Internships may be in Atlanta, Boston, Charlotte, Chicago, Cincinnati, Cleveland, Columbus, Dallas, Denver, Detroit, Hartford, Houston, Indianapolis, Kansas City, Los Angeles, Memphis, Miami, Milwaukee, Minneapolis/St. Paul, Nashville, New Jersey, New Orleans, New York, Omaha, Philadelphia, Pittsburgh, St. Louis, San Francisco, Seattle, Stamford, Tampa, and Washington, DC. Deadline: February 15 (summer); October 31 (winter).

629.

Arthur and Hazel Auer Scholarship Fund
Nobel County Community Foundation
209 North State Road 9
Albion, IN 46701

Numerous scholarships of varying amounts to graduating high school seniors at East Nobel High School. Contact counselor. Deadline: varies from mid-March to early April.

630.

Arthur C. and Florence S. Boehmer Scholarship Fund
228 West Pine Street
Lodi, CA 95240
(209) 369-2781

53 scholarships ranging from $500 to $700 to high school graduates in the Lodi, California, unified school district. May enter any California two- or four-year undergraduate, graduate, or professional school (though Stanford University is preferred). Preference given to students entering medical fields. Request applications after March 1. Deadline: June 15.

631.

Arthur C. and Lucia S. Palmer Foundation, Inc.
471 Pennsylvania Avenue
Waverly, NY 14892
(607) 565-4603

25 scholarships ranging from $300 to $5,000 to high school seniors and high school graduates who are residents of Waverly, New York, or Sayre or Athens, Pennsylvania. Deadline: May 1.

632.

Art of the Northeast USA Exhibition
Silvermine Guild Arts Center
1037 Silvermine Road
New Canaan, CT 06840
(203) 966-5617

Awards ranging from $4,000 to $8,000 to artists for paintings, drawings, mixed media, and sculptures. Artists must reside in Connecticut, Maine, Massachusetts, New Hampshire, New Jersey, New York, Pennsylvania, Rhode Island, or Vermont. There is an entry fee of $20/slide. The exhibition run varies, generally May through June. For prospectus, send a #10 self-addressed, stamped envelope to above address. Deadline: late March.

633.

Arts Recognition and Talent Search ("ARTS")
National Foundation for Advancement in the Arts
Dance Component
800 Brickell Avenue
Miami, FL 33131
(305) 377-1140

Scholarships of varying amounts totaling $3,000,000 and internships to students who will be seventeen or eighteen years old as of December 1 of the program year. Applicants may be high school seniors, high school graduates who haven't enrolled in college, or college freshmen. The dance component has categories in ballet, jazz, modern, tap, other cultural dance forms, and choreography. Applicants may enter more than one category, but must submit separate applications and videotapes for each. Applicants in dance performance must include a videotape of up to two minutes of technique and two minutes of a solo performance. Applicants in choreography must submit videotapes of no more than ten minutes in length. The tape may present more than one piece. Dances may be either group or solo performances. Specifications for performance content, apparel, and the preparation of the videotapes, plus additional rules, can be found by consulting the ARTS Reference Manual for the current year. There is a $25 registration fee. Deadline: June 1 (early registration); October 1 (regular).

634.

Arts Recognition and Talent Search ("ARTS")
National Foundation for Advancement in the Arts
Jazz Music Component
800 Brickell Avenue
Miami, FL 33131
(305) 377-1140

Scholarships of varying amounts totaling $3,000,000 and internships to students who will be seventeen or eighteen years old as of December 1 of the program year. Applicants may be high school seniors, high school graduates who haven't enrolled in college, or college freshmen. The jazz music component has categories in jazz instrumentalist, jazz drummer, and jazz vocalist. Evaluations are based on applicant's ability in improvisation, tone production, technique, diction, rhythm, intonation, interpretation, and phrasing. For guidelines, consult the ARTS manual. There is a $25 registration fee. Deadline: June 1 (early registration); October 1 (regular).

635.

Arts Recognition and Talent Search ("ARTS")
National Foundation for Advancement in the Arts
Music Component
800 Brickell Avenue
Miami, FL 33131
(305) 377-1140

Scholarships of varying amounts totaling $3,000,000 and internships to students who will be seventeen or eighteen years old as of December 1 of the program year. Applicants may be high school seniors, high school graduates who haven't enrolled in college, or college freshmen. This component has the following categories: classical voice, keyboard instruments, orchestral instruments (each instrument is considered a separate category), popular (piano or vocal), and composition. Applicants must submit an audiotape of selected performances. Audiotapes must not be less than twenty minutes or more than thirty minutes in length, except for classical voice (fifteen-minute tape is acceptable) and composition (no maximum length). A score must be submitted for each work. For guidelines, consult the ARTS manual. There is a $25 registration fee. Deadline: June 1 (early registration); October 1 (regular).

636.
Arts Recognition and Talent Search ("ARTS")
National Foundation for Advancement in the Arts
Theater Component
800 Brickell Avenue
Miami, FL 33131
(305) 377-1140

Scholarships of varying amounts totaling $3,000,000 and internships to students who will be seventeen or eighteen years old as of December 1 of the program year. Applicants may be high school seniors, high school graduates who haven't enrolled in college, or college freshmen. Acting (spoken acting and musical theater acting) is the only category in the theater component. Applicants must submit a videotape with two short, contrasting solo pieces (of not more than two minutes). One piece must be from a work published before 1910 and the other from a play or musical published after 1910. Props can be no more than a stool, two chairs, and a table. Selections will be judged on the basis of the actor's ability to demonstrate concentration, control of material, flexibility, and versatility of voice, movement, and expression. There is a $25 registration fee. Deadline: June 1 (early registration); October 1 (regular).

637.
Arts Recognition and Talent Search ("ARTS")
National Foundation for Advancement in the Arts
Visual Arts Component
800 Brickell Avenue
Miami, FL 33131
(305) 377-1140

Scholarships of varying amounts totaling $3,000,000 and internships to students who will be seventeen or eighteen years old as of December 1 of the program year. Applicants may be high school seniors, high school graduates who haven't enrolled in college, or college freshmen. This component has categories in ceramics, costume design, drawing, film, graphic design, jewelry making, painting, photography, prints, sculpture, textile and fiber design, theater set design, video, and "other." Film and video are considered two separate categories. For entry guidelines, consult the ARTS manual. There is a $25 registration fee. Deadline: June 1 (early registration); October 1 (regular).

638.
Arts Recognition and Talent Search ("ARTS")
National Foundation for Advancement in the Arts
Writing Component
800 Brickell Avenue
Miami, FL 33131
(305) 377-1140

Scholarships of varying amounts totaling $3,000,000 and internships to students who will be seventeen or eighteen years old as of December 1 of the program year. Applicants may be high school seniors, high school graduates who haven't enrolled in college, or college freshmen. This component has categories in poetry (from seven to fifteen poems), short stories, a section of a novel, a script for a dramatic performance in any medium, and expository prose (autobiographical material, discussion, or argument written from a personal point of view). Term papers are not eligible. There is a $25 registration fee. Deadline: June 1 (early registration); October 1 (regular).

639.
Asbury Park Press Scholarships for Minority Students
Editorial Department
Asbury Park Press
3601 Highway 66
P.O. Box 1550
Neptune, NJ 07754

2 scholarships of $1,500 available, one to a graduating high school student from Monmouth County, New Jersey, the other to a student from Ocean County, New Jersey, who will enter college seeking a career in the field of communications (including reporting, broadcasting, marketing, and advertising). Renewable for a total of four years with continued satisfactory progress. Deadline: varies.

640.
Asian American Journalists Association
1765 Sutter Street, Room 1000
San Francisco, CA 94115
(415) 346-2051

Scholarships ranging from $250 to $2,500 to Asian American students pursuing a career in broadcast or print journalism. Must be high school seniors, undergraduates, or graduate students. Based on academic achievement, community involvement, demonstrated journalistic ability, and a desire to pursue a news media career. Deadline: mid-April.

641.
ASM International
ASM Undergraduate Scholarships
Attn: Scholarship Committee
9639 Kinsman Road
Materials Park, OH 44073-0002
(440) 338-5151
(440) 338-4634 Fax
http://www.asm-intl.org/

Up to 34 scholarships of $500 awarded to students interested in metallurgy/materials science. Deadline: June 15.

642.

ASM International
N. J. Grant
Attn: Scholarship Committee
9639 Kinsman Road
Materials Park, OH 44073-0002
(440) 338-5151
(440) 338-4634 Fax
http://www.asm-intl.org/

1 full tuition scholarship awarded, based on financial need. Must be at least a sophomore college student enrolled in the department of materials science or materials engineering in metallurgy. Based on interest in metallurgy, academic achievement, letters of recommendation, and potential for success in metallurgy. Must be citizen of U.S., Canada, or Mexico and attending an institution in any of these countries. Renewable for one more year. Deadline: June 15.

643.

ASM International
Outstanding Scholar Awards
Attn: Scholarship Committee
9639 Kinsman Road
Materials Park, OH 44073-0002
(440) 338-5151
(440) 338-4634 Fax
http://www.asm-intl.org/

Up to 3 awards of $2,000 to undergraduate students interested in metallurgy, materials science, ceramic engineering, materials engineering, or metallurgical engineering. Must maintain at least a 3.0 GPA. Other restrictions may apply. Deadline: none.

644.

Aspen Center for Environmental Studies
Education Coordinator
Summer Naturalist Intern Program
P.O. Box 8777
Aspen, CO 81612
(970) 925-5756

11 twelve- to thirteen-week summer internships in Aspen, Colorado, providing $100/week plus housing to undergraduate juniors, seniors, recent graduates, and graduate students. The Center prefers students majoring in the natural sciences, environmental studies, or related fields. Knowledge of Rocky Mountain flora and fauna is not required. First Aid Certification is required. Interns lead interpretive walks, learn animal rehabilitation, and teach children about the environment. Deadline: March 1.

645.

Aspen Music School
Music Association of Aspen Scholarships
P.O. Box AA
Aspen, CO 81611
(303) 925-3254

800 partial- to full-tuition scholarships and fellowships to aspiring young and professional musicians. Must enroll in the nine-week summer session at the Aspen Music School for undergraduate or graduate credit. Between June and August, write above address. Between September and May, write to Aspen Music School, Office of Student Service, 250 W. 25th, 10th Floor East, New York, NY 10019. Deadline: varies.

646.

Assistant Directors Training Program
Attn: Administrator
15503 Ventura Boulevard
Encino, CA 91436-3140
(818) 556-6853

8 to 20 internships lasting 400 working days and providing a salary ranging from $400 to $500 per week to undergraduate students and recent college graduates. Interns work with cast and crew members and learn about set operations and the collective bargaining agreements of over twenty entertainment guilds and unions. Interns who complete the program are then placed on the Southern California Area Qualification List for employment as assistant directors. Relevant work experience may be used in place of college work. International applicants are eligible. Deadline: December 16.

647.

Associated General Contractors Education and
Research Foundation
G. E. Byrne Memorial Scholarships
Director of Programs
1957 E Street, N.W.
Washington, DC 20006
(202) 393-2040
(202) 347-4004 Fax

Numerous scholarships of $1,500 to high school seniors and undergraduate freshmen, sophomores, or juniors (attending or planning to attend either two- or four-year institutions). Applicants must be full-time students majoring in either construction or civil engineering and preparing for a career in construction. Must be U.S. citizens or permanent residents. Based on academic record, recommendation, and career goals. Renewable up to $6,000 over a four-year period. Deadline: November 15.

648.

Associated General Contractors Education and
Research Foundation
James L. Allhands Essay Competition
Director of Programs
1957 E Street, N.W.
Washington, DC 20006
(202) 393-2040
(202) 347-4004 Fax

Prizes of $500, $300, and $200 to full-time undergraduate seniors in an accredited four-year program. Based on essays relating to construction and /or general contracting. Should be general management-related rather than technical. Essay theme varies from year to year. Deadline: December 1.

649.

Associated General Contractors Education and
Research Foundation
Robert B. McEachern
Director of Programs
1957 E Street, N.W.
Washington, DC 20006
(202) 393-2040
(202) 347-4004 Fax

Numerous scholarships of $1,500 for high school seniors and undergraduate freshmen, sophomores, or juniors (attending or planning to attend either two- or four-year institutions). Must be full-time students majoring in either construction or civil engineering and preparing for a career in construction. Must be U.S. citizens or permanent residents. Based on academic record, recommendations, extracurricular activities, employment background, career goals, and financial need. Renewable for up to $6,000 over a four-year period. Deadline: November 15.

650.
Associated General Contractors Education and Research Foundation
Stanley F. Pepper Memorial Scholarships
Director of Programs
1957 E Street, N.W.
Washington, DC 20006
(202) 393-2040
(202) 347-4004 Fax

Numerous scholarships of $1,500 to high school seniors and undergraduate freshmen, sophomores, or juniors attending or planning to attend either two- or four-year college or university. Must be full-time students majoring in either construction or civil engineering and preparing for a career in construction. Must be U.S. citizens or permanent residents. Based on academic record, recommendations, extracurricular activities, employment background, career goals, and financial need. Renewable to $6,000 over a four-year period. Deadline: November 15.

651.
Associated General Contractors Education and Research Foundation
Undergraduate Scholarship Program
Director of Programs
1957 E Street, N.W.
Washington, DC 20006
(202) 393-2040
(202) 347-4004 Fax

50 to 60 scholarships of $1,500 to high school seniors, college freshmen, sophomores, and juniors enrolled in or planning to enroll in a two- or four-year college or university. Must be full-time students majoring in either construction or civil engineering and preparing for a career in construction. Must be U.S. citizens or permanent residents. Based on GPA, extracurricular activities, employment experience, financial need, and desire for a construction career. Request applications in writing or by fax after September 1. Renewable for up to four years. Deadline: November 15.

652.
Associated Male Choruses of America Scholarship Fund
c/o Bill Bates
Cedar Glen, Box 106
Dunsford, Ontario KOM ILO
Canada
(507) 354-5893

Scholarships of $300 to deserving male undergraduate vocal students to further their training while in college. Write for more details. Deadline: February 1.

653.
Associated Press Television–Radio Association of California/Nevada
APTRA–CLETE Roberts Memorial Journalism Scholarship Awards
Rachel Ambrose
Associated Press
221 South Figueroa Street, #300
Los Angeles, CA 90012
(213) 626-1200

Scholarships of $1,500 to undergraduate or graduate students pursuing careers in broadcast journalism. Must be attending an accredited institution in California or Nevada. Other restrictions may apply. Deadline: December 16.

654.
Associated Universities, Inc.
AUI Trustee Scholarships
1400 16th Street, N.W., Suite 730
Washington, DC 20036-2001
(202) 462-1676

Numerous $1,700 scholarships to graduating high school seniors who are dependents of members or employees. Based on SAT scores and extracurricular activities. Renewable for up to four years. Deadline: second week in November.

655.
Associated Western Universities, Inc.
AWU–DOE Student Research Fellowships
4190 South Highland Drive, Suite 211
Salt Lake City, UT 84124
(801) 278-0799

Various research fellowships for undergraduates and graduates to work during the summer on nonthesis research in an energy-related science or engineering project. Preference given to students with at least two years of college. Must have at least a 3.0 GPA on a 4.0 scale. Contact above address to obtain a list of the participating laboratories. Deadline: March 1; February 1 (for laboratories requiring security clearance).

656.
Association for American Indian Affairs, Inc.
95 Madison Avenue
New York, NY 10016

Numerous scholarships ranging from $50 to $300 to Native American Indians. Based on financial need; limited by the availability of funds. Sequoyah fellowships of $1,500 are available to Native Americans at the graduate level. Deadline: varies.

657.
Association for Education and Rehabilitation of the Blind and Visually Impaired Telesensory Scholarship
4600 Duke Street, Suite 430
P.O. Box 22397
Alexandria, VA 22314
(703) 823-9690

1 scholarship of $1,000 to a legally blind college student who is pursuing a career that will service blind and

visually impaired individuals. Must be a member of the association. Based on application, certificate of visual status, and career goals. Deadline: April 15.

658.

Association for Education and Rehabilitation of the Blind and Visually Impaired William and Dorothy Ferrell Scholarships
4600 Duke Street, Suite 430
P.O. Box 22397
Alexandria, VA 22314
(703) 823-9690

Numerous scholarships of varying amounts to legally blind college students pursuing careers that will service blind and visually impaired individuals. Based on application, certificate of visual status, and career goals. Deadline: April 15.

659.

Association for Education in Journalism & Mass Communication
Correspondence Fund Scholarships
c/o College of Journalism
University of South Carolina
Columbia, SC 29208
(803) 777-2005

8 to 15 scholarships of up to $2,000 to children of print or broadcast journalists who are foreign correspondents for U.S. media. For undergraduate, graduate, or postgraduate study at any accredited U.S. institution. Must submit two letters of recommendation, a résumé, and a brief letter outlining research interests and career plans. Renewable. Deadline: April 30.

660.

Association for Education in Journalism & Mass Communication
Foreign Correspondents Scholarship
c/o College of Journalism
University of South Carolina
Columbia, SC 29208
(803) 777-2005

1 scholarship of up to $2,000 to son or daughter of present or former foreign correspondent who wishes to study journalism at a U.S. college or university. Preference given to children of U.S. citizens working or who have worked for a bona fide news organization in the print or broadcast media as a foreign correspondent, in either American and non-American news organizations. Children of non-U.S. citizens working as foreign correspondents for American news organizations will also be considered. Deadline: April 15.

661.

Association for Education in Journalism & Mass Communication
Summer Journalism Internship for Minorities
c/o College of Journalism
University of South Carolina
Columbia, SC 29208
(803) 777-2005

Ten-week summer internship for minority students completing their junior year of college. For students interested in mass communications, providing information

on working conditions, job and graduate school opportunities, and experience. Most internships are in New York City area, though companies nationwide participate. Program offers $200 per week plus payment of tuition for the course. Room and board are not provided. Deadline: December 3.

662.

Association for Information and Image Management
AIIM–Chicago Scholarships
Scholarship Administrator
821 North Stratford Road
Arlington Heights, IL 60004
(312) 443-4339

Varying numbers of scholarships ranging from $300 to $1,000 to undergraduate students pursuing careers in records management. Must be residents of Cook County, Illinois. Other restrictions may apply. Deadline: January 31.

663.

Association for International Practical Training (AIPT)
10 Corporate Center, Suite 250
10400 Little Patuxent Parkway
Columbia, MD 21044-3510
(410) 997-3069

Periodically offers scholarships of varying amounts to undergraduate students majoring in a hotel/motel management, hospitality, and/or tourism-related major. Funds are subject to fluctuations in finances. For more information, contact above address. Other restrictions may apply. Deadline: varies.

664.

Association for International Practical Training (AIPT) Hospitality/Tourism Exchange
10400 Little Patuxent Parkway, Suite 250
Columbia, MD 21044-3510
(410) 997-3069
(410) 997-5186 Fax

610 twelve-week to eighteen-month internships providing living expenses of approximately $300 per week to undergraduate juniors, seniors, recent college graduates (under age thirty-five), and international students. The program arranges for students to work abroad in the hospitality and tourism industries. U.S. students are placed in organizations abroad, from Taj International Hotels and Japan Airlines to Queen's Flores Corporation and Pastries of Denmark. Though locations vary each year, the most common destinations for U.S. students have been in Switzerland and Germany. Deadline: rolling.

665.

Association for Library & Information Science Education
Research Grants
Attn: Research Committee
4101 Lake Boone Trail, Suite 201
Raleigh, NC 27607
(919) 787-5181

Varying numbers of grants totaling $2,500 to undergraduate, graduate, and doctoral students in library and information science. Must not be used for doctoral dissertation research. Selection based on previous work and quality of proposed research. Other restrictions may apply. Deadline: October 1.

666.
Association for Retarded Citizens–Brazoria County Scholarships
Brazoria County Association for Retarded Citizens, Inc.
Highway 20004 and 332
Lake Jackson, TX 77566

2 scholarships of $150 to graduating high school seniors from Brazoria County area. Must be used toward degree in special education. Contact high school counselor or above address. Deadline: varies.

667.
Association for Women in Science
Internships
1522 K Street, N.W., Suite 820
Washington, DC 20005
(202) 408-0742
(202) 408-8321 Fax

10 three-month internships per year providing a stipend. Internships are part-time and full-time year-round. Open to high school graduates, undergraduates, graduates, persons reentering the work force, and retired persons. Interest in science, science education, and women's issues required. Promotes participation of women in science through programs, publications, seminars, lobbying, and coordination of fifty local chapters nationwide. Interns assist with national and chapter-based programs, write articles for magazines, develop and monitor chapter activities, provide services for national members, participate in press and public relations activities, conduct research on status of women in sciences, and develop original projects to aid women and girls in the sciences. Office experience and strong writing skills preferred. Submit letter outlining interests and résumé. Interviews are conducted by phone. Deadline: open.

668.
Association of Certified Fraud Examiners
Attn: Education Committee
716 West Avenue
Austin, TX 78701
(800) 245-3321
(512) 478-9070
(512) 478-9297 Fax

Numerous scholarships of $500 to undergraduate and graduate students who are majoring in accounting or criminal justice. Based on academic achievement, recommendation letters (one letter must be from a Certified Fraud Examiner or a local CFE Chapter), and a 250-word essay explaining why the applicant deserves to win the scholarship and how awareness of fraud will affect his/her professional career development. Students who don't know a Certified Fraud Examiner will be referred to a representative of the nearest CFE Chapter. Deadline: April 1.

669.
Association of Former Agents of the U.S. Secret Service
J. Clifford Dietrich Scholarships
P.O. Box 848
Annandale, VA 22003
(703) 256-0188

Several scholarships ranging from $500 to $1,500 to undergraduate sophomores, juniors, seniors, or graduate students working toward an advanced degree in law enforcement or police administration. Must be U.S. citizens. Selection based on academic achievement, demonstrated leadership abilities, transcript, biography, recommendation letters, essay, and financial need. Deadline: April 15.

670.
Association of Former Agents of the U.S. Secret Service
Julie Y. Cross Scholarship
P.O. Box 848
Annandale, VA 22003
(703) 256-0188

1 scholarship of $1,000 to an undergraduate sophomore, junior, senior, or graduate student working toward an advanced degree in law enforcement or police administration. Must be a U.S. citizen. Selection based on academic achievement, demonstrated leadership abilities, transcript, biography, recommendation letters, essay, and financial need. Deadline: April 15.

671.
Association of Former Agents of the U.S. Secret Service
Law Enforcement Career Scholarships
P.O. Box 848
Annandale, VA 22003
(703) 256-0188

2 to 4 scholarships ranging from $500 to $1,500 to undergraduate sophomores, juniors, seniors, or graduate students majoring in law enforcement or police administration. Must be U.S. citizens. Must be enrolled at an accredited four-year institution and have an interest in leadership. Selection is based on academic achievement, demonstrated leadership abilities, transcript, autobiography, recommendation letters, essay, and financial need. Other restrictions may apply. Deadline: April 15.

672.
Association of Former Agents of the U.S. Secret Service
Manly Scholarship
P.O. Box 848
Annandale, VA 22003
(703) 256-0188

1 scholarship ranging from $500 to $1,500 to an undergraduate sophomore, junior, senior, or graduate student majoring in law enforcement or police administration. Must be a U.S. citizen. Must be enrolled at an accredited four-year institution and have an interest in leadership. Selection is based on academic achievement, demonstrated leadership abilities, transcript, autobiography,

recommendation letters, essay, and financial need. Other restrictions may apply. Deadline: April 15.

673.

Association of Graduates of the U.S. Air Force Academy

Vice-President
USAF Academy
Colorado Springs, CO 80840-6600
(800) 433-9266

7 scholarships ranging from $600 to $1,200 to students who are children of graduates of the U.S. Air Force Academy. Must be full-time students at an accredited institution and have at least a 3.0 GPA on a 4.0 scale for the six most recent full-time academic semesters. Based on academic record, SAT/ACT scores, career goals, extracurricular activities, employment history, and financial need. Deadline: March 1.

674.

Association of Official Analytical Chemists
Harvey W. Wiley Scholarship Awards

481 North Frederick Avenue, Suite 500
Gaithersburg, MD 20877-2417
(301) 924-7077
(301) 924-7089 Fax
http://www.aoac.org/
aoac@aoac.org

Scholarships of $500 per year for two years to students majoring in chemistry, microbiology, food technology, pharmaceutical sciences, forensic sciences, and related subjects. Students should apply during their sophomore year, have at least a B average, and have financial need. Prefer students planning on graduate study or proposing to work in an area of public health or agriculture. Awards are used during junior or senior year. Students majoring in pre-med, pre-dent, nursing, etc., are not eligible. Deadline: May 1.

675.

Association of Oilwell Servicing Contractors

6060 North Central Expressway, Suite 428
Dallas, TX 75206
(214) 692-0771

15 to 16 scholarships of $1,000 to employees and their dependents. Must be employees or legal dependents of an employee of a member company. Based on academic record, SAT/ACT scores, essay, and financial need. Obtain application through the member company. Deadline: April 15.

676.

Association of Old Crows

AOC Building
1000 North Payne Street
Washington, DC 22314-1686
(703) 549-1600

Scholarships of varying amounts to undergraduate students and noncommissioned officers (NCOs) returning for an undergraduate degree majoring in engineering, mathematics, or computer science. Some chapters provide a network for summer employment. Contact local chapter or college's

financial aid office or send a self-addressed, stamped envelope to above address to obtain the address of the nearest chapter. Deadline: varies by chapter.

677.

Association of Operating Room Nurses
AORN Scholarship Program

Credentialing Division
10170 East Mississippi Avenue
Denver, CO 80231
(303) 755-6300

Awards of tuition and fees for nursing undergraduate, graduate, or doctoral students. Must be active or associate AORN members for at least one consecutive year prior to deadline date. For full- or part-time study. Deadline: May 1.

678.

Association of Records Managers & Administrators (ARMA)
ARMA International Scholarships

Citizen's Scholarship Foundation of America
P.O. Box 297
St. Peter, MN 56082

2 scholarships of $1,500 and 2 scholarships of $750 to undergraduate students who are majoring in business administration or records/information management. Applicants must be attending Austin Community College (TX), Central Michigan University (MI), Chemeketa Community College (OR), Chippewa Valley Technical College (WI), Detroit College of Business (MI), Emporia State University (KS), Miami Dade Community College (FL), Mount Royal College (Alberta), North Harris County College (TX), Orange County Community College (NY), Pima Community College (AZ), Phoenix College (AZ), Ryerson Polytechnic Institute (Ontario), San Antonio College (TX), Southwest Missouri State University (MO), Stark Technical College (OH), State University of New York at Albany (NY), Tulsa Junior College (OK), University of Akron (OH), University of Cincinnati–Clermont College (OH), University of North Dakota (ND), Western Michigan University (MI), or Western Washington University (WA). Selection based on academic achievement, school and community involvement, work experience, goals, recommendation letters, and financial need. Request applications between January 15 and March 15. Deadline: April 1.

679.

Association of State Dam Safety Officials
ASDSO Scholarship

P.O. Box 55270
Lexington, KY 40555
(606) 257-5146

1 scholarship of $2,500 to a student who has excelled and is excelling in engineering and plans to pursue a career in dam safety engineering. Deadline: varies.

680.

Association of the Sons of Poland Grant Program

591 Summit Avenue, Room 702
Jersey City, NJ 07306
(201) 653-1163

Scholarships ranging from $50 to $500 to high school seniors for all areas of study. Must have been an association member for at least two years and must be insured by the association. Must plan to attend an accredited institution in September of the year of graduation from high school. Deadline: varies.

681.
Association of Trial Lawyers of America
Intern Coordinator
1050 31st Street, N.W.
Washington, DC 20007
(800) 424-2725

15 ten-week summer internships providing $8.50/hour in Washington, D.C. Open to high school seniors, undergraduates, recent graduates, and graduate students. Rolling submission of applications, but those submitted before May 1 are given preference. Internships are in Public Affairs, Legal Affairs, Education, State Relations, Communications, Meetings and Services, and *Trial* magazine. Some departments give interns experience in legal research. ATLA is located in the heart of Georgetown.

682.
Association of Women's Health, Obstetric, and Neonatal Nurses
Professional Development Division
700 N.W. 14th Street
Washington, DC 20005
(202) 662-1600

Fellowships ranging from $1,500 to $3,000 to undergraduate or graduate students in nursing or a related field, or a nurse practitioner or midwifery certificate. Must be full or associate members for at least one year prior to applying. Contact after January 1 and include your membership number. Formerly known as NAACOG. Other restrictions may apply. Deadline: April 5.

683.
Asthma Athlete Scholarship Program
Schering-Plough Corporation
Attn: Maureen Tice
2000 Galloping Hill Road
Kenilworth, NJ 07033
(908) 298-4000

5 scholarships of $1,000 and 10 scholarships of $3,500 to graduating high school seniors who have participated on high school athletic teams, with at least one year on a high school varsity team. Based on athletic achievement, extracurricular activities, and grade point average. Request applications after September 1. Deadline: March 31.

684.
Astrae Foundation
Margot Karle Scholarship
666 Broadway, Room 610
New York, NY 10012
(212) 857-2849

1 scholarship of $500 to a female undergraduate student at one of the schools in the New York City University system who demonstrates political and/or social commitment in actively fighting for gay and lesbian civil rights, much like Margot Karle did as an attorney. Deadline: November 30; May 31.

685.
AT&T Undergraduate Scholarships
Foundation for Public Relations Research and Education
310 Madison Avenue, #1710
New York, NY 10017
(212) 370-9353

Numerous scholarships of $2,000 to undergraduate sophomores, juniors, and seniors majoring in public relations studies. Must have at least a 3.0 GPA. May attend any U.S. college or university. Deadline: March 31.

686.
A. T. Brightwell School, Inc.
254 Oakland Avenue
Athens, GA 30606
(404) 543-6450

18 grants ranging from $1,500 to $6,000 to unmarried or divorced students under thirty years of age who live in the Maxeys, Georgia, area. Applicants' parents must also live in Maxeys area during the time of the scholarship. Deadline: varies.

687.
Augustus and Kathleen Barrows Memorial and Trust Fund
271 South Union Street
Burlington, VT 05401
(802) 863-4531

27 scholarships ranging from $200 to $400 to female high school seniors or undergraduate students who are residents of Vermont and under the age of twenty-five. Contact for more details. Deadline: varies.

688.
August W. Klingelhoefer Needy Student Assistance Fund
c/o Fredericksburg ISD
300 B West Main Street
Fredericksburg, TX 78624

12 scholarships of $400 to residents of Gillespie County, Texas. Contact: Fredericksburg High School principal. Selection based on academic achievement, extracurricular activities, and financial need. Deadline: May 1.

689.
The Aurora Foundation
111 West Downer Place, Suite 312
Aurora, IL 60506-5136
(708) 896-7800

Over $134,000 in scholarships to graduating high school seniors and undergraduate students. Must be residents of the Aurora, Illinois, area. Based on financial need. Deadline: varies.

690.
Austin Community Foundation
P.O. Box 5159
Austin, TX 78763
(512) 472-4483

Numerous scholarships to students who are residents of Travis County, Texas. Students should be high school seniors or higher. Write an introductory letter briefly describing educational and financial situation. Deadline: varies.

691.
Automotive Hall of Fame
Educational Funds
P.O. Box 1727
Midland, MI 48641-1727
(517) 631-5760

16 to 23 scholarships ranging from $250 to $2,000 to undergraduate freshmen and sophomores attending a two- or four-year institution. Must be pursuing an automotive career. Based on academic record and career goals. Deadline: June 30.

692.
Automotive Hall of Fame
Larry H. Averill Memorial Scholarships
P.O. Box 1727
Midland, MI 48641-1727
(517) 631-5760

3 scholarships ranging from $500 to $1,500 to undergraduate juniors and seniors attending a two- or four-year institution. Must be pursuing an automotive career regardless of major. Based on academic achievement, career goals, and financial need. Deadline: June 30.

693.
Automotive Hall of Fame
Universal Underwriters Scholarships
P.O. Box 1727
Midland, MI 48641-1727
(517) 631-5760

4 scholarships of $2,000 to full-time undergraduate juniors and seniors attending one of Northwood Institute's campuses. Must be pursuing an automotive career. Based on academic record and career goals. Deadline: June 30.

694.
Automotive Hall of Fame
Walter W. Stillman Scholarships
P.O. Box 1727
Midland, MI 48641-1727
(517) 631-5760

Up to 3 scholarships ranging from $666 to $2,000 to undergraduate juniors or seniors attending one of Northwood Institute's campuses. Must be pursuing an automotive career. Based on academic achievement, career goals, and financial need. Preference given to students from New Jersey. Deadline: June 30.

695.
Auxiliary of the American Association of Osteopathic Specialists
Jarri Miller Memorial Scholarships
804-10 Main Street, #D
Forest Park, GA 30050
(404) 363-8263

Scholarships ranging from $750 to $1,000 to students accepted to or enrolled in an accredited nursing program,

with a minimum 3.0 GPA. Applicants must have an AAOS auxiliary member as a sponsor before requesting information. Deadline: May 31.

696.
Auxiliary to Sons of Union Veterans of the Civil War
616 West Summit
Alliance, OH 44601
(216) 823-6919

1 scholarship of $300 to a high school junior or senior who plans to major in history and is a descendant of a Civil War veteran. Deadline: June 1.

697.
Aviation Boatswains Mates Association Scholarship
Cdr. Robert Gillen, USN, Retired
Chairperson, Scholarship Committee
13775 Paseo Cevera
San Diego, CA 92129
(written inquiries only)

1 scholarship of varying amount to the son or daughter of an active or deceased member in good standing of the association for the preceding two years prior to application (decreased member must have been in good standing at the time of death). All active, retired, discharged, or separated Aviation Boatswains Mates are eligible for membership. Based on academic record, character, motivation, potential for success and financial need. Deadline: June 1.

698.
Aviation Distributors and Manufacturers Association (ADMA)
ADMA Scholarship Program
1900 Arch Street
Philadelphia, PA 19103
(215) 564-3484

2 scholarships of $750 to graduating high school seniors or high school graduates who haven't attended college. One goes to an individual working toward a flight major and one to an individual working toward an aviation management career. Applicants must contact an ADMA member company for an application. Deadline: April 1.

699.
Aviation Insurance Association Scholarship
AIA Screening Committee
c/o Aviation Department
Broward Community College
7200 Hollywood Boulevard
Pembroke Pines, FL 33024

1 scholarship of $1,000 to an undergraduate or graduate student with at least thirty college credits (fifteen hours must be in aviation). Student must have at least a 2.5 GPA on a 4.0 scale or higher, be a U.S. citizen, and submit a letter describing activities, indicating leadership qualities, goals, and reason for applying, and at least one letter of recommendation from an employer or instructor. A transcript must accompany the application. Deadline: September 30.

700.
Aviation Maintenance Educational Fund
P.O. Box 2826
Redmond, WA 98073

14 to 18 scholarships of $250 and $500 to full-time students at a Certified Aviation Maintenance Technician School. Based on academic grades and comments from the schools. Only available to students already in the program. Deadline: varies.

701.
Aviation–Space Writers Association
AWA Writing Awards
17 South High Street, #1200
Columbus, OH 43215
(614) 221-1900

21 scholarships ranging from $100 to $500 to undergraduate and graduate students who have published articles on aviation and/or space during the year preceding the award. Awards are given in the following categories: newspapers, magazines, television, radio, books, and still photography. Deadline: February 14.

702.
Avon Products, Inc.
Attn: Personnel Manager
9 West 57th Street
New York, NY 10019
(800) 858-8000

8 scholarships of $3,000 (renewable up to three years) to sons or daughters of current employees of Avon Products with a minimum of six months of continuous service. Must be used at an accredited U.S. college or university. Deadline: November 1.

703.
Avon Products, Inc.
Avon–Kansas City, MO, School District, and
**   Center School District Scholarship**
83rd and College
Kansas City, MO 64141
(816) 361-8480

1 scholarship of $2,000 (renewable up to three years) to a high school senior who has been a resident of Kansas City, Missouri, school district or the Center school district since the second semester of high school junior year. Must be in the top 50 percent of class. Based on academic record, SAT scores, and financial need. May be used at any accredited U.S. college or university. Deadline: November 1.

704.
Avon Products, Inc.
Avon–Newark, Delaware, Scholarship Program
9 West 57th Street
New York, NY 10019
(212) 546-6729

1 scholarship of $3,000 (renewable up to three years) to a high school senior in the Newark school district in Delaware since the second semester of high school junior year. Applicants must be in the upper third of their class. Based on academic record, SAT, and financial need. May be

used at any accredited U.S. institutions. Deadline: November 1.

705.
Avon Products, Inc.
Avon–Pasadena Scholarship Program
2940 East Foothill Boulevard
Pasadena, CA 91121

1 scholarship of $3,000 (renewable up to three years) to a high school senior who has been a resident of the Pasadena Unified school district during his or her entire senior year. Must be in the top third of class. Based on academic record, SAT scores, and financial need. Deadline: November 1.

706.
Avon Products, Inc.
Avon–Seffern Scholarship Program
9 West 57th Street
New York, NY 10019

1 scholarship of $1,000 (renewable up to three years) to a high school senior who has been a resident of the Ramapo Central school district in the Suffern, New York, area since the second semester of his or her junior year. Must be in the top 10 percent of class. Based on academic record, SAT scores, and financial need. Deadline: November 2.

707.
Avon Products, Inc.
Avon–Springdale Scholarship Program
175 Progress Place
Springdale, OH 45246

1 scholarship of $2,000 (renewable up to three years) to a high school senior who has been a resident of the Princeton school district since the second semester of his or her junior year. Must be in the top 10 percent of class. Based on academic record, SAT scores, and financial need. Deadline: November 15.

708.
Awards of Excellence
Attn: Key Account Representative
Pacific Coca-Cola, in cooperation with Thriftway Stores
1150 124th Avenue, N.E.
P.O. Box C-93346
Bellevue, WA 98009-3346

16 scholarships of $1,500 to high school seniors and graduates in the Yakima and Wenatchee, Washington, area. Must be planning to attend Pacific Lutheran University, Seattle Pacific University, Seattle University, University of Washington, or Western Washington University. Must have at least a 3.5 GPA. Apply directly to admissions director at the chosen school. Deadline: April 20.

709.
Awards to Student Composers
Broadcast Music, Inc.
320 West 57th Street
New York, NY 10019
(212) 586-2000

Awards ranging from $500 to $2,500 to graduating high school seniors, high school graduates, undergraduates, and graduate students who are young composers. Must be citizens or permanent residents of the Western Hemisphere (North, Central and South American and Caribbean nations) who were under twenty-six on December 31 of the award year. Awarded to encourage young composers in the creation of concert music. Deadline: early February.

710.
A. W. Bodine Sunkist Memorial Scholarships
Attn: Scholarship Officer
P.O. Box 7888
Van Nuys, CA 91409
(818) 379-7510

Varying numbers of scholarships of $1,000 to high school seniors and current undergraduates who come from an agricultural background. Must be planning to major in agriculture. Must be residents of California. Applicants must maintain at least a 2.7 GPA and demonstrate financial need. Deadline: March 1.

711.
Ayn Rand Institute
Essay Competition
P.O. Box 6099
Inglewood, CA 90312
(310) 306-9232

20 third-prize awards of $100, 10 second-prize awards of $200, and 1 first-prize award of $1,000 in an essay competition open to all high school freshmen and sophomores. Assigned topics vary annually. Essays must be at least double-spaced, typewritten, and not longer than three pages. Information on contest is mailed to high schools each fall. If high school has not provided the information by November, contact the Institute directly. Deadline: March 30.

712.
Ayn Rand Institute
Essay Competition
P.O. Box 6099
Inglewood, CA 90312
(310) 306-9232

Contest for most outstanding essays on Ayn Rand's novel *The Fountainhead*, with ten $500 third prizes, five $1,000 second prizes, and one $5,000 first prize. Open to all high school juniors and seniors interested in English, literature, philosophy, and psychology. Information on contest is mailed to high schools each fall. If your high school has not provided the information by November, contact the institute directly. Deadline: April 15.

713.
Backer Spielvogel Bates
Internship Program
The Chrysler Building
405 Lexington Avenue
New York, NY 10174
(212) 297-7000

5 to 10 ten- to twelve-week summer, fall, and spring internships with no compensation, though there is a possible bonus stipend. Open to undergraduate juniors, seniors, and graduate students with exceptional writing

skills and at least a 3.0 GPA. Students are placed in Strategic Planning, which researches consumer attitudes and trends. This company developed both "Soup Is Good Food" (Campbell's Soup) and "Get Out of the Old, Get into the Cold" (Miller Genuine Draft). It is the world's fifth largest advertising agency. Deadline: late May (summer); late August (fall); late December (spring).

714.
Bagby Foundation for the Musical Arts
501 Fifth Avenue
New York, NY 10017
(212) 986-6094

4 scholarship grants ranging from $400 to $2,840 to high school seniors or graduates or undergraduate or graduate students. Must be majoring in music. Based on talent and financial need. Deadline: varies.

715.
Bailey Foundation
c/o State Street Bank and Trust Company
225 Franklin
Boston, MA 02110

1 scholarship covering tuition, books, supplies, and lab fees for four years and 4 scholarships of $1,250 to high school seniors or graduates of Amesbury, Massachusetts, high schools. Must be residents of Amesbury, Massachusetts. Deadline: varies.

716.
Bailey Foundation
Mercer Silas Bailey Memorial Scholarships
Administrator
P.O. Box 1276
Clinton, SC 29325-1276
(803) 833-1910

Scholarships of up to $3,000 (paid over a four-year period) to graduating high school seniors attending an accredited Laurens and Clinton High School in South Carolina and accepted to an accredited U.S. college or university. Submit the application to either the guidance counselor or to the foundation. Deadline: varies.

717.
Baker Boyer National Bank
P.O. Box 1796
Walla Walla, WA 99362
(509) 525-2000 ext. 314

Approximately 60 scholarships ranging from $1,000 to $1,800 to high school seniors or graduates who are residents of Walla Walla County. Must have at least a 2.0 GPA and be unmarried. May be used at any two- or four-year institution. Deadline: April 1.

718.
Bakery and Confectionery Workers International Union Scholarships
Scholarship Program
10401 Connecticut Avenue
Kensington, MD 20895-3961

8 scholarships of $4,000 to high school seniors who are dependents of members. Unrestricted fields of study.

Request application from local union office or above
address. Deadline: December 31 (endorsed application);
March 31 (all other materials).

719.
Baking School Scholarships
American Institute of Baking Scholarships
Allied Trades of the Banking Industry, Inc.
Attn: Secretary-Treasurer
Anderson Clayton/Humko Products, Inc.
P.O. Box 398
Memphis, TN 38101
(800) 238-5765
(901) 766-2441

14 scholarships of $1,000 and 1 scholarship of $750 to high
school seniors or undergraduate students who are pursuing
a career in the baking industry. Contact above address or
the American Institute of Baking, Registrar, 1213 Bakers
Way, Manhattan, KS 66502. Deadline: varies.

720.
Baking School Scholarships
William Hood Dunwoody Industry Institute
  Scholarships & Loans
Allied Trades of the Baking Industry, Inc.
Attn: Secretary-Treasurer
Anderson Clayton/Humko Products, Inc.
P.O. Box 398
Memphis, TN 38101
(800) 238-5765
(901) 766-2441

Numerous scholarships of varying amounts and a loan
plan to high school seniors and undergraduate students
pursuing a career in baking. Contact: Coordinator of
Admissions, 818 Wayzata Boulevard, Minneapolis, MN
55403. Deadline: varies.

721.
Balso Foundation
493 West Main Street
Cheshire, CT 06410
(203) 272-5361

Numerous scholarships ranging from $500 to $1,500 to
high school seniors or college undergraduates. Must be
residents of Cheshire, Connecticut, or surrounding areas.
Deadline: April 10.

722.
Baltimore Opera Annual Vocal Competition
527 North Charles Street
Baltimore, MD 21201-5030
(301) 727-0592

A vocal competition with prizes ranging from $1,000 to
$10,000 to undergraduate, graduate, and professional
singers. The top three finalists also receive contract support
for an engagement with the Baltimore Opera Company.
Must be between the ages of twenty and thirty-five.
Awards must be used to further voice training, learn
operatic roles, develop dramatic ability, and/or perfect
foreign languages. Deadline: May 1.

723.
Bankboston
Andover Service Men's Memorial Scholarship
  Fund
Attn: Trust Officer
P.O. Box 422TA
7 New England Executive Park
Burlington, MA 01803
(617) 434-2200

Numerous scholarships of varying amounts to students
who are children of Andover, Massachusetts, veterans who
served in the Armed Forces or Merchant Marines from
September 15, 1940, through July 25, 1947. If no students
fitting these qualifications apply, other students may be
considered. Award is good for any field of study. Deadline:
April-May.

724.
Bankboston
Betsey W. Taber Scholarship Fund
Attn: Trust Officer
P.O. Box 422TA
7 New England Executive Park
Burlington, MA 01803
(617) 434-2200

50 scholarships from $250 and up to graduating high
school seniors attending school in the greater New Bedford,
Massachusetts, area. Award is good for any field of study.
Renewable. Deadline: April.

725.
Bankboston
Carrie May Lyman Scholarship Fund
Attn: Trust Officer
P.O. Box 422TA
7 New England Executive Park
Burlington, MA 01803
(617) 434-2200

Numerous scholarships of varying amounts to graduating
high school seniors at Methuen High School in
Massachusetts. Award is good for any field of study.
Deadline: April-May.

726.
Bankboston
Charles H. Gray Scholarship Fund/Alice E.
  Rounds Memorial Scholarship Fund
Attn: Trust Officer
P.O. Box 422TA
7 New England Executive Park
Burlington, MA 01803
(617) 434-2200

Numerous scholarships of varying amounts to graduating
high school seniors at Dedham High School or Stoughton
High Schools in Massachusetts. Award is good for any field
of study. Renewable for all four undergraduate college
years. Deadline: April-May.

727.
Bankboston
Frank D. Hamilton Educational Fund
Attn: Trust Officer
P.O. Box 422TA
7 New England Executive Park
Burlington, MA 01803
(617) 434-2200

15 scholarships of varying amounts to graduating high school seniors from the Chester, Massachusetts, school system. Award is good for any field of study. Deadline: April-May.

728.
Bankboston
Lieutenant Stafford Leighton Brown Memorial Scholarship Fund
Attn: Trust Officer
P.O. Box 422TA
7 New England Executive Park
Burlington, MA 01803
(617) 434-2200

Varying numbers of scholarships of varying amounts to graduating male high school seniors in Newton, Massachusetts. Award is good for any field of study, though preference is given to theology majors. Deadline: May.

729.
Bankboston
Margaret Fenwick Hinchcliffe Scholarship Fund
Attn: Trust Officer
P.O. Box 422TA
7 New England Executive Park
Burlington, MA 01803
(617) 434-2200

Numerous scholarships of varying amounts to graduating high school seniors at Andover High School or Framingham High School in Massachusetts. Award is good for any field of study. Deadline: April-May.

730.
Bankboston
Nash Scholarship Fund
Attn: Trust Office
P.O. Box 422TA
7 New England Executive Park
Burlington, MA 01803
(617) 434-2200

Numerous scholarships of varying amounts to graduating high school seniors at Weymouth North High School or Weymouth South High School in Massachusetts. Recommendations by high school principals and superintendents are made to the trustees. Award is good for any field of study. Renewable for all four undergraduate college years. Deadline: April-May.

731.
Bankboston
Olga E. Blasser Scholarship Fund
Bernadette Stephan
P.O. Box 422TA
7 New England Executive Park
Burlington, MA 01803
(617) 434-2200

Numerous scholarships of $500 to female graduating high school seniors at Brookline High School. Must be planning to study economics or political science. Applications available through Brookline High School counselors. Deadline: April-May.

732.
Bankboston
Orr Foundation Scholarships
Attn: Trust Officer
P.O. Box 422TA
7 New England Executive Park
Burlington, MA 01803
(617) 434-2200

Numerous scholarships of varying amounts to graduating male high school seniors at the two high schools in Newton, Massachusetts. Award is good for any field of study. Renewable for all four undergraduate college years. Deadline: April.

733.
Bankboston
Steinhard Student Scholarship Fund
Attn: Trust Officer
P.O. Box 422TA
7 New England Executive Park
Burlington, MA 01803
(617) 434-2200

Numerous scholarships of varying amounts to graduating high school seniors from Chester High School in Chester, Massachusetts. Award is good for any field of study. Deadline: April-May.

734.
Bankboston
Warren Scholarship Fund
Attn: Trust Officer
P.O. Box 422TA
7 New England Executive Park
Burlington, MA 01803
(617) 434-2200

Numerous scholarships of varying amounts to graduating female high school seniors at the two high schools in Newton, Massachusetts. Award is good for any field of study. Deadline: April.

735.
Bankboston Connecticut
Charles F. Mitchell Scholarships
81 West Main Street
Waterbury, CT 06702
(203) 574-7114

3 scholarships of $1,000 per semester and 4 scholarships of $750 per semester to male high school seniors and

graduates. Must have been Waterbury, Connecticut, residents for the last five years. Deadline: May 25.

736.
Bank of America Achievement Awards Program
Corporate Community Development
Department #3246
P.O. Box 37000
San Francisco, CA 94137

320 cash awards, totaling $250,000, to high school seniors who are California residents. Student Achievement Award winners are chosen by their high schools and then compete for plaques. The plaque winners compete for regional awards. Students should contact high school counselors or above address. Deadline: varies.

737.
Bank of New England, N.A.
James W. Colgan Fund Loans
P.O. Box 9003
Springfield, MA 01101
(413) 787-8562

Various $2,000 loans to undergraduate students who are Massachusetts residents. Must be under thirty years of age and attending a two- or four-year institution or vocational/technical school. Repayment begins upon graduation. Deadline: June 1.

738.
Bank One, Marion Indiana, N.A.
Peter G. Flinn Scholarships
Trust Department
P.O. Box 68
Marion, IN 46952
(317) 668-3525

5 scholarships of varying amounts for high school seniors who have been residents of Grant County, Indiana, for at least one year. Apply between March and April. Deadline: April 1.

739.
Bank Street College of Education
Fellowship Program
Center for Children and Technology
610 West 112th Street
New York, NY 10025

Fellowships of varying amounts to minority undergraduate students. Must be enrolled in a two-year associate program in educational technology research and development. Must be New York State residents. Other restrictions may apply.

740.
Baptist General Convention of Texas
Scholarships for Ministerial Students
Attn: Jerry Dawson
333 North Washington Street, Suite 371
Dallas, TX 75246-1798
(214) 828-5100

Scholarships of varying amounts to high school seniors or undergraduate students who are pursuing a ministerial

career. Must be active members of a Baptist Church, have at least a 2.0 GPA on a 4.0 scale, have been Texas residents for at least twelve months, and must attend a Texas Baptist institution or an approved Baptist institution. Based on recommendations, academic record, and interview. Renewable.

741.
Baptist General Convention of Texas
Texas Black Scholarships
Black Church Relations Sector
333 North Washington Street, Suite 371
Dallas, TX 75246-1798
(214) 828-5131

Scholarships of $800 to African American high school seniors or graduates who are active members of a Baptist church. Must have at least a 2.0 GPA on a 4.0 scale and have been Texas residents for at least twelve months. Must attend a Texas Baptist college or university or an approved Baptist college or university. No restrictions on intended field of study. Based on recommendations, academic record, and interview. Renewable. Deadline: varies.

742.
Baptist General Convention of Texas
Texas Hispanic Scholarships
Attn: Jimmy Garcia
333 North Washington Street, Suite 371
Dallas, TX 75246-1798
(214) 828-5100

Awards of varying amounts to deserving Hispanic graduating high school seniors and undergraduate students who are unable to finance a college education. Awards are made to help finance training at a Baptist college or university. Must meet certain academic criteria. Deadline: none specified.

743.
Baptist Life Association Scholarship Grants
Scholarship Committee
Baptist Life Association
8555 Main Street
Buffalo, New York 14221-7494

Scholarships of $500 to students whose families are insured members of Baptist Life and who are applying to an accredited college or university. Write to above address for application instructions. Deadline: January 15.

744.
Barker Foundation, Inc.
P.O. Box 328
Nashua, NH 03061
(603) 889-1763

Numerous scholarships, totaling $42,000, to high school seniors or undergraduate college students. Must be New Hampshire residents. Deadline: varies.

745.
Barnum Festival Jenny Lind Contest
Barnum Festival, Inc.
1070 Main Street
Bridgeport, CT 06604
(203) 367-8495

1 scholarship of $2,000 and an all-expense-paid concert tour in Sweden to a female vocalist who is a high school graduate, undergraduate, or graduate student. Must be between the ages of twenty and twenty-seven by May 1 of the application year. Must have received formal voice training but not be professional. Auditions are required in operatic, classical, or light classical (not "pop"). Based on appearance, singing potential, personality, poise, delivery, and voice quality. Concerts are held in June. Deadline: May 15.

746.
Barwood Productions
Internship Coordinator
330 West 58th Street, Suite 301
New York, NY 10019
(212) 765-7191
(212) 765-6988 Fax

4 internships providing daily transportation reimbursement and free lunch are open to undergraduates, recent college graduates, and graduate students. International students may apply. Barwood Productions is Barbra Streisand's official production company. Interns work in the Development department. Internships last from twelve weeks to six months. Barwood produces Streisand and non-Streisand projects, including made-for-television movies. Deadline: rolling.

747.
Baumberger Endowment
7701 Broadway, Suite 206
P.O. Box 6067
San Antonio, TX 78209
(210) 822-8915

Numerous scholarships of varying amounts for high school seniors who are residents of Bexar County, Texas, and who will be attending a college or university in Texas. Contact the foundation office or high school counselor for guidelines and application forms. Request applications before January 31. Deadline: February 15, may vary.

748.
Bay De Noc Indian Culture Association
Charles Mouz Pamp Memorial Fund
2112 South Hill Road
Gladstone, MI 49837

Financial assistance to high school seniors, graduates, or undergraduates who are Native Americans. Must live in Michigan or Wisconsin, regardless of tribal affiliation. Deadline: varies.

749.
Baywatch Production Company
Internship Coordinator
Bonann Productions
5433 Beethoven Street
Los Angeles, CA 90066
(310) 302-9199 Fax

3 to 4 internships lasting from sixteen to twenty-two weeks (no compensation) are open to high school seniors, high school graduates, undergraduates, recent college graduates, and graduate students. International students may apply. Interns work as production assistants and runners in production, casting, and postproduction (editing). Must submit a résumé, cover letter, and recommendation. Deadline: rolling.

750.
B. C. & Addie Brookshire Kleberg County
Charitable Foundation
c/o Texas Commerce Bank-Trust Department
P.O. Drawer 749
Corpus Christi, TX 78403
(512) 883-3621

Numerous scholarships of varying amounts to students who are residents of Kleberg County, Texas. Students should be high school seniors or higher. Students should write an introductory letter briefly describing their educational and financial situation. Contact high school counselor or above address. Deadline: varies.

751.
Beatrice National Foundation
Beatrice National Merit Scholarships
Two North LaSalle Street
Chicago, IL 60602
(312) 558-4000

10 scholarships ranging from $1,000 to $2,500 to graduating high school seniors who are children of an employee of the Beatrice Company. The scholarship program is administered by the National Merit Corporation. Based on the PSAT, which is taken in the junior year. Renewable for four years. No application.

752.
Bechtel Corporation
College Recruiting
P.O. Box 193965
San Francisco, CA 94119-3965
(415) 768-1234

30 to 60 internships providing a salary ranging from $300 to $500 per week to undergraduate sophomores, juniors, seniors, and graduate students who are majoring in architecture, architectural engineering, construction, or related areas. Student interns are accepted into the areas of civil engineering, automation technology/CADD production, engineering technologies, mechanical engineering, research and development, financing services, accounting, and human resources. Internships range from four to twelve weeks. Deadline: rolling.

753.

Belle Smith Scholarship Fund
1119 Pacific Avenue
Tacoma, WA 98901

13 scholarships, totaling $14,000, to high school seniors from high schools in Purdy Washington. Contact high school counselor or above address. Deadline: varies.

754.

Bement Educational Grants Committee
Bement Undergraduate Grants
37 Chestnut Street
Springfield, MA 01103
(413) 737-4786

50 to 60 scholarship grants ranging from $200 to $750 to undergraduate students. Must be active Episcopalians in the diocese of western Massachusetts. Based on academic achievement and financial need. Request applications after November 1. Deadline: February 1.

755.

Bend Foundation
Attn: Trustee
416 Northeast Greenwood
Bend, OR 97701

18 scholarships, totaling $25,500, to high school seniors or graduates or undergraduate students. Must be residents of Deschutes County, Oregon. Deadline: none.

756.

Benjamin and Fedora Wolf Foundation
Attn: Administrator
Park Towne Place-North Building 1205
Parkway at 22nd Street
Philadelphia, PA 19130
(215) 787-6079

196 scholarships ranging from $250 to $625 to graduating high school seniors. Must be residents of Philadelphia, Pennsylvania, area. Students must be recommended by high school principal or counselor. Deadline: June 1.

757.

Berkeley Minor and Susan Fontaine Minor
   Foundation
c/o John L. Ray
1210 One Valley Square
Charleston, WV 25301

18 scholarship grants ranging from $1,000 to $6,800 to high school seniors or graduates or undergraduate students. Must be West Virginia residents and attend certain colleges. Deadline: varies.

758.

Berkeley Repertory Theater
Internship Coordinator
2025 Addison Street
Berkeley, CA 94704

6 to 12 ten-month internships providing a salary of $75 per week plus housing is open to undergraduates, recent college graduates, and graduate students. Interns live in an apartment building within a mile of the theater. Interns work in artistic administration and company management, costumes, development and marketing/PR, lighting, literary/dramaturgy, properties, scenic construction, scenic painting, sound, or stage management. Interns attend seminars on press and public relations, costuming, casting, and personnel management. Deadline: March 15 (state management); April 15 (all other departments).

759.

Bermuda Biological Station for Research
Ferry Reach, St. George's
GE01, Bermuda
(809) 297-1880
(809) 297-1839 Fax
(WSP): hlitz@bbsr.edu
(GIP): fred@bbsr.edu

10 to 20 summer Work-Study Programs (WSP) providing free room and board. The programs allow students to conduct research in the areas of the atmosphere and marine life, from coral reef ecology to oceanography. Research topics have included global climate change, use of optics for sea study, ocean carbon, nitrogen cycling, coral symbiosis, effects of oil spills and smokestack emissions on tropical environments, and larval marine animals. WSP is open to undergraduate juniors, seniors, and recent college graduates. Students obtain free scuba diving lessons and access to a sixteen-foot boat for marine data collection. Open to both U.S. citizens and international students. The WSP is a sixteen-week program offered in the summer, fall, and winter. Deadline, WSP: February 1 (summer); June 1 (fall); and October 1 (winter).

760.

Bernard Daly Educational Fund
c/o Lynch, Spencer
P.O. Box 351
Lakeview, OR 97630
(503) 947-2196

49 scholarships, totaling $93,000, to high school seniors or graduates or undergraduate students. Must be residents of Lake County, Oregon. Must attend a public Oregon college, university, or technical school. Renewable. Deadline: April 15.

761.

Bernice A. B. Keyes Trust
c/o Puget Sound National Bank, Trust Division
P.O. Box 11500, MS 8262
Tacoma, WA 98411-5052
(206) 593-3832

35 scholarships of $1,500 to high school seniors or graduates and undergraduate college students. Must be Tacoma, Washington, area residents. Deadline: varies.

762.

Bernstein-Rein Advertising, Inc.
Internship Coordinator
4600 Madison, Suite 1500
Kansas City, MO 64112
(816) 756-0640
(816) 756-1753

7 ten-week internships providing a salary of $188 per week are open to undergraduate college seniors. International

students may apply. Interns work in account service, creative, public relations, and media. Interns work on group project and make a final presentation to the company's CEO, Robert Bernstein. Deadline: February 20.

763.
Bertelsmann Music Group
Alternative Marketing Program
Manager of Training and Development
1540 Broadway, 38th Floor
New York, NY 10036
(212) 930-4000
(212) 930-4862 Fax

30 ongoing internships running from six months to two and a half years and averaging twenty hours per week with a salary of $6/hour and $220/month for field expenses. Open to undergraduates, preferably sophomores and juniors, though freshmen and seniors are also chosen. Graduate students are eligible for the longer internships. Interns are chosen based on creativity, intellectual abilities, social abilities, passion for music, and experience in the music business. Deadline: none.

764.
Beryl Buck Institute for Education
Marin County American Revolution Bicentennial
Scholarship
Executive Director
18 Commercial Boulevard
Novato, CA 94949
(415) 883-0122

1 or more awards ranging from $500 to $2,000 to high school seniors or graduates or undergraduate college students. Must have been residents of Marin County, California, since September 1 of the year prior to the application. Good at any two- or four-year institution. Request applications after January 1. Deadline: March 31.

765.
Beta Sigma Phi
Dorothy and Walter Ross Memorial Scholarship
1800 West 91st Place
P.O. Box 8500
Kansas City, MO 64114-0500

1 scholarship of $1,000 to a member of BSP or a dependent who is a high school senior, high school graduate, or college student. Based on character, academic record, SAT, and recommendations. Deadline: February 1.

766.
Beta Theta Pi Fraternity
Founders Fund Scholarship–Leadership Awards
Scholarship Committee Chairman
208 East High Street
P.O. Box 6277
Oxford, OH 45056
(513) 523-7591

35 scholarships ranging from $750 to $1,500 to undergraduate or graduate student members of Beta Theta

Pi Fraternity. Based on service to Beta Theta Pi, academic achievement, potential for success, character, and financial need. Good at any four-year college or university. Deadline: April 15.

767.
Beta Theta Pi Fraternity
Seth R. Brooks and Corinne H. Brooks
Scholarship Fund Award
Scholarship Committee Chairman
208 East High Street
Oxford, OH 45056
(513) 523-7591

1 scholarship of varying amounts to an undergraduate dependent of a member of BTP. May be single or married. Based on extracurricular activities, goals, academic record, and financial need. Deadline: May 15.

768.
Beverly Hills Theatre Guild
Julie Harris Playwright Award Competition
2815 N. Beachwood Drive
Los Angeles, CA 90068
(213) 465-2703

Awards of $500 third prize, $1,000 second prize, and $5,000 first prize in an annual competition for full-length (ninety minutes) unpublished, unproduced plays written for the theater. Open to undergraduate, graduate, or professional writers. Musicals, one-act plays, adaptations, translations, and plays entered in other competitions are not eligible. Plays may be co-written. Open to U.S. citizens only. Deadline: November 1.

769.
B. F. and Rose H. Perkins Foundation
P.O. Box 1064
Sheridan, WY 82801
(307) 674-8871

5 scholarship grants ranging from $100 to $200 and 137 loans ranging from $500 to $3,150 to high school seniors or graduates of Sheridan County High School. Must be under twenty years of age. Must be residents of Wyoming. Based on financial need. Deadline: June 1.

770.
Black American Cinema Society
Filmmakers Grants Program
3617 Mont Clair Street
Los Angeles, CA 90018
(213) 737-3292

Grants of $1,500 to African American filmmakers who are undergraduate, graduate, or doctoral students or young professionals. Applications must be in the name of the person with primary creative responsibility. Only one project per grant cycle. Project must be in 16mm or 3/4-in. video. Must be U.S. citizens or legal residents. Deadline: January 15.

771.
Black & Veatch
Internship Coordinator
P.O. Box 8405
Kansas City, MO 64114
(913) 458-2000

10 to 40 summer internships lasting from ten to fourteen weeks, providing a salary ranging from $300 to $500 to undergraduate juniors and seniors who are majoring in computer science or engineering (chemical, civil, electrical, mechanical) and have at least a 2.75 GPA. Interns at the headquarters location work in environmental areas, federal and industrial areas, power, and B&V waste science. Interns at one of the regional offices in Alabama, Arizona, California, Colorado, Florida, Georgia, Illinois, Massachusetts, Maryland, Michigan, Missouri, Nevada, New York, North Carolina, Ohio, Oklahoma, Oregon, Pennsylvania, South Carolina, Texas, Virginia, or Washington work on local construction projects. Deadline: April 1.

772.
Blackfeet Tribal Education Grant
Blackfeet Tribal Education Department
P.O. Box 850
Browning, MT 59417

Financial assistance for undergraduate or graduate education to members of the Blackfeet Tribe. Based on academic record and financial need. Deadline: varies.

773.
Black Student Fund
3636 16th Street, Suite AG 23
Washington, DC 20010

The fund helps African American students enter and finance private secondary-school education. It also helps schools recruit minority teachers to diversify their staffs.

774.
Blackwelder Foundation
P.O. Box 1431
Lenoir, NC 28645
(704) 757-9469

10 scholarships ranging from $550 to $1,000 to high school seniors or undergraduate students. Must be residents of North Carolina. Preference given to Caldwell County, North Carolina. Deadline: July.

775.
Blaine House Scholars Program
State House Station #119
Augusta, ME 04333
(800) 228-3734 in-state
(207) 287-2183

400 interest-free loans of $1,500 to high school seniors, undergraduates, and teachers returning for another degree. Individuals may be in any field of study, but preference is given to education majors. Loans are awarded on a competitive basis based on academic achievement, relevance of field of study, etc. Must be Maine residents. Renewable. Deadline: April 1.

776.
Blanche and Thomas Hope Fund
c/o Third National Bank
P.O. Box 1270
Ashland, KY 41105
(606) 329-2900

100 scholarships ranging from $90 to $2,900 to graduating high school seniors. Must be residents of Boyd or Greenup counties, Kentucky, or Lawrence County, Ohio. Deadline: March 1.

777.
Blinded Veterans Association
Kathern F. Gruber Scholarships
477 H Street, N.W.
Washington, DC 20001
(202) 371-8880

8 scholarships of $1,500 to dependent children or spouses of a blinded veteran. Veteran need not be a member of the association, and blindness may be service or nonservice connected. Good at any accredited two- or four-year institution, business, secretarial, or vocational training school. Based on academic record, extracurricular activities, references, career goals, and essay. Deadline: May 1.

778.
Blind Service Association Scholarship Awards
22 W. Monroe, 11th Floor
Chicago, IL 60603-2501
(312) 236-0808

Numerous $2,500 scholarships to high school seniors or graduates or undergraduate college students. Must be legally blind residents of the metropolitan Chicago area who are enrolled in or accepted to a college or university. Award is to promote the independence of blind and visually impaired individuals. Based on certification of visual status, academic record, and recommendations. Deadline: mid-March, but may vary.

779.
Blue Mountain Area Foundation
Attn: Administrator
P.O. Box 603
Walla Walla, WA 99362
(509) 529-4371

21 scholarships totaling $13,201 to high school graduates from the Blue Mountain area, including Benton, Columbia, Franklin, Garfield, and Walla Walla counties in southeastern Washington, and Umatilla County in Oregon. Deadline: April 14 or June 1.

780.
Blues Heaven Foundation
Muddy Waters Scholarship
249 North Brand
Glendale, CA 91203
(818) 507-7613

1 scholarship of varying amount to an undergraduate or graduate student attending a Chicago-area institution and

majoring in African American studies, history, journalism, or a related field. Based on academic record and financial need.

781.

B. M. Woltman Foundation
Lutheran Church Synod
7900 U.S. 290 East
Austin, TX 78724
(512) 926-4272

47 scholarships ranging from $500 to $2,400 to high school seniors or undergraduate or graduate students who are pursuing a career in the Lutheran ministry or plan to teach in a Lutheran school. Must be Texas residents attending a Texas college or university. Deadline: before start of academic year.

782.

Bodenwein Fellowships
Editor and Publisher
The Day Publishing Company
47 Eugene O'Neill Drive
New London, CT 06320

Fellowships from September to June to minorities who live or attend college in New England or New York State. Recipients work as reporter, copyeditor, photographer, or graphics artist in the newsroom of *The Day* and will work with schools and community groups throughout southeastern Connecticut to stimulate interest in print journalism as a career among minority students. Fellowship pays $350 a week. Send a résumé and a short essay explaining why you should be chosen. Deadline: varies.

783.

Boeing
College Relations
P.O. Box 3707
MS 6H-PR
Seattle, WA 98124
(206) 237-3639

100 to 250 ten- to fourteen-week summer or six-month winter/summer or summer/fall internships providing $440 per week plus travel allowance and a $1,000 housing allowance to undergraduate juniors or seniors. Internships available in accounting, communications, computer science, engineering, information systems, marketing, public relations, and other related fields. Finalists are interviewed by phone. Deadline: rolling.

784.

Boettcher Foundation
1670 Broadway, Suite 330
Denver, CO 80202
(303) 831-1938

40 scholarships covering tuition, fees, and books, plus a stipend, are given to high school seniors who are Colorado residents. Must plan on attending a Colorado college or university. Must be in the upper 7 percent of class and have at least a 3.0 GPA. Contact high school counselor or Foundation. Deadline: February 15.

785.

Borrego Springs Educational Scholarships Committee
Attn: Chairperson
P.O. Box 59
Borrego Springs, CA 92004
(619) 767-5314

9 scholarships, totaling $10,350, to high school seniors or graduates from Borrego Springs High School. Contact high school counselor or committee. Deadline: varies.

786.

Bour Memorial Scholarship Trust
P.O. Box 28
Kansas City, MO 64141

28 scholarships of $1,000 to high school seniors or graduates from Lafayette County, Missouri. Must attend a Missouri college or university. Based on financial need. Contact: Boatman's Bank of Lexington, 1016 Main Street, Lexington, MO 64067. Deadline: April 15.

787.

Bowerman Foundation
825 East Park Street
Eugene, OR 97401

8 scholarships ranging from $500 to $1,270 to high school seniors or graduates. Must be residents of the Eugene, Oregon, area. Deadline: varies.

788.

**Bowfin Memorial Scholarship
Academic Scholarships**
Bowfin Memorial Scholarship Committee
Submarine Officers' Wives Club
Lockwood Hall
Pearl Harbor, HI 96860

Scholarships of varying amounts to students who are children of active or retired Submarine Force personnel who live in Hawaii or whose surviving parent lives in Hawaii. Student must be under twenty-three years of age when applying. Based on academic merit and financial need. Renewable with reapplication. Deadline: March 1.

789.

**Bowfin Memorial Scholarship
Continuing Education Scholarships**
Bowfin Memorial Scholarship Committee
Submarine Officers' Wives Club
Lockwood Hall
Pearl Harbor, HI 96860

Scholarships of varying amounts to active or retired Submarine Force personnel, their children, or the dependents of deceased Submarine Force personnel. Students must be returning to school after a period of interruption and now want to continue, retrain, or reenter the work force. Applicants must live in Hawaii at the time of application and must intend to live in Hawaii during the scholarship award year. Based on leadership, community involvement, motivation, career goals, and financial need. Renewable with reapplication. Deadline: March 1.

790.
Bowler & Associates
Internship Coordinator
1000 S.W. Broadway, Suite 1600
Portland, OR 97205
(503) 248-9468
(503) 274-7689 Fax

4 thirteen-week internships providing a salary of $80 per week to college seniors and recent college graduates with majors in communications, journalism, marketing, or public relations. Interns assist staff with account work, recommending strategies for clients, create media lists, produce press kits, draft press releases, and clip articles. Deadline: June 15 (summer); September 15 (fall); December 15 (winter); March 15 (spring).

791.
Boye Scholarship Trust
c/o Wells Fargo Bank
400 Capitol Mall
Sacramento, CA 95814
(916) 440-4342

3 scholarships ranging from $3,000 to $10,560 to high school seniors or graduates or undergraduate college students. Must be residents of Sacramento County, California. Preference given to students majoring in an agriculture-related area.

792.
Boynton Gillespie Memorial Fund
Heritage Federal Building
Sparta, IL 62286
(618) 443-4430

104 scholarships ranging from $475 to $500 to high school seniors or graduates. Must be Sparta, Illinois, area residents. Contact high school counselor or above address. Deadline: May 1.

793.
Boys and Girls Clubs of Chicago
Allstate Foundation Citizenship Scholarships
625 W. Jackson Boulevard, Suite 300
Chicago, IL 60606
(312) 648-1666

20 scholarships of $1,000 to high school seniors who are members or past members of the Boys and Girls Club of Chicago only. Based on academic record, leadership abilities, academic potential, essay, interview, and financial need. Each Chicago Boys and Girls Club nominates up to three candidates. Deadline: March 1.

794.
Boys and Girls Clubs of Chicago
Boys and Girls Clubs Woman's Board
  Scholarships
625 W. Jackson Boulevard, Suite 300
Chicago, IL 60606
(312) 648-1666

Numerous scholarships ranging from $500 to $1,500 to high school seniors who are members or past members of Boys and Girls Clubs of Chicago only. Based on academic record, leadership abilities, academic potential, essay,

interview, and financial need. Each Chicago Boys and Girls Club may nominate up to three candidates. Deadline: March 1.

795.
Boys Club of San Diego
Spence Reese Scholarship Fund
#1 Administration Office
3760 Fourth Avenue
San Diego, CA 92103

4 scholarships of $2,000 per year (renewable for up to four years) to help high school seniors planning on a career in medicine, law, engineering, or political science. Preference given to students who live within 250-mile radius of San Diego. Based on ability, academic standing, financial need, and potential for good citizenship. Interview in San Diego is required. Boys Club affiliation not required. Must be U.S. citizens. Enclose a self-addressed, stamped envelope. Deadline: May 15.

796.
Boy Scouts of America
Eisenhower Memorial Scholarship Foundation
303 North Curry Pike
Bloomington, IN 47401

Numerous $2,500 scholarships to high school seniors or graduates who have never attended college. Based on academic achievement and leadership; must have an open and inquiring mind, faith in a Divine Being, and a firm belief in the free enterprise system and the American way of life. Renewable. Good at certain Indiana colleges. Deadline: varies.

797.
Boy Scouts of America
Elks National Foundation Eagle Scout
  Scholarships
1325 West Walnut Hill Lane
P.O. Box 152079
Irving, TX 75015-2079
(972) 580-2000

6 scholarships of $2,000 to graduating high school seniors. Must be active Boy Scouts who are Eagle Scouts (one from each BSA region). Based on academic record, SAT/ACT score, goals, recommendations, and financial need. Renewable for four years. Deadline: February 28.

798.
Boy Scouts of America
E. Urner Goodman Scholarship
1325 West Walnut Hill Lane
P.O. Box 152079
Irving, TX 75015-2079
(972) 580-2000

1 or more $2,000 scholarships to high school seniors. Must be members of the Order of the Arrow and planning on a career in the professional service of the Boy Scouts of America. Based on academic record, scouting record, reason for career goal, and recommendations. Deadline: January 15.

799.
Boy Scouts of America
Explorer/Crosman National Air Rifle
  Championship Scholarships
Crosman Airguns
Routes 5 and 20
East Bloomfield, NY 14443

Numerous awards to registered Explorers who participate
in the air rifle shooting competition. Area winners compete
in national competitions, with expenses paid. Based on
three-position shooting, aggregate, and international match
scores. Deadline: varies.

800.
Boy Scouts of America
Former Agents of the FBI Scholarships
1325 West Walnut Hill Lane
P.O. Box 152079
Irving, TX 75015-2079
(972) 580-2000

6 scholarships of $500 to high school seniors. Must be
Explorers interested in a career in law, law enforcement, or
criminal justice. Apply at your local Scout council or above
address. Deadline: varies.

801.
Boy Scouts of America
Fred A. Bryan Collegiate Students Fund (Tri–
  Valley Council)
The National Bank
112 West Jefferson Boulevard
South Bend, IN 44601

1 scholarship of $1,000 to a high school senior who is a
South Bend, Indiana, Boy Scout. Good at any college or
university.

802.
Boy Scouts of America
Greater New York City Councils' Scholarships
345 Hudson Street
New York, NY 10014

Numerous scholarships of varying amounts to high school
seniors. Must have been New York City Boy Scouts or
Explorer Scouts for the last two years. Based on academic
excellence, financial need, service to Greater New York City
councils, and strong scouting history. Request applications
after January 1. Deadline: June 1.

803.
Boy Scouts of America
Dr. Harry Britenstool Scholarship Fund
Greater New York Councils
345 Hudson Street
New York, NY 10014
(212) 242-1100

Scholarships of varying amounts to high school seniors.
Must have been Boy Scouts or employees of the Greater
New York Councils, Boy Scouts of America, for at least two

years. Based on academic record, goals, scouting
background, financial need, and other pertinent
information. Request applications after January 1. Deadline:
June 1.

804.
Boy Scouts of America
Henry E. Warren Loan Fund
Algonquin Council
34 Deloss Street
P.O. Box 149
Framingham, MA 01781
(617) 872-6551

Numerous loans of $800 to high school seniors or
undergraduate students. Must be Boy Scouts or Explorers
who are registered members of the Algonquin Council.
Must have been a member for at least three years. Based
on academic record and financial need. Deadline: varies.

805.
Boy Scouts of America
Illinois American Legion Scholarships
P.O. Box 2910
Bloomington, IL 61701

1 scholarship of $500 and 4 scholarships of $100 to high
school seniors. Must be qualified Boy Scouts or Explorers
from an Illinois Scout troop. Illinois residency not required.
Based on an essay. Deadline: March 15.

806.
Boy Scouts of America
J. Edgar Hoover Foundation Scholarships
1325 West Walnut Hill Lane
P.O. Box 152079
Irving, TX 75015-2079
(972) 580-2000

6 scholarships of $1,000 (one from each region) to high
school seniors who are Explorer Scouts. Must be active in a
post specializing in law enforcement and have a desire to
pursue a career in law enforcement. Based on academic
record and reasons for career goals. Deadline: March 31.

807.
Boy Scouts of America
Law Enforcement Assistance Award
1325 West Walnut Hill Lane
P.O. Box 152079
Irving, TX 75015-2079
(972) 580-2000

1 scholarship of $1,000 to a high school senior. Must be an
Explorer who assists law enforcement agencies with
meaningful and exceptional service. Must have performed
"an act which assisted in the prevention or solution of a
serious crime, or an act which assisted in leading to the
apprehension of a felony suspect wanted by a law

enforcement agency." The awards, a certificate, a medal, and special lapel pin, are presented by the Retired Agents Society of Secret Service.

808.
Boy Scouts of America
Marjorie S. Carter Boy Scout Scholarship Trust
Administrative Secretary
P.O. Box 527
West Chatham, MA 02669
(508) 945-1225

Approximately 35 scholarships of $1,000 to high school seniors who are worthy New England Scouts who have demonstrated leadership ability. Must be either Scouts or Explorers from Vermont, New Hampshire, Maine, Massachusetts, Connecticut, or Rhode Island. Recipients may attend any college or university. Recommendations from Scout Executive and high school counselor required. Renewable for four years. Deadline: April 15.

809.
Boy Scouts of America
Military Service Scholarships

Scholarships covering all tuition, books, and lab fees and a monthly stipend for living expenses to high school seniors or graduates who have been Boy Scouts. Upon completion of a bachelor's degree (often in engineering), students are commissioned in the Army, Air Force, Navy, or Marine Corps. Contact any local military recruiting office of the branch of the service you prefer. Deadline: none.

810.
Boy Scouts of America
National Eagle Scout Scholarships
1325 West Walnut Hill Lane
P.O. Box 152079
Irving, TX 75015-2079
(972) 580-2000

5 scholarships of $3,000 and 6 scholarships of $1,000 in each of the six Boy Scout regions. Any Eagle Scout may apply. Each applicant must provide a letter of recommendation from his Scoutmaster or other volunteer Scout leader who can attest to his character and leadership qualities. Based on financial need, scholastic achievements, scouting activities, and community and school activities. Renewable based on academic standing, participation in college, scouting, and community activities, and continued financial need. Deadline: varies according to region.

811.
Boy Scouts of America
National Society of the Sons of the American
  Revolution Scholarship
1000 South 4th Street
Louisville, KY 40703

1 scholarship of $2,000 to a graduating high school senior who is an Eagle Scout. Write for application forms and information. Please include a self-addressed, stamped envelope. Deadline: varies.

812.
Boy Scouts of America
Navy Dependents Scholarships
Commander
Naval Military Personnel Command (NMPC 121D)
Department of the Navy
Washington, DC 20370-5121

Several scholarships to high school seniors who are dependent children of active or retired members of the U.S. Navy. Must have been Boy Scouts. Based on academic achievement, character, and financial need.

813.
Boy Scouts of America
Pickard Scholarship
Del-Mar-Va Council
Eighth & Washington Streets
Wilmington, DE 19801
(302) 652-3741

1 scholarship of $500 to a graduating high school senior. Must be an Explorer or Senior Scout in the Del-Mar-Va Council. Must be a Delaware, Maryland, or Virginia resident. Must be recommended by the Scout executive and approved by the Scholarship Committee. Preference given to Eagle Scouts and Explorers. Renewable. Deadline: varies.

814.
Boy Scouts of America
Scouting Career Scholarships
Scholarship Coordinator
345 Hudson Street
New York, NY 10014

Numerous $1,000 scholarships to graduating high school seniors who are New York City Scouts. Must be pursuing a career as a professional Scout leader. Based on service to the Greater New York City Councils summer camp staff in the year the scholarship is to be used and financial need. Request applications after January 1. Deadline: June 1.

815.
Boy Scouts of America
Sheryl A. Horak Law Enforcement Explorer
  Memorial Scholarship
1325 West Walnut Hill Lane
P.O. Box 152079
Irving, TX 75015-2079

1 (or more) $1,000 scholarship is available to an Explorer Scout who is a graduating high school senior and is interested in a career in law enforcement. Based on academic record, career goals, and recommendations. Deadline: March 31.

816.
Boy Scouts of America National Office
1325 West Walnut Hill Lane
P.O. Box 152079
Irving, TX 75015-2079
(972) 580-2000

Numerous scholarships to high school seniors who are Boy Scouts. Write for complete details.

817.
Bozell Worldwide Public Relations
Internship Coordinator
800 Blackstone Centre
302 South 36th Street
Omaha, NE 68131-2453
(402) 345-3400
(402) 978-4193 Fax
knickels@omaha.bozell.com

30 internships providing a salary ranging from $150 to $200 per week to undergraduates, recent college graduates, and graduate students. Interns are designated "public relations interns" and are involved in writing, researching, and interacting with the media. Internships take place in Costa Mesa, CA; Detroit, MI; Minneapolis, MN; Omaha, NE; New York, NY; London, England; or Milan, Italy. Deadline: rolling.

818.
BP America Scholarships
10-3655-E
200 Public Square
Cleveland, OH 44114-2375
(216) 586-5667

20 scholarships ranging from $1,000 to $4,000 to high school seniors who are children of full-time employees (active, retired, or deceased) of BP America. Must have been selected as National Merit Semifinalists and have their scores sent by the National Merit Corporation. Renewable. Deadline: December 31.

819.
Broadcast Education Association
Broadcast Pioneers Scholarships
Attn: Membership Services Assistant
1771 N Street, N.W.
Washington, DC 20036
(202) 429-5354

2 scholarships of $1,250 to undergraduate juniors, seniors, graduate, or doctoral students majoring in broadcasting. Must be attending a BEA-member institution. Based on academic achievement and potential for success in journalism or communications. Must have a high degree of integrity and sense of responsibility. Deadline: January 15.

820.
Broadcast Education Association
Harold E. Fellows Scholarships
Attn: Membership Services Assistant
1771 N Street, N.W.
Washington, DC 20036
(202) 429-5354

4 scholarships of $1,250 to undergraduate juniors, seniors, graduate, or doctoral students majoring in broadcasting. Must be attending a BEA-member institution. Based on academic achievement and potential for success in journalism. Must have a high degree of integrity and sense of responsibility. Must supply proof of employment or internship at a National Association of Broadcasters station. Deadline: January 15.

821.
Broadcast Education Association
James Lawrence Fly Scholarship
Attn: Membership Services Assistant
1771 N Street, N.W.
Washington, DC 20036
(202) 429-5354

1 scholarship of $2,500 to undergraduate juniors, seniors, graduate, or doctoral students who have an interest in the general field of broadcasting. Must be attending a BEA-member institution. Based on academic achievement and potential for success in journalism. Must have a high degree of integrity and sense of responsibility. Scholarship must be used for the study of media law or policy. Deadline: January 15.

822.
Broadcast Education Association
Shane Media Scholarship
Attn: Membership Services Assistant
1771 N Street, N.W.
Washington, DC 20036
(202) 429-5354

1 scholarship of $3,000 to undergraduate juniors, seniors, graduate, or doctoral students who have an interest in radio. Must be attending a BEA-member institution. Based on academic achievement and potential for success in journalism. Must have a high degree of integrity and sense of responsibility. Scholarship must be used for the study of media law or policy. Deadline: January 15.

823.
Broadcast Education Association
Vincent T. Wasilewski Scholarship
Attn: Membership Services Assistant
1771 N Street, N.W.
Washington, DC 20036
(202) 429-5354

1 scholarship of $2,500 to undergraduate juniors, seniors, graduate, or doctoral students who have an interest in the general field of broadcasting. Must be attending a BEA-member institution. Based on academic achievement and potential for success in journalism. Must have a high degree of integrity and sense of responsibility. Scholarship must be used for the study of media law or policy. Deadline: January 15.

824.
Broadcast Education Association
Walter Patterson Scholarships
Attn: Membership Services Assistant
1771 N Street, N.W.
Washington, DC 20036
(202) 429-5354

2 scholarships of $1,250 to undergraduate juniors, seniors, graduate, or doctoral students who have an interest in radio. Must be attending a BEA-member institution. Based on academic achievement and potential for success in journalism. Must have a high degree of integrity and sense of responsibility. Scholarship must be used for the study of media law or policy. Deadline: January 15.

825.
Broadcast Music, Inc.
Music Awards to Student Composers
Attn: Director
320 West 57th Street
New York, NY 10019
(212) 586-2000

Awards ranging from $500 to $3,000 to students of up to age twenty-six in a music composition contest. Students must create a piece of music for any type of instrument and of any length. The style of the work is open-ended. Students may submit only one composition. Past recipients have ranged from students ages eight to twenty-five. Students must be citizens of the Western Hemisphere (including North, Central, and South America, and the Caribbean Islands). May be studying privately with a recognized and established teacher or enrolled in an accredited secondary school, college, or conservatory. Deadline: early February.

826.
Broadcast News Networks
253 5th Avenue, 6th Floor
New York, NY 10016
(212) 779-0500
(212) 532-5554 Fax

10 to 12 production assistant internships, 1 administrative internship, and 2 marketing trainee internships open to high school graduates, undergraduate and graduate students, career changers, and those reentering the work force. None of the internships provides monetary compensation, but travel expenses are reimbursed. BNN is a television production and program development facility that produces two weekly syndicated news magazines. Production intern responsibilities include assisting with audio and lighting for television news magazine field shoots. The administrative interns operate computers, file, handle telephones, and learn how to run an office. The marketing intern responsibilities include performing departmental support and research, writing press releases, and making pitches. All internships last four months. Interns may receive academic credit for their work. All individuals completing their internships are provided with placement assistance, including recommendation letters and names of contacts. Deadline: none specified.

827.
Brookfield Zoo
Intern Program
Coordinator
3300 South Golf Road
Brooksfield, IL 60513
(708) 485-0263

20 summer and 5 fall and spring internships providing no compensation are open to undergraduate juniors, seniors, graduate students, and college graduates of any age. Must have at least a 2.0 GPA. Interns are assigned to the Small Mammal House, Seven Seas Panorama, Australia House, Animal Hospital, Children's Zoo, Conservation Biology, Birds, Hoofed Stock, Primates, Animal Commissary, or Fragile Kingdom. There are also openings in non-animal departments, such as education, graphic arts, human resources, marketing, and public relations. Interns learn how to maintain an animal's health and well-being and assist visitors by directing them to exhibits and answering their questions on animals; helping people find demonstrations, or helping them understand zoo services like the Parent's Program. Applicants must have completed at least two years of college before starting the internship. Zoo experience and a science background aren't required, but helpful. Deadline: February 1 (summer) and one week prior to fall or spring term (fall and spring).

828.
Brookhaven Women in Science
Renate W. Chasman Scholarships
P.O. Box 183
Upton, NY 11973
(516) 282-7226

Numerous $1,000 scholarships to female undergraduate juniors or seniors or first-year graduate students pursuing a career in science, engineering, or mathematics but whose education was interrupted because of family, financial, or other problems. Must be reentry women, U.S. citizens, or permanent resident aliens who are residents of Nassau or Suffolk counties of Long Island, New York. Recipients who do not complete two consecutive semesters or quarters in good academic standing will have the award reclaimed by the Brookhaven Women in Science. Deadline: June 1.

829.
The Brookings Institute
Internship Coordinator
(Name of Program)
1775 Massachusetts Avenue, N.W.
Washington, DC 20036-2188
(202) 797-6050

6 twelve-week summer, fall, and winter/spring internships for undergraduate juniors, seniors, and graduate students majoring in political science, history, public policy, and law. Internships are in governmental studies in this think tank, which researches public policies facing America in areas such as health care and budget deficits. Though predominantly liberal, it does publish middle-of-the-road books. Deadline: April 15 (summer); August 15 (fall); December 15 (winter/spring).

830.
Bruce L. Crary Foundation, Inc.
Attn: President
Hand House, River Street
P.O. Box 396
Elizabethtown, NY 12932
(518) 873-6496

313 scholarships ranging from $250 to $800 to graduating high school seniors. Must be residents of Clinton, Essex, Franklin, Hamilton, or Warren counties, New York. Contact high school counselor or above address. Deadline: March 31.

831.
Bryan International String Competition
Music Performance Awards
North Carolina Symphony
P.O. Box 28026
Raleigh, NC 27611
(919) 733-2750

Prizes of $3,000, $6,000, and $12,000 in a music performance competition open to graduating high school seniors, high school graduates who haven't attended college, undergraduates, graduates, and professional musicians. Must be violinists, violists, or cellists. Must be between the ages of eighteen and thirty years of age. Open to all nationalities and held every four years. The next competition will be in 2000. Deadline: January 2.

832.
Buffalo Foundation
Attn: Director
237 Main Street
Buffalo, NY 14203
(716) 852-2857

429 scholarships, totaling over $258,000, to graduating high school seniors. Must be residents of Buffalo or Erie City, New York. Based on financial need. Deadline: May 25.

833.
Bureau of Indian Affairs Higher Education Grant
    Programs
Bureau of Indian Affairs Higher Education
    Grants
Office of Indian Education Programs
Code 522-Room 3512
19th and C Streets, N.W.
Washington, DC 20240

Numerous scholarship grants of varying amounts to high school seniors or graduates or undergraduate college students. Must have a Certificate of Degree of Indian Blood and tribal enrollment. Need not live on a reservation but must have a tribal affiliation. Deadline: April 1.

834.
Burger King Company
P.O. Box 520783
Miami, FL 33152

Scholarships of $200 per month ($2,000 maximum) to students who are Burger King employees, sixteen years or older, and have worked in a Burger King fast food outlet for over three months for at least fifteen hours per week. Must maintain at least a C average to retain scholarship. Contact the Burger King where employed. Deadline: May 1.

835.
Burlington Educational Loan Fund
Student Loan Coordinator, Treasurer's Department
Burlington Industries
P.O. Box 21207
Greensboro, NC 27420

Employees and their dependent children may participate in the following Corporate Reserve Program of the United

States Aid Fund (USAF): United Student Aid Funds Loan Plan for Parents and the USAF Loan Plan for Students. The Burlington Foundation no longer offers loan funds.

836.
Burlington Northern Scholarship Program
Employee Relations
Burlington Northern Railroad
3000 Continental Plaza Building
777 Main Street
Fort Worth, TX 76102

25 scholarships of $1,500 to high school seniors who are children of Burlington Northern Railroad active, retired, or deceased employees who have at least two consecutive years of employment. Must be in the upper third of the class and entering an accredited institution in the fall term after graduation. Must plan to attend four consecutive years of college. Renewable with transcript review. Request applications before November 30. Deadline: December.

837.
Burson-Marsteller
Internship Coordinator
230 Park Avenue South
New York, NY 10003
(212) 614-4000

8 to 12 ten-week internships providing a salary of $275 per week open to undergraduate seniors with at least a 3.0 GPA. International students may apply. Interns work in corporate/public affairs, consumer marketing, technology/telecommunications, health care, or video/event management. Internships take place in either Chicago or New York. Deadline: February 17.

838.
Burt Snyder Educational Foundation
620 North First Street
Lakeview, OR 97630
(503) 947-2196

4 scholarships ranging from $1,680 to $2,520 to graduating high school seniors from Lake County, Oregon, area high schools. Must be Oregon residents. Contact high school counselors. Deadline: varies.

839.
Business and Professional Women's Foundation
2012 Massachusetts Avenue, N.W.
Washington, DC 20036
(202) 293-1200

The foundation assists women at critical points in their lives financially. Whether reentry women, women with years of work experience, or women presently in undergraduate programs, the majority of these women face a common problem—the need for financial assistance. The Career Advancement Scholarship, BPW Loans for Women in Engineering Studies, and the New York Life Foundation Scholarship for Women in Health Professions provide funds for tuition, fees, and related expenses. Eligibility requirements, program deadlines, and career information are listed in program literature. Deadline: May 1.

840.
Business and Professional Women's Foundation Avon Products Foundation Scholarships for Women in Business Studies
2012 Massachusetts Avenue, N.W.
Washington, DC 20036
(202) 293-1200

Scholarships of $1,000 to female undergraduate or graduate students in business. Must be within twenty-four months of completing an undergraduate or graduate program in the U.S. Selection based on financial need. Award may not be used for doctoral studies, study abroad, or correspondence courses. Must be U.S. citizens. Applications must be requested between October 1 and April 1. Other restrictions may apply. Deadline: April 15.

841.
Business and Professional Women's Foundation BPW Career Advancement Scholarships
Attn: Assistant Director, Education and Training
Scholarship Department
2012 Massachusetts Avenue, N.W.
Washington, DC 20036
(202) 293-1200

400 scholarships of $1,000 to female undergraduate or graduate students in all areas of study, with emphasis on computer science, education science, and paralegal training. Must be within twenty-four months of completing an undergraduate or graduate program in the U.S. Selection based on financial need. Must be at least thirty years of age. Award may not be used for doctoral studies, study abroad, or correspondence courses. Must be U.S. citizens. Applications must be requested between October 1 and April 1. Deadline: April 15.

842.
Business and Professional Women's Foundation Clairol Loving Care Scholarship Program
Scholarship Department
2012 Massachusetts Avenue, N.W.
Washington, DC 20036
(202) 293-1200

Numerous scholarships of up to $1,000 to women over the age of thirty who need financial assistance to upgrade their skills or finish their education or for career advancement. Training must be completed within twenty-four months. Must furnish information and costs of specific course of study at an accredited school and must be officially accepted into a school. Request pre-application screening form between September 1 and November 30. If you fulfill requirements, you will be sent an application, which is due by February 28. Send a self-addressed, stamped envelope (legal size #10) for pre-application information. Deadline: February 28.

843.
Business and Professional Women's Foundation Florence Morse Scholarships
2012 Massachusetts Avenue, N.W.
Washington, DC 20036
(202) 293-1200

Numerous scholarships of varying amounts to women at least twenty-five years of age. Must be U.S. citizens and in their junior year of senior year of business school at a college or university accredited by the American Assembly of Collegiate Schools of Business. Must have financial need. Deadline: May 1; October 1.

844.
Business and Professional Women's Foundation Kelly Services Second Career Scholarships
2012 Massachusetts Avenue, N.W.
Washington, DC 20036
(202) 293-1200

Numerous scholarships of up to $1,000 to women who are at least twenty-five years old, who have spent five or more years in full-time housekeeping, and are seeking employment due to the death of a spouse or dissolution of a marriage. Deadline: February 15; July 15.

845.
Business and Professional Women's Foundation New York Life Foundation
Scholarships for Women in the Health Professions
2012 Massachusetts Avenue, N.W.
Washington, DC 20037
(202) 293-1200

50 scholarships ranging from $500 to $1,000 for women twenty-five years or older who are college juniors or seniors or master's candidates and are seeking the education necessary for a career in a health-care field. Must demonstrate critical financial need. Deadline: varies.

846.
Butterfield & Butterfield Internship Program
220 San Bruno Avenue
San Francisco, CA 94103
(415) 861-7500

12 ten-week internships providing a $10 daily stipend to undergraduate juniors, seniors, or graduate students, or college graduates of any age. Interns are assigned to Painting, Asian Art, Prints, Fine Photographs, Furniture and Decorative Arts, American Indian/Ethnographic, Oriental Rugs, Rare Books, Public Relations, or Marketing. Students work at least sixteen hours per week. Applicants must have taken at least two semesters of art history, though some are accepted for positions in less art-oriented areas, such as marketing and public relations. Interns are able to learn in general about the auction business and in particular about a type of art or antique. Interns working with Butterfield are able to handle pieces that would be inaccessible in a museum environment. Deadline: March 15 (summer); July 15 (fall); October 15 (spring).

847.
California Chicano News Media Association Joel Garcia Memorial Scholarships
Educational Programs Coordinator
c/o USC School of Journalism (GFS 315)
University of Southern California
Los Angeles, CA 90089
(213) 743-7158

10 scholarships ranging from $500 to $2,000 to Latino undergraduate students interested in a career in journalism or communications. Journalism or communications major

not required. May be used at any accredited institution in California. Must be U.S. citizen. Deadline: March 30.

848.
California Community Colleges

The Extended Opportunity Program offers students special support for study in any community college in California. Seeks to serve full-time (twelve hours or more) students from depressed areas and high-total-unemployment areas or students from families with a low total income. Offers financial assistance in the form of grants and loans as well as services such as tutorial assistance, peer counseling, and active recruitment help. Contact California community college financial aid offices.

849.
California Congress of Parents and Teachers, Inc.
Early Childhood/Elementary/Secondary Teacher
  Education Scholarships
930 Georgia Street
Los Angeles, CA 90015
(213) 620-1100

Numerous $750 scholarships to full-time undergraduate juniors or seniors or graduate students preparing to teach in field of early childhood education in California public schools. Must be residents of California. Must also be attending an accredited California college where the scholarships are available. List available upon request.

850.
California Congress of Parents and Teachers, Inc.
Health Services Scholarships at Community
  Colleges
930 Georgia Street
Los Angeles, CA 90015
(213) 620-1100

25 scholarships of $150 to full-time students who have completed the first year in an associate's degree program in a health-care services field. Must attend a California community college. Must be California residents. Apply through the community college.

851.
California Department of Education
Maple Creek Willie Scholarships
721 Capitol Mall
Sacramento, CA 95814

Scholarships of up to $1,250 to high school seniors or graduates who are Native Americans. Must be California residents. May attend a community or junior college, four-year college or university, or a vocational school. Deadline: varies.

852.
California Department of Veterans Affairs
Division of Veteran Services
College Fee Waiver
P.O. Box 942895
Sacramento, CA 94295-0001
(916) 445-2334

All fees are waived by universities for children of service-connected disabled or deceased veterans. Disability should be 10 percent or greater. Dependents of MIAs or POWs are eligible to have their fees paid by the department, not have their fees waived. Deadline: none.

853.
California Department of Veterans Affairs
Division of Veteran Services
College Stipend Program
P.O. Box 942895
Sacramento, CA 94295-0001
(916) 445-2334

Monthly payments for high school and college students, plus some tuition assistance. Applicants must be dependents of a veteran (with at least a 30 percent service-connected disability or who is deceased). Veteran must have been a native Californian and a resident when he or she entered or reentered active military duty during WWI, WWII, Korean War, or Vietnam War. High school students must be at least fourteen years of age and in the ninth grade. College students are assisted until they reach twenty-seven years of age or they receive their bachelor's degree (whichever comes first). Widows, widowers, and wives receive a maximum of forty-eight months of training. Dependents are eligible after all other federal benefits are exhausted.

854.
California Farm Bureau Scholarships
California Farm Bureau Scholarship Foundation
1601 Exposition Boulevard
Sacramento, CA 95815

Sscholarships of $1,000 to high school seniors or graduates entering California colleges or universities and majoring in agriculture or home economics. Based on scholarship, career goals, leadership, and determination. Deadline: March 1.

855.
California Governor's Committee for
  Employment of Disabled Persons
Employment Department
Hal Connolly Scholar–Athlete Awards
MIC 41
800 Capitol Mall, Room 5067
P.O. Box 972880
Sacramento, CA 94280-0001

2 first prizes of $1,000, 2 second prizes of $500, and 2 prizes of $250 (one each for a male and one each for a female) are available to high school seniors under age nineteen who have participated in athletics, although disabled. Must be California residents. Based on academic record, high school athletic activity, and recommendation letters. Contact high school counselor. Deadline: March 31.

856.
California–Hawaii Elks Major Project, Inc.
California–Hawaii Elks Disabled Student
  Scholarships
5450 East Lamona
Fresno, CA 93727

Scholarships of $2,000 renewable for up to four years to high school seniors or undergraduate college students who are physically disabled, visually disabled, hard of hearing, deaf, speech/language or neurologically impaired. Based on academic record, recommendations, career goals, and financial need. Applications accepted after January 1. Deadline: March 15.

857.
California Mason Foundation
Amaranth Funds Awards
1111 California Street
San Francisco, CA 94108
(415) 776-7000

Awards of up to $1,000 are available to female students under twenty-one years of age. Must be California residents living in California and attending a California institution. Must be U.S. citizens. Based on academic record, goals, recommendation letters, and financial need. Deadline: varies.

858.
California Masonic Foundation
General Fund Awards
1111 California Street
San Francisco, CA 94108
(415) 776-7000

Numerous scholarships ranging from $500 to $1,000 to undergraduate students. Must be California or Hawaii residents. May attend any accredited college or technical school. Based on academic record, goals, recommendation letters, and financial need. Deadline: varies.

859.
California Newspaper Carrier Foundation
Scholarships
General Manager
1010 Hurley Way, Suite 300
Sacramento, CA 95825

Scholarships of $500 to newspaper carriers whose newspapers are members of the CNCF. Must have delivered newspapers for at least one year (March 1 to March 1) during the year of the award. Based on delivery, collection, and sales record, newspaper's recommendation, academic achievement, and principal's recommendation. Nomination papers are sent to newspapers in January. Deadline: March.

860.
California Society of Professional Engineers
1006 12th Street, Suite J
Sacramento, CA 95814
(916) 442-9777

Scholarships of $1,000 to high school seniors planning to enter into an engineering curriculum. Some scholarships may require attendance at a certain college or university. For California residents only. Deadline: late November; local chapters may vary.

861.
California Society of Professional Journalists
Bill Farr Scholarship
Scholarship Committee Chairman
Los Angeles SPJ
4310 Coronet Drive
Encino, CA 91316

1 scholarship of $1,000 to an undergraduate senior or graduate student who is a journalism major with emphasis on news-editorial. Must be attending a Los Angeles County college or university or be a resident of Los Angeles County attending an out-of-state institution. Based on academic achievement, potential for success, and financial need. Deadline; November 15.

862.
California Society of Professional Journalists
Carl Greenberg Prize
Scholarship Committee Chairman
Los Angeles SPJ
4310 Coronet Drive
Encino, CA 91316

1 scholarship of $1,000 to undergraduate juniors or seniors who are journalism majors with emphasis on news-editorial. Must be attending a Los Angeles County college or university or be a resident of Los Angeles County attending an out-of-state institution. Based on demonstrated accomplishment in political or investigative reporting. Deadline: November 15.

863.
California State Department of Rehabilitation
California Vocational Rehabilitation for Persons
with Disabilities
830 K Street Mall
Sacramento, CA 95814

Students whose disability limits them from obtaining a suitable job or threatens their present employment are eligible for assistance depending on their financial and physical needs. Students should contact the local Rehabilitation Office.

864.
California State PTA Student Loan Fund
Student Loan Chairman
California Congress of Parents, Teachers and Students, Inc.
P.O. Box 15015
Los Angeles, CA 90015

Loans of varying amounts to California residents who will be attending a California college, university, community college, technical, or trade school. Deadline: May 15.

865.
California State University System
Educational Opportunity Program
P.O. Box 1590
Long Beach, CA 90801

Assists disadvantaged low-income students by actively recruiting them, helping them go through the process of admissions, and providing financial aid, tutoring, and housing. Operates at all nineteen California State University campuses. Must be California residents. Deadline: none.

866.
California Student Aid Commission
Assumption Program of Loans for Education
  (APLE)
P.O. Box 419026
Rancho Cordova, CA 95741-9026
(916) 526-7590
(916) 526-8002 Fax
http://www.csac.ca.gov/about.html

Offers relief from educational loans after a student has graduated and has obtained teaching certification. After one year of teaching, up to $2,000 in the first year in student loan payments will be assumed by California; after the second year, $3,000; and after the third, another $3,000 (with a maximum of $8,000).

867.
California Student Aid Commission
Bilingual Teacher Grants
P.O. Box 419026
Rancho Cordova, CA 95741-9026
(916) 526-7590
(916) 526-8002 Fax
http://www.csac.ca.gov/about.html

1,000 scholarships ranging from $300 to $3,800 to students who are certified by the dean of the school of education as being language-competent in a second language. Must have been California residents for at least twelve months and be U.S. citizens. May be used at any institution. Based on financial need. Deadline: early February.

868.
California Student Aid Commission
Cal Grant A
P.O. Box 419026
Rancho Cordova, CA 95741-9026
(916) 526-7590
(916) 526-8002 Fax
http://www.csac.ca.gov/about.html

Over 17,000 grants of varying amounts to high school seniors and graduates. Must attend schools and colleges labeled "A" on the California College Code list attached to the Student Aid Application for California. Deadline: varies.

869.
California Student Aid Commission
Cal Grant B
P.O. Box 419026
Rancho Cordova, CA 95741-9026
(916) 526-7590
(916) 526-8002 Fax
http://www.csac.ca.gov/about.html

Grants of varying amounts to assist with living expenses, books, supplies, transportation, etc. Students may be classified as disadvantaged due to finances, education, culture, language, home, community, environment, and other conditions that make gaining further education difficult. The average income of Cal Grant B recipients for a family of four is $7,519. Students with family income in excess of $20,000 are unlikely to qualify. Deadline: varies.

870.
California Student Aid Commission
Cal Grant C
P.O. Box 419026
Rancho Cordova, CA 95741-9026
(916) 526-7590
(916) 526-8002 Fax
http://www.csac.ca.gov/about.html

1,570 grants provide financial assistance to students who are in postsecondary vocational education and training. Award covers tuition and training-related costs, such as special clothing, tools, equipment, books, supplies, and transportation. Deadline: varies.

871.
California Student Aid Commission
Law Enforcement Personnel Dependents
  Scholarships
P.O. Box 419026
Rancho Cordova, CA 95741-9026
(916) 526-7590
(916) 526-8002 Fax
http://www.csac.ca.gov/about.html

Scholarships ranging from $100 to $1,500 per year, with a maximum of $6,000 in a six-year period, to dependents of California law enforcement officers killed or totally disabled in the line of duty. Applications must be requested before March 2. Deadline: March.

872.
California Student Aid Commission
Robert C. Byrd Honors Scholarships
P.O. Box 419026
Rancho Cordova, CA 95741-9026
(916) 526-7590
(916) 526-8002 Fax
http://www.csac.ca.gov/about.html

450 nonrenewable scholarships of $1,500 to high school seniors enrolled in public or private schools. Must be California residents attending a California college or university. Based on outstanding academic record; must be in the upper 5 percent of class, have at least a 3.5 GPA, and have at least an 1100 on SAT or 27 on ACT. Apply after January 1. Deadline: April 1.

873.
California Teachers Association (CTA)
1705 Murchison Drive
P.O. Box 921
Burlingame, CA 94011-1400
(415) 697-1400

3 scholarships of $2,000 to student members of CTA. Request applications after October 1 from the CTA Human Rights Department in Burlingame or any CTA Regional Resource Center Office. Deadline: February 15.

874.
The Callahan Group
Internship Coordinator
219 East 31st Street
New York, NY 10016
(212) 685-5520
(212) 685-5549 Fax

5 internships in public relations providing a salary of $50 per week are open to undergraduate juniors and seniors, recent college graduates, and graduate students. Interns assist account executives by performing clerical work, calling media contacts, and writing press releases. Applicants must submit a résumé, cover letter, and writing samples. Deadline: March 30 (summer); August 1 (fall); February 1 (spring).

875.
Canaan Public Relations
Internship Coordinator
301 East 47th Street, Suite 10M
New York, NY 10017
(212) 223-0100
(212) 223-3737 Fax

6 sixteen-week internships providing a salary of $50 per week are open to undergraduates and college graduates. Interns work in all areas of public relations in business, entertainment, fashion, and hospitality industry. Internships take place in summer, fall, or spring. Deadline: rolling.

876.
Canadian Association of Broadcasters
Jim Allard Broadcast Journalism Scholarships
P.O. Box 527, Station B
Ottawa, Ontario, Canada K1P 5S2

Varying numbers of scholarships in varying amounts to students enrolled in a broadcast journalism program at a Canadian institution. Based on character, leadership qualities, and career goals. Deadline: June 30.

877.
Canadian Association of Broadcasters
Ruth Hancock Scholarships
P.O. Box 527, Station B
Ottawa, Ontario, Canada K1P 5S2

3 scholarships of $2,000 to Canadian students enrolled in a recognized communications program in a Canadian institution. Based on recommendations, character, leadership qualities, and career goals. Deadline: June 30.

878.
Canadian Aviation Historical Society
Silver Dart Aviation History Award
National Headquarters
P.O. Box 224, Station A
Willowdale, ON, Canada M2N 5S8
(416) 488-2247

A $500 cash prize to a student attending a technical college, aviation school, or university. Based on a 5,000-word essay on Canadian aviation history. Papers will be published in the society's journal. Runners-up are awarded books. All

winners receive a one-year membership to the society. Deadline: March 15.

879.
Canadian Nurses Foundation (CNF)
c/o Judith A. Oulton, Secretary-Treasurer
50 The Driveway
Ottawa, ON, Canada K2P 1E2
(613) 237-2133

Scholarships ranging from $1,500 to $2,000 to registered nurses in a baccalaureate program. Must be members of CNF and Canadian Nurses Association (CNA). Must agree to work in a nursing position in Canada for one year for each year of assistance received. Must be Canadian citizens or immigrants. Based on academic ability, leadership, potential, and nursing ability. Request applications after November 1. Deadline: April 15.

880.
Cargill Scholarships for Rural America
Cargill, Inc.
P.O. Box 9300
Minneapolis, MN 55440
(612) 475-6201

Scholarships of varying amounts to high school seniors from farm families. Must be U.S. citizens and planning to attend a two- or four-year college, university, or vocational school. Must be Minnesota residents. Deadline: March 1.

881.
Carl and Florence King Foundation
5956 Sherry Lane, Suite 620
Dallas, TX 75225
(214) 750-1884

69 grants, totaling $73,600, and 56 loans, totaling $110,000, through certain colleges (Texas, A&M, University of North Texas, and Southern Methodist University), to students going into teaching math, science, or English. A separate program open only to students who are residents of Dallas County, through the YMCA of Dallas. Applicants must be Texas residents. Deadline: varies by school.

882.
Carle C. Conway Scholarship Foundation, Inc.
800 Connecticut Avenue
P.O. Box 5410
Norwalk, CT 06856
(203) 855-5055

20 scholarships of up to $3,500 per year (but not more than the cost of tuition and fees for four years) to high school seniors who are children of Continental Can employees who have had at least six months of continuous employment. Based on academic record, SAT scores, extracurricular activities, recommendations, and biographical information. SAT must be taken no later than December of the senior year. Deadline: mid-November.

883.
Carolina Telephone Scholarships
North Carolina Department of Community Colleges
Caswell Building
200 West Jones Street
Raleigh, NC 27603-1337
(919) 733-7051 ext. 319

56 scholarships of $500 to high school seniors, high school graduates, or full-time students enrolled in the North Carolina community college system. Must be pursuing a technical or vocational degree and be North Carolina residents. Preference is given to African Americans, Hispanic Americans, Native Americans, Asian Americans, or anyone who has lost a job because of inadequate job skills or for economic reasons.

884.
Carrie S. Camp Foundation, Inc.
Attn: Executive Director
P.O. Box 813
Franklin, VA 23851
Written inquiries only

27 scholarships, totaling $60,000, to high school seniors and graduates from Southampton, Isle of Wight, or Tidewater counties, Virginia, and northeastern North Carolina. Deadline: February 26 (for students to apply to high school principals); March 15 (for principals to file with the foundation).

885.
The Carter Center
Internship Program
One Copenhill Avenue
Atlanta, GA 30307
(404) 420-5151

25 internships with no compensation open to undergraduate juniors, seniors, and graduate students. Internships last for twelve weeks during summer, fall, and spring, with a six-week Winter Break internship also available. The Carter Center, founded by President Jimmy Carter in 1982, is a think tank established to improve the quality of life for people around the world. Interns are assigned to any one of a variety of programs: Latin American and Caribbean Studies, African Governance, Human Rights, Global 2000 (a large-scale project to improve health care and agriculture in developing countries), Domestic and International Health Policy, the Atlanta Project (a local program working on social problems associated with poverty in urban areas), Task Force for Child Survival and Development, and Conflict Resolution. There are also positions in administrative offices, such as public information, development, and conferencing. Interns research specific issues, monitor daily events, and write articles for in-house publications. Deadline: July 15 (fall); October 15 (spring); March 15 (summer).

886.
Catholic Workman
Catholic Workman College Scholarships
P.O. Box 47
New Prague, MN 56071
(612) 758-2229

22 scholarships, totaling $15,000, to undergraduate students enrolled in an accredited college or university. Must be members of its fraternal life insurance society. Based on SAT/ACT scores for freshmen and college transcripts for sophomores, recommendations, and involvement in the society, community, or parish. Deadline: July 1.

887.
CBS News
Internships
Attn: Manager of Professional Advancement and
  Internships
524 West 57th Street
New York, NY 10019
(212) 975-5567
(212) 975-8798 Fax

Varying numbers of internships to undergraduate and graduate students. Internships last for one semester and occur during the fall, spring, and summer. No monetary compensation is provided, but sponsor is willing to complete any necessary paperwork required for the intern to receive academic credit. Intern responsibilities include performing duties involving journalism, broadcasting, and communications in one of their offices in New York, Dallas, Los Angeles, Miami, or Washington, DC. Applicants must be full-time students and have an interest in journalism, broadcasting, and communications. Must send a résumé, two letters of recommendation, and a personal essay. Deadline: March 15 (summer); June 15 (fall); October 15 (spring).

888.
Cecil Armstrong Foundation
c/o Lake City Bank
P.O. Box 1387
Warsaw, IN 46581-1387
(219) 267-9110

50 scholarship grants ranging from $16 to $300 to high school seniors, undergraduate, or graduate students living in Warsaw, Indiana, area. Deadline: varies.

889.
Center for American Indian Alternative
  Education
P.O. Box 18285, Capitol Hill Station
Denver, CO 80218

Financial assistance to outstanding Native American high school seniors interested in pursuing postsecondary education. Must have one-quarter or more Indian blood and must currently reside in Arizona, New Mexico, Colorado, Oklahoma, Kansas, or San Bernardino County, California. Stipend amount is dependent upon family financial circumstances and cost of attending college. Deadline: none.

890.
Center for Coastal Studies
Internship Review Committee
59 Commercial Studies
P.O. Box 1036
Provincetown, MA 02657
(508) 487-3622
(508) 487-4495 Fax

4 internships providing $75 per week plus free housing to undergraduate juniors, seniors, recent college graduates, and graduate students with backgrounds in biology, zoology, or wildlife ecology. Interns conduct research projects, education, and conservation programs on coastal and marine environments. Includes field trips, off-shore research cruises, free T-shirts, and discounts at the CCS shop. Internships last for twelve weeks in the summer. Open to U.S. citizens and non-U.S. citizens who are legal residents. Deadline: January 31.

891.
Center for Defense Information Internships
Attn: Program Coordinator
1500 Massachusetts Avenue, N.W.
Washington, DC 20005
(202) 862-0700

Varying numbers of internships paying $700 per month to undergraduate and graduate students interested in political science and public policy as related to military issues. Internships last at least four months for full-time work as research and outreach assistants at CDI. Selection based on academic achievement and interest in U.S. military policy and related public policy. Applicants should have good writing skills. Deadline: April 1; July 1; November 1.

892.
Center for Health Services
Station 17, Vanderbilt University
Nashville, TN 37232
(615) 322-4773

Varying numbers of internships providing stipends and housing for summer interns. Open to undergraduate and graduate students, and individuals with a background in liberal arts, science, medical, or environmental areas. Interns organize summer and year-round programs, provide community follow-up and technical assistance to community groups, conduct fund-raising, and administer budgets. Programs sponsored by the Center include Service Training for Environmental Progress, Student Health Coalition, and Action Research. Interns can work part- or full-time. Submit letter detailing interests, résumé, and an application. An interview must be conducted. Deadline: March 21 (summer).

893.
Center for Investigative Reporting, Inc.
c/o Communications Directors
568 Howard Street, Fifth Floor
San Francisco, CA 94105-3008
(415) 543-1200

6 to 10 six-month internships providing $100 per month to students, and college graduates of any age. Interns are assigned to a senior reporter who guides them in gathering information for stories, making phone calls, conducting interviews, searching through public records, and organizing library and on-line searches. Interns are able to learn investigative techniques, ethics, writing, and journalistic skills by attending weekly seminars. Though the program is open to any major, applicants must have strong writing skills. Applicants who are unpublished must supply writing samples. Deadline: December 1 (winter/spring); May 1 (summer/fall).

894.
Center for Marine Conservation (CMC)
Internship Coordinator
1725 DeSales Street, N.W., Suite 500
Washington, DC 20036
(202) 429-5609

15 three-month internships providing no compensation for undergraduates and a stipend ranging from $200 to $1,000 plus reimbursement for daily travel expenses to graduate students. Students respond to public requests for information, make local presentations, research and write educational material, and summarize legislation. The CMC is dedicated to protecting marine life, especially marine mammals, sea turtles, fishes, and their habitats. The internships are conducted in Hampton, Virginia; Marathon and St. Petersburg, Florida; San Francisco, California; and Washington, DC. Deadline: May 17 (summer); August 2 (fall); December 7 (winter); March 8 (spring).

895.
Center for Talented Youth
CTY Summer Programs Employment
The Johns Hopkins University
3400 North Charles Street
Baltimore, MD 21218
(410) 516-0191

350 internships providing $850 for three weeks, room and board for resident advisors (RA) and teaching assistants (TA); and $750 for three weeks, room and board to laboratory assistants (LA). Positions are open to undergraduate and graduate students, and college graduates who graduated within one year. International applicants are also eligible. There are programs for teaching students in grades 2 through 6 and another teaching students in grades 7 and up. Interns work at Johns Hopkins (Baltimore, MD), Hampshire College (Amherst, MA), Dickinson College (Carlisle, PA), Skidmore College (Saratoga Springs, NY), Franklin and Marshall College (Lancaster, PA), or Loyola Marymount University (Los Angeles, CA). Interns may work one or two three-week sessions. RAs supervise recreational activities and are social facilitators. TAs and LAs help instructors carry out their classroom work, perform clerical duties, tutor students, and proctor evening study halls. Students sign up for one course per session, choosing from mathematics, science, humanities, or writing. Deadline: March 1 (resident advisors); February 1 (teaching assistants and laboratory assistants).

896.
Central Intelligence Agency
Career Trainee Internship Program
Recruitment Center
P.O. Box 12727, Dept STU-1
Arlington, VA 22209-8727
(703) 613-8388
http://www.odci.gov/cia/ciahome.html

Scholarships covering tuition for one year and summer programs providing a salary to undergraduate students interested in a career with the Agency in overseas intelligence operations. Program is during the summer between an undergraduate student's junior and senior year or first and second year of graduate school. Must be majoring in accounting, architecture, business administration, cartography, chemistry, computer science, economics, engineering, finance, geography, graphic design, international studies, languages (Russian, Chinese, or Japanese), law, mathematics, personnel administration, photo sciences, physics, political science, or printing/photography. Based on academic achievement, leadership, character, goals, and recommendations. Contact in August. Deadline: varies; usually early in the fall semester.

897.
Central Intelligence Agency
Minority Undergraduate Studies Program
Recruitment Center
P.O. Box 12727, Dept STU-1
Arlington, VA 22209-8727
(703) 613-8388
http://www.odci.gov/cia/ciahome.html

Tuition assistance plus a salary provided during summer employment with the Agency to minority undergraduate students. Must be majoring in accounting, architecture, business administration, cartography, chemistry, computer science, economics, engineering, finance, geography, graphic design, international studies, languages (Russian, Chinese, or Japanese), law, mathematics, personnel administration, photo sciences, physics, political science, and printing/photography. Based on academic achievement, leadership, character, goals, and recommendations. Contact in August. Deadline: varies; usually early in the fall semester.

898.
Central Intelligence Agency
Undergraduate Scholar Program
Recruitment Center
P.O. Box 12727, Dept STU-1
Arlington, VA 2209-8727
(703) 613-8388
http://www.odci.gov/cia/ciahome.html

Tuition assistance and a salary throughout college career to graduating high school seniors, particularly minorities. Students work during the summer at the Agency in Washington, DC. Must be majoring in accounting, architecture, business administration, cartography, chemistry, computer science, economics, engineering, finance, geography, graphic design, international studies, languages (Russian, Chinese, or Japanese), law, mathematics, personnel administration, photo sciences, physics, political science, or printing/photography. Based on academic achievement, leadership, character, goals, and

recommendations. Contact in August. Deadline: varies; usually early in the fall semester.

899.
Central Intelligence Agency
Undergraduate Student Trainee Program
Recruitment Center
P.O. Box 12727, Dept STU-1
Arlington, VA 22209-8727
(703) 613-8388
http://www.odci.gov/cia/ciahome.html

Tuition assistance and employment on alternating semester or quarter basis at the Agency to highly motivated undergraduates. Must be majoring in accounting, architecture, business administration, cartography, chemistry, computer science, economics, engineering, finance, geography, graphic design, international studies, languages (Russian, Chinese, or Japanese), law, mathematics, personnel administration, photo sciences, physics, political science, or printing/photography. Based on academic achievement, leadership, character, goals, and recommendations. Contact in August. Deadline: varies; usually early in the fall semester.

900.
Central Newspapers, Inc.
Pulliam Journalism Fellowships
c/o Editor
The Indianapolis News
Indianapolis, IN 46206
(317) 633-9208

20 awards providing a $3,250 stipend to recent graduates and undergraduate seniors who will receive their bachelor's degree in June. Award pays for a ten-week internship at one of CMI's newspapers in Indianapolis or Phoenix. Internships include sessions with a writing coach and seminars with local and national journalists. Deadline: March 1.

901.
C. G. Fuller Foundation
c/o National Bank-South Carolina
P.O. Box 1457
Columbia, SC 29202
(803) 256-6300

41 scholarships ranging from $750 to $2,000 to high school seniors or undergraduate college students. Must be South Carolina residents attending a college or university in South Carolina. Deadline: varies.

902.
CH2M Hill
Corporate Staffing
P.O. Box 221111
Denver, CO 80222-9998
(303) 771-0900

3 to 12 internships providing $175 per week to high school students and from $250 to $450 to undergraduate students to work at the largest U.S. environmental engineering firm. Students assist engineers with proposal creation, administrative work, surveying, engineering calculations, and drafting. Students are assigned to work in Phoenix,

AZ; Oakland, CA; Denver, CO; Atlanta, GA; Gainsville, FL; Portland, OR; or Milwaukee, WI. Interns work from twelve to fourteen weeks during the summer. Deadline: rolling.

903.
Charles A. Winans Memorial Trust
c/o Trust Department
P.O. Box 1359
Carlsbad, NM 88220

4 scholarships ranging from $500 to $650 to Beaumont, California, high school graduates. Contact: counseling office at Beaumont High School. Deadline: January 15.

904.
Charles B. Keesee Educational Fund Inc.,
  Scholarships
P.O. Box 431
Martinsville, VA 24114

750 scholarships of varying amounts to high school seniors or undergraduate college students. Must be residents of Virginia or North Carolina and attend a Virginia college affiliated with Virginia Baptist General Association or a Seminary of Southern Baptist Convention. Deadline: March 1.

905.
Charles Drew Memorial Scholarships
Careers in Health Program
1621 East 120th Street
Los Angeles, CA 90059
(213) 563-4800

Provides tutoring, housing stipend, and other assistance to train economically and educationally disadvantaged students who are about to take the Medical College Admissions Test (MCAT). Other restrictions may apply.

906.
Charles Drew Memorial Scholarships
Executive Secretary
Omega Psi Phi Fraternity
1231 Harvard Street, N.W.
Washington, DC 20009

Numerous scholarships of $300 to undergraduate sophomores, juniors, seniors, and graduate students. Must be used at a four-year college or university. Must have at least a B average. Open to all areas of study. Deadline: March 31.

907.
Charles E. Saak Trust
c/o Wells Fargo Bank, Trust Department
618 East Shaw Avenue
Fresno, CA 93710
(209) 442-6232

111 scholarships ranging from $9 to $500 to high school seniors or undergraduate college students. Must be residents of the Porterville-Poplar area of Tulare County, California. Students must be under twenty-one years of age and have financial need. Deadline: March 31.

908.
Charles H. Berry Trust Fund
P.O. Box 2036
Rochester, NH 03867
(603) 322-1670

3 scholarship grants ranging from $400 to $1,000 to male high school seniors. Must be residents of New Durham, Farmington, or Rochester, New Hampshire. Must attend a college in Strafford County, New Hampshire. Based on academic record and financial need. Contact high school counselor. Deadline: varies.

909.
Charles H. Bond Fund
c/o First Bank of Boston
100 Federal Street, 7th Floor
Boston, MA 02110
(617) 434-2102

8 scholarships ranging from $500 to $750 to high school seniors who are Massachusetts residents. Contact high school counselor or above address. Deadline: varies.

910.
Charles K. Blandin Foundation
100 Pokegama Avenue North
Grand Rapids, MN 55744
(218) 326-0523

474 scholarships ranging from $500 to $2,800 for graduates of Itasca County, Hill City, or Remer, Minnesota, high schools. Must be under twenty-two years of age. Deadline: May 1.

911.
Charles Kilburger Scholarship Fund
P.O. Drawer 869
Athens, OH 45701
(614) 653-0461

83 scholarships ranging from $470 to $6,000 to graduating high school seniors. Must be residents of Fairfield County, Ohio. Must be recommended by high school counselor. Deadline: varies.

912.
Charles Lyons Memorial Foundation, Inc.
2420 Pershing Road, Suite 400
Kansas City, MO 64108

74 scholarships ranging from $500 from $1,000 to Lafayette County, Missouri, high school graduates. Must be residents of Lafayette County at the time of application. Deadline: April 1.

913.
Charles M. Bair Memorial Trust
Attn: Trustee
c/o U.S. Bank Montana National
303 North Broadway, 2nd Floor
Billings, MT 59101
(406) 657-8124

38 scholarships, totaling $114,225, to graduates of Meagher and Wheatland counties, Harlowtown High School, or

White Sulphur Springs High School in Montana. Deadline: varies.

914.
Mr. & Mrs. Charles N. Flint Scholarship Foundation Fund
743 S. Lucern Boulevard
Los Angeles, CA 90005

63 scholarships, totaling $30,000, to undergraduate sophomores, juniors, seniors, and graduate students attending an accredited college or university in Los Angeles County. Applicants must be legal residents of L.A. County, U.S. citizens, registered voters, and have a 3.25 GPA while completing twelve units per semester. Applications can be picked up at the financial aid office of your school. Other restrictions may apply. Deadline: May 1.

915.
Charleston Evening Post, The News and Courier Post–Courier College Scholarship
134 Columbus Street
Charleston, SC 29403-4800

Grants of $1,400 or more to high school seniors who are newspaper carriers. Once in college, students will be awarded extra money for maintaining a high grade point average. An extra $50 per semester for a 3.0 GPA; $75 per semester for a 3.5 GPA. Deadline: spring.

916.
Charles W. Frees, Jr., Educational Fund
508 Coeur de Royale
Creve Coeur, MO 63141
(314) 993-5982

50 scholarships ranging from $900 to $1,200 to male high school seniors who will graduate from a St. Louis County, Missouri, high school. Must be in the top 20 percent of class, with at least a 3.0 GPA. May be used at a two- or four-year college. Based on academic record, SAT/ACT scores, and financial need. Request applications after February 1. Deadline: April 1.

917.
Charter Fund Scholarships
Grants Administrator
511 16th Street, Suite 700
Denver, CO 80202
(303) 572-1727

55 scholarships ranging from $200 to $2,000 are available to high school graduates from the Denver area. Based on SAT/ACT scores and financial need. Deadline: May 15.

918.
Chautauqua Institution Scholarships
Schools Office
P.O. Box 1098
Chautauqua, NY 14722
(716) 357-6234

250 scholarships, totaling $225,000, for summer school only to undergraduate students. Must be majoring in art, dance, music, or theater. Based on auditions (portfolio in art) indicating proficiency; financial need is also taken into

consideration. Some auditions are required in person, but taped auditions are also acceptable. Deadline: April 1.

919.
Chautauqua Region Community Foundation, Inc.
Attn: Director
104 Hotel Jamestown Building
Jamestown NY 14701
(716) 661-3390

43 scholarships, totaling over $18,000, to high school seniors. Must be residents of Chautauqua school district. Deadline: April 30.

920.
Chemists' Club
Chemists' Club Undergraduate Scholarship Award
295 Madison Avenue, 27th Floor
New York, NY 10017
(212) 532-7649

1 scholarship of $3,000 (renewable up to three years) for undergraduate chemistry student who is attending an American Chemical Society (ACS)-accredited college or university. Based on academic record, recommendations, and financial need. Deadline: May 1.

921.
Cherokee Nation of Oklahoma
P.O. Box 948
Tahlequah, OK 74465
(800) 722-4325 or (918) 456-0671

500 scholarships of varying amounts to high school seniors and undergraduate and graduate college students. Must be one-quarter or more Cherokee Indian. Amount awarded dependent upon educational requirements and financial needs of recipient. May be used at any U.S. institution. Deadline: April 1.

922.
Cheyenne–Arapahoe Tribal Scholarships
Higher Education Assistance Program
P.O. Box 38
Concho, OK 73022
(405) 262-0345

Scholarships of at least $100 to high school seniors or graduates or undergraduate college students who are Cheyenne-Arapahoe tribal members and are interested in pursuing postsecondary education. May be either enrolled or planning to enroll in a postsecondary school. Renewable. Deadline: none.

923.
Chicago and Northeast Illinois District Council of Carpenters
Ted Kennedy Memorial Scholarships
12 East Erie Street
Chicago, IL 60611

4 scholarships of $1,000 to high school seniors who are sons or daughters of union members in good standing of any local affiliated union. May be used at any accredited

U.S. college or university. Based on academic record, SAT/ACT score, and extracurricular activities. Deadline: July 1.

924.
Chicago Association of Black Journalists Scholarships
c/o Dept. of Journalism
Northern Illinois University
DeKalb, IL 60115
(815) 753-7017

Scholarships ranging from $1,000 to $2,000 to minority undergraduate juniors and seniors and graduate students. Must be enrolled in an accredited print- or broadcast-journalism program at a Chicago institution. Deadline: February.

925.
Chi Eta Phi Sorority
Aliene Ewell Scholarship Award
3029 13th Street, N.W.
Washington, DC 20009
(202) 232-3858

1 scholarship of varying amount to a nursing student. Preference given to students beginning their initial nursing education. Based on academic record, recommendations, career goals, and financial need. Deadline: March 1.

926.
Children's Foundation of Lake Wales, Florida, Inc.
402 East Park Avenue
Lake Wales, FL 33853
(813) 676-5456

14 grants ranging from $300 to $400 to high school seniors from Lake Wales, Florida, high school district. Deadline: May 15.

927.
Chilton Company
Attn: Manager Employment/EEO
201 King of Prussia Road
Radnor, PA 19089
(215) 964-4218

6 to 8 part-time internships lasting three to four months open to undergraduate juniors and seniors who are English, communications, or journalism majors. Interns are awarded a $500 stipend. Interns conduct research, write, interview, and interface with customers and learn about magazine photo and art layout production. Openings occur year-round. Submit a letter outlining interests, résumé, letters of recommendation, and writing samples. Deadline: open.

928.
Chinese Professional Club of Houston Scholarships
11302 Fallbrook Drive, Suite 304
Houston, TX 77065
(713) 955-0115

10 scholarships ranging from $600 to $1,500 to high school seniors or graduates or undergraduate college students.

Must be residents of Houston, Texas, metropolitan area and of Chinese descent. Deadline: November 15.

929.
Chi Psi Educational Trust
Clifford H. Williams Scholarship
1705 Washtenaw Avenue
P.O. Box 1344
Ann Arbor, MI 48106
(313) 663-9302

I award of $300 in each of the five Chi Psi regions to an undergraduate or graduate student. Must be a member of the fraternity. Deadline: May 1.

930.
Christa McAuliffe Fellowships
Department of Education
400 Maryland Avenue, S.W.
Washington, DC 20202
(202) 708-5366

Varying numbers of fellowships of $25,000 to undergraduate and graduate students. Must attend an accredited institution. Selection based on financial need. Contact state student loan office. Deadline: January.

931.
Christian Appalachian Project
Community Service Scholarships
322 Crab Orchard Road
Lancaster, KY 40446
(606) 792-3051

Numerous $1,000 and $1,500 scholarships to high school seniors from thirty-two eastern Kentucky counties. Must be entering a college, university, or vocational school the fall after high school graduation. Based on community involvement. Academic achievement and financial need are secondary considerations. Deadline: varies from county to county.

932.
Christian Record Braille Foundation Scholarships
4444 South 52nd Street
Lincoln, NE 68506
(402) 488-0981

5 to 10 scholarships of $1,000 to high school seniors and undergraduate students who are legally blind. Loans are sometimes available. Loan repayment begins upon graduation or completion of course. Based on financial need. Deadline: May 1.

933.
Churches Home Foundation, Inc.
c/o Bank South, Personal Trust Department
P.O. Box 4387 (MC 678)
Atlanta, GA 30302
(404) 529-4111

Numerous grants, totaling $124,086, to undergraduate students who are residents of Georgia. Based on academic record and financial need. Contact: Duncan G. Peek, President, 1100 Spring Street, N.W., Suite 600, Atlanta, GA 30367.

934.
CINTAS Fellowship Program
Arts International–Institute of International Education
809 United Nations Plaza
New York, NY 10017
(212) 984-5374

5 to 15 fellowships of $10,000 to undergraduate and graduate students and individuals to foster and encourage professional development and recognize talented creative artists in architecture, music composition, painting, printmaking, sculpture, and writing. For people of Cuban citizenship or Cuban ancestry (at least one Cuban parent). Deadline: March 1.

935.
C. I. Rowan Charitable and Educational Fund, Inc.
1918 Commerce Building
Fort Worth, TX 76102
(817) 322-2327

4 scholarships ranging from $79 to $14,275 to high school seniors from the Fort Worth area. Must be Texas residents and attend a Texas college or university. Contact high school counselor or above address. Deadline: varies.

936.
Civil Air Patrol (CAP) Scholarships
Attn: National Headquarters/TT
Maxwell AFB, AL 36112-5572
(205) 293-5332

Numerous scholarships of varying amounts to high school seniors or graduates or undergraduate college students. Must be majoring in or planning on majoring in aerospace-engineering, science, humanities, education, and also technical-vocational training. Must be current active members of Civil Air Patrol. Applications submitted on CAP Form 95 through squadron and wing commanders to arrive at National Headquarters. Deadline: April 1.

937.
Civitan International Foundation
P.O. Box 130744
Birmingham, AL 35222-0744
(205) 591-8910

Numerous scholarships of up to $2,000 for one year of study in history, political science, economics, or education to high school seniors planning a career in teaching. Deadline: May 1.

938.
Clarke & Company
Operations & Benefits Manager
535 Boylston Street
Boston, MA 02116
(617) 536-3003
(617) 536-8524 Fax

9 to 10 internships ranging from twelve to twenty weeks providing a salary of $240 per week to undergraduate juniors and seniors and first-year graduate students in public relations. Interns assist account coordinators by writing press releases, generating media lists, conducting research for specific clients, setting up for events, archiving client flies, and delivering packages to the media. Applicants must submit a résumé and cover letter. Deadline: April 1 (summer); June 1 (fall); November 1 (spring).

939.
The Clark Foundation Scholarship Program
30 Wall Street
New York, NY 10005
(212) 269-1833

684 renewable scholarships ranging from $300 to $3,000 to high school seniors or graduates. Must plan to attend or be attending a two- or four-year undergraduate college or university or graduate or professional school. Must be attending a high school in any of the following school districts in and around Cooperstown, New York: Cherry Valley, Cooperstown, Edmeston, Laurens, Milford, Richfield Springs, Scenevus, Springfield, Van Hornsville, West Winfield, or Worchester. Must have been in the upper one-third of class and have had at least a 3.0 GPA. Transportation, housing, and food allowances for student, spouse, and dependents. Deadline: none.

940.
Claude and Ina Brey Memorial Endowment Fund
c/o The Merchants National Bank of Topeka
P.O. Box 178
Topeka, KS 66601
(913) 291-1000

11 scholarships of $680 to graduating high school seniors, high school graduates who haven't attended college, and undergraduate students. Must be dependents of fourth-degree Kansas Grange members. Write a letter briefly detailing your educational and financial situation. Selection based on academic achievement, extracurricular activities, and financial need. Other restrictions may apply. Deadline: July 1.

941.
The Clemens Foundation
P.O. Box 427
Philomath, OR 97370
(503) 929-3541

359 scholarships, totaling $414,451, to high school seniors or graduates or undergraduate students. Must be residents of Pilomath, Eddyville, Crane, or Alsea, Oregon. Can be used at a college, university, or vocational school. Deadline: varies.

942.
Clem Jaunich Education Trust (Scholarships)
Attn: Trustee
5353 Gamble Drive, Suite 110
Minneapolis, MN 55416
(612) 546-1555

4 scholarships ranging from $500 to $5,000 to students who have attended public or private school in the Delano, Minnesota, school district or currently reside within seven miles of the city of Delano, Minnesota. Awards support undergraduate or graduate study in theology or medicine. Deadline: July 15.

943.
Cleveland Foundation
Harry Coulby Scholarships
c/o Pickands Mather & Co.
1100 Superior Avenue
Cleveland, OH 44114
Written inquiries only

2 scholarships of up to $6,000 to high school seniors or high school graduates (who have never attended college) who are children of Pickands Mather & Co. employees. Based on SAT score. Renewable for up to four years. Good for study of any major. Deadline: January 15.

944.
Cleveland Hispanic Scholarship Fund, Inc.
May-Dugan Multiservice Center
4115 Bridge Avenue
Cleveland, OH 44113

Financial assistance to Hispanic graduating high school seniors or graduates accepted at or enrolled in a college or university, a trade apprenticeship program, or an accredited technical institute who otherwise would be deprived of the advantages of such enrollment because of financial limitations. Must have graduated from a high school within the Cleveland metropolitan area and must be between seventeen and twenty-five years of age. Deadline: varies.

945.
Cleveland Scholarship Program, Inc.
2000 East 9th Street, Suite 1020
Cleveland, OH 44115

Scholarships ranging from $300 to $800 to high school graduates from certain schools in the greater Cleveland area. Must be or plan to be full-time students. Based on academic record, SAT/ACT score, and recommendation. No direct application. Students are selected through advisory staff referral. Awards can be used at a college or vocational school. Deadline: varies.

946.
Clinical Directors Network of Region II, Inc.
8 West 19th Street, 8th Floor
New York, NY 10011
(212) 255-3841
(212) 255-5227 Fax

2 to 3 internships lasting from three to six months providing local transportation expenses to undergraduates, college graduates, graduate students, persons reentering the work force, or retired persons. Positions are available in New York and New Jersey. Interns must be computer literate and have an interest in and commitment to public and community health. Preference given to bilingual applicants. Interns assist community health centers in launching outreach activities, help design and pretest research instruments for Cancer Control Project and HIV/AIDS Clinical Trials Projects, help develop a comprehensive resource guide for community health centers, assist with general administrative duties, and help develop a nutrition-oriented therapy for patients with HIV/AIDS. Submit a letter detailing interests, résumé, and references. An

interview is conducted in person or by telephone. Deadline: open.

947.
Clinton O. & Lura Curtis Jones Memorial Trust
66 West Street, 3rd Floor
Pittsfield, MA 01201
(413) 443-4771

Numerous scholarships, totaling $70,500, to high school seniors or graduates. Must be residents of Berkshire County, Massachusetts. Deadline: April 15.

948.
Close Up Foundation
Citizen Bee
44 Canal Center Plaza
Alexandria, VA 22314
(800) 336-5479 ext. 649

15 scholarships ranging from $2,000 to $12,000 to high school students in grades 9 through 12. Ask high school counselor or social studies teacher to write and obtain information on how your high school can participate in the Citizen Bee (students are asked questions, much like a spelling bee). Schools must contact the Close Up Foundation in September. Competitions begin in January.

949.
Clyde A. Erwin Scholarships
Chairman
Vocational Education Scholarship Committee
North Carolina Department of Public Instruction
116 West Edenton Street, Education Building
Raleigh, NC 27603-1712

5 scholarships of $500 to high school seniors who are planning to become teachers of vocational education. Must be North Carolina residents. Must be nominated for these awards. Based on leadership, academic record, community involvement, character, and financial need. Deadline: March 1.

950.
Coastal Advertising Federation
Scholarship Program
Mary Miller, Scholarship Chairman
P.O. Box 1414
Myrtle Beach, SC 29578
(803) 449-7121

Numerous $1,000 scholarships to undergraduate college students. Must be residents of Horry, Georgetown County, and have completed at least sophomore year of study at any accredited four-year college or university. Must have a 3.0 GPA or better. Deadline: March 31.

951.
Coastal Bend Community Foundation
860 Mercantile Tower-MT 276
Corpus Christi, TX 78477
(512) 882-9745

Numerous scholarships of varying amounts to high school seniors. Must be residents of Aransas, Bee, Jim Wells,

Kleberg, Nueces, Refugio, or San Patricio counties, Texas. Students should write an introductory letter briefly describing their educational and financial situation. Deadline: varies.

952.
Coastal Bend Community Foundation
Sue Kay Lay Memorial Scholarships
Contact: 2345
860 Mercantile Tower–MT 276
Corpus Christi, TX 78477
(512) 882-9745

10 to 15 scholarships ranging from $400 to $1,500 to high school seniors graduating from a Texas high school at the end of the spring semester. Must be residents of Aransas, Bee, Jim Wells, Kleberg, Nueces, Refugio, or San Patricio counties, Texas. Applicants must have a cumulative GPA of 90 or higher (through fall semester of senior year). Must plan to enroll full-time in the fall semester following graduation in a program leading toward an associate or bachelor's degree. Based on academics and need. Deadline: March 1.

953.
Coastal Bend Community Foundation
Talbert Family Memorial Fund Scholarship
Coordinator
Contact: 2345
860 Mercantile Tower–MT 276
Corpus Christi, TX 78477
(512) 882-9745

5 scholarships of $2,000 to full-time undergraduate juniors majoring in accounting. Must be permanent residents of and have graduated from a high school in Aransas, Bee, Jim Wells, Kleberg, Nueces, Refugio, or San Patricio counties, Texas. Must have a cumulative 3.25 GPA on a 4.0 scale. Deadline: March 27.

954.
Coca–Cola Scholars Program
Coca-Cola Scholars Foundation, Inc.
P.O. Box 442
Atlanta, GA 30301
(404) 733-5420

50 four-year $20,000 and 100 one-year $1,000 scholarships to graduating high school seniors. Must be U.S. citizens, full-time secondary school students graduating in current academic year, and planning to pursue a degree at a college or university. Based on character, personal merit, leadership in school, civic, and extracurricular activities, academic achievement, and motivation to succeed. Applications must be requested by a school official from the closest Coca-Cola Bottling Company or above address. Parents of home-schooled students should contact the National Foundation to open a file for the student. Deadline: October 31.

955.
Coffey Foundation, Inc.
P.O. Box 1170
Lenoir, SC 28645

Numerous grants of varying amounts, totaling $91,800, and 1 loan of $1,000 to high school seniors or undergraduate

students. Must be residents of Caldwell County, North Carolina. Based on academic record and financial need. Deadline: April 15.

956.
Cogswell Benevolent Trust
875 Elm Street
Manchester, NH 03101

Numerous scholarships of varying amounts, totaling $208,000, to high school seniors. Must be New Hampshire residents. Deadline: varies.

957.
Colburn–Pledge Music Scholarship Foundation
Secretary
510 Petroleum Commerce Building
San Antonio, TX 78205

Several scholarships totaling $3,000 to high school seniors or undergraduate students studying a string instrument (violin, viola, cello, bass) in classical music with the intention of becoming a professional musician. Must be in need of financial aid and possess musical talent. Must be Texas residents. Annual auditions of selected applicants held in San Antonio on or about June 1. Deadline: April 23 (audition applications).

958.
College Board's Engineering and Business
Administration
Scholarship Program for Minority Community
College Graduates
Edith Edmonds
College Scholarship Service
The College Board
45 Columbus Avenue
New York, NY 10023

Scholarships of varying amounts to undergraduate sophomore students. Must be completing second year at a two-year college and have at least a 3.0 GPA. Must be nominated by a school official. Deadline: November 15.

959.
College Connections
Internship Coordinator
329 East 82nd Street
New York, NY 10028-4103
(212) 734-2190

2 internships providing a salary ranging from $240 to $400 per week to undergraduate and graduate students in public relations. International students may apply. Internship takes place in New York City. Interns assist the staff in writing press releases, pitching stories to various media, and conducting mass mailings. Some of the clients for College Connections are Baylor University, College Board, Council for Undergraduate Research, Duke University, Monmouth College, *Rolling Stone*, Summerbridge National, and UNICEF. Applicants must submit a résumé and a cover letter. Deadline: rolling.

960.
College Foundation, Inc.
North Carolina Student Incentive Grants
P.O. Box 12100
Raleigh, NC 27605
(919) 821-4771

4,500 grants of $1,500 to undergraduate college students. Must be North Carolina residents and U.S. citizens. Must have substantial financial need and must be attending an eligible North Carolina college or university. Based on financial need. Deadline: March 15.

961.
Collins-McDonald Trust Fund
Attn: Trustee
203 South 2nd Avenue
Lakeview, OR 51246
(712) 472-2581

26 scholarships ranging from $610 to $2,520 to graduates of Lake County, Oregon, high schools. Must be residents of Lake County, Oregon. Contact high school counselor or above address. Deadline: May 14.

962.
Colonial Dames of America Scholarships
421 East 61st Street
New York, NY 10021
(212) 838-5489

Numerous scholarships of $1,000 to undergraduate and graduate students who are of qualified colonial descent. May attend any two- or four-year U.S. institution. Based on academic record, goals, recommendations, and financial need. Deadline: April 1.

963.
Colorado AFL-CIO
Americo Toffoli Scholarship Awards
Attn: Secretary-Treasurer
360 Acoma Street, Room 300
Denver, CO 80235
(303) 698-0001

Up to 6 scholarships ranging from $500 to $1,000 to graduating high school seniors. Must be dependents of AFL-CIO members and residents of Colorado. Selection based on academic and financial criteria. Other restrictions may apply. Deadline: April 22.

964.
Colorado Commission on Higher Education
Dependents Tuition Assistance Program
1300 Broadway, 2nd Floor
Denver, CO 80203
(303) 866-2723
http://www.state.co.us/cche-dir/hecche.html

Assistance in the form of paid tuition to graduating high school seniors or undergraduate students. Must be dependents of Colorado law enforcement officers, fire, or national guard personnel killed or disabled in the line of duty, or dependents of prisoners of war or service

personnel listed as missing in action. Dependents of disabled personnel must have demonstrated financial need for the assistance. Obtain applications from above address.

965.
Colorado Commission on Higher Education
Diversity Grants
1300 Broadway, 2nd Floor
Denver, CO 80203
(303) 866-2723
http://www.state.co.us/cche-dir/hecche.html

Grants of varying amounts to graduating high school seniors and undergraduate students. Must be members of underrepresented groups in the Colorado public higher education system. Must be Colorado residents and attend accredited Colorado institutions. Must file FAFSA. Deadline: varies by school.

966.
Colorado Commission on Higher Education
Nursing Scholarships
1300 Broadway, 2nd Floor
Denver, CO 80203
(303) 866-2723
http://www.state.co.us/cche-dir/hecche.html

Grants of varying amounts to graduating high school seniors and undergraduate students. Must be pursuing careers in nursing and intend to practice in Colorado. Must be Colorado residents and attend accredited Colorado institutions. Must file FAFSA. Deadline: varies by school.

967.
Colorado Commission on Higher Education
Student Grants
Coordinator
1300 Broadway, 2nd Floor
Denver, CO 80203
(303) 866-2723
http://www.state.co.us/cche-dir/hecche.html

Numerous scholarships of up to $2,000 to undergraduate students. Must be Colorado residents. Based on financial need. Colorado Graduate Grants and Fellowships also are offered for graduate study. Deadline: varies.

968.
Colorado Commission on Higher Education
Student Incentive Grants
Coordinator
1300 Broadway, 2nd Floor
Denver, CO 80203
(303) 866-2723
http://www.state.co.us/cche-dir/hecche.html

Grants of up to $2,500 grants to undergraduate students. Must be Colorado residents. Based on financial need. Deadline: varies.

969.
Colorado Commission on Higher Education Undergraduate Scholarships
Coordinator
1300 Broadway, 2nd Floor
Denver, CO 80203
(303) 866-2723
http://www.state.co.us/cche-dir/hecche.html

Scholarships of amounts up to the total cost of tuition and fees to high school seniors or undergraduate students. Must be Colorado residents. Based on academic achievement. Deadline: varies.

970.
Colorado Commission on Higher Education Veteran Tuition Assistance Programs
Coordinator
1300 Broadway, 2nd Floor
Denver, CO 80203
(303) 866-2723
http://www.state.co.us/cche-dir/hecche.html

Tuition assistance equal to one-half the weighted average resident tuition at state-supported colleges or universities to students who served in the military between August 1964 and May 1975. Applicants must have been Colorado residents when they entered the military and must currently be Colorado residents. Must have completed their time in the military less than eight years ago. Deadline: none.

971.
Colorado Masons Benevolent Fund Association
1614 Welton Street
Denver, CO 80202

70 scholarships of varying amounts, totaling $209,000, to high school seniors or graduates of Colorado high schools. Must be children of a member.

972.
(Colorado) Professional Engineers of Colorado
3161 South Josephine Street
Denver, CO 80210
(303) 756-9777

Scholarships of $1,000 to high school seniors planning to enter into an engineering curriculum. Some scholarships may require attendance at a certain college or university. For Colorado residents only. Deadline: late November; local chapters may vary.

973.
Colorado Society of CPA's
Educational Foundation Scholarships for HS Seniors
7720 East Belleview Avenue, Building 46B
Englewood, CO 80111
(303) 773-2877

5 to 10 scholarships of $750 to high school seniors. Must be Colorado residents, with at least a 3.75 GPA. Must intend to major in accounting at one of the eleven Colorado colleges and universities that offer an accounting major. Based on academic achievement. Deadline: March 1.

974.
Colorado Society of CPA's
Educational Foundation Scholarships for Undergraduates
7720 East Belleview Avenue, Building 46B
Englewood, CO 80111

Scholarships of up to $1,000 to undergraduate sophomore, junior, or senior students. Must be Colorado residents, with at least a 3.75 GPA. Must be accounting majors at one of the eleven Colorado colleges and universities that offer an accounting major. Renewable. Deadline: June 1 (fall); November 30 (spring).

975.
Columbia Journalism Review
Internships Program
700 Journalism Building
Columbia University
New York, NY 10027
(212) 854-1881

Varying numbers of internships lasting varying amounts of time are open to undergraduates and recent college graduates who have demonstrated an interest in news and public affairs. Interns answer phones, conduct research, fact-check, write, and report. Openings occur year-round. No monetary stipend is provided, though interns are paid free-lance rates for any work published in the magazine. Submit a letter detailing interests, résumé, writing samples, and the names and phone numbers of two appropriate references. Deadline: open.

976.
Cominco Ltd.
Higher Education Awards
200 Granville Street
Vancouver, BC V6C 2R2
Canada
(604) 682-0611

Approximately 40 scholarships ranging from $700 to $1,000 to high school seniors who are children or wards of active or retired Cominco Ltd. employees. Good for all fields of study. Deadline: August 31.

977.
Commission for Racial Justice
Special Higher Education Program
United Church of Christ
Attn: Carmen Williams, Coordinator
700 Prospect Avenue
Cleveland, OH 44115-1100
(216) 736-3786

65 scholarships ranging from $500 to $2,000 to nonwhite undergraduates in financial need. Preference given to members of the United Church of Christ. Based on academic record and an essay on how their interests, extracurricular activities, and future aims relate to the commission's goals. Deadline: January 1 and August 1.

978.
Commonwealth National Bank
Leon Lowengard Scholarships/Ray Shoemaker
   Scholarships
Trust Department
P.O. Box 1010
10 South Market Square
Harrisburg, PA 17108
(717) 780-3050

Numerous scholarships of $2,000 to graduating high school seniors or high school graduates. May have graduated from any high school in the Harrisburg, Pennsylvania, area. Applicants must be of the Jewish faith. Award is for full-time undergraduate study. Must be Pennsylvania residents and either U.S. citizens or legal residents. Deadline: none.

979.
Commonwealth Scholarship Fund
501 Carnell Hall
Temple University
Philadelphia, PA 18122

Scholarships of varying amounts to graduating high school seniors, high school graduates who haven't attended college, and undergraduates. Priority is given to students attending one of the state's two predominantly black institutions: Lincoln University and Cheyney State University. Selection based on financial need.

980.
Communications Workers of America (CWA)
Local Union Office

Varying numbers of scholarships of $1,000 to graduating high school seniors. Must be children of CWA members. Awards are only for certain fields of study. Selection based on academic achievement. Other restrictions may apply. Deadline: varies locally.

981.
Communications Workers of America (CWA)
Ray Hackney Scholarship Fund
c/o CWA Padonia Center
30 East Padonia Road, Suite 205
Timonium, MD 21930

8 scholarships of $1,000 per year for four years to graduating high school seniors or high school graduates who are children of CWA members. CWA members may also apply. Award is good for any field of study. Deadline: May 1.

982.
Community Foundation for Monterey County
Attn: Executive Director
P.O. Box 1384
Monterey, CA 93942
(408) 375-9712

2 scholarships of $2,000 to high school seniors and high school graduates. Must be residents of Monterey County, California. Selection based on academic achievement and financial need. Contact high school counselor or write a

letter briefly detailing your educational and financial situation. Other restrictions may apply.

983.
Community Scholarship Program
Community Service Center Building, Room 602
200 North Vineyard Boulevard
Honolulu, HI 96817
(808) 521-3861

Scholarships and loans ranging from $200 to $2,000 to high school seniors or undergraduate or graduate college students. Must be residents of Hawaii. Awards may be used by students studying the arts, business, education, health, the humanities, social concerns, science, engineering, and some areas where students may have special talents. Loans are interest-free and repayment begins thirteen months after graduation. Based on academic record, recommendations, employment, career goals, and financial need. Deadline: March 1.

984.
Concerned Media Professionals Scholarships
c/o Armando V. Durazo
Tucson Daily Star
P.O. Box 26807
Tucson, AZ 85726

6 scholarships ranging from $500 to $1,000 to minority undergraduate college students majoring in media fields. Deadline: April.

985.
Congressional Hispanic Caucus
504 C Street, N.E.
Washington, DC 20002
(800) 367-5273

Offers Hispanic students the chance to gain hands-on experience in the operation of the American governmental system. Summer internships are open to high school and college students, and nine-month appointments are available for recent bachelor's graduates and for current graduate students. Interns receive a stipend of $1,000 a month, plus housing and travel expenses. Must submit a completed application, high school or college transcript, and letters of reference from teachers or employers. Deadline: April 10.

986.
Connecticut AFL-CIO
Hank Kerschner Scholarship
Attn: President
30 Sherman Street
West Hartford, CT 06107

1 scholarship of $500 to graduating high school senior. Must be dependent of member of AFL-CIO and resident of Connecticut. Selection based on at least a 2.5 GPA, other academic criteria, and financial need. Renewable. Deadline: May 1.

987.
Connecticut Department of Higher Education Aid for Public College Students (CAPS)
61 Woodland Street
Hartford, CT 06105-2391
(860) 947-1800
(860) 947-1310 Fax
http://ctdhe.commnet.edu/dheweb/dhea.htm

Grants of varying amounts to Connecticut residents enrolled in state-supported Connecticut colleges or universities. The award can't exceed calculated financial need. Based on academic progress and financial need. Deadline: varies.

988.
Connecticut Department of Higher Education Aid to Dependents of Deceased/Disabled Veterans
61 Woodland Street
Hartford, CT 06105-2391
(860) 947-1800
(860) 947-1310 Fax
http://ctdhe.commnet.edu/dheweb/dhea.htm

Grants of $400 to students who are children of deceased or disabled veterans. Applicants must be between sixteen and twenty-three years of age. Must have financial need. Deadline: none.

989.
Connecticut Department of Higher Education Family Education Loan
61 Woodland Street
Hartford, CT 06105-2391
(860) 947-1800
(860) 947-1310 Fax
http://ctdhe.commnet.edu/dheweb/dhea.htm

Loans ranging from $2,000 to $20,000 per year to undergraduate students. May be either full- or part-time students at a Connecticut nonprofit college or be Connecticut residents and either a full- or part-time student enrolled at any U.S. nonprofit college. Based on applicant's ability to repay the loan. Deadline: none.

990.
Connecticut Department of Higher Education Independent College Student Grant Program (CICS)
61 Woodland Street
Hartford, CT 06105
(860) 947-1800
(860) 947-1310 Fax
http://ctdhe.commnet.edu/dheweb/dhea.htm

Grants of varying amounts to high school seniors or undergraduate college students. Must be Connecticut residents who are attending or have been accepted to a private Connecticut college or university. Must have financial need. Deadline: varies.

991.
Connecticut Department of Higher Education Nursing Scholarship
61 Woodland Street
Hartford, CT 06105
(860) 947-1800
(860) 947-1310 Fax
http://ctdhe.commnet.edu/dheweb/dhea.htm

Scholarships of varying amounts to high school seniors or undergraduate students pursuing a career in nursing. Must be Connecticut residents who are full-time students in a three-year hospital school of nursing program in Connecticut or a two- or four-year nursing program at a Connecticut college. Based on academic record and financial need. Deadline: varies.

992.
Connecticut Department of Higher Education Scholastic Achievement Grants
61 Woodland Street
Hartford, CT 06105
(860) 947-1800
(860) 947-1310 Fax
http://ctdhe.commnet.edu/dheweb/dhea.htm

Scholarships ranging from $100 to $2,000 to high school seniors or graduates who haven't attended college. Must be in the top 20 percent of class or have at least a 1200 SAT score. May be used at any approved Connecticut college or university or in a reciprocating state. Must be Connecticut residents and U.S. citizens. Based on academic promise. Deadline: February 15.

993.
Connecticut Department of Higher Education Tuition Aid for Needy Students
61 Woodland Street
Hartford, CT 06105
(860) 947-1800
(860) 947-1310 Fax
http://ctdhe.commnet.edu/dheweb/dhea.htm

Financial assistance of amounts up to unmet financial need to students attending public Connecticut colleges. Based on financial need.

994.
Connecticut Department of Higher Education Tuition Waiver for Senior Citizens
61 Woodland Street
Hartford, CT 06105
(860) 947-1800
(860) 947-1310 Fax
http://ctdhe.commnet.edu/dheweb/dhea.htm

Tuition costs are waived for any Connecticut resident over the age of sixty-two who is attending a public Connecticut college. Deadline: none.

995.
Connecticut Department of Higher Education Tuition Waiver for Veterans
61 Woodland Street
Hartford, CT 06105
(860) 947-1800
(860) 947-1310 Fax
http: //ctdhe.commnet.edu/dheweb/dhea.htm

Tuition costs are waived for any veteran who is a Connecticut resident at time of enrolling in college or when he or she entered the Armed Forces or for children of Vietnam veterans who have been declared as missing in action or prisoners of war. Student must be enrolled in a public Connecticut college.

996.
Connecticut League for Nursing Scholarships
P.O. Box 365
Wallingford, CT 06492
(203) 265-4248

2 scholarships of $500 to undergraduate college students in an NLN-accredited Connecticut school of nursing that is a CLN agency member. Must be pursuing a BSN; must have completed third year of four. Students in a diploma program must have completed second year of a three-year program or first year of a two-year program. Students in an RN program must be entering senior year. Must be Connecticut residents. Based on academic record and financial need. Deadline: October 20.

997.
Connecticut Library Association (CLA) Program for Education Grants
231 Capitol Avenue
Hartford, CT 06106
(203) 278-6685

4 to 5 educational grants of varying amounts to library employees, volunteer trustees, or friends of the library in the state of Connecticut. Must be members of CLA to be eligible. Deadline: none.

998.
Connecticut Society of Professional Engineers
2600 Dixwell Avenue
Hamden, CT 06514
(203) 281-4322

Scholarships of $1,000 to high school seniors planning to enter into an engineering curriculum. Some scholarships may require attendance at a certain college or university. For Connecticut residents only. Deadline: late November; local chapters may vary.

999.
Conrail Women's Aid Scholarships
c/o Resource Development Department
Consolidated Rail Corporation
Six Penn Center, Room 1010
Philadelphia, PA 19103-2959

Scholarships ranging from $500 to $1,500 per year for four years to children of present Conrail employees or former

Penn Central employees who were transferred to Amtrak or Penn Central Corp. Based on SAT/ACT, achievement tests, academic record, and financial need. Deadline: April 1.

1000.
Consortium of College and University Media Centers
Research Awards
c/o Don Rieck
121 Pearson Hall-MRC
Iowa State University
Ames, IA 50011
(515) 294-8022

Awards of varying amounts to undergraduate and graduate students, and to faculty or staff persons in a member organization of the Consortium. Research must be conducted within eighteen months of submission of proposal. Based on proposed study and how it relates to the needs or opportunities in the production, selection, cataloging, distribution, and/or utilization of educational sound motion picture/video. Application must include a one- to two-page description of the study, a proposed budget, and a résumé of the investigator. Deadline: May 15.

1001.
Consulting Engineers Council of Metropolitan Washington Scholarship
8811 Colesville Road
Silver Spring, MD 20910
(301) 588-6616

Scholarships ranging from $1,000 to $6,000 to high school seniors. Must be residents of metropolitan Washington, DC, area, which includes DC, Virginia, and Maryland. Teacher must send for application; DC states specific criteria. Contact: Publications Coordinator. Deadline: early fall.

1002.
Consulting Engineers Council of Metropolitan Washington–Virginia Scholarships
8811 Colesville Road, Suite 225
Silver Spring, MD 20910
(301) 588-6616

Awards ranging from $1,000 to $6,000 to undergraduate juniors pursuing careers in engineering. Must be in the top 40 percent of their class. Applicants must be residents of Alexandria County, Virginia. Other restrictions may apply. Contact: Publications Coordinator. Deadline: early February.

1003.
Consulting Engineers Council of New Jersey
Louis Goldberg Scholarship Fund
66 Morris Avenue
Springfield, NJ 07081
(201) 379-1100

Scholarships of $1,000 to undergraduate students who have completed at least two years of study at an Accrediting Board for Engineering and Technology (ABET)–accredited college or university in New Jersey. Must be in the top half of class and be pursuing a career in consulting engineering. Recipients will then be eligible for an American Consulting

Engineers Council National Scholarship from $2,000 to $5,000. Deadline: January 27.

1004.
Continental Grain Company–Wayne Feed Division
Scholarship Program
10 South Riverside Plaza
Chicago, IL 60606

Scholarships of $1,000 for high school seniors or undergraduate students majoring in animal science or a related field. Must be present or former 4-H members with at least one year of 4-H work. Must be U.S. citizens or legal residents. Contact your local or state 4-H organization or write to the above address. Deadline: October 1.

1005.
Continental Grain Foundation
277 Park Avenue
New York, NY 10172
(212) 207-5100

5 grants ranging from $500 to $1,000 to assist students in an exchange program with other countries.

1006.
The Cooking Contest Chronicle
c/o Karen Martis
P.O. Box 10792
Merrillville, IN 46411

"The Cooking Contest Chronicle" is a newsletter with a comprehensive list of best-recipe contests sponsored by product makers and even state fairs. It lists national and regional contests. To receive the newsletter, send a check or money order for $19.95.

1007.
Cooking Contest Newsletter
P.O. Box 339
Summerville, SC 29484

This newsletter lists cooking and recipe contests from around the country. To receive a sample copy, send a check or money order for $2 to the above address.

1008.
Cook Scholarship Fund
William J. Cook Scholarship Fund
5020 South Lake Shore Drive
Chicago, IL 60615

Scholarships of varying amounts to males graduating from high school in Cook County, Illinois (the Chicago area). Must be nominated by high school administrator. Based on financial need, scholastic record, character, potential for leadership, and strong interest in going to college. Deadline: January 15.

1009.
Coor's Brewing Company
311 Tenth Street
Mail No. NH210
c/o College Recruiting Representative
Golden, CO 80401
(303) 279-6565

40 to 75 nine- to twelve-week fall, spring, and summer internships providing salaries ranging from $390 to $430 per week for undergraduates and from $390 to $580 per week for graduates. Open to undergraduate sophomores, juniors, seniors, and graduate students who have at least one more semester. Internships are in accounting, biology, microbiology, chemistry, distributor development, engineering, journalism, public relations, purchasing, sensory analysis, project management, telecommunications, and the Wellness Center/Recreation. Eligibility requirements vary with the department offering the internship. Internships take place in Golden, Colorado. Deadline: March 1.

1010.
Cora W. Wood Scholarship Fund
c/o Bank One Colorado
P.O. Box 1699
Colorado Springs, CO 80942
(719) 471-4990

3 scholarships of $1,600 to graduating high school seniors who reside in the Pike's Peak region. Must attend a state-supported Colorado college or university. Deadline: April 30.

1011.
Cordelia Lunceford Beatty Trust
c/o Jim Rogers Law Office
P.O. Box 514
Blackwell, OK 74631
(580) 363-3684

15 scholarships ranging from $12 to $1,000 to students who are permanent residents of Blackwell, Oklahoma. Must be under nineteen years of age. Deadline: Prior to start of academic school year.

1012.
Cornell University Summer College: Explorations– The Business World
B 12 Ives Hall
Box 904
Ithaca, NY 14853-3901
(607) 255-6203

800 openings in a six-week summer program open to students between the ages of fifteen and eighteen who have completed the 11th or 12th grade to find out about marketing, finance, manufacturing, labor relations, and international business. Students are able to interact with business people and faculty and discuss such topics as business ethics, responsibility of business to consumers, regulation, effects of federal policies, and looking at the post-industrial future. Students participate in macroeconomics or principles of accounting, plus one other course of their

choice. Students live in supervised dorms. The cost of the program is $3,050, with limited partial to full scholarships. Deadline: April 20.

1013.
Corti Family Agricultural Fund
c/o Wells Fargo Bank, Trust Department
618 East Shaw Avenue
Fresno, CA 93710
(209) 442-6232

133 scholarships, totaling $24,605, to students who are graduates of Kern County, California, high schools. Must be planning on majoring in agriculture. Deadline: varies.

1014.
Council of Energy Resource Tribes (CERT)
Internship Coordinator
1999 Broadway, Suite 2600
Denver, CO 80202
(303) 297-2378
(303) 297-5690 Fax

10 to 14 ten-week summer internships providing $400 per week, free housing, and round-trip travel to undergraduate sophomores, juniors, and seniors, graduate students, and recent graduates to work on projects that can focus on tribal water quality studies, tribal/state and local government cooperative planning on environmental issues, hazardous waste operations training, and biodiversity. Interns work with senior CERT staff, tribal leaders, and host companies on technical and scientific issues, policies, and projects. Interested students must submit a résumé, cover letter, writing samples, college transcript, recommendations (from tribal officials, employers, or professors), and, if applicable, tribal affiliation documentation (this last item is not a requirement). Deadline: March 15.

1015.
Court Theatre–University of Chicago
Charles A. Sergel Drama Prize
5706 South University
Chicago, IL 60637
(312) 702-7005

A $1,500 prize for best original full-length play that has not been published or produced. Previous winners are not eligible. Playwright retains all rights. Deadline: June 1.

1016.
Cox Newspapers
Minority Journalism Scholarship Program
P.O. Box 4689
Atlanta, GA 30302
(404) 526-5091

Scholarships of full tuition for four years to Atlanta-area minority high school seniors with at least a B average who are interested in a journalism career. May be used at Georgia State University or at one of the colleges in the Atlanta University Center. Includes a paid internship. Deadline: April 30.

1017.
Creede Repertory Theater
Internship Coordinator
P.O. Box 269
Creede, CO 81130
(719) 658-2541
(719) 658-2343 Fax

10 fifteen-week summer internships providing a salary of $100 per week and free housing to high school graduates, undergraduates, college graduates, and graduate students. International students may apply. Interns work in Creede, Colorado, in the areas of set construction, light/sound, costume construction, stage management, and business management. Deadline: March 1.

1018.
C. Reiss Coal Company Scholarships
P.O. Box 688
Sheboygan, WI 53082-0688
(414) 457-4411

4 scholarships of $1,000 to graduating high school seniors from a Sheboygan area high school. Must be Wisconsin residents. Based on academic record and financial need. Contact high school counselor. Deadline: varies.

1019.
Creole Ethnic Association, Inc.
Creole Scholarship Fund
P.O. Box 2666, Church Street Station
New York, NY 10008
Written inquiries only

5 Annual Genealogy, Language, or Culture Research awards of $1,000 to undergraduate or graduate students who are at least $1/32$ African American. Must be U.S. citizens. Must include a genealogical chart going back at least five generations. Deadline: June 30.

1020.
Croatian Fraternal Union Scholarships
Secretary-Treasurer
100 Delaney Drive
Pittsburgh, PA 15235

Numerous scholarships of varying amounts to full-time undergraduate students who have been members of the Croatian Fraternal Union for at least three years. Good for all majors but only for undergraduate study. Based on academic record and financial need. Deadline: September 30.

1021.
Crosset Charitable Trust
205 Central Avenue
Cincinnati, OH 45202

13 scholarships, totaling $7,000, to high school seniors. Must be Cincinnati-area residents. Based on academic record and financial need. Contact high school counselors. Deadline: varies.

1022.
Crow Canyon Archeological Center
Internship Program
23390 County Road K
Cortez, CO 81321
(303) 565-8975

4 to 6 eleven-week internships providing room, board, and a small stipend to undergraduate juniors, seniors, and graduate students. Internships are conducted four times a year from mid-May to early August, early August to mid-October, mid-October to mid-December, and early January to mid-March. Students interested in a field internship must have prior field experience. Lab and Environmental Archeology positions require no field experience but do require some course work in archeology, anthropology, ethnobotany, botany, or museum studies. Deadline: March 15.

1023.
Crown Princess Sonja International Piano Competition
P.O. Box 1568 VIKA
N-0116 Oslo 1 Norway
+ 47 2 41 60 65

Approximately $40,000 in total prize money to undergraduate or graduate students or professional pianists. Must be between the ages of eighteen and thirty years. The top six finalists receive cash awards and the board of directors endeavors to provide them with solo engagements in various Nordic cities. Deadline: February 1.

1024.
Crystal Foundation
Sun Trust Bank, Chattanooga, N.A.
P.O. Box 1638
Chattanooga, TN 37401
(423) 757-3204

11 scholarships, totaling $7,500, to high school seniors or undergraduate students. Must be attending or plan to attend a Tennessee college or university. Based on academic record and financial need. Deadline: varies.

1025.
CSX Scholarship Program
c/o RASP Scholarship Service
P.O. Box 5151
Richmond, VA 23220-8151
(804) 353-4832

Scholarships of $1,000 to high school seniors and undergraduate college students who are dependents of a CSX employee (employed for at least one year). If the parent is deceased, he or she must have been employed for at least three years at the time of death. Must have at least a 2.5 GPA. Based on academic record and financial need. Deadline: May 1.

1026.
Cummins Engine Foundation
P.O. Box 3005
Columbus, IN 47202-3005

Scholarships ranging from $300 to $3,000 to graduating high school seniors and undergraduate college students who are dependents of employees. Must be in the upper 20 percent of class and be enrolled or planning to enroll in a regionally accredited four-year college or university. Based on academic record, leadership ability, SAT/ACT scores, recommendations, financial need, and interviews. Renewable. Deadline: February 15.

1027.
Curry Summer Internships
Illinois Governor's Office
Stratton Office Building, Room 107
Springfield, IL 62706
(217) 782-5213

100 summer internships lasting eight weeks for undergraduate and graduate college students. Must be pursuing a career in public service. Undergraduates earn $850 per month, and graduates earn $950 per month. Deadline: varies.

1028.
D. A. Biglane Foundation
P.O. Box 966
Natchez, MS 39121

6 scholarship grants ranging from $750 to $1,800 to high school seniors. Must be residents of the Natchez, Mississippi, area. Based on academic record and financial need. Deadline: varies.

1029.
D. D. Hachar Foundation
1102 Victoria Street
Laredo, TX 78040

50 scholarships of varying amounts, totaling $25,000, to high school seniors and undergraduate college students. Must be residents of Laredo or Webb counties, Texas, and attend or plan to attend college in Texas. Renewable when certain academic requirements are met. Deadline: last Friday in April and October.

1030.
Dairy Shrine Scholarships
Secretary
21st Century Genetics
Shawano, WI 54166
(715) 526-2141

3 scholarships ranging from $500 to $1,000 to undergraduate sophomores, juniors, and seniors majoring in dairy science, animal science, agricultural economics, agricultural education, agriculture, or food science technology/nutrition. Must have an interest in milk marketing, have a minimum 2.5 GPA, and a letter of recommendation from a faculty member in major department. Based on academic achievement, leadership, extracurricular activities, and reasons for interest in dairy product marketing. Deadline: April 1.

1031.
Dallas–Fort Worth Association of Black Communicators
Attn: Scholarship Committee
c/o Dallas Morning News, Communication Center
P.O. Box 22745
Dallas, TX 75222

10 scholarships of $1,500 to African American high school seniors, undergraduate freshmen, and sophomores. Must be planning to major or majoring in journalism, radio/TV broadcasting, photojournalism, graphic arts, or public relations. Must be Texas residents and attending college in Texas. Selection based on academic achievement, goals, and financial need. Deadline: March 1.

1032.
Dane G. Hansen Foundation
P.O. Box 187
Logan, KS 67646
(913) 689-4816

104 scholarships ranging from $250 to $3,500 to high school seniors or undergraduate students. Must be residents of central or northwest Kansas. Deadline: September and October.

1033.
D'Angelo Young Artist Competition
Mercyhurst College
Glenwood Hills
Erie, PA 16546
(814) 825-0363

Awards of $3,000, $5,000, and $10,000 and performance contracts to musicians in a competition (voice, strings, and piano) on a rotating basis. Send a self-addressed, stamped envelope for application and repertoire criteria in the fall. Other restrictions may apply. Deadline: January 15.

1034.
Daniel Ashley & Irene Houston Jewell Memorial Foundation
Sun Trust Bank, Chattanooga, N.A.
P.O. Box 1638
Chattanooga, TN 37401
(423) 757-3204

4 scholarships of $1,000 to undergraduate students. Must be residents of Tennessee or Georgia. Based on academic record and financial need. Deadline: varies.

1035.
Daniel Foundation of South Carolina
P.O. Box 9278
Greenville, SC 29604
(803) 271-7503

Numerous scholarships ranging from $500 to $1,000 to high school seniors who are children of Daniel employees. Employee must have worked for at least one year with the company. Deadline: March 31.

1036.
Danish Brotherhood in America Scholarships
3717 Harney Street
Omaha, NE 68131-3844
(403) 341-5049

16 scholarships of $1,000 to high school seniors and undergraduates who are insured members in good standing of Danish Brotherhood. 4 scholarships may go to vocational/technical school applicants. Based on academic record, extracurricular activities, lodge involvement, and financial need. Deadline: February 15.

1037.
Danish Sisterhood of America Scholarships
2916 North 121st Street
Milwaukee, WI 53222
(414) 453-8375
Written inquiries only

Scholarships of varying amounts to members of the sisterhood and their dependents. The awards may be used for undergraduate or graduate study at an accredited institution. Based on academic achievement. Deadline: varies.

1038.
Datapoint Corporation Merit Scholarship Program
Datapoint Corporation
9725 Datapoint Drive HO8
San Antonio, TX 78284
(210) 593-7000

Scholarships of varying amounts available to graduating high school seniors who are children of full-time Datapoint employees. Based on academic achievement and SAT/ACT scores. Deadline: varies.

1039.
Daughters of Penelope
ALTIS No. 85 Scholarship Fund
Mr. George Klotsas
32 Ashford Road
Longmeadow, MA 01106
(413) 739-9065

Up to 14 scholarships ranging from $200 to $700 to graduating female high school seniors. Must be of Greek descent, dependents of a member of Daughters of Penelope, and residents of Massachusetts. Other restrictions may apply. Deadline: May 15.

1040.
Daughters of Penelope
Order of Ahepa Springfield Chapter Scholarships
34 Chapin Terrace
Springfield, MA 01101

Up to 14 scholarships ranging from $200 to $700 to graduating female high school seniors. Must be of Greek descent, dependents of a member of Daughters of Penelope, and residents of Massachusetts. Other restrictions may apply. Deadline: May 15.

1041.
Daughters of Penelope National Scholarships
Alexandra Apostolides Sonenfeld Awards
AHEPA Senior Women's Auxiliary
1909 Q Street, N.W., Suite 500
Washington, DC 20009

2 or more $1,000 scholarships (renewable for up to three years) to female high school seniors or graduates or undergraduate college students. Must be of Greek descent, related to an AHEPAN or a Daughter of Penelope, or be a member of the Maids of Athens. Must be sponsored by her local or nearest Daughters of Penelope chapter. Must be citizens of the U.S., Canada, Greece, or any country in which there is an established Daughters of Penelope chapter. Based on academic merit and SAT/ACT. Financial need and other scholarships received are not considered. Deadline: early June.

1042.
Daughters of Penelope National Scholarships
Past Grand Presidents Awards
AHEPA Senior Women's Auxiliary
1909 Q Street, N.W., Suite 500
Washington, DC 20009

2 or more $500 scholarships (renewable for up to three years) to female high school seniors or graduates or undergraduate college students. Must be of Greek descent, related to an AHEPAN or a Daughter of Penelope, or be a member of the Maids of Athens. Must be sponsored by her local or nearest Daughters of Penelope chapter. Must be citizens of the U.S., Canada, Greece, or any country in which there is an established Daughters of Penelope chapter. Based on academic merit and SAT/ACT. Financial need and other scholarships received are not considered. Deadline: early June.

1043.
Daughters of the Cincinnati
122 East 58th Street
New York, NY 10022
(212) 319-6915

80 renewable scholarships ranging from $250 to $750 to high school female seniors who are daughters of regular Air Force, Army, Coast Guard, Marines, or Navy officers. Based on academic record, SAT/ACT scores, and financial need. Deadline: April 15.

1044.
Dave Cameron Educational Foundation
P.O. Box 181
York, SC 29745
(803) 684-4968

25 scholarships ranging from $500 to $2,000 to undergraduate students. Must be from York, South Carolina. Must maintain at least a 2.0 GPA. Based on academic record and financial need. Deadline: varies.

1045.
David and Eula Winterman Foundation
Attn: Daniel Thornton
P.O. Box 337
Eagle Lake, TX 77434
(409) 234-5551

3 scholarships ranging from $1,000 to $2,000 to high school seniors planning on studying medicine. Must be residents of Eagle Lake, Texas, and attend school within the Rice consolidated school district. Contact high school counselor for information and an application. Based on academic record and financial need. Deadline: April.

1046.
David James Ellis Memorial Award
Theatre Americana
P.O. Box 245
Altadena, CA 91001

Award of $500 for best unpublished full-length two- or three-act play (preferably on an American theme) submitted to the selection committee each season. No entry fee and no entry form to fill out. Deadline: April 1.

1047.
David R. Godine, Publisher, Inc.
P.O. Box 9103
9 Lewin Street
Lincoln, MA 01773
(617) 259-0700
(617) 259-9198 Fax

5 to 6 general upaid internships lasting from six to twelve weeks are open to high school graduates, undergraduates, college graduates, and graduate students. Interns perform duties from filing to corresponding with authors, sales, and performing publicity, editorial, and general administration tasks. Applicants should have writing ability and interest in books. Applicants must send two writing samples to the publicity director. In-person interview required.

1048.
David S. Blount Educational Foundation
Scholarships
c/o Crestar Bank—Trust Department
P.O. Box 13888
Roanoke, VA 24038
(703) 982-3200

8 scholarships of varying amounts to undergraduate and graduate students. Must be residents of Virginia and attending a Virginia institution. Contact school's financial aid officer. Deadline: May 31.

1049.
David Wasserman Scholarship Fund, Inc.
107 Division Street
Amsterdam, NY 12010
(518) 843-2800

70 scholarships of varying amounts, totaling $21,000, to high school seniors or undergraduate college students. Must be residents of Montgomery County, New York. Based on academic record and financial need. Deadline: April 15.

1050.
Davis–Hays and Co.
Internship Coordinator
930 Spring Valley Road
Maywood, NJ 07607
(201) 368-2288
(201) 368-1505 Fax

1 to 2 internships lasting six weeks, providing a salary of $240 per week to undergraduates, college graduates, and graduate students. Interns work in all areas of public relations from preparing press releases and writing short articles to coordinating special events. Must submit a résumé and cover letter. Deadline: rolling.

1051.
Davis–Roberts Scholarship Fund, Inc.
116 Lummis Court
Cheyenne, WY 82007
(307) 632-2948

11 scholarships of $350 to high school seniors or undergraduate college students who are members of a DeMolay or Job's Daughters, Bethel, in Wyoming. Must be full-time students. Based on academic record, recommendation, essay, and financial need. Interview may be required. Deadline: June 15.

1052.
DCAT Scholarship Awards
Drug, Chemical and Allied Trades Association, Inc.
Scholarship Awards Committee
Two Roosevelt Avenue
Syosset, NY 11791
(516) 496-3317

10 scholarships of $500 per year for four years to children of members of the Graphic Communications International Union. Members must have been in good standing for at least two continuous years prior to October 1 of the application year. May be used at any accredited institution. Open to high school seniors or first-semester freshmen. Based on SAT or ACT, Achievement Tests, academic achievement, essay, transcript, and recommendations. Deadline: April 14.

1053.
Deke Foundation
35 McKinley Place
Grosse Point, MI 48236
(313) 986-6320

5 scholarships ranging from $500 to $1,020 to undergraduate members of the Delta Kappa Epsilon fraternity. Contact local chapter. Deadline: varies.

1054.
Delaware Engineering Society, Inc.
1210 Arundel Drive
Wilmington, DE 19808
(302) 577-6500

Scholarships of $1,000 to high school seniors planning to enter into an engineering curriculum. Some scholarships may require attendance at a certain college or university.

For Delaware residents only. Deadline: late November; local chapters may vary.

1055.
Delaware Higher Education Commission
Delaware Nursing Incentive Scholarship/Loan
820 North French Street
Wilmington, DE 19801
(800) 292-7935
(302) 577-3240
(302) 577-6765 Fax
http://www.state.de.us/high-ed

Scholarship/loans of varying amounts to graduating high school seniors, high school graduates who haven't attended college, GED recipients, or undergraduate students who are pursuing careers in nursing. Must have graduated in the upper half of high school class, have at least a 2.5 GPA (GED recipients must have received at least 250 on GED), and be Delaware residents. Applicants who are employees of State of Delaware with five years of service may attend school part- or full-time; all other applicants must attend full-time. Loan is repaid through nursing service in a Delaware state hospital. Renewable up to four years with satisfactory academic progress. Deadline: March 31.

1056.
Delaware Higher Education Commission
Diamond State Scholarships
820 North French Street
Wilmington, DE 19801
(800) 292-7935
(302) 577-3240
(302) 577-6765 Fax
http://www.state.de.us/high-ed

Approximately 50 scholarships of $1,250 to graduating high school seniors, high school graduates who haven't attended college, or GED recipients. High school graduates must rank in the upper fourth of their class (GED recipients must score at least 300), have at least a 1200 on SAT or 27 on ACT, plan to be full-time students, and be Delaware residents. Renewable with satisfactory academic progress. Request applications after January 1 from high school counselor or above address. Deadline: March 31.

1057.
Delaware Higher Education Commission
Educational Benefits for Children of Deceased
**   Veterans and Others**
820 North French Street
Wilmington, DE 19801
(800) 292-7935
(302) 577-3240
(302) 577-6765 Fax
http://www.state.de.us/high-ed

Awards of up to full tuition and fees to graduating high school seniors and undergraduates. Must be children of deceased Delaware military veterans or State Police Officers whose cause of death was service related, or children of prisoners of war or those declared missing in action. Applicants must be Delaware residents and between the ages of sixteen and twenty-four. May attend full- or part-time at a state-supported institution, unless major is offered only at a private institution in Delaware or out-of-state school. Amount of award is adjusted for other colleges. Renewable up to four years with satisfactory academic progress. Request applications after January 1 from above address. Deadline: three weeks before classes begin.

1058.
Delaware Higher Education Commission
Governor's Workforce Development Grant
820 North French Street
Wilmington, DE 19801
(800) 292-7935
(302) 577-3240
(302) 577-6765 Fax
http://www.state.de.us/high-ed

Grants of up to $1,000 to part-time (carrying eleven or fewer credits) undergraduate students who are employed by a small business (100 or fewer employees). Must be between eighteen and twenty-four years of age during the last twelve months. Renewable with satisfactory academic progress. Must be Delaware residents, file FAFSA, and meet financial eligibility requirements. Obtain applications from above address. Deadline: due by end of drop/add each semester.

1059.
Delaware Higher Education Commission
Robert C. Byrd Honors Scholarships
820 North French Street
Wilmington, DE 19801
(800) 292-7935
(302) 577-3240
(302) 577-6765 Fax
http://www.state.de.us/high-ed

Approximately 15 scholarships of $1,000 to graduating high school seniors, high school graduates who haven't attended college, or GED recipients. High school seniors or graduates must rank in upper fourth of class (GED recipients must have at least a score of 300), have at least a 1200 on SAT or 27 on ACT, enroll at least half-time in an accredited Delaware college or university, and be Delaware residents. This is a federally funded program. Application for this award varies; some high school counselors nominate students without an application process. High school graduates and GED recipients must contact above address after January 1. Deadline: March 31.

1060.
Delaware Higher Education Commission
Scholarship Incentive Program (ScIP)
820 North French Street
Wilmington, DE 19801
(800) 292-7935
(302) 577-3240
(302) 577-6765 Fax
http://www.state.de.us/high-ed

Scholarships of up to tuition, fees, and books to graduating high school seniors and undergraduate students. Must have at least a 2.5 GPA. Must attend or plan to attend on a full-time basis a Delaware or Pennsylvania accredited college or university. At times, undergraduates and graduate students attending college in other states may be considered. Must be Delaware residents. Must file FAFSA before April 15.

1061.
Delius Association of North Florida Inc.
Delius Composition Contest
W. McNeiland, Chairman
c/o College of Fine Arts
Jacksonville University
Jacksonville, FL 32211
(904) 744-3950 ext. 3370

Awards of up to $500 are given in this music composition contest. Three genre categories (keyboard, vocal, and chamber music). High-school-age composers receive $200 and $100 awards. Grand prize is $500. Open to all age groups. Previous winners may reenter. Six awards per year.

1062.
Delta Gamma Foundation
Delta Gamma Foundation Senior Scholarships
3250 Riverside Drive
Columbus, OH 43221
(614) 481-8169

Numerous $400 scholarships to members who have completed five semesters or seven quarters and have at least a B average. Based on academic record, chapter and school activities, and financial need. Deadline: varies.

1063.
Delta Kappa Gamma
Epsilon Pi Chapter Scholarship
c/o Maureen Johannsen
1566 I Street
Arcata, CA 95521

1 scholarship of $250 to a high school senior or undergraduate college student. Must be majoring in education. Must be living in Humboldt or Del Norte counties, California, or attending Humboldt State University in Arcata or College of Redwood in Eureka. Deadline: May 1.

1064.
Delta Omicron International Music Fraternity
Composition Competition–Triennial
656 Berry Lane
Lexington, KY 40502
(606) 266-1215

Award of $500 and premiere performance in this music-composition competition. Open only to Delta Omicron members. Open to music composers of college age and over, for a work of ten to fifteen minutes in duration in the category selected for the particular competition. Deadline: August 1 every second year.

1065.
Delta Sigma Theta Sorority
Direct Search for Talent
1707 New Hampshire Avenue, N.W.
Washington, DC 20009
(202) 986-2400

Recruits, counsels, and motivates students in grades 10, 11, and 12. Also assists out-of-school young adults and veterans. The program operates as an information center on college admissions, college financial aid, and career opportunities. It provides counseling, college tours, recreational and enrichment activities, and a peer-buddy system.

1066.
Delta Sigma Theta Sorority
Julia Bumry Jones Scholarship
1707 New Hampshire Avenue, N.W.
Washington, DC 20009
(202) 986-2400

1 scholarship ranging from $1,000 to $2,000 to a student majoring in journalism or an area of communications. Applicant must be active, dues-paying member of Delta Sigma Theta. Deadline: March 1.

1067.
Delta Sigma Theta Sorority
Myra Davis Hemmings Scholarship
1707 New Hampshire Avenue, N.W.
Washington, DC 20009
(202) 986-2400

Awards are given for tuition and school expenses for one school year only in the areas of art and performing art. Open to dues-paying members of Delta Sigma Theta. Submit transcripts of all college records. Based on academic achievement. Deadline: March 1.

1068.
Delta Sigma Theta Sorority
Non-Member Scholarships
1707 New Hampshire Avenue, N.W.
Washington, DC 20009
(202) 986-2400

Numerous scholarships of varying amounts to either female or male undergraduate students (who have completed at least one semester) or graduate students in any area of study. May apply and receive financial assistance for no more than two years. Deadline: March 1.

1069.
Delta Sigma Theta Sorority
Sadie T. M. Alexander Scholarship
1707 New Hampshire Avenue, N.W.
Washington, DC 20009
(202) 986-2400

1 scholarship of varying amount to an undergraduate member of Delta Sigma Theta. Must be majoring in law or pre-law. Must submit transcripts. Based on academic achievement. Deadline: March 1.

1070.
Delta Tau Delta Educational Fund
8250 Haverstick Road, Suite 150
Indianapolis, IN 46240
(317) 259-1187

43 grants ranging from $50 to $1,500 and 33 loans, totaling $49,000, to undergraduate students who are members of Delta Tau Delta. Contact local chapter. Deadline: varies.

1071.
DeMolay Foundation
Frank S. Land Scholarships
Executive Director
10200 North Executive Hills Boulevard
Kansas City, MO 64153

30 scholarships of $800 to graduating high school seniors and undergraduate students. Preference given to members or past members of the Order of DeMolay. Inquire at local lodge or at above address. Deadline: May 1 and October 1.

1072.
Dental Laboratory Technology Scholarships
American Fund for Dental Health
211 East Chicago Avenue, Suite 820
Chicago, IL 60611
(312) 787-6270

Numerous scholarships of $500 and $600 to high school seniors or graduates enrolled in or admitted to an accredited dental laboratory technology program. Based on academic achievement, financial need, and potential. Deadline: June 1.

1073.
Denver Area Labor Federation, AFL-CIO
Cletus E. Ludden Memorial Scholarships
202 Denver Labor Center
360 Acoma Street
Denver, CO 80223
(303) 722-1300

Several scholarships ranging from $250 to $1,000 to high school seniors or graduates who are members of or children of members of a local union AFL-CIO affiliate with jurisdiction in Adams, Arapahoe, Denver, Douglas, or Jefferson counties, Colorado. Deadline: varies.

1074.
Deo B. Colburn Educational Foundation
63 Saranac Avenue
Lake Placid, NY 12946
Written inquiries only

29 scholarship grants of varying amounts, totaling $46,500, to high school seniors, undergraduates, and graduate students. May be used for any area of study. Must be residents of northern New York State. Write an introductory letter briefly detailing your educational and financial situation. Selection based on academic achievement, extracurricular activities, and financial need. Other restrictions may apply. Deadline: none specified.

1075.
Department of the Navy
Commander, Navy Military Personnel Command
NMPC-641D, Navy Department
Washington, DC 20370-5641

Scholarships of varying amounts to dependents of members of the U.S. Navy, Marine Corps, and Coast Guard. Based on financial need. Deadline: varies.

1076.

Descendants of the Signers of the Declaration of Independence, Inc.
William Penn Annex
P.O. Box 54145
Ninth and Chestnut Streets
Philadelphia, PA 19105

6 to 8 scholarships ranging from $1,500 to $2,000 to undergraduate and graduate students who are descendants of a signer of the Declaration of Independence. Based on GPA, recommendation letters, and financial need. Contact: Chairman; 7997 Windsail Court, Frederick, MD 21701. Telephone: (301) 695-3935. Deadline: May 15.

1077.

Detroit District Metropolitan Opera Auditions Awards
Auditions Director
32005 Alameda
Farmington Hills, MI 48018

Scholarships of $1,000 to undergraduate or graduate students. Must be Michigan residents for at least one year; or of Lucas, Fulton, or Ottawa counties, Ohio; or a nonresident who has been studying in these areas. Must be pursuing a career in opera. Students must be sopranos, mezzos, or contraltos, nineteen to thirty-three years old; or baritones or basses, twenty to thirty-three years old. Applicants must be sponsored by a school, college, music club, or voice teacher. Audition required. Deadline: varies.

1078.

Detroit District Metropolitan Opera Auditions Maccabees Award
Auditions Director
32005 Alameda
Farmington Hills, MI 48018

1 scholarship of $500 to an undergraduate or graduate student. Must be Michigan resident for at least one year; or of Lucas, Fulton, or Ottawa counties, Ohio; or a nonresident who has been studying in these areas. Must be pursuing a career in opera. Student must be a soprano, mezzo, or contralto, nineteen to thirty-three years old; or a baritone or bass, twenty to thirty-three years old. Applicants must be sponsored by a school, college, music club, or voice teacher. Audition required. Deadline: varies.

1079.

Detroit District Metropolitan Opera Auditions Walter Gerrke Award
Auditions Director
32005 Alameda
Farmington Hills, MI 48018

1 scholarship of $1,200 to an undergraduate or graduate student. Must be Michigan resident for at least one year; or of Lucas, Fulton, or Ottawa counties, Ohio; or a nonresident who has been studying in these areas. Must be pursuing a career in opera. Student must be a soprano, mezzo, or contralto, nineteen to thirty-three years old; or a baritone or bass, twenty to thirty-three years old. Applicants must be sponsored by a school, college, music club, or voice teacher. Audition required. Deadline: varies.

1080.

Detroit Free Press
Minority Journalism Scholarship
Publishers Office
321 West Lafayette Boulevard
Detroit, MI 48226
(800) 678-6400

3 awards of $20,000, 2 awards of $1,000, and 1 award of $750 to minority high school seniors who live within the *Free Press* circulation area. Must be of African American, Asian American, Hispanic American, or Native American ancestry. Must be pursuing a career in journalism (writers, editors, photojournalists). Based on academic record, SAT/ACT, essay, extracurricular activities (especially related to journalism), and recommendations. Must maintain a 3.0 GPA. Deadline: January 6.

1081.

Devry, Inc. Scholarship Program
2201 West Howard Street
Evanston, IL 60202
(800) 323-4256
(312) 328-8100

40 full-tuition and 80 half-tuition scholarships to high school graduates who enroll at a Devry Institute and major in electronics engineering technology, computer information systems, business operations, or telecommunications management. Renewable if a 2.5 GPA is maintained. Must be U.S. citizens. Deadline: March 23.

1082.

Diet Center National Scholarship
Executive Nutritionist
Diet Center, Inc.
220 South Second West
Rexburg, ID 83440
(208) 356-9381

10 scholarships of $3,000 to undergraduate juniors and seniors who are majoring in nutrition. Based on academic record, career goals, and financial need. Deadline: February 15.

1083.

Digital Equipment Corporation
U.S. Minority Education Scholarship
2500 West Union Hills Drive
Phoenix, AZ 85027

Scholarships ranging from $5,500 to $6,500 (renewable up to four years) to Arizona high school seniors. May be used at any Arizona university or college. Must have at least a 2.75 GPA. A separate scholarship, for full-time students entering their junior year and majoring in computer science or in electrical, mechanical, or industrial engineering, is also available.

1084.

Disciples of Christ Homeland Ministries
Black Scholarship Fund
P.O. Box 1986
Indianapolis, IN 56208
(317) 353-1491

Scholarships of varying amounts to African American undergraduate students pursuing a career in the ministry.

Must be members of the Disciples of Christ. Deadline: April 15.

1085.
Discover Card Tribute Awards
American Association of School Administrators
P.O. Box 9338
Arlington, VA 22219
(703) 875-0708

3 state awards of $500, 3 state awards of $1,250, and 3 state awards of $2,500 in each state and 3 national awards of $10,000, 3 national awards of $15,000, and 3 national awards $20,000 to high school juniors. Students may be nominated by themselves or by another person. Based on obstacles overcome, unique endeavors, community service, special talents, and leadership. May be used for tuition, books, room, board, transportation expenses, etc. May be used for any type of continuing education (vocational/technical schools, job training schools, two- or four-year colleges and universities). Deadline: early January.

1086.
Distributive Education Clubs of America (DECA)
Harry A. Applegate Scholarships
1908 Association Drive
Reston, VA 22091-1594
(703) 860-5000

Several scholarships of up to $1,000 to high school seniors or graduates or undergraduates who are or were DECA members and studying marketing, merchandising, and marketing education at any two- or four-year institution. Contact DECA chapter early in the year at above address. Based on SAT/ACT, academic record, recommendations, and application. Renewable. Deadline: second Monday in March.

1087.
District of Columbia Natural Gas
Mayoral/Council Scholarship Program
1100 H Street, N.W.
Washington, DC 20080
(202) 624-6758

8 Council Scholarships of $1,500 to high school seniors, 5 scholarships of $1,500 to college sophomores, and 2 Mayoral Scholarships of $1,500 to college seniors who will be attending graduate school. Must be pursuing a career in business or science. Based on academic record, recommendations, and community involvement. Deadline: February 26.

1088.
District of Columbia Office of Postsecondary
Education, Research, and Assistance
State Student Incentive Grant Program
2100 Martin L. King Jr. Avenue, S.E., Suite 401
Washington, DC 20020
(202) 727-3688
http://www.ci.washington.dc.us/OPERA/

Grants ranging from $400 to $1,500 to undergraduate students. Must be Washington, DC, residents. Must have documented substantial financial need. Deadline: varies.

1089.
District of Columbia Public Schools—Carvers
Administration Services
Martha V. Johnson Memorial Scholarships
Director of Student Affairs
4501 Lee Street, N.E.
Washington, DC 20019
(202) 724-4934

Numerous scholarships of varying amounts to high school seniors attending public school in the District of Columbia. Based on academic record and financial need. Contact high school counselor. Deadline: none.

1090.
District of Columbia Society of Professional
Engineers
3010 Legation Street, N.W.
Washington, DC 20015
(202) 686-3891

Scholarships of $1,000 to high school seniors planning to enter into an engineering curriculum. Some scholarships may require attendance at a certain college or university. For District of Columbia residents only. Deadline: late November; local chapters may vary.

1091.
Dog Writers' Educational Trust Scholarships
47 Kielwasser Road
Washington Depot, CT 06794
(203) 868-2863

10 scholarships of $1,000 to undergraduate, graduate, or professional students who are interested in or have a close relative who has a present or past interest in the world of dogs or has participated as exhibitor, breeder, handler, judge, club officer, or in other activities in the U.S. or Canada. Preference given to students planning on a career in veterinary medicine, animal welfare, or journalism. Based on academics, potential, leadership, and financial need; must be in upper third of class. As much importance is given to character, humane attitudes, and high marks in school records. Include a self-addressed, stamped envelope for application. Deadline: December 31.

1092.
Dolphin Scholarship Program
c/o West Virginia House
405 Dillingham Boulevard
Norfolk Naval Station
Norfolk, VA 23511

Numerous tuition scholarships to children of members or former members of the Submarine Service who have qualified in submarines, served in the Submarine Force for at least five years after qualification, or served in Submarine support activities (submarine bases, tenders, and rescue vessels) for at least six years. Children of Submarine personnel who died while on active duty in the Submarine Force have no time-period restrictions. Awards is for undergraduate study in any major. Based on academic merit, character, ability, and financial need. Deadline: April 15.

1093.
Donald & Evelyn Peters Foundation
421 Birchwood Road
Hinsdale, IL 60521

Up to 12 scholarships of varying amounts, totaling $11,500, to graduating high school seniors, high school graduates who haven't attended college, or undergraduate students. Must be Illinois residents. Write a brief letter detailing your financial and educational situation. Other restrictions may apply. Deadline: none specified.

1094.
Donald W. Reynolds Foundation, Inc.
Cleatis R. Carroll
P.O. Box 1359
Fort Smith, AR 72902
(501) 785-7815

20 scholarships of $5,000 to undergraduate college juniors majoring in journalism or communications. Must be attending one of ten select universities. Award is paid $2,500 during junior year and $2,500 during senior year. Students must be nominated by their school of journalism and entering their junior year. Applications must be made during the student's sophomore year. Deadline: varies.

1095.
Dougherty Foundation, Inc.
3620 North Third Street
Phoenix, AZ 85012
(602) 264-3751

Approximately 290 scholarships of $1,000 and 1,100 loans of $2,000 to high school seniors and undergraduate students. Must be Arizona residents. Based on financial need. Request applications after January 1. Deadline: April.

1096.
Dow Jones Newspaper Fund
High School Journalism Workshops for
Minorities
P.O. Box 300
Princeton, NJ 08543-0300
(609) 452-2820

Co-sponsored by the Newspaper Fund and local newspaper and journalism organizations, these summer workshops provide hands-on experience in reporting, writing, and producing a laboratory newspaper. Participants are eligible for two other programs sponsored by the Dow Jones Newspaper Fund: the National Youth News Correspondent Program and the Summer Workshops Writing Competition Scholarships. Deadline: varies.

1097.
Dow Jones Newspaper Fund
Minority Reporting Scholarships
P.O. Box 300
Princeton, NJ 08543-0300
(609) 452-2820

20 scholarships of $1,000 to minority undergraduate sophomores who complete a reporting internship during the summer after the sophomore year. Students must be nominated by newspaper supervisor. Students must find their own internships from the list of newspapers willing to accept reporting interns. Deadline: September 1.

1098.
Dow Jones Newspaper Fund
Newspaper Editing Intern Program
P.O. Box 300
Princeton, NJ 08543-0300
(609) 452-2820

40 scholarships of $1,000 to undergraduate juniors or seniors or graduates who work on their college newspapers and who have an interest in professional newspaper work. Internship program is conducted during the summer between junior and senior years. Interns receive regular wages and receive a $1,000 scholarship for use the following year (if student isn't returning to college, the award may be used to pay an outstanding loan). Based on academic record, professional interest in journalism, and professional promise. Application available September 1 through November 1 of junior year. Deadline: November 15.

1099.
Dupage Medical Society Foundation
Scholarship Program
498 Hillside Avenue
Glen Ellyn, IL 60137
(630) 858-9603

10 scholarships of $1,000 to undergraduate students who are enrolled or about to enroll in a health professions program (dental hygiene, medical transcription, nursing, medical school, dental school, etc.). Must be registered voters and residents of Dupage County, Illinois. Must be pursuing a health-related career in an accredited health professions program. Pre-med and pre-dental students are not eligible. Students must already be enrolled in or accepted to the professional program. Renewable. Other restrictions may apply. Deadline: December and March.

1100.
Duxbury Yacht Club Charitable Foundation
c/o State Street Bank and Trust Company
P.O. Box 351
Boston, MA 02101

9 scholarships of $500 to graduating high school seniors or graduates of Duxbury, Massachusetts, high schools.

1101.
The Eagle Art Gallery
Murray State University
MSU Box 9
Murray, KY 42071-0009

Call for proposals for exhibitions. Areas of high interest are in performance and/or installation and fiber but not to the exclusion of other media; of low interest is photography. For complete information, write: Albert Sperath, Eagle Art Gallery, MSU Box, 9, Murray, KY 42071-0009. Deadline: March 22.

1102.
Eagles Memorial Foundation, Inc.
4710 14th Street West
Bradenton, FL 34207
(813) 758-5456

Grants, totaling $56,000, to children of deceased members of the Fraternal Order of Eagle, law officers, firefighters, and graduates of Home on the Range for Boys in Sentinel Butte, North Dakota; High Sky Girls Ranch in Midland, Texas; or Bob Hope High School in Port Arthur, Texas. Based on academic record and financial need. Deadline: varies.

1103.
Eagleton War Memorial Scholarship Fund, Inc.
Attn: President
c/o Bridgehampton National Bank
P.O. Box 3005
Bridgehampton, NY 11932
(516) 537-1000

8 scholarships ranging from $500 to $1,750 to students who are graduates of Bridgehampton High School. Must be New York residents. Based on academic record and financial need. Deadline: varies.

1104.
The EAR Foundation
Minnie Pearl Scholarship Fund
Attn: Executive Director
2000 Church Street
P.O. Box 111
Nashville, TN 37236
(615) 329-7809

Numerous scholarships of $2,000 to hearing-impaired high school seniors. Must have at least a 3.0 GPA or better. Must be U.S. citizens. Based on academic record, financial need and recommendations; must have significant bilateral hearing impairment. Deadline: March.

1105.
Earthwatch Career Training Scholarship Program
P.O. Box 403T
680 Mount Auburn Street
Watertown, MA 02172
(617) 926-8200

200 awards ranging from $100 to $2,000 to high school students and teachers. Winners aren't given cash awards; rather, varying amounts of expenses are paid to allow the student or teacher to work in the field for two to three weeks with a professional scientist on a research expedition in the areas of archeology, anthropology, environmental studies, biology, and marine science. Deadline: March 31.

1106.
Easter Seal Society of Iowa
E. L. Peterson Memorial Scholarships
P.O. Box 4002
Des Moines, IA 50333
(515) 289-1933

10 scholarships of $1,000 to full-time undergraduate sophomores, juniors, seniors, or graduate students at accredited institutions planning a career in the broad field of rehabilitation. Must be Iowa residents. Must be in the top 40 percent of class and have a permanent disability. Based on financial need and academic record. Renewable. Deadline: April 15.

1107.
East Texas Historical Association
Ottis Lock Endowment Scholarship
c/o Dr. Archie P. McDonald
P.O. Box 6223, SFA Station
Nacogdoches, TX 75962
(409) 569-2407

1 scholarship of $500 to a graduating high school senior or undergraduate college student attending a college or university in East Texas. Based on academic record, recommendations, and financial need or interest in furthering his or her education. Deadline: May 1.

1108.
East-West Center
Undergraduate Fellowships for Pacific Islanders
1777 East-West Road
Room JAB 2066
Honolulu, HI 96848
(808) 944-7736
Written inquiries only

Ten- to twelve-month fellowships of varying amounts to undergraduate students. Must be Pacific Islanders who are pursuing majors in Asian Pacific Studies. Selection based on academic achievement and desire to broaden knowledge of the Pacific, Asia, and the U.S. Deadline: January 14.

1109.
Eaton Literary Agency
Attn: Richard Lawrence
Awards Program
P.O. Box 49795
Sarasota, FL 33578
(813) 355-4561

2 awards of $3,000 per year. Awards are given for novels, nonfiction books, short stories, and articles. Deadline: August 31 (book-length award); March 31 (short story/article award).

1110.
Ebell of Los Angeles Scholarship Endowment
Fund and the Mrs. Charles N. Flint Scholarship
Endowment Fund
Scholarship Chairperson
743 South Lucerne Boulevard
Los Angeles, CA 90005
(213) 931-1277

55 scholarships paying $200 per month for a ten-month school year to college undergraduate sophomores, juniors, or seniors attending an institution in Los Angeles County. Must be residents of Los Angeles County. Must be young, unmarried, and have financial need. Deadline: none.

1111.
Ed E. and Gladys Hurley Foundation
c/o Bank One, Trust
P.O. Box 21116
Shreveport, LA 71154
(318) 226-2211

Numerous scholarships, totaling $25,495, to students
attending Scaritt College for Christian Workers in Tennessee.
Numerous loans, totaling $85,733, to students who are
residents of Arkansas, Louisiana, and Texas. Loan recipients
may attend any U.S. college or university. Deadline:
May 31.

1112.
Edelman Worldwide Public Relations
Internship Coordinator
211 East Ontario
Chicago, IL 60611
(312) 280-7000

135 twelve-week internships providing approximately $250
per week to undergraduate students, college graduates, and
graduate students. International students may also apply.
Internships are conducted during the summer, fall, and
spring. Interns might be assigned to offices in Chicago, New
York, or twenty-five other offices worldwide. Interns work
in consumer marketing (food and nutrition), medical/health
care, business and industrial, technology, travel, event
marketing, investor and financial relations, public affairs,
corporate counsel, and media/video production. Interns
must submit a résumé, cover letter, and (optional) writing
samples. Deadline: rolling.

1113.
**Edgar Clay and Mary Cheery Doyle Memorial
   Fund**
Attn: Director
P.O. Box 1465
Greenville, SC 29687-1465

Numerous scholarship grants, totaling $61,000, to
graduating seniors of Oconee County, South Carolina, high
schools. For undergraduate study. Based on academic
record and financial need. Contact high school counselor or
above address. Deadline : March 1.

1114.
Edgar Lee Masters Awards
Caravan Press
15445 Ventura Boulevard, Suite 279
Sherman Oaks, CA 91403
(818) 377-4301

2 second prizes of $750 and 1 first prize of $2,500 for
published and unpublished poetry, fiction, and creative
nonfiction. Send a self-addressed, stamped #10 envelope for
guidelines. Charges an entry fee. Deadline: February 28.

1115.
Edith Grace Reynolds Estate Residuary Trust
c/o Key Bank Trust Company
35 State Street
Albany, NY 12207
(518) 486-8500

Numerous grants, totaling $137,050, to graduating high
school seniors of South District 1, in Rensselaer County,

New York. Based on academic record and financial need.
Deadline: February 15.

1116.
Edson's Raiders Association Scholarships
Attn: Chairperson
Scholarship Committee
2412 Carey Lane
Vienna, VA 22180

Numerous scholarships of varying amounts to dependent
children of members of the Edson's Raiders (also known as
The First Marine Raider Battalion-FMRB). Based on SAT
scores, which must be sent by the National Merit
Corporation. Deadline: varies.

1117.
**Educational and Cultural Fund of the Electrical
   Industry
Dr. Martin Luther King, Jr., Memorial
   Scholarship**
158-11 Jewel Avenue
Flushing, NY 11365

1 scholarship of $2,000 (renewable for four years) to a high
school senior who is a child of a member of this union.
Based on academic record and financial need. Deadline:
varies.

1118.
**Educational and Cultural Fund of the Electrical
   Industry Scholarship Program**
158-11 Jewel Avenue
Flushing, NY 11365

At least 20 scholarships covering full expense of tuition and
fees of up to $2,000, or 50 percent of the expense of up to
$5,000, to children of employees (for at least five years
before application). Must be graduating high school seniors
or have graduated within a year of filing the application.
Based on eligibility, academic achievement, and
extracurricular activities. Deadline: varies.

1119.
**Educational Communications, Inc.
National Dean's List Scholarships**
721 North McKinley Road
Lake Forest, IL 60045
(708) 295-6650

25 scholarships of $1,000 to undergraduate and graduate
students. Must be recommended by their college dean or a
faculty member. Based on academic record, extracurricular
activities, essay, recommendation, and financial need.
Request applications in June, July, and August. There is a
$2.50 processing fee. Deadline: mid-December.

1120.
**Educational Communications, Inc.
Scholarship Foundation**
721 North McKinley Road
Lake Forest, IL 60045
(708) 295-6650

65 scholarships of $1,000 awarded to high school seniors
who scored at least 30 on ACT or 1250 on SAT. Based on

academic ability, SAT scores, performance, extracurricular activities, awards, and work experience. When requesting application, include year of graduation and GPA. A processing fee is required when filing the application. Deadline: June 1.

1121.
Educational Council of the Graphic Arts Industry
National Scholarship Trust Fund
4615 Forbes Avenue
Pittsburgh, PA 15213
(412) 621-6941 ext. 229

Numerous renewable scholarships ranging from $250 to $1,000 to high school seniors and undergraduate freshmen, sophomores, and juniors pursuing a graphic communications career. There are also a limited number of scholarships to children of employees. Based on academic record, SAT, and recommendations. Deadline: January 15.

1122.
Educational Foundation of the National
Restaurant Association
Gold Plate Scholarships
250 South Wacker Drive, Suite 1400
Chicago, IL 60606-5834
(312) 715-1010

100 scholarships of $750 to full-time undergraduate students of food service, food management, or related fields. Must be U.S. citizens or legal residents. Based on academic record, career goals, and financial need. Request applications after December 1. Deadline: March 1.

1123.
Educational Foundation of the National
Restaurant Association
Griffith Lab Scholarships
250 South Wacker Drive, Suite 1400
Chicago, IL 60606-5834
(312) 715-1010

1 scholarship of $3,000 over two years to a culinary arts major in a junior or community college and 1 scholarship of $3,000 over two years to a food technology major attending a four-year college/university. Must be U.S. citizens or legal residents. Based on academic record, career goals, and financial need. Request applications after December 1. Deadline: March 1.

1124.
Educational Foundation of the National
Restaurant Association
Nestlé Scholarships
250 South Wacker Drive, Suite 1400
Chicago, IL 60606-5834
(312) 715-1010

1 scholarship of $1,500 and 1 scholarship of $1,200 to culinary arts majors enrolled in a junior or community college. Must be U.S. citizens or legal residents. Based on academic record, career goals, and financial need. Request applications after December 1. Deadline: March 1.

1125.
Educational Foundation of the National
Restaurant Association
Undergraduate Scholarships
250 South Wacker Drive, Suite 1400
Chicago, IL 60606-5834
(312) 715-1010

100 scholarships ranging from $500 to $1,000 to full-time undergraduate students with a 3.2 GPA or higher who are enrolled in an accredited food-service/hospitality or related programs (nutrition/dietetics) that will result in either an associate's or bachelor's degree. Must be U.S. citizens or legal residents. Based on academic record, career goals, and financial need. Renewal. Request applications after December 1. Deadline: March 1.

1126.
Educational Institute of the American Hotel &
Motel Association
1407 South Harrison Road
East Lansing, MI 48826
(517) 353-5500

Periodically offers scholarships of varying amounts to undergraduate students (associate, bachelor's, and certification programs) majoring in a hotel/motel management, hospitality, and/or tourism-related major. Funds are subject to fluctuations in finances. For more information, contact above address. Other restrictions may apply. Deadline: varies.

1127.
Edward Arthur Mellinger Educational
Foundation, Inc.
Scholarship Committee
1025 East Broadway
Monmouth, IL 61462
(309) 734-2419

Approximately 300 renewable scholarships of up to $750 to undergraduate students. First preference to students residing in western Illinois and eastern Iowa who attend college in those states. Second preference goes to students from states that border Illinois and Iowa. Final consideration given to students from other states. Request applications after February 1. Deadline: May 1.

1128.
Edward Bangs and Eliza Kelley Foundation
Scholarship Program
243 South Street
Hyannis, MA 02601
(508) 775-3117

35 to 40 scholarships of up to $2,000 to high school seniors or undergraduate, graduate, or professional school students. Must be residents of Barnstable County, Massachusetts. Scholarships are intended to benefit health welfare of inhabitants of Barnstable County. Must be pursuing a career in medicine, nursing, health sciences, or related areas. Deadline: April 30.

1129.
Edward Rutledge Charity
404 North Ridge Street
P.O. Box 758
Chippewa Falls, WI 54729
(715) 723-6618

34 scholarships, totaling $29,217, to graduating high school seniors. Must be Chippewa County, Wisconsin, residents. Based on academic record and financial need. Deadline: varies.

1130.
Edward Wagner and George Hosser Scholarship Fund Trust
c/o Citizens Bank of NH
875 Elm Street, #1
Manchester, NH 03108
(603) 624-9330

113 grants ranging from $500 to $3,000 to male high school seniors or undergraduate or graduate students. Must be residents of Manchester, New Hampshire. Based on academic record and financial need. Deadline: April 30.

1131.
Edwin H. Eddy Family Foundation
Attn: Trustee
c/o Northwest Bank Duluth, Trust Department
Duluth, MN 55802
(218) 723-2773

15 scholarships ranging from $333 to $1,500 to undergraduate students who are Duluth residents, or nonresidents attending the University of Minnesota at Duluth, and majoring in communication disorders. Based on academic record, career goals, and financial need. Deadline: varies.

1132.
Edwin L. and Louis B. McCallay Educational Trust Fund
Trust Division
c/o First National Bank of Southwestern Ohio
300 High Street
Hamilton, OH 45011
(513) 867-5571

20 scholarships ranging from $100 to $800 to graduating high school seniors and graduates of Middletown, Ohio, High School District. Based on academic record and financial need. Deadline: varies.

1133.
E. H. Kilbourne Residuary Charitable Trust
c/o Norwest Bank, Trust Department
P.O. Box 960
Fort Wayne, IN 46801-6632
(219) 461-6451

287 scholarship grants ranging from $100 to $1,500 to graduating high school seniors from Allen County, Indiana. Contact high school counselor or above address. Based on academic record and financial need. Deadline: April 15.

1134.
Eighth Mountain Press
Poetry Prize
624 Southeast 29 Avenue
Portland, OR 97214-3026
(503) 233-3936

1 prize of $1,000 given to recognize the importance of the feminist movement. Manuscripts of 50 to 120 pages by a woman writer may be submitted during January. Send self-addressed, stamped envelope for guidelines and further information. Deadline: January 31.

1135.
Eisenhower Memorial Scholarship Foundation, Inc.
Executive Director
303 North Curry Pike
Bloomington, IN 47401-1202
(812) 332-2257

Scholarships ranging from $2,500 to $10,000 over a four-year period to students who are graduates of Indiana high schools and who have never attended college before. Students who have already graduated from high school must submit: a biographical sketch, career goals, essay, transcripts, and recommendations. Based on high school academic achievement, extracurricular activities, essay, and interview. Must believe in a Divine Being and be willing to defend the free enterprise system and the American way of life. Not based on financial need. The foundation hopes to expand this to other states in the future. Deadline: varies.

1136.
E. K. and Lillian F. Bishop Foundation
Sea First Bank/Bank of America
Trust Department
P.O. Box 24565
Seattle, WA 98124-0565
(206) 358-3763

60 scholarships ranging from $500 to $3,500 to graduating high school seniors and undergraduate college students. Must have been residents of Grays Harbor County, Washington, for at least a year. Contact high school counselor or send a self-addressed, stamped envelope to above address. Deadline: June 1.

1137.
Eleanor Association
Eleanor Scholar Grants
1550 North Dearborn Parkway
Chicago, IL 60610
(312) 664-8245

10 scholarships of $5,000 to female undergraduate juniors currently attending: Elmhurst College, Lake Forest College, North Central College, Loyola University of Chicago, Wheaton College, Mundelein College, Rosary College, Northwestern University, University of Chicago, or University of Illinois at Chicago. Award must be used during senior year. Based on academic record, community or school activities, nomination by school official, and financial need. Finalists are interviewed. Deadline: March 1.

1138.
Eleanor Brackenridge Scholarship Committee
Attn: Scholarship Chairperson
c/o Women's Club
1717 San Pedro
San Antonio, TX 78212

1 scholarship to a male or female high school senior from a private or public school in San Antonio, Texas. Either request an application or include a short biographical sketch with financial need included. Send three letters of recommendation, name and address of school, and an official transcript. Deadline: May 1.

1139.
Eleanor Brackenridge Scholarship Committee
Attn: Scholarship Chairperson
c/o Women's Club
1717 San Pedro
San Antonio, TX 78212

1 scholarship of $500 to a woman who is continuing her education in nursing, teaching, or other such professions. Must be San Antonio, Texas, resident. Either request an application or include a short biographical sketch, with financial need included. Send three letters of recommendation, name and address of school, and an official transcript. Deadline: May 1.

1140.
Eleanor M. Webster Testamentary Trust
Key Bank Trust Department
127 Public Square
Cleveland, OH 44114
(216) 689-0969

8 scholarships of $350 and 8 loans of $300 to undergraduate sophomore, junior, or senior students. Must be from Stark County, Ohio. Must have completed one year at an Ohio college or university. Based on academic record and financial need. Deadline: varies.

1141.
Eleanor White Trust
c/o Richard S. Smith
P.O. Box 280
Rutland, VT 05701
(802) 775-7141

23 scholarships ranging from $250 to $4,000 to graduating high school seniors. Must be residents of Fair Haven, Vermont. Based on academic record and financial need. Deadline: varies.

1142.
Electronic Industries Foundation Scholarship Fund
1901 Pennsylvania Avenue, N.W., Suite 700
Washington, DC 20006
(202) 955-5810

6 scholarships of $2,000 to disabled high school seniors or undergraduate or graduate students. Must be pursuing career in aeronautics, computer science, electrical engineering, engineering technology, applied mathematics, or microbiology. Deadline: February 1.

1143.
Electron Microscopy Society of America (EMSA) Presidential Scholarships
P.O. Box EM
Woods Hole, MA 02543
(508) 540-7639

20 scholarships of varying amounts to full-time undergraduate students pursuing a career in the biological or physical sciences which relate to electron microscopy. Students must be sponsored by an EMSA member and submit an abstract on a paper written about research or a project. The award will include registration fees for the International Congress of EMSA, and reimbursement for round-trip travel expenses. Students must attend the meeting and present their papers. Deadline: March 15.

1144.
Electron Microscopy Society of America (EMSA) Undergraduate Scholarships
P.O. Box EM
Woods Hole, MA 02543
(508) 504-7639

Numerous scholarships of up to $3,000 to full-time undergraduate students pursuing a career in electron microscopy. Must be U.S. citizens or resident aliens (green card required). At least one scholarship is to a minority student. Preference given to student proposals utilizing a facility other than the one in which the student is currently enrolled. May receive the award only once. Based on a research proposal, recommendations, previous electron microscopy experience, and academic record. Deadline: November 15.

1145.
E. Leo and Louise F. Spain Scholarship Foundation
c/o Robert J. O'Brian
83 Bay Street
P.O. Box 785
Glens Falls, NY 12801
(518) 793-5173

6 scholarships of $500 to students of St. Mary's Academy in Glens Falls, New York, or to students from another school in Glens Falls, New York. Based on worthiness and financial need. Deadline: varies.

1146.
E. L. Gibson Foundation
201 South Edwards
Enterprise, AL 36330
(205) 393-4553

32 scholarships ranging from $46 to $1,000 to high school seniors or undergraduate college students. Must be residents of Coffee County, Alabama. Must be pursuing a health-related career. Based on academic record, career goals, and financial need. Deadline: varies.

1147.

Elias Lieberman Student Poetry Award
Attn: Award Director
Poetry Society of America
15 Gramercy Park South
New York, NY 10003

Contest with award of varying amounts for unpublished poems by students in grades 9 through 12. Charges a $5 fee. When requesting information, include a self-addressed, stamped envelope for rules. Deadline: December 31.

1148.

Elisha Leavenworth Foundation
35 Park Place
Waterbury, CT 06702

11 scholarships of varying amounts, totaling $8,000, to female high school seniors from Waterbury, Connecticut. Based on financial need. Contact high school counselor or above address. Deadline: varies.

1149.

Elite Model Management Corporation
111 East 22nd Street
New York, NY 10010
(212) 529-9700

13 to 18 internships providing no compensation, though a bonus is possible, to undergraduate students. Interns begin by answering phones, opening mail, sifting through unsolicited photographs, and creating possible leads for scouts to follow up, and don't assume responsibilities of Elite booking agents until well into their internships. Founded by John Casablancas. Though not limited to any major, some interns have majored in political science, women's studies, fashion merchandising, business, and advertising. Internships are available year-round and last at least three months. There are also branches in Atlanta, Beverly Hills, Chicago, and Miami Beach. Deadline: rolling.

1150.

Elizabeth City Foundation
P.O. Box 574
Elizabeth City, NC 27909

43 scholarship grants of varying amounts, totaling $32,500, to high school seniors or undergraduate students. Must be residents of Camden County, North Carolina. Based on academic record and financial need. Deadline: April 1; October 1.

1151.

**Elk's "Most Valuable Student" Scholarship/
  Leadership Awards**
Grand Lodge BPO Elks
Office of the Grand Secretary
2750 Lake View Drive
Chicago, IL 60614
(312) 477-2750
http://www.elks.org

500 renewable scholarships ranging from $1,000 to $5,000 and 1,585 one-time $800 scholarships to graduating high school seniors. Based on academic achievement, character, leadership, extracurricular activities, community involvement, recommendations, and financial need. Contact local lodge or above address for lodge nearest you. Deadline: mid-January; exact date varies.

1152.

**Elk's National Foundation
Vocational/Technical Grants**
2750 Lake View Avenue
Chicago, IL 60614
(312) 477-2750
http://www.elks.org

250 grants of $1,000 a year for two years to high school seniors or graduates planning to enroll in or already enrolled in a vocational/technical program. Contact local lodge. Membership isn't required. Deadline: November 26; may vary.

1153.

Elk's State Association Annual Essay Contest
Local Elk's Lodge

Many State Elk's Lodges sponsor an essay contest for all high school students from that specific state. The essay must be a minimum of 1,000 words and a maximum of 1,500 in length. Topics vary from year to year. Contact your local Elk's Lodge. Deadline: February 21; may vary.

1154.

Ella G. McKee Foundation
c/o First National Bank
432 West Gallatin Street
Vandalia, IL 62471
(618) 283-1141

63 scholarship grants ranging from $140 to $1,800 are available to high school seniors. Must have been residents of Fagette County, Illinois, for at least four years. Based on academic record and financial need. Deadline: varies.

1155.

Elmer O. and Ida Preston Educational Trust
801 Grand Avenue, Suite 3700
Des Moines, IA 50309
(515) 243-4191

35 scholarship grants ranging from $500 to $700 to male Protestant undergraduate or graduate students who live in Iowa. Must be attending a college or university in Iowa. Deadline: varies.

1156.

Emma Winkleman Trust B
Arm Securities Corporation
100 North Minnesota Street
New Ulm, MN 56073
(507) 354-2144

19 scholarships ranging from $325 to $770 to high school seniors or graduates or undergraduate students. Must have graduated from high school or live within thirty miles of Fairfax, Minnesota. Deadline: varies.

1157.
Endowment Fund of Phi Kappa Psi Fraternity, Inc.
510 Lokerbie Street
Indianapolis, IN 46202
(317) 632-5647

Scholarships ranging from $100 to $3,000 to undergraduate students, with preference given to Phi Kappa Psi fraternity members. Contact local chapter. Based on academic record, service to Phi Kappa Psi fraternity, and financial need. Deadline: varies.

1158.
Ennis William Cosby Foundation
c/o William Morris Agency
Attn: Norman Brokaw
151 El Camino Drive
Beverly Hills, CA 90212

Awards scholarships of varying amounts to graduating high school seniors, high school graduates who haven't attended college, and undergraduate students. Write a brief letter detailing your educational and financial situation; include a self-addressed, stamped envelope. Selection based on academic achievement and financial need. Other restrictions may apply.

1159.
Entomological Society of America (ESA)
ESA Undergraduate Scholarships
9301 Annapolis Road
Lanham, MD 20706-3115
(301) 731-4535
http://www.entsoc.org

1 scholarship of $1,000 and 1 scholarship of $500 to undergraduate students majoring in entomology, zoology, biology, or a related science in an institution in the U.S., Mexico, or Canada. Must have already completed thirty semester hours when the award is presented. Based on essay detailing interest in entomology, academic record, recommendations, and financial need.

1160.
The Environmental Careers Organization (ECO)
Internship Program
286 Congress Street
Boston, MA 02210-1009
(617) 426-4375

450 internships (approximately 325 in the Environmental Placement Services–EPS, and 140 for minority students in the Diversity Initiative Program) providing a salary ranging from $200 to $800 per week. The DI Program is open to undergraduate minority students and the EPS Program is open to undergraduate juniors, seniors, graduate students, and college graduates of any age. Students can be assigned to individuals from a variety of corporations, such as IBM, Ford, Boeing, Polaroid, Pacific Gas & Electric, etc. Interns might work in a department like environmental health and safety, where they compile reports or evaluate power produced by alternative-energy sources. Deadline: May 14 (DI); rolling (EPS).

1161.
Environmental Protection Agency
National Network for Environmental
Management Studies
Attn: National Program Manager
US EPA (1707)
401 M Street, S.W.
Washington, DC 20460
(202) 260-4965
http://www.epa.gov/

75 to 100 internships providing a grant ranging from $4,000 to $6,000 to undergraduate or graduate students. Interns work in the following areas: environmental policy, regulations, and law; environmental management and administration; environmental science; public relations and media; and computer programming and development. Internships are available at the headquarters in Washington, DC; Atlanta; Boston; Chicago; Dallas; Denver; Kansas City; New York; Philadelphia; San Francisco; and Seattle. Deadline: December 20.

1162.
Epilepsy Foundation of America
Behavioral Sciences Student Fellowships
Research Administration
4351 Garden City Drive, Suite 406
Landover, MD 20785
(301) 459-3700

Numerous grants of $1,500 to undergraduate and graduate students in nursing, psychology, and related areas to conduct epilepsy-related study or training projects. Must propose a three-month epilepsy-related project to be carried out in a U.S. institution at which there are ongoing epilepsy research, service, or training programs. Project must be conducted during a free period in the student's year. Other restrictions may apply. Deadline: March 2.

1163.
Epilepsy Foundation of America
Mary Litty Memorial Fellowship
Research and Professional Education
4351 Garden City Drive, Suite 406
Landover, MD 20785
(301) 459-3700

1 fellowship of $1,500 to graduating high school seniors and undergraduate students pursuing two- and four-year degrees in vocational rehabilitation or social science. Selection based on three-month proposed study plan related to epilepsy rehabilitation, service, training, or research. Write for more information. Deadline: March 1.

1164.
Epilepsy Scholarship Program
CNS Product Management
Parke-Davis
Division of Warner-Lambert Company
201 Tabor Road
Morris Plains, NJ 07950
(201) 540-2000

14 scholarships of $3,000 to high school seniors and undergraduate freshmen, sophomores, and juniors who are under a physician's care for epilepsy. Based on academic

record, extracurricular activities, and recommendation
letters. Deadline: varies.

1165.
Erie Community Foundation
Attn: Chairman
502 G. Daniel Baldwin Building
Erie, PA 16501
(814) 454-0843

5 scholarships of varying amounts, totaling $4,500, to
graduating high school seniors from four public high
schools in Erie County, Pennsylvania. Must be Erie County,
Pennsylvania, residents. Based on academic record and
financial need. Contact high school counselor or above
address. Deadline: varies.

1166.
Ernst and Whinney Foundation Scholarship
2000 National City Center
Cleveland, OH 44114
(216) 861-5000

5 to 6 scholarships of varying amounts, totaling $18,000, for
undergraduate students who are majoring in accounting or
teaching/education and plan on teaching after completion
of studies. Must have three years of experience working in
the U.S. in accounting. Deadline: June 1.

1167.
ESPN, Inc.
ESPN Plaza
935 Middle Street
Bristol, CT 06010
(203) 585-2000
http://espn.sportszone.com/
ESPNET1@espn.com

2 scholarships of $5,000 (1 male and 1 female) and 4
scholarships of $500 (2 male and 2 female) to high school
seniors attending public or private schools. May be used
for any area of study. Must be a U.S. citizen and not be an
immediate family member of a Capital Cities/ABC Inc. or
Hearst Corporation employee. Based on academic record,
participation in sports, and extracurricular school and
community activities. Request applications after November
1. Deadline: March 15.

1168.
Esther Vance Music Scholarship Fund
Trust Department
c/o Bank One
P.O. Box 1699
Colorado Springs, CO 80942
(719) 227-6435

3 scholarship grants ranging from $850 to $1,700 to
graduating high school seniors. Must be residents of the
Colorado Springs, Colorado, area. Must plan to major in
music. Based on academic record, talent, career goals, and
financial need. Deadline: May 15.

1169.
Ethel H. and George W. Tweed Scholarship
Endowment Trust
c/o First Florida Bank, N.A.
7500 Gulf Boulevard
St. Petersburg Beach, FL 33706
(813) 367-2786

9 scholarship grants ranging from $375 to $1,250 to
graduating high school seniors. Must be residents within
the corporate limits of St. Petersburg, Florida. Based on
academic record and financial need. Deadline: April 30.

1170.
Ethel N. Bowen Foundation
c/o First Century Bank National
500 Federal Street
Bluefield, WV 24701
(304) 325-8181

85 scholarships ranging from $500 to $5,000, mainly for
undergraduate study, though some graduate awards are
provided. Open to residents of southern West Virginia and
southwestern Virginia coalfields. Based on academic record
and financial need. Deadline: April 30.

1171.
Etude Music Club of Santa Rosa
Music Competition for Instrumentalists
P.O. Box 823
Santa Rosa, CA 95402
(707) 538-5325

5 awards of $600 (first place) and 5 awards of $300 (second
place) to high school seniors in this classical instrumentalist
competition. Must be residents of Sonoma, Napa, or
Mendocino counties, California. Must be studying music
with a private teacher of music or be recommended by
their school's music department. Deadline: December 25.

1172.
Etude Music Club of Santa Rosa
Music Competition for Vocalists
P.O. Box 823
Santa Rosa, CA 95402
(707) 538-5325

5 awards of $600 (first place) and 5 awards of $300 (second
place) to high school seniors in this classical vocalist
competition. Must be residents of Sonoma, Napa, or
Mendocino counties, California. Must be studying music
with a private teacher of music or be recommended by
their school's music department. Deadline: December 25.

1173.
Eugene Dozzi Charitable Foundation
Attn: Trustee
2000 Lincoln Road
Pittsburgh, PA 15235
(412) 361-4500

1 scholarship of $2,900 to a high school senior. Must be a
Pennsylvania resident, with preference given to Pittsburgh
residents. Based on academic record and financial need.
Deadline: varies.

1174.
Evans Scholarships
Western Golf Association Scholarship Committee
1 Briar Road
Golf, IL 60029

200 renewable scholarships paying full tuition and room costs to high school seniors who have been golf caddies for at least two years. Must be in the upper 25 percent of class. Must submit SAT scores, FAFSA, and recommendations. Good at fourteen universities (Colorado, Illinois, Indiana, Marquette, Miami (Ohio), Michigan, Michigan State, Ohio State, Minnesota, Missouri, Northern Illinois, Northwestern, Purdue, and Wisconsin) or candidates' state university. Obtain applications from Caddies Master, Chairman of Caddie Committee at the club, or by writing the above address. Apply after July 1 of junior year.

1175.
Evrytanian Association "Velouchi" of America
121 Greenwich Road
Charlotte, NC 28211
(704) 366-6571

8 scholarships of $1,200 to students of Evrytanian ancestry (with origins in Evrytania, Greece). 10 scholarships providing room and board to students from Greece to study in Greece. Greek students wanting to study in Greece must contact the Velouchi Association in Greece. Students from Greece wanting to study in the U.S. must contact the U.S. association. Deadline: June 1 (for U.S. and Greek students to study in U.S.).

1176.
Ewald Foundation
15175 East Jefferson Avenue
Grosse Pointe, MI 48230

38 scholarships of varying amounts, totaling $41,000, to high school seniors from the Detroit area. Must be Michigan residents. Based on academic record and financial need. Deadline: varies.

1177.
**Executive Women International (EWI)
    Scholarship Program**
Director of Administration
EWI, Spring Run Executive Plaza
965 East 4800 South, Suite I
Salt Lake City, UT 84117

Numerous scholarships ranging from $100 to $10,000 to high school juniors pursuing a career in business. Scholarships are awarded at the local, regional, and national levels. Must be under nineteen years of age. Can be used only at four-year institutions. Based on academic record, leadership ability, work experience, character, interview, and recommendations. For the address of local EWI chapters, send a self-addressed, stamped envelope. Deadline: April 15.

1178.
**Experimental Aircraft Association/EAA Aviation
    Foundation**
Scholarship Program
P.O. Box 3065
Oshkosh, WI 54903-3065
(414) 426-4815
http://www.aviation.uiuc.edu/

Various awards and scholarships ranging from $200 to full tuition, books, and equipment to students seeking careers in aviation. Send a self-addressed, stamped envelope for information on the ten scholarship programs offered by EAA. Selection based on academic achievement, career goals, and financial need. Other restrictions may apply.

1179.
**Experimental Aircraft Association Foundation
    (EAA)**
Herbert L. Cox Memorial Scholarship
P.O. Box 3065
Oshkosh, WI 54903-3065
(414) 426-4815
http://www.aviation.uiuc.edu/

1 scholarship of at least $800 to a high school senior or undergraduate. Must be accepted to or attending a four-year accredited college or university in pursuit of a degree leading to an aviation profession. Must remain in good standing, but GPA will not be more important than other criteria in making the selection. Must show unmet financial needs for educational expenses. Deadline: April 1.

1180.
**Experimental Aircraft Association Foundation
    (EAA)**
The Richard Lee Vernon Aviation Scholarship
Scholarship Program
P.O. Box 3065
Oshkosh, WI 54903-3065
(414) 426-4815
http://www.aviation.uiuc.edu/

1 scholarship of $800 to a graduating high school senior or high school graduate accepted to a two- or four-year accredited college, university, or aviation technical school. Must have demonstrated the ability to complete the course of training and attain acceptable grades, and must show financial need. Sponsored by EAA and the Richard Lee Vernon Family. Deadline: May 1.

1181.
**Experimental Aircraft Association Foundation
    (EAA)**
Rick Leonard Memorial Scholarship
EAA Chapter 474
P.O. Box 3065
Oshkosh, WI 54903-3065
(414) 426-4815
http://www.aviation.uiuc.edu/

1 scholarship of $5,000 to an undergraduate or graduate student. Must demonstrate a continuing level of quality in personal, academic, and aviation pursuits. May be applied toward the achievement of any aviation-related formal education or training. Deadline: April 1.

1182.
Experimental Aircraft Association Foundation (EAA)
Teledyne Continental Aviation Excellence Scholarship
Scholarship Program
P.O. Box 3065
Oshkosh, WI 54903-3065
(414) 426-4815
http://www.aviation.uiuc.edu/

1 scholarship of $500 to undergraduate students pursuing careers in an aviation-related field. Based on excellence in personal and aviation accomplishments and on individual's potential to become a professional in any field of aviation. Not based on endowment funds and sometimes not available. Deadline: depends on funding availability, generally April 1.

1183.
Explorers Club
Youth Activity Grant Fund
46 East 70th Street
New York, NY 10021
(212) 628-8383

Numerous grants ranging from $200 to $1,000 to high school and undergraduate students. Grants help with travel costs and expenses to assist them in participating in field natural science research anywhere in the world. Must be U.S. citizens or legal residents. Deadline: April 15.

1184.
Fahrney Education Foundation
c/o Firstar Bank
123 East Third Street
Ottumwa, IA 52501
(515) 683-1641

Numerous scholarship grants of varying amounts, totaling $104,000, to high school seniors or undergraduate students. Must be residents of Wapello County, Iowa. Deadline: February 15.

1185.
Fairfax County Medical Society Scholarships
Executive Director
200 Little Falls Street
Falls Church, VA 22046

11 scholarships of $1,000 to high school seniors. Must be legal residents of Fairfax County, Virginia. Renewable. Deadline: May 1.

1186.
Farm Foundation
Farm Foundation Extension Fellowships
1211 West 22nd Street
Oak Brook, IL 60521
(312) 986-9393

Scholarships of up to $4,000 to agriculture extension workers for undergraduate study. Priority is given to those on the administrative level. Those presently being trained to assume administrative responsibility are also considered. Major fields covered are social science, education, political science, agriculture, and business administration. Deadline: March 1.

1187.
Faught Memorial Scholarships
Attn: Trustee Officer
c/o Chittenden Bank
P.O. Box 399, 81 Atkinson Street
Bellows Falls, VT 05101
(802) 463-4524

5 scholarships ranging from $500 to $1,000 to graduating high school seniors. Must attend Union High School District 27 in Bellows Falls, Vermont. Write a brief letter detailing your educational and financial situation; include a self-addressed, stamped envelope. Selection based on academic achievement, extracurricular activities, and financial need. Other restrictions may apply.

1188.
Fay T. Barnes Scholarship Trust
P.O. Box 550
Austin, TX 78789-0001

Scholarships ranging from $1,250 to $2,500 to graduating high school seniors. Must be residents of Williamson or Travis counties, Texas, and planning to attend a college or university in Texas. Must submit application through high school counselor or principal. Deadline: January 15.

1189.
Federal Bureau of Investigation (FBI)
Honors Internship Program
FBI HQ
Room 6329
10th and Pennsylvania Avenue, N.W.
Washington, DC 20535
(202) 324-4991
http://www.fbi.gov/academy/academy.htm

50 to 70 ten-week summer internships to undergraduate seniors and graduate students in the area of domestic intelligence and criminal investigation. Internships are conducted at Washington, DC, and Quantico, Virginia. Interns work on projects related to ongoing investigations. Interns work in Personnel Resources, Behavioral Science Services, Criminal Informant, Accounting and Budget Analysis, Legal Forfeiture, European/Asian/Money Laundering, Undercover and Sensitive Operations, and Audit. They have access to Special Agents and tour field offices, DNA labs, and the Quantico Academy. Upon completion of the internship, interns are highly recruited. Must have at least a 3.0 GPA and must be U.S. citizens. Deadline: November 15.

1190.
Federal Employee Education and Assistance Fund
FEEA Loan Program
8441 W. Bowles Avenue, Suite 200
Littleton, CO 80123
(800) 323-4140
(303) 933-7580
(303) 933-7587 Fax

FEEA provides four different loan programs (PEP, TERI, Parent Loans for Undergraduate Students, and Stafford

Loans) to all active civilian, federal, and postal employees (with at least three years of service) and their dependents. May be used for undergraduate, graduate, or professional school, or postgraduate study at an accredited two- or four-year institution. Loans are made through Signet Bank, (800) 955-0005. For more information on any or all of the loan programs, contact Signet Bank. Deadline: none.

1191.
Federal Employee Education and Assistance Fund FEEA Retired Scholarship Program
8441 West Bowles Avenue, Suite 200
Littleton, CO 80123
(800) 323-4140
(303) 933-7580
(303) 933-7587 Fax

100 to 250 scholarships from $300 to $1,500 to high school seniors, undergraduates, or graduate students. Must be retired civilian federal or postal employees (with at least three years of service) and their dependents. For study at a two- or four-year institution. Must have at least a 3.0 GPA. Based on academic achievement, extracurricular activities, and community activities. Send a #10 self-addressed, stamped envelope for details after January 1. Deadline: first Friday in June.

1192.
Federal Employee Education and Assistance Fund FEEA Scholarship Program
8441 West Bowles Avenue, Suite 200
Littleton, CO 80123
(800) 323-4140
(303) 933-7580
(303) 933-7587 Fax

100 to 250 scholarships ranging from $500 to $2,500 to all federal employees (with at least three years of service) and their dependents. For undergraduate, graduate, or postgraduate study at a two- or four-year institution. Minimum 2.5 GPA. Send self-addressed, stamped envelope for details. Deadline: June 5.

1193.
Federal Employee Education and Assistance Fund TERI Loan Program
8441 W. Bowles Avenue, Suite 200
Littleton, CO 80123
(800) 323-4140
(303) 933-7580
(303) 933-7587 Fax

Numerous loans ranging from $2,000 to $15,000 per year to federal employees (with at least three years of service) and their dependents. For undergraduate, graduate, or postgraduate study at any two- or four-year institution. Send self-addressed, stamped envelope for details. Deadline: none.

1194.
Federal Government Cooperative Education Program
Contact Personnel Office of Agency of interest, or look for the "Federal Career Directory" in a career planning office.

18,000 internships per year, lasting from one to two years, full-time or part-time. Openings are year-round and provide a salary, health insurance, retirement and investment plans, vacation, holidays, and sick leave. Open to high school students, high school graduates, undergraduates, and graduate students. All majors welcome. Interns must be enrolled in their schools' cooperative education program and meet the academic requirements. Must be U.S. citizens or nationals. Internships are in accounting and budgeting; administration and office support; arts and communications; biological sciences; business and industry; computer science; engineering and architecture; mathematics and statistics; medical, dental, hospital, and public health; personnel management and industrial relations; physical sciences; social science and psychology; transportation and supply; and trades and crafts. Deadline: set by individual schools and federal agencies.

1195.
Fellowship of United Methodists in Worship, Music, and Other Arts
Committee on Memorial Scholarship Fund
P.O. Box 840
Nashville, TN 37202
(615) 340-7453

4 scholarships of at least $500 to graduating high school seniors or undergraduate students. Must be full-time music majors or theology majors with worship emphasis. Must be members of the United Methodist Church for at least one year before applying. Based on talent, leadership, and promise. Contact above address or: The Fellowship, 159 Ralph McGill Boulevard, NE, Atlanta, GA 30308. Deadline: June 15.

1196.
The Feminist Majority
8105 West Third Street, Suite 1
Los Angeles, CA 90048
(213) 651-0495
and
1600 Wilson Boulevard, Suite 801
Arlington, VA 22209
(703) 522-2214

20 internships providing only limited stipends to high school, undergraduate, and graduate students. Students can work either part- or full-time for at least two months in either Los Angeles or Washington, DC. The Feminist Majority strives to place feminists in public office or college-campus leadership positions, and encourages women to seek top positions in their professions. Interns monitor press conferences and congressional hearings, analyze policy, write position papers, and conduct research on women's issues. Deadline: rolling.

1197.
Ferree Education and Welfare Fund
101 Sunset Avenue
P.O. Box 2207
Asheboro, NC 27204-2207
(919) 629-2960

25 scholarship grants ranging from $1,000 to $1,500 and 68 loans ranging from $400 to $1,000 to high school seniors or graduates or undergraduate college students. Must be

residents of Randolph County, North Carolina. Must request application before May 1. Deadline: June 15.

1198.

Fifth Marine Division Association Scholarship Fund

Secretary-Treasurer
260 South Norwinden Drive
Springfield, PA 19064
(215) 543-4660

10 scholarships of up to $1,000 per year for four years to children of Marine or Navy veterans of the Fifth Marine Division. Parent must be member of the Fifth Marine Division Association. Based on financial need, SAT/ACT scores, and academic achievement. Award may be used at any accredited institution. Deadline: June 1.

1199.

Fight for Sight, Inc.
FFS–NSPB Student Fellowships

Attn: Research Awards Coordinator
500 East Remington Road
Schaumburg, IL 60173-4557
(708) 843-2020

Numerous fellowships of up to $500 per month for sixty to ninety days of summer research in eye-related clinical or basic research. Applicants may be undergraduate, medical, or graduate students. Renewable for two years. Deadline: March 1.

1200.

FINA/Dallas Morning News All–State–Scholar–Athlete Team Scholarships

Public Relations Division
P.O. Box 2159
Dallas, TX 75221
(214) 750-4111

28 scholarships of $500 and 12 scholarships of $4,000 to graduating high school seniors. Must have received a varsity letter in a U.I.L. sport, have a 90 GPA (3.6 on a 4.0 scale/4.5 on a 5.0 scale) or above, and be in the top 10 percent of high school class. Must be Texas residents. Based on academic achievement, leadership, and service. U.I.L. sports are baseball, basketball, cross–country running, football, golf, soccer, softball, swimming, tennis, track & field, volleyball, and wrestling. Open to all majors. The program is jointly sponsored by FINA Oil, Dallas Morning News, WFAA TV, Staubach Co., and Southwest Airlines. Obtain applications from high school principals, counselors, or coaches, or from above address. Deadline: early December.

1201.

Finnish Centre for International Exchange Programs
Reciprocal Scholarships

P.O. Box 343
SF-00531 Helsinki, Finland
90-7061

Scholarships of approximately $685 per month to citizens of thirty-seven countries (including the U.S.) to study the Finnish language and other subjects related to Finland.

Based on bilateral cultural agreements and programs of cultural exchange. University tuition is free to scholarship recipients. Travel within the country that is related to the study program will be paid by the program. Must be proficient in the Finnish language. Must have been born after January 1, 1957. Deadline: March 1.

1202.

Finnish Centre for International Exchange Programs
Scholarships for Study and Research in Finland

P.O. Box 343
SF-00531 Helsinki, Finland
90-7061

Scholarships of approximately $685 per month to citizens of all countries to study the Finnish language and other subjects related to Finland. University tuition is free to scholarship recipients. Travel within the country that is related to the study program will be paid by the program. Must be proficient in the Finnish language. Must have been born after January 1, 1957. Deadline: February 1.

1203.

Firestone Scholarships

Ms. Frances C. Houser, Contributions Coordinator
The Firestone Tire & Rubber Co.
1200 Firestone Parkway
Akron, OH 44317

Numerous renewable scholarships ranging from $1,000 to $4,000 to children of full-time hourly or salaried Firestone employees with one year of service. Children of retired or deceased employees on payroll at time of death are also eligible. Deadline: varies.

1204.

First Catholic Slovak Ladies Association
Fraternal Scholarship Awards

Director of Fraternal Scholarship Aid
24950 Chagrin Boulevard
Beachwood, OH 44122
(216) 464-8015

60 scholarships of $750 to members of the association who have been members for at least three years prior to the date of application on a $1,000 legal research certificate or a $5,000 participating estate certificate. 13 awards are for undergraduate freshmen, 13 for sophomores, 6 for juniors, 5 for seniors, and 5 for graduate students. Based on academic record, essay, and SAT/ACT. Deadline: March 1.

1205.

First Cavalry Division Association Scholarships

32 North Main
Copperas Cove, TX 76522-1799
(817) 547-6537

Numerous scholarships of $650 (renewable for four years) to dependents or orphans of veterans of the First Cavalry Division. Award may be used at any accredited institution and for any purpose (tuition, books, clothing, room, board, etc.). Applicant must be the child of a soldier who died while in the First Cavalry Division during or since the Vietnam War or of a soldier who was 100 percent disabled due to injuries during his military duty during the Vietnam War. Deadline: spring.

1206.
First Bank of Denver, N.A.
Freeman E. Fairfield–Meeker Charitable Trust
P.O. Box 5825
Denver, CO 80217

Numerous scholarships of $650 to high school seniors or undergraduates. Must be residents of Meeker or Rio Blanco counties, Colorado. No restrictions regarding race, sex, religion, national origin, or where the scholarship may be used.

1207.
First Marine Division Association (FMDA), Inc.
FMDA Grants
Executive Secretary
1704 Florida Avenue
Woodbridge, VA 22191

Scholarships of varying amounts to dependents of a deceased or 100 percent disabled person who was in the First Marine Division or a unit attached to it. May be used for any type of postsecondary higher education. Vocational/technical school applicants will be considered. Based on academic record and financial need. Deadline: varies.

1208.
First Mississippi Corporation Foundation, Inc.
700 North Street
P.O. Box 1249
Jackson, MS 39215-1249
(601) 948-7550

15 scholarship grants of $1,000 to graduating high school seniors in Pascagoula County, Mississippi. Must be Mississippi residents. Based on academic record and financial need. Contact high school counselor or above address. Deadline: varies.

1209.
Fitzgerald Memorial Fund Scholarships
First of America Bank, Trust Department
301 S.W. Adams Street
Peoria, IL 61631
(309) 655-5000

Scholarships of varying amounts to undergraduate students. Must be preparing for the priesthood at a Catholic institution. Based on academic record, career goal, and financial need. Deadline: none.

1210.
The Flannery O'Connor Award for Short Fiction
The University of Georgia Press
Terrell Hall
Athens, GA 30602
(404) 542-0601

Awards of varying amounts for short fiction. Charges $10 fee. Manuscripts will not be returned. Send self-addressed, stamped envelope for rules and information. Submit after June 1. Deadline: July 31.

1211.
Fleet Reserve Association (FRA)
Fleet Reserve Association Scholarship
National Executive Secretary
125 Northwest Street
Alexandria, VA 22314
(703) 683-1400
http://www.fra.org/fra

1 scholarship of varying amount to a child of an active-duty, retired-with-pay, or deceased (while on active duty) member of the U.S. Navy, Marine Corps, or Coast Guard. Deadline: April 15.

1212.
Fleet Reserve Association (FRA)
Oliver and Esther R. Howard Scholarship
National Executive Secretary
125 Northwest Street
Alexandria, VA 22314
(703) 683-1400
http://www.fra.org/fra

1 scholarship of varying amount to a child of a member of FRA or members of the FRA Ladies Auxiliary. Members must have been in good standing since April 1 of the award year. Awarded to daughters on even-numbered years and to sons on odd-numbered years. Based on academic record, character, leadership ability, and financial need. Deadline: April 15.

1213.
Fleet Reserve Association (FRA)
Schuyler S. Pyle Scholarship
National Executive Secretary
125 Northwest Street
Alexandria, VA 22314
(703) 683-1400
http://www.fra.org/fra

1 scholarship of varying amount to a child of a member of the FRA. Member must have been in good standing since April 1 of the award year. Members may be active, retired with pay, or deceased (while on active duty) officers or enlisted personnel of the U.S. Navy, Marine Corps, or Coast Guard. Deadline: April 15.

1214.
Fleet Reserve Association (FRA)
Stanley A. Doran Memorial Scholarships
National Executive Secretary
125 Northwest Street
Alexandria, VA 22314
(703) 683-1400
http://www.fra.org/fra

3 scholarships of varying amounts to children of members of the FRA. Members must have been in good standing since April 1 of the award year. Members may be active, retired-with-pay, or deceased (while on active duty) officers or enlisted personnel of the U.S. Navy, Marine Corps, or Coast Guard. Deadline: April 15.

1215.
Flexographic Technical Association Foundation
Flexography Scholarships
900 Marconi Avenue
Ronkonkoma, NY 11779
(516) 737-6026

14 renewable scholarships of $500 to high school graduates
who have been accepted to or are enrolled in a recognized
vocational program, two-year technical program, or four-
year undergraduate program and pursuing a career in
graphic arts. Deadline: March 31.

1216.
**Florence B. Stouch and Clyde W. Stouch
    Foundation**
Bank One of Eastern Ohio
Attn: Trust Department
P.O. Box 1428
Steubenville, OH 43952
(740) 283-8434

Varying numbers of scholarships of $1,000 to high school
seniors and undergraduates for all fields of study. Must be
residents of Jefferson, Ohio, or York counties, Pennsylvania.
Must demonstrate financial need. Contact high school
counselor or send a self-addressed, stamped envelope to
above address. Deadline: January.

1217.
Florence Evans Bushee Foundation, Inc.
Palmer and Dodge
One Beacon Street, Room 200
Boston, MA 021208
(617) 573-0100

118 scholarship grants of varying amounts, totaling
$110,050, to undergraduate students. Must be residents of
Newburyport, Massachusetts. Write a letter briefly detailing
your educational and financial situation. Other restrictions
may apply. Deadline: May 1.

1218.
**Florida Arts Council
Individual Artists Fellowships**
Division of Cultural Affairs
Florida Department of State
The Capitol
Tallahassee, FL 32301
(904) 488-3976

30 scholarships of up to $5,000 to artists for further work
(not their studies) in the following areas: music, theater,
dance, literature, media, folk, and unusual arts. Must be
Florida residents, over eighteen years old, and U.S. citizens.
Deadline: February 9.

1219.
**Florida Dental Association
Dental Hygiene Scholarship Program**
3021 Swann Avenue
Tampa, FL 33609
(813) 877-7597

Scholarships of varying amounts to Florida residents who
have been accepted in an accredited dental hygiene

program in Florida. Preference given to applicants from
areas in Florida with dental hygienist shortages. Deadline:
July 1; December 1; April 1.

1220.
**Florida Department of Education
Bright Futures Scholarship Program**
Office of Student Financial Assistance
255 Collins Building
Tallahassee, FL 32399-0400
(888) 827-2004 Hotline
(850) 488-4095
(850) 488-3612 Fax
http://www.firn.edu/doe/

Lottery-funded scholarships of varying amounts to
graduating high school seniors and high school graduates.
Must demonstrate high academic achievement. There are
three award levels: Florida Academic Scholars Award,
Florida Merit Scholars Awards, and the Florida Gold Seal
Vocational Scholars Award. Each program has different
academic criteria for eligibility and receives a different
award amount. Obtain applications from high school
counselor or above address. Renewable with satisfactory
academic progress. Deadline: February 15 and April 1.

1221.
**Florida Department of Education
"Chappie" James Most Promising Teacher
Scholarship/Loan Program**
Office of Student Financial Assistance
255 Collins Building
Tallahassee, FL 32399-0400
(888) 827-2004 Hotline
(850) 488-4095
(850) 488-3612 Fax
http://www.firn.edu/doe/

Approximately 480 scholarship/loans of up to $1,500 to
graduating high school seniors and 150 loans of up to
$4,000 to undergraduate juniors or seniors. Must have at
least a 2.5 GPA on a 4.0 scale. Must be Florida residents
and graduating from a Florida high school. May be
pursuing any area of study, but must be planning on a
teaching career in Florida and be in the upper fourth of
class. Must enroll full-time at an eligible Florida institution.
Loan is repaid by teaching in Florida after graduation.
Award is for two years. One student per public high school
and about the same number from private high school are
selected. Deadline: March 1 (high school students to
principals); April 1 (all others).

1222.
**Florida Department of Education
Critical Teacher Shortage Student Loan
    Forgiveness Program**
Office of Student Financial Assistance
255 Collins Building
Tallahassee, FL 32399-0400
(888) 827-2004 Hotline
(850) 488-4095
(850) 488-3612 Fax
http://www.firm.edu/doe/

Loan forgiveness awards of $2,500 per year for
undergraduates and $5,000 per year for graduate students.

This program repays up to $10,000 of the principal balance of student loans in an effort to attract certified graduates to teach in critical teacher shortage areas in Florida. The teacher must be a graduate of an approved education program, be certified in a designated critical teacher shortage area, and be teaching for the first time in a critical teacher shortage area in a Florida public school. Must be employed for at least 180 days. Deadline: March 1.

1223.
Florida Department of Education
Critical Teacher Shortage Tuition
   Reimbursement
Office of Student Financial Assistance
255 Collins Building
Tallahassee, FL 32399-0400
(888) 827-2004 Hotline
(850) 488-4095
(850) 488-3612 Fax
http://www.firn.edu/doe/

Scholarships of tuition reimbursement for up to nine semester hours are available to full-time certified teachers who are teaching in Florida. Must maintain a minimum 3.0 GPA in all courses. Deadline: none.

1224.
Florida Department of Education
Florida Resident Access Grants (FRAG)
Office of Student Financial Assistance
255 Collins Building
Tallahassee, FL 32399-0400
(888) 827-2004 Hotline
(850) 488-4095
(850) 488-3612 Fax
http://www.firn.edu/doe/

Approximately 18,000 grants of varying amounts to graduating high school seniors or undergraduates attending eligible independent nonprofit Florida colleges and universities. Not based on financial need. Amount of award depends on funding and number of eligible students. Deadline: set by individual schools.

1225.
Florida Department of Education
Florida Student Assistance Grants (FSAG)
Office of Student Financial Assistance
255 Collins Building
Tallahassee, FL 32399-0400
(888) 827-2004 Hotline
(850) 488-4095
(850) 488-3612 Fax
http://www.firn.edu/doe/

Grants ranging from $200 to $1,500 to full-time undergraduate students. Must have been residents of Florida for at least twenty-four consecutive months prior to beginning classes, and either U.S. citizens or permanent residents. Must maintain a 2.0 GPA on a 4.0 scale and have financial need. Must file FAFSA by May 15. Deadline: April 15; September 15 (community college students).

1226.
Florida Department of Education
Florida Work Experience Program
Office of Student Financial Assistance
255 Collins Building
Tallahassee, FL 32399-0400
(888) 827-2004 Hotline
(850) 488-4095
(850) 488-3612 Fax
http://www.firn.edu/doe/

Provides off-campus jobs in an undergraduate student's academic major or career interest. Applicants must not have received a bachelor's degree and must be a Florida resident for at least one year prior to entering college, have registered with the Selective Service System, and taken part in the college-level communications and computation testing (CLAST) program. Must be at least half-time students. Not all institutions participate in this program. Obtain applications from school's financial aid office. Must file FAFSA. Deadline: varies with institution.

1227.
Florida Department of Education
José Martí Scholarship Challenge Grant
   Fund
Office of Student Financial Assistance
255 Collins Building
Tallahassee, FL 32399-0400
(888) 827-2004 Hotline

Scholarships of $2,000 per year for up to eight semesters of undergraduate or four semesters of graduate study to students who are Hispanic or are of Spanish culture with origins in Mexico, South America, Central America, or the Caribbean (regardless of race). Must maintain a 3.0 GPA on a 4.0 scale during college study and be a full-time student. Based on academic record and financial need. Deadline: April 15.

1228.
Florida Department of Education
Limited Access Competitive Grants
Office of Student Financial Assistance
255 Collins Building
Tallahassee, FL 32399-0400
(888) 827-2004 Hotline
(850) 488-4095
(850) 488-3612 Fax
http://www.firn.edu/doe/

Approximately 300 grants of up to 50 percent of in-state public institution tuition to community college graduates or transfer students from state universities. Must enroll in one of the designated limited access programs at eligible private colleges or universities in Florida. Preference given to Florida residents from Florida high schools or community colleges. Deadline: set by each school.

1229.
Florida Department of Education
Mary McLeod Bethune Scholarship Challenge
  Grants
Office of Student Financial Assistance
255 Collins Building
Tallahassee, FL 32399-0400
(888) 827-2004 Hotline
(850) 488-4095
(850) 488-3612 Fax
http://www.firn.edu/doe/

Numerous scholarships of $3,000 to high school seniors.
Must be used for full-time undergraduate study at Florida
Agricultural and Mechanical University, Bethune-Cookman
College, Edward Waters College, or Florida Memorial
College. Students must have been residents of Florida for at
least one year prior to starting college and must register
with the Selective Service System. Based on academic record
(3.0 GPA on a 4.0 scale for high school seniors, and 2.0
GPA on a 4.0 scale for renewal), SAT/ACT, and financial
need. Deadline: April 15 (need analysis forms); April 30
(scholarship application).

1230.
Florida Department of Education
Occupational & Physical Therapist Scholarship/
  Loan Program
Office of Student Financial Assistance
255 Collins Building
Tallahassee, FL 32399-0400
(888) 827-2004 Hotline
(850) 488-4095
(850) 488-3612 Fax
http://www.firn.edu/doe/

Approximately 24 scholarship/loans of up to $4,000 to
undergraduate and graduate students pursuing careers as
occupational therapists or therapy assistants, or physical
therapists or therapist assistants. The loan is repaid by
employment for at least three years as therapists in Florida
public schools. If recipient doesn't work full-time in Florida
public schools for the required time period, the loan must
be repaid. Contact: Florida Department of Education,
Bureau of Instructional Support and Community Services,
Florida Education Center; 325 West Gaines Street, Suite 601;
Tallahassee, FL 32399-0400. Deadline: April 15.

1231.
Florida Department of Education
Robert C. Byrd Scholarships
Office of Student Financial Assistance
255 Collins Building
Tallahassee, FL 32399-0400
(888) 827-2004 Hotline
(850) 488-4095
(850) 488-3612 Fax
http://www.firn.edu/doe/

200 nonrenewable scholarships of $1,500 to high school
seniors. Must be Florida residents (for other than
educational purposes) for at least six months, register with
the Selective Service System, and enroll in a Florida public
or private nonprofit college or university. Based on
outstanding academic record; must have at least a 3.85 GPA
and SAT/ACT scores in the upper 75 percent. Apply after

January 1. Each Florida public or private high school may
nominate one student.

1232.
Florida Department of Education
Rosewood Family Scholarship Fund
Office of Student Financial Assistance
255 Collins Building
Tallahassee, FL 32399-0400
(888) 827-2004 Hotline
(850) 488-4095
(850) 488-3612 Fax
http://www.firn.edu/doe/

25 scholarships of up to $4,000 to high school seniors or
undergraduates who are descendants of affected African
American Rosewood families. Must attend or plan to attend
an eligible state-supported two- or four-year college or
university or a public vocational/technical school in
Florida. Scholarship must be used for full-time study. Must
file FAFSA in time to be processed by May 15. Deadline:
May 15.

1233.
Florida Department of Education
Seminole–Miccosukee Indian Scholarship
  Program
Office of Student Financial Assistance
255 Collins Building
Tallahassee, FL 32399-0400
(888) 827-2004 Hotline
(850) 488-4095
(850) 488-3612 Fax
http://www.firn.edu/doe/

Scholarships of varying amounts to students who are
Seminole or Miccosukee Indians, are Florida residents, and
are graduating high school seniors. Students must be
attending a two- or four-year Florida postsecondary
institution and maintain at least a 2.0 GPA. Deadline: none.

1234.
Florida Department of Education
Undergraduate Scholar's Fund
Office of Student Financial Assistance
255 Collins Building
Tallahassee, FL 32399-0400
(888) 827-2004 Hotline

Renewable scholarships from $1,000 to $2,500 for high
school seniors. Must 1) be a National Merit Scholar or
Finalist, 2) have a minimum 3.5 GPA and a combined SAT
score of at least 1200 or composite ACT score of at least 28,
3) be designated by the State Board of Education as a
Florida Academic Scholar, or 4) have been awarded an
International Baccalaureate Diploma from the International
Baccalaureate Office. Must have a Florida high school
diploma or its equivalent, have maintained residency in
Florida for a minimum of twenty-four months before
beginning classes, and be enrolled full-time at an eligible
Florida college or university. Minimum 3.2 GPA for twenty-
four semester hours or thirty-six quarter hours is required
for renewal. Obtain application from high school counselor.
Deadline: April 1.

1235.
Florida Engineering Society
125 S. Gadsden Street
P.O. Box 750
Tallahassee, FL 32302
(904) 224-0177

Scholarships of $1,000 to high school seniors planning to enter into an engineering curriculum. Some scholarships may require attendance at a certain college or university. For Florida residents only. Deadline: late November; local chapters may vary.

1236.
Ford Fund Student Loan Program
Ford Motor Company Fund
The American Road
Dearborn, MI 48121

Scholarships of varying amounts to children, adopted children, or stepchildren of a person who is (or immediately prior to death or retirement was) on the direct payroll of Ford Motor Company.

1237.
Ford Howard Paper Foundation, Inc.
Scholarship Selection Committee
1919 Broadway
Green Bay, WI 54304-1919
(414) 435-8821

3 scholarships ranging from $2,500 to $5,000 to graduating high school seniors. Must be residents of Brown County, Wisconsin. Based on academic record and financial need. Deadline: November 1.

1238.
Ford Scholars Program
San Antonio, TX

130 scholarships ranging from $500 to $1,000 to graduating high school seniors who are residents of San Antonio. Scholarships are awarded in ten different areas: science, English, vocational technology, etc. Students must contact their counselors and inquire how their school is taking applications. From one to ten students are nominated from each San Antonio high school. Deadline: late February (to submit to counselors); February 28 (for counselors to submit nominated students).

1239.
Fort Pierce Memorial Hospital Scholarship
  Foundation
c/o Lawnwood Medical Center
P.O. Box 188
1700 South 23rd Street
Fort Pierce, FL 34950
(407) 461-4000

Numerous scholarships ranging from $2,500 to $15,000 to undergraduate and graduate students from St. Lucie County, Florida. Must be pursuing a career in a health field. Undergraduate students must be unmarried. Deadline: April 15.

1240.
Forty Acres and A Mule Filmworks, Inc.
Internship Program
124 Dekalb Avenue
Brooklyn, NY 11217
(718) 624-3703

15 internships open to high school seniors, high school graduates, undergraduates, college graduates, and graduate students who are interested in the film industry. This company is owned by Spike Lee. The internships are not limited to any ethnic group, though the majority of the interns are African American. Interns work in wardrobe, props, extras casting, accounting, director's assistant, production, and editing. The internships last from eight to eleven weeks to coincide with production dates and are conducted in Brooklyn, New York. Deadline: rolling.

1241.
Foster City Annual Writers Contest
Foster City Committee for the Arts
650 Shell Boulevard
Foster City, CA 94404

Contest offering $1,500 in prizes for unpublished fiction, poetry, humor, and children's stories. Include a self-addressed, stamped envelope for rules. Deadline: April 1–August 31.

1242.
Foundation for Amateur Radio (FAR), Inc.
FAR Scholarships
6903 Rhode Island Avenue
College Park, MD 20740

Numerous scholarships of varying amounts to active licensed radio amateurs. Obtain information from amateur radio journals such as *QST, CQ, 73,* or *World Radio.* Deadline: varies.

1243.
Foundation for European Language and
  Educational Centers
Intensive European Language Courses
  Scholarships
Attn: Students' Assistance Department
Scholarship Department
Eurocentres
Seestrasse 247
Zurich CH-8038
Switzerland
(01) 482-10-65

Varying numbers of scholarships of Sf1,500, which covers part of the tuition for a three-month foreign language course in English, French, German, Italian, or Spanish to graduating high school seniors, undergraduate or graduate students, or other individuals. Must have at least two years of professional experience in any field. Selection based on financial need and prior knowledge of language to be studied. Course is conducted in the country where language is spoken. Applicants must be between eighteen and thirty years of age. Deadline: January 15; March 31; June 15; October 15.

1244.
Foundation for Exceptional Children
Stanley E. Jackson Scholarships for the
Handicapped
1920 Association Drive
Reston, VA 22091
(703) 620-1054

1 scholarship of $1,000 each to a disabled, a disabled
minority, a disabled gifted, and a disabled gifted minority
student. Other scholarships are awarded if funds are
available. Must have a handicapping disability and intend
to enroll as a full-time student in a two- or four-year
undergraduate program or vocational training program.
Based on academic record, recommendations, essay, and
financial need. Deadline: January 16.

1245.
Foundation for the Carolinas
301 South Brevard Street
Charlotte, NC 28202

40 scholarship grants, totaling $34,545, to high school
seniors. Must be residents of either North Carolina or
South Carolina. Based on academic record and financial
need. Deadline: varies.

1246.
Foundation of the National Student Nurses'
Association
555 West 57th Street, Suite 1325
New York, NY 10019

80 scholarships ranging from $1,000 to $2,500 to
undergraduate students in nursing programs. For
information send a self-addressed, stamped envelope with
58¢ postage. There is a $5 application fee. Scholarships are
awarded in the spring for use in summer school and the
ensuing academic year. Application are available between
September 15 and January 15. Deadline: February 1.

1247.
Foundation of the Wall & Ceiling Industry
Scholarship Program
1600 Cameron Street, 2nd floor
Alexandria, VA 22314
(703) 684-2924

15 awards of $500 are available to undergraduate
sophomores, juniors, or seniors who are construction
majors and enrolled in a two- or four-year program at an
accredited U.S. institution. Deadline: December 1.

1248.
Fourteenth Air Force Association, Inc.
General Claire Lee Chennault Scholarships
Scholarship Committee
1212 West High Street
Haddon Heights, NJ 08035

Scholarships of varying amounts to students who are
dependents or descendants of a member or a deceased
member of the 14th Air Force (Flying Tigers) Association
who is in good standing (or was at the time of death), who
served in the American Volunteer Group or China Air Task
Force or the 14th Air Force or was attached to any of those

groups. Based on personal qualifications and financial need.
Include a self-addressed, stamped envelope. Deadline:
varies.

1249.
Fourth Infantry Division Scholarships
Secretary
4th Infantry Division Association
937 Bowman Road, #337
Mt. Pleasant, SC 29464

Scholarships ranging from $1,500 to $4,500 to the eldest
two surviving children of deceased members of the 4th
Infantry Division who died while serving in Vietnam
between 8/1/66 and 12/31/77. Students may be attending
any two- or four-year institution or a vocational/technical
school. If the eldest children cannot accept, another child
may be designated by the surviving spouse or guardian.

1250.
Fourth Marine Division Association
General Clifton B. Cates Memorial Scholarships
Attn: Scholarship Committee
2854 South 44th Street
Milwaukee, WI 53219
(414) 543-3474

Numerous scholarships of up to $2,400 to high school
seniors, high school graduates, or undergraduate college
students. Parent must have been in active duty with the
Fourth Marine Division or an attached unit in WWII and
must be either deceased or totally disabled. May be used at
a two- or four-year college or university. Deadline: June 1.

1251.
Fox Educational Foundation
P.O. Box 29
Rehoboth Valley
Belle Vernon, PA 15012

Scholarship loans of varying amounts to high school
seniors or graduates. Must be dependent children of active
or former employee of the Fox Grocery Company and its
affiliates. Based on academic record, character, leadership,
and financial need.

1252.
Fox, Inc.
(Insert Name of Fox Company)
Personnel Department
P.O. Box 900
Beverly Hills, CA 90213
(310) FOX-1000

60 to 90 internships ranging from eight to sixteen weeks
during the summer, spring, and fall, and providing a salary
of $300 per week to undergraduates and $450 per week to
graduate students. International students studying in the
U.S. may apply. Internships are conducted in Dallas, TX;
Los Angeles, CA; and New York, NY, during the summer,
fall, and spring. There are nineteen separate entertainment
companies: Fox Broadcasting, Fox Television Network,
Cable Channels fX and fXM, Twentieth Television
(syndicates Fox television shows), Morning Studies, Fox
Sports, Fox Children's Network, Fox Latin America Channel,
Twentieth Century Fox, Twentieth Century Fox TV,

Twentieth Century Fox Licensing and Merchandising, and Fox Searchlight Pictures. Interns may work in any of the companies in the following departments: accounting, finance, legal, production, programming, research, and sales and marketing. Interns must receive academic credit for unpaid positions. Must submit a résumé and cover letter. Deadline: rolling.

1253.
Francis Nathaniel and Katheryn Padgett Kennedy Foundation
P.O. Box 1178
Greenwood, SC 29648
(803) 942-1400

48 scholarships ranging from $400 to $1,000 to undergraduate students from South Carolina. Award is for study as a Southern Baptist minister, for foreign mission work, or for Christian education in applicant's local church. Deadline: May 15.

1254.
Francis Ouimet Scholarship Fund
Caddie Scholarships
Scholarship Director
190 Park Road
Weston, MA 02193-3401

Renewable scholarships ranging from $500 to $5,000 to high school seniors. Must have been golf caddy, bag room/ pro shop attendant, or grounds crew worker for at least three years in Massachusetts. Award can be used at a four-year institution or a vocational/technical school. Based on academic record, SAT/ACT scores, essay, financial need, and recommendations. Deadline: December 1.

1255.
Francis S. Viele Scholarship Fund
502 Torro Canyon Road, Suite A
Santa Barbara, CA 93108
(213) 629-3571

28 scholarships ranging from $2,500 to $4,000 to members of Sigma Phi Society. Based on academic record, service to Sigma Phi, and financial need. Contact local chapter or above address.

1256.
Frank and Bea Wood Foundation
Attn: President
2304 Midwestern Parkway, Suite 204
Wichita Falls, TX 76308

7 scholarships ranging from $250 to $500 to high school seniors. Must be residents of the Wichita Falls, Texas, area. Based on academic record and financial need. Deadline: varies.

1257.
Frank and Lydia Bergen Foundation
Philanthropic Services Group
c/o First Union National Bank
765 Broad Street
Newark, NJ 07102
(973) 430-4500

Numerous scholarship grants, totaling $36,000, to high school seniors or graduates or undergraduate college

students. Must be majoring in or planning to major in music. Must be New Jersey residents. Based on academic record, career goals, and financial need. Deadline: September 15 and January 15.

1258.
Frank Family Memorial Scholarship Fund
Norwest Bank
636 Wisconsin Avenue
Sheboygan, WI 53081

131 scholarships of varying amounts, totaling $116,000, to high school seniors from Homestead High School in Mequon, Wisconsin. Based on academic record and financial need. Deadline: varies.

1259.
Frank F. Bentley Trust
Key Bank Trust Department
127 Public Square
Cleveland, OH 44114
(216) 689-0969

Numerous scholarship grants of varying amounts, totaling $22,436, to high school seniors or high school graduates of Trumbull County, Ohio. Contact high school counselor or write a letter briefly detailing your educational and financial situation. Other restrictions may apply. Contact: Joyce A. May, c/o Turner and May, 800 Second National Bank Building, Warren, OH 44481, (216) 399-8801. Deadline: mid-summer.

1260.
Frank Gannett Newspaper Carrier Scholarships
Lincoln Tower, 15th Floor
Rochester, NY 14604
(716) 258-2647

7 scholarships of $1,000 to high school seniors who have delivered any Gannett newspaper in the Rochester area by December of senior year. Based on academic record, recommendation, and financial need. Deadline: varies.

1261.
Frank P. and Clara R. Williams Scholarships
Attn: Administrator
P.O. Box 374
Oil City, PA 16301
(814) 677-5085

150 scholarship grants ranging from $100 to $1,200 to high school seniors or high school graduates. Must be residents of Venango County, Pennsylvania. Based on financial need. Contact high school counselor or write a letter briefly detailing your educational and financial situation. Other restrictions may apply. Deadline: April 15.

1262.
Frank Roswell Fuller Scholarships
Attn: Manager
300 Summit Street
Hartford, CT 06106
(203) 297-2046

16 scholarship grants ranging from $1,500 to $3,500 to graduating high school seniors or high school graduates

who haven't attended college. Must be graduates of a Hartford County, Connecticut, school. Must be members of the Congregational Church and have financial need. Deadline: May 15.

1263.
Fraternal Order UDT/SEAL Educational Grants
Chairperson, Scholarship Committee
Fraternal Order of UDT/SEAL, Inc.
P.O. Box 5365
Virginia Beach, VA 23455

Varying numbers of grants of varying amounts to children of regular or associated members in good standing of the Fraternal Order of UDT/SEAL, Inc., for at least three years. Members may be active, retired, discharged, or separated enlisted or officer personnel of the Armed Forces who have served with a Navy Combat Demolition Unit (NCDU), Underwater Demolition Team (UDT), or Seal Team (SEAL). Based on academic merit, character, and financial need. Deadline: April 15.

1264.
Fred Forsythe Educational Trust Fund
c/o Fleet Bank of Maine
80 Exchange Street, #3
Bangor, ME 04401
(207) 941-6000

37 scholarship grants, totaling $21,100, to high school seniors and graduates of Bucksport High School in Maine. Contact high school counselor or above address. Deadline: varies.

1265.
Fred W. Wells Trust Fund
Fleet National Bank
Trust Department
378 Federal Street
Greenfield, MA 01301
(413) 773-8853

Numerous grants ranging from $250 to $1,000 to high school seniors or undergraduate students. Must be residents of Ashfield, Bernardston, Buckland, Charlemont, Conway, Deerfield, Gill, Greenfield, Hawley, Heath, Leyden, Monroe, Montague, Northfield, Rowe, or Shelburne, Massachusetts. Deadline: May 1.

1266.
The Freedom Forum
Journalism Scholarships
1101 Wilson Boulevard
Arlington, VA 22209
(703) 528-0800

Renewable scholarships of $2,500 to undergraduate and graduate journalism or communications majors at an accredited four-year institution. Must be in the upper 50 percent of class, have at least a C+ average, and submit three samples of writing. Based on academic record, SAT/ACT scores, essay, and recommendations. Deadline: January 31.

1267.
Freedom from Religion Foundation
Saul Jakel Memorial Awards
P.O. Box 750
Madison, WI 53701
(608) 356-8900

Scholarships ranging from $100 to $1,000 to undergraduate and graduate students. Based on an essay relating to church and state separation or free thought. Send information on college year and major and permanent and school addresses and telephone numbers. Deadline: August 1.

1268.
Freedom's Foundation National Awards Program
   for Youth
Awards Department
Freedom's Foundation at Valley Forge
Route 23
P.O. Box 706
Valley Forge, PA 19482-0706

Awards of $100 U.S. Savings Bonds and framed George Washington Honor Medal to students in grades K–12 who carry out efforts of responsible citizenship in forms such as humanitarian, patriotic, educational, or community-related projects. Students write an essay about the basic values our country was built upon and their personal experiences with patriotism. If they wish, the essay can be replaced with an entry in the form of a scrapbook, ring binder, or photo album of substantiating material (such as news clippings or any material describing students' efforts). All entries must be done by individual students. An official nomination form must be included with the entry. Send a self-addressed, stamped envelope for guidelines and an entry form. This is not a scholarship competition, but merely a writing competition that provides awards of U.S. Savings Bonds. Deadline: January 15; May 1.

1269.
Free Sons of Israel
Free Sons Scholarship Fund
180 Varick Street
New York, NY 10014
(212) 924-6566

Numerous scholarships of varying amounts to members and children of members. Members must be of the Jewish faith. Based on financial need.

1270.
Fresno Philharmonic
Rotary Young Artists Awards Competition
1300 North Fresno Street, Suite 201B
Fresno, CA 93703
(209) 485-3020

1 first prize of $1,250 and 1 second prize of $700 are available to music students between the ages of twenty and thirty-four who are residents of or enrolled in an accredited music program in Alaska, California, Colorado, Hawaii, Indiana, New Mexico, Nevada, Montana, Oregon, Washington, or Wyoming. Competition is on a rotating basis (piano-1993; vocal-1994; instrumental-1995, etc.). A $20 nonrefundable registration fee is required if applicant's entry is accepted. Deadline: January 2.

1271.
Friendship Fund, Inc.
c/o Boston Safe Deposit and Trust Company
1 Boston Place, OBP-2
Boston, MA 02108
(617) 722-7000

1 scholarship of $3,000 to a high school senior or
undergraduate student. Must be a resident of
Massachusetts. Based on academic record and financial
need. Deadline: May 31.

1272.
Friends of the National Zoo
Graphics & Horticulture Traineeships
3000 Connecticut Avenue, N.W.
Washington, DC 20008
(202) 673-4717

Twelve-week summer or fall internships that provide a
$2,400 stipend to upper-level undergraduates and recent
graduates whose major was either graphic arts or
horticulture. Based on interest, academic achievement,
relevant experience, and recommendations. All internships
are at the National Zoological Park in Washington, DC.
Deadline: February 17.

1273.
Friends of the National Zoo
Research Traineeship Program
3000 Connecticut Avenue, N.W.
Washington, DC 20008
(202) 673-4717

Awards of up to $2,400 to undergraduate and graduate
students in zoology to participate in a twelve-week summer
or fall internship. Selection based on academic achievement,
statement of interest, relevant experience, and
recommendation letters. Other restrictions may apply.
Deadline: February 17.

1274.
Frito Lay, Inc.
Minority Internship Program
Staffing
7701 Legacy Drive
Plano, TX 75024-4099
(214) 334-7000

25 twelve-week summer internships providing a salary
ranging from $460 to $600 per week for undergraduates,
$540 to $820 per week for graduates, plus a $500 relocation
stipend and a $1,000 bonus. Open to minority
undergraduate sophomores, juniors, seniors, and graduate
students. Interns work in sales, marketing, finance,
manufacturing, purchasing, logistics, engineering,
management systems, research and development,
communications, and human resources at the corporate
headquarters in Plano, TX, or at the divisional headquarters
in Texas, Georgia, or California. Some interns take field
assignments in sales, operations, manufacturing, and
distributions in Phoenix, AZ; Los Angeles, CA; Chicago, IL;
and Beloit or Milwaukee, WI. Interns working in technical
positions develop packaging graphics, install new seasoning
systems, develop hardware and software, and track
seasoning-usage fluctuations. Interns in nontechnical

positions evaluate competitor products, and sell and
produce chips and dips, write articles, and even interview
employees. Deadline: April 15.

1275.
Frontier Nursing Service
Courier Program
Wendover, KY 41775
(606) 672-2317

25 six-week internships, conducted year-round, are open to
anyone at least eighteen years of age. Any major is
accepted, but experience in CPR, in first aid, and on
Macintosh computers is helpful. Couriers must hold valid
driver's licenses. Couriers experience rural life in Kentucky
working in FNS, an organization founded in 1925 by Mary
Breckinridge following the deaths of her children. FNS
provides quality health care to many of Leslie County's
poor, rural residents. This internship program is an
excellent opportunity for anyone interested in teaching and/
or health care. Couriers selected to participate in the
program receive no monetary compensation but do receive
free room and board. They may visit hospitals to pick up
mail, medicine, supplies, and prenatal equipment; take
medical histories of patients; take vital signs, and even
participate in various surgical procedures. Applicants must
submit a $100 application fee, an application form, a cover
letter explaining interest in program, and a résumé. Deadline:
rolling.

1276.
Frozen Food Association of New England
Scholarship Program
99 South Bedford Street, Suite 200
Burlington, MA 01803
(617) 270-5054

12 scholarships of $1,000 to undergraduate students who
are residents of any of the six New England states and are
planning on a career in the food industry (including
nutrition and dietetics). Awards can be used at two- or four-
year colleges. Deadline: April 1.

1277.
Fukunaga Scholarship Foundation
P.O. Box 2788
Honolulu, HI 96813
(808) 521-6511

8 scholarships of $1,000 to undergraduate and graduate
students majoring in business administration who rank in
the upper 25 percent of high school class, have a total 3.0
GPA in high school, and have financial need. Must be
residents of Hawaii. Based on ability, industriousness,
dependability, and determination. Must be pursuing a
career in business within the Pacific Basin area. Deadline:
March 15.

1278.
Fuller E. Callaway Foundation
Hatton Lovejoy Scholarship Plan
209 Broome Street
P.O. Box 790
LaGrange, GA 30241
(404) 884-7348

10 scholarships of $1,100 per quarter or $1,650 per semester
($13,200 total or total college costs—whichever is smaller)

to high school seniors who have been residents of Troup County, Georgia, for at least two years. Must be in the upper 25 percent of class. Based on academic record, SAT/ACT scores, extracurricular activities, community involvement, leadership qualities, and interview.

1279.
Fund for American Studies
Institute on Comparative Political & Economic Systems
1526 18th Street, N.W.
Washington, DC 20036
(202) 986-0384

Approximately 80 awards of up to $2,500 to undergraduates to attend annual six-week summer institute held at Georgetown University offering the following courses (worth six credits): Washington Internships, Foreign Policy Lectures, Media Dialogue Series, Site Briefings and Career Days. Must be majoring in political science, economics, or journalism. Preference given to sophomores or juniors. Deadline: March 12.

1280.
Furnas Foundation, Inc.
1000 McKee Street
Batavia, IL 60510
(708) 879-6000

77 grants averaging $1,000 (totaling $76,538) to high school seniors or undergraduate students. Must be residents of Batavia, Illinois, or Clarke County, Iowa. Based on academic record and financial need. Deadline: March 1.

1281.
Future Homemakers of America
Raye Virginia Allen State President's Scholarship
Youth/Adult Leadership Coordinator
1910 Association Drive
Reston, VA 22091
(703) 476-4900

1 scholarship of $2,000 to a member of Future Homemakers of America who served as a state president but who has not held a national FHA office. Based on academic record, volunteer activities, and leadership. Deadline: February 1.

1282.
Future Homemakers of America (FHA), Texas Association
Adams Extract Scholarship
P.O. Box 9616
Austin, TX 78766-9616

1 scholarship of $500 to a high school senior based on a 500-word essay on "Creative Use of Adams Extract in Foods." Must be Texas resident and member of Texas FHA. High school seniors may apply for only one Adams scholarship, either Extract or Spices. Other restrictions may apply. Deadline: March 1.

1283.
Future Homemakers of America (FHA), Texas Association
Adams Spices Scholarship
P.O. Box 9616
Austin, TX 78766-9616

1 scholarship of $500 to a high school senior based on a 500-word essay on "Creative Use of Adams Spices in Foods." High school seniors may apply for only one Adams scholarship, either Extract or Spices. Must be Texas resident and member of Texas FHA. Other restrictions may apply. Deadline: March 1.

1284.
Future Homemakers of America (FHA), Texas Association
C. J. Davidson Scholarships
P.O. Box 9616
Austin, TX 78766-9616

10 scholarships of $1,800 to graduating high school seniors planning on majoring in home economics. Must have at least an 85 GPA, be a member of the Texas Chapter of FHA for at least two years, have completed one or more years of home economics in high school, and be a Texas resident. Selection based on academic achievement, involvement in FHA, test scores, essay, and plans to teach Home Economics. The 500-word essay should be on topic of students' choice related to Home Economics or Future Homemakers of America. Award can be used at only one of eleven approved Texas universities. Send a self-addressed, stamped envelope for an application. Deadline: March 1.

1285.
Future Homemakers of America (FHA), Texas Association
Favorite Recipes Press
P.O. Box 9616
Austin, TX 78766-9616

1 scholarship of $500 to high school seniors. Based on a 500-word essay on topic of student's choice related to Home Economics or Future Homemakers of America. Must be a member of the Texas Chapter of FHA and a Texas resident. Send a self-addressed, stamped envelope for an application. Deadline: March 1.

1286.
Future Homemakers of America (FHA), Texas Association
Institutional Financing Services
P.O. Box 9616
Austin, TX 78766-9616

1 scholarship of varying amount to a graduating high school senior. Must be a member of the Texas Chapter of FHA and a Texas resident. Must have participated in an IFS fund-raising program. The amount of the award is determined by royalties from FHA/HERO sales of IFS products. Must attach a statement to the application showing evidence of involvement with IFS. Send a self-addressed, stamped envelope for an application. Deadline: March 1.

1287.
Future Homemakers of America (FHA), Texas Association
Regional Scholarships
P.O. Box 9616
Austin, TX 78766-9616

5 scholarships of varying amounts to members of Texas chapters of FHA. Must be Texas residents, graduating from a Texas high school. Based on 500-word essay on how involvement with FHA or Vocational Home Economics has prepared you for your future. Deadline: March 1.

1288.
Future Homemakers of America (FHA), Texas Association
San Antonio Livestock Exposition, Inc. Scholarships
P.O. Box 9616
Austin, TX 78766-9616

Varying numbers of scholarships of $2,500 to graduating high school seniors. Must be residents of Bexar County, Texas, and members of the Texas Chapter of FHA. Must be planning to major in agriculture or a related field. Recipients are selected by FHA, Texas Association. Must submit a 200-word essay on how agriculture or a closely related field relates to home economics. Send a self-addressed, stamped envelope for an application. Deadline: March 1.

1289.
Future Homemakers of America (FHA), Texas Association
Texas Farm Bureau
P.O. Box 9616
Austin, TX 78766-9616

1 scholarship of $1,000 to a graduating high school senior. Must be a Texas resident, graduating from a Texas high school, and member of a Texas chapter of FHA. Must have been an area, regional, or state FHA/HERO Officer and planning to teach home economics in Texas. Attach two copies of an autobiography. Deadline: March 1.

1290.
Future Teachers Scholarships
Texas State Teachers Association
316 West 12th Street
Austin, TX 78701

2 Teacher Preparation scholarships of $1,000 awarded annually to members from the Texas Future Teachers of America chapters. Based on academic record, career goals, and financial need. Deadline: March 1.

1291.
Gamma Iota Sigma Scholarships
Griffith Foundation for Insurance Education
1775 College Road
Columbus, OH 43210
(614) 292-2061

Scholarships ranging from $500 to $6,000 to undergraduate juniors or seniors and graduate students. May be majoring

in insurance/risk management or actuarial science. Support is provided at schools with Gamma Iota Sigma fraternity chapters. Renewable. Deadline: none.

1292.
Gannett Foundation
Scholarships Administrator
1101 Wilson Boulevard
Arlington, VA 22234
(703) 285-6000

50 scholarships ranging from $500 to $3,000 undergraduate and graduate students. Students must be interested in a career in newspaper or broadcast journalism and be majoring in news/editorial broadcasting or advertising. Deadline: January.

1293.
Garden Club of America
Awards for Summer Environmental Studies
Conservation Committee
598 Madison Avenue
New York, NY 10022

Scholarship awards of $1,500 to undergraduate and graduate students majoring in ecology or related fields. The award is meant for use to cover a summer course in environmental studies. Preference given to undergraduates. Send a self-addressed, stamped envelope to M. Freeman at above address for an application. Deadline: February 15.

1294.
Gardener Foundation
500 Thornhill Lane
Middletown, OH 45042
(513) 422-5363

24 scholarships of $3,500 to graduating high school seniors. Must be residents of Middletown or Hamilton counties, Ohio. Based on academic record and financial need. Contact high school counselor or above address. Deadline: April 1.

1295.
Gemco Charitable and Scholarship Fund
6565 Knott Avenue
Buena Park, CA 90620

Numerous scholarships of varying amounts, totaling $140,000, to graduating high school seniors in areas where Gemco stores are located. Based on a written competition in which knowledge of economics and the free enterprise system is demonstrated. Deadline: varies.

1296.
GEM National Center for Graduate Education for Minorities, Inc.
P.O. Box 537
Notre Dame, IN 46556

Fellowships ranging from $6,000 to $12,000 to minority undergraduate and graduate students in engineering. Must attend one of the GEM universities. Other restrictions may apply.

1297.
Gemological Institute of America (GIA)
Arthur F. Gleim Jr. Scholarships
1600 Stewart Street
P.O. Box 2110
Santa Monica, CA 90404

Numerous tuition scholarships ranging from $275 to $750 to students in correspondence courses in gemology. Must be studying GIA home-study courses in diamond, colored stone, gem identification, jewelry design, jewelry retailing, or creative jewelry display. Write a letter briefly describing educational background, experience in gemology, career goals, and financial situation. Must be sponsored and/or recommended by a jeweler who is a member of a state retail jewelers' association, the Diamond Manufacturers and Importers Association, or the American Gem Society. Sponsor's membership affiliation must be indicated in the recommendation letter. Deadline: March 31.

1298.
Genentech
Human Resources
Summer Internship Program
P.O. Box 1950
South San Francisco, CA 94083-1950
(650) 225-1000
http://www.gene.com
Written inquiries only

85 ten- to twelve-week summer internships providing $400 per week to undergraduate sophomores, juniors, and seniors, and $475 per week to graduate students. Internships are available in business, corporate communications, manufacturing, marketing, medical affairs, quality control, and research. Those students applying for biotechnology research must have a science background (biology, chemistry, chemical engineering, etc.). Finalists are interviewed in person or by telephone. Deadline: March 15.

1299.
General Educational Fund, Inc.
c/o Merchants Trust Co.
P.O. Box 1009
164 College Street
Burlington, VT 05402
(802) 865-1887

382 scholarships ranging from $300 to $1,000 to graduating high school seniors or graduates or undergraduate students. Must be residents of Vermont. Based on academic record and financial need.

1300.
General Electric Foundation
GE Foundation Minority Student Scholarships
Fairfield, CT 06431

Numerous scholarships of varying amounts, totaling $1 million, to minority students majoring in engineering and business. Awards are made directly to the colleges and universities, which then select the recipients. Contact school's financial aid office or the engineering or business department at the institution you will be attending. Do not contact the foundation. Deadline: varies by school.

1301.
Gensler and Associates/Architects
Intern Coordinator
600 California Street, Suite 1000
San Francisco, CA 94108
(415) 433-3700

12 or more internships lasting from two months to a year, providing a salary of $9 per hour and possible scholarship, is open to undergraduate sophomores, juniors, seniors, and graduate students. Students work in New York, Washington, DC, San Francisco, Los Angeles, Denver, or Houston. Most positions are in architecture, though a few are available in support departments, such as marketing or the library. Interns are assigned to an architect or a team of architects and are exposed to a variety of educational and cultural programs. Though most interns have taken at least one or two architectural courses, there are no academic prerequisites. Send résumé, cover letter, and examples of your work, which will not be returned. Deadline: February 1 (summer); rolling (fall and spring).

1302.
George Abrahamian Foundation
945 Admiral Street
Providence, RI 02904
(401) 831-2887

5 scholarships ranging from $600 to $900 to high school graduates. Must be residents of Rhode Island and of Armenian lineage. Must be U.S. citizens, members of an Armenian church, and have at least a 3.0 GPA. Can be used at a two- or four-year institution in Rhode Island. Renewable. Deadline: September.

1303.
George E. Stifel Scholarship Fund
Bank One
1114 Market Street
Wheeling, WV 26003
Written inquiries only

33 awards ranging from $280 to $2,000 to public high school seniors or graduates from Wheeling, West Virginia. Must be legal residents of Ohio County, West Virginia. Students must be between seventeen and twenty-five. Deadline: spring.

1304.
George Grotefend Scholarship Fund
Grotefend Scholarship Board
c/o Wells Fargo Bank, Trust Department
1644 Magnolia Avenue
Redding, CA 96001
(800) 869-3557

300 scholarships ranging from $50 to $400 to students who received their entire high school education in Shasta County, California. Based on financial need. Deadline: May 1.

1305.
George J. Record School Foundation
P.O. Box 581
Conneaut, OH 44030
(216) 599-8283

Numerous scholarships of approximately $2,000 to undergraduate students. Must be residents of Ashtabula County, Ohio. Must be attending an approved private institution and have completed at least six quarter hours of study in religion. Deadline: May 20 (freshmen); June 20 (all others).

1306.
George Lurcy Charitable and Educational Trust
c/o LeBoeuf, Lamb, Leiby, & Macrae
520 Madison Avenue
New York, NY 10022
(212) 715-8000

Scholarships of varying amounts for U.S. college students to study in France and for French college students to study in the U.S. Based on academic record, career goals, reason for wanting to study outside the country, and financial need. Deadline: varies.

1307.
George M. Pullman Educational Foundation
3604-N
5020 South Lake Shore Drive, Suite 307
Chicago, IL 60615
(773) 363-6191

563 scholarships of varying amounts, totaling $325,000, to high school seniors. Must be Cook County residents or descendants of a student of the Pullman Free School of Manual Training. Based on financial need. Must be nominated by counselor. Deadline: January 1.

1308.
George T. Welch Testamentary Trust
c/o Baker-Boyer Bancorp.
P.O. Box 1796
Walla Walla, WA 99362
(509) 525-2000

95 scholarships ranging from $150 to $1,700 to high school seniors or graduates or undergraduate students. Must be unmarried residents of Walla Walla County and enrolled in Washington schools. Based on financial need. Deadline: April 1.

1309.
Georgia Society of Professional Engineers
One Park Place, Suite 226
1900 Emery Street, N.W.
Atlanta, GA 30318
(404) 355-0177

$1,000 scholarships to high school seniors planning to enter into an engineering curriculum. Some scholarships may require attendance at a certain college or university. For Georgia residents only. Deadline: late November; local chapters may vary.

1310.
Georgia Student Finance Commission
Georgia Charles McDaniel Teacher Scholarships
2082 East Exchange Place, Suite 200
Tucker, GA 30084
(800) 546-HOPE
(770) 414-3085
http://www.gsfc.org/gsfc

Numerous scholarships of $1,000 to graduates of Georgia high schools. Must have at least a 3.25 GPA on a 4.0 scale. Based on academic record and financial need. Contact high school counselor or above address. Deadline: varies.

1311.
Georgia Student Finance Commission
Georgia Governor's Scholarship Program
2082 East Exchange Place, Suite 200
Tucker, GA 30084
(800) 546-HOPE
(770) 414-3085
http://www.gsfc.org/gsfc

Scholarships of up to $1,461 per year to graduating Georgia high school seniors with exceptional academic achievement. Must be planning to enroll as a full-time college student. Must have been a legal resident of Georgia for at least twelve consecutive months. May not receive any other nonrepayable federal, state, college, university, or privately funded scholarships or grant aid that totals more than college costs. Students chosen Georgia Scholars will automatically receive an application. Renewable until receipt of bachelor's degree. Deadline: April.

1312.
Georgia Student Finance Commission
Georgia Law Enforcement Personnel Dependents Grants
2082 East Exchange Place, Suite 200
Tucker, GA 30084
(800) 546-HOPE
(770) 414-3085
http://www.gsfc.org/gsfc

Numerous scholarships of up to $2,000 per year for up to four years are available to children of Georgia law enforcement officers, firemen, and prison guards who died or were permanently disabled while in the line of duty. Must be Georgia residents. Deadline: August 1.

1313.
Georgia Student Finance Commission
Georgia State Regents Scholarship Program
2082 East Exchange Place, Suite 200
Tucker, GA 30084
(800) 546-HOPE
(770) 414-3085
http://www.gsfc.org/gsfc

The following scholarships are available: $500 to students in junior colleges; $750 to students in four-year institutions; and $1,000 to graduate students. Awards are repaid by working in the state of Georgia for one year for each $1,000 received, or in cash with 3 percent interest. Must be Georgia residents and full-time students in a University System of Georgia institution. Based on academic record,

SAT score, and financial need; must be in upper 25 percent of class. Deadline: May 1.

1314.

Georgia Student Finance Commission
Georgia Student Incentive Grants
2082 East Exchange Place, Suite 200
Tucker, GA 30084
(800) 546-HOPE
(770) 414-3085
http://www.gsfc.org/gsfc

Numerous $150 to $450 scholarships to high school seniors or undergraduate students. Must be Georgia residents enrolled full-time in an eligible Georgia college, vocational/technical, or hospital school. Must demonstrate financial need. Renewable. Deadline: June 1.

1315.

German Academic Exchange Service (DAAD)
"Deutschlandkundlicher Sommerkurs"–German
Studies Summer Course
Attn: Deutscher Akademischer Austauschdienst
950 Third Avenue, 19th Floor
New York, NY 10022
(212) 758-3223

Varying numbers of grants providing full tuition, room, partial board, and excursions to undergraduate juniors, seniors, and graduate students to participate in a six-week summer research/study program in the German language, or historical, cultural, and economic aspects of contemporary Germany at the University of Regensburg in Germany. Must be between the ages of eighteen and thirty-two, have taken at least two years of college-level German, and be either U.S. or Canadian citizens. Students with previous study experience in Germany are ineligible. Selection based on academic achievement. Write for more information. Deadline: January 31.

1316.

German Academic Exchange Service (DAAD)
German Sur Place Grants
Attn: Deutscher Akademischer Austauschdienst
950 Third Avenue, 19th Floor
New York, NY 10022
(212) 758-3223

Varying numbers of grants offsetting tuition and research costs or summer earnings requirements to undergraduate juniors, seniors, or graduate students in German studies for the study of German affairs from a multidisciplinary perspective. Applicants must have completed at least two years of college-level German and at least three courses in German studies. Must be nominated by department/program chairpersons at U.S. universities only. Deadline: May 1; November 1.

1317.

German Academic Exchange Service (DAAD)
Hochschulferienkurs
950 Third Avenue, 19th Floor
New York, NY 10022
(212) 758-3223

2 scholarships of varying amounts to undergraduate students. Provides assistance at a German university for study in the field of German studies (particularly language and literature). Request applications up to January 15. Deadline: January 31.

1318.

German Academic Exchange Service (DAAD)
"Hochschulsommerkurse"–German Studies and
Language Courses at German Universities
Scholarships
Attn: Deutscher Akademischer Austauschdienst
950 Third Avenue, 19th Floor
New York, NY 10022
(212) 758-3223

Varying numbers of grants providing full tuition and fees, partial living expenses, and travel subsidy to undergraduate juniors, seniors, and graduate students for the study of German language or German studies in all disciplines. Must be between the ages of nineteen and twenty-one, be enrolled in an accredited U.S. university, have at least two years of college-level German with adequate reading and speaking knowledge, and be U.S. citizens. Deadline: January 31.

1319.

German Academic Exchange Service (DAAD)
Summer Language Study Grants at Goethe
Institutes for Undergraduate and Graduate
Students
Attn: Deutscher Akademischer Austauschdienst
950 Third Avenue, 19th Floor
New York, NY 10022
(212) 758-3223

Varying numbers of grants providing tuition, fees, room, and partial board to undergraduate juniors, seniors, and graduate students to take a two-month intensive German language course at the Goethe Institute in Germany. Must have a basic knowledge of German, with three semesters of college-level German preferred, be between ages eighteen and thirty-two, be U.S. citizens, and be enrolled full-time in an accredited U.S. institution. Individuals with previous study experience in Germany, who previously received a language scholarship, or who are majoring in modern languages and literature, are ineligible. No travel allowance is provided. Deadline: January 31.

1320.

Gertrude D. Curran Trust FBO Curran Music
School
c/o Trust Department Marine Midland Bank
P.O. Box 803
Buffalo, NY 14240
(716) 841-2424

Numerous scholarships of varying amounts, totaling $9,000, to undergraduate students. Must be music majors. Must be residents of Utica, New York. Based on academic record, talent, career goals, and financial need. Deadline: varies.

1321.

Gilman Paper Company Foundation, Inc.
Contribution Committee
111 West 50th Street
New York, NY 10020
(212) 246-3300

16 scholarships of $4,000 to graduating high school seniors. Must be children of employee. Scholarship must be used

for postsecondary education. Based on academic record and financial need. Deadline: varies.

1322.
Gina Bacháuer International Piano Competition Award
c/o Utah Symphony
P.O. Box 11664
Salt Lake City, UT 84147
(801) 521-9200

Award of up to $5,000 to undergraduate or graduate students or young professionals. Must be between nineteen and thirty-three years of age. May be of any nationality. Must submit an audition tape. Deadline: March 1.

1323.
Glass Bottle Blowers Association
608 East Baltimore Pike
P.O. Box 607
Media, PA 19063

4 renewable scholarships of $2,500 to high school seniors who are children of active, retired, or deceased members of the Glass, Molders, Pottery, Plastics, and Allied Workers International Union (AFL-CIO, CLC). Children of deceased members must apply within three years of parent's death. Students must be in the upper 25 percent of class. Children of officers and employees of the international union are not eligible. Based on academic record, SAT, extracurricular activities, leadership qualities, recommendations, and essay. Deadline: November (application at the College Scholarship Service); December (for taking SAT).

1324.
Gleaner Life Insurance Society Scholarship Awards
Attn: Coordinator, Personnel Services
5200 West U.S. 223
P.O. Box 1894
Adrian, MI 49221
(517) 263-2244

8 scholarships of $1,000 and 1 scholarship of $250 to members and dependents of members who are high school graduates and full-time students. Based on academic record, extracurricular school and community activities, and financial need. Deadline: April 30.

1325.
Glenn Miller Birthplace Society
Scholarship Competition
711 N. 14th Street
Clarinda, IA 51632
(712) 542-4439

Scholarships ranging from $400 to $650 to high school seniors and undergraduate freshmen attending or planning to attend a recognized college, university, or music school.

Based on instrumental music performance competition. Auditions required. Winners perform at Clarinda's Glenn Miller Festival in June. Write for complete details. Deadline: April 2.

1326.
Glimmer Train Press
Northwest Short Story Award for New Writers
710 Southwest Madison Street, Suite 504
Portland, OR 97205
(503) 221-0836
(530) 221-0837 Fax
http://www.glimmertrain.com

1 first prize of $1,200 and publication to first-place winner and an award of $500 to the first runner-up for a short story written by a writer whose fiction hasn't been published in a nationally distributed publication. May enter up to two short stories between 1,200 and 6,000 words. $10 reading fee per entry. Submit manuscripts between February 1 and March 31. Send a self-addressed, stamped envelope or see website for guidelines. Deadline: March 31 (postmark).

1327.
Golden Gate Restaurant Association
David Rubenstein Memorial Scholarship Foundation Awards
291 Geary Street, Suite 600
San Francisco, CA 94102
(415) 781-5348

10 scholarships of $1,000 to high school seniors. Must have a minimum 2.75 GPA and plan to enroll full-time in hotel-and-restaurant management or food science at any accredited college or university in U.S. Send a stamped, self-addressed envelope with 74¢ postage. Must be interviewed in San Francisco. Deadline: March 31.

1328.
Golden State Minority Foundation
Minority Foundation Scholarships
1055 Wilshire Boulevard, Suite 1115
Los Angeles, CA 90017
(213) 482-6300

75 scholarships of up to $2,000 to minority undergraduate juniors or seniors or graduate students majoring in business administration. Must be California residents attending a California college or university. Must maintain a 3.0 GPA or better. Include a self-addressed, stamped envelope with request for information. Deadline: varies.

1329.
Goldstein Scottish Rite Trust
P.O. Box 021194
Juneau, AK 99802

10 scholarships ranging from $900 to $2,000 to students who are graduates of local Juneau, Alaska, high schools. Based on financial need. Deadline: May 15.

1330.
Golf Course Superintendents Association of America
Essay Contest
1421 Research Park Drive
Lawrence, KS 66049-3859
(800) 472-7878
(913) 841-2240
http://www.gcsaa.org

Awards of varying amounts totaling $2,000 to undergraduate and graduate students pursuing a degree in turfgrass science, agronomy, or any field related to golf course management. Essay must be seven to twelve pages and focus on the relationship between golf courses and the environment. Deadline: March 31.

1331.
Golf Course Superintendents Association of America
Legacy Awards
1421 Research Park Drive
Lawrence, KS 66049
(800) 472-7878
(913) 841-2240
http://www.gcsaa.org

Scholarships of $1,500 to high school seniors or undergraduate students. Must be the children or grandchildren of GCSAA members who have been active members for five or more years. Must be studying a field unrelated to golf-course management. Must attend or plan to attend full-time. Deadline: April 15.

1332.
Golf Course Superintendents Association of America
O. M. Scott Scholarship/Internship Program
1421 Research Park Drive
Lawrence, KS 66049
(800) 472-7878
(913) 841-2240
http://www.gcsaa.org

5 summer internships providing $500 award and the opportunity to complete for 2 scholarships of $2,500 to graduating high school seniors, undergraduate freshmen, sophomores, or juniors. Program offers work experience and an opportunity to compete for financial aid awards. Selection is based on academic achievement and interest in being golf course superintendents and in a "green industry" career. Other restrictions may apply. Deadline: March 1.

1333.
Golf Course Superintendents Association of America
Scholars Program
1421 Research Park Drive
Lawrence, KS 66049
(800) 472-7878
(913) 841-2240
http://www.gcsaa.org

Awards ranging from $1,500 to $3,500 to undergraduate students majoring in a field related to golf/turf management. Must have completed at least twenty-four credit hours or the equivalent of one year of full-time study in an appropriate major. Selection based on academic achievement. Deadline: June 1.

1334.
Golf Course Superintendents Association of America
Valderrama Award
1421 Research Park Drive
Lawrence, KS 66049
(800) 472-7878
(913) 841-2240
http://www.gcsaa.org

1 scholarship of $7,000 to an undergraduate student. Must be a citizen of Spain who wishes to study golf/turfgrass management in the U.S. Selection based on academic achievement, professional interest, and leadership potential.

1335.
Good Samaritan Foundation
Nursing Scholarships
5615 Kirby Drive, Suite 308
Houston, TX 77005
(713) 529-4647

600 scholarships of varying amounts to all nursing students attending a Texas school who have attained the clinical level of their nursing education. Awards support full-time study in all accredited nursing programs (LVN, Diploma, ADN, RN, and BSN). Must be U.S. citizens or legal residents. Must apply at least six months before the start of the clinical courses. Deadline: none.

1336.
Gould Farm
Internship Coordinator
Box 157
Monterey, MA 01245-0157
(413) 528-1084
(413) 528-5051 Fax

10 to 12 internships lasting from six months to a year on an ongoing basis, which provide a weekly salary, free room and board, and medical benefits to undergraduates, recent college graduates, graduate students, and college graduates of any age. International applicants are eligible. Interns work in the kitchen, recreation, gardens/grounds, clinical, farm (dairy and other livestock care), and business office. Interns are able to participate in extensive recreational opportunities (maple syrup production, wood cutting, pottery, weaving, furniture making), use of art room and weaving studio. Close to skiing and to Tanglewood and other music festivals. The farm owns and operates The Roadside Store & Café, featuring vegetables, bread, and dairy products produced on the farm. Interns must submit a résumé, cover letter, and three references. Deadline: rolling.

1337.

Grace Margaret Watterson Trust
c/o First Union National Bank of Florida
130 North Ridgewood Avenue
P.O. Drawer 2720
Daytona Beach, FL 32115
(904) 254-1783

73 grants ranging from $1,000 to $4,000 to high school seniors from Daytona Beach, Florida, or Peterborough, Ontario, Canada. Based on academic record and financial need. Deadline: December 31.

1338.

Graham–Fancher Scholarship Fund
Attn: Trustee
149 Josephine Street, Suite A
Santa Cruz, CA 95060
(408) 423-3640

Numerous scholarships of varying amounts to high school seniors or graduates from a high school in northern Santa Cruz County, California. Must be residents of northern Santa Cruz County. Based on academic record and financial need. Deadline: May 15.

1339.

Graham Memorial Fund
Attn: Chairperson
308 West Main Street
Bennettsville, SC 29512

31 scholarships ranging from $250 to $600 to high school seniors. Must be residents of Marlboro County, South Carolina. Based on academic record and financial need. Deadline: May 15.

1340.

Grand Army of the Republic Living Memorial Scholarships
National Headquarters
Daughters of the Union Veterans of the Civil War 1861–1865
441 Elmwood Drive
Marion, OH 43302
http://pages.prodigy.com/CGBD86A/garhp.htm

Numerous scholarships of up to $500 to undergraduate sophomores, juniors, or seniors who are lineal descendants of the Union Veterans of the Civil War. Must have a photocopy of their ancestor's war record, transcripts, and two recommendation letters. Based on academic record and character and must believe in the U.S. form of government. Deadline: April 30.

1341.

Grand Rapids Foundation
161 Ottawa, N.W., Suite 209c
Grand Rapids, MI 49503

Numerous scholarships and loans of varying amounts, totaling $108,000, to high school seniors or undergraduate students. Must be Kent County, Michigan, residents. Based on academic record and financial need. Deadline: varies.

1342.

Greater Kanawha Valley Foundation
Executive Director
P.O. Box 3041
Charleston, WV 25331
(304) 346-3620

314 scholarships of varying amounts, totaling over $392,000, to high school seniors or undergraduate college students. Must be West Virginia residents. Based on financial need. Deadline: April 1; July 1; October 1; December 1.

1343.

Great Projects Film Company Internship Program
584 Ninth Avenue
New York, NY 10036
(212) 581-1700
(212) 581-3157 Fax

2 to 4 internships running from ten to twenty weeks providing a salary ranging from $50 to $200 per week to undergraduates, college graduates, and graduate students. International students may apply. Interns work in New York, New York, in all aspects of the company from answering phones to typing, logging tapes, writing proposals, editing films, and bookkeeping. Interns are able to see how documentaries are produced, from research and fund-raising to production and promotion. Internships are conducted throughout the year. Deadline: rolling.

1344.

Gregg–Graniteville Foundation, Inc.
William Gregg Scholarships
P.O. Box 418
Graniteville, SC 29829

Numerous scholarships of $2,500 to high school seniors or graduates who are children of current employees of Graniteville Company who have been employees for at least one year. If employee is deceased, employee must have had twenty-five years or more of employment and have died while still employed. Employee must not be an official of the company. Applicants must be unmarried and have, or have had, at least an 80 average. Deadline: June 15.

1345.

Grey Forest Utilities
P.O. Box 258
Helotes, TX 78023
(210) 695-8781

5 or more scholarships of $1,000 to Grey Forest Utilities customers and their dependents and 1 scholarship of $1,000 to a Grey Forest community resident or dependent. Based on academic achievement, potential, extracurricular activities, essay, and financial need. Award is administered by CRM Scholarship Foundation, in San Antonio, Texas. Applications are requested from Grey Forest Utilities but submitted to CRM Scholarship Foundation. Deadline: varies.

1346.
Groves Fund
P.O. Box 1267
10000 Highway 55 West
Minneapolis, MN 55440

22 scholarships of varying amounts, totaling $18,000, to high school seniors. Must be residents, of Minneapolis, Minnesota. Based on academic record and financial need. Deadline: varies.

1347.
Guam Society of Professional Engineers
c/o OICC Marianas
FPO San Francisco, CA 96630
(707) 333-2925

Scholarships of varying amounts to high school seniors planning to enter into an engineering curriculum. Some scholarships may require attendance at a certain college or university. For Guam residents only. Deadline: late November; local chapters may vary.

1348.
Guideposts Youth Writing Contest
Guideposts Magazine
16 East 34th Street
New York, NY 10016
(212) 251-8100

25 scholarships from $1,000 to $8,000 to high school juniors and seniors. Must submit an original manuscript in the first person on a true, personal, moving, or memorable experience. Experience must demonstrate that student's beliefs (in self, family, God, etc.) were strengthened in some way. Top twenty-five winners receive a typewriter. Deadline: First Monday after Thanksgiving.

1349.
G. William Klemstine Foundation
c/o PNC Bank
One Oliver Plaza
Pittsburgh, PA 15265
(412) 762-3706

34 loans ranging from $125 to $1,500 to high school seniors or undergraduate students. Must be residents of Cambria or Somerset counties, in western Pennsylvania. Based on financial need. Deadline: none.

1350.
Hackney Literary Awards
Birmingham-Southern College
Box A-3
Birmingham, AL 35254
(205) 226-4921

1 prize of $2,000 for an original, unpublished novel of any length. Winning novel will be considered for publication by a major publishing house. Enclose a self-addressed, stamped envelope for return of manuscript. $15 entry fee. Deadline: September 30.

1351.
Hallmark Cards
College Relations/Internship Program
Mail Drop #112
P.O. Box 41980
Kansas City, MO 64141-6580
(816) 274-5111
http://www.hallmark.com/ourcompany

30 to 35 summer internships providing a salary ranging from $1,300 to $2,300 for undergraduate seniors and from $2,400 to $3,400 for graduate students. Interns may choose from a variety of positions: accounting/finance, business research, engineering, human resources, business services, international, manufacturing, marketing, management information systems, public affairs, and sales programming. Applicants must demonstrate academic achievement, leadership abilities, excellent communication skills, and the ability to relate to a wide variety of people and disciplines. Deadline: February 1.

1352.
Hallmark–CRWEB
Creative Writing Summer Intern Competition
Creative Staffing and Development #444
250 McGee
Kansas City, MO 64141-6580
(816) 274-5111
http://www.hallmark.com/ourcompany

Internships are assigned through a nationwide language arts (writing/editorial/copywriting) competition held each spring to upper-level undergraduate and graduate students. Minorities and multicultural students are strongly encouraged to apply. Deadline: late March.

1353.
Harness Horsemen International (HHI) Foundation
Jerome L. Hauch Scholarships
525 Highway 33, Suite 3
Englishtown, NJ 07726
(908) 446-3346

Numerous scholarships of $1,000 to high school seniors or graduates who are children of a full-time groom or children of a member of an HHI association. Based on academic record, extracurricular school and community activities, leadership, recommendations, and financial need. Deadline: June 1.

1354.
Harness Horse Youth Foundation
Charles Bradley Scholarship
14950 Greyhound Court, Suite 210
Carmel, IN 46032
(317) 848-5132
http://www.ustrotting.com/newsroom/hhyfbrad.htm

1 scholarship of varying amount to a graduating high school senior or undergraduate student who is the child or relative of a racing official who is a member of the North American Judges & Stewards Association (NAJSA) and/or licensed by USTA officials as presiding, associate, or paddock judge or a parimutuel starter. Award may be used

for any field of study. Request applications before April 1.
Deadline: April 30.

1355.
Harness Horse Youth Foundation
Critchfield–Oviatt Memorial Scholarship
14950 Greyhound Court, Suite 210
Carmel, IN 46032
(317) 848-5132
http://www.ustrotting.com/newsroom/

1 or more scholarships of varying amounts, totaling
$15,000, to high school seniors or graduates or
undergraduate college students who are pursuing or
planning on pursuing a horse-related career. Based on
academic record, experience with horses, potential,
character, recommendations, and financial need. Deadline:
April 30.

1356.
Harness Horse Youth Foundation
Francis McKinzie Memorial Scholarship
14950 Greyhounds Court, Suite 210
Carmel, IN 46032
(317) 848-5132
http://www.ustrotting.com/newsroom/

1 or more scholarships of varying amounts, totaling
$15,000, to high school seniors or graduates or
undergraduate college students who are pursuing or
planning on pursuing a horse-related career. Based on
academic record, experience with horses, potential,
character, recommendations, and financial need. Deadline:
April 30.

1357.
Harness Horse Youth Foundation
Margot Taylor Scholarship
14950 Greyhound Court, Suite 210
Carmel, IN 46032
(317) 848-5132
http://www.ustrotting.com/newsroom/

1 or more scholarships of varying amounts, totaling
$15,000, to high school seniors or graduates or
undergraduate college students who are pursuing or
planning on pursuing a horse-related career. Based on
academic record, experience with horses, potential,
character, recommendations, and financial need. Deadline:
April 30.

1358.
Harness Tracks of America (HTA)
Harry M. Stevens and Peter Houghton Memorial
   Scholarships
HTA Scholarship Committee
35 Airport Road
Morristown, NJ 07960
(201) 285-9090

5 scholarships of $3,000 to high school seniors whose
parents are affiliated with harness racing or are licensed full-
time harness racing drivers, trainers, caretakers, owners, or
breeders. Students who are involved in harness racing are
also eligible to apply. Based on academic record, essay,

goals, industry involvement, recommendations, and
financial need. Deadline: May 31.

1359.
Harold and Sara Wetherbee Foundation
c/o Regions Bank
P.O. Box 8
Albany, GA 31703
(912) 432-8000

37 scholarships grants ranging from $500 to $2,000 to high
school seniors from Dougherty County, Georgia. Based on
financial need. Deadline: April 15.

1360.
Harry S. Truman Memorial Scholarship Program
712 Jackson Place, N.W.
Washington, DC 20006

Scholarships providing tuition, fees, books, room and
board, or $5,000 (whichever is less) to college juniors who
demonstrate outstanding potential for and who plan to
pursue a career in public service. Must be college juniors in
the initial year of the award. Renewable for up to four
years. Deadline: varies.

1361.
Harry S. Truman Scholarship Program
712 Jackson Place, N.W.
Washington, DC 20006

Up to 85 scholarships ranging from $3,000 to $13,500 to
upper-level undergraduates or graduate students pursuing a
career in public or government service. May be majoring in
agriculture, biology, economics, education, engineering/
techology, history, legal services, math, physical sciences,
political science, or social sciences. Must be enrolled in an
accredited four-year institution, have had experience in
community service, and have an interest in leadership.
Selection based on academic achievement, autobiography,
interview, and an essay. Deadline: December 1.

1362.
Harvey and Bernice Jones Foundation
Attn: Director
P.O. Box 233
Springdale, AR 72765
(501) 756-0611

44 scholarships ranging from $500 to $1,000 to high school
seniors. Must be residents of Springdale, Arkansas. Must be
pursuing a nursing career. Based on financial need.
Deadline: none.

1363.
Harvey Foundation, Inc.
First Federal Building, Suite 507
1519 Ponce de Leon Avenue
Santurce, PR 00909

6 scholarships from $2,000 to $6,000 for high school
seniors. Must be residents of Puerto Rico. Based on
academic record and financial need. Deadline: varies.

1364.
Hastings Center
Internship Program
255 Elm Road
Briarcliff Manor, NY 10510
(914) 762-8500
(914) 762-2124 Fax

4 full-time, four-week internships open to undergraduates, college graduates, graduate, and professional school students who are majoring in philosophy, theology, law, or medicine. Must be able to work independently. Interns conduct a self-designed research project that examines ethical issues in medicine, the life sciences, or the environment. Submit an application form, résumé, letters of recommendation, transcript, writing sample, and a three- to five-page project proposal. Deadline: open.

1365.
Hatterscheidt Foundation
c/o US Bank
320 South First Street
Aberdeen, SD 57401
(800) 846-4646
(605) 225-9400

39 scholarships of varying amounts, totaling $100,500, to high school seniors or graduates. Must be residents of South Dakota or Jamestown, North Dakota. Must be in the upper 25 percent of class. Based on academic record and financial need. Deadline: April 1.

1366.
The Hauss–Helms Foundation
Fifth Third Bank
1311 Bellefontaine Street
Wapakoneta, OH 45895
(419) 738-9617

1,262 scholarships ranging from $97 to $4,000 to graduating high school seniors or graduates. Must be residents of Allen or Auglaize counties. Award can be used at a vocational/technical school, or two- or four-year college. Renewable. Request applications after January 1. Deadline: April 15.

1367.
Hawaii Department of Education
Hawaii Student Incentive Grants (HSIG)
P.O. Box 2360
Honolulu, HI 96804
(808) 733-9124
http://www.state.hi.us/

Numerous grants of varying amounts to high school seniors. Must have been Hawaii residents for at least one year. Must have been accepted for admission into an eligible institution and eligible for a Pell Grant. Based on academic record, residency, and financial need. Deadline: May 1.

1368.
Hawaii Department of Education
Hawaii Tuition Waiver Program
P.O. Box 2360
Honolulu, HI 96804
(808) 733-9124
http://www.state.hi.us/

Tuition waivers for up to eight semesters to undergraduate or graduate students. Tuition waivers are available in the areas of athletics, band, merit, or orchestra. Must be legal residents of Hawaii, be enrolled in or accepted to a University of Hawaii System campus, or be transferring from a two-year community college. Based on academic record, talent, and financial need. Those waivers awarded for merit don't have to have financial need.

1369.
Hawaiian Trust Company Limited
AIEA General Hospital Association Scholarship
Fund
P.O. Box 3170
Honolulu, HI 96802
(808) 525-6512

Numerous scholarships of varying amounts for high school seniors. Must be residents of Leeward-Oahu-Hawaii who plan to pursue a course of study leading to a career in a health-related field at an accredited college or university. Deadline: March 1.

1370.
Hawaiian Trust Company Limited
Gertrude S. Straub Trust—M. M. Scott Scholarship
Fund
P.O. Box 3170
Honolulu, HI 96802
(808) 525-6512

Scholarships of varying amounts to graduates of Hawaii public schools who are undergraduate or graduate students attending an accredited mainland college or university. Studies should be in areas that will promote international understanding, cooperation, and world peace. The following majors are acceptable: history, government, international relations, political science, anthropology, economics, geography, law, psychology, philosophy, or sociology. Deadline: March 1.

1371.
Hawaiian Trust Company Limited
Hans & Clara Zimmerman Foundation
P.O. Box 3170
Honolulu, HI 96802
(808) 525-6512

Scholarships to high school seniors or undergraduate or graduate students. Must be Hawaii residents planning to pursue a course of study leading to a career in a health-related field at an accredited college or university. Preference given to undergraduate students, but graduate students may apply. Deadline: March 1.

1372.
Health Educational Fund
Department SSU
P.O. Box 40200
Jacksonville, FL 32203-0200
(800) 457-6417

4 scholarships ranging from $1,000 to $3,500 to male high school graduates from southeastern U.S. Must be pursuing a career in the ministry, missionary activities, or social work. Based on academic record, career goals, and financial need. Deadline: varies.

1373.
Health Resource Center
One Dupont Circle, NW, Suite 670
Washington DC 20036-1193
(800) 544-3284

Clearinghouse for financial aid and educational programs for disabled children and students. Provides a free quarterly newsletter on current programs of interest to students with physical or mental disabilities, and for their parents.

1374.
Hebrew Free Loan Society
205 E. 42nd Street
New York, NY 10017
(212) 687-0188
or
717 Market Street, Suite 555
San Francisco, CA 94103
(415) 546-9902

No-interest short-term loans of up to $750, for up to ten months, for high school seniors or undergraduate, graduate, or professional school students. Nearly a million borrowers in over ninety years of service. Deadline: none.

1375.
H. E. Butt Foundation
P.O. Box 670
Kerrville, TX 78029
(210) 896-2505

Numerous scholarships of varying amounts to students who work for the H.E.B. grocery and video store chain. Must meet certain criteria and work at least 300 hours per year for the company. Contact store manager or the company's main headquarters, at Human Resources, Employee Benefits, 646 South Main Avenue, San Antonio, TX 78204. Deadline: varies.

1376.
Helen Martha Schiff Foundation
c/o Union Bank of California, Private Bank
910 4th Avenue, 4th Floor
Seattle, WA 98164
(206) 587-3691

5 scholarships ranging from $668 to $1,670 to high school seniors. Must be Washington residents. Based on academic record and financial need. Deadline: varies.

1377.
**Hemingway Days Festival
Short Story Writers Competition**
P.O. Box 4045
Key West, FL 33041

1 award of $1,000 and 2 awards of $500 in a contest for unpublished short stories. May be any form or style and must be 2,500 words or less. $10 fee. Send self-addressed, stamped envelope for rules, specific deadline, and entry form. Deadline: late June.

1378.
**Hemingway Days Festival
Young Writer's Scholarships**
P.O. Box 4045
Key West, FL 33041

2 scholarships of $1,000 to high school juniors and seniors who are preparing to attend college. Based on exceptional talent in the craft of writing in the areas of fiction, nonfiction, and poetry. One of the scholarships is only for Florida residents; the other is open to students living anywhere in the U.S. Send a self-addressed, stamped envelope for rules and entry form. Deadline: May 1.

1379.
**Henry E. and Florence W. Snayberger Memorial
    Foundation**
c/o Pennsylvania National Bank and Trust Company
1 South Centre Street
Pottsville, PA 17901
(717) 622-4200

571 scholarships ranging from $250 to $700 to high school seniors or graduates or undergraduate college students. Must be residents of Schuylkill, Pennsylvania. Based on academic record and financial need. Deadline: February 28.

1380.
**Herb Society of America
Herb Society of America Research and Education
    Grant**
9019 Kirtland Chardon Road
Mentor, OH 44060
(216) 256-0514

1 to 3 grants of $5,000 for undergraduate or graduate students. Must submit a 500-word outline for an herbal research project. Proposed budget must be included. Projects must be supervised by the Chairman of the Grants Committee, consultants, or designers. Request applications after February 1. Deadline: January 31.

1381.
**The Hermitage
Internship Program**
4580 Rachel's Lane
Hermitage, TN 37076-1331
(615) 889-2941

10 internships providing $1,000 per session, housing, and $50 per week food stipend to undergraduate juniors and seniors, graduate students, and recent graduates. Interns must have academic background in historical archeology.

A field course in archeology is good, but not required. The internship is conducted in Hermitage, Tennessee, at the home of Andrew Jackson. Interns conduct diggings to find artifacts that help reconstruct life at the Hermitage during Jackson's days. Deadline: April 10.

1382.

Herschel C. Price Educational Foundation

Attn: Trustee
P.O. Box 412
Huntington, WV 25708-0412
(304) 529-3852

190 scholarships ranging from $250 to $1,500 to high school seniors or graduates or undergraduates. Must be residents of West Virginia attending a West Virginia college or university. Based on financial need and academic record. Deadline: October 1; April 1.

1383.

Hewlett–Packard

SEED Program
3000 Hanover Street
Palo Alto, CA 94304
(605) 857-2092
http://www.jobs.external.hp.com/USA/college/internship

300 to 500 ten- to fourteen-week summer internships providing round-trip travel, relocation allowance, and salaries ranging from $450 to $625 per week for undergraduates and from $700 to $950 per week for graduate students. Open to undergraduate sophomores, juniors, seniors, and graduate students. Internships are in California, Colorado, Delaware, Georgia, Idaho, Massachusetts, New Hampshire, New Jersey, Oregon, and Washington. Internships are open to the following majors: accounting, business administration, computer science, engineering (computer, electrical, industrial, mechanical, etc.), finance, information technology, and operations research. Deadline: April 30.

1384.

H. Fletcher Brown Fund Scholarships

PNC Bank
3840 Kennett Pike
Wilmington, DE 19899
(302) 429-1166

Numerous scholarships to high school seniors or graduates or undergraduate or graduate students. Must have been born in Delaware, graduated from a Delaware high school, and still be a resident of Delaware. Must be pursuing a career in medicine, dentistry, law, engineering, or chemistry. Based on scholastic achievement, moral character, and financial need. Renewable. Deadline: April 15.

1385.

Hill & Knowlton

Internship Coordinator
420 Lexington Avenue
New York, NY 10017
(212) 697-5600
http://www.hillandknowlton.com/

10 to 15 internships providing $6 per hour to undergraduate juniors, seniors, and graduate students.

Internships introduce students to the day-to-day work in a public relations agency and assist them in developing written and oral communication skills. Interns are assigned to accounts where they write media lists, prepare press releases, and compose pitch letters. Though applications are accepted year-round, preference is given to applications submitted before April 1. Deadline: rolling.

1386.

Hill, Holliday, Conners, Cosmopulos Advertising, Inc.

Internship Coordinator
200 Clarendon Street
Boston, MA 02116
(617) 572-3418
http://clarendon.hhcc.com/

25 to 35 internships providing $250 per week to students participating during summer internships, but no compensation during fall, winter, or spring internships. Open to undergraduate sophomores, juniors, seniors, and graduate students. Interns work in virtually all departments: accounting, account service, administration, art, broadcast, community relations, copy, corporate, design, direct marketing, human resources, market research, mechanical art, media, management information systems, new accounts, and traffic. Interns work full-time for eight weeks during the summer, full-time for four weeks during the winter, or fifteen to twenty weeks part-time during the fall or spring. Deadline: rolling (at least two weeks before beginning the internship).

1387.

Hilton Head Jazz Society

P.O. Box 6705
Hilton Head Island, SC 29938
(803) 689-3367

1 or more scholarships of $1,000 to undergraduate juniors, seniors, or graduate students (when using the award) in a music/jazz studies program at an accredited college or university in the U.S. Must be proficient in jazz. Application period: January 15 to April 15. Deadline: April 30.

1388.

Hispanic College Fund, Inc.

One Thomas Circle, N.W., Suite 375
Washington, DC 20005
(202) 296-5400
(202) 296-3774 Fax
http://hispanicfund.org/
Hispanic.Fund@InternetMCI.com

Varying numbers of scholarships of varying amounts to full-time undergraduate students majoring or concentrating in business. Must have at least a cumulative 3.0 GPA on a 4.0 scale. Must demonstrate financial need. Close attention will be given to students who demonstrate leadership qualities through involvement and participation in extracurricular activities. Deadline: April 15.

1389.
Historic Savage Mill Art Guild
Annual Regional Juried Show
Box 2007 Savage Mill
Savage, MD 20763
(301) 490-0187

Awards of $1,000 and up in the Annual Regional Juried Show for original oil, acrylic, watercolor, pastel, collage, mixed media, photography, and sculpture. Must be residents of Delaware, District of Columbia, Maryland, Pennsylvania, and Virginia. Charges an entry fee of $20 for up to three slides. The show runs from May through June. For prospectus, send a #10 self-addressed, stamped envelope to above address. Deadline: varies.

1390.
Home Box Office
Internship Program
Room 3-14A
1100 Sixth Avenue
New York, NY 10036
(212) 512-1000
(212) 512-1520 Fax
No telephone calls

100 internships lasting from twelve to sixteen weeks during the summer, fall, and spring provide a $500 stipend at the end of the internship, which is open to undergraduates and graduate students in the areas of television and film. International students may apply, but will work only in the finance or international departments. U.S. interns work in accounting, advertising, film programming, finance, human resources, international, marketing, original programming, production, public relations, or sports. All students must receive academic credit for the internship. Interns are provided with placement assistance, including letters of recommendation. Submit a résumé, cover letter, and writing samples. Deadline: March 31 (summer); August 31 (fall); November 30 (spring).

1391.
Hooked on Sports Scholarship Program
FOOTACTION USA
c/o Bustin & Co.
717 North Harwood, Suite 1600
Dallas, TX 75201
(800) 527-2723
http://www.footaction.com/scholarship/index.html

4 grand prize scholarships of $5,000 and 20 scholarships of $1,500 to graduating high school seniors, which can be used for tuition, fees, on-campus room and board, or books. Must be planning to attend a two- or four-year accredited U.S. college or university as a full-time student. Selection is based on academic achievement, financial need, and a written essay on how sports and education have positively influenced the applicant's life. The grand prize winners also receive a three-day, two-night trip for two to the FootAction USA NFL Quarterback Challenge. FootAction provides round-trip coach airfare from the nearest major airport to the winner's home, double-occupancy accommodations, and transportation to the event. Applications may be obtained at any FootAction store. Deadline: late March, may vary.

1392.
Hope Pierce Tartt Scholarship Fund
P.O. Box 1964
Marshall, TX 75670

200 scholarships of varying amounts, totaling $150,000, to high school seniors or graduates or undergraduate college students. Must be residents of East Texas and attending a private college or university in Texas or Louisiana.

1393.
Horace Mann Companies
Scholarship Program
P.O. Box 20490
Springfield, IL 62708
http://www.horacemann.com/html/educator/escholar.html
hmadmin@horacemann.com

10 scholarships of $1,000, 5 scholarships of $4,000, and 1 scholarship of $20,000 to graduating high school seniors who are children of public school employees. Open to all majors. Applicants must have at least a 3.0 GPA or "B" average, and have scored at least 23 on the ACT, or 1100 on the SAT. Deadline: February 28.

1394.
Horace Smith Fund
Walter S. Barr Scholarship Fellowship & Loan
   Fund
P.O. Box 3034
1441 Main Street
Springfield, MA 01101
(413) 739-4222

Scholarships of varying amounts to high school seniors and fellowships and loans for undergraduate and graduate students in all areas of study. High school seniors must be graduating from Agawam, Chicopee, East Longmeadow, Longmeadow, Ludlow, Springfield, West Springfield, or Wilbraham high schools. Applicants must be residents of Hampden County, Massachusetts. Scholarship and fellowship applications are available after September 1. Loan applications are available after April 1. Renewable. Financial need is primary concern. Deadline: December 31 (scholarships); February 1 (fellowships); July 1 (loans).

1395.
Horbach Fund
c/o Bank of New York
385 Rifel Camp Road
West Paterson, NJ 07424
(973) 357-7000

Numerous scholarships of varying amounts, totaling $7,500, to high school seniors or graduates or undergraduate students. Must be residents of Connecticut, Massachusetts, New Jersey, New York, or Rhode Island. Must be under age twenty. Based on academic record and financial need. Deadline: August 1.

1396.

Horse Cave Theater

Internships

Box 215

Horse Cave, KY 42749

(502) 786-1200

4 full-time internships providing a small stipend to undergraduate or graduate students, and persons with career work experience in a professional theater that produces comedy, drama, classics, and new works by Kentucky playwrights. Interns are able to work with professional artists and managers, attend classes taught by directors, and perform supporting and understudy roles. Openings are from June through December. If an intern is cast in a play, the intern is enrolled as a membership candidate in Actors Equity Association. Applicants should have extensive knowledge in their area of interest, including acting, scenery, costumes, props, lighting, stage management, public relations and marketing, development, administration, box office, or house management. Applicants should have at least college-level theater experience. Submit application, résumé, references, photograph, and audition (if applicable). Deadline: April 1.

1397.

Horticultural Research Institute

Grants

1250 I Street, Suite 500

Washington, DC 20005

(202) 789-2900

2 scholarship grants of $2,500 to undergraduate juniors, seniors, or graduate students who are majoring in agribusiness, agriculture, floriculture, horticulture, landscape architecture, or natural resources. Must be attending an accredited institute in Connecticut, Massachusetts, Maine, New Hampshire, Rhode Island, or Vermont and be residents of one of these states. Must be U.S. citizens or permanent residents. Selection based on academic achievement, financial need, recommendation letters, and an essay. Deadline: May 1.

1398.

Hospitality Sales and Marketing Association International (HSMAI)

1300 L Street, N.W., Suite 840

Washington, DC 20005

(202) 789-0089

Local chapters offer scholarships of varying amounts to undergraduate students majoring in a hospitality and/or tourism-related major. Funds are subject to fluctuations in the chapter's finances. For the address of a local chapter, contact above address. Deadline: varies by chapter.

1399.

Hostelling International–American Youth Hostels

Internship Program

733 15th Street, N.W., #840

Washington, DC 20005

(202) 783-6161

11 twenty-week internships in summer, fall, or spring providing $100 per week to undergraduates and $150 per week to graduate students, plus free housing at local hostels and $200 for relocation to undergraduates, recent college graduates, college graduates of any age, and graduate students. Interns work in programs and education, marketing, hostel services, and hostel development. Must be fluent in English. Must submit résumé, cover letter, transcript, and three recommendations. Deadline: April 1 (summer); August 1 (fall); February 1 (spring).

1400.

Houston Underwater Club

Seaspace Scholarships

P.O. Box 3753

Houston, TX 77253

(713) 467-6675

9 awards of approximately $1,000 to undergraduate juniors, seniors, or graduate students majoring in marine sciences, marine biology or geology, nautical archeology, biological oceanography, ocean and fishery sciences, naval/marine engineering, or naval science. Must be pursuing a career in marine science and attend an accredited institution in the U.S. Undergraduates must have at least a 3.5 GPA and graduate students must have at least a 3.0 GPA. Selection is based on career goals, academic achievement, and financial need. Send a self-addressed, stamped envelope for an application. Deadline: March 15.

1401.

Howard and Mamie Nichols Scholarship Trust Scholarships

Wells Fargo Bank Trust Department

P.O. Box 2511

Sacramento, CA 95812

(800) 352-3705

(916) 440-4719

Written inquiries only

Approximately 100 scholarships of varying amounts to students for use for full-time undergraduate or graduate study in all areas of study. Must be graduates of Kern County, California, high schools, have financial need, and have at least a 2.0 GPA or better. Renewable with reapplication. Other restrictions may apply. Deadline: February 28.

1402.

Howard Memorial Fund

Scholarship Chairperson

500 East 62nd Street

New York, NY 10021

51 scholarships ranging from $300 to $450 to graduating high school seniors. Must be residents of greater metropolitan New York City. Must be at least fourteen years of age and have financial need. Contact high school counselor or write a letter briefly detailing your educational and financial situation and include a self-addressed, stamped envelope. Other restrictions may apply. Deadline: May 30.

1403.
Hoyt Foundation
c/o First Western Bank
P.O. Box 1488
New Castle, PA 16103
(724) 652-5511

122 scholarships ranging from $100 to $4,400 to high school seniors. Must be residents of Lawrence County, Pennsylvania. Based on academic record and financial need. Deadline: July 15; December 15.

1404.
H. T. Ewald Foundation
H. T. Ewald Scholarship
15175 East Jefferson Avenue
Grosse Pointe, MI 48230
(313) 821-2000

1 scholarship ranging from $500 to $2,500 per year for four years to a high school senior. Must be a resident of metropolitan Detroit. Based on academic record, essay, extracurricular activities, SAT/ACT, interview, and financial need. Deadline: May 1.

1405.
Hualapai Tribal Council
Scholarship Program
P.O. Box 179
Peach Springs, AZ 86434
(602) 769-2216

Varying numbers of scholarships of $700 to full-time undergraduate or graduate students in all fields of study. Must be members of the Hualapai tribe. Must maintain passing grades. Other restrictions may apply. Deadline: two weeks before each semester.

1406.
Hughes Aircraft Company
Bachelor of Science Scholarship
Corporate Fellowship Office (B168)
P.O. Box 45066
Los Angeles, CA 90045-0066
(213) 568-6711

Numerous scholarships paying tuition, book allowance, and fees to junior or senior undergraduates or students with an associate's degree majoring in electrical or mechanical systems, aerospace engineering, computer science, mathematics, or physics. Must attend the University of California at Los Angeles, Riverside, or Irvine, University of Southern California, Loyola Marymont University, one of the California State Universities, the University of Arizona, or any Accreditation Board of Engineering and Technology (ABET)-accredited university. Recipients also receive salaries, company benefits, and relocation expenses. Based on academic record. Deadline: March.

1407.
Humboldt State University
Raymond Carver Short Story Contest
Attn: Patricia Roller
English Department
Humboldt State University
Arcata, CA 95521-4957
(707) 826-3758

A $500 prize awarded annually for a short story of up to twenty-five pages. Submission should be made in duplicate and be accompanied by a $7.50 entry fee. Deadline: November 19.

1408.
Hunt Manufacturing Company Foundation
Foundation Scholarships
230 South Broad Street
Philadelphia, PA 19102
(215) 732-7700

4 to 6 renewable scholarships ranging from $1,000 to $2,000 to high school seniors who are children of Hunt Manufacturing employees. Based on academic record, extracurricular activities, and financial need. Deadline: April 15.

1409.
Idaho Society for Medical Technology
Internships
c/o Magic Valley Memorial Hospital
Twin Falls, ID 83301
(208) 737-2000

3 medical-technology internships per year are available to fourth-year undergraduates or graduate students. Must be recommended by a teaching supervisor in a clinical area, by supervising pathologists, and by two professors in science courses at the undergraduate level. Amount of funding varies. Deadline: varies.

1410.
Idaho State Board of Education
Robert C. Byrd Scholarship
P.O. Box 83720
Boise, ID 83720-0027
(208) 332-6800
http://www.sde.state.id.us/DEPT/

Varying numbers of scholarships of $1,500 to graduating high school seniors for use the first year of study in a college or university within the state. Administered by each state's educating agency. Obtain applications from state agency or high school counselor.

1411.
Idaho State Board of Education
Scholarships for Children of POW/MIAs
P.O. Box 83720
Boise, ID 83720-0027
(208) 332-6800
http://www.sde.state.id.us/DEPT/

Scholarships of varying amounts to graduating high school seniors or undergraduate students. Must be the spouse or dependent child of a veteran or serviceperson who has been declared a prisoner of war, missing in action, who died as a result of a service-connected disability, or who was 100 percent permanently disabled from a service-connected injury. Veteran or serviceperson must have been a resident of Idaho at the time of entering the service. Eligible children must be under twenty-six years of age.

1412.
Illinois AMVETS
AMVETS Auxiliary Department of Illinois Memorial Scholarship
Executive Director
2206 South Sixth Street
Springfield, IL 62703-3496
(217) 528-4713

1 scholarship of $500 to a high school senior. Must be an Illinois resident. Must submit family's financial statement and actual need. Must be unmarried. Based on academic record (30 percent), personality (20 percent), goals (10 percent), and financial need (40 percent). Contact high school counselor or above address. Deadline: varies.

1413.
Illinois AMVETS
AMVETS Auxiliary WORCHID Scholarships
Executive Director
2206 South Sixth Street
Springfield, IL 62703-3496
(217) 528-4713

Numerous $500 scholarships to high school seniors who are children of deceased veterans. Veteran need not have been killed in action or as a result of a service-connected injury. Applicants must be Illinois residents. Must submit family's financial statement and actual need. Based on academic record (30 percent), personality (20 percent), goals (10 percent), and financial need (40 percent). Contact high school counselor or above address. Deadline: varies.

1414.
Illinois AMVETS
AMVETS Sad Sacks Nursing Scholarships
Executive Director
2206 South Sixth Street
Springfield, IL 62703-3496
(217) 528-4713

Numerous $500 scholarships to high school seniors or graduates who have been accepted to an approved nursing school in Illinois. Preference given to students who are dependents of deceased or disabled veterans. Applicants must be Illinois residents. Must submit family's financial statement and actual need. Based on academic record (30 percent), personality (20 percent), goals (10 percent), and financial need (40 percent). Contact high school counselor or above address. Deadline: March 1.

1415.
Illinois AMVETS
AMVETS Service Foundation Scholarship Award
Executive Director
2206 South Sixth Street
Springfield, IL 62703-3496
(217) 528-4713

1 scholarship of $500 to a high school senior who is a child of a veteran who served after September 15, 1940,

and was honorably discharged. Must be Illinois resident and unmarried. Must submit family's financial statement and actual need. Based on academic record (30 percent), personality (20 percent), goals (10 percent), and financial need (40 percent). Contact high school counselor or above address. Deadline: March 1.

1416.
Illinois AMVETS
Clarence Newlun Memorial Scholarship Award
Executive Director
2206 South Sixth Street
Springfield, IL 62703-3496
(217) 528-4713

1 scholarship of $500 to a high school senior who is a child of a war veteran who served after September 15, 1940, and was honorably discharged. Must be Illinois resident and unmarried. Must submit family's financial statement and actual need. Based on academic record (30 percent), personality (20 percent), goals (10 percent), and financial need (40 percent). Contact high school counselor or above address. Deadline: March 1.

1417.
Illinois AMVETS
Paul Powell Memorial AMVETS Scholarship
Executive Director
2206 South Sixth Street
Springfield, IL 62703-3496
(217) 528-4713

1 scholarship of $500 to a high school senior who is the child of a veteran. Must have taken the ACT. Must be Illinois resident and unmarried. Must submit family's financial statement and actual need. Based on academic record (30 percent), personality (20 percent), goals (10 percent), and financial need (40 percent). Contact high school counselor or above address. Deadline: March 1.

1418.
Illinois Congress of Parents and Teachers
Illinois PTA Lillian E. Glover Scholarships
901 South Spring Street
Springfield, IL 62704
(217) 528-9617

26 scholarships of $1,000 and 26 scholarships of $500 to graduating high school seniors. Must be in the upper 20 percent of class and enrolled in a public high school. Must major in education. Contact high school counselor. Deadline: March 1.

1419.
Illinois Department of Veterans Affairs
Illinois MIA/POW Scholarships
P.O. Box 19432
Springfield, IL 62794-9432

Waiver of tuition and some fees at any state-supported college or university to any spouse or dependent child of a veteran or serviceperson who has been declared a prisoner of war, missing in action, who died as a result of a service-connected disability, or who was 100 percent permanently disabled from a service-connected injury. Veteran or serviceperson must have been a resident of Illinois at the time of entering the service. Eligible children must be under twenty-six years of age. Eligible spouse must use the funds within ten years of eligibility date. Contact nearest office of Illinois Department of Veterans Affairs or above address.

1420.

Illinois Department of Veterans Affairs
Illinois Veterans' Children Educational
    Opportunities Act
P.O. Box 5054
Springfield, IL 62705

Up to $250 per child per year to students who are dependent children of serviceperson or veteran permanently 100 percent disabled or who was killed in action or died as a result of a service-connected injury while in the Armed Forces and engaged in a period of war during specific time periods, including those who were draft inductees between 9/16/40 and 5/7/75. Students must attend an Illinois school, be between ten and eighteen years of age, and be a resident of Illinois for at least one year. May be used for private elementary, secondary, business, vocational schools, or colleges or universities.

1421.

Illinois Pilot Association Scholarship
IPA State Headquarters
801½ South 4th Street, Apt. A
Springfield, IL 62703

1 scholarship of $500 to undergraduate students in an aviation degree program. Must be Illinois residents. Other restrictions may apply. Deadline: varies.

1422.

Illinois Restaurant Association Scholarship Fund
120 North Wacker Drive
Chicago, IL 60606
(312) 372-6200

Various scholarships of varying amounts for undergraduate students. Must be Illinois residents majoring in food service management, culinary arts, food processing, or related areas (nutrition and dietetics) at an accredited school in the U.S. Deadline: varies.

1423.

Illinois Student Assistance Commission
Bonus Incentive Grant (BIG)
500 West Monroe, 3rd Floor
Springfield, IL 62704-1876
(217) 782-6767
(217) 524-1858 Fax
http://www.state.il.us/agency/edu/default.htm

Grants ranging from $15 to $440 to students who are holders of Illinois College Savings Bonds if the bond proceeds are used to pay for educational expenses at an eligible Illinois institution. Must have owned the bond for at least twelve months preceding the date of maturity. Must be enrolled at least half-time an any approved Illinois two- or four-year public or private institution. May not be used in an academic program of divinity for any religious denomination or to pursue a career as a minister, priest, rabbi, or other professional person in the field of religion.

Apply between August 1 and May 30 of the academic year immediately following the redemption.

1424.

Illinois Student Assistance Commission
David A. DeBolt Teacher Shortage Scholarship
    Program
500 West Monroe, 3rd Floor
Springfield, IL 62704-1876
(217) 782-6767
(217) 524-1858 Fax
http://www.state.il.us/agency/edu/default.htm

Scholarships of up to $5,000 to undergraduate sophomores or above in a Teacher Education program at a public or private eligible institute and pursuing course work to teach in an approved specialized teacher shortage program. If student doesn't fulfill teaching commitment, the award must be repaid with interest. Deadline: May 1.

1425.

Illinois Student Assistance Commission
Grant Program for Dependents of Correctional
    Officers
500 West Monroe, 3rd Floor
Springfield, IL 62704-1876
(217) 782-6767
(217) 524-1858 Fax
http://www.state.il.us/agency/edu/default.htm

Grants of varying amounts up to tuition and fees to graduating high school seniors, undergraduate, or graduate students who are children or spouse of a State of Illinois Department of Corrections officer killed or 90 percent disabled in the line of duty. Applicants need not be Illinois residents to receive the grant but must attend an approved Illinois institution. Renewable up to four years with satisfactory academic progress. Must be a U.S. citizen or eligible noncitizen. Deadline: none specified.

1426.

Illinois Student Assistance Commission
Grant Program for Dependents of Police or Fire
    Officers
500 West Monroe, 3rd Floor
Springfield, IL 62704-1876
(217) 782-6767
(217) 524-1858 Fax
http://www.state.il.us/agency/edu/default.htm

Grants of varying amounts up to tuition and fees to graduating high school seniors, undergraduate, or graduate students who are children or spouse of an Illinois police or fire officer killed or 90 percent disabled in the line of duty. Applicants need not be Illinois residents to receive the grant but must attend an approved Illinois institution. Renewable up to four years with satisfactory academic progress. Must be U.S. citizens or eligible noncitizens. Deadline: none specified.

1427.

Illinois Student Assistance Commission
Illinois Incentive for Access (IIA) Program
500 West Monroe, 3rd Floor
Springfield, IL 62704-1876
(217) 782-6767
(217) 524-1858 Fax
http://www.state.il.us/agency/edu/default.htm

Grants of up to $500 to graduating high school seniors, high school graduates who haven't attended college, or undergraduate freshmen. Must be enrolled at least half-time at an IIA-participating school. Students must have been evaluated on the SAR to have a zero (0) EFC. Must maintain satisfactory academic progress and be Illinois residents. Deadline: ASAP after January 1.

1428.

Illinois Student Assistance Commission (ISAC)
Merit Recognition Scholarships
500 West Monroe, 3rd Floor
Springfield, IL 62704-1876
(217) 782-6767
(217) 524-1858 Fax
http://www.state.il.us/agency/edu/default.htm

Numerous scholarships of $1,000 to graduating high school seniors. Must be Illinois residents. Must be U.S. citizens or eligible noncitizens, be in the upper 5 percent of class, plan to attend an approved Illinois college or university, and register with the Selective Service System. Must maintain a 2.5 GPA on a 4.0 scale. Deadline: one year after high school graduation.

1429.

Illinois Student Assistance Commission
Minority Teacher of Illinois Scholarship Program
500 West Monroe, 3rd Floor
Springfield, IL 62704-1876
(217) 782-6767
(217) 524-1858 Fax
http://www.state.il.us/agency/edu/default.htm

Scholarships of up to $5,000 to minority full-time undergraduate sophomores or above who are pursuing a career in education at the preschool, elementary, or secondary level. Must have at least a 2.5 GPA on a 4.0 scale, be Illinois residents, and either U.S. citizens or eligible noncitizens. May not be in default on any student loan or owe a refund on any state or federal grant. Must attend an accredited Illinois institution and file FAFSA. Deadline: August 1.

1430.

Illinois Student Assistance Commission (ISAC)
Monetary Award Program
500 West Monroe, 3rd Floor
Springfield, IL 62704-1876
(217) 782-6767
(217) 524-1858 Fax
http://www.state.il.us/agency/edu/default.htm

Renewable scholarships of up to $3,100 to high school seniors or graduates. Must be Illinois residents. Must be U.S. citizens or eligible noncitizens. May attend a public or private college or university in Illinois. Based on financial need; academic record is not considered. Deadline: October 1 (students who haven't attended college); June 1 (college students); March 15 (spring term only).

1431.

Illinois Student Assistance Commission (ISAC)
Programs for National Guard
500 West Monroe, 3rd Floor
Springfield, IL 62704-1876
(217) 782-6767
(217) 524-1858 Fax
http://www.state.il.us/agency/edu/default.htm

Exemptions from certain tuition and fee charges at all public colleges to children of National Guard personnel. Financial need is not considered. Contact financial-aid officer of the public college or university in which you will be or are enrolled. Deadline: varies.

1432.

Illinois Student Assistance Commission
Robert C. Byrd Scholarship Program
500 West Monroe, 3rd Floor
Springfield, IL 62704-1876
(217) 782-6767
(217) 524-1858 Fax
http://www.state.il.us/agency/edu/default.htm

Varying numbers of scholarships of up to $1,500 to graduating high school seniors for use the first year of study in a college or university within the state. Administered by each state's educating agency. Obtain applications from state agency or high school counselor. Deadline: varies.

1433.

Illinois Student Assistance Commission
Special Education Teacher Tuition Waiver
  Program
500 West Monroe, 3rd Floor
Springfield, IL 62704-1876
(217) 782-6767
(217) 524-1858 Fax
http://www.state.il.us/agency/edu/default.htm

Tuition and fee waivers to graduating high school seniors, undergraduates, or graduate students who are preparing to teach handicapped students or students with learning disabilities. Must be in the upper half of their class, be attending on a full-time basis, be Illinois residents, and attend an accredited Illinois institution. Renewable up to four years. Submit application to the Deerfield office. Deadline: February 15.

1434.

Illuminating Engineering Society of North
  America
Robert Thunen Memorial Education Fund
  Scholarships
345 East 47th Street
New York, NY 10017
(212) 705-7511

Scholarships of varying amounts to students who are in their third or fourth undergraduate year at an accredited institution in northern California, Oregon, Washington, or northern Nevada. Must be majoring in architecture, architectural engineering, electrical engineering, interior design, or theater. Deadline: none.

1435.
"Images" Competition
Central PA Festival of the Arts
Box 1023
State College, PA 16804

Awards of $2,000 to artists from Pennsylvania and the mid-Atlantic region. Juried 2-D and 3-D, any media. Entry fee of $20. Runs from late June through early July. For prospectus, send a self-addressed, stamped envelope to: Central PA Festival of the Arts, Box 1023, State College, PA 16804. Deadline: varies.

1436.
Independent Accounting International
Educational Foundation
Robert Kaufman Memorial Scholarship Fund
9200 South Dadeland Boulevard, Suite 510
Miami, FL 33156
(305) 661-3580

20 scholarships of up to $5,000 to high school seniors or full-time undergraduate students pursuing a career in accounting. Several $250 honorary awards to be used to purchase textbooks only to full-time undergraduate students in accounting. May attend an accredited school anywhere in the world. Payment is made directly to the recipient, but applicant must provide proof of enrollment. Must be sponsored by a member firm. Write to the foundation for a list of local member firms; include a self-addressed, stamped envelope. Send an introductory letter and résumé to the nearest firm. Deadline: February 28.

1437.
Indianapolis Press Club
Maurice and Robert Early Scholarships
150 West Market Street
Indianapolis, IN 46204

Numerous $600 scholarships to undergraduate students majoring in journalism or broadcast journalism. Based on journalistic competence, career potential, recommendations, and financial need. Deadline: June 1.

1438.
Indiana Society of Professional Engineers
P.O. Box 20806
Indianapolis, IN 46220
(317) 255-2267
(317) 255-2530 Fax

Scholarships of varying amounts to undergraduate students majoring in engineering. Designated engineering scholarships requiring that a specific university be attended or a specific program of engineering study be pursued are also offered. Must be Indiana residents. Other restrictions may apply. Deadline: varies.

1439.
Indiana State Student Assistance Commission
Higher Education Grant Program
150 West Market Street
Indianapolis, IN 46204
(317) 232-2350
http://www.state.in.us/ssaci/
grants@ssaci.state.in.us

Grants ranging from $100 to $1,476 to students attending state-supported institutions and ranging from $1,749 to $3,707 to students at independent institutions and nursing schools. Must be Indiana residents, attending or planning to attend an eligible Indiana institution, be at least full-time undergraduates, and have financial need. Deadline: March 1.

1440.
Indiana State Student Assistance Commission
Hoosier Scholar Program
150 West Market Street
Indianapolis, IN 46204
(317) 232-2350
http://www.state.in.us/ssaci/
grants@ssaci.state.in.us

Scholarships of $500 to graduating high school seniors who will be attending an eligible Indiana institution. Up to three students from each Indiana high school are nominated by principals and counselors. Must be in the upper 20 percent of class. There is no application. Students are nominated for this award. Deadline: none.

1441.
Indiana State Student Assistance Commission
Minority Teacher & Special Education
Scholarships
150 West Market Street
Indianapolis, IN 46204
(317) 232-2350
http://www.state.in.us/ssaci/
grants@ssaci.state.in.us

Scholarships of up to $1,000 to African American or Hispanic American students pursuing a teaching career or any student pursuing a special education teaching certificate. Must be Indiana residents, have at least a 2.0 GPA on a 4.0 scale, and attend an Indiana institution. Must plan to be a full-time student. Obtain an application from high school counselor, college financial-aid office, or above address. Deadline: varies.

1442.
Indiana State Student Assistance Commission
Nursing Scholarships
150 West Market Street
Indianapolis, IN 46204
(317) 232-2350
http://www.state.in.us/ssaci/
grants@ssaci.state.in.us

Scholarships of up to $5,000 to students in a nursing program in Indiana. May be full-time or part-time students;

must have at least a 2.0 GPA on a 4.0 scale and be Indiana residents. Must work as a nurse in Indiana for at least two years and complete the nursing program within six years of the first scholarship received. Deadline: none.

1443.
Indiana State Student Assistance Commission
Robert C. Byrd Scholarships
150 West Market Street
Indianapolis, IN 46204
http://www.state.in.us/ssaci/
grants@ssaci.state.in.us

Varying numbers of scholarships of up to $1,121 to graduating high school seniors for use the first year of study in a college or university within the state. Must have scored at least 1300 on SAT or 31 on ACT. Administered by each state's educating agency. Obtain applications from state agency or high school counselor. Deadline: varies.

1444.
Indiana State Student Assistance Commission
Summer State Work–Study Program
150 West Market Street
Indianapolis, IN 46204-1088
(317) 232-2350
http://www.state.in.us/ssaci/

Summer work-study program for students attending Indiana institutions who received an Indiana Higher Education Grant and/or Lilly Endowment Education Award. Students must locate the position from the list of participating employers provided by the ISSAC. Students may work part- or full-time. The state of Indiana reimburses the employer one-half of the student's wages.

1445.
Indiana State Student Assistance Commission
Twenty–First Century Scholars Program
State Student Assistance Commission
150 West Market Street
Indianapolis, IN 46204
(317) 232-2350
http://www.state.in.us/ssaci/
grants@ssaci.state.in.us

Scholarships providing tuition and fees to students who meet certain criteria. Eighth-grade students who qualify for free or reduced-price lunches may enroll in the program. Must be Indiana residents and attend Indiana institutions. Contact: (800) 992-2076.

1446.
Indian Health Employees Scholarship Fund
Attn: Executive Secretary
Federal Building, Room 215
Aberdeen, SD 57401

Scholarships of varying amounts to Native Americans for study in health fields. Other fields are considered if funds allow. Based on academic record, seriousness of purpose, and financial need. Deadline: January 1; June 1; October 1.

1447.
Inroads, Inc.
Internships
10 South Broadway, Suite 700
St. Louis, MO 63102
(314) 241-7880
http://www.inroadsinc.org/
info@notes.inroadsinc.org

800 to 1,000 internships providing a salary ranging from $170 to $750 per week to minority high school juniors, seniors, and undergraduate freshmen and sophomores to train for management positions in business, engineering, and science. Internships are available in Birmingham, AL; Phoenix, AZ; Los Angeles, San Diego, and San Francisco, CA; Denver, CO; Hartford and Stamford, CT; Jacksonville, Miami, and Tampa Bay, FL; Atlanta, GA; Chicago, IL; Indianapolis, IN; New Orleans, LA; Boston, MA; Baltimore, MD; Detroit, MI; St. Paul, MN; Kansas City and St. Louis, MO; Charlotte and Raleigh, NC; New Brunswick and Newark, NJ; New York City, Rochester, and Syracuse, NY; Cincinnati, Cleveland, Columbus, and Toledo, OH; Philadelphia and Pittsburgh, PA; Memphis and Nashville, TN; Dallas and Houston, TX; Richmond, VA; Charleston, WV; Beloit and Milwaukee, WI; and Washington, DC. Students work for companies such as AT&T, American Express, 3M, Johnson & Johnson, Anheuser-Busch, Nestlé, Federal Express, and Federal Reserve Banks. Students attend business workshops, conduct public service projects, receive academic counseling, and are paired with mentors. Deadline: December 31.

1448.
Institute for Education in Journalism
AEJ Summer Internships for Minorities
New York University
Institute of Afro-American Affairs
289 Mercer Street, Suite 601
New York, NY 10003
(212) 998-2130

Summer ten-week internships paying $200 a week for undergraduate minority students. Preference given to full-time juniors or seniors planning on going to graduate school. Based on career goals, academic record, transcript, writing samples, and recommendations. Deadline: mid-December.

1449.
Institute for Humane Studies—George Mason University
IHS Excellence in Liberty Prizes
4400 University Drive
Fairfax, VA 22030-4444
(703) 323-1055

2 awards of $500 for term papers written by undergraduate and graduate students. Papers may be in history, political theory, sociology, literature, or economics. Deadline: June 1.

1450.

Institute for Local Self–Reliance
Internship Coordinator
2425 18th Street, N.W.
Washington, DC 20009-2096
(202) 232-4108
(202) 332-0463 Fax

4 to 10 internships that last at least six months and provide $230 per week to undergraduates and $280 per week to graduate students, plus health insurance to work in environmental and public policy efforts with grassroots community groups, government leaders, and business entrepreneurs. Interns work conducting research, creating policy initiatives, coalition building, and providing technical assistance. Interns work in either Minneapolis, Minnesota, or Washington, DC. Internships are conducted on an ongoing basis. Deadline: rolling.

1451.

Institute for the Advancement of Engineering Scholarships
P.O. Box 1305
Woodland Hills, CA 91365
(818) 992-8292

Scholarships of varying amounts to undergraduate engineering students attending one of thirteen California institutions. Based on academic record in engineering and mathematics. May be used at student's discretion. Deadline: November 1.

1452.

Institute of Business Designers
Student Design Competition Scholarships
1155 Merchandise Mart
Chicago, IL 60654
(312) 467-1950

1 national and 6 regional awards of $1,000 to undergraduate students in a design competition. Students must solve a design problem. Presentations may be on a total of four design boards. Problems change from year to year. Inquire through participating schools. Deadline: varies by school.

1453.

Institute of European Studies
700 North Rush Street
Chicago, IL 60611

Numerous scholarships of $1,300 to college juniors and seniors for up to one year of study at one of seven European locations. Some part-time employment is available at most locations to supplement the $1,300 award. Deadline: varies.

1454.

Institute of Food Technologists (IFT)
Freshman/Sophomore Scholarships
221 North LaSalle, Suite 300
Chicago, IL 60601-1291
(312) 782-8424/(312) 782-8348 Fax
http://www.ift.org/
info@ift.org

33 scholarships of $500 to high school seniors or graduates who will be entering college for the first time or undergraduate sophomores. Must be enrolled in an IFT-approved curriculum in food technology, food science, food engineering, or nutrition. Undergraduate sophomores must have at least a 2.5 GPA for the first semester or first two quarters of college. Obtain an application after October 1. Deadline: February 15 (first year); March 15 (sophomores).

1455.

Institute of Food Technologists (IFT)
Junior/Senior Scholarships
221 North LaSalle, Suite 300
Chicago, IL 60601-1291
(312) 782-8424/(312) 782-8348 Fax
http://www.ift.org
info@ift.org

5 scholarships of $2,000, 2 scholarships of $1,500, 1 scholarship of $1,000, and 10 scholarships of $750 to sophomore or junior students in an institution with an approved IFT program. Based on academic achievement, professional promise, and well-rounded personality. Request applications before December 31. Deadline: February 1.

1456.

Institute of Industrial Engineers (IIE)
IIE, Scholarships
25 Technology Part/Atlanta
Norcross, GA 30092
(770) 449-0460

Scholarships of varying amounts to undergraduate and graduate students who are industrial engineering majors. Must be active IIE members with at least one full year of study remaining at an accredited U.S. or Canadian institution. Must have at least a 3.4 GPA on a 4.0 scale. Applications mailed only to students who have been nominated by the department head. Deadline: November 1 (nominations); February 15 (applications).

1457.

Intel Corporation
Staffing Department
FM4-145
P.O. Box 1141
Folsom, CA 95763-1141
(916) 356-8080
http://www.intel.com/intel/other/research/

750 to 800 summer, fall, and spring internships providing relocation allowance ranging from $500 to $700, round-trip travel, and salaries ranging from $450 to $750 per week for undergraduates and from $750 to $1,000 per week for graduates. Summer internships are from eight to fifteen weeks; fall and spring range from four to eight months. Open to undergraduate, graduate, and doctoral students with at least a 3.0 GPA, and who are majoring in accounting, business, computer science, education, engineering (chemical, computer, electrical, or industrial), finance, human resources, materials science, or mathematics. Deadline: rolling (majority filed by March 1).

1458.
Intermural Research Training Award
Summer Intern Program
Office of Education
Building 10, Room IC-129
10 Center Drive
Mail Stop Code 1158
Bethesda, MD 20892-1158
(301) 496-2427
http://www.training.nih.gov

Summer internship program providing a stipend to
undergraduate, graduate, or medical students. The program
provides an opportunity to acquire hands-on research
training and experience in the neurosciences. For more
information, which changes on a yearly basis, contact the
website. Deadline: varies.

1459.
International Association of Arson Investigators
(IAAI)
John Charles Wilson Scholarship Fund
P.O. Box 91119
Louisville, KY 40291
(502) 491-7482

Numerous scholarships of $1,000 to undergraduate students
who are IAAI members, family members, or nonmembers
who are sponsored and recommended by members in
good standing. Must be majoring in police science or fire
science. Deadline: February 15.

1460.
International Association of Bridge, Structural,
and Ornamental Iron Workers
John H. Lyons Sr. Scholarship Program
1750 New York Avenue, N.W., Suite 400
Washington, DC 20006

2 scholarships of $1,500 to adopted, natural, or stepchildren
of active members of this association for five or more
years. Children of deceased members may apply if the
member was in good standing at the time of death. Based
on academic record, SAT/ACT, extracurricular activities,
leadership, recommendations, and character. Award may be
used at any accredited institution in the U.S. or Canada.
Deadline: March.

1461.
International Association of Fire Chiefs
4025 Fair Ridge Drive
Fairfax VA 22033-2868
(703) 273-0911
http://www.iafc.org/

1 scholarship of $2,500 (renewable up to four consecutive
years) to sons, daughters, or legally adopted children of firefighters who died in the line of duty. Parent must have
been a member in good standing of the International
Association of Fire Fighters, AFL-CIO/CLC, at time of death.
Based on financial need, transcript, recommendation, and
essay about goals. Deadline: varies.

1462.
International Association of Fire Chiefs
Foundation
Scholarship Program
4025 Fair Ridge Drive
Fairfax, VA 22033-2868
(703) 273-0911
http://www.iafc.org/

18 scholarships of $250 to members of a fire service of a
state, county, provincial, municipal, community, industrial,
or federal fire department. Must be majoring in business or
urban administration, engineering, or fire science. Deadline:
August 15.

1463.
International Association of Hospitality
Accountants Scholarships
Scholarship Committee Chairperson
P.O. Box 203008
Austin, TX 78720
(512) 346-4242

3 scholarships of $1,000 and 1 scholarship of $1,500 to
students pursuing a career in hospitality management or
accounting at any accredited institution. Must be endorsed
by local IAHA chapter. Based on academic record,
employment experience, and recommendations. Deadline:
July 15.

1464.
International Association of Machinists and
Aerospace Workers
IAM Scholarships
1300 Connecticut Avenue, N.W.
Washington, DC 20036
(202) 857-5215

Scholarships of $2,000 to members and $1,000 to adopted,
natural, or stepchildren of members of this association.
Members must have been in good standing for at least two
years. Members may be entering freshmen or current
undergraduates. Children of members must be high school
seniors and not be attending or have attended college.
Based on academic record, goals, SAT/ACT,
recommendations, extracurricular activities, and local lodge
responsibilities. Deadline: December 1.

1465.
International Association of Y's Men's Clubs
Alexander Scholarship/Loans
3815 5th Avenue South
Great Falls, MT 59405

10 to 15 scholarship/loans of $1,500 per year to
undergraduate men majoring in business administration or
youth leadership. Scholarship/loan repayment is waived if
you agree to work for YMCA after graduation for at least
one year for each year of funding. History of previous
YMCA participation is helpful. Include a self-addressed,
stamped envelope with application request. Deadline:
May 1.

1466.
International Brotherhood of Teamsters
Scholarship Program
25 Louisiana Avenue, N.W.
Washington, DC 20001
(202) 624-8735

Numerous scholarships to high school seniors who are children of Teamster members. Obtain application from parent's local union or directly from the above address, September through November. Deadline: November 30.

1467.
International Brotherhood of Teamsters—Local 317, IBT
Attn: Administrative Assistant
566 Spencer Street
Syracuse, NY 13204
(315) 471-4164

1 scholarship of $1,000 to a high school senior who is a child of an active or retired Teamster member. Based on academic record, SAT/ACT, goals, and extracurricular activities. Deadline: May 30.

1468.
International Brotherhood of Teamsters— Minnesota
Teamsters Joint Council No. 32 Scholarship Awards
3001 University Avenue, S.E.
Minneapolis, MN 55414
(612) 331-6767

8 scholarships of $1,000 to high school seniors within the jurisdiction of Minnesota Teamsters Joint Council No. 32. Applicants must be members or children of active or deceased member and have at least a 3.0 GPA on a 4.0 scale. Award may be used at any Minnesota college, university, or vocational or technical school. Deadline: April 30.

1469.
International Chiropractors Association (ICA)
King Koil Spinal Guard Student Scholarships
1110 North Glebe Road, Suite 1000
Arlington, VA 22201
(800) 423-4690
(703) 528-5000
http://www.chiropractic.org/

Awards of varying amounts to undergraduate and graduate students who are student members of ICA and pursuing chiropractic medicine. Number of awards (and amount) determined on an individual basis. Based on academic achievement and service. Awards are good at schools with ICA chapters. Not available for freshmen. Deadline: spring.

1470.
International Chiropractors Association Women's Auxiliary (WAICA) Scholarships
1110 North Glebe Road, Suite 1000
Arlington, VA 22201
(703) 528-5000

Scholarships of varying amounts to undergraduate and graduate students who are student members of ICA and pursuing chiropractic medicine. Number of awards (and amount) determined on an individual basis. Based on academic achievement and service. Awards are good at schools with ICA chapters. Not available for freshmen. Deadline: spring.

1471.
International Furnishings and Design Association—Editorial Foundation
IFDA Student Design Competition
107 World Trade Center
P.O. Box 58045
Dallas, TX 75258
(214) 747-2406

3 awards of $2,000 and 1 award of $3,500 to second-, third-, or fourth-year undergraduate or graduate design students. First-place winner's school receives a $2,000 grant and each runner-up's school receives $1,000. Design-competition categories change each year. Based on storage-living-space innovations, creativity of design, practicality, aesthetic value, and adherence to requirements. Deadline: March 1.

1472.
International Food Service Editorial Council
IFEC Scholarships
82 Osborne Lane
East Hampton, NY 11937
(516) 324-2725

Scholarships of $1,000 for undergraduate and graduate students enrolled in a food service communications program at an accredited college or university. Based on academic record and financial need. Renewable. Deadline: May 1.

1473.
International Food Service Executives Association Scholarships
IFSEA Worthy Goal Scholarships
1100 South State Road 7, Suite 103
Margate, FL 33068-4033
(954) 977-0767/(954) 977-0874 Fax
http://www.ifsea.org/scholarship.htm
hq@ifsea.org

4 scholarships ranging from $300 to $3,000 to students pursuing a career in commercial food service training. Individual scholarships range from $100 to $500. Students must be endorsed by a local branch of the IFSEA. Applicants must submit a transcript, letter of enrollment from the college, and three letters of recommendation (at least one from an employer). Based on financial need, academic achievement, and professional intentions. Write to address above or get an application from a local IFSEA branch. Deadline: varies.

1474.
International Ladies Garment Workers' Union
ILGWU Local 23–25 College Textbook Scholarships
275 Seventh Avenue, 4th Floor
New York, NY 16001
(212) 229-9221

Numerous scholarships of $250 per year for four years to graduating high school seniors who are children of members. Members may be active, retired, permanently disabled, or deceased. Students must have at least an 80 average. Based on academic record, extracurricular activities, and community involvement. Deadline: January 15.

1475.
International Ladies Garment Workers' Union
ILGWU National Scholarship Fund
275 Seventh Avenue, 4th Floor
New York, NY 16001
(212) 229-9221
http://www.fieldtrip.com/ny/

10 four-year scholarships providing $550 the first year, $600 the second year, $650 the third year, and $700 the fourth year for dependents of present members of the ILGWU with three years of good standing in the union. Based on academic record, class rank, and SAT/ACT. Deadline: December 31.

1476.
International Ladies Garment Workers' Union
ILGWU Scholarships
275 Seventh Avenue, 4th Floor
New York, NY 10001
(212) 229-9221
http://www.fieldtrip.com/ny/

Numerous scholarships of $600 for high school seniors or graduates of one year who are children of members of the Philadelphia South Jersey District Council since April 15 of the award year. If parent is deceased, he or she must have died within two years of application. Recipient may use the award for any major in any approved college or university. Based on academic record, recommendation, SAT, Achievement Test scores, and essay. Deadline: April 15.

1477.
International League of Women Composers
Search for New Music Award
Chairperson
P.O. Box 42
Three Mile Bay, NY 13693
(315) 649-5086

$250 first prize and $150 second prize to female student composers in a music composition contest. May be of any age and nationality. Award can be used anywhere. Deadline: October 15.

1478.
International Ministers' Wives and Widows
Association
E. C. Bouey Memorial Scholarship Awards
Gladden–Johnson Awards
c/o Dr. Muriel L. Johnson
128 Pennsylvania Avenue
Roosevelt, NY 11575
(516) 379-2795

Numerous $500 scholarships to undergraduate students majoring in theology. Must be members of a religious community and be recommended by a wife of a minister. Based on academic record. Deadline: varies.

1479.
International Order of Alhambra
Scholarship Committee Chairperson
4200 Leeds Avenue
Baltimore, MD 21229
(301) 242-0660

1 grant of $400 per quarter (renewable up to four quarters, for a total of $1,600) to students who are at least in their third year of college. Must be majoring in a field involving the handicapped and retarded. Send a short résumé stating year in college and the courses being pursued. Deadline: none.

1480.
International Order of King's Daughters/Sons
Health Scholarships
Office Manager
P.O. Box 1017
Chautauqua, NY 14722
(716) 357-6200

20 to 30 scholarships ranging from $500 to $1,000 to undergraduate students. Must be studying in a health field, such as medicine, dentistry, nursing, physical therapy, occupational therapy, or medical technologies. RN applicants must be in the second year of their program and BA candidates in at least the third year. Enclose self-addressed, stamped envelope (legal size) with inquiries to: Mrs. J. F. Sellew, 514 Colonial Avenue, Norfolk, VA 23507. (804) 622-1583. Deadline: April 1.

1481.
International Order of King's Daughters/Sons
North American Indian Scholarships
13 Boardman Street
Middlebury, VT 05753

Scholarships of varying amounts to high school seniors who are Native Americans. May be used for any major. Send self-addressed, stamped envelope for application. Deadline: none.

1482.
International Order of King's Daughters/Sons
Student Ministry Scholarship Fund
Headquarters
P.O. Box 1017
34 Vincent Avenue
Chautauqua, NY 14722
(716) 357-6200

18 to 25 scholarships of $1,000 to undergraduate seniors or graduate students majoring in Christian leadership education or theology. Must have a "B" or better GPA. Must have been accepted to or enrolled in an accredited U.S. or Canadian graduate school or seminary. Must be preparing for a full-time religious vocation. Must be U.S. or Canadian citizens. Send a self-addressed, stamped envelope to obtain name and address of current director. Deadline: April 30.

1483.
International Radio & Television Society
IRTS Summer Fellowship Program
420 Lexington Avenue, Room 1714
New York, NY 10170
(212) 867-6650

Fellowships providing housing, travel expenses, and a stipend for undergraduate juniors and seniors who have an interest in communications or broadcasting. The program is a nine-week summer program in New York City. Deadline: November 30.

1484.
International Society for Clinical Laboratory
Technology
Scholarships
818 Olive Street, # 918
St. Louis, MO 63101
(314) 241-1445

Scholarships of varying amounts to graduating high school seniors and undergraduates for all fields of study. Must either be ISCLT members or be dependent children of members to apply. Must have graduated from or will graduate from an accredited high school or equivalent before award begins. Must be U.S. citizens or legal residents. Other restrictions may apply. Deadline: July 31.

1485.
International Society for Optical Engineering
Scholarships & Grants
Chairman SPIE Education Committee
P.O. Box 10
Bellingham, WA 98227
(206) 676-3290

Numerous scholarships ranging from $500 to $5,000 to undergraduate students majoring in optical engineering. Based on assessment of the student's potential contribution to optics and optical engineering. Deadline: May 14.

1486.
International Union of Bricklayers and Allied
Craftsmen
Harry C. Bates Merit Scholarships
Education Department
815 15th Street, N.W.
Washington, DC 20005

1 United States Bates Scholarship of $2,000 and 1 $400 and 1 $600 Canadian Bates Scholarships to high school seniors who are children of current, retired, or deceased members. Applicants must take the PSAT in October of junior year in high school. Based on SAT score and National Merit Semifinalist standing. Deadline: varies.

1487.
International Union of Electronic, Electrical,
Salaried Machine, & Furniture Workers,
AFL-CIO
1126 16th Street, N.W.
Washington, DC 20036
(202) 296-1200

9 scholarships worth $1,000 to sons or daughters of active or deceased members of IUE-AFL-CIO. May be used at a two- or four-year college or vocational/occupational schools. Based on financial need, recommendation letters, transcript, and SAT/ACT scores. Payment is made to recipients. Request applications between February and April. Deadline: April 15.

1488.
Investor-Owned Electric Utilities of Texas
State FHA/HERO Advisor
Texas Education Agency
1701 North Congress
Austin, TX 78701

Scholarships of $1,000 to a high school senior. Attach a typewritten two-page summary of activities related to conserving energy in the home. Based on essay. Deadline: March 1.

1489.
Iota Sigma Pi Award Program
Gladys Anderson Emerson Scholarship
Department of Chemistry B-003
University of California
La Jolla, CA 92093
(619) 534-6479

1 scholarship of $1,000 to a female undergraduate junior or senior or graduate student majoring in chemistry or biochemistry. May be used at any accredited college or university; student need not be a member of Iota Sigma Pi. Based on academic achievement. Contact: Dr. Martha Thompson, Department of Physiology and Pharmacology, Oregon Health Sciences University, School of Dentistry, 611 SW Campus Drive, Portland, OR 97201. Deadline: January 1.

1490.
Iota Sigma Pi Award Program
ISP Undergraduate Award for Excellence in
Chemistry
Department of Chemistry B-003
University of California
La Jolla, CA 92093
(619) 534-6479

1 scholarship of $300 to a female undergraduate senior for excellence in chemistry. Award is good at any accredited college or university. Need not be a member of Iota Sigma Pi. Based on academic achievement. Deadline: February 1.

1491.
Iowa College Student Aid Commission
Iowa Grants
200 10th Street, 4th Floor
Des Moines, IA 50309-2036
(800) 383-4222
(515) 281-3501
http://www.state.ia.us/government/icsac/
icsac@max.state.ia.us

Grants of up to $1,000 to graduating high school seniors or undergraduate students. Must be enrolled or plan to enroll at least part-time in an undergraduate degree program in an accredited Iowa institution. Must be Iowa residents and either U.S. citizens or legal residents. Must file an FAFSA.

1492.

Iowa College Student Aid Commission
Robert C. Byrd Scholarships
200 10th Street, 4th Floor
Des Moines, IA 50309-2036
(800) 383-4222
(515) 281-3501
http://www.state.ia.us/government/icsac/
icsac@max.state.ia.us

Varying numbers of scholarships of up to $1,110 to graduating high school seniors for use the first year of study in a college or university within the state. Selection based on academic achievement. Must be Iowa residents and attend an Iowa institution. Obtain applications from state agency or high school counselor. Deadline: April 15.

1493.

Iowa College Student Aid Commission
State of Iowa Scholarship Program
200 10th Street, 4th Floor
Des Moines, IA 50309-2036
(800) 383-4222
(515) 281-3501
http://www.state.ia.us/government/icsac/
icsac@max.state.ia.us

Scholarships of up to $500 to Iowa high school seniors. Must be selected State of Iowa Scholars and attend an eligible Iowa institution. Must take the ACT by October of senior year. Must be in upper 15 percent of class at the end of junior year. Based on academic record and ACT, not financial need. Renewal of awards is based on academic record and financial need; must maintain at least a B average. Deadline: mid-November.

1494.

Iowa College Student Aid Commission
Tuition Grants
200 10th Street, 4th Floor
Des Moines, IA 50309-2036
(800) 383-4222
(515) 281-3501
http://www.state.ia.us/government/icsac/
icsac@max.state.ia.us

Grants of up to $2,225 for full-time and up to $1,225 for part-time undergraduate study. Must be residents of Iowa and be enrolled or planning to enroll at a private college, university, nursing, or business college in Iowa. Based on financial need. Deadline: April.

1495.

Iowa College Student Aid Commission
Vocational–Technical Tuition Grants
200 10th Street, 4th Floor
Des Moines, IA 50309-2036
(800) 383-4222
(515) 281-3501
http://www.state.ia.us/government/icsac/
icsac@max.state.ia.us

Grants of up to $450 to students enrolled in or planning to enroll in a full-time vocational or technical program at an Iowa area school. Based on Iowa residency and financial need. Deadline: April 15.

1496.

Iowa Program for War Orphans
Veterans Affairs Division
Department of Public Defense
7700 NW Beaver Drive, Camp Dodge
Johnston, IA 50131-1902

$400 scholarships (renewable up to $2,000) for students whose parents died in the Armed Forces or as a result of a service-connected injury. War orphans of the National Guardsmen and other members of the Reserve Components are also eligible. This is awarded without regard to academic record, financial need, age, or marital status. Deadline: none.

1497.

Iowa Vocational Rehabilitation
Bureau Chief for Client Services
Division of Vocational Rehabilitation Services
510 East 12th Street
Des Moines, IA 50319

Scholarships of varying amounts (based on individual's needs) to students with a disability that is a handicap for employment. Must be residents of Iowa. Deadline: none.

1498.

Irish American Cultural Institute
Irish Way Scholarships
Attn: James Bohen, Administrative Asst.
P.O. Box 5026
2115 Summit Avenue
St. Paul, MN 55105

25 scholarships ranging from $250 to $1,000 per year to high school students in grades 9 through 11 to take part in a summer study and recreation program in Ireland. Must be U.S. citizens. Deadline: April.

1499.

Italian–American Chamber of Commerce of
 Chicago Scholarships
126 West Grand Avenue
Chicago, IL 60610
(312) 661-1336

Numerous scholarships of $1,000 to high school seniors and undergraduate students who are of Italian ancestry. Based on academic record, recommendations, essay, and goals. Deadline: April 30.

1500.

Italian Catholic Federation Scholarships
1801 Van Ness Avenue, Suite 330
San Francisco, CA 94109
(415) 673-8240

190 renewable scholarships of $350 to students who are of Italian ancestry and Catholic. Must be residents of California, Nevada, or Illinois. Must have a 3.0 GPA. Request applications after January 1. Deadline: March 15.

1501.
Jackie Robinson Foundation
Attn: Scholarship Program
3 W. 35th Street, 11th Floor
New York, NY 10001
(212) 290-8600

Four-year scholarships of up to $5,000 per year to minority high school seniors. Must be accepted to a four-year accredited college or university and be U.S. citizens. Based on academic achievements, SAT scores, leadership potential, and financial need. Only written requests for the application are accepted. Deadline: March 30.

1502.
Jack in the Box
Essay and Photo Competition
Anderson Communications Company, Inc.
3 Corporate Plaza, Suite 200
Newport Beach, CA 92660

25 scholarships of $1,000 (2 in Arizona, 10 in California, 2 in Hawaii, 2 in Missouri, 6 in Texas, and 3 in Washington State) to high school seniors. Students must submit an essay written about a picture (8 ×10) that represents something about their heritage. Competition may vary. Send a self-addressed, stamped envelope in the fall for information. Deadline: March 1.

1503.
Jackson Laboratory
Summer Student Program
Training & Education Office
600 Main Street
Bar Harbor, ME 04609-1500
(207) 288-6250
http://www.jax.org/
training@jax.org

Scholarships of varying amounts to assist with the cost of room and board during the nine-week internships open to high school juniors or undergraduate students. College students receive a scholarship to cover the program fee plus a stipend of $2,500. High school students may apply for scholarships, which are awarded based on financial need. The program fee is $2,850, which includes room and board. Interns participate in an existing research program on mammalian genetics. Students must live at Highseas, located on the East Coast adjoining Acadia National Park. Selection is based on interest, written statement for applying, recommendations, scientific ability and curiosity, and academic achievement. High school students must be at least fifteen years of age. All students must be U.S. citizens or permanent residents. Deadline: mid-February.

1504.
Jacksonville University Biannual Playwriting
Contest
Attn: Director
College of Fine Arts
Department of Theatre Arts
Jacksonville, FL 32211
(904) 744-3950

Top cash award of $1,000 to playwrights for best original, unproduced, full-length or one-act play or musical. The award is presented at the premier production. This is a cash award and not a scholarship. Applications are available only in September of odd-numbered years. For rules, send a #10 self-addressed, stamped envelope after September 1 of odd-numbered years. Deadline: varies.

1505.
Jacques Weber Foundation
1460 Broadway
New York, NY 10036
(212) 784-7701

17 scholarships ranging from $950 to $5,700 to high school seniors who live within seventy miles of Bloomsburg, Pennsylvania, for textile studies, or are residents of Abbeville, South Carolina, and surrounding area. Contact: Jacques Weber Foundation, Inc., Scholarship Committee, P.O. Box 420, Bloomsburg, PA 17815. Deadline: November 30.

1506.
James B. Black College Scholarship Program
Administrator, Scholarship Program
Pacific Gas & Electric Company
77 Beale Street, Room 2825 F
San Francisco, CA 94106
(415) 973-1338

18 scholarships of $4,000, 12 scholarships of $2,000, and 6 scholarships of $1,000 to high school seniors residing in one of six regions (each region receives 3 of $4,000, 2 of $2,000, and 1 of $1,000). Applicants who reside in one region and attend school in another region compete in the region where the school is located. Must reside or attend school in a PG & E service region. Based on academic achievement, extracurricular activities, SAT scores, application, essays, and school report. Test scores should be sent to PG & E in October, November, or December. Deadline: November 15.

1507.
James F. Byrnes Foundation
P.O. Box 9596
Columbia, SC 29290
(803) 776-1211
(803) 776-3372

Numerous renewable scholarships of $1,500 to high school seniors who are orphaned or have only one surviving parent. Must be South Carolina residents. Deadline: February 15.

1508.
James F. Lincoln Arc Welding Foundation
Awards Program
Attn: Secretary
P.O. Box 17035
Cleveland, OH 44117
(216) 481-4300

17 undergraduate and 12 graduate scholarships of up to $2,000 to students of engineering and technology who solve design engineering or fabrication problems involving the knowledge or application of arc welding. Deadline: June 15.

1509.
James Gordon Bennett Memorial Corporation
c/o Patrick Finnegan
200 Park Avenue, Room 4320
New York, NY 10166

85 scholarships of varying amounts, totaling $99,000, to
students who have worked on New York City daily
newspapers for at least ten years. Deadline: varies.

1510.
James H. Hoffman Scholarship Trust
c/o Southtrust Bank
P.O. Box 1000
Anniston, AL 36202
(205) 238-1000

32 scholarships of $500 to students who are graduates of
Calhoun County, Alabama, high schools. Must be residents
of Calhoun County, Alabama. Based on academic record
and financial need. Deadline: March.

1511.
James J. Bloomer Trust
Chemung Canal Trust Co.
P.O. Box 1522
Elmira, NY 14902
(607) 737-3711

10 scholarships of varying amounts, totaling $7,300, to high
school seniors who are of the Catholic faith. Must be
residents of Elmira, New York. Based on academic record
and financial need. Deadline: varies.

1512.
James J. Kerrigan Memorial Scholarships
Attn: Human Resources
Merck & Company, Inc.
P.O. Box 2000
Rahway, NJ 07065-0900

16 scholarships ranging from $1,500 to full tuition and
expenses (depending on family's financial need) for natural,
adopted, or stepchildren of active, retired, or deceased
employees residing in the U.S. Children of company
officials are not eligible. Based on academic standing,
leadership, character, and financial need. Deadline:
November 15.

1513.
James S. Kemper Foundation Scholarships
Kemper Insurance Center
Long Grove, IL 60049

15 scholarships ranging from $1,000 to $3,500 to
undergraduate freshman students at participating colleges
and universities who are majoring in business
administration or insurance. List of campuses is available
upon request. Based on academic record. Deadline: varies.

1514.
James Z. Naurison Scholarship Fund
Fleet National Bank
P.O. Box 9006
Springfield, MA 01102-9006
(413) 787-8745

450 scholarship grants, totaling $227,800, for students from
Berkshire, Franklin, Hampden, or Hampshire counties,
Massachusetts, or Enfield or Suffield counties, Connecticut.
Deadline: May 1.

1515.
Janesville Foundation, Inc.
Attn: Executive Director
121 North Parker Drive
P.O. Box 1492
Janesville, WI 53545
(608) 752-1032

34 scholarships of varying amounts, totaling over $33,000,
to students. Must be residents of Janesville, Wisconsin.
Deadline: March 1; June 1; September 1; December 1.

1516.
Japan–America Society of Washington
U. Alexis Johnson Scholarship
606 18th Street, N.W.
Washington, DC 20006-5293
(202) 289-8290

1 or more $3,000 scholarships and/or air travel to Japan for
an undergraduate or graduate student of Japanese language
and culture. Award provides support to study in Japan.
Must be full-time student at institution in the District of
Columbia, Maryland, Virginia, or West Virginia. Based on
academic record, motivation, and financial need. Deadline:
March 1.

1517.
Japanese American Citizens League (JACL)
Freshmen Awards
National Headquarters
1765 Sutter Street
San Francisco, CA 94115

Scholarships of varying amounts to graduating high school
seniors or undergraduate or graduate students. May be
used at a trade school, business school, college, or
university. Must be JACL members, their children, or any
American citizen of Japanese ancestry. Request applications
and additional information from local JACL Chapters,
Regional Offices, or send self-addressed, stamped envelope
to the above address. Deadline: March 1.

1518.
JayCee War Memorial Fund Scholarships
Scholarship, Chair
War Memorial Fund, U.S. Jaycees
P.O. Box 7
Tulsa, OK 74121-0007

8 national scholarships of $1,000 to high school seniors
preparing to enter college as first-semester freshmen. Based
on academics, need, and leadership. Request information

and application between July 1 and February 15. Deadline: March 1; (state) March 15 (national).

1519.

Jeannette Rankin Foundation
Scholarship Awards
P.O. Box 6653
Athens, GA 30604-6653
http://www.wmst.unt.edu/jrf/apply.htm
odendhal@mail2.theonramp.net

25 or more awards of $1,500 to women thirty-five years or older who have been accepted or enrolled at a school to pursue an undergraduate degree or vocational or technical training course. Financial need is a primary factor. Must be U.S. citizens. When requesting an application write a letter indicating your gender, age, and level of study or training. Include a #10 self-addressed, stamped envelope; in the lower left-hand corner, write "JRF (insert year of application)." Deadline: March 1.

1520.

Jennie and Pearl Abell Education Trust
723½ Main Street
P.O. Box 487
Ashland, KS 67831

113 scholarships of varying amounts, totaling $116,000, to high school seniors or graduates of Clark County high schools. Must be residents of Clark County, Kansas. Deadline: varies.

1521.

Jesse Klicka Foundation
Wells Fargo Trust Department
101 W. Broadway, Suite 301
San Diego, CA 92101

18 scholarships of varying amounts, totaling $25,000, to graduates of San Diego County and city high schools. Based on academic record and financial need. Deadline: April 15.

1522.

Jessie H. Baker Educational Fund
c/o Marine Midland Bank
P.O. Box 719
Binghamton, NY 13902
(607) 772-5521

Numerous scholarships of varying amounts, totaling $109,850, to graduating high school seniors from Broome County, New York, high schools. For use in an undergraduate college or university. Based on academic record and financial need. Deadline: varies.

1523.

Jewish Family & Children Services
Stanley Olson Youth Scholarship Fund
1600 Scott Street
San Francisco, CA 94115
(415) 561-1226
(415) 567-8860

Scholarships of up to $2,500 to undergraduate and graduate students accepted to or enrolled in a college or university for all areas of study, with preference given to liberal arts majors. Award may be used for studies, personal, business, or professional purposes. Must be Jewish students, under twenty-five years of age, and residents of San Francisco, San Mateo, Santa Clara, Marin, or Sonoma County, California. Based on academic achievement and financial need. Must be U.S. citizens. Write a letter briefly detailing your educational and financial situation and include a self-addressed, stamped envelope. Other restrictions may apply. Deadline: none.

1524.

Jewish Federation of Metropolitan Chicago
Jewish Federation of Metropolitan Chicago
  Scholarships
Levie Educational Fund Scholarships
Scholarship Secretary
1 South Franklin Street
Chicago, IL 60606
(312) 346-6700

60 to 80 renewable scholarships from $1,000 to $5,000 per year to Jewish students living in the metropolitan area of Chicago. For the Levie scholarships, students must be Cook County residents. Must be majoring in medicine, nursing, social work, dentistry, or other "helping professions" and enrolled in or planning to enroll in a vocational/occupational school or a two- or four-year undergraduate institution, graduate, or professional school. Request applications after December 1. Deadline: March 1.

1525.

Jewish Foundation for Education of Women
Scholarships
Attn: Executive Director
330 West 58th Street
New York, NY 10019
(212) 265-2565

Scholarships ranging from $500 to $3,500 to full-time undergraduate female students who live within fifty miles of New York City, including New Jersey and Long Island. Deadline: January 31.

1526.

Jewish Social Service Agency
Irene Stambler Vocational Opportunities Grant
  Program
6123 Montrose Road
Rockville, MD 20852
(301) 881-3700
(301) 816-2676

Varying numbers of grants of up to $2,000 to female Jewish undergraduate students for any field of study. Must be residents of the Washington metropolitan area who are seeking to improve their earning potential because of divorce, separation, or death of their spouse. Award may be used to complete an educational or vocational program or to start or expand a small business. Based on financial need. Must be U.S. citizens or permanent residents seeking citizenship. Deadline: none.

1527.
Jewish Social Service Agency
Jewish Undergraduate Scholarship
6123 Montrose Road
Rockville, MD 20852
(301) 816-2676

1 scholarship of $3,500 to a Jewish undergraduate student
from the Washington metropolitan area. Student must be
less than thirty years of age. Must have financial need.
Deadline: June.

1528.
Jewish Vocational Service
6715 Minnetonka Boulevard
St. Louis Park, MN 55426

Various scholarship/loans of $2,500 to undergraduate
juniors, seniors, or graduate students in certain fields,
including Jewish education, social work, or the rabbinate.
Recipients either repay the amount at low interest or work
one year for each year scholarship awarded.

1529.
Jewish Vocational Service
Encouragement Scholarships
1500 South Lilac Drive, Suite 311
Minneapolis, MN 55416

Scholarships of up to $1,000 to students who are enrolled
in or accepted to an accredited college, university, rabbinical
seminary, or teacher-training institution. Applicants may
submit their own applications. Must be of Jewish
background and pursue Jewish educational studies during
the award year. Based on academic achievement,
recommendations, aptitude, and financial need. Deadline:
April 1.

1530.
Jewish Vocational Service
Marcus & Theresa Levie Educational Fund
    Scholarships
1 South Franklin Street
Chicago, IL 60606
(312) 346-6700

85 to 100 scholarships of $5,000 to high school seniors or
undergraduate or graduate students. Must be Cook County
residents of the Jewish faith. Must be enrolled or entering an
accredited institution or vocational training program to study
social work, medicine, dentistry, nursing, or other related
helping professions and vocations. Deadline: March 1.

1531.
Jewish Vocational Service
Recruitment Scholarships
1500 South Lilac Drive, Suite 311
Minneapolis, MN 55416

Numerous scholarships of up to $2,500 to high school
seniors or undergraduate students. Must be enrolled in or
accepted to an accredited postsecondary institution,
rabbinical seminary, or teacher-training institution. Must be
sponsored and approved by a community agency or
institution. Must be of Jewish background; must pursue
Jewish educational studies while receiving the award. Based

on academic achievement, recommendations, aptitude, and
financial need. Deadline: April 1.

1532.
Jewish War Veterans of the USA
National Scholarship Chairman
1811 R Street, N.W.
Washington, DC 20009

1 scholarship of $1,000, 1 scholarship of $500, 1 scholarship
of $250, and 3 scholarships of $100 to members or the
children or grandchildren of members in good standing. If
the child or grandchild is of a deceased member, the
member must have been in good standing at the time of
death. Must be entering freshmen year in a four-year
college or university or entering a three-year school of
nursing. Based on academic record, SAT, achievement test
scores, and extracurricular activities. Deadline: June 1.

1533.
Jewish Welfare Board
15 East 26th Street
New York, NY 10010
(212) 532-4949

Grants from $1,000 to $4,000 per year to undergraduate
juniors or seniors or graduate students who are committed
to the work of Jewish Community Centers, the YMHA, or
the YWHA, and are majoring in social work, adult
education, early childhood education, health education,
physical education, cultural studies, or Jewish education.
Must complete a year of field work in a Jewish Community
Center setting. Deadline: February 1.

1534.
J. Hugh and Earle W. Fellows Memorial Fund
Scholarships and Loans
c/o Pensacola Junior College
Academic Affairs
1000 College Boulevard
Pensacola, FL 32504
(904) 484-1706

5 to 10 scholarships and loans of varying amounts to
undergraduate and graduate students. Must be residents of
Escambia, Santa Rosa, Okaloosa, or Walton counties,
Florida, who have been admitted to or are enrolled in an
accredited school studying medicine, nursing, medical
technology, or theology. Must have a 2.5 GPA and a
commitment to return to the four-county area for at least
five years after graduation. Renewable. Loans must have
one endorser for each $10,000 loan commitment. Deadline:
none.

1535.
Jim Henson Productions
Internships
Attn: Assistant to the Executive Office
117 East 69th Street
New York, NY 10021
No telephone calls

1 to 6 internships open to undergraduate students. No
monetary compensation is provided. Intern responsibilities
include faxing, photocopying, filing, running errands, and
answering correspondence in one of the following

departments: production, public relations, archives/photo library, Jim Henson Foundation, consumer products, or studio. Interns must keep a weekly journal and provide an evaluation. Length of internship is flexible. Familiarity with WordPerfect is helpful. Sponsor is willing to complete any necessary paperwork required for intern to receive academic credit. In-person interview is required. Deadline: none.

1536.
Jimmie Ullery Charitable Trust Scholarship Grants
c/o First National Bank & Trust Company of Tulsa
Trust Department
P.O. Box 1
Tulsa, OK 74193
(918) 586-5845

6 to 8 scholarships ranging from $1,000 to $1,200 to undergraduate or graduate Presbyterian students who are preparing for full-time Christian service. The scholarships are usually (but not always) awarded for study at Presbyterian Theological Seminaries. Deadline: none.

1537.
Job Training Partnership
Public Affairs Office, Room S-2322
Employment and Training Administration
U.S. Department of Labor
200 Constitution Avenue, N.W.
Washington, DC 20210

Program providing job training to disadvantaged jobless youth (between the ages of sixteen and twenty-one) and dislocated workers. Provides a special employment and training program for service-connected disabled veterans, veterans of the Vietnam era, and veterans recently separated from military service. There are also programs for Native Americans and migrant and seasonal farmworkers. Applicants are trained in classrooms or in the business and factories. The Job Corps provides in-residence training programs, as well as food, clothing, shelter, health services, and recreation as a part of the education and job training program.

1538.
Joe Beirne Scholarships
SWA/TSEU 6186
1412 West 6th
Austin, TX 78703

25 scholarships of up to $3,000 to high school seniors or undergraduate or graduate students who are dependents of current or retired members of Communications Workers of America #6186. Students planning careers in education, rehabilitation, special education, and labor studies are encouraged to apply. Based on academic record and financial need. Deadline: varies.

1539.
Joe W. and Dorothy Dorsett Brown Foundation
1801 Pere Marquette Building
New Orleans, LA 70112
(504) 522-4233

8 scholarship grants ranging from $2,600 to $10,000 to high school seniors or undergraduate students. Must be residents of Louisiana or Mississippi. Contact high school counselor or write a letter briefly detailing your educational and financial situation and include a self-addressed, stamped envelope. Other restrictions may apply. Deadline: varies.

1540.
John Bayliss Broadcast Foundation Scholarships
P.O. Box 221070
Carmel, CA 93922
(408) 624-1536

Scholarships of $2,000 to undergraduate juniors, seniors, and graduate students who are pursuing a career in radio. Must have at least a 3.0 GPA. Financial need is a consideration. Must be U.S. citizens or legal residents. For more information, send a self-addressed, stamped envelope. Other restrictions may apply. Deadline: April 30.

1541.
John Cowles Frautschy Scholarship Fund Trust
First National Bank of Monroe
P.O. Box 30
Monroe, WI 53566

10 scholarships of varying amounts, totaling $7,000, to male Protestant graduates of Monroe High School. Must be residents of Monroe, Wisconsin. Based on academic record and financial need. Deadline: varies.

1542.
John Edgar Thomson Foundation
Director
The Rittenhouse Claridge, Suite 318
Philadelphia, PA 19103
(215) 545-6083

144 scholarship grants ranging from $500 to $4,400 to high school seniors who are daughters of deceased railroad employees to attend a postsecondary institution. Based on academic record and financial need. Deadline: varies.

1543.
John Gyles Education Scholarships
P.O. Box 4808
712 Riverside Drive
Fredericton, New Brunswick E3B 5G4
Canada
(506) 459-7460

Several scholarships of up to $3,000 to undergraduate and graduate students in any area of study. Must be attending a two- or four-year accredited institution in either the U.S. or Canada. Must maintain at least a 2.75 GPA. Must be citizens of either the U.S. or Canada. Deadline: April 15; June 15; November 1.

1544.
John McIntire Educational Fund
c/o Banc First Ohio Corporation
422 Main Street
Zanesville, OH 43701
(740) 452-8444

150 scholarships ranging from $250 to $1,600 to high school seniors or undergraduate students. Must live in

Zanesville, Ohio. Must be under twenty-one years of age. Based on academic record and financial need. Deadline: varies.

1545.

John Q. Shunk Association
P.O. Box 625
Bucyrus, OH 44820

Numerous scholarships, totaling $75,500, to high school seniors or graduates. Must have graduated from Bucyrus, Colonel Crawford, Wynford, or Buckeye Central, Ohio, high schools. Contact: Jane C. Peppard, 1201 Timber Lane, Marion, OH 43302, (614) 389-3132. Deadline: varies.

1546.

John Wiley & Sons, Inc.
Internship Program
605 Third Avenue
New York, NY 10158
(212) 850-6000

6 to 8 ten-week summer internships providing $250 per week to undergraduate sophomores, juniors, and seniors interested in the publishing industry. Interns work in editorial, marketing, finance, or production departments. Though most interns are English majors, the internships are not limited to certain majors. Deadline: rolling.

1547.

John W. Landis Scholarship Trust
c/o D. Williams Evans, Jr.
1670 Christmas Run Boulevard
Wooster, OH 44691

7 scholarships ranging from $400 to $500 to high school graduates or undergraduate students. Must be residents of Wayne County, Ohio. Must be majoring in or planning to major in agriculture, animal husbandry, farm economics, forestry, home economics, horticulture, or soil or water conservation. Contact: Wayne County Superintendent of Schools, 2534 Burbank Road, Wooster, OH 44691. Deadline: March 15.

1548.

Jordon Foundation Trust
First State Bank & Trust Co.
P.O. Box 360, 116 West 6th Street
Larned, KS 67550

29 scholarships of varying amounts, totaling $25,000, to high school seniors or graduates. Must be residents of Pawnee County, Kansas. Based on academic record and financial need. Deadline: varies.

1549.

Joseph Frasca Excellence in Aviation
  Scholarships
The Frasca Family and the University Aviation
  Association (UAA)
Dr. David A. Newmyer
c/o College of Technical Careers
Southern Illinois University at Carbondale
Carbondale, IL 62901-6621

4 scholarships of $500 (2 to pilots and 2 to mechanics) to undergraduate juniors or seniors enrolled in a UAA

member institution. Must show evidence of excellence in activities, studies, events, organizations, etc., related to aviation. Must have at least a 3.0 on a 4.0 scale overall grade point average and Federal Aviation Administration certification/qualifications in either Aviation Maintenance or Flight. Membership in aviation organizations, such as Alpha Eta Rho, NIFA Flying Team, Experimental Aircraft Association, Warbirds of America, etc. Aviation activities, projects, events, etc., will demonstrate an interest and an enthusiasm for aviation. Awards are presented at the National Intercollegiate Flying Association National Flying Championships banquet. Deadline: April 15.

1550.

Joseph H. Bearns Prize in Music
Department of Music
703 Dodge Hall
Columbia University
New York, NY 10027
(212) 854-3825

$2,500 and $3,500 awards to composers between the ages of eighteen and twenty-five. Two categories of competition: $3,500 for larger composition forms and $2,500 for smaller composition forms. May submit only one entry; must be U.S. citizen. Deadline: February 1 (odd-numbered years).

1551.

Joseph Tauber Scholarship Program
National Benefit Fund
310 West 43rd Street
New York, NY 10036

Scholarships ranging from $175 to $3,000 to high school seniors or graduates who are dependents of members or who are National Benefit Fund for Hospital and Health Care Employees. Members must be in Benefit Wage Class One. Amount of award depends on the financial need of the student. Based on financial need and academic achievement. Request applications between December 1 and January 30. Deadline: March 13.

1552.

Josten's Foundation
P.O. Box 297
St. Peter, MN 56082
(507) 931-1682

Numerous scholarships of $1,000 to high school seniors. Must be Minnesota residents. Preference given to residents of Twin Cities, Minnesota, area. Based on academic record and financial need. Deadline: November 15.

1553.

Josten's Foundation
Jack M. Holt Memorial Scholarship
5501 Norman Center Drive
Minneapolis, MN 55437

1 scholarship of $1,500 to a high school senior who is a child of a Josten employee or sales representative. Renewable for up to four years. Based on academic record.

1554.

Josten's Foundation
Josten's Employee Scholarships
5501 Norman Center Drive
Minneapolis, MN 55437

15 scholarships of $1,000 to high school seniors who are children of Josten employees or sales representatives. Based on academic record.

1555.

Journalism Association of Community Colleges
JACC Scholarships
c/o Paul DeBolt
Contra Costa College
2600 Mission Bell Drive
San Pablo, CA 94806
(415) 235-7800

6 scholarships of $1,200 to undergraduate students majoring in journalism or a related field. Must be attending a member institution. Based on academic record, college publications, and recommendations. Deadline: early March.

1556.

Journalism Education Association (JEA)
National High School Journalists of the Year
Scholarships
Kansas State University
Manhattan, KN 66506

1 first-place scholarship of $1,000, 1 second-place scholarship of $500, and 1 third-place scholarship of $300 to high school students nominated through state Journalists of the Year competitions. Directors of state chapters of JEA must send the names of the winners by April 1 to the JEA national headquarters at above address. Deadline: April 1.

1557.

Journalism Foundation of Metropolitan St. Louis
Scholarships
Attn: Scholarship Chairperson
c/o Patrick Gaven
900 North Tucker Boulevard
St. Louis, MO 63101
(314) 340-8000

17 or more scholarships ranging from $750 to $2,500 to undergraduate juniors, seniors, or graduate students pursuing a career in journalism. Must have writing talent (samples). Must be St. Louis residents. Deadline: February 28.

1558.

J P Morgan & Co., Incorporated
60 Wall Street
New York, NY 10260
(212) 648-9909

75 eight-to-twelve-week summer internships providing approximately $500 per week to undergraduate juniors and seniors who will be returning to school. There are four programs: Management Services Summer Internship Program, Global Technology and Operations Summer Internship Program, Audit and Financial Management Summer Internship Program, and Global Markets Summer Internship Programs. Send a résumé, cover letter, and transcript to only one program. Deadline: January 31.

1559.

Junior Achievement (JA), Inc.
Disney Foundation Scholarships
Education Department
45 East Clubhouse Drive
Colorado Springs, CO 80906
(719) 540-8000

Full-tuition scholarships for four years to exceptional high school seniors. Must be members of a JA company or applied economics class. Can be used at any accredited university. May major in business administration or fine arts. Based on academics and extracurricular activities. Contact nearest JA office or above address for complete details. Deadline: June 1.

1560.

Junior Achievement (JA), Inc.
Richard S. Maurer Scholarship
Education Department
45 East Clubhouse Drive
Colorado Springs, CO 80906
(719) 540-8000

1 scholarship of $1,000 to a high school senior from Alabama, Florida, Georgia, North or South Carolina, or eastern Tennessee who has participated in Junior Achievement's JA Company or Applied Economics course. Must plan to be a full-time business major at an accredited institution. Based on academic record and Junior Achievement involvement. Deadline: April 6.

1561.

Junior Engineering Technical Society (JETS), Inc.
1420 King Street, Suite 405
Alexandria, VA 22314-2794
(703) 548-5387

National competition open to high school students with prizes of scientific equipment, calculators, computer supplies, and guidance materials. Students compete in state competitions by solving problems and answering questions in math, chemistry, physics, engineering sciences, biology, English, and computer science as related to engineering problems. Winners in each of eight state divisions move on to the national competition.

1562.

Junior Engineering Technical Society (JETS), Inc.
National Engineering Aptitude Search
The American College Testing Program
Contract Administration
P.O. Box 168
Iowa City, IA 52244-9986

The NEAS testing program determines a student's aptitude and qualifications toward engineering at the college level. It doesn't replace ACT or SAT. It doesn't provide any scholarship money, but some colleges will use the NEAS scores in the selection process for scholarship awards. NEAS testing is open to students in grades 9 through 12, who are interested in an engineering career.

1563.
Junior League of Northern Virginia Scholarships
7921 Jones Branch Drive, #320
McLean, VA 22102
(703) 893-0258

8 to 10 awards ranging from $500 to $2,000 to female undergraduate or graduate students who have been accepted to or enrolled in an accredited institution. Open to all fields of study. Must be over twenty-three years of age, residents of northern Virginia, U.S. citizens, and have financial need. Deadline: December 1.

1564.
**Juvenile Diabetes Foundation International
Summer Student Program**
432 Park Avenue South
New York, NY 10016
(212) 889-7575

$1,250 stipend to undergraduate, graduate, or medical school students for an eight-week summer research internship to do research work in diabetes. Based on career interest. Deadline: varies.

1565.
Kahlil Gibran Educational Fund Scholarships
Kahlil Gibran Educational Fund, Inc.
Four Longfellow Place, Suite 3802
Boston, MA 02114
(617) 523-4455

Scholarships ranging from $500 to $2,000 to high school seniors. Must be of Lebanese ancestry. Based on financial need. Deadline: June 1.

1566.
**Kansas Department of Education
Kansas Robert C. Byrd Scholarship Program**
120 S.E. 10th Avenue
Topeka, KS 66612-1182
(785) 296-3517
http://www.ksbe.state.us/
tlowe@smtpgw.ksbe.state.ks.us

Varying numbers of scholarships of up to $1,500 to graduating high school seniors for use the first year of study in a college or university within the state. Selection based on academic achievement. Must be Kansas residents. Administered by each state's educating agency. Obtain information from state agency or high school counselor.

1567.
Kansas Department of Education (Scholarships)
120 S.E. 10th Avenue
Topeka, KS 66612-1182
(785) 296-3517
http://www.ksbe.state.us/
tlowe@smtpgw.ksbe.state.ks.us

Grants of up to $1,000 per year to high school seniors or undergraduate students attending Kansas public two- or four-year colleges or universities, public area vocational-technical schools, or eligible independent colleges. Based on financial need. Deadline: May 1.

1568.
**Kansas Department of Education
Vocational Education Scholarship**
Director of Student Financial Aid
120 S.E. 10th Avenue
Topeka, KS 66612-1182
(785) 296-3517
http://www.ksbe.state.us/
tlowe@smtpgw.ksbe.state.ks.us

100 awards ranging from $390 to $500 to first- and second-year vocational/technical students. Must register to take the vocational education exam given twice a year; selection is based on test score.

1569.
**Kansas State Program of Benefits for Dependents
of POWs and MIAs**
Director, Kansas Commission on Veterans' Affairs
Jayhawk Towers, Suite 701
700 S.W. Jackson Street
Topeka, KS 66603

Waiver of tuition and fees for up to six years to high school seniors and undergraduate students who are dependents of Armed Forces personnel who have been listed as prisoner of war (POW) or missing in action (MIA). May attend any state-supported college, university, community junior college, or vocational school. Deadline: none.

1570.
**Kappa Kappa Gamma
Undergraduate/Graduate Rehabilitation
Scholarships**
530 East Town Street
Columbus, OH 43216
(614) 228-6515

Approximately 20 scholarships of $1,000 to female undergraduate juniors or seniors or graduate or doctoral students. Must be majoring in rehabilitation or related fields: occupational, speech, or hearing therapy, or mental health therapy. Undergraduates must have completed first two years of study at an institution with a KKG chapter and must plan on completing a master's or doctoral degree in rehabilitation. Graduate students must be conducting their work on a campus with a KKG chapter. Deadline: February 15.

1571.
**Kappa Kappa Gamma
Undergraduate Rehabilitation Scholarships**
530 East Town Street
Columbus, OH 43216
(614) 228-6515

Various scholarships or $750 to female junior or senior undergraduate students. Must be majoring in rehabilitation, special education, or social work. Undergraduates must have completed at least two years of study at an institution with a KKG chapter. Deadline: February 15.

1572.
Kathleen S. Anderson Award
P.O. Box 1770
Manomet, MA 02345

1 or 2 research awards of $1,000 to undergraduate and graduate students majoring in animal science, biology, or veterinary science. Awards are made to assist research projects involving the ecological and behavioral activities of birds. Preference is given to projects relevant to bird conservation. Selection is based on application, essay, and recommendations. Must submit two copies of proposal with budget and references. Award is not renewable. Deadline: December 1.

1573.
Kathryn M. Whitten Trust
Farmers & Merchants Company of Long Beach
302 Pine Avenue
Long Beach, CA 90802
(562) 437-0011

25 scholarships of varying amounts, totaling $20,000, to high school seniors. Must be residents of Long Beach, California. Based on academic record and financial need. Deadline: varies.

1574.
Kawabe Memorial Fund
c/o SeaFirst Bank Trust Department
701 5th Avenue, FL 56
Seattle, WA 98124
(206) 358-7800

2 scholarships of $2,000 to high school seniors. Must be residents of Alaska. Based on academic record and financial need.

1575.
**Kennedy Center Alliance for Art Education
    Network**
JFK Center for Performing Arts
Internship Program Manager
Washington, DC 20566
(202) 416-8845

20 twelve- to sixteen-week internships (summer, fall, winter/spring) providing $500 per month to undergraduates, recent graduates, graduate students, and teachers of the arts. Internships are open to students from all majors. Positions are available in Advertising, Alliance for Arts Education, Kennedy Center American College Theater Festival, Community Outreach, Cultural Diversity Affairs, Development, Education Administration, Events for Teachers, Government Liaison, Marketing, National Symphony Orchestra, Performance Plus, Press Office, Programming, Public Relations, Special Events, Subscriptions, and Theater for Young People. Internships in the American College Theater Festival and the Press Office offer the unique ability to meet big-name festival judges (such as casting directors from Paramount Studios and head of daytime casting for ABC). Deadline: March 1; June 1; November 1.

1576.
**Kentucky Center for Veterans Affairs
Benefits for Veterans & Their Dependents**
545 South 3rd Street, Room 123
Louisville, KY 40202
(501) 595-4447

Financial assistance of varying amounts to high school seniors or undergraduate students. Must be dependent children, spouses, or non-remarried widows of permanently and 100 percent disabled war veterans who served during periods of federally recognized hostilities, or who were MIAs or POWs. Veteran must be Kentucky residents or, if deceased, must have been residents at the time of death. May be used for all areas of study. Deadline: none.

1577.
**Kentucky Council on Postsecondary Education
Grants**
1024 Capitol Center Drive, Suite 320
Frankfort, KY 40601
(502) 573-1554
http://www.kheaa.state.ky.us
linda.robinson@mail.state.ky.us

Grants from $200 to $1,700 per year to undergraduate full-time students in an approved college, university, hospital school of nursing, or vocational or business school in Kentucky. Must be U.S. citizens or permanent residents and Kentucky residents; must not have a bachelor's degree; must have financial need. Must apply for a Pell Grant. Deadline: April 1.

1578.
**Kentucky Council on Postsecondary Education
Robert C. Byrd Scholarships**
1024 Capitol Center Drive, Suite 320
Frankfort, KY 40601
(502) 573-1554
http://www.kheaa.state.ky.us
linda.robinson@mail.state.ky.us

Varying numbers of scholarships of up to $1,500 to graduating high school seniors for use the first year of study in a college or university within the state. Selection based on academic achievement. Must be Kentucky residents. Administered by each state's educating agency. Obtain information from state agency or high school counselor.

1579.
**Kentucky Department of Agriculture
Kentucky Rural Rehabilitation Fund Student
    Loan Program**
KRRF Student Loan Officer
Capital Plaza Tower
Frankfort, KY 40601
(502) 564-7135

Student loans of up to $2,625 for the first two years of undergraduate study; $4,000 for the last two years of undergraduate study; and $7,500 for graduate study to students who are farmers or farm laborers or to members of their families. Applicants must be residents of Kentucky, be at least half-time students, maintain at least a C average, and have financial need. Must apply for a Pell Grant.

1580.
Kentucky Society of Professional Engineers
Attn: Mr. George M. Binder
160 Democrat Drive
Frankfort, KY 40601
(502) 695-5680
(502) 695-0738 Fax

Scholarships of varying amounts to graduating high school seniors interested in an engineering career. Must be Kentucky residents. Applicants are encouraged to apply early so there will be enough time to allow for an interview. Other restrictions may apply. Deadline: generally, early December.

1581.
Kentucky Vocational Rehabilitation Services
Program Administrator
Division of Field Services
Capital Plaza Tower, Ninth Floor
Frankfort, KY 40601
(800) 372-7172

Scholarships of varying amounts (based on individual's needs) are available to students with a disability that is a handicap for employment. Must be a resident of Kentucky. Deadline: none.

1582.
King's Daughters of Wisconsin Foundation
Scholarship Committee
4010 West Spencer
Appleton, WI 54914
(414) 739-6311

9 scholarships ranging from $500 to $11,500 to high school seniors. Must be residents of Appleton, Kaunauna, Lake Mills, Menasha, Neenah, Sheboygan, or Sheboygan Falls, Wisconsin; for study at a Wisconsin college or university. Based on academic record and financial need. Deadline: March 1.

1583.
Kittie Fairey Educational Fund
c/o Wachouia Bank
1401 Main Street
Columbia, SC 29226
(803) 771-3945

20 scholarships of varying amounts totaling $60,360 to graduating high school seniors. Must be South Carolina residents who are planning on attending South Carolina colleges or universities. Write an introductory letter briefly describing educational and financial situation. Other restrictions may apply.

1584.
Knights of Columbus Canadian Scholarships
Director of Scholarship Aid
P.O. Drawer 1670
New Haven, CT 06507

Numerous scholarships of $1,000 (renewable for four years) to Canadian members in good standing or their children. If member is deceased, he or she must have been in good standing at time of death. Applicants must be entering freshmen and scholarship must be used at a Canadian university. Deadline: May 1.

1585.
Knights of Columbus Pro Dea Et Pro Patria Scholarships
Director of Scholarship Aid
Knights of Columbus
P.O. Drawer 1670
New Haven, CT 06507

12 awards of $1,000 to members in good standing, their children, or children of deceased members (who were in good standing at time of death). Renewable. May be used at a Catholic college of the student's choice. A similar scholarship is available to a member of the Columbian Squires. Deadline: March 1.

1586.
Knights of Columbus Student Loan Committee
Knights of Columbus
P.O. Drawer 1670
New Haven, CT 06507

Numerous loans to cover a full academic year are available to students who are wives, widows, sons, or daughters of members in good standing. Must be at least a part-time student. Deadline: none.

1587.
Knights Templar Educational Foundation Special Low-Interest Loans
Attn: Grand Recorder-Secretary
5097 N. Elston Avenue, #101
Chicago, IL 60630
(312) 777-3300

Loans of up to $6,000 to vocational/technical students, undergraduate juniors, seniors, and graduate students. Interest rate is 5 percent and must be repaid within four years after graduation. Open to all areas of study. Write to the individual Grand Recorder of your state. If the state address is not known, it may be obtained from above address. Must be U.S. citizens or legal residents. Deadline: none specified.

1588.
Kohler Foundation, Inc.
Attn: Executive Director
104 Orchard Road
Kohler, WI 53044
(414) 458-1972

Numerous scholarships of varying amounts to high school seniors from Sheboygan, Wisconsin, high schools. Must be nominated by high school's administrator. Deadline: April 15.

1589.
The Kosciuszko Foundation Chopin Piano Competition
15 East 65th Street
New York, NY 10021

1 award of $2,500, 1 award of $1,500, and 1 award of $1,000 to students. Must be between the ages of sixteen and

twenty-two as of the opening date of the competition. Based on national competition. Write for further details. Deadline: April 30.

1590.
Kosciuszko Foundation Music Scholarships
Music Competitions
15 East 65th Street
New York, NY 10021

Scholarships ranging from $1,000 to $2,500 to undergraduate (2) and graduate (remaining) students. 2 scholarships for piano and for piano and violin are open to talented youth who have not yet reached advanced levels in college. Must be prepared to perform in auditions at the Kosciuszko Foundation House in New York City in May or June. Deadline: March 31.

1591.
Kraft General Foods Corporate University Relations
Three Lakes Drive
Northfield, IL 60093
(708) 646-2000
http://www.kraftfoods.com/careers/college/intern.html

100 to 150 twelve-week summer internships providing salaries ranging from $400 to $600 per week to undergraduates and from $800 to $900 per week for graduate students with possible majors in engineering (chemical, mechanical, industrial, electrical, etc.), information systems, food science, biology, chemistry, microbiology, biochemistry, and liberal arts (for business areas). Internships are conducted in Glenview, IL; Northfield, IL; White Plains, NY; and Tarrytown, NY. Interns at Kraft USA may work in beverages, desserts, dinners and enhancers, Post cereals, and Maxwell House Coffee; at Kraft General Foods USA, where they may conduct research in any KGF product; and at corporate headquarters, as well as all other locations, in corporate affairs, sales, finance, and human resources. Deadline: March 31.

1592.
Ladies Auxiliary of the Fleet Reserve Association Program I, I, III
National Executive Secretary
Fleet Reserve Association
125 Northwest Street
Alexandria, VA 22314
(703) 683-1400
http://www.fra.org/fra

$500 scholarships in each category: 1) children of members (in good standing as of April 1 of award year) of the Fleet Reserve Association. Members may be active duty, retired with pay, or deceased (while on active duty or retired with pay) of the U.S. Navy, Marine Corps, or Coast Guard personnel; 2) children of FRA members and service members of the U.S. Navy, Marine Corps, or Coast Guard, as in group 1; or 3) children of deceased FRA members. Preference is given to group 3. Deadline: April 15.

1593.
Ladies of Northants Scholarships
P.O. Box 6609
Coddingtown, CA 95406
Written inquiries only

Scholarships of $250 to female undergraduate or graduate students pursuing careers in nuclear engineering. Must be over age forty. Applicants must have immigrated to the United States from Northamptonshire, England, with preference given to individuals of the village of Podington. Must have at least a 3.75 GPA on a 4.0 scale and demonstrate financial need. Send a self-addressed, stamped envelope for more information. Deadline: early February.

1594.
Lake City Writers' Forum Annual Contest
c/o Lynda Rivers
Lake City Writers' Forum
Lake City, CO 81235

An award of $50 and publication in *Timberlines* for unpublished fiction and poetry. Honorable mentions are also published. Promotes good writing, especially among new writers. Send a self-addressed, stamped #10 envelope for rules and entry forms. Entry fee of $6 per submission. Deadline: October 1.

1595.
Lalitta Nash McKaig Foundation
Attn: Vice-President
c/o Pittsburgh National Bank-PNC
1 Oliver Plaza, 28th Floor
Pittsburgh, PA 15265
(412) 762-2000

283 scholarships ranging from $50 to $3,000 to graduating high school seniors. Must be residents of Bedford or Somerset counties, Pennsylvania; Mineral or Hamshir counties, West Virginia; or Allegheny or Garrett counties, Maryland. Based on academic record and financial need. Deadline: May 1.

1596.
Lamont–Doherty Earth Observatory Summer Internship Program for Undergraduates
Palisades, NY 10964
(212) 365-8482
dallas@ideo.columbia.edu

10 ten-week summer internships providing $200 per week, free housing, daily transportation to LDEO, and round-trip travel reimbursement if more than 200 miles away to undergraduate juniors and seniors who are studying oceanography, geology, physics, chemistry, math, biology, engineering, or environmental-related areas. Interns are supervised by scientists in a wide variety of subject areas: marine geochemistry, marine geophysics, micropaleontology, petrology, and seismology. Internships are conducted at LDEO in New York, New York. Deadline: March 10.

1597.
Land Improvement Foundation for Education Life Scholarship Program
Ms. Mary Ellen Bushnell
1300 Maybrook Drive
P.O. Box 9
Maywood, IL 60153

Up to 3 scholarships of $1,000 to undergraduate or graduate students pursuing careers in natural resources and/or conservation construction. Based on a short essay (300 words or less) and recommendations. Other restrictions may apply. Deadline: March 15.

1598.
**Landscape Architecture Foundation
The Coxe Group Scholarship**
American Society of Landscape Architecture
636 Eye Street, N.W.
Washington, DC 20001
(202) 898-2444
(202) 898-1185 Fax
http://www.asla.org/

1 scholarship of $1,000 to an undergraduate or graduate student who is in his or her fourth, fifth, or sixth year in a landscape architectural degree program. Selection based on ability and financial need. Send a self-addressed, stamped envelope for information. Deadline: May 4.

1599.
**Landscape Architecture Foundation
Edith H. Henderson Scholarship**
American Society of Landscape Architecture
636 Eye Street, N.W.
Washington, DC 20001
(202) 898-2444
(202) 898-1185 Fax
http://www.asla.org/

1 scholarship of $1,000 to an undergraduate or graduate student who is in his or her beginning or final year of undergraduate study or any graduate year of study in a landscape architectural degree program. Selection based on ability and financial need. Send a self-addressed, stamped envelope for information. Deadline: May 4.

1600.
**Landscape Architecture Foundation
Grace & Robert Fraser Landscape Award**
American Society of Landscape Architecture
636 Eye Street, N.W.
Washington, DC 20001
(202) 898-2444
(202) 898-1185 Fax
http://www.asla.org/

1 award of $500 to an undergraduate or graduate student to recognize innovative horticultural research or design relating to landscape architecture. Selection based on ability and financial need. Send a self-addressed, stamped envelope for information. Deadline: May 4.

1601.
**Landscape Architecture Foundation
Harriett Barnhart Wimmer Scholarship**
American Society of Landscape Architecture
636 Eye Street, N.W.
Washington, DC 20001-3736
(202) 898-2444
(202) 898-1185 Fax
http://www.asla.org/

1 scholarship of $500 to a female student in her final undergraduate year at a U.S. or Canadian institution. Based on academics, design ability, sensitivity to the environment, and quality of life. Deadline: April 15-May 15.

1602.
**Landscape Architecture Foundation
LANDCADD Inc. Scholarship Fund**
American Society of Landscape Architecture
636 Eye Street, N.W.
Washington, DC 20001
(202) 898-2444
(202) 898-1185 Fax
http://www.asla.org/

Scholarships of $500 to undergraduate and graduate students majoring in landscape architecture and who wish to use computer-aided design, video imaging, and/or telecommunications in their career. Selection based on ability and financial need. Send a self-addressed, stamped envelope for information. Deadline: May 4.

1603.
**Landscape Architecture Foundation
Lester Walls III Endowment Scholarship**
American Society of Landscape Architecture
636 Eye Street, N.W.
Washington, DC 20001
(202) 898-2444/(202) 898-1185 Fax
http://www.asla.org/

1 scholarship of $500 to a disabled undergraduate or graduate student pursuing a career in landscape architecture or for research on barrier-free design for the disabled. Send a self-addressed, stamped envelope for information. Deadline: May 4.

1604.
**Landscape Architecture Foundation
Raymond E. Page Scholarship Fund**
American Society of Landscape Architecture
636 Eye Street, N.W.
Washington, DC 20001
(202) 898-2444
(202) 898-1185 Fax
http://www.asla.org/

Scholarships of $700 to undergraduate or graduate students who have financial need, regardless of academics. Must submit a two-page explanation describing financial need and how money will be used. Three letters of recommendation from previous or current professors or employers are required. Deadline: April 15-May 15.

1605.
Landscape Architecture Foundation
Student Research Grants
American Society of Landscape Architecture
636 Eye Street, N.W.
Washington, DC 20001
(202) 898-2444
(202) 898-1185 Fax
http://www.asla.org/

Grants of $1,000 to undergraduate and graduate students, to encourage practical educational research that will benefit the profession and the general public. Also allows students to expand their field of interest and propose creative, innovative projects. Deadline: April 15–May 15.

1606.
Landscape Architecture Foundation
William Locklin Scholarship
American Society of Landscape Architecture
636 Eye Street, N.W.
Washington, DC 20001
(202) 898-2444
(202) 898-1185 Fax
http://www.asla.org/

1 scholarship of $500 to undergraduate and graduate students in landscape architectural degree with emphasis in lighting design. Purpose is to stress the importance of twenty-four-hour lighting in landscape design. Send a self-addressed, stamped envelope for information. Deadline: May 4.

1607.
Late Show with David Letterman
Internship Coordinator
1697 Broadway
New York, NY 10019
(212) 975-5300

10 ten-week summer, fall, and spring internships to undergraduate and graduate students who will receive academic credit for the internship. There is no compensation for this internship. Open to all majors. Interns are placed in talent, research, production, writing, music, producer's office, and as David Letterman's assistant.

1608.
Laurel & Hardy Sons of the Desert Scholarship
  Fund
Attn: Trust Administrator
c/o Wells Fargo Bank
P.O. Box X-1013
San Diego, CA 92112
(619) 622-6958

Scholarships of up to $1,500 to full-time students who are attending an accredited two- or four-year institution in San Diego County. Preference given to students who excel in comedy and/or pantomime. Deadline: none.

1609.
League of United Latin American Citizens
  (LULAC) National Scholarship Fund
National Education Service Center
1133 20th Street, N.W., Suite 750
Washington DC 20036
(202) 408-0060

Numerous scholarships of varying amounts to Hispanic high school seniors or to those who graduated within one year of application. Selection handled by local LULAC councils. Contact above address for address of the nearest council; send a self-addressed, stamped envelope to the above address. Deadline: varies according to each LULAC council.

1610.
Leidy–Rhodes Foundation Trust Scholarships
Boyertown Area School District
Attn: Anne McCaffrey
Education Center
911 Montgomery Avenue
Boyertown, PA 19512
(610) 367-6031

52 scholarships ranging from $600 to $900 to graduating high school seniors. Must be residents of Boyertown, Pennsylvania. Based on academic record and financial need. Send a #10 stamped, self-addressed envelope. Deadline: varies.

1611.
LEK Alcar Consulting Group
Internships
12100 Wilshire Boulevard, Suite 1700
Los Angeles, CA 90025
(310) 442-6500
(310) 207-4210 Fax

4 to 6 summer internships of at least eight weeks to undergraduate seniors to work at a management consulting firm specializing in corporate strategy, value-based planning, mergers and acquisitions, and advice to business start-ups. Interns work in all areas in either Los Angeles, CA; Boston, MA; or Chicago, IL. Students receive a week of classes in accounting and finance, and general training in Lotus, WordPerfect, on-line databases, and other office equipment. There isn't any limit on possible majors, but applicants must have at least a 3.4 GPA. There are two other addresses: 5215 Old Orchard Road, Suite 600, Skokie, IL 60077-1035, (708) 581-2200, (708) 581-2201 Fax; and 101 Federal Street, 27th Floor, Boston, MA 02110, (617) 951-9500, (617) 951-9392 Fax. Deadline: late February or early March.

1612.
Levi Strauss & Co.
College Intern Program
P.O. Box 7215
San Francisco, CA 94120-6914
(415) 544-7000

30 summer internships providing a salary ranging from $320 to $600 per week for undergraduate juniors and seniors, and from $400 to $600 to graduate students. Internships last from eight to twelve weeks, with part-time work available, and are held in San Francisco, California.

Students can be assigned to merchandising, treasury (accounting), operations, design, telemarketing, claims administration, retail marketing, retail relations, consumer affairs, LeviLink (Information Resource), and fabric purchasing. There is also a Summer Youth Program for high school students, where students learn office procedures and improve their clerical skills. Internship applicants must have at least a 2.5 GPA. Information is sent to colleges after January 1. Deadline: varies.

1613.
Liederkranz Foundation Awards for Piano
Music Director
6 East 87th Street
New York, NY 10128
(212) 534-0880

Awards ranging from $1,000 to $3,500 in cash, tuition payment, or a combination; may be used anywhere. Pianists must be between twenty and thirty years of age, with proven training and experience. Deadline: December 1; may vary.

1614.
Liederkranz Foundation Awards for Voice
Music Director
6 East 87th Street
New York, NY 10128
(212) 534-0880

Awards ranging from $1,000 to $3,500 in cash, tuition payment, or a combination; may be used anywhere. Singers must be between twenty and thirty-five years of age, with proven vocal training and experience. Deadline: December 1; may vary.

1615.
Lilly Endowment, Inc.
P.O. Box 88068
Indianapolis, IN 46208-0068
(317) 924-5471

Numerous awards of varying amounts for graduating high school seniors and undergraduate students. Must be Indiana residents and full-time students. Based on financial need. Deadline: March 1.

1616.
Lincoln–Lane Foundation
112 Granby Street, Suite 300
Norfolk, VA 23510
(757) 622-2557

127 scholarship grants ranging from $500 to $2,500 to college students living in and around Norfolk or Virginia Beach, Virginia, area. Provides college scholarships to students who are permanent residents of the Tidewater, Virginia, area. Request applications after October 1. Deadline: October 31.

1617.
Linguistic Society of America
Summer Fellowships at the Linguistic Institute
1325 18th Street, N.W., Suite 211
Washington, DC 20036
(202) 835-1714

125 fellowships of varying amounts to undergraduate and graduate students to attend the Linguistic Society of America Institute, which is held during the summer of odd-numbered years. Must be majoring in linguistics. Deadline: February 11 of odd-numbered years.

1618.
Liz Claiborne
Internship Coordinator
1441 Broadway
New York, NY 10018
(212) 354-4900

20 to 25 internships providing $7 per hour to undergraduates interested in apparel and fashion accessories. Internships last from three to six months and are conducted during the summer, fall, and winter/spring in New York, New York, and North Bergen, New Jersey. Some part-time work is available. Internships are in creative resources, marketing, textile design, apparel design, merchandising, and sales groups. Deadline: May 15 (summer); July 31 (fall); November 15 (winter/spring).

1619.
Lloyd D. Sweet Scholarship Foundation
Scholarships
Box 217
Chinook, MT 59523
(406) 357-3374

Approximately 100 scholarships of varying amounts to undergraduate or graduate students. Must be graduates of Chinook High School in Chinook, Montana. May be used at any U.S. accredited institution for any field of study. Selection based on academic achievement and financial need. Deadline: March 2.

1620.
Loren L. Zachary Society for the Performing Arts
Annual Opera Awards National Vocal
  Competition
2250 Gloaming Way
Beverly Hills, CA 90210
(213) 276-2731

10 awards of up to $20,000, plus travel expenses, are awarded in an annual vocal competition open to young (females twenty-one to thirty-three; males twenty-one to thirty-five) opera singers. Request applications after December 1; include a self-addressed, stamped envelope. Deadline: February (New York competition); April-May (Los Angeles competition).

1621.
Los Angeles Times
Editorial Internships
Times Mirror Square
Los Angeles, CA 90053
(800) 283-NEWS ext. 74487

10 to 25 eleven-week summer (full-time) and seventeen-week fall or spring (part-time) internships providing $480 per week (summer) or $6 per hour (fall and spring) open to undergraduates and recent graduates (within six months). Internships are in Los Angeles, Orange County, San Diego, San Fernando Valley, Ventura, San Gabriel Valley, South Bay, Southeast, and Westside, California, and Washington, D.C. Finalists are interviewed in person or by phone. Deadline: December 1 (summer); June 1 (fall); October 1 (spring).

1622.
Louisiana Department of Veterans Affairs
P.O. Box 94095 Capitol Station
Baton Rouge, LA 70804-9095
(504) 342-5863

Numerous free tuition scholarships, plus an allowance, are available to children (ages sixteen to twenty-five) or widows of deceased veterans or 100 percent disabled veterans. Deceased veterans must have been Louisiana resident for at least one year before entering the service. Living, disabled veterans must be Louisiana resident for at least two years before student enters a college or university. Students must be attending a state-supported school; must apply at least six weeks before school begins. Deadline: none.

1623.
Louisiana Literature Prize for Poetry
Attn: Contest Director
Box 792
Southeastern Louisiana University
Hammond, LA 70402

Contest with varying cash prizes for unpublished poetry. Must deal with some aspect of Louisiana. Send a self-addressed, stamped envelope for rules. Deadline: February 15.

1624.
Louisiana Student Financial Assistance Commission
Honors Scholarships
Department of Education
Attn: Scholarships and Grants
P.O. Box 94064
Baton Rouge, LA 70804-9064
(504) 342-4411
http://www.doe.state.la.us/
webteam@mail.doe.state.la.us

Scholarships of public school tuition costs to graduating high school seniors or undergraduate students. Must have been in the upper 5 percent of their class, be residents of Louisiana for at least one year prior to application, and plan to attend a Louisiana institution. Renewable with full-time status and at least a 3.0 GPA on a 4.0 scale. Deadline: varies.

1625.
Louisiana Student Financial Assistance Commission
Robert C. Byrd Scholarship
Department of Education
Attn: Scholarships and Grants
P.O. Box 94064
Baton Rouge, LA 70804-9064
(504) 342-2098
http://www.doe.state.la.us/
webteam@mail.doe.state.la.us

Varying numbers of scholarships of up to $1,500 to graduating high school seniors for use the first year of study in a college or university within the state. Selection based on academic achievement. Must be Louisiana residents. Administered by each state's educating agency. Obtain information from state agency or high school counselor.

1626.
Louisiana Student Financial Assistance Commission
Rockefeller Wildlife Scholarship
Department of Education
P.O. Box 94064
Baton Rouge, LA 70804-9064
(504) 342-4411
http://www.doe.state.la.us/
webteam@mail.doe.state.la.us

1 scholarship of $1,000 to a Louisiana undergraduate or graduate student. Must be majoring in forestry, wildlife, fisheries, or marine sciences at Nicholls University, Louisiana Tech, LSU in Baton Rouge, McNeese University, Northeast University, Northwestern University, Southwestern, or University of New Orleans. Must have at least a B average. Based on academic record, extracurricular activities, and Louisiana residency. Must maintain a 2.5 GPA in major courses. If student fails to complete the course work, the scholarship reverts to a loan and must be repaid. Deadline: May 1.

1627.
Louisiana Student Financial Assistance Commission
State Student Incentive Grants (SSIG)
Department of Education
P.O. Box 94064
Baton Rouge, LA 70804-9064
(504) 342-4411
http://www.doe.state.la.us/
webteam@mail.doe.state.la.us

2,000 grants ranging from $200 to $2,000 to undergraduate students. Eligibility determined by individual colleges and universities. Renewable. Based on financial need. Deadline: May 1.

1628.
**Louisiana Student Financial Assistance
    Commission
Tuition Assistance Plan (TAP)**
Department of Education
P.O. Box 94064
Baton Rouge, LA 70804-9064
(504) 342-4411
http://www.doe.state.la.us/
webteam@mail.doe.state.la.us

Full-tuition scholarships to high school seniors or
undergraduate students. Must have lived in Louisiana for
twenty-four months before enrolling in an institution and
have a parent or guardian who is a Louisiana resident.
Must have a 2.5 GPA. Based on academic criteria and
financial need. Must be U.S. citizens. Deadline: April 1.

1629.
Louisiana Vocational Rehabilitation
Attn: Executive Director
Division of Rehabilitation Services
P.O. Box 94381
Baton Rouge, LA 70804

Scholarships of varying amounts (based on individual's
needs) to undergraduate students with a mental or physical
disability that is a handicap for employment. Must be
residents of Louisiana. Deadline: none.

1630.
**Luby's Cafeterias
Rising Star Scholarship Awards**
Attn: Scholarships
P.O. Box 33069
San Antonio, TX 78265
(210) 654-9000

10 scholarships of $1,000 to high school seniors attending
public or private high schools in Bexar County, Texas.
Based on academic achievement, extracurricular activities,
volunteerism, and career goals. Obtain applications from
high school counselors. Applicants must plan to attend a
two- or four-year college or university as full-time students
in the fall. Deadline: mid-February.

1631.
LucasFilm
Human Resources–Intern Department
P.O. Box 2009
San Rafael, CA 94912
(415) 662-1999

15 to 20 internships ranging from nine to twelve weeks
during the summer, fall, and spring to undergraduate
juniors, seniors, and graduate students who will be
returning to school after the internship ends. Open to all
majors. Compensation of minimum wage is available only
during the summer internships. Program looks for students
with professionalism and maturity. Applicants for the fall
and spring internships must obtain a letter from their
college verifying they will receive academic credit for the
internship. Deadline: March 30 (summer); July 30 (fall);
November 15 (spring).

1632.
**Lupus Foundation of America
Gina Finzi Memorial Student Summer
    Fellowships for Research**
4 Research Place, Suite 180
Rockville, MD 20850
(310) 670-9292
(310) 670-9486 Fax
http://internet-plaza.net/lupus

Varying numbers of fellowships of up to $2,000 to
undergraduate, graduate, or medical students to conduct a
summer research project on lupus erythematosus. Project
must be sponsored and supervised by an established
investigator. Applicants must submit an application form, a
five-page narrative of the research project, a proposed
budget, a lay-language abstract, a biographical sketch,
evidence of compliance with government regulations, a
statement of concurrent support from other sources, and a
statement of support by a sponsor. Deadline: February 1.

1633.
**Lupus Foundation of America
Student Summer Fellowship Program**
4 Research Place, Suite 180
Rockville, MD 20850
(310) 670-9292
(310) 670-9486 Fax
http://internet-plaza.net/lupus

10 awards of $2,000 to undergraduate, graduate, and post-
graduate students to pursue lupus erythematosus research.
Preference given to individuals already having a college
degree. Research may be conducted at any recognized
institution in the U.S. Applications are evaluated NIH-style.
Application materials are available in November. Deadline:
February 1.

1634.
Lutheran Brotherhood Member Scholarships
Financial Aid Coordinator
625 Fourth Avenue South
P.O. Box 857
Minneapolis, MN 55415
(800) 383-7168
(612) 340-8028
http://www.luthbro.com/

Renewable scholarships ranging from $500 to $2,000 to high
school seniors or undergraduate students. Must be Lutheran
Brotherhood members; for undergraduate study only. Based
on academic achievement, SAT/ACT scores, essay, transcripts,
and recommendations. Deadline: February 13.

1635.
**Lutheran Brotherhood Senior College
    Scholarships**
Financial Aid Coordinator
625 Fourth Avenue South
P.O. Box 857
Minneapolis, MN 55415
(800) 383-7168
(612) 340-8028
http://www.luthbro.com/

Renewable scholarships ranging from $800 to $1,500 to
Lutheran high school seniors. Must be planning to attend a

four-year undergraduate Lutheran college. Awards are based on financial need. Contact individual colleges. Deadline: varies by school.

1636.
Lutheran Campus Scholarship Program
Attn: Scholarships
4321 North Ballard Road
Appleton, WI 54919

Scholarships of varying amounts to undergraduate students for use at Lutheran colleges or universities or Bible institutes. Contact participating institutions for further information. Deadline: varies by school.

1637.
Lutheran Church of America
Attn: Administrator
Unified Education Fund
2900 Queen Lane
Philadelphia, PA 19129

Scholarships grants of varying amounts to Native Americans. Must be of the Lutheran faith. There are also grants to students who are preparing to serve or are serving in a leadership position in the Lutheran Church of America. Deadline: March 15.

1638.
Luso–American Education Foundation
General Scholarships
P.O. Box 1768
Oakland, CA 94604
(415) 452-4465

Scholarships of varying amounts to high school seniors or graduates. Must be of Portuguese descent, be planning to take Portuguese language classes, or be a member of an organization whose scholarships are administered by the Luso-American Foundation. Must be California residents under the age of twenty-one who plan to enroll full-time in a four-year program. Must have a 3.0 GPA. Deadline: March 1.

1639.
MacCurdy–Salisbury Educational Foundation, Inc.
9 Monserwood Road
Old Lyme, CT 06371
(203) 434-7983

158 scholarship grants ranging from $240 to $750, totaling $78,000, to students who are residents of Lyme and Old Lyme, Connecticut. Based on academic record and financial need. Deadline: April 30 (first semester); November 15 (second semester).

1640.
MacNeil/Lehrer Productions
Internship Coordinator
Attn: Caitlin Gross
2700 South Quincy Street, Suite 250
Arlington, VA 22206
(703) 998-2170

4 twelve- to sixteen-week internships during summer, fall, or spring with no monetary compensation to

undergraduate juniors, seniors, and recent graduates. Interns assist with production of the show, answer telephones, run errands, conduct research, and assist producers and production assistants. Open to all majors; students must have knowledge of domestic and foreign policy issues. Internships last up to one semester. Applicants should have a working knowledge of domestic and foreign issues. Deadline: July 31 (fall); October 31 (spring); March 31 (summer).

1641.
Madison Scholarship Committee
Attn: Applications Chairperson
4 Vinton Road
Madison, NJ 07940

33 scholarship grants ranging from $300 to $500, totaling $18,500, to graduates of Madison, New Jersey, high schools. Based on academic record and financial need. Deadline: February 15.

1642.
Maine Bureau of Veterans Services
Veterans Benefits
117 State House Station
Augusta, ME 04333
(207) 626-4464

Numerous scholarship grants of up to $300 to students who are children, wives, or widows of a 100 percent disabled or deceased serviceman. Serviceman or veteran must have been a resident of Maine at the time of entry into the service or the dependent must have been a Maine resident for at least five years prior to applying. Children must be high school graduates, between sixteen and twenty-one years when they entered college. Students attending a state-supported institution, any University of Maine, vocational/technical schools, or the Maine Maritime Academy at Castine can receive full tuition.

1643.
Maine Bureau of Veterans Services
Veterans Benefits/G.I. Bill
117 State House Station
Augusta, ME 04333
(800) 827-1000/(800) 829-4833 TDD
(207) 623-8000

Scholarships of free tuition to students attending state-supported institutions in Maine or up to $300 per year for four years to students attending public or private institutions in or out of Maine. Students must be veterans.

1644.
Maine Division of Educational Services
Robert C. Byrd Scholarships
25 State House
Augusta, ME 04333
(207) 289-2183
(800) 228-3734 (in-state)
http://www.state.me.us/education

Varying numbers of scholarships of up to $1,500 to graduating high school seniors for use the first year of study in a college or university within the state. Selection based on academic achievement. Must be Maine residents.

Administered by each state's educating agency. Obtain information from state agency or high school counselor. Renewable with satisfactory academic progress. Deadline: April 15.

1645.
Maine Division of Educational Services Student Incentive Scholarship Program
Director, Higher Education Services
25 State House Station
Augusta, ME 04333
(207) 623-3263
800 228-3734 (in-state)
http://www.state.me.us/education

3,000 scholarships ranging from $500 to $1,000 to Maine high school graduates. Must be full-time students enrolled in a public or private institution in Maine or New England. Selection based on financial need. Must submit FAFSA. Deadline: April 15.

1646.
Maine Division of Educational Services Teachers for Maine Program
25 State House
Augusta, ME 04333
(207) 289-2183
(800) 228-3734 (in-state)
http://www.state.me.us/education

Scholarship/loans of up to $3,000 to graduating high school seniors, high school graduates, and undergraduates, and up to $1,500 for graduate students. Must have graduated from a Maine high school, be in the top 25 percent of class, with at least a 3.0 GPA on a 4.0 scale, and plan to be full-time students enrolled in a public or private institution in Maine or New England. Full-time undergraduate students must have at least a 3.0 GPA on a 4.0 scale and be attending an accredited institution. Graduate students must have a bachelor's degree, have at least a 3.0 GPA on a 4.0 scale, and plan to teach upon completion of degree. Selection based on academic achievement or financial need. Loans are forgiven by teaching in Maine upon graduating. Renewable with satisfactory academic progress. Deadline: May 1.

1647.
(Maine) Finance Authority of Maine (FAME) National Service Scholarship Program
83 Western Avenue
P.O. Box 949
Augusta, ME 04332-0949
(207) 623-3263
(207) 623-0095 Fax
(207) 626-2717 TDD
http://www.famemaine.com/
info@famemaine.com

Scholarships of at least $1,000 to juniors and seniors in public or private high schools. Selection is based on outstanding service or service-learning within their community for at least a year. Must demonstrate sustained commitment of at least 100 hours of service in a year. Deadline: April 10.

1648.
Maine Vocational–Technical Institutes Scholarship Program
Maine VTIS Office
323 State Street
Augusta, ME 04330

Scholarships of up to one semester of tuition in any one year to students who are enrolled in a vocational or technical school in Maine. Must be Maine residents. Based on financial need. Deadline: varies.

1649.
Makarios Scholarship Fund, Inc. Scholarships
13 East 40th Street
New York, NY 10016
(212) 696-4590

Scholarships of approximately $1,000 to graduating high school seniors, high school graduates who haven't attended college, and undergraduate or graduate students. May be used for any field of full-time study at an accredited U.S. institution. Applicants must be residents of Cyprus with a student visa and have financial need. Other restrictions may apply. Deadline: May 31.

1650.
Maple Creek Willie Indian Scholarship Fund for California Indian Students
Maple Creek Willie Scholarship Selection Board
Department of Education
721 Capitol Mall
Sacramento, CA 95814

Scholarships of up to $1,250 to high school seniors or graduates. Must be Native Americans and California residents. Must have at least one-quarter degree Indian blood of an Indian tribe in the U.S. May be used at a public or private two- or four-year college, university, or vocational school. Based on financial need. Deadline: July 1.

1651.
Marcus and Theresa Levie Educational Fund
One South Franklin Street
Chicago, IL 60606

50 scholarships of varying amounts, totaling $104,000, to high school seniors, undergraduates, or graduate students. Must be of the Jewish faith and residents of Cook County, Illinois. Must be preparing for a helping profession. Deadline: varies.

1652.
Margaret and Irvin Lesher Foundation Scholarships
Lesher Foundation
National Transit Building, Room 27-C
P.O. Box 374
Oil City, PA 16301
(814) 677-5085

80 scholarships of $1,500 per year for four years, or $2,000 per year for two years, to students who are graduates of Union Joint School District high schools. Based on financial

need. Must have a minimum of 25 GPA for renewal. Deadline: April 15.

1653.
Marie–Louise D'Esternaux Student Poetry Contest
Contest Chairperson
The Brooklyn Poetry Circle
2550 Independence Avenue, #3V
Bronx, NY 10463

Contest with prizes of varying amounts for poetry written by students between sixteen and twenty-one years of age. Contact above address for rules; send a self-addressed, stamped envelope. Deadline: April 15.

1654.
Marina Maher Communications
Internship Coordinator
400 Park Avenue, 4th Floor
New York, NY 10022
(212) 759-7543
(212) 355-6318 Fax

6 to 8 internships providing a salary ranging from $200 to $320 per week to graduating high school seniors, high school graduates, undergraduates, college graduates, and graduate students interested in public relations. International students may apply. MMC generates publicity for clients and develops special events, promotional videos, trade campaigns, consumer brochures, and point-of-sale materials. Interns work in accounting and account management. Submit a résumé, a cover letter, optional writing samples, and a transcript. Deadline: May 1 (summer); August 1 (fall); December 1 (spring).

1655.
Marine Corps Historical Center
College Internships
Building 58
Washington Navy Yard
Washington, DC 20374-0580

Summer internships providing small grants for daily expenses are available to undergraduate students majoring in history, political science, data processing, art, music, museology, or American studies. Interns perform as beginning professional-level reference and research historians, curators' assistants, and work catalogers. The student's academic institution must agree to grant credit for the internship.

1656.
Marine Corps Scholarship Foundation
James Forrestal Campus
P.O. Box 3008
Princeton, NJ 08540-3008
(609) 921-3534

Approximately 300 undergraduate scholarships ranging from $500 to $2,500 to high school seniors who are sons and daughters of current, former, or reservist Marines. Family income must not exceed $35,000 per year. Based on financial need, transcript, SAT/ACT scores, and essay. Request applications in the fall. Deadline: February 1.

1657.
Marin Educational Foundation
Marin Educational Grants
1010 B Street, Suite 300
San Rafael, CA 94901
(415) 459-4240

Grants ranging from $200 to $2,700 to high school seniors or graduates. Dependent students must be Marin County high school graduates or residents of Marin County, California, since September 1 of the application year. Independent students must be residents of Marin County for an additional two years. All applicants must be U.S. citizens or of permanent resident alien or asylum status, and male students must have registered with the Selective Service System. Must be enrolled or planning to enroll in a two- or four-year institution or a vocational/technical school anywhere in the U.S. Based on financial need. Deadline: March 2.

1658.
Marin Educational Foundation
Marin Outstanding Student Achievement Awards
1010 B Street, Suite 300
San Rafael, CA 94901
(415) 459-4240

Several $1,000 or $5,000 scholarships for Marin County high school seniors. Must have attended the school for at least two years and be residents of Marin County. Students may be nominated in one of two areas: specific achievement (any academic subject; business, home, and industrial arts; or community service) and personal achievement (outstanding personal achievement despite adversity; must have perseverance, courage, commitment, and potential for success). Based on demonstrated achievement, not financial need; academic achievement without a specific or personal achievement; or athletics. Any person, other than the student or a family member, may nominate a student. Nominees must provide evidence of their achievement and a 500-word essay or oral tape supporting their achievements. Deadline: early November.

1659.
Marin Educational Foundation
Short–Term and Long–Term Occupational Study
 Grants
1010 B Street, Suite 300
San Rafael, CA 94901
(415) 459-4240

Grants ranging from $200 to $2,700 for high school seniors or graduates from Marin County. Independent students must have been residents of Marin County for three years. Dependent students, wards of the court, and/or those in foster homes must be high school graduates from a Marin County high school and/or be residents for at least one year prior to application. All applicants must be U.S. citizens or eligible noncitizens and be accepted by a vocational training school in an eighteen-week or shorter program for a short-term grant or eighteen weeks to two years for a long-term grant. Must be able to maintain living expenses while in training and have financial need for educational costs. Deadline: for short-term grants—none; long-term grants—February 28, May 31, August 31, and November 30.

1660.

**Marion and Ed Peeples Memorial Foundation
  Scholarships**
Bank One Trust Group—Franklin, Indiana
P.O. Box 369
Franklin, IN 46131
(317) 736-2498

20 to 30 scholarships ranging from $300 to $3,000 to high
school seniors who graduated from an Indiana high school
or persons with a General Equivalency Diploma (GED)
equivalent. Must be current residents of Indiana. Based on
SAT scores, academic record, and interview. Applications
available after November 1. Deadline: March 15.

1661.

Marvel Comics
Internship Program
387 Park Avenue South
New York, NY 10016
(212) 696-0808

30 internships providing no compensation are open to
undergraduate juniors and seniors. Interns must receive
academic credit for the internships, which last from three to
four months during the spring, fall, and summer. Interns
are assigned to editors and do anything that needs to be
done, including photocopying, retrieving mail, sending out
complimentary comic books, filing, typing fan mail
responses, and answering fan inquiries over the phone.
Once interns have demonstrated their skills, some begin
editing, writing, and critiquing scripts. Deadline: rolling.

1662.

**Maryland Higher Education Commission
Distinguished Scholar Teacher Education Awards**
State Scholarship Administration
16 Francis Street
Annapolis, MD 21401-1781
(410) 974-5370/(800) 735-2258 TDD
http://www.state.md.us/
ssamail@mhec.state.md.us

Scholarships of $3,000 to graduating high school seniors
and undergraduate students who are pursuing careers as
teachers. Must already have received a Distinguished
Scholar Award, attend a Maryland institution as a full-time
student, have at least a 3.0 GPA, and promise to teach full-
time in a Maryland public school, or recipients must repay
the award with interest. Renewable up to three times with
satisfactory academic progress. Parents of dependent
students must be Maryland residents. Students who are
eligible are sent applications.

1663.

**Maryland Higher Education Commission
Educational Access Grant**
State Scholarship Administration
16 Francis Street
Annapolis, MD 21401-1781
(410) 974-5370/(800) 735-2258 TDD
http://www.state.md.us
ssamail@mhec.state.md.us

Grants ranging from $200 to $3,000 to graduating high
school seniors or undergraduate students. Applicants must
be residents of Maryland, be full-time students at a
Maryland institution, have at least a 2.0 GPA, and
demonstrate financial need. Must file FAFSA. Parents of
dependent student applicants must also be Maryland
residents. Deadline: March 1.

1664.

**Maryland Higher Education Commission
Edward T. Conroy Memorial Scholarships**
State Scholarship Administration
16 Francis Street
Annapolis, MD 21401-1781
(410) 974-5370/(800) 735-2258 TDD
http://www.state.md.us/
ssamail@mhec.state.md.us

Scholarships providing up to in-state public school tuition
and mandatory fee costs to graduating high school seniors.
Must be dependent children of veterans who are deceased
or were 100 percent disabled in the line of duty after
December 7, 1941, or who were MIAs or POWs during the
Vietnam Conflict. Veterans must have been Maryland
residents at the time of disability or death. Applicants must
be Maryland residents and U.S. citizens. Also eligible to
apply are spouses, who have not remarried, of a state or
local public safety officer, and individuals who have been
100 percent disabled in the line of duty serving as a state or
public safety officer. May be used for full-time or part-time
study in any area at a Maryland college or private career
school. Deadline: July 15.

1665.

**Maryland Higher Education Commission
Guaranteed Access Grants**
State Scholarship Administration
16 Francis Street
Annapolis, MD 21401-1781
(410) 974-5370/(800) 735-2258 TDD
http://www.state.md.us/
ssamail@mhec.state.md.us

Grants of up to $8,300 to graduating high school seniors.
Must currently have at least a 2.5 GPA on a 4.0 scale, be
Maryland residents, be under twenty-two years of age, and
begin college within one year after high school graduation.
Must plan to be full-time undergraduate students at a
Maryland institution. Parents must also be Maryland
residents. Renewable up to three times with 2.0 GPA.
Selection based on financial need. Must file FAFSA.
Deadline: March 1.

1666.

**Maryland Higher Education Commission
Part-Time Grants**
State Scholarship Administration
16 Francis Street
Annapolis, MD 21401-1781
(410) 974-5370/(800) 735-2258 TDD
http://www.state.md.us/
ssamail@mhec.state.md.us

Grants ranging from $200 to $1,000 to undergraduate
students attending college on a part-time basis. Must be
Maryland residents and demonstrate financial need. Must
file FAFSA. Deadline: varies by college.

1667.
Maryland Higher Education Commission
Physical and Occupational Therapists and
**   Assistants Grants**
State Scholarship Administration
16 Francis Street
Annapolis, MD 21401-1781
(410) 974-5370/(800) 735-2258 TDD
http://www.state.md.us
ssamail@mhec.state.md.us

Grants of up to $2,000 to graduating high school seniors or
undergraduate students. Must be Maryland residents, attend
a Maryland institution on a full-time basis, and plan to be
or be enrolled in a professional program leading to a
license in physical therapy, physical therapy assistant,
occupational therapist, or occupational therapy assistant.
Must sign a promissory note agreeing to work one year in
a Maryland public school for each year assistance is
received, or must repay the assistance with interest.
Deadline: July 1.

1668.
Maryland State Scholarship Administration
Distinguished Scholar Program
The Jeffrey Building
16 Francis Street
Annapolis, MD 21401
(410) 974-5370/(800) 735-2258 TDD
http://www.state.md.us
ssamail@mhec.state.md.us

Scholarships of $3,000 to graduating high school seniors.
Students who are finalists in the National Merit Scholarship
or National Achievement Scholarship Program are offered
scholarships if attending a Maryland institution. High
schools nominate five students for auditions in visual art,
instrumental music, vocal music, dance, or drama. Officially
designated magnet school of the arts nominate ten students.
Nominated students in the arts must audition in person or
submit a portfolio review to a panel of judges. Students
may also apply if they have at least a 3.7 GPA on a 4.0
scale, and submit SAT or ACT scores. Renewable with
satisfactory academic progress and if parents maintain
Maryland residency. Students must apply during high
school junior year. Nominations must be made while
student is a high school junior.

1669.
Maryland State Scholarship Administration
Fire Fighters, Ambulance, and Rescue Squad
**   Members Reimbursement Program**
The Jeffrey Building
16 Francis Street
Annapolis, MD 21401
(410) 974-5370
(800) 735-2258 TDD
ssamail@mhec.state.md.us

Scholarships of full-tuition costs to students pursuing a
degree in "fire service technology" or paramedics in
"emergency medical technology" programs. Recipients must
be employed as or be volunteer firemen in an organized
state fire department. Must be Maryland residents.
Renewable. Deadline: July 1.

1670.
Maryland State Scholarship Administration
Maryland Delegate Scholarships
The Jeffrey Building
16 Francis Street
Annapolis, MD 21401
(410) 974-5370
(800) 735-2258 TDD
ssamail@mhec.state.md.us

Scholarships of at least $200 to students chosen by their
delegate. Must be full-time students in Maryland.
Applicants may not be General State Award recipients. May
be used for undergraduate, graduate, or professional-school
study; but scholarship will only pay undergraduate rates.
Contact your district delegate to the state legislature or
above address.

1671.
Maryland State Scholarship Administration
Senatorial Scholarships
The Jeffrey Building
16 Francis Street
Annapolis, MD 21401
(410) 974-5370
(800) 735-2258 TDD
ssamail@mhec.state.md.us

Numerous scholarships ranging from $200 to $1,500 to
Maryland high school seniors or high school graduates for
study in Maryland. Students must be U.S. citizens or legal
residents. Renewable with 3.0 GPA. Deadline: February 15
and July 15.

1672.
Maryland State Scholarship Administration
Sharon Christa McAuliffe Teacher Education
**   Awards**
The Jeffrey Building
16 Francis Street
Annapolis, MD 21401
(410) 974-5370
(800) 735-2258 TDD
ssamail@mhec.state.md.us

Scholarships of $2,000 (commuting students) and $10,000
(on-campus) to students and teachers pursuing a career in
teaching. Undergraduate students and teachers must be full-
time; degreed nonteachers may be half-time. Must have at
least a 3.0 GPA on a 4.0 scale and be seeking certification
for teaching in a critical shortage area. Must teach full-time
for one-and-a-half years for each year of financial support.
Based on academic record, writing, and work experience.
Financial need is not considered. Deadline: December 31.

1673.
Maryland State Scholarship Administration
State Nursing Scholarships & Living Expenses
**   Grants**
The Jeffrey Building
16 Francis Street
Annapolis, MD 21401
(410) 974-5370

Scholarships of up to $2,400 providing tuition and fees to
students for full- or part-time nursing study. Must be

Maryland residents, attend a Maryland institution, and have at least a 3.0 GPA. Must sign a surety bond agreeing to complete the program and work full-time for one year for each year of assistance. Students who do not fulfill the agreement must repay the amount of the assistance received. Based on academic record, recommendations, essay on nursing goals, and community involvement in a nursing activity. Financial need is considered. Only for Living Expenses Grants of up to $2,400. Deadline: June 30.

1674.
Maryland State Scholarship Administration
Tolbert Grants
The Jeffrey Building
16 Francis Street
Annapolis, MD 21401
(410) 974-5370

Grants ranging from $200 to $1,500 to high school seniors or graduates. Must be attending or planning to attend a private Maryland career school. Based on financial need. Deadline: May 1.

1675.
Maryland Veterans Grants
Maryland State Scholarship Board
2100 Guildford Avenue
Baltimore, MD 21218-5888

Free tuition and fees to veterans attending any state-supported two- or four-year Maryland institution. Must have been a resident upon induction in the Armed Forces and have been declared a prisoner of war as a result of conflict in Southeast Asia on or after January 1, 1960. Deadline: none.

1676.
Massachusetts Office of Student Financial
Assistance
Christian A. Herter Memorial Scholarships
330 Stuart Street, Suite 304
Boston, MA 02116
(617) 727-9420
(617) 727-0667 Fax
http://www.osfa.mass.edu

Scholarships of up to 50 percent of financial need to graduating high school seniors or undergraduate students. Must be permanent Massachusetts residents, plan to enroll or be enrolled in a Massachusetts institution, and exhibit extreme personal or family difficulties or medical problems or have overcome a personal obstacle or hardship. Request information and application after January 1 from above address.

1677.
Massachusetts Office of Student Financial
Assistance
Gilbert Grants
330 Stuart Street, Suite 304
Boston, MA 02116
(617) 727-9420
(617) 727-0661 Fax
http://www.osfa.mass.edu

Scholarships to students who are Massachusetts residents for at least one year and are enrolled full-time in an independent, regionally accredited school in Massachusetts. Amount is determined by the school's financial-aid office. Must file FAFSA.

1678.
Massachusetts Office of Student Financial
Assistance
MASSGrants
330 Stuart Street, Suite 304
Boston, MA 02116
(617) 727-9420
(617) 727-0667 Fax
http://www.osfa.mass.edu

Scholarships ranging from $200 to $2,500 to graduating high school seniors or undergraduate students. Must have been permanent residents of Massachusetts for at least twelve months before the beginning of the academic year for which the scholarship is awarded. Full-time students may attend a state-approved institution in Massachusetts or a reciprocal state: Connecticut, Maine, Maryland, New Hampshire, Pennsylvania, Rhode Island, Vermont, or the District of Columbia. Students must file FAFSA. Renewable with satisfactory academic progress. Deadline: May 1.

1679.
Massachusetts Office of Student Financial
Assistance
Part–Time Student Grants
330 Stuart Street, Suite 304
Boston, MA 02116
(617) 727-9420/(617) 727-0661 Fax
http://www.osfa.mass.edu

Grants of varying amounts for part-time undergraduate students enrolled for three to eleven credit hours at a Massachusetts institution. Must be Massachusetts residents. Contact school's financial-aid office. Must file FAFSA. Deadline: varies by school.

1680.
Massachusetts Office of Student Financial
Assistance
Performance Bonus Grants
330 Stuart Street, Suite 304
Boston, MA 02116
(617) 727-9420
(617) 727-0667 Fax
http://www.osfa.mass.edu

Grants ranging from $350 to $500 to MASSGrant recipients. Must have at least a 3.0 GPA and an Expected Family Contribution (EFC) of zero. Students and parents of dependent students must be Massachusetts residents and attend a Massachusetts institution. Must file FAFSA. Deadline: May 1.

1681.
Massachusetts Office of Student Financial
Assistance
Public Service Scholarships
330 Stuart Street, Suite 304
Boston, MA 02116
(617) 727-9420/(617) 727-0661 Fax
http://www.osfa.mass.edu

Scholarships providing tuition costs to graduating high school seniors or high school graduates. Must be children of deceased police officers, correctional officers, firemen, or veterans listed as prisoners of war, missing in action, or deceased while on active duty. Widowed spouses of deceased police officers, correctional officers, or firemen are also eligible. Students must attend an accredited Massachusetts institution on a full-time basis. Other criteria may apply.

1682.
Massachusetts Office of Student Financial Assistance
Tuition Waivers/Cash Grants
330 Stuart Street, Suite 304
Boston, MA 02116
(617) 727-9420
(617) 727-0667 Fax
http://www.osfa.mass.edu

Awards of up to tuition costs to graduating high school seniors or undergraduate students. Must be Massachusetts residents and attend an accredited public Massachusetts institution. Must file FAFSA.

1683.
Massachusetts State Federation of Women's Clubs
Undergraduate Scholarship Program
245 Dutton Road
Sudbury, MA 01776
(617) 443-4569

Scholarships ranging from $350 to $500 to undergraduate students majoring in art or music who are Massachusetts residents. Must have a letter of endorsement from a local Women's Club president; must submit a transcript. Deadline: February 15.

1684.
Materials Handling Education Foundation Scholarships
8720 Red Oak Boulevard, #201
Charlotte, NC 28210
(704) 522-8644

15 scholarships ranging from $1,000 to $2,500 to undergraduate students who have completed at least two years of study or graduate or transferring students majoring in materials handling. Award can be used at eligible accredited U.S. colleges or universities. Deadline: May 1.

1685.
Mathcounts National Competition
1420 King Street
Alexandria, VA 22314-2794

9 awards ranging from $2,000 to $8,000 in a math competition open to 7th- and 8th-grade students. Points are scored on written and oral rounds in series of local, regional, then national competitions. Application materials available from junior high math teacher at participating schools. There is a $40 application fee for each school. Awards are for college tuition and will be distributed on a yearly basis over applicant's undergraduate tenure. Award is for use for full-time undergraduate study at any accredited two- or four-year U.S. college, university, or vocational/technical school. Must be U.S. citizens or

permanent residents. Obtain information from middle school counselor or math teacher. Deadline: November 15.

1686.
Matred Carlton Olliff Foundation
P.O. Box 385
Wauchula, FL 33873
(813) 773-4131

103 scholarship grants ranging from $40 to $2,000 and totaling $64,000 to high school seniors, undergraduates, and graduate students. Must be Florida residents. Open to all majors. Write an introductory letter briefly detailing your educational and financial situation. Other restrictions may apply. Deadline: July 1.

1687.
The Matt Garcia Foundation Scholarships
310 South St. Mary's
San Antonio, TX 78205
(210) 225-0449

Numerous scholarships of varying amounts to Hispanic high school seniors or undergraduate, graduate, or professional-school students who are residents of San Antonio and who will be attending St. Mary's University. Must submit a personal statement, three letters of recommendation, transcript, and photograph and have at least a 2.75 GPA. Deadline: June 15.

1688.
Maud Glover Folsom Foundation
Attn: Leon A. Francisco
P.O. Box 151
Harwinton, CT 06791
(203) 485-0405 or (718) 474-0006

30 scholarships of varying amounts, totaling $75,000, to fourth-generation male Americans of Anglo-Saxon or German descent. When requesting application, include a self-addressed, stamped envelope. Deadline: varies.

1689.
Maxwell House Coffee
Minority Scholarships
250 North Street
White Plains, NY 10625
(914) 335-2361

5 scholarships of $1,000 (renewable up to four years) to minority high school seniors or recent graduates from Baltimore, Chicago, Detroit, New York, Newark, St. Louis/ East St. Louis, or Philadelphia who will be attending a historically black institution that participates in the Maxwell House-sponsored black-college fairs. Based on academic record, class rank, GPA, community activities, and financial need. Deadline: mid-April.

1690.
Maxwell Macmillan Scholarship Program
College Scholarship Service
Sponsored Scholarship Programs
P.O. Box 6730
Princeton, NJ 08541
(609) 951-6806

Numerous scholarships of up to $2,500 for graduating high school seniors who are dependents of full-time, permanent employees of the Maxwell Macmillan, Inc., or any of its U.S. subsidiaries. Parent must have been employed full-time for at least three years by the application deadline. Based on SAT scores, academic achievement, leadership, extracurricular activities, and financial need. Amount of scholarship is determined by financial need and cost of education. Renewable for up to four years. Application procedures are administered by the College Scholarship Service. Deadline: November 30.

1691.
McDonald's HACER Foundation
NHSF Selection Committee
HACER Scholarship
P.O. Box 748
San Francisco, CA 94101

Numerous scholarships of $1,000 to graduating high school seniors of Hispanic American background who are in the top 15 percent of their class. Only available in Arizona, California, Florida, New Jersey, New Mexico, New York, or Texas. Request applications after December 1. Applications can be requested from local McDonald's between dates given. Deadline: February 1.

1692.
**McDonald's
Internship Program**
432 North 44th Street, Suite 250
Phoenix, AZ 85008
(602) 273-0230

30 internships lasting from two to three years that provide from $8 to $12 per hour, health insurance, and $1,000 per year educational stipend to undergraduate college juniors. Interns work at McDonald's restaurants as manager trainees, learning how to operate work stations, plan and schedule shifts, order supplies, and keep the restaurant sanitized. Interns may take classes in management skills and take training classes at McDonald's Hamburger University, plus enjoy employee benefits (stock plan, profit sharing, paid vacations, matching gifts program, and McSave program). Applicants must have at least a 2.0 GPA. Submit a résumé and cover letter directly to the region of interest. Additional regions: 21300 Victory Boulevard, Suite 800, Woodland Hills, CA 91367, (818) 594-0525; 1750 How Avenue, Suite 550, Sacramento, CA 95825, (916) 649-9797; or 4370 La Jolla Village Drive, Suite 800, San Diego, CA 92122, (619) 535-8900.

1693.
McDonnell Douglas Scholarship Foundation
3855 Lakewood Boulevard
M/C 802-11
Long Beach, CA 90846
(213) 593-2612

Scholarships ranging from $1,500 to $4,000 to high school seniors who are the dependent adopted, natural, or stepchildren of an active, retired, or deceased employee of an MDC component company or subsidiary that participates in the McDonnell Douglas-West Employees Community Fund, Inc. Students must be graduating seniors in the upper one-third of their class or graduates in the upper one-third of their class. Not based on financial need. Deadline: first Friday in March.

1694.
The McFarland Charitable Foundation
Havana National Bank
112 South Orange Street, Box 489
Havana, IL 62644
(309) 543-3361

6 to 10 scholarships ranging from $1,200 to $3,000 to high school seniors or graduates. Must be accepted into an accredited nursing school program at a vocational/occupational school or a two- or four-year institution. Must have at least a 2.0 GPA and be a U.S. citizen. Students agree to return to Havana, Illinois, to work as a registered nurse for a number of years after graduation. Failure to fulfill the work requirement results in the scholarship converting into a loan plus interest, which must be repaid. Deadline: May 31.

1695.
McLean Hospital
Attn: Director, Volunteer Services
115 Mill Street
Belmont, MA 02178
(617) 855-2118

Varying numbers of internships lasting three months, with openings year-round, are open to undergraduate juniors and seniors and to graduate or professional school students. Applicants should have an interest in a medical career, mental health, or mental health research, and should have strong interpersonal skills. Interns talk with patients and assist with activities in inpatient units, group residencies, or day treatment programs. Interns may also assist children and adolescent patients with schoolwork, or assist staff in clinical or basic research. No monetary compensation is required. Submit a letter detailing interests, an application form, a résumé, and references. An interview is required. Deadline: open.

1696.
McMannis Educational Trust Fund
Executive Director
Marine Bank Trust Division
P.O. Box 8480
Erie, PA 16553
(814) 871-9324

114 renewable scholarships ranging from $500 to $2,000 to high school seniors or undergraduate, graduate, or professional school students. Can be used for any major. Must be U.S. citizens and attend a U.S. institution. Based on academic record and financial need. Request applications after September 1. Deadline: January 15.

1697.
**Memphis State University
River City Writing Awards in Fiction**
Attn: Editor
Department of English
Memphis State University
Memphis, TN 38152
(901) 678-2651

1 first prize of $2,000 and 1 second prize of $500 awarded for unpublished short stories. Write to above address for

rules; include a self-addressed, stamped envelope. Deadline: December 6.

1698.
Merit Shop Foundation
Associated Builders & Contractors Scholarship
  Program
729 15th Street, N.W.
Washington, DC 20005
(202) 637-8800

20 scholarships ranging from $500 to $2,000 to undergraduate students majoring in construction at an accredited four-year degree program. Must have completed their first year of study and be pursuing a career in the construction industry. Applications available after October 1. Deadline: December 15.

1699.
Metro–Goldwyn/United Artists
Internship Coordinator
2500 Broadway Street
Santa Monica, CA 90404
(310) 449-3000

30 internships providing in Santa Monica and New York to undergraduate and graduate students. U.S. internships provide no salary. Internships in Canada provide a salary of $125 and are open to graduate students, college graduates, undergraduates, and high school graduates. Must have an interest in advertising, communications, film, journalism, or related fields. Interns work in Story & Development (New York and Los Angeles) and Publicity/Promotions. Internships range from three to six months and are conducted during the summer, fall, and spring. Open to U.S. or Canadian citizens. Deadline: rolling.

1700.
Metropolitan Business League (MBL)
214 East Clay Street
P.O. Box 26751
Richmond, VA 23261

1 scholarship of varying amount to a deserving college student from Virginia. MBL serves as an information clearinghouse, counseling assistance center, and skills bank. Based on academic record, career goal, and financial need. Deadline: varies.

1701.
Metropolitan Museum of Art
Internship Program–Education Dept.
1000 Fifth Avenue
New York, NY 10028-0198
(212) 570-3710
or
The Cloisters
Fort Tryon Park
New York, NY 10040
(212) 923-3700

22 undergraduate and 10 graduate internships providing compensation of $2,200 for Met undergraduates, $2,500 for Met graduate students, and $2,000 for Cloister undergraduates in a summer internship program lasting from nine to ten weeks. Interns are assigned to administration, conservation, library, and curatorial departments (Arts of Africa, Oceania, and the Americas; American Art; Ancient Near Eastern Art; Arms and Armor; Asian Art; the Costume Institute; European Paintings; Greek and Roman Art; Islamic Art; Musical Instruments; Photographs; Prints and Illustrated Books; and 20th Century Art). The Cloisters is the Medieval Arts branch of the Met, and offers a formal nine-week internship in European art of the Middle Ages. Deadline: January 21 (Met undergraduates); January 28 (Met graduate students); February 4 (Cloisters).

1702.
Metropolitan Opera
National Council Regional Award
National Council Auditions
Lincoln Center
New York, NY 10023
(212) 799-3100

1 to 5 awards ranging from $200 to $10,000 to undergraduate and graduate students majoring in music or vocal music. Applicants must audition. Renewable. Deadline: varies.

1703.
Michigan Department of Higher Education
Adult Part–time Grant Program
608 West Allegan Street
Lansing, MI 48933
(517) 373-3394

Grants of up to $600 per year for two years to undergraduate students. Must be enrolled on a part-time basis (three to eleven credit hours) as undergraduate students at a participating Michigan degree-granting college or university. Must be self-supporting students, be out of high school, be Michigan residents, and be U.S. citizens or residents. Must not be in a program leading to a degree in theology or divinity or be in default on a loan guaranteed by Michigan Higher Education Assistance Authority. Based on financial need. Contact your college's financial-aid office.

1704.
Michigan Department of Higher Education
Carl D. Perkins Vocational & Applied Technology
  Education Act
608 West Allegan Street
Lansing, MI 48933
(517) 373-3394

Tuition assistance and support services to undergraduate students. Must be either single parents, single pregnant women, displaced homemakers, or sex equity occupational students. Must be Michigan residents and attend a Michigan community college or State Board of Education–approved four-year institution offering a two-year degree in occupational education. Contact school's financial aid office for more information.

1705.
Michigan Department of Higher Education
Indian Tuition Waivers
608 West Allegan Street
Lansing, MI 48933
(517) 373-3394

Tuition waivers to high school seniors or graduates who are Native North American Indians. Must be planning to attend or attending a state-supported public two- or four-year college or university. Must be Michigan residents for at least twelve consecutive months and at least one-quarter Native American Indian certified by the Michigan Commission on Indian Affairs.

1706.
Michigan Department of Higher Education
Michigan Competitive Scholarships
608 West Allegan Street
Lansing, MI 48933
(517) 373-3394

Numerous renewable scholarships ranging from $100 to $1,200 to high school seniors or graduates. Must be used for tuition and fees at a Michigan institution. Must be Michigan residents for at least five years. Must be U.S. citizens, permanent residents, or refugees. Based on ACT and financial need; must have at least a 2.0 GPA and maintain satisfactory academic progress. Deadline: February 15.

1707.
Michigan Department of Higher Education
Michigan Educational Opportunity Grants
608 West Allegan Street
Lansing, MI 48933
(517) 373-3394

Grants of up to $1,000 to graduating high school seniors or undergraduate students. Must be enrolled or planning to enroll at least on a half-time basis at an accredited Michigan college or university and demonstrate financial need. Must be U.S. citizens or permanent residents, Michigan residents, and not be in default of a loan. Deadline: varies by institution.

1708.
Michigan Department of Higher Education
Michigan Tuition Grants
608 West Allegan Street
Lansing, MI 48933
(517) 373-3394

Numerous renewable grants ranging from $100 to $2,300 to full-time students who are Michigan residents and attending an independent nonprofit Michigan institution. Based on financial need. Deadline: varies.

1709.
Michigan Department of Higher Education
Police Officer's and Fire Fighter's Survivors
** Tuition Act**
608 West Allegan Street
Lansing, MI 48933
(517) 373-3394

Tuition waivers at public institutions to graduating high school seniors or undergraduate students. Must be children under age twenty-one or surviving spouse of a Michigan police officer or firefighter killed in the line of duty. Contact the Department of State Police. Officials in that department determine eligibility and contact the appropriate institution concerning applicant's status. Deadline: varies by institution.

1710.
Michigan Department of Higher Education
Tuition Incentive Program (TIP)
608 West Allegon Street
Lansing, MI 48933
(517) 373-3394
(800) 243-2847

Assistance of varying amounts to help pay tuition and fees to graduating high school seniors and GED recipients. Must apply anytime after completing the sixth grade but before high school graduation or GED completion. Must be Michigan residents, under age twenty, receiving or have received Medicaid, and U.S. citizens. Must begin college within two years following graduation or GED completion. Must be enrolled at least part-time in an associate's or certificate program. May be able to assist with benefits for study beyond an associate's degree.

1711.
Michigan United Conservation Clubs
MUCC/MICHCON Natural Resources Scholarships
P.O. Box 30235
2101 Wood Street
Lansing, MI 48912
(517) 371-1041

5 scholarships of $1,000 and seven of $350 to high school juniors or seniors. Must be Michigan residents. Must be planning to study natural resources, conservation, or a related field. Based on best conservation-related project proposals. Deadline: March 11.

1712.
Michigan Veterans' Affairs
Tuition Grants Program
477 Michigan Avenue
Detroit, MI 48826
(800) 827-1000

Numerous tuition grants to high school seniors or graduate or undergraduate students who are children of a Michigan veteran who was killed in action, died of other causes during wartime, was totally disabled, or has since died due to wartime causes. Applicant must have been Michigan resident for at least twelve months. Must be between sixteen and twenty-six years of age. Must attend or plan to attend a Michigan tax-supported college or university. Deadline: none.

1713.
Microsoft
Attn: Recruiting Department
CN05i-0101
One Microsoft Way
Redmond, WA 98052-6399
(206) 882-8080
http://www.microsoft.com/college/work.htm

350 twelve- to sixteen-week summer internships providing round-trip travel, subsidized housing, rental car, and salaries ranging from $320 to $480 per week to undergraduate sophomores, juniors, and seniors. Internships are in software testing, program management, program development, product marketing, and finance.

Most interns have a solid background in computer science. Deadline: rolling.

1714.
Microsoft
Attn: Scholarships
One Microsoft Way
Redmond, WA 98052-6399
(206) 882-8080

Some scholarships of varying amounts to undergraduate and graduate students who are computer science majors. Scholarships are only at certain colleges and universities. Students must contact their school's financial aid or scholarship office and inquire whether their school participates in the Microsoft Scholarship Program. If Microsoft Scholarships are offered, the student may inquire further. Those students whose schools don't participate should not contact Microsoft.

1715.
Migrant Dropout Reconnection Program
Gloria and Joseph Mattera National Scholarship
    for Migrant Children
Scholarship Coordinator
BOCES Geneseo Migrant Center
Holcomb Building, Room 210
Geneseo, NY 14454
(716) 245-5681

60 scholarships ranging from $100 to $250 to students who are children of migrant workers or to migrant workers enrolled in or accepted at a public or private college or university or vocational/technical school. Applicant must be a dropout or potentially a dropout who shows the potential to continue school. Deadline: varies.

1716.
Military Order of the Purple Heart
Adjutant General
5413-B Backlick Road
Springfield, VA 22151-3960
(703) 642-5360

3 to 5 scholarships of $1,000 to high school seniors or graduates who are children or grandchildren of a member of the Military Order of the Purple Heart. Must have at least a 2.5 GPA and submit SAT/ACT scores. Renewable up to four years. Request applications after January 1. Deadline: August 1.

1717.
Minerals, Metals & Materials Society
Scholarships
420 Commonwealth Drive
Warrendale, PA 15086
(724) 776-9000
(724) 776-3770 Fax
http://www.tms.org/Society/society.html
tmsgeneral@tms.org

6 different scholarships ranging from $1,000 to $4,000 to undergraduate students majoring in metallurgical engineering, materials science and engineering, minerals processing/extraction programs, or physical metallurgy. Must be student members of TMS. Preference given to full-time undergraduate juniors or seniors. Obtain application through student chapter, above address, or via the Internet. Deadline: June 30 (received).

1718.
Minnesota Chippewa Tribe Scholarship Fund
Education Division
P.O. Box 217
Cass Lake, MN 56633
(218) 335-2252

Scholarships of up to $3,000 to high school seniors or graduates. Must be one-quarter Native American Indian and enrolled members of the Minnesota Chippewa Tribe or eligible for enrollment. Must have applied for all available financial aid through the college. Based on financial need. Deadline: January.

1719.
Minnesota Foundation
55 East Fifth Street
St. Paul, MN 55101
(651) 224-5463

7 scholarships ranging from $500 to $5,900 to high school seniors. Must be residents of Minnesota. Based on academic record and financial need. Deadline: varies.

1720.
Minnesota Higher Education Services Office
Academic Excellence Scholarships
1450 Energy Park Drive, Suite 350
St. Paul, MN 55108-5227
(800) 657-3866
(651) 642-0533
(651) 297-8880 Fax
http://www.heso.state.mn.us/
info@heso.state.mn.us

Scholarships to cover public school tuition and fees to graduating high school seniors or high school graduates. May attend a public or private accredited four-year Minnesota institution. Renewable up to three more times with satisfactory academic progress. Implementation of program depends on availability of funds.

1721.
Minnesota Higher Education Services Office
Child Care Grants
1450 Energy Park Drive, Suite 350
St. Paul, MN 55108-5227
(800) 657-3866
(651) 642-0533
(651) 297-8880 Fax
http://www.heso.state.mn.us/
info@heso.state.mn.us/

Financial assistance of up to $2,000 for each eligible child to enrolled undergraduate students who have a child twelve years old or younger or fourteen years old or younger who is handicapped. Student may be either part-time or full-time and not receiving Aid to Families with Dependent Children or Minnesota Family Investment Program–Statewide (MFIP-S). Assistance may cover up to forty hours per eligible child. Contact school's financial aid office.

1722.

**Minnesota Higher Education Services Office
Dean's Scholars Program**
1450 Energy Park Drive, Suite 350
St. Paul, MN 55108-5227
(800) 657-3866
(651) 642-0533
(651) 297-8880 Fax
http://www.heso.state.mn.us/
info@heso.state.mn.us

Scholarships ranging from $1,000 to $4,000 to graduating high school seniors, high school graduates who haven't attended college, and undergraduate students. Must be in the upper 10 percent of their class, with at least a 3.25 GPA, be Minnesota residents, and attend an accredited Minnesota institution. Deadline: January 15.

1723.

**Minnesota Higher Education Services Office
Dislocated Rural Workers Grant**
1450 Energy Park Drive, Suite 350
St. Paul, MN 55108-5227
(800) 657-3866
(651) 642-0533
(651) 297-8880 Fax
http://www.heso.state.mn.us/
info@heso.state.mn.us/

Grants of varying amounts to students who are rural Minnesotans enrolled in an adult farm management program or an employment preparation program. Must have lost their job, be a displaced homemaker, or be a farmer with severe financial need. Spouses are eligible. Contact school's financial-aid office.

1724.

**Minnesota Higher Education Services Office
Farm Families Assistance**
1450 Energy Park Drive, Suite 350
St. Paul, MN 55108-5227
(800) 657-3866
(651) 642-0533
(651) 297-8880 Fax
http://www.heso.state.mn.us/
info@heso.state.mn.us/

Assistance of varying amounts to graduating high school seniors and undergraduate students who are from farm families. Selection based on academic achievement. Must be in the upper 10 percent of their class, with at least a 3.25 GPA, and be Minnesota residents. Deadline: January 15.

1725.

**Minnesota Higher Education Services Office
Indian Scholarship**
1450 Energy Park Drive, Suite 350
St. Paul, MN 55108-5227
(800) 657-3866
(651) 642-0533
(651) 297-8880 Fax
http://www.heso.state.mn.us/
info@heso.state.mn.us/

Numerous $1,450 scholarships to high school seniors or graduates or persons with a General Equivalency Diploma (GED). Must be members of a recognized Indian tribe. Must be of at least one-quarter Indian ancestry, be high school graduates or have a GED, and be Minnesota residents. Contact: Joe Aitken, Scholarship Office, Indian Education, 1819 Bemidji, MN 56601. Deadline: varies.

1726.

**Minnesota Higher Education Services Office
National Guard Benefits**
1450 Energy Park Drive, Suite 350
St. Paul, MN 55108-5227
(800) 657-3866
(651) 642-0533
(651) 297-8880 Fax
http://www.heso.state.mn.us/
info@heso.state.mn.us

Tuition reimbursement ranging from $25 to $46 per quarter credit hour to undergraduate and graduate students. Must be active members of the Minnesota Army or Air National Guard. Students may also receive tuition reimbursement for out-of-state colleges. May use this program in addition to the federal GI Bill benefits. For more information, contact the Minnesota National Guard Education Services Office at (612) 282-4590 or write to: Department of Military Affairs, Education Services, Veterans Service Building, St. Paul, MN 55155-2098. Their website address is: http://www.dma.state.mn.us.

1727.

**Minnesota Higher Education Services Office
National Service Scholars Program**
1450 Energy Park Drive, Suite 350
St. Paul, MN 55108-5227
(800) 657-3866
(651) 642-0533
(651) 297-8880 Fax
http://www.heso.state.mn.us/
info@heso.state.mn.us

Scholarships of at least $1,000 to high school juniors or seniors who have performed community service for at least a year. Nominations are made by high school principals in late spring. For more information, contact your high school principal or above address.

1728.

**Minnesota Higher Education Services Office
Nursing Grants for Persons of Color**
1450 Energy Park Drive, Suite 350
St. Paul, MN 55108-5227
(800) 657-3866
(651) 642-0533
(651) 297-8880 Fax
http://www.heso.state.mn.us/
info@heso.state.mn.us/

Scholarships ranging from $2,000 to $4,000 to minority high school graduates. Must be in a Minnesota program leading to an LPN or RN. Must be Minnesota residents. Must agree to work at least three of the first five years in a designated rural area. Based on career goal and financial need. Deadline: August 1.

1729.
Minnesota Higher Education Services Office
Robert C. Byrd Scholarships
1450 Energy Park Drive, Suite 350
St. Paul, MN 55108-5227
(800) 657-3866
(651) 642-0533
(651) 297-8880 Fax
http://www.heso.state.mn.us/
info@heso.state.mn.us/

Scholarships of $1,500 for high school seniors. Must be a Minnesota resident (for other than educational purposes) for at least six months, register with the Selective Service System, and enroll in a Minnesota public or private nonprofit college or university. Based on outstanding academic record; must have at least a 3.85 GPA and SAT/ACT scores in the upper 75 percent. High school principals nominate one or two students who are in the upper 5 percent of their class. Deadline: March 1.

1730.
Minnesota Higher Education Services Office
Safety Officer's Survivor Program
1450 Energy Park Drive, Suite 350
St. Paul, MN 55108-5227
(800) 657-3866
(651) 642-0533
(651) 297-8880 Fax
http://www.heso.state.mn.us/
info@heso.state.mn.us/

Scholarships providing tuition and fees to high school seniors or undergraduate students who are dependent children or spouses of public safety officers killed in the line of duty on or after January 1, 1973. Must be under twenty-three years of age (except spouses) and enrolled in an undergraduate program in a public or private Minnesota institution. Must submit an eligibility certificate from the Department of Public Safety, 211 Transportation Building, St. Paul, MN 55155. Deadline: varies.

1731.
Minnesota Higher Education Services Office
Scholarship and Grant Program
1450 Energy Park Drive, Suite 350
St. Paul, MN 55108-5227
(800) 657-3866
(651) 642-0533
(651) 297-8880 Fax
http://www.heso.state.mn.us/
info@heso.state.mn.us/

65,000 scholarships ranging from $100 to $4,115 to high school seniors or undergraduate students. Must be Minnesota residents and attending a Minnesota college or university. Must be U.S. citizens or legal residents. Deadline: May 31.

1732.
Minnesota Higher Education Services Office
State Grant Program
1450 Energy Park Drive, Suite 350
St. Paul, MN 55108-5227
(800) 657-3866
(651) 642-0533
(651) 297-8880 Fax
http://www.heso.state.mn.us/
info@heso.state.mn.us/

Scholarships ranging from $1,200 to $2,501 to undergraduate students attending a two-year institution or $5,564 to students at a private four-year institution. Must be high school graduates, over seventeen years of age, and at least half-time undergraduates. Must contribute at least 50 percent of education cost. Deadline: varies.

1733.
Minnesota Higher Education Services Office
State Veterans' Dependents Assistance
1450 Energy Park Drive, Suite 350
St. Paul, MN 55108-5227
(800) 657-3866 (in-state)
(651) 642-0533
(651) 297-8880 Fax
http://www.heso.state.mn.us/
info@heso.state.mn.us/

Grants of up to $250 to help pay for tuition and fees to graduating high school seniors or undergraduate students who are dependents of veterans listed as prisoners of war or missing in action after August 1, 1958. Contact school's financial aid office. Deadline: none.

1734.
Minnesota Higher Education Services Office
Summer Scholarships for Academic Enrichment
1450 Energy Park Drive, Suite 350
St. Paul, MN 55108-5227
(800) 657-3866
(651) 642-0533
(651) 297-8880 Fax
http://www.heso.state.mn.us/
info@heso.state.mn.us

Scholarships of up to $1,000 to students in grades 7 through 12 to attend eligible college summer academic programs. Must be Minnesota residents, nineteen years of age or younger, earned at least a B average in the subject areas of the enrichment course, and demonstrate financial need. Program subjects include communications, humanities, social studies, sciences, mathematics, fine or performing arts, and foreign language. Must be U.S. citizens or legal residents. Obtain application for the program and scholarship from the college or university sponsoring the program. Deadline: not specified.

1735.
Minority Scholarship Program
Wells Fargo Bank
3550 Wilshire Boulevard
Los Angeles, CA 90017

5 scholarships of $2,000 to undergraduate minority college students. Students also get a part-time job in a nearby

branch office. Based on career goals, academic record, and financial need. Deadline: varies.

1736.
Miss America Pageant
Karen E. Aarons, Administrative Officer
P.O. Box 119
Atlantic City, NJ 08404
http://www.missamerica.org

Awards ranging from $2,000 to $35,000 to females between the ages of seventeen and twenty-six on Labor Day. Must be high school graduates, never married, and U.S. citizens. Contact local organization or write to above address to obtain information.

1737.
Mississippi Office of State Student Financial Aid
Gulf Coast Research Laboratory Minority
**   Summer Grant Program**
3825 Ridgewood Road
P.O. Box 2336
Jackson, MS 39211-6453
(601) 982-6570
(800) 327-2980
http://www.state.ms.us/

Grants providing from $750 to $1,800 to the institution and from $100 to $250 to the recipient for the four-, five-, or ten-week programs. Open to minority students enrolled as full-time students at the Gulf Coast Research Laboratory. There are no service or repayment requirements. Awards are made on a first-come, first-serve basis. Deadline: May 18.

1738.
Mississippi Office of State Student Financial Aid
Higher Education Legislative Plan for Needy
**   Students (HELP Scholarship)**
3825 Ridgewood Road
P.O. Box 2336
Jackson, MS 39211-6453
(601) 982-6570
(800) 327-2980
http://www.state.ms.us/

Scholarships of full tuition to graduating high school seniors or undergraduate students. Must demonstrate financial need, have at least a 2.5 GPA on a 4.0 scale, and have scored at least 20 on ACT. There are specific financial need requirements. Must file FAFSA. Deadline: May 1.

1739.
Mississippi Office of State Student Financial Aid
Law Enforcement Officers and Firemen
**   Scholarships**
3825 Ridgewood Road
P.O. Box 2336
Jackson, MS 39211-6453
(601) 982-6570
(800) 327-2980
http://www.state.ms.us/

Tuition scholarships to high school seniors or undergraduate students who are children of full-time Mississippi law enforcement officers and firemen who died

or were permanently 100 percent disabled due to a service-connected injury. The scholarship is for up to eight semesters. Deadline: varies.

1740.
Mississippi Office of State Student Financial Aid
Mississippi Eminent Scholars Grant (MESG)
**   Program**
3825 Ridgewood Road
P.O. Box 2336
Jackson, MS 39211-6453
(601) 982-6570
(800) 327-2980
http://www.state.ms.us/

Grants of up to $2,500 to graduating high school seniors, high school graduates who haven't attended college, or GED recipients. Must apply as a "first-time-in-college" student or be a renewal applicant. Must be a semifinalist or finalist in the National Merit Scholarship Corporation or the National Achievement Scholarship Program; or have scored at least a 1280 on SAT or 29 on ACT, and have at least a 3.5 GPA on a 4.0 scale; or have completed the Home Education Program and scored at least a 1280 on SAT or 29 on ACT. Renewable with a 3.5 GPA on a 4.0 scale. Must be a Mississippi resident for no less than four years prior to the award. Deadline: April 1.

1741.
Mississippi Office of State Student Financial Aid
Mississippi Resident Tuition Assistance Grant
**   (MTAG) Program**
3825 Ridgewood Road
P.O. Box 2336
Jackson, MS 39211-6453
(601) 982-6570
(800) 327-2980
http://www.state.ms.us/

Grants of up to $500 for undergraduate freshmen or sophomores or up to $1,000 to undergraduate juniors or seniors. High school graduates must have at least a 2.5 GPA on a 4.0 scale and scored at least a 15 on ACT. GED recipients must have completed the GED and scored at least a 15 on ACT. Home-schooled students must have completed the Home Education Program and scored at least a 15 on ACT. Undergraduates must have scored at least a 2.5 GPA on a 4.0 scale, regardless of high school performance. Renewable with 2.5 GPA on a 4.0 scale. Deadline: April 1.

1742.
Mississippi Office of State Student Financial Aid
Nursing Education Scholarship/Loan Program
3825 Ridgewood Road
P.O. Box 2336
Jackson, MS 39211-6453
(601) 982-6570
(800) 327-2980
http://www.state.ms.us/

Scholarships/loans of up to $3,000 to upper-level undergraduate or graduate students. Must be enrolled in a baccalaureate or graduate degree program. Must be

Mississippi residents at least one year and attending an accredited Mississippi institution. Renewable with 2.5 GPA for undergraduates and 3.0 GPA for graduate students on a 4.0 scale. Loan is repaid through full-time service in nursing in Mississippi for one year's scholarship/loan. Period of service shall not be less than twelve consecutive months. If student fails to fulfill the service obligation, repayment of principal and interest is required. Deadline: April 30.

1743.
Mississippi Office of State Student Financial Aid Psychology Apprenticeship Program
3825 Ridgewood Road
P.O. Box 2336
Jackson, MS 39211-6453
(601) 982-6570
(800) 327-2980
http://www.state.ms.us/

Varying numbers of apprenticeships providing a stipend of $500 per month to undergraduate students and $1,000 per month to graduate students to participate in a three-month summer program. Must be enrolled full-time, have at least a 3.0 GPA on a 4.0 scale, and be majoring in psychology. Preference given to economically, educationally, and/or socially disadvantaged students. Deadline: April 1.

1744.
Mississippi Office of State Student Financial Aid Robert C. Byrd Scholarship Program
3825 Ridgewood Road
P.O. Box 2336
Jackson, MS 39211-6453
(601) 982-6570
(800) 327-2980
http://www.state.ms.us/

Scholarships of $1,500 to graduating high school seniors for use the first year of study in a college or university within the state. Administered by each state's educating agency. Obtain applications from state agency or high school counselor.

1745.
Mississippi Office of State Student Financial Aid Southeast Asia POW/MIA Scholarship Program
3825 Ridgewood Road
P.O. Box 2336
Jackson, MS 39211-6453
(601) 982-6570
(800) 327-2980
http://www.state.ms.us/

Tuition scholarships to children of veterans presently or formerly listed as prisoners of war or as missing in action in Southeast Asia or who were prisoners of a foreign government as a result of the action against the U.S.S. *Pueblo*. The scholarship is for up to eight semesters, excluding books, food, supplies, materials, or extracurricular activity fees.

1746.
Mississippi Office of State Student Financial Aid State Student Incentive Grants
3825 Ridgewood Road
P.O. Box 2336
Jackson, MS 39211-6453
(601) 982-6570
(800) 327-2980
http://www.state.ms.us/

Grants ranging from $100 to $1,500 to full-time undergraduate students to attend a Mississippi institution. The federal government pays half the cost, and the state the other half. Based on financial need.

1747.
Mississippi Office of State Student Financial Aid William Winter Teacher Scholar Loan Program
3825 Ridgewood Road
P.O. Box 2336
Jackson, MS 39211-6453
(601) 982-6570
(800) 327-2980
http://www.state.ms.us/

Scholarship/loans of up to $1,000 to undergraduate freshmen and sophomores and up to $3,000 to undergraduate juniors and seniors. Must be pursuing careers in teaching, be Mississippi residents, and be full-time students. Entering freshmen must have scored at least 21 on ACT and a 3.0 GPA on a 4.0 scale. Undergraduate students must maintain a 2.5 GPA on a 4.0 scale. Repayment may be done on the basis of two years' teaching service forgiveness for one year's teaching service. Must teach in a teacher shortage geographic area in Mississippi. Deadline: April 1.

1748.
Missouri League for Nursing, Inc. Meinecke Scholarship
1804 Southwest Boulevard, Suite E
Jefferson City, MO 65101

Scholarships of $200 to students who have completed their freshman year and are enrolled in a nursing education program in Missouri that has current accreditation from the National League for Nursing. Must be Missouri residents. Each school may submit only one candidate. Based on academic record, extracurricular activities, and financial need. Deadline: September 30.

1749.
Missouri Review Editor's Prize
1507 Hillcrest Hall, UMC
Columbia, MO 65211

1 first prize of $1,000 plus publication for short fiction and nonfiction essays and 1 first prize of $500 for poetry (up to ten pages). Entries must be unpublished. Entries will not be returned. Entry fee of $15. Send a stamped, self-addressed envelope for rules. Deadline: October 1.

1750.

Missouri Student Assistance Resource Services
Charles Gallagher Student Financial Assistance
   Program
3515 Amazonas Drive
Jefferson City, MO 65109-5717
(314) 751-3940
(800) 473-6757
http://www.mocbhe.gov/mostars/fin.menu.htm

Scholarships of one-half school's previous year's tuition,
$1,500, or student's financial need for full-time
undergraduate students. Must have financial need, be
working toward first undergraduate degree, and be
attending a participating Missouri institution. Theology and
divinity students are not eligible. Based on financial need.
Must be legal residents of Missouri. Must be U.S. citizens
or permanent residents. Apply after January 1. Deadline:
April 30.

1751.

Missouri Student Assistance Resource Services
Marguerite Ross Barnett Memorial Scholarship
   Program
3515 Amazonas Drive
Jefferson City, MO 65109-5717
(314) 751-3940
(800) 473-6757
http://www.mocbhe.gov/mostars/fin.menu.htm

Scholarships of varying amounts to graduating high school
seniors or undergraduate students. Must be Missouri
residents, be enrolled part-time, be employed for twenty or
more hours per week, be at least eighteen years of age, and
demonstrate financial need.

1752.

Missouri Student Assistance Resource Services
Minority Teacher Education Scholarships
Department of Elementary and Secondary Education
P.O. Box 480
Jefferson City, MO 65102
(573) 751-1668
http://www.mocbhe.gov/mostars/fin.menu.htm

Scholarships of varying amounts to minority graduating
high school seniors and undergraduate students. Must be
pursuing a teaching career. Other restrictions may apply.

1753.

Missouri Student Assistance Resource Services
Missouri Higher Education Academic
   Scholarships
3515 Amazonas Drive
Jefferson City, MO 65109-5717
(314) 751-3940
(800) 473-6757
http://www.mocbhe.gov/mostars/fin.menu.htm

Numerous $2,000 scholarships to graduating high school
seniors. Must be planning to enroll full-time at a
participating Missouri postsecondary institution. SAT or
ACT score must be in the top 3 percent of all Missouri
students taking the tests. Renewable. Deadline: July.

1754.

Missouri Student Assistance Resource Services
Missouri National Guard Association
   Scholarships
2007 Retention Drive
Jefferson City, MO 65101
(800) 972-1164
http://www.mocbhe.gov/mostars/fin.menu.htm

Scholarships of varying amounts to undergraduate
students. Must be members of the Missouri National
Guard, Missouri residents, and attend an accredited
Missouri institution. Other restrictions may apply.

1755.

Missouri Student Assistance Resource Services
Missouri Public Service Officer or Employee's
   Child Survivor Grants
3515 Amazonas Drive
Jefferson City, MO 65109-5717
(314) 751-3940
(800) 473-6757
http://www.mocbhe.gov/mostars/fin.menu.htm

Tuition scholarships to high school seniors or
undergraduate students who are dependent children of
public safety officers or employees of the Department of
Highways and Transportation (construction or maintenance
of the state's highways, roads, and bridges) who were killed
in the line of duty. Must be enrolled or planning to enroll
as full-time undergraduate students in a program leading to
a certificate, associate, or baccalaureate degree at a
participating Missouri institution. Must be U.S. citizens or
permanent residents of the U.S. and Missouri residents.

1756.

Missouri Student Assistance Resource Services
Missouri Student Grants
3515 Amazonas Drive
Jefferson City, MO 65109-5717
(314) 751-3940
(800) 473-6757
http://www.mocbhe.gov/mostars/fin.menu.htm

Scholarships of one-half school's previous year's tuition,
$1,500, or student's financial need are available. Must be
U.S. citizens or permanent residents. Must be legal residents
of Missouri. Full-time students must have financial need, be
working toward first undergraduate degree, and be
attending a participating Missouri institution. Theology and
divinity students are not eligible. Based on financial need.
Apply after January 1. Deadline: April 30.

1757.

Missouri Student Assistance Resource Services
Missouri Teacher Education Scholarships
Department of Elementary and Secondary Education
P.O. Box 480
Jefferson City, MO 65102
(573) 751-1668
http://www.mocbhe.gov/mostars/fin.menu.htm

Scholarships of varying amounts to graduating high school
seniors and undergraduate students. Must be pursuing a
teaching career. Must be Missouri residents and attend an
accredited Missouri institution. Other restrictions may
apply.

1758.
Missouri Student Assistance Resource Services Robert C. Byrd Scholarship Program
3515 Amazonas Drive
Jefferson City, MO 65109-5717
(314) 751-3940
(800) 473-6757
http://www.mocbhe.gov/mostars/fin.menu.htm

Scholarships of $1,500 to graduating high school seniors. For use the first year of study in a college or university within the state. Must be Missouri residents and attend an accredited Missouri institution. Administered by each state's educating agency. Obtain applications from state agency or high school counselor.

1759.
Missouri Student Assistance Resource Services Vietnam Veteran's Survivor Grant Program
3515 Amazonas Drive
Jefferson City, MO 65109-5717
(314) 751-3940
(800) 473-6757
http://www.mocbhe.gov/mostars/fin.menu.htm

Grants providing tuition costs to graduating high school seniors or undergraduate students. Must be children or spouse of a Vietnam veteran whose death was attributed or caused by exposure to toxic chemicals during the Vietnam conflict. Must maintain satisfactory academic progress. Renewable with maintained academic progress. Must be Missouri residents and attend an accredited Missouri institution. Deadline: none specified.

1760.
Miss Teenage America Awards
Miss Teenage America National Headquarters
c/o Teen Magazine
8490 Sunset Boulevard
Los Angeles, CA 90405

1 scholarship of $15,000 to female student between thirteen and eighteen years. Must be U.S. citizen, unmarried, and in grades 8-12 in current school year. Based on scholastic achievement, awareness, poise, appearance, and individual accomplishment. Deadline: varies.

1761.
Mitchell Field Thrift Shop Scholarship
Scholarship Committee
Building 19
West Road, Mitchell Field
Garden City, NY 11530-6711

1 scholarship of varying amount to a graduating high school senior who is a dependent of an active-duty Armed Forces personnel member (U.S. Army, Air Force, Coast Guard, Marine Corps, or Navy) stationed in the New York area (Brooklyn, Bronx, Manhattan, Queens, Staten Island, Nassau County, or Suffolk County). Must submit a copy of college or university acceptance letter, recommendation, and transcripts. Deadline: May 15.

1762.
Modern Woodmen of America Scholarship Program
Undergraduate Scholarships
Fraternal Scholarship Administrator
1701 1st Avenue
P.O. Box 2005
Rock Island, IL 61205-2005
(309) 793-5630
http://www.modern-woodmen.org/
ssnawerd@modern-woodmen.org

35 four-year scholarships ranging from $750 to $2,000 to high school seniors who are members of the Modern Woodmen of America. Must be high school seniors who have been a member for at least two years and be in the upper 50 percent of class. Based on academic record, SAT/ACT scores, character, leadership, extracurricular activities, and potential. Deadline: January 1.

1763.
Modern Woodmen of America Scholarship Program
Vocational/Technical Scholarships
Fraternal Scholarship Administrator
1701 1st Avenue
P.O. Box 2005
Rock Island, IL 61205-2005
(309) 793-5630
http://www.modern-woodmen.org/
ssnawerd@modern-woodmen.org

12 scholarships of $600 or $1,000 to high school seniors who have been members for at least two years and are in the upper half of their class. Based on academic record, SAT/ACT scores, character, leadership, extracurricular activities, and potential. Deadline: January 1.

1764.
Montana Commission of Higher Education High School Honor Scholarship Program
2500 Broadway
P.O. Box 203101
Helena, MT 59620-3101
(406) 444-6570
(406) 444-1469 Fax
http://www.montana.edu/wwwoche/
scholars@mgslp.state.mt.us

Scholarships of varying amounts to graduating high school seniors. Must meet certain academic criteria, be Montana residents, and attend a Montana institution. Contact high school counselor or above address for more information.

1765.
Montana Commission of Higher Education Indian Fees Waiver Program
2500 Broadway
P.O. Box 203101
Helena, MT 59620
(406) 444-6594
http://www.montana.edu/wwwoche/

500 waivers of registration and incidental fees to graduating high school seniors or undergraduate students. May be used for any field of study. Must be of one-quarter or

more Indian blood and Montana residents for at least one year before enrolling in a Montana university. Must demonstrate financial need. Each school in the system makes its own rules for selection. Deadline: none.

1766.
Montana Commission of Higher Education
Robert C. Byrd Scholarship Program
2500 Broadway
P.O. Box 203101
Helena, MT 59620
(406) 444-6570
(406) 444-1469 Fax
http://www.montana.edu/wwwoche/
scholars@mgslp.state.mt.us

Scholarships of $1,500 to graduating high school seniors. For use the first year of study in a college or university within the state. Must be Missouri residents and attend an accredited Montana institution. Administered by each state's educating agency. Obtain applications from state agency or high school counselor.

1767.
Montana Commission of Higher Education
State Student Incentive Grants
Director of Special Projects
2500 Broadway
P.O. Box 203101
Helena, MT 59620-3101
(406) 444-6570
http://www.montana.edu/wwwoche

Incentive grants of $600 to students who are Montana residents. Must be full-time undergraduates and have financial need. There are also programs offering fee waivers to athletic grants-in-aid, community college honors students, custodial students, dependents of POWs and MIAs, dependents of faculty and staff, high school honors scholarships, honorably discharged veterans, honor scholarships for National Merit Semifinalists, Indian students, nonresidents of Montana, resident senior citizens, residents of Montana, war orphans, and work-study-program participants. Contact above address for more information.

1768.
Montana Commission of Higher Education
University System Fee Waivers
2500 Broadway
P.O. Box 203101
Helena, MT 59620-3101
(406) 444-6570
http://www.montana.edu/wwwoche

The following programs offer exemptions from certain tuition charges and fees at all state-supported public colleges to athletic grants-in-aid, community college honors students, custodial students (residents of the Montana Children's Center, Twin Bridges; Mountain View School, Helena; or Pine Hills School, Miles City), dependents of POWs or MIAs, dependents of faculty and staff, high school honors students, honorably discharged veterans, National Merit Semifinalists, Indian students, nonresidents of Montana, resident senior citizens, and war orphans. Deadline: varies.

1769.
Montana Department of Social and
   Rehabilitation Services
Rehabilitative/Visual Services Division
P.O. Box 4210
Helena, MT 59604

Financial assistance is provided to students who are vocationally handicapped. Must be residents of Montana, of employable age, have a physical or mental disability, and have financial need.

1770.
Montgomery G.I. Bill—Active Duty
Veterans Administration Central Office
810 Vermont Avenue, N.W.
Washington, DC 20420
(800) 368-5896

Benefits of up to $300 per month for up to thirty-six months are available to full-time students who served in the Armed Forces for two years. Must be high school graduates or have a General Equivalency Diploma (GED) and be on active duty, in the reserves, or honorably discharged. For more information, contact above address. Deadline: none.

1771.
Moody Foundation Scholarships
Moody Scholars Program
Nelda Davis Scholarship Administrator
704 Moody National Bank Building
Galveston, TX 77568

Approximately 300 scholarships ranging from $500 to $2,000 to incoming freshmen based on financial need and academic achievement. Must be residents of Galveston County and be planning to attend a Texas college or university. Renewable. Deadline: varies.

1772.
Moorman Agriculture Scholarships
Secretary
Moorman Company Fund
1000 North 30th Street
Quincy, IL 62301-3496

4 scholarships of $1,000 for high school seniors admitted to schools of agriculture. Must be majoring in some branch of agriculture at certain universities. Based on academics; leadership in school, church, community, and/or youth groups; financial need; and interest in some aspect of agriculture.

1773.
Mote Marine Laboratory
Internship Coordinator
Mote Marine Library
1600 Ken Thompson Parkway
Sarasota, FL 34236
(813) 388-4441
(813) 388-4312 Fax

55 internships lasting from eight to sixteen weeks, providing no compensation, are open to undergraduates, recent college graduates, and graduate students. Interns work in

research (biomedical, chemical fate and effects, coastal resources, environmental assessment and enhancement, fisheries and aquaculture, marine mammals, sea turtles, Southwest Florida Coast Research, and shark biology), as well as in support programs in aquarium, education, communications, graphics, and business. Deadline: rolling.

1774.
Mother Joseph Rogan Marymount Foundation
Grants and Loans
Scholarship Chairperson
2217 Clayville Court
St. Louis, MO 63017
(314) 391-6248

Grants and loans of up to $750 to high school seniors. Must be residents of the St. Louis, Missouri, metropolitan area. Must maintain average grades. Based on academic record and financial need. Deadline: May 1.

1775.
MTV: Music Television
Intern Coordinator
1515 Broadway, 22nd Floor
New York, NY 11036
(212) 258-8000

150 ten- to thirteen-week summer, fall, or spring internships providing no compensation. Open to high school, undergraduate, and graduate students. Students must receive academic credit for internship. Internships are in advertising, art promotions, graphics, international programming, marketing, on-air talent, press and public relations, programming, talent relations, video library, or a particular MTV program. Deadline: rolling.

1776.
Music Assistance Fund
Director
New York Philharmonic, Avery Fisher Hall
10 Lincoln Center Plaza
New York, NY 10023-6973
(212) 580-8700

Grants ranging from $250 to $2,500 are made to minority undergraduate students in major conservatories and schools of music throughout the U.S. Must be seeking a career as a member of a symphony orchestra. Also, African Americans enrolled in a music program are eligible for renewable scholarships ranging from $500 to $2,500. Students may be undergraduate or graduate students majoring in music (orchestral instruments only; no piano). The fund offers scholarships to music students of all ages and sometimes funds private study. Based on exceptional talent and financial need. Deadline: December 1.

1777.
Nancy Jo Abels Scholarship Fund
1055 Bedford Road
Pleasantville, NY 10570

39 grants of varying amounts, totaling $39,050, to undergraduate or graduate students. Must be residents of New York State or attending college in New York State. Open to all majors. Write a brief letter detailing your

financial and educational situation. Other restrictions may apply. Deadline: varies.

1778.
NAPA Valley Symphony Association
Robert Mondavi International Music
Achievement Awards
2407 California Boulevard
Napa, CA 94558
(707) 226-6872

Cash awards of $500, $1,000, and $2,000 in a music performance competition. Musicians must be between the ages of eighteen and twenty-five. The competitions will be piano in 1997, strings in 1999, piano in 2001, and strings in 2003. Must submit an audio recording and a $25 nonrefundable entry fee. Send a self-addressed, stamped envelope for information. Deadline: February 12.

1779.
National Academy for Nuclear Training
Scholarship Program
P.O. Box 6302
Princeton, NJ 08541
(800) 828-5489

275 scholarships of $2,500 to undergraduate students majoring in engineering (chemical, electrical, or mechanical) or physics. Must be in the top 20 percent of their class and be U.S. citizens. Renewable with satisfactory academic progress. Deadline: February 3.

1780.
National Achievement Program for Outstanding
Negro Students & National Merit Scholarship
Program
One American Plaza
1560 Sherman Avenue, Suite 200
Evanston, IL 60201

350 scholarships ranging from $250 to $8,000 (many are renewable) to African American high school seniors taking the Preliminary Scholastic Aptitude Test (PSAT) National Merit Scholarship qualifying test. African American students who wish to be considered can check a box on the test. Semifinalists are selected on the basis of test scores. Students should take the PSAT in the junior year. Students do not apply; they become eligible by receiving a certain score or better on the Preliminary Scholastic Aptitude Test. Must be U.S. citizens.

1781.
National Action Council for Minorities in
Engineering (NACME), Inc.
Incentive Grants Program
3 West 35th Street
New York, NY 10001
(212) 279-2626

Numerous grants ranging from $250 to $2,500 to entering freshmen or transfer students who are Native American Indian, African American, Mexican American, or Puerto Rican. Must be majoring in engineering. Must demonstrate need or be designated to receive a merit award. Deadline: varies by college or university.

1782.

National Aeronautics and Space Administration
NASA Headquarters
Higher Education Branch
Mail Code FEH
Washington, DC 20546
(202) 358-0000
(650) 604-4584 TDD
http://www.arc.nasa.gov

1,000 six-week or four-month summer internships
providing salaries ranging from $100 to $400 per week for
undergraduates and from $400 to $700 per week for
graduates. Internship sites are in Alabama, California,
Florida, Maryland, Mississippi, Ohio, Texas, and Virginia.
Open to high school students (at least sixteen years old),
undergraduates, and graduate or professional school
students. Internships are in accounting, budgeting,
engineering, mathematics, procurement, and science. There
are some internships that are specifically for minorities,
while others have no restrictions. Deadline: range from
December 31 to April 1, depending on program.

1783.

National Aeronautics and Space Administration
Undergraduate Student Researchers Program
http://www.arc.nasa.gov

50 summer research positions paying $8,000 per year (for
tuition, books, fees, room, and board) to undergraduate
freshman or sophomore students who are African
American, Hispanic American, Native American, Pacific
Islander, or disabled at colleges and universities across the
country. Must be math, science, or engineering majors.
Program seeks talented students at the beginning of their
undergraduate studies in order to increase the number of
minorities and persons with disabilities receiving degrees in
science and engineering. Must have at least a 3.0 GPA on a
4.0 scale, have scored at least 1000 on SAT or equivalent on
ACT, have taken at least three years of science in high
school, and have successfully completed college prep
courses in high school. Program pays institution $2,000 per
student to cover administrative, advisory, counseling, and
mentorship functions. $2,000 per student is also available to
cover travel, association membership dues and meets, and
summer research experience. Positions are renewable if
student maintains a 3.0 average and remains a math,
science, or engineering major. If selected student transfers to
another school, the grant may also be transferred. Contact
the science, math, or engineering department at your school
for information. Deadline: varies with individual college or
university.

1784.

National Air Transport Association
Foundation Pioneers of Flight Scholarship
Manager Public Relations
4226 King Street
Alexandria, VA 22302

4 renewable scholarships of $2,500 for undergraduate
juniors or seniors. Must be pursuing an aviation-related
career. Selection based on academic achievement, goals, and
other criteria. Other restrictions may apply. Deadline: varies.

1785.

National Amateur Baseball Federation
Ronald & Irene Mcminn Scholarships
P.O. Box 705
Bowie, MD 20718

10 scholarships of $500 to high school seniors and
undergraduates. Must be used at an accredited college or
university and have participated in an NABF event and be
sponsored by an NABF-member association. Selection
based on financial need and academic achievement.
Deadline: none specified.

1786.

National and Community Service
The Corporation for National and Community Service
1100 Vermont Avenue, N.W.
Washington, DC 20525
(800) 942-2677

A program that provides $4,725 a year for up to two years
of community service in one of four priority areas:
education, human services, the environment, or public
safety. Open to anyone of any age interested in earning
assistance to cover educational costs by completing
community service. A person must complete 1,700 hours of
service work per year. Work can be completed before or
after the person has attended a vocational/trade school, an
undergraduate college or university, or a graduate school.
Funds are used to pay current educational expenses or to
repay federal student loans. The program provides a living
allowance of at least $7,400 per year and, if necessary,
health care and child care allowances.

1787.

National Art Materials Trade Association
NAMTA Scholarships
178 Lakeview Avenue
Clifton, NJ 07011
(201) 546-6400

Numerous scholarships of varying amounts to
undergraduate or graduate students who are employees, or
employee dependents or relatives, or to individuals in an
organization related to art or the art materials industry.
Must be used for study in the visual arts. Selection based
on academic achievement, extracurricular activities, interests,
career goals, and financial need. Deadline: March 15.

1788.

National Association for Campus Activities
    Educational Foundation
NACA Multi-Cultural Scholarships
13 Herbison Way
Columbia, SC 29212-3401
(803) 732-6222
(803) 749-1047 Fax

Up to three scholarships for registration to NACA-
sponsored training workshops, regional conferences, and
national conventions to undergraduate and graduate
students. Travel is not included. Open to African American,
Hispanic American, Native American, Pacific Islander, or
Asian American ethnic minority groups who are interested
in training in campus activities. Must have financial need.

Send a self-addressed, stamped envelope for guidelines.
Deadline: May 1.

1789.
**National Association for Campus Activities
    Educational Foundation
NACA Prize Papers Competition**
13 Herbison Way
Columbia, SC 29212-3401
(803) 732-6222

6 prizes of $250 and 6 prizes of $150 to undergraduate or
graduate students, faculty, or staff at a college or university.
Applicants submit an eight- to fifteen-page original paper
on an aspect of campus-activities programming including
management, volunteerism, leadership training, travel,
recreation, etc. Deadline: August 1.

1790.
**National Association for Campus Activities
    Educational Foundation
NACA Scholarships for Student Leaders**
13 Herbison Way
Columbia, SC 29212-3401
(803) 732-6222

Scholarships ranging from $200 to $240 to full-time
undergraduate students who have demonstrated
outstanding leadership abilities and made significant
campus contributions. Deadline: November 1.

1791.
National Association for Sickle Cell Disease
Lonzie L. Jones Jr. Essay Contest
3345 Wilshire Boulevard, Suite 1106
Los Angeles, CA 90010

1 first-place award of $2,500, 1 second-place award of
$1,500, and 1 third-place award of $1,000 to graduating
high school seniors. Based on a 700-to-750-word essay on
a specific theme concerning Sickle Cell Disease. Theme
varies from year to year. Deadline: February 28.

1792.
**National Association for the Advancement of
    Colored People (NAACP)
Agnes Jones Jackson Scholarships**
4805 Mt. Hope Drive
Baltimore, MD 21215-3297
(301) 358-8900
http://www.iwc.pair.com/scholarshipage/org/NAACP.html

Scholarships of $1,500 (undergraduate) and $2,500
(graduate) to minority students. Students must be NAACP
members for at least one year or fully paid life members,
under the age of twenty-five by April 30, and have a
minimum 2.5 GPA (undergraduate) or 3.0 GPA (graduate).
Send legal-size self-addressed, stamped envelope for an
application. Deadline: April 30.

1793.
**National Association for the Advancement of
    Colored People (NAACP)
Roy Wilkins Scholarship**
4805 Mount Hope Drive
Baltimore, MD 21215-3297
(301) 358-8900
http://www.iwc.pair.com/scholarshipage/org/NAACP.html

1 scholarship of $1,000 to a graduating high school senior
who is a member of the NAACP. Applicants must have at
least a 2.5 GPA (C+) average. Include a self-addressed,
stamped envelope. Deadline: April 30.

1794.
**National Association for the Advancement of
    Colored People (NAACP)
Willems Scholarships**
Education Department
4805 Mt. Hope Drive
Baltimore, MD 21215
(301) 358-8900
http://www.iwc.pair.com/scholarshipage/org/NAACP.html

20 scholarships of $2,000 to undergraduates students
majoring in engineering, chemistry, physics, computer or
mathematical sciences. Must have been NAACP member for
one year or more and have at least a 3.0 GPA. Request
between January 1 and April 15. Deadline: April 30.

1795.
**National Association of American Business Clubs
Scholarships**
P.O. Box 5127
High Point, NC 27262
(919) 869-2166

400 to 500 scholarships ranging from $300 to $1,000 to
undergraduate college juniors or seniors or graduate
students majoring in music therapy, physical therapy,
occupational therapy, rehabilitation, speech-language
pathology, hearing-audiology, special education, and related
areas. Based on academic achievement, financial need, and
eligibility requirements. Renewable. Deadline: May 1.

1796.
**National Association of Black Accountants
    (NABA)**
7249-A Hanover Parkway
Greenbelt, MD 20770
(301) 474-NABA
(301) 474-3114 Fax
http://www.wam.umd.edu/

Scholarships ranging from $1,000 to $2,000 to minority
undergraduate and graduate students. Must be in good
academic standing and be paid members of a NABA
student chapter. Applications are available in the summer.

1797.
National Association of Black Journalists
Scholarship Award
P.O. Box 17212
Washington, DC 20041

1 scholarship of $2,500 to an undergraduate or graduate
journalism major enrolled in a four-year accredited college

or university. Must write a 500-to-800-word essay on a black journalist and submit three samples of writing. Check with local NABJ chapters for additional scholarships. Write for an application in the fall.

1798.
National Association of Broadcasters
1771 N Street, N.W.
Washington, DC 20036
(202) 429-5300/(202) 429-5343 Fax
http://www.nab.org

10 grants of up to $1,400 to undergraduate, graduate, or doctoral students for study of the social, political, and economic aspects of broadcasting. Deadline: varies.

1799.
National Association of College Broadcasters
71 George Street
Box 1824
Providence, RI 02912
(401) 863-2225/(401) 863-2221 Fax

8 to 10 internships lasting three to four months providing transportation expenses and a possible stipend to undergraduate students, preferably with some experience in college radio or television station operations. Internships can be part- or full-time, with openings occurring year-round. Interns work in the association, publications, or university network divisions, or possibly with WLNE-TV (local CBS affiliate) in sales, marketing, and research; with WJAR-TV (local NBC affiliate) in news; with WPRI-TV (local ABC affiliate) in production, or with WNAC-TV (local Fox affiliate) in programming. Applicants will work hard and must be comfortable with phone work and have strong writing skills. Submit a letter detailing interests, résumé, and writing sample, and have an interview in person or by phone. Deadline: open.

1800.
National Association of Colored Women's Clubs
Hallie Brown Scholarship Fund
5808 16th Street, N.W.
Washington, DC 20506
(202) 726-2044

Varying numbers of scholarships of $1,000 to undergraduate and graduate African American, Hispanic American, or Native American female students. Write an introductory letter briefly explaining your educational and financial situation. Other restrictions may apply. Student must be recommended by a member of the organization. The organization does not disseminate member information. Applicant must contact a local chapter and ask for an introduction in order to obtain a recommendation letter. We recommend students look in their local phone books for chapters and initiate the procedure. Deadline: April of even-numbered years.

1801.
National Association of Educational Office
Personnel
7223 Lee Highway, Suite 301
Falls Church, VA 22046
(703) 533-0810

3 scholarships of $500 to graduating high school seniors or graduates who will be attending or are now attending a two- or four-year college or vocational/occupational school. Must be pursuing a career in the secretarial business profession. Must have taken two or more business courses (bookkeeping, shorthand, typing, office practices or procedures, etc.). Must maintain a 2.8 GPA during the scholarship year. Contact above address for address of nearest sponsoring association. Deadline: March 15.

1802.
National Association of Hispanic Journalists
(NAHJ)
NAHJ Scholarship Program
1193 National Press Building, Suite 1193
529 14th Street, N.W.
Washington, DC 20045
(202) 662-7145

Scholarships of varying amounts to high school seniors and undergraduate students who are committed to pursuing a career in print or broadcast journalism. Need not major in these areas to be eligible. Hispanic ancestry not required. Good at any accredited U.S. college or university. Deadline: varies.

1803.
National Association of Letter Carriers
Scholarships
100 Indiana Avenue, N.W.
Washington, DC 20001-2144
(202) 393-4695
http://www.nalc.org/
halcinf@access.digex.net

Scholarships of varying amounts to high school seniors who are sons or daughters of active, retired, or deceased letter carriers of the National Association of Letter Carriers, Branch 46. Legally adopted stepchildren, children, and widows are eligible. Based on academic merit. Renewable. Deadline: varies.

1804.
National Association of Letter Carriers
William C. Doherty Scholarships
100 Indiana Ave, N.W.
Washington, DC 20001-2144
(202) 393-4695
http://www.nalc.org/
halcinf@access.digex.net

15 scholarships of $800 to high school seniors who are children or legally adopted stepchildren of active, retired, or deceased letter carriers. Parent or guardian must be employee in good standing for one year prior to application. Applications available only in July through November issues of the *Postal Record*. SAT scores are among requirements. Based on academic merit. Renewable if recipient maintains satisfactory grades. Deadline: varies.

1805.
National Association of Plumbing–Heating–Cooling Contractors (Scholarships)
P.O. Box 6808
Falls Church, VA 22046
(703) 237-8100

Numerous scholarships of $2,500 renewable for up to four years to high school seniors or undergraduate students with background in the plumbing-heating-cooling industry and a specialized academic background. Must be sponsored by NAPHCC member. Deadline: April 1.

1806.
National Association of Real Estate Editors
Charlie Evans Memorial Undergraduate Scholarship
P.O. Box 324
North Olmsted, OH 44070
(216) 779-1624

1 scholarship of $500 to an undergraduate student who is studying to become a real estate/business writer, editor, or broadcaster. Can be used at any college or university. Deadline: May 1.

1807.
National Association of Realtors
Herbert U. Nelson Memorial Fund
430 North Michigan Avenue
Chicago, IL 60611
(312) 329-8296

Scholarships ranging from $500 to $1,500 per semester to undergraduate and graduate students who intend to pursue a career in real estate at any accredited institution. Renewable. Deadline: December 15; April 15; October 15.

1808.
National Association of Returning Students (NARS)
NARS Scholarship Program
P.O. Box 3283
Salem, OR 97302

6 to 9 scholarships ranging from $75 to $500 to undergraduate, graduate, postgraduate, or professional school students. Must be over the age of twenty-five and active student members of NARS. Based on essay. NARS student membership is $15 per year and includes a monthly newsletter, college course, career selection database access, and other services. Deadline: varies.

1809.
National Association of Secondary School Principals (NASSP)
Century III Leaders Scholarships
1904 Association Drive
Reston, VA 22091
(703) 860-0200
http://www.nassp.org

153 scholarships ranging from $100 to $11,500 to graduating high school seniors. Students representing their school are selected by academic achievement, extracurricular activities, community service, and awareness of world events. Must take a current events test and write an essay. Application packets are sent to principals in late August. Obtain applications through high school principal. Deadline: mid-October; may vary.

1810.
National Association of Secondary School Principals (NASSP)
NASSP Principal's Leadership Award (PLA)
1904 Association Drive
Reston, VA 22091
(703) 860-0200
http://www.nassp.org

250 scholarships of $1,000 to high school seniors chosen to represent the senior class as a leader. School winners receive a certificate of merit and are considered semifinalists. Principals receive application packets in mid-October. For information, contact high school counselor or principal.

1811.
National Association of Secondary School Principals (NASSP)
National Honor Society Scholarship Program
1904 Association Drive
Reston, VA 22091
(703) 860-0200
http://www.nassp.org

250 scholarships of $1,000 for graduating high school seniors who are members of the National Honor Society. Applicants must be nominated by their local Honor Society. NHS advisers have applications. Essay theme changes annually. Based on academic record, leadership, character, service, and essay. Deadline: February 2.

1812.
National Association of Social Workers
Arizona Chapter of NASW Scholarships
750 First Street, N.E., Suite 700
Washington, DC 20002
(800) 638-8799 ext. 287

Varying numbers of scholarships of varying amounts for undergraduate and graduate students pursuing degrees in social work. Must be attending an Arizona college or university. Contact the schools directly for more information. Selection based on academic achievement, goals, and financial need. Deadline: varies by school.

1813.
National Association of Teachers of Singing Foundation
Artists Awards Competition
2800 University Boulevard, North
Jacksonville, FL 32211
(904) 744-9022

6 awards ranging from $2,500 to $5,000 to singers between the ages of twenty-one and thirty-five who have studied with a NATS teacher for at least one year. Award is used to assist young singers who are ready for professional careers. Six awards every eighteen months. Deadline: varies.

1814.
National Association of Teachers of Singing Foundation
NATS Foundation Award for Vocal Excellence
3352 Flowerdale Road
Springfield, OH 45504

6 scholarships of $500 that are matched by institutions for undergraduate students who have completed their junior year as a voice major. Request applications after June 1. Deadline: September 1.

1815.
National Association of Water Companies—New Jersey Chapter
Scholarships
c/o NJ-American Water Company
66 Shrewsbury Avenue
Shrewsbury, NJ 07702
(908) 842-6900
(908) 842-7541 Fax

Numerous scholarships of $2,500 to undergraduate or graduate students majoring in biology, business/consumer services, communications, computer science/data processing, earth science, economics, engineering/technology, legal services, natural resources, physical sciences, math, or trade/technical specialties. Must be attending a two- or four-year college or university in New Jersey. Applicants must be pursuing a career in the investor-owned water utility industry. Must have a 3.0 GPA or better. Selection based on application, academic achievement, career goals, essay, transcript, and recommendation letters. Deadline: April 1.

1816.
National Association of Women in Construction
El Camino Real Chapter #158 Scholarships
550 Sunol Street
San Jose, CA 95126
(408) 379-3280

Scholarships of $1,000 to full-time female undergraduate sophomores attending a four-year institution in California. Must be majoring in civil engineering, construction, architecture, or architectural engineering. Can be used during the junior year. Deadline: May 1.

1817.
National Athletic Trainer's Association
NATA Undergraduate Scholarships
Committee on Grants and Scholarships
1001 East Fourth Street
Greenville, NC 27858
(919) 446-2794

25 scholarships of $1,500 to undergraduate sophomores, juniors, seniors, or graduate students. Must have distinguished themselves academically, and performed with distinction as members of the Student Athletic Trainer Program. Students must intend to pursue the profession of athletic training, must conduct themselves, both on and off the field, in a manner that brings credit to themselves, their institution, intercollegiate athletics, and to the ideals and objectives of American higher education. Award is based on academic record, participation in campus activities,

leadership, and record as student athletic trainers. Need is not a factor. Must be nominated by a Certified Athletic Trainer. For more information, write to above address. Deadline: February 1.

1818.
National Audubon Society
Government Affairs Internship Program
666 Pennsylvania Avenue, S.E.
Washington, DC 20003
(202) 547-9009

15 twelve-week summer internships and 3 to 8 twelve-to-twenty-week fall and winter internships providing no compensation. Open to undergraduate juniors, seniors, recent graduates, and graduate students. Internships may be in Washington D.C., Milwaukee, WI; Santa Fe, NM; Elgin, AZ; Trabuco Canyon, CA; Sharon, CT; Naples, FL; Frankfort, KY; Monson, ME; Garrison, NY; Ithaca, NY; or Harleyville, SC. No environmental experience is necessary, but must have interest in environment. Finalists are interviewed by phone. Interns build displays, lead nature walks, and collect field data. Deadline: April 1 (summer); August 1 (fall); January 1 (winter).

1819.
National Audubon Society
Wildlife Management Internships
Attn: Human Resource Department

700 Broadway
New York, NY 10003
(212) 979-3000

15 twelve-week summer internships and 3 to 8 twelve-to-twenty-week fall and winter internships providing no compensation to undergraduate juniors, seniors, recent graduates, and graduate students. Internships may be in Washington D.C., Milwaukee, WI; Santa Fe, NM; Elgin, AZ; Trabuco Canyon, CA; Sharon, CT; Naples, FL; Frankfort, KY; Monson, ME; Garrison, NY; Ithaca, NY; or Harleyville, SC. No environmental experience is necessary. Finalists are interviewed by phone. Deadline: varies.

1820.
National Baptist Convention U.S.A., Inc.
General Scholarships
356 East Boulevard
Baton Rouge, LA 70802

Scholarships of $1,000 to students who are active members of National Baptist Convention USA, Inc., churches. Based on financial need. Apply before the fall semester of each year. Deadline: varies.

1821.
National Basketball Association
Intern Coordinator
645 Fifth Avenue
New York, NY 10022
(212) 826-7000
http://www.nba.com

8 to 12 internships selected for summer, fall, and spring programs that provide $200 per week stipend to undergraduate sophomores, juniors, and seniors. Interns

must receive academic credit for the internship. Internships are in New York, NY, and Secaucus, NJ. Students are assigned to NBA Entertainment in New Jersey, and to broadcasting, consumer products, team services (marketing), and public relations in New York. Submit a résumé, a cover letter outlining relevant background and department to which you are applying, and a letter from your college or university explaining that you will receive at least six semester credits for the NBA internship. Candidates must travel to New York (at student's expense) for an on-site visit and interview. Deadline: April 15 (summer); August 15 (fall); December 15 (spring).

1822.
National Black Nurses' Association
Dr. Lauranne Sams Scholarships
P.O. Box 1823
Washington, DC 20013
(202) 393-6870

Scholarships ranging from $1,000 to $4,000 to undergraduate students enrolled in a nursing program (associate's diploma, bachelor of science in nursing, or LPN/LVN) in good scholastic standing. Association members given preference. Based on academic record, nursing commitment, involvement in black community, integrity, and financial need. Renewable. Deadline: April 15.

1823.
National Black Police Association Scholarship
Alphonso Deal Scholarship Award
Attn: Executive Director
3251 Mount Pleasant, N.W., 2nd Floor
Washington, DC 20010
(202) 986-2070

1 scholarship of $500 to a minority high school senior graduating from any high school in the U.S. Student should express an interest in criminal justice, law, or related career and must have at least a 2.5 GPA. Based on recommendations, academics, and extracurricular activities. Deadline: June 1.

1824.
National Business Aircraft Association
Scholarships
Education Programs
1200 Eighteenth Street, N.W.
Second Floor, Suite 200
Washington, DC 20036-2598
(202) 783-9000

10 scholarships of $500 to undergraduate sophomores, juniors, or seniors who will be continuing in school the following academic year. Must be U.S. citizens and enrolled in an aviation-related program at an NBAA member institution. Must have a cumulative GPA of 3.0 or higher. Submit with application a 250-word paper describing your interest in a career in aviation and a written request for detailed purpose and objective of scholarship. Deadline: October 15.

1825.
National Campers and Hikers Association
Scholarships
Scholarship Director
74 West Genesee Street
Skaneateles, NY 13152

8 scholarships ranging from $500 to $2,000 to high school seniors and undergraduate students attending two- or four-year institutions and majoring in conservation, forestry, wildlife management, geology, or related fields. High school seniors must be in the upper 40 percent of their class, with at least a 1000 SAT score. College students must have at least a 3.0 GPA. Deadline: April 15.

1826.
National Center for Indian Education
Santa Fe Pacific Railway Foundation Grant
Program
P.O. Box 18239, Capitol Hill Station
Denver, CO 80218
(303) 861-1052

Scholarships of up to $2,000 per year for four years to high school seniors with one-quarter degree or more Indian blood. Must be residents of Kansas, Oklahoma, Colorado, Arizona, or San Bernadino County, California. Must major in business, engineering, science, or medicine. Based on academic performance and need. Deadline: March 15.

1827.
National Collegiate Athletic Association (NCAA)
NCAA Degree Completion Grant
6201 College Boulevard
Overland Park, KS 66211-2422
(913) 339-1906

Full athletic grants to full-time students and grants covering tuition and book allowance to part-time students. Full-time students may be funded for two semesters and part-time students for five semester hours. Must have completed their athletics eligibility at a Division I member institution at least one year before application and be within thirty semester hours of graduating. Deadline: October 10 (fall); May 15 (spring).

1828.
National Commercial Finance Association
A. Van Biema Essay Award
225 West 34th Street, Suite 1815
New York, NY 10001
(212) 594-3490

$1,500 award to an undergraduate or graduate student in a commercial finance field at an accredited university. Award given for best essay (not to exceed 5,000 words) on a subject in asset-based lending. Essays must be typed, double-spaced, on one side of plain white paper. Deadline: June 28; may vary.

1829.
National Council of Jewish Women (NCJW)
Amelia Greenbaum Scholarship Fund
Administrative Director
Greater Boston Section
75 Harvard Avenue
Allston, MA 02134

Scholarships of varying amounts to female students of the Jewish faith who are Greater Boston-area residents. Must be attending or planning to attend a Massachusetts institution. Priority given to women returning to school after at least a five-year absence or new Americans with English competency who intend to study an area related to NCJW (social work, public policy, administration, law, or early childhood education). Amount of scholarship is based on student's need. Deadline: April 30.

1830.
National Council of State Garden Clubs, Inc.
Scholarships
4401 Magnolia Avenue
St. Louis, MO 63110-3492

30 scholarships of $3,500 to undergraduate juniors, seniors, or graduate students pursuing a career in agriculture, biology, botany, floriculture, forestry, horticulture, natural resources, or related areas. Must have at least a 3.0 GPA and be nominated by their home state's Garden Club. Selection based on academic achievement, financial need, and recommendation letters. Deadline: March 1.

1831.
National Electronic Distributor Association
(NEDA) Education Foundation
NEDA Scholarships
35 East Wacker Drive, Suite 3202
Chicago, IL 60601

20 to 25 scholarships of $1,000 to full-time undergraduate students majoring in a discipline related to electronic distribution (industrial distribution, business administration, or marketing). Can be used at any accredited college or university. Renewable up to four years. Deadline: June 1.

1832.
National Executive Housekeepers Educational
Foundation
National Scholarship Chairperson
1001 Eastwind Drive, Suite 301
Westerville, OH 43081

Scholarships of varying amounts to students enrolled in a National Executive Housekeepers Association (NEHA)-participating postsecondary institution. Must be majoring in institutional housekeeping management. Based on financial need, potential, and enthusiasm. Deadline: January and September.

1833.
National Federation of Music Clubs
Chairman, Scholarship Department
NFMC Headquarters
1336 North Delaware Street
Indianapolis, IN 46202
(317) 638-4003

About $138,000 is awarded annually, in a diversity of music scholarships ranging from $100 to $5,000, by affiliated music clubs. Latest information can be obtained through subscription to appropriate publications, YAI Young Artist Auditions Bulletins ($1.75 each) and SAI Student Auditions Bulletin ($1.75 each). These may be ordered from address above. Based on musical talent and promise. Request scholarship and awards charts at the above address and request "SC3" (40¢ each). Include two first-class stamps for postage.

1834.
National Federation of Music Clubs
Hazel Heffner Becchnina Award in Voice
740 Chestnut Street
Camden, AR 71701

1 award of $1,500 to a student between the ages of eighteen and twenty-six (by March 1 of the audition year) who is majoring in vocal music. Must be a member of the National Federation of Music Clubs. Awarded only in odd-numbered years. Contact: Wanda Fantz, Scholarship Chairperson, 37 Meadow Lane, Stuttgart, AR 72160. Deadline: November 15.

1835.
National Federation of Music Clubs
Hinda Honigman Scholarship for the Blind
Headquarters Office
Chairman, Scholarship Department
1336 North Delaware Street
Indianapolis, IN 46202
(317) 638-4003

1 scholarship of $250 and 1 scholarship of $500 to high school and undergraduate students between sixteen and twenty-six years of age. Must be legally blind. Include a self-addressed, stamped envelope to obtain an application and information. Deadline: March 15.

1836.
National Federation of Music Clubs
Irene S. Muir Voice Awards
740 Chestnut Street
Camden, AR 71701

2 scholarships of $1,000 to undergraduate vocal music majors. One award each for a male and a female. Must be between eighteen and twenty-five years old and a member of the National Federation of Music Clubs. Awarded only in odd-numbered years. Contact: Wanda Fantz, Scholarship Chairperson, 37 Meadow Lane, Stuttgart, AR 72160. Deadline: November 15.

1837.
National Federation of Music Clubs (NFMC) Junior Festivals
1336 North Delaware Street
Indianapolis, IN 46202
(317) 638-4003

Awards of gold cups and special certificates to students up to the age of nineteen in a music competition in 21 categories: electronic organ, percussion, hand bells, hymn playing, piano (solo, duets, quartets, and concertos), strings, woodwinds, brass, vocal art–musical theater, and musicianship. Some states also hold auditions in ballet, theater dance, and tap. Festivals are held in the forty-one states where the Federation has active senior clubs. Notices of festival sites and dates are sent to music teachers who are members. Students must be club members or special members. Students may enter as an individual or group and play two pieces. The first piece is an American patriotic or folk song composition; the second piece may be chosen by the student or group. The required pieces are at different levels. Students are not judged against each other, but rather rated as superior, excellent, very good, good, or fair. Send a self-addressed, stamped envelope for information on how to join NFMC and about the festivals. Deadline: varies by festival.

1838.
National Federation of Music Clubs NFMC Music for the Blind
Chairman, Scholarship Department
1336 North Delaware Street
Indianapolis, IN 46202
(317) 638-4003

1 scholarship of $200 to undergraduate and graduate students between nineteen and thirty-one years in the area of musical composition. Must be legally blind. Include a self-addressed, stamped envelope for application and information. Deadline: March 30.

1839.
National Federation of Music Clubs Virginia Peace Mackey–Althouse Voice Award
740 Chestnut Street
Camden, AR 71701

1 scholarship of $1,200 to a female student between the ages of eighteen and twenty-six who is majoring in vocal music. Must be a member of the National Federation of Music Clubs. Only awarded during odd-numbered years. Contact: Wanda Fantz, Scholarship Chairperson, 37 Meadow Lane, Stuttgart, AR 72160. Deadline: November 15.

1840.
National Federation of Music Clubs Vivian Nelson Scholarship for the Handicapped
Chairman, Scholarship Department
1336 North Delaware Street
Indianapolis, IN 46202
(317) 638-4003

1 scholarship worth $1,000 to an undergraduate or graduate student between the ages of twenty-five and thirty-five. Must be handicapped in some way. Award may be used for undergraduate or professional study. Include a self-addressed, stamped envelope for application and information. Deadline: March 15.

1841.
National Federation of Music Clubs Young Artist Auditions
740 Chestnut Street
Camden, AR 71701

8 scholarships ranging from $500 to $5,000 to instrumentalists and vocalists. Instrumentalists must be between the ages of eighteen and twenty-nine (by March 1 of the year of auditions); vocalists must be between the ages of twenty-three and thirty-four. Awarded in odd-numbered years. Contact: Mrs. Donald A. Morton, NFMC Chairperson, 1704 Varner Avenue, McLean, VA 22101. Deadline: November 15.

1842.
National Federation of Press Women
Helen Miller Malloch Scholarship
4510 West 89th Street, Suite 110
Prairie Village, KS 66207-2282
(913) 341-2715
(913) 342-0165 Fax

1 scholarship of $1,000 to a female college junior or senior or graduate student majoring in communications. Based on scholarship, professional intent, and financial need. Deadline: varies.

1843.
National Federation of Press Women
NFPW Junior/Senior Scholarship
4510 West 89th Street, Suite 110
Prairie Village, KS 66207-2282
(913) 341-2715
(913) 342-0165 Fax

1 scholarship of $1,000 to a female high school junior or senior planning to major in journalism. Recipient may use award at the college or university of her choice.

1844.
National Federation of State Poetry Societies, Inc. Scholarship Fund for Poets
c/o G. F. Walker
915 Aberdeen Avenue
Baton Rouge, LA 70808
(504) 334-9932

Numerous $500 scholarships to undergraduate college juniors and seniors in the area of poetry at accredited U.S. institutions. Send self-addressed, stamped envelope for complete information. Deadline: February 1.

1845.
National Federation of the Blind (NFB) Scholarships
1800 Johnson Street
Baltimore, MD 21230
(301) 659-9314
http://www.nfb.org
epc@roudley.com

3 scholarships worth $4,000, 4 scholarships worth $2,500, and 10 scholarships worth $2,000 to undergraduate students in any major field of study. Must be legally blind. Must attend national convention to accept award. Must be accepted for full-time study at an accredited college or university. Request applications after July 1; enclose a self-addressed, stamped envelope. Deadline: March 31.

1846.
National Federation of the Blind (NFB) Scholarships
American Brotherhood for the Blind Scholarship
Chairperson
1800 Johnson Street
Baltimore, MD 21230
(301) 659-9314
http://www.nfb.org
epc@roudley.com

1 scholarship of $6,000 to a blind undergraduate or graduate student. Open to both male and female students entering any field of study. Based on academic achievements, service to the community, and financial need. Deadline: March 31.

1847.
National Federation of the Blind (NFB) Scholarships
Blind Educator of Tomorrow Award
1800 Johnson Street
Baltimore, MD 21230
(301) 659-9314
http://www.nfb.org
epc@roudley.com

1 scholarship worth $2,500 to a legally blind undergraduate student pursuing a career in elementary, secondary, or postsecondary education. Request an application after July 1 and enclose a self-addressed, stamped envelope for an application and information. Deadline: March 31.

1848.
National Federation of the Blind (NFB) Scholarships
Distinguished Scholar
1800 Johnson Street
Baltimore, MD 21230
(301) 659-9314
http://www.nfb.org
epc@roudley.com

1 scholarship worth $20,000 to a graduating high school senior or high school graduate who has been accepted to an accredited two- or four-year college or university for full-time study in any major. Must be legally blind and attend the annual convention to receive award. Request an application after July 1 and include a self-addressed, stamped envelope for application and information. Deadline: March 31.

1849.
National Federation of the Blind (NFB) Scholarships
Esra Davis Memorial Scholarship
Chairperson
1800 Johnson Street
Baltimore, MD 21230
(301) 659-9314
http://www.nfb.org
epc@roudley.com

1 scholarship of $10,000 to a legally blind male or female student enrolled in or planning to enroll in a college or university. For all college levels and fields of interest. Based on academic achievements, service to the community, and financial need. Request applications after July 1. Deadline: March 31.

1850.
National Federation of the Blind (NFB) Scholarships
Francis Urbanek Memorial Scholarship
Chairperson
1800 Johnson Street
Baltimore, MD 21230
(301) 659-9314
http://www.nfb.org
epc@roudley.com

1 scholarship of $2,000 to a legally blind high school graduate about to enter the freshman year at college. Good for any major at any college or university. Based on academic achievements, service to the community, and financial need. Deadline: March 31.

1851.
National Federation of the Blind (NFB) Scholarships
Frank Walton Horn Memorial Scholarship
Chairperson
1800 Johnson Street
Baltimore, MD 21230
(301) 659-9314
http://www.nfb.org
epc@roudley.com

1 scholarship of $2,500 to a legally blind student at any college or university. Preference given to students majoring in architecture or engineering. Based on academic achievements, service to the community, and financial need. Deadline: March 31.

1852.
National Federation of the Blind (NFB) Scholarships
Hermione Grant Calhoun Scholarship
Chairperson
1800 Johnson Street
Baltimore, MD 21230
(301) 659-9314
http://www.nfb.org
epc@roudley.com

2 scholarships of $2,500 to blind female students majoring in education at an accredited college or university. Based on

academic achievements, service to the community, and financial need. Deadline: March 31.

1853.
National Federation of the Blind (NFB) Scholarships
Howard Brown Rickard Scholarship
1800 Johnson Street
Baltimore, MD 21230
(301) 659-9314
http://www.nfb.org

1 scholarship of $2,500 to a blind student majoring in law, medicine, engineering, architecture, or the natural sciences. Based on academic achievements, service to the community, and financial need. Deadline: March 31.

1854.
National Federation of the Blind (NFB) Scholarships
Humanities Scholarship
1800 Johnson Street
Baltimore, MD 21230
(301) 659-9314
http://www.nfb.org

1 scholarship worth $2,500 to a legally blind undergraduate student majoring in art, English, foreign languages, history, philosophy, or religion. Must be accepted for full-time humanities study at an accredited college or university. Enclose a self-addressed, stamped envelope for an application and information. Deadline: March 31.

1855.
National Federation of the Blind (NFB) Scholarships
Melva T. Owen Memorial Scholarship
1800 Johnson Street
Baltimore, MD 21230
(301) 659-9314
http://www.nfb.org

1 scholarship of $1,800 to a blind student going into any field of study except religion. Must be attending a college or university in order to become financially independent and not only to further general or cultural education. Based on academic achievements, service to the community, and financial need. Request applications after July 1. Deadline: March 31.

1856.
National Federation of the Blind (NFB) Scholarships
Merit Scholarships
1800 Johnson Street
Baltimore, MD 21230
(301) 659-9314
http://www.nfb.org

3 scholarships of $4,000, 7 scholarships of $2,500, and 9 scholarships of $1,800 to blind male and female students. May be used for any field of study at an accredited college or university. Based on academic achievements, service to the community, and financial need. Request applications

after July 1 and enclose a self-addressed, stamped envelope. Deadline: March 31.

1857.
National Federation of the Blind (NFB) Scholarships
Oracle Corporation Scholarship
1800 Johnson Street
Baltimore, MD 21230
(301) 659-9314
http://www.nfb.org

1 scholarship worth $2,500 to a legally blind undergraduate student majoring in computer science, engineering, or technical writing. Must be accepted for full-time study at an accredited college or university. Must attend annual convention to accept award. Request applications after July 1 and enclose a self-addressed, stamped envelope. Deadline: March 31.

1858.
National Foster Parent Association
Benjamin Eaton Scholarship Trust Fund
Scholarship Chair
Information and Services Office
226 Kilts Drive
Houston, TX 77024
(713) 467-1850

Scholarships for foster children or birth children in foster homes to attend a postsecondary institution. Must be foster children, adopted children, or birth children in foster homes affiliated with the NFPA. Amount of the scholarships is determined by the trust fund. Deadline: March 1.

1859.
National 4–H Awards Scholarships
National 4–H Council
7100 Connecticut Avenue
Chevy Chase, MD 20815
(301) 961-2800

Numerous scholarships of $1,000 to high school seniors or undergraduate college freshmen going into farming, farm management, business and industry, research and industry, processing, marketing, advertising, and conservation. Submit National Report Form, high school transcript, and the original and two copies of "My 4-H Story." Deadline: April 1; may vary.

1860.
National Frozen Food Association
Attn: Neven Montgomery
4755 Linglestown Road, 300
Harrisburg, PA 17112
(717) 657-8601
http://www.nffa.org

12 scholarships of $1,000 to undergraduate students who are residents of any of the six New England states and who are planning on a career in the food industry (including nutrition and dietetics). Awards can be used at two- or four-year colleges. Deadline: April 1.

1861.
National Future Farmers of America (FFA) Center
Ag Radio Network, Inc.
Executive Director
5632 Mount Vernon Memorial Highway
P.O. Box 15160
Alexandria, VA 22309-0160
(703) 360-3600
(703) 360-5524 Fax
http://www.ffa.org/

1 scholarship of $500 to a high school senior who is an
FFA member. Must be planning to major in agriculture in a
two-year program. Must be a resident of Connecticut,
Maine, Massachusetts, New Hampshire, New York, Rhode
Island, or Vermont. Deadline: March 1.

1862.
National Future Farmers of America (FFA) Center
Agricultural Scholarship
P.O. Box 5117
310 North Midvale Boulevard
Madison, WI 53705

1 scholarship of varying amount to a high school senior or
college freshman majoring in agriculture or veterinary
medicine. Must be member of FFA and club leader. Write
for complete details. Deadline: March 1.

1863.
National Future Farmers of America (FFA) Center
Allflex/Vet Brand, Inc.
Executive Director
5632 Mount Vernon Memorial Highway
P.O. Box 15160
Alexandria, VA 22309-0160
(703) 360-3600
(703) 360-5524 Fax
http://www.ffa.org/

1 scholarship of $1,000 to a high school senior who is an
FFA member. Must be planning to major in animal science
at a four-year college or university. Must be a member of
FFA. Deadline: March 1.

1864.
National Future Farmers of America (FFA) Center
Alpha Gamma Rho Educational Foundation
    Scholarship
Executive Director
5632 Mount Vernon Memorial Highway
P.O. Box 15160
Alexandria, VA 22309-0160
(703) 360-3600
(703) 360-5524 Fax
http://www.ffa.org/

1 scholarship of $1,000 to a male high school graduate who
is an FFA member. Must be enrolled or planning to enroll
in an agricultural, forestry, or veterinary medicine degree
program. Must be FFA member and nominated by the State
Supervisor of Agricultural Education. Based on academic
record and extracurricular activities. Deadline: March 1.

1865.
National Future Farmers of America (FFA) Center
American Dairy Goat Association
Executive Director
5632 Mount Vernon Memorial Highway
P.O. Box 15160
Alexandria, VA 22309-0160
(703) 360-3600
(703) 360-5524 Fax
http://www.ffa.org/

3 scholarships of $1,000 to high school seniors who are
FFA members. Must be planning on majoring in agriculture/
agribusiness. Must have used dairy goats as part of the FFA
Supervised Occupational Experience Program. Preference
given to students who have competitively shown dairy
goats at fairs, rodeos, etc. Deadline: March 1.

1866.
National Future Farmers of America (FFA) Center
American Floral Endowment
Executive Director
5632 Mount Vernon Memorial Highway
P.O. Box 15160
Alexandria, VA 22309-0160
(703) 360-3600
(703) 360-5524 Fax
http://www.ffa.org/

1 scholarship of $1,000 to a high school senior who is an
FFA member. Must be planning to major in floriculture and/
or environmental horticulture and obtain a bachelor's
degree. Deadline: March 1.

1867.
National Future Farmers of America (FFA) Center
American Morgan Horse Institute
Executive Director
5632 Mount Vernon Memorial Highway
P.O. Box 15160
Alexandria, VA 22309-0160
(703) 360-3600
(703) 360-5524 Fax
http://www.ffa.org/

2 scholarships of $1,000 at a four-year institution and 1
scholarship of $500 at a two-year institution to high school
seniors who were FFA members. Must be planning to
major in animal science, with an equine emphasis. Deadline:
March 1.

1868.
National Future Farmers of America (FFA) Center
Association Milk Products, Inc.–Babson Brothers,
    Co./SURGE
Executive Director
5632 Mount Vernon Memorial Highway
P.O. Box 15160
Alexandria, VA 22309-0160
(703) 360-3600
(703) 360-5524 Fax
http://www.ffa.org/

5 scholarships of $1,000 to high school seniors who were FFA members. Must attend a four-year college or university and major in dairy science. Must have competed in the Dairy contest at the local, state, and national level. 8 scholarships of $1,000 to high-scoring students in the National FFA Dairy Contest. Deadline: March 1.

1869.
National Future Farmers of America (FFA) Center
Barlett and Company
Executive Director
5632 Mount Vernon Memorial Highway
P.O. Box 15160
Alexandria, VA 22309-0160
(703) 360-3600
(703) 360-5524 Fax
http://www.ffa.org/

1 scholarship of $500 to a high school senior or graduate planning to major in agriculture at a two-year college in Kansas. Must have been in the upper 20 percent of class. Based on academic record, leadership, and financial need. Deadline: March 1.

1870.
National Future Farmers of America (FFA) Center
Building Rural Initiative for Disabled Through
   Group Effort (B.R.I.D.G.E.)
Executive Director
5632 Mount Vernon Memorial Highway
P.O. Box 15160
Alexandria, VA 22309-0160
(703) 360-3600
(703) 360-5524 Fax
http://www.ffa.org/

1 scholarship of $1,000 to a high school senior who was an FFA member. Must be physically disabled. Must be planning to major in agriculture at a four-year university. Deadline: March 1.

1871.
National Future Farmers of America (FFA) Center
Building Rural Initiative for Disabled Through
   Group Effort (B.R.I.D.G.E.) Sponsored by
   Quaker Oats Foundation
Executive Director
5632 Mount Vernon Memorial Highway
P.O. Box 15160
Alexandria, VA 22309-0160
(703) 360-3600
(703) 360-5524 Fax
http://www.ffa.org

1 scholarship of $1,000 to a high school senior who was an FFA member. Must be physically disabled. Must be planning to major in agriculture at a four-year university. Deadline: March 1.

1872.
National Future Farmers of America (FFA) Center
Bunge Corporation
Executive Director
5632 Mount Vernon Memorial Highway
P.O. Box 15160
Alexandria, VA 22309-0160
(703) 360-3600
(703) 360-5524 Fax
http://www.ffa.org

1 scholarship of $1,000 to a high school senior who was an FFA member. Must be planning to major in agriculture at a four-year institution. Deadline: March 1.

1873.
National Future Farmers of America (FFA) Center
Business Men's Assurance Company of America
Executive Director
5632 Mount Vernon Memorial Highway
P.O. Box 15160
Alexandria, VA 22309-0160
(703) 360-3600
(703) 360-5524 Fax
http://www.ffa.org/

5 scholarships of $1,000 to high school seniors who were FFA members. Must be planning to major in some area of agriculture at a four-year institution. Must be residents of Alabama, Arizona, Arkansas, California, Colorado, Delaware, Florida, Georgia, Idaho, Illinois, Indiana, Iowa, Kansas, Kentucky, Louisiana, Maryland, Michigan, Minnesota, Mississippi, Missouri, Montana, Nebraska, Nevada, New Mexico, North Carolina, North Dakota, Ohio, Oklahoma, Oregon, Pennsylvania, South Carolina, South Dakota, Tennessee, Texas, Utah, Virginia, Washington, West Virginia, Wisconsin, or Wyoming. Deadline: March 1.

1874.
National Future Farmers of America (FFA) Center
Capital Agricultural Property Service
Executive Director
5632 Mount Vernon Memorial Highway
P.O. Box 15160
Alexandria, VA 22309-0160
(703) 360-3600
(703) 360-5524 Fax
http://www.ffa.org/

1 scholarship of $1,000 to a high school senior who was an FFA member. Must be pursuing a four-year degree in agricultural economics. Deadline: March 1.

1875.
National Future Farmers of America (FFA) Center
Carhartt, Inc.
Executive Director
5632 Mount Vernon Memorial Highway
P.O. Box 15160
Alexandria, VA 22309-0160
(703) 360-3600
(703) 360-5524 Fax
http://www.ffa.org/

1 scholarship of $1,000 to a high school senior who was an FFA member. Must be pursuing a four-year degree in agricultural education. Deadline: March 1.

1876.
National Future Farmers of America (FFA) Center
CarQuest Corporation
Executive Director
5632 Mount Vernon Memorial Highway
P.O. Box 15160
Alexandria, VA 22309-0160
(703) 360-3600
(703) 360-5524 Fax
http://www.ffa.org/

4 scholarships of $1,000 to high school seniors who were FFA members. Must have been a member of FFA chapter with a CarQuest store within twenty-five miles. Good for any major. Deadline: March 1.

1877.
National Future Farmers of America (FFA) Center
Casey's General Stores, Inc.
Executive Director
5632 Mount Vernon Memorial Highway
P.O. Box 15160
Alexandria, VA 22309-0160
(703) 360-3600
(703) 360-5524 Fax
http://www.ffa.org/

3 scholarships of $500 to high school seniors who were FFA members. Must be pursuing an agricultural or agribusiness career at a two-year institution. One scholarship each in Illinois, Iowa, and Missouri. Based on academic record, leadership, and financial need. Deadline: March 1.

1878.
National Future Farmers of America (FFA) Center
Chevron U.S.A., Inc.
Executive Director
5632 Mount Vernon Memorial Highway
P.O. Box 15160
Alexandria, VA 22309-0160
(703) 360-3600
(703) 360-5524 Fax
http://www.ffa.org/

1 scholarship of $1,000 to an undergraduate college student attending a four-year college or university in Georgia or Florida majoring in agriculture or agribusiness. Must be an FFA member. Preference given to students with outstanding leadership abilities. Deadline: March 1.

1879.
National Future Farmers of America (FFA) Center
Chicago and Northwestern Transportation Company
Executive Director
5632 Mount Vernon Memorial Highway
P.O. Box 15160
Alexandria, VA 22309-0160
(703) 360-3600
(703) 360-5524 Fax
http://www.ffa.org/

1 scholarship of $1,000 to an undergraduate student who has been an FFA member. Must be majoring in agricultural education at a four-year college or university. Deadline: March 1.

1880.
National Future Farmers of America (FFA) Center
Chicago Mercantile Exchange
Executive Director
5632 Mount Vernon Memorial Highway
P.O. Box 15160
Alexandria, VA 22309-0160
(703) 360-3600
(703) 360-5524 Fax
http://www.ffa.org/

4 scholarships of $1,000 to undergraduate college students who have been FFA members. Must be majoring in agricultural economics, animal science (cows and hogs), production management, or agricultural education. Deadline: March 1.

1881.
National Future Farmers of America (FFA) Center
Chief Industries, Inc.
Executive Director
5632 Mount Vernon Memorial Highway
P.O. Box 15160
Alexandria, VA 22309-0160
(703) 360-3600
(703) 360-5524 Fax
http://www.ffa.org/

1 scholarship of $1,000 to a high school senior who will attend a four-year institution, and 1 scholarship of $500 to a high school senior who will attend a two-year institution. Both recipients must be from Nebraska, FFA members, and planning to major in agriculture. Deadline: March 1.

1882.
National Future Farmers of America (FFA) Center
ConAgra, Inc.
Executive Director
5632 Mount Vernon Memorial Highway
P.O. Box 15160
Alexandria, VA 22309-0160
(703) 360-3600
(703) 360-5524 Fax
http://www.ffa.org/

2 scholarships of $1,500 per year for four years (totaling $6,000) to graduating high school seniors. Must be planning to attend the University of Nebraska-Lincoln and major in agribusiness. Must be in the upper 15 percent of class. Renewable if a 3.2 GPA on a 4.0 scale is maintained. Deadline: March 1.

1883.
National Future Farmers of America (FFA) Center
Coopers Animal Health, Inc.
Executive Director
5632 Mount Vernon Memorial Highway
P.O. Box 15160
Alexandria, VA 22309-0160
(703) 360-3600
(703) 360-5524 Fax
http://www.ffa.org/

1 scholarship of $1,000 to an undergraduate college student
majoring in pre-veterinary medicine. Must have been an
FFA member. Deadline: March 1.

1884.
National Future Farmers of America (FFA) Center
Cornhusker Farms
Executive Director
5632 Mount Vernon Memorial Highway
P.O. Box 15160
Alexandria, VA 22309-0160
(703) 360-3600
(703) 360-5524 Fax
http://www.ffa.org/

1 scholarship of $1,000 to an undergraduate college student
majoring in an agriculture-related field at a four-year
college or university. Must be an FFA member. Must have
worked in an area of swine production. Must be a resident
of Iowa, Kansas, Minnesota, Nebraska, or South Dakota.
Deadline: March 1.

1885.
National Future Farmers of America (FFA) Center
Data Transmission Network Corporation
Executive Director
5632 Mount Vernon Memorial Highway
P.O. Box 15160
Alexandria, VA 22309-0160
(703) 360-3600
(703) 360-5524 Fax
http://www.ffa.org/

1 scholarship of $1,000 scholarship to a high school senior
who was an FFA member. May major in any agriculture-
related area at a four-year institution. Deadline: March 1.

1886.
National Future Farmers of America (FFA) Center
Eastern Agriculture Society of North America
Executive Director
5632 Mount Vernon Memorial Highway
P.O. Box 15160
Alexandria, VA 22309-0160
(703) 360-3600
(703) 360-5524 Fax
http://www.ffa.org/

1 scholarship of $500 to an undergraduate college student
attending a two-year college or vocational/technical school
and majoring in agribusiness or an agriculture-related area.

Must have been an FFA member. College or vocational/
technical school must be in Connecticut, Delaware, Maine,
Maryland, Massachusetts, New Hampshire, New Jersey,
New York, North Carolina, Ohio, Pennsylvania, Rhode
Island, Tennessee, Vermont, Virginia, West Virginia, or the
District of Columbia. Deadline: March 1.

1887.
National Future Farmers of America (FFA) Center
Edward D. Jones & Co. Scholarship
Executive Director
5632 Mount Vernon Memorial Highway
P.O. Box 15160
Alexandria, VA 22309-0160
(703) 360-3600
(703) 360-5524 Fax
http://www.ffa.org/

1 scholarship of $500 to a high school senior who is an
FFA member and planning to enroll as a freshman
majoring in agriculture economics or education at a four-
year undergraduate program at any accredited U.S. college
or university. Must be a resident of Illinois or Missouri.
Deadline: April 1.

1888.
National Future Farmers of America (FFA) Center
Ellen Nielsen Cooperative
Executive Director
5632 Mount Vernon Memorial Highway
P.O. Box 15160
Alexandria, VA 22309-0160
(703) 360-3600
(703) 360-5524 Fax
http://www.ffa.org/

4 scholarships of $500 to undergraduate college students
majoring in an agriculture-related field. Must have been
FFA members. Must be residents of and attending a four-
year college or university in one of the following states:
Colorado, Illinois, Iowa, Kansas, Minnesota, Missouri,
Nebraska, North Dakota, Oklahoma, South Dakota, Texas,
Wisconsin, or Wyoming. Based on financial need. Deadline:
March 1.

1889.
National Future Farmers of America (FFA) Center
Farm Aid
Executive Director
5632 Mount Vernon Memorial Highway
P.O. Box 15160
Alexandria, VA 22309-0160
(703) 360-3600
(703) 360-5524 Fax
http://www.ffa.org/

9 scholarships of $3,000 ($1,500 during freshman year;
$1,000 during sophomore year; and $500 during junior
year) for high school seniors who were FFA members.
Must be planning to major in an agriculture-related area.

Must be from a farm family and have at least a 2.0 GPA on a 4.0 scale. Based on academic record, career goal, and financial need. Deadline: March 1.

1890.
National Future Farmers of America (FFA) Center Farmers Hybrid Companies, Inc.
Executive Director
5632 Mount Vernon Memorial Highway
P.O. Box 15160
Alexandria, VA 22309-0160
(703) 360-3600
(703) 360-5524 Fax
http://www.ffa.org/

2 scholarships of $1,000 to undergraduate college students majoring in animal science at a four-year college or university. Must have been FFA members. Deadline: March 1.

1891.
National Future Farmers of America (FFA) Center Farmers Mutual Hail Insurance Company of Iowa
Executive Director
5632 Mount Vernon Memorial Highway
P.O. Box 15160
Alexandria, VA 22309-0160
(703) 360-3600
(703) 360-5524 Fax
http://www.ffa.org/

1 scholarship of $1,000 to an undergraduate college student majoring in agronomy or animal science at any four-year college or university. Must be an Iowa FFA member and resident. 2 scholarships of $1,000 to undergraduate college students majoring in agronomy or animal science at any four-year college or university. Must be an FFA member. Must be a resident of Arkansas, Colorado, Illinois, Indiana, Michigan, Minnesota, Missouri, Nebraska, North Dakota, Ohio, South Dakota, or Wisconsin. Deadline: March 1.

1892.
National Future Farmers of America (FFA) Center Firestone Agricultural Mechanics
Executive Director
5632 Mount Vernon Memorial Highway
P.O. Box 15160
Alexandria, VA 22309-0160
(703) 360-3600
(703) 360-5524 Fax
http://www.ffa.org/

10 scholarships of $500 to students attending either a four-year college or university or a vocational/technical school. Must be FFA members. Must have competed in agricultural mechanics in a state FFA contest. 10 other $500 scholarships to high-scoring students in the National FFA Agricultural Mechanics Contest. Deadline: March 1.

1893.
National Future Farmers of America (FFA) Center First Mississippi Corporation
Executive Director
5632 Mount Vernon Memorial Highway
P.O. Box 15160
Alexandria, VA 22309-0160
(703) 360-3600
(703) 360-5524 Fax
http://www.ffa.org/

1 scholarship of $1,000 to an undergraduate student and 1 scholarship of $500 to a student attending a vocational/technical school. Recipients must be FFA members from Mississippi or Louisiana. Deadline: March 1.

1894.
National Future Farmers of America (FFA) Center Ford New Holland, Inc.
Executive Director
5632 Mount Vernon Memorial Highway
P.O. Box 15160
Alexandria, VA 22309-0160
(703) 360-3600
(703) 360-5524 Fax
http://www.ffa.org/

2 scholarships of $1,200 to graduating high school seniors who are planning to major in agricultural machinery engineering at a four-year college or university. Must be FFA members. Deadline: March 1.

1895.
National Future Farmers of America (FFA) Center Harold Davis Memorial
Executive Director
5632 Mount Vernon Memorial Highway
P.O. Box 15160
Alexandria, VA 22309-0160
(703) 360-3600
(703) 360-5524 Fax
http://www.ffa.org/

1 scholarship of $750 to an undergraduate college student who has been an FFA member. Must have experience in swine, beef, or dairy livestock. Preference given to student majoring in animal agriculture (livestock or dairy), agricultural education, or agribusiness. Will also consider financial need. Deadline: March 1.

1896.
National Future Farmers of America (FFA) Center Helena Chemical Company Scholarship
Scholarship Office
P.O. Box 15160
Alexandria, VA 22309-0160
(703) 360-3600
(703) 360-5524 Fax
http://www.ffa.org/

1 scholarship of $1,000 to a graduating high school senior planning to major in agriculture economics or education at

a four-year accredited U.S. college or university. Must be an FFA member. Must be a resident of Alabama, Arizona, Arkansas, California, Delaware, Florida, Georgia, Kansas, Louisiana, Michigan, Minnesota, Mississippi, Missouri, Nebraska, New Jersey, New Mexico, New York, North Carolina, Ohio, Oklahoma, Oregon, Pennsylvania, South Carolina, Tennessee, Texas, Virginia, or Washington. Deadline: April 1.

1897.
**National Future Farmers of America (FFA) Center
IBP Foundation, Inc.**
Executive Director
5632 Mount Vernon Memorial Highway
P.O. Box 15160
Alexandria, VA 22309-0160
(703) 360-3600
(703) 360-5524 Fax
http://www.ffa.org/

5 scholarships of $1,000 to undergraduate students who were FFA members. One scholarship to a student from each of the following states: Illinois, Iowa, Kansas, Nebraska, and Texas. Must be an animal science major at a land grant university. Deadline: March 1.

1898.
**National Future Farmers of America (FFA) Center
Illinois Farmers Union**
Executive Director
5632 Mount Vernon Memorial Highway
P.O. Box 15160
Alexandria, VA 22309-0160
(703) 360-3600
(703) 360-5524 Fax
http://www.ffa.org/

1 scholarship of $500 to a student attending a two-year vocational/technical school and studying any agriculture production-related area. Must have been an Illinois FFA member. Deadline: March 1.

1899.
**National Future Farmers of America (FFA) Center
Jacques Seed Company**
Executive Director
5632 Mount Vernon Memorial Highway
P.O. Box 15160
Alexandria, VA 22309-0160
(703) 360-3600
(703) 360-5524 Fax
http://www.ffa.org/

15 scholarships of $500 to undergraduate college students majoring in an agriculture-related field at a four-year college or university. Must be FFA members. Must be from a farm family or have had agriculture production experience from the Supervised Occupational Experience Program. Deadline: March 1.

1900.
**National Future Farmers of America (FFA) Center
Kansas City Southern Industries, Inc.**
Executive Director
5632 Mount Vernon Memorial Highway
P.O. Box 15160
Alexandria, VA 22309-0160
(703) 360-3600
(703) 360-5524 Fax
http://www.ffa.org/

1 scholarship of $1,000 to a high school senior who is an FFA member. Must be a resident of Arkansas, Kansas, Louisiana, Missouri, Oklahoma, or Texas. Must be majoring in an agriculture-related area. Deadline: March 1.

1901.
**National Future Farmers of America (FFA) Center
Livestock Marketing Association**
Executive Director
5632 Mount Vernon Memorial Highway
P.O. Box 15160
Alexandria, VA 22309-0160
(703) 360-3600
(703) 360-5524 Fax
http://www.ffa.org/

1 scholarship of $1,000 to an undergraduate student at a four-year college or university and 1 scholarship of $500 to a student in a one- or two-year vocational/technical school. Must be an FFA member. Students must be studying animal science and industry and pursuing a career based on livestock production. Deadline: March 1.

1902.
**National Future Farmers of America (FFA) Center
Louis Dreyfus Corporation**
Executive Director
5632 Mount Vernon Memorial Highway
P.O. Box 15160
Alexandria, VA 22309-0160
(703) 360-3600
(703) 360-5524 Fax
http://www.ffa.org/

1 scholarship of $1,000 to a high school senior who is an FFA member. May be majoring in any area of agriculture at a four-year institution. Deadline: March 1.

1903.
**National Future Farmers of America (FFA) Center
Manna Pro Corporation**
Executive Director
5632 Mount Vernon Memorial Highway
P.O. Box 15160
Alexandria, VA 22309-0160
(703) 360-3600
(703) 360-5524 Fax
http://www.ffa.org/

2 scholarships of $2,000 to undergraduate students who were FFA members. Must be majoring in animal science, with preference given to equine animal science. Based on leadership, financial need, and academic achievement. Deadline: March 1.

1904.
**National Future Farmers of America (FFA) Center
Miller Meester Advertising, Inc.**
Executive Director
5632 Mount Vernon Memorial Highway
P.O. Box 15160
Alexandria, VA 22309-0160
(703) 360-3600
(703) 360-5524 Fax
http://www.ffa.org/

1 scholarship of $1,000 to a junior undergraduate student.
Must be a communications major at a four-year institution.
Deadline: March 1.

1905.
**National Future Farmers of America (FFA) Center
Minnesota Wheat Research and Promotion
   Council**
Executive Director
5632 Mount Vernon Memorial Highway
P.O. Box 15160
Alexandria, VA 22309-0160
(703) 360-3600
(703) 360-5524 Fax
http://www.ffa.org/

1 scholarship of $500 to an undergraduate student majoring
in an agriculture-related field at a four-year institution.
Preference given to minor or emphasis on international
trade, marketing, or international relations. May have raised
wheat as part of the Supervised Occupational Experience
Program or be the son or daughter of an active wheat
farmer or a family in grain production. Deadline: March 1.

1906.
**National Future Farmers of America (FFA) Center
Mississippi Farm Bureau Federation**
Executive Director
5632 Mount Vernon Memorial Highway
P.O. Box 15160
Alexandria, VA 22309-0160
(703) 360-3600
(703) 360-5524 Fax
http://www.ffa.org/

1 scholarship of $500 to a student attending a two-year
vocational/technical school. Must be an FFA member and
be studying agriculture or agribusiness. Must be a
Mississippi resident. Deadline: March 1.

1907.
**National Future Farmers of America (FFA) Center
Monravia Nursery Company**
Executive Director
5632 Mount Vernon Memorial Highway
P.O. Box 15160
Alexandria, VA 22309-0160
(703) 360-3600
(703) 360-5524 Fax
http://www.ffa.org/

1 scholarship of $1,000 to an undergraduate college student
majoring in ornamental horticulture. Must have been an
FFA member. Deadline: March 1.

1908.
**National Future Farmers of America (FFA) Center
National Pork Producers Council**
Executive Director
5632 Mount Vernon Memorial Highway
P.O. Box 15160
Alexandria, VA 22309-0160
(703) 360-3600
(703) 360-5524 Fax
http://www.ffa.org/

1 scholarship of $1,000 to an undergraduate college student
majoring in any agriculture-related field at a four-year
college or university. Must be an FFA member. Must be
from a swine-producing family or have been involved in a
swine-producing enterprise. Deadline: March 1.

1909.
**National Future Farmers of America (FFA) Center
National Suffolk Sheep Association**
Executive Director
5632 Mount Vernon Memorial Highway
P.O. Box 15160
Alexandria, VA 22309-0160
(703) 360-3600
(703) 360-5524 Fax
http://www.ffa.org/

2 scholarships of $500 to undergraduate students attending
any two-year institution and majoring in an agriculture-
related field. Must be FFA members with sheep-related
experience. Based on leadership and experience. Deadline:
March 1.

1910.
**National Future Farmers of America (FFA) Center
Norfolk Southern Corporation**
Executive Director
5632 Mount Vernon Memorial Highway
P.O. Box 15160
Alexandria, VA 22309-0160
(703) 360-3600
(703) 360-5524 Fax
http://www.ffa.org/

3 scholarships of $1,000 to undergraduate students at four-
year colleges or universities and 1 scholarship of $500 to an
undergraduate student. Must be majoring in agricultural
education at a four-year institution. Must be FFA members.
Deadline: March 1.

1911.
**National Future Farmers of America (FFA) Center
Pennsylvania Pork Producers Council**
Executive Director
5632 Mount Vernon Memorial Highway
P.O. Box 15160
Alexandria, VA 22309-0160
(703) 360-3600
(703) 360-5524 Fax
http://www.ffa.org/

1 scholarship of $500 to an undergraduate college student
at Penn State University majoring in meat and animal
science (with swine emphasis). Must be a Pennsylvania FFA
member. Deadline: March 1.

1912.
National Future Farmers of America (FFA) Center
Prairie Farms Dairy, Inc.
Executive Director
5632 Mount Vernon Memorial Highway
P.O. Box 15160
Alexandria, VA 22309-0160
(703) 360-3600
(703) 360-5524 Fax
http://www.ffa.org/

1 scholarship of $500 to an undergraduate student studying
dairy science at a two-year vocational or technical school.
Must be an FFA member. Must be a resident of Illinois,
Iowa, or Missouri. Deadline: March 1.

1913.
National Future Farmers of America (FFA) Center
Professional Products, Inc.
Executive Director
5632 Mount Vernon Memorial Highway
P.O. Box 15160
Alexandria, VA 22309-0160
(703) 360-3600
(703) 360-5524 Fax
http://www.ffa.org/

1 scholarship of $500 to an undergraduate college student
pursuing a career in livestock production. Must have been
an FFA member. Deadline: March 1.

1914.
National Future Farmers of America (FFA) Center
Rhone-Poulenc Ag Company, Animal Nutrition
** Division**
Executive Director
5632 Mount Vernon Memorial Highway
P.O. Box 15160
Alexandria, VA 22309-0160
(703) 360-3600
(703) 360-5524 Fax
http://www.ffa.org/

2 scholarships of $1,000 to undergraduate college students
majoring in animal or poultry science. Must be an FFA
member. Must be residents of and attending a four-year
college or university in any of the following states:
Alabama, Arkansas, California, Florida, Georgia, or North
Carolina. Deadline: March 1.

1915.
National Future Farmers of America (FFA) Center
Ritchie Industries, Inc.
Executive Director
5632 Mount Vernon Memorial Highway
P.O. Box 15160
Alexandria, VA 22309-0160
(703) 360-3600
(703) 360-5524 Fax
http://www.ffa.org/

1 scholarship of $1,000 to an undergraduate college student
majoring in an agriculture-related area at a four-year
institution. Must be an FFA member. Deadline: March 1.

1916.
National Future Farmers of America (FFA) Center
Sandoz Crop Protection Corporation
Executive Director
5632 Mount Vernon Memorial Highway
P.O. Box 15160
Alexandria, VA 22309-0160
(703) 360-3600
(703) 360-5524 Fax
http://www.ffa.org/

2 scholarships of $2,000 to undergraduate college students
attending any of the following: Cornell University, Iowa
University, Kansas State University, Michigan State
University, North Dakota State University, Oklahoma
State University, Purdue University, Rutgers University,
South Dakota State University, Texas A&M University,
University of Illinois, University of Minnesota, University
of Nebraska at Lincoln, University of Wisconsin at
Madison, Virginia Polytechnic Institute, Western Kentucky
University, or West Virginia University. Deadline: March 1.

1917.
National Future Farmers of America (FFA) Center
Santa Fe Pacific Foundation Scholarships
Executive Director
5632 Mount Vernon Memorial Highway
P.O. Box 15160
Alexandria, VA 22309-0160
(703) 360-3600
(703) 360-5524 Fax
http://www.ffa.org/

2 scholarships of $1,000 to students who are FFA members
in Arizona, California, Colorado, Illinois, Kansas, Missouri,
Minnesota, Oklahoma, or Texas. 4 Educational Merit
Awards are also granted in each state to FFA students.
Awards funded by the Santa Fe Pacific Foundation.

1918.
National Future Farmers of America (FFA) Center
Seaboard Farms
Executive Director
5632 Mount Vernon Memorial Highway
P.O. Box 15160
Alexandria, VA 22309-0160
(703) 360-3600
(703) 360-5524 Fax
http://www.ffa.org/

1 scholarship of $1,000 to an undergraduate college student
majoring in poultry science. Must be an FFA member and a
resident of Georgia. Deadline: March 1.

1919.
National Future Farmers of America (FFA) Center
State Farm Companies Foundation
Executive Director
5632 Mount Vernon Memorial Highway
P.O. Box 15160
Alexandria, VA 22309-0160
(703) 360-3600
(703) 360-5524 Fax
http://www.ffa.org/

1 scholarship of $1,000 to an undergraduate college student majoring in agriculture or agribusiness at a four-year college or university. Must be an FFA member and an Illinois resident. Deadline: March 1.

1920.

National Future Farmers of America (FFA) Center Syntex Animal Health Division of Syntex Agribusiness, Inc.

Executive Director
5632 Mount Vernon Memorial Highway
P.O. Box 15160
Alexandria, VA 22309-0160
(703) 360-3600
(703) 360-5524 Fax
http://www.ffa.org/

1 scholarship of $1,000 (7 total) to an undergraduate FFA member majoring in animal science at each of one of the following: Colorado State University, Iowa State University, Kansas State University, Oklahoma State University, Texas A&M University, University of Missouri at Columbia, and University of Nebraska at Lincoln. Must have beef production as part of Supervised Occupational Experience Program. Must be a resident of Colorado, Iowa, Kansas, Missouri, Nebraska, Oklahoma, or Texas. Based on experience and financial need. Deadline: March 1.

1921.

National Future Farmers of America (FFA) Center 21st Century Genetics Cooperative (Shawano, Wisconsin)

Executive Director
5632 Mount Vernon Memorial Highway
P.O. Box 15160
Alexandria, VA 22309-0160
(703) 360-3600
(703) 360-5524 Fax
http://www.ffa.org/

2 scholarships of $1,000 to undergraduate college students majoring in dairy science at a four-year college or university. Must be FFA members from Iowa, Minnesota, or Wisconsin. Deadline: March 1.

1922.

National Future Farmers of America (FFA) Center Valmont Industries, Inc.

Executive Director
5632 Mount Vernon Memorial Highway
P.O. Box 15160
Alexandria, VA 22309-0160
(703) 360-3600
(703) 360-5524 Fax
http://www.ffa.org/

1 scholarship of $1,000 to an undergraduate student who is an FFA member. Must be an agriculture major at a four-year institution. Deadline: March 1.

1923.

National Future Farmers of America (FFA) Center Veratec Agricultural Products

Executive Director
5632 Mount Vernon Memorial Highway
P.O. Box 15160
Alexandria, VA 22309-0160
(703) 360-3600
(703) 360-5524 Fax
http://www.ffa.org/

1 scholarship of $1,000 to an undergraduate at a four-year college or university and 1 scholarship of $500 to a student attending a vocational/technical school. Must be FFA members. Must be majoring in dairy science. Deadline: March 1.

1924.

National Future Farmers of America (FFA) Center Vickers Scholarship

5632 Mount Vernon Memorial Highway
P.O. Box 15160
Alexandria, VA 22309-0160
(703) 360-3600
(703) 360-5524 Fax
http://www.ffa.org/

1 scholarship of $500 to an undergraduate student majoring in agricultural mechanics or agricultural engineering at a two- or four-year college or university. Must be an FFA member. Must be a resident of Arkansas, Illinois, Michigan, Missouri, or Nebraska. Request applications after December 1. Deadline: March 1.

1925.

National Future Farmers of America (FFA) Center Wal-Mart Scholarships

Executive Director
5632 Mount Vernon Memorial Highway
P.O. Box 15160
Alexandria, VA 22309-0160
(703) 360-3600
(703) 360-5524 Fax
http://www.ffa.org/

14 scholarships of $1,000 to high school seniors who were FFA members. Must be residents of Alabama, Arkansas, Arizona, Colorado, Florida, Georgia, Illinois, Indiana, Iowa, Kansas, Kentucky, Louisiana, Minnesota, Mississippi, Missouri, Nebraska, New Mexico, North Carolina, Oklahoma, South Carolina, Tennessee, Texas, Virginia, or Wisconsin. Deadline: March 1.

1926.

National Future Farmers of America (FFA) Center Wells Fargo Bank

Executive Director
5632 Mount Vernon Memorial Highway
P.O. Box 15160
Alexandria, VA 22309-0160
(703) 360-3600
(703) 360-5524 Fax
http://www.ffa.org/

1 scholarship of $750 to an undergraduate college student majoring in an agriculture-related field at a four-year college or university. Based on academic record, FFA leadership, and career goals. Deadline: March 1.

1927.
National Future Farmers of America (FFA) Center
Western Dairymen–John Elway–Melba FFA
   Scholarship
Executive Director
5632 Mount Vernon Memorial Highway
P.O. Box 15160
Alexandria, VA 22309-0160
(703) 360-3600
(703) 360-5524 Fax
http://www.ffa.org/

1 scholarship of $250 to a high school senior who is an FFA member. Must be planning to major in an agriculture-related area or agribusiness. Preference given to student from a Melba, Idaho, FFA chapter. Must have at least a 3.0 GPA. Based on academic record. Deadline: March 1.

1928.
National Future Farmers of America (FFA) Center
Western Seedmen's Association
Executive Director
5632 Mount Vernon Memorial Highway
P.O. Box 15160
Alexandria, VA 22309-0160
(703) 360-3600
(703) 360-5524 Fax
http://www.ffa.org/

1 scholarship of $1,000 to a high school senior who is an FFA member to study agricultural education at a four-year college or university. 1 scholarship of $500 to a high school senior who is an FFA member. For any agriculture-related major. Must be a resident of Arizona, California, Colorado, Idaho, Iowa, Kansas, Minnesota, Missouri, Montana, Nebraska, Nevada, New Mexico, North Dakota, Oklahoma, Oregon, South Dakota, Texas, Utah, Washington, or Wyoming.

1929.
National Future Farmers of America (FFA) Center
Who's Who Among American High School
   Students
Executive Director
5632 Mount Vernon Memorial Highway
P.O. Box 15160
Alexandria, VA 22309-0160
(703) 360-3600
(703) 360-5524 Fax
http://www.ffa.org/

1 scholarship of $1,000 to a high school senior who is an FFA member. Must be planning to major in agricultural education at a four-year college or university. Deadline: March 1.

1930.
National Future Farmers of America (FFA) Center
William Biggs/Gilmore Associates Scholarships
5632 Mount Vernon Memorial Highway
P.O. Box 15160
Alexandria, VA 22309-0160
(703) 360-3600
(703) 360-5524 Fax
htt://www.ffa.org/

5 scholarships of $1,250 to undergraduate juniors and seniors who are current or former FFA members. Must be majoring in agricultural communications or journalism. Must be attending Iowa State University, Michigan State University, Ohio State University, Texas Tech University, or the University of Illinois. Request applications after December 1. Deadline: March 1.

1931.
National Future Farmers of America (FFA) Center
Wolf's Head Oil Company
Executive Director
5632 Mount Vernon Memorial Highway
P.O. Box 15160
Alexandria, VA 22309-0160
(703) 360-3600
(703) 360-5524 Fax
http://www.ffa.org/

2 scholarships of $500 to high school seniors who are FFA members. Must major in agricultural mechanics at a two-year technical program. Must be residents of Connecticut, Delaware, Florida, Georgia, Illinois, Indiana, Kentucky, Maine, Maryland, Massachusetts, Michigan, Minnesota, Missouri, New Hampshire, New Jersey, New York, North Carolina, Ohio, Pennsylvania, Rhode Island, South Carolina, Tennessee, Vermont, Virginia, West Virginia, or Wisconsin. Deadline: March 1.

1932.
National Future Farmers of America (FFA) Center
Wyandot, Inc., Snacks and Popcorn
Executive Director
5632 Mount Vernon Memorial Highway
P.O. Box 15160
Alexandria, VA 22309-0160
(703) 360-3600
(703) 360-5524 Fax
http://www.ffa.org/

1 scholarship of $1,000 to a high school senior who is an FFA member from a chapter located in Marion or Wyandot counties, Ohio. May be used to study any agriculture-related field at a vocational/technical school or a four-year institution. Deadline: March 1.

1933.
National Geographic Society
Intern Programs for Geography Students
1145 17th Street, N.W.
Washington, DC 20036
(202) 828-5466
http://www.nationalgeographic.com/

Fourteen- to sixteen-week internships paying $385 per week, plus travel expenses, for junior and senior undergraduates and graduate students majoring in geography or cartography at a U.S. institution. Interns assist with editorial research, cartographic design, or cartographic production for magazines, books, or maps produced by National Geographic. Internships may be conducted in the spring—January to May; summer—May to August; or fall—August to December. Deadline: mid-October.

1934.
National Geographic Society (Scholarships)
1145 17th Street, N.W.
Washington, DC 20036
(202) 828-5466
http://www.nationalgeographic.com/

2 scholarships of $5,000 to students in grades 3–9 (one for 3–5 and one for 6–9). $5,000 in National Geographic educational materials awarded to the two schools the winners attend. Second- and third-place winners are awarded National Geographic products. The contest begins with clues published in the National Geographic *World* magazine from January through June. The second part of the contest is in June, when National Geographic *World* magazine publishes a puzzle that contains a secret message describing the final project. Students then use the clues to solve the puzzle. Students send their project to the address listed in the June issue. Deadline: listed in the June issue.

1935.
National Guild of Community Schools of the Arts
Young Composers Awards
40 North Van Brunt Street, Suite 32
Englewood, NJ 07631
(201) 871-3337

Awards of $500, $750, and $1,000 to students ages thirteen to eighteen (as of June 30 of award year) enrolled in a public or private secondary school or a recognized musical school or engaged in private study of music with an established teacher in the U.S. or Canada. Based on music composition. Deadline: April 1.

1936.
National Hispanic Scholarship Fund
Selection Committee
One Sansome Street, Suite 1000
San Francisco, CA 94104
(415) 445-9930
http://www.nhsf.org/

2,262 scholarships of $1,000 to Hispanic American full-time students enrolled in or attending a college or university in the U.S. Must have completed a minimum of fifteen units of college work. Request applications after April 1. For information, send a self-addressed, stamped envelope. Deadline: June 15.

1937.
National Institute for Architectural Education
Competition
30 West 22nd Street
New York, NY 10010
(212) 924-7000

Several different competitions with awards ranging from $500 to $8,000 to undergraduate students or individuals with degrees in architecture. Each competition poses a problem that students must solve. The themes vary each year. Top winners must travel and/or study abroad for between three and eight months. Write for information about rules and deadlines.

1938.
National Institute for Architectural Education
Competition
Design America Accessible Competition
30 West 22nd Street
New York, NY 10010
(212) 924-7000

Awards ranging from $150 to $2,500 to full- or part-time students enrolled in an architectural or engineering program in the U.S., except those in the final year of their first professional degree program. Students must address the practical aspects of designing structures that are accessible to all people. Deadline: mid-June.

1939.
National Institute for Architectural Education
Competition
William Van Alen Architect Memorial Fellowship
30 West 22nd Street
New York, NY 10010
(212) 924-7000

1 award of $6,000 to an undergraduate or graduate student enrolled in an accredited architectural or civil engineering program. Winner receives award for travel and study abroad. Must be U.S. citizen. Deadline: April 6.

1940.
National Institute for Music Theater
Internships
JFK Center for the Performing Arts
Washington, DC 20566
(202) 965-2800

Stipends ranging from $1,000 to $1,460 per month through internships in all aspects of music theater except instrumental playing. Preference is given to composers, lyricists, and librettists. Interns are generally in the early stages of their professional careers. Internships usually last from six months to one year. Write for complete details.

1941.
National Institute of Neurological and
Communicative Disorders and Stroke
Summer Programs in Biomedical Research
Building 31, Room 8A–19
Bethesda, MD 20892

Summer intern program (paying $5.28 to $6.63 per hour) designed to provide "academically talented" undergraduate students a unique opportunity to acquire valuable hands-on research training and experience in the neurosciences. Must have a 3.0 GPA or better. Deadline: March 16.

1942.
National Italian American Foundation (NIAF)
Agnes E. Vaghi–Cornaro Scholarship
Attn: Education Director
1860 19th Street, N.W.
Washington, DC 20009-5599
(202) 387-0600
http://www.niaf.org/

1 scholarship of $1,000 to an Italian American female undergraduate student pursuing any major. Other restrictions may apply. Include a #10 self-addressed, stamped envelope with request. Deadline: May 31.

1943.
National Italian American Foundation (NIAF)
A. P. Giannini Scholarship
Attn: Education Director
1860 19th Street, N.W.
Washington, DC 20009-5599
(202) 387-0600
http://www.niaf.org/

1 scholarship of $1,000 to an Italian American undergraduate or graduate student. Must be majoring in banking or international finance. Other restrictions may apply. Enclose a #10 self-addressed, stamped envelope. Deadline: May 31.

1944.
National Italian American Foundation
   Scholarship Program
Aracri Scholarship
Attn: Education Director
1860 19th Street, N.W.
Washington, DC 20009-5599
(202) 387-0600
http://www.niaf.org/

1 scholarship of $1,000 to an Italian American undergraduate or graduate student majoring in Italian art, literature, or theater. Award allows student to conduct research on Calabrese art, music, literature, and/or theater. Based on academic achievement, Italian descent, and financial need. Send a self-addressed, stamped envelope for an application. Other restrictions may apply. Deadline: May 31.

1945.
National Italian American Foundation (NIAF)
Bolla Wines Scholarship
Attn: Education Director
1860 19th Street, N.W.
Washington, DC 20009-5599
(202) 387-0600
http://www.niaf.org/

1 scholarship of $1,000 to an Italian American undergraduate or graduate student. Must be at least twenty-one years of age. Must have a background in international studies with emphasis on Italian business or Italian American history. Must have at least a 3.0 GPA. Must write an essay of approximately 1,000 words on "The Importance of Italy in Today's Business World." Enclose a #10 self-addressed, stamped envelope. For an application, contact: Bolla/NIAF Scholarships, P.O. Box 4819, Monticello, MN 55565-4819.

1946.
National Italian American Foundation (NIAF)
Capital Area Regional Scholarship
Attn: Education Director
1860 19th Street, N.W.
Washington, DC 20009-5599
(202) 387-0600
http://www.niaf.org/

1 scholarship of $1,000 to an Italian American high school senior or undergraduate student pursuing any major. Must be a resident of Maryland, Virginia, West Virginia, or Washington, D.C. Include a #10 self-addressed, stamped envelope with request. Other restrictions may apply. Deadline: May 31.

1947.
National Italian American Foundation (NIAF)
Communications Scholarship
Attn: Education Director
1860 19th Street, N.W.
Washington, DC 20009-5599
(202) 387-0600
http://www.niaf.org/

1 scholarship of $1,000 to an Italian American graduating high school senior or undergraduate student pursuing a journalism or communications major. Based on application and two samples of published or unpublished work. Include a #10 self-addressed, stamped envelope with request. Other restrictions may apply. Deadline: May 31.

1948.
National Italian American Foundation (NIAF)
FBI Honors Internship Program
Attn: Education Director
1860 19th Street, N.W.
Washington, DC 20009-5599
(202) 387-0600
http://www.niaf.org/

50 to 75 internships providing $4,800 to Italian American undergraduate juniors or graduate students with at least one more year of academic work. May be of any major. Internship should enhance area of study and research. Other restrictions may apply. Enclose a #10 self-addressed, stamped envelope. Deadline: May 31.

1949.
National Italian American Foundation (NIAF)
FIER/NIAF National Scholarship
Attn: Education Director
1860 19th Street, N.W.
Washington, DC 20009-5599
(202) 387-0600
http://www.niaf.org/

1 scholarship of $1,000 to an Italian American undergraduate student. Based on a three-page, double-spaced, typed essay on the topic "Italian American Entrepreneurs," about either a historical or modern-day figure. Enclose a #10 self-addressed, stamped envelope. Other restrictions may apply. Deadline: May 31.

1950.
**National Italian American Foundation (NIAF)
High School Senior Awards**
Education Director
1860 19th Street, N.W.
Washington, DC 20009-5599
(202) 387-0600
http://www.niaf.org/

5 scholarship awards of $100 to Italian American high school seniors studying Italian. Selection is based on a 500-word essay on the "Importance of Taking Italian in Today's Society." Students must include an application, letter of recommendation from Italian language teacher, and the essay. Send a #10 self-addressed, stamped envelope for information. Other restrictions may apply. Deadline: May 31.

1951.
**National Italian American Foundation (NIAF)
Italian Regional Scholarship**
Attn: Education Director
1860 19th Street, N.W.
Washington, DC 20009-5599
(202) 387-0600
http://www.niaf.org/

1 scholarship of $1,000 to an Italian American high school senior or undergraduate student. May be pursuing any major at an Italian university in Italy. Italian university credits must count toward undergraduate degree. Include a #10 self-addressed, stamped envelope with request. Other restrictions may apply. Deadline: May 31.

1952.
**National Italian American Foundation (NIAF)
James A. Scatena Memorial Scholarship**
Attn: Education Director
1860 19th Street, N.W.
Washington, DC 20009-5599
(202) 387-0600
http://www.niaf.org/

1 scholarship of $1,000 to an Italian American full-time undergraduate student pursuing any major. Must be a resident of northern California, Hawaii, or northern Nevada. Based on application, recommendation letters, and financial need. Include a #10 self-addressed, stamped envelope with request. Other restrictions may apply. Deadline: May 31.

1953.
**National Italian American Foundation (NIAF)
John Cabot University Scholarship**
Attn: Education Director
1860 19th Street, N.W.
Washington, DC 20009-5599
(202) 387-0600
http://www.niaf.org/

1 scholarship of approximately $10,000 (depending on exchange rate) to an Italian American undergraduate student pursuing art history, business administration, English literature, or international affairs. Must attend the John Cabot University in Rome. Selection is based on application, essay describing preparation for the program, letters of recommendation, and academic achievement.

Include a #10 self-addressed, stamped envelope with request. Other restrictions may apply. Deadline: May 31.

1954.
**National Italian American Foundation (NIAF)
Lower Mid–Atlantic Regional Scholarship**
Attn: Education Director
1860 19th Street, N.W.
Washington, DC 20009-5599
(202) 387-0600
http://www.niaf.org/

1 scholarship of $1,000 to an Italian American graduating high school senior or undergraduate student pursuing any major. Must be a resident of Delaware, southern New Jersey (Trenton and south of Trenton), or Pennsylvania. Include a #10 self-addressed stamped envelope with request. Other restrictions may apply. Deadline: May 31.

1955.
**National Italian American Foundation (NIAF)
Marinelli Scholarships**
Attn: Education Director
1860 19th Street, N.W.
Washington, DC 20009-5599
(202) 387-0600
http://www.niaf.org/

2 scholarships of $1,000 and 1 scholarship of $2,000 to Italian American high school seniors or undergraduate students pursuing any major. The $1,000 scholarship recipients must attend American University in Rome and the $2,000 scholarship recipient must attend Nova University in Florida. Include a #10 self-addressed, stamped envelope with request. Other restrictions may apply. Deadline: May 31.

1956.
**National Italian American Foundation (NIAF)
Mid–America Regional Scholarship**
Attn: Education Director
1860 19th Street, N.W.
Washington, DC 20009-5599
(202) 387-0600
http://www.niaf.org/

1 scholarship of $1,000 to an Italian American graduating high school senior or undergraduate student pursuing any major. Must be a resident of Arkansas, Colorado, Iowa, Kansas, Nebraska, Missouri, or Oklahoma. Include a #10 self-addressed, stamped envelope with request. Other restrictions may apply. Deadline: May 31.

1957.
**National Italian American Foundation (NIAF)
Mid–Pacific Regional Scholarship**
Attn: Education Director
1860 19th Street, N.W.
Washington, DC 20009-5599
(202) 387-0600
http://www.niaf.org/

1 scholarship of $1,000 to an Italian American graduating high school senior or undergraduate student pursuing any major. Must be a resident of northern California, Guam, Hawaii, northern Nevada (Reno), or Utah. Include a #10

self-addressed, stamped envelope with request. Other restrictions may apply. Deadline: May 31.

1958.
National Italian American Foundation (NIAF)
New England Regional Scholarship
Attn: Education Director
1860 19th Street, N.W.
Washington, DC 20009-5599
(202) 387-0600
http://www.niaf.org/

1 scholarship of $1,000 to an Italian American graduating high school senior or undergraduate student pursuing any major. Must be a resident of Connecticut, Maine, Massachusetts, New Hampshire, Rhode Island, or Vermont. Include a #10 self-addressed, stamped envelope with request. Other restrictions may apply. Deadline: May 31.

1959.
National Italian American Foundation (NIAF)
NIAF–Cornaro Scholarship
Attn: Education Director
1860 19th Street, N.W.
Washington, DC 20009-5599
(202) 387-0600
http://www.niaf.org/

1 scholarship of $1,000 to an Italian American female undergraduate student who is currently enrolled in or about to enter college and pursuing any major. Other restrictions may apply. Include a #10 self-addressed, stamped envelope with request. Other restrictions may apply. Deadline: May 31.

1960.
National Italian American Foundation (NIAF)
North Central Regional Scholarship
Attn: Education Director
1860 19th Street, N.W.
Washington, DC 20009-5599
(202) 387-0600
http://www.niaf.org/

1 scholarship of $1,000 to an Italian American graduating high school senior or undergraduate student pursuing any major. Must be a resident of Indiana, Illinois, Kentucky, Michigan, Ohio, or Wisconsin. Include a #10 self-addressed, stamped envelope with request. Other restrictions may apply. Deadline: May 31.

1961.
National Italian American Foundation (NIAF)
Northwest Regional Scholarship
Attn: Education Director
1860 19th Street, N.W.
Washington, DC 20009-5599
(202) 387-0600
http://www.niaf.org/

1 scholarship of $1,000 to an Italian American graduating high school senior or undergraduate student pursuing any major. Must be a resident of Alaska, Idaho, Montana, Oregon, Washington State, or Wyoming. Include a #10 self-addressed, stamped envelope with request. Other restrictions may apply. Deadline: May 31.

1962.
National Italian American Foundation (NIAF)
Piancone Family Agriculture Scholarship
Attn: Education Director
1860 19th Street, N.W.
Washington, DC 20009-5599
(202) 387-0600
http://www.niaf.org/

1 scholarship of $2,000 to an Italian American undergraduate or graduate student pursuing an agriculture major. Must be a resident of Delaware, Maryland, Massachusetts, New Jersey, New York, Pennsylvania, Virginia, or Washington, D.C. Include a #10 self-addressed, stamped envelope with request. Selection based on application, academic achievement, recommendation letters, and financial need. Other restrictions may apply. Deadline: May 31.

1963.
National Italian American Foundation (NIAF)
Robert J. DiPietro Scholarships
Attn: Education Director
1860 19th Street, N.W.
Washington, DC 20009-5599
(202) 387-0600
http://www.niaf.org/

2 scholarships of $1,000 to Italian American undergraduate or graduate students. Must not be over twenty-five years of age. Based on an essay ranging from 400 to 600 words on how the applicant intends to preserve and use his/her ethnicity throughout life. Must submit four copies of the essay with applicant's name and title of essay on each copy. Enclose a #10 self-addressed, stamped envelope for information. Deadline: May 31.

1964.
National Italian American Foundation (NIAF)
Rose Basile Green Scholarship
Attn: Education Director
1860 19th Street, N.W.
Washington, DC 20009-5599
(202) 387-0600
http://www.niaf.org/

1 scholarship of $1,000 to an Italian American undergraduate student whose emphasis is on Italian American studies. Other restrictions may apply. Include a #10 self-addressed, stamped envelope with request. Deadline: May 31.

1965.
National Italian American Foundation (NIAF)
Sarina Grande Scholarship
Attn: Education Director
1860 19th Street, N.W.
Washington, DC 20009-5599
(202) 387-0600
http://www.niaf.org/

1 scholarship of $1,000 to an Italian American undergraduate or graduate student. May have any major. Other restrictions may apply. Enclose a #10 self-addressed, stamped envelope with request. Deadline: May 31.

1966.

National Italian American Foundation (NIAF)
Sergio Franchi Music Scholarship in Voice
Performance
Attn: Education Director
1860 19th Street, N.W.
Washington, DC 20009–5599
(202) 387-0600
http://www.niaf.org/

1 scholarship of $1,000 to an Italian American high school graduate or undergraduate student. Must be majoring in vocal music. Include a #10 self-addressed, stamped envelope with request. Other restrictions may apply. Deadline: May 31.

1967.

National Italian American Foundation (NIAF)
Silvio Conte Internship
Attn: Education Director
1860 19th Street, N.W.
Washington, DC 20009–5599
(202) 387-0600
http://www.niaf.org/

1 internship providing $1,000 to an Italian American undergraduate or graduate student interested in working for one semester on Capitol Hill. Upon completion of internship, student must write a paper about the experience and the benefits to his/her career. Enclose a #10 self-addressed, stamped envelope with request. Other restrictions may apply. Deadline: May 31.

1968.

National Italian American Foundation (NIAF)
South Central Regional Undergraduate
Scholarship
Attn: Education Director
1860 19th Street, N.W.
Washington, DC 20009–5599
(202) 387-0600
http://www.niaf.org/

1 scholarship of $1,000 to an Italian American high school senior or undergraduate student pursuing any major. Must be a resident of Alabama, Louisiana, Mississippi, Tennessee, or Texas. Other restrictions may apply. Include a #10 self-addressed, stamped envelope with request. Deadline: May 31.

1969.

National Italian American Foundation (NIAF)
Southeast Regional Scholarship
Attn: Education Director
1860 19th Street, N.W.
Washington, DC 20009–5599
(202) 387-0600
http://www.niaf.org/

1 scholarship of $1,000 to an Italian American high school senior or undergraduate student pursuing any major. Must be a resident of Florida, Georgia, North Carolina, or South Carolina. Include a #10 self-addressed, stamped envelope with request. Other restrictions may apply. Deadline: May 31.

1970.

National Italian American Foundation (NIAF)
Southwest Regional Scholarship
Attn: Education Director
1860 19th Street, N.W.
Washington, DC 20009–5599
(202) 387-0600
http://www.niaf.org/

1 scholarship of $1,000 to an Italian American high school senior or undergraduate student pursuing any major. Must be a resident of Arizona, southern California, New Mexico, or southern Nevada (Las Vegas). Include a #10 self-addressed, stamped envelope with request. Other restrictions may apply. Deadline: May 31.

1971.

National Italian American Foundation (NIAF)
Stella Scholarship
Attn: Education Director
1860 19th Street, N.W.
Washington, DC 20009–5599
(202) 387-0600
http://www.niaf.org/

1 scholarship of $1,000 to an Italian American undergraduate or graduate student. Must be a business major. Other restrictions may apply. Enclose a #10 self-addressed, stamped envelope with request. Deadline: May 31.

1972.

National Italian American Foundation (NIAF)
Upper Mid–Atlantic Regional Scholarship
Attn: Education Director
1860 19th Street, N.W.
Washington, DC 20009–5599
(202) 387-0600
http://www.niaf.org/

1 scholarship of $1,000 to an Italian American high school senior or undergraduate student pursuing any major. Must be a resident of New York or northern New Jersey (north of Trenton). Include a #10 self-addressed, stamped envelope with request. Other restrictions may apply. Deadline: May 31.

1973.

National Italian American Foundation (NIAF)
William Toto Scholarship
Attn: Education Director
1860 19th Street, N.W.
Washington, DC 20009–5599
(202) 387-0600
http://www.niaf.org/

1 scholarship of $1,000 to an Italian American undergraduate who has completed the sophomore year. Must be majoring in either engineering or business management. Other restrictions may apply. Include a #10 self-addressed, stamped envelope with request. Deadline: May 31.

1974.
National Junior Classical League Scholarships
Miami University
Oxford, OH 45056
(513) 529-4116

Scholarships ranging from $500 to $1,000 to high school seniors who plan to study the classics (classics major isn't required). Preference given to students who are pursuing a teaching career in the classics. Deadline: May 1.

1975.
National Junior Horticultural Association (NJHA) Scottish Gardening Scholarship
441 East Pine Street
Fremont, MI 48412

1 scholarship awarded each year to a high school graduate with at least one summer's employment in ornamental horticulture. The scholarship provides the cost of transportation to the Threave School of Gardening in Scotland, food, tuition, and $100 per month while at the Threave School of Gardening. The course of study is one year in duration, beginning the second week of August. NJHA sponsors a variety of contests for a wide array of horticulture areas. Only plaques and certificates are awarded as prizes in these other competitions; no scholarships or cash awards. Deadline: December 31.

1976.
National Merit Corporation Scholarship Program
1560 Sherman Avenue
Evanston, IL 60201
(312) 866-5100

Approximately 5,000 to 6,000 scholarships to students selected as National Merit Scholars. Highest-scoring (on PSAT) high school seniors are selected as Semifinalists and are invited to submit applications, from which National Merit Finalists will be selected. All Merit Scholars are selected from the Finalist group. Selection is based on academics, extracurricular activities, test scores, nominations, and community involvement.

1977.
National Merit Corporation Scholarship Program Achievement Awards
1560 Sherman Avenue
Evanston, IL 60201
(312) 866-5100

Numerous scholarships of varying amounts to African American graduating high school seniors selected as National Merit Finalists. 15,000 high school seniors are selected as National Merit Semifinalists (from PSAT scores) and are invited to submit applications. All Merit Scholars are selected from the Finalist group. Selection is based on PSAT, SAT, academics, extracurricular activities, test scores, nominations, and community involvement.

1978.
National Merit Corporation Scholarship Program National Hispanic Scholar Award
1560 Sherman Avenue
Evanston, IL 60201
(312) 866-5100

Numerous awards to Hispanic American graduating high school seniors selected as National Merit Scholars. Approximately 15,000 high school seniors are selected as National Merit Semifinalists (from PSAT scores) and are invited to submit applications. All Merit Scholars are selected from the Finalist group. Selection is based on PSAT, SAT, academics, extracurricular activities, test scores, nominations, and community involvement.

1979.
National Music Camp Scholarships
Mary F. James, Director of Admissions
National Music Camp
Interlochen Center for the Arts
Interlochen, MI 49643
(616) 276-9221

Numerous partial scholarships at Interlochen for high school students to attend the National Music Camp. The camp has no assistance whatsoever for anyone seeking to finance a college or university education elsewhere. Do not apply to Interlochen for such aid. Scholarship listing available from the National Music Camp in the areas of music, art, dance (ballet), and drama can be obtained on request from above address. Up to, but no more than, one-half of the total camp fee. All scholarship applications submitted directly to the camp must be accompanied by the deposit of $225 (total of application and registration fee). $200 registration fee is refundable if a scholarship is not awarded and student cannot attend camp without financial aid. In music, applicant must be a very outstanding high school player of one of the more unusual band and orchestral instruments. In art, a portfolio of work must accompany the application for a scholarship. In dance, applicant must be recommended by a private dance teacher and must submit a videocassette tape demonstrating technique and movement. For drama, information about additional requirements will be sent upon request. Deadlines: vary.

1980.
National Newspaper Publishers Association (NNPA)
3200 13th Street, N.W.
Washington, DC 20010
(202) 588-8764

6 scholarships of $1,200 (renewable for four years) are awarded. Contact: Kenneth T. Stanley, Chairperson, NNPA Scholarship Committee, *The Louisville Defender*, 1720 Dixie Highway, Louisville, KY 40210.

1981.
National Office Products Association (NOPA)
Scholarship Fund
301 North Fairfax Street
Alexandria, VA 22314
(703) 549-9040

Numerous $2,000 scholarships (over a one-year period) to high school graduates who are employees or children of employees of a NOPA member firm or a group affiliated with the office products industry. Based on academic record, financial need, ambition, extracurricular activities, and self-help. Deadline: March 15.

1982.

National Press Foundation
529 14th Street, N.W., 13th Floor
Washington, DC 20045
(202) 662-7356
(202) 662-1232 Fax
http://npc.press.org/

Scholarships ranging from $250 to $1,000 to undergraduate juniors or seniors majoring in journalism. Must be recommended by the school they are attending. Deadline: June.

1983.

National Press Photographers Foundation
3200 Croasdaile, Suite 306
Durham, NC 27705
(919) 383-7246
http://sunsite.unc.edu/nppa/

Scholarships of $1,000 to undergraduate students pursuing a photojournalism career. Send a self-addressed, stamped envelope for more information. Deadline: varies.

1984.

National Press Photographers Foundation
Bob East Scholarship
3200 Croasdaile, Suite 306
Durham, NC 27705
(919) 383-7246
http://sunsite.unc.edu/nppa/

1 scholarship grant of $1,500 to an undergraduate or graduate student pursuing a career in newspaper photojournalism. Write an introductory letter briefly describing your educational and financial situation. Send a self-addressed, stamped envelope. Other restrictions may apply. Deadline: March 1.

1985.

National Press Photographers Foundation
College Photographer of the Year Competition
3200 Croasdaile, Suite 306
Durham, NC 27705
(919) 383-7246
http://sunsite.unc.edu/nppa/

1 Colonel William Lookadoo Scholarship grant of $1,000; 1 Milton Freier Award of $500 will be awarded to the first runner-up. For applications and details, write before February 15. Other restrictions may apply. Send a self-addressed, stamped envelope for more information. Deadline: March 29.

1986.

National Press Photographers Foundation
Joseph Ehrenreich–NPPF Scholarships
3200 Croasdaile, Suite 306
Durham, NC 27705
(919) 383-7246
http://sunsite.unc.edu/nppa/

5 scholarships of $1,000 to undergraduate students pursuing careers in photojournalism. Based on aptitude and potential for success in photojournalism. Other restrictions may apply. Send a self-addressed, stamped envelope for more information. Deadline: March 1.

1987.

National Press Photographers Foundation
NPPF Broadcast & Media Photojournalism
  Scholarships
3200 Croasdaile, Suite 306
Durham, NC 27705
(919) 383-7246
http://sunsite.unc.edu/nppa/

2 scholarships of $1,000 to an undergraduate pursuing a career in photojournalism. One award is based on aptitude and potential for success in use of photography as a communications tool and the other is based on aptitude and potential for success in electronic news photojournalism. Request information before February 1. Other restrictions may apply. Send a self-addressed, stamped envelope for more information. Deadline: March 1.

1988.

National Press Photographers Foundation
Reid Blackburn Scholarship
3200 Croasdaile, Suite 306
Durham, NC 27705
(919) 383-7246
http://sunsite.unc.edu/nppa/

1 scholarship of $1,000 to an undergraduate pursuing a career in photojournalism. Based on aptitude, potential for success, and financial need. Must be attending a two- or four-year college or university, not a trade school. Other restrictions may apply. Send a self-addressed, stamped envelope for more information. Deadline: March 1.

1989.

National PTA
Seniors' Reflections Scholarships
c/o Reflections Program
330. N. Wabash Avenue, Suite 2100
Chicago, IL 60611
(312) 670-6782
http://www.pta.org
info@pta.org

4 awards of $750 (one in each area) to high school seniors with talent and ability or an interest in literature, musical composition, photography, or visual arts. Based on ability, personal essay, and teacher recommendations. To obtain more information or an application, write the National PTA and include the six-digit local PTA Unit ID number. Requests without this ID number will not be responded to. Deadline: varies.

1990.

National Public Radio (NPR)
Internship Coordinator
635 Massachusetts Avenue
Washington, DC 20001-3753
(202) 414-2000
http://www.npr.org

20 to 30 internships providing a salary of $5 per hour to the first fifteen interns chosen (remaining interns receive no compensation). Open to undergraduate juniors, seniors, and graduate students interested in pursuing careers in radio. Internships are conducted in Washington, DC. Interns are assigned to specific departments, such as news and

information, events unit, cultural programming, promotion and public affairs, development, personnel, representation, legal, marketing, engineering and operations, or audio engineering, or to one of NPR's programs. Internships last from eight to twelve weeks during the summer, fall, or winter/spring, and interns work from sixteen to forty hours per week. Deadline: March 30 (summer); August 15 (fall); December 15 (winter/spring).

1991.
National Radio Astronomy Observatory Summer Research Assistantships
520 Edgemont Road
Charlottesville, VA 22903-2475
(804) 296-0211
(804) 246-0278 Fax
http://www.cv.nrao.edu/html/

20 assistantships of $1,500 per month, plus travel expenses, to undergraduate students with at least three years of study and graduate students who have completed no more than two years of study. Students must be majoring in astronomy, physics, computer science, or electrical engineering. Deadline: February 1.

1992.
National Rifle Association (NRA)
Jeanne E. Bray Memorial Scholarship
Attn: Megan A. O'Hara
11250 Waples Mill Road
Fairfax, VA 22030
(703) 267-1400
http://www.nra.org

3 scholarships of $2,000 to any high school senior, undergraduate, or graduate student whose parent is an active or retired law enforcement officer and member of the National Rifle Association, or a nonmember law enforcement officer killed in the line of duty. Applicants must write an essay on the second amendment and have at least a 3.0 GPA, and high school seniors must have at least a 750 SAT I or a 20 ACT score. Award may be used at any accredited U.S. two- or four-year college, university, or graduate school. Must be U.S. citizens. Award is renewable. Deadline: November 15.

1993.
National Roofing Foundation
NRF Scholarship Awards Program
O'Hare International Center
10255 West Higgins Road, Suite 600
Rosemont, IL 60018
(708) 299-9070

Awards of $2,000 to high school seniors, undergraduate, or graduate students pursuing careers in architecture or construction as related to the roofing industry. Must be U.S. citizens. Scholarships must be used for full-time study at an accredited four-year college or university. Send a #10 self-addressed, stamped envelope to receive an application. Deadline: January 15.

1994.
National Scholarship Trust Fund
TAGA/NSTF Fellowships
4615 Forbes Avenue
Pittsburgh, PA 15213
(412) 621-6941

Numerous fellowships ranging from $1,500 to $3,000 to undergraduate seniors or graduate students with no less than one year of study remaining. Must be pursing a career in the graphic communications industries. Request applications after September 1. Deadline: January 10.

1995.
National Science Teachers Association
Duracell/NSTA Scholarship Competition
Space Science and Technology
1840 Wilson Boulevard
Arlington, VA 22201-3000
(202) 358-1529
http://www.nsta.org/

1 scholarship of $20,000, 2 scholarships of $10,000, 5 scholarships of $1,000, 12 scholarships of $500, and 30 scholarships of $200 (all are U.S. Series EE Savings Bonds) to students in grades 7 through 9 and in grades 10 through 12. Must be U.S. citizens or reside in a U.S. Territory. Students may enter individually or in pairs. Students must design and build a working device that runs on Duracell batteries. Sponsoring teachers also win prizes. Deadline: mid-January.

1996.
National Science Teachers Association
NASA/NSTA Space Student Involvement Program
Space Science and Technology
1840 Wilson Boulevard
Arlington, VA 22201-3000
(202) 358-1529
http://www.nsta.org/

Five different competitions involving art and essays open to students in 3rd through 12th grade. (1) Future Aircraft/Spacecraft Design Team Competition for grades 3–5, (2) Mission to Planet Earth Team Project for grades 6–8, (3) Mars Scientific Experiment Proposal for grades 9–12, (4) Aerospace Internships for grades 9–12, and (5) Intergalactic Art Competition for grades 3–12. Top awards include all-expense-paid trips to the National Space Science Symposium and trips to Space Camp. Sponsoring teachers also win awards. Deadline: early January (for all competitions).

1997.
National Science Teachers Association
Toshiba/NSTA ExploraVision
National Science Teachers Association
1840 Wilson Boulevard
Arlington, VA 22201
(800) EXPLOR9/(800) 397-5679
http://www.nsta.org/

Awards ranging from $5,000 and $10,000 to students in grades K through 12 who enter this competition. Students must conduct some literature research and envision what a certain technology will be like in twenty years. Theme may vary. Students can use their imaginations to create simple drawings and provide information on current technology. Sponsoring teachers also win awards. Deadline: early February.

1998.
National Science Teachers Association
Young Inventors Awards Program
Space Science and Technology
1840 Wilson Boulevard
Arlington, VA 22201-3000
(202) 358-1529
http://www.nsta.org/

11 awards of $5,000 and 1 award of $10,000 in the form of U.S. Series EE Savings Bonds to students in grades 3 through 8. Must be students in the U.S. or the U.S. Territories. Students conceive and design a tool invention; an adult (parent or teacher) may provide some guidance. The tool must perform a practical function, such as mending, making life easier or safer, entertaining, or solving an everyday problem. Deadline: mid-March.

1999.
National Security Agency (NSA)
College Summer Employment Program
S232–Suite 6840
Ft. Meade, MD 20755-6840
(800) 962-9398
http://www.nsa.gov:8080/

Employment for up to twelve weeks to undergraduate students. Must be majoring in electrical or computer engineering, computer science, mathematics, or languages (Far Eastern, Middle Eastern, or Slavic, but not Russian). Participants also receive round-trip travel expenses. Must have at least a 3.0 GPA on a 4.0 scale for all majors except mathematics, for which students must have at least a 3.5 GPA on a 4.0 scale. Must be U.S. citizens; immediate family members must also be U.S. citizens.

2000.
National Security Agency (NSA)
Undergraduate Scholarships
S232–Suite 6840
Ft. Meade, MD 20755-6840
(800) 962-9398
http://www.nsa.gov:8080/

Numerous scholarships providing full tuition costs to undergraduate juniors, particularly minorities, to use during undergraduate senior year. Must be majoring in computer science; electrical engineering; computer engineering; Asian, Middle Eastern, or Slavic languages; or mathematics. Award includes reimbursement for books and certain fees and a year-round salary. Recipients are employed during the summer. A housing allowance and travel expenses are provided during the summer employment. Based on academic achievement, leadership abilities, and extracurricular activities. Student and immediate family must be U.S. citizens. Deadline: early November.

2001.
National Society of Professional Engineers
Education Foundation
NSPE Undergraduate Scholarships for Enrolled
College Students
1420 King Street
Alexandria, VA 22314
(703) 684-2830
http://www.nspe.org/

Scholarships of $1,000 to undergraduate students majoring in engineering. Must have at least a 3.0 GPA. Must be enrolled in an accredited bachelor's degree program in engineering. Must be U.S. citizens. Deadline: February 1.

2002.
National Society of Professional Engineers
Educational Foundation
NSPE Undergraduate Scholarship for Enrolled
College Students Presidential Scholarship
1420 King Street
Alexandria, VA 22314
(703) 684-2858
http://www.nspe.org/

1 scholarship of $1,000 awarded every other year to an undergraduate student majoring in engineering. Must be enrolled in an Accreditation Board for Engineering and Technology (ABET)-accredited program in New Mexico. Based on academics and recommendations. Deadline: December 1.

2003.
National Society of Public Accountants
1010 North Fairfax Street
Alexandria, VA 22309
(703) 549-6400

22 scholarships of $900 awards to undergraduate students majoring in accounting. Must be enrolled in accredited night school or two- or four-year school. Students at four-year school may apply for third and fourth year only. The most outstanding applicant will be awarded an additional $200 Charles Earp Memorial Scholar Award. Deadline: March 20.

2004.
National Society of the Colonial Dames of
America
Colonial Dames Indian Nurse Scholarships
2305 Gillette Drive
Wilmington, NC 28403
(919) 763-6013

10 to 14 scholarships of $500 to students who are Native American Indians. Must be pursuing a nursing career related to the needs of Native American Indians. May be enrolled in a vocational/occupational school or a two- or four-year undergraduate or graduate school nursing program. Recipients of the Indian Health Service Scholarships are not eligible. Deadline: July 1; January 1.

2005.
**National Society of the Daughters of the
   American Revolution
American History Scholarships**
NSDAR Administration Building
1776 D Street, N.W.
Washington, DC 20006-5303
(202) 628-1776
http://www.dar.org

2 awards ranging from $1,000 to $2,000 to graduating high
school seniors in the top third of their class who intend to
major in American history. No affiliation or relationship
with the DAR is necessary to qualify. Must be U.S. citizens.
Transcripts are reviewed annually for continued renewal.
Deadline: February 1 (state chairperson).

2006.
**National Society of the Daughters of the
   American Revolution
Caroline Holt Nursing Scholarship**
NSDAR Administration Building
1776 D Street, N.W.
Washington, DC 20006-5303
(202) 628-1776
http://www.dar.org

1 scholarship awarded for first year of undergraduate study
in an accredited school of nursing. Applications must be
sent to the national chairman. Deadline: February 15;
August 15.

2007.
**National Society of the Daughters of the
   American Revolution
Enid Hall Griswold Memorial Scholarship
   Program**
NSDAR Administration Building
1776 D Street, N.W.
Washington, DC 20006-5303
(202) 628-1776
http://www.dar.org

1 scholarship of $1,000 to a junior or senior attending an
accredited college or university and majoring in history,
political science, government, or economics. Applicant must
be sponsored by a DAR chapter. Deadline: February 15.

2008.
**National Society of the Daughters of the
   American Revolution
Lillian and Arthur Dunn Scholarship**
NSDAR Administration Building
1776 D Street, N.W.
Washington, DC 20006-5303
(202) 628-1776
http://www.dar.org

1 scholarship of $1,000 (renewable for four years) to a
graduating high school senior who is a dependent of an
active DAR member. Must be planning to attend a college
or university in the U.S. Minimum 3.0 GPA required. Must
be U.S. citizen. Renewable with annual transcript review.
Deadline: February 20.

2009.
**National Society of the Daughters of the
   American Revolution
Longman–Harris Scholarship**
NSDAR Administration Building
1776 D Street, N.W.
Washington, DC 20006-5303
(202) 628-1776
http://www.dar.org

1 scholarship of $2,000 (renewable for four years) to a
graduating high school senior of Kate Duncan Smith DAR
School. Transcript review required for renewal. Obtain
applications through school. Deadline: February 15.

2010.
**National Society of the Daughters of the
   American Revolution
Madeline Picket (Halbert) Cogswell Nursing
   Scholarship**
NSDAR Administration Building
1776 D Street, N.W.
Washington, DC 20006-5303
(202) 628-1776
http://www.dar.org

1 scholarship of $500 to a student currently enrolled in an
accredited school of nursing for undergraduate study who
is a DAR member, is eligible for membership, or is related
to a member of NSDAR, SR, or C.A.R. Applications must be
sent to the national chairman. Deadline: February 20;
August 20.

2011.
**National Society of the Daughters of the
   American Revolution
Margaret Howard Hamilton Scholarship**
NSDAR Administration Building
1776 D Street, N.W.
Washington, DC 20006-5303
(202) 628-1776
http://www.dar.org

1 scholarship of $1,000 (renewable for four years) to a
graduating high school senior who has been accepted to
the Ben Caudle Learning Center, University of the Ozarks.
Applications must be requested directly from the Learning
Center upon acceptance into program for learning-disabled
students. Deadline: February 15.

2012.
**National Society of the Daughters of the
   American Revolution
National Chairman American Indian Committee**
NSDAR Administration Building
1776 D Street, N.W.
Washington, DC 20006-5303
(202) 628-1776
http://www.dar.org

1 scholarship of $450 to an undergraduate student who is a
Native American Indian. Deadline: February 15.

2013.
National Society of the Daughters of the American Revolution
Occupational Therapy Scholarship
NSDAR Administration Building
1776 D Street, N.W.
Washington, DC 2006-5303
(202) 628-1776
http://www.dar.org

1 scholarship of $500 to a student pursuing a career in occupational or physical therapy. Must be recommended by nearest DAR chapter. Deadline: February 20 and August 20.

2014.
National Society of the Sons of the American Revolution
George and Stella M. Knight Essay Contest
1000 South Fourth Street
Louisville, KY 40203
(502) 589-1776

Scholarships ranging from local awards to state-level scholarships and a national first prize of $2,000 to high school juniors and seniors. Must submit original essay of not more than 500 words (excluding title page and bibliography). The topic must deal with a personality, event, philosophy, or ideal associated with the American Revolutionary War, the Declaration of Independence, or the Framing of the United States Constitution. Essays will be judged for historical accuracy, clarity of thought, organization, grammar and spelling, and creativity. Contact high school counselor for more information and an application. Deadline: early to mid-November.

2015.
National Space Club
Dr. Robert H. Goddard Space Science and Engineering Scholarships
655 15th Street, N.W., #300
Washington, DC 20005
(202) 639-4210

Scholarships of $7,500 to college juniors and seniors for study leading to increased knowledge of space research and exploration. Must be planning to pursue a career in aerospace sciences and technology. Deadline: January.

2016.
National Speakers Association
NSA Scholarships
1500 South Priest Drive
Tempe, AZ 85281
(602) 968-2552
(602) 968-0911 Fax

4 scholarship awards of $2,500 to full-time undergraduate juniors, seniors, or graduate students majoring or minoring in speech, oral communications, or a directly related area. Must have at least a 3.0 GPA on a 4.0 scale. Must be well-rounded students demonstrating leadership abilities and potential to make an impact by using oral communications. Deadline: June 3.

2017.
National Strength & Conditioning Association Challenge Scholarships
P.O. Box 81410
Lincoln, NE 68501
(402) 472-3000

Scholarships of $1,000 to undergraduate and graduate students in areas related to strength and conditioning. Must be members of the National Strength & Conditioning Association. Must be attending an accredited institution. Deadline: March 1.

2018.
National Student Nurses Association
555 West 57th Street, Suite 1327
New York, NY 10019
(212) 581-2215

5 scholarships of $1,500 to undergraduate students pursuing a nursing career. Based on financial need, academic achievement, and community activities. There is a $5 processing fee. Send a #10 self-addressed, stamped envelope with two stamps. Deadline: February 1.

2019.
National Student Nurses Association Foundation
Non–Member Regular Scholarship Program
555 West 57th Street, Suite 1327
New York, NY 10019
(212) 581-2215

Scholarships of varying amounts for students enrolled in accredited two-year pre-nursing, four-year nursing, diploma, or generic (not diploma) graduate nursing programs. Based on academics, activities, and financial need. Send a self-addressed, stamped envelope with 58¢ postage. Deadline: fall; may vary.

2020.
National Tropical Botanical Garden
Internship Program
P.O. Box 340
Lawai Kauai, HI 96765
(805) 332-7361

6 internships providing $240 per week to undergraduate juniors, seniors, graduate students, and college graduates of any age. Internships last from ten to eighteen weeks during the summer, fall, and spring in Kauai, HI. Interns work in a different department each week at Lawai Gardens, such as in Living Collections, Research, Administration, the Visitor's Center, and the Hawaii Plant Conservation Center. Though many interns have a background in botany and horticulture, there are no academic requirements for selection, but students should have a serious interest in plants. Deadline: March 1.

2021.
National Union of Hospital and Health Care Employees
District 1199C Training and Upgrading Fund
1319 Locust Street, 1st Floor
Philadelphia, PA 19107

Scholarship and stipend to a high school senior who is a dependent of a full-time union member working for a contributing employer. Based on seniority and acceptance into a full-time program in a college or university in a health-related field. Deadline: varies.

2022.
National Urban League Inc.
NUL–Draft Scholarship & Intern Program for
**   Minority Students**
c/o Director of Education
500 East 62nd Street
New York, NY 11021

5 scholarship of $10,000 ($5,000 per year for two years) and 10 scholarships of $1,000 to outstanding minority undergraduate juniors. Provide students with summer internships within large corporations. Students must be classified as college juniors during the time the scholarship award commences, must be within the top 25 percent of their class, and must major in engineering, sales, marketing, manufacturing operations, finance, or business administration. Request applications after January 1. Deadline: April 15.

2023.
National Women's Health Network
Internship Coordinator
1325 G Street, N.W.
Washington, DC 20005
(202) 347-1140

5 twelve-week internships open to undergraduates, college graduates, and graduate students to work in the only public-interest organization devoted to women and health. Interns work on federal health care projects, such as writing testimony for FDA hearings, and conduct research in response to written and telephone requests for information. Internships offer no compensation and take place in summer, fall, or spring. Deadline: April 15 (summer); May 15 (fall); November 15 (spring).

2024.
National Zoological Park
Minority Traineeships
3001 Connecticut Avenue, N.W.
Washington, DC 20008
(202) 673-4950

Twelve-week summer or fall internships providing a stipend of at least $2,400 to minority undergraduate, graduate, veterinary students, and recent college graduates. Interns work in one of the following programs: animal behavior; reproductive physiology; nutrition; genetics; husbandry; exotic animal medicine; veterinary pathology; interpretive exhibition development, design, and evaluation; Appalachian Mountain ecosystem studies; public affairs; education; biopark horticulture collections; facilities design; landscaping; and zoo photography. Intern responsibilities may include working on ongoing and special projects, animal observation and handling, data recording, laboratory analysis, data processing, and report writing. Selection is based on statement of interest, academic achievement, relevant experience, and letters of reference. Interns must make their own lodging arrangements. Send a self-addressed, stamped envelope for specific application requirements. Deadline: February 1.

2025.
National Zoological Park
Research Traineeships
3001 Connecticut Avenue, N.W.
Washington, DC 20008
(202) 673-4950

Varying numbers of twelve-week summer or fall traineeships providing a stipend of up to $2,400 to undergraduate and veterinary students and recent college graduates. Students could work in one of various animal research areas: behavior and ecology, reproductive physiology, nutrition, genetics, husbandry and exhibit interpretation, exotic animal medicine, veterinary pathology, or Appalachian Mountain ecosystem studies. Selection is based on statement of interest, academic achievement, relevant experience, and letters of reference. Trainees must make their own lodging arrangements. Send a self-addressed, stamped envelope for specific application requirements. Deadline: February 1.

2026.
National Zoological Park
Traineeship in BioPark Horticulture
3001 Connecticut Avenue, N.W.
Washington, DC 20008
(202) 673-4950

Varying numbers of twelve-week summer or fall traineeships providing a stipend of up to $2,400 to undergraduate and veterinary students, and recent college graduates with a biology, forestry, or horticulture background. Trainees assist with ongoing inventory of the arboriculture collection, field observation, literature research, and data entry. Selection is based on statement of interest, academic achievement, relevant experience, and letters of reference. Trainees must make their own lodging arrangements. Send a self-addressed, stamped envelope for specific application requirements. Deadline: mid- to late February.

2027.
National Zoological Park
Traineeship in Education
3001 Connecticut Avenue, N.W.
Washington, DC 20008
(202) 673-4950

Varying numbers of twelve-week summer or fall traineeships providing a stipend of up to $2,400 to undergraduate and graduate students and recent college graduates. Trainees assist with the development and running of the Reptile Discovery Center and the Amazonia Exhibit. Trainees are able to work on projects that experiment with varying educational approaches by interpreters of animal and plant exhibits. Selection is based on statement of interest, academic achievement, relevant experience, and letters of reference. Trainees must make their own lodging arrangements. Send a self-addressed, stamped envelope for specific application requirements. Deadline: mid-February; varies.

2028.
National Zoological Park
Traineeship in Exhibit Interpretation
3001 Connecticut Avenue, N.W.
Washington, DC 20008
(202) 673-4950

Varying numbers of twelve-week summer or fall traineeships providing a stipend of up to $2,400 to undergraduate and graduate students and recent college graduates. Trainees assist with the development and designing of graphic exhibits to complement and enhance other zoo exhibits. Trainees may work on projects that focus on the zoo visitor experience by interviewing visitors, assessing the results of the survey, assess the impact of the Native American and African American Heritage Gardens, or finding out what visitors know about the Amazon. Selection is based on statement of interest, academic achievement, relevant experience, and letters of reference. Trainees must make their own lodging arrangements. Send a self-addressed, stamped envelope for specific application requirements. Deadline: mid-February; varies.

2029.
National Zoological Park
Traineeship in Facilities Design
3001 Connecticut Avenue, N.W.
Washington, DC 20008
(202) 673-4950

Varying numbers of twelve-week summer or fall traineeships providing a stipend of up to $2,400 to undergraduate and graduate students and recent college graduates in the areas of architectural or engineering programs who have an interest in zoo/museum facilities. Trainees work in facilities design concerning zoo facilities planning and construction. Trainees spend time on field observation, literature research, and data entry. Selection is based on statement of interest, academic achievement, relevant experience, and letters of reference. Trainees must make their own lodging arrangements. Send a self-addressed, stamped envelope for specific application requirements. Deadline: mid-February; varies.

2030.
National Zoological Park
Traineeship in Landscaping
3001 Connecticut Avenue, N.W.
Washington, DC 20008
(202) 673-4950

Varying numbers of twelve-week summer or fall traineeships providing a stipend of up to $2,400 to undergraduate and graduate students and recent college graduates in the area of landscaping. Trainees assist with the zoo's landscaping program, educational plant exhibits, plant-animal interactions, and exhibit landscaping. Selection is based on statement of interest, academic achievement, relevant experience, and letters of reference. Trainees must make their own lodging arrangements. Send a self-addressed, stamped envelope for specific application requirements. Deadline: mid-February; varies.

2031.
National Zoological Park
Traineeship in Public Affairs
3001 Connecticut Avenue, N.W.
Washington, DC 20008
(202) 673-4950

Varying numbers of twelve-week summer or fall traineeships providing a stipend of up to $2,400 to undergraduate and graduate students and recent college graduates. Trainees assist in developing, implementing, and evaluating programs. Selection is based on statement of interest, academic achievement, relevant experience, and letters of reference. Trainees must make their own lodging arrangements. Send a self-addressed, stamped envelope for specific application requirements. Deadline: mid-February; varies.

2032.
National Zoological Park
Traineeship in Zoo Photography
3001 Connecticut Avenue, N.W.
Washington, DC 20008
(202) 673-4950

Varying numbers of twelve-week summer or fall traineeships providing a stipend of up to $2,400 to undergraduate and graduate students and recent college graduates. Trainees assist in zoo photography. Selection is based on statement of interest, academic achievement, relevant experience, and letters of reference. Trainees must make their own lodging arrangements. Send a self-addressed, stamped envelope for specific application requirements. Deadline: mid-February; varies.

2033.
Native Daughters of the Golden West
Annie L. Adair Scholarships
543 Baker Street
San Francisco, CA 94117-1405
(415) 563-9091

2 scholarships of $1,300 to high school seniors, high school graduates, or undergraduate freshmen who are dependents of members in good standing and are majoring in business or social welfare education. Grandchildren of members are eligible if the parent is ineligible for membership. Junior Native Daughters are eligible provided they become affiliated with the Native Daughters of the Golden West. Must have at least a 3.0 GPA or better. Must submit a letter bearing the Seal of the Parlor sponsoring the applicant, three letters of recommendation, and official transcript. Deadline: May 1.

2034.
Native Daughters of the Golden West
Bertha A. Briggs Veteran Scholarships
543 Baker Street
San Francisco, CA 94117-1405
(415) 563-9091

6 scholarships of $750 to high school seniors, high school graduates, or undergraduate freshmen who are veterans or dependents of veterans. Students must be affiliated with the Native Daughters of the Golden West. Must have at least a 3.0 GPA on a 4.0 scale and be California residents. Must submit a letter bearing the Seal of the Parlor sponsoring the applicant, three letters of recommendation, and official transcript. Deadline: May 1.

2035.
Native Daughters of the Golden West
Junior Native Daughter Scholarships
543 Baker Street
San Francisco, CA 94117-1405
(415) 563-9091

Numerous $100 scholarships for high school seniors who have been members of the Junior Native Daughters since October 12, 1985. Must have at least a 2.5 GPA on a 4.0 scale and have a letter of acceptance from a vocational or trade school or a two- or four-year college or university. Must submit a letter bearing the Seal of the Parlor sponsoring the applicant, three letters of recommendation, and official transcript. Deadline: May 1.

2036.
Native Daughters of the Golden West
Native Daughters Nursing Scholarships
543 Baker Street
San Francisco, CA 94117-1405
(415) 563-9091

3 scholarships of $400 ($200 per semester) to high school seniors who plan to pursue a career in nursing. Need not be members of the Daughters of the Golden West. Must submit a letter bearing the Seal of the Parlor sponsoring the applicant, three letters of recommendation, and official transcript. Deadline: May 1.

2037.
Native Daughters of the Golden West
Sue J. Irwin Scholarships
543 Baker Street
San Francisco, CA 94117-1405
(415) 563-9091

4 scholarships of $1,000 to high school seniors, high school graduates, or undergraduate freshmen attending a California vocational or trade school or college or university who are members or children of members in good standing (only when mother is not eligible for membership). Junior Native Daughters are eligible provided they become affiliated with the Native Daughters of the Golden West. Must have a 3.0 GPA or better. Must submit a letter bearing the Seal of the Parlor sponsoring the applicant, three letters of recommendation, and official transcript. Deadline: May 1.

2038.
Native Sons of the Golden West
Public Speaking Contest
Grand Secretary
Native Sons of the Golden West
414 Mason Street
San Francisco, CA 94102
(415) 392-1223

Awards ranging from $500 to $1,000 to California high school students under the age of twenty in a public-speaking contest offered to foster an interest in the romantic and interesting story of California. Contact above address for more information. Deadline: January.

2039.
Natural Sciences and Engineering Research
Council of Canada
Undergraduate Student Research Awards
200 Kent Street
Ottawa, Ontario K1A 1H5
Canada
(613) 996-3769

Numerous scholarships of Canadian $750 for up to four months to undergraduate students to conduct research at universities or industrial labs in the fields of agriculture, biology, computer science, engineering, food science, forestry, geography, and geology. Award is presented to encourage students to undertake graduate studies. Award may be used during the academic year or summer session. Must conduct the research at a university or industrial lab in Canada. Deadline: set by individual schools.

2040.
The Nature Conservancy (TNC)
Internship Coordinator
Home Office
1815 North Lynn Street
Arlington, VA 22209
(703) 841-5300
(703) 247-3721 Hotline

130 to 150 internships providing from minimum wage to $6 per hour plus free housing for most positions on preserves to high school graduates, undergraduates, graduate students, and recent graduates to work at an environmental internship. Interns can work at headquarters in botany, fund-raising, communications, or legal, and in field offices in stewardship or as natural or environmental scientists on any of The Nature Conservancy's (TNC) preserves. Locations available are at Arlington, VA (HQ), or fifty field and eight regional offices in all fifty states, or preserves in AZ, CA, CO, FL, GA, IL, ME, MN, NC, NY, or SD. Internships last from eight weeks to six months during the summer or on an ongoing basis. Deadline: rolling.

2041.
Naval Reserve Officers Training Corps
Commander, Navy Recruiting Command
Attn: Code 314
4015 Wilson Boulevard
Arlington, VA 22203

The NROTC trains and educates young men and women to enter as commissioned officers in the Navy or Marine Corps. All college majors are accepted. Covers tuition, books, fees, uniforms, a $100 monthly allowance for forty months to assist with room and board; student receives pay during their summer involvement on ships. Applicant must be U.S. citizen, between seventeen and twenty-one years of age, physically fit, at least a second-semester high school junior, and be prepared to serve his time upon graduation from college. Based on high school record, college potential, and potential for a career in the Navy. Contact your local Navy Recruiting Office or above address. Deadline: December 1.

2042.
Navy–Marine Corps Relief Society
Education Program
801 North Randolph Street, Room 1228
Arlington, VA 22203-1989
(202) 696-4960

Unlimited numbers of loans are available to spouses or unmarried dependent children of regular, retired (twenty years), or deceased Navy and Marine Corps personnel. Applicants must be high school graduates and under twenty-three years of age prior to entering college (age requirement is waived for graduate and professional students within five years after undergraduate degree).

Spouses may be enrolled half-time; dependents must be full-time students. The NMCRS pays the expense of the guarantee fee. Amount of loan is dependent on the federal regulation of the Stafford Student Loans.

2043.
Navy–Marine Corps Relief Society
Active Duty Commissioning Programs (ADCP)
801 North Randolph Street, Room 1228
Arlington, VA 22203
(703) 696-4904

Scholarships of up to $1,000 to undergraduate students. Must be enrolled in a Commissioning Program (NROTC, ECP, NESEP, MECAP, EEAP, etc.). Apply through the Professor of Naval Science or administrative commanding officer. Interest-free loans also available. Based on financial need. Deadline: 30 days before end of spring semester before grant is made.

2044.
Navy–Marine Corps Relief Society
Battleship *Iowa* Memorial Scholarships
801 North Randolph Street, Room 1228
Arlington, VA 22203
(703) 696-4904

Scholarships of varying amounts to children and widows of deceased crewmembers of the U.S.S. *Iowa* who died in the April 19, 1989, turret explosion. Deadline: 30 days before end of spring semester before grant is made.

2045.
Navy–Marine Corps Relief Society
Children of Deceased Active Duty (CDAD)
801 North Randolph Street, Room 1228
Arlington, VA 22203
(703) 696-4904

Scholarships grants and interest-free loans to high school graduates who are children, including stepchildren and legally adopted children, of Navy and Marine Corps members who died while on active duty for undergraduate studies and vocational training. Based on financial need. Obtain applications from NMRCS headquarters. Deadline: 30 days before end of spring semester before grant is made.

2046.
Navy–Marine Corps Relief Society
Children of Deceased, Retired Servicemembers
  (CDR) Grants
801 North Randolph Street, Room 1228
Arlington, VA 22203
(703) 696-4904

Up to 1,000 grants of varying amounts to children, stepchildren, and legally adopted children of Navy or Marine Corps members who died in retirement. Amount of grant is based on college costs, federal grants, Veteran Administration (VA) benefits, and scholarships. For undergraduate studies and vocational training. Obtain applications from NMRCS headquarters. Deadline: 30 days before end of spring semester before grant is made.

2047.
Navy–Marine Corps Relief Society
U.S. Navy–Marine Corps Stafford Student Loans
801 North Randolph Street, Room 1228
Arlington, VA 22203
(703) 696-4904

Full-time students who are children, stepchildren, or legally adopted children of Navy or Marine Corps members who are active, reserve, retired, or deceased are eligible to borrow funds. Must be unmarried and under twenty-three years of age. Freshmen may borrow up to $2,625 per year; sophomores may borrow up to $3,500 per year; and juniors or seniors may borrow up to $4,000 per year. Deadline: 30 days before end of spring semester before grant is made.

2048.
Navy–Marine Corps Relief Society
U.S.S. *Stark* Memorial Scholarships
801 North Randolph Street, Room 1228
Arlington, VA 22203
(703) 696-4904

Scholarships of varying amounts to children and widows of deceased crewmembers of the U.S.S. *Stark* as a result of the Persian Gulf missile attack on May 17, 1987. Deadline: 30 days before end of spring semester before grant is made.

2049.
Navy–Marine Corps Relief Society
U.S.S. *Tennessee* Scholarships
801 North Randolph Street, Room 1228
Arlington, VA 22203
(703) 696-4904

Scholarships of varying amounts to children of active-duty personnel on or previously assigned to the U.S.S. *Tennessee*. Deadline: 30 days before end of spring semester before grant is made.

2050.
Navy Relief Society
801 N. Randolph Street, Suite 1228
Arlington, VA 22203

Loans (no interest while in school, low interest thereafter) for unmarried dependent children of present or former Navy and Marine personnel. Funds are available for undergraduate, graduate, and vocational education.

2051.
Navy Supply Corps Foundation Scholarships
Scholarship Chairman
Navy Supply Corps School
Athens, GA 30606-9988
(404) 354-4111

Scholarships of $2,000 for dependents of active-duty, reserve, or deceased Navy Supply Corps enlisted personnel. Must be single, in upper 50 percent of class, and have at least a C+ average; can be either undergraduates or graduates at a two- or four-year institution. Based on academic record, character, and leadership potential. Deadline: February 15.

2052.
**Nebraska Coordinating Commission for
 Postsecondary Education**
Postsecondary Education Award Program
P.O. Box 95005
Lincoln, NE 68509-5005
(402) 471-2847/(402) 471-2886 Fax
http://nol.org/NEspostsecondaryed/

Scholarships of varying amounts to graduating high school
seniors and undergraduate students. Must be Nebraska
residents and attend an accredited Nebraska institution.
Selection based on financial need. Must file FAFSA.

2053.
**Nebraska Coordinating Commission for
 Postsecondary Education**
Robert C. Byrd Scholarships
P.O. Box 95005
Lincoln, NE 68509-5005
(402) 471-2847/(402) 471-2886 Fax
http://nol.org/NEspostsecondaryed/

Scholarships of up to $1,500 to graduating high school
seniors. For use the first year of study in a college or
university within the state. Must be a Nebraska resident
and attend an accredited Nebraska institution. Administered
by each state's educating agency. Obtain applications from
state agency or high school counselor.

2054.
**Nebraska Coordinating Commission for
 Postsecondary Education**
Scholarship Assistance Program
P.O. Box 95005
Lincoln, NE 68509-5005
(402) 471-2847/(402) 471-2886 Fax
http://nol.org/NEspostsecondaryed/

Scholarships of varying amounts to graduating high school
seniors and undergraduate students. Must be Nebraska
residents and attend an accredited Nebraska institution.
Selection based on financial need. Must file FAFSA.

2055.
**Nebraska Coordinating Commission for
 Postsecondary Education**
Scholarship Award Program
P.O. Box 95005
Lincoln, NE 68509-5005
(402) 471-2847/(402) 471-2886 Fax
http://nol.org/NEspostsecondaryed/

Scholarships of varying amounts to graduating high school
seniors and undergraduate students. Must be Nebraska
residents and attend an accredited Nebraska institution.
Selection based on financial need. Must file FAFSA.

2056.
Nebraska Department of Veterans' Affairs
Nebraska Active Selected Reserve Tuition Credit
P.O. Box 95083
State Office Building
Lincoln, NE 68509
(402) 471-2458

Tuition credit of up to 50 percent of tuition charges at any
state-supported Nebraska institution. Must be Nebraska
resident and an enlisted member of a Nebraska reserve unit
of the U.S. Armed Forces, with at least two more years
remaining. Must not have completed ten years of service in
the Armed Forces.

2057.
Nebraska National Guard Tuition Credit
Military Department
1300 Military Road
Lincoln, NE 68508
(402) 473-1133

Tuition credit of up to 75 percent to students who are
members of the Nebraska National Guard and attending
any state-supported Nebraska college, university, or
technical community college.

2058.
**Nebraska Tuition Waivers for Veterans'
 Dependents**
Nebraska Department of Veterans' Affairs
P.O. Box 95083
State Office Building
Lincoln, NE 68509
(403) 471-2458

Tuition scholarships to spouses, widows, widowers, or
dependent children under twenty-six years of age of a
veteran who died from a service-connected injury before or
after leaving the service since WWI or was listed as a
prisoner of war or as missing in action since December 7,
1941. Deadline: beginning of term.

2059.
Negro Educational Emergency Drive
Need Scholarship Program
Midtown Towers.
643 Liberty Avenue, 17th Floor
Pittsburgh, PA 15222
(412) 566-2760

400 renewable scholarships ranging from $100 to $1,000 to
African American students who are residents of Allegany,
Armstrong, Beaver, Butler, Washington, or Westmoreland
counties, Pennsylvania. Students must have a high school
diploma or a GED. Deadline: May 13.

2060.
Nellie Martin Carman Scholarship Trust
Secretary, Carman Scholarship Committee
1121 244th Street, S.W., No. 65
Bothell, WA 98021
(206) 486-6575

Renewable awards of up to $1,000 per year to graduates of
public high schools in King, Sonomish, or Pierce counties
who plan to attend colleges in Washington. Each high
school nominates one student for this award (or if senior
class is over 400, two are nominated). Open to all majors
except drawing, home economics, interior design, music,
and sculpture. Deadline: March 15.

2061.
Nevada State Board of Education
Robert C. Byrd Scholarships
1850 East Sahara, Suite 200
Las Vegas, NV 89104
(702) 486-6455
http://www.nsn.k12.nv.us/nvdoe/

Scholarships of up to $1,500 to graduating high school
seniors. For use the first year of study in a college or
university within the state. Must be a Nevada resident and
attend an accredited Nevada institution. Administered by
each state's educating agency. Obtain applications from state
agency or high school counselor.

2062.
Nevada State Board of Education
Student Incentive Grant Program
1850 East Sahara, Suite 200
Las Vegas, NV 89104
(702) 486-6455
http://www.nsn.k12.nv.us/nvdoe/

Grants ranging from $200 to $5,000 to undergraduate
students. Must be Nevada residents attending Nevada
colleges or universities. Contact school's financial-aid office.
Deadline: May 1.

2063.
New England Board of Higher Education
New England Regional Student Program
45 Temple Place
Boston, MA 02111
(617) 357-9620

Reduced tuition rates of 50 percent above in-state tuition to
students from Connecticut, Maine, Massachusetts, New
Hampshire, Rhode Island, or Vermont who attend a school
outside their own state because an in-state institution
doesn't carry their degree program. Students from
Connecticut, Massachusetts, Rhode Island, and Vermont
whose degree program is offered in-state may attend an out-
of-state institution if it's closer to the student's residence.

2064.
New Hampshire Charitable Foundation
37 Pleasant Street
P.O. Box 1335
Concord, NH 03301
(603) 225-6641

Grants averaging $1,100, totaling $460,805, and loans
totaling $221,145, to students who are residents of New
Hampshire. Deadline: varies.

2065.
New Hampshire Department of Education
Nursing Education Assistance Grants
101 Pleasant Street
Concord, NH 03494
(603) 271-3493
(603) 271-1953 Fax
http://www.state.nh.us/doe/about.htm

110 grants ranging from $600 to $2,000 to graduating high
school seniors or undergraduate students. Must be accepted

to or enrolled in an approved nursing program in New
Hampshire. Must be U.S. citizens or legal residents. Must
demonstrate financial need. Deadline: June 1; December 15.

2066.
New Hampshire Department of Education
Robert C. Byrd Honors Scholarships
101 Pleasant Street
Concord, NH 03494
(603) 271-3493
(603) 271-1953 Fax
http://www.state.nh.us/doe/about.htm

Scholarships of up to $1,500 to graduating high school
seniors. For use the first year of study in a college or
university within the state. Must be New Hampshire
residents and attend an accredited New Hampshire
institution. Administered by each state's educating agency.
Obtain applications from state agency or high school
counselor.

2067.
New Hampshire Department of Education
Scholarships for Orphans of Veterans
101 Pleasant Street
Concord, NH
(603) 271-3493
(603) 271-1953 Fax
http://www.state.nh.us/doe/about.htm

Scholarships providing tuition and $1,000 toward room,
board, books, and supplies to a student whose parent died
in a service-connected injury in the U.S. Armed Forces in
WWI, WWII, Korea, or the Southeast Asia conflict. Must be
between the ages of sixteen and twenty-five and New
Hampshire residents.

2068.
New Hampshire Department of Education
State Incentive Grants
101 Pleasant Street
Concord, NH
(603) 271-3493
(603) 271-1953 Fax
http://www.state.nh.us/doe/about.htm

Grants ranging from $100 to $1,500 to students who are
New Hampshire residents and attending a college or
university in New Hampshire, Connecticut, Maine,
Massachusetts, Rhode Island, or Vermont. Student must
apply for a Pell Grant. Deadline: May 1.

2069.
New Hampshire Rural Rehabilitation
  Corporation Grants
c/o Office of Associate Dean
College of Life Science and Agriculture
Room 201, Taylor Hall
University of New Hampshire
Durham, NH 03824

Grants of up to $500 per year to students who are from
current or former New Hampshire farm families, attending
a postsecondary institution, and majoring in life science and/
or agriculture. Students from communities of less than
5,000 population without farm connections may apply if

they are majoring in life science or agriculture. Must be New Hampshire residents either transferring from a community college or a junior or senior undergraduate at a four-year institution, and be attending a New Hampshire institution. Deadline: July 15.

2070.
New Hampshire State Department of Education
New Hampshire State Tuition Waivers
State House Annex
Concord, NH 03301

Waivers of tuition to students whose parent was listed as missing in action or was captured by the enemy during the Southeast Asia conflict. Must be attending a vocational or technical school.

2071.
New Jersey Department of Higher Education
Distinguished Scholars Program
Office of Student Assistance
4 Quakerbridge Plaza CN 540
Trenton, NJ 08625
(800) 792-8670
(609) 984-2709
http://www.state.nj.us/

Scholarships ranging from $1,000 to $2,000 per year for four undergraduate years to high school seniors selected as Scholars. Must be New Jersey residents and full-time undergraduates at a New Jersey institution. Based on SAT scores, academic record, and financial need. Deadline: January 1.

2072.
New Jersey Department of Higher Education
Educational Opportunity Fund (EOF) Grants
Office of Student Assistance
4 Quakerbridge Plaza CN 540
Trenton, NJ 08625
(800) 792-8670
(609) 984-2709
http://www.state.nj.us/

Grants ranging from $200 to $1,950 to undergraduate and $4,000 to graduate students who have been New Jersey residents for at least one year. Must be full-time students at a New Jersey institution. For eligibility, students must be inadmissable by regular admissions standards, have standardized test scores below institutional norms, and have a high school record suggesting deficiencies in basic skills, yet hold a high school diploma or GED. Deadline: March 15.

2073.
New Jersey Department of Higher Education
Garden State Schools (GSS) Program
Office of Student Assistance
4 Quakerbridge Plaza CN 540
Trenton, NJ 08625
(800) 792-8670
(609) 984-2709
http://www.state.nj.us/

Scholarships of $500 per year and an additional $500 for students with exceptional financial need. Open to all

undergraduate full-time students attending an approved New Jersey institution. Based on academic record, SAT scores, and financial need. Deadline: January 1.

2074.
New Jersey Department of Higher Education
MIA/POW Program
Office of Student Assistance
4 Quakerbridge Plaza CN 540
Trenton, NJ 08625
(800) 792-8670
(609) 984-2709
http://www.state.nj.us/

Tuition grants to undergraduate students who are New Jersey residents and who are children of members of the Armed Forces who were declared as missing in action or prisoners of war after January 1, 1960. May attend any public or independent undergraduate institution in New Jersey. Deadline: October 1; March 1.

2075.
New Jersey Department of Higher Education
Public Tuition Benefits Program
Office of Student Assistance
4 Quakerbridge Plaza CN 540
Trenton, NJ 08625
(800) 792-8670
(609) 984-2709
http://www.state.nj.us/

Full tuition benefits to students who are children or surviving spouses of emergency service personnel or law enforcement officers who died of a service-connected injury. Must be within eight years of the member's death for a spouse attending college and within eight years after the date of high school graduation for a child attending college. Must be New Jersey residents attending a New Jersey institution. Deadline: October 1; March 1.

2076.
New Jersey Department of Higher Education
Tuition Aid Grants (TAG)
Office of Student Assistance
4 Quakerbridge Plaza CN 540
Trenton, NJ 08625
(800) 792-8670
(609) 984-2709
http://www.state.nj.us/

Grants ranging from $400 to $3,700 to undergraduate students attending New Jersey public or independent institutions. Must be residents of New Jersey for at least twelve months; must file a New Jersey Financial Aid Form (NJFAF). Based on financial need. Deadline: October 1 (fall and spring); March 1 (spring only).

2077.
New Jersey Department of Military Affairs
Veterans Tuition Credit Program
Attn: DCVA-FO
Eggert Crossing Road
P.O. Box 340
Trenton, NJ 08625-0340
(609) 530-6961

Tuition credits of $400 to full-time and $200 for half-time students who are qualified veterans from New Jersey. Students may attend any postsecondary institution anywhere in the U.S. Must have served in the Armed Forces between December 31, 1960, and August 1, 1974. Deadline: October 1 (fall term); March 1 (spring term).

2078.
New Jersey Job Training Partnership Act Women Working Technical
540 Hudson Street
Hackensack, NJ 07601
(201) 329-9600 ext. 5500

Tuition sponsorship to females to prepare for employment in electronic and mechanical jobs. Recipients must be economically disadvantaged, dislocated workers, or displaced homemakers. Must be at least eighteen years of age and residents of Bergen County, New Jersey.

2079.
New Jersey Society of Professional Engineers
Joseph A. Simonetta
196 West State Street
Trenton, NJ 08608
(609) 393-0099
(609) 396-5361 Fax

Scholarships of varying amounts to graduating high school seniors wanting to pursue an engineering career. Must be New Jersey residents. Applicants are encouraged to apply early so there will be enough time to allow for an interview. Other restrictions may apply. Deadline: December 15.

2080.
New Letters Literary Awards
University of Missouri-Kansas City
Kansas City, MO 64110
(816) 235-1168

A $750 award for best short story; a $750 award for the best group of three to six poems; and a $500 award for the best expository nonfiction. A $10 reading fee is charged for each entry. Each entry must be mailed in a separate envelope. Two cover sheets (one with complete name, address, category, and title of the story, essay, or poem; and the second with the title only). Name and address cannot appear anywhere else on the entry. Send a self-addressed, stamped envelope postcard for notification of receipt and entry number. Include self-addressed, stamped envelope for a list of the winners. Fiction and essay must not exceed 5,000 words. All entries must be unpublished work. Deadline: May 15 (postmark).

2081.
New Mexico Commission on Higher Education Incentive Grant
P.O. Box 15910
Albuquerque, NM 87606-5910
(505) 827-7383
http://www.nmche.org/
highered@che.state.nm.us

Grants ranging from $200 to $2,500 to students attending public or private institutions in New Mexico. Must be U.S.

citizens and New Mexico residents; must be either full- or part-time students. Contact school's financial aid office.

2082.
New Mexico Commission on Higher Education Lottery Scholarships
P.O. Box 15910
Santa Fe, NM 87606-5910
(505) 827-7383
(505) 827-7392 Fax
(800) 279-9777
http://www.nmche.org/
highered@che.state.nm.us

Varying numbers of scholarships to graduating high school seniors. Must be New Mexico residents, planning to attend an accredited eligible New Mexico institution, and planning to enroll the first regular semester after high school graduation. Must maintain at least a 2.5 GPA while in college. Contact above address for more information.

2083.
New Mexico Commission on Higher Education Scholars Program
P.O. Box 15910
Albuquerque, NM 87606-5910
(505) 827-7383
http://www.nmche.org/
highered@che.state.nm.us

Scholarships providing tuition, fees, and books to students who graduated from a New Mexico high school the same year the award is presented. Must have graduated in the upper 5 percent of class, have at least a 1020 on SAT or 25 on ACT, and be U.S. citizens. Family income cannot exceed $30,000 per year. Renewable for up to four years, depending on academic progress.

2084.
New Mexico Commission on Higher Education Student Choice Grants
P.O. Box 15910
Albuquerque NM 87606-5910
(505) 827-7383
http://www.nmche.org/
highered@che.state.nm.us

Grants of varying amounts for full-time and half-time students attending public and private New Mexico institutions. Must be U.S. citizens, New Mexico residents, and attending College of Sante Fe, St. John's College in Sante Fe, or the College of the Southwest in Hobbs. Contact school's financial aid office.

2085.
New Mexico Commission on Higher Education Vietnam Veteran's Scholarships
P.O. Box 15910
Albuquerque, NM 87606-5910
(505) 827-7383
http://www.nmche.org/
highered@che.state.nm.us

Limited number of scholarships providing tuition and fees to Vietnam veterans. Must be New Mexico residents;

eligibility must be certified by the New Mexico Veterans' Service Commission. Contact school's financial aid office.

2086.
New Mexico Society of Professional Engineers
Ms. Kate Warder
1615 University, N.E.
Albuquerque, NM 87102
(505) 247-9376

Scholarships of varying amounts to graduating high school seniors wanting to pursue an engineering career. Must be New Mexico residents. Applicants are encouraged to apply early so there will be enough time to allow for an interview. Other restrictions may apply. Deadline: December 15.

2087.
New Mexico Veterans' Service Commission Scholarships
P.O. Box 2324
Santa Fe, NM 87504
(505) 827-6300

Students who are children of deceased New Mexican veterans who were New Mexico residents at the time of entering the military are eligible. Veterans must have died during WWI, WWII, or any action in which U.S. military forces were in armed conflict. Students are eligible for free tuition at any state-supported postsecondary school plus assistance (up to $300 per year per child) with fees, room and board, books, and supplies. Other eligible students may be children of deceased members of the New Mexico National Guard or State Police who were killed while on duty.

2088.
New York Arts Program
305 West 29th Street
New York, NY 10001
(212) 563-0255

100 internships and off-campus program in affiliation with twelve liberal arts colleges in the Midwest are open to undergraduate juniors and seniors. International students may also apply. Interns work as apprentices to architects, actors, directors, composers, photographers, studio artists, or fashion designers or with museums, theaters, dance companies, symphonies, television and radio stations, film and video companies, advertising agencies, magazines, publishing houses, and literary journals. Internships last from ten to fifteen weeks during the spring or fifteen weeks in the fall. Deadline: March 31 (fall); October 31 (spring).

2089.
New York Bureau of Higher Education Opportunity Programs
Aid for Part-Time Study
Scholarship Unit
Cultural Center, Room 5A55, CEC
Albany, NY 12230
(518) 474-5642
http://www.higher.nysed.gov/
HEOP1@higher.nysed.gov

Scholarships of up to $2,000 or tuition, whichever is less, to undergraduate students attending an accredited program in a New York institution on a part-time basis. Students must be New York residents, U.S. citizens, permanent resident aliens, or refugees. Based on academic record and financial need. Contact school's financial aid office.

2090.
New York Bureau of Higher Education Opportunity Programs
Children of Veteran Awards
Scholarship Unit
Cultural Center, Room 5A55, CEC
Albany, NY 12230
(518) 474-5642
http://www.higher.nysed.gov/
HEOP1@higher.nysed.gov

Grants of $450 to graduating high school seniors or undergraduate students. Must be children of a veteran who either died or was 50 percent disabled as a result of a service-connected injury. Must be residents of New York and U.S. citizens, attending a public or private New York institution on a full-time basis. Veteran must have served during WWI, WWII, Korean conflict, or between October 1, 1961, and May 7, 1975. Contact NYSHESC, Student Information, Albany, NY 12255.

2091.
New York Bureau of Higher Education Opportunity Programs
Health Service Corps Scholarship
Scholarship Unit
Cultural Center, Room 5A55, CEC
Albany, NY 12230
(518) 474-5642
http://www.higher.nysed.gov/
HEOP1@higher.nysed.gov

250 scholarships of up to $15,000 to full-time undergraduate students. Must be within two years of being eligible for a New York State license in their chosen field. Students may be enrolled in dental hygiene, nurse practitioner, occupational therapy, pharmacy, physical therapy, physician assisting, nursing, or speech pathology. Based on academic achievement, work experience, and interest in working with institutionalized patients. Recipients must work eighteen months in a state-operated facility or participating voluntary agency for each year of financial support. Contact: New York State Health Service Corps, Coming Tower, Room 1602, Empire State Plaza, Albany, NY 12237, (518) 473-7019. Deadline: February.

2092.
New York Bureau of Higher Education Opportunity Programs
Higher Education Opportunity Program
Scholarship Unit
Cultural Center, Room 5A55, CEC
Albany, NY 12230
(518) 474-5642
http://www.higher.nysed.gov/
HEOP1@higher.nysed.gov

Approximately 6,544 $3,000 scholarships to graduating high school seniors who are academically and economically disadvantaged. Academic disadvantage is based on inability to gain admission to a program at an independent New York State institution. Economic disadvantage is based on income levels set by the Regents of the State of New York. Contact: Bureau Chief, Higher Education Opportunity Program, NYS Education Department, Room 5A55, Cultural Education Center, Albany, NY 12230, (518) 474-5313.

2093.
New York Bureau of Higher Education
    Opportunity Programs
Regent College Scholarships
Scholarship Unit
Cultural Center, Room 5A55, CEC
Albany, NY 12230
(518) 474-5642
http://www.higher.nysed.gov/
HEOP1@higher.nysed.gov

1,000 scholarships of up to $250 to graduating high school seniors or undergraduate students. Must be New York residents in approved degree programs in a New York State institution. Must be legal residents of New York for at least one year. Based on ACT or SAT. Renewable up to four or five years with satisfactory academic progress. Deadline: November 5.

2094.
New York Bureau of Higher Education
    Opportunity Programs
Regents Professional Education in Nursing
Scholarship Unit
Cultural Center, Room 5A55, CEC
Albany, NY 12230
(518) 474-5642
http://www.higher.nysed.gov/
HEOP1@higher.nysed.gov

800 scholarships of $250 to graduating high school seniors or high school graduates entering a professional nursing program in an approved New York postsecondary institution. Must be New York State residents. Must be U.S. citizens, permanent residents, or refugees. Based on SAT/ACT and academic record. Must take SAT or ACT by October of their senior year. Renewable with satisfactory academic progress. Deadline: November 5.

2095.
New York Bureau of Higher Education
    Opportunity Programs
Regents Professional Opportunity Scholarships
Scholarship Unit
Cultural Center, Room 5A55, CEC
Albany, NY 12230
(518) 474-5642
http://www.higher.nysed.gov/
HEOP1@higher.nysed.gov

Scholarships from $1,000 to $5,000 to graduating high school seniors, undergraduates, or graduate students. Must be enrolled in or about to enroll in an approved professional field. Preference is given to minority or economically disadvantaged students. Must be New York State residents, U.S. citizens, permanent residents, or refugees. Must not have defaulted on a student loan. Students may be entering or enrolled in one of the

following professions: ASSOCIATES LEVEL—dental hygiene, occupational therapy assistant, ophthalmic dispensing, or physician's assistant; BACCALAUREATE LEVEL—accounting, architecture, engineering, landscape architecture, nursing, occupational therapy, physical therapy, or physician's assistant; MASTER'S—architecture, landscape architecture, occupational therapy, physical therapy, social work, or speech language pathology/audiology; DOCTORATE—chiropractic, law, optometry, podiatry, psychology, or veterinary medicine. Deadline: January 15.

2096.
New York Bureau of Higher Education
    Opportunity Programs
Robert C. Byrd Honors Scholarships
Scholarship Unit
Cultural Center, Room 5A55, CEC
Albany, NY 12230
(518) 474-5642
http://www.higher.nysed.gov/
HEOP1@higher.nysed.gov

At least 340 scholarships of $1,500 to graduating high school seniors. Must be New York residents who meet two of these three requirements: rank in the top 5 percent of their class, have at least a 3.5 GPA, or have at least an 1100 on SAT or 27 on ACT. Contact high school counselor or above address. Deadline: May 1.

2097.
New York Bureau of Higher Education
    Opportunity Programs
Tuition Assistance Program (TAP)
Scholarship Unit
Cultural Center, Room 5A55, CEC
Albany, NY 12230
(518) 474-5642
http://www.higher.nysed.gov/
HEOP1@higher.nysed.gov

Tuition assistance of up to $4,125 per year to graduating high school seniors or undergraduate students. Must be enrolled in or planning to enroll for full-time study in a postsecondary institution, hospital nursing program, two-year business school, or vocational/technical school. Must be a U.S. citizens, permanent residents, or refugees and legal New York residents for at least one year. Based on family's financial need, number of family members enrolled in college, tuition costs, and prior TAP payments. Deadline: May 1.

2098.
New York Bureau of Higher Education
    Opportunity Programs
Vietnam Veterans Tuition Awards (VVTA)
Scholarship Unit
Cultural Center, Room 5A55, CEC
Albany, NY 12230
(518) 474-5642
http://www.higher.nysed.gov/
HEOP1@higher.nysed.gov

Tuition awards of $1,000 to full-time and $500 to part-time undergraduate students. Must be veterans who served in the Armed Forces in Indochina between January 1, 1963, and May 7, 1975. Must have been a New York resident on

April 20, 1984, or have been one at the time entering the service and resumed residency on or before September 1, 1990. Students can't receive more than $10,000 total. Deadline: September 1.

2099.
New York City Department of Health
Health Research Training Program
346 Broadway, Room 712
New York, NY 10013
(212) 442-3380
(212) 442-3385 Fax

Over 200 internships lasting from three to six months, part- or full-time, year-round, and providing from $200 to $350 per week to undergraduate, graduate, and professional school students with federal work-study grants. Open to all majors, though applicants should have an interest in public health. Interns work within the five boroughs of New York City by working in ongoing ad hoc research or administration of public health projects. Interns may conduct lab or survey work, biostatistics, or health education. Interns prepare a brief report of project accomplishments that could result in a co-authored publication. Submit an application form and transcript. Deadline: March 15 (summer); all other times are open.

2100.
New York City Department of Personnel
Government Scholars Internship Program
2 Washington Street, 19th Floor
New York, NY 10004
(212) 487-5698

24 to 30 urban fellows (UF) and 24 to 30 government scholars (GS) providing $250 per week (GS) to undergraduate sophomores, juniors, and seniors and recent graduates and $460 per week (UF) to graduate students. Interns have daily contact with people. Applicants must be interested in a public service career, but may have any major. Must demonstrate leadership and be willing to look at issues with an open mind. Internships are conducted in New York City. Students must go to office and pick up applications. Do not call. Deadline: January 27 (GS); January 20 (UF).

2101.
New York City Department of Personnel
Urban Fellows Program
2 Washington Street, 19th Floor
New York, NY 10004
(212) 487-5698

Fellowships providing $18,000 to undergraduate seniors and recent college graduates pursuing careers in public administration, urban planning, government, public service, or urban affairs. Program covers one academic year (nine months) of full-time work experience in urban government. Must be U.S. citizens. Students must go to office and pick up applications. Do not call. Deadline: January 20.

2102.
New York City YWCA
Department of ReEntry Employment
610 Lexington Avenue
New York, NY 10022
(212) 735-9726

Financial assistance and counseling to female undergraduate and graduate students. Women must be separated, divorced, or widowed and reentering the job market. Funded by the New York State Department of Labor.

2103.
New York Financial Writer's Association
Scholarship Program
P.O. Box 20281
Greeley Square Station
New York, NY 10001
(800) 533-7551

Scholarships of $2,000 to undergraduate and graduate students who are pursuing a financial or business journalism career. Must be enrolled in an accredited college or university in metropolitan New York City. Other restrictions may apply. Deadline: March 1.

2104.
New York Hospital–Cornell Medical Center
Pre-Career Practicum
Westchester Division
21 Bloomingdale Road
White Plains, NY 10605
(914) 997-5780

50 to 60 eight-week summer internships providing no compensation to undergraduates and graduate students. Interns are assigned to nursing, therapeutic activities, social services, marketing, psychology, and research. Internships take place in White Plains, New York. Deadline: April 1.

2105.
New York State Assembly
NYSA Session Internships Committee
Attn: Jim Murphy
Legislative Office Building 104A
Albany, NY 12248
(518) 455-4100

150 internships from January through mid-May (thirty hours per week) to undergraduate juniors or seniors at New York institutions. Provides a $2,500 stipend to defray living and transportation costs. Must have at least a 2.5 GPA, be New York residents, and have a strong interest in state government; may have any academic field of study. Some institutions offer supplementary stipends, temporary loans, tuition waivers, or work-study funds to students in the program. Contact school's liaison officer. Deadline: November 1.

2106.
New York State Assembly
NYSA Summer Internships Committee
Attn: Jim Murphy
Legislative Office Building 104A
Albany, NY 12248
(518) 455-4100

Ten-week summer internships providing a $3,000 stipend (travel costs are not provided or reimbursed) to undergraduate students who are New York residents attending in- or out-of state colleges or out-of-state residents attending a New York college or university. Interns work on research projects with Assembly staff.

Students who have participated in either the Assembly Session or Summer Intern Program are not eligible to apply. Deadline: March 15.

2107.
New York State Education Department
AMS Science and Technology Energy Programs
State & Federal Scholarship & Fellowship Unit
Room 1071, EBA
Albany, NY 12234
(518) 474-5313

Provides a program for high school juniors and seniors interested in a health profession. Provides academic instruction in science and math, tutoring assistance, counseling, field trips, and mentoring by medical school students and health professionals. There is a full-time summer program ranging from four to six weeks at nine medical schools. There is also an after-school and Saturday program at ten medical sites.

2108.
New York State Grange
Howard and Marjories DeNise Memorial
**   Scholarships**
100 Grange Place
Cortland, NY 13045

Scholarships providing tuition, room, and board to high school seniors and college undergraduate students pursuing a career in agriculture. Must be New York State residents and agriculture majors; must maintain a B average. Upon completion of degree, recipients must remain in some area of agriculture for at least ten years or must repay 10 percent plus interest of the scholarship received for each year less than the ten-year minimum. Each year of mandatory military commitment counts as a year toward the ten-year agriculture-work requirement. Based on academic record, involvement in agricultural youth organizations, potential, recommendation, SAT/ACT scores, CEEB, and financial need. Deadline: April 15.

2109.
New York State Grange
Susan W. Freestone Vocational Education Awards
100 Grange Place
Cortland, NY 13045

10 awards of $100 to high school seniors who are members in good standing of the New York State Junior Grange and of a subordinate Grange. Students must attend an approved two- or four-year New York institution. A second $100 scholarship is available to students maintaining satisfactory academic performance. Based on academic records and extracurricular activities. Contact any Junior Deputy or State Director of Junior Granges. Deadline: May 1.

2110.
New York State Senate
Legislative Fellows Program; R. J. Roth
Journalism Fellowship; R. A. Weibe Public
**   Service Fellowship**
State Capitol, Room 500A
Albany, NY 12247
(518) 455-2611

14 fellowships of $22,575 to sophomore, junior, or senior undergraduates or graduate students who are New York State residents. Applicants can be majoring in any of the following areas: political science, government, public service, journalism, or public relations. Recipients work as regular legislative staff members of the offices to which they are assigned. Deadline: November 1 (undergraduates); May 10 (graduates).

2111.
New York State Senate
Senate Sessions Assistance Program
Senate Students Programs Office
State Capitol, Room 500A
Albany, NY 12247

Up to 61 positions paying $1,200 for five months (to defray living expenses) to work as session assistants. Students must live in Albany, be U.S. citizens, New York residents, and full-time undergraduate sophomores, juniors, or seniors attending New York institutions. Undergraduate freshmen are ineligible. All majors are accepted, though a career goal in public service is required. Based on academic record and research, and communication skills; there must be a balance in academic affiliation, equal opportunity, and geographic representation. The session runs from January to May. Contact school's Liaison Officer or Director. Deadline: mid-October.

2112.
Niccum Educational Trust Foundation
National Bank of Detroit, Trustee
401 South Main
P.O. Box 27
Goshen, IN 46526
(219) 538-5840

Numerous scholarships ranging from $800 to $1,500 to public high school seniors or students who have graduated within two years of applying. Must be in the upper third of class. Students must be residents of Elkhart, St. Joseph, Marshall, Noble, Kosciusko, or LaGrange counties, Indiana. SAT scores must be submitted. Deadline: April 15.

2113.
Nightline
Intern Coordinator
1717 Desales Street, N.W., 3rd Floor
Washington, DC 20036
(202) 887-7360
http://www.abcnews.com

5 twelve-week internships providing no compensation to undergraduate juniors and seniors, who must be able to receive academic credit. Internships are part-time (two to three days per week) during the summer, fall, or spring. Interns send faxes, make photocopies, scan newspapers for relevant articles, answer phones, and get to brainstorm for ideas for the night's shows. Deadline: rolling.

2114.
Nike
Internship Program
One Bowerman Drive
Beaverton, OR 97005
(503) 671-6453
(800) 890-6453
http://www.info.nike.com

15 ten-week summer internships to minority undergraduate sophomores, juniors, seniors, and graduate students. Must have at least a 3.0 GPA on a 4.0 scale. Interns can work in marketing, finance/accounting, records management, international division, customer service, retail resources, human resources, research design and development, and film/video. Students should be willing to ask for additional work, be flexible, have a passion to be the best, and have an appreciation for sports and fitness. Deadline: January 15.

2115.
Ninety–Nines, Inc.
Amelia Earhart Memorial Research Grant
Box 965
7100 Terminal Drive
Oklahoma City, OK 73159-0965
(800) 994-1929
(405) 685-7969
(405) 685-7985 Fax

1 research grant of varying amount to individuals wanting to conduct research on women's issues in aviation. Must have private license to join organization. Must be a member of The Ninety-Nines for two years prior to application. Must be a resident of Oklahoma City, Oklahoma. Other restrictions may apply. Deadline: December 31.

2116.
Ninety–Nines, Inc.
Amelia Earhart Memorial Scholarship Committee
Box 965
7100 Terminal Drive
Oklahoma City, OK 73159-0965
(800) 994-1929
(405) 685-7969
(405) 685-7985 Fax

17 scholarships of varying amounts to females working on an additional rating. 1 scholarship is to individuals wanting to work on a Flight Engineer rating. Must have private license to join organization. Must be members of The Ninety-Nines for two years prior to application. Must be residents of Oklahoma City, Oklahoma. Other restrictions may apply. Deadline: December 31.

2117.
Ninety–Nines, Inc.
Majorie Van Vliet Aviation Memorial
    Scholarships
Eastern New England Ninety-Nines, Inc.
P.O. Box 19
Waterford, VT 05848
(617) 259-0222

Scholarships of $2,000 to female high school seniors, undergraduates, or graduate students to use for tuition and/or flight training. May be majoring or planning to major in aeronautics, aviation maintenance, or flight training. Must live in one of the New England states, be planning a career in aviation, and have applied to an aviation-related education or training program. Selection based on goals and demonstrated financial need. Deadline: January 31.

2118.
Ninety–Nines, Inc.
Marion Barnick Memorial Scholarship
Attn: Judy Williams, Chairperson
Marion Barnick Scholarship Committee
5 No Name Road
Los Gatos, CA 95030

1 scholarship of $1,000 to a female private pilot who is either a member of the Ninety-Nines or a student at San Jose State, Gavilian College, Foothill College, or West Valley College in California. Other restrictions may apply. Deadline: June 1.

2119.
Nissan Focus Awards
Filmmaking Awards
1140 Avenue of the Americas, 5th Floor
New York, NY 10036
(212) 575-0270

Cash and prizes, totaling $60,000, in nine different categories for films made by students enrolled in a U.S. institution, art institution, or film school on a noncommercial basis. The nine categories cover all areas of filmmaking (writing, editing, sound, etc.). Films must be 16mm; silent or optical sound; color or black and white. Deadline: varies.

2120.
Noble Educational Fund
Noble Scholarships
P.O. Box 2180
Ardmore, OK 73402
(405) 223-5810

Numerous $2,000 renewable scholarships to high school graduates who are children of employees of the Samuel Roberts Noble Foundation, Inc., Noble Affiliates, Inc., Noble Drilling Corporation, or Samedan Oil Corporation. Must be under twenty-five years of age. Based on academic record, character, leadership, seriousness of purpose, SAT/ACT scores, and financial need. May be used at any two- or four-year institution, vocational, technical, or other school approved by the scholarship committee. Renewal based on academic progress. Deadline: March 1.

2121.
Non–Commissioned Officers Association
Betsy Ross Educational Fund
P.O. Box 33610
San Antonio, TX 78265
(210) 653-6161

12 scholarships of $250 per quarter to students attending local business or technical schools. Applicants must be a spouse of an NCOA member and a member of the NCOA International Auxiliary. An NCOA International Auxiliary membership application may accompany the scholarship application letter. State why you need the grant; courses you wish to take; name, address, and phone number of the school; and total cost. Deadline: 30 days prior to new quarter.

2122.
Non–Commissioned Officers Association (NCOA)
Mary Barraco Scholarship
P.O. Box 33610
San Antonio, TX 78265
(210) 653-6161

1 scholarship of $1,000 to a spouse or child of a member of the NCOA. Children must be under twenty-five years of age when applying for the initial assistance. Based on academic record, SAT/ACT (vocational students are exempt from SAT/ACT requirement), recommendations, patriotism, and essay on "Americanism." Deadline: March 31.

2123.
Non–Commissioned Officers Association
NCOA Scholarships
P.O. Box 33610
San Antonio, TX 78265
(210) 653-6161

8 academic and 4 vocational scholarships of $750 for undergraduate and graduate studies to sons and daughters, and 2 academic scholarships of $750 to spouses of members of the Non-Commissioned Officers Association. Awards are for study at accredited colleges, universities, and vocational training institutes. Must be under the age of twenty-five (with the exception of spouses). Renewable by reapplication; minimum of fifteen credit hours per semester; must maintain a B average. Based on recommendation, academic record, SAT/ACT (vocational students are exempt from SAT/ACT requirement), patriotism, and essay on "Americanism." Deadline: March 31.

2124.
Non–Commissioned Officers Association
William T. Green Scholarship
P.O. Box 33610
San Antonio, TX 78265
(210) 653-6161

1 scholarship of $1,000 to a child or spouse of an NCOA member. Applicants must be under twenty-five years of age upon initial application for award (with the exception of spouses). Award is for study at an accredited college, university, or vocational training institute. Based on recommendation, academic record, SAT/ACT (vocational students are exempt from SAT/ACT requirement), patriotism, and essay on "Americanism." Deadline: March 31.

2125.
North American Baptist Seminary
Canadian Student Awards
1525 South Grange Avenue
Sioux Falls, SD 57105
(605) 336-6588

Varying numbers of grants of varying amounts to full-time undergraduate students. Must be preparing for a church-related career. Must be Canadian citizens or legal permanent residents. Other restrictions may apply. Deadline: none specified.

2126.
North American Baptist Seminary
Financial Aid Grants
1525 South Grange Avenue
Sioux Falls, SD 57105
(605) 336-6588

Up to 70 grants of up to $2,100 to undergraduate students. Must be used for full-time study. Student must be enrolled in a North American Baptist Seminary and preparing for a church-related career. Applications must be submitted before the first week of the semester for which financial assistance is needed. Other restrictions may apply. Deadline: none.

2127.
North American Die Casting Association
David Laine Memorial Scholarships
9701 West Higgins Road, Suite 880
Rosemont, IL 60018
(708) 292-3600

Scholarships of $2,000 to undergraduate and graduate students enrolled in an engineering college affiliated with the Foundry Educational Foundation (FEF) and registered with FEF for the current year. Must be U.S. citizens. Other restrictions may apply. Deadline: May 1.

2128.
North Carolina Bar Association (NCBA)
Scholarships
P.O. Box 12806
Raleigh, NC 27605
(919) 828-0561

Numerous renewable scholarships of $2,000 to children (natural or adopted) of North Carolina law enforcement officers killed or permanently disabled in a service-connected injury. Student must be under twenty-seven years and attend a postsecondary institution approved by the Young Lawyers Division of NCBA. Open to all majors. Deadline: November 1.

2129.
North Carolina Chapter of NSPE
Professional Engineers of North Carolina
4000 Wake Forest Road, Suite 108
Raleigh, NC 27609
(919) 872-0683
(919) 872-9748 Fax

Scholarships of varying amounts to graduating high school seniors wanting to pursue an engineering career. Must be North Carolina residents. Applicants are encouraged to apply early so there will be enough time to allow for an interview. Other restrictions may apply. Deadline: December 15.

2130.
North Carolina Department of Administration–
Division of Veterans Affairs
Scholarships for Children of War Veterans
Albemarle Building, Suite 1065
325 North Salisbury Street
Raleigh, NC 27603
(919) 733-3851

Scholarships to students attending public community or technical colleges or institutes or two- or four-year colleges. Students must have been born in North Carolina or be children of veterans who were North Carolina residents at the time they entered the Armed Forces. Birth requirement is waived in some circumstances if mothers were native-born North Carolinians. Scholarship categories are as follows: Class I-A is for children whose veteran parent may have died or been killed due to a service-connected incident; Class I-B is for those whose veteran parent was rated as 100 percent disabled due to a service-connected injury; Class II is for those whose veteran parent was rated at least 20 percent but less than 100 percent disabled or was given a statutory award for arrested pulmonary tuberculosis and was or is currently receiving compensation; Class III is for those whose veteran parent is or was at time of death receiving a pension for total, permanent disability or who is deceased or honorably discharged, but doesn't qualify under other provisions, if student is under twenty-three years of age; Class IV is for those whose parents were listed as prisoners of war or missing in action. Class I-A and Class IV receive free tuition and room and board allowance; fees are waived to students at public community or technical schools or $3,000 to students at two- or four-year colleges. Class I-B provides free tuition and some fees are waived to students attending public community or technical schools or $1,200 to students at two- or four-year colleges. Class II and III provide 100 scholarships with the same services as Class I-A. Deadline: May 31.

2131.
North Carolina Department of Community Colleges
Law Enforcement Women's Association Criminal Justice Scholarship
Caswell Building
200 West Jones Street
Raleigh, NC 27603-1337
(919) 733-7051 ext. 319

1 scholarship of $300 to a student planning on enrolling in or enrolled full-time in a program leading to a degree in criminal justice, juvenile justice, corrections science, or police science. The student should be attending a community college and be a North Carolina resident. Deadline: August 1.

2132.
North Carolina Department of Public Instruction
Robert C. Byrd Scholarships
301 North Wilmington Street
Raleigh, NC 27601-2825
(919) 715-1018
http://www.dpi.state.nc.us/

Scholarships of up to $1,500 to graduating high school seniors. For use the first year of study in a college or university within the state. Must be North Carolina residents and attend an accredited North Carolina institution. Administered by each state's educating agency. Obtain applications from state agency or high school counselor.

2133.
North Carolina Department of Public Instruction
Scholarship Loan Program for Prospective Teachers
Office of Teacher Recruitment
301 North Wilmington Street
Raleigh, NC 27601-2825
(919) 733-4736

200 loans of up to $2,000 to undergraduate and graduate students pursuing careers in education and teaching. Must be North Carolina residents and plan to teach in North Carolina public schools. Selection is based on academic achievement, standardized test scores, class rank, congressional district, and recommendation. Must be U.S. citizens. Deadline: February 15.

2134.
North Carolina Department of Public Instruction
Student Incentive Grants
301 North Wilmington Street
Raleigh, NC 27601-2825
(919) 715-1018
http://www.dpi.state.nc.us/

Grants of up to $1,500 per academic year or half of student's unmet need (whichever is less) to high school seniors, graduates, or undergraduates who do not have a bachelor's degree. Must be North Carolina residents, U.S. citizens, or permanent resident aliens. Cannot owe a refund on any type of grant or student loan. Must be full-time students for at least nine months leading to a degree, diploma, or certificate. May not be pursuing a religious career. Must apply for a Pell Grant and have financial need.

2135.
North Carolina Division of Services for the Blind
Rehabilitation Assistance for Visually Handicapped
309 Ashe Avenue
Raleigh, NC 27606
(919) 733-9700

Awards providing tuition, fees, books, and supplies to undergraduate and graduate students in any field of study. Must be North Carolina residents who are legally blind or who have a progressive eye condition that may result in blindness and will create an employment handicap. Must attend a North Carolina institution. Other restrictions may apply. Deadline: none.

2136.
North Carolina Office of Budget and Management
NC Health/Sciences & Math Scholarship–Loans
116 West Jones Street, #2054
Raleigh, NC 27611
(919) 733-2164

Scholarships ranging from $500 to $6,000 to residents of North Carolina who are seeking careers as health professionals, science teachers, or math teachers. Students may be undergraduates or graduates and attending an accredited institution anywhere in the U.S. There are also low-interest loans available. These are repayable after graduation or they may be retired after graduation if student works one year for each loan at designated institutions. Deadline: varies.

2137.
North Carolina Office of Budget and Management
North Carolina Student Loan Program for Health, Science, & Mathematics
3824 Barrett Drive, Suite 304
Raleigh, NC 27619
(919) 733-2164

Low-interest loans ranging from $2,500 to $7,500 to undergraduate or graduate students majoring in a health profession, science, or engineering. Must be North Carolina residents for at least one year. Repayable after graduation, or may be retired after graduation by working one year for each loan at designated institutions. Deadline: early January to early May.

2138.
North Carolina Prospective Vocational Teacher Scholarships
Chairperson
Vocational Education Scholarship Committee
Education Building, Room 542
116 East Edenton Street
Raleigh, NC 27603-1712

Scholarships of up to $2,000 to high school seniors and vocational education teachers in an approved teacher education program in North Carolina. Must be North Carolina residents. Based on academic record, character, goals, leadership, and financial need. Deadline: March 15.

2139.
North Carolina State Contractual Scholarship Fund
North Carolina General Administration
P.O. Box 2688
Chapel Hill, NC 27515-2688

Scholarships of varying amounts to undergraduate students who have not received a bachelor's degree and who are residents of North Carolina and attending any one of the thirty-seven private junior or senior North Carolina institutes. Amount of scholarship varies from college to college. May be either full-time or part-time students in any course of study except those leading to a religious career. Based on financial need. Contact school's financial aid office or above address.

2140.
North Carolina Symphony
Bryan Young Artists Competition
P.O. Box 28026
Raleigh, NC 27611
Written inquiries only

Awards of up to $3,000 to music performers (piano, vocal, or strings) under thirty years of age (time will be deducted for any applicant who has served in the military) who are North Carolina residents and who are attending school in the U.S. Deadline: November 2.

2141.
North Dakota Aid Program for Veterans and Their Dependents
Engineering and Technician Scholarships
Commissioner of Veteran Affairs
15 Broadway, Suite 613
Fargo, ND 58102

Scholarships of up to $800 per year ($2,400 total) to students who are veterans or their spouses or children pursuing careers in civil engineering, civil engineering technology, industrial drafting, or design technology in a North Dakota institute. Veterans must have been North Dakota residents at the time of service. Veteran status refers to servicepersons who were killed in action, died from a service-connected injury, or are 100 percent disabled as a result of a service-connected injury.

2142.
North Dakota Aid Program for Veterans and Their Dependents
National Guard Tuition Waivers
Commissioner of Veteran Affairs
15 Broadway, Suite 613
Fargo, ND 58102

Tuition waivers of up to 75 percent to any member of the North Dakota National Guard in a state-supported institution. Must have been in the National Guard for at least one year; must maintain satisfactory academic progress.

2143.
North Dakota Aid Program for Veterans and Their Dependents
POW/MIA Dependents Education
Commissioner of Veteran Affairs
15 Broadway, Suite 613
Fargo, ND 58102

Four years of tuition exemption to dependents of service personnel listed as prisoners of war or missing in action. Students must be in an undergraduate program in a state-supported college, university, or vocation/technical school. Students cannot be deprived of tuition exemption benefits because of serviceperson's return. Veterans must have been North Dakota residents at the time of service.

2144.
North Dakota Aid Program for Veterans and Their Dependents
Veterans Aid Loan Program
Commissioner of Veteran Affairs
15 Broadway, Suite 613
Fargo, ND 58102

Loans of up to $2,000, with 10 percent interest, to veterans attending a postsecondary educational institution. Must be North Dakota residents and have been in the service during WWII (December 7, 1941, to December 31, 1945), the Korean conflict (June 27, 1950, to January 31, 1955), or the Vietnam War (August 5, 1964, to May 7, 1975). If loan is repaid within two years (allowed time period), one half of the interest paid is refunded.

2145.
North Dakota Department of Public Instruction
Robert C. Byrd Scholarships
600 East Boulevard Avenue
Bismarck, ND 58505-0440
(701) 328-2260
(701) 328-2461 Fax
http://www.state.nd.us/

Scholarships of up to $1,500 to graduating high school seniors. For use the first year of study in a college or university within the state. Must be North Dakota residents and attend an accredited North Dakota institution. Administered by each state's educating agency. Obtain applications from state agency or high school counselor.

2146.
North Dakota Indian Affairs Commission
North Dakota Indian College Scholarship
  Program
State Capitol Building, Judicial Wing, 1st Floor
600 East Boulevard
Bismarck, ND 58505-0300
(701) 224-2428

Scholarships from $200 to $2,000 to students with certification of Indian blood or tribal enrollment who are planning to attend a North Dakota institution. Must have at least a 2.0 GPA; students having a 3.0 GPA or better are given priority. Based on academic record, recommendations, financial need, and number of applicants. Renewable with reapplication. Deadline: June 30.

2147.
North Dakota Society of Professional Engineers
P.O. Box 14262
Grand Forks, ND 58202-4262
(701) 777-3795
(701) 777-2339 Fax

Scholarships of varying amounts to graduating high school seniors wanting to pursue an engineering career. Must be North Dakota residents. Applicants are encouraged to apply early to allow enough time for an interview. Other restrictions may apply. Deadline: December 15.

2148.
North Dakota State Highways Department
  Scholarships
Human Resources Division
608 East Boulevard Avenue
Bismarck, ND 58505
(701) 224-2574

2 to 4 scholarships of $800 per year to undergraduate students attending accredited institutions in North Dakota. Applicants must have completed at least one year of study in civil engineering or civil engineering technology. Deadline: February 15.

2149.
Northeastern Loggers' Association (NELA)
NELA Scholarships
P.O. Box 69
Old Forge, NY 13429
(315) 369-3078

2 scholarships of $2,000 and 2 scholarships of $1,000 to junior undergraduate students in a four-year forestry and wood technology program and to second-year students in a two-year forestry and wood technology program. Based on essay, academic record, and work experience. Deadline: January 15.

2150.
Northern California Scholarship Foundation
Helen Wegman Parmalee Educational
  Foundation Scholarships
1547 Lakeside Drive
Oakland, CA 94612
(510) 451-1906

Scholarships of $3,000 per year (renewable for four years) to northern and central California public high school seniors. Students attending a two-year college and living at home may receive less financial support, but it will be increased if they transfer to a four-year institute. May major in any field of study. Based on academic record, SAT, and financial need; must be willing to help pay for part of college expenses. Must be nominated by high school principal or counselor. Contact high school principal in January. Deadline: March 17.

2151.
Northern California Scholarship Foundation
Herbert Frank and Bertha Maude Lairde
  Memorial Foundation
1547 Lakeside Drive
Oakland, CA 94612
(510) 451-1906

Scholarships of $3,000 per year (renewable for four years) to northern and central California public high school seniors. Students attending a two-year college and living at home may receive less financial support, but it will be increased when they transfer to a four-year institute. Preference given to students pursuing an engineering career. Based on academic record, SAT, and financial need; must be willing to help pay for part of college expenses. Must be nominated by high school principal or counselor. Contact high school principal in January. Deadline: March 17.

2152.
Northern California Scholarship Foundation
NCSF Alumni Association Foundation
  Scholarships
1547 Lakeside Drive
Oakland, CA 94612
(510) 451-1906

Scholarships of $3,000 per year (renewable for four years) to northern and central California public high school seniors. Students attending a two-year college and living at home may receive less financial support, but it will be increased when they transfer to a four-year institution. May major in any field of study. Based on academic record, SAT, and financial need; must be willing to help pay for part of college expenses. Must be nominated by high school principal or counselor. Contact high school principal in January. Deadline: March 17.

2153.
Northern California Scholarship Foundation
Scaife Foundation Scholarships
1547 Lakeside Drive
Oakland, CA 94612
(510) 451-1906

Scholarships of $3,000 per year (renewable for four years) to northern and central California public high school seniors. Students attending a two-year college and living at home may receive less financial support, but it will be increased when they transfer to a four-year institution. Must be the son of American-born parents or major in medicine or theology. Based on academic record, SAT, financial need; must be willing to help pay for part of college expenses. Must be nominated by high school principal or counselor. Contact high school principal in January. Deadline: March 17.

2154.
Northern Virginia Board of Realtors, Inc.
Ebner R. Duncun Scholarship Program
8411 Arlington Boulevard
Fairfax, VA 22116
(703) 207-3200

Scholarships ranging from $500 to $1,000 to students who are residents of northern Virginia only. This program recognizes and encourages serious students with potential for professional development and contributions to the real estate community to continue their college education. Awards good at recognized colleges and universities in northern Virginia. Deadline: April 30.

2155.
Nucor Foundation, Inc.
2100 Rexford Road
Charlotte, NC 28211
(706) 366-7000

129 scholarship grants ranging from $104 to $3,000 to high school seniors who are children of Nucor, Inc., employees from Alabama, Arizona, Indiana, Nebraska, North Carolina, South Carolina, Texas, or Utah. Based on academic record and financial need. Deadline: March 31.

2156.
Nurses' Educational Fund, Inc.
Frances Tompkins Nursing Scholarship Program
555 West 57th Street
New York, NY 10019
(212) 582-8820

Scholarships ranging from $1,000 to $2,000 to students enrolled in a nursing or pre-nursing program in state-approved schools of nursing. Based on academic record, community involvement related to health care, involvement in nursing student organizations, and financial need. Deadline: February 1.

2157.
Nursing Scholarships
Director School of Nursing
Baptist Memorial Hospital System
111 Dallas Street
San Antonio, TX 78205

Numerous scholarship/loans at Baptist Memorial Hospital System School of Nursing. Students borrow the full amount needed to obtain their diploma. Upon receiving their diploma after completing the course and qualifying for state certification, if the nurse serves in the profession at the Baptist Memorial Hospital System for at least one year (twelve months), the first $2,000 of the loan will be canceled; the remainder of the loan received will be canceled at the rate of $200 per month if employed beyond the first year.

2158.
Oakland Scottish Rite Scaife Scholarship
  Foundation
1547 Lakeside Drive
Oakland, CA 94612
(510) 451-1906

94 scholarships of varying amounts, totaling $87,000, to male high school seniors. Must attend high school and be residents of northern California. Parents must be American-born. Deadline: varies.

2159.
Oak Ridge Institute for Science & Education
University Programs Division
Oak Ridge Associated Universities
P.O. Box 117
Oak Ridge, TN 37831
(423) 576-2600
(423) 576-8293 Fax

Research stipends of $200 per week to undergraduates and from $800 to $1,000 to graduate students for use in research, development, and demonstration programs at Department of Energy Laboratories or Energy Research Centers (usually for ten weeks during the summer). Students must be undergraduate juniors or beginning graduate students majoring in physical, life, or environmental science or engineering or mathematics. Based on academic achievement, interest in research, recommendations, and appropriateness of proposed projects to ongoing research at the DOE sites. Deadline: mid-January.

2160.
Ohio Arts Council Scholarship Program
727 East Main Street
Columbus, OH 43205
(614) 446-2613

Scholarships of varying amounts are open to high school seniors wishing to pursue a career in dance, music, theater arts, visual arts, or writing at an accredited institution in Ohio. Students should apply during their junior year in high school. Must be Ohio residents. Deadline: varies.

2161.
Ohio Board of Regents
Nurse Education Assistance Loan Program
State Grants and Scholarships
P.O. Box 182452
Columbus, OH 43218-2452
(888) 833-1133
(614) 466-7420/(614) 752-5903 Fax
http://www.bor.ohio.gov/sgs/

Awards of up to $3,000 to graduating high school seniors
or undergraduate students pursuing a career in nursing.
Selection based on financial need and goals. Must be Ohio
residents and attend an accredited Ohio institution. Award
may be canceled at a rate of 20 percent per year for up to
four years if the recipient is employed in the clinical
practice of nursing in Ohio. May cancel up to 80 percent of
Award. Deadline: June 1.

2162.
Ohio Board of Regents
Ohio Academic Scholarships
State Grants & Scholarships
P.O. Box 182452
Columbus, OH 43218-2452
(888) 833-1133
(614) 466-7420/(614) 752-5903 Fax
http://www.bor.ohio.gov/sgs/

Scholarships of $1,000 to students who are Ohio residents
and among the top five graduating seniors. Based on ACT
scores and academics. Renewable for up to four years.
Contact high school counselor. Deadline: February.

2163.
Ohio Board of Regents
Ohio Instructional Grants
State Grants & Scholarships
P.O. Box 182452
Columbus, OH 43218-2452
(888) 833-1133
(614) 466-7420/(614) 752-5903 Fax
http://www.bor.ohio.gov/sgs/

Scholarships of varying amounts to students who are Ohio
residents and are attending an Ohio institution full-time.
Based on family's income, which must be below $27,000.
Deadline: last Friday in September.

2164.
Ohio Board of Regents
Ohio Part-Time Student Instructional Grant
　　Program
State Grants & Scholarships
P.O. Box 182452
Columbus, OH 43218-2452
(888) 833-1133
(614) 466-7420/(614) 752-5903 Fax
http://www.bor.ohio.gov/sgs/

Grants of varying amounts to students who are enrolled
for part-time undergraduate study at an eligible Ohio
institution. Selection is based on financial need. Must
submit FAFSA and be Ohio residents and U.S. citizens.
Contact school's financial aid office. Deadline: set by
individual schools.

2165.
Ohio Board of Regents
Ohio Robert C. Byrd Scholarship Program
State Grants & Scholarships
P.O. Box 182452
Columbus, OH 43218-2452
(888) 833-1133
(614) 466-7420/(614) 752-5903 Fax
http://www.bor.ohio.gov/sgs/

Scholarships of $1,500 to graduating high school seniors.
Must be used for the first year of study in a college or
university within the state. Must meet two of these three
requirements: rank in the top 5 percent of their class, have
at least a 3.5 GPA, or have at least an 1100 on SAT or 27
on ACT. Administered by each state's educating agency.
Obtain applications from state agency or high school
counselor. Some states offer no direct application; students
are nominated by high school counselor. Deadline: varies,
by state.

2166.
Ohio Board of Regents
Ohio Safety Officers College Memorial Fund
State Grants & Scholarships
P.O. Box 182452
Columbus, OH 43218-2452
(888) 833-1133
(614) 466-7420/(614) 752-5903 Fax
http://www.bor.ohio.gov/sgs/

Scholarships of varying amounts to graduating high school
seniors or undergraduate students. Must be children or
spouses of Ohio peace officers, firefighters, or certain other
safety officers who died in the line of duty. May be used
for part- or full-time study for any field of study. Contact
school's financial aid office, or above address.

2167.
Ohio Board of Regents
Ohio Student Choice Grant
State Grants & Scholarships
P.O. Box 182452
Columbus, OH 43215-2452
(888) 833-1133
(614) 466-7420/(614) 752-5903 Fax
http://www.bor.ohio.gov/sgs/

Scholarships of varying amounts to students in an
approved Ohio institution. Must be Ohio residents and
enrolled in a bachelor's degree program; must not have
attended any postsecondary institution full-time before July
1, 1984. No application, though some institutions may have
their own application. Deadline: varies with each institution.

2168.
Ohio Board of Regents
Ohio War Orphans Scholarship
State Grants & Scholarships
P.O. Box 182452
Columbus, OH 43215-2452
(888) 833-1133
(614) 466-7420/(614) 752-5903 Fax
http://www.bor.ohio.gov/sgs/

Scholarships of varying amounts to students who are children of a veteran who served at least ninety days during a period of war and was killed in action, is below 60 percent disabled from a service-connected injury, or is 100 percent disabled from a non-service-connected injury. Disabled veterans must be receiving disability benefits from the VA. Deadline: July 1.

2169.
Ohio League for Nursing
Grants and Loans
Student Aid Committee
2800 Euclid Avenue, Suite 235
Cleveland, OH 44115
(216) 781-7222

20 to 25 scholarships of varying amounts to undergraduate and graduate students in accredited nursing programs. Must be residents of Greater Cleveland area (Cuyahoga, Grauga, Lake, or Lorain counties). Must agree to work in a health care facility in that area for at least a year after graduation. Must be U.S. citizens or legal residents. Deadline: May 15.

2170.
Ohio National Guard
Tuition Grant
Adjutant General's Department, AGOH-TG
2825 West Granville Road
Columbus, OH 43235
(614) 889-7032

Scholarships to high school graduates working on their first undergraduate degree. Financial assistance is 60 percent of tuition and fees at a state-supported college or university or equal to 60 percent of the tuition costs at a state-supported institution for proprietary degrees. Must be Ohio residents and enlisted in the Ohio National Guard for at least six years; must successfully complete the advanced military training. Must submit AGOH-Form 621-1 and 621-2 (obtained from military unit); 621-3 is used for renewal applications. Deadline: July 1 (fall); November 1 (winter); February 1 (spring); April 1 (summer).

2171.
Ohio Society for Medical Technology
Clinical Laboratory Science Scholarships
Attn: Chairperson
4373 River Ridge Road
Dayton, OH 45415

Scholarships of $300 to undergraduate students attending an Ohio institution who are clinical laboratory science majors (CLT/MLT or CLS/MT). Based on academic record and financial need. Request application in the fall. Deadline: January.

2172.
Ohio Society of Professional Engineers
445 King Avenue
Columbus, OH 43201
(614) 424-6640
(614) 421-1257 Fax

Scholarships of varying amounts to graduating high school seniors wanting to pursue an engineering career. Must be

Ohio residents. Applicants are encouraged to apply early so there will be enough time to allow for an interview. Other restrictions may apply. Deadline: December 15.

2173.
Oklahoma Society of Professional Engineers
201 North East 27th Street, Room 125
Oklahoma City, OK 73105
(405) 528-1435
(405) 557-1820 Fax

Scholarships of varying amounts to graduating high school seniors wanting to pursue an engineering career. Must be Oklahoma residents. Applicants are encouraged to apply early so there will be enough time to allow for an interview. Other restrictions may apply. Deadline: December 15.

2174.
Oklahoma State Regents for Higher Education
Academic Scholars Program
500 Education Building, State Capitol Complex
Oklahoma City, OK 73105
(800) 858-1840 Hotline
(405) 524-9100
(405) 524-9230 Fax
http://www.okhighered.org/
studentinfo@osrhe.edu

Awards of varying amounts to graduating high school seniors. Must meet specified academic criteria, be Oklahoma residents, and attend an accredited Oklahoma institution. Not based on financial need.

2175.
Oklahoma State Regents for Higher Education
Future Teachers Scholarship Program
500 Education Building, State Capitol Complex
Oklahoma City, OK 73105
(800) 858-1840 Hotline
(405) 524-9100
(405) 524-9230 Fax
http://www.okhighered.org/
studentinfo@osrhe.edu

Scholarships of varying amounts to graduating high school seniors and undergraduate students who are pursuing careers in teaching with emphasis in the areas of special education, counseling, library/media, science, early childhood education, speech/language pathology, foreign language, language arts, or math. Must be Oklahoma residents, attend an Oklahoma institution, and teach in Oklahoma.

2176.
Oklahoma State Regents for Higher Education
Oklahoma Higher Learning Access Program
500 Education Building, State Capitol Complex
Oklahoma City, OK 73105
(800) 858-1840 Hotline
(405) 524-9100
(405) 524-9230 Fax
http://www.okhighered.org/
studentinfo@osrhe.edu

Scholarships of varying amounts to students who will be pursuing an undergraduate course of study. Must have financial need; students wanting to participate must enroll in the program during the ninth or tenth grade. Students must take certain high school courses and maintain a certain GPA.

2177.
Oklahoma State Regents for Higher Education Oklahoma Robert C. Byrd Honors Scholarship Program
500 Education Building, State Capitol Complex
Oklahoma City, OK 73105
(800) 858-1840 Hotline
(405) 524-9100/(405) 524-9230 Fax
http://www.okhighered.org/
studentinfo@osrhe.edu

Scholarships of $1,500 to graduating high school seniors for use the first year of study in a college or university within the state. Must be Oklahoma residents and attend an accredited Oklahoma institution. Administered by each state's educating agency. Obtain applications from state agency or high school counselor. Some states offer no direct application; students are nominated by high school counselor. Deadline: varies by state.

2178.
Oklahoma State Regents for Higher Education Oklahoma Tuition Aid Grant Program
500 Education Building, State Capitol Complex
Oklahoma City, OK 73105
(405) 524-9100/(405) 524-9230 Fax
http://www.okhighered.org/

Grants of up to $1,000 to undergraduate students, based on financial need. If a family's income is less than $15,000 per year, a student is eligible for assistance. If income is between $15,000 and $20,000, there might be a limited grant. If the income is over $20,000, the student shouldn't apply unless there are special circumstances. Must be residents of Oklahoma and attending an Oklahoma institution. May transfer to other Oklahoma schools, but the grant money doesn't transfer to an out-of-state institution. Apply after January 1. Deadline: March 1.

2179.
Oncology Nursing Foundation Undergraduate Scholarship
1016 Greentree Road
Pittsburgh, PA 15220-3125
(412) 921-7373

10 scholarships of $1,000 to students who are licensed to practice as registered nurses. Must be in an undergraduate nursing degree program in an NLN-accredited school of nursing. Deadline: January 15.

2180.
101st Airborne Division Association Chappie Hall Memorial Scholarship
204 Charlemagne Boulevard
Clarkesville, TN 37042

1 or more scholarships of varying amounts to students who are sons, grandsons, wives, or widows of a regular member of the 101st Airborne Division Association. Must have had at least a C average in the previous year. Based on academic record, career goals, recommendations, and financial need.

2181.
102nd Infantry Division Association
Chairman
Scholarship Committee
1821 Shackleford Road
Nashville, TN 37215

3 scholarships of $1,200, 3 scholarships of $500, and 1 scholarship of $200 to children or grandchildren of a dues-paying member of the 102nd Infantry Division Association. If the veteran is deceased, he must have been a dues-paying member at time of death. Applicants may be high school graduates or college freshmen or sophomores. Deadline: May 15.

2182.
Operating Engineers (IUOE), Local Union No. 3 Scholarship Awards
474 Valencia Street
San Francisco, CA 94103
(415) 431-1568

2 scholarships of up to $1,000 and 2 scholarships of up to $500 to high school seniors who are children of members of Local No. 3. Parent must have been a member for at least one year just prior to application. Must have at least a 3.0 GPA. Award may be used at any U.S. college or university and for any major. Must submit an application, high school report, recommendation letters, transcript, and recent photograph. Submit applications after January 1. Deadline: March 1.

2183.
Opportunities for Women in Broadcasting Program
P.O. Box 297
St. Peter, MN 56082
(507) 931-1682

Numerous scholarships from $500 to $2,000 to female undergraduate students pursuing a career in some area of radio and television. Must be U.S. citizens or legal residents. Deadline: varies.

2184.
Optimist International Essay Scholarship
Project Manager, Activities Department
Optimist International
4494 Lindell Boulevard
St. Louis, MO 63108
(314) 371-6000

Scholarships of $2,000, $3,000, and $5,000 to top three essay winners. Essay topics vary, but must be 400 to 500 words in length. Contact local club. Deadline: December 1.

2185.
**Optimist International Oratorical Scholarship
Contest**
Project Manager, Activities Department
Optimist International
4494 Lindell Boulevard
St. Louis, MO 63108
(314) 371-6000

Essay contest is open to all high school sophomores,
juniors, and seniors under the age of sixteen. 100
scholarships of $1,500 are awarded yearly. Contestants must
deliver a four-to-five-minute oration on an official subject.
For more information and entrance to contests, contact the
Optimist Club nearest you.

2186.
Order of Alhambra Scholarship
Attn: Executive Secretary
4200 Leeds Avenue
Baltimore, MD 21229
(301) 242-0660

1 scholarship of $400 to an undergraduate junior or senior
student pursuing a career in special education, including
mental, physical, or emotional handicaps. Student attending
a California institution or clergy can receive the scholarship
for postgraduate study. Must submit a Scholarship Report
Form to the Supreme Office. Deadline: January, March, and
July.

2187.
Oregon AFL-CIO Asat-May Darling Scholarship
Oregon AFL-CIO
2110 State Street
Salem, OR 97301
(503) 585-6320

1 scholarship each of $600, $750, $1,000, and $3,000 to
students graduating from an Oregon high school. Must be
Oregon residents. Based on academic record, interview,
financial need, and written labor history exam. Deadline:
March 1.

2188.
**Oregon Association of Broadcasters
Thomas R. Dargan Minority Scholarship**
449, 111 West 7th Street, Suite 230
Eugene, OR 97440-0449
(503) 343-2101

1 scholarship of $3,500 to a minority undergraduate
freshman, sophomore, or junior student majoring in
broadcasting. Must be attending an institution in Oregon or
Washington and have at least a 3.0 GPA. Deadline: April 30.

2189.
**Oregon Chapter of NSPE
Professional Engineers of Oregon**
530 North Columbia River Highway, Suite C
St. Helens, OR 97051
(503) 228-2701
(503) 241-9029 Fax

Scholarships of varying amounts to graduating high school
seniors wanting to pursue an engineering career. Must be

Oregon residents. Applicants are encouraged to apply early
so there will be enough time to allow for an interview.
Other restrictions may apply. Deadline: December 15.

2190.
Oregon Department of Veterans' Affairs
Educational Scholarship Aid for Oregon Veterans
700 Sumner Street, N.E., Suite 150
Salem, OR 97310-1201
(800) 692-9666
(503) 373-2085

30 scholarship grants from $35 to $50 per month to
students who served at least ninety days in the Armed
Forces during the Korean War or received the Armed
Forces Expeditionary Medal or the Vietnam Service Medal
after July 1, 1958. Students must have been an Oregon
resident for one year prior to entering the Armed Forces
and must currently be an Oregon resident. Must be U.S.
citizens. Contact registrar's office.

2191.
**Oregon PTA
Teacher Education Scholarships**
531 S.E. 14th Avenue, Room 205
Portland, OR 97214

Scholarships of $250 per year for two years to students
who are Oregon high school seniors, have a GED, or are
attending a public Oregon postsecondary institution and
preparing for a teaching career at the elementary or
secondary level. Must be Oregon residents and plan to
teach in Oregon. Deadline: March 1.

2192.
**Oregon State Scholarship Commission
AFL-CIO Scholarships**
1500 Valley River Drive, Suite 100
Eugene, OR 97401-2130
(541) 687-7400
http://www.ossc.state.or.us/

1 scholarship of $3,000 (renewable for four years) to a
graduating high school senior. Must be an Oregon resident
and must have taken the AFL-CIO Exam. Based on
academic record, AFL-CIO Exam score, and financial need.
Contact high school counselor, principal, social studies
teacher, or the Oregon AFL-CIO, 1990 Hines, S.E., Salem,
OR 97302. Deadline: February 20.

2193.
**Oregon State Scholarship Commission
Alpha Delta Kappa Scholarship**
1500 Valley River Drive, Suite 100
Eugene, OR 97401-2130
(541) 687-7400
http://www.ossc.state.or.us/

Usually, 2 scholarships ranging from $300 to $500 are
awarded each year to Oregon students who will be college
seniors during the award year. Must be in a program
leading to a degree in elementary or secondary education.
Must be Oregon residents. Deadline: June 1.

2194.
Oregon State Scholarship Commission
Barber and Hairdressers (B & H) Grants
1500 Valley River Drive, Suite 100
Eugene, OR 97401-2130
(541) 687-7400
http://www.ossc.state.or.us/

Grants ranging from $200 to $1,000 to full-time students who are enrolled in a school of barbering, hair design, cosmetology, or manicure. School must be located in and licensed by the state of Oregon. Renewable for duration of training program if maintaining satisfactory academic progress.

2195.
Oregon State Scholarship Commission
Bertha P. Singer Nurses Scholarships
1500 Valley River Drive, Suite 100
Eugene, OR 97401-2130
(541) 687-7400
http://www.ossc.state.or.us/

Scholarships of varying amounts to full-time undergraduate or graduate students. Must have graduated from an accredited Oregon high school or be an Oregon resident for one full year. Must attend any accredited school of nursing or nursing program within the state of Oregon that is affiliated with a two- or four-year college or university or hospital. Must have at least a 3.0 GPA. Selection based on academic record and financial need. Deadline: December.

2196.
Oregon State Scholarship Commission
Bowerman Foundation Scholarships
1500 Valley River Drive, Suite 100
Eugene, OR 97401-2130
(541) 687-7400
http://www.ossc.state.or.us/

Open to Oregon students in final year of undergraduate or graduate school. Number and amount of awards vary from year to year. Specify whether undergraduate or graduate student.

2197.
Oregon State Scholarship Commission
Cash Awards Program
1500 Valley River Drive, Suite 100
Eugene, OR 97401-2130
(541) 687-7400
http://www.ossc.state.or.us/

A cash award of $804 to an Oregon student who is enrolled in an Oregon two-year or four-year public or private degree-granting institution accredited by the Northwest Association of Secondary and Higher Schools. May be transferred from one eligible institution to another. Renewable for up to four years. Applicant must be enrolled as an entering freshman or sophomore in an approved Oregon college or university.

2198.
Oregon State Scholarship Commission
Children of Deceased Peace Officers
1500 Valley River Drive, Suite 100
Eugene, OR 97401-2130
(541) 687-7400
http://www.ossc.state.or.us/

Grants providing tuition and fees to high school students or undergraduate students who are children of Oregon peace officers killed or permanently disabled by a service-connected injury. Student must attend a state-supported college or university in Oregon. Deadline: varies.

2199.
Oregon State Scholarship Commission
Flora M. Von Der Ahe Scholarships
1500 Valley River Drive, Suite 100
Eugene, OR 97401-2130
(541) 687-7400
http://www.ossc.state.or.us/

Scholarships of varying amounts to full-time undergraduate or graduate students in any area of study. Must be residents of Umatilla County, Oregon. Must attend an accredited two- or four-year college, university, or vocational/technical school in Oregon. Must have at least a 2.5 GPA or meet the school's admission standard. Based on financial need. Deadline: December.

2200.
Oregon State Scholarship Commission
G. Russell Morgan Law Scholarship Fund
1500 Valley River Drive, Suite 100
Eugene, OR 97401-2130
(541) 687-7400
http://www.ossc.state.or.us/

Scholarships of varying amounts to graduating high school seniors, undergraduates, or law school students. Must have graduated from either Hillsboro or Glencoe High School and be interested in attending law school and becoming a practicing attorney in Oregon. Must show sincerity of purpose, morality, and integrity. Must attend an accredited college, university, or law school, and upon graduation apply for membership in the Oregon State Bar and practice law in Oregon. Deadline: December.

2201.
Oregon State Scholarship Commission
Harley and Mertie Stevens Memorial Fund
1500 Valley River Drive, Suite 100
Eugene, OR 97401-2130
(541) 687-7400
http://www.ossc.state.or.us/

Scholarships of varying amounts to full-time undergraduate students. Must be Oregon residents and graduates of a Clackamas County, Oregon, high school. May attend an accredited state-supported or private, Protestant-owned college or university. Must have at least a 3.5 GPA. Deadline: December.

2202.
Oregon State Scholarship Commission
Ida M. Crawford Scholarship Fund
1500 Valley River Drive, Suite 100
Eugene, OR 97401-2130
(541) 687-7400
http://www.ossc.state.or.us/

Scholarships of varying amounts to graduating high school seniors, undergraduates, or graduate students. Must attend a two- or four-year college or university or vocational/ technical school anywhere in the U.S. Scholarships cannot be used for study in medicine (including acupuncture, chiropractic, and naturopathic studies), law, theology, teaching, or music. If in high school, students must have at least a 3.5 GPA. If an undergraduate or graduate student, must have at least a 3.5 GPA. Deadline: December.

2203.
Oregon State Scholarship Commission
Jenkins Scholarship Fund
1500 Valley River Drive, Suite 100
Eugene, OR 97401-2130
(541) 687-7400
http://www.ossc.state.or.us/

Scholarships of varying amounts to full-time undergraduate or graduate students. Must have graduated from a high school in the Portland Public School District #1. Scholarships may be used for any area of study. Students must attend an accredited college or university in the U.S. If a graduating high school senior, must have at least a 3.5 GPA. If in college, must have at least a 3.0 GPA. Deadline: December.

2204.
Oregon State Scholarship Commission
Jerome B. Steinbach Scholarships
1500 Valley River Drive, Suite 100
Eugene, OR 97401-2130
(541) 687-7400
http://www.ossc.state.or.us/

Scholarships of varying amounts to full-time undergraduate students. Must be Oregon residents and American citizens by birth. Must attend an accredited two- or four-year college, university, or vocational/technical school. Must have at least a 3.25 GPA. Selection based on academic achievement and financial need. Graduate students are ineligible. Deadline: December.

2205.
Oregon State Scholarship Commission
John Lamar Cooper Scholarship Fund
1500 Valley River Drive, Suite 100
Eugene, OR 97401-2130
(541) 687-7375
http://www.ossc.state.or.us/

Scholarships of varying amounts to graduating high school seniors, high school graduates, undergraduates, or graduate students. Must be Hood River residents who are Oregon high school graduates or students who obtained a GED. Scholarships may be used for full-time undergraduate or graduate study in any major or to attend a two- or four-year Oregon college, university, or vocational/technical

school. If in high school, students must have at least a 3.0 GPA. If in college, must have at least a 2.5 GPA. Write an introductory letter detailing financial and educational situation. Other restrictions may apply. Deadline: December.

2206.
Oregon State Scholarship Commission
KGON Radio Scholarships
1500 Valley River Drive, Suite 100
Eugene, OR 97401-2130-2130
(541) 687-7400
http://www.ossc.state.or.us/

For residents of Clackamas, Clark, Multnomah, Washington, or Yamhill counties, Oregon, who are enrolled as full-time undergraduate students in the field of broadcasting or journalism. Deadline: April 15.

2207.
Oregon State Scholarship Commission
Maria C. Jackson & General George A. White
Scholarship Fund
1500 Valley River Drive, Suite 100
Eugene, OR 97401-2130
(541) 687-7400
http://www.ossc.state.or.us/

Scholarships of varying amounts to graduating high school seniors, high school graduates, or undergraduates. Must be Oregon residents. Must have served or have parents who are serving or have served in the U.S. Armed Forces, Army Coast Guard, Marines, Navy, National Guard, or Reserves. Students who have been, or whose parents have been, in the Merchant Marines or civil servants employed by the U.S. Army Transport Service or Naval Transportation Service and are considered "active duty" are also eligible. Must file official proof of active duty (DD Form 93) or discharge (DD Form 214) verifying military service. Must be U.S. citizens by birth and attend an accredited two- or four-year college or university in Oregon eligible to participate in the federal Title IV student financial aid program. Must have at least a 3.75 GPA or meet a technical school's academic standards. Deadline: December.

2208.
Oregon State Scholarship Commission
Need Grant Awards
1500 Valley River Drive, Suite 100
Eugene, OR 97401-2130-2130
(541) 687-7400
http://www.ossc.state.or.us/

These awards are made under essentially the same rules and regulations as the Cash Awards. Awards vary from $222 to $1,710, depending on the student's cost of education and financial need.

2209.
Oregon State Scholarship Commission
Robert C. Byrd Scholarship Program
1500 Valley River Drive, Suite 100
Eugene, OR 97401-2130
(541) 687-7400
http://www.ossc.state.or.us/

Scholarships of $1,500 to graduating high school seniors for use the first year of study in a college or university within the state. Administered by each state's educating agency. Obtain applications from state agency or high school counselor. Some states offer no direct application; students are nominated by high school counselor. Deadline: varies by state.

2210.
Oregon State Scholarship Commission
Walter C. and Marie C. Schmidt Foundation Fund
1500 Valley River Drive, Suite 100
Eugene, OR 97401-2130
(541) 687-7400
http://www.ossc.state.or.us/

Scholarships of varying amounts for tuition only to undergraduate nursing students. Must be at least half-time students at any accredited school of nursing or nursing program affiliated with a two- or four-year college or university or hospital. Recipients must state in writing the desire to work in geriatric health care. Selection based on academic achievement, essay, and financial need. Priority is given to (1) students attending Lane Community College, (2) students in a two-year college nursing program, or (3) students attending a state or private college or university. Must be Oregon residents, with first preference given to those who intend to work in nonprofit nursing homes and hospitals in Lane County, and then in other parts of the state of Oregon. May not be used for room, board, or living expenses. Deadline: December.

2211.
Oregon State Scholarship Commission
Walter Davies Scholarships
1500 Valley River Drive, Suite 100
Eugene, OR 97401-2130
(541) 687-7400
http://www.ossc.state.or.us/

Scholarships of varying amounts to graduating high school seniors or undergraduate students. Must be employees, or natural or adopted children of employees, of U.S. Bancorp. Must have graduated from an Oregon high school. Must attend or plan to attend full-time a two- or four-year college, university, or vocational/technical school. May be working toward a bachelor's degree, an academic award, or a certificate. Deadline: December.

2212.
Oregon State Scholarship Commission
W. C. and Pearl Campbell Non-Linfield
  Scholarship Fund
1500 Valley River Drive, Suite 100
Eugene, OR 97401-2130
(541) 687-7400
http://www.ossc.state.or.us/

Scholarships of varying amounts to graduating high school seniors, undergraduate, and graduate students in any area of study. Must attend a college or university (other than Linfield College) in the state of Oregon. If in high school, must have at least a 3.75 GPA and an 1100 SAT. If an undergraduate or graduate, must have at least a 3.75 GPA. Other restrictions may apply. Deadline: December.

2213.
Oregon State Scholarship Commission
Woodie and Mabel Best Scholarship Fund
1500 Valley River Drive, Suite 100
Eugene, OR 97401-2130
(541) 687-7400
http://www.ossc.state.or.us/

Scholarships of varying amounts to graduating high school seniors, high school graduates, or undergraduates. Must have graduated from a public high school in Harney County, Oregon. Scholarships may be used for any major. Graduating high school seniors must have at least a 3.0 GPA, and current undergraduate students must have at least a 2.75 GPA. Deadline: December.

2214.
Orphan Foundation of America Scholarship
  Program
1500 Massachusetts Avenue, N.W., Suite 448
P.O. Box 14261
Washington, DC 20064-4261
(202) 861-0762

Over 100 scholarships of $300, $500, and $800 to students to use in any major at any accredited undergraduate college or university or vocational/technical school. Must be "orphans" by the standards used by the Orphan Foundation of America. Must be U.S. citizens or legal residents. Deadline: April 15.

2215.
Our World–Underwater Scholarship
P.O. Box 4428
Chicago, IL 60680

A $7,500 award to nationally certified SCUBA divers who are high school seniors or undergraduate or graduate students between the ages of eighteen and twenty-five. Applicants must have high academic achievement and interest in the underwater world. The award is used to cover the cost of spending one year investigating career possibilities in underwater and water-related fields. The award covers travel and per diem expenses for the period, which usually lasts thirty-five to forty weeks. Request applications in the fall. Deadline: December 1 (preliminary application); December 15 (letters of recommendation); January 1 (final application).

2216.
Outdoor Writers Association of America
Scholarship Awards
2017 Cato Avenue, Suite 101
State College, PA 16801
(814) 234-1011

10 scholarships of at least $1,400 to students pursuing a career in outdoor writing, broadcasting, photography, art, or related fields. Must be undergraduate juniors or seniors or graduate students majoring in journalism or mass communication and attending an accredited school listed in the Association for Education in Journalism and Mass Communications or those listed on the Outdoor Writers Association application. Only one student per school may apply each year. Institution nominates the student. Based

on academic record, writing samples, career goals, and recommendations. Deadline: March 1.

2217.
Panama Canal Society of Professional Engineers
Panama Canal Commission
Dredging Division, Unit 2300
Engrng Section Unit 2300
APO AA 34011-2300
(507) 276-6742
(507) 276-6387 Fax
crodgers@pancanal.com

Scholarships of varying amounts to graduating high school seniors wanting to pursue an engineering career. Must be Panama Canal residents. Applicants are encouraged to apply early to allow enough time for an interview. Other restrictions may apply. Deadline: December 15.

2218.
Parapsychology Foundation
Eileen J. Garrett Research Scholarships
228 East 71st Street
New York, NY 10021
(212) 628-1550

15 scholarships of $3,000 to undergraduate or graduate students attending an accredited college or university and studying any area of parapsychology (telepathy, precognition, psychokinesis, related phenomena). Deadline: July 15.

2219.
Parents Without Partners
International Scholarships
401 North Michigan Avenue
Chicago, IL 60611-4267
(800) 637-7974

Scholarships to students who are children of Parents Without Partners members. Must be high school seniors or undergraduates under twenty-five years of age. Deadline: March 15.

2220.
Parkinson's Disease Foundation
Summer Fellowship
William Black Medical Research Building
Columbia-Presbyterian Medical Center
650 West 168th Street
New York, NY 10032
(212) 923-4700

Fellowships providing stipends to undergraduate and medical students to conduct research under the supervision of a research investigator. Deadline: April 1.

2221.
Paul and Mary Haas Foundation
Executive Director
600 Leopard Street
P.O. Box 2928
Corpus Christi, TX 78403
(512) 888-9301

Unlimited number of $750-per-year scholarships to undergraduate students who are Corpus Christi residents. Applicants may be attending a vocational/technical school or a two- or four-year institution. Students must apply within at least two months before the start of the semester.

2222.
Pemco Foundation
325 Eastlake Avenue
Seattle, WA 98109
(206) 628-4000

94 scholarships ranging from $150 to $900 totaling $43,950 to high school seniors and undergraduates. Must be Washington State residents. Write an introductory letter detailing your educational and financial situation. Other restrictions may apply. Deadline: none specified.

2223.
Pennsylvania AFL-CIO Scholarships
Attn: Secretary-Treasurer
230 State Street
Harrisburg, PA 17105
(717) 238-9351

8 scholarships ranging from $50 to $1,000 to graduating high school seniors and undergraduate students. Must be dependents of AFL-CIO members and be residents of Pennsylvania. Selection is based on academic and financial criteria. Other restrictions may apply. Deadline: December 31.

2224.
Pennsylvania Department of Military Affairs
Bureau of Veterans Affairs (Scholarships)
Fort Indianatown Gap
Annville, PA 17003-5002
(717) 865-8904

70 renewable scholarships ranging from $200 to $1,600 to students who have been Pennsylvania residents for at least five years prior to applying and whose parent died or was totally disabled as a result of a WWII, Korea, or Vietnam service. Must be between sixteen and twenty-one years of age. Based on financial need.

2225.
Pennsylvania Department of Military Affairs
Pennsylvania Educational Allowance for
**   Veterans' Children**
Commonwealth of Pennsylvania
Fort Indiantown Gap
Annville, PA 17003-5002
(717) 865-8904

Students who are children of a deceased or totally disabled veteran of specified war service are eligible. An eligible student can receive up to $500 per semester, paid to the educational institution attended, which will help cover the cost of matriculation fee, other fees, tuition, room, board, books, and supplies. Limited to four academic years or the duration of the course, whichever is less. Maximum amount is $4,000. The student must be a resident of Pennsylvania; must attend school in Pennsylvania.

2226.
**Pennsylvania Higher Education Assistance
 Agency (PHEAA)**
**Pennsylvania Grants for Veterans and POW/MIA
 Dependents**
P.O. Box 8114
Harrisburg, PA 17105-8114
(717) 720-3600
http://www.pheaa.org:80/

Students who are qualified veterans or the dependents of
veterans listed as prisoners of war (POWs) or missing in
action (MIA) are eligible for assistance during enrollment as
full-time or part-time students. Open to Pennsylvania
residents. Grants to veterans only cover up to 80 percent of
the tuition and fees, not to exceed $2,000 in a Pennsylvania
school or $800 at an out-of-state school. Grants to POW/
MIA dependents can't exceed $1,200 for Pennsylvania
schools or $800 for out-of-state schools. Deadline: May 1.

2227.
**Pennsylvania Higher Education Assistance
 Agency (PHEAA)**
Robert C. Byrd Scholarships
P.O. Box 8114
Harrisburg, PA 17105-8114
(717) 720-3600
http://www.pheaa.org:80/

230 scholarships of $1,500 to students who are
Pennsylvania residents and who meet two of these three
requirements: rank in the top 5 percent of their class, have
at least a 3.5 GPA, or have at least 1100 on SAT or 27 on
ACT. Deadline: May 1.

2228.
**Pennsylvania Higher Education Assistance
 Agency (PHEAA)**
Pennsylvania Scholars in Education Awards
P.O. Box 8114
Harrisburg, PA 17105-8114
(717) 720-3600
http://www.pheaa.org:80/

Scholarships ranging from $1,500 to $5,000 or 50 percent of
the annual tuition (whichever is less) to students with
superior abilities and achievement in high school. Students
receiving these awards are the best qualified from the
applicant pool; the number of awards is limited by
availability of funds. Students must agree to teach or to
repay the grant as a loan. Students must plan to attend or
attend as a full-time undergraduate at a Pennsylvania
school; must rank in the top one-fifth of class; must have
at least a 3.0 GPA; and must have scored at least 1000 on
SAT or 22 on ACT.

2229.
**Pennsylvania Higher Education Assistance
 Agency (PHEAA)**
Pennsylvania State Higher Education Grants
P.O. Box 8114
Harrisburg, PA 17105-8114
(717) 720-3600
http://www.pheaa.org:80/

Grants for undergraduate study at a two-year Pennsylvania
school or any four-year school in the U.S.; another is for
study at a business, trade, or technical school, or a hospital
school of nursing. Open to Pennsylvania residents. Based
on financial need. Students are expected to help with
expenses through a combination of loans, work-study, and
parental assistance.

2230.
Pennsylvania Society of Professional Engineers
4303 Derry Street
Harrisburg, PA 17111
(717) 561-0590
(717) 561-0529 Fax

Scholarships of varying amounts to graduating high school
seniors wanting to pursue an engineering career. Must be
Pennsylvania residents. Applicants are encouraged to apply
early to allow enough time for an interview. Other
restrictions may apply. Deadline: December 15.

2231.
Percy B. Ferebee Endowment
Charitable Funds Management Section
Wachovia Bank and Trust Company
P.O. Box 3099
Winston-Salem, NC 27103

39 scholarships of varying amounts, totaling $37,000, to
graduating high school seniors. Must be residents of certain
counties in North Carolina. Must plan to enroll in a North
Carolina college or university. Deadline: varies.

2232.
Petro-Canada, Inc.
**Petro-Canada Education Awards for Native
 Students**
Native Development Advisor
P.O. Box 2844
Calgary, AB, Canada T2P 3E3

Numerous $5,000 scholarships to students who are of
Canadian or Inuit ancestry. Must be pursuing a career in
the oil and gas industry. Deadline: varies.

2233.
**PFLAG/New Orleans Chapter
 Scholarships**
Selection Committee
P.O. Box 15515
New Orleans, LA 70175
(504) 866-1705
(504) 895-3936
http://www.backdoor.com

15 or more scholarships of $1,000 to graduating high
school seniors or undergraduate students. Must be gay
youth who are seventeen years or older as of March 31 of
the award year and are planning to attend or attending an
accredited postsecondary education. Must be residents of
Louisiana. Selection based on affirmation of one's identity,
integrity and honesty, extracurricular activities, potential to
achieve goals, and financial need. Cannot be a prior winner
of this award. Deadline: mid-February.

2234.
PGA Tour
Minority Internship Program
112 TPC Boulevard
Ponte Vedra Beach, FL 32082
(904) 285-3700

15 to 20 nine-week summer internships providing $250 per week, round-trip travel, and a housing stipend to undergraduate and graduate minority students. Internships are available in Los Angeles, CA; Trumbull, CT; Jacksonville, FL; Ponte Vedra Beach, FL (HQ); or Atlanta, GA. Depending on placement, interns arrange banquets at the TPC club, conduct research for upcoming tournaments, assist with architectural design of golf courses, contact corporate sponsors, teach golf lessons, manage the TPC driving range, collect Nielsen ratings data, and write for *Golf Digest*. 10 unpaid internships year-round for nonminority and minority undergraduates, recent college graduates, and graduate students in creative services, productions, corporate marketing, and business development. Must submit résumé and cover letter when requesting an application. Deadline: February 15.

2235.
Phi Delta Kappa, Inc.
Scholarship Grants for Prospective Teachers
Attn: Scholarship Grants
P.O. Box 789
8th and Union Avenue
Bloomington, IN 47402
(812) 339-1156

33 scholarships ranging from $1,000 to $2,000 to high school seniors in upper one-third of class who plan to pursue a career as teacher or educator. Based on academic achievement, extracurricular activities, community involvement, recommendations, and an essay. Deadline: January 31.

2236.
Phi Eta Sigma Founders Fund Scholarships
228 J. E. Foy Union Building
Auburn University, AL 36849
(205) 826-5856

22 scholarships of $1,000 to undergraduate students and 10 scholarships of $2,000 to first-year graduate, PES members entering first year of graduate, professional, or undergraduate studies. Other criteria may apply. Deadline: March 1.

2237.
Phi Gamma Nu National Fraternity
Scholarships & Grants
6745 Cheryl Ann Drive
Seven Hills, OH 44131
(216) 524-0934

Scholarships of $300 to undergraduate juniors and seniors who are members in good standing of Phi Gamma Nu National Business Fraternity. Must be majoring in business administration. Deadline: October 31.

2238.
Phi Gamma Nu National Fraternity
Scholastic Achievement Awards
6745 Cheryl Ann Drive
Seven Hills, OH 44131
(216) 524-0934

2 scholarships of $150 to undergraduate Phi Gamma Nu members who have had the largest improvement in grade point average during the last year in comparison to the year before. Deadline: October 31.

2239.
Phi Kappa Theta National Foundation
National Scholarships
c/o Gregory Stein
111-55 77th Avenue
Forest Hills, NY 11375
(718) 793-2193

6 to 8 scholarships ranging from $300 to $1,000 to undergraduate student members of Phi Kappa Theta. Based on academic record and financial need. Applications are sent to chapters by February 15. Deadline: April 15.

2240.
Phillips Petroleum Company Scholarships
Director of Educational Funds
180 Plaza Building
Bartlesville, OK 74004

Scholarships of $1,000 per year for four years to high school seniors who haven't attended college. Applicants must be children of a direct employee of the Phillips Petroleum Co. Based on academic achievement, character, citizenship, and financial need. Deadline: January 1.

2241.
Phi Sigma Iota Scholarships Contest
Attn: Santiago Velas
Administrative Director
5211 Essen Lane, Suite 2
Baton Rouge, LA 70809
(504) 769-7100

Scholarships of $500 to members of Phi Sigma Iota for study by both undergraduate and graduate students specializing in foreign languages. Also, the Quebec Government will grant Phi Sigma Iota a scholarship (covering tuition, fees, room and board) for six or eight weeks in Quebec. Students must be nominated by a faculty advisor. Request applications before March. Deadline: March 15.

2242.
Phi Theta Kappa International Honor Society
Guistwhite Scholar Program
P.O. Box Drawer 13729
Jackson, MS 39236-3729
(601) 957-2241

10 scholarships of $2,500 per year for two years to undergraduate students who are PTK members and have completed an associate's degree. Based on academic record, recommendations, and essay. Deadline: November.

2243.

Phi Theta Kappa International Honor Society
Phi Theta Kappa Executive Committee
 Scholarships
P.O. Box Drawer 13729
Jackson, MS 39236-3729
(601) 957-2241

5 scholarships of $2,000 to students who are Phi Theta
Kappa members and have been elected to the Executive
Committee at the annual convention. No application
process.

2244.

Phi Theta Kappa International Honor Society
Steve Orlowski Memorial Scholarships
P.O. Box Drawer 13729
Jackson, MS 39236-3729
(601) 957-2241

5 scholarships of $2,000 to undergraduate students who are
Phi Theta Kappa members and candidates for the Executive
Committee. Contact local chapter. Deadline: varies.

2245.

Phi Theta Kappa International Honor Society
USA Today/American Association of Community
 & Technical Colleges
Phi Theta Kappa Academic All-American Team
 Scholarship Stipends
P.O. Box Drawer 13729
Jackson, MS 39236-3729
(601) 957-2241

20 stipends of $2,500 to students attending a two-year
community or junior college or a technical school that is a
member of the American Association of Community and
Junior Colleges (AACJC). Must be nominated by college
president; must complete an associate's degree with the
academic year. Based on nomination, academic record,
recommendations, and a 500-word essay. Deadline:
November 30.

2246.

Phi Upsilon Omicron National Office
Janice Cory Bullock Scholarships
208 Mount Hall
1050 Carmack Road
Columbus, OH 43210
(614) 421-7860

Scholarships of $500 to undergraduate or graduate students
in home economics who are Phi Upsilon Omicron
homemakers. Applicants must be updating their education
so they are able to be gainfully employed or for career
advancement. Other restrictions may apply. Deadline:
March 1.

2247.

Photographic Art & Science Foundation
Paul Linwood and Evelyn May Gittings Loan
 Fund
c/o F. Quellmalz
111 Stratford Road
Des Plaines, IL 60016
(312) 824-6855

Loans of varying amounts are available to high school
graduates who have only two semesters of formal
portraiture photography study remaining, intend to pursue
a career as a professional, and are recommended by the
dean of their school. Open to U.S. and Canadian citizens.
Loans are good at one of three schools. Deadline:
February 1.

2248.

Photographic Society of America Scholarship
PSA Educational/Scholarship Committee
3000 United Founders Boulevard, Suite 103
Oklahoma City, OK 73112

1 scholarship of $1,500 (plus membership in the society) is
available to applicants who graduated from high school
within last two years (not counting military service). For
more information, send a self-addressed, stamped envelope.

2249.

Photography Contest
c/o Parade/Kodak
P.O. Box 4719, Grand Central Station
New York, NY 10163-4719

100 awards of $100 cash and an award certificate in this
annual photography competition. If a winner's photograph
is published in December issue of *Parade*, contestant will be
awarded an additional $200. Theme varies every year.
Anyone is eligible to enter this contest, except employees of
Parade Publications, Inc., or Eastman Kodak Co., and their
families. There is no entry fee. All entries must be received
by mid-September and winners are announced in *Parade*
magazine in early December. Entries must be taken by
contestant. Deadline: mid-September.

2250.

Physical Therapy Awards
Excalibur Foundation
Round Table International
3430 Baker Street
San Francisco, CA 94123

1 scholarship of $1,000 to a college junior or senior in a
physical therapy program who hasn't received a bachelor's
degree. For more information, send a self-addressed,
stamped envelope. Deadline: March 31.

2251.

Physical Therapy Education Awards
Mary McMillan Scholarships
American Physical Therapy Association
Patricia Yarbrough, PhD, Director
Department of Education
1111 North Fairfax Street
Alexandria, VA 22314
(703) 684-7343

Numerous scholarships of varying amounts to students
who are in their final year of study in a physical therapy
program. Faculty members nominate individuals. For more
information, send a self-addressed, stamped envelope.

2252.
Physician Assistant Foundation of the American Academy of Physician Assistants
Undergraduate or Graduate Educational Program
950 North Washington Street
Alexandria, VA 22314
(703) 836-2271

Numerous $1,000, $2,000, and $5,000 scholarships to undergraduate and graduate students in a physician-assistant program. Based on academic record, extracurricular school activities, community involvement, and financial need. Deadline: January 15.

2253.
Pilot International Foundation (PIF)
PIF/Lifeline Scholarship Program
P.O. Box 5600
244 College Street
Macon, GA 31208

Open to any applicant seeking retraining for a "second career" working with persons with disabilities or training those who will or seeking to improve his or her professional skills in current occupation of working with persons with disabilities or training those who will. Renewable for up to three years. Send a self-addressed, stamped envelope to above address to find the location of the nearest Pilot Club. Deadline: April 1.

2254.
Pilot International Foundation (PIF)
PIF Scholarship Program
P.O. Box 5600
244 College Street
Macon, GA 31208

1 scholarship of $1,500 per year open to any undergraduate student preparing for a career working directly with persons with disabilities or training those who will. Local Pilot Club sponsorship in your country required. Send a self-addressed, stamped envelope to above address to find the location of the nearest Pilot Club. Deadline: April 1.

2255.
Pipe Line Contractors Association of Canada
Cal Callahan Memorial Bursary
698 Seymour Street, Suite 203
Vancouver, BC, Canada V6B 3K6

Scholarships totaling $2,000 to undergraduate dependent children of persons whose principal income is obtained from the pipeline industry (employers must be members of the association). Deadline: varies.

2256.
Pitney Bowes, Inc. (Scholarships)
Scholarship Committee (51-11)
World Headquarters
One Elmcroft
Stamford, CT 06926-0700

30 scholarships of $2,500 for four years to high school seniors who are children of Pitney-Bowes, Inc., employees who have been full-time employees for one year as of December 1 of the application year, or one year prior to

retirement, long-term disability, or death. Students must be in the upper third of their class. Must submit SAT in October (if in California, Florida, New York, or Texas) or October, November, or December (if from any other area), and Financial Aid Form (FAF). FAF must be sent to 7231 Towne Place, Middletown, CT 06457. Deadline: December 31.

2257.
Pittsburgh New Music Ensemble
Harvey Gaul Composition Contest
600 Forbes Avenue
Pittsburgh, PA 15219
(412) 261-0554

Awards of $3,000 to undergraduate or graduate students or professionals for an original music competition. Awards are for new works scored for five to fifteen instruments. There is an entry fee that must accompany submissions. Applicants may enter more than one competition. Must be U.S. citizens. Other restrictions may apply. Deadline: April 15.

2258.
Playwright's Center
Midwest Playlabs
2301 Franklin Avenue East
Minneapolis, MN 55406
(612) 332-7481
(612) 332-6037 Fax

4 to 6 playwrights receive honoraria, travel expenses, and room and board to attend a two-week workshop. Playwrights must be unpublished and submit unproduced full-length plays. Each play receives a public reading followed by an audience discussion of the work. Selection based on an open script competition. Applications available after October 1. Must be U.S. citizens. Deadline: December 1.

2259.
Poetry Society of America
Cash Awards
15 Gramercy Park
New York, NY 10003
(212) 254-9628

Cash awards of $100 in an annual competition aimed at advancing excellence in poetry and encouraging skill in traditional forms, as well as experimentation in contemporary forms. These are cash awards, not scholarships. Send a self-addressed, stamped envelope for contest rules brochure. Deadline: December 31.

2260.
Poetry Society of America
Contests Open to PSA Members
15 Gramercy Park
New York, NY 10003
(212) 254-9628

Various contests with varying amounts of awards are available to PSA members. Only one submission per contest. Entries must be unpublished on date of entry and not scheduled for publication by the date of the PSA awards ceremony, held in the spring. For contest rules, send a self-addressed, stamped envelope. Deadline: December 31.

2261.
Poets and Patrons of Chicago
Attn: Richard Calisch
1725 North Patton Avenue
Arlington Heights, IL 60004

Prizes of $75 and $25 awarded for original, unpublished poems of up to forty lines. There is no entry fee. Send a self-addressed, stamped envelope for rules. Deadline: September 1.

2262.
Portuguese Continental Union Scholarships
Cultural and Scholarship Committee
899 Boylston Street
Boston, MA 02115
(617) 536-2916

Scholarships of $500 to $1,000 to graduating high school seniors or undergraduates who are members of the Portuguese Continental Union with at least one year of membership and currently in good standing. Based on character, academic achievement, and SAT/ACT scores. Deadline: February 15.

2263.
The Poynter Fund
P.O. Box 1121
St. Petersburg, FL 33731

Numerous $2,500 scholarships to high school seniors or undergraduate students for the study of journalism and newspaper management at any school. Based on academic record, goals, and aptitude for publishing. Recipients are invited to donate to the Poynter Fund for future scholarships. Once donations reach $500, a scholarship will be awarded in the name of the donor. Deadline: July 1.

2264.
Prairie Schooner
Bernice Slote Award
201 Andrews
University of Nebraska
Lincoln, NE 68588-0334
(402) 472-4636

An award of $500 for best work by a beginning writer published in the *Prairie Schooner*. Winner announced in the spring issue of the following year. Send a self-addressed, stamped envelope for rules. No entry or reading fee.

2265.
Prairie Schooner
Lawrence Foundation Award
201 Andrews
University of Nebraska
Lincoln, NE 68588-0334
(402) 472-4636

1 award of $500 for best short story published in the *Prairie Schooner*. Winner announced in the spring issue of the following year. Send a self-addressed, stamped envelope for guidelines. No entry or reading fee.

2266.
Prairie Schooner
Readers' Choice Award
201 Andrews
University of Nebraska
Lincoln, NE 68588-0334
(402) 472-4636

Several awards of $250 for work published in the *Prairie Schooner*. Winners announced in the spring issue of the following year. Send a self-addressed, stamped envelope for guidelines. No entry or reading fee.

2267.
Prairie Schooner
Virginia Faulkner Award for Excellence in
  Writing
201 Andrews
University of Nebraska
Lincoln, NE 68588-0334
(402) 472-4636

1 award of $1,000 to the best short story, poetry, or nonfiction article published in the *Prairie Schooner*. All genres eligible. No entry or reading fee. Send a self-addressed, stamped envelope for guidelines.

2268.
Presbyterian Church (USA)
Ethnic Minority Student Opportunity
  Scholarships
Financial Aid for Studies
100 Witherspoon Street
Louisville, KY 40202-1396
(502) 569-5745
http://www.pcusa.org/

Scholarships ranging from $100 to $1,400 to minority students who are communicant members of the Presbyterian Church. Students must be entering freshmen in the fall and must have applied for financial aid at the colleges to which they are applying. Deadline: April 1.

2269.
Presbyterian Church (USA)
National Presbyterian College Scholarships
100 Witherspoon Street
Louisville, KY 40202-1396
(502) 569-5745
http://www.pcusa.org/

Renewable scholarships ranging from $500 to $1,400 to high school seniors who are communicant members of the Presbyterian Church (USA) and who plan on attending a Presbyterian-related four-year undergraduate institution. Students must be in the upper 50 percent of their class, have at least a 3.0 GPA on a 4.0 scale, and be under twenty-one years of age. Based on academic record, SAT/ACT scores, financial need, and recommendations. Deadline: December 1.

2270.
Presbyterian Church (USA)
Native American Education Grant
100 Witherspoon Street
Louisville, KY 40202-1396
(502) 569-5745
http://www.pcusa.org/

40 to 45 awards ranging from $200 to $1,500 to Native American Indians, Aleuts, and Eskimos who have completed at least one semester of work at an accredited institution. Preference given to Presbyterian undergraduate students. Renewal based on continued financial need and satisfactory academic progress.

2271.
Presbyterian Church (USA)
Presbyterian Study Grants
Financial Aid for Studies
100 Witherspoon Street
Louisville, KY 40202-1396
(502) 569-5745
http://www.pcusa.org/

Varying numbers of grants of varying amounts according to financial need and available funds. Applicants must be under care of the presbytery of the Presbyterian Church or in the "inquiry" stage, be U.S. citizens, or preparing for a church occupation. Based on academic record, financial need, professional goals, and character.

2272.
Presbyterian Church (USA)
Samuel Robinson Scholarship
475 Riverside Drive, Room 430
New York, NY 10027

1 award of $1,000 to undergraduate student enrolled in a Presbyterian-related college. Applicants must take a test and write an essay. Apply at college. Deadline: April 1.

2273.
Presbyterian Church (USA)
Student Loan Fund
100 Witherspoon Street
Louisville, KY 40202-1396
(502) 569-5745
http://www.pcusa.org/

Renewable loans ranging from $200 to $2,000 to communicant members of the Presbyterian Church. May be undergraduate students at a regionally accredited college or university, theology students preparing for a church occupation at any regionally accredited college, university, or seminary accredited by the Association of Theological Schools in the U.S. or Canada, and in a program approved by the presbytery for their first degree. Christian education students must be pursuing a career in the Presbyterian Church (USA). Also available to continuing-education Presbyterian ministers or lay professionals who already have a first degree. Applicants must maintain a C average and have financial need that isn't met by other resources. Undergraduates may borrow up to $4,000; and graduates, $2,000. This award can only be used at four-year

institutions. Based on financial need, academic record, and recommendations.

2274.
President's Committee on Employment of People with Disabilities
Nike Scholarship
Chairman
1111 20th Street, N.W., Suite 636
Washington, DC 20036
(202) 376-6200
(202) 376-6219 Fax
(202) 376-6206 TDD
Written inquiries only
http://www.pcepd.gov/
info@pcepd.gov

1 scholarship of $2,500 to a graduating high school or undergraduate student attending a four-year college or university. Must have a disability and be a U.S. citizen. The disability should be a physical or mental impairment that limits one or more major life activities. Student should have a record of such an impairment or be regarded as having such as impairment. Deadline: late May.

2275.
President's Committee on Employment of People with Disabilities
Nordstrom Scholarships
Chairman
1111 20th Street, N.W., Suite 636
Washington, DC 20036
(202) 376-6200
(202) 376-6219 Fax
(202) 376-6206 TDD
Written inquiries only
http://www.pcedpd.gov/
info@pcepd.gov

5 scholarships of $2,000 to graduating high school seniors or undergraduate students attending a four-year college or university and pursuing a business degree. Must have a disability and be U.S. citizens. The disability should be a physical or mental impairment that limits one or more major life activities. Students should have a record of such an impairment or be regarded as having such as impairment. Deadline: late May.

2276.
President's Committee on Employment of People with Disabilities
Sprint Scholarships
Chairman
1111 20th Street, N.W., Suite 636
Washington, DC 20036
(202) 376-6200
(202) 376-6219 Fax
(202) 376-6206 TDD
Written inquiries only
http://www.pcepd.gov/
info@pcepd.gov

3 scholarship of $2,500 to graduating high school seniors or undergraduate students attending a four-year college or

university. Must have a disability, be pursuing a business degree, and be U.S. citizens. The disability should be a physical or mental impairment that limits one or more major life activities. Students should have a record of such an impairment or be regarded as having such as impairment. Deadline: late May.

2277.
**Press Club of Houston
Educational Foundation**
P.O. Box 541038
Houston, TX 77254-1038
(713) 867-8847

Scholarships of varying amounts to undergraduate juniors or seniors majoring in broadcasting, communications, or journalism and pursuing careers in those majors. Must be residents of Harris County or a contiguous county or attending a college or university in Harris County or a contiguous county. Must be passing all courses in major field of study and be in good scholastic standing.

2278.
**Pro Bono Advocates
Internship Program**
165 North Canal, Suite 1020
Chicago, IL 60606
(312) 906-8013
(312) 906-8298 Fax
http://www.tripod.cod/

15 internships lasting three months are open to high school students, college students, and graduate law students. This organization works as advocates on behalf of women, especially battered women, by providing free civil legal services to victims of domestic violence. Interns interview clients, monitor case progress, and place cases with volunteer attorneys. Interns may work part- or full-time, with openings occurring year-round. Submit a letter detailing interests, a résumé, and references. Deadline: open.

2279.
**Procter & Gamble Co.
Internships**
Recruiting Service
P.O. Box 599
Cincinnati, OH 45201
(513) 983-1100
http://www.pg.com/docCareers/
careers@pg.com

300 summer internships providing salaries ranging from $450 to $675 for undergraduate sophomores, juniors, and seniors, and from $700 to $1,150 to graduate students, plus relocation expenses and round-trip travel expenses. Internships last from nine to fourteen weeks. Interns are assigned to Brand Management; Product Supply; Financial Management; Market Research and Management Systems; Cosmetics and Fragrances; Pharmaceuticals; Product Supply/ Manufacturing; and Engineering and Research and Product Development in Baltimore, MD; Cincinnati, OH; or in any one of forty-nine different sites across the country. Deadline: February 1.

2280.
Professional Aviation Maintenance Association
PAMA Scholarship Committee
500 N.W. Plaza, Suite 912
St. Ann, MO 63074

1 annual scholarship of varying amount to a student pursuing an A&P license. Other restrictions may apply. Deadline: varies.

2281.
**Professional Horsemen's Association of America,
Inc.
Financial Assistance**
Attn: Scholarship Committee Chairperson
P.O. Box 572
Long Hill Road
New Vernon, NJ 07976
(201) 538-3797

Assistance of $500 to undergraduate students in any field of study. Students who are members or dependents of members of the Association receive first priority. Award may be used for a vocational school, college, or university. Deadline: May 1.

2282.
Professional Secretaries International
Dora M. Murders, CPS
Texas-Louisiana Division President
527 Fraser
Houston, TX 77007-2704

1 scholarship of $500 to a deserving student pursuing a two- or four-year business degree relating to a secretarial field. The student must be a full-time student, have and maintain a 3.0 GPA, and have completed at least one year toward degree. Based on educational objectives, financial need, academics, and character. Deadline: March 31.

2283.
**Professional Secretaries International
Professional Secretaries Scholarship**
P.O. Box 20404
Kansas City, MO 64195-0404
(816) 891-6600
http://www.psi.org/

Scholarships ranging from $500 to $2,000 to high school seniors planning to major in secretarial sciences in a two- or four-year business or secretarial school. Must be members of Future Secretaries Association. Based on educational goals, academics, character, and financial need. Apply through local chapters in the U.S. or Canada. Deadline: March 31.

2284.
**Public Employees Roundtable
Public Service Scholarship**
P.O. Box 44801
Washington, DC 20026-4801
(202) 401-4324

1 scholarship of $1,000 to an undergraduate sophomore, junior, or senior preparing for a public service career at the federal, state, or local level. Based on career goals and essay.

Include a self-addressed, stamped envelope with application request. Deadline: May.

2285.
Public Housing Authorities Directors Association
Stephen J. Bollinger Scholarship Awards
511 Capitol Court, N.E., Suite 200
Washington, DC 20002
(202) 546-5445

Scholarships of varying amounts to high school seniors who are public housing residents. Must have maintained at least a 2.5 GPA during junior and senior high school years and been recommended by Executive Director. Based on academic record, recommendations, and goals.

2286.
Puerto Rico Home Economics Program
Director, Home Economics Program
Department of Education
Commonwealth of Puerto Rico
G.P.O. Box 759
Hato Rey, Puerto Rico 00919

Scholarships of $500 per year for the first two years and $1,000 for the next two years to students pursuing a career as a home-economics teacher. Recipients must repay one half of the financial assistance received. Must have completed high school in Puerto Rico; must maintain a 3.0 GPA or higher. Based on goals, behavior in school and community, and financial need.

2287.
Puerto Rico Public Employees Scholarship
Program
Public Service Personnel Development Institute
G.P.O. Box 8476, Fernàdez Juncos Station
Santurce, Puerto Rico 00910

Scholarships ranging from $4,500 to $12,500 providing tuition and a monthly stipend to students enrolled in or accepted to the Center of Studies. Must be an American citizen; must work in the U.S.; must be able to speak, read, and write English fluently. Based on academic record, interview, and other criteria.

2288.
Quaker Chemical Foundation
Elm and Lee Streets
Conshohocken, PA 19428
(610) 832-4000

Numerous scholarships of $4,000 to students who are children of employees. May be pursuing an undergraduate degree or a nonbaccalaureate degree. Deadline: December.

2289.
Queen Marie Jose Musical Prize Contest
Box 19
CH-1252 Meinier
Geneva, Switzerland
Written inquiries only

An award of 10,000 Swiss francs in a competition open to composers of all nationalities without age limits. Musical

scores, preferably written in ink, together with a tape recording of the work are required. Send a self-addressed, stamped envelope for specific information. Deadline: May 31.

2290.
Quill & Scroll Foundation
Edward J. Nell Memorial Scholarships
School of Journalism & Mass Communication
University of Iowa
Iowa City, IA 52242
(319) 335-5795

10 scholarships of $500 to high school seniors planning to enroll in an accredited journalism program. May be winners in the national Writing/Photo Contest sponsored by Quill & Scroll or National Gold Key winners (award may have been won in sophomore, junior, or senior high school year). Deadline: May 10.

2291.
Quincy Writer's Guild Annual Creative Writing
Contest
c/o Natalie Miller Rotunda
P.O. Box 112
Quincy, IL 62306-0112
(217) 223-3117

Awards for unpublished poetry, short stories, and nonfiction. Entry fee: $2 per poem and $4 for short stories and articles. Send a self-addressed, stamped envelope for guidelines. Deadline: April 15.

2292.
Quota International Fund Fellowships
1420 21st Street, N.W.
Washington, DC 20036
(202) 331-9694

6 to 8 scholarship grants ranging from $500 to $3,000 to undergraduate or graduate students majoring in education for the hearing-impaired. Renewable. Deadline: May 15.

2293.
Racine Environment Committee Educational
Fund
Executive Director
310 5th Street, Room 101
Racine, WI 53403
(414) 631-5600

110 scholarships ranging from $100 to $1,000 to Racine, Wisconsin, residents who are either low-income or minority students. Applicants must be high school graduates and attend college full-time. Students must maintain at least a 2.0 GPA. Deadline: June 10 (fall); October 31 (spring).

2294.
Radio and Television News Directors Foundation
Broadcast Journalism Scholarship Awards
1717 K Street, N.W., Suite 615
Washington, DC 20006
(202) 737-8657

6 scholarships of $1,000 to college sophomore, junior, senior, or graduate students whose objective is broadcast

news. Awards are renewable. For more information, send a self-addressed, stamped envelope. Deadline: varies.

2295.
Radio Free Europe/Radio Liberty
Electrical Engineering Internship
Mr. Alan Dodds, Director Professional Development
1201 Connecticut Avenue, N.W.
Washington, DC 20036
(202) 457-6900

1 or 2 summer internships in Germany for undergraduate juniors or seniors or graduate students majoring in electrical engineering. Preference given to students who have completed course work relevant to technical aspects of international radio broadcasting, such as electronics, electromagnetics, antenna, radio propagation, communication theory, digital technology, and computer science. Basic ability to speak German is preferred. Deadline: February 22.

2296.
Radio Free Europe/Radio Liberty
Media & Opinion Research on Eastern Europe &
the Former Soviet Union
Director Professional Development
1201 Connecticut Avenue, N.W.
Washington, DC 20036
(202) 457-6900

Internships providing a daily stipend of forty-eight German marks plus accommodations to exceptional undergraduates or graduate students majoring in communications, market research, statistics, sociology, social psychology, or East European studies. Must demonstrate knowledge or quantitative research methods, computer applications, and public opinion survey techniques. Proficiency in East European language skills is a plus. Deadline: February 22.

2297.
Radio Technical Commission for Aeronautics
William E. Jackson Award
1140 Connecticut Avenue, N.W., Suite 1020
Washington, DC 20036
(202) 833-9339
(202) 833-9434 Fax

1 scholarship of $2,000 through a competition open to undergraduate and graduate students in aviation electronics, aviation, or telecommunications. Based on a written report, which may be in the form of an essay, thesis, or paper that has been completed within the last three years. Students must also submit a one-to-two-page summary, biographical information, and an endorsement letter by student's instructor, professor, or department head to the Commission. Award is based on the paper. Deadline: June 30.

2298.
Ralph McGill Scholarship Fund
Scholarship Program
P.O. Box 4689
Atlanta, GA 30302
(404) 526-5526

12 to 14 scholarships of up to $2,000 to undergraduate juniors and seniors whose roots lie in the southern states

and who intend to pursue a career in daily or weekly newspaper work. Minimum 3.0 GPA on a 4.0 scale. Deadline: May 1.

2299.
Random House, Inc.
Internship Program
201 East 50th Street
New York, NY 10022
(212) 572-2610

7 ten-week summer internships providing $250 per week to undergraduate juniors, seniors, or graduate students. Interns are placed in one of the company's five major publishing groups—Crown, Ballantine, Knopf, Random House, or Juvenile Merchandise—and rotate through publicity, marketing, production, and editorial. Other restrictions may apply. Deadline: April 15.

2300.
Raychem
Human Resources Recruiters Department
M/S 111/8201
300 Constitution Drive
Menlo Park, CA 94025-1164
(650) 361-4999

40 summer internships providing a salary ranging from $400 to $500 per week for undergraduates and from $700 to $1,000 per week for graduate students, plus round-trip travel to undergraduate sophomores, juniors, seniors, or graduate students. Internships last from ten to twelve weeks, and interns must have at least a 3.0 GPA. Interns are assigned to engineering, research & development (R&D), product design, manufacturing, marketing, finance, human resources, and accounting. Deadline: March 1.

2301.
Real Estate Educators Association
Harwood Scholarship Program
1 Illinois Center, No. 200
111 East Wacker Drive
Chicago, IL 60601
(312) 616-0800

10 scholarships of $500 to undergraduate students who have completed at least two semesters and to graduate students. Students attending a two-year college must have completed two real estate courses. If attending a four-year institution, students must have completed one real estate course. Must be full-time students with at least a 3.2 GPA and intend to pursue a career in real estate. Students must submit a transcript, a letter of recommendation from a professor of a real estate course, and a letter of support from a REEA member. If students don't know a member, the association will provide the name of a member. Deadline: December 4.

2302.
Rebekah Assembly of Texas
Irma Gesche Scholarship Committee
Attn: Scholarship Chairperson
P.O. Box 1434
Baytown, TX 77501

1 scholarship of $1,000 to a graduating high school senior. Must be a Texas resident. Based on academic record, community involvement, character, leadership, and financial need. Deadline: December 1.

2303.
Recording for the Blind
Learning Through Listening
Attn: Lorraine Grestry
20 Rozelle Road
Princeton, NJ 08540
(609) 452-0606

3 scholarships of $3,000 to high school seniors who have learning disabilities. Based on academic achievement, leadership, enterprise, and service to others. Financial need is not a factor. Deadline: February 1.

2304.
Record-Journal Publishing Co.
Record-Journal Carrier Scholarships
Crown St. Square
Meriden, CT 06450
(203) 235-1661

Numerous scholarships of varying amounts to students who are present or former *Record-Journal* carriers. Based on academic record, recommendations, career goals, character, community service, and financial need. Contact public high schools in Cheshire, Meriden, Middlefield, Southington, or Wallingford, Connecticut, or the *Record-Journal* offices in Meriden or Wallingford. Deadline: April 1.

2305.
Red River Valley Fighter Pilots Association
Red River Valley Scholarship Foundation
6237 South Greenwich Road
Derby, KS 67037

Numerous scholarships of varying amounts to sons or daughters of air-crew members in Southeast Asia who were killed in action or are listed as missing in action; children of men who died as the result of the aborted raid into Iran to rescue hostages in April 1980; and children of air-crew members killed during the Libyan air strikes. Based on need and academic achievement. Funds are released to college of choice to satisfy tuition, fees, books, room and board, in order listed. Amount varies with college expenses. Deadline: April 1.

2306.
Reebok
c/o College Relations Program
100 Technology Center Drive
Stoughton, MA 02072
(617) 341-5000

10 ten-to-twelve-week summer internships providing $460 per week for undergraduates, and from $625 to $690 per week for graduates and NFL players. Internships are at Stoughton, MA; Irvine, CA; Atlanta, GA; and Chicago, IL. Applicants must have at least a 3.0 GPA and be enrolled full-time at the time of application. Acceptable areas: liberal arts, business, economics, management information systems, and accounting. Applicants must send a résumé, cover letter, and two professional references (letters of

recommendation or addresses and phone numbers). Deadline: May 15.

2307.
Renew America
Internship Coordinator
1400 16th Street, N.W., Suite 710
Washington, DC 20036
(202) 232-2252
(202) 232-2617 Fax

6 internships providing $250 per week to high school graduates, undergraduates, recent college graduates, and graduate students to work in Washington, DC, in the area of the environment. Renew America collects and promotes information on successful environmental programs developed by community groups, nonprofit organizations, government agencies, and businesses. Interns work with local grassroots environmental organizations to identify and verify projects for inclusion in the "Index." Summer internships last for twelve weeks. Six-month internships are conducted on an ongoing basis. Deadline: April 1 (summer); rolling (ongoing).

2308.
Reserve Officers Association of the United States
Henry J. Reilly Memorial Scholarship—
   Undergraduate Program for College Students
1 Constitution Avenue, N.E.
Washington, DC 20002-5624
(202) 479-2200

Numerous scholarships of up to $500 to students who are active or associate ROA or ROAL members or the children and grandchildren of members. Children and grandchildren of active or associate members must be twenty-six years or younger. Children and grandchildren of deceased members must be twenty-one years or younger. Spouses who are ROA or ROAL members are eligible. ROTC members are not eligible to be sponsors. Applicants must have registered with the Selective Service System and be full-time undergraduate students at a four-year institution in the U.S. Freshmen must have at least a 3.3 GPA on a 4.0 scale in high school. Sophomores and above must have a 3.0 GPA on a 4.0 scale in college and complete at least thirty semester or forty-eight quarter credit hours per year. Based on eligibility, academic record, and SAT or ACT. Deadline: April 30.

2309.
Reserve Officers Association of the United States
Henry J. Reilly Memorial Scholarship—
   Undergraduate Program for High School
   Students
1 Constitution Avenue, N.E.
Washington, DC 20002-5624
(202) 479-2200

Numerous scholarships of up to $500 to children and grandchildren of members, twenty-one years or younger, who are graduating high school seniors accepted for full-time undergraduate study at a four-year institution in the U.S. Applicants must be in the upper quarter of their class. Based on eligibility, academic record, essay, and SAT or ACT. Deadline: April 30.

2310.
Retired Officers Association
General John Paul Ratay Grant
201 North Washington Street
Alexandria, VA 22314

Scholarships not exceeding total tuition and room and board costs to students who are dependent children of deceased retired officers. Deadline: January 15.

2311.
Retired Officers Association—Cape Canaveral Chapter
Cape Canaveral Chapter Scholarship
P.O. Box 4186
Patrick AFB, FL 32925

2 scholarships of $1,500 to dependents of officers or enlisted active, reserve, retired with pay, or deceased members of the Armed Forces. Students must be Brevard County, Florida, residents about to enter their junior year at a four-year institution and majoring in science, engineering, mathematics, or liberal arts. First two years may have been earned at either a two- or a four-year college. Based on academic record, character, citizenship, leadership, and extracurricular activities. Deadline: June 30.

2312.
Rhode Island Commission on State Government Summer Internships
Program Coordinator
8AA State House
Providence, RI 02903
(401) 277-6782

Numerous two-month internships to undergraduate sophomores, juniors, seniors, graduate students, and law students. Must be Rhode Island residents attending an out-of-state four-year university or disabled students attending either a two- or four-year college or university. Must have at least a 2.5 GPA on a 4.0 scale. Students intern in a department or agency that is related to the intern's major. Stipends are paid on a monthly basis. Internships are for thirty-five-hour weeks in July and August. There is also a spring internship that only provides class credit. Deadline: May 15.

2313.
Rhode Island Higher Education Assistance Authority
Rhode Island Higher Education Grants
301 Promenade Street
Providence, RI 02908
(401) 277-2080
(401) 277-2545 Fax
http://www.state.ri.us/

Grants ranging from $250 to $2,000 to high school seniors and undergraduate students who are Rhode Island residents. Must be U.S. citizens and have financial need. Deadline: March 1.

2314.
Rhode Island Higher Education Assistance Authority
Rhode Island Robert C. Byrd Honors Scholarship Program
301 Promenade Street
Providence, RI 02908
(401) 277-2080
(401) 277-2545 Fax
http://www.state.ri.us/

Varying numbers of scholarships of $1,500 to graduating high school seniors who are Rhode Island residents and who meet two of these three requirements: rank in the top 5 percent of their class, have at least a 3.5 GPA, or have at least an 1100 on SAT or 27 on ACT. Some states offer no direct application; students are nominated by high school counselor. Deadline: May 1.

2315.
Rhode Island Society of Professional Engineers
Russell J. Morgan
139 Little Rest Road
Kingston, RI 02881-1610
(401) 421-4140
(401) 435-5569 Fax

Scholarships of varying amounts to high school seniors and undergraduates. High school seniors must have scored at least 1200 on SAT. Undergraduates must fulfill other academic criteria. Scholarships offered by the National Society of Professional Engineers are administered at the state level. Other restrictions may apply. Deadline: November 15 (high school seniors) and varies (undergraduates).

2316.
Rhode Island Vocational Rehabilitation Training Grants
Division of Community Services
Department of Human Services
40 Fountain Street
Providence, RI 02903

Scholarships of varying amounts (based on individual's needs) for students with a mental or physical disability that is a handicap for employment. Priority given to persons with severe disabilities (paraplegic, quadriplegic, multiple amputees, etc.). Must be residents of Rhode Island. Deadline: none.

2317.
Richard Eberhart Prize in Poetry
Florida State University
English Department
Tallahassee, FL 32306

1 prize of $300 and publication in "Sun Dog: The Southeast Review" to the best original, unpublished poem of thirty to 100 lines. Send a self-addressed, stamped envelope for rules. Deadline: September 1.

2318.
Robert Mondavi Winery
Internship Program
P.O. Box 106
Oakville, CA 94562
(707) 963-9611

13 internships providing a salary ranging from $10 to $12 per hour to undergraduate juniors, seniors, graduate students, and recent graduates who have a science background and are at least twenty-one years of age. Internships last from three to six months from July to December, with some part-time work available. Interns must have an interest in the wine-making industry. Deadline: rolling.

2319.
Roberts Writing Awards
P.O. Box 1868
Pittsburg, KS 66762

1 first prize of $500, 1 second prize of $200, 1 third prize of $100, and 1 honorable mention of $25 awarded in poetry, short fiction, and informal essays. Charges a $6 entry fee, plus $1 for each additional poem over five. Manuscripts will not be returned. This is a cash award and not a scholarship competition. For rules, send a self-addressed, stamped envelope. Deadline: September 15.

2320.
Rolling Stone Internships
Editorial Department
1290 Avenue of the Americas
New York, NY 10104
(212) 484-1616

4 to 6 twelve-week summer, fall, and spring internships providing no compensation. 2 scholarships of $3,000 for minority undergraduate or graduate students during the summer session only. Open to students from any major. Interns must be outgoing, self-motivated, and have an interest in rock-and-roll. The best interns want to learn every aspect of magazine publishing and are inquisitive and enthusiastic. Interns are placed in a variety of departments, such as advertising, editorial, and publicity. Applicants must send in a résumé, transcript, letter of recommendation from a professor or professional, and cover letter stating why they are applying for the internship and want to work at *Rolling Stone.* Finalists are interviewed in person or by phone. Deadline: rolling.

2321.
Rosalie Tilles Nonsectarian Charity Fund
c/o Mercantile Bank of St. Louis, N.A.
P.O. Box 387
St. Louis, MO 63166
(314) 425-2525

65 scholarship grants ranging from $100 to $4,150 to high school seniors. Must be residents of the city and county of St. Louis, MO. Students must be planning to attend St. Louis University; the University of Missouri at Columbia, Rolla, or St. Louis; or Washington University. Contact high school counselor or above address. Include a self-addressed, stamped envelope. Deadline: February 1.

2322.
Rosenbluth International
Internship Program
1911 Arch Street
Philadelphia, PA 19103
(215) 557-8700

5 ten-week internships providing no compensation to undergraduate and graduate students and to recent graduates. Internships are held during the summer, fall, and spring in Philadelphia. Interns are assigned to Industry Relations, M.Power, and Human Resources as they apply to advertising, public relations, internal communications, and sports marketing. Students should have excellent writing skills, poise, and maturity, and the ability to handle pressure and responsibilities and to meet deadlines. Deadline: rolling.

2323.
Rotary Club (Downtown) of San Antonio
Diploma Plus
2120 Tower Life Building
San Antonio, TX 78205
(210) 222-8242

62 Diploma Plus awards of $50 per month for nine months and an extra $50 upon graduation. Students must have at least a 2.5 GPA on a 4.0 scale, 95 percent attendance, and extreme financial need. Contact high school counselor for application and information. Students in other communities should contact local Rotary Clubs and inquire whether they sponsor a Diploma Plus program.

2324.
Rotary Foundation Scholarships for
  International Understanding
Journalism Scholarships
1600 Ridge Avenue
Evanston, IL 60201

Journalism scholarships to high school graduates to study journalism in a country where there are Rotary Clubs. Must be between the ages of twenty-one and fifty and have at least two years of experience as a professional journalist; may be married.

2325.
Rotary Foundation Scholarships for
  International Understanding
Teachers of the Handicapped
1600 Ridge Avenue
Evanston, IL 60201

Scholarships of varying amounts to undergraduate or graduate students pursuing a career as teacher of the handicapped in a country where there are Rotary Clubs. Must be between the ages of twenty-one and fifty and have at least two years of experience as a teacher of the handicapped; may be married. Other restrictions may apply.

2326.
Rotary Foundation Scholarships for
  International Understanding
Undergraduate Scholarships
1600 Ridge Avenue
Evanston, IL 60201

Undergraduate scholarships of varying amounts to students with at least two years of college prior to commencement of scholarship studies. Scholarships are for study in foreign countries where Rotary Clubs are located. Applicants must be between the ages of eighteen and twenty-four and must be single during the duration of scholarship.

2327.
Rotary Foundation Scholarships for International Understanding Vocational Scholarships
1600 Ridge Avenue
Evanston, IL 60201

Vocational scholarships to students enrolled in or accepted to a vocational school program in a foreign country where Rotary Clubs are located. Must be between twenty-one and fifty years of age; may be married; must have at least two years of work experience.

2328.
Royal Neighbors of America (RNA)
Fraternal Scholarship Committee
230 16th Street
Rock Island, IL 61201
(309) 788-4561

10 renewable scholarships of $2,000 and 19 nonrenewable scholarships of $500 are awarded each year to high school seniors. For the $2,000 award, students must be in the top 25 percent of class or be recommended by the school principal. Must have been a member of RNA for at least two years, be recommended by the local lodge and field representative of that area, and submit SAT/ACT scores. For the $500 award, students must be in the top 25 percent of class, submit SAT/ACT scores, and be members in a lodge or territory that is offering the grant for at least two years. Deadline: third Friday in September.

2329.
Roy and Roxie Campanella Physical Therapy Scholarship Foundation
7657 Winnitka Avenue, Suite 534
Canoga Park, CA 91306
(818) 716-0206
(818) 340-9663 Fax

Scholarships of varying amounts to undergraduate students who are majoring in physical therapy. Write an introductory letter briefly describing your educational and financial situation. Other restrictions may apply. Deadline: none specified.

2330.
Ruiz Food Products Scholarships
501 South Alta Avenue
P.O. Box 37
Dinuba, CA 93618
(209) 591-5510

Approximately 20 scholarships of $250 per year (for two years) to high school seniors attending a high school in Tulare County or who are children of employees. May occasionally assist high school seniors with exceptional financial need from neighboring counties. Students must plan to attend a two- or four-year college or university.

Contact high school counselor or Human Resources at above address. Deadline: May.

2331.
Ruritan National Foundation Educational Grant and Loan Program
P.O. Box 487
Ruritan Road
Dublin, VA 24084
(703) 674-5431

Limited grants of $750 to graduating high school seniors and undergraduate students, with preference given to college freshmen and sophomores. Based on financial need, character, scholarship, and academic promise. Must have two letters of recommendation from Ruritan members. Must live in a community with a Ruritan chapter. Deadline: April 1.

2332.
Ruth Eleanor and John Bamberger Memorial Foundation
1201 Walker Center
Salt Lake City, UT 84111
(801) 364-2045

66 scholarship grants ranging from $75 to $1,877 to high school seniors, undergraduates, and graduate students. Must be Utah residents. Preference is given to students majoring in nursing, though all majors are welcome. Write an introductory letter briefly detailing your educational and financial situation. Other restrictions may apply. Deadline: none specified.

2333.
Ruth Hindman Foundation
H. E. Francis Short Story Competition
Attn: Patricia Sammon
Department of English
University of Alabama
Huntsville, AL 35899
(205) 539-3320

1 prize of $1,000 and publication in the regional magazine *Hometown Press* offered to an original unpublished manuscript not exceeding 5,000 words. Writers may submit more than one story. Reading fee of $15 is required. Deadline: September 30.

2334.
Sachs Foundation Professional Award
Norwest Bank
90 South Cascade Avenue, #400
Colorado Springs, CO 80903
(719) 633-1361

Approximately 40 scholarships of $3,000 to African American residents of Colorado for undergraduate, graduate, and medical school students. Applicants must have at least a 3.4 GPA. Applications available after January 1. Deadline: March 1.

2335.
Sachs Foundation Undergraduate Grants
Norwest Bank
90 South Cascade Avenue, #400
Colorado Springs, CO 80903
(719) 633-1361

Numerous grants of $3,000 per year to African American residents of Colorado. Must have a 3.4 GPA or better. Preference given to high school seniors, but college students can apply as well. Renewable. Applications are available after January 1 each year. Deadline: March 15.

2336.
Sacramento Scottish Rite of Freemasonry
Charles M. Goethe Memorial Scholarships
6151 H Street
P.O. Box 19497
Sacramento, CA 95819
(916) 452-5881

Numerous scholarships of varying amounts to high school seniors who are children of members or deceased members of a California Masonic Lodge on register of the Grand Lodge F. & A.M. of California or a Senior Member of the Order of Demolay. Payment is made to the student. Deadline: June 10.

2337.
SAE Educational Relations
400 Commonwealth Drive
Warrendale, PA 15096
(412) 776-4841

2 scholarships of $2,000 to high school seniors graduating from a Michigan high school and planning to major in engineering at an Accreditation Board for Engineering and Technology (ABET)-accredited institution. Must have at least a 3.0 GPA and rank in the top 75 percent for both math and verbal SAT or ACT scores. Deadline: December 15.

2338.
St. David's Hospital Auxiliary
Junior Volunteers Scholarships
St. David's Hospital Auxiliary
Attn: Scholarship Committee
P.O. Box 4039
Austin, TX 78765

Varying numbers of scholarships of $600 per semester to undergraduate or graduate students who are St. David's Junior Volunteers pursuing any major. Preference is given to students pursuing degrees in a field directly or indirectly related to medical services. Awards may be used for tuition, fees, and books. Must be used in a Texas institution. Renewable up to four years with reapplication. Deadline: varies.

2339.
St. David's Hospital Auxiliary
Upper Division Scholarships
St. David's Hospital Auxiliary
Attn: Scholarship Committee
P.O. Box 4039
Austin, TX 78765

Varying numbers of scholarships of $600 per semester to undergraduate juniors or seniors pursuing degrees in a field directly or indirectly related to medical services. Awards may be used for tuition, fees, and books. Must be used in a Texas institution. Renewable with reapplication. Deadline: varies.

2340.
St. David's Hospital Auxiliary
Vocational Scholarships
St. David's Hospital Auxiliary
Attn: Scholarship Committee
P.O. Box 4039
Austin, TX 78765

Varying numbers of scholarships of $400 per class, session, or semester pursuing degrees related to health care. Awards may be used for tuition, fees, and books, but are limited to one year of study per student. Must be used in a Texas institution. Programs that are non-degree-granting but award certification upon completion are eligible. Deadline: varies.

2341.
Sales Association of the Chemical Industry
One-Year Scholarship
1 Gail Court
Piscataway, NJ 08854
(908) 463-1540

1 scholarship of $500 per year (for four years) to a high school senior who is a resident of New Jersey. Must be majoring in chemistry at an accredited college or university. Based on academic achievement and extracurricular activities. Deadline: May 30.

2342.
Samuel S. Johnson Foundation
P.O. Box 356
Redmond, OR 97756
(503) 548-8104

9 scholarship grants ranging from $500 to $1,000 and 2 loans totaling $1,500 to graduating high school seniors or undergraduate students who will be or are attending a college or university in the Pacific Northwest or northern California. Deadline: June 1; December 1.

2343.
San Antonio Area Foundation
405 North St. Mary's, Suite 808
San Antonio, TX 78205
(210) 225-2243

Numerous scholarships of varying amounts to high school seniors from Bexar and Clemens counties, Texas. There are thirty different programs in a variety of majors. Some of the scholarships are for use only in San Antonio colleges or in Texas, but others can be used by any student in any major at any school. Apply through the Bexar County Clearinghouse. Only students who are in the top 25 percent of their class are eligible and only 10 percent of an entire class can apply. For more information, contact your high school counselor. Deadline: varies.

2344.
San Antonio Women's Celebration and Hall of Fame
Attn: Cynthia Ruiz McKee
Scholarship Chairperson
1633 Babcock Road, Suite 425
San Antonio, TX 78229

From 1 to 10 scholarships ranging from $500 to $1,000 to female students at all levels: graduating high school seniors, nontraditional students returning to school, undergraduate, graduate, or professional school students. Must be Bexar County, Texas, residents. Awards are good for any major at any accredited four-year U.S. institution. In January, send a #10 self-addressed, stamped envelope with two stamps for an application. Request applications by March 1. Deadline: mid-March.

2345.
Sandee Thompson Memorial Foundation Scholarship
1211 Napoleon Manor, N.E.
Lawrenceville, GA 30243
(615) 365-9951

1 scholarship of $500 to an undergraduate or graduate student who has an interest in serving humanity and relieving human suffering. Applicant may be majoring in physical therapy, nursing, medicine, or a religious career and have at least a 3.0 GPA on a 4.0 scale. Must attend an accredited college or university. Preference given to applicants with Christian background. Request applications after January 1; include a #10 self-addressed, stamped envelope. Deadline: March 15.

2346.
S&H Foundation
330 Madison Avenue
New York, NY 10017
(202) 924-9585

280 scholarships of varying amounts, totaling $200,000, to high school seniors who are children of employees of the Sperry & Hutchinson Company, and also to high school seniors whose parents own or work for a business that gives S&H Green Stamps to its customers. Deadline: varies.

2347.
Sanford Adler Scholarship Fund
Baker School District 5J
2090 Fourth Street
Baker City, OR 97814
(503) 523-5814
(503) 523-6111 Fax

Scholarships of varying amounts to graduating high school seniors, undergraduates, or graduate students who are majoring in any field of study. Must be residents of Baker County, Oregon. Must attend a two- or four-year college or university in Oregon. Selection based on academic achievement, activities, character, and financial need. Other restrictions may apply. Deadline: December.

2348.
San Francisco Bay Area Chapter—National Defense Transportation Association (NDTA)
NDTA Scholarship
P.O. Box 24676
Oakland, CA 94623
(703) 751-5011

1 scholarship of $1,000 to a student studying in the field of transportation, physical distribution, or business logistics in preparation for pursuit of a career in transportation. For study in San Francisco Bay Area colleges and universities. Deadline: May 1.

2349.
San Francisco Symphony
Pepsi Young Musician Awards
Louise M. Davies Symphony Hall
San Francisco, CA 94102
(415) 552-8000

$1,000 music competition for students in grades 7–12 in public, private, or parochial schools within northern California. Categories are brass, piano, string, and woodwinds. Deadline: date varies.

2350.
Sansum Medical Reserve Fund
Research Foundation Student Internships
2219 Bath Street
Santa Barbara, CA 93105
(805) 682-7638
(805) 682-3332 Fax

Varying numbers of ten-week full-time research internships providing $125 per week, with a travel allowance of up to $500 to out-of-state interns. Program is open to undergraduate and graduate students who have a strong background in biology and chemistry. Selection based on academic achievement, laboratory skills, familiarity with assays and/or equipment, and letter of recommendation. Send a self-addressed, stamped envelope for an application. Deadline: mid-March.

2351.
Santa Barbara Foundation
Mary & Edith Pillsbury Foundation Scholarships
Student Aid Director
15 East Carrillo Street
Santa Barbara, CA 93101
(805) 963-1873

28 to 35 scholarships ranging from $400 to $2,500 to undergraduate and graduate students of all ages in the area of music performance and music composition. Applicants must be Santa Barbara County residents or have strong ties to the county. Awards may be used for music lessons, camps, or college tuition. Selection based on recommendations, financial need, interviews, and auditions. Renewable. Other restrictions may apply. Deadline: May 15.

2352.
Santa Barbara Scholarship Foundation
Student Aid Director
P.O. Box 1403
Santa Barbara, CA 93102-1403
(805) 965-7212

420 scholarships (averaging $1,200) to graduates of greater Santa Barbara high schools (the region from Carpinteria to Goleta). Must have a 2.5 GPA or better and maintain at least a 2.0 GPA while in college. Awards are good for students in vocational/occupational schools or two- or four-year undergraduate, graduate, or professional schools. Request applications after December 1. Deadline: February 12.

2353.
Santa Fe Pacific Foundation Scholarships
American Indian Scholarships
Executive Director
1700 East Gulf Road
Schaumburg, IL 60173-5860
(708) 995-6000

6 scholarships ranging from $1,000 to $2,500 to outstanding high school students who are at least one quarter Native American Indians, with preference given to students living in Arizona, Colorado, Kansas, New Mexico, Oklahoma, or San Bernardino County, California. Two scholarships are for members of the Navajo tribe. Based on academic achievement. Preference given to students planning to major in engineering, other natural resource-related professions, business-related fields, and educational administration. Contact: American Indian Science and Engineering Society, 1085 14th Street, Suite 1506, Boulder, CO 80302-7309. Deadline: varies.

2354.
Santa Fe Pacific Foundation Scholarships
Hispanic American Scholarships
Executive Director
1700 East Gulf Road
Schaumburg, IL 60173-5860
(708) 995-6000

3 types of scholarship awards are available: National Scholastic Achievement Award (outstanding academic achievement); Honors Awards (for students with less than outstanding academic achievement, but who have potential of graduating from a postsecondary institution); and Need Awards (for students with academic potential and financial need). The value of the award is determined by LULAC. Contact: League of United Latin American Citizens (LULAC), National Educational Service Centers, Inc., 400 First Street, N.W., Washington, DC 20001.

2355.
Santa Fe Pacific Foundation Scholarships
National Merit Scholarships
Executive Director
1700 East Gulf Road
Schaumburg, IL 60173-5860
(708) 995-6000

4 scholarships of $2,000 to high school seniors from the Santa Fe Pacific Foundation. These awards go to finalists who are enrolled as full-time students in accredited U.S. institutions.

2356.
Santa Fe Pacific Foundation Scholarships
Outstanding African American Scholarships
Executive Director
1700 East Golf Road
Schaumburg, IL 60173-5860
(708) 995-6000

Varying numbers of scholarships of varying amounts to graduating high school seniors who are National Merit Finalists. Must be dependents of Santa Fe Pacific employees. These awards go to finalists who enroll as full-time students in accredited U.S. institutions. Selection is based on academic achievement, leadership abilities, extracurricular activities, recommendations, essay, and test scores. Financial need is not considered.

2357.
Santa Fe Pacific Foundation Scholarships
Sons and Daughters National Merit Scholarships
Executive Director
1700 East Gulf Road
Schaumburg, IL 60173-5860
(708) 995-6000

10 scholarships ranging from $2,000 to $3,500 (depending on financial need) to high school seniors who are sons or daughters of employees and were selected as National Merit Scholarship Semifinalists and Finalists. All phases of the competition are handled by the National Merit Scholarship Corporation.

2358.
Sara Lee Foundation
Nathan Cummings—Sara Lee Corporation
  Scholarship Program
3 First National Plaza
Chicago, IL 60602-4260
(312) 588-8448

10 scholarships of varying amounts to high school seniors who are children of U.S. employees and 2 scholarships of varying amounts for high school seniors who are children of Canadian employees. U.S. students are chosen by the National Merit Corporation, based on the PSAT. Canadian students are chosen by the Association of Universities and Colleges of Canada. There is 1 scholarship of unspecified amount for an African American high school student who is a child of a U.S. employee. This student is also chosen by the National Merit Corporation. There is also an educational loan program available for employees, spouses, or children of employees.

2359.
Scholarship Foundation of St. Louis
8215 Clayton Road
St. Louis, MO 63117
(314) 725-7990

680 scholarships of up to $3,000 to students at all levels of education (high school seniors, vocational/technical students, two- or four-year undergraduate, graduate, professional, and postdoctoral) and for all majors. Must be residents of St. Louis and have at least a 2.0 GPA. Request applications after January 1. Deadline: April 15.

2360.
Scholarship Fund of Game Wardens of Vietnam
  Association, Inc.
Attn: John Williams
P.O. Box 5523
Virginia Beach, VA 23455

1 scholarship of $400, 1 scholarship of $500, and 1 scholarship of $600 to high school seniors or graduates or undergraduate, graduate, or professional students who are children of veterans from the River Patrol Force (also known as the Brown Water Navy). No restrictions on age or marital status of student. Based on academic record and financial need. Deadline: April 15.

2361.
Scholarship Program for Seamen
Seafarers' Welfare Plan
5201 Auth Way
Camp Springs, MD 20746

Scholarships ranging from $6,000 to $15,000 to high school graduates and undergraduates. Must be seamen who have credit for two years of employment with an employer who is obligated to make contributions to the Seafarers' Welfare Plan on the employer's behalf prior to the date of application. Open to all areas of study. Must have at least 120 days of employment with some days from the previous calendar year. Applicants must be a high school graduate or its equivalent. Deadline: April 16.

2362.
**Scholarships for Children of American Military
    Personnel**
SCAMP Grants
136 South Fuller Avenue
Los Angeles, CA 90036

Numerous grants ranging from $3,500 to $5,500 to graduating high school seniors. Must be children of armed service personnel who were killed in action, missing in action, or a prisoner of war during the Vietnam conflict. Children of any man or woman who gave their lives to the challenge of Space, and children of Desert Storm Armed Forces personnel. Deadline: none specified.

2363.
Scholarships for Handicapped Students
4747 North Ocean Drive
Suite 240
Fort Lauderdale, FL 33302

20 to 25 scholarships of up to $4,000 to undergraduate and graduate severely handicapped students in any area of study. Must be residents of Broward County, Florida. Amount based on need according to financial statement submitted by applicant. Renewable if student maintains a 2.5 GPA on a 4.0 scale. Deadline: none.

2364.
School for Field Studies
**Environmental Science Training, Education, &
    Research Program**
376 Hale Street
Beverly, MA 01915
(617) 927-7777

150 grants and loans for month-long and semester-long research expeditions to high school students and undergraduates to study problems and issues in wildlife studies, marine studies, botany, and environmental studies.

Academic credit can be arranged. Deadline: February 1; February 15; March 1; March 15; April 1; April 15; May 1.

2365.
Schramm Foundation
Attn: Personnel Officer
800 East Virginia Avenue
West Chester, PA 19380
(215) 696-2500

12 scholarships of $300 to students who are graduates from high schools in the West Chester, Pennsylvania, area. Must be majoring in business or engineering. Based on financial need. Deadline: varies.

2366.
Schwab Foundation
c/o Wright and Sawyer
P.O. Box 3247
Enid, OK 73702
(405) 233-4455

6 grants ranging from $384 to $11,035 to graduating high school seniors, undergraduate, or graduate students who are majoring in any field of study. Must be residents of either Joplin, Missouri, or Enid, Oklahoma. Write an introductory letter detailing your educational and financial situation. Other restrictions may apply. Deadline: none specified.

2367.
Science Essay Awards Program
c/o General Learning Corporation
60 Revere Drive, Suite 200
Northbrook, IL 60062
(708) 205-3000

54 scholarships ranging from $50 to $1,500 to students in grades seven through twelve who submit original essays of 600–1000 words on a science topic important to humankind. Teacher's signature required on essay submission. Deadline: late January.

2368.
Screen Actors Guild Foundation
John L. Dales Scholarship Fund
5757 Wilshire Boulevard
Los Angeles, CA 90036-3600
(213) 954-1600
http://www.sag.com/

Scholarships of $2,000 to undergraduate, graduate, and post-graduate students in any field of study. Must be SAG members for at least five years or dependents of members of at least eight years. Financial need is a consideration. Renewable with reapplication and continued satisfactory academic progress. Deadline: April 30.

2369.
Scripps Howard Foundation Scholarship
Charles M. Schulz Awards
P.O. Box 5380
Cincinnati, OH 45201-5380
(513) 977-3035
http://www.scripps.com/foundation

Awards of varying amounts to full-time undergraduate and graduate students who are college cartoonists. Awards are given to encourage their professional careers. Students must work on a college newspaper or magazine in the U.S. or its territories. Request applications during the fall months. Send a self-addressed, stamped envelope for an application or download application from the Internet. Deadline: mid-January.

2370.
Scripps Institution of Oceanography/USD
Summer Undergraduate Research Fellowship
9500 Gilman Drive
La Jolla, CA 92093-0003
(619) 534-3555
(619) 534-3868 Fax

30 ten-week summer internships providing $250 per week, housing, and round-trip travel to minority undergraduate juniors and seniors who are majoring in biology, chemistry, computer science, engineering, geology, mathematics, or physics. Interns engage in laboratory research with a faculty member in the areas of geochemistry, marine geology, geophysics, marine biology, climatology, space science, and physical oceanography. Open to U.S. citizens and international students. Deadline: February 15.

2371.
Sear's/Seventeen Magazine Essay Contest

Awards of $1,500 and $10,000 to females between the ages of thirteen and twenty-one. Students must write a 150-word essay on a specific theme that focuses on their educational goals and why those goals will make a difference in the student's life. Essay theme varies. Obtain applications from the computer or junior department at Sears stores in July or August. Due: early October.

2372.
Second Marine Division Association Memorial Scholarship Fund
Chairperson, Board of Trustees
20082 Ferglen Drive
Yorba Linda, CA 92686

Scholarships for high school seniors, high school graduates, and undergraduate students who are sons or daughters of a Marine who served in or is serving with the Second Marine Division, U.S. Marine Corps. Deadline: April 1.

2373.
Seminole Tribe of Florida
Higher Education Awards
6073 Stirling Road
Hollywood, FL 33024
(305) 584-0400, ext. 154

Awards of varying amounts to undergraduate and graduate students in all fields of study at any U.S. accredited institution. Must be enrolled members of the Seminole Tribe of Florida or eligible to become a member. Renewable. Other restrictions may apply. Deadline: April 15; July 15; November 15.

2374.
Seneca Nation Higher Education
Education Grants
Box 231
Salamanca, NY 14779
(716) 945-1790

Awards of up to $5,000 to undergraduate, graduate, and doctoral students in all fields of study at accredited U.S. institutions. Must be enrolled members of the Seneca Nation of Indians. Based on financial need. Other restrictions may apply. Deadline: July 15; December 15; May 20.

2375.
Senior Award
International Society of Dramatists
P.O. Box 1310
Miami, FL 33153

Contest with cash awards for previously unpublished scripts (any media or length) written by college students. Winner's script gets staged and read for possible future production. Send self-addressed, stamped envelope for rules. Deadline: May 1.

2376.
Serbian Singing Federation
Paul S. Bielich Scholarship Award
26356 John R. Road
Madison Heights, MI 48071
(248) 542-4004

1 scholarship of $1,000 to a graduating high school senior. Must be a member of the Serbian Singing Federation. Selection based on membership and talent. Other restrictions apply. Deadline: May 1.

2377.
Serb National Federation
SNF Scholarship Program
c/o SNF Home Office
One Fifth Avenue, 7th Floor
Pittsburgh, PA 15222
http://www.serbnationalfederation.org
snf@serbnationalfederation.org

12 scholarships of $1,000 (3 scholarships per four regions— East, Midwest, Far West, and Canada) to graduating high school seniors or high school graduates. Must have been SNF members on or before January 1 of the application year. The award will be $250 per year for four years provided the recipient is still a member. Selection is based solely on merit. Deadline: April 15.

2378.
Service League of Northern Virginia
5012 Lee Highway
Arlington, VA 22207
(703) 522-1993

Awards of up to $5,000 to female undergraduate or graduate students in all fields of study. Must be over thirty years of age and residents of northern Virginia. May be part-time or full-time students. Based on financial need. Other restrictions may apply. Deadline: none specified.

2379.
Service Merchandise Scholarships
Service Merchandise Company, Inc.
Scholarship Program
P.O. Box 2810
Cherry Hill, NJ 08034

100 scholarships of $500 to graduating high school seniors or high school graduates who haven't attended college. Must be planning to attend a four-year college on a full-time basis. Open to students majoring in business, merchandising, marketing, economics, or accounting. Stop by your local Service Merchandise store after October 15 to pick up an application/brochure. Deadline: mid-January.

2380.
Shell Oil Companies Foundation
Two Shell Plaza
P.O. Box 2099
Houston, TX 77001
(713) 241-4511

50 scholarships of varying amounts to minority undergraduate students pursuing a career in business or a technical field. Must be U.S. citizens. May attend any accredited postsecondary institution in the U.S. Contact school's financial aid office or business department, not the foundation.

2381.
Sico Foundation
15 Mount Joy Street
Mount Joy, PA 17552
(717) 653-1411

Numerous scholarships of $1,000 to undergraduate students who attend specific schools in Delaware, Pennsylvania, or Maryland. Write an introductory letter briefly describing your educational and financial situation. Other restrictions may apply. Deadline: February 15.

2382.
Sigma Nu Educational Foundation, Inc.
P.O. Box 1869
Lexington, VA 24450
(703) 463-2164

22 scholarship grants ranging from $50 to $1,000 to students who are members of Sigma Nu. Emergency Aid Grants are based on financial need, and Academic Encouragement Awards are based on academic achievement.

2383.
Sigma Xi—The Scientific Research Society Research Grants
P.O. Box 13975
99 Alexandria Drive
Research Triangle Park, NC 27709
(919) 549-4691

Awards ranging from $100 to $2,500 to undergraduate or graduate students, postdoctoral fellows, or scientists to conduct research. Students must be majoring in animal science, astronomy, atmospheric sciences, biology, earth science, eye/vision research, health sciences, mathematics, medical sciences, meteorology, natural resources, physical sciences, or physics. Awards must be used to conduct research in any field of science. Preference is given to scientists in the early stages of their careers. Contact for more information. Deadline: February 1; May 1; November 1.

2384.
Sisters of Salisaw Foundation Scholarship
911 Bartlett Place
Windsor, CA 95492
Written inquiries only

1 scholarship of $500 to an undergraduate or graduate student who is a child of a migrant farm laborer. Award may be used for any field of study. Student must be residing in Windsor, California, and student's family must have migrated to California from Salisaw, Oklahoma, during the Dust Bowl era of the 1930s. The family must have worked at least six months in the Hernesto Onexioca Vineyards. Other restrictions may apply. Deadline: August 1.

2385.
Skidmore Owings & Merrill Foundation Travelling Fellowship Program
224 South Michigan Avenue, Suite 1000
Chicago, IL 60604
(312) 554-9090
(312) 360-4545 Fax

1 fellowship of $10,000 to undergraduate and graduate students majoring in architecture. Must be U.S. citizens. For information or an application, send a self-addressed, stamped envelope. Deadline: none specified.

2386.
Skirball Essay Contest
Skirball Institute on American Values
635 South Harvard Boulevard, Suite 214
Los Angeles, CA 90005-2511
(213) 381-1819

50 third prizes of $100, 1 second prize of $500, 1 first prize of $1,000, and 1 grand prize of $5,000 plus a trip to Washington, DC, for the winner and the sponsoring teacher. Open to high school sophomores, juniors, and seniors. Selection based on essay written on a specific theme. The 1996 theme was "What does U.S. history teach us about the role of immigration in the creation of American society?" The first 100 teachers who submit their students' essays in a group as a class project will receive a copy of the *American Heritage Dictionary*, Second College Edition, as a gift from the Houghton Mifflin Company. Winners are announced in early May. Deadline: mid-March.

2387.
Slovene National Benefit Society Scholarship Awards
Scholarship Chairperson
166 Shore Drive
Burr Ridge, IL 60521

Renewable $500 scholarships to undergraduate and graduate students who have been members for at least two years of the Slovene Benefit Society. Must be in the top 50 percent of class, with at least a 2.5 GPA on a 4.0 scale. Award is good at two- and four-year institutions. Based on academic record, financial need, and recommendations. Deadline: August 1.

2388.
Smithsonian Environmental Research Center
Work/Learn Program
P.O. Box 28
Edgewater, MD 21037

A twelve-week program that allows undergraduate and graduate students the opportunity to work on specific projects involving long-range study of the local watershed and its estuary. Undergraduate students receive $75 per week and living accommodations. Graduate students receive $90 per week and living accommodations. Based on academic achievements, professional promise, relevant training and experience, and letters of recommendation. Deadline: July 1 (fall semester); December 1 (spring semester); April 1 (summer sessions).

2389.
Smithsonian Institution
Cooper–Hewitt Museum of Design Academic Year
  Internships
Cooper-Hewitt Museum
2 East 91st Street
New York, NY 10128
(212) 860-6868
http://www.si.edu/organiza/office/musstud/intern.htm

Full-academic-year internships at the Cooper-Hewitt Museum are open to undergraduate and graduate students who are enrolled in an accredited institution and majoring in art, design, architecture, or museum studies. Minimum term is one month. Deadline: none.

2390.
Smithsonian Institution
Cooper–Hewitt Museum of Design Summer
  Internships
Cooper-Hewitt Museum
2 East 91st Street
New York, NY 10128
(212) 860-6868
http://ww.si.edu/organiza/office/musstud/intern.htm

Fellowships of varying amounts are awarded to cover ten-week summer internships at the Cooper-Hewitt Museum. Undergraduate students who have completed at least two years of study in either art, design, architecture, or museum studies at an accredited institution are eligible for the fellowships. Deadline: March 31.

2391.
Smithsonian Institution
Intern
Office of Elementary & Secondary Education
A&I Building, Room 2283
MRC 444
Washington, DC 20560
(202) 357-4542
http://www.si.edu/organiza/office/musstud/intern.htm

Numerous six-week internships for graduating high school seniors. Fellowships pay for transportation, lodging, and a small allowance. Internships are in art, biology, computer science, history, journalism, library science, photography, and veterinary science. Internship begins June 24 and ends August 5. Request applications by March 1; send a self-addressed, stamped envelope or download the application via the Internet. Deadline: mid-March.

2392.
Smithsonian Institution
Internship Coordinator
Office of Museum Programs
Arts & Industries Building
Suite 2235, MRC 427
Washington, DC 20560
(202) 357-3102
http://www.si.edu/organiza/office/musstud/intern.htm

700 internships providing no compensation, though a few positions may offer stipends, to high school seniors, undergraduate and graduate students, and recent graduates. Some positions have specific requirements. Request "Internships and Fellowships," a free brochure listing museum addresses and position descriptions, or send a $5 check and request "Internship Opportunities at the Smithsonian Institution." Internships last from two months to one year, and students work at least twenty hours per week during the summer, fall, or spring. Deadline: February 15 (summer); June 15 (fall); October 15 (spring).

2393.
Smithsonian Institution
Minority Undergraduate & Graduate Fellowships
Office of Fellowships and Grants
L'Enfant Plaza, Room 3300
Washington, DC 20560
(212) 860-6868

Fellowships providing $200 per week plus travel to minority undergraduates and $250 per week plus travel to minority graduates are available to minority students to fund research and study at the Smithsonian or the Cooper-Hewitt Museum of Design in New York City. Students must be studying design, architecture, art, or museum studies. Deadline: March 1; July 1; October 15.

2394.
Smithsonian Institution
National Air & Space Museum Internships
  Program
Attn: NASM Intern Program Director, Room P700
Washington, DC 20560
(202) 357-1504
http://www.si.edu/organiza/office/musstud/intern.htm

$115- to $150-per-week stipend or academic credit to undergraduate and graduate students. Internships available in areas such as aviation, astronomy, geology, space science, art, and all aspects of museum and library operations from artifact registration and history to public relations. Applications are considered quarterly. Write for complete details.

2395.
Smithsonian Institution
National Museum of African Art Internships
950 Independence Avenue, S.W.
Washington, DC 20560
(202) 357-4600
http://www.si.edu/organiza/office/musstud/intern.htm

Internships for the academic year and for the summer are available to undergraduate juniors and seniors and graduate students majoring in African studies, Afro-American studies, art history, or museum studies. Interns work for ten weeks in one of several museums. Internships don't always include financial aid. Request financial aid information at initial inquiry. Deadline: December 15 and April 1.

2396.
Smithsonian Institution
Peter Krueger Summer Internship Program
Cooper-Hewitt Museum
2 East 91st Street
New York, NY 10128
(212) 860-6868
(212) 860-6909 Fax
http://www.si.edu/organiza/office/musstud/intern.htm

Ten-week summer internships at the Cooper-Hewitt Museum open to undergraduate and graduate students who are enrolled in an accredited institution and majoring in art history, design, or architectural history. Internships commence in June and end in August. Housing is not provided. Deadline: March 31.

2397.
Soaring Society of America
Youth Soaring Scholarship
CADET Scholarship
P.O. Box E
Hobbs, NM 88241
(505) 392-1177

1 scholarship of $600 toward sailplane flying lessons, and lesser prizes of textbooks and memberships, awarded to young persons between ages fourteen and twenty-two who are not holders of any FAA pilot license. Application forms are available at gliderports only.

2398.
Sociedad Honoraria Hispanica (SHH)
Joseph Adams Scholarships
Glendale Community College
6000 West Olive Avenue
Glendale, AZ 85302

8 scholarships of $1,000 and 20 scholarships of $500 to graduating high school seniors who are members of SHH and studying either Spanish or Portuguese. Each chapter enters one student and a national selection committee selects the recipients. Application packets are sent to the chapters in December. Deadline: February 15.

2399.
Society for Exploration Geophysicists
SEG Education Foundation
8801 South Yale Avenue
P.O. Box 702740
Tulsa, OK 74101
(918) 497-5500
http://www.seg.org/

60 to 100 scholarships ranging from $500 to $3,000 to high school seniors, undergraduates, and graduate students who are pursuing a career in geophysics or a related earth science. Must be accepted to or enrolled in an accredited institution in the U.S. or its possessions. Applicants must be in the upper third of their class and have at least a B average. Based on academic record, standardized test scores, financial need, and recommendations. Renewable. Deadline: March 1.

2400.
Society for Imaging Science and Technology
Raymond Davis Scholarships
7003 Kilworth Lane
Springfield, VA 22151
(703) 642-9090
(703) 642-9094

Scholarships of $1,000 to full-time undergraduate juniors, seniors, or graduate students majoring in photographic science or engineering. Award is to assist in continuing studies in the theory or practice of photographic science, including any type of image formation initiated by radiant energy. Other restrictions may apply. Deadline: December 15.

2401.
Society for Range Management
Masonic–Range Science Scholarships
Office of the Executive Vice President
1839 York Street
Denver, CO 80206

Scholarships of varying amounts to graduating high school seniors and current freshmen who are majoring in range science. Other restrictions may apply. Send a self-addressed, stamped envelope for an application. Deadline: January 15.

2402.
Society for Technical Communication
Undergraduate Scholarships
901 N. Stuart Street, Suite 904
Arlington, VA 22203
(703) 522-4114
http://www.stc-va.org

4 scholarships of $1,500 to full-time undergraduate students having completed at least one year of study and enrolled in a two-year or four-year degree program for a career in any area of technical communication. Awards are good at any college or university. Deadline: February 15.

2403.
Society for the Advancement of Material and
**   Process Engineering**
SAMPE–Scholarship Awards
P.O. Box 2459
Covina, CA 91722
(818) 331-0616

18 scholarships of $1,000 to undergraduate freshmen, sophomores, and juniors who are recommended by their adviser or department head. Not available to seniors. Students must be majoring in material sciences, metallurgy, chemistry, chemical engineering, or physics. Must submit transcript of all college grades and letters of reference. Deadline: January 31.

2404.
Society for the Protection of Ancient Buildings Memorial Trusts Scholarships
37 Spital Square
London E1 6DY, England
01-377-1644

2 to 3 scholarships of 3,200 British pounds to undergraduate and graduate students to travel for nine months to research conservation architecture to be used in the United Kingdom. Emphasis on practical training, traditional building, and modern and traditional repairs. Open to students of all nationalities attending accredited institutions. Deadline: December 31.

2405.
Society of Actuaries Scholarships for Minority Students
500 Park Boulevard
Itasca, IL 60143
(312) 773-3010

15 scholarships of $4,000 to minority high school seniors or undergraduate students enrolled or accepted in a program in actuarial science. Amount varies according to student's financial need and credentials. Based on financial need. Deadline: May 1.

2406.
Society of Architectural Historians Annual Domestic Tours
Attn: Executive Director
1232 Pine Street
Philadelphia, PA 19107
(215) 735-0224
(215) 635-0246 Fax

2 awards of varying amounts to undergraduate and graduate students to participate in an architectural study tour conducted by regional experts. Must be student members of SAH. There is also a competition to award a scholarship to a student to attend annual domestic tour. Other restrictions may apply. Deadline: none specified.

2407.
Society of Architectural Historians Annual Meeting Award
Attn: Executive Director
1232 Pine Street
Philadelphia, PA 19107
(215) 735-0224
(215) 635-0246

1 award of varying amount to undergraduate and graduate students to attend the annual meeting of SAH. Must be student members of SAH. Other restrictions may apply. Deadline: none specified.

2408.
Society of Daughters of the United States Army Scholarships
P.O. Box 78
West Point, NY 10096
(800) 890-8253
(914) 446-0566
(914) 446-3031 Fax
http://www.pojonews.com/enjoy/locnums

8 scholarships of $750 to daughters, stepdaughters, adopted daughters, or granddaughters of career U.S. Army commissioned or warrant officers on active duty, retired, or deceased. Good at any accredited vocational school, college, or professional school. Renewable. Based on academic record and financial need. Deadline: March 31.

2409.
Society of Environmental Graphic Designers Student Scholarship Awards
47 Third Street
Cambridge, MA 02141
(617) 577-8225

Scholarships ranging from $1,000 to $3,000 to undergraduate and graduate students who are majoring in graphic design (preference given to this major), environmental design, landscape architecture, architecture, interior design, or industrial design. Can be used at any accredited institution. Given to encourage students to pursue a career in environmental graphic design. Deadline: March 18.

2410.
Society of Hispanic Professional Engineers Foundation Educational Grants
5400 East Olympic Boulevard, Suite 306
Los Angeles, CA 90022

90 awards ranging from $500 to $3,000 to full-time undergraduate and graduate students majoring in engineering and science. Students must have completed algebra, geometry, trigonometry, chemistry, and physics. Recipients must submit application for renewal. Deadline: April 15.

2411.
Society of Illustrators Scholarships Annual Student Scholarship Show
Director
Society of Illustrators
128 East 63rd Street
New York, NY 10021
Written inquiries only

1 full-tuition, fees, and materials scholarship and 30 cash awards ranging from $500 to $2,500 to college-level students attending an art school, college, or university and pursuing a career in illustration. Based on artistic ability. The Society relies on college instructors to make the preliminary evaluations and then submit nominations. Deadline: none.

2412.
Society of Illustrators Scholarships
Charles Dana Gibson Memorial Scholarship
Director
Society of Illustrators
128 East 63rd Street
New York, NY 10021
(212) 838-3560
Written inquiries only

1 scholarship of full tuition, fees, and materials to an undergraduate or graduate student attending an art school, college, or university and pursuing a career in illustration. Based on artistic ability. The Society relies on college instructors to make the preliminary evaluations and then submit nominations. Other restrictions may apply. Deadline: none.

2413.
Society of Manufacturing Engineering Education Foundation
Alfred V. Bodine/SME Award
One SME Drive
P.O. Box 930
Dearborn, MI 48121-0930
(800) 733-4763
(313) 271-1500
http://www.sme.org./

1 award of $5,000 to a student majoring in manufacturing engineering, industrial engineering, or machine tool economics who writes the best graduate-student paper on machine tool justification and its relationship to manufacturing productivity. A $1,500 award is given to the student's major professor. Open to U.S. or Canadian students. Deadline: February 1.

2414.
Society of Manufacturing Engineering Education Foundation
MTM Association for Standards & Research Undergrad Scholarship Fund
One SME Drive
P.O. Box 930
Dearborn, MI 48121-0930
(800) 733-4763
(313) 271-1500
http://www.sme.org/

1 scholarship of $1,000 to a full-time undergraduate student majoring in manufacturing engineering or industrial engineering at an accredited school. Based on interest in work measurement and productivity improvement; must have at least a 3.2 GPA. Deadline: February 1.

2415.
Society of Manufacturing Engineering Education Foundation
Myrtle and Earl Walker Scholarship Fund
One SME Drive
P.O. Box 930
Dearborn, MI 48121-0930
(800) 733-4763
(313) 271-1500
http://www.sme.org/

20 scholarships of $500 to full-time undergraduate students majoring in electrical or electronic engineering, engineering technology, mechanical engineering, or a trade/technical specialty. Must be attending a two- or four-year accredited institution. Applicants must be pursuing a career in manufacturing, robotics, or automated systems, have at least a 3.5 GPA on a 4.0 scale, and have completed at least thirty credit hours. Selection based on application, academic achievement, transcript, essay, and recommendation letters. Open to U.S. and non–U.S. citizens. Other restrictions may apply. Deadline: March 1.

2416.
Society of Manufacturing Engineering Education Foundation
St. Louis Chapter No. 17 Scholarship Fund
One SME Drive
P.O. Box 930
Dearborn, MI 48121-0930
(800) 733-4763
(313) 271-1500
http://www.sme.org/

4 scholarships of $1,000 to undergraduate students majoring in engineering, engineering technology, manufacturing engineering, or industrial engineering. Must be enrolled in a two- or four-year SME-approved institution with an SME student chapter sponsored by St. Louis Chapter No. 17. Selection based on academic achievement, application, transcript, essay, career goals, and recommendation letters. Open to U.S. and non–U.S. citizens. Other restrictions may apply. Deadline: March 1.

2417.
Society of Manufacturing Engineering Education Foundation
Wayne Kay Scholarship
One SME Drive
P.O. Box 930
Dearborn, MI 48121-0930
(800) 733-4763
(313) 271-1500
http://www.sme.org/

10 scholarships of $2,500 to undergraduate students majoring in manufacturing engineering or manufacturing technology. Must have completed thirty credit hours and be student members of SME. Must submit prescribed cover sheet, statement letter, transcript, résumé, essay, and two recommendation letters. Must be enrolled in a two- or four-year SME-approved accredited institution. Open to U.S. and non–U.S. citizens. Other restrictions may apply. Deadline: March 1.

2418.
Society of Manufacturing Engineering Education Foundation
William E. Weisel Scholarship Fund
One SME Drive
P.O. Box 930
Dearborn, MI 48121-0930
(800) 733-4763
(313) 271-1500
http://www.sme.org/

1 scholarship of $1,000 to a full-time undergraduate student majoring in electrical or electronic engineering, engineering technology, mechanical engineering, or a trade/technical specialty. Must be attending a two- or four-year SME-approved accredited institution. Applicant must be pursuing a career in manufacturing, robotics, or automated systems, have at least a 3.5 GPA on a 4.0 scale, and have completed at least thirty credit hours in manufacturing, robotics, or automated systems. Must be a student member of SME. Selection based on application, academic achievement, transcript, essay, and recommendation letters. Open to U.S. and non–U.S. citizens. Other restrictions may apply. Deadline: March 1.

2419.
Society of Mining, Metallurgy & Exploration Coal Division Scholarships
P.O. Box 625002
8307 S. Shaffer Parkway
Littleton, CO 80162-5002
(800) 763-3132
(303) 973-9550
http://www.smenet.org/

Scholarships of up to $1,000 to undergraduate-student SME members who are majoring in mining engineering with an emphasis on coal. Good only at U.S. institutions that are Accreditation Board for Engineering Technology (ABET)-accredited. Must be involved in coal-related activities. Contact the department head of Mining Engineering at the college or university. Deadline: varies.

2420.
Society of Mining, Metallurgy & Exploration Eugene P. Pfleider Memorial Scholarships
P.O. Box 625002
8307 S. Shaffer Parkway
Littleton, CO 80162-5002
(800) 763-3132
(303) 973-9550
http://www.smenet.org/

Scholarships of up to $1,000 to undergraduate sophomores majoring in mining engineering at any U.S. accredited institution that offers a bachelor's degree in mining engineering. Deadline: November 30.

2421.
Society of Mining, Metallurgy & Exploration Industrial Minerals Division Scholarships
P.O. Box 625002
8307 S. Shaffer Parkway
Littleton, CO 80162-5002
(800) 763-3132
(303) 973-9550
http://www.smenet.org/

Scholarships of up to $2,000 to undergraduate juniors or seniors or graduate students majoring in mining engineering, geology, or minerals economics. Good at any U.S. accredited institution offering a bachelor's, master's, or doctorate. Deadline: November 30.

2422.
Society of Mining, Metallurgy & Exploration Mineral & Metallurgical Division Scholarships
P.O. Box 625002
8307 S. Shaffer Parkway
Littleton, CO 80162-5002
(800) 763-3132
(303) 973-9550
http://www.smenet.org/

6 scholarships ranging from $1,000 to $2,000 to undergraduate juniors or seniors majoring in materials science or metallurgy who want a career in the minerals industry. Applicant must have a minimum 2.5 GPA on a 4.0 scale. Good at any U.S. institution accredited by Accreditation Board for Engineering and Technology. Deadline: October 1.

2423.
Society of Mining, Metallurgy & Exploration Mining & Exploration Division Scholarships
P.O. Box 625002
8307 S. Shaffer Parkway
Littleton, CO 80162-5002
(800) 763-3132
(303) 973-9550
http://www.smenet.org/

Amount of award varies. Open to undergraduate students majoring in materials science, metallurgy, mining engineering, geology, or a related area who want a career in the minerals industry. Good at any U.S. accredited institution. Open to U.S. citizens or legal residents. Deadline: November 30.

2424.
Society of Naval Architects and Marine Engineers Scholarships
Robert G. Meade
Executive Director
601 Pavonia Avenue
Jersey City, NJ 07306
(201) 798-4800

Scholarships of $1,000 to undergraduates and from $3,000 and up to graduate students. The society encourages careers in naval architecture, marine engineering, and ocean engineering, but graduate scholarships aren't limited to these areas. Applicant must be U.S. or Canadian citizens. Awards are good at University of California (Berkeley), Florida Atlantic University (Boca Raton), Massachusetts Institute of Technology (Cambridge), University of Michigan (Ann Arbor), University of Newfoundland (St. John's), and the State University of New York Maritime College (Fort Schuyler). Contact the university, not the society. Based on academic achievement, professional promise, and leadership. Deadline: February 1.

2425.
Society of Physics Students (SPS) SPS Scholarships
One Physics Ellipse
College Park, MD 20740
(301) 209-3007
(301) 209-0839 Fax
http://www.aip.org/education/sps/sps.htm
sps@aip.org

3 scholarships of $1,000 for final undergraduate year of full-time study leading to a B.S. degree in physics. Must be SPS members. Based on high scholastic performance, potential for continued scholastic development in physics, and active SPS participation. Deadline: January 31.

2426.
Society of Professional Journalists
Barney Kilgore Freedom of Information Award
16 South Jackson Street
Greencastle, IN 46135-1514
(765) 653-3333
(765) 653-4631 Fax
http://www.spj.org/spjhome.htm

An internship providing $300 per week for eight weeks. The internship is open to undergraduate seniors, journalism graduate students, or law students with a journalism background. The intern may choose the time for the internship. Interns work with members of the Society's Freedom of Information Network. Request applications after November 1. Deadline: January 10.

2427.
Society of the First Infantry Division Foundation Scholarships
5 East Montgomery Avenue
Philadelphia, PA 19118
(215) 233-5444

2 scholarships of $1,000 to high school seniors or undergraduate college students who are children or grandchildren of a First Division veteran. Deadline: August 1.

2428.
Society of Women Engineers
Attn: Executive Assistant
120 Wall Street, 11th Floor
New York, NY 10005-3902
(212) 509-9577
http://www.swe.org/
hq@swe.org

35 scholarships of $1,000 to $2,500 to women in any year (freshman, sophomore, junior, senior, or graduate) of college. Must be majoring in engineering at an Accreditation Board for Engineering and Technology (ABET)-accredited institution.

2429.
Society of Women Engineers
Admiral Grace Murray Hopper Memorial Scholarships
Attn: Executive Assistant
120 Wall Street, 11th Floor
New York, NY 10005-3902
(212) 509-9577
http://www.swe.org/
hq@swe.org

5 scholarships of $1,000 to female entering freshman students majoring in computer science/data processing or engineering/technology. Must be attending a four-year ABET-accredited or SWE-approved institution. Must have at least a 3.5 GPA. Selection based on application, academic achievement, transcript, test scores, career goals, and essay. Must be U.S. citizens. Send a self-addressed, stamped envelope with information request. Other restrictions may apply. Nonrenewable. Deadline: March 15.

2430.
Society of Women Engineers
Anne Maureen Whitney Barrow Memorial Scholarship
Attn: Executive Assistant
120 Wall Street, 11th Floor
New York, NY 10005-3902
(212) 509-9577
http://www.swe.org/
hq@swe.org

1 scholarship of $5,000 to female undergraduate students majoring in engineering or engineering technology. Must be attending a four-year ABET-accredited or SWE-approved institution. Must have at least a 3.5 GPA and be active contributors and supporters of SWE. Selection based on application, academic achievement, transcript, test scores, career goals, and essay. Must be U.S. citizens. Send a self-addressed, stamped envelope with information request. Renewable until bachelor's degree is completed. Other restrictions may apply. Deadline: March 15.

2431.
Society of Women Engineers
Chevron Scholarships
Attn: Executive Assistant
120 Wall Street, 11th Floor
New York, NY 10005-3902
(212) 509-9577
http://www.swe.org/
hq@swe.org

2 scholarships of $2,000 to female students who will be undergraduate sophomores or juniors majoring in engineering (chemical, mechanical, petroleum, or technology). Must be attending a four-year ABET-accredited or SWE-approved institution. Must have at least a 3.5 GPA. Selection based on application, academic achievement, transcript, test scores, career goals, and essay. Must be U.S. citizens. Send a self-addressed, stamped envelope with information request. Nonrenewable. Deadline: February 1.

2432.
Society of Women Engineers
Chrysler Corporation Scholarship
Attn: Executive Assistant
120 Wall Street, 11th Floor
New York, NY 10005-3902
(212) 509-9577
http://www.swe.org/
hq@swe.org

1 scholarship of $1,750 to a female minority student who will be an undergraduate junior or senior majoring in engineering or computer science. Must be active contributor and supporter of SWE. Must be attending a four-year ABET-accredited or SWE-approved institution. Must have at least a 3.5 GPA. Selection based on application, academic achievement, transcript, test scores, career goals, and essay. Must be a U.S. citizen. Send a self-addressed, stamped

envelope with information request. Nonrenewable. Deadline: February 1.

2433.
Society of Women Engineers
David Sarnoff Research Center Scholarship
Attn: Executive Assistant
120 Wall Street, 11th Floor
New York, NY 10005-3902
(212) 509-9577
http://www.swe.org/
hq@swe.org

1 scholarship of $1,500 to a female undergraduate junior who is majoring in electrical, mechanical, or computer engineering at an accredited institution in U.S. Deadline: February 1.

2434.
Society of Women Engineers
Drommond/Grummon Scholarships
Attn: Executive Assistant
120 Wall Street, 11th Floor
New York, NY 10005-3902
(212) 509-9577
http://www.swe.org/
hq@swe.org

2 scholarships of $1,000 and 1 of $1,500 to female juniors or seniors majoring in engineering at accredited institutions in U.S. Deadline: February 1.

2435.
Society of Women Engineers
Dorothy Lemke Howarth Scholarships
Attn: Executive Assistant
120 Wall Street, 11th Floor
New York, NY 10005-3902
(212) 509-9577
http://www.swe.org/
hq@swe.org

5 scholarships of $2,000 to female undergraduate sophomores majoring in engineering or engineering technology. Must be attending a four-year ABET-accredited or SWE-approved institution. Must be active contributors and supporters of SWE. Selection based on application, academic achievement, transcript, test scores, career goals, and essay. Must be U.S. citizens. Send a self-addressed, stamped envelope. Nonrenewable. Other restrictions may apply. Deadline: February 1.

2436.
Society of Women Engineers
General Electric Foundation Scholarship
Attn: Executive Assistant
120 Wall Street, 11th Floor
New York, NY 10005-3902
(212) 509-9577
http://www.swe.org/
hq@swe.org

3 scholarships of $1,000 to outstanding female students who will be incoming freshmen and majoring in engineering. Applications available March through June. When requesting application, enclose a self-addressed,

stamped envelope. Renewable for up to three years. Deadline: July 1.

2437.
Society of Women Engineers
General Motors Foundation Freshmen
  Scholarships
Attn: Executive Assistant
120 Wall Street, 11th Floor
New York, NY 10005-3902
(212) 509-9577
http://www.swe.org/
hq@swe.org

2 scholarships of $1,500 to female undergraduate juniors who are majoring in engineering/technology. Must be enrolled in a four-year ABET-accredited or SWE-approved U.S. institution. Send a self-addressed, stamped envelope with information request. Renewable with continuing academic achievement. Must be U.S. citizens. Other restrictions may apply. Deadline: May 15.

2438.
Society of Women Engineers
GTE Foundation Scholarships
Attn: Executive Assistant
120 Wall Street, 11th Floor
New York, NY 10005-3902
(212) 509-9577
http://www.swe.org/
hq@swe.org

9 scholarships of $1,000 to female students who will be undergraduate sophomores or juniors majoring in electrical engineering or computer science. Must be attending a four-year ABET-accredited or SWE-approved institution. Must have at least a 3.5 GPA, and be active contributors and supporters of SWE. Selection based on application, academic achievement, transcript, test scores, career goals, and essay. Must be U.S. citizens. Applications available March through June. Send a self-addressed, stamped envelope with information request. Nonrenewable. Deadline: February 1.

2439.
Society of Women Engineers
Ivy Parker Memorial Scholarship
Attn: Executive Assistant
120 Wall Street, 11th Floor
New York, NY 10005-3902
(212) 509-9577
http://www.swe.org/
hq@swe.org

1 scholarship of $1,000 to an outstanding female undergraduate junior or senior majoring in engineering. Applications available October through January. Send a self-addressed, stamped envelope with information request. Renewable. Deadline: February 1.

2440.
Society of Women Engineers
Judith Resnik Memorial Scholarship
Attn: Executive Assistant
120 Wall Street, 11th Floor
New York, NY 10005
(212) 509-0224

1 scholarship of $2,000 to female rising senior who is majoring in a space-related engineering field. Must be planning to pursue a career in space industry. Must be a student member of SWE with at least a 3.5 GPA on a 4.0 scale. Selection based on academic achievement, discipline, leadership abilities, and career interest. Must attend a four-year ABET-accredited institution. Must be a U.S. citizen. Applications available from October to January. Send a self-addressed, stamped envelope with information request. Other restrictions may apply. Deadline: February 1.

2441.
Society of Women Engineers
Lillian M. Gilbreth
Attn: Executive Assistant
120 Wall Street, 11th Floor
New York, NY 10005-3902
(212) 509-9577
http://www.swe.org/
hq@swe.org

Scholarships ranging from $750 to $2,500 to women students who are juniors or seniors majoring in engineering at accredited institutions in U.S. Deadline: February 1.

2442.
Society of Women Engineers
MASWE Memorial Scholarships
Attn: Executive Assistant
120 Wall Street, 11th Floor
New York, NY 10005-3902
(212) 509-9577
http://www.swe.org/
hq@swe.org

Scholarships ranging from $750 to $2,500 to female juniors or seniors majoring in engineering at accredited institutions in U.S. Deadline: February 1.

2443.
Society of Women Engineers
Microsoft Corporation Undergraduate
**   Scholarships**
Attn: Executive Assistant
120 Wall Street, 11th Floor
New York, NY 10005
(212) 509-0224
http://www.swe.org/

10 scholarships of $1,000 to female rising undergraduate sophomores or juniors majoring in computer science, computer engineering, or engineering technology. Must exhibit a career interest in the field of computer software. Must be attending a four-year ABET-accredited or SWE-approved institution. Must have at least a 3.5 GPA and be active contributors and supporters of SWE. Selection based on application, academic achievement, transcript, test scores, career goals, and essay. Must be U.S. citizens. Applications available March through June. Send a self-addressed, stamped envelope with information request. Nonrenewable. Other restrictions may apply. Deadline: February 1.

2444.
Society of Women Engineers
NALCO Foundation Scholarship
Attn: Executive Assistant
120 Wall Street, 11th Floor
New York, NY 10005-3902
(212) 509-9577
http://www.swe.org/
hq@swe.org

1 scholarship of $1,000 to an outstanding female college sophomore majoring in engineering. Applications available October through January. Send a self-addressed, stamped envelope with information request. Renewable. Deadline: February 1.

2445.
Society of Women Engineers
Olive Lynn Salembier Scholarship
Attn: Executive Assistant
120 Wall Street, 11th Floor
New York, NY 10005-3902
(212) 509-9577
http://www.swe.org/
hq@swe.org

1 scholarship of $2,000 to a female undergraduate or graduate student who has been out of the engineering job market for a minimum of two years to aid in obtaining the credentials necessary to reenter the job market as an engineer. Must have employment experience in an engineering career field. Must be attending a four-year ABET-accredited or SWE-approved U.S. institution. Selection based on application, academic achievement, transcript, test scores, career goals, and essay. Must be a U.S. citizen. Send a self-addressed, stamped envelope with information request. Nonrenewable. Other restrictions may apply. Deadline: May 15.

2446.
Society of Women Engineers
Rockwell International Corporation Scholarships
Attn: Executive Assistant
120 Wall Street, 11th Floor
New York, NY 10005-3902
(212) 509-9577
http://www.swe.org/
hq@swe.org

2 scholarships of $3,000 to female juniors majoring in engineering at accredited institutions in U.S. Deadline: February 1.

2447.
Society of Women Engineers
SWE Founders Scholarships
Attn: Executive Assistant
120 Wall Street, 11th Floor
New York, NY 10005-3902
(212) 509-9577
http://www.swe.org/
hq@swe.org

Scholarships ranging from $500 to $1,000 to female undergraduate sophomores majoring in engineering at accredited institutions in U.S. Must be student members. Deadline: February 1.

2448.
Society of Women Engineers
SWE Hewlett–Packard Scholarships
Attn: Executive Assistant
120 Wall Street, 11th Floor
New York, NY 10005-3902
(212) 509-9577
http://www.swe.org/
hq@swe.org

7 scholarships of $1,000 to female rising undergraduate juniors or seniors majoring in computer science, computer engineering, or engineering technology. Must be attending a four-year ABET-accredited or SWE-approved institution. Must have at least a 3.5 GPA and be active contributors and supporters of SWE. Selection based on application, academic achievement, transcript, test scores, career goals, and essay. Must be U.S. citizens. Applications available March through June. Send a self-addressed, stamped envelope with information request. Nonrenewable. Other restrictions may apply. Deadline: February 1.

2449.
Society of Women Engineers
Texaco Foundation Scholarships
Attn: Executive Assistant
120 Wall Street, 11th Floor
New York, NY 10005-3902
(212) 509-9577
http://www.swe.org/
hq@swe.org

2 scholarships of $2,000 to outstanding female rising undergraduate juniors majoring in chemical or mechanical engineering. Must be enrolled in a four-year ABET-accredited institution, be student members of SWE, and be in the upper 20 percent of their class. Applications available March through June. Send a self-addressed, stamped envelope with information request. Renewable for two years if class standing is maintained. Other restrictions may apply. Deadline: February 1.

2450.
Society of Women Engineers
TRW Scholarships
Attn: Executive Assistant
120 Wall Street, 11th Floor
New York, NY 10005-3902
(212) 509-9577
http://www.swe.org/
hq@swe.org

10 scholarships ranging from $100 to $500 to female entering undergraduate freshmen planning to major in engineering/technology. Must be planning to enroll in a four-year ABET-accredited or SWE-approved U.S. institution. Send a self-addressed, stamped envelope with information request. Selection based on Best National, Regional, and New Student sections. Nonrenewable. Other restrictions may apply. Deadline: May 15.

2451.
Society of Women Engineers
United Technologies Corporation Scholarships
Attn: Executive Assistant
120 Wall Street, 11th Floor
New York, NY 10005-3902
(212) 509-9577
http://www.swe.org/
hq@swe.org

2 scholarships of $1,000 to sophomore female engineering students to continue their education. Applications available October through January. Send a self-addressed, stamped envelope with information request. Renewable for two years. Deadline: February 1.

2452.
Society of Women Engineers
Westinghouse Scholarships
Attn: Executive Assistant
120 Wall Street, 11th Floor
New York, NY 10005-3902
(212) 509-9577
http://www.swe.org/
hq@swe.org

3 scholarships of $1,000 to female incoming freshmen majoring in engineering. Applications available March through June. Send a self-addressed, stamped envelope with information request. Renewable. Deadline: July 1.

2453.
Soil and Water Conservation Society of America
Donald A. Williams Scholarships
7515 Northeast Ankeny Road
Ankeny, IA 50021-9764
(800) THE SOIL
(515) 289-2331
(515) 289-1227 Fax

Varying numbers of scholarships of $1,200 to society members who are employed in a natural resource-related field and who wish to return to school to improve their technical or administrative skills in the area of business administration/conservation. Attainment of degree isn't required. Send a self-addressed, stamped envelope for information. Deadline: April 1.

2454.
Soil Conservation Society of America
Scholarships
7515 Northeast Ankeny Road
Ankeny, IA 50021-9764
(800) THE SOIL or (515) 289-2331

9 scholarships of $1,000 to students who have completed at least two years of study at an accredited college or university, have at least a 2.5 GPA, and are enrolled in an agricultural or natural-resource-related curriculum. The following majors are accepted: agronomy, soil science, range management, forestry, geography journalism, agricultural education, wildlife management, and other related fields. Deadline: April 1.

2455.
Solomon R. Guggenheim Foundation
Summer Volunteer Internship Program
1071 Fifth Avenue
New York, NY 10128
(212) 360-3540

Stipends provide 35 (ten-week) internships to students majoring in arts administration or art history who have completed at least two years of undergraduate study and are recent graduates or first-year graduate students. Deadline: March 15.

2456.
Sons of Italy Foundation
National Leadership Grants
219 E Street, N.E.
Washington, DC 20002
(202) 547-2900

Grants ranging from $2,000 to $5,000 to full-time undergraduate and graduate students in all areas of study at accredited U.S. institutions. Must be of Italian heritage and demonstrate leadership abilities. Contact local and state lodges for an application and information. To locate local and state lodges, send a self-addressed, stamped envelope with request. Other restrictions may apply. Deadline: March 15.

2457.
Sons of Norway Foundation
King Olav V Norwegian–American Heritage Fund
1455 West Lake Street
Minneapolis, MN 55408
(612) 827-3611

12 awards ranging from $250 to $3,000 to students, eighteen years or older, who have an interest in Norwegian studies or U.S. studies. Good at any recognized institution. Applicant can be U.S., Canadian, or Norwegian citizen. Deadline: March 1.

2458.
Sony Music Entertainment, Inc.
Credited Internship
550 Madison Avenue, 2nd Floor
New York, NY 10022-3211
(212) 833-8000

70 to 80 ten-week summer, fall, and spring internships providing no compensation. Open to undergraduate and graduate students who will be returning to school after the internship and must receive academic credit for the internship. All majors are accepted, but an interest in the music business is an asset. Interns are placed in promotions, publicity, retail marketing, artists and repertoire (A&R), A&R administration, and business affairs. Applicants must submit a cover letter and résumé. Finalists are interviewed in person or by phone. Deadline: rolling.

2459.
Sony Music Entertainment, Inc.
Attn: Department 13-5
Minority Internship
550 Madison Avenue, 13th Floor
New York, NY 10022-3211
(212) 833-8000

45 ten-week summer, fall, and spring internships with compensation varying with the position. Open to minority (African American, Hispanic American, Asian-American, and American Indian) undergraduate and graduate students who will be returning to school after the internship, must receive academic credit for the internship, and have at least a 3.0 GPA. All majors are accepted, but an interest in the music business is an asset. Interns are placed in promotions, publicity, retail marketing, artists and repertoire (A&R), A&R administration, and business affairs. Applicants must submit a cover letter and résumé. Finalists are interviewed in person or by phone. Deadline: April 1.

2460.
Soroptimist International of the Americas
Handicapped Student Scholarships
Two Penn Center Plaza, Suite 1000
Philadelphia, PA 19102-1883
http://www.siahq.com/

Awards of varying amounts to physically disabled young persons between fifteen and thirty-five years of age. May be used in all areas of study at any undergraduate or graduate program of study at any accredited institution. Write for complete details; include a self-addressed, stamped envelope.

2461.
Sotheby's
Internship Program
1334 York Avenue
New York, NY 10021
(212) 606-7000

40 to 50 eight-week summer internships in New York providing no compensation are open to undergraduate juniors and seniors, and recent graduates. Interns are assigned to a client-service department, such as the press office, graphics, or marketing, or in one of thirty-three expert departments, such as American paintings or Chinese works of arts. Interns may be from any major but must have an interest in the auction business. Deadline: March 15.

2462.
Sourisseau Academy for State and Local History
Research Grants
c/o San Jose State University
San Jose, CA 95192
(408) 924-6510
(408) 227-2657

5 to 10 awards of $500 to undergraduate and graduate students to conduct research on California history. Must be attending an accredited U.S. institution. Preference is given to research on Santa Clara County history. Awards are made to help defray project expenses. Other restrictions may apply. Deadline: April 1; November 1.

2463.
South Carolina Higher Education Tuition Grants
Commission
Academic Common Market
P.O. Box 12159
1310 Lady Street
Columbia, SC 29211
(830) 734-1200
(830) 734-1426 Fax
http://www.state.sc.us/edu/

Out-of-state tuition difference is waived for students who are South Carolina residents attending a participating public college or university in a southeastern state. Open to all fields of majors.

2464.
South Carolina Higher Education Tuition Grants Commission
South Carolina National Guard Tuition Assistance
P.O. Box 12159
1310 Lady Street
Columbia, SC 29211
(830) 734-1200
(830) 734-1426 Fax
http://www.state.sc/us/edu/

Up to $500 per year tuition assistance for four years to any member of the South Carolina National Guard or Air National Guard enrolled in a South Carolina institute approved by the State Department of Education. Contact National Guard Armory or the Adjutant General of South Carolina, Rembert C. Dennis Building, 1000 Assembly Street, Columbia, SC 29201.

2465.
South Carolina Higher Education Tuition Grants Commission
Robert C. Byrd Honors Scholarship Program
P.O. Box 12159
1310 Lady Street
Columbia, SC 29211
(830) 734-1200
(830) 734-1426 Fax
http://www.state.sc/us/edu/

Varying numbers of scholarships of $1,500 to graduating high school seniors who are South Carolina residents and who meet two of these three requirements: rank in the top 5 percent of their class, have at least a 3.5 GPA, or have at least an 1100 on SAT or 27 on ACT. Some states offer no direct application; students are nominated by high school counselor. Deadline: May 1.

2466.
South Carolina Higher Education Tuition Grants Commission
South Carolina Tuition Exemptions
P.O. Box 12159
1310 Lady Street
Columbia, SC 29211
(830) 734-1200
(830) 734-1426 Fax
http://www.state.sc/us/edu/

Tuition exemption to students who are dependents of deceased or disabled South Carolina firemen, law officers, members of Civil Air Patrol, or Organized Rescue Squad. Must be attending a public institution in South Carolina. Not based on financial need.

2467.
South Carolina Higher Education Tuition Grants Commission
South Carolina Tuition Grants
P.O. Box 12159
1310 Lady Street
Columbia, SC 29211
(830) 734-1200
(830) 734-1426 Fax
http://www.state.sc/us/edu/

Grants ranging from $100 to $3,000 or tuition (whichever is less) to South Carolina residents accepted for full-time enrollment in a private institution. Contact Tuition Grants Committee, P.O. Box 11638, Columbia, SC 29211.

2468.
South Carolina Higher Education Tuition Grants Commission
Vocational Rehabilitation Benefits
P.O. Box 12159
1310 Lady Street
Columbia, SC 29211
(830) 734-1200
(830) 734-1426 Fax
http://www.state.sc/us/edu/

Scholarships of up to $1,040 to students with a mental or physical disability that is a handicap for employment. Must be residents of South Carolina. Additional funds are available for special services. Based on financial need. Contact nearest Vocational Rehabilitation Office. Deadline: none.

2469.
South Carolina Department of Veterans Affairs
1205 Pendleton Street
Columbia, SC 29201
(803) 765-5198

Tuition waivers to children of war veterans who were residents of South Carolina when they entered the Armed Forces or have resided in South Carolina for eighteen years. Children must be twenty-six years or younger (or up to thirty-first birthday if students were in the Armed Forces, or the veteran parent became eligible between the child's twenty-first and twenty-sixth birthday). Veteran may be alive, disabled due to a service-connected injury, or deceased due to a service-connected injury, or while in combat, may have been a prisoner of war, or have received the Congressional Medal of Honor. If veteran parent is alive, he or she must reside in South Carolina. If veteran parent was a POW, parent may reside anywhere, but must have been a South Carolina resident when entering the service.

2470.
South Carolina Student Loan Corporation
P.O. Box 21487
Columbia, SC 29221
(803) 798-0916
http://www.slc.sc.edu/

Loans of varying amounts to undergraduate and graduate students in all areas of study. Must be enrolled at or accepted to an eligible U.S.-accredited insitution. Open to

U.S. citizens and eligible non-citizens. Amount of loan is determined by cost of education and financial need. The loan must be renewed annually. Deadline: 30 days before end of loan period.

2471.
**South Dakota Department of Education and
 Cultural Affairs**
Incentive Grant Program
Office of the Secretary
700 Governors Drive
Pierre, SD 57501-2291
(605) 773-3134/(605) 773-6139 Fax
http://www.state.sd.us/state

Grants ranging from $100 to $600 to students who are South Dakota residents attending a South Dakota postsecondary institution at least on a half-time basis. Must not owe a refund on any grant or have defaulted on a student loan.

2472.
**South Dakota Department of Education and
 Cultural Affairs**
Robert C. Byrd Honors Scholarship Program
Office of the Secretary
700 Governors Drive
Pierre, SD 57501-2291
(605) 773-3134/(605) 773-6139 Fax
http://www.state.sd.us/state

$1,500 scholarships to students who are South Dakota residents and who meet two of these three requirements: rank in the top 5 percent of class, have at least a 3.5 GPA, or have at least an 1100 on SAT or 27 on ACT. Deadline: May 1.

2473.
**South Dakota Department of Education and
 Cultural Affairs**
Superior Scholar Program
Office of the Secretary
700 Governors Drive
Pierre, SD 57501-2291
(605) 773-3134/(605) 773-6139 Fax
http://www.state.sd.us/state

Scholarships of up to $1,500 per year for four years to students who are selected as National Merit Semifinalists. Must be South Dakota residents attending a South Dakota college. For renewal, students must complete fifteen credit hours per semester and maintain a 3.0 GPA. Deadline: June 1.

2474.
**South Dakota Department of Education and
 Cultural Affairs**
Tuition Equalization Grant Program
Office of the Secretary
700 Governors Drive
Pierre, SD 57501-2291
(605) 773-3134/(605) 773-6139 Fax
http://www.state.sd.us/state

Grants ranging from $100 to $250 or tuition and fees (whichever is less) to undergraduate students who are

South Dakota residents attending a private South Dakota institution. Good for any field of study except theology or religious education. Must not be receiving an athletic scholarship or a South Dakota Student Incentive Grant.

2475.
South Dakota State Board of Regents
Assistance to POW/MIA Dependents
207 East Capitol Avenue
Pierre, SD 57501-2408
(605) 773-3455

Financial assistance providing tuition and fees to dependents of service persons who were listed as prisoners of war or missing in action after January 1, 1940. Must have been a South Dakota resident when entering the Armed Forces or during the time serving in the Armed Forces.

2476.
South Dakota State Board of Regents
Benefits for Visually Impaired Persons
207 East Capitol Avenue
Pierre, SD 57501-2408
(605) 773-3455

Financial assistance providing tuition, library fees, registration fees, and other mandatory fees at any state-supported institution to South Dakota residents who are visually impaired. Will provide benefits up to, but no more than, 225 semester hours.

2477.
**South Dakota State Department of Military and
 Veteran Affairs**
National Guard Educational Benefits
Director of Personnel
2823 West Main
Rapid City, SD 57702-8186

A variety of programs to members of the South Dakota Army and Air National Guard. Includes Army Continuing Education System, Montgomery GI Bill, State 50 percent Free Tuition, Student Loan Repayment, and Simultaneous Membership.

2478.
**South Dakota State University Spring Science
 and Technology Camp**
Biology Department
Brookings, SD 57007
(605) 688-4566
(605) 688-6141

40 different five-day-long science-oriented activities open to students who have completed 6th through 12th grade. Students reside in supervised dormitories. Faculty lead classes in animal science, biology, microbiology, chemistry, physics, computer science, engineering, dairy science, veterinary science, psychology, health, nutrition, pharmacy, plant science, water resources, wildlife, and fisheries. Cost is $163 for residents and $85 for commuters, with limited partial to full scholarships. Deadline: June 1.

2479.
South Seas Plantation
Internship Coordinator
Recreation Department
P.O. Box 194
Captiva Island, FL 33924
(813) 472-5111
(813) 472-7541 Fax

16 fifteen-week internships during the summer, fall, or spring providing $30 per week, free housing, and one free meal per day to undergraduate seniors, recent college graduates, college graduates of any age, and graduate students. International applicants are eligible. Interns work in the recreation department, where they plan social activities, supervise bike and boat rentals, supervise the fitness center, and assist in the coordination of special events such as wine tastings, fun runs, and magic shows. Interns are also exposed to other departments. Deadline: rolling.

2480.
Southwest Review Awards
Elizabeth Matchett Stover Award
Southern Methodist University
6410 Airline Road
Dallas, TX 75275

A $250 award to the author of the best poem published in the magazine during the preceding year. Poetry is not submitted directly for the award but simply for publication in the magazine. From among the poetry published in each two-year period, the judges select the best poetry for the Stover award.

2481.
Southwest Review Awards
John H. McGinnis Memorial Award
Southern Methodist University
6410 Airline Road
Dallas, TX 75275

1 award of $1,000 given each year for the fiction and nonfiction articles selected as the best that have been published in the *Southwest Review* in the previous year. Stories or articles are not submitted directly for the award but simply for publication in the magazine. From among those published in each two-year period, the judges select the best story for the McGinnis award.

2482.
The Sow's Ear Poetry Review
245 McDowell Street
Bristol, TN
(703) 628-2651

1 prize of $500, and publication, is given in poetry. Entries may consist of one to five unpublished poems. No multiple submissions. Reading fee of $2 per poem must be included. Entries must be postmarked in September or October. Deadline: October 31.

2483.
Spense Reese Foundation
Security Pacific National Bank
P.O. Box 3189, Terminal Annex
Los Angeles, CA 90051

14 scholarships of varying amounts, totaling $28,000, to male undergraduate and graduate students. Must be majoring in political science, engineering, medicine, or law. Must be attending an accredited U.S. institution in California. Must be California residents and U.S. citizens. Other restrictions may apply. Deadline: none specified.

2484.
Sponsors for Educational Opportunity
Internship Program
23 Gramercy Park South
New York, NY 10003
(212) 979-2040

125 to 175 summer internships lasting at least ten weeks to minority undergraduate juniors and seniors with at least a 3.0 GPA. The accounting summer program is only open to students with at least three accounting courses. No particular major is required, though the program is looking for students with demonstrated leadership, professionalism, academic excellence, and maturity. Deadline: February 15.

2485.
Spy Internship Program
The SPY Building
5 Union Square West
New York, NY 10003
(212) 633-6550

4 internships providing $50 per week to undergraduate juniors, seniors, graduate students, and recent graduates. Internships last from twelve to twenty-four weeks during the summer, fall, or spring in New York City. Interns at the magazine run errands, photocopy, and are given research assignments where they gather articles and check stories. Though journalism is not a required major, applicants should have gained some writing experience from working on a college publication. Deadline: rolling.

2486.
Stanley Drama Award
Playwriting Awards Competition
c/o Wagner College, Drama Department
631 Howard Avenue
Staten Island, NY 10301
(718) 390-3100

An annual $1,000 award given to the best play or musical submitted to the competition. Script must be unpublished and unproduced and be recommended by a theater professional. Application must accompany script. Previous winners are ineligible. Deadline: June 1.

2487.
State Farm Companies Foundation Scholarships
One State Farm Plaza
Bloomington IL 61710
(309) 766-2039
http://www.state.farm.com/

40 scholarships ranging from $2,000 to $5,000 to students who are children of State Farm agents or employees. Must have been selected as National Merit Finalist by the National Merit Corporation, based on the PSAT/NMSQT. Based on PSAT score, academic record, extracurricular activities, recommendations, and essay. Deadline: December 31.

2488.
State Farm Companies Foundation Scholarships
Exceptional Student Fellowship
One State Farm Plaza
Bloomington, IL 61710
(309) 766-2039
http://www.state.farm.com/

40 scholarships of $3,000 to exceptional full-time junior or senior college students in a business-related field (accounting, statistics, business administration, actuarial science, finance, insurance, investments, marketing), computer science, pre-law, or mathematics. Must be U.S. citizens. Must be nominated by dean or department head. Deadline: February 28.

2489.
Statler Foundation Scholarships
New Hampshire Lodging Association
P.O. Box 1175
Concord, NH 03302-1175
(603) 228-9585

900 scholarships of $500 to undergraduate and graduate students who are accepted to or enrolled full-time at a U.S. institution in an accredited program of study in food management, culinary arts, or hotel-motel management. Renewable. Deadline: April 15.

2490.
Story Line Press
Nicholas Roerich Poetry Prize
Three Oaks Farm
Brownsville, OR 97327-9718
(503) 466-5352

1 prize of $2,000 and publication to a full-length poetry manuscript. Entries must be at least forty-eight pages in length. Writers who have published chapbooks of under thirty-two pages are eligible to submit. Each submission must include a one-paragraph biographical statement, $15 entry fee, and a self-addressed, stamped envelope for manuscript return. Deadline: October 15.

2491.
Stratton Arts Festival
Janeway Fellowship & Juror's Awards
P.O. Box 576
Stratton Mountain, VT 05155
(802) 297-2200

4 fellowships and 6 juror's awards of $500 and $1,000 to undergraduate and graduate students majoring in fine arts, photography, or crafts. Must be Vermont residents and either U.S. citizens or legal residents. Deadline: September 5.

2492.
Student Press Law Center
Internship Program
1735 I Street, N.W., Suite 504
Washington, DC 20006
(202) 466-5242
(202) 466-6326 Fax

8 to 12 internships lasting three months providing a stipend are open to undergraduate students who are journalism or political science majors and law students. Journalism interns produce the *Report*, a thrice-yearly magazine documenting student press cases and controversies and related legislation. Law interns research and write opinion letters, memoranda and briefs on current legal disputes, and articles on completed research. All interns participate in a series of seminars conducted by SPLC and the Reporters Committee on Freedom of the Press. The positions are part- or full-time, with openings year-round. Submit a letter detailing interests, a résumé, and writing samples; must be interviewed by phone. Deadline: June 1 (fall); November 15 (spring); March 1 (summer).

2493.
Sucarnochee Review Poetry/Fiction Award
The Sucarnochee Review
Station 22
Livingston University
Livingston, AL 35470
(205) 652-9661

1 prize of $50 and publication for unpublished work. All submissions to the magazine are considered for the competition. Send a self-addressed, stamped envelope for guidelines. Deadline: None.

2494.
Summerbridge National Internship Program
3101 Washington Street
San Francisco, CA 94115
(415) 749-2037

450 to 500 eight-week summer internships providing a stipend ranging from $750 to $1,500 for undergraduates and $500 for high school sophomores, juniors, and seniors. The internship is meant to introduce students to teaching. Interns teach courses in a variety of areas. Internships are conducted in San Francisco, San Diego, and Ross, CA; New Haven, CT; Miami, FL; Louisville, KY; New Orleans, LA; Cambridge and Concord, MA; Kansas City, MO; Manchester, NH; Bronx, NY; Cincinnati, OH; Portland, OR; Lehigh Valley, PA; Providence, RI; and Hong Kong. Deadline: March 1.

2495.
Supercomputing Program for Undergraduate
 Research (SPUR)
Cornell Theory Center
427 Rhodes Hall
Ithaca, NY 14853-3801
(607) 254-8813
(607) 254-8888 Fax
http://www.tc.cornell.edu/EDU/SPUR
spur@tc.cornell.edu

Stipends of $2,000 plus a travel allowance to undergraduate students to conduct a nine-week training and research program in computational science. Must be U.S. citizens or permanent residents. Must have relevant course work for their research area, as well as course work or programming experience in Fortran or C. Previous SPUR participants are ineligible. Information and applications can be obtained on the Internet. Deadline: February 28.

2496.
Supreme Court of the United States
Judicial Internship Program
Office of the Administrative Assistant of the Chief Justice
Room 5
Washington, DC 20543
(202) 479-3374

2 three-to-four-month summer, fall, or winter internships to undergraduate juniors, seniors, and recent graduates. Students from all majors may apply, but should have taken some course work on constitutional law or the Supreme Court. Though interns answer to the administrative assistant, students typically work with a Judicial Fellow who is a lawyer or professor serving a year-long Judicial Fellowship at the Court. Deadline: March 10 (summer); June 1 (fall); October 10 (winter).

2497.
Surfrider Foundation
Internship Program
122 South El Camino Real, Number 67
San Clemente, CA 92672
(800) 743-SURF

12 internships providing no compensation are open to high school, undergraduate, and graduate students, and recent college graduates to work in environmental activism projects. Internship can last from eight weeks to one year and are conducted year-round in San Clemente. Deadline: rolling (at least three weeks before starting date).

2498.
The Swiss Benevolent Society of Chicago
P.O. Box 2137
Chicago, IL 60690

34 scholarships of $750 to high school seniors of Swiss descent. Must be residents of Illinois, Indiana, Iowa, Michigan, or Wisconsin. Deadline: March 31.

2499.
Synod of the Trinity Appalachian Scholarship
Program
3040 Market Street
Camp Hill, PA 17011
(717) 737-0421

225 scholarships ranging from $300 to $800 to students of Pennsylvania, West Virginia, or parts of Ohio who are Presbyterian or attend Synod-related schools (Beaver, Davis and Elkins, Grove City College, Lafayette, Waynesburg, Westminister, or Wilson). Deadline: March 1.

2500.
Tailhook Association
Captain Grant L. Donnelly & Admiral Jimmy
  Thach Memorial Scholarship Awards
P.O. Box 40
Bonita, CA 92002
(619) 479-8525

4 scholarships of $1,000 are available to members, dependents, or individuals sponsored by members who are accepted at an accredited four-year program in aerospace education. Based on academic achievement and citizenship. Deadline: July 15.

2501.
Tandy Technology Scholars
Scholarship Coordinator
P.O. Box 32897, TCU Station
Fort Worth, TX 76129

100 scholarships of $1,000 to graduating high school seniors who have excelled in math, science, or computer science. Must be nominated by high school principal. Cannot apply directly. Nominated students must be in the upper 25 percent of their class, have at least a 3.0 GPA, and be under twenty-one years of age. Can only be used for undergraduate study. Based on academic achievement, SAT/ACT scores, essay, and recommendations. Deadline: October 1.

2502.
Tanglewood Music Center Fellowship Program
Symphony Hall
Boston, MA 02115
(617) 266-5241

Tuition costs for an entire summer session at Tanglewood are available. Depending on financial need, some applicants are also provided room and board in the center's dormitories. Those who can will be asked to pay their own dorm fees. In addition, students may qualify (upon special application) for one of a limited number of stipends available in cases of extreme financial need. Designed to meet the needs of young instrumentalists, singers, composers, and conductors who have completed most of their formal training and who are active performers, focusing on performance in chamber music, orchestral music, and contemporary music. Must be competent musicians and active performers. Applicants must be at least eighteen years of age.

2503.
Target All-Around Scholarship Program

1,490 scholarships of $1,000 and 1 scholarship of $10,000 to graduating high school seniors who will be attending a two- or four-year college, university, or vocational or technical school in the U.S. Awards are based on community service, a one-page essay on volunteer service, activities résumé, recommendation letter, and at least a "C" average GPA. Obtain a copy of the application form from local Target stores. Deadline: varies from late October to mid-December.

2504.
TBWA
Internship Program
TBWA House
292 Madison Avenue
New York, NY 10017
(212) 725-1150

8 to 12 ten-week summer internships providing $225 per week are open to undergraduate students in any major. Applicants must demonstrate a consuming interest in the advertising business and have a point of view about it. Selection is based on work experience, extracurricular work, and personal interests. Interns work in market research (investigating potential clients and what the agency can do for them), account management (the agency's billing and budgeting department), and media (projects determine the best media—television, newspaper, magazines, etc.) for TBWA's clients. Students must submit a résumé and a cover letter explaining why they are seeking the job. Live interviews are mandatory for all but overseas students. Deadline: April 1.

2505.
Technical Marketing Society of America (TMSA) Scholarship
3711 Long Beach Boulevard, Suite 609
Long Beach, CA 90807
(213) 595-0254

$750 scholarship to a dependent of a member or to a member of TMSA who is enrolled in an undergraduate degree program in marketing, business, or engineering at an accredited four-year college or university. Must maintain a 3.0 GPA. Deadline: October 31.

2506.
Tennessee Higher Education Commission
Tennessee Academic Scholars Program
Parkway Towers, Suite 1900
404 James Robertson Parkway
Nashville, TN 37219
(800) 342-1663 or (615) 741-1346
http://www.state.tn.us/edu.htm

Scholarships of up to $4,000 (50 percent provided by the state and 50 percent provided by the institution) to Tennessee-resident students who are attending a Tennessee institution. Must have scored in at least the 95th percentile of the SAT or ACT and have at least a 3.5 GPA in high school. Based on academic record, SAT, and leadership. Deadline: February 15.

2507.
Tennessee Higher Education Commission
Tennessee Benefits for Children of Veterans
Parkway Towers, Suite 1900
404 James Robertson Parkway
Nashville, TN 37219
(800) 342-1663 or (615) 741-1346
http://www.state.tn.us/edu.htm

Free tuition and fees to children of veterans who were killed in action, died from a service-connected injury, or were listed as a prisoner of war or missing in action during the Vietnam War. Veteran parent must have been a Tennessee resident when entering the service. Students must be Tennessee residents and under twenty-one years of age.

2508.
Tennessee Higher Education Commission
Tennessee Minority Teaching Fellows Program
Parkway Towers, Suite 1900
404 James Robertson Parkway
Nashville, TN 37219
(800) 342-1663
(615) 741-1346
http://www.state.tn.us/edu.htm

Fellowships of $5,000 per year to minority graduating high school seniors and undergraduate students. High school seniors must have at least a 2.75 GPA on a 4.0 scale. Undergraduate students must have at least a 2.5 GPA on a 4.0 scale. All applicants must have scored at least 850 on SAT or 18 on ACT, be in the top 25 percent of their high school class, be Tennessee residents, and attend a Tennessee institution. Recipients must agree to teach a K-12 level in a Tennessee public school one year for each year the award is received. Renewable with satisfactory academic progress. Obtain application from high school counselor, college financial aid office, or above address. Deadline: April 15.

2509.
Tennessee Higher Education Commission
Tennessee Ned McWherter Scholars Program
Parkway Towers, Suite 1900
404 James Robertson Parkway
Nashville, TN 37219
(800) 342-1663
(615) 741-1346
http://www.state.tn.us/edu.htm

Scholarships of up to $6,000 to graduating high school seniors. Must have at least a 3.5 GPA and at least 1280 on SAT or 29 on ACT. Must be a Tennessee resident and attend an eligible Tennessee institution. Selection is based on academic achievement, goals, leadership abilities, and potential, and is highly competitive. Obtain applications from high school counselor or above address. Deadline: February 15.

2510.
Tennessee Higher Education Commission
Tennessee Robert C. Byrd Scholarship Program
Parkway Towers, Suite 1900
404 James Robertson Parkway
Nashville, TN 37219
(800) 342-1663
(615) 741-1346
http://www.state.tn.us/edu.htm

Scholarships of up to $1,500 to graduating high school seniors or GED recipients. The award must be utilized the same year of graduation or receipt of GED. Must have at least a 3.5 GPA on a 4.0 scale or have scored at least 57 on GED. Students with at least a 3.0 GPA in high school must have scored at least a 1090 on SAT or 24 on ACT. Must be Tennessee residents and attend a Tennessee institution. Renewable up to four years. Deadline: April 1.

2511.
Tennessee Higher Education Commission
Tennessee Student Assistance Awards
Parkway Towers, Suite 1900
404 James Robertson Parkway
Nashville, TN 37219
(800) 342-1663
(615) 741-1346
http://www.state.tn.us/edu.htm

Grants of up to $1,530 to part-time or up to $3,450 to full-time students are open to graduating high school seniors and undergraduate students. Must be Tennessee residents, attending an eligible Tennessee institution, eligible for a Pell Grant, and U.S. citizens. Selection based on financial need. Must file FAFSA. Obtain application from high school counselor, college/university financial aid office, or above address. Deadline: May 1.

2512.
Tennessee Higher Education Commission
Tennessee Teaching Scholars Program
Parkway Towers, Suite 1900
404 James Robertson Parkway
Nashville, TN 37219
(800) 342-1663
(615) 741-1346
http://www.state.tn.us/edu.htm

Forgivable loans of up to $3,000 to undergraduate juniors, seniors, and postgraduate students admitted to state-approved teacher education programs. Must be Tennessee residents, attending an eligible Tennessee institution, U.S. citizens, and have at least a 2.75 GPA. Must promise to teach at a public preschool, elementary, or secondary school in Tennessee one year for each year the award is received or award must be repaid. Obtain applications from Teacher Education Program, financial aid office, or above address. Deadline: April 15.

2513.
Texas AFL–CIO Scholarships
P.O. Box 12727
1106 Lavaca
Austin, TX 78711
(512) 477-6195

Up to 15 scholarships of $1,000 to high school seniors who are children of members of affiliated AFL-CIO unions. Selection based on academic and financial criteria and Texas residency. Contact local Central Labor Councils. Deadline: January 31.

2514.
Texas Baptist Ethnic Missions Scholarship
    Program
Ethnic Missions
Ethnic Missions Scholarship Committee
333 North Washington
Dallas, TX 75246-1798

Scholarships of varying amounts to minority students attending a Texas Baptist University. Must be U.S. citizens, have at least a 3.0 GPA for last three high school years, and be a member of a Southern Baptist Church or Mission.

2515.
Texas Central Labor Council
Raymond J. Beal Scholarship/Steward W. "Red"
    Goble Scholarship
Smith County Central Labor Council
Route 11, P.O. Box 258
Tyler, TX 75709

2 scholarships of $250 to high school seniors who are children of members of affiliates of the Smith County Central Labor Council. Must be entering first year of college or trade school. Deadline: early fall.

2516.
Texas Department of Transportation
Conditional Grant Program
Attn: Faye Bomar
Division of Civil Rights D-14
125 East 11th Street
Austin, TX 78701-2483
(512) 475-3116

Approximately 35 scholarships providing tuition and fees up to $2,500 (depending on student's financial need) to minority students showing an aptitude for engineering and who meet other criteria. In exchange for the scholarship, student agrees to work for the department for two years after graduation. Deadline: March 1.

2517.
Texas Floral Endowment
Alamo Area Allied Florist Association Scholarship
P.O. Box 140255
8309 Cross Park Drive
Austin, TX 78714

1 scholarship of $500 to any individual who has been employed for at least a year as a retail or wholesale florist or in the growers profession. The award may be used at any accredited floral design school, state association credentialed class, community college, or four-year university. A 500-word essay is required on the individual's goals and how the award would be utilized in assisting him/her in attaining those goals. Preference will be given to San Antonio residents. Award must be used within two years. Deadline: June 1.

2518.
Texas Floral Endowment
Allied Florist of Dallas Scholarship
P.O. Box 140255
8309 Cross Park Drive
Austin, TX 78714

1 scholarship of $750 to any floral industry person to attend the Texas State Florists' Association Texas Certified Florist Program, which is conducted annually. Preference will be given to Dallas residents. Award must be used within two years. Deadline: June 1.

2519.
Texas Floral Endowment
Allied Florist of Houston Scholarship
P.O. Box 140255
8309 Cross Park Drive
Austin, TX 78714

1 scholarship of $765 to any floral industry person to attend the Texas State Florists' Association Texas Certified Florist Program, conducted annually. Selection based on criteria established by the Texas Certified Florist Program. Preference will be given to Houston residents. Award must be used within two years. Deadline: June 1.

2520.
Texas Floral Endowment
Bud and Marian Montague Memorial
  Scholarship
P.O. Box 140255
8309 Cross Park Drive
Austin, TX 78714

1 scholarship of $250 to any high school senior who will be entering Texas A&M University and is interested in the field of floristry. The award is a tribute to Bud and Marian Montague of East Texas Foliage of Fort Worth, Texas. Award must be used within two years. Deadline: June 1.

2521.
Texas Floral Endowment
Fort Worth Florist Association Scholarship
P.O. Box 140255
8309 Cross Park Drive
Austin, TX 78714

1 scholarship of $500 to any individual who has been employed for at least a year as a retail or wholesale florist or in the growers profession. The award may be used at any accredited floral design school, state association credentialed class, community college, or four-year university. A 500-word essay is required on the individual's goals and how the award would be utilized in assisting him/her in attaining those goals. Preference will be given to Fort Worth residence. Award must be used within two years. Deadline: June 1.

2522.
Texas Floral Endowment
James A. Kana Memorial Scholarship
P.O. Box 140255
8309 Cross Park Drive
Austin, TX 78714

1 scholarship of $600 to any person employed in a florist shop who is thirty years or older and is pursuing a career in the floral industry. The award may be applied toward the course of his/her choice at the Buddy Benz School. This award is funded by Tom Crow, President of Alamo Plants and Petals, Inc., in memory of James A. Kana, who had a strong belief in education. Award must be used within two years. Deadline: June 1.

2523.
Texas Floral Endowment
James A. Kana Texas Cup Memorial Scholarship
P.O. Box 140255
8309 Cross Park Drive
Austin, TX 78714

1 scholarship of $500 to the current year's Texas State Florists' Association Texas Cup Winner, to be used as a full registration for the AIFD National Symposium. This award is funded by Tom Crow, President of Alamo Plants and Petals, Inc., in memory of James A. Kana, who had a strong belief in education and who was a former Texas Cup Winner. Award must be used within two years. Deadline: June 1.

2524.
Texas Floral Endowment
Lunn Larry McLean Scholarship
P.O. Box 140255
8309 Cross Park Drive
Austin, TX 78714

1 scholarship of $500 to any individual who is pursuing a floral career. The award may be used at any accredited floral design school, state association credentialed class, community college, or four-year university. Award must be used within two years. Deadline: June 1.

2525.
Texas Floral Endowment
North Texas Telefora Unit Scholarship
P.O. Box 140255
8309 Cross Park Drive
Austin, TX 78714

1 scholarship of $525 to any floral industry person to further the applicant's education in horticulture and/or floriculture. The award may be used at any accredited floral design school, state technical school, state association credentialed class, community college, or four-year university. A 500-word essay is required on the individual's goals and how the award would be utilized in assisting him/her in attaining those goals. Award must be used within two years. Deadline: June 1.

2526.
Texas Floral Endowment
Redbook Florist Services Scholarship
P.O. Box 140255
8309 Cross Park Drive
Austin, TX 78714

1 scholarship of $1,000 to any individual affiliated with Redbook Florist Services. The purpose is to assist the individual's education in horticulture and floriculture. The award may be used at a regional, state, or national Floral Industry Convention, any accredited floral design school, state association credentialed class, community college, or four-year university. Award may not be used at any wire service program not associated with Redbook Florist Services. Award must be used within two years. Deadline: June 1.

2527.
Texas Floral Endowment
Seymour Carren Memorial Scholarship
P.O. Box 140255
8309 Cross Park Drive
Austin, TX 78714

1 scholarship of $500 to any deserving high school student who is interested in entering the field of floristry. The award may be used at any accredited floral design school, state association credentialed class, community college, or four-year university. The award is a tribute to the late Mr. Seymour Carren of Carren's Flowers in Dallas, Texas, by

Teleflora. Award must be used within two years. Deadline: June 1.

2528.
Texas Floral Endowment
Texas State Florists Association Past President's Scholarship
P.O. Box 140255
8309 Cross Park Drive
Austin, TX 78714

1 scholarship of $500 to any floral industry person to attend the Texas State Florists' Association Texas Certified Florist Program. Applicants must meet certain criteria established by the Texas Certified Florist Program. Award must be used within two years. Deadline: June 1.

2529.
Texas Floral Endowment
Wolfe Greenhouse Scholarship
P.O. Box 140255
8309 Cross Park Drive
Austin, TX 78714

1 scholarship of $500 to any deserving high school senior or undergraduate who is interested in a career in floriculture. Applicant must be studying in the fields of floral design or horticulture. This award may be used at any accredited floral design school, state association credentialed class, community college, or four-year university. Must submit a short essay on the individual's goals in floriculture, how the award would be utilized in assisting him/her in attaining those goals, and why the student is deserving of this scholarship. Award must be used within two years. Deadline: June 1.

2530.
Texas Hearing Aid Association Memorial Scholarship Fund
Mr. Jim Wilson, Executive Secretary
Texas Hearing Aid Association
222 North Riverside
Fort Worth, TX 76111

1 scholarship of varying amount to a graduating high school senior. Must be a child or stepchild of a deceased or current member of the Texas Hearing Aid Association who meets certain criteria. Write for more information. Deadline: July 31.

2531.
Texas Higher Education Coordinating Board
Early High School Graduation Scholarships
P.O. Box 12788, Capitol Station
Austin, TX 78711
(512) 483-6101
(512) 483-6169 Fax
http://www.state.tx.us/agency

Scholarships of varying amounts to students who graduate from a public high school in no more than thirty-six consecutive months. Must have attended a Texas public high school, be Texas residents, and attend a Texas college or university. May enroll on a part- or full-time basis.

2532.
Texas Higher Education Coordinating Board
Fifth Year Accountancy Scholarship Program
P.O. Box 12788, Capitol Station
Austin, TX 78711
(512) 483-6101
(512) 483-6169 Fax
http://www.state.tx.us/agency

Scholarships of up to $3,000 or student's financial need (whichever is less) to undergraduate students who are fifth-year accounting students and enrolled at least part-time. Must intend to take the CPA exam. GPA must equal that which is required for graduation. May be Texas residents or nonresidents. Obtain information from school's financial aid office.

2533.
Texas Higher Education Coordinating Board
General Scholarships for Nursing Students
P.O. Box 12788, Capitol Station
Austin, TX 78711
(512) 483-6101
(512) 483-6169 Fax
http://www.state.tx.us/agency

Scholarships of $1,500 for LVN students and $2,000 for ADN, BSN, or graduate nursing students are open to undergraduate and graduate students enrolled at least part-time. Must be Texas residents and attending an eligible Texas institution. Obtain guidelines from school's director of financial aid.

2534.
Texas Higher Education Coordinating Board
Outstanding Rural Scholar Program
P.O. Box 12788, Capitol Station
Austin, TX 78711
(512) 483-6101
(512) 483-6169 Fax
http://www.state.tx.us/agency

Loans of varying amounts to graduating high school seniors and undergraduate or graduate students who are pursuing a health-related program. Must be in the top 25 percent of their class, have at least a 3.0 GPA, and enroll, at least, on a part-time basis. Must be Texas residents and promise to work one year for a sponsoring community for each year of support while in college. Sponsoring community must be located in a non-metropolitan county in Texas. Selection is based on academic achievement, personal credentials, and career goals. For an application, contact: Center for Rural Health Initiatives, 211 East 7th Street, Suite 915, Austin, TX 78701, or call (512) 479-8891.

2535.
Texas Higher Education Coordinating Board
Robert C. Byrd Honors Scholarships
P.O. Box 12788, Capitol Station
Austin, TX 78711
(512) 483-6101
(512) 483-6169 Fax
http://www.state.tx.us/agency

Scholarships of $1,500 to graduating high school seniors or GED recipients. Based on outstanding academic record,

GPA, rank in class or GED equivalent, SAT/ACT scores, and school recommendation. Students are unable to apply directly. High school counselors or GED training center directors nominate three of the most academically eligible candidates to the Texas Higher Education Coordinating Board.

2536.
Texas Higher Education Coordinating Board Scholarships for Ethnic Minorities in Nursing
P.O. Box 12788, Capitol Station
Austin, TX 78711
(512) 483-6101
(512) 483-6169 Fax
http://www.state.tx.us/agency

Scholarships of $1,500 for licensed vocational nursing students and $2,000 for an associate's degree, bachelor's, or master's degree nursing students are open to minority graduating high school seniors, high school graduates, undergraduate, and graduate students enrolled at least part-time. Must be Texas residents and attending an eligible Texas institution. Obtain guidelines from school's director of financial aid.

2537.
Texas Higher Education Coordinating Board Scholarships for Rural BSN or Graduate Nursing Students
P.O. Box 12788, Capitol Station
Austin, TX 78711
(512) 483-6101
(512) 483-6169 Fax
http://www.state.tx.us/agency

Scholarships of $2,500 for undergraduate or graduate students pursuing a professional nursing degree and enrolled at least part-time. Must be Texas residents, attending an eligible Texas institution, and from a rural county in Texas. Obtain guidelines from school's director of financial aid.

2538.
Texas Higher Education Coordinating Board Scholarships for Rural Nursing Students
P.O. Box 12788, Capitol Station
Austin, TX 78711
(512) 483-6101
(512) 483-6169 Fax
http://www.state.tx.us/agency

Scholarships of $1,500 for licensed vocational nursing students, $1,500 for an associate's degree program, and $2,000 for bachelor's or master's degree nursing students are open to minority graduating high school seniors, high school graduates, undergraduate, and graduate students enrolled at least part-time. Must be Texas residents, attending an eligible Texas institution, and from a rural county in Texas. Obtain guidelines from school's director of financial aid.

2539.
Texas Higher Education Coordination Board State Scholarship for Ethnic Recruitment (SSER) Program
P.O. Box 12788, Capitol Station
Austin TX 78711
(512) 483-6101
(512) 483-6169 Fax
http://www.state.tx.us/agency

Scholarships of up to $2,000 to minority graduating high school seniors. Must be members of an ethnic group that comprises less than 40 percent of the enrollment at a public four-year Texas institution. Students must score at least a 750 on SAT or 17 on ACT. Transfer students must have at least a 2.5 GPA on a 4.0 scale. Must have recommendation of admissions officer or minority affairs officer. Texas residency required. Contact above address or financial aid officer at the public institution in which enrollment is planned.

2540.
Texas Higher Education Coordinating Board State Student Incentive Grant Program (SSIG)
P.O. Box 12788, Capitol Station
Austin, TX 78711
(512) 483-6101
(512) 483-6169 Fax
http://www.state.tx.us/agency

Grants of approximately $323 for students at public schools or $748 for students at independent, private schools. If attending a public Texas school, students must receive a SIG; if at a private school, must receive a TEG of equal or greater amount.

2541.
Texas Higher Education Coordination Board Student Incentive Grant (SIG) Program
P.O. Box 12788, Capitol Station
Austin, TX 78711
(512) 483-6101
(512) 483-6169 Fax
http://www.state.tx.us/agency

Grants of up to $1,250 or student's financial need, whichever is less, to graduating high school seniors, undergraduate, or graduate students. Students must either be Texas residents or National Merit Scholars and be enrolled at least half-time in an accredited public college or university in Texas. Students must demonstrate financial need. Student cannot be on an athletic scholarship or enrolled in a religion-degree program. Obtain guidelines from school's financial aid office.

2542.
Texas Higher Education Coordinating Board Texas Public Education Grant (TPEG)
P.O. Box 12788, Capitol Station
Austin, TX 78711
(512) 483-6101
(512) 483-6169 Fax
http://www.state.tx.us/agency

Grants of varying amounts to graduating high school seniors, undergraduate, and graduate students. Based on financial need. Must be Texas residents, attending eligible Texas institutions, and demonstrate financial need. Must file FAFSA. Obtain guidelines from school's financial aid office.

2543.
Texas Higher Education Coordinating Board
Texas Tuition Assistance Grant Program (TTAG)
P.O. Box 12788, Capitol Station
Austin, TX 78711
(512) 483-6101
(512) 483-6169 Fax
http://www.state.tx.us/agency

Grants of varying amounts to graduating high school seniors, high school graduates who graduated within the last two years, and undergraduate students. Must be Texas residents, attending an eligible Texas institution. High school GPA must have been at least 80 on a 100 scale. Renewable with 2.5 GPA on a 4.0 scale. Must not have a conviction on a felony or a crime involving moral turpitude. Amount of award is the lesser of the student's financial need or amount of public school tuition. Obtain information from school's financial aid office.

2544.
Texas Higher Education Coordination Board
Texas Waivers of Nonresident Tuition
P.O. Box 12788, Capitol Station
Austin, TX 78711
(512) 483-6101
(512) 483-6169 Fax
http://www.state.tx.us/agency

This program is different from the Tuition Exemption Program. It allows those students who would be subject to nonresident tuition fees to qualify for resident fees. The following categories qualify for such consideration: Aliens under Permanent Residence Visa; Competitive Scholarship Winners; Faculty, Staff and Dependents; Junior College and Upper Level University Students in Reciprocity Areas of their states; Military personnel and dependents; and students paying real estate taxes in a junior college district.

2545.
Texas Higher Education Coordination Board
Tuition and/or Fee Exemption Programs
P.O. Box 12788, Capitol Station
Austin, TX 78711
(512) 483-6101
(512) 483-6169 Fax
http://www.state.tx.us/agency

The following programs offer exemptions from certain tuition and fee charges at all state-supported public colleges: AFDC Students, Children of Disabled Firemen and Policemen, Children of Prisoners of War or Persons Missing in Action, Deaf and/or Blind Persons, Firemen Enrolled in Fire Science Courses, Foster Care Students, Highest Ranking High School Graduate, ROTC/National Guard Students, Students from Other Nations of the American Hemisphere, Senior Citizens, Veterans and Dependents. To apply for any of these programs, contact the financial aid officer of the public college or university in which you will be or are enrolled.

2546.
Texas Higher Education Coordinating Board
Tuition Equalization Grant (TEG)
P.O. Box 12788, Capitol Station
Austin, TX 78711
(512) 483-6101
(512) 483-6169 Fax
http://www.state.tx.us/agency

Grants of up to $2,640 or student's financial need (whichever is less) to graduating high school seniors, undergraduate, and graduate students. Based on financial need. Must be Texas residents, attending eligible independent Texas institutions, and demonstrate financial need. Must file FAFSA. May not be on athletic scholarship or pursuing a theology or religion major. Obtain guidelines from school's financial aid office.

2547.
Texas Library Association
CULD Research Grant
3355 Bee Cave Road, Suite 401
Austin, TX 78746

1 grant of varying amount to an undergraduate student majoring in library science. Must be a Texas resident. Other restrictions may apply. Send a self-addressed, stamped envelope for more information. Deadline: February 1.

2548.
Texas Library Association
TLA Research Grant
3355 Bee Cave Road, Suite 401
Austin, TX 78746

1 research grant of up to $2,000 to an undergraduate student majoring in library science. Must be a Texas resident. Other restrictions may apply. Send a self-addressed, stamped envelope for more information. Deadline: February 1.

2549.
Texas Restaurant Association for Food
  Service Scholarships
W. Price Jr. Scholarships
Attn: Educational Director
Texas Restaurant Association
P.O. Box 1429
Austin TX 78767
(512) 472-3666

Scholarships of varying amounts to assist in covering tuition and fees to undergraduate students pursuing careers in restaurant management, hotel/motel management, or a food-related area. Must be Texas residents. Must attend a specific institution in Texas. Other restrictions may apply. Deadline: April 10.

2550.
Texas Society for Biomedical Research (TSBR) Art/Essay Contest
401 West 15th Street, Suite #690
Austin, TX 78701
(512) 370-1660

2 prizes of $500 and 3 prizes of $250 awarded to junior and senior Texas high school students who write an essay or design a poster on "Why Animals Are Important to Biomedical Research." Based on form and content. Judging will be done by TSBR Board of Scientific Advisors, the Texas Education Agency, and Texas Medical Association staff. Deadline: early February (postmark).

2551.
Texas Society of Professional Engineers
P.O. Box 2145
Austin, TX 78768

Scholarships of $1,000 and $2,000 for an engineering curriculum. Designated engineering scholarships requiring that a specific university be attended or a specific program of engineering study be pursued are also offered. Must be Texas resident. Deadline: mid-November; may vary.

2552.
Texas State Council Knights of Columbus Scholarships
2500 Columbus Drive
Austin, TX 78746

10 grants of $1,000 to high school seniors and undergraduate students who are members or sons, daughters, or wives of members. Application requests should be sent to above address. Deadline: March 31.

2553.
Texas State Firemen and Fire Marshals Association
Attn: Scholarship Chairperson
1000 Brazos Street
Austin, TX 78701-2446
(512) 454-3473
http://www.tsaff.org

2 scholarships of $200 to graduating high school seniors. Must be dependents of members of the Ladies Auxiliary who are in good standing and have been members for at least one year. Also available to dependents of deceased or disabled Texas firefighters. Father must be or have been in good standing with the Texas Fire Fighters Labor Union. SAT or ACT required. When requesting an application, send a #10 self-addressed, stamped envelope and request it be sent to the scholarship chairperson. Deadline May 1.

2554.
Theta Delta Chi Educational Foundation Scholarships
135 Bay State Road
Boston, MA 02215
Written inquiries only

Scholarships of $1,000 to undergraduate and graduate students in all areas of study who are active members of TDC. Based on academic achievement, service to fraternity, extracurricular activities, promise of success, and financial need. Deadline: April 30.

2555.
Third Marine Division Association Memorial Scholarships
Memorial Scholarship Fund
P.O. Box 634
Inverness, FL 32651

Grants from $400 to $2,400 to students who are children of marine and naval personnel who died or were 100 percent permanently disabled while in the 3rd Marine Division in Vietnam during the Vietnam War, or dependent children of a regular (living or deceased) member of the association for at least two years.

2556.
Thirty-Seventh Division Veterans Association Scholarships
Headquarters
65 South Front Street, Room 717
Columbus, OH 43215
(614) 228-3788

At least 2 scholarships of $500 to students who are dependents of veterans of the 37th Division during WWI, WWII, or the Korean War. Based on financial need. Deadline: April 1.

2557.
3M
Staffing & College Relations
224 1W-02
3M Center
St. Paul, MN 55144-1000
(800) 328-1343
http://www.mmm.com

200 fourteen-week summer internships providing a stipend ranging from $425 to $500 per week for undergraduates and from $550 to $650 for graduate students. Students can work in St. Paul, MN; Austin, TX; or in one of eighty plants throughout the country (one is located in North Carolina). Majors accepted: biology, chemistry, computer science, engineering (chemical, electrical, mechanical, industrial, and ceramic), materials science, and physics. For finance positions, applicants must be seniors in accounting or business, though a few sophomores, juniors, and MBA candidates have been accepted. For marketing positions, applicants must be seniors pursuing marketing-related degrees, including communications, journalism, or advertising; MBA candidates are also eligible. All students must have at least a 3.0 GPA. Deadline: December 1.

2558.
Tower Hill Botanic Garden Scholarship Program
Worcester County Horticulture Society
Boylston, MA 01505
(508) 869-611

Scholarships ranging from $500 to $2,000 to undergraduate juniors, seniors, or graduate students majoring in horticulture or a horticulture-related area. Must reside in New England or attend a college or university in New

England. Selection based on interest in horticulture, purpose, academic achievement, and financial need. Send a self-addressed, stamped envelope for information. Deadline: May 1.

2559.
Transportation Clubs International (TCI)
Scholarship Committee Chairperson
1275 Kamus Drive, Suite 101
Fox Island, WA 98333
(206) 549-2257

Scholarships of $1,000 to students attending vocational/ technical school who are TCI members or dependents. Applicants for either award must be pursuing a career in transportation or traffic management. Please include a self-addressed, stamped envelope with application request. Deadline: March 31.

2560.
Transportation Clubs International (TCI)
Charlotte Woods Memorial Scholarship
Scholarship Committee Chairperson
1275 Kamus Drive, Suite 101
Fox Island, WA 98333
(206) 549-2257

1 scholarship of $1,000 to a student who is a TCI member or a dependent of a member. Must be in a degree program in the fields of transportation, traffic management, or other related areas (such as marketing economics, etc.), and in pursuit of a career in transportation. Deadline: April 15.

2561.
Transportation Clubs International
Emma Kentz Memorial Scholarship
Scholarship Committee Chairperson
1275 Kamus Drive, Suite 101
Fox Island, WA 98333
(206) 549-2257

1 scholarship of up to $1,000 is available to a female student enrolled in an accredited institution that offers a degree program in transportation, traffic management, or related fields. Student must be pursuing a career in one of these areas. Based on academic record, potential, professional interest, references, and financial need. Deadline: April 15.

2562.
Transportation Clubs International
Hooper Memorial Scholarship
Scholarship Committee Chairperson
1275 Kamus Drive, Suite 101
Fox Island, WA 98333
(206) 549-2257

1 scholarship of $1,000 to a student enrolled in an accredited institution of higher learning in a degree or vocational program in the fields of transportation, traffic management, or other related areas (i.e., marketing, economics, etc.) in preparation for a career in transportation. Based on scholastic ability, potential, professional interest, character, and financial need. Deadline: April 15.

2563.
Transportation Clubs International
Mexico Scholarship
Scholarship Committee Chairperson
1275 Kamus Drive, Suite 101
Fox Island, WA 98333
(206) 549-2257

1 scholarship of $500 to a student enrolled in an accredited institution in Mexico that offers a degree program in transportation, traffic management, or related fields. Student must be pursuing a career in these areas. Based on academic record, potential, professional interest, references, and financial need. Deadline: April 15.

2564.
Transportation Clubs International
Michigan Transportation Scholarship
Scholarship Committee Chairperson
1275 Kamus Drive, Suite 101
Fox Island, WA 98333
(206) 549-2257

1 scholarship of $1,500 to a student who was enrolled in a school in Michigan during some phase of his or her education (elementary, secondary, or college). Must be in a degree program in the field of transportation, traffic, management, or other related areas (such as marketing, economics, etc.) and in pursuit of a career in transportation. Deadline: April 15.

2565.
Transportation Clubs International
Roger Gerlinger Memorial Scholarship
Scholarship Committee Chairperson
1275 Kamus Drive, Suite 101
Fox Island, WA 98333
(206) 549-2257

1 scholarship of $1,000 to a male student enrolled in an accredited institution that offers a degree program in transportation, traffic management, or related fields. Student must be pursuing a career in one of these areas. Based on academic record, potential, professional interest, references, and financial need. Deadline: April 15.

2566.
Transportation Clubs International
Texas Traffic and Transportation Scholarship
Scholarship Committee Chairperson
1275 Kamus Drive, Suite 101
Fox Island, WA 98333
(206) 549-2257

1 scholarship of $1,000 to a student who has graduated from a Texas senior high school. Must be in a degree program in the field of transportation, traffic management, or other related areas (such as marketing, economics, etc.) in preparation for a career in transportation. Deadline: April 15.

2567.
Transport Workers Unions of America
Michael Quill Scholarship Committee
1980 Broadway
New York, NY 10023

Scholarships of varying amounts to students who are children of union members. Recipients must have been accepted to an approved health professions school. Must maintain satisfactory academic progress. Based on financial need and academic achievement. Other restrictions may apply. Deadline: none specified.

2568.
Treacy Company
Box 1700
Helena, MT 59624
(406) 442-3632

80 scholarships averaging $500 and totaling up to $22,500 to high school seniors and undergraduates. Must be residents of or attending an institution in Idaho, Montana, North Dakota, South Dakota, or Washington. Write an introductory letter detailing your educational and financial situation. Other restrictions may apply. Deadline: June 15.

2569.
Tupperware Home Parties Scholarships
P.O. Box 2353
Orlando, FL 32802

Numerous scholarships of varying amounts to high school seniors who are children of independent Tupperware dealers or managers and their dependent children. Good for any area of study at any recognized college or university.

2570.
Tuskegee Airmen Scholarships
Tuskegee Airmen
East Coast Chapter
P.O. Box 62404
Washington, DC 20029-2404

10 scholarships of $500 to graduates from high schools in Maryland, Washington, DC, or Virginia area. Based on financial need. A minimum 3.0 GPA is required. Deadline: January-February.

2571.
Twin City Area Urban Corps
Internship Program
111 City Hall
350 5th Street South
Minneapolis, MN 55415
(612) 673-3027

700 internships lasting from ten weeks to one year and providing an hourly wage for work-study students and $20 per week for others. Internships are open to undergraduate and graduate students. Interns work in governmental and nonprofit agencies; responsibilities vary. Submit an application form and have an in-person interview. Positions are filled on a first-come, first-served basis. Deadline: open.

2572.
Two/Ten Charity Trust Scholarship Program
56 Main Street
Watertown, MA 02172
(800) FIND-210

Scholarships ranging from $500 to $2,000 to high school seniors, high school graduates within the last four years, or fill-time college students through junior year. Must be planning to attend or attending any two- or four-year college or nursing program, vocational/technical school, or business program in the U.S. Must be a dependent of a parent currently employed in the footwear, leather, or allied industries for at least two consecutive years or a student who has worked not less than five hundred hours in the above industries. Request application after September 1. Deadline: December 16.

2573.
Ty Cobb Educational Foundation
P.O. Box 725
Forest Park, GA 30051

223 scholarships ranging from $400 to $1,000 to undergraduate students who have completed forty-five quarter hours or thirty semester hours and have at least a 3.0 GPA. Must be Georgia residents. Good for various fields, including: law, medicine, veterinary medicine, and dentistry. May attend any U.S. institution.

2574.
Tylenol Scholarships
McNeiLab, Inc.
Fort Washington, PA 19034
(215) 233-8505

500 scholarships of $1,000 and 10 scholarships of $10,000 to high school seniors, undergraduate college students (of all ages), and students attending vocational/technical schools. Applications are available starting in September. Ask local drug stores; or if you're unable to find copies of the application, call Tylenol Customer Service and they will send you an application. Deadline: November 15 (may vary).

2575.
Tyson Foundation, Inc.
P.O. Box 2020
Springdale, AR 72765-2020
(501) 756-4955

Numerous $1,000 scholarships to high school graduates. Must have at least a 2.5 GPA, be U.S. citizens, and live in the vicinity of one of the Tyson Foundation facilities. Must be full-time students and work to earn part of own expenses. Though this is a scholarship, students are asked to sign an application that states they will either pay the money back or help another student (not related by blood or marriage) to obtain a college degree. Deadline: June 21 (fall); January 1 (spring).

2576.
Union Pacific Railroad Employee Dependent
Scholarships
Scholarship Administrator
1416 Dodge Street, Room 320
Omaha, NE 68179

Scholarships of $750 per semester to high school seniors who are sons or daughters of Union Pacific Railroad employees. Must be in the top 25 percent of their class.

Renewable for eight semesters in a five-year period with a 2.75 GPA. Deadline: February 1.

2577.
Unitarian Universalist Association
Scholarships and Awards
25 Beacon Street
Boston, MA 02108
(617) 742-2100

Scholarships ranging from $100 to $700 to undergraduate students majoring in art, poetry, or music who are members of or sponsored by members of the Unitarian Universalist Society. Contact Unitarian Universalists Musicians Network, 4190 Front Street, San Diego, CA 92103. Deadline: March.

2578.
Unitarian Universalist Association
Stanfield Scholarship Program
25 Beacon Street
Boston, MA 02108
(617) 742-2100
Written inquiries only

Scholarships of varying amounts to graduating high school seniors, undergraduate, or graduate students. Must be children of Unitarian ministers. Must have been accepted to an approved health professions school (nursing, medical, dental, etc). Based on academic achievement and financial need. Must maintain satisfactory academic progress. Deadline: none specified.

2579.
United Agribusiness League
UAL Scholarship Program
54 Corporate Park
Irvine, CA 92714
(714) 975-1424

Varying numbers of scholarships ranging from $2,000 to $3,500 to undergraduate or graduate students majoring in agriculture or agribusiness. Must be UAL member employees or their dependent children. Must be enrolled in an accredited college or university. Send a self-addressed, stamped envelope for information. Renewable with maintained academic progress. Deadline: March 31.

2580.
United Commercial Travelers of America
Retarded Citizens Teacher Scholarships
632 North Park Street
P.O. Box 159019
Columbus, OH 43215-8619
(614) 228-3276

500 scholarships of $750 to undergraduate juniors, seniors, graduate students, teachers, or persons who plan to vocationally teach the mentally retarded. Awards are good at any U.S. or Canadian accredited institution. Preference given to UTC members. Deadline: none.

2581.
United Daughters of the Confederacy
Scholarships
Committee on Education
Memorial Building
328 North Boulevard
Richmond, VA 23220
(804) 355-1636

Approximately 72 scholarships ranging from $400 to $800 (renewable for up to four years) to students who are lineal descendants of a worthy Confederate or collateral descendant who is a member of the Children of the Confederacy or the United Daughters of the Confederacy. Must have proof of Confederate record of one ancestor, with the company and regiment in which he served. Certified proof can be obtained from any state capitol with Archives of Confederate Records, or the National Archives and Records Service in Washington DC; or the UDC will supply it (enclose a $3.00 check or money order made out to the Treasury General, UDC). For more information, send a self-addressed, stamped envelope. Deadline: February 15.

2582.
United Federation of Teachers College
Scholarship Fund
UFT Undergraduate College Scholarships
260 Park Avenue South
New York, NY 10010

Varying numbers of scholarships ranging from $1,000 to $4,000 to graduates of a New York City public vocational, academic, or alternative high school, or to students having received a high school equivalency diploma from public evening schools or other New York City Board of Education alternative educational programs. Can be used for any major. Based on financial need. Renewable for up to four years. Deadline: December 15.

2583.
United Food & Commercial Workers (UFCW)
Scholarship Program
1775 K Street, N.W.
Washington, DC 20006
(202) 684-2822

Scholarships of varying amounts to members in good standing or their unmarried children who are graduating high school seniors planning to enroll in an accredited college/university. Parent or individual must have been a member in good standing for no less than one year prior to graduation. Deadline: December 31.

2584.
United Methodist Church
Ernest & Eurice Miller Bass Scholarship Fund
Office of Loans & Scholarships
P.O. Box 871
Nashville, TN 37202
(615) 327-2700
http://www.netins.net/showcase/umsource/

Scholarships of up to $1,000 to undergraduate students who are members of the United Methodist Church. Must be preparing for the ministry or other full-time religious careers. Deadline: June 1.

2585.
United Methodist Church
Georgia Harkness Scholarships
Office of Loans & Scholarships
P.O. Box 871
Nashville, TN 37202
(615) 327-2700
http://www.netins.net/showcase/umsource/

Scholarships of up to $1,000 to female undergraduate students who are members of the United Methodist Church. Must be over the age of thirty-five and preparing for the ministry as a second career. Deadline: March 1.

2586.
United Methodist Scholarship Program
Office of Loans and Scholarships
Board of Higher Education-Ministry
P.O. Box 871
Nashville, TN 37202
(615) 327-2700
http://www.netins.net/showcase/umsource/

Scholarships of varying amounts to members of the United Methodist Church for at least one year prior to applying. Several scholarships available to attend a United Methodist-related college. There are also scholarships to attend other accredited colleges and universities and minority scholarships.

2587.
United Methodist Undergraduate Scholarships
Office of Loans and Scholarships
Board of Higher Education and Ministry
The United Methodist Church
P.O. Box 871
Nashville, TN 37202
(615) 327-2700
http://www.netins.net/showcase/umsource/

Scholarships of up to $500 and student loans of $900 to $1,000 are available. Incoming freshmen must, at the end of seven semesters in high school, have had a B average or better. An undergraduate student must have a B average or better in the year preceding the one for which award is to be used. Based on academic achievement, leadership ability, promise of usefulness, Christian philosophy, and financial need. Good at more than one hundred United Methodist colleges and universities. Deadline: varies.

2588.
United Nations Association of the USA
Intern Coordinator
485 Fifth Avenue
New York, NY 10017
(212) 697-3232
http://www.unausa.org/

20 internships providing no compensation to high school students, undergraduate and graduate students, and recent graduates who have an interest in international affairs. Internships last from ten to twelve weeks during the summer, fall, and spring and can either be part- or full-time. Interns are assigned to communications (only open to undergraduate seniors and above), Congressional and corporate programs, the field department, and Model UN and Youth Departments, multilateral studies, Policy Studies (requires foreign language skill), and public studies. Deadline: April 1 (summer); August 1 (fall); January 15 (spring).

2589.
United Negro College Fund, Inc.
500 East 62nd Street
New York, NY 10021
(212) 326-1238
http://www.unc.org/

1,000 scholarships of approximately $1,200 to high school seniors to attend a UNCF college or university. Based on financial need, SAT/ACT scores, and academic record. Many are renewable if student maintains a 3.0 GPA. Deadline: September 30.

2590.
United Presbyterian Church
Office of Financial Aid for Studies
475 Riverside Drive, Room 420
New York, NY 10115

150 scholarships of up to $1,400 per year to communicant members of the church attending certain affiliated schools. Also 25 scholarships of $500 based on a competitive essay contest. Additional scholarships for minority incoming freshmen who are church members.

2591.
United States Air Force Office of Scientific Research
High School Apprentice Program
Universal Energy Systems, Inc.
4401 Dayton-Xenia Road
Dayton, OH 45432
(513) 426-6900

100 eight-week summer apprenticeships providing approximately $1,000 to students who have finished 10th, 11th, or 12th grades. Students are assigned to an Air Force research lab near their homes, so that students reside at home. Students conduct a segment of their mentor's ongoing research. Students attend seminars, field trips, and other enrichment activities. Fields (may vary by site): physics, chemistry, computer science, mathematics, microbiology, engineering, meteorology, environmental science, psychology, and optics. Some labs require a final oral report. Selection is based on academic achievement based on transcript, test scores, personal statement, and one recommendation. Deadline: April 1.

2592.
United States Association for Blind Athletes (USABA)
Arthur E. and Helen Copeland Scholarships
33 North Institute Street
Colorado Springs, CO 80903
(719) 630-0422

1 scholarship of $500 each to a male and female student. Applicants should be scholars/athletes who have participated in USABA activities for at least two years and have been accepted into a postsecondary institution. Based on academic record, extracurricular activities, goals, and USABA involvement. Deadline: May 10.

2593.

United States Department of Commerce Internships
Bureau of the Census
Federal Building 3, Room 3124
Suitland, MD 20233
(301) 457-3371

Varying numbers of internships in volunteer programs and Co-op and Student Employment (SE) Programs that pay from $275 to $500 per week and last from two weeks to four months open to high school students, undergraduates, and graduate students. Students must be able to receive academic credit. The program is conducted in Washington, DC. Deadline: rolling.

2594.

United States Department of Commerce Internships
International Trade Administration
Personnel, Room 4814
14th and Constitution Avenue, N.W.
Washington, DC 20230
(202) 482-2262
(202) 482-1903 Fax

120 eight-week internships providing no compensation open to undergraduate and graduate students in Washington, DC. Students involved in a co-op semester-long internship do receive some compensation. This internship provides opportunities to work on programs involving ways to increase American competitiveness abroad, open foreign markets, eliminate unfair trade practices, identify trade and investment opportunities for U.S. exporters, advise U.S. businesses on overseas economic developments, monitor imports, and sponsor trade fairs and missions. Interns work in Trade Development, the Office of the Undersecretary, International Policy, and Import Administration. Internships are conducted on an ongoing basis. Deadline: rolling.

2595.

United States Department of Commerce Internships
National Institute of Standards & Technology
Administration Building
Room A-123
Gaithersburg, MD 20899
(301) 975-3026

Varying numbers of internships in volunteer programs and Co-op and Student Employment (SE) Programs that pay from $275 to $500 per week and last from two weeks to four months open to high school students, undergraduates, and graduate students. Students must be able to receive academic credit. The program is conducted in Washington, DC. Deadline: rolling.

2596.

United States Department of Commerce Internships
National Oceanic & Atmospheric Administration
Personnel Office
SSMC #2 OA215, Room 01230
Silver Spring, MD 20910
(301) 713-0534

500 to 1,000 volunteer programs lasting from two weeks to four months open to high school students, undergraduates, and graduate students. Students must be able to receive academic credit. The program is conducted in Washington, DC. Deadline: rolling.

2597.

United States Department of Commerce Internships, Office of the Secretary
Office of Personnel Operations
Room 1069
14th and Constitution Avenue, N.W.
Washington, DC 20230
(202) 482-2560

Varying numbers of internships in volunteer programs and Co-op and Student Employment (SE) Programs that pay from $275 to $500 per week and last from two weeks to four months open to high school students, undergraduates, and graduate students. Students might be assigned to one of the following agencies: Bureau of Economic Analysis, Bureau of Export Administration, Economics & Statistics Administration, Economic Development Administration, Minority Business Development Agency, National Technical Information Service, National Telecommunications & Information Administration, Technology Administration, or the U.S. Travel & Tourism Administration. Students must be able to receive academic credit. The program is conducted in Washington, DC. Deadline: rolling.

2598.

United States Department of Commerce Internships
Office of Inspector General
Room 7713 HCHB
Washington, DC 20230
(202) 482-3006

Varying numbers of internships in volunteer programs and Co-op and Student Employment (SE) Programs that pay from $275 to $500 per week and last from two weeks to four months open to high school students, undergraduates, and graduate students in all areas of study. Students must be able to receive academic credit. The program is conducted in Washington, DC. Deadline: rolling.

2599.

United States Department of Commerce Internships
Patent & Trademark Office
2011 Crystal Drive
Crystal Park One, Suite 700
Washington, DC 22202
(703) 305-8434

Varying numbers of internships in volunteer programs and Co-op and Student Employment (SE) Programs that pay from $275 to $500 per week and last from two weeks to four months open to high school students, undergraduates, and graduate students. Students must be able to receive academic credit. The program is conducted in Washington, DC. Deadline: rolling.

2600.

United States Department of Defense
Student Employment Program (SEP) or Stay–in–
**   School Program**
Staffing Division
Personnel & Security Directorate
1155 Defense Pentagon
Washington, DC 20301-1155

Up to 40 employment opportunities providing a weekly salary ranging from $240 to $275 to high school students, $350 to $400 to undergraduates, and from $450 to $575 to graduate students within one year of graduation. Students should live or attend school within the Washington, DC, Maryland, and Virginia area. Students work within the Office of the Secretary of Defense in departments such as Ballistic Missile Defense Operations, Staffing, Budget & Finance, Real Estate & Facilities, Executive Classification, Military Personnel, Personnel Systems & Evaluation, and Equal Employment Opportunities. Program lasts from twelve to sixteen weeks. Deadline: rolling (at least four months prior to starting date).

2601.

United States Department of Defense
Student Volunteer Program
Employee Career Development & Training Division
Washington Headquarters Service
Personnel & Security Directorate
1155 Defense Pentagon
Washington, DC 20301-1155

Up to 300 student (nonpaid) volunteer positions to undergraduate students. Students should live or attend school within the Washington, DC, Maryland, and Virginia area. Students work within the Office of the Secretary of Defense in departments such as Ballistic Missile Defense Operations, Staffing, Budget & Finance, Real Estate & Facilities, Executive Classification, Military Personnel, Personnel Systems & Evaluation, and Equal Employment Opportunities. Must receive academic credit. Positions last from two weeks to one year and occur throughout the year. Deadline: rolling (four months prior to starting date).

2602.

United States Department of Education
Indian Business, Engineering, Natural Resources
**   Fellowships**
Room 2177, Mail Stop 6267
400 Maryland Avenue, S.W.
Washington, DC 20202
(202) 732-1909

Fellowships ranging from $600 to $24,000 available to American Indian or Alaskan native students who are U.S. citizens seeking an undergraduate or graduate degree in business administration, engineering, natural resources, and related areas. Renewable up to four years. Deadline: varies.

2603.

United States Department of Education
Indian Education & Psychology Fellowships
Room 2177, Mail Stop 6267
400 Maryland Avenue, S.W.
Washington, DC 20202
(202) 732-1924

Fellowships ranging from $600 to $24,000 to American Indian or Alaskan native students who are U.S. citizens and seeking an undergraduate or graduate degree in education, psychology, and related areas. Up to 10 percent of the fellowships shall be awarded on a priority basis to applicants who indicate they plan to receive training in guidance counseling with a specialty in alcohol and substance abuse counseling and education. Deadline: varies.

2604.

United States Department of Education
Training Personnel for the Education of the
**   Handicapped (CFDA 84.029)**
Room 2177, Mail Stop 6267
400 Maryland Avenue, S.W.
Washington, DC 20202
(202) 401-1902

Numerous awards of varying amounts to students at two- or four-year undergraduate, graduate, and professional schools. The awards assist students who are training in special education, adaptive physical education, therapeutic recreation, speech pathologists, audiologists, infant specialists, transition specialists, related services personnel, and parent training. Students must be preparing to work with disabled children and youth as a teacher, supervisor, administrator, researcher, physical educator, recreation, or related services personnel. Deadline: September.

2605.

United States Department of Energy—Office of
**   Energy Research**
DOE Student Research Participation
1000 Independence Avenue, S.W.
Washington, DC 20585
(202) 586-8800

1,100 undergraduate, 200 graduate, and 200 faculty Summer Research Awards are made each year. The program may last from ten weeks up to one year. The amount of stipend depends on the level of the appointment. Students and faculty must be majoring or teaching in the fields of science and engineering. Must be U.S. citizens or permanent residents. Deadline: December to January.

2606.

United States Department of Health & Human
**   Services**
American Physiological Society Travel
**   Fellowships for Minority Physiologists**
NIH Employment Office
Building 31, Room B3C15
Bethesda, MD 20892
(301) 496-2403

Fellowships of varying amounts to minority undergraduate students involved in biomedical research to attend either the annual spring meeting of the Federation of American Societies for Experimental Biology or the APS annual fall meeting. Fellows are assigned to mentors who guide them through the symposia, tutorials, workshops, and poster sessions. Deadline: none specified.

2607.

United States Department of Health & Human
**   Services**
National Institute of Health 1040 Hours Program
NIH Employment Office
Building 31, Room B3C15
Bethesda, MD 20892
(301) 496-2403

Awards of approximately $12,385 to undergraduate and graduate students to work a maximum of 1,040 hours in assisting scientific, professional, and technical staff in research projects. U.S. citizens and noncitizens with permanent visa status who are from countries allied with the U.S. may apply. Appointments are made between October 1 and May 12. Deadline: open.

2608.

United States Department of Health & Human Services

National Institute of Health Summer Internship Program
Coordinator
Office of Education
Building 10, Room 1C129
9000 Rockville Pike
Bethesda, MD 20892
(301) 402-2176

100 high school internships, 550 undergraduate and recent graduate internships, and 200 graduate or professional school internships providing $800 per month to high school students, $1,000 to $1,400 per month to undergraduates, and from $1,600 to $2,000 per month to graduate and professional school students. Internships are eight weeks long during the summer. Acceptable majors are biology, biochemistry, chemistry, computer science, engineering, mathematics, psychology, physics, and liberal arts. Deadline: February 1.

2609.

United States Department of State
Intern Coordinator
Recruitment Division
P.O. Box 9317
Arlington, VA 22219

Numerous paid and unpaid internships for undergraduate juniors, seniors, and graduate students. Accepted majors: accounting, architecture, business, communications, criminal justice, economics, engineering, environmental studies, history, information systems, international relations, law, linguistics, natural sciences, nursing and medical technology, personnel management, political science, procurement, and public administration and policy. Interns gain firsthand knowledge of how U.S. diplomacy works and develop relationships with professionals in the field. Apply early. Deadline: November 1 (summer paid and unpaid internships); March 1 (fall work study internships); July 1 (spring work study internships).

2610.

United States Department of Veterans Affairs— Central Office

Veterans Affairs Health Professionals Scholarship Awards
810 Vermont Avenue, N.W.
Washington, DC 20420

Scholarships providing tuition, fees, and a monthly stipend of $621 to students accepted for enrollment in or enrolled in a course of training for bachelor's or master's degree in nursing or occupational or physical therapy. Must be juniors or seniors in a nursing, occupational, or physical

therapy program or in first or second year of master's program. Deadline: May.

2611.

United States Department of Veterans Affairs— Central Office

Veterans Affairs Health Professionals Scholarship Reserve Member Stipend Awards
810 Vermont Avenue, N.W.
Washington, DC 20420

Tax-free $400 monthly stipends to full-time students enrolled in nursing, occupational therapy, and physical therapy programs. Must be U.S. citizens, members of the Selected Ready Reserves, eligible for the Reserve G.I. Bill, and have scored above 50 percent on the Armed Forces Qualification Test. Based on academic record, goals, recommendation, and military/work/volunteer service. Deadline: May.

2612.

United States Hispanic Chamber of Commerce
1030 15th Street, N.W., Suite 206
Washington, DC 20005
(202) 842-1212

Numerous scholarships of varying amounts to Hispanic undergraduate, graduate, or professional school students enrolled in colleges, universities, or vocational programs in any area of study. Awards are based on academic achievement, community service, and financial need. Send a self-addressed, stamped envelope for more information. Deadline: July; varies.

2613.

United States Information Agency
Internship Coordinator
M/PDP Room 518
301 Fourth Street, S.W.
Washington, DC 20547
(202) 619-4659
(202) 205-0496 Fax

80 to 100 internships providing no compensation open to undergraduate students with an interest in the government, the arts, or foreign affairs. The internships last from five to twelve weeks on an ongoing basis in Los Angeles, CA; New York, NY; Washington, DC; and occasionally overseas. The U.S. Information Agency is a division of the U.S. Executive Branch. The Agency explains and supports American foreign policy and promotes mutual understanding between the U.S. and other nations by conducting educational and cultural activities through programs such as the Fulbright Exchange Program, Arts America, and Worldnet. Interns in Washington, DC, work in Educational & Cultural Exchange, Information Management, Public Liaison, Research, General Counsel, or the Foreign Service Press Center. Interns in California or New York work in those cities' Foreign Service Press Center. Deadline: March 17 (summer); rolling (all other times).

2614.

United States Institute of Peace
National Peace Essay Contest
1550 M Street, N.W., Suite 700
Washington, DC 20005
(703) 457-1700

Scholarships ranging from $100 to $10,000 to all public and private high school students, grades 9–12, in the U.S., U.S. territories, and schools in other countries. Students must consider the United States' role in the world in light of the dramatic changes that have taken place over the last several years. The first-place state winners will be invited to a week-long Awards Program in Washington, DC, where they will meet national and international leaders, participate in an international negotiation simulation, and visit many sites in the capital. Deadline: February 1.

2615.
United States Marine Corps Historical Center College Internships
Washington Navy Yard, Building 58
Washington, DC 20374
(202) 433-3859

Approximately $500 for daily expenses to undergraduate students at a college or university that will grant academic credit for work experience as an intern at address above or Marine Corps Airground Museum in Quantico, Virginia. All internships are regarded as beginning professional-level historian, curator, librarian, or archivist positions.

2616.
United States Marine Corps Scholarship Foundation
P.O. Box 3008
Princeton, NJ 08543-3008
(609) 921-3534

Scholarships ranging from $500 to $2,500 to students who are children of active, deceased, honorably or medically discharged, or retired Marines or Marine Reservists. Students must be high school seniors or graduates or enrolled in an undergraduate college or vocational program. Family income must not exceed $33,000 per year. Based on eligibility and extracurricular school or community involvement. Deadline: February 1.

2617.
United States Naval Institute Arleigh Burke Essay Contest
118 Maryland Avenue
Annapolis, MD 21402-5035
(410) 268-6110
(410) 269-7940 Fax
http://www.usni.org/Membership/CONTESTS.htm

3 awards of $2,000 per year for best essay on a topic that relates to the objective of the U.S. Naval Institute, "The Advancement of Professional Literary and Scientific Knowledge in the Naval and Maritime Services and the Advancement of the Knowledge of Sea Power." Essay must not exceed 4,000 words. Deadline: December 1.

2618.
United States Naval Institute Coast Guard Essay Contest
118 Maryland Avenue
Annapolis, MD 21402-5035
(410) 268-6110
(410) 269-7940 Fax
http://www.usni.org/Membership/CONTESTS.htm

1 award each of $1,000, $750, and $500 for best essays on current issues and new directions for the Coast Guard. This competition is open to anyone, but the essay must be of the same level as those printed in *Proceedings*. For specific guidelines, rules, and updates, send a self-addressed, stamped envelope to above address. Winning essays are published in the December issue of *Proceedings*. Essay must not exceed 3,500 words. Deadline: June 1.

2619.
United States Naval Institute Colin L. Powell Joint Warfighting Essay Contest
118 Maryland Avenue
Annapolis, MD 21402-5035
(410) 268-6110
(410) 269-7940 Fax
http://www.usni.org/Membership/CONTESTS.htm

1 award each of $2,500, $2,000, and $1,000 for best essays on combat readiness with key issues involving two or more services. Must be heavy in uni-service detail, but must have joint application in tactics, strategy, weaponry, combat training, force structure, doctrine, operations, organization for combat, or interoperability of hardware, software, and procedures. Open to both civilians and military professionals. For specific guidelines, rules, and updates, send a self-addressed, stamped envelope to above address. Winning essays are published in July issue of *Proceedings*. Deadline: April 1.

2620.
United States Naval Institute Enlisted Essay Contest
118 Maryland Avenue
Annapolis, MD 21402-5035
(410) 268-6110
(410) 269-7940 Fax
http://www.usni.org/Membership/CONTESTS.htm

1 award each of $1,000, $750, and $500 for best essays on a topic that relates to the objective of the U.S. Naval Institute, "The Advancement of Professional Literary and Scientific Knowledge in the Naval and Maritime Services and the Advancement of the Knowledge of Sea Power." This competition is open to anyone, but the essay must be of the same level as those printed in *Proceedings*. For specific guidelines, rules, and updates, send a self-addressed, stamped envelope to above address. Winning essays are published in the February issue of *Proceedings*. Essay must not exceed 3,500 words. Deadline: September 1.

2621.
United States Naval Institute International Navies Essay Contest
118 Maryland Avenue
Annapolis, MD 21402-5035
(410) 268-6110
(410) 269-7940 Fax
http://www.usni.org/Membership/CONTESTS.htm

1 award each of $1,000, $750, and $500 for the best essays discussing strategic, geographic, and cultural influences on individual or regional navies, their commitments and capabilities, and relationships with other navies. Open to all nationalities. For specific guidelines, rules, and updates send a self-addressed, stamped envelope to above address.

Winning essays are published in the March issue of *Proceedings*. Deadline: August 1.

2622.
United States Naval Institute
International Navies Photo Contest
118 Maryland Avenue
Annapolis, MD 21402-5035
(410) 268-6110
(410) 269-7940 Fax
http://www.usni.org/Membership/CONTESTS.htm

1 award each of $200, $100, and $50 for best photos of images of international naval and maritime subjects (from countries other than the United States). Amateur and professional photographers are eligible to enter up to five entries per person. For specific guidelines, rules, and updates, send a self-addressed, stamped envelope to above address. Winning photos are published in the March International Navies issue of *Proceedings*. Deadline: August 1.

2623.
United States Naval Institute
Marine Corps Essay Contest
118 Maryland Avenue
Annapolis, MD 21402-5035
(410) 268-6110
(410) 269-7940 Fax

1 award each of $1,000, $750, and $500 for best essays on current issues and new directions for the Marine Corps. This competition is open to anyone, but the essay must be of the same level as those printed in *Proceedings*. For specific guidelines, rules, and updates, send a self-addressed, stamped envelope to above address. Winning essays are published in the November issue of *Proceedings*. Essay must not exceed 3,500 words. Deadline: May 1.

2624.
United States Naval Institute
Marine Corps Photo Contest
118 Maryland Avenue
Annapolis, MD 21402-5035
(410) 268-6110
(410) 269-7940 Fax
http://www.usni.org/Membership/CONTESTS.htm

1 award of $500, 2 awards of $200, and 3 awards of $100 for best photo pertaining to Marine Corps subjects. This competition is open to all photographers—military or civilian, amateur or professional. Limited to five entries per person. For specific guidelines, rules, and updates send a self-addressed, stamped envelope to above address. Winning photos are published in the November issue of *Proceedings*. Deadline: May 1.

2625.
United States Naval Institute
Naval and Maritime Photo Contest
118 Maryland Avenue
Annapolis, MD 21402-5035
(410) 268-6110
(410) 269-7940 Fax
http://www.usni.org/Membership/CONTESTS.htm

1 award each of $500, $350, and $250, and 15 awards of $100 for best photos on naval or maritime subjects. Amateur and professional photographers are eligible to enter up to five entries per person. For specific guidelines, rules, and updates, send a self-addressed, stamped envelope to above address. Winning photos are published in the April issue of *Proceedings*. Deadline: December 31.

2626.
United States Navy—Navy, Marine Corps, Coast
** Guard Dependents' Scholarship Program**
Naval Military Personnel Command
NMPC 641 D
Navy Department
Washington, DC 20370-5641

A variety of Navy-oriented organizations provide scholarships to dependents of current or former members of the Navy, Marine Corps, or Coast Guard. May be based on academic record, character, and financial need. Deadline: March 15; may vary.

2627.
United States Olympic Committee
Intern Coordinator
One Olympic Plaza
Colorado Springs, CO 80909-5760
(719) 632-5551
(719) 578-4817 Fax

25 to 30 internships during the summer, fall, and spring open to undergraduate juniors, seniors, recent graduates, and graduate students. Internship pays $45 per week plus room and board. Interns are assigned to positions in Colorado Springs, CO; Lake Placid, NY; or Marquette, MI. Internships are in broadcasting, accounting, journalism, computer science, sports administration, public relations, marketing, fund-raising, and athlete performance. Previous interns have written for "Olympic Coach," arranged job interviews and employment for athletes, studied athletes' job training and job transition, and designed exercise programs for high school and college volleyball players. Students must submit a résumé, transcript, completed application form, and three faculty references. Students may also enclose up to three letters of recommendation and other relevant information (but not in page protectors or binders). Applicants to the journalism program must submit six recent writing samples photocopied onto 8½" × 11" paper. Deadline: June 1 (fall); February 15 (summer); and October 1 (winter/spring).

2628.
United States Secret Service
Student Volunteer (Intern) Program
Personnel Department
1800 G Street, N.W., Room 912
Washington, DC 20223
(202) 435-5800

200 to 400 internships open to undergraduate and graduate students with an interest in government. Internships last from ten to sixteen weeks during the summer, fall, and spring. Interns working at the main headquarters are assigned in Counterfeit, Financial Crimes, Forensic Services, Special Agent Training & Employee Development, Intelligence, Dignitary Protective, Asset Forfeiture, and

Administrative Operations. Twenty to fifty students work at the main headquarters in Washington, DC, and from four to nine students per department in field offices. Field offices are located in Mobile, AL; Los Angeles and San José, CA; Jacksonville, Miami, Orlando, and Tampa, FL; Atlanta, GA; Chicago, IL; New Orleans, LA; Baltimore, MD; Boston, MA; Detroit and Saginaw, MI; St. Louis, MO; Charlotte, NC; Newark, NJ; Buffalo, Rochester, Syracuse, and White Plains, NY; Cleveland, Columbus, and Toledo, OH; Pittsburgh, PA; San Juan, PR; Dallas, El Paso, Houston, and San Antonio, TX; Richmond, VA; Seattle, WA; and Charleston, WV. Interns at field offices conduct research and do clerical work for the local forgery, counterfeit, and fraud units. Prior to starting internship, applicants undergo a thorough background investigation that takes about three months to complete. Deadline: rolling (three months prior to starting date).

2629.
United States Senate Youth Programs
William Randolph Hearst Foundation
90 New Montgomery Street, Suite 1212
San Francisco, CA 94105

Over 100 scholarships of $2,000 to high school juniors and seniors who are student government officers with demonstrated leadership capabilities. Delegates for awards are determined by a standardized test on the American government system. It includes a one-week stay in Washington, DC, with all transportation and accommodations paid by the foundation. Contact high school principal or write to above address. Deadline: early autumn.

2630.
United Steel Workers of America, District 37 Paul Montemayor Scholarship
12821 Industrial Road
Houston, TX 77015

1 scholarship of $1,000 sponsored by the American Income Life Insurance Company to a son or daughter of a Mexican-American member of the United Steel Workers of America, District 37, Southwest Texas Sub-District. All Mexican-Americans who apply for the Philip Murray Scholarship will automatically have applied for the Paul Montemayor Scholarship. Deadline: April 15.

2631.
United Steel Workers of America, District 37 Philip Murray Memorial Scholarship
Scholarship Committee
12821 Industrial Road
Houston, TX 77015

5 scholarships of $800 to graduating high school seniors, high school graduates, and undergraduate students. Must be members, sons, daughters, or legal wards of members of Local Unions affiliated with the Existence and Education Council District 37, United Steel Workers of America. Selection based on academic achievement, goals, and financial need. Contact local union for applications. Other restrictions may apply. Deadline: April 15.

2632.
University Film and Video Association (Grants)
c/o Loren Cocking
Department of Cinema & Photography
Southern Illinois University
Carbondale, IL 62901
(618) 453-2365

$1,500 grants to undergraduate and graduate students majoring in film and video who are sponsored by a faculty member who is active in the Film and Video Association. Deadline: June 15.

2633.
University Film and Video Association Development Grants
Department of Drama and Communications
University of New Orleans, Lakefront
New Orleans, LA 70122

1 development grant of $1,500 awarded to an undergraduate or graduate student for support in a film and video production, and historical, critical, theoretical, or experimental studies in film and video. Applicant must be recommended or sponsored by a faculty member who is an active member of the University Film and Video Association. Applicant must present a report on the project at the next annual meeting of the association. Applicant must submit a proposal, résumé, script, budget, and a faculty feasibility statement that indicates willingness to serve as the faculty supervisor or consultant. Deadline: June 15.

2634.
University Film and Video Foundation Scholarships and Fellowships
c/o Dr. R. W. Wagner
Department of Photography & Cinema
Ohio State University
Columbus, OH 43210
(614) 292-4920

Scholarships and fellowships of varying amounts to undergraduate and graduate students enrolled in a film and video program at any accredited institution. Deadline: varies.

2635.
University of Alabama at Birmingham Ruby Lloyd Apsey Playwriting Competition
School of Arts & Humanities
Department of Theatre & Dance
University Station
Birmingham, AL 35294
(205) 934-3236

1 award of varying amount. Playwriting competition for talented new American playwrights. Entries must be original, unproduced, unpublished, and full-length. UAB reserves the rights for the premier production of the winning play, without royalties. Applicant must be U.S. citizen. Deadline: January 1.

2636.
University of Maryland International Piano Festival & William Kapell Competition
College of Summer & Special Programs
College Park, MD 20742
(301) 454-5276

15 awards ranging from $5,000 to $20,000 through a piano competition. Contestants must be between eighteen and thirty-three years of age. Award is in the form of cash and recital engagements. Interested applicants must submit a taped audition. Deadline: April 1.

2637.
Urann Foundation
Attn: Administrator
P.O. Box 1788
Brockton, MA 02403
(508) 588-7744

Scholarships of varying amounts to high school seniors who are children of cranberry growers in Massachusetts. Deadline: varies.

2638.
USAA Dependent Scholarship Program
Employee Education, B-2-F
9800 Fredericksburg Road
San Antonio, TX 78288
(210) 498-1532

Numerous awards of $1,500 to high school seniors who are planning to enroll in a full-time course of study leading to a baccalaureate degree. Must be naturally born or legally adopted dependent children of full-time USAA employees with one year of employment as of the application deadline date. Must have at least a 3.0 GPA on a 4.0 scale. Must attend an accredited four-year college or university. Must be U.S. citizens. Renewable for three years with satisfactory academic progress and continued parental employment by USAA. Contact USAA Education Office. Deadline: November 30.

2639.
USAA Dependent Scholarship Program Scholarships to Students from Specific High Schools
Employee Education, B-2-F
9800 Fredericksburg Road
San Antonio, TX 78288
(210) 498-1532

At least four awards of $1,500 to graduating high school seniors from Health Careers High School or Business Careers High School, both in San Antonio. Must be planning to enroll in a full-time course of study leading to a baccalaureate degree. Must be naturally born or legally adopted dependent children of full-time USAA employees with one year of employment as of the application deadline date. Must have at least a 3.0 GPA on a 4.0 scale. Must attend an accredited four-year college or university. Must be U.S. citizens. Renewable for three years if student maintains at least a 2.5 GPA on a 4.0 scale and with continued parental employment by USAA. Obtain

application from high school counselor or USAA Education Office. Deadline: November 30.

2640.
USAA National Merit Scholarship Program
Employee Education, B-2-F
9800 Fredericksburg Road
San Antonio, TX 78288
(210) 498-1532

Numerous awards of $2,000 to high school seniors who achieved the Semifinalist stage of the National Merit Scholarship Program. Must be planning to enroll in a full-time course of study leading to a baccalaureate degree. Must be naturally born or legally adopted dependent children of full-time USAA employees with one year of employment as of the application deadline date. Must attend an accredited four-year college or university. Must be U.S. citizens. Renewable for three years if student maintains satisfactory academic progress and continued parental employment by USAA. Obtain information from Employee Education Office. Deadline: November 30.

2641.
U.S. Bank of Oregon Foundation Team Ben Selling Scholarship/Loan Fund
111 S.W. Fifth Avenue, T-6
P.O. Box 3168
Portland, OR 97208-3168
(503) 275-4456
(503) 275-4177 Fax

20 loans ranging from $1,500 to $2,000 to undergraduate and graduate students. Must be residents of Oregon or attending an Oregon college or university. Must be attending Oregon state-supported or Protestant church-affiliated colleges or universities in Oregon. Based on academic record and financial need. Deadline: August 15.

2642.
U.S. Bank of Oregon Foundation Team Bill Selling Scholarship/Loan Fund
111 S.W. Fifth Avenue, T-6
P.O. Box 3168
Portland, OR 97208-3168
(503) 275-4456
(503) 275-4177 Fax

30 loans of varying amounts to undergraduate, graduate, and professional school students, especially those attending medical, dental, or nursing school. Must be Oregon residents and attending Oregon state-supported or Protestant church-affiliated colleges or universities in Oregon. Based on academic record and financial need. Deadline: varies.

2643.
U.S. Bank of Oregon Foundation Team Franks Foundation Fund
111 S.W. Fifth Avenue, T-6
P.O. Box 3168
Portland, OR 97208-3168
(503) 275-4456
(503) 275-4177 Fax

Scholarships of varying amounts of graduating high school seniors or high school graduates from public or private high schools in the Portland area. Must be or planning to be full-time students and majoring in nursing or ministry. May be used for undergraduate or graduate study. Special scholarships for the education and maintenance of handicapped, underprivileged, and disadvantaged people to obtain a postsecondary education. Special emphasis is placed on financial need. Priority is given to students from Deschutes, Crook, and Jefferson counties. Second preference to students from Harney, Lake Grant, and Klamath counties. Must maintain at least a 2.5 GPA. Deadline: none specified.

2644.
**U.S. Bank of Oregon Foundation Team
Harley and Mertie Stevens Memorial Fund**
111 S.W. Fifth Avenue, T-6
P.O. Box 3168
Portland, OR 97208-3168
(503) 275-4456
(503) 275-4177 Fax

32 scholarships ranging from $280 to $2,000 to high school graduates of Clackamas County, Oregon. Must be attending Oregon state-supported or Protestant church-affiliated colleges or universities in Oregon. Based on academic record and financial need. Deadline: May 1.

2645.
**U.S. Bank of Oregon Foundation Team
Joann Hamilton Memorial Fund**
111. S.W. Fifth Avenue, T-6
P.O. Box 3168
Portland, OR 97208-3168
(503) 275-4456
(503) 275-4177 Fax

Scholarships of varying amounts to graduating high school seniors or high school graduates who haven't attended college. Must be graduates of a Lincoln County high school, Newport High School in particular. Student must apply within five years of high school graduation and may receive assistance only four times. Awards may be used for tuition, fees, and other educational costs. May be used at a two- or four-year college or university or vocational/technical school. Selection based on academic performance, recommendation, SAT/ACT, aptitude for college work, and financial need. Deadline: none specified.

2646.
**Utah State Office of Education
Academic Scholarships**
250 East 500 South
Salt Lake City, UT 84111
(801) 538-7500
(801) 538-7521 Fax
http://www.state.ut.us/html/education.htm

Scholarships of varying amounts to graduating high school seniors. Selection is based on academic achievement and SAT/ACT scores. Must be Utah residents attending eligible Utah institutions. Deadline: varies. Obtain applications from high school counselors or specific school.

2647.
**Utah State Office of Education
Career Teaching Scholarships**
250 East 500 South
Salt Lake City, UT 84111
(801) 538-7500
(801) 538-7521 Fax
http://www.state.ut.us/html/education.htm

150 scholarships of full tuition and fees are available to Utah high school graduates and college freshmen who are residents, or undergraduate sophomores, juniors, or seniors who are residents or nonresidents but attending a Utah state institution, and pursuing a career in teaching. Deadline: March 1.

2648.
**Utah State Office of Education
Robert C. Byrd Honors Scholarships**
250 East 500 South
Salt Lake City, UT 84111
(801) 538-7500
(801) 538-7521 Fax
http://www.state.ut.us/html/education.htm

Varying numbers of scholarships of $1,500 to graduating high school seniors. Applicants must meet two of three requirements: rank in the top 5 percent of their class, have at least a 3.5 GPA, or have at least an 1100 on SAT or 27 on ACT. Must be Utah residents and attend eligible Utah institutions. Students are unable to apply directly. Students must be nominated by a school official. Deadline: May 1.

2649.
Utah State Office of Education
250 East 500 South
Salt Lake City, UT 84111
(801) 538-7500
(801) 538-7521 Fax
http://www.state.ut.us/html/education.htm

Scholarships of varying amounts to graduating high school seniors. Selection is based on academic achievement, SAT/ACT scores, potential for success, and some may be based on financial need. Must be Utah residents attending eligible Utah institutions. Deadline: varies.

2650.
**Utah State Office of Education
State Student Incentive Grants**
250 East 500 South
Salt Lake City, UT 8411
(801) 538-7500
(801) 538-7521 Fax
http://www.state.ut.us/html/education.htm

Scholarships of up to $2,500 to graduating high school seniors and undergraduate students attending a participating Utah institution. Selection based on financial need. Must be Utah residents. Contact school's financial aid office.

2651.
Van Buren Foundation, Inc.
Scholarship Program
Community First Bank
Trust Department
714 First Street
Keosauqua, IA 52565
(319) 293-3794

1 scholarship of varying amount to a student entering or pursuing a conservation-related field (ecology, wildlife, etc.) and 1 loan of varying amount for a nursing student. The loan is forgiven if the student works in a Van Buren County hospital upon completion of nursing degree. Applicants must be residents of Van Buren County, Iowa, and graduates of a Van Buren County high school. Nursing applicants must request applications from the hospital in Keosauqua. Students may attend any accredited U.S. college or university. Deadline: none.

2652.
Vermont Department of Education
Vermont Incentive Grants
120 State Street
Montpelier, VT 05620-2501
(802) 828-3174
(802) 828-3140 Fax
http://www.state.vt.us/edu/

Grants ranging from $500 to $5,200 to students who are Vermont residents attending a public institution in- or out-of-state. Must not have received a bachelor's degree. Must have financial need. Deadline: March 1.

2653.
Vermont Department of Education
Vermont Part-Time Student Grants
120 State Street
Montpelier, VT 05620-2501
(802) 828-3174
(802) 828-3140 Fax
http://www.state.vt.us/edu/

Grants ranging from $150 to $3,600 to students enrolled for fewer than twelve credit hours per semester. Student must be Vermont residents accepted to or enrolled in an undergraduate program awarding a degree, diploma, or certificate. Based on financial need. Deadline: January 31.

2654.
Vermont Department of Education
Vermont Robert C. Byrd Scholarships
120 State Street
Montpelier, VT 05620-2501
(802) 828-3174
(802) 828-3140 Fax
http://www.state.vt.us/edu/

Varying numbers of scholarships of $1,500 to graduating high school seniors. Generally must meet two of three requirements: rank in the top 5 percent of their class, have at least a 3.5 GPA, or have at least an 1100 on SAT or 27 on ACT. Must be Vermont residents and attend eligible Vermont institutions. Students are unable to apply directly. Students must be nominated by a school official. Deadline: May 1.

2655.
Vermont Society of Professional Engineers
Perminder Grewal
207 South Union #4
Burlington, VT 05401
(802) 860-6065
(802) 860-6076 Fax

Scholarships of varying amounts to graduating high school seniors or undergraduate students majoring in engineering. Designated engineering scholarships requiring that a specific university be attended or a specific program of engineering study be pursued are also offered. Must be Vermont residents. Other restrictions may apply. Deadline: varies.

2656.
Vertical Flight Foundation
Undergraduate/Graduate Scholarships
217 North Washington Street
Alexandria, VA 22314
(703) 684-6777

9 scholarships of approximately $2,000 to undergraduate and graduate students who are majoring in mechanical engineering, electrical engineering, or aerospace engineering and interested in helicopter or vertical flight. Scholarships are good at any accredited U.S. college or university. Deadline: February 1.

2657.
VFW Ladies Auxiliary National Patriotic Creative
   Art Competition
Ladies Auxiliary to the VFW National Headquarters
406 West 34th Street
Kansas City, MO 64111
(816) 756-3390

Open to all high school students (grades 9, 10, 11, and 12). Awards range from $200 to $1,500. Obtain more information and entry blank from a local chapter or from above address. Deadline: May 1.

2658.
VFW Voice of Democracy Scholarship Program
Veterans of Foreign Wars of the United States
VFW Building, 406 West 34th Street
Kansas City, MO 64111

Awards ranging from $1,000 to $18,000 in a national broadcasting scriptwriting program for students in grades 10, 11, and 12. Students must submit a tape recording of a three-to-five-minute essay on a selected topic. Contact school principal or local VFW post. Deadline: November 15.

2659.
Vikki Carr Scholarship Foundation
P.O. Box 5126
Beverly Hills, CA 90210
(213) 278-5665

1 to 10 scholarships ranging from $100 to $2,000 to high school graduates between the ages of seventeen and twenty-five. Must be Mexican-American, California residents, and U.S. citizens. Award may be used for undergraduate, graduate, professional, advanced professional, and

postdoctoral study. May be used at two- or four-year colleges, universities, or vocational/technical schools. Deadline: April 1.

2660.
Vikki Carr Scholarship Foundation
P.O. Box 780968
San Antonio, TX 78278

1 to 10 scholarships ranging from $100 to $2,000 to high school seniors or high school graduates between the ages of seventeen and twenty-five. Must be Mexican-American, Texas residents, and U.S. citizens. Award may be used for undergraduate, graduate, professional, advanced professional, and postdoctoral study. May be used at two- or four-year colleges, universities, or vocational/technical schools. Deadline: late March.

2661.
Virginia Airport Operators Council Aviation (VAOC) Scholarships
c/o Herbert B. Armstrong
Airway Science Program
Hampton University
Hampton, VA 23688

1 scholarship of $500 and 2 scholarships of $50 to entering college freshmen pursuing a career in aviation and who have been accepted by an accredited college. Award is good at any accredited institution with an aviation program. Other restrictions may apply. Deadline: varies.

2662.
Virginia Baptist General Board
Baptist Ministerial Undergraduate Student Aid
P.O. Box 8568
Richmond, VA 23226
Written inquiries only

50 awards of varying amounts to undergraduate students who are Virginia residents, enrolled in a Southern Baptist Convention school, studying to become a Southern Baptist minister, and members of a church associated with a Baptist General Association of Virginia. Loans are nonrepayable if recipient works in a Christian-related service for two years. Deadline: August.

2663.
Virginia Commonwealth Department of Veterans' Affairs
War Orphans Education Program
270 Franklin Road, S.W., Room 1012
Poff Federal Building
Roanoke, VA 24011-2215
(703) 857-7104

Awards of tuition plus required fees to graduating high school seniors, high school graduates, or undergraduates. Must be surviving, dependent children of U.S. military personnel who were or are Virginia residents and lost their life or were disabled as a result of war/armed conflict or were listed as prisoners of war or missing in action. Students must be between the ages of sixteen and twenty-five. Recipients must attend a state-supported secondary or postsecondary educational institution. Must be accepted to

or enrolled in a vocational, technical, undergraduate, or graduate program. Deadline: none.

2664.
Virginia Council of Higher Education
College Scholarship Assistance
James Monroe Building, 9th Floor
101 North 14th Street
Richmond, VA 23219
(804) 225-2137
(804) 371-8017 TDD
http://www.schev.edu/wufinaid

Scholarships ranging from $400 to $2,000 to undergraduate students who are residents of Virginia. Must be enrolled for at least six credit hours in a public or private Virginia institution and in any field of study except religious training or theological education.

2665.
Virginia Council of Higher Education
College Scholarship Assistance Grants
Coordinator of Financial Aid Programs
James Monroe Building, 9th Floor
101 North 14th Street
Richmond, VA 23219
(804) 225-2137/(804) 371-8017 TDD
http://www.schev.edu/wufinaid

Grants ranging from $400 to $1,000 per year to eligible Virginia residents, for full-time undergraduate work only (up to four years on a yearly basis), who demonstrate sufficient financial need. Write to the Virginia college you plan to attend for application forms and instructions, or secure them from the State Council. Deadline: varies.

2666.
Virginia Council of Higher Education
Eastern Shore Tuition Assistance Program
James Monroe Building, 9th Floor
101 North 14th Street
Richmond, VA 23219
(804) 225-2137/(804) 371-8017 TDD
http://www.schev.edu/wufinaid

Grants of $1,350 to students who are full-time undergraduate, graduate, or first-professional-degree students. Must be Virginia residents attending an approved private Virginia institution. Not based on financial need.

2667.
Virginia Council of Higher Education
Robert C. Byrd Scholarships
Coordinator of Financial Aid Programs
James Monroe Building, 9th Floor
101 North 14th Street
Richmond, VA 23219
(804) 225-2137/(804) 371-8017 TDD
http://www.schev.edu/wufinaid

Scholarships of $1,500 to graduating high school seniors or GED recipients. Based on outstanding academic record, GPA, rank in class or GED equivalent, SAT/ACT scores, and school recommendation. Students are unable to apply directly. High school counselors nominate varying numbers of the most academically eligible candidates. Must be Virginia residents and attend eligible Virginia institutions.

2668.
Virginia Council of Higher Education
Transfer Grants
James Monroe Building, 9th Floor
101 North 14th Street
Richmond, VA 23219
(804) 225-2137/(804) 371-8017 TDD
http://www.shev.edu/wufinaid

Grants providing tuition and fees or amount of financial need (whichever is less) to students who are in the minority in a traditionally white or black public four-year Virginia institution. Students must meet certain academic criteria and be entering as first-year transfer students.

2669.
Virginia Council of Higher Education
Undergraduate Student Financial Assistance (Last Dollar)
James Monroe Building, 9th Floor
101 North 14th Street
Richmond, VA 23219
http:www.shev.edu/wufinaid

Grants of at least $200 to undergraduate African American students who are residents of Virginia. Must be at least half-time students at a state-supported Virginia institution. Based on financial need.

2670.
Virginia Department of Health—Public Health Nursing
Mary Marshall Nursing Scholarships
1500 East Main Street, Room 108
Richmond, VA 23218
(804) 371-4088

Scholarships ranging from $150 to $4,000 to undergraduate or graduate students who are Virginia residents. May be entering or enrolled in a nursing program in Virginia and agree to engage in full-time nursing practice in Virginia upon graduation. Must have at least a 3.0 GPA. Based on financial need. Deadline: July 30.

2671.
Virginia Department of Health—Public Health Nursing
Virginia General Assembly Nursing Scholarships
1500 East Main Street, Room 108
Richmond, VA 23218
(804) 371-4088

Scholarships ranging from $150 to $2,000 to high school seniors or graduates or college undergraduate or graduate students who are Virginia residents. May be entering or enrolled in a nursing program in Virginia. If already in a program, must have at least a 2.5 GPA. Graduate students may attend a program outside the state if it isn't offered in Virginia. Based on financial need. Deadline: April 30 (enrolled students); June 30 (entering students).

2672.
Virginia Forestry Association
Forestry Scholarship
Executive Vice President
1205 East Main Street
Richmond, VA 23219
(804) 644-8462

4 scholarships of $500 to undergraduate students majoring in forestry or any curriculum in the School of Forestry at Virginia Polytechnic Institute and State University. Based on academic achievement, motivation, potential for contribution to the forestry profession, extracurricular activities, leadership qualities, and financial need. Deadline: March 15.

2673.
Virginia Museum of Fine Arts
Undergraduate/Graduate & Professional Fellowships
Virginia Museum Boulevard & Grove Avenue
Richmond, VA 23221
(804) 257-0824

12 to 18 fellowships of up to $4,000 are available to undergraduate or graduate students majoring in art, fine art, art history, architecture, photography, film, or video. Professional Artist Fellowships are also available. Applicants must be Virginia residents (for at least five of the last ten years) and U.S. citizens or legal residents. Deadline: March 9.

2674.
Virginia Society of Professional Engineers
Heritage Building, Suite 625
1001 East Main Street
Richmond, VA 23219

Scholarships of $1,000 and $2,000 for an engineering curriculum. Designated engineering scholarships requiring that a specific university be attended or a specific program of engineering study be pursued are also offered. For Virginia residents only. Deadline: December 3; local chapters may vary.

2675.
Virginia State Assistance for Physically Disabled Students
Deputy Commissioner
Department of Rehabilitative Services
4901 Fitzhugh Avenue
P.O. Box 11045
Richmond, VA 23230

The Virginia Department of Rehabilitative Services strives to assure males and females that a disability isn't a handicap in making a living. Impairment must be determined to be a vocational handicap that limits the fields of work in which the person may engage successfully. Students must be physically disabled (amputated or impaired arm or leg, seriously impaired hearing, certain heart and lung conditions, etc.) or have a mental or emotional disability.

2676.
Virginia State Assistance to Children of Veterans
Samuel Black
Director of VA Department of Veterans' Affairs
P.O. Box 809
Roanoke, VA 24004

Applicant must be a son or daughter of a veteran who was 1) a citizen of Virginia at the time of entering war service; 2) a Virginia citizen for at least ten years immediately prior to application for financial assistance in sending student to college; or 3) (if deceased) a Virginia citizen on date of death and for at least ten years immediately prior to death. Student must be between sixteen and twenty-five years old. Must continue making satisfactory progress in college.

2677.
Virgin Islands Board of Education
Music Scholarship
P.O. Box 11900
St. Thomas, VI 00801
(809) 774-4546

1 scholarship of $2,000 to a Virgin Island resident enrolled in an accredited music program at a postsecondary institution. Renewable if recipient maintains at least a 2.5 GPA. Deadline: March 31.

2678.
Virgin Islands Board of Education
Territorial Loan/Grant Program and Special
Legislative Grants
P.O. Box 11900
St. Thomas, VI 00801
(809) 774-4546

Grants and loans of varying amounts to students who are residents of the Virgin Islands. Must be maintaining a C average or better and be accepted to an accredited postsecondary institution. Deadline: March 31 (fall); October 31 (spring).

2679.
Volkswagen of America, Inc.
Internship Program
Staffing Department
3800 Hamlin Road
Auburn Hills, MI 48326
(313) 349-5000

13 internships providing no compensation to undergraduates in any major. Interns are assigned to every division: Volkswagen United States, Audi of America Sales & Marketing, Public Affairs, Human Resources, Finance, VW Credit, Inc., Parts and Information Organization, and Corporate Staffing. The internships last from one to six months and are conducted year-round. Deadline: rolling.

2680.
Von Trotha Educational Trust
Union Colony Bank, Asset Management Officer
920 54th Avenue
Greeley, CO 80632
(970) 356-7000

20 scholarships of $400 per year to graduating high school seniors from a Weld County, Colorado, high school. Must be in the top 33 percent of class. May be used at a two- or four-year college. Based on SAT/ACT scores. Request applications after June 1 before the senior year. Deadline: March 30.

2681.
Wall Street Journal
Internship Program
c/o Assistant Managing Editor
200 Liberty Street
New York, NY 10281

15 to 18 ten-week summer internships to undergraduates, recent graduates, and graduate students providing $500 per week salary. Internships are in Atlanta, GA; Chicago, IL; Dallas, TX; New York, NY; and Washington, D.C. Half of the internships are for minority students. Most interns have a solid journalism background. Deadline: Thanksgiving.

2682.
Wal-Mart Foundation

1 scholarship of $1,000 to graduating high school seniors who live in a community with a Wal-Mart store. Based on academic achievement, SAT/ACT, extracurricular activities, community involvement, and financial need. For information, contact high school counselors. High school counselors need to request applications from local Wal-Mart stores in January. Deadline: varies by community.

2683.
Walt Disney Studios
Internship Program Administrator
500 South Buena Vista Street
Burbank, CA 91521-0880
(818) 560-6335

20 three-month summer internships paying $200 per week are open to undergraduates with any major, though a relevant background is helpful. Internships are in production (reads scripts, determines locations, and analyzes film footage), marketing (advertising, promotions, and press junkets), finance (budget), and feature animation (administrative, not for would-be animators). Students should send transcript, résumé, and a cover letter that details their qualifications, goals, and what they wish to gain from the internship. Deadline: March 31.

2684.
WAMSCO Young Artist Competition
1111 Nicollet Mall
Minneapolis, MN 55403
(612) 371-5654

Numerous prizes and scholarships of varying amounts are available to both undergraduate and graduate students (performing on the piano or orchestral instruments) in schools in Iowa, Minnesota, Missouri, Nebraska, North Dakota, South Dakota, Wisconsin, Manitoba, or Ontario. Must not be older than twenty-six as of December 1 of application year. Please indicate instrument when requesting a list of repertoires and information. Deadline: August 17.

2685.

Washington Center for Internships and Academic Seminars

1101 14th Street, N.W., Suite 500
Washington, DC 20005
(800) 486-8921
INFO@TWC.edu

175 to 210 internships lasting from ten to fifteen weeks and providing a $2,500 program fee, housing fee; some offer a stipend. Scholarships are available for certain programs. Open to undergraduate sophomores, juniors, seniors, recent college graduates, and graduate students. Open to U.S. citizens and international students. Internships are in government, public policy, public service, foreign affairs, journalism, law, women's studies, health care, science, and the environment. There is a $60 application fee. Internships take place in a variety of places within Washington, DC. Deadline: varies with program.

2686.

Washington Congress of Parents and Teachers

Financial Grant Foundation Program
2003 65th Avenue West
Tacoma, WA 98466

60 awards ranging from $500 to $1,000 to Washington State residents. Assist high school seniors and graduates who will be entering freshmen at accredited colleges or universities. May be used for any area of study. Deadline: March 1.

2687.

Washington International Competition

Charlotte Wesley Holloman
1824 Taylor Street, N.W.
Washington, DC 20011
(202) 726-7415

The foundation has assisted the advanced training of gifted young concert-ready singers, pianists, and string players (violinists, violists, and cellists) since it was organized in 1948. This competition is designed for young performing artists at a high level of professionalism. Age limited to eighteen through thirty-two. This is not a college scholarship program. Deadline: January 10.

2688.

Washington Internships for Students of Engineering

1899 L Street, N.W., Suite 500
Washington, DC 20036
(202) 466-8744

15 ten-week summer internships providing travel allowance and a $2,700 stipend to undergraduate seniors majoring in engineering. Applicants must have completed their undergraduate junior year by the time internship begins and plan to return to school for at least one more semester. Interns are introduced to technical public policy issues and attend twenty to thirty meetings. Interns are housed in a George Washington University dormitory (for which students must pay from the stipend). Deadline: December 20.

2689.

Washington Post
Internship Program

1150 15th Street, N.W.
Washington, DC 20071-5508
(202) 334-6000
http://www.washingtonpost.com/

15 to 20 twelve-week summer internships providing $730 per week are open to undergraduate juniors, seniors, and graduate students. Applicants must have previous journalism experience. Interns are assigned to national, metro, business, sports, or style departments to work as reporters. Deadline: November 15.

2690.

Washington Post
Thomas Ewing Memorial Educational Grants for Newspaper Carriers

1150 15th Street, N.W.
Washington, DC 20071-5508
(202) 334-5799
(202) 334-6000

25 to 35 scholarship grants ranging from $1,000 to $2,000 to graduating high school seniors or undergraduate students. Must be current *Post* carriers who have been on-route for the past eighteen months. Students may be in any area of study. Award is made to encourage pursuit of higher education. Deadline: last Friday in January.

2691.

Washington Press Association
Scholarship Awards

217 Ninth Avenue, North
Seattle, WA 98109

1 or more scholarships of at least $500 to undergraduate juniors or seniors majoring in communications at a two- or four-year institution. Washington Press Association members wanting additional formal educational training are also eligible. Based on academic achievement in communications, financial need, and career potential or performance. Deadline: none specified.

2692.

Washington Society of Professional Engineers

530 North Columbia River Highway, Suite C
St. Helens, OR 97051
(503) 366-2851
(503) 366-2850 Fax
http://www.nspe.org/
peo@hevanet.com

Scholarships of varying amounts to students in an engineering curriculum. Designated engineering scholarships requiring that a specific university be attended or a specific program of engineering study be pursued are also offered. For Washington residents only. Deadline: mid-November; may vary.

2693.

Washington Society of Professional Journalists/ Western WA Chapter
Betterment of Journalism Scholarship

217 Ninth Avenue, North
Seattle, WA 98109

1 scholarship of at least $500 to an undergraduate or graduate student majoring in broadcast or print journalism. Must be attending a Washington State institution with a journalism program. Based on financial need and potential to become a working journalist. Preference given to minority students.

2694.
Washington State Higher Education Coordinating Board
Washington State Benefits to Blind Students
917 Lakeridge Way
P.O. Box 43430
Olympia, WA 98504-3430
(360) 753-7800
http://HECB.wa.gov/

Available only to blind students who are residents of Washington State. Amounts vary with students. For more information, write to above address.

2695.
Washington State Higher Education Coordinating Board
Washington State Need Grant Program
917 Lakeridge Way
P.O. Box 43430
Olympia, WA 98504-3430
(360) 753-7800
http://HECB.wa.gov/

To assist needy and disadvantaged students to obtain higher education. Available only to residents of Washington State.

2696.
Washington State Higher Education Coordinating Board
Washington State Robert C. Byrd Program
917 Lakeridge Way
P.O. Box 43430
Olympia, WA 98504-3430
(360) 753-7800
http://HECB.wa.gov/

Varying numbers of scholarships of $1,500 to graduating high school seniors who are Washington residents and who meet two of these three requirements: rank in the top 5 percent of their class, have at least a 3.5 GPA, or have at least an 1100 on SAT or 27 on ACT. Students are unable to apply directly. Must be nominated by a school official. Deadline: May 1.

2697.
Washington State Higher Education Coordinating Board
Washington State Tuition Waiver Program
917 Lakeridge Way
P.O. Box 43430
Olympia, WA 98504-3430
(360) 753-7800
http://HECB.wa.gov/

The state's public two- and four-year colleges and universities will waive all or part of the tuition and fees of needy and disadvantaged students up to a level of 3 percent of the total tuition and fees. Only available to state residents.

2698.
Washington State Higher Education Coordinating Board
Washington State Work Study Program
917 Lakeridge Way
P.O. Box 43430
Olympia, WA 98504-3430
(360) 753-7800
http://HECB.wa.gov/

Provides employment opportunities to needy students attending public or private postsecondary educational institutions in the state of Washington. Based on financial need.

2699.
Water Environment Federation
Student Paper Competition
601 Wythe Street
Alexandria, VA 22314
(703) 684-2407

Awards of $250, $500, and $1,000 in each of four categories for papers written by undergraduate and graduate students on water pollution. Must submit 500-to-1,000-word abstracts on papers dealing with water pollution control, water quality problems, water-related concerns, or hazardous wastes. Individuals who have graduated within one calendar year are also eligible. Send a self-addressed, stamped envelope for guidelines. Deadline: January 1.

2700.
Waverly Community House, Inc.
F. Lammont Belin Arts Scholarships
Scholarships Selection Committee
Waverly, PA 18471
(717) 586-8191

Awards of $8,000 are made to artists in the following areas: painting, sculpture, music, drama, dance, literature, architecture, photography, printmaking, or film. Preference given to residents of Abington or Pocono Northeastern Region of Pennsylvania. In absence of suitable candidates from these areas, residents of other regions of the country are considered. Must furnish proof of ability. Deadline: December 15.

2701.
Welsh Society of Philadelphia
Cymdeithas Gymreig/Philadelphia Scholarships
c/o Daniel E. Williams
450 Broadway
Camden, NJ 08103
(609) 964-0891

Usually, 6 scholarships ranging from $500 to $1,000 to graduating high school seniors of Welsh descent. Must live within, or intend to go to a college or university within, 150 miles of metropolitan Philadelphia. Other students may be considered if there are no suitable applicants within the 150-mile radius. Based on SAT/ACT scores, academic record, potential, career goals, extracurricular activities, recommendations, and participation in or membership in a Welsh organization or church. Contact: Daniel E. Williams, Ysgrifennydd, at above address. Deadline: none specified.

2702.
Western Interstate Commission for Higher Education
WICHE Student Exchange Program
P.O. Drawer P
Boulder, CO 80301-9752

Allows out-of-state students to pay in-state resident fees. Students must be residents of Alaska, Arizona, California, Colorado, Hawaii, Idaho, Montana, Nevada, New Mexico, Oregon, Utah, Washington, or Wyoming and seeking a program not available in their home state. Only available for certain professional degrees. Contact above address for a list of states and participating schools.

2703.
Westinghouse Electric Corporation
Family Scholarship Program
c/o Manager of University Relations
Pittsburgh, PA 15521

Scholarships of varying amounts to graduating high school seniors. Must be dependents of employees. Recipients must have been accepted to an approved health professions school. Based on academic achievement and financial need. Other restrictions may apply.

2704.
Westinghouse Science Talent Search Scholarships
Science Service, Inc.
1719 North Street, N.W.
Washington, DC 20036

40 scholarships ranging from $1,000 to $20,000 to students who submit a 1,000-word report on an independent research project in the field of science, mathematics, or engineering, along with an application, transcript, test scores, and teacher recommendation. High school official must request applications. Deadline: December 15.

2705.
Westin Hotels & Resorts
Internship Coordinator
22001 Sixth Avenue, 13th Floor
Seattle, WA 98121
(206) 443-5000
(206) 443-8997 Fax

70 to 90 internships lasting from ten to twelve weeks to undergraduates, recent college graduates, and graduate students. International students are also eligible. Westin Hotels & Resorts operates over eighty hotels in sixteen countries worldwide. Interns work at the corporate headquarters in Seattle or directly at a Westin Hotel, including the Westin La Paloma in Tucson, the Westin Mission Hills Resort in Rancho Mirage, the Westin Bonaventure and the Century Plaza Hotel in Los Angeles, the Westin St. Francis in San Francisco, the Westin Maui in Hawaii, the Westin Hotel in Waltham, the Algonquin in New York, the Westin Hotel in Dallas, the Westin Galleria & Oaks in Houston, or the Westin Hotel in Seattle. Depending on the location, interns may work in public relations/marketing, special events, or promotions. Submit a résumé, cover letter, writing samples, and recommendations. Internships may be conducted in the summer, fall, or spring. Deadline: rolling.

2706.
West Virginia Department of Veterans' Affairs
West Virginia War Orphans Educational Benefits
1321 Plaza East, No. 101
Charleston, WV 25301-1405
(304) 348-3661

Financial assistance providing $225 per semester to high school students and $250 per semester to college students who are children of war veterans who died while on active duty or as a result of a service-connected injury. Must maintain a 2.0 GPA. Deadline: third Monday in July (fall); first Monday in December (spring).

2707.
West Virginia Department of Education
Central Office
1018 Kanawha Boulevard East, Suite 700
Charleston, WV 25301
(304) 558-4618
http://www.scusco.wvnet.edu

Approximately 5,700 grants ranging from $350 to $1,650 (not exceeding tuition and fees) to undergraduate students who are West Virginia residents in an approved postsecondary institution. Must be U.S. citizens. For entering freshmen, based on academic record, SAT/ACT, and financial need. For college students, based on college academic record and financial need. Deadline: March 1.

2708.
West Virginia Department of Education
Robert C. Byrd Scholarship Program
Central Office
1018 Kanawha Boulevard East, Suite 700
Charleston, WV 25301
(304) 558-4618
http://www.scusco.wvnet.edu

Varying numbers of scholarships of $1,500 to graduating high school seniors who are West Virginia residents and who meet two of these three requirements: rank in the top 5 percent of their class, have at least a 3.5 GPA, or have at least an 1100 on SAT or 27 on ACT. Students are unable to apply directly. Students must be nominated by a school official. Deadline: May 1.

2709.
West Virginia Department of Education
Underwood–Smith Teacher Scholarship Program
Central Office
1018 Kanawha Boulevard East, Suite 700
Charleston, WV 25301
(304) 558-4618
http://www.scusco.wvnet.edu

Scholarships of up to $5,000 to high school seniors or graduates who graduated in the top 10 percent of their class or scored in the top 10 percent statewide in ACT, or who have a 3.2 GPA after completing two years of course work at an approved institute in West Virginia and who are pursuing a career in education. Students must agree to teach at the preschool, elementary, or secondary school level in West Virginia for two years for each year of assistance, unless entering a teacher-shortage area, an exceptional children's program, or an economically disadvantaged area as designated by the West Virginia Board of Education. Students failing to fulfill obligation must repay the loan, with interest and collection fees. Deadline: April 1.

2710.
West Virginia Society of Professional Engineers
179 Summers Street, Suite 804
Charleston, WV 25301-2131
(304) 346-2100

Scholarships of varying amounts to students in an engineering curriculum. Designated engineering scholarships requiring that a specific university be attended or a specific program of engineering study be pursued are also offered. For West Virginia residents only. Deadline: varies.

2711.
Weyerhaeuser
Information Technology Intern Program
PC2-18
Tacoma, WA 98477
(206) 924-4403

35 to 40 six-month summer/fall and winter/spring internships providing round-trip travel and a salary ranging from $280 to $400 per week for undergraduates and from $440 to $560 per week for graduate students. Internships are at the Tacoma, Washington, office and at 250 offices and plants nationwide. Undergraduate juniors, seniors, and graduate students must be majoring in computer science, management information systems, computer information systems, industrial engineering, electrical engineering, or physics. Undergraduate freshmen and sophomores may apply only for summer positions. Deadline: January 10 (summer/fall); October 1 (winter/spring).

2712.
Weyerhaeuser
Recruiting and Staffing
CH1 J26
Tacoma, WA 98477
(206) 924-2602

210 three-month summer internships providing round-trip travel and a salary ranging from $280 to $400 per week for undergraduates and from $440 to $560 per week for graduate students. Internships are at the Tacoma, Washington, office and at 250 offices and plants nationwide. Open to undergraduate freshmen, sophomores, juniors, and seniors, and graduate students who are majoring in engineering (mechanical, chemical, electrical, or industrial), pulp and paper science, accounting, forestry, environmental science, or communications. High school students are hired to do clerical work. Deadline: rolling.

2713.
Whirly–Girls Memorial Scholarship
Organization of Women Helicopter Pilots
1619 Duke Street
Alexandria, VA
(703) 683-4646

1 scholarship of $4,000 to a female commercial airplane pilot to obtain an initial or additional helicopter rating. Based on financial need and career goals. Must hold a valid FAA pilot's license for an airplane, balloon, or glider. Award

may only be used for helicopter flight training. Other restrictions may apply. Deadline: October 31.

2714.
White House Fellowships
Intern Program
Office of Presidential Personnel
Old Executive Office Building
Room 151
Washington, DC 20500
(202) 456-6676

200 internships providing no compensation to undergraduate and graduate students and recent graduates interested in government. Interns are placed in twenty-two different White House offices: Advance, Cabinet Affairs, Chief of Staff, Communications, Correspondence, Domestic Policy, Office of the Executive Clerk, First Lady's Office, General Counsel, Intergovernmental Affairs, Legislative Affairs, Management/Administration/Operations, National Economic Council, Office of National Service, Photography Office, Political Affairs, Presidential Personnel, Public Liaison, Scheduling, Staff Secretary, Vice President's Office, and Visitors' Office. Deadline: April 15 (summer); June 1 (fall); November 15 (spring).

2715.
Whitney Museum of American Art
Internship Program
Personnel Office
945 Madison Avenue
New York, NY 10021
(212) 570-3600

20 internships providing no compensation to undergraduate juniors, seniors, and graduate students interested in art museums. Interns are assigned to curatorial, development, education, film and video, library, operations, public relations, publications, and registrar in New York City or Stamford, Connecticut. Internships last for eight weeks full-time during the summer and from ten to sixteen weeks part-time during the fall and spring. Deadline: March 1 (summer); rolling (fall and spring).

2716.
Wichita Eagle
Internship
825 East Douglas
Wichita, KS 67202
(316) 268-6426
(316) 268-6627 Fax

6 full-time internships lasting ten to thirteen weeks providing $340 per week to undergraduate juniors and graduate students who have at least one semester of study after completion of internship. Interns work as staff photographers, reporters, copy editors, and graphic artists. Submit a letter detailing interests, résumé, references, and work sample appropriate to area of interest; interview by person or phone. Deadline: December 15.

2717.
Wichita State University Playwriting Contest
Wichita State University Theatre
WSU, Box 31
Wichita, KS 67208

Awards are presented to two or three short, unpublished, unproduced plays or full-length plays by undergraduate or graduate U.S. college students. Include a self-addressed, stamped envelope when requesting information. Deadline: February 15.

2718.
The Widmeyer Group, Inc.
Internship Program
1875 Connecticut Avenue, N.W., Suite 640
Washington, DC 20009
(202) 667-0901

5 internships providing no compensation open to undergraduate students and fellowships providing $200 per week to graduate students with public relations experience and to recent graduates. Applicants should have an enthusiastic interest in the public relations profession. Interns photocopy reports, fax press releases, answer phones, clip newspaper articles, and are given assignments directly related to public relations. Deadline: May 1 (summer); August 1 (fall); December 1 (winter/spring).

2719.
Wildlife Habitat Council
Internship Coordinator
1010 Wayne Avenue, Suite 920
Silver Spring, MD 20910
(301) 588-8994

10 internships providing no compensation to undergraduates and $245 per week to recent college graduates. WHC is dedicated to protecting and enhancing wildlife habitat on corporate lands. Undergraduates write pamphlets on wildlife species, conduct research in the WHC library, and contact state agencies. Older interns work as research assistants, helping biologists research, write, and produce wildlife-management reports and maps. Undergraduate internships last for three months during the summer, and for recent college graduates they last six months and are conducted on an ongoing basis. Deadline: rolling.

2720.
The Wildlife Society
Internship Coordinator
5410 Grosvenor Lane, Suite 200
Bethesda, MD 20814
(301) 897-9770
(301) 530-2471 Fax
TWS@clark.net

2 internships providing $250 per week to undergraduates, recent college graduates, and graduate students to work in Bethesda. The Wildlife Society is a nonprofit organization dedicated to enhancing the scientific, technical, managerial, and educational capability of wildlife professionals. Interns work in the wildlife policy department, where they research conservation issues, prepare background information for use in testimony or comments, and assist with the preparation of Society publications. Internships last for twenty-four weeks and are conducted from January to June, or July to December. Deadline: December 5 (January-June); June 5 (July-December).

2721.
Wildwood Prize in Poetry
Attn: Director
Rose Lehrman Arts Center 213-E
Harrisburg Area Community College
3300 Cameron Street Road
Harrisburg, PA 17110
(717) 780-2487

1 prize of $500, and publication, is given each year for the best poem under 100 lines. Submit one to three poems in duplicate (one copy should state author's name, address, and telephone number). A $5 reading fee is required. Send self-addressed, stamped envelope for guidelines. Submit after September 30. Deadline: November 30.

2722.
William M. Grupe Foundation, Inc.
Scholarships
P.O. Box 775
Livingston, NJ 07039

50 to 100 scholarships per year ranging from $500 to $2,000 to residents of Bergen, Essex, or Hudson counties, New Jersey. Students may major in medicine, nursing, or paramedical fields. Applicants should indicate desire to practice in New Jersey. Students may apply every year.

2723.
William Randolph Hearst Foundation
888 Seventh Avenue
New York, NY 10019

Scholarships are awarded annually to undergraduate journalism majors with matching grants to college or universities.

2724.
William Randolph Hearst Foundation
Broadcast News Competition
90 New Montgomery Street, #1212
San Francisco, CA 94105
(415) 543-4057

Awards ranging from $300 to $2,000 to undergraduate journalism students at one of eighty-eight member colleges and universities of the Association of Schools of Journalism and Mass Communication. Must be full-time students. Must submit an audio (radio) or video (television) tape and scripts. Based on writing quality, clarity, depth, focus, editing, content, appropriate use of unique qualities of either medium, and broadcast skills.

2725.
William Randolph Hearst Foundation
Photojournalism Competition
90 New Montgomery Street, #1212
San Francisco, CA 94105
(415) 543-4057

Awards ranging from $300 to $2,000 to undergraduate journalism students at one of eighty-eight member colleges and universities of the Association of Schools of Journalism and Mass Communication. Must be full-time students. Must submit a portfolio of no more than six entries (one slide per single photograph and up to ten slides per picture story or series). Must include each of the following categories: news, features, sports, and portrait/personality. Based on photographic quality, versatility, consistency, human interest, news value, and originality.

2726.
William Randolph Hearst Foundation Writing Competition
90 New Montgomery Street, #1212
San Francisco, CA 94105
(415) 543-4057

Awards ranging from $300 to $2,000 to undergraduate journalism students at one of eighty-eight member colleges and universities of the Association of Schools of Journalism and Mass Communication. Must be full-time students. Students must submit a single article written by them and printed in their campus or professional publication. Based on writing quality, clarity, depth of reporting, focus, editing, content, color, and construction.

2727.
Wilson Ornithological Society Research Grants Margaret Morse Nice Awards
c/o Museum of Zoology
University of Michigan
Ann Arbor, MI 48109-1079

1 grant of $200 to an independent researcher without access to funds and facilities at colleges, universities, or governmental agencies. Must be amateur, including high school student. May conduct any kind of avian research. Deadline: March 1.

2728.
Wilson Ornithological Society Research Grants Paul A. Steward Awards
c/o Museum of Zoology
University of Michigan
Ann Arbor, MI 48109-1079

Several awards of up to several hundred dollars to anyone conducting avian studies. Preference is given to, but not limited to, those studying bird movements based on banding, analysis of recoveries and returns of banded birds, or on economic ornithology. Deadline: March 1.

2729.
Wisconsin Congress Parents and Teachers, Inc. Brookmire-Hastings Scholarships
223 North Baldwin
Madison, WI 53707
(608) 256-1312

2 scholarships of $250 per year for four years to Wisconsin graduating high school seniors in public high schools. Recipients must be outstanding high school graduates who are pursuing a career in child care or education. Deadline: March 15.

2730.
Wisconsin Department of Public Instruction Academic Scholarships
125 South Webster
P.O. Box 7841
Madison, WI 53707-4563
(800) 441-4563
(608) 267-2206
(608) 267-2808 Fax
http://www.state.wi.us/

Scholarships of up to $2,100 to high school seniors attending a University of Wisconsin-system campus or a Wisconsin technical school. Students must be pupils with the highest grade point averages in their schools. Renewable for up to three years if attending a four-year institution.

2731.
Wisconsin Department of Public Instruction Higher Education Grant Program
125 South Webster
P.O. Box 7841
Madison, WI 53707-4563
(800) 441-4563
(608) 267-2206
(608) 267-2808 Fax
http://www.state.wi.us/

Grants of up to $1,800 per year to high school seniors attending a state vocational school or the University of Wisconsin. Must be at least half-time students, be residents of Wisconsin, and have financial need.

2732.
Wisconsin Department of Public Instruction Minority Retention Grants
125 South Webster
P.O. Box 7841
Madison, WI 53707-4563
(800) 441-4563
(608) 267-2206
(608) 267-2808 Fax
http://www.state.wi.us/

Financial assistance provided to African American, Hispanic American, or Native American students and those admitted to the U.S. before December 31, 1975, who are former citizens of Laos, Vietnam, or Cambodia, or whose ancestor was a citizen of one of those countries. Students may attend public or private Wisconsin institutions.

2733.
Wisconsin Department of Public Instruction Native American Grant Program
125 South Webster
P.O. Box 7841
Madison, WI 53707-4563
(800) 441-4563
(608) 267-2206
(608) 267-2808 Fax
http://badger.state.wi.us/education/

Grants of up to $1,800 per academic year to Native American Indians who are Wisconsin residents attending either an in-state or out-of-state institution. Renewable for up to five years. Must be at least one-quarter or more Native American, certified by an appropriate Indian Agency. Based on financial need.

2734.
Wisconsin Department of Public Instruction Part-Time Student Grants for Veterans and Certain Eligible Dependents
125 South Webster
P.O. Box 7841
Madison, WI 53707-4563
(800) 441-4563
(608) 267-2206
(608) 267-2808 Fax
http://badger.state.wi.us/education

Grants providing tuition, fees, and up to $270 per course ($1,000 maximum) for books. Must be eligible veteran or unmarried widow, widower, or minor or dependent child of a deceased veteran. Applicants must be Wisconsin residents currently living in Wisconsin. Only for a first-time undergraduate degree. Deadline: 60 days after official completion of the course.

2735.
Wisconsin Department of Public Instruction
Robert C. Byrd Honors Scholarship Program
125 South Webster
P.O. Box 7841
Madison, WI 53707-4563
(800) 441-4563
(608) 267-2206
(608) 267-2808 Fax
http://badger.state.wi.us/education

Varying numbers of scholarships of $1,500 to graduating high school seniors. Selection is based on outstanding academic achievement. Must be Wisconsin residents and attend a eligible Wisconsin institution. Students are unable to apply directly. Students must be nominated by a school official. Deadline: May 1.

2736.
Wisconsin Department of Public Instruction
Talent Incentive Program
125 South Webster
P.O. Box 7841
Madison, WI 53707-4563
(800) 441-4563
(608) 267-2206
(608) 267-2808 Fax
http://badger.state.wi.us/education

Scholarships of up to $1,800 to nontraditional undergraduate students. Must have financial need. Contact the Wisconsin Educational Opportunity Program, 223 West Galina Court, Suite 104, Milwaukee, WI 53212.

2737.
Wisconsin Department of Public Instruction
Tuition Grant Program
125 South Webster
P.O. Box 7841
Madison, WI 53707-4563
(800) 441-4563
(608) 267-2206
(608) 267-2808 Fax
http://badger.state.wi.us/education

Grants of $2,172 to students who are Wisconsin residents and are attending a college, university, or nursing program in Wisconsin. Tuition must be in excess of that at the University of Wisconsin. May be full- or half-time students. Based on financial need. Deadline: none.

2738.
Wisconsin Department of Public Instruction
Visual and Hearing Impaired Grants
125 South Webster
P.O. Box 7841
Madison, WI 53707-4563
(800) 441-4563
(608) 267-2206
(608) 267-2808 Fax
http://badger.state.wi.us/education

Grants of up to $1,800 to students who are Wisconsin residents and legally deaf or blind. If the impairment prevents the student from studying in a Wisconsin program, he or she may attend an out-of-state school specializing in teaching the blind or deaf.

2739.
Wisconsin Department of Veterans' Affairs
Full-Time Education Grants
P.O. Box 7843
Madison, WI 53707-7843
(608) 266-1309

Grants of up to $400 to married veterans or veterans with dependents, and $200 for single veterans, who are full-time undergraduate students at a Wisconsin institution. Veteran must have served for ninety days or more, for other than training, in the Armed Forces between August 5, 1964, and July 1, 1975, or been eligible for an Expeditionary Medal for service in Lebanon between August 1, 1982, and August 1, 1984, or Grenada from October 23, 1983, to November 21, 1983, or other periods of conflict. Not available to dependents or veterans of other wars. Contact school's financial aid office or above address.

2740.
Wisconsin League for Nursing, Inc.
Scholarships
2121 East Newport Avenue
Milwaukee, WI 53211
(414) 332-6271

Scholarships of $500 to undergraduate and graduate students pursuing a diploma or degree (ADN diploma, RN seeking BSN, BSN-RN seeking MSN) in an accredited program in Wisconsin. Must be halfway through academic program. Must have at least a 3.0 GPA and demonstrate financial need. Must be recommended by dean or director at NLN-accredited school. Contact financial aid office or nursing department for an application. Must be Wisconsin residents. Deadline: February 28.

2741.
Wisconsin Society of Professional Engineers
6501 Watts Road, Suite 112
Madison, WI 53719
(608) 278-7000
(608) 278-7005 Fax
http://www.nspe.org/
wspe1@aol.com

Scholarships of varying amounts to students in an engineering curriculum. Designated engineering scholarships requiring that a specific university be attended or a specific program of engineering study be pursued are also offered. For Wisconsin residents only. Deadline: varies.

2742.
Wisconsin State Vocational Rehabilitation
Division of Rehabilitation
1 West Wilson Street, 8th Floor
P.O. Box 7852
Madison, WI 53707
(800) 362-9611

Scholarships of varying amounts (based on individual's needs) are available to students with a mental or physical disability that is a handicap for employment. Priority is given to, but not limited to, persons with severe disabilities (paraplegic, quadriplegic, multiple amputees, etc.). Must be residents of Wisconsin. Deadline: none.

2743.
WJBK–TV
College Internship Program
Attn: Intern Coordinator
Box 2000
Southfield, MI 48037
(313) 557-2000
(313) 557-0280 Fax

45 internships lasting twelve to sixteen weeks to undergraduate juniors and seniors, and graduate students. Must be majoring in advertising, communications, English, journalism, public relations, or related fields. Interns work at the CBS affiliate in various departments: news, program, creative services, graphic arts, public affairs, public relations, research, or marketing. Internships can be part- or full-time, during June to August, January to May, or September to December. Must receive college credit for internship. Submit letter detailing interests, application, résumé, and letters of recommendation from school intern coordinator, and have an in-person interview. Deadline: six weeks before internship period begins.

2744.
WMAL Radio
Internship Program
4400 Jenifer Street, N.W.
Washington, DC 20015
(202) 686-3100
(202) 244-2700 Fax

30 to 40 internships lasting three months to undergraduate juniors or seniors, or graduate students who must be majoring in marketing, newspaper journalism, writing, or other relevant experience. Interns work in various departments: advertising, marketing, news, or promotions. Interns can work part- or full-time, with openings occurring year-round. Submit an application form, résumé, and course verification form. Deadline: open.

2745.
WNBC–TV
Internships
Attn: Administrator of Employee Relations
30 Rockefeller Plaza, Suite 1175
New York, NY 10112
(212) 664-4228
(212) 664-6449 Fax

20 to 24 internships to undergraduate sophomores, juniors, and seniors interested in broadcasting, journalism, computer science, engineering, electronics, public relations, marketing, or finance. All applicants should have a high level of interpersonal communication skills and experience with Microsoft Word or WordPerfect. No monetary compensation is provided, but travel expenses are reimbursed. Sponsor is willing to complete any necessary paperwork required for intern to receive academic credit. Interns are provided with placement assistance, letters of

recommendation, names of contacts, job counseling, and résumé writing assistance. Internships are in News-4, creative services, press and publicity, public affairs, public service, visions, engineering and operations, Hispanic public affairs programming, African-American public affairs programming, TV research and marketing, and computer systems. Internships last one semester and are conducted during fall, winter/spring, and summer. Deadline: November 1 (winter/spring); April 1 (summer); August 1 (fall).

2746.
WNET–TV
College Internship Program
356 West 58th Street
New York, NY 10019
(212) 560-6865 Fax
Written inquiries only

Varying numbers of internships lasting one semester open to undergraduate juniors and seniors, and graduate students. No monetary compensation, though travel expenses are reimbursed and lunch is provided. Sponsor is willing to complete necessary paperwork required for academic credit. Interns work in broadcast management, educational service, marketing, program information, programming, production, public affairs, or management information systems. Interns perform research, typing, word processing, photocopying, and clerical duties. Applicants should have a working knowledge of computer applications, such as Microsoft Word for Windows, and be full-time students. Interns are provided with placement assistance, letters of recommendation, and names of contacts. In-person interviews are recommended. Deadline: April 12 (summer); July 12 (fall); October 11 (winter); December 13 (spring).

2747.
WNYC–TV
Internships
Attn: Human Resources Assistant
One Centre Street
New York, NY 10007
(212) 669-7711
(212) 669-8986 Fax

7 internships open to undergraduate and graduate students interested in broadcast journalism, marketing, and space planning. Interns work in television programming, radio programming, marketing and communications, membership department, or facilities and construction. Internships last for one semester, but offer no monetary compensation except for travel expenses reimbursement. Sponsor is willing to complete necessary paperwork for intern to receive academic credit. Placement assistance and recommendation letters are provided upon completion of the internship. In-person interview is required. Deadline: none specified.

2748.
WNYW–FOX Television
Internships
Attn: Personnel Manager
205 East 67th Street
New York, NY 10021
(212) 452-5700

Varying numbers of internships open to undergraduate juniors and seniors who are majoring in communications and/or journalism. Interns receive a $5-per-day travel stipend and are able to attend seminars and workshops. Interns must receive academic credit or have a statement from the school that the internship will be recorded on the student's transcript. Interns are assigned to work in human resources, "McCreary Report," "A Current Affair," publicity, community affairs, sales, traffic research, 10 o'clock evening news, "Good Day New York," programming, or newsroom research. Duration of internship varies. Deadline: late summer for fall semester; late November for spring semester; April for summer semester.

2749.
Wolf Trap Foundation for the Performing Arts
Intern Coordinator
1624 Trap Road
Vienna, VA 22182
(703) 255-1900

20 twelve-week internships during the summer (full-time), fall (part-time), and spring (part-time) providing $150 per week compensation, open to undergraduate sophomores, juniors, seniors, recent graduates, and graduate students. Though open to all majors, two departments have some prerequisities. Interns gain valuable theater-operations experience and a taste of the footlights. Deadline: March 10 (summer); rolling (fall and spring).

2750.
Woman's Auxiliary of the American Institute of Mining, Metallurgical and Petroleum Engineers, Inc.
345 East 47th Street, 4th Floor
New York, NY 10017
(212) 705-7605

All or part of the educational expenses of the recipient are offered as a scholarship/loan. Recipient is expected to repay only 50 percent of the monies received from the fund, with no interest charges, commencing six months after graduation. Open to any student majoring in engineering (mining, metallurgy, geology, geophysics, petroleum, mineral science, geological oceanograpy, materials engineering, materials science, and mining economics). Contact the local Section Scholarship Chairman. For information about local Section Scholarship Chairman, contact above address. Deadline: March 15.

2751.
Woman's Auxiliary of the American Institute of Mining, Metallurgical and Petroleum Engineers
Scholarship-Loan Fund Chairman
345 East 47th Street, 14th Floor
New York, NY 10017
(212) 705-7605

Scholarship/loan amounts vary. Open to undergraduate juniors or seniors majoring in earth sciences, mining engineering, or petroleum engineering. Applicants receive a scholarship loan to cover all or part of their education. Recipients only repay one-half of the interest-free loan. Repayment begins six months after graduation. Deadline: March 15.

2752.
Women and Foundations/Corporate Philanthropy (WAF/CP)
Diversity Internship Program
322 Eighth Avenue, Suite 702
New York, NY 10001
(202) 463-9934
(202) 463-9417 Fax

36 internships per year lasting three to four months, either full-time or part-time from September to May, providing an average salary of $10 per hour. Open to undergraduate juniors, seniors, college graduates, graduate students, mid-career persons, and persons reentering the work force. All majors welcome. Positions are in Boston, MA: New York, NY; Minneapolis/St. Paul, MN; San Francisco Bay area, and throughout North Carolina. Strong written and oral communication skills required. Understanding of nonprofit sector, research experience, and previous community service preferred. Program is for those with a desire to assume leadership positions in philanthropic organizations. Works to increase funding for programs serving all women and girls, and to promote the leadership of women and people of color in philanthropy. Submit application form, letter outlining interests, résumé, letters of recommendation, and writing sample. Interview in person. Deadline: June (fall); December (spring).

2753.
Women Athletes' Voice of Encouragement (WAVE)
WAVE Excellency Awards, WAVE Grants and WAVE Scholarships
(800) 662-3263

Numerous grants, awards, and scholarships of varying amounts, totaling $143,000, to high schools and outstanding female high school athletes. The program's goals are to increase participation in women's high school sports and to teach good nutrition to teenage women. The WAVE Excellency Awards honor outstanding women's sports programs. The WAVE Grants assist female high school athletic programs in need of funding. Coaches, teachers, and parents can nominate senior high school female athletes for WAVE Scholarships. Contact in January. Deadline: April 1.

2754.
Women Band Directors National Association
Kathryn G. Siphers Scholarship
344 Overlook Drive
West Lafayette, IN 47906
(317) 463-1738

1 scholarship to a young female college student pursuing a career as a band director. Must be instrumental-music major working toward a degree in music education. Deadline: December 1.

2755.
Women Band Directors National Association
Virginia Volkwein Memorial Scholarship
344 Overlook Drive
West Lafayette, IN 47906
(317) 463-1738

1 scholarship to a young female college student pursuing a career as a band director. Must be instrumental-music major working toward a degree in music education. Deadline: December 1.

2756.
Women Grocers of America
Mary Macey Scholarship Program
1825 Samuel Morse Drive
Reston, VA 22090-5317
(703) 437-5300

1 scholarship of at least $1,000 to an undergraduate or graduate student in management or food science. Must be pursuing a career in a food industry–related career. Must be used at a recognized, accredited U.S. college or university. Must be U.S. citizens or permanent residents. Other restrictions may apply. Deadline: June 1.

2757.
Women in Communications, Inc.—Akron Chapter
250 Mistwood Drive
Tallmadge, OH 44278
http://www.womcom.org/prochap_about.htm/

1 or 2 scholarships of $1,000 to students at Kent State University, Mt. Union College, Malone College, or the University of Akron. Must be majoring in journalism and completing sophomore year. Based on academic record, journalism-related activities, and financial need.

2758.
Women in Communications, Inc.—Columbus
1554 Abraham Woods Road
Columbus, OH 48232
http://www.womcom.org/prochap_about.htm/

2 scholarships of $1,000 to students majoring in journalism or communications at Ohio State University or Otterbein or Ohio University. Based on academic record, ability, and financial need. 1 award of $1,000 to a student who is a central Ohio resident majoring in journalism or communications at an accredited institution. 1 award of $500 to a mature adult returning to school and majoring in journalism or communication. Must be a central Ohio resident.

2759.
Women in Communications, Inc.—Columbus
 Non–Traditional Student Scholarship
1554 Abraham Woods Road
Columbus, OH 48232
http://www.womcom.org/prochap_about.htm/

1 scholarship of $500 to a nontraditional undergraduate or graduate student in journalism or communications. Must attend a four-year accredited institution. Must be an Ohio resident and a U.S. citizen. Based on academic record, ability, and financial need. Other restrictions may apply. Deadline: varies.

2760.
Women in Communications, Inc.—Dallas Chapter
Helen Jane Wamboldt Memorial Scholarship
Attn: Scholarship Chair
411 East Highway 67
Duncanville, TX 75137
(817) 267-8643 Hotline
(214) 890-2991
http://www.womcom.org/prochap_about.htm/

1 or 2 scholarships of $500 to undergraduate students with at least one semester remaining. Must be students members of WIC. Must be taking at least fifteen credit hours per semester and be majoring in communications. Other restrictions may apply. Deadline: late January.

2761.
Women in Communications, Inc.—Dallas Chapter
Members Scholarship
411 East Highway 67
Duncanville, TX 75137
(817) 267-8643 Hotline
(214) 890-2991
http://www.womcom.org/prochap_about.htm/

Reimbursement assistance of up to half of tuition to undergraduate and graduate students in communications. Award is meant to assist members of WIC, Dallas Chapter, in furthering their education. Must be Texas residents and attend a Texas institution. Must be U.S. citizens. Other restrictions may apply. Deadline: none.

2762.
Women in Communications, Inc.—Detroit
 Chapter
Lenore Upton Scholarship
2134 Mortenson Boulevard
Berkley, MI 48072-1965
(248) 559-2362

1 scholarship of $1,000 to a female Michigan resident who is an undergraduate junior or senior or graduate student attending a Michigan institution and majoring in journalism or communications. Must be recommended by a faculty member or department chairperson. Based on academic record, communication skills, and financial need. Deadline: early April.

2763.
Women in Communications, Inc.—Detroit
 Chapter
Lucy Corbet Scholarship
2134 Mortenson Boulevard
Berkley, MI 48072-1965
(248) 559-2362

1 scholarship ranging from $500 to $1,000 to a female upper-level undergraduate or graduate student majoring in communications, journalism, or TV/radio broadcasting. Must be a Michigan resident and attend an accredited four-year Michigan institution. Must be recommended by a faculty member or department chairperson. Based on academic record, communication skills, and financial need. Must be a U.S. citizen. Nonrenewable. Deadline: April 1.

2764.
Women in Communications, Inc.—Detroit
 Chapter
Mary Butler Scholarship
2134 Mortenson Boulevard
Berkley, MI 48072-1965
(248) 559-2362

1 scholarship of $500 to a female Michigan resident who is an undergraduate junior or senior or graduate student

attending a Michigan institution and majoring in journalism or communications. Must be recommended by a faculty member or department chairperson. Based on academic record, communication skills, and financial need. Deadline: early April.

2765.
Women in Communications, Inc.—Fort Worth
P.O. Box 3611, 4SM
Fort Worth, TX 75235-1611
(214) 792-4127

25 scholarships ranging from $300 to $1,500 to undergraduate or graduate students who are residents of Tarrant, Hood, Johnson, or Parker counties, Texas. Must be majoring in journalism or communications. Based on academic record and financial need. Deadline: January 1.

2766.
Women in Communications, Inc.—Houston
1110 Ferndale Court
Sugarland, TX 77479
(713) 227-5050 Hotline

Numerous scholarships for female journalism or communications majors attending Texas institutions. Deadline: varies.

2767.
Women in Communications, Inc.—Indianapolis
Scholarship Chairperson
2051 South 600 West
New Palestine, IN 46163-9791
(317) 861-0550

Grants of at least $200 to students attending accredited Indiana institutions who will be either undergraduate juniors or seniors during the award year. Based on academic record, extracurricular activities, and financial need. Deadline: April 1.

2768.
Women in Communications, Inc.—Los Angeles
21821 Burbank Boulevard
Los Angeles, CA 91367
(310) 228-1103 Hotline

Scholarships ranging from $100 to $2,500 to undergraduate or graduate students who are majoring in journalism or communications at an accredited Los Angeles institution. Deadline: varies.

2769.
Women in Communications, Inc.—New York
355 Lexington Avenue, 17th Floor
New York, NY 10017-6603
(212) 661-4737 Hotline

1 scholarship of $1,000 to a student attending a New York area institution majoring in communications. Based on academic record, involvement in communication-related activities, recommendations, and financial need. Deadline: April 15.

2770.
Women in Communications, National Offices
1244 Ritchie Highway, Suite 6
Arnold, MD 21012-1887
(410) 544-7442/(410) 544-4640 Fax
http://www.womcom.org/

There are 70 chapters throughout the United States. Most chapters offer scholarships of varying amounts. Check the website to find out if there is a chapter in or near your community and send a self-addressed, stamped envelope for information. Deadline: varies by chapter.

2771.
Women in Communications, Inc.—San Antonio
P.O. Box 780382
San Antonio, TX 72287
(210) 231-5799
http://www.wicsa.org

Scholarships of $200 and up are awarded to Bexar County residents who are college sophomores or higher. Based on academic achievement, need, and dedication to the profession of journalism or communications.

2772.
Women in Communications, Inc.—Seattle/ Western Washington Chapter
1412 S.W. 102nd Street, #224
Seattle, WA 98146
(206) 553-7620

1 to 4 scholarships ranging from $500 to $1,000 to students who are Washington residents, attending a Washington institution, and majoring in communications. Deadline: March 1.

2773.
Women in Communications, Inc.—Spokane
13224 Fourth Avenue
Spokane, WA 99216

1 scholarship of $500 to an undergraduate junior or senior majoring in journalism or communications and attending an institution in eastern Washington, northern Idaho, or western Montana. Deadline: June 1.

2774.
Women in Communications, Inc.—Toledo Chapter
Attn: Scholarship Chairperson
P.O. Box 1395
Toledo, OH 43603

2 scholarships of $750 to undergraduate students who are pursuing careers in communications, such as: marketing, public relations, journalism, graphic design, etc. One is awarded to a student attending or accepted to Bowling Green University and the other to a student attending or accepted to the University of Toledo. Selection is based on grade point average, cooperative education/internship participation, community involvement, and stated goals after graduation. Candidates must also have at least one semester remaining before graduation. Must be residents of the Toledo area. Contact chapter in the spring or summer for information and an application. Awarded in the fall. Deadline: varies.

2775.
Women in Communications, Inc.—Tulsa Chapter
110 East 2nd Street
Tulsa, OK 74103
(918) 596-2367

1 (or more) $500 scholarship to a student entering the junior year and pursuing a career in communications. Based on academic record, extracurricular activities, and writing samples. Must attend an Oklahoma four-year institution. Deadline: March 1.

2776.
Women Marines Association
WMA Scholarships
282 San Dimas Avenue
Oceanside, CA 92056
(619) 439-1447

Scholarships of $500 to high school seniors or undergraduate students who are sponsored by a WMA member for at least two years. High school students must have maintained a B average during the last three years in high school. College students must maintain a B average while in a two- or four-year institution. Deadline: March 31.

2777.
Women of the Evangelical Lutheran Church in America
Women of the ELC Scholarship
8765 West Higgins Road
Chicago, IL 60631-4189

1 scholarship ranging from $500 to $3,000 to a female college student who is twenty-one years of age or older (cannot be a high school senior) and has had at least a two-year interruption in her education. Cannot be studying for ordination, deaconess, or a church-related career. Based on goals, academic record beyond high school, Christian commitment, and financial need. Deadline: February.

2778.
Women Seamen's Friends Society of Connecticut
74 Forbes Avenue
New Haven, CT 06512
(203) 467-3887

91 scholarships, totaling $55,000, to Connecticut residents to study maritime sciences or to dependents of Connecticut merchant seamen for any field of study. Renewable with reapplication. Deadline: April 1 (summer studies); May 15 (fall and spring semesters).

2779.
Women's Equity Action League (WEAL)
WEAL Washington Intern Program
Intern Program Director
1250 I Street, N.W., Suite 305
Washington, DC 20005
(202) 898-1588

Internships to undergraduate, graduate, or law school students pursuing degrees in education, employment, the military, economics, women's studies, women's economic issues, pension, taxation, budget, and insurance. Students must be seeking reentry into the job market, changing careers, or upgrading credentials. Must be U.S. citizens or permanent residents. Other restrictions may apply. Deadline: early May (summer); early August (fall); early December (intersession).

2780.
Women's Sports Foundation
Travel & Training Grants
Eisenhower Park
East Meadow, NY 11554
(800) 227-3988 or (516) 542-4700

40 scholarships of up to $1,500 are awarded each year to help female athletes to reach higher ranking and achievement within their sport. The scholarship is for travel to competitions and for training. Based on financial need. Deadline: March 15; July 15; November 15.

2781.
Women's Transportation Seminar (WTS)
Undergraduate Scholarship
808 17th Street, N.W., Suite 200
Washington, DC 20006-3953
(202) 223-9669

1 scholarship of $2,000 to an undergraduate female student majoring in a transportation-related field. Must have a 3.0 GPA or higher. Obtain and submit applications from WTS chapters in home state. Each chapter may nominate one student. If there is no chapter in student's home state, contact the national headquarters for an application. Deadline: February.

2782.
Women's Western Golf Foundation Scholarships
Mrs. Peter C. Marshall
348 Granville Road
Cedarburg, WI 53012

12 scholarships of $1,500 to female high school seniors. Based on academics, financial need, excellence of character, and involvement or interest in golf. Skill or excellence in golf is not a criterion. Deadline: April 1.

2783.
Woods Hole Oceanographic Institution
Summer Student Fellowship
Fellowships Coordinator
Woods Hole, MA 02543
(508) 548-1400 ext. 2219

Fellowships providing a $3,080 stipend and travel allowance are provided to selected students participating in a summer oceanographic study at the Woods Hole Oceanographic Institution. Open to undergraduate juniors and seniors with an interest in oceanography and a major in any area of science or engineering. Deadline: March 1.

2784.
Worcester County Horticultural Society
Scholarships
Tower Hill Botanic Garden
11 French Drive
P.O. Box 598
Boylston, MA 01505-0598

2 scholarships ranging from $500 to $2,000 to undergraduate juniors, seniors, or graduate students majoring in agriculture, floriculture, horticulture, landscape architecture, or a related field. Must be U.S. citizens or permanent residents and be attending an accredited four-year college or university. Selection based on academic achievement, application,

recommendation letters, and financial need. Other restrictions may apply. Deadline: May 1.

2785.
World Federalist Association (WFA)
Internship Program
418 7th Street, S.E.
Washington, DC 20003
(202) 546-3950
(202) 546-3749 Fax

10 to 15 internships lasting three months providing $25 per week to undergraduate and graduate students who are majoring in communications, environmental studies, international law, political science, philosophy, or related areas. Internships take place in Washington, DC, nationwide, or Amsterdam, Netherlands. Interns conduct research on world order and U.N. reform issues. They assist with writing, editing, and layout for newsletters and publications. They also assist with lobbying activities, coordinate college campus programs, organize conferences, write news releases, promote WFA ideas and events to the media, and work with grassroots activists. Applicants must have strong written and oral communication skills, be extremely self-motivated and directed, and be able to work on a number of projects simultaneously. Submit a letter detailing interests, a résumé, writing samples, and have an interview in person or by phone. Deadline: open.

2786.
World's Best Short Story Contest
Writing Program, English Department
Florida State University
Tallahassee, FL 32306

Annual award for unpublished short story (no more than 250 words). Send a self-addressed, stamped envelope for rules. Deadline: February 15.

2787.
Writer's Digest Writing Competition
Attn: Contest Director
Writer's Digest Magazine
1507 Dana Avenue
Cincinnatti, OH 45207

Submissions must be unpublished. Send self-addressed, stamped envelope for rules. Deadline: May 31.

2788.
WUSA-TV
Channel 9 Internships
4100 Wisconsin Avenue, N.W.
Washington, DC 20016
(202) 895-5754

35 unpaid internships lasting from three to four months open to undergraduate juniors, seniors, and college graduates. All applicants should have an interest in broadcasting. Interns assist producers in news, sports, programming, and on-air promotion. Application process is through open interviews held at the station. Must provide a letter from the school that verifies enrollment and eligibility for credit. Interviews are conducted in November (for spring and summer) and in April (for summer and fall).

2789.
Wyoming Department of Education
Robert C. Byrd Scholarships
2300 Capitol Avenue
Hathaway Building, 2nd Floor
Cheyenne, WY 82002-0050
(307) 777-7674/(307) 777-6234 Fax
http://www.state.wy.us/

Varying numbers of scholarships of $1,500 to graduating high school seniors. Selection is based on outstanding academic achievement. Must be Wyoming residents and attend on eligible Wyoming institution. Students are unable to apply directly. Must be nominated by a school official. Deadline: May 1.

2790.
Wyoming Peace Officers Association
Wyoming Peace Officers Association Scholarship
P.O. Box 787
Cheyenne, WY 82001

1 scholarship of $750 to a dependent of an active, retired, or deceased law enforcement officer, or to someone currently working as a law enforcement officer, or to a student enrolled in a law enforcement program at the University of Wyoming or a Wyoming community college. Applications may be requested between June and September. Deadline: September 10.

2791.
Wyoming Society of Professional Engineers
Dr. John W. Steadman, P.E.
University of Wyoming
College of Engineering
Box 3295
Laramie, WY 82071
(307) 766-2240/(307) 766-4444 Fax

Scholarships of varying amounts to students in an engineering curriculum. Designated engineering scholarships requiring that a specific university be attended or a specific program of engineering study be pursued are also offered. For Wyoming residents only. Deadline: varies.

2792.
Xerox Corporation
P.O. Box 1600
Stamford, CT 06904

Scholarships of up to $4,000 to minority undergraduate students in engineering or science. Paid summer employment also available. Write an introductory letter explaining your educational situation. Other restrictions may apply. Deadline: none specified.

2793.
Yakima Indian Nation Scholarship Program
P.O. Box 151
Toppenish, WA 98948
(509) 865-5121

200 scholarships of $1,000 to undergraduate and graduate students in all fields of study. Must be enrolled members of

the Yakima Indian Nation. May be used at any accredited institution. Other restrictions may apply. Deadline: July 1.

2794.
Y•E•S to Jobs
1416 North La Brea Avenue
Hollywood, CA 90028
(213) 469-2411

300 to 400 ten-week summer internships providing $200 per week to minority high school students at least sixteen years old or older. International students attending school in the U.S. may apply. Internships and jobs are in artist development, creative, development, film, finance, graphics, legal, mail room, marketing, MIS, personnel, promotion, public relations agencies, publicity, record labels, sales, telecommunications, and television. Students can be employed at various locations: Los Angeles and San Francisco, CA; Miami, FL; Atlanta, GA; Chicago, IL; Indianapolis, IN; Detroit, MI; Minneapolis, MN; NJ; New York, NY; Cleveland, OH; Nashville, TN; Dallas, TX; and Washington, DC. Deadline: April 1.

2795.
Yosemite Association Student Internship
National Park Service
P.O. Box 2027
Wawona, CA 95389
(209) 372-0563

25 to 30 internships providing $35 per week, $1,000 bonus at end of program, free housing, and round-trip travel to undergraduate sophomores, juniors, and seniors, and graduate students. International students may apply. Interns work in two sections, Natural/Cultural Resources Interpretation and Wilderness Management. Interns in Interpretation prepare nature walks, talks, and campfire programs in the areas of geology, plants, forest ecology, astronomy, and pioneer history. Interns in Management issue backcountry permits and discuss weather conditions, equipment, and trail conditions with hikers. Internships last from ten to twelve weeks and are conducted during the summer, fall, or spring. Deadline: February 15.

2796.
Yoshiyama Award
P.O. Box 19247
Washington, DC 20036
(202) 457-0588

6 to 8 awards of $5,000 over two years to high school seniors. This is not a scholarship and students may not nominate themselves. Based on outstanding community service by high school students. Not based on academic achievement and student need not attend college. There are no restrictions on how the award can be used. Student's parent or other adult should contact above address and ask about the award. Deadline: April 1.

2797.
Young Menswear Association
1328 Broadway
New York, NY 10001
(212) 594-6422

1 scholarship of $2,000 per year to a student attending the Fashion Institute of Technology; Pratt Institute; North Carolina State, College of Textiles; or Philadelphia College of Textiles. Must be planning on a career in men's or women's apparel and/or textiles. Renewable up to four years.

2798.
Youth Foundation, Inc.
Alexander & Maude Hadden Scholarships
36 West 44th Street
New York, NY 10036
(212) 840-6291

90 renewable scholarships of $1,000 to high school seniors and undergraduate, graduate, and professional students. Contact this foundation in early fall. Send a self-addressed, stamped envelope. Student should write a letter briefly explaining educational plans and financial situation. Deadline: April 15.

2799.
Zeta Phi Beta Sorority
Deborah Partridge Wolfe International
   Fellowship
National Educational Foundation
1734 New Hampshire Avenue, N.W.
Washington, DC 20009
(202) 387-3103

1 scholarship ranging from $500 to $1,000 to an undergraduate or graduate student in any area of study. Must either be a U.S. citizen wanting to conduct full-time undergraduate or graduate study abroad or an undergraduate foreign student wanting to study full-time within the U.S. Must submit an application, transcript, and letters of recommendation. Other restrictions may apply. Deadline: February 1.

2800.
Zeta Phi Beta Sorority
General Undergraduate Scholarships
National Educational Foundation
1734 New Hampshire Avenue, N.W.
Washington, DC 20009
(202) 387-3103

Scholarships ranging from $500 to $1,000 to current female high school seniors and undergraduate freshmen, sophomores, and juniors. Must be full-time students in any major. No affiliation with Zeta Phi Beta is required. Award length is one year. Send a stamped, self-addressed envelope to the national headquarters for further information. Deadline: February 1.

2801.
Zeta Phi Beta Sorority
Isabel M. Henson Scholarship in Education
National Educational Foundation
1734 New Hampshire Avenue, N.W.
Washington, DC 20009
(202) 387-3103

1 scholarship ranging from $500 to $1,000 to a female undergraduate or graduate student in an accredited program of elementary or secondary education. Must submit an application, transcript, and letters of recommendation. Other restrictions may apply. Deadline: February 1.

2802.
Zeta Phi Beta Sorority
Lullelia W. Harrison Scholarship in Counseling
National Educational Foundation
1734 New Hampshire Avenue, N.W.
Washington, DC 20009
(202) 387-3103

Scholarships ranging from $500 to $1,000 to female full-time undergraduate or graduate students in counseling or counseling psychology. Must attend an accredited institution. Award length is one year. No affiliation with Zeta Phi Beta is required. Send a stamped, self-addressed envelope to the national headquarters. Other restrictions may apply. Deadline: February 1.

SCHOLARSHIPS TO SPECIFIC COLLEGES AND UNIVERSITIES

Unless noted, all entries require that students meet additional academic criteria as established by the college or university. Though not all schools offer athletic scholarships, the sports may be listed to provide additional information.

ALABAMA

Alabama A&M University
P.O. Box 1357
Normal, AL 35762
(205) 851-5000
http://www.aamu.edu/
aboyle@asnaam.aama.edu

2803. **Academic** Numerous scholarships ranging from $200 to $3,200 to students with at least a 3.0 GPA and scoring at least 720 on SAT or 16 on ACT. Renewable with a 3.0 GPA.

2804. **Academic** Numerous scholarships ranging from $200 to $3,200 to students with at least a 2.0 GPA and scoring at least 720 on SAT or 16 on ACT. Renewable with a 2.0 GPA.

2805. **Athletic (Men)** Basketball, cross-country, football, soccer, swimming, tennis, and track and field scholarships. Contact Athletic Director.

2806. **Athletic (Women)** Basketball, swimming and diving, track and field, and volleyball scholarships.

Alabama State University
915 South Jackson Street
Montgomery, AL 36104
(205) 293-4100
http://www.alasu.edu
drcump@asunet.alasu.edu

2807. **Athletic (Men)** Basketball, baseball, cross-country, football, golf, indoor track, tennis, and track and field scholarships. Contact Athletic Director.

2808. **Athletic (Women)** Basketball scholarships.

2809. **Presidential** 152 scholarships ranging from $3,000 to $4,000 to entering freshmen scoring at least 20 on ACT or 840 on SAT; with a minimum 3.5 GPA or a junior college transfer of at least a 3.5 GPA after completing twenty-four semester hours. Renewable with a 3.0 GPA.

2810. **University Scholar** 45 scholarships ranging from $2,900 to $4,900 to students with at least a 3.5 GPA and scoring at least 840 on SAT or 20 on ACT. Renewable with a 3.0 GPA.

Auburn University
Auburn, AL 36849
(205) 844-4000
http://www.auburn.edu/
admissions@mail.auburn.edu

2811. **Alumni Academic** 40 scholarships of $800 to students with at least a 3.5 GPA and scoring at least 1250 on SAT or 29 on ACT.

2812. **Athletic (Men)** Baseball, basketball, soccer, and tennis scholarships. Contact Athletic Director.

2813. **Athletic (Women)** Basketball, golf, gymnastics, swimming and diving, tennis, track and field, and volleyball scholarships.

2814. **Blount Presidential** 1 scholarship of $5,000 to a student with at least a 3.5 GPA and scoring at least 1360 on SAT or 31 on ACT. Renewable with a 3.0 GPA.

2815. **Dudley Academic** 50 scholarships of $1,250 to students with at least a 3.5 GPA and scoring at least 1250 on SAT or 29 on ACT.

2816. **Dudley Achievement** 10 scholarships of $500 to students with at least a 3.5 GPA and scoring at least 1250 on SAT or 29 on ACT. Renewable with a 3.0 GPA.

2817. **Dudley Opportunity** 15 scholarships of $1,250 to students with at least a 3.5 GPA and scoring at least 1250 on SAT or 29 on ACT. Renewable with a 3.0 GPA.

2818. **McWane Foundation** 1 scholarship of $6,000 to a student with at least a 3.5 GPA and scoring at least 1410 on SAT or 32 on ACT. Renewable with a 3.0 GPA.

2819. **Phi Eta Sigma Freshman Honor Society** 22 grants of $1,000 for entering freshman who meet certain criteria. Contact: Faculty Advisor of local chapter. Deadline: March 1.

2820. **Presidential Opportunity** Numerous $1,250 scholarships to students with at least a 3.5 GPA and at least 1250 on SAT or 29 on ACT. Renewable with a 3.0 GPA.

2821. **President's Scholar** 25 scholarships of $1,250 scholarships to students with at least a 3.5 GPA and at least 1250 on SAT or 29 on ACT. Renewable with a 3.0 GPA.

2822. **Tuition Waivers** Numerous partial- to full-tuition waivers to students who are employees or children of employees.

2823. **Vulcan/Presidential** 1 scholarship of $6,600 to a student with at least a 3.5 GPA and scoring at least 1410 on SAT or 32 on ACT. Renewable.

Auburn University at Montgomery
P.O. Box 244023
Montgomery, AL 36124
(334) 244-3000/(800) 227-2649
http://www.aum.edu/home/
auminfo@mickey.aum.edu

2824. **Athletic (Men)** Baseball, basketball, soccer, and tennis scholarships.

2825. **Athletic (Women)** Basketball and tennis scholarships.

2826. **Merit Scholarship** 140 scholarships ranging from $600 to $1,500 to students meeting certain state-residency criteria. Renewable with at least a 3.5 GPA.

Birmingham-Southern College
900 Arkadelphia Road
Birmingham, AL 35254
(205) 226-4600
http://www.bsc.edu/
admissions@bsc.edu

2827. **AMI Honors Nursing** 3 scholarships ranging from $3,000 to $8,000 to nursing students. Renewable with a 2.5 GPA.

2828. **Athletic (Men)** Baseball, basketball, soccer, and tennis scholarships.

2829. **Athletic (Women)** 5 full tennis scholarships.

2830. **Bicentennial** Numerous scholarships ranging from $2,000 to $3,000. Renewable with a 2.0 GPA.

2831. **BSC National Merit** Numerous scholarships ranging from $500 to $2,000. Renewable with a 2.0 GPA.

2832. **Christian Vocations** Numerous scholarships covering 15 percent of tuition to students entering Christian vocations. Renewable with a 2.0 GPA.

2833. **Church** Numerous scholarships ranging from $500 to $1,500 to students pursuing a church-related career. Renewable with a 2.0 GPA.

2834. **Eagle Scout** 3 scholarships of $1,000. Renewable with a 3.0 GPA.

2835. **Fine Arts** Numerous scholarships ranging from $1,000 to $3,000. Renewable with a 2.0 GPA.

2836. **Gorgas** 1 full-tuition scholarship. Renewable with a 3.0 GPA.

2837. **Health Careers** 10 scholarships toward tuition to students in the top 10 percent of their class. Renewable with a 3.0 GPA.

2838. **Hess Computer Science** 2 scholarships covering 50 percent of tuition. Renewable with a 3.0 GPA.

2839. **Honors Finalists** 6 scholarships of $5,000 to students in the top 10 percent of their class. Renewable with a 3.0 GPA.

2840. **Honors Semifinalists** 40 scholarships of $2,500 to students in the top 10 percent of their class. Renewable with a 3.0 GPA.

2841. **Junior College** 6 scholarships of half tuition to junior-college transfer students. Renewable with a 2.0 GPA.

2842. **McWane Finalists** 4 scholarships of up to $7,700 to students in the top 10 percent of their class. Renewable with a 3.0 GPA.

2843. **McWane Honors** 1 scholarship of up to $15,200 to a student in the top 10 percent of class. Renewable with a 3.0 GPA.

2844. **Model Senate** 4 scholarships from $1,000 to $3,000. Renewable with a 3.0 GPA.

2845. **Other Faiths** Numerous scholarships up to $930 for students of other faiths. Renewable with a 2.0 GPA.

2846. **Phi Beta Kappa** 4 tuition scholarships for students in the top 10 percent of their class. Renewable with a 3.0 GPA.

2847. **Presidential** 50 scholarships of $1,000. Renewable with a 2.0 GPA.

2848. **Small Business Career** 1 scholarship of $2,000. Renewable with a 3.0 GPA.

2849. **UMC Ministerial** Numerous scholarships up to $1,500 for ministerial students. Renewable with a 2.0 GPA.

Chattahoochee Valley Community College
2602 Savage Drive
Phoenix City, AL 36867
(205) 347-2623

2850. **Athletic (Men)** Baseball, basketball, and golf scholarships.

2851. **Athletic (Women)** 12 basketball and 18 softball scholarships. Contact Athletic Director.

2852. **Need-Based Assistance** Numerous need-based scholarships, loans, and work-study programs open to anyone accepted for admission with financial need. Contact the financial aid office.

Enterprise State Junior College
P.O. Box 1300
Enterprise, AL 36330
(205) 297-4981

2853. **Athletic (Men)** Baseball and basketball scholarships.

2854. **Athletic (Women)** 12 partial basketball scholarships. Contact Athletic Director.

2855. **Need-Based Assistance** Numerous need-based scholarships, loans, and work-study programs open to anyone accepted for admission with financial need. Contact the financial aid office.

Gadsden State Junior College
George Wallace Drive
Gadsden, AL 35999
(205) 546-0484

2856. **Athletic (Men)** Baseball and basketball scholarships.

2857. **Athletic (Women)** 12 basketball and 18 softball scholarships. Contact Athletic Director.

2858. **Need-Based Assistance** Numerous need-based scholarships, loans, and work-study programs open to anyone accepted for admission with financial need. Contact the financial aid office.

Huntingdon College
1550 East Fairview Avenue
Montgomery, AL 36106
(334) 833-4497
http://www.huntingdon.edu
admiss@huntingdon.edu

2859. **Academic Competitive** Unlimited number of scholarships ranging from $500 to all costs. Students must have at least a 2.5 GPA and at least 850 on SAT or 10 on ACT. Renewable with a 2.0 GPA.

2860. **Visual & Performing Arts Honors Program** Numerous $4,000 scholarships to students with at least a 2.25 GPA and scoring at least 800 on SAT or 18 on ACT. Renewable with a 2.0 GPA.

International Bible College
P.O. Box IBC
Florence, AL 35630
(205) 766-6610

2861. **Academic "Honors Program"** Numerous scholarships providing 50 percent of tuition to students who are first or second in their class.

Jacksonville State University
Jacksonville, AL 36265
(256) 782-5400
http://www.jsu.edu/
info@jsucc.jsu.edu

2862. **Athletic (Men)** Baseball, basketball, crew, cross-country, golf, riflery, soccer, and tennis scholarships.

2863. **Athletic (Women)** 8 basketball, 5 softball, 3 tennis, and 5 volleyball scholarships. Contact Athletic Director.

2864. **Faculty Scholars** 100 scholarships of $1,000 to students scoring at least 1230 on SAT or 26 on ACT. Renewable with a 2.5 GPA.

2865. **Leadership** 200 full-tuition scholarships.

2866. **Tuition Waivers** Numerous partial- to full-tuition waivers to students who are employees or children of employees.

Jefferson Davis State Junior College
P.O. Box 958
Brewton, AL 36427-0958
(205) 867-4832

2867. **Athletic (Men)** Baseball, basketball, and tennis scholarships.

2868. **Athletic (Women)** 8 partial tennis scholarships.

2869. **Need-Based Assistance** Numerous need-based scholarships, loans, and work-study programs open to anyone accepted for admission with financial need. Contact the financial aid office.

Jefferson State Community College
2601 Carson Road
Birmingham, AL 35215
(205) 853-1200

2870. **Athletic (Men)** Baseball, basketball, or tennis scholarships.

2871. **Athletic (Women)** 8 partial tennis scholarships. Contact Women's Varsity Coach.

2872. **Need-Based Assistance** Numerous need-based scholarships, loans, and work-study programs open to anyone accepted for admission with financial need. Contact the financial aid office.

Judson College
P.O. Box 120
Marion, AL 36756
(334) 683-6161
http://home.judson.edu
admissions@future.judson.edu

2873. **Athletic (Men)** Baseball, basketball, cross-country, soccer, and tennis scholarships.

2874. **Athletic (Women)** Basketball, softball, and volleyball scholarships.

2875. **Garner Webb Honor** 5 full-tuition scholarships for students scoring at least 29 on ACT. Renewable.

2876. **Lockhart** 6 scholarships from $500 to full tuition. Renewable.

2877. **Music** 3 scholarships of $1,500 for music majors. Renewable.

Livingston University
Livingston, AL 35470
(205) 652-9661

2878. **Athletic (Men)** Baseball, basketball, football, golf, and tennis scholarships.

2879. **Athletic (Women)** Basketball, softball, tennis, and volleyball scholarships. Contact Athletic Director.

2880. **Leadership** 25 scholarships ranging from $250 to $1,500. Renewable.

2881. **Trustees** 130 scholarships ranging from $250 to $2,500 to students with at least a 3.2 GPA and scoring at least 20 on ACT. Renewable with a 2.75 GPA.

2882. **Tuition Waivers** Numerous partial- to full-tuition waivers to students who are employees or children of employees.

Lurleen Wallace State Junior College
P.O. Box 1418
Andalusia, AL 36420
(205) 222-6591

2883. **Athletic (Women)** Basketball and softball scholarships.

2884. **Need-Based Assistance** Numerous need-based scholarships, loans, and work-study programs open to anyone accepted for admission with financial need. Contact the financial aid office.

Oakwood College
Huntsville, AL 35896
(256) 726-7000
http://www.oakwood.edu
admissions@oakwood.edu

2885. **Academic** Number of $1,500 scholarships varies; must have at least a 3.0 GPA. Renewable.

2886. **Valedictorian/Salutatorian** Number of $1,200 scholarships varies; for students who were class valedictorian or saluatorian. Renewable.

Samford University
800 Lakeshore Drive
Birmingham, AL 35229
(800) 888-7218
http://www.samford.edu/
admiss@mailbox.samford.edu

2887. **Academic** 50 scholarships ranging from $500 to $3,000 to students in the top 10 percent of their class, with at least a 3.25 GPA, and who scored at least 1200 on SAT or 27 on ACT. Renewable with 3.0 GPA.

SCHOLARSHIP LISTING / 473

2888. **Athletic (Men)** Basketball, cross-country running, football, golf, tennis, and track and field.

2889. **Athletic (Women)** Cross-country running, golf, softball, track, track and field, and volleyball.

2890. **Honors** 25 scholarships of varying amounts open to students in the top 20 percent of their class, with at least a 3.0 GPA. Renewable with a 3.0 GPA.

2891. **Leadership** 30 scholarships of $1,000 to students in the top 50 percent of their class, with at least a 3.0 GPA, and who scored at least 1000 on SAT or 22 on ACT. Renewable with 2.5 GPA.

2892. **Ministerial** Varying numbers of scholarships of varying amounts to students who are pursuing careers in the clergy.

2893. **Minister's Dependents Awards** Varying numbers of scholarships of varying amounts to students who are dependents of ministers and who meet other criteria.

2894. **Music Awards** Varying numbers of scholarships of varying amounts to students meeting certain criteria who are music majors.

2895. **National Merit** Varying numbers of scholarships of varying amounts to students who received National Merit designation.

2896. **Presidential** 15 scholarships ranging from $1,000 to $4,672 to students in the top 10 percent of their class, with at least a 3.5 GPA, scoring at least 1250 on SAT or 28 on ACT. Renewable with a 3.0 GPA.

2897. **Tuition Waivers** Numerous partial- to full-tuition waivers to students who are employees or children of employees.

Southern Union State Junior College
Wadley, AL 36276
(205) 395-2211

2898. **Athletic (Men)** Baseball and basketball scholarships.

2899. **Athletic (Women)** basketball, diving, softball, and volleyball scholarships.

2900. **Need-Based Assistance** Numerous need-based scholarships, loans, and work-study programs open to anyone accepted for admission with financial need. Contact the financial aid office.

Spring Hill College
4000 Dauphin Street
Mobile, AL 36608
(334) 380-3030
http://www.shc.ed
admit@she.edu

2901. **Achievement** Numerous scholarships ranging from $500 to $2,500 to students in the top 50 percent of class, with at least a 2.5 GPA, scoring at least 1000 on SAT or 24 on ACT. Renewable with a 2.5 GPA.

2902. **Athletic (Men)** Baseball, basketball, golf, softball, and tennis scholarships.

2903. **Athletic (Women)** 3 basketball and 2 tennis partial scholarships; and 4 full basketball scholarships.

2904. **Metropolitan** Numerous scholarships ranging from $1,500 to $2,500 to students in top 50 percent of class, with at least a 2.5 GPA, and scoring at least 915 on SAT or 20 on ACT. Renewable with a 2.0 GPA.

2905. **Miller LeJeune** 4 scholarships of $11,000 to students in the top 20 percent of class, with a 3.0 GPA, and scoring at least 1125 on SAT or 27 on ACT. Renewable with a 3.0 GPA.

2906. **Presidential** 50 scholarships ranging from $500 to $7,300 to students in the top 30 percent of their class, with a 3.0 GPA, and scoring at least 1075 on SAT or 26 on ACT. Renewable with 3.0 GPA.

2907. **Presidential Honors** 6 scholarships of $7,300 to students in the top 20 percent of class, with a 3.0 GPA, and scoring at least 1125 on SAT or 27 on ACT. Renewable with a 3.0 GPA.

2908. **Transfer** Numerous scholarships ranging from $1,000 to $3,000 to students with at least a 2.0 GPA. Renewable with a 3.0 GPA.

Stillman College
P.O. Box 1430
Tuscaloosa, AL 35403
(205) 366-8816

2909. **Bellingrath** 8 scholarships covering all costs for students in the top 5 percent of their class, with at least a 3.5 GPA, and scoring at least 1000 on SAT or 22 on ACT. Renewable.

2910. **Stillman Scholar** 20 scholarships of $2,400 to students with at least a 3.0 GPA and scoring 800 on their SAT or 18 on their ACT.

Talladega College
627 West Battle Street
Talladega, AL 35160
(800) 633-2440

2911. **Academic** 100 scholarships ranging from $1,000 to $5,000 to students in the upper 25 percent of their class with at least a 3.0 GPA and scoring at least 742 on SAT or 16 on ACT.

2912. **Athletic (Men)** Baseball, basketball, indoor track, and track and field scholarships.

2913. **Athletic (Women)** Basketball scholarships.

Troy State University
University Avenue
Troy, AL 36082
(334) 670-3179
http://www.troyst.edu
jhutto@trojan.troyst.edu

2914. **Athletic (Men)** Baseball, basketball, cross-country, football, golf, tennis, and track and field scholarships.

2915. **Athletic (Women)** Basketball, softball, tennis, track and field, and volleyball scholarships.

2916. **G. C. Wallace** Unlimited scholarships ranging from $100 to $1,805 to students with at least a B+ average and scoring at least 1200 on SAT or 25 on ACT.

2917. **Tuition Waivers** Numerous partial- to full-tuition waivers to students who are employees or children of employees.

Tuskegee University
Tuskegee, AL 36088
(334) 727-8500
http://www.tusk.edu/

2918. **Athletic (Men)** Baseball, basketball, football, tennis, and track and field scholarships.

2919. **Athletic (Women)** Baseball, basketball, tennis, track and field, and volleyball scholarships.

2920. **Need-Based Assistance** Numerous need-based scholarships, loans, and work-study programs open to anyone accepted for admission with financial need. Contact the financial aid office.

University of Alabama at Birmingham
UAB Station
Birmingham, AL 35294
(205) 934-4011
http://www.uab.edu
uabadmit@aubdpo.dpo.uab.edu

2921. **Alumni Society** 5 scholarships of varying amounts to students meeting certain academic criteria who have demonstrated leadership abilities.

2922. **Athletic (Men)** Baseball, basketball, cross-country, golf, soccer, swimming, and tennis scholarships.

2923. **Athletic (Women)** Basketball, cross-country, swimming, tennis, track and field, and volleyball scholarships.

2924. **BE&K** 1 scholarship of varying amount to a student meeting certain academic criteria who is an engineering major.

2925. **Birmingham News/Hanson** 1 scholarship of varying amount to a local and in-state student meeting certain academic criteria.

2926. **Charles W. Ireland** Varying numbers of scholarships of varying amounts to students meeting certain academic criteria.

2927. **David Lloyd** 1 scholarship of varying amount to a student meeting certain criteria and majoring in theater or dance.

2928. **Francis J. Dupuis** 10 scholarships of varying amounts to students meeting certain academic criteria who are engineering majors.

2929. **Goodfellow** 2 scholarships of varying amounts to local and in-state students meeting certain academic criteria.

2930. **Hess-Abroms** 5 scholarships of varying amounts to students meeting certain academic criteria.

2931. **Minority Presidential** Varying numbers of scholarships of varying amounts to students meeting certain academic criteria.

2932. **Need-Based Assistance** Numerous need-based scholarships, loans, and work-study programs open to anyone accepted for admission with financial need. Contact the financial aid office.

2933. **Pizitz** 1 scholarship of varying amount to a student meeting certain academic criteria.

2934. **Poinsettia Men's Club** 1 scholarship of varying amount to a student meeting certain academic criteria majoring in a performing art.

2935. **Rime** 1 scholarship of varying amount to a student meeting certain academic criteria who is a business major.

2936. **Special Achievement/Activities Award** Varying numbers of scholarships of varying amounts to students meeting certain criteria and participating in certain activities.

2937. **S. Richarson Hill** 15 scholarships of varying amounts to students meeting certain academic criteria.

2938. **Steele Piano** 1 scholarship of varying amount to a student meeting certain criteria. Based on talent on piano.

2939. **Theatre and Dance** 20 renewable scholarships of $1,000 to entering freshmen with above-average GPA and theater and dance talent. Recipients will appear in various performances and touring groups. Contact Department Chairperson.

2940. **Tuition Waivers** Numerous partial- to full-tuition waivers to students who are employees or children of employees.

2941. **UAB Honors** 30 scholarships of $1,250 to students in the top 10 percent of their class, with a 3.5 GPA, and scoring at least 1250 on their SAT or 27 on their ACT. Renewable with a 3.0 GPA.

2942. **University Scholars Award** 13 scholarships of varying amounts to students meeting certain academic criteria.

2943. **Virginia & Anna Praytor** 2 scholarships of varying amounts to local and in-state students meeting certain academic criteria.

University of Alabama in Huntsville
Huntsville, AL 35899
(256) 890-6070
http://www.uah.edu/
admitme@email.uah.edu

2944. **Athletic (Men)** Basketball, crew, cross-country, golf, ice hockey, soccer, or tennis scholarships.

2945. **Athletic (Women)** 12 basketball, 1 crew, 1 tennis, and 3 volleyball scholarships.

2946. **National Society of Professional Engineers** 3 scholarships (1 unrestricted, 1 female, and 1 minority) of $1,750 for four years to students in the top quarter of their class with a minimum 3.0

GPA and scoring a verbal SAT of 500 and math SAT of 600 (English ACT score of 22 and math score of 29). Must apply early in senior year so that interviews can be conducted in November. Deadline: December 15.

2947. **University Honors** 20 tuition scholarships. Renewable.

University of Alabama at Tuscaloosa
P.O. Box 870132
Tuscaloosa, AL 35487-0132
(205) 348-6010
http://www.ua.edu

2948. **Air Force ROTC** Scholarships covering tuition, laboratory and incidental fees, textbooks, and $150 tax-free monthly allowance to students based on ACT or SAT scores, GPA, personal interviews, and leadership ability. Awards renewable for two, three, or four years. Recipients agree to a specified time commitment to the Air Force. Deadline: December 1.

2949. **Alumni Honors** 20 scholarships of $4,680 to students in the top 10 percent of their class, with at least a 3.5 GPA, and who scored at least 1240 on SAT or 30 on ACT.

2950. **Alumni Leadership** 50 scholarships of $2,068 to students in the top 20 percent of their class, with at least a 3.0 GPA, and who scored at least 920 on SAT or 22 on ACT.

2951. **Army ROTC** Scholarships covering tuition, laboratory and incidental fees, textbooks, and $1,500 tax-free yearly allowance to students based on ACT or SAT scores, GPA, personal interviews, extracurricular leadership and athletic activities. Awards renewable for two, three, or four years. Recipients agree to a specified time commitment to the Air Force. Contact high school counselor or Army ROTC unit. Deadline: December 1.

2952. **Athletic (Men)** Baseball, basketball, cross-country, football, golf, swimming and diving, tennis, and track and field scholarships.

2953. **Athletic (Women)** Basketball, cross-country, golf, gymnastics, swimming and diving, tennis, track and field, and volleyball scholarships. Contact Assistant Athletic Director.

2954. **Barrett C. and Tolly Gilmer Shelton Honors Program** 1 scholarship of $1,200 to a student accepted into the University Honors Program and who isn't receiving any other scholarship aid from the university. Renewable up to four years with continued excellent performance.

2955. **Blount** 1 scholarship of $6,000 to a student with at least a 3.8 GPA, at least a 32 on ACT or 1400 on

SAT, and a broad base of leadership experiences. Student must be pursuing a course of study in the College of Arts and Sciences, the College of Commerce and Business Administration, or the College of Engineering. Must be an Alabama resident. An essay and interview are required. Renewable up to four years with 3.0 GPA. Deadline: January 15.

2956. **College of Arts and Sciences** Several scholarships of varying amounts to undergraduate and graduate students in the College of Arts and Sciences who meet certain academic and financial criteria. Jointly sponsored by the university and the College of Arts & Sciences. Deadline: January 15.

2957. **College of Commerce and Business Administration** Several scholarships of varying amounts to undergraduate and graduate students in the College of Commerce and Business Administration who meet certain academic and financial criteria. Jointly sponsored by the university and the College of CBA. Deadline: January 15.

2958. **College of Communication** Several scholarships of varying amounts to undergraduate and graduate students in the College of Communication who meet certain academic and financial criteria. Jointly sponsored by the university and the College of Communication. Deadline: January 15.

2959. **College of Education** Several scholarships of varying amounts to undergraduate and graduate students in the College of Education who meet certain academic and financial criteria. Jointly sponsored by the university and the College of Education. Deadline: January 15.

2960. **College of Engineering** Several scholarships of varying amounts to undergraduate and graduate students in the College of Engineering who meet certain academic and financial criteria. Jointly sponsored by the university and the College of Engineering. Deadline: January 15.

2961. **College of Human Environmental Sciences** Several scholarships of varying amounts to undergraduate and graduate students in the College of Human Environmental Sciences who meet certain academic and financial criteria. Jointly sponsored by the university and the College of HES. Deadline: January 15.

2962. **College of Nursing** Several scholarships of varying amounts to undergraduate and graduate students in the College of Nursing who meet certain academic and financial criteria. Jointly sponsored by the university and the College of Nursing. Deadline: January 15.

2963. **College of Social Work** Several scholarships of varying amounts to undergraduate and graduate students in the College of Social Work who meet certain academic and financial criteria. Jointly sponsored by the university and the College of Social Work Deadline: January 15.

2964. **Computer–Based Honors Program** 6 scholarships of $2,500 to students in the top 10 percent of their class, with at least a 3.9 GPA, and who scored at least 1400 on SAT or 32 on ACT. Renewable with continued superior performance in UA and CBHP. Contact: Computer–Based Honors Program. Deadline: January 15.

2965. **Crimson** At least 1 scholarship providing tuition, housing allowance, book grant, and an educational enrichment allowance to students with at least a 32 on ACT or 1400 on SAT, at least a 3.8 GPA, and in the top 2 percent of their class. Renewable up to four years if 3.0 GPA is maintained. Deadline: December 3.

2966. **Edwin F. Averyt Memorial** 1 scholarship of $2,000 to a student with an ACT or SAT score in the top percentile. Selection is made by the Alumni Honors Scholarship Committee from the Alumni Honors applications. Renewable for up to four years with a 3.0 GPA. Deadline: January 15.

2967. **Elizabeth Coleman Honors** 2 scholarships of $2,000 to outstanding undergraduate students who meet certain academic criteria. Renewable with a 3.0 GPA. Deadline January 15.

2968. **Honors Program** Numerous scholarships ranging from $1,500 to $7,300 to students in the top 10 percent of their class, with at least a 3.5 GPA, and scoring at least 1200 on their SAT or 29 on ACT.

2969. **Human Nutrition and Hospitality Management Department** Several scholarships of varying amounts to undergraduate and graduate students in the HNHM Department who meet certain academic and financial criteria.

2970. **Jo Nell Usrey Stephens Honors Program** 1 scholarship of $1,200 to a student accepted into the University Honors Program and not currently receiving any other scholarship aid from the university. Renewable for up to four years with acceptable academic performance. Deadline: June 1.

2971. **Junior College Honors** 5 scholarships of tuition to transfer students with at least a 3.5 GPA. Must be transferring from a two–year community college. Renewable up to two years with a 3.0 GPA. Deadline: January 15.

2972. **National Alumni Association Honors** 30 scholarships of in-state tuition and a yearly housing allowance to students with at least a 30 ACT or 1320 SAT score and at least a B average. Renewable for four years with 3.0 GPA. Deadline: December 3.

2973. **National Alumni Association Junior College Honors** 10 scholarships of $1,500 to transfer students with at least a college 3.0 GPA and strong leadership activities. Must be transferring from a two-year community college. Renewable for up to two years. Deadline: January 15.

2974. **National Alumni Association Leadership Awards** 60 scholarships of in-state tuition costs to students with at least a 24 ACT or 1090 SAT score, and at least a B average. Must demonstrate unique leadership ability in elected positions in school organizations and have volunteered for or been elected to activities that benefit their school, community, or state. Nonrenewable. Deadline: December 3.

2975. **National Merit/Achievement/ Hispanic** Scholarships of tuition, plus $750 if the student doesn't receive a corporate or other Merit/Achievement/Hispanic Scholarship. Awards can be increased up to $2,000 based on financial need. Students who list UA as their first-choice school will receive a personal laptop computer upon enrollment. Renewable up to four years.

2976. **Presidential** 100 scholarships of current tuition costs to students in the top 10 percent of their class, with at least a 3.5 GPA, and who scored at least 1170 on SAT or 26 on ACT. Leadership activities and other achievements are also considered. Deadline: January 15.

2977. **UA Professor of Military Science** Varying numbers of scholarships of $2,000 to students who are Army four-year and three-year advanced designee winners. Contact high school counselor or Army ROTC unit. Deadline: February 1.

2978. **Vulcan** 1 scholarship of tuition plus $30,000 over four years to a student in the top 1 percent of his/her class, with at least a 3.8 GPA, who scored at least 1400 on SAT or 32 on ACT and has a broad base of leadership experiences. An essay and interview are required. Deadline: January 15.

University of Mobile
P.O. Box 13220
Mobile, AL 36663
(334) 675-5990
http://www.umobile.edu
adminfo@umobile.edu

2979. **Athletic (Men)** Baseball, basketball, cross-country, golf, soccer, and tennis.

2980. **Athletic (Women)** Basketball, softball, and tennis.

2981. **Need-Based Assistance** Numerous need-based scholarships, loans, and work-study programs open to anyone accepted for admission with financial need. Contact the financial aid office.

2982. **Presidential** Numerous scholarships of $1,000 for students who scored at least 26 on ACT. Renewable with 3.5 GPA.

University of Montevallo
Station #6030
Montevallo, AL 35115
(205) 665-6000
http://www.montevallo.edu
admissions@um.montevallo.edu

2983. **Athletic (Men)** Baseball, basketball, and golf scholarships.

2984. **Athletic** Basketball and volleyball scholarships.

2985. **Leadership** 20 scholarships covering tuition and fees for students with a 3.0 GPA and scoring at least 26 on their ACT. Renewable with a 3.0 GPA.

2986. **Presidential Merit "Honors Program"** Numerous scholarships covering all costs. Renewable with a 3.5 GPA.

University of North Alabama
Wesleyan Avenue
Florence, AL 35632-0001
(256) 760-4100
http://www.una.edu
admis1@unanov.una.edu

2987. **Academic** 12 scholarships ranging from $500 to $1,000 are available to students in the top 10 percent of their class, with at least a 3.5 GPA, and scoring at least 990 on SAT or 24 on ACT. Renewable with a 2.25 GPA.

2988. **Academic** 24 scholarships of $500 to students in the top 10 percent of their class, with at least a 3.5 GPA, and scoring at least 990 on SAT or 24 on ACT.

2989. **Athletic (Men)** Baseball, basketball, cross-country, football, golf, riflery, and tennis scholarships.

2990. **Athletic (Women)** Basketball, cross-country, golf, track and field, tennis, and volleyball scholarships.

University of South Alabama
307 University Boulevard
Mobile, AL 36688
(234) 460-6141
(800) 872-5247
http://www.usouthal.edu
admiss@jaguar1.usouthal.edu

2991. **Athletic (Men)** Baseball, basketball, golf, soccer, tennis, and track and field scholarships. Contact Athletic Director.

2992. **Athletic (Women)** Basketball, tennis, track and field, and volleyball scholarships. Contact Athletic Director.

2993. **Creative Arts/Performance Awards** Numerous awards of varying amounts to students majoring in music, theater, or drama.

2994. **Drama** 8 scholarship grants of $1,300 to students meeting certain criteria for the study of drama. Selection is done by university faculty. Contact: Drama Department.

2995. **Presidential/Achievement** 134 scholarships ranging from $800 to $4,200 to students with at least a 3.5 GPA and scoring at least a 24 on ACT. Renewable with a 3.0 GPA.

2996. **Tuition Waivers** Numerous partial- to full-tuition waivers to students who are employees or children of employees.

Wallace State Community College
801 Main Street
Hanceville, AL 35079
(205) 352-6403

2997. **Athletic (Men)** Baseball, basketball, or golf scholarships.

2998. **Athletic (Women)** Basketball and softball scholarships.

2999. **Need-Based Assistance** Numerous need-based scholarships, loans, and work-study programs open to anyone accepted for admission with financial need. Contact the financial aid office.

ALASKA

Alaska Pacific University
4101 University Drive
Anchorage, AK 99508
(800) 252-7528
http://www.alaska.net
apu@corecom.net

3000. **Achievement/National** Numerous scholarships covering 50 percent tuition. Renewable.

3001. **Alaska Native and American Indian Awards** 10 scholarships of $3,780 to students meeting certain criteria and whose ethnic origins are either Alaska Natives or American Indians.

3002. **Alaska Awards** 20 scholarships of $1,000 to graduating high school seniors who graduated from an Alaskan high school.

3003. **Department Awards** 6 scholarships of $1,000 to students meeting certain academic criteria and who are majoring in certain fields.

3004. **Distinguished Scholar** 10 tuition scholarships for students with a 3.5 GPA. Renewable with a 3.2 GPA.

3005. **Travel Awards** Up to 8 scholarships of $750 to students who are non-Alaska residents.

3006. **Trustee** 25 scholarships providing one-third of tuition costs to students with at least a 3.25 GPA. Renewable with 3.25 GPA.

3007. **Tuition Waivers** numerous partial- to full-tuition waivers to students who are employees, children of employees, or senior citizens.

3008. **United Methodist Conference** 4 scholarships of $3,780 to students who are church members and who meet certain criteria.

3009. **University Award** 20 scholarships providing one-third of tuition costs to students with at least a 3.0 GPA and who scored at least 1000 on SAT or 22 on ACT.

Sheldon Jackson College
801 Lincoln Street
Sitka, AK 99835
(800) 478-4556
http://www.sheldonjackson.edu
tndac@acad1.alaska.edu

3010. **Academic** 100 to 125 scholarships ranging from $1,250 to $6,000 to students in the upper 50 percent of class and with at least a 3.0 GPA.

3011. **Incentive** 40 scholarships ranging from $500 to $750 to students with at least a 3.0 GPA.

3012. **Need–Based Assistance** Numerous need-based scholarships, loans, and work-study programs open to anyone accepted for admission with financial need. Contact the financial aid office.

University of Alaska
3211 Providence Drive
Anchorage, AK 99508
(907) 786-1480
http://www.uaa.alaska.edu/

3013. **Achievement Awards** 110 scholarships of varying amounts to students who meet certain academic criteria.

3014. **Anchorage Daily News** 1 scholarship of $1,000 to a minority undergraduate student pursuing a career in journalism. Must have at least a 2.0 GPA and financial need. Apply during the spring semester.

3015. **Alaska Press Club** 1 scholarship of $1,000 to an undergraduate junior or senior with an interest in journalism. Based on academic achievement and financial need.

3016. **Athletic (Men)** Basketball, cross-country, ice hockey; skiing (cross country), skiing (downhill); swimming; or swimming and diving scholarships.

3017. **Athletic (Women)** Basketball, gymnastics, skiing, and volleyball scholarships.

3018. **Creative Arts/Performance Awards** Varying numbers of scholarships of varying amounts to students who meet certain criteria. Based on talent.

3019. **Emily Ivanoff Brown** 1 scholarship of $250 to an undergraduate student who is an Alaskan Native (Eskimo, Indian, or Aleut) pursuing a career in journalism. Based on financial need.

3020. **Forbes Baker** 1 scholarship of $500 to an undergraduate with an interest in journalism. Based on academic achievement and financial need.

3021. **Joann Wold** 1 scholarship of $500 to an undergraduate with an interest in journalism. Based on academic achievement and financial need.

3022. **Marian and W. F. Thompson** 1 scholarship of $1,000 to an undergraduate from Alaska with an interest in journalism. Deadline: February 1.

3023. **Need–Based Assistance** Numerous need-based scholarships, loans, and work-study programs open to anyone accepted for admission with financial need. Contact the financial aid office.

3024. **Special Characteristics Awards** Varying numbers of scholarships of varying amounts to students who meet certain criteria.

3025. **Tuition Waiver** 15 scholarships ranging from $1,000 to $2,700 to students with at least a 2.5 GPA. Renewable.

University of Alaska
Fairbanks, AK 99775-0240
(907) 474-7521
http://www.uaf.edu
fyapply@aurora.alaska.edu

3026. **Academic/Talent** 101 scholarships ranging from $720 to $1,920 to students with at least a 3.7 GPA and scoring at least 28 on their ACT.

3027. **Athletic (Men)** Basketball, cross country, cross-country skiing, diving, ice hockey, riflery, and swimming scholarships.

3028. **Athletic (Women)** Basketball, cross country, skiing, and 2 volleyball scholarships.

3029. **Need–Based Assistance** Numerous need-based scholarships, loans, and work-study programs open to anyone accepted for admission with financial need. Contact the financial aid office.

3030. **Tuition Waivers** Numerous partial- to full-tuition waivers to students who are employees, children of employees, children of alumni, or senior citizens.

University of Alaska, Southeast
11120 Glacier Highway
Juneau, AK 99801-8694
(907) 465-6460
http://www.jun.alaska.edu
jngaw@acadl.alaska.edu

3031. **Need–Based Assistance** Numerous need-based scholarships, loans, and work-study programs open to anyone accepted for admission with financial need. Contact the financial aid office.

3032. **University** 25 scholarships ranging from $100 to $3,000 to students with at least a 2.0 GPA. Renewable with a 2.0 GPA.

ARIZONA

Arizona State University
Tempe, AZ 85287-0112
(602) 965-9011
http://www.asu.edu
ugradadm@asuvm.inre.asu.edu

3033. **ASU Academic** 1,500 tuition scholarships to students in top 4 percent of their graduating class. Renewable.

3034. **Athletic (Men)** Archery, badminton, baseball, basketball, cross-country, diving, football, golf, gymnastics, swimming, swimming and diving, tennis, track and field, and wrestling scholarships.

3035. **Athletic (Women)** Archery, badminton, basketball, cross-country, golf, gymnastics, softball, swimming and diving, tennis, track and field, and volleyball scholarships.

3036. **Charles A. Stauffer Journalism** 1 scholarship of $350 to an undergraduate junior or senior journalism major. Based on ability.

3037. **Eugene C. Pulliam Memorial Journalism** 5 scholarships of $1,500 to undergraduate juniors for use during senior year.

3038. **Leadership** 15 scholarships for tuition. Renewable.

3039. **Medallion Merit** 120 tuition scholarships.

3040. **National Merit** 25 scholarships of $500 to incoming freshmen who received National Merit designation and who are Arizona residents.

3041. **Phoenix Press Club Foundation—ASU Foundation** 16 scholarships of $500 to undergraduate sophomores, juniors, and seniors who are journalism majors. Based on ability.

3042. **Phoenix Press Club Foundation—ASU Foundation Minority Scholarships** 16 scholarships of $500 to minority undergraduate sophomores, juniors, and seniors who are journalism majors. Based on ability.

3043. **Phoenix Professional Chapter of WICI Gladys Bagley Schaefer Achievement Award** 1 scholarship of $200 to an undergraduate journalism student. Based on outstanding achievement in journalism.

3044. **Private Donor** $3,500 scholarships of $1,000 to entering freshmen, undergraduates, and graduate students who meet certain criteria. Renewable. Deadline: March 15.

3045. **Regents Registration Fee** 3,150 scholarships of $1,528 to entering freshmen, undergraduate, and graduate students. Based on academic achievement, financal need, ethnic ancestry, gender, field of interest, physical disability, and organizational affiliation. Renewable. Deadline: March 15.

3046. **Regents Tuition** 830 scholarships of $5,406 to entering freshmen, undergraduate, and graduate students based on academic achievement, financial need, ethnic ancestry, gender, field of interest, physical disability, and organizational affiliation. Renewable. Deadline: March 15.

3047. **Robert Lance Memorial** 1 scholarship of $350 to an undergraduate sophomore, junior, or senior journalism student.

3048. **Steve Allen Mass Communications** 1 scholarship of $250 to a student majoring in mass communications.

3049. **Tuition Waivers** Numerous partial- to full-tuition waivers to students who are employees or children of employees.

Arizona State University
Box 929
Yuma, AZ 85287
(602) 965-3856
http://www.asu.edu
ugradadm@asuvm.inre.asu.edu

3050. **Athletic (Women)** 7 softball and 4 volleyball partial scholarships; 2 softball and 2 volleyball full scholarships.

3051. **Need-Based Assistance** Numerous need-based scholarships, loans, and work-study programs open to anyone accepted for admission with financial need. Contact the financial aid office.

Central Arizona College
Woodruff at Overfield Road
Coolidge, AZ 85228
(602) 426-4304

3052. **Athletic (Women)** Basketball, rodeo, softball, and volleyball scholarships. Contact the Women's Basketball Coach.

3053. **Need-Based Assistance** There are many need-based scholarships, loans, and work-study programs open to anyone accepted for admission. Many factors, other than family income, are considered. Contact the financial aid office.

Grand Canyon University
3300 West Camelback Road
Phoenix, AZ 85017
(800) 800-9776
http://www.grand-canyon.edu
admiss@grand-canyon.edu

3054. **Academic** 50 scholarships of $1,000 to students in the top 10 percent of their class and with SAT/ACT score above the 95th percentile. Renewable.

3055. **Alumni** Varying numbers of scholarships of varying amounts to students who meet certain criteria.

3056. **Art Awards** Varying numbers of scholarships of varying amounts to students who meet certain criteria and who are majoring in applied art or design, and are members of NAHS.

3057. **Athletic (Men)** Baseball, basketball, golf, soccer, and tennis scholarships.

3058. **Athletic (Women)** 6 basketball, 1 cross-country, 4 tennis, and 4 volleyball scholarships.

3059. **Business Awards** Varying numbers of scholarships of varying amounts to students who meet certain criteria and who are business majors.

3060. **Drama Awards** Varying numbers of scholarships of varying amounts to students who meet certain criteria and who are drama majors.

3061. **Faculty/Staff Awards** Varying numbers of scholarships of varying amounts to students who meet certain criteria and who are dependents of faculty or staff.

3062. **Music Awards** Varying numbers of scholarships of varying amounts to students who meet certain criteria and who are music majors.

3063. **Need-Based Assistance** Numerous need-based scholarships, loans, and work-study programs open to anyone accepted for admission with financial need. Contact the financial aid office.

3064. **Nursing Awards** Varying numbers of scholarships of varying amounts to students who meet certain criteria and who are nursing majors.

3065. **Presidential** A $300-per-year grant for up to 3 three years for any Eagle Scout.

3066. **Presidential Awards** Scholarships of varying amounts to students who are relatives of clergy or out-of-state residents.

3067. **Scholars' 100** Varying numbers of scholarships providing full tuition costs to students meeting certain academic criteria.

3068. **Theater Awards** Varying numbers of scholarships of varying amounts to students who meet certain criteria and who are theater majors.

3069. **Top Five Academic** Varying numbers of scholarships providing 50 percent of tuition costs to students who meet certain academic criteria.

3070. **Top Ten Academic** Varying numbers of scholarships providing 25 percent of tuition costs to students who meet other academic criteria.

3071. **Transfer** A varying number of $700 awards to students with a 3.5 GPA. Renewable.

Northern Arizona University
Box 4084
Flagstaff, AZ 86011-4084
(520) 523-5511
http://www.hau.edu/
undergraduate.admissions@nau.edu

3072. **Arizona Republic/Phoenix Gazette Scholarship** 3 scholarships of $1,000 to undergraduate journalism majors. Deadline: March 1.

3073. **Athletic (Men)** Basketball, cross-country, football, indoor track, swimming and diving, tennis, and track and field scholarships.

3074. **Athletic (Women)** Basketball, cross-country, golf, swimming and diving, tennis, track and field, and volleyball scholarships.

Phoenix College
1202 West Thomas Road
Phoenix, AZ 85013
(602) 264-2492

3075. **Athletic (Men)** Baseball, basketball, cross-country, football, golf, soccer, tennis, track and field, and wrestling scholarships.

3076. **Athletic (Women)** Basketball, cross-country, soccer, softball, tennis, track and field, and volleyball scholarships.

Pima Community College
2202 West Anklam Road
Tucson, AZ 85709
(602) 884-6005

3077. **Arizona Daily Star Frank E. Johnson** 1
scholarship of $500 to a minority undergraduate
student. Selection based on scholarship, need, and
interest in journalism. Contact the Department of
Journalism. Deadline: varies.

3078. **Athletic (Men)** Baseball, basketball, cross-
country, golf, soccer, tennis, and track and field
scholarships.

3079. **Athletic (Women)** Basketball, cross-country,
softball, tennis, track and field, and volleyball
scholarships.

Prescott College
220 Grove Avenue
Prescott, AZ 86301
(520) 776-5180
http://aztec.asu.edu/prescott.col
applypc@aztec.asu.edu

3080. **Prescott** 5 awards ranging from $250 to $500.

Scottsdale Community College
9000 East Chaparral Road
Scottsdale, AZ 85253
(602) 941-0999

3081. **Athletic (Men)** Archery, baseball, basketball,
bowling, cross-country, fencing, football, golf,
racquetball, soccer, tennis, and track and field
scholarships.

3082. **Athletic (Women)** Archery, basketball, cross-
country, softball, tennis, track and field, and
volleyball scholarships.

South Mountain Community College
7050 South 24th Street
Phoenix, AZ 85040
(602) 243-6661

3083. **Athletic (Women)** Basketball, cross-country,
softball, tennis, track and field, and volleyball
scholarships.

Southwestern College
Phoenix, AZ 85032
(602) 992-6101

3084. **Demonstrated Need + Excellence** 4 awards of
$1,650 to students with a 3.3 GPA. Renewable
with a 3.3 GPA.

3085. **Excellence** 4 scholarships of $3,300 to students
with a 3.75 GPA. Renewable with a 3.75 GPA.

University of Arizona
Tucson, AZ 85721
(520) 621-3237
http://www.arizona.edu/
appinfo@arizona.edu

3086. **Academic Preparedness Awards** 10 awards of
varying amounts to students meeting certain
criteria.

3087. **Academic Waivers** 597 tuition waivers to
students meeting certain academic criteria who
are Arizona residents.

3088. **Arizona Daily Star Scholarships for
Minority Students** 1 to 4 scholarships of $3,000
to minority students who are journalism majors.
Based on academic achievement and financial
need. Renewable.

3089. **Athletic (Men)** Baseball, basketball, cross-
country, football, golf, swimming and diving,
tennis, and track and field scholarships.

3090. **Athletic (Women)** Basketball, cross-country,
golf, gymnastics, softball, swimming and diving,
tennis, track and field, and volleyball
scholarships.

3091. **Calf-roping** $500 a year for people with high
marks and calf-roping experience.

3092. **Citizens Beginning Minority Journalism** 1
scholarship of $500 to minority journalism majors
pursuing a career as a news professional.

3093. **Creative Arts/Performance Awards** 205
scholarships of varying amounts totaling $429,073
to students majoring in a creative or performance
art. Based on talent.

3094. **Don Schellie Journalism** 1 scholarship of $500
to an undergraduate junior or senior who has a
3.0 GPA or better. Financial need is sometimes a
factor.

3095. **Doug Martin Journalism Fund** Numerous
scholarship grants of up to $500 to undergraduate
journalism majors. Based on financial need.

3096. **Ed Emerine Journalism** 1 scholarship of $500
to undergraduate or graduate journalism
students. Based on academic achievement and
sometimes on financial need.

3097. **Edith Auslander Minority Journalism** 1
scholarship of $500 to undergraduate minority
students who are journalism majors and have at
least a 3.0 GPA and financial need.

3098. **Eugene C. Pulliam Memorial Journalism** 5 scholarships of $1,500 to undergraduate juniors for use during senior year. Must be pursuing careers as newspaper journalists. Based on journalism faculty recommendation.

3099. **Exchange Scholarships to Autonomous University of Guadalajara, Mexico** 2 scholarships providing tuition waivers to students interested in Latin American journalism.

3100. **John Barnett** 3 scholarships of $600 to undergraduate student editors working on the *Tombstone Epitaph*.

3101. **Lois Whisler Journalism** 1 to 2 scholarships of $250 to undergraduate or graduate journalism students. Based on academic achievement and sometimes on financial need.

3102. **Mildred and Gordon Gordon "Darn Cat"** 2 to 3 scholarships of at least $400 to undergraduate and graduate journalism students. Based on academic promise, financial need, and demonstrated potential for print news.

3103. **Minority** 293 scholarships of varying amounts to minority students who meet certain academic criteria.

3104. **Minority Waivers** 43 tuition waivers to minority students who meet certain academic criteria.

3105. **President's** Numerous scholarships of varying amounts. Renewable with a 3.5 GPA.

3106. **Regents** 1,890 scholarships covering all fees to students in the top 5 percent of their graduating class. Renewable with a 3.2 GPA.

3107. **Roy Drachman Minority** 1 to 2 scholarships of $1,000 to minority undergraduate or graduate students who are Arizona residents. Based on academic achievement and financial need.

3108. **Schaefer** 25 scholarships of $1,000. Renewable with a 3.5 GPA.

3109. **Study Abroad** 1 scholarship of varying amount to a student who will be studying abroad for a year.

3110. **Tucson Citizen Minority** 1 scholarship of $500 to an undergraduate junior or senior student pursuing a career as a news professional.

3111. **Tuition Waivers** Numerous partial- to full-tuition waivers to students who are employees, children of employees, or minority students.

Yavapai Community College
1100 East Sheldon
Prescott, AZ 86301
(602) 445-7300

3112. **Athletic (Men)** Baseball scholarships.

3113. **Athletic (Women)** 7 basketball, 7 cross-country, and 9 volleyball scholarships.

ARKANSAS

Arkansas State University
Box 1630
State University, AR 72467
(800) 643-0080
http://www.astate.edu
admissions@chickasaw.astate.edu

3114. **Academic** Varying numbers of scholarships of $900 to students in the top 10 percent of their class, with at least a 3.0 GPA, and who scored at least 24 on ACT. Renewable with 3.0 GPA.

3115. **Academic Distinction** Unlimited numbers of scholarships ranging from $1,536 to $2,160 to students in the top 10 percent of their class, with at least a 3.0 GPA, and who scored at least 1010 on SAT or 24 on ACT. Renewable with 3.0 GPA.

3116. **Athletic (Men)** Baseball, basketball, cross-country, football, golf, indoor track, and track and field scholarships.

3117. **Athletic (Women)** Basketball, cross-country, softball, tennis, track and field, and volleyball scholarships.

3118. **Need-Based Assistance** Numerous need-based scholarships, loans, and work-study programs open to anyone accepted for admission with financial need. Contact the financial aid office.

3119. **President's** Unlimited numbers of scholarships ranging from $1,536 to $2,160 to students who scored at least 1090 on SAT or 26 on ACT. Renewable with 3.0 GPA.

3120. **Trustee's "Honors Program"** Unlimited numbers of scholarships ranging from $3,936 to $5,640 to students who scored at least 1260 on SAT or 30 on ACT. Renewable with 3.5 GPA.

3121. **Tuition Waivers** Numerous partial- to full-tuition waivers to students who are alumni, employees, children of employees, or senior citizens.

Arkansas Tech University
Russellville, AR 72801
(501) 968-0343
http://www.atu.edu
adhc@atuvm.atu.edu

3122. **Athletic (Men)** Baseball, basketball, cross-country, football, golf, indoor track, tennis, or track and field scholarships.

3123. **Athletic (Women)** 12 basketball and 12 volleyball full scholarships.

3124. **Honors** 150 scholarships of $1,050 to students scoring at least 23 on ACT. Renewable with a 3.25 GPA.

3125. **Music** 25 scholarships ranging from $525 to $1,050 to students, based on audition. Renewable with a 2.25 GPA.

Garland County Community College
#1 College Drive
Hot Springs, AR 71913
(501) 767-9371

3126. **Athletic (Men)** Baseball, basketball, and tennis scholarships.

3127. **Athletic (Women)** 12 basketball and 6 tennis scholarships.

Harding University
900 East Center
Searcy, AR 72143
(800) 477-4407
http://www.harding.edu
mwilliams@harding.edu

3128. **Academic** Numerous scholarships ranging from $400 to $3,800 to students scoring at least 840 on SAT or 20 on ACT. Renewable with a 3.0 GPA.

3129. **Athletic (Men)** Baseball, basketball, cross-country, football, golf, swimming, swimming and diving, or tennis scholarships.

3130. **Athletic (Women)** 12 basketball and 12 volleyball partial scholarships.

3131. **Trustee** 15 scholarships of $3,500 to students with at least a 3.2 GPA who scored at least 1260 on SAT or 30 on ACT. Renewable with a 3.0 GPA.

Henderson State University
1100 Henderson Street
Arkadelphia, AR 71999
(870) 230-5028
http://www.hsu.edu
gattint@oaks.hsu.edu

3132. **Academic** 150 tuition scholarships to students in top 10 percent of their class and scoring at least 23 on ACT. Renewable.

3133. **Alumni** 60 scholarships ranging from $200 to $400 to students with a 3.0 GPA who scored at least 22 on ACT. Renewable with a 3.0 GPA.

3134. **Athletic (Men)** Baseball, basketball, football, golf, swimming and diving, and tennis scholarships.

3135. **Athletic (Women)** Basketball, cross-country, diving, swimming, tennis, track and field, and volleyball scholarships.

3136. **Board of Trustees** 10 scholarships ranging from $790 to $2,062 to students in the top 10 percent of their class and scoring at least 30 on ACT. Renewable with a 3.5 GPA.

3137. **Presidential** 50 scholarships ranging from $790 to $2,062 to students in top 10 percent of the class and scoring at least 25 on ACT. Renewable with a 3.25 GPA.

Hendrix College
Conway, AR 72032
(800) 277-9017
http://www.hendrix.edu
adm@hendrix.edu

3138. **Academic** Numerous scholarships covering 50 percent tuition to students with at least a 3.25 GPA and scoring at least 1150 on SAT or 28 on ACT. Renewable.

3139. **Athletic (Men)** Baseball, basketball, cross-country, golf, soccer, swimming and diving, tennis, and track and field scholarships.

3140. **Athletic (Women)** Basketball, cross-country, soccer, swimming and diving, track and field, and volleyball scholarships.

John Brown University
Siloam Springs, AR 72761
(501) 524-7157
http://www.jbu.edu
jbuinfo@acc.jbu.edu

3141. **Academic** 150 scholarships ranging from $800 to $1,250 to students with at least a 3.25 GPA and scoring at least in the 80th percentile on the SAT or ACT. Renewable with a 3.25 GPA.

3142. **Divisional "Honors Program, Honors College"** 25 scholarships of 50 percent tuition to students in the top 10 percent of their class, with at least a 3.5 GPA, and scoring in the 90th percentile of the SAT or ACT. Renewable with a 3.2 GPA.

3143. **High Ability** 30 scholarships ranging from $1,500 to $3,780 to students in the top 10 percent of their class, with at least a 3.5 GPA and scoring above the 90th percentile on the SAT or ACT. Renewable with a 3.5 GPA.

3144. **Presidential** 10 scholarships toward tuition for students in top 5 percent of class, with at least a 3.9 GPA, and scoring above the 95th percentile on the SAT or ACT. Renewable with a 3.4 GPA.

Lyon College
P.O. Box 2317
Batesville, AR 72503
(800) 423-2542
http://www.lyon.edu

3145. **Athletic (Men)** Basketball, cross-country, golf, and track and field scholarships.

3146. **Athletic (Women)** Basketball scholarships.

3147. **Brown** 5 scholarships of $4,810 for students with a 3.75 GPA, scoring at least 1250 on SAT or 27 on ACT. Renewable with 3.25 GPA.

3148. **$1,800 Endowed** Various numbers of scholarships of $1,800 for students with at least 3.5 GPA and scoring at least 1030 on SAT or 22 on ACT. Renewable with 2.8 GPA.

3149. **$1,300 Endowed** Numerous scholarships of $1,300 for students with at least 3.0 GPA, scoring at least 970 on SAT or 20 on ACT. Renewable with 2.6 GPA.

3150. **$900 Endowed "Honors Program" Awards** Numerous scholarships of $900 for students with at least 2.5 GPA, scoring at least 970 on SAT or 20 on ACT. Renewable with 2.4 GPA.

3151. **Need-Based Assistance** Numerous need-based scholarships, loans, and work-study programs open to anyone accepted for admission with financial need. Contact the financial aid office.

Ouachita Baptist University
410 Ouachita
Arkadelphia, AR 71998
(870) 245-5110
http://www.obu.edu
jones@sigma.obu.edu

3152. **Athletic (Men)** Baseball, basketball, cross-country, diving, football, golf, indoor track, swimming, swimming and diving, tennis, or track and field scholarships.

3153. **Athletic (Women)** Basketball, cross-country, swimming and diving, tennis, and volleyball scholarships.

3154. **Centennial** 7 scholarships of $4,000. Renewable.

3155. **Honor Grad** Unlimited number of $500 scholarships to students in the top 3 percent of their class.

3156. **Scholastic Excellence** Unlimited number of scholarships ranging from $400 to $1,200 to students scoring at least 940 on SAT or 23 on ACT. Renewable with a 2.5 GPA.

3157. **Second Century** Unlimited number of tuition scholarships to students with at least a 3.5 GPA and scoring at least 30 on ACT. Renewable.

Southern Arkansas University
Box 9382
Magnolia, AR 71753
(870) 235-4040
http://www.saumag.edu
addonna@saumag.edu

3158. **Academic** Unlimited number of $1,050 scholarships to students in the top 10 percent of their class, with at least a 3.0 GPA, and scoring at least 23 on ACT. Renewable with a 3.0 GPA.

3159. **Athletic (Men)** Baseball, basketball, cross-country, football, golf, indoor track, rodeo, tennis, and track and field scholarships.

3160. **Athletic (Women)** 2 partial and 11 full basketball, and 13 volleyball scholarships.

3161. **Presidential** 25 scholarships of $1,050 for students in the top 10 percent of their class with at least a 3.5 GPA and scoring at least 23 on ACT. Renewable with a 3.0 GPA.

University of Arkansas
Fayetteville, AR 72701
(800) 377-8632
http://www.uark.edu
uafadmis@comp.uark.edu

3162. **Athletic (Men)** Baseball, basketball, cross-country running, football, golf, soccer, swimming and diving, tennis, and track and field scholarships.

3163. **Athletic (Women)** Full basketball, cross-country, swimming and diving, tennis, and track and field; and 9 partial soccer scholarships.

3164. **Chancellors Scholarships** Varying numbers of scholarships of $8,828 to students with at least a 3.5 GPA who scored at least 1400 on SAT or 33 on ACT. Renewable with 3.2 GPA.

3165. **Freshman Academic** Numerous tuition scholarships to students in top 10 percent of their class and with at least a 3.0 GPA. Renewable with a 3.0 GPA.

3166. **Music Awards** 191 scholarships of varying amounts to students meeting certain criteria who are music majors. Based on talent.

3167. **Nonresident Awards** 63 scholarships of varying amounts to students who are not Arkansas residents and who meet certain academic criteria.

3168. **Sturgis** Varying numbers of scholarships of $10,000 to students meeting certain academic criteria. Renewable.

3169. **Tuition Waivers** Numerous partial- to full-tuition waivers to students who are employees, children of employees, or senior citizens.

3170. **University** Varying numbers of scholarships of $2,228 to students with at least a 3.25 GPA and who scored at least 1130 on SAT or 27 on ACT. Renewable with 3.2 GPA.

3171. **VAL/SAL** Unlimited number of full-tuition scholarships to students in top 1–2 percent of their class. Renewable with a 2.0 GPA.

University of Arkansas
2801 South University Avenue
Little Rock, AR 72204
(501) 569-3000
http://www.ualr.edu
admissions@ualr.edu

3172. **Academic Scholarships** 200 scholarships ranging from $1,270 to $1,650 to entering freshmen who are Arkansas residents. Students must score at least 23 on ACT and rank in the top 10 percent of their class. Renewable with a 3.25 GPA. Deadline: March 15.

3173. **Athletic (Men)** Baseball, basketball, diving, golf, soccer, swimming, tennis, and water polo scholarships.

3174. **Athletic (Women)** Basketball, soccer, swimming and diving, and tennis scholarships.

University of Arkansas
1100 North University Drive
Pine Bluff, AR 71601
(501) 541-6500
http://www.uapb.edu
uafadmis@com.uark.edu

3175. **Academic** 96 scholarships ranging from $100 to $700 to students in the top 10 percent of their class, with a 3.0 GPA. Renewable with a 3.0 GPA.

3176. **Athletic (Men)** Basketball, football, and track and field scholarships.

3177. **Athletic (Women)** Basketball and volleyball scholarships.

3178. **Band/Choir "Honors College"** 120 scholarships ranging from $100 to $3,600 to students with at least a 2.0 GPA. Renewable with a 2.0 GPA.

University of Central Arkansas
201 Donaghey Avenue
Conway, AR 72035
(800) 243-8245
http://www.uca.edu/
admissions@ecom.uca.edu

3179. **Academic** 350 scholarships of $1,500 to students with at least a 3.0 GPA who scored at least 23 on ACT. Renewable with a 3.25 GPA.

3180. **Athletic (Men)** Basketball and football scholarships.

3181. **Athletic (Women)** Basketball and volleyball scholarships.

3182. **Music, Art, Speech** 150 scholarships toward tuition. Renewable with a 2.0 GPA.

University of the Ozarks
415 College Avenue
Clarksville, AR 72830
(501) 979-1227
http://www.ozarks.edu
admiss@dobson.ozark.edu

3183. **Recognition** Numerous scholarships ranging from $400 to $2,000 to students with at least a 3.5 GPA and scoring at least 23 on ACT. Renewable with a 3.0 GPA.

CALIFORNIA

Art Center College of Design
1700 Lida Street
Pasadena, CA 91103-1999
(626) 396-2373
http://www.artcenter.edu
admissions@artcenter.edu

3184. **Photographic Society of America Grant** 2 $250 awards to undergraduate seniors to help them complete the year. Contact the financial aid office or: PSA Educational Scholarship Committee, 3000 United Founders Boulevard, Suite 103, Oklahoma City, OK 73112.

Azusa Pacific University
901 East Alosta
Azusa, CA 91702-7000
(800) TALK-APU
http://www.apu.edu
admissions@apu.edu

3185. **Athletic (Men)** Baseball, basketball, cross-country, football, indoor track, soccer, or track and field scholarhips.

3186. **Athletic (Women)** Basketball, tennis, and volleyball scholarships.

3187. **Dean's** Numerous scholarships from $1,000 to $1,800 for students with at least a 3.6 GPA. Renewable with 3.6 GPA.

3188. **Presidential** Unlimited number of scholarships ranging from $2,000 to $3,000 to students with at least a 3.9 GPA. Renewable.

Bethany Bible College
800 Bethany Drive
Santa Cruz, CA 95066-2989
(800) 843-9410
http://www.bethany.edu

3189. **Academic** Unlimited number of scholarships ranging from $430 to $645 to students with at least a 3.5 GPA. Renewable with a 3.5 GPA.

Biola University
13800 Biola Avenue
La Mirada, CA 90639-0001
(562) 903-6000
http://www.biola.edu/
admissions@biola.edu

3190. **Athletic (Men)** Baseball, basketball, cross-country, soccer, and track and field scholarships.

3191. **Athletic (Women)** 5 basketball, 2 tennis, and 5 volleyball partial- to full- scholarships.

3192. **Honors** 38 scholarships providing 50 percent tuition to students with at least a 3.95 GPA and who scored at least 1000 on SAT. Renewable with a 3.6 GPA.

California Baptist College
8432 Magnolia Avenue
Riverside, CA 92504-3297
(800) 782-3382
http://www.calbaptist.edu

3193. **Academic** Unlimited number of scholarships that pay 35 percent of tuition to students with at least a 3.5 GPA and scoring at least 750 on SAT or 16 on ACT. Renewable with a 3.0 GPA.

3194. **Athletic (Men)** Baseball, basketball, and soccer scholarships.

3195. **Athletic (Women)** Basketball, soccer, softball, tennis, and volleyball scholarships.

3196. **Church-Related Vocation Awards** 8 scholarships of $1,000 to students who meet certain academic criteria, who are religion majors, and who are Southern Baptists.

3197. **Drama Awards** 7 scholarships of at least $1,000 to students who meet certain criteria and who are drama majors. Based on talent.

3198. **Music** Numerous scholarships paying 20 to 50 percent of tuition costs. Must be music major.

3199. **Valedictorian/Salutatorian** Unlimited number of tuition scholarships to students who were class valedictorians or salutatorians and scored at least 750 on SAT or 16 on ACT. Renewable with a 3.3 GPA.

California College of Arts & Crafts
450 Irwin Street
San Francisco, CA 94107
(800) 653-8113
(415) 703-9500
http://www.ccac-art.edu
enroll@ccacsf.edu

3200. **AICA** Numerous scholarships ranging from $500 to $7,700 to students with at least a 3.0 GPA. Based on essay, portfolio/audition, leadership, recommendation, and interview.

3201. **CCAC** Up to 270 scholarship grants ranging from $1,000 to $8,600 to undergraduate and graduate students based on academic achievement and financial need. Contact the Associate Director, Enrollment. Deadline: March 1.

3202. **Presidential** 2 scholarships of $3,000 to students with a 3.5 GPA. Based on essay, portfolio/audition, leadership, recommendation, and interview. Renewable with a 3.0 GPA.

California Institute of Technology
1200 East California Boulevard
Pasadena, CA 91125
(800) LOV-TECH
(626) 395-6341
http://www.caltech.edu/
ugadmissions@caltech.edu

3203. **Athletic (Men)** Baseball, basketball, cross-country, fencing, golf, sailing soccer, softball, swimming and diving, tennis, track and field, water–polo, and wrestling scholarships.

3204. **Athletic (Women)** Cross-country, fencing, golf, sailing, soccer, swimming and diving, tennis, track and field, and water–polo scholarships.

3205. **Caltech Prize** 10 awards of tuition. Renewable.

3206. **Carnation** 25 awards of tuition. Renewable.

3207. **Millikan** 12 scholarships of varying amounts to students meeting certain academic criteria.

3208. **Need–Based Assistance** Numerous need-based scholarships, loans, and work–study programs open to anyone accepted for admission with financial need. Contact the financial aid office.

3209. **Tuition Waivers** Numerous partial– to full–tuition waivers to students who are employees or children of employees.

California Lutheran University
60 West Olsen Road
Thousand Oaks, CA 91360
(800) 252-5884
(805) 493-3135
http://www.clunet.edu
cluadm@robles.clunet.edu

3210. **Academic** 200 scholarships ranging from $500 to $2,450 to students who are in the top 25 percent of their class, have at least a 3.25 GPA, and scored at least 800 on SAT. Renewable.

3211. **Athletic (Men)** Baseball, basketball, cross-country, football, golf, soccer, tennis, and track and field scholarships.

3212. **Athletic (Women)** Basketball, cross-country, softball, tennis, track and field, and volleyball scholarships.

3213. **Pederson Merit** 200 scholarships ranging from $100 to $1,500 to students in the top 50 percent of their class who have at least a 2.65 GPA and scored at least 800 on SAT. Deadline: July 1.

California Polytechnic State University
San Luis Obispo, CA 93407
(805) 756-2311
http://www.calpoly.edu
dp141@calpoly.edu

3214. **A. Anderson & Co. Outstanding Junior** Varying numbers of scholarships of $200 to undergraduate juniors with at least a 3.0 GPA who are majoring in industrial engineering.

3215. **Academic** Varying numbers of scholarships of varying amounts to students meeting certain academic criteria.

3216. **Air Energy Conservation** Varying numbers of scholarships of $600 to undergraduate seniors who are majoring in engineering or mechanical engineering.

3217. **Army ROTC Scholarship** Scholarships ranging from $4,000 to $6,000 to freshmen who are U.S. citizens, have good moral character and leadership potential, and are medically qualified to enroll in ROTC. Minimum 2.5 GPA; scores of at least 850 on SAT or 17 on ACT are required. Renewable.

3218. **Arthur Anderson** Varying numbers of scholarships of $200 to students with at least a 3.0 GPA who are majoring in mathematics. Must be members of Kappa Epsilon.

3219. **ASHRAE—San Jose Chapter** Varying numbers of scholarships of $1,000 to undergraduate juniors with at least a 3.0 GPA who are majoring in mechanical engineering or technology engineering and are student members of ASHRAE.

3220. **Athletic (Men)** Baseball, basketball, cross-country, football, soccer, swimming and diving, tennis, track and field, and wrestling scholarships.

3221. **Athletic (Women)** 9 basketball, 5 softball, 2 tennis, 10 track and field, and 12 volleyball scholarships.

3222. **Boeing Company** Varying numbers of scholarships of $1,500 to students with at least a 3.0 GPA and who will be or are majoring in aerospace or aeronautical engineering, or aerospace engineering. Deadline: March 1.

3223. **Boyd Judd** Varying numbers of scholarships of $100 to students with at least a 3.0 GPA, who are majoring in mathematics, and who are members of Kappa Epsilon. Deadline: March 1.

3224. **California State Grange** Varying numbers of scholarships of $250 to incoming freshmen with at least a 3.0 GPA who will be majoring in agribusiness, animal science, or dairy science. Must be a member of Future Farmers of America, Grange. Deadline: March 1.

3225. **Callmat Company** Varying numbers of scholarships of $1,000 to undergraduates who have at least a 3.0 GPA and are majoring in architecture, construction, architectural engineering, construction engineering, or construction management. Deadline: March 1.

3226. **Chester O. McCorkle Memorial Scholarship** 1 scholarship of $1,000 to an upper-level agriculture student. Based on financial need. Minimum 3.2 GPA required. Deadline: March 1.

3227. **Chevron USA, Inc.** Varying numbers of scholarships of varying amounts to undergraduate students who meet certain academic criteria and are majoring in electrical or mechanical engineering. Deadline: March 1.

3228. **Class Fund** Scholarships ranging from $500 to $2,000 to students of landscape architecture. Based on financial need and promise/commitment to landscape architecture. Only for study at California Polytechnic Institute (Pomona or San Luis Obispo) and for those enrolled in the extension programs at UCLA or UC Irvine. Must be residents of Southern California. Contact: Landscape Architecture Foundation, 4401 Connecticut Avenue, N.W., Fifth Floor, Washington, DC 20008-2369, (202) 686-2752. Deadline: April 15 to May 15.

3229. **CPSU** Varying numbers of scholarships of $1,000 to undergraduate juniors with at least a 3.3 GPA, and who are majoring in aerospace engineering.

3230. **Glen Hubbard Memorial** Varying numbers of scholarships of $300 to undergraduate juniors with at least a 3.0 GPA, who are majoring in aerospace engineering and have an interest in aviation. Deadline: March 1.

3231. **Knudson Foundation Scholarship** 1 to 2 scholarships of $1,500 to junior or senior students majoring in dairy science technology. Must have a minimum 3.0 GPA and financial need. Deadline: March 1.

3232. **Jacob Loeb Memorial** Varying numbers of scholarships of $250 to undergraduates majoring in graphic arts and pursuing careers in printing or publishing.

3233. **Jean Eddy Sander/Rodeo Queen Awards** Varying numbers of scholarships of varying amounts to students with at least a 3.0 GPA who are majoring in agriculture and are members of the Rodeo Club.

3234. **Karl Gulbrand Memorial** Varying numbers of scholarships of varying amounts to students who have at least a 3.0 GPA, are majoring in mechanical engineering, and are members of Tau Beta Pi. Deadline: March 1.

3235. **Paul Etchechury Memorial** Varying numbers of scholarships of $300 to undergraduate seniors who have at least a 3.0 GPA and who are majoring in agricultural engineering. Must be residents of Kern County, California. Deadline: March 1.

3236. **Roy N. Pooge Memorial** Varying numbers of scholarships of $500 to students with at least a 3.0 GPA who meet other academic criteria and are majoring in engineering, environmental engineering, or mechanical engineering. Deadline: March 1.

3237. **Tuition Waivers** Numerous partial- to full-tuition waivers to students who are employees, children of employees, or senior citizens.

3238. **War Veterans** Varying numbers of scholarships of varying amounts to minority undergraduate students who have at least a 3.0 GPA and are majoring in agribusiness, agriculture, and animal science. Deadline: March 1.

California State Polytechnic University
3801 West Temple Avenue
Pomona, CA 91768-4003
(909) 869-7659
http://www.csupomona.edu/
cspadmit@csupomona.edu

3239. **Athletic (Men)** Baseball, basketball, cross-country, soccer, tennis, and track and field scholarships.

3240. **Athletic (Women)** 11 basketball, 8 soccer, 14 softball, 7 tennis, 14 track and field, or 13 volleyball scholarships.

3241. **Class Fund** Scholarships ranging from $500 to $2,000 to students of landscape architecture. Based on financial need and promise/commitment to landscape architecture. Only for study at California Polytechnic Institute (Pomona or San Luis Obispo) and for those enrolled in the extension programs at UCLA or UC Irvine. Must be residents of Southern California. Contact:

Landscape Architecture Foundation, 4401 Connecticut Avenue, N.W., Fifth Floor, Washington DC 20008–2369, (202) 686–2752. Deadline: April 15 to May 15.

California State University at Bakersfield
9001 Stockdale Highway
Bakersfield, CA 93311–1099
(805) 664–3036
http://www.csubak.edu/
hmontaluo@scubak.edu

3242. **Academic "Honors Program"** 317 scholarships ranging from $50 to $2,500 to students in the top 33 percent of their class and with at least a 3.0 GPA.

3243. **Alfred Moore** 8 scholarships of $1,200 to students with at least a 3.5 GPA. Renewable.

3244. **Athletic (Women)** Softball, tennis, track and field, and volleyball scholarships.

California State University at Chico
First and Normal Street
Chico, CA 95929
(800) 542–4426
http://www.csuchico.edu
info@oavax.scuchico.edu

3245. **Academic "Honors Program"** 250 scholarships ranging from $100 to $1,000.

California State University at Dominguez Hills
1000 E. Victoria Street
Carson, CA 90747
(310) 243–3300
(310) 243–3696
http://www.csudh/edu/
admit@csudh.edu

3246. **Alumni "Honors Program"** 8 to 10 scholarships from $755 to $2,000 for students in the upper 33 percent of their class, who have at least a 3.0 GPA. Renewable with 3.0 GPA.

3247. **Athletic (Men)** Baseball, basketball, golf, and soccer scholarships.

3248. **Athletic (Women)** Basketball, soccer, softball, and volleyball scholarships.

3249. **CSU African–American** 5 scholarships of $1,000 to African American students meeting certain criteria.

3250. **CSU Hispanic Alumni** 10 scholarships of $1,000 to Hispanic students meeting certain criteria.

3251. **CSU National Hispanic** 20 scholarships of $1,000 to Hispanic undergraduate students who have at least a 3.0 GPA. Renewable with 3.0 GPA.

3252. **Kaiser Permanente** 2 scholarships of $500 to undergraduate students who are disabled and are majoring in health or medicine.

3253. **Loker Scholarship "Honors Program"** 1 scholarship of $2,000 to a student with at least a 3.0 GPA who meets other criteria. Renewable with 3.0 GPA.

3254. **Presidential** 5 scholarships of $2,000 for students in the top 33 percent of their class who have at least a 3.4 GPA. Renewable with 3.4 GPA.

3255. **University Merit** 4 scholarships providing all fees to students with at least a 3.0 GPA who meet other academic criteria.

3256. **Tuition Waivers** Numerous partial– to full-tuition waivers to students who are employees or children of employees.

California State University at Fresno
5150 North Maple Avenue
Fresno, CA 93740–0057
(209) 278–4240
http://www.csufresno.edu
josephina@csufresno.edu

3257. **Academic** 600 scholarships ranging from $50 to $1,000 to students in the top 46 percent of their class with at least a 3.0 GPA.

3258. **Athletic (Men)** Baseball, basketball, cross-country, football, golf, soccer, swimming and diving, tennis, track and field, and wrestling scholarships.

3259. **Athletic (Women)** Basketball, gymnastics, softball, swimming and diving, tennis, and volleyball scholarships.

California State University at Fullerton
800 North State College Boulevard
Fullerton, CA 92634
(714) 733–2011
http://www.fullerton.edu/
admrec@fullerton.edu

3260. **American Society of Civil Engineers, Orange County Branch** 2 scholarships ranging from $1,000 to $2,000 to an undergraduate junior or senior civil engineering major who has been a member of ASCE for at least one year. Based on academic achievement and essay.

3261. **Athletic (Men)** Baseball, basketball, cross-country, fencing, football, gymnastics, soccer, track and field, and wrestling scholarships.

3262. **Athletic (Women)** Basketball, cross-country, fencing, gymnastics, softball, tennis, track and field, and volleyball scholarships.

3263. **Golf Writer's Association of America** 1 scholarship of $3,000 to an undergraduate sophomore for use during junior year. Must be a communications major in print journalism. Based on academic achievement and financial need.

3264. **President's** 10 scholarships of $750 to students in top 33 percent of class with a 3.5 GPA and scoring at least 1050 on SAT or 24 on ACT. Renewable with a 3.5 GPA.

3265. **President's Opportunity** 2 scholarships of $750 to students in top 33 percent of class with a 3.5 GPA and scoring at least 900 on SAT or 20 on ACT. Renewable with a 3.2 GPA.

3266. **Trustee's Award for Outstanding Achievement** 1 scholarship of $2,500 to an undergraduate sophomore, junior, or senior. Based on academic achievement, community involvement, and personal achievement.

3267. **TRW** 3 scholarships ranging from $500 to $1,500 to undergraduate sophomores, juniors, or seniors majoring in management science or management information systems. Based on academic achievement, goals, and outstanding scholarship in management science and management information systems.

3268. **Tuition Waivers** Numerous partial- to full-tuition waivers to students who are employees, children of employees, or minority students.

3269. **Western Association of Food Chains** 5 scholarships of $1,000 to students majoring in business administration management. Based on academic achievement and financial need.

California State University at Long Beach
1250 Beltflower Boulevard
Long Beach, CA 90840-0119
(310) 985-4111
http://www.csulb.edu

3270. **Alumni** Varying numbers of scholarships of varying amounts to students who meet certain academic criteria.

3271. **Brotman** Varying numbers of scholarships of varying amounts to students who meet certain academic criteria.

3272. **Copley Newspapers** 1 scholarship of $1,000 to an undergraduate student meeting certain criteria and who is a journalism major.

3273. **Don Brackenbury Award** 1 award of $200 to an undergraduate junior or senior who is a news-editorial major. Based on outstanding examples of general reporting. Deadline: April 30.

3274. **Edison Institute** 1 to 2 scholarships of $250 to undergraduate sophomores and juniors who are journalism majors. Based on academic achievement and potential.

3275. **Greater Los Angeles Press Club** 5 to 7 scholarships of $200 to undergraduate sophomores and juniors who are journalism majors. Based on financial need. Deadline: April 15.

3276. **Richard A. Cross Photojournalism Memorial** 1 scholarship of $300 to a female undergraduate student who is pursuing a career in photojournalism.

3277. **Robert A. Steffes Photojournalism Award** 1 award of $300 to a student pursuing a career in photojournalism. Based on ability, potential for success, and financial need. Renewable.

3278. **Tuition Waivers** Numerous partial- to full-tuition waivers to students who are employees or children of employees.

California State University at Los Angeles
5151 State University Drive
Los Angeles, CA 90032
(213) 343-3000
http://www.calstatela.edu/
admissions@cslanet.calstatela.edu

3279. **Athletic (Men)** Basketball, cross-country, soccer, swimming and diving, tennis, and track and field scholarships.

3280. **Athletic (Women)** Basketball, cross-country, swimming and diving, tennis, track and field, and volleyball scholarships.

3281. **CSU Scholarships for African-American Students** Up to 10 scholarships of $1,000 to African American students meeting certain criteria.

3282. **CSU Scholarships for Hispanic Students** Up to 20 scholarships of $1,000 to Hispanic students meeting certain criteria.

3283. **Dalby Proudfoot** 2 scholarships of $400 to students meeting certain academic criteria who are pre-nursing majors.

3284. **Freshman Honors** 5 scholarships of $500 to students with at least a 3.5 GPA. Renewable.

3285. **Gardner Power** 5 scholarships of $250 to male students meeting certain criteria who are education majors.

3286. **General Education Honors Awards** Varying numbers of scholarships ranging from $500 to $2,500 to students with at least a 3.0 GPA who meet certain academic criteria.

3287. **Journalism Grants–in–Aid** Up to 15 scholarship grants of $1,500 to undergraduate sophomores or above who work on the *University Times* (student newspaper) and are enrolled in J–391. Renewable with the same qualification. Deadline: before registration.

3288. **Mattel** 1 scholarship of $800 to an undergraduate student who meets certain academic criteria.

3289. **Outstanding Freshman** 5 scholarships of $300 to students with at least a 3.3 GPA.

3290. **Samuel Freeman Memorial** 4 scholarships of $500 to Hispanic students with at least a 3.0 GPA who meet certain criteria.

3291. **Tuition Waivers** Numerous partial- to full-tuition waivers to students who are employees or children of employees.

California State University at Northridge
18111 Nordhoff Street
Northridge, CA 91220-0001
(818) 677-3700
http://www.csun.edu

3292. **Athletic (Men)** Baseball, basketball, cross-country, football, golf, soccer, swimming and diving, track and field, and volleyball scholarships.

3293. **Athletic (Women)** Basketball, cross-country, softball, swimming and diving, tennis, track and field, and volleyball scholarships.

3294. **CSUN** 325 scholarships ranging from $250 to $1,550 to students with at least a 3.0 GPA. Renewable.

3295. **Departmental "Honors Program"** 250 scholarships ranging from $500 to $1,500.

California State University at Sacramento
6000 J Street
Sacramento, CA 95819
(916) 278-3901
http://www.csus.edu

3296. **Athletic (Men)** Baseball, basketball, football, golf, swimming and diving, tennis, and track and field scholarships.

3297. **Athletic (Women)** 12 basketball, 15 softball, swimming and diving, tennis, track and field, and 10 volleyball scholarships.

3298. **Auburn Journal Award** 1 scholarship of $300 to an undergraduate student interested in pursuing a career in journalism who meets certain criteria. Contact the Department of Journalism.

3299. **Freedom of Information Journalism** 1 scholarship of $1,000 to an undergraduate student demonstrating outstanding achievement by a government–journalism major. Contact the Department of Journalism. Deadline: April 15.

3300. **Friends of Journalism Department** 1 scholarship of $1,000 to an undergraduate junior or senior demonstrating excellence in a journalism field (news, editorial, photography, or graphics). Contact the Department of Journalism.

3301. **Harlin D. Smith Jr. Journalism Award** 1 scholarship of $400 to a student demonstrating excellence in a journalism field (including photography). Contact the Department of Journalism. Deadline: late April.

3302. **Kathlynn Knudsen Scholarship Fund** 1 scholarship of $500 to an undergraduate junior majoring in journalism who has demonstrated potential for a journalism career. Contact the Department of Journalism.

3303. **Margaret McKoane Photography** 1 scholarship of $200 to an undergraduate junior or senior demonstrating a personal commitment to photography. Contact the Department of Journalism.

3304. **Patrick and Sheila Marsh Scholarships in Photography** 2 scholarships of $500 to undergraduate students (one to the most promising beginning student and one for an established photography student). Preference given to minority students. Contact the Department of Journalism.

3305. **Sacramento Bee** 5 scholarships of $500 to undergraduate juniors and seniors meeting certain criteria who are majoring in journalism. Contact the Department of Journalism. Deadline: April.

3306. **Sacramento Press Club Squire Behrens Journalism** 1 scholarship of $2,500 to an undergraduate junior or senior based on academic achievement, past endeavors, interest in journalism career, and financial need. Contact: Scholarship Chairperson, Sacramento Press Club, 1961 Seventh Avenue, Sacramento, CA 95818. Deadline: May 15.

3307. **Spectrum Photography** 1 scholarship of $500 to an undergraduate student meeting certain criteria who demonstrates a personal commitment to photography. Contact the Department of Journalism.

3308. **Stephen Kyle Memorial** 1 scholarship of $400 to a student interested in pursuing a career in journalism. Contact the Department of Journalism.

3309. **Tuition Waivers** Numerous partial- to full-tuition waivers to students who are employees, children of employees, or senior citizens.

California State University at Stanislaus
801 West Monte Vista Avenue
Turlock, CA 95382
(209) 667-3122
http://www.csustan.edu

3310. **Academic** Numerous scholarships ranging from $100 up to total fees. Renewable with a 3.0 GPA.

3311. **Need "Honors Program"** Numerous scholarships ranging from $50 to $2,000 per year.

Chapman College
333 North Glassell
Orange, CA 92666
(714) 997-6611
http://www.chapman.edu
iow@chapman.edu

3312. **Academic** 100 scholarships ranging from $800 to $4,000 to students with at least a 3.0 GPA. Renewable with a 2.75 GPA.

3313. **Athletic (Men)** Baseball and basketball partial scholarships.

3314. **Athletic (Women)** Basketball, softball, and volleyball partial scholarships.

3315. **Performance** 100 scholarships ranging from $800 to $4,000 to students with at least a 2.5 GPA. Renewable with a 2.25 GPA.

3316. **Tuition Awards** Awards providing tuition costs to graduate students meeting certain academic and financial criteria.

3317. **Tuition Waivers** Numerous partial- to full-tuition waivers to students who are employees, children of employees, or children of alumni.

Christ College Irvine
1530 Concordia
Irvine, CA 92715-3299
(714) 854-8002

3318. **Athletic (Men)** Baseball, basketball, cross-country, and soccer scholarships.

3319. **Athletic (Women)** Basketball, cross-country, softball, and volleyball scholarships.

3320. **President's** 5 scholarships of $3,900 to students in the top 10 percent of their class with a 3.75 GPA. Renewable with a 3.75 GPA.

3321. **Scholar Award** Unlimited number of scholarships ranging from $500 to $1,000 to students in the top 10 percent of their class who have at least a 3.75 GPA and score at least 1200 on SAT or 26 on ACT. Renewable with a 3.5 GPA.

3322. **Scholarship** Unlimited number of scholarships ranging from $500 to $1,000 to students in the top 10 percent of their class with at least a 3.5 GPA. Renewable with a 3.5 GPA.

Christian Heritage College
2100 Greenfield Drive
El Cajon, CA 92019
(619) 588-7747
http://www.christianheritage.edu

3323. **Academic** Numerous scholarships ranging from $250 to $4,000 to students in the top 5 percent of their class, with at least a 3.5 GPA, who meet other criteria. Renewable.

3324. **Academic Merit** 2 scholarships ranging from $500 to $4,500 for students in the top 10 percent of their class, with at least a 4.0 GPA, and scoring at least 1250 on SAT or 28 on ACT.

3325. **Assistance "Honors Program"** Unlimited number of scholarships ranging from $500 to $2,000. Renewable with a 2.0 GPA.

3326. **Athletic (Men)** Basketball and soccer scholarships.

3327. **Athletic (Women)** Volleyball scholarships.

3328. **Christian Service** Unlimited number of scholarships ranging from $500 to $1,000.

3329. **Honors** Unlimited number of scholarships ranging from $500 to $2,000 to students in the top 20 percent of their class, with at least a 3.5 GPA, and scoring at least 1100 on SAT or 26 on ACT.

Claremont McKenna College

890 Columbia Avenue
Claremont, CA 91711
(909) 621-8088
http://www.mckenna.edu/
admission@mckenna.edu

3330. **McKenna** 25 scholarships of $2,500 to students in the top 10 percent of their class and scoring at least 1200 on SAT.

Cogswell College

10420 Bubb Road
Cupertino, CA 95014
(408) 252-5550

3331. **Academic** Numerous scholarships ranging from $100 to $2,880 to students with at least a 3.2 GPA. Renewable with a 3.0 GPA.

3332. **Academic** Numerous scholarships ranging from $100 to $2,880 to students with at least a 3.0 GPA. Renewable with a 3.0 GPA.

College of Notre Dame

1500 Ralston Avenue
Belmont, CA 94002
(650) 508-3607
http://www.cnd.edu
admiss@cnd.edu

3333. **Freshmen/Transfer Students** 6 programs with scholarships ranging from $1,000 to $2,000. Financial need isn't considered.

3334. **Honors at Entrance** 10 scholarships of $1,000 to students with at least a 3.0 GPA. Renewable with a 3.0 GPA.

3335. **Regents** 6 scholarships of $2,000 to students with at least a 3.0 GPA who meet certain criteria. Renewable with a 3.0 GPA.

Dominican College of San Rafael

50 Acacia Avenue
San Rafael, CA 94901
(800) 788-3522
http://www.dominican.edu
enroll@dominican.edu

3336. **Award for Academic Excellence** 9 awards of $1,000 to undergraduate students who demonstrate academic excellence. Minimum of 3.2 GPA required for renewal.

3337. **D. C. Merit** Numerous scholarships ranging from $1,000 to $2,000 to students in top 25 percent of class with a 3.0 GPA. Renewable.

3338. **O. P. Merit Award** 16 awards ranging from $500 to $3,000 to students with a strictly academic major. Minimum 3.2 GPA for renewal.

3339. **Presidential** 1 award of $6,200 to a student in top 10 percent of class with a 3.5 GPA. Renewable with a 3.4 GPA.

Fresno Pacific College

1717 South Chestnut
Fresno, CA 93702
(209) 453-2000
http://www.fresno.edu
ugadmis@fresno.edu

3340. **Athletic (Men)** Basketball, cross-country, soccer, and track and field scholarships.

3341. **Athletic (Women)** Basketball, cross-country, softball, swimming and diving, and track and field scholarships.

3342. **Top 5 Percent** 20 scholarships ranging from $200 to $2,000 to students in the top 5 percent of their class with at least a 3.44 GPA. Renewable with a 3.5 GPA.

3343. **Valedictorian/Salutatorian** 20 scholarships ranging from $200 to $3,000 to high school class valedictorians and salutatorians. Must have at least a 3.64 GPA.

Golden Gate University

536 Mission Street
San Francisco, CA 94105-2968
(415) 442-7800
http://www.ggu.edu
info@ggu.edu

3344. **GGU Community College** Numerous full-tuition scholarships to students with at least a 3.25 GPA. Renewable.

3345. **GGU High School** 8 tuition scholarships. Renewable.

Holy Names College

3500 Mountain Boulevard
Oakland, CA 94619-1699
(510) 436-1321
http://www.hnc.edu
admissions@admin.hnc.edu

3346. **Alumni** 7 scholarships ranging from $200 to $1,000 to students with at least a 3.3 GPA. Renewable with a 3.0 GPA.

3347. **President's** Numerous scholarships ranging from $500 to $3,650 to students with at least a 3.0 GPA. Renewable with a 3.0 GPA.

3348. **Regent's** 3 tuition scholarships to students with at least a 3.6 GPA. Renewable with a 3.0 GPA.

Humboldt State University
Arcata, CA 95521
(707) 826-4402
http://www.humboldt.edu/
hsuinfo@laurel.humboldt.edu

3349. **University** 240 scholarships ranging from $100 to $1,500 to students with at least a 3.0 GPA.

3350. **Von Humboldt** 12 scholarships of $500 to students with at least a 3.75 GPA and scoring at least 1200 on SAT. Renewable with a 3.0 GPA.

Loyola Marymount University
7900 Loyola Boulevard at W. 80th Street
Los Angeles, CA 90045
(310) 338-2750
http://www.lmu.edu/
admissions@lmumail.mu.edu

3351. **Alpha Gamma Sigma** Numerous scholarships ranging from $800 to $1,000 to students with at least a 3.25 GPA and scoring at least 1200 on SAT. Renewable.

3352. **Chevron** 1 scholarship of $2,000 to a student with at least a 3.5 GPA and scoring at least 1250 on SAT. Renewable.

3353. **CSF** 4 scholarships ranging from $500 to $2,000. Renewable.

3354. **Debate** Varying numbers of scholarships of varying amounts to students who participate in debate.

3355. **Father Kilp Memorial Alumni** Varying numbers of scholarships of varying amounts to students meeting certain criteria.

3356. **Jesuit and Marymount High School** Up to 10 scholarships of $6,600 to students who graduated from Jesuit and Marymount High School.

3357. **Jesuit Community** Up to 5 scholarships of $3,500 to students meeting certain criteria and who have participated in community service and religious activities. Renewable.

3358. **Leadership** Up to 25 scholarships of $5,000 to students meeting certain academic criteria. Renewable with 3.0 GPA.

3359. **National Merit** 3 scholarships ranging from $500 to $2,000. Renewable.

3360. **Presidential** 10 scholarships of $2,000 to students with at least a 3.5 GPA and scoring at least 1250 on SAT. Renewable.

3361. **Trustee "Honors Program"** Up to 10 scholarships providing tuition costs to students with at least a 3.5 GPA and who scored at least 1200 on SAT or 29 on ACT. Renewable with 3.25 GPA.

3362. **Tuition Waivers** Numerous partial- to full-tuition waivers to students who are employees or children of employees.

The Master's College
21726 West Placerita Canyon Road
P.O. Box 878
Newhall, CA 91332-0878
(800) 568-6248
http://www.masters.edu
enrollment@masters.edu

3363. **Academic** Unlimited scholarships toward tuition to students with at least a 3.6 GPA and scoring at least 1000 on SAT and in 75th percentile on ACT. Renewable with a 3.6 GPA.

3364. **Athletic (Men)** Baseball, basketball, cross-country, and soccer scholarships.

3365. **Athletic (Women)** Basketball, cross-country, and volleyball scholarships.

3366. **Music/Talent** 10 scholarships ranging from $300 to $1,800 to students meeting certain criteria.

Mills College
5000 MacArthur Boulevard
Oakland, CA 94613
(510) 430-2135
http://www.mills.edu/
admissions@mills.edu

3367. **Native Daughters of the Golden West** One $1,000 scholarship to an entering student, who need not be a member, with at least a 3.0 GPA. Based on a written exam by Mills College. Must be a California resident. Obtain forms from the Chairperson of the Committee on Education and Scholarships or from the Grand Parlor Office of the Native Daughters of the Golden West. Deadline: May 1.

3368. **Regional** 18 scholarships of $2,000 to students with at least a 3.5 GPA. Renewable with a 3.5 GPA.

3369. **Transfer** 6 scholarships of $2,000 to transfer students with at least a 3.5 GPA. Renewable with a 3.5 GPA.

3370. **Trustee** 5 scholarships of $8,400 to students with at least a 3.5 GPA and scoring at least 1200 on SAT. Renewable with a 3.6 GPA.

Mount St. Mary's College
12001 Chalon Road
Los Angeles, CA 90049
(310) 954-4250
http://www.msmc.la.edu
admmsmc@aol.com

3371. **Dean's** Numerous scholarships from $100 to
$1,000 to students with at least a 3.0 GPA.
Renewable with a 3.0 GPA.

3372. **National Merit** Numerous scholarships of up to
full tuition. Renewable with a 3.5 GPA.

3373. **President's** Numerous scholarships ranging
from $1,000 up to full tuition to students in the
top 10 percent of their class, with at least a 3.7
GPA, and scoring at least 1100 on SAT or 24 on
ACT. Renewable with a 3.5 GPA.

National University
4025 Camino del Rio South
San Diego, CA 92108-4194
(619) 563-7100
http://www.nu.edu
pcasey@unic.nu.edu

3374. **Collegiate Honors Scholarships** 100
scholarships of $1,000 to students with at least a
3.5 GPA who meet certain other academic criteria.

3375. **Eagle Scouts** Unlimited $1,000 scholarships to
students who are Eagle Scouts and who meet
certain criteria.

3376. **Gold Awardees "Honors Program"** Unlimited
number of $1,000 scholarships.

3377. **Leadership** 250 scholarships of $1,000 to
students meeting certain criteria who have
demonstrated leadership abilities.

3378. **NU President's Honors Program** 75
scholarships of $2,500 to students with at least a
2.4 GPA who meet other academic criteria.
Renewable.

New College of California
50 Fell Street
San Francisco, CA 94102
(415) 626-0884
http://www.newcollege.edu

3379. **Academic** Number and amount of scholarships
varies.

3380. **Law/Academic** Numerous scholarships ranging
from $300 to $600 to students meeting certain
academic criteria. Renewable.

Northrop University
5800 West Arbor Vitae Street
Los Angeles, CA 90045-4770
(213) 337-4440

3381. **James L. McKinley** 3 tuition scholarships to
students in the top 5 percent of their class who
have at least a 3.5 GPA. Renewable with a 3.0
GPA.

3382. **John K. Northrop** Numerous scholarships
paying up to 50 percent of tuition to students in
the top 10 percent of their class. Renewable with
a 3.5 GPA.

Occidental College
1600 Campus Road
Los Angeles, CA 90041
(213) 259-2500
http://www.oxy.edu
admission@oxy.edu

3383. **Carnation** 63 scholarships ranging from $1,000
to $5,000. Renewable with a 3.0 GPA.

3384. **Dean's** Varying numbers of scholarships of
varying amounts to students meeting certain
academic criteria.

3385. **Irvin** Varying numbers of scholarships of
varying amounts to students meeting certain
academic criteria who are Los Angeles residents.

3386. **Margaret Bundy Scott** 11 scholarships of
$10,000. Renewable with a 3.0 GPA.

3387. **Occidental Centennial** 3 scholarships of
varying amounts. Based on academic merit.

3388. **Presidential** Varying numbers of scholarships
of varying amounts to students meeting certain
academic criteria.

3389. **Swan Music Awards** Varying numbers of
scholarships of varying amounts to students
meeting certain criteria who are music majors.
Based on talent.

3390. **Trustee** Varying numbers of scholarships of
varying amounts to students meeting certain
academic criteria.

3391. **Tuition Waivers** Numerous partial- to full-
tuition waivers to students who are employees or
children of employees.

3392. **Uhlman Awards** 2 scholarships of varying
amounts. Based on academic merit.

Otis/Parsons School of Art and Design
9045 Lincoln Boulevard
Los Angeles, CA 90045
(310) 665-6800
http://www.otisart.edu
otisart@otisart.edu

3393. **Art and Design** Number and amount of scholarships varies; to students in the top 25 percent of their class who have at least a 3.0 GPA. Renewable.

3394. **Dean's Scholars** 10 scholarships ranging from $1,000 to $2,000 to students in the top 10 percent of their class who have at least a 3.0 GPA and scored at least 1000 on SAT or 24 on ACT. Renewable.

Pacific Christian College
2500 East Nutwood Avenue
Fullerton, CA 92631
(714) 879-3901
http://www.pacificcc.edu

3395. **Honors/DAHSS/DCHSS** 20 scholarships of 50 percent tuition to students with at least a 3.5 GPA. Renewable with a 3.0 GPA.

Pacific Union College
Angwin, CA 94508-9707
(707) 965-6336
http://www.puc.edu/

3396. **Honor Award** Unlimited number of $750 scholarships to students in the top 10 percent of their class.

3397. **National Merit** Unlimited number of $9,390 scholarships to students designated National Merit Scholars. Renewable.

Pepperdine University
24255 Pacific Coast Highway
Malibu, CA 90263
(310) 456-4000
http://www.pepperdine.edu
admission-seaver@pepperdine.edu

3398. **Athletic (Men)** Baseball, basketball, golf, tennis, volleyball, and water-polo scholarships.

3399. **Athletic (Women)** Basketball, golf, soccer, swimming and diving, tennis, and volleyball scholarships.

3400. **Dean's** 25 awards ranging from $1,000 to $3,500 to students in the top 10 percent of their class, with a 3.75 GPA, and scoring at least 1200 on SAT or 28 on ACT. Renewable with a 3.25 GPA.

3401. **James S. Copley Foundation—Talmage A. Campbell** 2 scholarships of $500 each to continuing journalism students. Based on financial need and potential. Deadline: April 1.

3402. **Music Awards** Varying numbers of scholarships of varying amounts to students who meet certain criteria. Based on talent.

3403. **Pepperdine Grants** Varying numbers of scholarships of varying amounts to students meeting certain academic criteria.

3404. **Presidential** 25 awards ranging from $1,500 to $4,500 to students in the top 5 percent of their class, with a 3.9 GPA, and scoring at least 1300 on SAT or 30 on ACT.

3405. **Special Achievement Awards** Varying numbers of scholarships of up to $2,500 per semester to continuing and incoming transfer students. Based on financial need and past accomplishments in the field of journalism. Awards can be increased when a journalism student assumes a position such as editor of a publication or manager of a TV or radio station. Deadline: May 1.

3406. **Special Characteristics Awards** Varying numbers of scholarships of varying amounts to students who meet certain criteria.

3407. **Student Publications Awards** Varying numbers of scholarships of varying amounts to students who work on a student publication.

3408. **Theater Awards** Varying numbers of scholarships of varying amounts to students who are theater majors. Based on talent.

3409. **Tuition Waivers** Numerous partial- to full-tuition waivers to students who are employees or children of employees.

Pitzer College
1050 North Mills Avenue
Claremont, CA 92711-6114
(919) 621-8000
http://www.pitzer.edu
admissions@pitzer.edu

3410. **Chevron Merit** 1 scholarship of $2,000 to a student in the top 10 percent of class, with at least a 3.5 GPA, and scoring at least 1100 on SAT.

3411. **Pacific Telesis Foundation** 1 scholarship of $2,000 to a student in the top 10 percent of class, with at least a 3.5 GPA, and scoring at least 1100 on SAT. Renewable with a 3.0 GPA.

Point Loma Nazarene College
3900 Lomaland Drive
San Diego, CA 92106-2899
(619) 221-2200
http://www.ptloma.edu
billyyoung@ptloma.edu

3412. **Athletic (Men)** Baseball, basketball, cross-country, golf, soccer, tennis, and track and field scholarships.

3413. **Athletic (Women)** Basketball, cross-country, tennis, track and field, and volleyball scholarships.

3414. **PLN College** Numerous $599 scholarships. Renewable.

3415. **President's** Numerous $684 scholarships. Renewable.

3416. **Valedictorian** Numerous scholarships ranging from $2,050 to $4,104 to students who are among the top three of their class.

Pomona College
333 North College Way
Claremont, CA 91711-6312
(909) 621-8000
http://www.pomona.edu
admission@pomona.edu

3417. **Chevron** 1 scholarship of $2,000 to a student in the top 10 percent of class, with at least a 3.5 GPA, and scoring at least 1200 on SAT or 28 on ACT.

3418. **National Merit** 6 scholarships of $750 to students in the top 10 percent of their class, with at least a 3.5 GPA, and scoring at least 1200 on SAT or 28 on ACT.

3419. **Uhlmann** 3 scholarships of $1,000 to students in the top 15 percent of their class, with at least a 3.0 GPA, and scoring at least 1200 on SAT or 28 on ACT.

St. Mary's College of California
1928 St. Mary's Road
Moraga, CA 94575
(510) 631-4224
(510) 631-4000
http://www.stmarys-ca.edu
admissions@stmarys-ca.edu

3420. **Academic Dean's** Varying numbers of scholarships of varying amounts to students meeting certain academic criteria.

3421. **Athletic (Men)** Baseball, basketball, crew, cross-country running, football, golf, rugby, soccer, and tennis.

3422. **Athletic (Women)** Basketball, crew, cross-country running, soccer, softball, tennis, and volleyball scholarships.

3423. **Catholic High School Graduate Grants** Varying numbers of scholarships of varying amounts to students meeting certain academic criteria who graduated from a Catholic high school.

3424. **President's Leadership** Varying numbers of scholarships of varying amounts to students meeting certain academic criteria.

3425. **St. Mary's College Departmental Awards** Varying numbers of scholarships of varying amounts to students meeting certain academic criteria.

3426. **St. Mary's Scholar Awards** Varying numbers of scholarships of varying amounts to students meeting certain academic criteria.

3427. **Tuition Waivers** Numerous partial- to full-tuition waivers to students who are employees or children of employees.

San Diego State University
San Diego, CA 92182-0420
(619) 594-5200
http://www.sdsu.edu/
admissions@sdsu.edu

3428. **Academic Achievement** Number and amount of scholarships vary. There are also many need-based scholarships, loans, and work-study programs open to anyone accepted for admission and having financial need. Contact the financial aid office.

3429. **Athletic (Men)** Basketball, cross-country, football, golf, soccer, tennis, track and field, and volleyball scholarships.

3430. **Athletic (Women)** Basketball, cross-country, golf, gymnastics, softball, tennis, track and field, and volleyball scholarships.

3431. **Copley Newspapers** Varying numbers of scholarships of $2,500 to students majoring in journalism and meeting certain criteria.

3432. **Creative Arts/Performance Awards** Numerous scholarships of varying amounts to students majoring in music.

3433. **Foster S. Post Memorial** 1 scholarship of $200 to an undergraduate student who is a journalism major meeting certain criteria.

3434. **General** Varying numbers of scholarships of varying amounts to first-time freshmen who meet certain academic criteria.

3435. **Johnny Johnson—Society of Professional Journalists Memorial** 1 scholarship of $200 to an undergraduate student majoring in journalism based on academic achievement, financial need, and service to and probable success in journalism. Apply in October or February to: SPJ Scholarship Committee Chairperson, Department of Journalism.

3436. **San Diego Professional Chapter Society of Professional Journalists** 10 scholarships of up to $200 to undergraduate students majoring in journalism. Based on financial need and interest in journalism. Renewable.

3437. **Tuition Waivers** Numerous partial- to full-tuition waivers to students who are employees or children of employees, children of alumni, minority students, or senior citizens.

3438. **Union–Tribune Publishing Company Charities** 3 scholarships of $200 to undergraduate juniors and 1 scholarship of $300 to an undergraduate senior who are journalism majors. Based on faculty recommendations.

San Jose State University
1 Washington Square
San Jose, CA 95192-0017
(408) 924-1000
http://www.sjsu.edu
contact@anrnet.sjsu.edu

3439. **Athletic (Men)** Basketball, football, golf, soccer, and tennis scholarships.

3440. **Athletic (Women)** Basketball, golf, gymnastics, softball, swimming and diving, tennis, and volleyball scholarships.

3441. **Scholarships** 450 scholarships ranging from $50 to $1,000 to students in all areas of study. Based on academic record and financial need. Deadline: January 1–March 1.

Santa Clara University
500 El Camino Real
Santa Clara, CA 95053
(408) 554-4764
http://www.scu.edu
ugadmissions@scu.edu

3442. **Athletic (Men)** Baseball, basketball, and football scholarships.

3443. **Athletic (Women)** Basketball, soccer, and volleyball scholarships.

3444. **Bruscher Theatre Arts** 10 to 20 scholarships ranging from $200 to tuition plus some other fees. Renewable with a 2.0 GPA.

3445. **Honor's Program** 50 scholarships ranging from $500 up to tuition to students in the top 25 percent of their class, with at least a 3.5 GPA, and scoring at least 1350 on SAT. Renewable with a 3.0 GPA.

3446. **Music** 5 to 8 scholarships ranging from $200 to $2,500 to students meeting certain criteria. Renewable with a 2.0 GPA.

3447. **Presidential** 25 to 30 scholarships ranging from $200 to $2,500 to students with at least a 3.5 GPA who meet certain other criteria.

3448. **Schmidt** 1 scholarship that covers all costs to a student in the top 2 percent of class, with at least a 3.8 GPA, and scoring at least 1400 on SAT. Renewable with a 3.5 GPA.

Scripps College
1030 Columbia Avenue
Claremont, CA 91711
(800) 770-1333
http://www.scrippscol.edu
admofc@ad.scrippscol.edu

3449. **Alice Shapiro Award** 1 scholarship of varying amount to a student majoring in music.

3450. **Chevron Merit** 1 award of $2,000; student must have scored at least 1100 on SAT.

3451. **Dean's Award** 29 scholarships of varying amounts. Based on academic standing.

3452. **Dorothy Drake** 25 scholarships of varying amounts. Based on academic merit.

3453. **Jaqua Harden** 2 scholarships of varying amounts for students majoring in music.

3454. **J. E. Scripps** 5 awards of $5,000 to students who are in top 10 percent of class and score at least 1250 on SAT.

3455. **Pacific Telesis Foundation** 2 awards of $2,000; students must have scored at least 1100 on SAT.

Sonoma State University
1801 East Cotati Avenue
Rohnert Park, CA 94928
(707) 664-2778
http://www.sonoma.edu
admitme@sonoma.edu

3456. **University** 60 to 75 scholarships ranging from $200 to $1,000 to students with at least a 3.5 GPA.

Southern California College
55 Fair Drive
Costa Mesa, CA 92626
(714) 556-3610
http://www.sccu.edu

3457. **Academic** Numerous scholarships of $1,200. Renewable.

3458. **Athletic (Men)** Baseball, basketball, cross-country, and soccer scholarships.

3459. **Athletic (Women)** Basketball, cross-country, softball, and volleyball scholarships.

Stanford University
Stanford, CA 94305-3005
(415) 723-2091
http://www.stanford.edu
admissions@stanford.edu

3460. **Athletic (Men)** Baseball, basektball, crew, cross-country, football, golf, gymnastics, soccer, swimming and diving, tennis, track and field, volleyball, water-polo, and wrestling scholarships.

3461. **Athletic (Women)** Basketball, golf, gymnastics, soccer, swimming and diving, tennis, track, and volleyball scholarships.

3462. **Dofflemyer Honors Scholarship** Amount varies. Eagle Scouts within Region 12 (Arizona, California, Hawaii, West Virginia, and Rock Springs, Wyoming). Based on recommendation and financial need.

University of California at Berkeley
110 Sproul Hall, #5800
Berkeley, CA 94720
(510) 642-3175
http://www.berkeley.edu
ovars@uclink.berkeley.edu

3463. **Alumni** 420 scholarships of varying amounts to students who meet certain academic criteria.

3464. **Athletic (Men)** Baseball, basketball, crew, cross-country, football, golf, gymnastics, rugby, soccer, swimming and diving, tennis, track and field, and water-polo scholarships.

3465. **Athletic (Women)** Basketball, cross-country, field hockey, gymnastics, soccer, softball, swimming and diving, tennis, track and field, and volleyball scholarships.

3466. **Honorary** 1,200 scholarships ranging from $300 to $500 to students with at least a 3.88 GPA.

3467. **Mary C. and William G. Drake** 10 scholarships of varying amounts to students meeting certain academic criteria who are mechanical engineering majors.

3468. **Native Daughters of the Golden West** 3 scholarships of $1,350 to entering students who are members or daughters or granddaughters of a member and have at least a 3.0 GPA. Obtain forms from the Chairperson of the Committee on Education and Scholarships or from the Grand Parlor Office of the Native Daughters of the Golden West. Renewable. Deadline: May 1.

3469. **Regents and Chancelors** 220 scholarships ranging from $500 to $12,000 to students in the top 5 percent of their class, with at least a 4.0 GPA and scoring at least 1400 on SAT. Renewable with a 3.0 GPA.

3470. **Tuition Waivers** Numerous partial- to full-tuition waivers to students who are employees or children of employees.

3471. **University Honorary** 3 scholarships of varying amounts to students meeting certain academic criteria.

University of California at Davis
Davis, CA 95616-8678
(916) 752-2971
(916) 752-1011
http://www.ucdavis.edu/
thinkucd@ucdavis.edu

3472. **Agricultural Fraternity of CALPHA** 3 scholarships ranging from $1,000 to $2,000 to undergraduate sophomores, juniors, or seniors majoring in agriculture or environmental science.

3473. **Alice C. Bridge Memorial** 1 scholarship of $5,000 to undergraduate students majoring in food science or food technology.

3474. **Alumni** 100 scholarships of $500 to students with at least a 3.5 GPA. Based on academic achievement, essay, leadership abilities, community involvement, and recommendations.

3475. **Boeing Company** 2 scholarships of $2,000 to undergraduate juniors or seniors who are majoring in engineering, computer science, or mechanical engineering.

3476. **Cal Aggie Alumni Association** 54 scholarships of $1,000 to entering freshmen who have demonstrated leadership ability.

3477. **E. A. Boyd** 2 scholarships of $1,000 to undergraduate students who are residents of Northern California.

3478. **Elmer Hughes** 4 scholarships of $1,000 to entering freshmen who will be majoring in animal science.

3479. **Farmers Insurance** 1 scholarships of $2,000 to an undergraduate junior or senior interested in pursuing a career in the insurance industry.

3480. **Farm Home** 2 scholarships ranging from $1,000 to $2,700 to undergraduate students who are majoring in home economics.

3481. **Frank A. Mespie Memorial** 3 scholarships of $2,000 to undergraduate juniors or seniors who are political science majors.

3482. **Gail E. and Ruth M. Oliver** 35 scholarships of $2,000 to undergraduate students majoring in agriculture or environmental science.

3483. **General Dillingham Produce Industry** 2 scholarships of $1,200 to undergraduate juniors or seniors pursuing careers in the produce industry who have at least a 3.25 GPA. Renewable with continued interest in the produce industry.

3484. **George W. Pierce** 6 scholarships of $2,000 to undergraduate students majoring in agriculture or environmental science.

3485. **Guild Wineries and Distilleries** 1 scholarship of $1,000 to undergraduate juniors or seniors who are enology or viticulture majors.

3486. **Henry Jastro** 25 to 37 scholarships ranging from $2,000 to $2,700 to students with at least a 3.5 GPA who are agriculture or environmental science majors. Based on academic achievement, essay, leadership abilities, community involvement, and recommendations. Renewable with 3.25 GPA.

3487. **Howard R. Murphy** 1 scholarship of $2,500 to an undergraduate student majoring in agricultural engineering.

3488. **Hubert H. Wakeham** 3 scholarships of $3,000 to entering freshmen who meet certain criteria.

3489. **Jack Messick Memorial** 2 scholarships of $1,500 to undergraduate juniors or seniors who are pursuing careers in agribusiness.

3490. **Jack T. Picket Agriculture** 4 scholarships of $3,000 to entering freshmen who are pursuing careers in agriculture. Must have demonstrated leadership abilities in 4–H or FFA.

3491. **James and Leta Fulmore** 20 to 70 scholarships of $2,000 to students who meet certain academic criteria and who are pursuing careers in any major in the College of Letters or Science. Renewable with 3.25 GPA.

3492. **James Bonnheim** 16 scholarships ranging from $1,000 to $9,608 to undergraduate students between the ages of sixteen and nineteen at the time of first application.

3493. **Jarena D. Wright** 15 scholarships of $1,000 to undergraduate students who are residents of Santa Rosa.

3494. **Lewis Clark Starr** 4 scholarships ranging from $1,000 to $2,100 to undergraduate students majoring in animal science.

3495. **Luther and Marie Davis** 100 scholarships ranging from $200 to $1,800 to undergraduate students majoring in agriculture or environmental science.

3496. **Mabel Wilson Richards** 3 scholarships of $1,667 to female undergraduate students with financial need who are residents of Los Angeles.

3497. **Matilda Newsom Fowler** 4 scholarships of $1,000 to undergraduate students majoring in home economics who have financial need.

3498. **McBeth Memorial** 2 scholarships of $3,000 to undergraduate entomology students who meet certain criteria.

3499. **Modesto High School** 4 scholarships of $1,000 to undergraduate students who are graduates of Modesto High School and have financial need.

3500. **National Merit** 20 scholarships of varying amounts to students receiving National Merit standing.

3501. **Peter J. Shields** 4 scholarships of $2,000 to undergraduate students who are agriculture or environmental science majors.

3502. **R. E. and Hilda M. Sparling** 29 scholarships ranging from $1,000 to $11,400 to undergraduate students who are graduates of Dixon High School and have financial need. Renewable.

3503. **Regents** 50 scholarships of varying amounts to students who meet certain academic criteria.

3504. **Robert and Louise Jameson** 4 scholarships ranging from $1,000 to $2,100 to undergraduate students majoring in agriculture or environmental science.

3505. **Robert Lawrence Balzer** 1 scholarship of $1,000 to undergraduate senior or graduate students majoring in enology or viticulture.

3506. **Tracy and Ruth Storer** 13 scholarships of $1,000 to undergraduate sophomores, juniors, or seniors who are interested in or intend to do graduate study or research in an animal–related science or the biology of an animal system.

3507. **Tuition Waivers** Numerous full- or partial–tuition waivers to students who are employees or children of employees.

3508. **William B. Jameson** 3 scholarships of $1,000 to undergraduate sophomores with any major in the College of Letters and Science.

University of California at Irvine
Irvine, CA 92717
(714) 856-6345
http://www.uci.edu
oars@uci.edu

3509. **Alumni** Varying numbers of scholarships of $350 to students with at least a 3.75 GPA, who scored at least 1250 on SAT and meet other criteria. Renewable with 3.0 GPA.

3510. **Athletic (Men)** Basketball, cross-country, golf, swimming and diving, tennis, and track and field scholarships.

3511. **Athletic (Women)** Basketball, cross–country, swimming and diving, tennis, track and field, and volleyball scholarships.

3512. **Chancellor's Club** Varying numbers of scholarships of $1,000 to students with at least a 3.75 GPA, who scored at least a 1250 on SAT and who meet other criteria. Renewable with 3.0 GPA.

3513. **Class Fund** Scholarships ranging from $500 to $2,000 to students studying landscape architecture. Based on financial need and promise/commitment to landscape architecture. Only for study at California Polytechnic Institute (Pomona or San Luis Obispo) and for those enrolled in the extension programs at UCLA or UC Irvine. Must be residents of Southern California. Contact: Landscape Architecture Foundation, 4401 Connecticut Avenue, N.W., Fifth Floor, Washington DC 20008-2369, (202) 686-2752. Deadline: April 15 to May 15.

3514. **Native Daughters of the Golden West** 1 scholarship of $1,350 to an entering student who is a member or daughter or granddaughter of a member and has at least a 3.0 GPA. Obtain forms from the Chairperson of the Committee on Education and Scholarships or from the Grand Parlor Office of the Native Daughters of the Golden West. Renewable. Deadline: May 1.

3515. **Regents Honorarium** Varying numbers of scholarships of varying amounts to students meeting certain academic criteria.

3516. **Restrictive Endowment** Varying numbers of scholarships ranging from $250 to $1,000 to students with at least a 3.0 GPA.

3517. **Settle** Varying numbers of scholarships ranging from $250 to $1,000 to students with at least a 3.0 GPA.

3518. **Strauss** Varying numbers of scholarships ranging from $250 to $1,000 to students with at least a 3.0 GPA.

3519. **Thurgood Marshall** Varying numbers of scholarships of varying amounts to students meeting certain academic criteria.

3520. **Tierney** Varying numbers of scholarships of $1,000 to students with at least a 3.0 GPA who meet other criteria.

3521. **Town and Gown** Varying numbers of scholarships of varying amounts to students with at least a 3.0 GPA who meet other criteria.

3522. **Tuition Waivers** Numerous partial- to full–tuition waivers to students who are employees or children of employees.

3523. **UCI Foundation** Varying numbers of scholarships of $250 to students with at least a 3.75 GPA, who scored at least a 1250 on SAT, and who meet other criteria.

3524. **University Scholarships** Varying numbers of scholarships of varying amounts to students who meet certain academic criteria.

University of California at Los Angeles
405 Hilgard Avenue
Los Angeles, CA 90024
(310) 825-4321
http://www.ucla.edu
admissions@saonet.ucla.edu

3525. **Alumni** 150 scholarships ranging from $1,000 to $3,500 are awarded to students with a 3.85 GPA who scored at least 1000 on SAT. Renewable.

3526. **Athletic (Men)** Baseball, basketball, crew, cross–country, diving, football, golf, gymnastics, indoor track, soccer, swimming, swimming and diving, tennis, track and field, volleyball, and water–polo scholarships.

3527. **Athletic (Women)** Basketball, cross-country, golf, gymnastics, softball, swimming and diving, tennis, track and field, and volleyball scholarships.

3528. **Class Fund Scholarships** Scholarships ranging from $500 to $2,000 to students studying landscape architecture. Based on financial need and promise/commitment to landscape architecture. Only for study at California Polytechnic Institute (Pomona or San Luis Obispo) and for those enrolled in the extension programs at UCLA or UC Irvine. Must be residents of Southern California. Contact: Landscape Architecture Foundation, 4401 Connecticut Avenue, N.W., Fifth Floor, Washington, DC 20008-2369, (202) 686-2752. Deadline: April 15 to May 15.

3529. **National Merit** Numerous scholarships ranging from $500 to $2,000 to students designated National Merit Scholars.

3530. **Native Daughters of the Golden West** 1 scholarship of $1,350 to an entering student who is a member or daughter or granddaughter of a member and has at least a 3.0 GPA. Obtain forms from the Chairperson of the Committee on Education and Scholarships or from the Grand Parlor Office of the Native Daughters of the Golden West. Renewable. Deadline: May 1.

3531. **Regents "Honors Program"** 100 scholarships ranging from $500 to $6,000 to students in top 3 percent of class, with a 4.0 average, and scoring at least 1350 on SAT. Renewable with a 3.0 GPA.

University of California at Riverside
900 University Avenue
Riverside, CA 92521-0118
(909) 787-1012
http://www.ucr.edu/
hsro@ucrac1.ucr.edu

3532. **Academic Excellence Scholarships** Varying numbers of scholarships of varying amounts to minority students meeting certain academic criteria.

3533. **Alumni Scholarships** Varying numbers of scholarships of varying amounts to students meeting certain academic criteria.

3534. **Athletic (Men)** Basketball and cross-country scholarships.

3535. **Athletic (Women)** 9 partial basketball and volleyball scholarships.

3536. **Brecht Scholarships** Varying numbers of scholarships of varying amounts to minority students meeting certain academic criteria.

3537. **Creative Writing Awards** Varying numbers of scholarships of varying amounts to minority students meeting certain criteria who are creative writing majors. Based on talent.

3538. **Dance Awards** Varying numbers of scholarships of varying amounts to minority students meeting certain criteria who are art majors. Based on talent.

3539. **Music Awards** Varying numbers of scholarships of varying amounts to minority students meeting certain criteria who are music majors. Based on talent.

3540. **Native Daughters of the Golden West** 1 scholarship of $1,350 to an entering student who is a member or daughter or granddaughter of a member and has at least a 3.0 GPA. Obtain forms from the Chairperson of the Committee on Education and Scholarships or from the Grand Parlor Office of the Native Daughters of the Golden West. Renewable. Deadline: May 1.

3541. **Studio Art Awards** Varying numbers of scholarships of varying amounts to minority students meeting certain criteria who are art majors. Based on talent.

3542. **Theater Arts Awards** Varying numbers of scholarships of varying amounts to minority students meeting certain criteria who are theater majors. Based on talent.

3543. **UC Riverside National Merit Awards** Varying numbers of scholarships of varying amounts to minority students meeting certain academic criteria who are designated as National Merit finalists.

University of California, San Diego
9500 Gilman Drive
La Jolla, CA 92093
(619) 534-4831
(619) 534-2230
http://www.ucsd.edu
admissionsinfo@ucsd.edu

3544. **Alumni** 10 scholarships of varying amounts to students meeting certain academic criteria.

3545. **Brace** 1 scholarship of varying amount to student meeting certain academic criteria.

3546. **National Merit Awards** 39 scholarships of varying amounts to students meeting certain academic criteria who received National Merit designation.

3547. **Ramsayer** 3 scholarships of varying amounts to students meeting certain academic criteria.

3548. **Regents Honor Awards** 69 scholarships ranging from $1,000 to $6,875 to students meeting certain academic criteria. Renewable.

3549. **Revelle** 2 scholarships of varying amounts to students meeting certain academic criteria.

3550. **Thelen** 2 scholarships of varying amounts to students meeting certain academic criteria.

3551. **UCSD Merit** 843 scholarships of $1,200 to students meeting certain academic criteria. Renewable.

University of California at Santa Barbara
Santa Barbara, CA 93106
(805) 893-2327
http://www.ucsb.edu

3552. **Athletic (Men)** Baseball, basketball, cross-country, gymnastics, soccer, swimming and diving, tennis, track and field, and volleyball scholarships.

3553. **Athletic (Women)** Basketball, cross-country, gymnastics, soccer, softball, swimming and diving, tennis, track and field, and volleyball scholarships.

3554. **Native Daughters of the Golden West** 1 scholarship of $1,350 to an entering student who is a member or daughter or granddaughter of a member and has at least a 3.0 GPA. Obtain forms from the Chairperson of the Committee on Education and Scholarships or from the Grand Parlor Office of the Native Daughters of the Golden West. Renewable. Deadline: May 1.

3555. **Regents** Numerous renewable scholarships ranging from $1,000 to $6,875.

3556. **University** Numerous renewable $1,200 scholarships.

University of Redlands
1200 East Colton Avenue
P.O. Box 3080
Redlands, CA 92373-0999
(800) 455-5069
http://www.uor.edu/
admit@uor.edu

3557. **California Scholarship Federation Awards** 18 scholarships of varying amounts to students from state public high schools who meet certain academic criteria.

3558. **Creative Arts/Performance Awards** Scholarhips of varying amounts to students based on talent in the following categories: 1 in art, 88 in music, 8 in debate, and 21 in creative writing.

3559. **Multicultural Awards** 98 scholarships of varying amounts to students meeting certain criteria.

3560. **National Merit Awards** 43 scholarships of varying amounts to students meeting certain academic criteria.

3561. **Presidential** 459 scholarships ranging from $500 to $1,500 to students with at least a 3.7 GPA, and who scored at least 1100 on SAT or 23 on ACT. Renewable with 3.5 GPA.

3562. **Special Achievement/Activities Awards** 129 scholarships of varying amounts totaling $227,100 to students meeting certain criteria.

3563. **Trustee Awards** 15 scholarships ranging from $500 to $5,000 to students with at least a 3.9 GPA, and who scored at least 1200 on SAT or 27 on ACT. Renewable with 3.5 GPA.

3564. **Tuition Waivers** Varying numbers of partial- to full-tuition waivers to students who are employees or children of employees.

3565. **UR Awards of Merit** 59 scholarships of varying amounts to students meeting certain academic criteria.

University of San Diego
5998 Alcala Pike
San Diego, CA 92110
(619) 260-4600
http://www.acusd.edu

3566. **Athletic (Men)** Basketball and tennis scholarships.

3567. **Athletic (Women)** Basketball, swimming and diving, tennis, or volleyball scholarships.

3568. **Catholic Leadership** Numerous scholarships ranging from $200 to $1,000 to students with at least a 2.8 GPA who are of the Catholic faith. Renewable with a 2.5 GPA.

3569. **Presidential** Numerous $4,100 scholarships to students with at least a 3.6 GPA and scoring at least 1170 on SAT. Renewable with a 3.25 GPA.

3570. **Trustee "Honors Program"** Numerous $5,300 scholarships to students with at least a 3.8 GPA and scoring at least 1220 on SAT. Renewable with a 3.45 GPA.

University of San Francisco
Ignatian Heights
San Francisco, CA 94117-1080
(800) CALL-USF
(415) 666-6292
http://www.usfca.edu/

3570. **Athletic (Men)** Basketball, soccer, and tennis scholarships.

3571. **Athletic (Women)** Basketball, golf, soccer, softball, tennis, and volleyball scholarships.

3572. **President's Honors Program** 15 to 20 scholarships ranging from $1,000 to $2,000 to students with at least a 3.5 GPA and scoring at least 1200 on SAT. Renewable with a 3.0 GPA.

3573. **Special Achievement/Activities Awards** Varying numbers of scholarships of varying amounts to students meeting certain criteria.

3574. **Tuition Waivers** Numerous partial- to full-tuition waivers to students who are employees or children of employees.

3575. **University Scholarships** Varying numbers of scholarships of varying amounts to students who meet certain academic criteria.

University of Southern California
University Park
Los Angeles, CA 90089-0911
(213) 740-1111
http://www.usc.edu

3576. **Alumni** 120 scholarships of $500 to students with a 3.0 GPA. Renewable.

3577. **Athletic (Men)** Baseball, basketball, cross-country, football, golf, tennis, track and field, and volleyball scholarships.

3578. **Athletic (Women)** Basketball, golf, swimming and diving, tennis, track and field, and volleyball scholarships.

3579. **Eagle Scout** Numerous $500 scholarships to students who are Eagle Scouts, with at least a 3.0 GPA on a 4.0 scale, and are admitted to the School of Engineering. Deadline: March 1.

3580. **Presidential** 275 scholarships of $500 to students with a 3.95 GPA who scored at least 1250 on SAT or 27 on ACT. Renewable.

3581. **Trustee** 25 to 30 scholarships of $1,500 to students with a 3.95 GPA and who scored at least 1250 on SAT or 27 on ACT. Renewable.

3582. **USC Associates** 30 to 50 scholarships ranging from $1,000 to $3,500 to students with a 3.5 GPA who scored at least 1150 on SAT. Renewable.

University of the Pacific
3601 Pacific Avenue
Stockton, CA 95211
(209) 946-2211
http://www.uop.edu
admissions@uop.edu

3583. **Athletic (Men)** Baseball, basketball, football, swimming and diving, and tennis scholarships.

3584. **Athletic (Women)** Basketball, cross-country, field hockey, softball, swimming and diving, tennis, and volleyball scholarships.

3585. **Freshman Honors** 50 scholarships ranging from $500 to $5,000 to students with at least a 3.5 GPA and scoring at least 1050 on SAT. Renewable.

Westmont College
955 La Paz Road
Santa Barbara, CA 93108
(800) 777-9011
http://www.westmont.edu
admissions@westmont.edu

3586. **Athletic (Men)** Basketball, cross-country, soccer, tennis, and track and field scholarships.

3587. **Athletic (Women)** Cross-country, soccer, tennis, track and field, and volleyball scholarships.

3588. **Presidential** 12 scholarships ranging from $1,000 to $4,000. Renewable.

Whittier College
Whittier, CA 90608
(562) 907-4238
http://www.whittier.edu
admissions@whittier.edu

3589. **George E. Wanberg** Varying numbers of scholarships ranging from $200 to $800 to young men pursuing a career in youth leadership (Boy Scouts, YMCA, and other youth organizations).

3590. **Gifford Eagle Scout** Scholarships ranging from $500 to $800 to Eagle Scouts who plan a career in youth leadership (such as scouting or the ministry).

3591. **Talent** 15 scholarships ranging from $250 to $3,750. Based on portfolio or audition, talent, and recommendations. Renewable.

3592. **WC Academic Merit** 49 scholarships ranging from $1,000 to $7,300 to students with at least a 3.25 GPA and scoring at least 1100 on the SAT. Renewable with a 3.25 GPA.

COLORADO

Adams State College
208 Edgemont Avenue
Alamosa, CO 81102
(719) 587-7712
http://www.adams.edu
ascadmit@adams.edu

3593. Athletic (Men) Basketball, cross–country, football, golf, indoor track, track and field, and wrestling scholarships. Contact the Athletic Director.

3594. Athletic (Women) Basketball, cross–country, gymnastics, track and field, and volleyball scholarships.

3595. Honors at Entrance 150 scholarships ranging from $1,405 to $1,750 to incoming freshmen who scored at least 19 on ACT, were in the top fifth of their class, and had a minimum 3.25 GPA. Deadline: March 15.

3596. National 200 scholarships of $1,473 to entering students who are in the top 40 percent of their class and scored at least 19 on ACT. Transfer students must have a minimum of a 2.5 GPA. Must live on campus and cannot be Colorado residents. Deadline: Aug. 15.

3597. President's 200 scholarships ranging from $400 to $750 to undergraduates who have a minimum 3.25 GPA and meet certain ACT criteria. Deadline: March 15.

3598. Woodward Memorial 35 scholarships of $2,600 to students with strong academic records and community involvement. Deadline: March 15.

Colorado Christian University
Lakewood, CO 80226
(800) 443-2484
http://www.ccu.edu
admissions@ccu.edu

3599. Alumni Incentive Grants Varying numbers of scholarships of varying amounts to students who are children of alumni.

3600. Athletic (Men) 7 scholarships averaging $1,728 to students in basketball, golf, soccer, and tennis.

3601. Athletic (Women) 13 scholarships averaging $3,700 to students in basketball, tennis, and volleyball.

3602. Church/College Matching Varying numbers of scholarships of varying amounts to students who meet certain criteria.

3603. Drama/Music 21 scholarships ranging from $200 to $1,000 to students who are majoring in performing arts, communications, or music. Selection based on talent.

3604. Family Allowance Awards Varying numbers of scholarships of varying amounts to students who are siblings of current students.

3605. Incentive 100 scholarships ranging from $300 to $500 to students who meet certain academic criteria.

3606. Ministerial Varying numbers of scholarships of varying amounts to students who meet certain criteria and are majoring in religion/biblical studies.

3607. Ministerial Dependent Awards Varying numbers of scholarships of varying amounts to students who meet certain criteria and are relatives of clergy.

3608. Presidential Excellence Awards Varying numbers of scholarships of varying amounts to students based on leadership and/or religious involvement.

3609. Spouse Half–Tuition Awards Varying numbers of scholarships of varying amounts to students who are spouses of current students.

3610. Tuition Waivers Numerous partial of full tuition waivers to students who are employees, children of employees, or children of alumni.

3611. Young Scholars Awards 150 scholarships ranging from $600 to $1,000 to students who meet certain academic criteria.

Colorado College
14 East Cache La Poudre
Colorado Springs, CO 80903-9972
(800) 542-7214
http://www.cc.colorado.edu
admissions@cc.colorado.edu

3612. Athletic (Women) 13 partial soccer scholarships.

3613. CC Faculty Minority 3 scholarships ranging from $100 to $1,500. Renewable.

3614. Colorado Merit 60 scholarships of $750 to students with a 3.6 GPA.

3615. **Harold C. Harmon** 1 scholarship of $4,000. Renewable.

3616. **Otis A. and Margaret T. Barnes Trust** 10 scholarships ranging from $1,800 to $8,840 for chemistry majors. Deadline: prior to high school graduation.

3617. **Women's Education Society** 5 scholarships of $1,750 to students, based on class standing. Renewable.

Colorado Institute of Art
200 East Ninth Avenue
Denver, CO 80203
(303) 837-0825
http://www.cia.aii.edu

3618. **Art Scholarships** 5 full-tuition scholarships to high school seniors pursuing a degree related to art, such as commercial art, interior design, photography, fashion merchandising, or the music and video businesses. Recipients must pay a one-time enrollment fee of $25 and a general fee of $230, as well as pay for a supply kit. Based on applicant's original artwork (or 35mm slides of artwork). Deadline: March 15.

Colorado School of Mines
1811 Elm Street
Golden, CO 80401
(800) 446-9488
http://www.mines.colorado.edu/
admit@mines.colorado.edu

3619. **Athletic (Men)** Baseball, basketball, cross-country, football, golf, lacrosse, skiing (cross-country), skiing (downhill), swimming and diving, tennis, track and field, and wrestling scholarships.

3620. **Athletic (Women)** Basketball, cross-country, golf, softball, swimming and diving, tennis, track and field, and volleyball scholarships.

3621. **Board of Trustees** 30 scholarships ranging from $3,000 to $8,000 to students in the top 10 percent of their class, with at least a 3.5 GPA, and scoring at least 1200 on SAT or 27 on ACT. Renewable with a 2.75 GPA.

3622. **BOT Scholarships** 40 scholarships of varying amounts to students who meet certain academic criteria.

3623. **Coors Scholarship** 1 scholarship of varying amount to a student meeting certain criteria.

3624. **Creative Arts/Performance Awards** 17 scholarships of varying amounts to students who will be participating in band or chorus and who meet certain criteria.

3625. **Dodge NSP Scholarship** 1 scholarship of varying amount to a student who meets certain academic criteria.

3626. **"E" Day Scholarships** 3 scholarships of varying amounts to Colorado State residents based on an essay contest.

3627. **Mines Medal of Achievement Scholarships** Varying numbers of scholarships of varying amounts to students who meet certain academic criteria.

3628. **Minority Scholarships** 40 scholarships of varying amounts to minority students who meet certain academic criteria.

3629. **NSP Keck Scholarships** 3 scholarships of varying amounts of out-of-state students who meet certain criteria.

3630. **Presidential** 20 scholarships ranging from $1,500 to $2,500 to students in the top 15 percent of their class, with at least a 3.3 GPA, and scoring at least 1100 on SAT or 24 on ACT. Renewable with a 2.5 GPA.

Colorado State University
Fort Collins, CO 80523-0015
(970) 491-6909
http://www.colostate.edu/
admissions@colstate.edu

3631. **Arts** 347 scholarships ranging from $100 to $1,000 to students with at least a 2.4 GPA. Renewable with a 2.4 GPA.

3632. **Athletic (Men)** Baseball, basketball, cross-country, football, and track and field scholarships.

3633. **Athletic (Women)** Basketball, cross-country, softball, swimming and diving, track and field; and volleyball scholarships.

3634. **Chevron USA Scholarship** 1 scholarship of $1,000 to an undergraduate junior or senior who is a print or broadcast major and who has completed at least six hours in economics and/or business and intends to take more.

3635. **Claude W. Wood Scholarships** 12 scholarships of $1,500 each to entering freshmen students with at least a 3.5 GPA who will be majoring in engineering.

3636. **Clyde E. Moffitt Memorial Fund Scholarships** 6 scholarships of at least $600 to students based on academic achievement, financial need, and dedication to journalism career. Renewable.

3637. **Colorado Scholars** 82 scholarships of $1,000 to students with at least a 3.0 GPA. Renewable.

3638. **Diversity** 40 scholarships of $1,000 to students with at least a 2.0 GPA. Renewable.

3639. **Honors** 58 scholarships of $1,000 to students with at least a 3.8 GPA. Not renewable.

3640. **Nonresident** 200 scholarships ranging from $800 to $1,000. Renewable if student maintains a 2.75 GPA.

3641. **Philip A. Connolly Scholarship** 5 scholarships of $1,000 to junior or senior undergraduate students majoring in forestry or natural resources. Based on financial need and leadership potential. Minimum 3.0 GPA required. Deadline: February 15.

3642. **President's** 410 scholarships of $1,000 to students in top 1 percent of class with a 3.8 GPA. Renewable with a 3.8 GPA.

Colorado Technical College
4435 North Chestnut Street
Colorado Springs, CO 80907-3896
(719) 598-0200
http://www.colotech.edu

3643. **Board of Governors** 5 scholarships of $1,000 to students with at least a 3.0 GPA. Renewable with a 3.0 GPA.

3644. **Colorado HS** 20 scholarships of $600 to students with at least a 2.5 GPA. Renewable with a 3.0 GPA.

3645. **Colorado Scholars** 20 scholarships ranging from $250 to $750. Renewable with a 3.0 GPA.

Fort Lewis College
1000 Rim Drive
Durango, CO 81301
(303) 247-7184
http://www.fortlewis.edu

3646. **Alumni** 6 scholarships of varying amounts to students meeting certain criteria.

3647. **Athletic (Men)** Basketball, football, soccer, and wrestling scholarships.

3648. **Athletic (Women)** Basketball, softball, and volleyball scholarships.

3649. **Bodo** 10 scholarships of varying amounts to students who meet certain criteria.

3650. **Craig–Dyer** 2 scholarships of varying amounts to students meeting certain criteria and are local residents.

3651. **Dalpra** 5 scholarships of varying amounts to students who meet certain academic criteria.

3652. **Dean's** Up to 189 scholarships of $600 to students with at least a 3.0 GPA who scored at least 24 on ACT.

3653. **First Generation Awards** 10 scholarships of varying amounts to students meeting certain criteria who are the children of parents who have not attended college.

3654. **Helen Kroeger–Faris** 7 scholarships of varying amounts to students who meet certain criteria.

3655. **New Mexico Reciprocal Tuition Awards** 10 scholarships of varying amounts to students meeting certain criteria who are residents of Northwestern New Mexico.

3656. **Performing Arts "Honors Program"** Numerous scholarships ranging from $800 to $1,400 to students with at least a 3.0 GPA. Renewable with a 3.0 GPA.

3657. **Presidential** 90 scholarships ranging from $500 to $1,000 to students in the top 20 percent of their class who have at least a 3.5 GPA.

3658. **Western Undergraduate Exchange Awards** 10 scholarships of varying amounts to students meeting certain criteria.

Mesa State College
P.O. Box 2647
Grand Junction, CO 81502
(303) 248-1020
http://www.mesastate.edu
stonewpogate.mesa.colorado.edu

3659. **Athletic (Men)** Basketball, football, and tennis scholarships.

3660. **Athletic (Women)** Basketball, cross–country, softball, tennis, and volleyball scholarships.

3661. **Colorado Scholars** 200 scholarships of $700 to students with at least a 3.0 GPA and scoring at least 19 on ACT. Renewable with a 3.0 GPA.

3662. **Drama Awards** 8 scholarships of varying amounts to students meeting certain criteria who are art majors.

3663. **Music Awards** 12 scholarships of varying amounts to students meeting certain criteria who are music majors.

3664. **Vocational Awards** 5 scholarships of varying amounts totaling $3,500 to students meeting certain criteria.

Metropolitan State College
1006 11th Street
P.O. Box 173362
Denver, CO 80217-3362
(303) 556-3058
http://www.msed.edu

3665. **Athletic (Men)** Basketball, soccer, swimming and diving, and tennis scholarships.

3666. **Athletic (Women)** Basketball, soccer, swimming and diving, tennis, and volleyball scholarships.

3667. **HS Presidential** 20 scholarships of $886 to students in the top 20 percent of their class, with at least a 3.0 GPA, and scoring at least 975 on SAT or 23 on ACT. Renewable with a 3.33 GPA.

3668. **Transfer Presidential** 10 scholarships ranging from $278 to $556 to students with at least a 3.33 GPA. Renewable with a 3.33 GPA.

Regis University
3333 Regis Boulevard
Denver, CO 80221
(303) 458-4100
http://www.regis.edu
regisadm@regis.edu

3669. **Academic** 30 scholarships of $2,000 to students in the top 20 percent of their class with at least a 3.3 GPA. Renewable with a 3.0 GPA.

3670. **Activity** 30 scholarships of $1,000. Renewable.

3671. **Athletic (Men)** Baseball, basketball, golf, soccer, and tennis scholarships.

3672. **Athletic (Women)** Basketball, golf, soccer, softball, tennis, and volleyball scholarships.

3673. **Natural Science** 12 tuition scholarships. Renewable with a 3.0 GPA.

3674. **Regis Academic Scholarships** Varying numbers of scholarships of varying amounts to students who meet certain academic criteria.

3675. **Second Century Scholarships** Varying numbers of scholarships of varying amounts to students who meet certain academic criteria.

3676. **Zarlengo Scholarships** Varying numbers of scholarships of varying amounts to students who meet certain academic criteria and are Colorado residents.

University of Colorado
Boulder, CO 80309
(303) 492-6301
http://www.colorado.edu/
apply@colorado.edu.

3677. **Alvin G. Flanagan Scholarships** 1 or more scholarship of at least $300 to undergraduate juniors or above who are journalism majors. Based on academic achievement and financial need. Renewable. Deadline: February 1.

3678. **Arnold National Scholarships** Varying numbers of scholarships of varying amounts to students based on leadership and activities.

3679. **Athletic (Men)** Basketball, cross-country, football, golf, skiing (cross-country), skiing (downhill), tennis, and track and field scholarships.

3680. **Athletic (Women)** Skiing, tennis, track and field, and volleyball partial scholarships, and basketball, skiing, tennis, track and field, and volleyball full scholarships.

3681. **Boulder Daily Camera—L. C. Paddock Journalism Scholarship** 1 scholarship providing in-state tuition and fees to a student interested in journalism. Preference given to children of Colorado newspaper familes. Deadline: February 1.

3682. **Boulder Press Club Scholarship** 1 scholarship of $300 to a senior who is a Colorado resident and a journalism major. Based on academic achievement and financial need. Deadline: February 1.

3683. **Boulder Scholars Awards** Varying numbers of scholarships of varying amounts to students meeting certain criteria.

3684. **Colorado Scholars Music Scholarships** 14 scholarships of varying amounts to students meeting certain criteria who are music majors.

3685. **Colorado Scholars Presidential Leadership Scholarships** 51 scholarships of varying amounts to students. Based on leadership abilities.

3686. **Colorado Scholars Regents Scholarships** 300 scholarships of $500 to students in top 3 percent of their class who meet certain other criteria. Must be Colorado residents.

3687. **CU Opportunity** Varying numbers of scholarships of varying amounts to minority students meeting certain criteria.

3688. **Dean's Scholars** 325 scholarships ranging from $100 to $1,200. Renewable.

3689. **Denver Woman's Press Club—Frances Belford Wayne Merit Award** 1 scholarship of $500 to a female undergraduate junior or senior journalism major. Based on outstanding academic achievement and talent. Renewable. Deadline: February 1.

3690. **Engineering Department** Varying numbers of scholarships of varying amounts to students meeting certain academic criteria who are majoring in engineering.

3691. **Faculty** 1 scholarship of at least $300 to an undergraduate junior based on outstanding journalistic performance.

3692. **Gene Cervi Memorial Award** 1 scholarship of $400 to a student majoring in journalism who is in a news–editorial sequence. Contact: School of Journalism and Communication. Deadline: February 1.

3693. **Gladys Van Vranken Parce** 1 scholarship of $400 to an undergraduate junior or senior, or a graduate print journalism major. Must have at least a 3.0 GPA and financial need. Renewable. Deadline: March 1.

3694. **J. Ember and Agnes P. Sterling Memorial** 1 scholarship of $300 to an undergraduate senior or a graduate news–editorial student. Based on academic achievement and financial need. Deadline: February 1.

3695. **Marcela Hertzog Memorial** 1 scholarship of $500 to an undergraduate junior, senior, or graduate student. Based on academic achievement and financial need. Deadline: February 1.

3696. **Mile–High Kennel Club—Denver Press Club** 1 scholarship providing in-state tuition and fees to students who are residents of Colorado, have satisfactory academic achievement, have financial need, and have a superior interest and aptitude in journalism. Renewable. Deadline: February 1.

3697. **Nonie Lann Journalism** 1 scholarship of $250 to an undergraduate junior or senior journalism major with at least a 3.0 GPA and financial need. Renewable. Deadline: March 1.

3698. **President's** 250 scholarships ranging from $200 to $1,000. Renewable.

3699. **Regents** 300 scholarships of $500 to students in top 3 percent of their class.

3700. **Tuition Waivers** Numerous partial- to full-tuition waivers to students who are senior citizens.

3701. **Winston C. Lemen Scholarship** 1 scholarship of $400 to an undergraduate junior, senior, or a graduate student majoring in journalism. Based on professional interest, promise, and "high ethical, moral standards." Deadline: February 1.

University of Colorado at Colorado Springs
P.O. Box 7150
Colorado Springs, CO 80933-7150
(719) 593-3000
http://www.uccs.edu
admrec@mail.ussc.edu

3702. **Athletic (Men)** Basketball, golf, and tennis scholarships.

3703. **Athletic (Women)** Basketball, softball, tennis, and volleyball scholarships.

3704. **Colorado Scholars** 120 scholarships ranging from $400 to $800 to students with at least a 3.0 GPA. Renewable.

3705. **H. A. Arnold** Numerous scholarships ranging from $600 to $1,200 to students in the top 50 percent of their class. Renewable with a 2.5 GPA.

3706. **Minority Graduate** Numerous scholarships ranging from $500 to $1,000. Renewable.

3707. **Regents** 50 scholarships ranging from $400 to $800 to students in the top 11 percent of their class and scoring at least 1050 on SAT or 24 on ACT.

University of Colorado at Denver
Admissions Office, Campus Box 167
Denver, CO 80217-3364
(303) 556-2704
http://www.cudenver.edu
admissions@castle.cudenver.edu

3708. **Regents** Numerous scholarships ranging from $303 to $1,018 to students in the top 25 percent of their class, with a 3.0 GPA, and scoring at least 1200 on SAT or 25 on ACT. Renewable with a 3.0 GPA.

University of Denver
University Hall, Room 155
Denver, CO 80208-0132
(800) 525-9495
http://www.du.edu/
admissions@du.edu/

3709. **Alumni** 6 scholarships of varying amounts to students meeting certain criteria.

3710. **Art** 5 scholarships of varying amounts to students meeting certain criteria who are art majors.

3711. **Athletic (Men)** Baseball, basketball, golf, ice hockey, lacrosse, soccer, swimming and diving, and tennis scholarships.

3712. **Athletic (Women)** Basketball, gymnastics, soccer, swimming and diving, tennis, and volleyball scholarships.

3713. **Honors Program** 100 scholarships covering 50 percent of tuition to students in the top 10 percent of their class and scoring at least 1200 on SAT or 28 on ACT. Renewable with a 3.0 GPA.

3714. **Minority Leadership Awards** 7 scholarships of varying amounts totaling $89,964 to minority students who meet certain criteria and who have demonstrated leadership abilities.

3715. **Music** 25 scholarships of varying amounts to students meeting certain criteria who are music majors.

3716. **Speech Awards** 5 scholarships of varying amounts to students who meet certain criteria and are speech majors.

3717. **Tuition Waivers** Numerous partial- to full-tuition waivers to students who are employees or children of employees.

University of Northern Colorado
Greeley, CO 80639
(970) 351-2881
http://www.univnorthco.edu
unc@mail.univnorthco.edu

3718. **Athletic (Men)** Basketball, football, tennis, track and field, and wrestling scholarships.

3719. **Athletic (Women)** Basketball, gymnastics, soccer, swimming and diving, tennis, track and field, and volleyball scholarships.

3720. **President's Honor** Number of scholarships and their amounts vary. Open to students in the top 10 percent of their class. Renewable.

University of Southern Colorado
2200 Bonforte Boulevard
Pueblo, CO 81001-4901
(719) 549-2461
http://www.uscolo.edu
vasquez@uscolo.edu

3721. **Athletic (Women)** Basketball, cross-country, rodeo, tennis, track and field, and volleyball scholarships.

3722. **President's Academic** Numerous scholarships ranging from $400 to $800 to students with at least a 3.0 GPA and scoring at least 22 on ACT. Renewable with a 3.0 GPA.

3723. **President's Talent** Numerous scholarships ranging from $400 to $800 to students with at least a 2.25 GPA. Renewable with a 2.25 GPA.

Western State College of Colorado
Gunnison, CO 81231
(970) 943-2119
http://www.western.edu/welcome.html
swadsworth@western.edu

3724. **Academic/Leadership** Varying numbers of scholarships of $1,400 to students with at least a 3.0 GPA. Renewable with 2.5 GPA.

3725. **Athletic (Men)** Basketball, cross-country, football, skiing, (cross-country), skiing (downhill), track and field, and wrestling scholarships.

3726. **Athletic (Women)** Basketball, cross-country, skiing, (cross-country), skiing (downhill), track and field, and volleyball scholarships.

3727. **Honors** 20 scholarships of $800 to students in the top 15 percent of their class scoring at least 22 on ACT. Renewable.

3728. **Presidential** 20 scholarships of $1,000 to students in the upper 5 percent of their class and scoring 25 on ACT. Renewable.

3729. **WSCS** 150 scholarships of $600 to students in the top 25 percent of their class, with at least a 3.0 GPA and scoring at least 20 on ACT. Renewable with a 3.2 GPA.

CONNECTICUT

Albertus Magnus College
700 Prospect Street
New Haven, CT 06511-1189
(203) 773-8550
http://www.albertus.edu
admissions@albertus.edu

3730. Dominican 1 scholarship of varying amount to a student meeting certain academic criteria who is a Dominican High School graduate.

3731. Honors Numerous scholarships ranging from $1,000 to $1,500 to students in the top 10 percent of their class, with at least a 3.25 GPA, and scoring at least 1100 on SAT or 25 on ACT.

3732. Mohun Varying numbers of scholarships of $4,000 to students who have at least a 3.0 GPA and scored at least 900 on SAT or 20 on ACT. Renewable with 3.0 GPA.

3733. New Haven Area Numerous scholarships ranging from $1,880 to $5,640 to students scoring at least 1100 on SAT or 25 on ACT. Renewable with a 3.0 GPA.

3734. Presidential Scholarships Varying numbers of scholarships providing one-third tuition costs to students in the top 20 percent of their class who scored at least 1000 on SAT or 23 on ACT. Renewable with 3.5 GPA.

3735. Transfer "Honors" Program Scholarships Varying numbers of scholarships of $1,500 to students with at least a 3.0 GPA. Renewable with 3.0 GPA.

3736. Tuition Waivers Numerous partial- to full-tuition waivers to students who are employees, children of employees, or senior citizens.

3737. Valedictorian/Salutatorian Scholarships Varying numbers providing one-half tuition costs to students who scored at least 1100 on SAT or 25 on ACT and meet other academic criteria. Renewable with 3.0 GPA.

Central Connecticut State University
Davidson Hall
1615 Stanley Street
New Britain, CT 06050
(860) 832-2278
http://www.csu.ctstateu.edu/
admission@ccsu.ctstateu.edu

3738. Athletic (Men) Baseball, basketball, cross-country running, football, golf, soccer, swimming and diving, tennis, track and field, and wrestling scholarships.

3739. Athletic (Women) Basketball, cross-country running, softball, swimming and diving, tennis, track and field, and volleyball scholarships.

3740. CCSU Foundation Varying numbers of scholarships of varying amounts to students meeting certain academic criteria.

3741. D & L Scholarships Varying numbers of scholarships of varying amounts to minority students meeting certain criteria.

3742. Honors Scholarships 24 scholarships of $1,865 to undergraduate freshmen and sophomores who meet certain academic criteria.

3743. Private Scholarships Varying numbers of scholarships of varying amounts to students meeting certain academic criteria. These scholarships are provided from external organizations.

3744. Stanley Works Scholarships Varying numbers of scholarships of varying amounts to minority students who meet certain criteria.

3745. Tuition Waivers Numerous partial- to full-tuition waivers to students who are employees, children of employees, or senior citizens.

Eastern Connecticut State University
83 Windham Street
Willimantic, CT 06226
(860) 456-5286
http://www.ecsu.ctstateu.edu/

3746. Competitive "Honors Program" 25 scholarships ranging from $250 to $1,500 to students in top 20 percent of class, with at least a 2.5 GPA, and scoring at least 1000 on SAT.

3747. Honors 10 scholarships of $1,500 to students in top 10 percent of class and scoring at least 1100 on SAT. Renewable.

Fairfield University
1073 North Benson Road
Fairfield, CT 06430-7524
(203) 254-4000
http://www.fairfield.edu

3748. Fairfield Scholars 129 scholarships ranging from $500 to $4,000 to students in the top 10 percent of their class, with at least a 3.0 GPA, and scoring at least 1100 on SAT. Renewable with a 3.0 GPA.

3749. **Glee Club/Drama** 18 scholarships ranging from $750 to $1,000.

3750. **Presidential** 36 tuition scholarships to students who were first in their class, with at least a 3.75 GPA, and scoring at least 1100 on their SAT. Renewable with a 2.0 GPA.

Quinnipiac College
275 Mt. Carmel Avenue
Hamden, CT 06518-0569
(800) 462-1944
http://www.quinnipiac.edu

3751. **Dean's** 80 scholarships of $3,180 to students in the top 25 percent of their class, with at least a 3.0 GPA, and scoring at least 1100 on SAT. Renewable with a 3.0 GPA.

3752. **Diversity Scholarship "Honors" Program** Varying numbers of scholarships ranging from $500 to $6,500 to students in the upper 50 percent of their class with at least a 2.7 GPA. Renewable with 3.0 GPA.

3753. **Leadership Scholarships** Varying numbers of scholarships of varying amounts to students in the upper 50 percent of their class who have demonstrated leadership abilities. Renewable with a 2.5 GPA.

3754. **Quinnipiac** 100 scholarships ranging from $500 to $3,000 to students in the top 10 percent of their class, with at least a 3.0 GPA, and scoring at least 1000 on SAT or 24 on ACT. Renewable with a 3.0 GPA.

Sacred Heart University
5151 Park Avenue
Fairfield, CT 06432-1000
(203) 371-7880
http://www.sacredheart.edu
enroll@sacredheart.edu

3755. **Diocesan Scholars Awards** Varying numbers of scholarships of varying amounts to students who are in their upper 25 percent of their class and are members of the Bridgeport Diocese.

3756. **Presidential** 25 scholarships ranging from $500 to $2,000 to students in the top 10 percent of their class, with at least a 3.5 GPA, and scoring at least 1100 on SAT or 24 on ACT. Renewable.

3757. **Student Activity Recognition Awards** 14 scholarships of varying amounts to students who have been on the yearbook staff or newspaper staff, members of student government, or involved in sports.

3758. **Tuition Waivers** Numerous full- to partial-tuition waivers to students who are employees, children of employees, or senior citizens.

3759. **Trustee Awards** Varying numbers of scholarships of varying amounts to students in the upper 25 percent of their class.

University of Bridgeport
380 University Avenue
Bridgeport, CT 06601
(203) 576-4000
http://www.bridgeport.edu
admit@cse.bridgeport.edu

3760. **Academic Excellence & Leadership "Honors" Program Scholarships** 50 scholarships ranging from $12,020 to $18,824 to students who are in the upper 20 percent of their class, with at least a 3.0 GPA, and who scored at least 1100 on SAT. Renewable with 3.0 GPA.

3761. **Athletic (Men)** Basketball and soccer scholarships.

3762. **Athletic (Women)** Basketball, gymnastics, soccer, softball, tennis, and volleyball scholarships.

3763. **Charles Stetson** 20 to 40 scholarships ranging from $1,000 to $2,000 to students with at least a 3.2 GPA and scoring at least 1000 on SAT or 26 on ACT.

3764. **Dean's Scholarships** Varying numbers of scholarships of varying amounts to students meeting certain criteria and based on community service.

3765. **Dunnacan Scholarships** Varying numbers of scholarships of varying amounts to students meeting certain academic criteria.

3766. **GE Scholarships** Varying numbers of scholarships of varying amounts to students meeting certain criteria and who have performed community service.

3767. **Music Scholarships** Varying numbers of scholarships of varying amounts to students meeting certain criteria who are music majors.

3768. **N. Donald Edwards Scholarship in Marketing** Varying numbers of scholarships of $1,000 to students in the top 10 percent of their class, and who completed Junior Achievement in applied economics or a company program. Contact the Director of Admissions/Junior Achievement Award. Deadline: April 1.

3769. **Project Choice Awards** Varying numbers of scholarships of varying amounts to students who meet certain criteria and are residents of Fairfield County.

3770. **Residential Leadership Scholarships** Varying numbers of scholarships of varying amounts to students who have demonstrated leadership abilities and based on community service.

University of Connecticut
Storrs, CT 06269
(860) 486-2000
http://www.uconn.edu
beahusky@uconnvm.uconn.edu

3771. **Alumni** 25 scholarships of $1,000 to students who have at least a 3.7 GPA. Interview required. Renewable.

3772. **Department of Dramatic Arts** 9 scholarships of varying amounts to undergraduate and graduate students majoring in dramatic arts, fine arts, music, or art.

3773. **University** 30 scholarships covering all fees to students who have at least a 3.7 GPA. Interview required. Renewable.

University of Hartford
200 Bloomfield Avenue
West Hartford, CT 06117
(860) 768-4296
http://www.hartford.edu
admission@uhavax.hartford.edu

3774. **Academic Merit** 100 scholarships ranging from $500 to $2,000 to students in the top 20 percent of their class, with a 3.5 GPA, and scoring at least 1050 on SAT. Renewable.

3775. **Leadership** Numerous renewable $2,000 scholarships.

3776. **President's** 28 scholarships of up to $4,000 to students in the top 10 percent of their class and scoring at least 1150 on SAT. Renewable.

3777. **Regent's** Numerous scholarships of up to $6,000 to students in the upper 5 percent of their class and scoring at least 1250 on SAT. Renewable.

University of New Haven
300 Orange Avenue
West Haven, CT 06516-0605
(203) 932-7000
http://www.newhaven.edu
admissions@newhaven.edu

3778. **Academic** 60 scholarships ranging from $500 to $2,000 to students in the upper 10 percent of their class. Renewable.

3779. **Cheseborough-Ponds Engineering Scholarships** 5 scholarships of $2,500 to minority students meeting certain academic criteria who are engineering majors.

3780. **Echlein Family Scholarships** 5 scholarships of $2,000 to students meeting certain academic criteria, who demonstrate financial need, and who are majoring in either engineering or business.

3781. **Presidential** 20 scholarships of $1,000 to students in the upper 15 percent of their class, with at least a 3.0 GPA, and scoring at least 1000 on SAT or 22 on ACT. Renewable with a 3.0 GPA.

3782. **University Excellence** 5 scholarships of $5,000 to students in the upper 10 percent of their class, with at least a 3.5 GPA, and scoring at least 1100 on SAT or 25 on ACT. Renewable with a 3.5 GPA.

Wesleyan University
High Street and Wyliss Avenue
Middletown, CT 06457
(860) 344-7900
http://www.wesleyan.edu
admission@wesleyan.edu

3783. **Adelphic Educational Fund, Inc.** 11 grants ranging from $200 to $850. Deadline: October 1.

3784. **Annual Eagle Scout** Scholarship for an Eagle Scout. Based on financial need. Renewable with B average.

3785. **Special Scholars "Honors Program"** 80 scholarships ranging from $500 to $10,000. Renewable.

Yale University
P.O. Box 208234
New Haven, CT 06520
(293) 432-4771
http://www.yale.edu/
admissions@yale.edu

3786. **Defores/Leavenworth** $1,000 scholarship for a person surnamed Defores or Leavenworth.

3787. **Need-Based Assistance** There are many need-based scholarships, loans, and work-study programs open to anyone accepted for admission. Many factors other than family income are considered. Contact the financial aid office.

DELAWARE

Goldey–Beacom College
4701 Limestone Road
Wilmington, DE 19808
(302) 998-8814
http://goldey.gbc.edu
gbc@goldey.gbc.edu

3788. **Americans for a Competitive Enterprise System** 1 scholarship of varying amount to an entering freshman majoring in business administration or management. Must be in the upper three-fifths of class and be a Delaware resident. Based on academic achievement and financial need. A 2.0 GPA with twenty-four credit hours per year is required for renewal. Deadline: March 31.

3789. **Ann Wright Hirons** 2 scholarships of $500 to freshmen pursuing an Executive Secretarial Associate Degree in Secretarial Studies. Based on academic achievement and financial need. Renewable for two years with a 2.0 GPA and twenty-four credits per year. Deadline: March 31.

3790. **A. Raymond Jackson Scholarship** 3 scholarships of $500 to entering freshmen planning to major in business administration. Based on academic achievement and financial need. Deadline: March 31.

3791. **A. Raymond Jackson Scholarship in Secretarial Studies** 1 scholarship of $500 to a freshman pursuing an Executive Secretarial Associate Degree or a degree in Information Processing or Secretarial Studies. Based on academic achievement and financial need. Renewable for two years with a 2.0 GPA and twenty-four credits per year. Deadline: March 31.

3792. **Brandywine Valley Press Club** 1 scholarship of $500 to a freshman marketing major with at least a 3.0 GPA and scoring at least 450 on the verbal SAT. Must have financial need. Renewable for four years with at least a 2.0 GPA and twenty-four credit hours per year. Contact high school counselor.

3793. **DuPont Secretarial Training Program** At least 30 scholarships of variable amounts to freshmen students majoring in secretarial studies. Contact high school business teacher or guidance counselor. Deadline: March 31.

3794. **Eunice C. Bounds Memorial Scholarship** 1 full-tuition ($500 average) scholarship to a freshman student majoring in secretarial studies who is a resident of the greater Wilmington, Delaware, area. Based on academic achievement and financial need. Renewable for two years if a 2.0 GPA is maintained, with twenty-four credit hours per year. Deadline: March 31.

3795. **H.F.S. Inc.** 1 scholarship of $500 to an entering freshman majoring in business or management. Preference given to a physically handicapped student. Deadline: March 31.

3796. **Merit** 10 scholarships of $3,750 to students in top 10 percent of their class, with at least a 3.5 GPA, and scoring at least 1150 on SAT. Renewable with a 2.0 GPA.

3797. **Presidential** 10 scholarships of $1,000 to students in the top 40 percent of their class, with at least a 3.0 GPA, and scoring at least 1000 on SAT. Renewable with a 2.0 GPA.

3798. **Sears Roebuck Foundation** 2 scholarships of $500 to undergraduates majoring in business administration. Renewable with a 2.0 GPA and twenty-four credit hours per year. Only awarded during even-numbered years. Deadline: March 31.

University of Delaware
U.S.P.S. 077580
Newark, DE 19716
(302) 831-8123
http://www.udel.edu/
ask.admissions@mvs.udel.edu

3799. **Academic Incentive** 50 scholarships of $1,000.

3800. **Agricultural Sciences General Scholarships** Varying numbers of scholarships of varying amounts to students meeting certain academic criteria and majoring in an agricultural science.

3801. **Alumni Merit Scholarships** Varying numbers of scholarships of varying amounts to students who are children of alumni.

3802. **Alumni Scholarships** Varying numbers of scholarships of varying amounts to students with demonstrated leadership abilities.

3803. **Art and Humanities Scholarships** Varying numbers of scholarships of varying amounts to students majoring in art, music, or history.

3804. **B. Bradford Barnes** 1 scholarship of full tuition, fees, room, and board to graduating high school seniors who are in the upper fourth of their class, with at least a 1200 on SAT or 27 on SAT.

Renewable with satisfactory academic progress. After January 1, contact: Delaware Higher Education Commission, 820 North French Street, Wilmington, DE 19801, (302) 577-3240, (302) 577-6765 Fax, (800) 292-7935 (in-state), http://www.state.de.us/high-ed or high school counselor. Deadline: February 6.

3805. **C. E. Davis Trust Scholarships** Varying numbers of scholarships of varying amounts to students meeting certain academic criteria who are Delaware residents and civil engineering majors.

3806. **Delaware Academic** 38 scholarships covering all costs. Renewable.

3807. **Delaware Secondary** 33 scholarships of $500 to students in the top 10 percent of their class, with at least a 3.2 GPA, and scoring at least 1200 on SAT. Renewable.

3808. **DuPont Distinguished** 10 scholarships covering all costs for students. Renewable.

3809. **Joseph C. Roger/CEPA Scholarship** 1 scholarship of $500 offered by the Society of Computer Applications in Engineering, Planning, and Architecture to undergraduate juniors and seniors majoring in computer science. Based on academic achievement and financial need.

Contact the Director of Scholarships and Financial Aid.

3810. **Minority Engineering** 25 scholarships covering room and board to minority students in the top 20 percent of their class, with at least a 3.3 GPA, and scoring at least 1000 on SAT or 23 on ACT. Renewable.

3811. **Paynter** 5 scholarships of $500 to students in the top 10 percent of their class, with at least a 3.6 GPA, and scoring at least 1400 on SAT. Renewable.

3812. **President's Achievement** 25 scholarships of $650 to students with at least a 3.0 GPA. Renewable.

3813. **Rodney Sharp** 25 scholarships of $1,000 to students in the top 10 percent of their class, with at least a 3.6 GPA, and scoring at least 1400 on SAT. Renewable.

3814. **University Honors** Numerous $1,000 scholarships to students meeting certain qualifying criteria.

3815. **University Merit** 40 tuition scholarships to students in the top 25 percent of their class, with at least a 3.3 GPA, and scoring at least 1000 on SAT or 23 on ACT. Renewable.

DISTRICT OF COLUMBIA

American University
4400 Massachusetts Avenue, N.W.
Washington, DC 20016-8001
(202) 885-1000
http://www.american.edu/
afa@american.edu

3816. **Athletic (Men)** Basketball, swimming and diving, and wrestling scholarships.

3817. **Athletic (Women)** Field hockey, swimming and diving, tennis, and volleyball scholarships.

3818. **AU Honor** Numerous scholarships providing amounts up to tuition to students with at least a 3.75 GPA and scoring at least 1300 on SAT. Renewable.

3819. **Presidential** Numerous $3,000 scholarships to students with at least a 3.3 GPA and scoring at least 1150 on SAT. Renewable with a 3.3 GPA.

Catholic University of America
Cardinal Station
Washington, DC 20064
(800) 673-2772
http://www.cua.edu/
cua-admissions@cua.edu

3820. **Archdiocesan** 30 tuition scholarships to students in the top 10 percent of their class, with at least a 3.5 GPA, and scoring at least 1200 on SAT. Renewable with a 2.5 GPA.

3821. **Cardinal Gibbons Awards** Varying numbers of scholarships of varying amounts to students meeting certain academic criteria.

3822. **Clyde C. Cowan** Varying numbers of scholarships of varying amounts to students meeting certain academic criteria.

3823. **Donald E. Marlo** Varying numbers of scholarships of varying amounts to students meeting certain academic criteria.

3824. **Family** Varying numbers of scholarships of varying amounts to students meeting certain criteria who are siblings or children of current students.

3825. **Farona** Varying numbers of scholarships of varying amounts to students meeting certain academic criteria who are parishioners of the Diocese of Albany.

3826. **Francis Owen Rice** Varying numbers of scholarships of varying amounts to students meeting certain academic criteria.

3827. **J. B. Ward** Varying numbers of scholarships of varying amounts to students meeting certain academic criteria.

3828. **Knights of Columbus Awards** Varying numbers of scholarships of varying amounts to students meeting certain criteria who are children of members.

3829. **Lurty Music** Numerous scholarships ranging from $500 to $2,000.

3830. **Martin McGuire Scholarships** Varying numbers of scholarships of varying amounts to students meeting certain academic criteria.

3831. **Mullen Scholarships** Varying numbers of scholarships of varying amounts to students meeting certain academic criteria.

3832. **Presidential Scholarships** Varying numbers of scholarships of varying amounts to students meeting certain academic criteria.

3833. **Quinn Scholarships** Varying numbers of scholarships of varying amounts to students meeting certain academic criteria.

3834. **Sister Olivia Gowan Scholarships** Varying numbers of scholarships of varying amounts to students meeting certain academic criteria.

3835. **Tuition Waivers** Numerous partial- to full-tuition waivers to students who are employees or children of employees.

Corcoran School of Art
500 17th Street, N.W.
Washington, DC 20006
(202) 628-9484
http://www.corcoran.edu
admofc@aol.com

3836. **Dean's Leadership** 20 scholarships ranging from $500 to $1,500 to students in the top 25 percent of their class, with at least a 3.0 GPA, and

scoring at least 1000 on SAT or 23 on ACT. Renewable.

3837. **Presidential Honor Scholarships** Varying numbers of scholarships ranging from $2,500 to full tuition to students who are in the top 20 percent of their class and scored at least 1200 on SAT or 29 on ACT. Renewable with 3.0 GPA.

Gallaudet University
800 Florida Avenue, N.E.
Washington, DC 20002
(202) 651-5000
http://www.gallaudet.edu
admissions@gallau.gallaudet.edu

3838. **Grants–in–Aid** Grants of $750 are available to undergraduate and graduate students. Based on financial need.

3839. **Scholarships** Numerous scholarships of varying amounts to selected undergraduate and graduate students. Based on academic record and financial need. Students must file a Form 2000, provided by Gallaudet.

Georgetown University
37th and O Streets, N.W.
Washington, DC 20057
(202) 687-3634
http://www.georgetown.edu
guadmiss@gunet.georgetown.edu

3840. **Athletic (Men)** Baseball, basketball, cross-country, lacrosse, and track and field scholarships.

3841. **Athletic (Women)** Basketball, cross-country, track and field, and volleyball scholarships.

3842. **Barbara Zackman Zuckwert Scholarship** 1 scholarship of varying amount to a blind part-time student.

3843. **George McCandlish Fellowship in American Literature** $2,500 plus 18 hours of tuition for the most promising graduate student in a master's or doctoral program in American literature. Must have a 3.25 GPA or better.

3844. **Presidential Academic** 2 scholarships of $1,500 to entering freshmen in the upper 20 percent of class, with at least a 3.9 GPA, and scoring at least 29 on ACT. Contact financial aid office. Deadline: March 1.

George Washington University
Washington, DC 20052
(202) 994-6040
http://www.gwu.edu
gwadm@gwisz.circ.gwu.edu

3845. **Academic** Numerous scholarships of varying amounts for entering freshmen in the top 10 percent of their class, with at least a 3.0 GPA, and scoring at least 1200 on SAT. Deadline: March 1.

3846. **Alumni** 382 scholarships of varying amounts, based on academic criteria.

3847. **Athletic (Men)** Baseball, basketball, crew, cross-country, diving, golf, soccer, swimming, swimming and diving, tennis, and water-polo scholarships.

3848. **Athletic (Women)** Badminton, basketball, crew, cross-country, diving, gymnastics, soccer, swimming, swimming and diving, tennis, and volleyball scholarships.

3849. **Debate** 3 scholarships of varying amounts to students participating in debate.

3850. **Engineering Honors** 20 scholarships paying 50 percent of tuition to students in the top 10 percent of their class, with at least a 3.4 GPA, and scoring at least 1250 on SAT or 30 on ACT. Renewable with a 3.0 GPA.

3851. **Engineering High Honors** 5 full-tuition scholarships to students in the top 5 percent of their class, with at least a 3.7 GPA, and scoring at least 1450 on SAT or 34 on ACT. Renewable with a 3.3 GPA.

3852. **Freshman Honors** 40 scholarships paying 50 percent of tuition to students in the top 10 percent of their class and scoring at least 1300 on SAT or 32 on ACT. Renewable with a 3.0 GPA.

3853. **Pep Band** 13 scholarships to students in Pep Band.

3854. **Presidential Honors** 382 scholarships of varying amounts, based on academic criteria.

3855. **Presidential Performing Arts** 16 scholarships to students majoring in the performing arts.

3856. **Special Achievement/Activities** 6 scholarships, totaling $18,000, for cheerleading.

3857. **21st Century Scholarships** 5 scholarships of varying amounts to students who are District of Columbia residents.

Howard University
2400 Sixth Street, N.W.
Washington, DC 20059
(202) 806-6100
http://www.howard.edu
admission@howard.edu

3858. **Athletic (Men)** Basketball, cross-country, football, soccer, swimming and diving, tennis, track and field, and wrestling scholarships.

3859. **Athletic (Women)** Basketball, cross-country, swimming and diving, tennis, track and field, and volleyball scholarships.

3860. **Chapman Scholarships** 6 scholarships ranging from $500 to $1,000 to students with at least a 2.75 GPA who meet other academic criteria. Renewable with 2.75 GPA.

3861. **Drama Scholarships** Varying numbers of scholarships of varying amounts to students meeting certain criteria who are drama majors. Based on talent.

3862. **Music Scholarships** Varying numbers of scholarships of varying amounts to students meeting certain criteria who are music majors. Based on talent.

3863. **National Competition** 100 scholarships of $5,243 to students with at least a 3.0 GPA and scoring at least 1000 on SAT. Renewable.

Strayer College
1100 16th Street, N.W.
Washington, DC 20036-3504
(202) 728-0048
http://www.strayer.edu

3864. **Academic Achievement** 20 to 30 scholarships ranging from $300 to $2,640 to students with at least a 3.2 GPA.

3865. **Presidential** 6 scholarships ranging from $1,320 to $2,640 to students. Renewable with a 3.0 GPA.

3866. **Regional** 36 scholarships of $1,000.

Trinity College
125 Michigan Avenue, N.E.
Washington, DC 20017-1094
(800) 492-6882
http://www.trinitydc.edu

3867. **Founders** 10 scholarships of $2,500 to students in the top 10 percent of their class, with a 3.4 GPA, and scoring at least 1100 on SAT or 26 on ACT. Renewable with a 3.0.

3868. **Patterson** Numerous scholarships from $3,000 to $8,000 for students in the top 10 percent of their class, with a 3.5 GPA, scoring at least 1125 on SAT. Renewable with a 3.0 GPA.

University of the District of Columbia
Van Ness Campus
4200 Connecticut Avenue, N.W.
Washington, DC 20008
(202) 728-0048
http://www.udc.edu

3869. **Miscellaneous "Honors Program"** 60 scholarships of varying amounts.

3870. **Presidential** Numerous $750 scholarships to students in the top 50 percent of their class with at least a 3.0 GPA. Renewable with 3.0 GPA.

FLORIDA

Barry University
11300 North East 2nd Avenue
Miami Shore, FL 33161-6695
(305) 899-3000
http://www.barry.edu
admissions@pcsaol.edu

3871. **Academic Achievement Scholarships** Varying numbers of scholarships of $4,000 to students in the top 15 percent of their class, with at least a 3.0 GPA, who scored at least 1000 on SAT or 24 on ACT. Renewable with 3.0 GPA.

3872. **Athletic (Men)** Baseball, basketball, cross-country, golf, soccer, and tennis scholarships.

3873. **Athletic (Women)** Basketball, cross-country, soccer, softball, tennis, and volleyball scholarships.

3874. **Focus on Excellence** 25 scholarships ranging from $3,000 to $5,400 to students in the top 10 percent of their class, with a 3.25 GPA, and scoring 1100 on SAT or 26 on ACT. Renewable.

3875. **Presidential** 25 scholarships ranging from $1,000 to $2,000 to students in the top 10 percent of their class, with a 3.5 GPA, and scoring 1100 on SAT or 26 on ACT. Renewable.

3876. **Transfer Scholarships** Varying numbers of scholarships ranging from $1,000 to $3,000 to students with at least a 3.0 GPA, who scored at least 1100 on SAT or 26 on ACT, and who are transfer students from two-year institutions. Renewable.

3877. **Trustee Scholarships** Varying numbers of scholarships providing tuition costs to students with at least a 3.5 GPA and who scored at least 1100 on SAT or 27 on ACT. Renewable with 3.3 GPA.

Bethune–Cookman College
640 Dr. Mary McLeod Bethune Boulevard
Daytona Beach, FL 32115
(800) 448-0228
http://www.bethune.cookman.edu

3878. **Academic Merit** 25 scholarships ranging from $1,000 to $2,000 to students in the top 15 percent of their class, with at least a 3.0 GPA, and scoring at least 860 on SAT or 17 on ACT. Renewable.

3879. **Athletic (Men)** Basketball and football scholarships.

3880. **Athletic (Women)** Basketball scholarships.

Clearwater Christian College
3400 Gulf-to-Bay Boulevard
Clearwater, FL 34619-9989
(813) 726-1153
http://www.clearwater.edu
cccadmissions@juno.com

3881. **President's** Numerous scholarships of $2,000 to students with at least a 3.5 GPA and scoring at least 1140 on SAT or 26 on ACT. Renewable with a 3.5 GPA.

Eckerd College
4200 54th Street South
St. Peterburg, FL 33711
(813) 864-8331
http://www.eckerd.edu
admissions@eckerd.edu

3882. **Athletic (Men)** Baseball, basketball, cross-country, golf, soccer, and tennis scholarships.

3883. **Athletic (Women)** Basketball, cross-country, softball, tennis, and volleyball scholarships.

3884. **Church & Campus** 50 scholarships of $2,400 to students in the top 33 percent of their class, with at least a 2.5 GPA, and scoring at least 1000 on SAT or 21 on ACT. Renewable with a 2.0 GPA.

3885. **Honors** 50 scholarships ranging from $2,000 to $4,000 to students in the upper 20 percent of their class, with at least a 3.2 GPA, and scoring at least 1000 on SAT or 24 on ACT. Renewable with a 3.0 GPA.

3886. **Junior Achievement, Inc.** 15 scholarships of $4,000 to entering freshmen who have taken part in Junior Achievement's JA Company or Applied Economics course. Must have scored at least 1000 on SAT or 22 on ACT.

3887. **Presidential** 20 scholarships of $6,000 to students in the top 10 percent of their class, with a 3.5 GPA, and scoring 1100 on SAT or 26 on ACT. Renewable with a 3.0 GPA.

3888. **Special Honors Program** 20 scholarships providing tuition to students in the top 10 percent of their class, with at least a 3.5 GPA, and scoring at least 1150 on SAT or 26 on ACT. Renewable with a 3.2 GPA.

Embry Riddle Aeronautical University
600 S. Clyde Morris Boulevard
Daytona Beach, FL 32114
(904) 226-6000
http://www.db.erau.edu
admit@db.erau.edu

3889. **Presidential Scholarships** 10 scholarships of $1,500 to entering students who meet certain academic criteria.

3890. **ROTC Awards** Scholarships providing room and board to students who are members of ROTC and who meet certain criteria.

3891. **Tuition Waivers** Numerous partial to full tuition waivers to students who are employees or children of employees.

Flagler College
74 King Street
P.O. Box 1027
St. Augustine, FL 32085-1027
(800) 304-4208
http://www.flagler.edu
admiss@flagler.edu

3892. **Athletic (Men)** Basketball, cross-country, golf, soccer, and tennis scholarships.

3893. **Athletic (Women)** Basketball, cross-country, tennis, and volleyball scholarships.

3894. **Lewis** 5 scholarships covering all costs to students in the top 15 percent of their class, with at least a 3.5 GPA, and in the 80th percentile on either SAT or ACT. Renewable.

3895. **Presidential** 50 scholarships ranging from $200 to $1,000. Renewable.

Florida A&M University
Tallahassee, FL 32307
(904) 599-3000
http://www.famu.edu
bcox@nsi.famu.edu

3896. **Alethia A. Lesesne Howard Award** 1 scholarship of $1,000 to a senior. Based on excellence in British literature, character, academic record, and personality.

3897. **Athletic (Men)** Cross-country, football, golf, swimming and diving, tennis, and track and field scholarships.

3898. **Athletic (Women)** Cross-country, golf, swimming and diving, tennis, track and field, and volleyball scholarships.

3899. **President's Merit** 5 scholarships ranging from $500 to $4,000 to students with at least a 3.5 GPA and scoring at least 1200 on SAT or 28 on ACT. Renewable with a 3.0 GPA.

3900. **President's Scholars** 25 scholarships ranging from $500 to $1,000 to students with at least a 3.3 GPA and scoring at least 950 on SAT or 21 on ACT. Renewable with a 3.0 GPA.

Florida Atlantic University
P.O. Box 3091
Boca Raton, FL 33431
(561) 367-3040
http://www.fau.edu
acc@fau.edu

3901. **FAU Alumni** 8 scholarships of $1,200 to students in the top 10 percent of their class. Renewable.

3902. **FAU Presidential** 20 scholarships of $1,600 to students in the upper 5 percent of their class. Renewable.

3903. **Hispanic** 5 scholarships of $1,200 to Hispanic students with at least a 3.0 GPA. Renewable with a 3.0 GPA.

3904. **Martin Luther King** 20 renewable scholarships of $1,000.

3905. **Min. Ed. Achievement** Numerous $1,200 scholarships to students with at least a 2.8 GPA. Renewable with a 2.8 GPA.

3906. **National Merit Finalist** Numerous $2,000 scholarships to students selected as National Merit Finalists, based on PSAT, SAT, and application. Renewable.

3907. **National Merit Semifinalist** Numerous $1,200 scholarships to students selected as National Merit Semifinalists, based on PSAT scores. Renewable.

3908. **Phi Theta Kappa** 30 scholarships of $1,200. Renewable.

3909. **Tuition Waivers** Numerous scholarships ranging from $300 to $1,200 to students with at least a 3.0 GPA. Renewable.

3910. **Valedictorian/Salutatorian** Numerous $1,000 scholarships to students who are their class valedictorians and salutatorians.

3911. **William Pollier Jr. Scholarship** 1 scholarship of $1,000 to an outstanding graduating senior with at least a 3.4 GPA who plans to enter the MBA program at the university. Based on academic achievement and community involvement. Deadline: March 1.

Florida Institute of Technology
150 West University Boulevard
Melbourne, FL 32901-6988
(407) 768-8000
http://www.fit.edu/
gmeyer@roo.fit.edu

3912. **Athletic (Men)** Basketball, crew, riflery, and soccer scholarships.

3913. **Athletic (Women)** Basketball, crew, riflery, and volleyball scholarships.

3914. **Departmental** 40 scholarships ranging from $600 to $1,500 to students scoring at least 1000 on SAT.

3915. **FITGAP** 110 or more scholarships ranging from $600 to $900 to students scoring from 900 to 1100 on SAT.

3916. **National Action Council** Numerous scholarships ranging from $250 to $2,500 to students with at least a 2.5 GPA. Renewable with a 2.5 GPA.

3917. **Women** 20 scholarships ranging from $600 to $1,500 to female students scoring 1100 on SAT.

Florida International University
University Park
Miami, FL 33199
(800) 888-4348
http://www.fiu.edu
admissions@nomadd.fiu.edu

3918. **Armando Badia Scholarship** 1 scholarship of $1,000 to a full-time Hispanic undergraduate

student with at least a 3.0 GPA. Preference given to science and administrative-related careers. Deadline: June 1.

3919. **Athletic (Men)** Baseball, basketball, crew, cross-country, golf, soccer, tennis, and track and field scholarships.

3920. **Athletic (Women)** Basketball, crew, cross-country, golf, soccer, tennis, track and field, and volleyball scholarships.

3921. **Gregory B. Wolfe/Student Government Association Scholarship** 1 scholarship of $500 to a full-time undergraduate junior or senior with at least a 3.0 GPA. Must be involved in a student organization to enhance the university experience. Contact the Student Government Association, (305) 554-2121. Deadline: April 1.

3922. **Judith Seymour Memorial Scholarship** 1 scholarship of $500 to an undergraduate sophomore, junior, or senior or a graduate student interested in historic preservation. Must have completed thirty semester hours. Contact financial aid office. Deadline: June 1.

3923. **Pearce Memorial Scholarship** 1 scholarship of $500 to an undergraduate junior or senior or graduate student majoring in plant science, biology, or environmental science. Applicants should be interested in plant science. Deadline: June 1.

3924. **Sara and Solomon Rosenberg Scholarship** 1 scholarship of $1,000 to a Native American or African American junior and senior undergraduate majoring in business, computer science, or engineering. Based on financial need.

3925. **Senator Gwen Margolis Scholarship** 1 scholarship of $750 to an African American undergraduate junior or senior majoring in communications. Must have financial need. Deadline: June 1.

3926. **Student Government Association Academic Excellence Scholarship** 1 scholarship of $500 to a full-time undergraduate or graduate student. Must have at least a 3.5 GPA and have financial need. Deadline: April 1. Contact the Student Government Association, (305) 554-2121.

3927. **Student Government Association Handicapped Student Scholarship** 1 scholarship of $500 to a full-time undergraduate or graduate student who is permanently physically disabled. Must have at least a 2.0 GPA and have financial need. Deadline: April 1.

3928. **Student Government Association Minority Scholarship** 1 scholarship of $500 to a full-time minority undergraduate junior or senior with at least a 2.5 GPA. Must be involved in a student organization that presents his or her ethnic culture to the university experience. Contact: Student Government Association, (305) 554-2121. Deadline: April 1.

3929. **Two Hundred Scholarship** 1 scholarship of $1,500 to a female resident of Dade County, Florida. Must be a U.S. citizen, have at least a 3.0 GPA, have completed at least one semester, and have at least one year of study remaining. Deadline: July 15.

Florida State University
Tallahassee, FL 32306
(904) 644-2525
http://www.fsu.edu
admissions@mailer.fsu.edu

3930. **Accounting Excellence** 28 scholarships of $500 to students with at least a 3.5 GPA and scoring at least 1200 on SAT or 28 on ACT. Renewable with a 3.0 GPA.

3931. **Athletic (Men)** Baseball, basketball, cross-country, football, golf, swimming and diving, tennis, and track and field scholarships.

3932. **Athletic (Women)** Basketball, cross-country, golf, softball, swimming and diving, tennis, track and field, and volleyball scholarships.

3933. **FSU Incentive** 50 scholarships of $750 to students with at least a 3.0 GPA and scoring 900 on SAT or 20 on ACT.

3934. **Honors Out-of-State** Numerous scholarships ranging from $800 to $1,000 to out-of-state students with at least a 3.5 GPA and scoring 1200 on SAT or 28 on ACT.

3935. **Marshall Hamilton** 48 scholarships of $600 to students with a 3.5 GPA. Renewable with a 3.0 GPA.

3936. **New Generation** 14 scholarships ranging from $300 to $600. Renewable with a 2.0 GPA.

3937. **Phi Chi Theta Scholarship** 3 scholarships of $1,000 to undergraduate and graduate female full-time students. Based on academic achievement, leadership, potential, motivation, and financial need. Contact: Phi Chi Theta Foundation, 314 RBA, (904) 644-3090.

3938. **Promising Accounting Scholar Award** 5 to 8 scholarships of $500 to entering freshmen (between sixteen and eighteen years) who will be majoring in accounting, who have at least a 3.5 GPA, and who scored at least 1200 on SAT or 28 on ACT. Renewable. Deadline: March 15.

3939. **Sam D. Mansfield Memorial Scholarship** 1 scholarship of $1,000 to undergraduate sophomores, juniors, or seniors pursuing a career in insurance, finance, or real estate. Florida residency and a 3.0 GPA required. Deadline: June 30.

3940. **T. Edwin White Memorial Scholarship** 1 scholarship of $1,500 to a student pursuing a career in financial services and majoring in finance. Preference given to residents of Leon and Wakulla counties. Deadline is the last day of exams in the spring semester.

Jacksonville University
2800 University Boulevard North
Jacksonville, FL 32211
(800) 225-2027
http://www.ju.edu/
admiss@junix.ju.edu

3941. **Alumni** 8 scholarships of $750 to students with a parent who graduated from Jacksonville University. Deadline: November 1.

3942. **Athletic (Men)** Basketball, crew, cross-country, golf, soccer, and tennis scholarships.

3943. **Athletic (Women)** Crew, cross-country, golf, tennis, and volleyball scholarships.

3944. **Junior College Honors Program** 30 scholarships of $1,200 to students transferring from a two-year community college. Renewable.

3945. **President's** 31 scholarships of $6,900 to students in the top 10 percent of their class and scoring at least 1060 on SAT. Deadline: January 30.

3946. **Trustees** 70 scholarships ranging from $500 to $6,900 to students in the top 20 percent of their class, with a 3.0 GPA, and scoring at least 1000 on SAT. Renewable with a 3.0 GPA.

Lynn University
3601 North Military Trail
Boca Raton, FL 33431
(800) 544-8035
http://www.lynn.edu
admission@lynnuniversity.edu

3947. **Academic Incentive** 10 scholarships ranging from $2,975 to $11,900 to students in the top 25 percent of their class with at least a 3.0 GPA, and who scored at least 900 on SAT or 24 on ACT. Renewable with 3.0 GPA.

3948. **Athletic (Men)** Baseball, golf, soccer, and tennis.

3949. **Athletic (Women)** Golf, soccer, and tennis.

3950. **Florida Resident Award** Unlimited numbers of scholarships providing one–half tuition to students in the upper 50 percent of their class, with at least a 3.5 GPA, who scored at least 850 on SAT or 20 on ACT. Must be Florida residents. Renewable with 2.75 GPA.

3951. **National Merit Finalists Awards** 10 scholarships of $10,000 to students designated as National Merit Finalists and meet certain academic criteria. Renewable with 2.75 GPA.

3952. **Presidential Scholarships** Unlimited numbers of scholarships ranging from $2,000 to $3,500 to students with at least a 3.5 GPA who scored at least 850 on SAT or 20 on ACT. Renewable with 2.75 GPA.

3953. **Top Ten Awards** 25 scholarships of $7,000 to students in the top 10 percent of their class and who meet other academic criteria. Renewable with 2.75 GPA.

3954. **Transfer Award "Honors Program"** Unlimited scholarships ranging from $2,000 to $2,500 to student with at least a 2.0 GPA. Renewable with 2.75 GPA.

3955. **Transfer** Varying numbers of scholarships ranging from $2,000 to $2,500 to transfer students meeting certain academic criteria. Renewable with 2.75 GPA.

3956. **Tuition Waivers** Numerous partial- to full-tuition waivers to students who are employees or children of employees.

New College of the University of South Florida
5700 North Tamiami Trail
Sarasota, FL 34243-2197
(941) 359-4269
http://www.sar.usf.edu/nc
ncadmissions@virtu.sar.usf.edu

3957. **Need–Based Assistance** Numerous need-based scholarships, loans, and work-study programs open to anyone accepted for admission with financial need. Contact the financial aid office.

3958. **NC Foundation Scholarships** 20 scholarships of $2,100 to students who meet certain academic criteria. Renewable.

3959. **Out-of-State Scholarships** 15 scholarships ranging from $5,500 to $6,000 to students who meet certain academic criteria. Renewable.

3960. **Pepsico Minority Scholarships** 2 scholarships ranging from $6,000 to $12,000 to students who meet certain academic criteria. Renewable.

3961. **Tuition Waivers** Numerous partial to full tuition waivers to students who are employees or children of employees.

3962. **Wardens "Honors College" Scholarships** 2 scholarships ranging from $6,000 to $12,000 to students who meet certain academic criteria. Renewable.

3963. **Yates Minority Scholarships** 2 scholarships ranging from $2,100 to $6,000 to students who meet certain academic criteria. Renewable.

Nova Southeastern University
3301 College Avenue
Ft. Lauderdale, FL 33314
(800) 338-4723, ext. 8000
http://www.nova.edu
acsinfo@polaris.acs.nova.edu

3964. **Athletic (Men)** Basketball, cross–country, golf, and soccer scholarships.

3965. **Athletic (Women)** Cross–country, tennis, and volleyball scholarships.

3966. **Community Service Awards** 10 scholarships of $1,000 to students who have demonstrated community service.

3967. **Honors Program** Numerous scholarships ranging from $500 to $3,000 to students with at least a 3.0 GPA and scoring at least 1000 on SAT. Renewable with a 3.0 GPA.

3968. **Minority Scholarships** 10 scholarships from $1,000 to $3,500 to minority students who meet certain academic criteria.

3969. **School of Psychology** Varying numbers of scholarships ranging from $1,000 to $1,500 to students with at least a 3.0 GPA who are psychology majors. Renewable with 3.0 GPA.

3970. **Tuition Waivers** Numerous partial- to full-tuition waivers to students who are employees or children of employees.

Palm Beach Atlantic College
901 South Flagler Avenue
P.O. Box 3353
West Palm Beach, FL 33401
(800) 238-3998
http://www.pbac.edu
admit@pbac.edu

3971. **Athletic (Men)** Baseball, basketball, and soccer scholarships.

3972. **Athletic (Women)** Volleyball scholarship.

3973. Christian Leadership Unlimited $1,000 scholarships. Renewable with a 2.0 GPA.

3974. Opportunity Unlimited scholarships ranging from $500 to $1,500. Renewable.

3975. Presidential Unlimited scholarships ranging from $500 to $1,000 to students scoring 930 on SAT or 23 on ACT. Renewable with a 3.0 GPA.

Pensacola Christian College
Box 18,000
Pensacola, FL 32523-9160
(800) PCC-INFO
(904) 478-8496
http://www.pcci.edu

3976. Academic Honors Numerous scholarships of $3,200 total ($800 per year for four years) to entering freshmen who were either class valedictorian or class salutatorian (in a class of six or more) or scored at least 25 on ACT or at least 1055 on SAT. Renewable.

3977. Art Numerous scholarships of $500 to undergraduate sophomores, juniors, and seniors who are majoring in commercial art or graphic design. Renewable.

3978. Christian Service Numerous scholarships of $1,000 to entering freshmen who have at least one parent in a full-time, approved Bible-believing ministry. Renewable.

3979. Ministerial Numerous scholarships of $1,000 to entering male freshmen who will be majoring in Bible with a concentration in evangelism, youth ministries, missions, or music ministries. Must have at least a C average in high school. Renewable.

3980. Music Numerous scholarships of $500 to first-time freshmen who are majoring in music, sacred music, or music education. Based on academic achievement and written recommendation from high school music or private music teacher. Renewable.

3981. Speech Numerous scholarships of $500 to first-time freshmen majoring in speech or speech education. Renewable.

3982. Teacher Education Numerous scholarships of $500 to first-time freshmen who are preparing to be teachers. Renewable.

3983. Work Assistance Program Financial assistance ranging from $910 to $1,750 to students who work from 8 ½ to 16 ½ hours per week. Students must be living in residence halls, with preference given to students with the greatest financial need.

Rollins College
Campus Box 2720
Winter Park, FL 32789
(407) 646-2000
http://www.rollins.edu
admissions@rollins.edu

3984. Alonzo Rollins 7 full-tuition scholarships to students in the top 5 percent of their class, with at least a 3.5 GPA, and scoring at least 1200 on SAT or 28 on ACT. Renewable with a 3.2 GPA.

3985. Athletic (Men) Baseball, basketball, golf, soccer, and tennis scholarships.

3986. Athletic (Women) Basketball, golf, tennis, and volleyball scholarships.

3987. Centennial 14 scholarships providing 50 percent of tuition to students in the top 10 percent of their class, with at least a 3.2 GPA, and scoring 1100 on SAT or 26 on ACT. Renewable with a 3.2 GPA.

St. Leo College
P.O. Box 2008
Saint Leo, FL 33574
(352) 588-8283
http://www.saintleo.edu
admissns@saintleo.edu

3988. Academic "Honors Program" Scholarships 55 scholarships ranging from $500 to $2,500 to students with at least a 3.0 GPA. Renewable with 3.0 GPA.

3989. Athletic (Men) Baseball, basketball, soccer, and tennis scholarships.

3990. Athletic (Women) Basketball, softball, tennis, and volleyball scholarships.

3991. Campus Ministries Awards Varying numbers of scholarships of varying amounts to students based on religious involvement.

3992. GTE Minority Scholarships Varying numbers of scholarships of varying amounts to minority students who meet certain criteria.

3993. Humanities Awards 27 scholarships of varying amounts to students majoring in theater or dance who meet certain criteria. Based on talent.

3994. Need-Based Assistance Numerous need-based scholarships, loans, and work-study programs open to anyone accepted for admission with financial need. Contact the financial aid office.

3995. Presidential Scholarships 12 scholarships ranging from $1,000 to $4,222 to students with at least a 3.25 GPA and who scored at least 1000 on SAT or 22 on ACT. Renewable with 3.25 GPA.

3996. **Trustees Scholarships** 10 scholarships ranging from $1,000 to $8,250 to students with at least a 3.5 GPA and who scored at least 1050 on SAT or 25 on ACT. Renewable with 3.5 GPA.

3997. **Tuition Remission Awards** Varying numbers of awards providing tuition remission to students who are children or spouses of school employees.

3998. **Tuition Waivers** Varying numbers of partial- to full-tuition waivers to students who are employees or children of employees.

St. Thomas University
16400 North West 32nd Avenue
Miami, FL 33054
(305) 628-6546
http://www.stu.edu
alightbo@stu.edu

3999. **Athletic (Men)** Baseball, basketball, golf, soccer, and tennis.

4000. **Athletic (Women)** Soccer, softball, tennis, and volleyball.

4001. **Bishop Roman Scholarships** Varying numbers of scholarships of varying amounts to students who meet certain criteria.

4002. **Catholic High School Awards** Up to 44 scholarships of $500 to students who meet certain academic criteria and graduated from a Catholic high school.

4003. **Freshman Achievement Awards** Up to 43 scholarships of up to $1,600 to incoming freshmen who meet certain academic criteria.

4004. **Golden Drum Minority Scholarships** 2 scholarships of up to $7,640 to African American students who meet certain academic criteria.

4005. **Need-Based Assistance** Numerous need-based scholarships, loans, and work-study programs open to anyone accepted for admission with financial need. Contact the financial aid office.

4006. **Presidential Scholarships** 50 scholarships ranging from $375 to $3,960 to students meeting certain criteria. Renewable.

4007. **St. Thomas Scholarships** 5 scholarships of $500 to students who meet certain academic criteria. Renewable.

4008. **Tuition Waivers** Numerous partial- to full-tuition waivers to students who are employees or children of employees.

Stetson University
421 North Woodland Boulevard
Deland, FL 32720
(800) 688-0101
http://www.stetson.edu
admissions@suvax1.stetson.edu

4009. **Athletic (Men)** Basketball, cross-country, golf, soccer, and tennis scholarships.

4010. **Athletic (Women)** Basketball, cross-country, golf, tennis, and volleyball scholarships.

4011. **Centennial** 2 scholarships providing total costs for students with at least a 3.5 GPA and scoring at least 1300 on SAT or 30 on ACT. Renewable with a 3.0 GPA.

4012. **Guilden** 1 scholarship of $1,500 to an entering freshman majoring in economics, business administration, or business management. Must have at least a 3.25 GPA and have scored at least 1200 on SAT. Renewable with a 3.0 GPA. Deadline: March 1.

4013. **Harrah** 2 scholarships ranging from $3,000 to $4,000 to students in the top 20 percent of their class, with at least a 3.5 GPA, and scoring at least 1200 on SAT or 28 on ACT. Renewable with a 3.0 GPA.

4014. **Jones** 2 scholarships of $800 to students with a 3.0 GPA and scoring at least 1100 on SAT or 26 on ACT. Renewable with a 3.0 GPA.

4015. **Landers** 4 scholarships ranging from $1,500 to $3,000 to students in the top 20 percent of their class, with at least a 3.5 GPA, and scoring at least 1200 on SAT or 28 on ACT. Renewable with a 3.0 GPA.

4016. **Presidential** 10 to 20 scholarships of $5,300 to students in the top 10 percent of their class, with at least a 3.5 GPA, and scoring at least 1300 on SAT or 30 on ACT. Renewable with a 3.0 GPA.

4017. **Selby** 15 to 20 scholarships of $1,000 to students with at least a 3.0 GPA and scoring at least 1150 on SAT or 26 on ACT. Renewable.

University of Central Florida
4000 Central Florida Boulevard
Orlando, FL 32816-0113
(407) 823-3200
http://www.ucf.edu
sburitt@pegasus.cc.ucf.edu
kcornett@pegasus.cc.ucf.edu

4018. **Academic Enrichment Awards** Varying numbers of scholarships of varying amounts to students who meet certain academic criteria.

4019. **Athletic (Men)** Baseball, basketball, cross-country, football, riflery, soccer, and tennis scholarships.

4020. **Athletic (Women)** Basketball, cross-country, riflery, soccer, tennis, and volleyball scholarships.

4021. **Equal Educational Opportunity** Up to 74 scholarships of approximately $1,387 to minority students who meet certain academic criteria and are Florida residents.

4022. **Florida Undergraduate** Varying numbers of scholarships of varying amounts to students who meet certain academic criteria and are Florida residents.

4023. **High Achievement "Honors Program"** Varying numbers of scholarships ranging from $500 to $1,500 to minority students who are their class valedictorian or salutatorian, with at least a 4.0 GPA, and who scored at least 1450 on SAT or 32 on ACT. Renewable with 3.0 GPA.

4024. **Music Lottery Awards** 24 scholarships of $616 to students meeting certain criteria who are music majors.

4025. **Music Service Awards** Varying numbers of scholarships of varying amounts to students who meet certain criteria and are music majors.

4026. **Polasek Foundation Awards** Varying numbers of scholarships of varying amounts to students who meet certain criteria and are art majors. Based on talent.

4027. **Presidential** Numerous scholarships ranging up to $1,500 to students who are in the top ten of their class, with at least a 3.7 GPA, and scoring at least 1300 on SAT or 29 on ACT. Renewable with 3.25 GPA.

4028. **Selby** Numerous scholarships ranging from $500 to $1,500 to students with at least a 3.25 GPA and scoring at least 1200 on SAT or 28 on ACT. Renewable with 3.25 GPA.

4029. **Tuition Waivers** Numerous partial- to full-tuition waivers to students who are employees or children of employees.

University of Florida
201 Criser Hall
Gainesville, FL 32611-2073
(352) 392-1365
http://www.ufl.edu/
spritz@nw.mail.uft.edu

4030. **Athletic (Men)** Baseball, basketball, cross-country running, football, golf, swimming and diving, tennis, and track and field.

4031. **Athletic (Women)** Basketball, cross-country running, golf, swimming and diving, tennis, track and field, and volleyball.

4032. **National Merit Scholarships** Numerous scholarships of varying amounts to students designated National Merit Finalists.

4033. **Out-of-State Scholarships** 50 scholarships ranging from $1,000 to $1,230 to students with at least a 3.5 GPA who scored at least 1260 on SAT or 29 on ACT.

4034. **Presidential Honors Scholarships** Varying numbers of scholarships of varying amounts to students meeting certain academic criteria.

4035. **Selby Scholarships** 35 scholarships ranging from $1,000 to $1,500 to students with at least a 3.5 GPA who scored at least 1200 on the SAT. Renewable.

4036. **Tuition Waivers** Varying numbers of partial- to full-tuition waivers to students who are employees, children of employees, or senior citizens.

4037. **Valedictorian Scholarships** Unlimited scholarships of $500 to students who are designated as the top graduating senior of their high school.

University of Miami
P.O. Box 248025
Coral Gables, FL 33124
(305) 284-2211
http://www.miami.edu
admission@admiss.msmail.miami.edu

4038. **Alumni Awards** Varying numbers of scholarships providing one-third of tuition costs (up to $6,667 per year) to students who are in the top 20 percent of their class, have at least a 3.5 GPA, scored at least 1180 SAT 1 or 26 on ACT. Must be Florida residents. Renewable up to four years.

4039. **Athletic (Men)** Baseball, basketball, cross-country, football, golf, swimming and diving, tennis, and track and field scholarships.

4040. **Athletic (Women)** Basketball, cross-country, golf, swimming and diving, tennis, and track and field scholarships.

4041. **Bowman F. Ashe** 250 scholarships ranging from $1,500 to $4,000 to students in the top 15 percent of their class and scoring at least 1100 on SAT or 27 on ACT. Based on academic merit and financial need. Renewable with a 3.0 GPA. Deadline: March 1.

4042. **City of Miami Awards** Varying numbers of scholarships of varying amounts to students who meet certain academic criteria and are residents of Miami.

4043. **Dade County Public Schools Awards** Varying numbers of scholarships of varying amounts to students who meet certain academic criteria and who graduated from a public high school in Dade County.

4044. **George Edgar Merrick Scholarships** Varying numbers of scholarships ranging up to $6,667 (one-third tuition costs) to students who are in the top 20 percent of their class, have at least a 3.5 GPA, and who scored at least 1180 on SAT 1 or 26 on ACT. Renewable up to four years.

4045. **Golden Drum Awards** Varying numbers of scholarships of varying amounts to students meeting certain academic criteria.

4046. **Henry K. Stanford "Honors Program"** 200 scholarships providing 50 percent of tuition to students in top 10 percent of class, with at least a 3.75 GPA, and scoring at least 1280 on SAT or a 29 on ACT. Renewable with a 3.0 GPA.

4047. **Isaac B. Singer** 18 scholarships of full tuition to students in top 2 percent of their class, with at least a 3.9 GPA, and scoring at least 1400 on SAT or 32 on ACT. Renewable with a 3.0 GPA.

4048. **Jay F. W. Pierson** 150 scholarships of $4,500 to students in the top 12 percent of their class and scoring at least 1150 on SAT or 27 on ACT. Renewable with a 3.0 GPA.

4049. **Marching Band Awards** Varying numbers of scholarships of varying amounts to students meeting certain criteria and who are members of the marching band.

4050. **Music Awards** Varying numbers of scholarships of varying amounts to students who meet certain criteria and are music majors. Based on talent.

4051. **Need-Based Assistance** Numerous need-based scholarships, loans, and work-study programs open to anyone accepted for admission with financial need. Contact the financial aid office.

4052. **ROTC Supplemental Grants** Varying numbers of scholarships of varying amounts to students meeting certain criteria who are members of ROTC.

4053. **Tuition Waivers** Numerous partial- to full-tuition waivers to students who are employees or children of employees.

University of North Florida
4567 St. Johns Bluff Road, South
Jacksonville, FL 32224
(904) 646-2624
http://www.unf.edu/
osprey@unf.edu

4054. **Alumni Achievement Scholarships** 18 scholarships of $500 to students in the upper 15 percent of the class, with at least a 3.3 GPA, and who scored at least 1100 on SAT or 25 on ACT.

4055. **Athletic (Men)** Baseball, basketball, cross-country running, golf, soccer, and tennis scholarships.

4056. **Athletic (Women)** Basketball, cross-country running, golf, softball, tennis, and volleyball scholarships.

4057. **Community College Scholarships** 5 scholarships of $1,000 to students with at least a 3.5 GPA who are transferring from a community college. Renewable.

4058. **Foundation Scholarships** 10 scholarships of $2,000 to students in the upper 10 percent of the class, with at least 3.5 GPA, and who scored at least 1200 on SAT or 27 on ACT. Renewable.

4059. **Minority Scholarships** 20 scholarships of $1,000 to students in the upper 15 percent of their class, with at least a 3.0 GPA, and who scored at least 1000 on SAT or 23 on ACT.

4060. **University Scholarships** 10 scholarships of $1,000 to students in the top 10 percent of their class, with at least a 3.5 GPA, and who scored at least 1200 on SAT or 27 on ACT. Renewable.

GEORGIA

Agnes Scott College
141 East College Avenue
Decatur, GA 30030-4298
(800) 868-8602
http://www.agnesscott.edu
admission@agnesscott.edu

4061. **Centennial** Numerous scholarships ranging from $2,000 to $3,500. Renewable.

4062. **Emma Baugh Music** 1 scholarship of $4,500 to a junior or senior music major. Auditions required.

4063. **Honors** 24 scholarships ranging from $5,000 to $9,500 to students. Based on high academic achievement and evidence of promise. Renewable.

4064. **Kemper Hatfield Music** 1 scholarship of $1,000 to a junior or senior music or keyboard music major. Audition required.

4065. **Nannette Hopkins Music** 4 scholarships of $2,000 to undergraduate music majors. Applicants must audition.

Augusta College
2500 Walton Way
Augusta, GA 30910
(706) 737-1400
http://www.ac.edu/
admissio@aug.edu

4066. **Athletics (Men)** Baseball, basketball, cross-country running, golf, soccer, and tennis scholarships.

4067. **Athletics (Women)** Basketball, cross-country running, softball, tennis, and volleyball scholarships.

4068. **Augusta College Leadership Scholarships** 2 scholarships of $1,327 to students meeting certain criteria who have demonstrated leadership abilities.

4069. **August Free School Scholarships** 10 scholarships of varying amounts to students with at least a 3.0 GPA and who scored at least a 1000 on SAT. Renewable with 3.0 GPA.

4070. **Clarke Cordle Endowment Fund Scholarships** Varying numbers of scholarships of varying amounts to students who are licensed ham radio operators and meet other criteria.

4071. **Faculty/Alumni Scholarship Fund** 8 scholarships ranging from $500 to all costs to students in the top 5 percent of their class, with at least a 3.0 GPA, and who scored at least 1000 on SAT. Renewable. 3.5 GPA.

4072. **Faculty Scholarships** 6 scholarships of varying amounts to students in the top 5 percent of their class, with at least a 3.0 GPA, and who scored at least 1000 on SAT.

4073. **Georgia Rotary Award** 1 scholarship of $1,632 to an international student meeting certain academic criteria.

4074. **Grover B. Williams Awards** 1 scholarship of approximately $1,000 to students meeting certain academic criteria who are mathematics majors.

4075. **Jack and Mary Craven Scholarship** 1 scholarship of $1,200 to students with at least a 3.0 GPA. Renewable with 3.0 GPA.

4076. **J. B. White Literary Award** 1 award of $666 to the first-place winner of a high school essay/poetry/fiction competition.

4077. **Katherine R. Pamplin** 3 scholarships ranging from $750 to $1,632 to students with at least a 3.0 GPA who meet other academic criteria. Renewable with 3.0 GPA.

4078. **Kelley Drake Scholarships** Varying numbers of scholarships of varying amounts to students meeting certain criteria in citizenship, dedication, and musical talent.

4079. **Louise Smith McCollum "Honors Program"** 1 scholarship of $1,429 to students with at least a 3.0 GPA and who meet other academic criteria. Renewable with 3.0 GPA.

4080. **Mary S. Byrd Fine Arts Awards** 2 scholarships of $1,000 to students meeting certain criteria and talent requirements. Must be majoring in fine arts.

4081. **Maxwell Music Scholarships** 3 scholarships of approximately $300 to students meeting certain academic criteria and either vocal or instrumental achievement.

4082. **Tuition Waivers** Varying numbers of partial to full tuition waivers to students who are employees, children of employees, or senior citizens.

4083. **Uptown Kiwanis Club Award** 1 scholarship of $1,632 to a student meeting certain academic criteria based on GPA.

4084. **W. Bruce McCollum Scholarship** 1 scholarship of $1,308 to students with at least a 3.0 GPA who meet other academic criteria. Renewable with 3.0 GPA.

4085. **William S. and Elizabeth Boyd Music Scholarships** 1 or more scholarships of varying amounts to students meeting certain criteria. Based on musical talent.

Covenant College
14049 Scenic Highway
Lookout Mountain, GA 37350
(706) 820-2398
http://www.covenant.edu
admissions@covenant.edu

4086. **Academic** Varying numbers of scholarships of varying amounts to students meeting certain academic criteria.

4087. **African American** Varying numbers of scholarships of varying amounts to African American students meeting certain academic criteria.

4088. **Chambliss** Varying numbers of scholarships of varying amounts to students meeting certain academic criteria.

4089. **Maclellan** 4 to 8 of scholarships of $5,800 to students with at least a 3.3 GPA and who scored at least 1100 on SAT or 25 on ACT. Renewable with 3.0 GPA.

4090. **Merit** varying numbers of scholarships ranging from $500 to $4,500 to students with at least a 3.0 GPA and who scored at least 1100 on SAT or 25 on ACT. Renewable with 3.0 GPA.

4091. **Music** Varying numbers of scholarships of varying amounts to students meeting certain criteria who are music majors.

4092. **Presbyterian Church Members Awards** Varying numbers of scholarships of varying amounts to students meeting certain criteria who are members of the Presbyterian Church.

Emory University
1380 South Oxford Road, N.E.
Atlanta, GA 30322
(404) 727-6013
http://www.emory.edu
admiss@emory.edu

4093. **Alben W. Barkley Debate** 2 scholarships ranging from $2,000 to $4,000 to students who are members of the debate team. Must maintain good academic standing. Renewable. Contact: the Director of Forensics. Deadline: March 1.

4094. **Alexander Means** 1 scholarship of varying amount. Based on academic merit.

4095. **Bowden Award** 2 scholarships of varying amounts. Based on academic merit.

4096. **Charles and Anne Duncan** 2 scholarships of varying amounts. Based on academic merit.

4097. **Chris A. Yannopoulous** 1 scholarship of varying amount. Based on academic merit.

4098. **Courtesy Scholarships** 27 scholarships of varying amounts. Based on academic merit and career interests.

4099. **David Potter** 1 scholarship of varying amount. Based on academic merit.

4100. **Dean's Scholarships** 3 scholarships of varying amounts. Based on academic merit.

4101. **Dumas Malone Award** 1 scholarship of varying amount. Based on academic merit and interests.

4102. **Emory National Merit Awards** 14 scholarships of varying amounts to students chosen as National Merit Finalists.

4103. **Flora Glenn Candler** 2 scholarships ranging from $2,000 to $4,000 are awarded to students with good academic standing who are majoring in the performing arts.

4104. **Goodrich C. White** 15 scholarships of varying amounts. Based on academic merit.

4105. **Ignatius Few** 2 scholarships of varying amounts. Based on academic merit.

4106. **John Gordon Stipe Society** 5 scholarships of $1,000 to students in the top 20 percent of their class. Must show ability in chosen major. Deadline: April 1.

4107. **Kemp Malone Award** 1 scholarship of varying amount. Based on academic merit.

4108. **Martin Luther King, Jr.** 6 scholarships of varying amounts. Based on academic merit.

4109. **Methodist Ministerial** 12 scholarships of varying amounts are available to students preparing for a Methodist ministerial career.

4110. **Pollard Turman Leadership Scholarships** 16 scholarships ranging from $250 to $500. Renewable.

4111. **Robert Woodruff Scholar** 12 scholarships covering all costs (up to $12,000) to students in top 20 percent of their class. Based on character, academic achievements, leadership, and clear potential. Renewable.

Georgia Institute of Technology
Atlanta, GA 30332-0320
(404) 894-4160
http://www.gatech.edu
admissions@success.gatech.edu

4112. **Athletic (Men)** Baseball, basketball, football, golf, swimming and diving, tennis, track and field, and wrestling scholarships.

4113. **Athletic (Women)** Basketball, swimming and diving, tennis, track and field, and volleyball scholarships.

4114. **Dean's Scholarships** Varying numbers of scholarships of varying amounts to students meeting certain academic criteria.

4115. **National Merit Awards** Varying numbers of scholarships of varying amounts to students designated National Merit Finalists.

4116. **President's Scholarships** 70 scholarships ranging from $1,100 to $7,000 to students with at least a 3.9 GPA and who scored at least 1350 on their SAT. Renewable with a 3.2 GPA.

Georgia State University
University Plaza
Atlanta, GA 30303
(404) 651-2000
http://www.gsu.edu/
admissions@gsu.edu

4117. **Athletic (Men)** Baseball, basketball, cross-country running, golf, soccer, tennis, and wrestling scholarships.

4118. **Athletic (Women)** Basketball, cross-country running, golf, softball, tennis, and volleyball scholarships.

4119. **Leadership Scholarships** Varying numbers of scholarships providing tuition costs to students with at least a 3.2 GPA on a 4.0 scale who scored at least 1000 on SAT. Renewable.

4120. **Tuition Waivers** Numerous partial- to full-tuition waivers to senior citizens.

LaGrange College
601 Broad Street
LaGrange, GA 30240-2999
(706) 812-7260
http://www.lgc.peachnet.edu
pdodson@mentor.lgc.peachnet.edu

4121. **Academic** Numerous scholarships ranging from $500 to $1,100. Based on academic merit.

4122. **Candler** Numerous scholarships of varying amounts. Based on academic merit.

4123. **Chevron** Scholarships of varying amounts to students who are science or mathematics majors.

4124. **Evelyn Powell Hoffman** 1 scholarship of varying amount to a student majoring in drama.

4125. **Honors** Numerous scholarships ranging from $500 to $1,100 to students with a 3.0 GPA and scoring 1100 on SAT.

4126. **Ingrid Bergman** 1 scholarship ranging from $3,690 to $4,000.

Morehouse College
830 Westview Drive, S.W.
Atlanta, GA 30314
(800) 851-1254
http://www.morehouse.edu

4127. **Academic** Numerous scholarships of up to half of tuition to students with at least a 3.0 GPA and scoring at least 1000 on SAT or 22 on ACT. Renewable.

4128. **Athletic (Men)** Basketball, cross-country, football, swimming and diving, tennis, and track and field scholarships.

4129. **Oprah Winfrey** Full scholarships for students with at least a 3.0 GPA. Contact financial aid office.

Savannah College of Art and Design
342 Bull Street
P.O. Box 3146
Savannah, GA 31402-3146
(912) 238-2400
http://www.scad.edu
admissions@scad.edu

4130. **Board of Trustee** Varying numbers of scholarships ranging from $2,000 to $5,000 to students who are their class valedictorian and who have a 4.0 GPA. Renewable with a 3.0 GPA.

4131. **Brook Reeve Jr.** 2 scholarships of varying amounts to students meeting certain criteria who are selected in a painting contest.

4132. **Corbin Flowers Memorial** 2 scholarships of varying amounts to visual arts students meeting certain criteria who are from Colorado.

4133. **Creative Arts/Performance Awards** Varying numbers of scholarships of varying amounts to students meeting certain criteria who are majoring in a creative or performance art. Based on talent.

4134. **E. C. Williams** Varying numbers of scholarships ranging from $2,000 to $5,000 to students who meet certain academic criteria. Renewable with a 3.0 GPA.

4135. **Elizabeth Cooksey Williams Awards** Varying numbers of scholarships of varying amounts to students meeting certain academic criteria.

4136. **Frances Larkin McCommon Awards** Varying numbers of scholarships of varying amounts to students competing in the ICSA contest.

4137. **Georgia Symposium Awards** Varying numbers of scholarships of varying amounts to students meeting certain criteria who are majoring in a fine art.

4138. **Gordon Lewis Academic Achievement Awards** 2 scholarships of varying amounts to students meeting certain academic criteria.

4139. **Henderson** Varying numbers of scholarships of $1,500 to students who meet certain academic criteria. Renewable with 3.0 GPA.

4140. **Hugh M. Dorsey III Awards** Varying numbers of scholarships of varying amounts to students meeting certain academic criteria.

4141. **International Competition** Varying numbers of scholarships ranging from $2,000 to $5,000 to students who meet certain criteria. Renewable with 3.0 GPA.

4142. **Irene Rousakis Memorial** 2 scholarships of varying amounts to students meeting certain academic criteria to provide assistance for off-campus programs in New York and Europe.

4143. **Mary Rene Nellings Whelan** Varying numbers of scholarships ranging from $2,000 to $5,000 to students who scored at least 1200 on SAT or 27 on ACT. Renewable with 3.0 GPA.

4144. **Portfolio** Varying numbers of scholarships ranging from $2,000 to $5,000 to students based on portfolio and talent. Renewable with 3.0 GPA.

4145. **Richard F. Abbitt Architecture Contest Awards** 2 scholarships of varying amounts to architectural students who have been selected through a competition.

4146. **Rose Kakish Friedman** Varying numbers of scholarships ranging from $4,000 to $10,000 to students who scored at least 1400 on SAT or 33 on ACT. Renewable with 3.0 GPA.

4147. **Tuition Waivers** Numerous partial to full tuition waivers to students who are employees or children of employees.

Spelman College
350 Spelman Lane, S.W.
Atlanta, GA 30314-4399
(404) 681-3643
http://www.spellman.edu
admiss@spelman.edu.

4148. **Academic Scholarships** Varying numbers of scholarships of varying amounts to students who meet certain academic criteria.

4149. **Admissions** Numerous scholarships ranging from $750 to $2,000 to students with a 3.0 GPA and scoring at least 950 on SAT or 20 on ACT.

4150. **Dean's Merit Scholarships** Varying numbers of scholarships of varying amounts to students who meet certain academic criteria.

4151. **Dewitt's Scholarships** Varying numbers of scholarships of varying amounts to students who meet certain academic criteria.

4152. **Honors** 60 awards ranging from $2,525 to $6,025 to students with at least a 3.0 GPA and scoring at least 1000 on SAT or 25 on ACT. Renewable with a 3.0 GPA.

4153. **Math Awards** Varying numbers of scholarships of varying amounts to students who meet certain academic criteria and will be majoring in math.

4154. **Penn Scholarships** Varying numbers of scholarships of varying amounts to students who meet certain academic criteria in the area of science.

4155. **Presidential Scholarships** Varying numbers of scholarships of varying amounts to students who meet certain academic criteria.

4156. **Spelman Academic** 271 scholarships, totaling $613,119. Based on academic merit.

4157. **Tuition Waivers** Numerous partial to full tuition waivers to students who are employees or children of employees.

4158. **WISE Scholarships** Varying numbers of scholarships of varying amounts to students who meet certain academic criteria in the area of science.

University of Georgia
Athens, GA 30602
(706) 542-2112
http://www.uga.edu
undergrad@admissions.uga.edu

4159. **Alumni Scholar** Unlimited number of scholarships worth $750 to students with a 3.2 GPA and scoring at least 1200 on SAT. Renewable.

4160. **Athletic (Men)** Baseball, basketball, cross-country, football, golf, swimming and diving, tennis, and track and field scholarships.

4161. **Athletic (Women)** Basketball, cross-country, golf, gymnastics, swimming and diving, tennis, track and field, and volleyball scholarships.

4162. **Atlanta Press Club Journalism Grant** 1 or more scholarships of at least $200 to a student who is a journalism or communications major attending an accredited Georgia college. Based on financial need and potential for contribution to the field of journalism or communications. Contact: Scholarship Committee Chairperson, Atlanta Press Club, P.O. Box 52756, Atlanta, GA 30355. Deadline: April 30.

4163. **August H. and Grace A. Barrett Scholarships** 1 or more scholarships ranging from $500 to $1,000 to currently enrolled students who are journalism or communications majors. Based on academic achievement, professional achievement, and potential. Renewable.

4164. **Foundation** 11 scholarships of $4,500 to students with a 3.2 GPA and scoring at least 1300 on SAT. Renewable.

4165. **Frank N. Hawkins Scholarship** 1 scholarship ranging from $500 to $1,000 to a current or transfer undergraduate junior majoring in newspaper.

4166. **George H. Boswell Scholarship Fund** 1 scholarship of full tuition for one year to a currently enrolled student in the College of Journalism and Mass Communication who is a Georgia resident.

4167. **Georgia Scholastic Press Association Awards—The Jon E. Drewry Scholarship** 1 scholarship of $350 to the highest ranked of the top five contestants in the annual Georgia Champion High School Journalism Contest who will be entering the University of Georgia as freshmen pre-journalism majors.

4168. **Jack McDonough Editorial Award** 1 award of $1,000 given in a competition to high school juniors and seniors based on the best editorial on free enterprise published in a school newspaper that is a member of the Georgia Scholastic Press Association. Award is given upon enrollment in UG as a pre-journalism major.

4169. **Julia Ellen Askew Stephens Scholarship** 1 scholarship ranging from $300 to $600 to an outstanding undergraduate junior or senior journalism major.

4170. **Kirk Sutlive Scholarship** 1 scholarship of $1,000 to an outstanding undergraduate junior or senior majoring in newspaper or public relations. Awarded in conjunction with the Georgia Press Educational Foundation.

4171. **Margaret Beasley Broun Scholarship** 1 or more scholarships ranging from $750 to $1,500 to undergraduate freshmen who are currently enrolled or transfer students. Must demonstrate outstanding academic and professional achievement and potential.

4172. **Marion Tyus Butler Scholarship** 1 scholarship of $1,000 to a journalism or pre-journalism student demonstrating a superior vocabulary, excellence in English grammar, and proven writing ability.

4173. **National Association of Media Women** Varying numbers of scholarships of at least $500 to undergraduate minority female students majoring in mass communications. Contact: Scholarship Chairperson, National Association of Media Women, Inc.; P.O. Box 4698, Atlanta, GA 30302. Deadline: April 16.

4174. **Paul Ashley Simon Memorial Scholarships** 1 or more scholarships ranging from $500 to $1,500 to incoming freshmen and currently enrolled or transfer undergraduate students pursuing newspaper careers. Must have at least a 3.0 GPA. Renewable.

4175. **Peyton T. Anderson Scholarships** 2 scholarships of $750 to freshmen students who are Georgia residents with an interest in a newspaper career. Based on outstanding potential and financial need.

4176. **Sanford–Burgess Scholarship Sponsored by the Northeast Georgia Professional Chapter, SPJA** 1 scholarship of $750 to an undergraduate junior or senior with demonstrated ability in news writing who is pursuing a career in newspaper journalism. Preference given to residents of northeast Georgia.

4177. **Terry F. Barker Journalism Scholarship** 1 scholarship of $2,000 to an undergraduate junior or senior student who is a Georgia resident. Preference given to Gwinnett County residents. Based on academic achievement, potential, and financial need.

4178. **Thomas H. Frier Scholarship** 1 scholarship of $600 to an outstanding newspaper journalism major who meets certain academic criteria.

4179. **Times–Mirror Co. of Los Angeles Scholarships** 2 scholarships ranging from $500 to $1,000 to freshmen Georgia residents who are interested in a career in newspaper journalism.

Based on outstanding potential and financial need.

4180. **Transfer** 10 scholarships of $750 to students with at least a 3.2 GPA.

4181. **Wilkins** 5 scholarships of $1200 to students with a 3.2 GPA who scored at least 1100 on SAT. Renewable.

4182. **William C. Rogers Scholarship** 1 scholarship of $1,000 to an undergraduate junior or senior pursuing a newspaper career. Given in conjunction with the Georgia Press Educational Foundation.

HAWAII

Brigham Young University–Hawaii Campus
55-220 Kulanui Street
A 153 A.S.B.
Laie Oahu, HI 96762
(808) 293-3738
http://www.byuh.edu

4183. **Academic** Numerous scholarships of up to $1,500 to students with at least a 3.5 GPA and scoring in the 90th percentile on either SAT or ACT. Renewable.

4184. **David O. McKay** 6 scholarships of $8,000 to students from the Asian Rim or South Pacific. Must be members of the Church of Latter–Day Saints. Must have at least a 3.7 GPA and score at least 25 on ACT. Contact: Scholarship Supervisor. Deadline: May 1 (Hawaii); September 1 (South Pacific).

Hawaii Pacific University
1164 Bishop Street
Honolulu, HI 96813
(808) 544-0200
http://www.hpu.edu
admissions@hpu.edu

4185. **Athletic Scholarships** 36 scholarships for women and 79 to men.

4186. **Band Scholarships** Varying numbers of scholarships of varying amounts to students meeting certain criteria who are members of the band. Based on talent.

4187. **Cheerleading Scholarships** Varying numbers of scholarships of varying amounts to students meeting certain criteria who are members of the cheerleading squad. Based on talent.

4188. **President's Scholarships** Varying numbers of scholarships providing up to tuition costs to students with at least a 3.0 GPA. Renewable.

4189. **Tuition Waivers** Numerous partial to full tuition waivers to students who are employees or children of employees.

University of Hawaii at Hilo
Hilo, HI 96720-4091
(808) 897-4456
http://www2.hawaii.edu/
uhhadm@hawaii.edu

4190. **Charles R. Hemenway Scholarship Trust** Various grants ranging from $200 to $2,000. Must be Hawaii residents and be committed to Hawaii and its people. Contact: c/o Hawaiian Trust Company, Ltd., Box 3170, Honolulu, HI 96802. Deadline: April 1.

4191. **Civic Associates** 1 full-tuition scholarship to a student who is full or part Filipino. Contact: Scholarship Committee, c/o Civic Associates, Nuuanu YMCA, 1441 Pali Highway, Honolulu, HI 96813. Deadline: May 15.

4192. **Talented Students** 25 tuition scholarships. Renewable.

University of Hawaii at Manoa
2444 Dole Street C200
Honolulu, HI 96822
(808) 956-8111
http://www.hawaii.edu/uhinfo.html

4193. **Athletic (Men)** Baseball, basketball, football, golf, swimming and diving, tennis, and volleyball scholarships.

4194. **Athletic (Women)** Basketball, cross-country, golf, swimming and diving, tennis, and volleyball scholarships.

4195. **Charles R. Hemenway Scholarship Trust** Various grants ranging from $200 to $2,000. Must be Hawaii residents and be committed to Hawaii and its people. Contact: c/o Hawaiian Trust Company, Ltd., Box 3170, Honolulu, HI 96802. Deadline: April 1.

4196. **Civic Associates** 1 full–tuition scholarship to a student who is full or part Filipino. Contact: Scholarship Committee, c/o Civic Associates, Nuuanu YMCA, 1441 Pali Highway, Honolulu, HI 96813. Deadline: May 15.

4197. **Pacific Asian "Honors Program"** Varying numbers of tuition scholarships to students with at least a 3.7 GPA. Renewable with a 3.7 GPA.

4198. **Presidential Achievement** 10 tuition plus $4,000 scholarships to students with at least a 3.7 GPA. Renewable.

4199. **Regents** 20 tuition plus $4,000 scholarships to students in the top 5 percent of their class, with at least a 3.7 GPA, and scoring at least 1200 on their SAT. Renewable.

4200. **Tuition Waiver** Varying numbers of tuition scholarships to students in the top 5 percent of their class who have at least a 3.5 GPA. Renewable with a 3.5 GPA.

IDAHO

Albertson College of Idaho
2112 Cleveland Boulevard
Caldwell, ID 83605
(800) 224-3246
http://www.acofi.edu

4201. **Honor Student** Unlimited number of scholarships ranging from $150 to $1,350 to students with at least a 3.0 GPA and scoring at least 1000 on SAT or 23 on ACT. Renewable with a 3.0 GPA.

4202. **Jeppesen Memorial** 1 scholarship of varying amount to a student with at least a 3.0 GPA. Renewable with a 3.0 GPA.

4203. **McCain Family** 1 scholarship of $9,370 to a student with at least a 3.0 GPA. Renewable with a 3.0 GPA.

4204. **Moore Cunningham** 20 scholarships of $2,000 to students with at least a 2.7 GPA. Renewable with a 2.7 GPA.

4205. **Performance "Honors Program"** Unlimited number of scholarships ranging from $100 to $9,600 to students with at least a 2.0 GPA. Renewable with a 2.0 GPA.

Idaho State University
741 South 7th Avenue
Pocatello, ID 83209-0009
(208) 236-0211
http://www.isu.edu
isuinfo@isu.edu

4206. **Athletic (Men)** Basketball, cross–country, football, and tennis scholarships.

4207. **Athletic (Women)** Basketball, cross–country, tennis, and volleyball scholarships.

4208. **Freshman** Numerous scholarships ranging from $200 to $2,500 to students with at least a 3.0 GPA and scoring 18 on ACT. Renewable with a 3.3 GPA.

4209. **Kasiska Scholarship** 1 scholarship ranging from $1,000 to $1,500 to a student at the School of Health Science who has at least a 3.0 GPA. Contact the Director of Enrollment Services.

4210. **Out-of-State Freshman** 10 scholarships ranging from $1,000 to $2,000 to out–of–state students with at least a 3.0 GPA and scoring 18 on ACT.

4211. **Transfer** Numerous scholarships of varying amounts to transfer students with at least a 3.0 GPA. Renewable.

University of Idaho
Moscow, ID 83843
(208) 885-6111
http://www.idaho.edu
admappl@uidaho.edu

4212. **A. E. Larson Scholarship** 4 or 5 scholarships of $500 to students enrolled in any major in the College of Mines. Preference given to students from the Coeur d'Alene Mining District. Deadline: March 14.

4213. **Athletic (Men)** Basketball, cross–country, football, golf, and tennis scholarships.

4214. **Athletic (Women)** Basketball, cross–country, golf, tennis, and volleyball scholarships.

4215. **Harold and Claudia Sterns Scholarship** Varying number of scholarships ranging from $250 to $500 to students majoring in geology. May be used for school or field-trip expenses. Deadline: March 14.

4216. **H. James Magnuson Scholarship** 1 scholarship of $300 to a junior or senior undergraduate enrolled in any major at the College of Mines. Deadline: March 14.

4217. **Idaho Mining Memorial Scholarship** Number of scholarships and their amounts vary, depending on funds available. Based on financial need. Open to entering freshmen and transfer students enrolled in any major at the College of Mines. Deadline: March 14.

4218. **Newton Scholarship** One scholarship of $700 to a sophomore, junior, or senior enrolled in any

major at the College of Mines. Must have at least a 2.5 GPA. May be a transfer student. Deadline: March 14.

4219. **Norman N. Smith Scholarship** 1 scholarship of $400 to an undergraduate student enrolled in any major at the College of Mines. Deadline: March 14.

4220. **Ziegler Education Foundation Scholarship** Numerous scholarships and loans of up to full college costs to students who are Idaho residents. Must be enrolled in or planning to enroll in the fields of metallurgical engineering or mining engineering. Deadline: March 14.

ILLINOIS

Augustana College
639 38th Street
Rock Island, IL 61201-2296
(800) 798-8100
(309) 794-7000
http://www.augustana.com
admissions@augustana.edu

4221. **Alumni** Numerous scholarships ranging from $500 to $1,000 to students in the top 20 percent of their class and scoring at least 1025 on SAT or 27 on ACT. Renewable with a 3.2 GPA.

4222. **Athletic (Men)** Basketball, cross-country, football, golf, and track and field scholarships.

4223. **Athletic (Women)** Basketball, cross-country, softball, track and field, and volleyball scholarships.

4224. **Honors** Numerous scholarships ranging from $300 to $2,000 for students in the top 10 percent of their class. Renewable.

4225. **Performance** Numerous scholarships ranging from $300 to $2,000. Renewable.

4226. **Presidential** 50 scholarships of $3,000 to students scoring at least 1260 on SAT or 30 on ACT. Renewable.

Blackburn College
700 College Avenue
Carlinville, IL 62626
(800) 233-3550
(217) 854-3231
http://www.blackburn.edu

4227. **Academic** Unlimited $500 scholarships to students with at least a 3.7 GPA. Renewable.

4228. **Honors Graduate** Unlimited $500 scholarships to students in the top 10 percent of their class. Renewable.

4229. **Leadership** 40 scholarships of $500 to students in the top 20 percent of their class and scoring at least 1100 on SAT or 24 on ACT. Renewable.

College of St. Francis
500 Wilcox Street
Joliet, IL 60435-6188
(800) 735-7500
(815) 740-3400
http://www.stfrancis.edu
admissions@vax.stfrancis.edu

4230. **Athletic (Men)** Baseball, basketball, golf, soccer, and tennis scholarships.

4231. **Athletic (Women)** Basketball, cross-country, softball, tennis, and volleyball scholarships.

4232. **Community College** 40 scholarships of $1,000 to transfer students with at least a 3.25 GPA after sixty credit hours. Renewal with a 3.25 GPA. Deadline: May 1.

4233. **Presidential** 20 scholarships of $500 to students in the top 25 percent of their class and scoring at least 1100 on SAT or 25 on ACT. Renewable.

4234. **President's Circle** 12 scholarships ranging from $500 to $1,000 to students, based on leadership activities. Deadline: March 1.

4235. **Trustee** 100 scholarships of $1,000 to students in the top 25 percent of their class and scoring at least 1100 on SAT or 25 on ACT. Renewable with a 3.25 GPA.

4236. **Valedictorian** 15 tuition scholarships to students who are their class valedictorians, have at least a 3.2 GPA, and score at least 1100 on SAT or 25 on ACT. Renewable with a 3.5 GPA.

DePaul University
1 East Jackson Boulevard
Chicago, IL 60604-2287
(312) 362-8000
http://www.depaul.edu
admitdpu@wppost.depaul.edu

4237. **Athletic (Men)** Basketball, cross-country, golf, riflery, soccer, tennis, and track and field scholarships.

4238. **Athletic (Women)** Basketball, cross-country, riflery, softball, tennis, track and field, and volleyball scholarships.

4239. **Bauer-Schmitt** 10 scholarships of $2,000 to students in the upper 2 percent of their class, with at least a 3.6 GPA and scoring at least 1200 on SAT or 30 on ACT. Renewable.

4240. **Competitive** Numerous scholarships ranging from $300 to total financial need of students in the top 10 percent of their class, with at least a 3.2 GPA and scoring at least 24 on ACT. Renewable.

4241. **Stanley** Numerous scholarships of $1,000 to students in the top 10 percent of their class, with at least a 3.6 GPA, and who scored at least 24 on ACT. Renewable.

Greenville College
315 East College Avenue
Greenville, IL 62246
(618) 664-1840
http://www.greenville.edu

4242. **Achievement** Numerous scholarships ranging from $500 to $1,000 to students with at least a 3.25 GPA. Renewable with a 3.3. GPA.

4243. **Honors** Numerous scholarships ranging from $500 to $1,500 to students in the top 10 percent of their class. Renewable with a 3.25 GPA.

4244. **Leadership** Numerous scholarships ranging from $500 to $1,000 to students in the top 20 percent of their class with at least a 3.0 GPA. Renewable with a 3.0 GPA.

4245. **Presidential "Honors Program"** 6 scholarships of $2,500 to students in the top 10 percent of their class with at least a 3.3 GPA. Renewable with a 3.3. GPA.

Knox College
Galesburg, IL 61401-4999
(309) 343-0112
(800) 678-5669
http://www.knox.edu
admission@knox.edu

4246. **Academic** Numerous scholarships ranging from $1,000 to $2,000 to students in the top 10 percent of their class and scoring at least 1100 on SAT or 25 on ACT. Renewable with a 3.0 GPA.

4247. **Creative Arts** 20 to 25 scholarships ranging from $500 to $1,500 to undergraduate students majoring in drama/theater, music, or creative writing. Based on auditions, interviews, and academic performance. Renewable with a 2.0 GPA.

4248. **Presidential** 10 to 15 scholarships of $5,000 to entering freshmen in the top 10 percent of their class and scoring at least 1100 on SAT or 25 on ACT. Based on leadership ability, talents, recommendation, interview, and an on-campus competition. Renewable with a 3.3 GPA.

4249. **Rothwell Stephens** 1 scholarship of $1,000 to an entering freshman student who will be majoring in mathematics. Must show exceptional ability in mathematics and take a mathematics exam at Knox College. Renewable with a 3.0 GPA.

Loyola University of Chicago
820 North Michigan Avenue
Chicago, IL 60611
(312) 915-6000
http://www.luc.edu
admission@luc.edu

4250. **Academic** Numerous scholarships ranging from $1,000 to tuition to students in the top 10 percent of their class and scoring at least 1150 on SAT or 27 on ACT. Renewable.

4251. **Athletic (Men)** Basketball, cross-country, golf, soccer, swimming and diving, and track and field scholarships.

4252. **Athletic (Women)** Basketball, cross-country, softball, track and field, and volleyball scholarships.

4253. **Condon** 2 tuition scholarships. Renewable.

4254. **Honorary** Numerous $1,000 scholarships to students in the top 10 percent of their class and scoring at least 1150 on SAT or 27 on ACT. Renewable.

4255. **Honors** 3 tuition scholarships. Renewable.

4256. **Placieniak** Numerous scholarships of varying amounts.

4257. **Public Accounting** 2 scholarships ranging from $1,000 to $4,000 to entering freshmen who will major in accounting. Renewable with a 3.0 GPA. Deadline is March 1.

4258. **Theater** Numerous scholarships of varying amounts. Renewable.

Northern Illinois University
DeKalb, IL 60115
(815) 753-1300
http://www.niu.edu/
admissions-info@niu.edu

4259. **Academic Finalist** 25 scholarships providing tuition plus $300 to students in the top 5 percent of their class and with at least a 3.5 GPA. Renewable with 3.0 GPA.

4260. **Alumni "Honors Program"** Numerous scholarships ranging from $600 to $1,200 to students in the top 10 percent of their class, with at least a 3.0 GPA, and who scored at least 25 in ACT.

4261. **Ann Nelson Nahas Scholarship** 1 scholarship of $300 to an undergraduate sophomore or higher or graduate students. Based on academic achievement.

4262. **Athletic (Men)** Baseball, basketball, football, golf, soccer, swimming and diving, tennis, and wrestling scholarships.

4263. **Athletic (Women)** Basketball, field hockey, golf, gymnastics, softball, swimming and diving, tennis, and volleyball scholarships.

4264. **Copley Newspaper Scholarship** 1 scholarship of $1,000 to journalism students meeting certain criteria.

4265. **Creative Arts/Performance Awards** 37 scholarships to students majoring in music, theater arts, or art. Based on talent.

4266. **Granville Price Award** 1 scholarship of $200 to a returning upper-class student majoring in print news who meets other criteria.

4267. **Hearst Foundation Scholarships** 2 or more scholarships of $300 to NIU journalism students in a national competition.

4268. **Illinois Journalist of the Year Scholarship** 1 scholarship of $1,000 to a returning upper-class student. Based on academic achievement and performance in journalism.

4269. **International Students** Numerous scholarships of varying amounts to international students meeting certain criteria.

4270. **Irvan Kummerfeldt Scholarship** 1 scholarship of $300 to an undergraduate or graduate student. Based on reporting skills.

4271. **Minority Awards** Numerous scholarships of varying amounts to minority students meeting certain criteria.

4272. **NIU Foundation Awards** Numerous scholarships of varying amounts to students meeting certain criteria.

4273. **Northern Illinois Newspaper Association Scholarship** 1 scholarship of up to $1,000 to an undergraduate sophomore or above who is majoring in news-editorial or photojournalism. Based on high academic achievement and performance in journalism.

4274. **Salner's Media Award** 1 scholarship of $300 to a journalism student based on academic achievement.

4275. **Scripps League Scholarship** 1 scholarship of $1,000 to a minority high school senior who was a member of high school publications or electronic news program and intends to major in journalism.

4276. **Scripps League Scholarship** 1 scholarship of $1,000 to a minority college student who was a member of community college publications or an electronic news program and is majoring in journalism.

4277. **Scripps League Scholarship** 1 scholarship of $500 to an undergraduate sophomore or higher. Based on academic achievement and performance in journalism.

4278. **Tuition Waiver** 220 scholarships providing tuition costs to students in the top 5 percent of their class and with at least a 2.0 GPA.

4279. **University Scholar** 5 scholarships providing all costs to students in the top 5 percent of their class, with at least a 3.5 GPA. Renewable with 3.3 GPA.

Northwestern University
P.O. Box 3060
1801 Hinman Avenue
Evanston, IL 60204-3060
(847) 491-7271
(847) 491-3741
http://www.nwu.edu
ug@admissionnwu.edu

4280. **Athletic (Men)** Baseball, football, golf, swimming and diving, tennis, and wrestling scholarships.

4281. **Athletic (Women)** Fencing, field hockey, softball, swimming and diving, tennis, and volleyball scholarships.

4282. **Coply Newspapers Scholarship** 1 scholarship of $750 to undergraduate journalism students.

4283. **Journalism Scholarships** Approximately 329 scholarships ranging from $250 to $13,000 to undergraduate students meeting certain academic criteria, with financial need, and who were majoring in journalism.

Southern Illinois University
Carbondale, IL 62901
(618) 453-2121
http://www.siu.edu/cwis/

4284. **Athletic (Men)** Baseball, basketball, cross-country, football, golf, softball, swimming and diving, tennis, and track and field scholarships.

4285. **Athletic (Women)** Basketball, cross-country, golf, swimming and diving, tennis, and track and field scholarships.

4286. **Presidential** Numerous scholarships providing tuition costs and $1,000 to students in the top 2 percent of their class and scoring at least 1260 on SAT or 30 on ACT. Renewable with a 3.5 GPA.

4287. **Presidential Minority** Numerous scholarships providing tuition costs and $1,000 to minority students in the top 2 percent of their class and scoring at least 1260 on SAT or 30 on ACT. Renewable with a 3.5 GPA.

4288. **SIU Academic** Numerous scholarships providing tuition to students in the top 10 percent of their class and scoring at least 1100 on SAT or 27 on ACT.

4289. **SIU Academic Minority** Numerous scholarships providing tuition to minority students in the top 10 percent of their class and scoring at least 840 on SAT or 20 on ACT.

4290. **SIU Academic Transfer** Numerous scholarships providing tuition to transfer students with at least a 3.5 GPA.

4291. **SIU Foundation** Numerous $500 scholarships to students in the top 10 percent of their class and scoring at least 1100 on SAT or 27 on ACT.

4292. **SIU Foundation Merit** Numerous scholarships of tuition plus $1,000. Based on academic merit. Renewable with a 3.5 GPA.

4293. **SIU Foundation Merit Minority Honors Program** Numerous scholarships of tuition plus $1,000 to minority students. Based on academic merit. Renewable with a 3.5 GPA.

Trinity Christian College
6601 West College Drive
Palos Heights, IL 60463
(800) 748-0085
(312) 597-3000
http://www.trnty.edu
admissions@trnty.edu

4294. **Alumni** 1 scholarship of $500 to a child of a Trinity alumnus. Renewable. Deadline: February 15.

4295. **Bergsman** 1 scholarship of $500 to a student from San Diego County, California. Application is automatic with acceptance.

4296. **Cable Business Award** 3 scholarships of $500 to undergraduates majoring in business administration. Deadline: February 15.

4297. **Evers-Lawson** 2 scholarships of $500 to students from the Illinois and Indiana area. Application is automatic with acceptance.

4298. **Heeren Memorial in Theology** 1 scholarship of $500 to an undergraduate student majoring in theology or religion. Not available every year. Deadline: February 15.

4299. **Honors** 15 scholarships ranging from $600 to $1,200 to students in the top 25 percent of their class, with at least a 3.0 GPA and scoring at least 870 on SAT or 21 on ACT. Renewable with a 3.0 GPA.

4300. **Leadership** 15 scholarships ranging from $500 to $1,000 to students who showed outstanding leadership qualities while in high school and will continue to do so in college. Deadline: February 15.

4301. **Mitchell Memorial** 2 scholarships of up to $2,000 to entering freshmen with outstanding leadership qualities. Deadline: February 15.

4302. President's Honors 6 scholarships of $2,500 to students who were valedictorians in a Christian Schools international high school. Must have at least a 3.4 GPA. Deadline: February 15.

4303. Vander Velde Science Honors Program 3 scholarships of $2,000 to students majoring in science.

4304. Vermeer 2 scholarships of $500 to students from the Pella, Iowa, area. Application is automatic with acceptance

University of Chicago
1116 East 59th Street
Chicago, IL 60637
(703) 702-8650
http://www.uchicago.edu
college.admissions@uchicago.edu

4305. College Honors Scholarships Varying numbers of scholarships of varying amounts to students who have demonstrated leadership abilities.

University of Illinois at Chicago
601 South Morgan
Chicago, IL 60680-5220
(312) 996-7000
http://www.uic.edu
uicadmit@uic.edu

4306. Academic Scholarships Varying numbers of scholarships of $1,000 to students who are in the top 15 percent of their class and scored at least 26 on ACT. Renewable.

4307. Chancellor's Scholarships 35 scholarships of $1,000 to students in the upper 15 percent of their class, who scored at least 690 on SAT or 18 on ACT.

4308. FMC Excellence "Honors Program, Honors College" Varying numbers of scholarships of $1,000 to students meeting certain academic criteria.

4309. Freshman Scholarships Unlimited numbers of scholarships of $1,000 to students who scored at least 1220 on SAT or 30 on ACT.

4310. National Merit Scholarships Varying numbers of scholarships of varying amounts to students who have been designated National Merit Finalists and Scholars.

4311. President's Scholarships Varying numbers of scholarships ranging from $500 to full tuition to students in the upper 50 percent of their class who scored at least 880 on SAT or 22 on ACT. Renewable.

4312. University Scholars Varying numbers of scholarships providing at least tuition to students who meet certain academic criteria. Renewable.

4313. Tuition Waivers Numerous partial to full tuition waivers to students who are senior citizens.

University of Illinois at Urbana–Champaign
506 South Wright Street
Urbana, IL 61801
(217) 333-0302
http://www.uiuc.edu

4314. Academic 221 scholarships ranging from $624 to $2,229. Renewable.

4315. Athletic (Men) Baseball, basketball, cross–country, fencing, football, golf, gymnastics, swimming and diving, tennis, track and field, and wrestling scholarships.

4316. Athletic (Women) Basketball, cross–country, golf, gymnastics, softball, swimming and diving, tennis, track and field, and volleyball scholarships.

4317. Lydia E. Parker Bates Scholarship 175 awards of varying amounts to students who maintain a 3.85 GPA or higher on a 5.0 scale. Must carry at least fifteen hours per semester and must be majoring in art, architecture, landscape architecture, urban planning, dance, or theater. Deadline: mid–March.

INDIANA

Ball State University
2000 University Avenue
Muncie, IN 47306-0855
(800) 482-4BSU
(765) 285-8300
http://www.bsu.edu/
askus@up.bsu.edu

4318. Academic Recognition Scholarships 75 scholarships providing N.R. fees to students in the top 50 percent of their class and have at least a 3.0 GPA. Renewable with 2.0 GPA.

4319. Alumni Awards Varying scholarships of varying amounts to students meeting certain academic criteria.

4320. **Athletic (Men)** Baseball, basketball, cross-country, football, golf, swimming and diving, tennis, track and field, and volleyball scholarships.

4321. **Athletic (Women)** Basketball, cross-country, gymnastics, swimming and diving, tennis, track and field, and volleyball scholarships.

4322. **Ball State** 500 scholarships ranging from $1,200 to $1,300 to students in the top 20 percent of their class, with at least a 3.0 GPA, and scoring at least 1030 on SAT or 23 on ACT. Renewable with a 2.6 GPA.

4323. **College/Departmental "Honors Program, Honors College"** Varying numbers of scholarships of varying amounts to students who meet certain academic criteria and have certain majors.

4324. **David Letterman Scholarship for C Students** 3 scholarships (first place—full tuition, room, and board; second place—50 percent of tuition, room, and board; third place—33 percent of tuition, room, and board) to undergraduate junior or senior students majoring in communications. Competition in any area of audio, video, or print. Based on creativity and originality. Academic record is not considered, but you must be at least a C student to enter. Contact the Department of Communications.

4325. **John R. Emens Scholarships** 5 scholarships providing in-state fees to students meeting certain academic criteria and who have demonstrated leadership abilities. Renewable.

4326. **National Merit Scholarships** Varying numbers of scholarships ranging from $500 to $2,000 to students who received National Merit designation. Renewable with 3.0 GPA.

4327. **Palmer Music Awards** Varying numbers of scholarships of varying amounts to students meeting certain criteria who are music majors. Based on talent.

4328. **Presidential Scholarships** 404 scholarships ranging from $1,432 to $3,622 to students in the top 20 percent of their class, who scored at least 1030 on SAT or 24 on ACT and are residents of Indiana. Renewable with 3.0 GPA.

4329. **Special Characteristics Awards** Varying numbers of scholarships providing fee remission to students who are employee dependents.

4330. **Tuition Waivers** Numerous partial to full tuition waivers to students who are employees, children of employees, or senior citizens.

4331. **Whitinger Scholarships** 10 scholarships providing fees, plus room and board, to students in the top 10 percent of their class who scored at least 1200 on SAT or 29 on ACT. Renewable with 3.0 GPA.

4332. **Young Artist Awards** Varying numbers of scholarships of varying amounts to students meeting certain criteria. Based on talent.

DePauw University
313 South Locust Street
Greencastle IN 46135-0037
(765) 658-4006
http://www.depauw.edu

4333. **Black Student Leadership Award** 15 scholarships of $5,000 to entering freshmen. Application is automatic with acceptance. Renewable.

4334. **Charles Grannon Scholarship** 3 scholarships of $4,000 to entering freshmen who will major in management. Renewable with a 3.4 GPA. Deadline: February 15.

4335. **Conduit Science** 8 scholarships of $2,500 to entering freshmen taking a science exam in December. Interview and science major required. Renewable with a 3.25 GPA.

4336. **Distinguished Rector** 20 scholarships of $5,500 to entering freshmen. Application is automatic with acceptance. Based on academic record, SAT/ACT scores, and achievement. Renewable with a 3.25 GPA.

4337. **Frees Nursing** 4 scholarships of $4,000 to entering freshmen planning to major in nursing. Based on academic record and career goals. Application is automatic with acceptance. Renewable with a 3.0 GPA.

4338. **Health Science** 4 scholarships of $2,500 to entering freshmen taking a science exam in December. Science major not required, but you must take numerous science and math courses. Renewable with a 3.5 GPA.

4339. **Presidential Rector** 5 scholarships of $6,500 to entering freshmen. Based on academic record and leadership potential. Application is automatic with acceptance. Renewable with a 3.25 GPA.

4340. **Rector Honors** 29 scholarships of $4,000 to entering freshmen. Based on academic record and potential for success. Application is automatic with acceptance. Renewable with a 3.25 GPA.

4341. **School of Music Honors Performance** 14 scholarships ranging from $500 to $5,000 to entering freshmen planning to major in music. Based on audition.

Franklin College
501 East Monroe Street
Franklin, IN 46131-2598
(317) 738-8000
http://www.franklincoll.edu
admissions@franklincoll.edu.

4342. **Ben Franklin** 61 scholarships ranging from $500 to $2,000 to entering freshmen in the upper 20 percent of class and scoring at least 1050 on SAT or 24 on ACT. Renewable.

4343. **Cummins Engine Company** 29 scholarships ranging from $500 to $2,000 (average $1,500) to entering freshmen who will major in accounting, business, or economics. Must have scored at least 1100 on SAT or 24 on ACT. Based on financial need and recommendations.

4344. **Maurice and Rose Johnson** 58 scholarships ranging from $500 to $1,000 to students in the upper 10 percent of their class. Based on financial need. Renewable.

4345. **Pulliam Journalism** 58 scholarships ranging from $500 to $3,000 to freshman journalism majors. Based on academic achievement and financial need. Renewable with a 3.0 GPA. Contact the Associate Director of Financial Aid. Deadline: December 15.

Indiana University–South Bend
1700 Mishawaka Avenue
P.O. Box 7111
South Bend, IN 46634-7111
(219) 237-4357
http://www.indiana.edu/

4346. **Dean's Scholarships** Unlimited numbers of scholarships providing half of tuition costs to students in the top 10 percent of their class, with at least a 3.5 GPA, and who scored at least 1100 on SAT. Renewable with 3.5 GPA.

4347. **Distinguished Scholarships** 4 scholarships of $1,000 to students in the top 10 percent of their class who scored at least 1300 on SAT. Renewable with 3.75 GPA.

4348. **Merit Scholarships** Unlimited numbers of scholarships ranging from $100 to $200 to students in the top 10 percent of their class, with at least a 3.3 GPA, and who scored at least 1000 on SAT. Renewable with 3.3 GPA.

Manchester College
604 East College Avenue
North Manchester, IN 46962-0365
(800) 852-3648
(219) 982-5000
http://www.manchester.edu
admissionsinfo@manchester.edu

4349. **Alumni** Unlimited number of $500 scholarships.

4350. **Church of the Brethren Honors Program** Unlimited number of $1,000 scholarships to students who are members of the Church of the Brethren.

4351. **Honors** 70 scholarships of $2,000 to students in the top 10 percent of their class and scoring 1100 on SAT or 27 on ACT. Renewable with a 3.3 GPA.

4352. **Manchester College** Unlimited number of scholarships ranging from $1,000 to $1,800 to students in the upper 20 percent of their class and scoring at least 1100 on SAT or 24 on ACT. Renewable with a 3.0 GPA.

4353. **Presidential** 45 scholarships of $2,500 to entering freshmen in the top 5 percent of their class, with at least 3.3 GPA, and scoring 1100 on SAT or 27 on ACT. Renewable with a 3.3 GPA.

Purdue University
West Lafayette, IN 47907
(765) 494-4600
http://www.purdue.edu
admissions@adms.purdue.edu

4354. **Academic "Honors Program"** Numerous scholarships of up to $1,500 to students in the top 10 percent of their class with a 3.5 GPA.

4355. **Athletic (Men)** Baseball, basketball, cross-country, football, golf, swimming and diving, tennis, track and field, and wrestling scholarships.

4356. **Athletic (Women)** Basketball, cross-country, golf, swimming and diving, tennis, track and field, and volleyball scholarships.

4357. **Departmental** Numerous scholarships of up to $2,000 to students in the top 15 percent of their class.

4358. **Merit** 50 scholarships ranging from $500 to $5,000 to students majoring in agriculture, consumer and family sciences, education, engineering, humanities, social sciences, management, pharmacy, or science. Based on merit. Must be in the top one-fifth of their class. Contact academic department for applications and information.

4359. **Minority Engineering Education Effort** 5 scholarships ranging from $250 to $2,500 to incoming minority freshmen majoring in engineering. Based on financial need. Contact the Assistant Director of Minority Engineering Program. Deadline: March 5.

4360. **Presidential Merit** Numerous scholarships providing all costs. Based on academic merit and financial need.

4361. **Presidential Honors** 5 scholarships ranging from $500 to $10,000 to students in top 1 percent of their class who have at least a 3.9 GPA and scored at least 1450 on SAT or 33 on ACT. Renewable with a 3.5 GPA.

4362. **Zada M. Cooper Undergraduate Scholarship** 4 scholarships of $500 to undergraduate pharmacy students who are members of Kappa Epsilon fraternity. Based on service to College of Pharmacy, completion of two semesters in the College of Pharmacy, and academic standing. Contact: Kappa Epsilon Fraternity, Room 162, School of Pharmacy, (317) 494–9015. Deadline: November 1.

Rose–Hulman Institute of Technology
5500 Wasash Avenue
Terre Haute, IN 47803
(800) 248-7448
(812) 877-1511
http://www.rose-hulman.edu/

4363. **Forrest G. Sherer Honorary Boy Scout Scholarship** 1 scholarship of $500 to active scout from the Wabash Valley Council.

4364. **Presidential Awards** Numerous scholarships of varying amounts. Based on leadership.

4365. **Rose–Hulman Scholarships** Numerous scholarships of varying amounts. Based on academic achievement.

University of Evansville
1800 Lincoln Avenue
Evansville, IN 47722-0329
(800) 423-8633
(812) 479-2000
http://www.evansville.edu/

4366. **Alumni Merit** Unlimited number of scholarships of $1,000 to students in the top 10 percent of their class who scored at least 1000 on SAT or 22 on ACT. Renewable.

4367. **Athletic (Men)** Baseball, basketball, cross-country, golf, soccer, swimming and diving, and tennis scholarships.

4368. **Athletic (Women)** Basketball, cross–country, swimming and diving, tennis, and volleyball scholarships.

4369. **President's** Unlimited number of scholarships of $2,000 to students in the top 5 percent of their class and scoring at least 1200 on SAT or 27 on ACT. Renewable.

University of Indianapolis
1400 East Hanna Avenue
Indianapolis, IN 46227
(800) 232-8634
(317) 788-3368
http://www.uindy.edu/

4370. **Alumni Scholarships** 38 scholarships providing 30 percent of tuition costs to students in the upper 15 percent of their class, who scored at least 1000 on SAT. Renewable with 2.7 GPA.

4371. **Art Scholarships** Varying numbers of scholarships of varying amounts to students meeting certain criteria who are art majors. Based on talent.

4372. **Bohn Scholarships** Varying numbers of scholarships of varying amounts to students meeting certain academic criteria.

4373. **Dean's Scholarships** 100 scholarships of one-half tuition costs to students in the top 5 to 7 percent of their class who scored at least 1200 on SAT. Renewable with 3.3 GPA.

4374. **Faculty/Staff Discounts** Discounts of varying amounts to students meeting certain criteria who are dependents of faculty/staff.

4375. **Foreign Student Grants** Varying numbers of scholarships of varying amounts to foreign students meeting certain criteria.

4376. **Ministerial Grant** Varying numbers of scholarships of varying amounts to students meeting certain criteria who are pursuing careers in the ministry.

4377. **Music Grants** 10 scholarships ranging from $1,000 to $3,000 to undergraduate and graduate students meeting certain criteria who are music majors. Based on talent. Auditions are required.

4378. **Presidential Scholarships** 12 scholarships providing tuition costs to students in the top 5 percent of their class who scored at least 1200 on SAT. Renewable with 3.3 GPA.

4379. **Service Award "Honors Program" Scholarships** Varying numbers of scholarships providing 30 percent of tuition costs to students meeting certain criteria who have participated in community service projects. Renewable with 2.0 GPA.

4380. **Theater Scholarships** Varying numbers of scholarships of varying amounts to students meeting certain criteria who are theater majors. Based on talent.

4381. **Tuition Waivers** Numerous partial to full tuition waivers to students who are employees, children of employees, or senior citizens.

4382. **United Methodist Scholarships** Unlimited numbers of scholarships providing 30 percent of tuition costs to students meeting certain criteria. Renewable with 2.0 GPA.

University of Notre Dame
Notre Dame, IN 46556
(219) 239-5000
http://www.nd.edu

4383. **Athletic (Men)** Basketball, cross-country, fencing, football, golf, ice hockey, soccer, swimming and diving, tennis, track and field, and wrestling scholarships.

4384. **Athletic (Women)** Basketball, cross-country, fencing, golf, soccer, softball, swimming and diving, tennis, track and field, and volleyball scholarships.

4385. **Holy Cross Awards** Several scholarship programs providing scholarships of varying amounts to minority students meeting certain academic criteria who demonstrate financial need.

4386. **Notre Dame Scholar Awards** Scholarships of varying amounts to students meeting certain academic criteria. Generally, 25 percent of all students accepted for admission receive scholar designation.

4387. **Tuition Waivers** Numerous partial to full tuition waivers to students who are employees or children of employees.

Valparaiso University
Valparaiso, IN 46383
(888) GO-VALPO
(219) 464-5011
http://www.valpo.edu/

4388. **AAL Scholarship** 63 scholarships ranging from $500 to $1,000 to undergraduate students who are Lutheran and members of the AAL. Based on academic achievement and/or financial need. Renewable with a 2.0 GPA. Contact the Director of Admissions. Deadline: March 1.

4389. **Ament-Brenner Nursing Scholarship** 1 scholarship ranging from 1,000 to $5,000 to an undergraduate majoring in nursing. Preference given to a Lutheran student from the St. Louis, Missouri, area. Deadline: March 1 (priority).

4390. **Angus Ward Foreign Service Scholarship** 1 award of $1,000 to an entering freshman pursuing a career in U.S. foreign service. Based on academic achievement and financial need. Renewable with a 2.0 GPA. Deadline: March 1.

4391. **Athletic (Men)** Baseball, basketball, cross-country, football, golf, soccer, swimming and diving, tennis, and wrestling scholarships.

4392. **Athletic (Women)** Basketball, cross-country, gymnastics, softball, swimming and diving, tennis, and volleyball scholarships.

4393. **Dow Scholarship** 1 scholarship of $2,500 to an entering freshman who intends to pursue a doctorate in chemistry. Renewable with a 3.0 GPA. Deadline: March 1.

4394. **Guild Scholarship** 7 scholarships of $2,000 to undergraduates who are the sons or daughters of a Valparaiso University Guild member. Renewable with a 2.0 GPA. Deadline: March 1.

4395. **Lutheran Brotherhood** 25 scholarships ranging from $500 to $1,000 to undergraduate students who are Lutheran and members of the Lutheran Brotherhood. Renewable with a 2.0 GPA. Deadline: March 1.

4396. **Lutheran HS Principal's Award** 150 scholarships ranging from $500 to $1,000 to entering freshmen. Renewable with a 2.0 GPA. Deadline: March 1.

4397. **Lutheran President's Award** 16 scholarships ranging from $1,000 to $2,000 to entering freshmen. Based on academic achievement and religious leadership. Renewable with a 2.0 GPA. Deadline: March 1.

4398. **Lutheran Principal's Award** 65 scholarships ranging from $500 to $1,500 to entering freshmen who have graduated from a Lutheran high school. Based on academic achievement. Renewable with a 2.0 GPA. Deadline: March 1.

4399. **Martin Luther Award** 295 scholarships ranging from $1,000 to $3,000 to undergraduates who are dependents of a full-time professional Lutheran church worker or have financial need. Renewable with a 2.0 GPA. Deadline: March 1.

4400. **Mechanical Engineering** Varying numbers of $2,000 scholarships to full-time undergraduate third- and fourth-year students majoring in mechanical engineering. Must have a minimum 3.8 GPA. Renewable. Contact the Mechanical Engineering Dept. Chairman. Deadline: April 1.

4401. **Minnesota Merit Scholarship** 2 scholarships ranging from $400 to $1,500 are available to undergraduates. Based on academic achievement or leadership. Applicants must be Minnesota residents. Renewable with a 3.0 GPA. Deadline: March 1.

4402. **Music** Numerous scholarships ranging from $200 to $1,000. Audition required. Renewable.

4403. **National Merit Scholarship** 44 awards ranging from $750 to $2,000 to undergraduates designated National Merit Finalists by the National Merit Corporation. Renewable with a 2.0 GPA. Deadline: March 1.

4404. **Presidential** 150 scholarships ranging from $500 to $2,500 to students in the top 5 percent of their class, who have at least a 3.5 GPA and scored at least 1250 on SAT or 28 on SAT. Renewable with a 3.0 GPA.

4405. **Presidential Law Scholarship** 1 full scholarship to a law student who is a graduate of a Lutheran institution. Minimum of a 3.6 GPA and at least a 37 on LSAT required. Renewable. Contact Assistant Dean of the Law School.

4406. **University Scholarship** 90 scholarships ranging from $500 to $1,000 to undergraduates. Based on academic achievement, high school transcript, and other criteria. Renewable with a 3.0 GPA. Deadline: March 1.

4407. **Wisconsin Merit Award** 2 scholarships of $1,500 to undergraduates. Based on academic achievement. Must be Wisconsin residents. Renewable. Deadline: March 1.

IOWA

Buena Vista College
4th and College Street
Storm Lake, IA 50588
(800) 383-9600
(712) 749-2235
http://www.bvu.edu
admissions@bvu.edu

4408. **Honors** Numerous scholarships ranging from $600 to $1,800 for students in the top 20 percent of their class, with at least a 3.2 GPA, and scoring at least 24 on ACT. Renewable.

4409. **Science—Math Honors Program** Numerous $1,000 scholarships to students majoring in science. Renewable with a 3.5 GPA.

4410. **Talent** Numerous $1,200 scholarships. Based on a written exam administered by Buena Vista College, essay, leadership qualities, and interview. Renewable with a 2.0 GPA.

Iowa State University of Science and Technology
100 Alumni Hall
Ames, IA 50011-2010
(800) 262-3810
(515) 294-4111
http://www.public.iastate.edu

4411. **Achievement Foundation** 20 scholarships of $2,500 to students who are valedictorian or salutatorian of their class. Renewable.

4412. **Athletic (Men)** Baseball, basketball, cross-country, football, golf, gymnastics, swimming and diving, tennis, track and field, and wrestling scholarships.

4413. **Athletic (Women)** Basketball, cross-country, golf, gymnastics, softball, swimming and diving, tennis, track and field, and volleyball scholarships.

4414. **Biotechnology Scholarship** Numerous full-tuition scholarships to entering students who plan to major in seed science, agriculture, animal ecology, biometry, food technology, genetics, or pest management. Must be U.S. citizens and graduates of an Iowa high school, with fourteen semesters of math and science courses. Must rank in the top 15 percent of the class, score in the 90th percentile on SAT or ACT, and have a minimum 3.5 GPA. Based on extracurricular activities and/or work experience. Deadline: December 1.

4415. **Casualty Actuarial Society** 1 scholarship of $500 to a student in the Department of Statistics and Actuarial Science.

4416. **Dean's** 8 tuition scholarships to students in the top 5 percent of their class. Renewable.

4417. **Recognition Honors Program** 80 scholarships of $1,000 to students in the top 5 percent of their class.

4418. **Scholarship for Excellence** 10 scholarships of $2,500 to students in the top 5 percent of their class, with at least a 3.0 GPA, who are U.S. citizens. Deadline: October 31.

Iowa Wesleyan College
601 North Main Street
Mount Pleasant, IA 52641
(319) 385-6231
http://www.iwc.edu

4419. **Athletic (Men)** Baseball, basketball, cross-country, football, golf, and track and field scholarships.

4420. **Athletic (Women)** Basketball, cross-country, golf, softball, track and field, and volleyball scholarships.

4421. **Merit** Numerous scholarships from $1,000 to $2,500 for students in the top 20 percent of their class. Renewable with a 3.0 GPA.

4422. **Presidential** Numerous scholarships from $3,500 to $5,500 for students in the top 15 percent of their class, with at least a 3.5 GPA and scoring at least 24 on ACT. Renewable with a 3.5 GPA.

University of Iowa
Iowa City, IA 52242
(319) 335-3847
http://www.uiowa.edu

4423. **Alumni and Media Scholarships** Varying numbers of scholarships of varying amounts to journalism majors who meet certain criteria.

4424. **A. W. Lee Scholarships** 4 scholarships of $1,000 to undergraduate juniors, seniors, and graduate students. Based on potential for a successful journalism career, academic achievement, journalistic competence, and extracurricular activities.

4425. **Creative/Performing Arts** 60 scholarships of $2,100 to entering freshmen or transfer students majoring in art, dance, music, or theater. Must be in the upper 20 percent of class. Deadline: March 1.

4426. **Dorothy Pownall Award** 1 scholarship of $500 to a female undergraduate senior demonstrating highest potential for success as a journalist.

4427. **Frank Luther Mott Undergraduate Scholarship** 1 scholarship of $1,000 to an undergraduate junior or senior journalism major. Based on magazine or newspaper reporting, investigating ability, purity of writing, and absence of news editorializing.

4428. **Fred Pownall Scholarship** 1 scholarship of $500 to a senior male student with great potential in journalism. Based on competence.

4429. **Freshman Engineering Scholarships** 80 scholarships of varying amounts to entering freshman students who will be majoring in engineering and who meet certain academic criteria.

4430. **Harry S. Bunker Scholarship** 1 scholarship of $2,000 awarded in the spring of junior year to a student with an aptitude and interest in a newspaper career.

4431. **Iowa Center for the Arts** 4 scholarships of $2,500 to entering freshmen students majoring in art, dance, music, or theater. Based on audition or portfolio. Deadline: March 1.

4432. **Jacob E. Reizenstein Award** 1 scholarship award of $250 to an undergraduate sophomore or above who has demonstrated outstanding enterprise and capability in news gathering and writing.

4433. **James Blackburn Scholarships** 2 scholarships of $1,000 to undergraduate students based on academic achievement, extracurricular activities, and character. Deadline: November 1.

4434. **Jerry Parker Feature Writing Award** 1 scholarships of $250 to a senior based on outstanding achievement in journalism-related assignments in feature writing, extracurricular feature writing, and overall academic achievement.

4435. **Jess Gorkin Magazine Scholarship** 1 scholarship of $2,000 to an undergraduate junior or senior journalism major. Based on potential for success in the magazine field.

4436. **J. F. K. Truth-in-Journalism Award** 1 scholarship award of $250 to an undergraduate journalism major who has achieved distinction in interpretive or investigating reporting.

4437. **John F. Murray Scholarships in Journalism** Varying numbers of scholarships of $500 to journalism students meeting certain criteria.

4438. **Judy Klemesrud Writing Award** 1 scholarship of $250 to an undergraduate with at least a 2.75 GPA who exhibits great potential for ability to write about social issues.

4439. **J. Y. Bryan Prize** 1 award of $500 to an undergraduate junior, senior, or graduate student in a competition in either interpretive photography or investigative reporting. Deadline: February 1.

4440. **Larence Fairall Scholarships in Journalism** Approximately 5 scholarships of $750 each to undergraduate juniors, seniors, or graduate students who were born and raised in Iowa and who are pursuing a career in newspaper or magazine writing or editing.

4441. **National Merit Scholarships** 31 scholarships of varying amounts of students selected as National Merit Finalists.

4442. **Opportunity at Iowa Minority Academic Scholarships** 10 scholarships of varying amounts to minority students who meet certain academic criteria.

4443. **Opportunity at Iowa Minority Achievement Scholarships** 20 scholarships of varying amounts to minority students who meet certain academic criteria.

4444. **Phillip D. Adler Journalist Award** 1 scholarship of $1,000 to an undergraduate junior journalism major. Based on leadership potential and editorial achievement in newspaper or broadcast journalism.

4445. **Presidential** 20 scholarships ranging from $1,800 to $7,400 to entering freshmen in the top 5 percent of their class and with at least 1200 on SAT or 29 on ACT. Renewable with a 3.6 GPA.

4446. **Quill and Scroll Scholarship** 1 scholarship of $500 to a high school senior who will be a journalism major. Deadline: April 1.

4447. **Ruth Baty and Maurice Barnett Jones Scholarship** 1 scholarship of up to $500 to a student based on academic achievement and character.

4448. **W. Earl Hall and Reeves E. Hall Awards** 2 scholarships of $250 each to undergraduate and graduate students who have demonstrated distinction in the field of interpretive writing during the academic year.

4449. **Westbrook Pegler Award** 1 award of $500 to an undergraduate junior or senior or graduate student who has demonstrated an interest in and awareness of the responsibility and immense power of the press.

KANSAS

Baker University
P.O. Box 65
Baldwin City, KS 66006
(800) 873-4282
(913) 594-6451
http://www.bakeru.edu
johnson@harvey.bakeru.edu

4450. **Achievement** Numerous scholarships ranging from $200 to $800 to students with at least a 2.0 GPA. Renewable with a 2.0 GPA.

4451. **Baker** Numerous scholarships ranging from $1,260 to $1,860 to students with at least a 2.5 GPA. Renewable with a 2.5 GPA.

4452. **Departmental** 36 scholarships of $3,000. Based on exam administered by Baker University. One each in accounting, art, biology, business, chemistry, computer information systems, computer science, economics, elementary education, English, fashion merchandising, French, German, history, instrumental music, international business, mass communications, math, music, music education, philosophy, physics, political science, psychology, religion, sociology, Spanish, speech/communications, theater, and vocal music. Renewable with a 3.0 GPA.

4453. **Nell A. Kimble** 1 scholarship of $5,820 to an entering freshman. Based on SAT/ACT score. Deadline: March 1.

4454. **Presidential** Numerous $3,000 scholarships to students with at least a 3.25 GPA and scoring at least 1090 on SAT or 25 on ACT. Renewable with a 3.0 GPA.

Kansas State University
Manhattan, KS 66506-0110
(785) 532-6250
http://www.ksu.edu

4455. **Athletic (Men)** Baseball, basketball, cross-country, football, golf, and track and field scholarships.

4456. **Athletic (Women)** Basketball, cross-country, golf, tennis, track and field, and volleyball scholarships.

4457. **Foundation** 103 scholarships ranging from $700 to $1,000 to students in the upper 15 percent of their class, with at least a 3.67 GPA, and scoring at least 30 on ACT. Renewable with a 3.0 GPA.

4458. **Leadership Honors Program** Numerous $500 scholarships to students scoring at least 26 on ACT.

4459. Putnam 246 scholarships ranging from $900 to $1,250 to students in the top 10 percent of their class, with a 3.75 GPA and scoring 30 on ACT. Renewable with a 3.0 GPA.

University of Kansas
Lawrence, KS 66045-1910
(785) 864-2700
http://www.ukans.edu/

4460. Athletic (Men) Baseball, basketball, cross-country, football, golf, swimming and diving, tennis, and track and field scholarships.

4461. Athletic (Women) Basketball, cross-country, golf, softball, swimming and diving, tennis, track and field, and volleyball scholarships.

4462. Departmental 1,200 scholarships ranging from $50 to $2,000.

4463. Endowment Merit 75 scholarships ranging from $300 to $1,000.

4464. Honors 600 scholarships ranging from $100 to $1500 to students in the top 10 percent of their class and scoring at least 30 on ACT.

4465. KU 800 scholarships ranging from $100 to $2,500.

4466. National Merit "Honors Program" 20 to 35 scholarships ranging from $250 to $2,000 to students selected as National Merit Finalists. Renewable.

KENTUCKY

Alice Lloyd College
100 Purpose Road
Pippa Passes, KY 41844
(888) 280-4252
(606) 368-2101
http://www.aikcu.org/colleges.html
admissions@alicelloyd.edu

4467. Athletic (Men) Baseball, basketball, and cross-country scholarships.

4468. Athletic (Women) Basketball and cross-country scholarships.

4469. Memorial 125 to 150 scholarships of $8,158 to students with at least a 3.5 GPA. Renewable with a 3.0 GPA.

Centre College
600 W. Walnut Street
Danville, KY 40422
(606) 238-5200
http://www.centre.edu
admission@centre.edu

4470. Academic Recognition Scholarships 31 scholarships of varying amounts to students who are in the upper 10 percent of their class, with at least a 3.5 GPA, and who scored at least 27 on ACT.

4471. Alumni Scholarships 10 scholarships of varying amounts to students meeting certain academic criteria.

4472. Colonel Scholarships Varying numbers of scholarships of $5,000 per year for four years to students from middle-income families meeting certain academic criteria who demonstrate potential for success.

4473. Day Scholarships 10 scholarships of $5,000 to students in the top 10 percent of their class, with at least a 3.5 GPA, and who scored at least 27 on ACT. Renewable with 2.7 GPA.

4474. Dean's Scholarships Varying numbers of scholarships of $9,000 per year for four years to students meeting certain academic criteria and who demonstrate potential for success. Renewable.

4475. Faculty Scholarship Varying numbers of scholarships of $6,000 per year for four years to students meeting certain academic criteria and who demonstrate potential for success. Renewable.

4476. Heritage Scholarships 20 scholarships of $7,500 to students who are in the top 10 percent of their class, with at least a 3.5 GPA, and scored at least 29 on ACT. Renewable with 3.4 GPA. Preference given to minority and Appalachian students.

4477. Honor Scholarships 100 scholarships of $2,500 per year for four years to students who are in the top 10 percent of their class, with at least a 3.5 GPA, who scored at least 27 on ACT, and who demonstrate potential for success. Renewable with 3.0 GPA.

4478. James Graham Brown Scholarships Varying numbers of scholarships of varying amounts to students meeting certain academic criteria. Must be residents of Kentucky.

4479. Presidential Scholarships 20 scholarships of $5,000 to students in the top 10 percent of their class, with at least a 3.5 GPA, and who scored at least 27 on ACT. Renewable with 3.0 GPA.

4480. **Recognition Scholarships** 100 scholarships of $1,500 to students in the top 10 percent of their class, with at least a 3.5 GPA, and who scored at least 27 on ACT. Renewable with 3.0 GPA.

4481. **Trustee Scholarships** 10 scholarships providing full four-year costs of up to $16,120 per year to students in the top 5 percent of their class, with at least a 3.5 GPA, and who scored at least 30 on ACT. Renewable with 3.4 GPA.

4482. **Tuition Waivers** Numerous partial to full tuition waivers to students who are employees or children of employees.

4483. **Union Pacific Scholarships** Varying numbers of scholarships of varying amounts to students meeting certain criteria who are residents of states with UPRR trackage.

Kentucky State University
400 East Main Street
Frankfort, KY 40601
(800) 325-1716
http://www.kysu.edu
idyson@gwmail.kysu.edu

4484. **Athletic (Men)** Basketball, cross-country running, football, golf, tennis, and track and field scholarships.

4485. **Athletic (Women)** Basketball, cross-country running, golf, tennis, track and field, and volleyball scholarships.

4486. **Band Awards** 78 scholarships ranging from $200 to $500 to students meeting certain criteria who will be members of the band. Based on talent.

4487. **Choir Awards** 48 scholarships of approximately $500 to students meeting certain criteria who are members of the choir. Based on talent.

4488. **Gospel Ensemble Awards** 27 scholarships of approximately $200 to students meeting certain criteria who are members of the Gospel Ensemble. Based on talent.

4489. **Honor Scholarships** 10 scholarships of approximately $4,900 to students meeting certain academic criteria.

4490. **Music Awards** 5 scholarships of approximately $500 to students meeting certain criteria who will be music majors. Based on talent.

4491. **Presidential Awards** 63 scholarships ranging from $1,000 to $4,000 to students meeting certain academic criteria.

4492. **Senior Citizen Scholarships** 53 scholarships of approximately $200 to students who are senior citizens.

4493. **Service Area Awards** 33 scholarships of approximately $3,000 to students meeting certain criteria who have demonstrated service to the community.

4494. **Tuition Waivers** Numerous partial to full tuition waivers to students who are senior citizens.

4495. **Vocational Rehabilitation Awards** 63 scholarships of approximately $1,200 to students meeting certain criteria who are physically disabled.

4496. **War Orphan Scholarships** 14 scholarships of approximately $1,000 to students whose parent died while on active duty during a period of war.

Kentucky Wesleyan College
3000 Frederica Street
P.O. Box 1039
Owensboro, KY 42302-1039
(800) 999-0592
(502) 926-3111
http://www.kwc.edu
admission@kwc.edu

4497. **Athletic (Men)** Baseball, basketball, cross-country, football, golf, and soccer scholarships.

4498. **Athletic (Women)** Basketball, tennis, and volleyball scholarships.

4499. **J. G. Brown** 20 scholarships of $5,000 to students in the top 10 percent of their class, with at least a 3.5 GPA and scoring at least 28 on ACT. Renewable with a 3.25 GPA.

4500. **Presidential** 125 to 150 scholarships ranging from $500 to $3,500 to students in the top 30 percent of their class, with at least a 3.0 GPA and scoring at least 21 on ACT.

University of Kentucky
Lexington, KY 40506-0032
(606) 257-9000
http://www.uky.edu/

4501. **Athletic (Men)** Basketball, cross-country, football, golf, swimming and diving, tennis, and track and field scholarships.

4502. **Athletic (Women)** Basketball, cross-country, golf, gymnastics, swimming and diving, tennis, track and field, and volleyball scholarships.

4503. **Band Awards** 45 scholarships of varying amounts to students who are members of the band. Based on talent.

4504. **Chancellor Scholarships** 250 scholarships of varying amounts to students meeting certain academic criteria.

4505. **Commonwealth** 100 tuition scholarships to students with at least a 3.0 GPA and scoring 1100 on SAT or 27 on ACT.

4506. **Human Environmental Sciences Awards** 8 scholarships of varying amounts to students meeting certain academic criteria and majoring in an environmental science.

4507. **Kentucky Valedictorian Scholarships** 56 scholarships of varying amounts to students who were their class valedictorian and are Kentucky residents.

4508. **Music Awards** 40 scholarships of varying amounts to students who are music majors. Based on talent.

4509. **National Merit Finalist Awards** 20 scholarships of varying amounts to students who have been designated National Merit Finalists.

4510. **Otis T. Singletary Scholarships** Varying numbers of scholarships of varying amounts to students meeting certain academic criteria.

4511. **Presidential** 50 tuition scholarships to students with at least a 3.0 GPA and scoring 1100 on SAT or 27 on ACT. Renewable with a 3.0 GPA.

4512. **Project Ahead/Continuing Education for Women** Scholarships of varying amounts and internships to female undergraduate sophomores, juniors, or seniors. Awarded to prepare women for transition from school to employment in business, government, or community service.

4513. **Singletary "Honors Program"** 10 scholarships providing all college costs to students with at least a 3.5 GPA and scoring at least 1260 on SAT or 30 on ACT. Renewable with a 3.3 GPA.

4514. **Tuition Waivers** Numerous partial to full tuition waivers to students who are employees or children of employees.

4515. **University Resident Minority Scholarships** 146 scholarships of varying amounts to minority students who are living on campus.

LOUISIANA

Centenary College of Louisiana
P.O. Box 41188
Shreveport, LA 71134-0188
(318) 869-5131
http://www.centenary.edu
admissions@beta.centenary.edu

4516. **Alumni** 2 scholarships of $5,400 to students with at least a 3.5 GPA and scoring at least 1300 on SAT or 30 on ACT. Renewable with a 3.5 GPA.

4517. **Athletic (Men)** Baseball, basketball, cross-country, golf, riflery, soccer, and tennis scholarships.

4518. **Athletic (Women)** Cross-country, gymnastics, riflery, softball, tennis, and volleyball scholarships.

4519. **Dean's** Numerous $1,350 scholarships to students with at least a 3.0 GPA and scoring at least 1100 on SAT or 24 on ACT.

4520. **Music** Numerous $250 to $5,000 scholarships to students who are music majors. Audition required. Renewable with a 3.0 GPA.

4521. **President's** Numerous $2,700 scholarships to students with at least a 3.0 GPA and scoring at least 1250 on SAT or 28 on ACT. Renewable with a 3.0 GPA.

4522. **Trustee's** 7 scholarships of $4,050 to students with at least a 3.5 GPA and scoring at least 1250 on SAT or 28 on ACT. Renewable with a 3.25 GPA.

Louisiana State University
One University Place
Shreveport, LA 71115
(318) 797-5000
http://www.lsus.edu
admissions@lsus.edu

4523. **Louisiana Library Association Scholarship** 1 scholarship of $1,000 to a student majoring in Library Science. Contact the following address for details: Louisiana Library Association, P.O. Box 3058, Baton Rouge, LA 70821; or call (504) 342-4928. Deadline: May 1.

4524. **LSUS** 25 scholarships of $1,700 to students with at least a 3.5 GPA and scoring at least 20 on ACT. Renewable with a 3.2 GPA.

4525. **Valedictorian** Numerous $1,200 scholarships to students who were valedictorian of their graduating class. Renewable with a 3.0 GPA.

Louisiana State University and A&M College
Baton Rouge, LA 70803
(504) 388-6977
http://www.lsu.edu

4526. **Alumni Federation** 100 scholarships ranging from $3,780 to $4,450.

4527. **Athletic (Men)** Baseball, basketball, cross-country, football, golf, swimming and diving, tennis, and track and field scholarships.

4528. **Athletic (Women)** Basketball, cross-country, swimming and diving, tennis, track and field, and volleyball scholarships.

4529. **Chancellor's** 5 to 7 scholarships ranging from $5,380 to $7,300. Renewable.

4530. **LSU Honors** 500 scholarships of $3,030. Renewable.

4531. **LSU Merit** 50 scholarships ranging from $3,780 to $4,450.

4532. **School of Music Awards** 74 scholarships of varying amounts to music students.

Loyola University
6363 St. Charles Avenue
P.O. Box 18
New Orleans, LA 70118
(800) 456-9652
http://www.loyno.edu
admit@beta.loyno.edu

4533. **Academic** 30 scholarships of $2,000 to students with at least a 3.0 GPA and scoring at least 1140 on SAT or 28 on ACT. Renewable.

4534. **Creative Arts/Performance Awards** Varying numbers of scholarships of varying amounts to students meeting certain criteria in the areas of music and band, drama/speech, and visual arts.

4535. **Presidential** 30 full-tuition scholarships to students with at least a 3.0 GPA and scoring at least 1140 on SAT or 28 on ACT. Renewable.

Northwestern State University of Louisiana
Natchitoches, LA 71497-9990
(800) 426-3754
(318) 357-4503
http://www.nsula.edu
maggio@nsula.edu

4536. **A. A. Fredericks Scholarship** 1 scholarship of $800 to an incoming freshman who has at least a 2.5 GPA, is in the top 40 percent of his/her class, is majoring in agriculture, and demonstrates financial need. Deadline: December 1.

4537. **Academic Achievement Awards** Varying numbers of scholarships of varying amounts to students who meet certain academic criteria and are Louisiana residents.

4538. **Academic Scholarships** 100 scholarships of $1,400 to students in the top 10 percent of their class, with at least a 3.5 GPA, and who scored at least 26 on ACT. Renewable with 3.0 GPA.

4539. **Adult Student Scholarships** Varying numbers of scholarships of varying amounts to students who are over age sixty-five.

4540. **Alumni Children and Siblings Scholarships** Varying numbers of scholarships of varying amounts to students who are children or siblings of alumni and meet certain criteria.

4541. **Biological Sciences Scholarships** Varying numbers of scholarships of varying amounts to students who meet certain academic criteria and are majoring in a biological science.

4542. **Business Scholarships** Varying numbers of scholarships of varying amounts to students who meet certain academic criteria and are business majors.

4543. **Catherine Winters Scholarship** 1 scholarship of varying amount to a female undergraduate junior with at least a 3.2 GPA who is majoring in teaching/education and demonstrates financial need. Deadline: December 1.

4544. **Cheerleader Scholarships** Varying numbers of scholarships of varying amounts to students who meet certain criteria and are members of the cheerleading squad.

4545. **Choral Scholarships** Varying numbers of scholarships ranging from $250 to $700 to students who meet certain criteria and are voice music majors. Based on talent. Renewable with 2.0 GPA.

4546. **Dance Scholarships** Varying numbers of scholarships ranging from $250 to $700 to students who meet certain criteria and are dance majors. Based on talent. Renewable with 2.0 GPA.

4547. Debate Team Scholarships Varying numbers of scholarships ranging from $250 to $700 to students who meet certain criteria and are members of the debate team. Based on talent. Renewable with 2.0 GPA.

4548. Demon Band Scholarships Varying numbers of scholarships ranging from $250 to $1,200 to students who meet certain criteria and are members of the band. Based on talent. Renewable with 2.0 GPA.

4549. Education Scholarships Varying numbers of scholarships of varying amounts to students who meet certain academic criteria and are education majors.

4550. FHA Scholarship 1 scholarship of $400 to an incoming freshman who has at least a 3.0 GPA, is majoring in either education or home economics, was a member of Future Homemakers of America, and is a Louisiana resident. Deadline: December 1.

4551. Health Field Scholarships Varying numbers of scholarships of varying amounts to students who meet certain academic criteria and are majoring in a health field.

4552. John & Jewell Jones Memorial Scholarship 1 scholarship of $800 to an undergraduate who is majoring in teaching/education. Deadline: December 1.

4553. J. W. Johnson/Kiwanis Scholarship 1 scholarship of $1,500 to an incoming freshman who has at least a 2.5 GPA, is majoring in business or management, and is a resident of Natchitoches County, Louisiana. Deadline: December 1.

4554. Leadership Scholarships Varying numbers of scholarships of varying amounts to students who meet certain criteria and demonstrate leadership abilities.

4555. Out-of-State Students Scholarships Varying numbers of scholarships of varying amounts to students who meet certain academic criteria and are out-of-state residents.

4556. Peoples Bank & Trust Scholarship 1 scholarship of $1,000 to an incoming freshman who is in the top 20 percent of his/her class, demonstrates financial need, is majoring in business or management, and is a resident of Natchitoches County, Louisiana. Deadline: December 1.

4557. Presidential Scholarships 100 scholarships of $500 to students in the top 10 percent of their class, with at least a 3.0 GPA, and scored at least 25 on ACT. Renewable with 3.0 GPA.

4558. Sarah Clapp Scholarship 1 scholarship of $200 to an undergraduate junior who is in the top 20 percent of his/her class, has at least a 3.3 GPA, and is majoring in teaching/education. Deadline: December 1.

4559. Social Sciences Scholarships Varying numbers of scholarships of varying amounts to students who meet certain academic criteria and are majoring in a social science.

4560. Theater Scholarships Varying numbers of scholarships ranging from $250 to $700 to students who meet certain criteria and are theater majors. Based on talent. Renewable with 2.0 GPA.

4561. Tuition Waivers Varying numbers of partial- to full-tuition waivers to students who are employees or children of employees.

4562. Work Service Awards Varying numbers of scholarships of $1,000 to incoming freshmen who have at least a 2.5 GPA, meet other academic criteria, are graduates of Los Angeles High School, have participated in community volunteer service, and are Louisiana residents. Deadline: December 1.

Tulane University
6823 St. Charles Avenue
New Orleans, LA 70118
(504) 865-5000
http://www.tulane.edu/

4563. Athletic (Men) Basketball, cross-country, football, golf, tennis, and track and field scholarships.

4564. Athletic (Women) Basketball, cross-country, golf, tennis, track and field, and volleyball scholarships.

4565. Dean's Honors Winners 80 to 110 full-tuition scholarships to students in top 5 percent of their class and scoring at least 1200 on SAT or 28 on ACT. Based on essay, talent, leadership, community service, and recommendation. Renewable with a 2.5 GPA.

4566. Founder's Scholarships 100 scholarships of varying amounts to students meeting certain academic criteria.

4567. Mayoral Scholarships Varying numbers of scholarships of varying amounts to students meeting certain criteria who are New Orleans parish residents.

4568. **Middle–Income Scholarships** 100 scholarships to students who come from middle–income families.

4569. **ROTC Scholarships** 152 scholarships of varying amounts, totaling $834,000, to students who will be participating in Air Force, Army, or Navy ROTC.

4570. **Tuition Exchange Scholarships** Varying numbers of scholarships providing tuition costs to students who are spouses or children of faculty/staff from participating schools.

4571. **Tuition Waivers** Numerous partial- to full-tuition waivers to students who are employees or children of employees.

4572. **Tulane Scholarships** 22 scholarships of varying amounts to students selected as National Merit Finalists.

MAINE

Husson College
1 College Circle
Bangor, ME 04401
(207) 941-7000
http://www.huson.edu

4573. **Academic** 10 scholarships of $1,000 to students in the top 10 percent of their class with at least a 3.0 GPA. Renewable with a 3.4 GPA.

4574. **Academic** 2 scholarships of $1,000 to students in the top 10 percent of their class with at least a 3.0 GPA. Renewable with a 3.4 GPA.

4575. **Athletic (Men)** Basketball, golf, and soccer scholarships.

4576. **Athletic (Women)** Basketball and soccer scholarships.

University of Maine
223 Chadbourne Hall
Orono, ME 04469
(207) 581-1561
http://www.maine.ed
um-admit@maine.maine.edu

4577. **Athletic (Men)** Baseball, basketball, cross-country, football, ice hockey, soccer, swimming and diving, and track and field scholarships.

4578. **Athletic (Women)** Basketball, cross-country, field hockey, swimming and diving, and track and field scholarships.

4579. **National Merit Scholarships** Varying numbers of scholarships of approximately $3,000 to students who meet certain criteria and receive National Merit designation.

4580. **Pulp and Paper Technology** 30 scholarships of $1,000 to first–year students and 110 in–state tuition scholarships to students interested in a paper–related career and majoring in either chemistry or chemical engineering.

MARYLAND

Bowie State University
14000 Jericho Park Road
Bowie, MD 20715
(301) 464-3000
http://www.bowiestate.edu

4581. **Harold Ferguson** Numerous $600 scholarships to students with at least a 3.0 GPA and scoring at least 800 on SAT. Renewable with a 3.0 GPA.

4582. **Litton Industries** Numerous $500 scholarships to students with at least a 3.0 GPA and scoring at least 800 on SAT. Renewable with a 3.0 GPA.

4583. **Mid–Atlantic Coca–Cola Bottling Company Scholarship** 3 scholarships of $1,000 to freshman minority students majoring in information systems, accounting, business, or marketing. Based on financial need. Renewable with a 2.5 GPA.

4584. **Tuition Waiver** 24 tuition waivers to students with at least a 3.0 GPA and scoring at least 1000 on SAT. Renewable with a 3.0 GPA.

Frostburg State University
Frostburg, MD 21532
(301) 689-4000
http://www.fsu.umd.edu

4585. **Academic Merit** 55 to 60 tuition scholarships to students with at least a 3.25 GPA and scoring at least 1100 on SAT. Renewable with a 3.75 GPA.

4586. **Aden Lewis Music** 1 scholarship of $350 to a music major.

4587. **Foundation Honors Program** 8 scholarships ranging from $500 to $2,000 to students with at least a 3.5 GPA and scoring at least 1200 on SAT.

4588. **HPER Scholarship** 1 scholarship of varying amount to a student majoring in physical education.

4589. **Kelly–Springfield Scholarship** 1 scholarship of $1,750 to an undergraduate junior or senior majoring in accounting, business, or economics. Must be a U.S. citizen and have financial need. Renewable.

4590. **Presidential** 25 scholarships of $500 to students with at least a 3.0 GPA and scoring at least 1000 on SAT. Renewable with a 3.25 GPA.

Johns Hopkins University
3400 North Charles Street
Baltimore, MD 21218
(410) 516-8171
http://www.jhu.edu

4591. **Beneficial Hodson** 20 awards of three–fifths tuition to students in top 20 percent of class, with a 3.8 GPA, and scoring at least 1400 on SAT. Renewable with a 3.0 GPA.

4592. **National Achievement Scholarship** 1 scholarship of varying amount. Based on academic merit.

4593. **National Merit** Numerous scholarships to students selected as National Merit Finalists.

4594. **National Society of Professional Engineers** 3 scholarships of varying amounts to students majoring in engineering.

Towson State University
Towson, MD 21204-7097
(410) 830-2000
http://www.towson.edu

4595. **Athletic (Men)** Baseball, basketball, cross-country, football, lacrosse, soccer, swimming and diving, tennis, and track and field scholarships.

4596. **Athletic (Women)** Basketball, cross-country, field hockey, gymnastics, lacrosse, softball, swimming and diving, tennis, track and field, and volleyball scholarships.

4597. **Board of Directors** Numerous scholarships providing tuition plus some fees to students with at least a 3.5 GPA and scoring at least 1200 on SAT. Renewable with a 3.25 GPA.

4598. **Dean's** Numerous $500 scholarships. Based on academic merit.

4599. **Handicapped Student** Numerous scholarships providing tuition and fees to handicapped students with at least a 3.0 GPA. Renewable with a 2.75 GPA.

4600. **Minority Merit Honors Program** 25 or more scholarships of $1,000 to minority students. Based on academic merit.

4601. **Provost's** 20 scholarships of $500 to students with at least a 3.25 GPA and scoring at least 1100 on SAT.

4602. **University** Numerous $1,000 scholarships to students with at least a 3.5 GPA and scoring at least 1200 on SAT.

University of Maryland
North Administration Boulevard
College Park, MD 20742-1672
(800) 422-5867
http://www.umd.edu
umadmit@uga.umd.edu

4603. **Alcoa Transportation** 1 scholarship of $1,000 to an undergraduate junior or senior pursuing a career in transportation or traffic management. Merit-based awards are for full-time students enrolled in the College of Business and Management. Contact the Chairperson, Transportation Department. Deadline: February.

4604. **Allied Scholarship Program Awards** Varying numbers of scholarships of varying amounts to students meeting certain academic criteria who will be majoring in business or management.

4605. **American Society of Heating, Refrigeration, and Air Conditioning** 2 scholarships ranging from $2,500 to $6,000 to undergraduate sophomores or above who are African American, Hispanic American, or Native American engineering majors. Deadline: December 15.

4606. **Applied Physics Lab Scholarships** Varying numbers of scholarships of varying amounts to students meeting certain criteria who are children of employees of Applied Physics Lab.

4607. **Baltimore Sun Papers Awards** Varying numbers of scholarships of varying amounts to students meeting certain criteria who are journalism majors.

4608. **Banneker** 20 full-tuition scholarships to students with at least a 3.0 GPA and scoring at least 1000 on SAT. Renewable.

4609. **Chancellor's** 25 full-tuition scholarships to students in the top 10 percent of their class with at least a 3.5 GPA. Renewable.

4610. **College of Journalism High School Senior Scholarship** 1 scholarship of $10,000 to an outstanding high school senior who will be majoring in print journalism. Must have graduated from a Maryland high school. Deadline: March 1.

4611. **Creative and Performance Arts Awards** 60 scholarships of $2,100 to entering freshmen and transfer students meeting certain criteria who will be majoring in art, music, dance, or drama. Based on talent.

4612. **General Honors** 80 scholarships of $500 to students in the top 10 percent of their class, with at least a 3.7 GPA, and scoring at least 1350 on SAT. Renewable.

4613. **George Hyman Construction Scholarships** Varying numbers of scholarships of varying amounts to students meeting certain academic criteria who will be majoring in construction or civil engineering.

4614. **Glenn L. Martin Awards** Varying numbers of scholarships of varying amounts to students meeting certain academic criteria.

4615. **Hecht Company Scholarships** Varying numbers of scholarships of varying amounts to students meeting certain academic criteria.

4616. **Helen Linthicum Scholarships** Varying numbers of scholarships of varying amounts to students meeting certain academic criteria.

4617. **John Hopkins University Scholarships** Varying numbers of scholarships of varying amounts to students meeting certain criteria who are children of employees of Johns Hopkins University.

4618. **Journalism Scholarships** Varying numbers of scholarships of varying amounts to undergraduate students meeting certain criteria who are journalism majors.

4619. **Kelly Award Scholarships** Varying numbers of scholarships of varying amounts to students meeting certain academic criteria.

4620. **Key Scholarships** 41 scholarships providing tuition plus fees to students in the top 5 percent of their class, who scored at least 1250 on SAT, and who have at least a 3.6 GPA. Renewable with a 3.2 GPA.

4621. **Math Competition Scholarships** Varying numbers of scholarships of varying amounts to students based on a math competition.

4622. **McCormick Scholarships** Varying numbers of scholarships of varying amounts to students meeting certain academic criteria who will be majoring in business or management.

4623. **Mobile Oil Scholarships** Varying numbers of scholarships of varying amounts to students meeting certain academic criteria who will be engineering majors.

4624. **National Achievement Awards** Varying numbers of scholarships of varying amounts to students meeting certain academic criteria.

4625. **National Action Council for Minorities in Engineering Awards** Varying numbers of scholarships of varying amounts to minority students meeting certain academic criteria who will be engineering majors.

4626. **National Merit Awards** Varying numbers of scholarships of varying amounts to students who received National Merit designations.

4627. **NUS Corp. for Black Engineering Minorities Awards** Varying numbers of scholarships of varying amounts to African American students meeting certain academic criteria who will be majoring in engineering.

4628. **Regents** Numerous scholarships covering all costs to students with a 4.0 GPA and scoring at least 1400 on SAT. Renewable with a 3.5 GPA.

4629. **Sigma Delta Chi Scholarships** Varying numbers of scholarships of varying amounts to students meeting certain criteria who are journalism majors.

4630. **Tuition Waivers** Numerous partial to full tuition waivers to students who are employees, children of employees, or senior citizens.

4631. **UM Band Scholarships** Varying numbers of scholarships of varying amounts to students meeting certain criteria and who are members of the UM Band.

4632. **University Honors Program Scholarships** 600 scholarships ranging from $200 to $2,500 to students with at least a 3.0 GPA who meet other academic criteria.

4633. **Winslow Foundation Scholarships** Varying numbers of scholarships of varying amounts to students meeting certain academic criteria who will be majoring in agriculture.

Western Maryland College
Westminister, MD 21157
(800) 638-5005
http://www.wmde.edu

4634. **Eagle Scout** $1,000 scholarships are guaranteed to Eagle Scouts.

4635. **General** Numerous scholarships ranging from $1,000 to $3,000 to students with at least a 3.5 GPA and scoring at least 1100 on SAT. Renewable with a 3.0 GPA.

4636. **Presidential Honors Program** 25 scholarships of up to tuition to students with at least a 3.5 GPA and scoring at least 1100 on SAT. Renewable with a 3.0 GPA.

MASSACHUSETTS

American International College
1000 State Street
Springfield, MA 01109-9183
(413) 747-7000
http://www.aic.edu

4637. **Athletic (Men)** Baseball, basketball, football, and ice hockey scholarships.

4638. **Athletic (Women)** Basketball, softball, and volleyball scholarships.

4639. **Freshman Academic** 60 scholarships ranging from $100 to $4,620 to students in the top 20 percent of their class. Renewable.

Boston College
Chestnut Hill, MA 02167
(617) 552-8000
http://www.bc.edu

4640. **Athletic (Men)** Basketball, cross-country, football, ice hockey, lacrosse, soccer, and track and field scholarships.

4641. **Athletic (Women)** Basketball, cross-country, soccer, softball, swimming and diving, tennis, track and field, and volleyball scholarships.

4642. **Boston College** Numerous scholarships of $500 to $9,900. Based on academic merit. Renewable with a 3.0 GPA.

4643. **Boston College Grant** Numerous grants of $500 to $9,900.

4644. **Presidential Scholarships** 11 scholarships of varying amounts to students meeting certain academic criteria.

4645. **Tuition Waivers** Numerous partial- to full-tuition waivers to students who are employees or children of employees.

Boston University
121 Bay State Road
Boston, MA 02215
(617) 353-2300
http://www.bu.edu

4646. **Athletic (Men)** Baseball, basketball, crew, football, ice hockey, soccer, swimming and diving, tennis, track and field, and wrestling scholarships.

4647. **Athletic (Women)** Basketball, crew, field hockey, softball, swimming and diving, tennis, and track and field scholarships.

4648. **Bookbuilders Scholarships** 1 or 2 scholarships ranging from $500 to $1,000 to graduate journalism students with an interest in publishing. Based on academic achievement and interest. Deadline: May 1.

4649. **City of Boston High School Scholars Awards** Varying numbers of scholarships of varying amounts to students who meet certain academic criteria.

4650. **Creative Arts/Performance Awards** 35 scholarships of varying amounts to students who meet certain criteria and are majoring in visual arts, music, or theater.

4651. **Dean's Scholarships** Varying numbers of scholarships of varying amounts to students who meet certain academic criteria.

4652. **Dennis Kauff Memorial Fellowship** 1 fellowship providing full tuition to an undergraduate senior or graduate student based on academic achievement.

4653. **Max Kase Scholarship** 1 scholarship of at least $1,000 to freshman journalism major who has outstanding academic achievement and financial need.

4654. **Nathan H. Miller Award** 1 scholarship award of $1,000 to an undergraduate junior who works on the school daily newspaper. Based on academic achievement and financial need.

4655. **National Merit Scholars Awards** Varying numbers of scholarships of varying amounts to students designated as National Merit Scholars.

4656. **RKO General Inc. Scholarships** 5 scholarships of up to full tuition ($14,950) to graduate minority students pursuing careers in communications. Contact the College of Communication, Department P.

4657. **ROTC Supplemental Grants** Varying numbers of supplemental grants of varying amounts to students who meet certain criteria and are members of ROTC.

4658. **School of Education President's Scholar's Awards** Varying numbers of scholarships of varying amounts to students who meet certain academic criteria.

4659. **School of Education Dean's Scholar's Awards** Varying numbers of scholarships of varying amounts to students who meet certain academic criteria.

4660. **Stern Spector Prize Fund** 1 scholarship award of at least $300 to an undergraduate junior or senior based on merit.

4661. **Trustee** 30 to 35 tuition scholarships to students in the top 5 percent of their class, with at least a 3.5 GPA, and scoring at least 1300 on SAT. Renewable with a 3.5 GPA.

Emerson College
100 Beacon Street
Boston, MA 02116
(617) 824-8600
http://www.emerson.edu

4662. **Dean's** 80 scholarships of varying amounts. Based on academic merit.

4663. **Restricted** 50 scholarships ranging from $300 to $3,000 to students with at least a 3.0 GPA. Renewable with a 3.0 GPA.

4664. **Trustee Awards** 20 scholarships of varying amounts. Based on academic merit.

Harvard University
8 Garden Street, Byerly Hall
Cambridge, MA 02138
(617) 495-2202
http://www.harvard.edu

4665. **Baxendale, Borden, Pennoyer, or Murphy** Any student with one of these surnames is eligible for a scholarship of varying amount.

4666. **Charles J. Paine Scholarship Fund Trust** 6 scholarship grants ranging from $1,500 to $3,500 to undergraduates. Submit a letter with financial situation and biographical information. Write to the Fund Trust, c/o Taylor, Granson, & Perrin, 160 Franklin Street, Boston, MA 02110 (617) 951-2777.

4667. **Grace T. Blanchard Trust and Flora T. Blanchard Scholarships** Grants of $2,000 to students who are Massachusetts residents. Contact: Gary A. Petersen, c/o Easton Bank & Trust Company, 225 Essex Street, Salem MA 01980-3728, (617) 599-2100.

4668. **Need-Based Assistance** Numerous need-based scholarships, loans, and work-study programs open to anyone accepted for admission who has financial need. Contact the financial aid office.

Massachusetts Institute of Technology
77 Massachusetts Avenue
Room 4-237 Communications
Cambridge, MA 02139-4301
(617) 253-1000
http://web.mit.edu

4669. **Charles J. Paine Scholarship Fund Trust** Varying numbers of scholarship grants ranging from $1,500 to $3,500 to students meeting certain criteria. Must write a letter detailing educational and financial information. Contact: Trustee, c/o Taylor, Granson & Perrin, 160 Franklin Street, Boston, MA 02110.

4670. **Gorman Foundation** 25 scholarship grants ranging from $1,250 to $3,000 to students who are residents of St. Louis and graduated from a St. Louis High School. Contact: c/o Wayne L. Millsap, P.C., 7777 Bonhomme Street, Suite 2300, Clayton, MO 06315. Deadline: November 1 (for spring semester); May 31 (for summer and fall semesters).

4671. **Tuition Waivers** numerous partial- to full-tuition waivers to students who are employees or children of employees.

Northeastern University
360 Huntington Avenue
Boston, MA 02115
(617) 437-2000
http://www.neu.edu/
admissions@neu.edu

4672. **Athletic (Men)** Baseball, basketball, crew, cross-country running, football, golf, ice hockey, soccer, swimming and diving, tennis, and track and field scholarships.

4673. **Athletic (Women)** Basketball, crew, cross-country running, field hockey, gymnastics, ice hockey, swimming and diving, track and field, and volleyball scholarships.

4674. **Boston Housing Authority Scholarships** 48 scholarships of varying amounts, totaling $476,640, to students who are local residents and meet certain criteria.

4675. **Carl Ell Scholarships** 45 scholarships covering all costs to students in the top 15 percent of their class who scored at least 1200 on SAT or 26 on ACT. Renewable with 3.25 GPA.

4676. **Community Scholarships** 88 scholarships of varying amounts to students meeting certain academic criteria who are local residents.

4677. **Merit Scholarships** Varying numbers of scholarships covering tuition costs to students in the top 15 percent of their class who meet other academic criteria. Renewable with a 3.25 GPA.

4678. **Ralph Bunche "Honors Program" Scholarships** 10 scholarships covering all costs to students in the top 15 percent of their class who scored at least 1000 on SAT or 26 on ACT. Renewable with a 3.25 GPA.

4679. **Tuition Waivers** Numerous partial- to full-tuition waivers to students who are employees, children of employees, or senior citizens.

Tufts University
Medford, MA 02155
(617) 381-3170
http://www.tufts.edu

4680. **National Merit** 13 scholarships averaging $1,400 to entering students who were selected as National Merit Finalists.

4681. **Need-Based Assistance** Numerous need-based scholarships, loans, and work-study programs open to anyone accepted for admission who has financial need. Contact the financial aid office.

University of Massachusetts
Whitmore Building
Amherst, MA 01003-0001
(413) 545-0222
http://www.umass.edu

4682. **Alumni Academic Scholarships** 50 scholarships of $4,000 to students in the top 10 percent of their class, with at least a 3.5 GPA, and who scored at least 1200 on SAT. Renewable.

4683. **Athletic (Men)** Baseball, basketball, cross-country running, football, gymnastics, ice hockey, lacrosse, skiing (downhill), soccer, swimming and diving, tennis, track and field, and water polo.

4684. **Athletic (Women)** Basketball, cross-country running, field hockey, gymnastics, lacrosse, skiing (downhill), soccer, softball, swimming and diving, tennis, track and field, and volleyball.

4685. **Chancellor's Academic Scholarships** 31 scholarships of tuition to students in the top 5 percent of their class who scored at least 1250 on SAT.

4686. **Chancellor's Arts Scholarships** 27 scholarships of tuition to students in the top 5 percent of their class, who scored at least 1250 on SAT, and who will be art majors.

MICHIGAN

Albion College
611 East Porter
Albion, MI 49224-1899
(800) 858-6770
(517) 629-0440
http://www.albion.edu
admissions@albion.Edu

4687. **Ford Institute** 22 scholarships of varying amounts. Based on academic achievement.

4688. **Music** 43 scholarships ranging from $300 to $1,000 to students who are music majors. Audition required. Renewable.

4689. **Presidential Recognition** 64 scholarships of $5,000 to students with at least a 3.9 GPA; must be one of the top ten students in class; must have scored at least 1200 on SAT or 26 on ACT. Deadline: April 1. Renewable.

4690. **Professional Management Scholarships** Numerous scholarships of varying amounts to students majoring in business.

4691. **Theatre Creative Arts** 10 scholarships of varying amounts to students majoring in theatre.

4692. **Trustee** 26 scholarships of varying amounts to students selected as National Merit Finalists.

4693. **Visual Arts/Creative Arts** 9 scholarships of varying amounts to students majoring in the visual arts.

4694. **Webster** 150 scholarships ranging from $300 to $2,500 to students in the top 10 percent of their class, with at least a 3.7 GPA, and scoring at least 1200 on SAT or 26 on ACT. Renewable.

GMI Engineering and Management Institute
1700 West Third Avenue
Flint, MI 48054-4898
(800) 955-4464
(810) 762-7865
http://www.gmi.edu
admissions@gmi.edu

4695. **AIM Scholarships** 2 scholarships of varying amounts to incoming freshmen who meet certain academic criteria.

4696. **ASPIRE Scholarships** Varying numbers of scholarships of varying amounts to students meeting certain academic criteria.

4697. **Co-op Program** Five-year 100 percent tuition to high school seniors or graduates interested in a bachelor's degree in engineering or management. Students alternate twelve-week periods of academics with twelve weeks of work experience. Two-phase admission process: academic acceptance and employment by corporate sponsor. Students are encouraged to apply early in their senior year.

4698. **Junior Achievement Inc.** Full tuition for the first year, and 50 percent tuition and co-op work thereafter for outstanding high school students who are members of a Junior Achievement applied-economics class.

4699. **LULAC Scholarships** Varying numbers of scholarships of varying amounts to students meeting certain academic criteria.

4700. **McKinnon Scholarships** Varying numbers of scholarships of varying amounts to students meeting certain criteria who are local county residents.

4701. **Michigan Society of Professional Engineers Scholarships** Varying numbers of scholarships of varying amounts to students meeting certain academic criteria.

4702. **Mott Scholarships** varying numbers of scholarships of varying amounts to students meeting certain academic criteria.

4703. **National Society of Professional Engineers** Varying numbers of scholarships of varying amounts to students meeting certain academic criteria who are engineering majors.

4704. **Odyssey of the Mind Scholarships** Varying numbers of scholarships of varying amounts to students meeting certain academic criteria.

4705. **PRIME Scholarships** Varying numbers of scholarships of varying amounts to students meeting certain academic criteria.

4706. **Provost** 2 scholarships providing $1,550 or 25 percent of tuition to students in the top 10 percent of their class, with at least a 3.8 GPA, and scoring at least 1250 on SAT or 30 on ACT.

4707. **Say Yes to GMI** 25 scholarships of $1,000 to students in the top 10 percent of their class, with at least a 3.0 GPA, and scoring at least 1200 on SAT or 27 on ACT.

4708. **Trustee** 2 scholarships providing $3,100 or 50 percent of tuition to students in the top 3 percent of their class, with at least a 3.9 GPA, and scoring 1300 on SAT or 32 on ACT.

Michigan State University
East Lansing, MI 48824-1046
(517) 355-1855
http://www.msu.edu
admis@msu.edu

4709. **Academic Excellence** 500 scholarships ranging from $300 to $500 to students in the top 5 percent of their class with at least a 3.85 GPA.

4710. **Alumni Distinguished** 10 scholarships ranging from $5,000 to $7,500 to students in the top 5 percent of their class, with at least a 3.72 GPA, and scoring at least 1300 on SAT or 30 on ACT. Renewable with a 3.2 GPA.

4711. **Athletic (Men)** Basketball, cross-country, football, golf, gymnastics, ice hockey, soccer, swimming and diving, tennis, track and field, and wrestling scholarships.

4712. **Athletic (Women)** Basketball, cross-country, field hockey, golf, gymnastics, swimming and diving, tennis, track and field, and volleyball scholarships.

4713. **Creative Arts** 20 scholarships of $500 to students who will be or are majoring in art, dance/drama, or music. Based on portfolio/audition and talent. Renewable.

4714. **Distinguished Freshman** 15 scholarships ranging from $2,000 to $5,000 to students in the top 5 percent of their class, with at least a 3.6 GPA and scoring at least 1300 on SAT or 30 on ACT. Renewable with a 3.2 GPA.

4715. **Distinguished Minority "Honors Program"** 15 scholarships of $2,000 to minority students in the top 20 percent of their class with at least a 3.0 GPA. Renewable.

University of Michigan
1220 Student Activities Building
Ann Arbor, MI 48109-1316
(734) 764-7433
http://www.umich.edu
usadmiss@umich.edu

4716. **Academic** 75 scholarships of $2,000. Based on academic merit.

4717. **American Indian Grants** 10 scholarships of varying amounts to students meeting certain criteria who are of Native American ancestry.

4718. **Art Awards** Numerous scholarships of varying amounts to students meeting certain criteria who are art majors. Based on talent.

4719. **Backham Undergraduate Scholarships** 4 scholarships of $1,000 to entering students who meet certain academic criteria. Must be Michigan residents. Honors students are invited to apply.

4720. **Bently Scholarships** 2 scholarships of $8,119 to entering freshman students who meet certain academic criteria; students must be interviewed.

4721. **Drama/Theater Awards** Varying numbers of scholarships of varying amounts to students who meet certain criteria and who are drama/theater majors. Based on talent.

4722. **Junior College** Numerous $500 scholarships to students transferring from a junior college.

4723. **Michigan Achievement** 200 scholarships of varying amounts to students in the top 10 percent of their class, with at least a 3.2 GPA, and scoring at least 1000 on SAT. Renewable.

4724. **Michigan Annual Giving** 225 scholarships of $1,500 to students with at least a 3.5 GPA and scoring at least 1000 on SAT or 23 on ACT.

4725. **Michigan Scholar Awards** 133 scholarships of varying amounts to minority students meeting certain criteria who are out-of-state residents.

4726. **National Achievement Scholarship** 1 scholarship of varying amount to a minority student who meets certain academic criteria.

4727. **Rackham** Numerous $1,000 renewable scholarships.

4728. **Regents Alumni** 335 scholarships of $1,000 to students in the top 1 percent of their class, with at least a 3.9 GPA, and scoring at least 1260 on SAT and 28 on ACT.

4729. **Scholar Recognition Awards** 70 scholarships of varying amounts to students meeting certain criteria.

4730. **School of Music Scholarships** 110 partial scholarships of varying amounts to graduate students who meet certain academic and financial criteria.

4731. **Slater** 8 to 12 scholarships of $2,000. Renewable.

4732. **Waltz** 4 to 12 scholarships of $1,000. Renewable.

MINNESOTA

Carleton College
One North College Street
Northfield, MN 55057
(507) 663-4000
http://www.carleton.edu
admissions@acs.carleton.edu

4733. **National Achievement** Numerous scholarships of varying amounts. Based on academic merit.

4734. **National Merit** Numerous scholarships ranging from $750 to $2,000 to students selected as National Merit Scholars. Renewable.

Concordia College
275 North Syndicate Street
St. Paul, MN 55104-5494
(612) 641-8278
http://www.csp.edu/
admiss@luther.csp.edu

4735. **Academic/Activity** Numerous scholarships ranging from $200 to $800 to students in top 30 percent of class, with at least a 3.25 GPA, and scoring at least 24 on ACT. Renewable with a 3.25 GPA.

4736. **Dean's Academic** 5 scholarships providing 25 percent of tuition. Renewable with a 3.25 GPA.

4737. **Dean's Leadership** 5 scholarships providing 25 percent of tuition. Renewable.

4738. **President's Academic** Numerous scholarships of 50 percent of tuition costs. Renewable with a 3.5 GPA.

4739. **President's Leadership** Numerous scholarships of 50 percent of tuition costs. Renewable.

Macalester College
1600 Grand Avenue
St. Paul, MN 55105-1899
(800) 231-7974
(651) 696-6000
http://www.macalstr.edu

4740. **Catherine Laeltad** Numerous $10,000 scholarships to students in the top 25 percent of their class. Must have been selected a National Merit Finalist. Renewable.

4741. **Dewitt Wallace** Numerous $10,000 scholarships to students in the top 15 percent of their class. Must have been selected a National Merit Finalist. Renewable.

University of Minnesota
231 Pillsbury Place, S.E., 240 Williamson Hall
Minneapolis, MN 55455
(612) 625-2008
http://www.umn.edu/tc/

4742. **Allis Honor Awards** Numerous scholarships of varying amounts to students majoring in liberal arts.

4743. **Athletic (Men)** Basketball, cross-country, football, golf, gymnastics, ice hockey, swimming and diving, tennis, track and field, and wrestling scholarships.

4744. **Athletic (Women)** Basketball, cross-country, golf, gymnastics, swimming and diving, tennis, track and field, and volleyball scholarships.

4745. **Katz Minority Scholarships** 50 scholarships ranging from $1,000 to $3,000 for Early Notification. Renewable.

4746. **National Merit** Numerous scholarships of varying amounts to students designated as National Merit Finalists.

4747. **Presidential Scholar** 175 scholarships ranging from $500 to $1,700 to students in the top 5 percent of their class. Renewable.

4748. **Searles Awards** Numerous scholarships of varying amounts to students who are home economics majors.

MISSISSIPPI

Belhaven College
1500 Peachtree Street
Jackson, MS 39202
(601) 968-5928
http://www.belhaven.edu

4749. **Academic** Numerous scholarships ranging from $1,350 to $5,900 to students with at least a 3.5 GPA and scoring 1000 on SAT or 24 on ACT. Renewable with a 3.25 GPA.

4750. **Art** Numerous scholarships ranging from $500 to $1,500. Based on portfolio. Renewable.

4751. **Athletic (Men)** Basketball, soccer, and tennis scholarships.

4752. **Athletic (Women)** Basketball scholarships.

4753. **Leadership** Numerous scholarships ranging from $300 to $1,000 to students with a 3.0 GPA and scoring at least 875 on SAT or 20 on ACT. Renewable with a 2.5 GPA.

4754. **Music Honors Program** Numerous scholarships ranging from $500 to $1,500 to students majoring in music. Audition required. Renewable.

Jackson State University
1400 J. R. Lynch Street
Jackson, MS 39217
(601) 968-2121
http://www.jsums.edu/

4755. **Academic** 150 scholarships ranging from $1,072 to $3,100 to students with at least a 3.0 GPA and scoring at least 810 on SAT or 18 on ACT. Renewable with a 3.0 GPA.

4756. **Academic Honors Program** Numerous scholarships ranging from $610 to $1,000 to students with at least a 3.0 GPA and scoring at least 700 on SAT or 14 on ACT.

4757. **Athletic (Men)** Baseball, basketball, football, golf, tennis, and track and field scholarships.

4758. **Athletic (Women)** Basketball and track and field scholarships.

University of Mississippi
University, MS 38677
(601) 232-7226
http://www.olemiss.edu
info@olemiss.edu

4759. **Academic Excellence** 150 to 200 scholarships ranging from $1,250 to $2,932 to students in the top 15 percent of their class, with at least a 3.6 GPA, and scoring at least 1120 on SAT or 27 on ACT. Renewable with a 3.0 GPA.

4760. **Athletic (Men)** Baseball, basketball, cross-country, football, golf, tennis, and track and field scholarships.

4761. **Athletic (Women)** Basketball, cross-country, tennis, track and field, and volleyball scholarships.

4762. **Band** 300 scholarships ranging from $100 up to tuition to students who are band and music majors. Audition required. Renewable.

4763. **Chancellor's** 40 scholarships of $750 to students with at least a 3.76 GPA. Renewable with a 3.5 GPA.

4764. **Fine Arts** 50 scholarships ranging from $100 to $2,282 to students majoring in fine arts. Renewable.

4765. **Junior College Achievement** 80 to 110 scholarships ranging from $800 to $1,900 to transfer students from community colleges. Must have at least a 3.5 GPA. Renewable with a 3.0 GPA.

4766. **Regional** 55 scholarships of $1,182 to students in the top 10 percent of their class and scoring at least 860 on SAT or 20 on ACT. Renewable with a 3.0 GPA.

MISSOURI

Central Missouri State University
Warrensburg, MO 64093-5222
(800) 956-0177
http://www.cmsu.edu
dhudson@cmsuvmb.cmsu.edu

4767. **Achievement Awards** Unlimited scholarships ranging from $200 to $600. Renewable.

4768. **Athletic (Men)** Basketball, cross-country, football, golf, track and field, and wrestling scholarships.

4769. **Athletic (Women)** Basketball, cross-country, track and field, and volleyball scholarships.

4770. **Distinguished** 35 scholarships providing total costs to students in the top 5 percent of their class, with at least a 3.75 GPA, and scoring at least 27 on ACT. Renewable with a 3.75 GPA.

4771. **Foundation Awards** Unlimited number of scholarships from $100 to $3,724. Renewable.

4772. **H.S. Recognition** 125 scholarships of $500 to students in the top 50 percent of their class.

4773. **Merit** Numerous $800 scholarships to students in the top 20 percent of their class. Renewable with a 3.25 GPA.

4774. **Regents** Numerous $800 scholarships to students in the top 10 percent of their class. Renewable with a 3.25 GPA.

Columbia College
1001 Rogers Street
Columbia, MO 65216
(573) 875-8700
http://www.ccis.edu
admissions@cclshp.ccis.edu

4775. **Achieving Curricular Excellence** Numerous scholarships of varying amounts. Based on extracurricular activities.

4776. **Athletic (Men)** Basketball and soccer scholarships.

4777. **Athletic (Women)** Volleyball scholarships.

4778. **Creative Arts/Performance Awards** 7 scholarships of varying amounts to students in fashion, music, applied art, and design.

4779. **Eagle Scout** A $500 scholarship for an Eagle Scout.

4780. **Valedictorian/Salutatorian** Numerous scholarships of varying amounts to students who were valedictorian or salutatorian of their graduating high school senior class.

Drury College
900 North Benton Avenue
Springfield, MO 65802
(417) 865-8731
http://www.drury.edu
druyad@lib.drury.edu

4781. **Academic** Numerous scholarships ranging from $1,000 to $2,500 to students with at least a 2.9 GPA and scoring at least 980 on SAT or 21 on ACT. Renewable with a 2.75 GPA.

4782. **Athletic (Men)** Basketball, golf, swimming and diving, and tennis scholarships.

4783. **Athletic (Women)** Swimming and diving, tennis, and volleyball scholarships.

4784. **Competitive** Numerous scholarships ranging from $600 to $800. Renewable with a 2.75 GPA.

4785. **Presidential** 4 scholarships of $3,000. Renewable with a 2.75 GPA.

4786. **Trustees** 1 full-tuition scholarship to a student who scored at least 1300 on SAT or 29 on ACT. Renewable with a 3.0 GPA.

Missouri Valley College
500 East College
Marshall, MO 65340
(660) 831-4114
http://www.murlin.com/
mo-valley@juno.com

4787. **Academic** 50 scholarships ranging from $800 to $2,800 to students in the top 33 percent of their class, with at least a 3.0 GPA, and scoring at least 1000 on SAT or 26 on ACT. Renewable with a 3.2 GPA.

4788. **Board of Trustees** 6 tuition scholarships to students in the top 10 percent of their class, with at least a 3.7 GPA, and scoring at least 1150 on SAT or 28 on ACT. Renewable with a 3.3 GPA.

4789. **Eagle Scouts, Explorers, and Brotherhood Members of the Order of the Arrow** Scholarships of $3,500 per year for four years and a $1,000 work-and-learn stipend.

4790. **Talent** 30 scholarships ranging from $500 to $2,000 to students in the top 50 percent of their class with at least a 2.0 GPA. Renewable with a 2.0 GPA.

Southwest Missouri State University
901 South National
Springfield, MO 65804
(800) 492-7900
http://www.smsu.edu

4791. **Alumni "Honors Program" Scholarships** Varying numbers of scholarships of $1,440 to students in the top 20 percent of their class who scored at least 23 on ACT. Renewable with 3.5 GPA.

4792. **Athletic (Men)** Baseball, basketball, cross-country running, football, golf, soccer, swimming and diving, tennis, track and field, and wrestling scholarships.

4793. **Athletic (Women)** Basketball, cross-country running, field hockey, golf, softball, tennis, track and field, and volleyball scholarships.

4794. **Emily Nelson Moseley Memorial Scholarships** 3 scholarship grants of $2,000 to undergraduate juniors, seniors, and graduate students in Special Education. Selection is based on academic achievement. Recipients must enroll in Reading and Special Education Department. Contact: Scholarship Coordinator. Deadline: May 1.

4795. **Florence C. Painter Memorial Scholarships** 2 scholarship grants of $2,000 to undergraduate seniors and graduate students in secondary education. Must have at least a 3.0 GPA and demonstrate financial need. Preference given to those students planning to teach Spanish. Contact the Scholarship Coordinator. Deadline: May 1.

4796. **Foreign Languages Regents Scholarships** 4 scholarship grants ranging from $1,000 to $1,200 to undergraduates with at least a 3.0 GPA, who have taken 12 credit hours of one language and earned an A in each course, and are majoring in foreign languages; must participate in departmental events. Contact the Scholarship Coordinator.

4797. **Freshman Academic Scholarships** 40 scholarships of varying amounts to students meeting certain academic criteria.

4798. **Inmon Memorial Scholarship** 10 scholarship grants ranging from $1,962 to $3,786 to undergraduate seniors or graduate students in business. Must carry at least 12 hours each semester, maintain at least a 3.2 GPA, and be U.S. citizens. Preference is given to Missouri natives. Contact the Scholarship Coordinator. Deadline: February 8.

4799. **In-School Players Scholarships** 6 grants ranging from $1,000 to $1,200 to undergraduate students majoring in dance or theater. Must have performance experience in acting and/or music. Contact the Scholarship Coordinator.

4800. **Junior and Community College President's Scholarships** 32 scholarship grants ranging from $2,326 to $4,186 to undergraduate students nominated by presidents of Missouri public junior and community colleges. Must have at least 30 credit hours. Contact the Scholarship Coordinator.

4801. **Junior and Community College Regents Scholarships** 16 scholarship grants ranging from $1,000 to $1,200 to transferring students who have associate degrees or sixty acceptable credit hours from a Missouri junior or community college and at least a cumulative 3.4 GPA. Must be Missouri residents. Contact the Scholarship Coordinator. Deadline: May 1.

4802. **Minority Leadership Scholarships** 31 scholarships providing certain fees to minority students in the upper 50 percent of their class who have demonstrated leadership abilities and community service. Renewable with a 2.0 GPA.

4803. **Music Regents Scholarships** 81 scholarships ranging from $1,000 to $1,200 to students meeting certain criteria who are music majors. Based on talent as shown in an audition. Contact the Scholarship Coordinator.

4804. **Presidential Leadership Council Scholarships** 20 scholarships providing certain fees to students in the upper 20 percent of their class who scored at least 23 on ACT and have demonstrated leadership abilities.

4805. **Presidential Scholarships** 50 scholarships providing total costs to students in the upper 10 percent of the class who scored at least 1240 on SAT or 30 on ACT. Renewable with a 3.5 GPA.

4806. **President's Scholarships** 24 scholarships of varying amounts to students designated as National Merit Finalists.

4807. **Regents Scholarships** 400 scholarships providing two-thirds of fees to students in the upper 10 percent of their class who scored at least 23 on ACT. Renewable with a 3.5 GPA.

4808. **Student Government Scholarships** 6 scholarships of varying amounts to students who have demonstrated leadership abilities and community service.

4809. **Theater and Dance Activity Regents Scholarships** 16 scholarship grants ranging from $1,000 to $1,200 to undergraduate students in theater or dance. Must have at least a 2.5 GPA,

have participated in related activities, and have departmental faculty recommendation. May reapply for renewal. Audition or interview required. Contact the Scholarship Coordinator. Deadline: February 20.

4810. **Tuition Waivers** Numerous partial- to full-tuition waivers to students who are employees, children of employees, or senior citizens.

4811. **Undergraduate Work Grants** 4 grants of $1,000 to undergraduates majoring in physics or astronomy. Selection is based on academic achievement and interest in science. Contact the Scholarship Coordinator.

4812. **University Scholarships** Varying numbers of scholarships providing fees to students in the upper 10 percent of their class who scored at least 1240 on SAT or 30 on ACT. Renewable with a 3.5 GPA.

4813. **Vocational Rehabilitation Scholarships** 47 scholarships of varying amounts to disabled students meeting certain criteria.

University of Missouri at Columbia
305 Jesse Hall
Columbia, MO 65211
(573) 882-7786
http://www.missouri.edu/

4814. **Agriculture Awards** Varying numbers of scholarships of varying amounts to students who meet certain criteria and are majoring in an area of agriculture.

4815. **Albert T. and Lilla W. Scroggins Jr. Scholarship** 1 scholarship of $500 to an undergraduate junior journalism major. Preference given to Alabama residents.

4816. **Ann M. Frank Scholarship** 1 scholarship of $1,000 to a graduate student in the Washington reporting program of the School of Journalism.

4817. **Benjamin Franklin Scholarships** 2 scholarships of $1,000 to undergraduate or graduate students who are journalism majors. Based on academic achievement, financial need, character, and interest in journalism.

4818. **Besse Marks Memorial Journalism Scholarship** 1 scholarship of $600 to an undergraduate or graduate journalism student. Based on academic achievement, financial need, character, and interest in journalism. Preference given to residents of Wayne County, NY, and Kansas City, MO.

4819. **Bob Goddard Memorial Scholarships** 1 scholarship of $1,500 to an undergraduate student majoring in print journalism.

4820. **Carol Jean Cherry Mehlberg Memorial Scholarship** 1 scholarship of $200 to an undergraduate or graduate journalism student who meets certain criteria.

4821. **Carol Jean Cherry Mehlberg Memorial Scholarship** 1 scholarship of $300 to a member of Alpha Mu chapter of Kappa Alpha Theta. Based on exceptional academic achievement and leadership in the School of Journalism.

4822. **Chancellor's Leadership Class Awards** Varying numbers of scholarships of varying amounts to students who have demonstrated leadership abilities.

4823. **Chevron U.S.A./B. J. "Jack" Werre Scholarships** 3 scholarships of $1,000 to undergraduate or graduate students in a business journalism program. Based on academic achievement and journalistic ability.

4824. **Communications Awards** Numerous scholarships of varying amounts to students majoring in communications.

4825. **Creative Arts/Performance Awards** Numerous scholarships of varying amounts to students of music and drama or with other special talents.

4826. **Curators** 300 scholarships of varying amounts to students in the top 3 percent of their class who scored in the 90th percentile on SAT and ACT. Must be Missouri high school graduates. Renewable.

4827. **David E. Dexter Scholarship** 1 scholarship of $500 to a student who is a journalism major and a varsity athlete in either football or wrestling. Must have at least a C average and financial need.

4828. **Donald W. Reynolds Foundations Scholarship** 1 scholarship of $5,000 a year for two years to a student majoring in journalism mass communication. Must apply in sophomore year. Awarded in junior year, and renewable for senior year.

4829. **Eugene Field Scholarship** 1 scholarship of $200 to a student majoring in journalism who is "well equipped in professional ideas and in general newspaper–making ability."

4830. **Eugene W. Sharp Scholarship** 1 scholarship of $1,000 to an undergraduate or graduate journalism major.

4831. **Excellence Awards** Numerous scholarships of varying amounts.

4932. **Fairchild Publications Scholarship** 1 scholarship of $2,500 to a student majoring in journalism or business and pursuing a career in business journalism who meets certain other criteria. Renewable.

4933. **G. Ellsworth Huggins** Numerous scholarships of varying amounts.

4934. **George Brooks Minority Scholarships** 34 scholarships of varying amounts to minority students who meet certain criteria.

4935. **Hal Boyle Scholarship** 1 scholarship of $2,000 to an undergraduate or graduate student based on journalism excellence.

4936. **H. S. Jewell Scholarship** 1 scholarship of $500 to an undergraduate or graduate journalism student who meets certain criteria.

4937. **Hullie G. Award in Journalism** 1 scholarship of $1,000 to an undergraduate junior. Based on excellence in journalism and "adherence to the Journalism Creed as set down by Walter Williams."

4938. **Inez Callaway Robb Scholarship** 1 scholarship of $1,000 to a female undergraduate or graduate journalism student.

4939. **INGAA Scholarships in Business Communications** 2 scholarships of $300 per semester to undergraduate or graduate journalism students. Based on financial need and interest and talent in business news writing. Deadline: October 1.

4940. **Jay L. Torrey Scholarship** 1 scholarship of $250 to a female undergraduate or graduate journalism student who is "considered well prepared to do the work of a journalist."

4941. **John P. Herrick Scholarships** 2 scholarships of $1,000 to undergraduate or graduate students. Based on academic achievement, financial need, character, and interest in journalism. Preference given to New York State residents. Renewable.

4942. **(Mrs.) John P. Herrick Scholarships** 2 scholarships of $1,000 to female undergraduate or graduate students. Based on financial need, character, and interest in journalism. Renewable.

4943. **John W. Jewell Scholarship** 1 scholarship of $500 to a graduate or undergraduate journalism student. Based on academic achievement and general merit.

4944. **Journalism Scholarships** 51 different scholarships from $250 to $5,000 to students majoring in journalism. Inquire with Journalism Department.

4945. **J. Richard Sage Scholarship** 1 scholarship of $300 to an undergraduate or graduate journalism student. Based on academic achievement and financial need.

4946. **Kansas City Press Club Scholarship** 1 scholarship of $500 to an undergraduate junior. Based on excellence in journalism.

4947. **Knight–Ridder Scholarships** 5 scholarships of $2,000 to minority undergraduate juniors who are majoring in journalism. Renewable.

4948. **Lafayette Young Scholarships** 2 scholarships of $1,000 to undergraduate or graduate journalism students. Based on academic achievement, character, financial need, and interest in journalism.

4949. **Lyle Wilson Scholarship** 1 scholarship of $1,000 provided by the Scripps–Howard Foundation to an undergraduate or graduate journalism student pursuing a course of study that will qualify him/her for a career in editorial, business, broadcasting, or newspapers who intends to pursue a career in one or more of these fields.

4950. **Margaret Ann Wheeler Gilbert Memorial Scholarships** 2 scholarships of $1,000 to undergraduate or graduate students who are journalism majors and meet certain other criteria.

4951. **Mary S. Pryor Scholarship** 1 scholarship of $500 to a female journalism student. Based on financial need, character, academic achievement, and interest in journalism.

4952. **Mildred L. Ayres Trust Scholarships** 5 scholarship grants ranging from $750 to $1,500 to graduate students pursuing theological or medical degrees. Must be Missouri residents. Preference is given to residents of metropolitan Kansas City. Contact: Mildred L. Ayres Trust, P.O. Box 419038, Kansas City, MO 64105, (816) 221–2800.

4953. **MU Scholars Awards** Varying numbers of scholarships of varying amounts to students who meet certain academic criteria.

4954. **National Merit/Achievement** Numerous scholarships of varying amounts to students selected as National Merit Finalists.

4955. **Norman Hurst Trenholm Journalism Scholarship** 1 scholarship of $250 to an undergraduate junior, senior, or graduate journalism student.

4956. **Olive Coates Memorial Scholarships** 8 scholarships of $1,000 to undergraduate or graduate students meeting certain criteria who are journalism majors.

4957. **Oliver K. Bovard Memorial Journalism Scholarship** 1 scholarship consisting of summer employment on the *St. Louis Post-Dispatch* plus $300 stipend to a student who has completed the first year as a journalism major. Must demonstrate exceptional journalistic ability and interest in newspaper reporting.

4958. **O. O. McIntyre Scholarship** 1 scholarship of $2,000 to an undergraduate junior who meets certain criteria and demonstrates financial need.

4959. **Phillip L. Blazer Memorial Scholarship** 1 scholarship of $500 to an undergraduate or graduate student who is a Missouri resident, is majoring in journalism, who meets certain other criteria.

4960. **Reader's Digest Excellence in Journalism Scholarships** 3 scholarships of $4,000 each to graduate journalism students. Based on academic achievement, writing skills, and leadership.

4961. **Robert M. Ibrahim Scholarship** 1 scholarship of $500 to an undergraduate or graduate journalism student demonstrating interest in work in Asia or the Middle East. Based on financial need.

4962. **Robert M. Jackson Fellowship** 1 fellowship of $250 to a graduate journalism student. Based on financial need and journalistic ability.

4963. **Sara Lockwood Williams Scholarships** 4 scholarships of $500 to undergraduate or graduate journalism students. Preference given to females.

4964. **Science Fair Scholarships** Varying numbers of scholarships of varying amounts to students based on science fair competitions.

4965. **Science Writing Scholarship** 1 scholarship of $600 to an undergraduate or graduate student for outstanding achievement in science writing.

4966. **St. Louis Business Journal/Alfred Fleishman Scholarship** 1 scholarship of $1,000 to an outstanding undergraduate or graduate student in business journalism.

4967. **St. Louis Post–Dispatch Scholarships** 1 to 4 scholarships of $1,800 each to minority students who are graduating high school seniors or students transferring from a junior college. Must be residents of Jefferson, St. Charles, or St. Louis, counties, Missouri. Renewable, based on academic achievement. Contact the Assistant Managing Editor, *St. Louis Post-Dispatch*. Deadline: April 1.

4968. **Theodore Roosevelt Scholarships** 2 scholarships of $1,000 to undergraduates or graduate journalism students. Based on financial need, character, and interest in journalism.

4969. **Tilghman R. Cloud Memorial Scholarships** 3 scholarships of $500 to undergraduate or graduate students who are Missouri residents and majoring in journalism. Based on journalistic ability and financial need as deemed by faculty.

4970. **Tuition Waivers** Numerous partial- to full-tuition waivers to students who are employees or children of employees.

4971. **UM Scholars Award** Numerous scholarships of varying amounts.

4972. **University** 600 scholarships of varying amounts to students with a 3.5 GPA. Renewable with a 3.5 GPA.

4973. **University Scholars** Unlimited number of scholarships of varying amounts to students with a 3.5 GPA. Renewable.

University of Missouri at Kansas City
5100 Rockhill Road
Kansas City, MO 64111-2499
(816) 235-1000
http://www.umkc.edu
admit@umkc.edu

4974. **Chancellor's Award** Varying numbers and amounts of scholarships to students. Based on leadership and talent.

4975. **Creative Arts/Performance Awards** 28 scholarships of varying amounts to students in the performing arts.

4976. **Curators** 300 scholarships of varying amounts to students in the top 3 percent of their class who scored in the 90th percentile on SAT or ACT. Must be Missouri high school graduates. Renewable.

4977. **Journalism Scholarships** 51 different scholarships ranging from $250 to $5,000 to students majoring in journalism. Inquire with Journalism Department.

4978. **UMKC Scholars Awards** Varying numbers and amounts of scholarships to students who are residents of the Kansas City area.

4979. **University** 600 scholarships of varying amounts to students with a 3.5 GPA. Renewable with a 3.5 GPA.

4980. **University Scholars** Unlimited numbers of scholarships of varying amounts to students with a 3.5 GPA. Renewable.

Washington University
One Brookings Drive
Campus Box 1089
St. Louis, MO 63130-4899
(800) 638-6700
(314) 889-5000
http://www.wustl.edu
admissions@wustl.edu

4981. **Compton** 4 scholarships of tuition to students in the top 10 percent of their class. Renewable.

4982. **Conway** 2 scholarships of $6,000 to students in the top 10 percent of their class. Renewable.

4983. **Honorary Fellowships** 3 scholarships of tuition to students in top 10 percent of their class. Renewable.

4984. **Landsdorf** 4 scholarships of tuition to students in the top 10 percent of their class. Renewable.

4985. **Lien** 3 scholarships of tuition to students in the top 10 percent of their class. Renewable.

4986. **Merit Fellowship** 1 scholarship of tuition. Renewable.

4987. **Mylonas** 3 scholarships of tuition to students in the top 10 percent of their class. Renewable.

4988. **Woodward** 20 scholarships of $4,500 to students in the top 10 percent of their class. Renewable.

MONTANA

Montana State University
P.O. Box 172190
Bozeman, MT 59717
(800) 662-6132
http://montana.edu
admissions@montana.edu

4989. Athletic (Men) Basketball, cross-country, football, tennis, and track and field scholarships.

4990. Athletic (Women) Basketball, cross-country, tennis, track and field, and volleyball scholarships.

4991. Fee Waivers Waivers of up to tuition to certain students. Renewable.

4992. High School Week 125 scholarships ranging from $200 to $1,000.

Northern Montana College
P.O. Box 7751
Havre, MT 59501-7751
(406) 265-3700

4993. Academic 60 scholarships of varying amounts.

4994. Athletic (Men) Basketball, track and field, and wrestling scholarships.

4995. Athletic (Women) Basketball, track and field, and volleyball scholarships.

4996. President's 20 scholarships of $500 to students in the top 10 percent of their class, with at least a 3.2 GPA, and scoring at least 1000 on SAT or 24 on ACT. Renewable with a 3.0 GPA.

4997. Talent 40 scholarships of varying amounts. Based on talent and essay.

University of Montana
101 Lodge, U of M
Missoula, MT 59812
(406) 243-0211
http://www.umt.edu/nss

4998. Butte Press Club Award 1 scholarship of $350 to an undergraduate junior, senior, or graduate student who will be a journalism major. Based on academic achievement and potential. Must be recommended by journalism faculty.

4999. C. C. Rochon Scholarship 1 scholarship of at least $200 to an entering freshman who will be majoring in journalism. Must have graduated from Anaconda High School.

5000. D. J. Shults Journalism Scholarships 1 or more scholarships of at least $200 to entering freshmen or transfer students who will be majoring in journalism. Must have graduated from Big Sandy High School. If a suitable recipient is not found at Big Sandy High School, applicants from Chouteau County will be considered. If suitable recipient still isn't found, then any Montana resident will be considered.

5001. Don Anderson Scholarship 1 scholarship of $1,000 to an undergraduate junior, senior, or graduate student who will be a journalism major. Based on academic achievement and potential. Must be recommended by journalism faculty.

5002. Dorcas Keach Northey Award 1 scholarship of $200 to an undergraduate junior, senior, or graduate student who will be a journalism major. Based on academic achievement and potential. Must be recommended by journalism faculty.

5003. Dorothy Rochon Powers Scholarship 1 scholarship of $1,200 to an undergraduate junior, senior, or graduate student who will be a journalism major. Based on academic achievement and potential. Must be recommended by journalism faculty.

5004. Freshman Numerous scholarships ranging from $300 to $1,200 to students in the top 25 percent of their class, with at least a 3.0 GPA, and scoring at least 870 on SAT or 20 on ACT.

5005. General 150 scholarships ranging from $100 to $2,000 to students with at least a 3.3 GPA.

5006. George E. Bright Memorial Fellowship 3 to 4 fellowships of $2,000 to students who are majoring in natural resource management and meet certain academic criteria and recommendations. Deadline: February 15. Contact financial aid office.

5007. Grace Crane Newman Award 1 scholarship of $200 to an undergraduate junior, senior, or graduate student who will be a journalism major. Based on academic achievement and potential. Must be recommended by journalism faculty.

5008. Great Falls Newspaper Guild Award 1 scholarship of $250 to an undergraduate junior, senior, or graduate student who will be a journalism major. Based on academic achievement and potential. Must be recommended by journalism faculty.

5009. **Great Falls Tribune Awards** 2 scholarships of $500 and 1 scholarship of $1,000 to undergraduate juniors, seniors, or graduate students who will be journalism majors. Based on academic achievement and potential. Must be recommended by journalism faculty.

5010. **Great Falls Tribune Native American Scholarship** 1 scholarship of $1,000 to an entering freshman or full-time undergraduate or graduate student majoring in journalism. Must be Native American as defined by the applicant's tribal regulations.

5011. **Guy Mooney Award** 1 scholarship of $250 to an undergraduate junior, senior, or graduate student who will be a journalism major. Based on academic achievement and potential. Must be recommended by journalism faculty.

5012. **Harry S. Truman Scholarship** 39 scholarships of $7,000 to undergraduate students who wish to pursue a career in public service. Based on academic achievement, interest, and commitment to future government service. Deadline: October 20.

5013. **Last Chance Press Club Award** 1 scholarship of $200 to an undergraduate junior, senior, or graduate student who will be a journalism major. Based on academic achievement and potential. Must be recommended by journalism faculty.

5014. **Lee Enterprises Native American Journalism Scholarship** 1 scholarship of at least $500 to an entering freshman or full-time undergraduate or graduate Native American student who is a journalism major. Renewable for up to four years with at least a 2.5 GPA. Deadline: February 1.

5015. **Montana Newspaper Association Dean Stone Award** 1 scholarship of $300 to an undergraduate junior, senior, or graduate student who will be a journalism major. Based on academic achievement and potential. Must be recommended by journalism faculty.

5016. **Music Scholarships** 32 scholarships of varying amounts, totaling $6,100, to students who meet certain criteria. Based on talent.

5017. **Myre–McGaugh Journalism Scholarship** 1 scholarship of $500 to an undergraduate junior, senior, or graduate student who will be a journalism major. Based on academic achievement and potential. Must be recommended by journalism faculty.

5018. **Norman A. Johnson Memorial Award** 1 scholarship of $400 to an undergraduate junior, senior, or graduate student who will be a journalism major. Based on academic achievement and potential. Must be recommended by journalism faculty.

5019. **Pacific Northwest Newspaper Association Scholarships** 1 or more scholarships of at least $200 to undergraduate and graduate students who are journalism majors. Must submit a transcript, writing samples, and letter of application discussing professional goals and a brief personal history. Deadline: February 1.

5020. **Presidential Honors Program** 10 scholarships of $1,500 to students in the top 10 percent of their class, with at least a 3.5 GPA, and scoring at least 1200 on SAT or 27 on ACT. Renewable with a 3.3 GPA.

5021. **Presidential Leadership Scholarships** 10 scholarships of varying amounts, totaling $25,000, for students meeting certain academic criteria who have demonstrated leadership abilities.

5022. **Tuition Waivers** Numerous partial to full tuition waivers to students who are minority students or senior citizens.

5023. **Warren J. Brier/PEMCO Scholarship** 1 scholarship of $600 to an incoming freshman or transfer student who will be majoring in journalism. Selection based on academic achievement, performance, and professional promise. Renewable for up to three years. Must submit transcript, writing samples, and letter of recommendation. Deadline: February 1.

NEBRASKA

Bellevue College
1000 Galvin Road South
Bellevue, NE 68005
(800) 756-7920
http://www.bellevue.edu

5024. **Athletic (Men)** Basketball scholarships.

5025. **Athletic (Women)** Volleyball scholarships.

5026. **Business Divisional Scholarships** 5 scholarships of $1,095 to full-time undergraduates with at least a 3.0 GPA who are majoring in accounting, business administration, economics, or information management. Deadline: May 15.

5027. New Horizon Scholarships 3 scholarships of $1,100 to junior or senior undergraduate students pursuing a career in management of human resources. Deadline: May 15.

5028. Professional Studies Ambassador Scholarship 8 scholarships of $1,000 to undergraduate juniors or seniors with at least a 3.5 GPA and an interest in management of human resources. Students must show professionalism in the workplace and/or have positively influenced others through community service and political involvement. Contact the Director of Financial Aid.

5029. Professional Studies Merit Awards 6 scholarships of $1,000 to undergraduate juniors or seniors interested in management of human resources. Contact the Director of Financial Aid.

Creighton University
2500 California Plaza
Omaha, NE 68178
(800) 282-5835
http://www.creighton.edu/
admissions@creighton.edu

5030. Campaign Creighton Scholarships Varying numbers of scholarships of $1,000 to students who are in the top 30 percent of their class and scored at least 25 on ACT. Renewable with 2.5 GPA.

5031. Centennial "Honors Program" Varying numbers of scholarships ranging from $500 to $750 to students in the top 30 percent of their class, with at least a 2.5 GPA, and who scored at least 25 on ACT. Renewable with 2.5 GPA.

5032. Honors Scholarships 30 scholarships ranging from $500 to $1,000 to students in the top 10 percent of their class who scored at least 24 on ACT. Renewable with 2.75 GPA.

5033. Presidential Scholarships 20 scholarships providing half of tuition costs to students in the upper 5 percent of their class who scored at least 29 on SAT. Renewable with a 3.3 GPA.

5034. Reinert/Condon Scholarships Varying numbers of scholarships of $2,500 to students in the upper 15 percent of their class who scored at least 1170 on SAT or 29 on ACT. Renewable with 3.0 GPA.

University of Nebraska at Lincoln
14th and R Street
Lincoln, NE 68588-0415
(800) 742-8800
(402) 472-3601
http://www.unl.edu

5035. Athletic (Men) Baseball, basketball, cross-country, football, golf, gymnastics, swimming and diving, tennis, track and field, and wrestling scholarships.

5036. Athletic (Women) Basketball, cross-country, golf, gymnastics, softball, swimming and diving, tennis, track and field, and volleyball scholarships.

5037. David Memorial Scholarships 150 scholarships of $1,500 to graduating in-state or out-of-state high school seniors in the top 25 percent of their class. Based on academic record and SAT/ACT score. Renewable.

NEVADA

University of Nevada at Las Vegas
4505 South Maryland Parkway
Las Vegas, NV 89154
(702) 739-3443
http://www.unlv.edu
witter@ccmail.nevada.edu

5038. Athletic (Men) Baseball, basketball, football, golf, soccer, swimming and diving, and tennis scholarships.

5039. Athletic (Women) Basketball, cross-country, softball, swimming and diving, tennis, and track and field scholarships.

5040. Continuing Students 300 to 800 scholarships ranging from $100 to $2,500 to students to continue their education. Must have at least a 3.0 GPA.

5041. Freshman Academic 100 to 300 scholarships ranging from $200 to $2,500 to students with at least a 3.4 GPA.

NEW HAMPSHIRE

Colby–Sawyer College
100 Main Street
New London, NH 03257
(800) 272-1015
http://www.colby-sawyer.edu
cdadmiss@colby-sawyer.edu

5042. **Adelaide B. Nichols Music Scholarships** 4 scholarships ranging from $500 to $3,000 to students meeting certain criteria who are music majors.

5043. **Athletic (Men)** Basketball, equestrian sports, skiing (downhill), soccer, and tennis scholarships.

5044. **Athletic (Women)** Basketball, equestrian sports, lacrosse, skiing (downhill), soccer, tennis, and volleyball scholarships.

5045. **Colby–Sawyer College Scholarships** Varying numbers of scholarships of varying amounts to students meeting certain criteria.

5046. **Tuition Waivers** Numerous partial- to full-tuition waivers to students who are employees or children of employees.

Notre Dame College
2321 Elm Street
Manchester, NH 03104
(603) 669-4298
http://www.notredame.edu

5047. **Commuter Honors** 10 scholarships of $1,000 to commuting students in the top 25 percent of their class, with at least a 3.0 GPA, and scoring at least 900 on SAT. Renewable with a 3.0 GPA.

5048. **Presidential Honors** 10 scholarships of $2,500 to students in the top 25 percent of their class, with at least a 3.0 GPA, and scoring at least 950 on SAT. Renewable with a 3.0 GPA.

5049. **Wheelock, Vermont Scholarship** 15 scholarship grants of up to $16,230 each to undergraduates who either were born in or are residents of Wheelock, Vermont. Must have financial need and remain in Wheelock to maintain eligibility. Contact the Director of Financial Aid. Deadline: February 15.

Keene State College
229 Main Street
Keene, NH 03431
(800) KSC-1909
(603) 358-2280
http://www.keene.edu/

5050. **Art Award** 1 scholarship of varying amount to a student who is an art major and meets certain criteria. Based on talent.

5051. **Challenge Scholarships** 15 scholarships of varying amounts to students who are New Jersey state residents and meet certain academic criteria.

5052. **Drama Award** 1 scholarship of varying amount to a student who is a drama major and meets certain criteria. Based on talent.

5053. **Music Awards** 3 scholarships of varying amounts to students who are music majors and meet certain criteria. Based on talent.

5054. **President's Scholarships** 2 scholarships of varying amounts to students who are New Jersey residents and meet certain academic criteria.

5055. **Tuition Waivers** Numerous partial- to full-tuition waivers to students who are employees, children of employees, or senior citizens.

University of New Hampshire
4 Garrison Avenue
Durham, NH 03824
(603) 862-1234
http://www.unh.edu

5056. **Creative Arts/Performance Awards** 10 scholarships of varying amounts to students meeting certain criteria and majoring in a creative or performing art.

5057. **Dean's Scholarships** Varying numbers of scholarships of varying amounts to students meeting certain academic criteria.

5058. **Granite State Honor** 15 scholarships ranging from $500 up to need. Renewable with a 3.0 GPA.

5059. **Special Achievement/Activities Award** 20 scholarships of varying amounts to students meeting certain criteria and involved in a particular activity.

NEW JERSEY

Bloomfield College
467 Franklin Street
Bloomfield, NJ 07003
(800) 848-4555
http://www.bloomfield.edu

5060. **Alumni Awards** 5 scholarships of varying amounts to students who are children of alumni and meet certain criteria.

5061. **Bloomfield Academic** 18 scholarships of $3,000 to students in the top 30 percent of their class and scoring at least 850 on SAT. Renewable with a 3.0 GPA.

5062. **Challenge** 21 scholarships of $1,000 to students in the top 50 percent of their class and scoring at least 750 on SAT. Renewable with a 3.0 GPA.

5063. **Family Scholarships** 3 scholarships of varying amounts to students who are relatives of current students and meet certain criteria.

5064. **Merit Scholarships** 30 scholarships of varying amounts, totaling $73,000, to students meeting certain academic criteria.

5065. **Presbyterian Ministers Awards** 2 scholarships of varying amounts to students who are children of Presbyterian ministers and meet certain criteria.

5066. **Tuition Waivers** Numerous partial to full tuition waivers to students who are children of alumni, employees, children of employees, adult nontraditional students, or senior citizens.

College of St. Elizabeth
2 Convent Road
Morristown, NJ 07960
(973) 290-4700
http://www.st-elizabeth.edu
apply@liza.st-elizabeth.edu

5067. **Academic Scholarships** 5 scholarships of tuition costs to students in the top 20 percent of their class, with at least a 3.0 GPA, and who scored at least 1200 on SAT. Renewable with a 3.0 GPA.

5068. **Children of Alumni Scholarships** 5 scholarships of approximately $500 to students who are children of alumni and meet certain criteria.

5069. **Elizabethan Scholarships** 50 scholarships providing half of tuition costs to students in the top 20 percent of their class, with at least a 3.0 GPA, and who scored at least 1100 on SAT. Renewable with 3.0 GPA.

5070. **Genevieve A. Walsh Scholarships** 2 scholarships ranging from $3,000 to $7,500 to female freshmen students with a visual, mobility, or auditory impairment due to a physical disability. Contact the Director of Financial Aid. Deadline: June 1.

5071. **Handicapped Students Scholarships** 2 scholarships of $10,900 to students with disabilities who meet certain criteria.

5072. **International Students Scholarships** 2 scholarships of $11,450 to international students who meet certain criteria.

5073. **Junior Miss Scholarship** 1 scholarship of $10,400 to a student selected in the Junior Miss Competition.

5074. **Leadership Scholarships** Varying numbers of scholarships ranging from $500 to $1,500 to students who have demonstrated leadership abilities.

5075. **Tuition Waivers** Numerous partial- to full-tuition waivers to students who are employees, children of employees, or senior citizens.

Princeton University
P.O. Box 430
Princeton, NJ 08544
(609) 258-3000
http://www.princeton.edu/

5076. **Class of 1926 Foundation** 1 scholarship of $5,000 to a student meeting certain criteria. Contact: Trustee, Cardinal Road, Greenwich, CT 06830, (203) 869-2382.

5077. **Need-Based Assistance** Numerous need-based scholarships, loans, and work-study programs open to anyone accepted for admission who has financial need. Contact the financial aid office.

5078. **Tuition Waivers** Numerous partial- to full-tuition waivers to students who are employees or children of employees.

Rutgers, The State University of New Jersey at New Brunswick
P.O. Box 2101
New Brunswick, NJ 08903-2101
(732) 932-4636
http://www.rutgers.edu

5079. **Bloustein Distinguished Scholars Awards** Varying numbers of scholarships of varying amounts to students who meet certain academic criteria.

5080. **Bloustein Distinguished Urban Scholars Awards** Varying numbers of scholarships of varying amounts to students who meet certain academic criteria.

5081. **Camden College of A&S** 2 scholarships ranging from $1,000 to $4,000 to students in the upper 10 percent of their class, with at least a 3.2 GPA, and scoring at least 1100 on their SAT. Renewable with a 3.0 GPA.

5082. **College Scholars Awards** Varying numbers of scholarships of varying amounts to students who meet certain academic criteria.

5083. **Cook College** 2 scholarships ranging from $500 to $4,000 to students in the upper 10 percent of their class, with at least a 3.2 GPA, and scoring at least 1100 on their SAT. Renewable with a 3.0 GPA.

5084. **County College** 5 scholarships ranging from $1,750 to $7,000 to students in the upper 10 percent of their class, with at least a 3.2 GPA, and scoring at least 1100 on their SAT. Renewable with a 3.0 GPA.

5085. **Douglass College** 10 scholarships ranging from $500 to $4,000 to students in the upper 10 percent of their class, with at least a 3.2 GPA, and scoring at least 1100 on their SAT. Renewable with a 3.0 GPA.

5086. **Engineering** 2 scholarships ranging from $500 to $4,000 to students in the upper 10 percent of their class, with at least a 3.2 GPA, and scoring at least 1100 on their SAT. Renewable with a 3.0 GPA.

5087. **James Dickson Car Scholarships** Up to 75 scholarships of $5,000 to minority students in the top 14 percent of their class, with at least a 3.2 GPA, and who scored at least 1100 on SAT. Renewable with 3.0 GPA.

5088. **Livingston College** 2 scholarships ranging from $500 to $4,000 to students in the upper 10 percent of their class, with at least a 3.2 GPA, and scoring at least 1100 on their SAT. Renewable with a 3.0 GPA.

5089. **National Achievement** 10 scholarships ranging from $1,000 to $4,000 to students in the upper 10 percent of their class, with at least a 3.2 GPA, and scoring at least 1100 on their SAT. Renewable with a 3.0 GPA.

5090. **National Merit** 10 scholarships ranging from $1,000 to $4,000 to students in the upper 10 percent of their class, with at least a 3.2 GPA, and scoring at least 1100 on their SAT. Renewable with a 3.0 GPA.

5091. **Minority** 60 scholarships of $1,000 to minority students in the upper 10 percent of their class, with a 3.2 GPA, and scoring at least 1100 on their SAT. Renewable with a 3.0 GPA.

5092. **Newark College of A&S** 10 scholarships ranging from $500 to $4,000 to students in the upper 10 percent of their class, with at least a 3.2 GPA, and scoring at least 1100 on their SAT. Renewable with a 3.0 GPA.

5093. **Nursing** 2 scholarships ranging from $500 to $4,000 to students in the upper 10 percent of their class, with at least a 3.2 GPA, and scoring at least 1100 on their SAT. Must be pursuing a career in nursing. Renewable with a 3.0 GPA.

5094. **Pharmacy** 2 scholarships ranging from $500 to $4,000 to students in the upper 10 percent of their class, with at least a 3.2 GPA, and scoring at least 1100 on their SAT. Renewable with a 3.0 GPA.

5095. **Presidential Scholar** 15 scholarships ranging from $18,000 to $22,500 to students in the upper 10 percent of their class, with at least a 3.2 GPA, and scoring at least 1100 on their SAT. Renewable with a 3.0 GPA.

5096. **Rutgers College** 5 scholarships ranging from $500 to $4,000 to students in the upper 10 percent of their class, with at least a 3.2 GPA, and scoring at least 1100 on their SAT. Renewable with a 3.0 GPA.

NEW MEXICO

New Mexico Institute of Mining and Technology
Socorro, NM 87801
(505) 835-5425
http://www.nmt.edu.
admission@admin.nmt.edu

5097. **Competitive Scholarship** 15 awards ranging from $200 to $700 to out-of-state freshmen or transfer students. Renewable.

5098. **Counselor's Choice Award** 85 scholarships of $1,000 to students who are New Mexico residents, with at least a 2.5 GPA, and scoring at least 19 on ACT. Only one scholarship awarded per high school. Renewable.

5099. **Presidential Scholarship** 121 awards of $2,000 to entering students with at least a 3.0 GPA and scoring at least 26 on ACT.

5100. **President's Associates Scholarship** 1 scholarship of $1,500.

5101. **Regents Scholarship** 86 scholarships of $1,250 to students with at least a 3.0 GPA and scoring at least 24 on ACT. 1 scholarship for a transfer student with the same test scores.

New Mexico State University
P.O. Box 30001
Las Cruces, NM 88003-0001
(505) 646-0111
http://www.nmsu.edu/
admissions@nmsu.edu

5102. **Adrian Berryhill Family Agricultural Scholarship** 2 awards of $1,000 to junior or senior students majoring in range management, animal science, or farming/ranching. Must be New Mexico residents. Deadline: March 1.

5103. **Alumni Scholarships** 100 scholarships ranging from $100 to $4,652 to students with at least a 3.5 GPA who scored at least 980 on SAT or 12 on ACT. Renewable with a 3.5 GPA.

5104. **Dollar Rent-a-Car Scholarships** 4 scholarship grants of $1,000 to undergraduate students who are civil engineering majors. Selection is based on academic achievement and financial need. Deadline: March 1. Contact the Dean of Engineering.

5105. **Duke V. Layton Memorial Award** 2 scholarships of $1,000 to undergraduates majoring in entomology or plant sciences who plan to pursue a career in scientific agriculture. Deadline: March 1.

5106. **El Paso Natural Gas Company Scholarships** 4 scholarships ranging from $1,000 to $1,250 to undergraduate students who will be majoring in computer science, management information systems, chemical or mechanical engineering, or accounting. Preference is given to Hispanic students. Selection is based on academic achievement and academic potential. Deadline: March 1.

5107. **Garden Club Inc. Scholarship** 1 scholarship of $1,000 to a junior or senior or a graduate student majoring in horticulture or botany. Must have at least a 3.0 GPA, be a U.S. citizen and resident of New Mexico, and have financial need. Deadline: March 1.

5108. **Hutchinson Fruit Company Scholarship** 1 scholarship of $1,000 to a student pursuing a career in food crop production. Recipient must be a U.S. citizen and New Mexico resident. Renewable.

5109. **Presidential Associates Honors Scholarships** 5 scholarships of $4,980 to students with at least a 3.5 GPA who scored at least 1100 on SAT or 26 on ACT. Renewable with a 3.5 GPA.

5110. **President Associates' Scholarships** 10 scholarships of $2,200 to students with at least a 3.5 GPA who scored at least 1100 on SAT or 25 on ACT. Renewable with a 3.5 GPA.

5111. **Ocle Gray Memorial Scholarship** 2 scholarships of $800 to juniors or seniors majoring in animal science, fisheries, or wildlife resources/management. Based on financial need, academic achievement, and participation in wildlife conservation. Deadline: March 1.

5112. **Regents' Scholarships** 350 scholarships of $1,980 to students in the top 10 percent of their class who scored at least 940 on SAT or 23 on ACT. Renewable with 3.5 GPA.

5113. **Tony Lama Scholarship** 1 scholarship of $1,000 for an undergraduate junior or senior agricultural student. Deadline: March 1.

5114. **Tuition Waivers** Numerous partial to full tuition waivers to students who are senior citizens.

5115. **William S. May Scholarship** 1 scholarship of $1,000 to a junior or senior student majoring in an agricultural finance–related field. Deadline: March 1.

University of New Mexico
Albuquerque, NM 87131-2039
(505) 277-2446
http://www.unm.edu
apply@unm.edu

5116. **Activity Scholarships** 55 scholarships of varying amounts to students meeting certain criteria and participating in certain activities.

5117. **Alumni Scholarships** 16 scholarships of varying amounts to students meeting certain criteria.

5118. **Amigo Scholarships** 77 scholarships of varying amounts to students meeting certain academic criteria. Must be out–of–state residents.

5119. **Distributive Education Clubs of America Awards** 5 scholarships of varying amounts to students meeting certain criteria who are members of DECA and are business or marketing majors.

5120. **Fine Arts Awards** 6 scholarships of varying amounts to students meeting certain academic criteria who will be fine arts majors.

5121. **Friends of Music Awards** 6 scholarships of varying amounts to students meeting certain criteria and who are music majors.

5122. **General Motors Awards** 8 scholarships of varying amounts to undergraduate students meeting certain academic criteria.

5123. **Johanna Fishe Award** 1 scholarship of varying amount to a student meeting certain academic criteria who will be a music major.

5124. **NASA Scholarships** 20 scholarships of varying amounts to students meeting certain academic criteria who will be engineering majors.

5125. **National Action Council for Minorities in Engineering Awards** 11 scholarships of varying amounts to minority students meeting certain academic criteria who are engineering majors.

5126. **New Mexico Mathematics Contest Award** 1 scholarship of varying amount to a student competing in the NM Mathematics Contest.

5127. **New Mexico Scholars Awards** Up to 300 scholarships of $1,953 to students with at least a 3.2 GPA, who scored at least 1020 on SAT or 25 on ACT, and who have financial need. Must be New Mexico residents. Renewable with a 3.0 GPA.

5128. **NW Science Fair Awards** 10 scholarships of varying amounts to students meeting certain criteria who were winners in the NW Science Fair.

5129. **Presidential** 200 scholarships of $1,000 to students in the top 10 percent of their class who have at least a 3.0 GPA. Renewable.

5130. **Regents Awards** 15 scholarships of $5,400 to students who are in the top 5 percent of their class, with at least a 3.9 GPA, and who scored at least 30 on ACT. Renewable with a 3.5 GPA.

5131. **University of New Mexico Scholars Awards** 300 scholarships of varying amounts to students meeting certain academic criteria.

5132. **Valedictorian, Excel, Regents, and Sterling** Over 800 scholarships ranging from $1,000 to full tuition.

5133. **Zia/Activity Scholarships** 200 scholarships ranging from $250 to $700 to students with at least a 3.0 GPA and who scored at least 20 on ACT. Renewable with 3.0 GPA.

NEW YORK

Adirondack Community College
Bay Road
Queensbury, NY 12804
(518) 793-4491

5134. **Academic Excellence** 6 awards ranging from $500 to $1,450 to students in the top 10 percent of their high school class in Warren County, Washington County, or northern Saratoga County, New York. Deadline: May 1.

5135. **ACC** 41 scholarships ranging from $100 to $625 to freshman and sophomore students majoring in accounting, broadcasting, business administration, criminal justice, liberal arts, nursing, or tourism. Must have at least a 2.5 GPA, extracurricular activities, and financial need. Deadline: September 1.

5136. **Beeman** 5 scholarships ranging from $500 to $1,070 to students in the top 10 percent of their class. High school must be in Warren County, Washington County, or Saratoga County, New York. Deadline: May 1.

5137. **Bryan** 1 scholarship ranging from $500 to $1,070 to a student in the top 10 percent of high school class; school must be in Warren County, Washington County, or Saratoga County, New York. Deadline: May 1.

5138. **Freed** 3 scholarships ranging from $500 to $1,070 to students in the top 10 percent of their high school class; school must be in Warren County, Washington County, or Saratoga County, New York. Deadline: May 1.

5139. **Hill** 5 scholarships ranging from $500 to $1,070 to freshman and sophomore students with at least a 2.5 GPA or a high school average of 80. Must be graduates of Fort Edward High School, in Fort Edward, New York. Renewable. Deadline: May 1.

Alfred University
Associate Director of Admissions
P.O. Box 765
Alfred, NY 14082
(800) 541-9229 or (607) 871-2115
http://www.alfred.edu/

5140. **Art Portfolio Scholarships** 6 scholarships providing one-half tuition to students majoring in art. Based on art portfolio. Renewable.

5141. **Association of Women** 2 scholarships of $500; one is awarded to a student who is a resident of Allegany County, New York, and the other to a resident of Steuben County, New York. Deadline: April 1.

5142. **Competition Scholarships** 10 scholarships of $1,000 to students meeting certain academic criteria. Renewable.

5143. **Ernest and Fern Snyder Memorial Scholarship** 1 scholarship of $500 to a high school senior who graduated from a school in western New York State and will be majoring in agricultural technologies, with an interest in the dairy industry.

5144. **Junior Achievement Scholarship** 1 scholarship of $4,000 per year (for four years) to an entering freshman majoring in business administration or accounting. Must have been a member of a Junior Achievement applied economics class. Must have scored at least 1000 on SAT or be in the top 20 percent of class; must have completed sixteen college–prep courses; must have at least a 3.0 GPA. Deadline: February 1.

5145. **M. A. and C. A. Graham Nursing** 2 scholarships of $500 to freshman nursing students; preference given to graduates from LeRoy or Warsaw, New York, high school or other Wyoming County, New York, high schools. Deadline: April 1.

5146. **Merit Scholarships** Varying numbers of scholarships ranging from $5,029 to $11,725 to students meeting certain academic criteria.

5147. **President's Honors** 55 scholarships of $1,350 to students who are in the top 10 percent of their class from a high school in one of the following western New York counties: Allegheny, Cattaraugus, Chautauqua, Erie, Genesee, Livingston, Monroe, Niagara, Ontario, Orleans, Steuben, and Wyoming. Renewable with a 3.25 GPA. Deadline: April 1.

5148. **Robert S. Sweeney Scholarship** 1 scholarship of $500 to an entering freshman who graduated from a Steuben County, New York, high school. Student must be majoring in business technology. Deadline: April 1.

5149. **Sorrento Inc.** 1 scholarship of $1,350 to a student majoring in agriculture, chemical technology, business administration, truck and diesel, or secretarial studies. Preference given to a Hamburg, New York, student; if no one is eligible, scholarship is awarded to a southern Erie County, New York, high school graduate. Deadline: April 1.

5150. **Southern Tier Scholarships** Varying numbers of scholarships of $4,000 to students in the top 10 percent of their class with at least a 90 average. Renewable with 3.0 GPA.

Bard College
Annandale-on-Hudson, NY 12504
(914) 758-6822
http://www.bard.edu/

5151. **Bard** 400 scholarships ranging from $500 to $6,500. Renewable with a 2.0 GPA.

5152. **Distinguishing Science Scholarships** 24 scholarships providing tuition costs to students meeting certain academic criteria who will be majoring in either a biological or physical science. Renewable with a 3.0 GPA.

5153. **Excellence** 50 scholarships of varying amounts; students must be in the top 10 percent of their class. Renewable with a 3.0 GPA.

5154. **Tuition Waivers** Numerous partial– to full-tuition waivers to students who are employees or children of employees.

CUNY (City University of New York)
CUNY Bernard M. Baruch College
17 Lexington Avenue
New York, NY 10010
(212) 447-3000
http://www.baruch.cuny.edu
udgbb@cunyvm.cuny.edu

5155. **Baruch Scholars Awards** 60 scholarships of $3,000 to students in the top 10 percent of their class, with at least an 87 GPA, and who scored at least 1100 on SAT. Renewable with 3.25 GPA.

5156. **Excellence Award** Varying numbers of scholarships of approximately $3,300 to incoming freshmen with at least a 90 GPA, who scored at least 1300 on SAT. Based on academic criteria, essay, and recommendation letters. Renewable with 3.25 GPA. Contact the Scholarship Coordinator. Deadline: February 15.

5157. **Rosenberg Scholars "Honors Program" Scholarships** 10 scholarships of $4,000 to students with at least a 90 GPA who scored at least 1300 on SAT. Renewable with a 3.25 GPA.

5158. **Tuition Waivers** Numerous partial- to full-tuition waivers to students who are employees, children of employees, or senior citizens.

Columbia University
212 Hamilton Hall
New York, NY 10027
(212) 854-2521
http://www.columbia.edu
ugrad-admiss@columbia.edu

5159. **Ann O'Hare McCormick Memorial Fund, Inc.** 6 grants ranging from $300 to $3,100 to women accepted to the Columbia School of Journalism. Based on academic achievement and financial need. No journalism experience necessary. Contact: Foundation Trustees, c/o Newswomen's Club of New York, 15 Gramercy Park, New York, NY 10003, (212) 777-1610.

5160. **Endowed Scholarships** 50 scholarship grants ranging from $1,000 to $14,000 to undergraduates majoring in engineering. Based on financial need and academic achievement. Deadline: March 1.

5161. **Joseph H. Bearns Prize in Music** A music-composition competition open to young composers ages eighteen to twenty-five. Two categories: $3,500 for larger forms and $2,500 for smaller forms. Applicants may enter only one composition. Contact: Bearns Prize Committee, Dept. of Music, (212) 854-3825. Only offered every other year. Deadline: February 1 of odd-numbered years.

5162. **Tuition Waivers** Numerous partial- to full-tuition waivers to students who are employees or children of employees.

Cooper Union
Cooper Square
New York, NY 10003-7183
(212) 353-4120
http://www.cooper.edu
admissions@cooper.edu

5163. **For the Advancement of Science and Art** Free tuition for accepted students. Room and board is $3,650. Students must be majoring in engineering, architecture, or fine art. Based on SAT and CEEB scores.

Cornell University
410 Thurston Avenue
Ithaca, NY 14850-2488
(607) 255-2000
http://www.cornell.edu/
admissions@cornell.edu

5164. **National Book Scholarship** Award of $250. For additional information, write directly to the Director of Financial Aid.

5165. **National Scholarship Program** Scholarships of $1,500 to students designated National Merit Finalists. Based on academic and extracurricular achievements and community involvement.

5166. **Outstanding Junior** Scholarship of $1,000 to a junior student majoring in journalism.

5167. **Outstanding Senior** Scholarship of $1,000 to a senior student majoring in journalism.

5168. **Regents Scholarship** At least 61 scholarships ranging from $100 to $1,000, renewable for four to five years. Based on SAT/ACT, GPA, and financial need. Must be U.S. citizens, permanent residents, or refugees.

5169. **Scholastic Magazine** Scholarship of $1,000 and summer internship to a journalism student.

5170. **Sheila Turner Seed Memorial Scholarship** Scholarship of $1,000 to a female undergraduate junior. Based on interest and ability in magazine journalism or audio-visual presentation.

Culinary Institute of America
433 Albany Post Road
Hyde Park, NY 12538-1499
(800) CULINARY
(914) 452-9430

5171. **Edward T. Hanley Scholarship** Scholarships of tuition, fees, and room and board (valued over

$6,500) to students who are Hotel Employees & Restaurant Employees (HERE) International Union members of at least one year or who have been recommended by a union member. Applications are by the vice–presidential district in which member lives. Those in odd–numbered districts apply in odd–numbered years, even–numbered districts in even–numbered years. Applications are published in "Catering Industry Employee" in January, February, and March. Funded by HERE. Deadline: April 1.

5172. **Merit Scholarships** 16 scholarships of approximately $500 to students who meet certain academic criteria.

Fordham University
441 East Fordham Road
Bronx, NY 10458
(800) FORDHAM
(718) 817-1000
http://www.fordham.edu
ad_buckley@lars.fordham.edu

5173. **Athletic (Men)** Baseball, basketball, cross-country running, football, golf, soccer, squash, swimming and diving, tennis, track and field, and water polo scholarships.

5174. **Athletic (Women)** Basketball, cross–country running, softball, swimming and diving, tennis, track and field, and volleyball scholarships.

5175. **Band Awards** Up to 11 scholarships of approximately $500 to students who meet certain criteria and are or will be band members. Based on talent.

5176. **Class of 1940 Award** 1 scholarship of varying amount to an entering student meeting certain academic criteria.

5177. **Dean's Scholarships** 200 to 300 scholarships ranging from $5,000 to $10,000 to students meeting certain academic and financial criteria. Renewable.

5178. **Fordham College Alumni Scholarships** scholarships of varying amounts to students who are children of alumni and meet certain other criteria.

5179. **Presidential Scholarships** Up to 15 scholarships providing tuition plus additional funds to students who are in the top 10 percent of their class and scored at least 1300 on SAT. Renewable.

5180. **Tuition Waivers** Numerous partial to full tuition waivers to students who are employees or children of employees.

New York University
22 Washington Square North
New York, NY 10011
(212) 998-4636
http://www.nyu.edu
nyu.admit@nyu.edu

5181. **Journalism** 8 scholarships ranging from $1,000 to $2,500. Inquire with journalism department for requirements.

5182. **Presidential** 15 scholarships ranging from $2,000 to $5,000 to students in the top 1 percent of their class, with at least a 3.8 GPA, scoring at least 1250 on SAT. Renewable with a 3.5 GPA.

5183. **Scholars in Education** 50 scholarships of $2,000 to students in top 10 percent of class, with at least a 3.0 GPA, and scoring at least 1100 on SAT. Renewable with a 3.0 GPA.

5184. **Silverstein** 5 scholarships of $2,500 to students in top 5 percent of class, with a 3.8 GPA, and scoring at least 1250 on SAT. Renewable with a 3.5 GPA.

5185. **Trustees** 300 scholarships of $1,000 to students in top 5 percent of class, with at least a 3.6 GPA, and scoring at least 1200 on SAT. Renewable with a 3.0 GPA.

5186. **University** 100 scholarships ranging from $750 to $5,000 to students in top 5 percent of class, with at least 3.7 GPA, and scoring at least 1200 on SAT. Renewable.

Rochester Institute of Technology
One Lomb Memorial Drive
Rochester, NY 14623-0887
(716) 475-2400
http://www.rit.edu
admissions@rit.edu

5187. **Hirosato Scholarship** 1 scholarship of varying amount to a student who is a resident of Bucks County and will be majoring in graphic art, printing, or photography.

5188. **International Student Scholarships** 50 scholarships of varying amounts to international students who meet certain criteria.

5189. **National Merit Awards** 2 scholarships of varying amounts to students designated as National Merit Finalists.

5190. **Outstanding Transfer Student Scholarships** 50 scholarships ranging from $3,300 to $6,600 to students with at least a 3.2 GPA. Renewable with 3.0 GPA.

5191. **Presidential Scholars** 131 scholarships of varying amounts. Based on academic merit.

5192. **PSA Scholarship** Awards of $750 to high school seniors (or students who graduated within the past two years) who will study photography at Rochester Institute of Technology; must submit portfolio. Contact: Photographic Society of America, PSA Education/Scholarship Committee, 3000 United Founders Blvd., Suite 103, Oklahoma City, OK 73112. Deadline: March 15.

5193. **RIT Merit Awards** 63 scholarships of varying amounts. Based on academic merit.

5194. **RIT/Urban League Scholarships** 50 scholarships of $2,500 to students in the upper 50 percent of their class who have at least a 3.0 GPA. Renewable with 2.0 GPA.

5195. **ROTC Room Scholarships** 12 scholarships providing dormitory costs to students who are members of ROTC and meet certain criteria.

5196. **ROTC Tuition Subsidies** 9 scholarships providing tuition costs to students who are members of ROTC and meet certain criteria.

5197. **Scholastic Art Award** 1 scholarship award of varying amount to a student meeting certain criteria.

5198. **Scholastic Photo Award** 1 scholarship award of varying amount to a student meeting certain criteria.

5199. **Society of Automotive Engineers** 1 scholarship of varying amount to a student majoring in automotive engineering.

5200. **Special** 140 scholarships of $1,500 to people born on June 17, 1979.

5201. **Tuition Waivers** numerous partial- to full-tuition waivers to students who are employees or children of employees.

5202. **Young Printing Executives Club Scholarship Fund** Scholarships of $2,500 to undergraduate students majoring in printing management. Must be residents of NY, NJ, or CT and enrolled at the Rochester Institute of Technology. Applicants must have at least a 3.0 GPA and be pursuing a career in the tri-state area. Renewable for four years. Contact: Young Printing Executives Club, Scholarship Fund, 5 Penn Plaza, New York NY 10001, (212) 279-2100. Deadline: varies from May 15 to June 1.

Syracuse University
201 Administration Building
Syracuse NY 13244-1120
(315) 443-1870
http://www.syr.edu/

5203. **Army–Air Force ROTC Awards** Varying numbers of scholarships of varying amounts to students meeting certain criteria who are members of either Army or Air Force ROTC.

5204. **Art/Drama Awards** Varying numbers of scholarships of varying amounts to students meeting certain criteria who will be or are majoring in art or drama. Based on talent.

5205. **Citizenship Education Awards** Varying numbers of scholarships of varying amounts to students meeting certain academic criteria who are majoring in a social science.

5206. **Dollars for Scholars Awards** Varying numbers of scholarships of varying amounts to students meeting certain academic criteria.

5207. **Herald Journal Awards** Varying numbers of scholarships of varying amounts to students meeting certain academic criteria.

5208. **Junior Achievement Awards** Varying numbers of scholarships of varying amounts to students who are members of Junior Achievement.

5209. **Music Awards** Varying numbers of scholarships of varying amounts to students meeting certain criteria who are or will be music majors. Based on talent.

5210. **National Merit Scholars Awards** Varying numbers of scholarships of varying amounts to students receiving National Merit designation.

5211. **University "Honors College"** 45 scholarships ranging from $1,000 to $8,000. Renewable with a 2.5 GPA.

University of Rochester
Rochester NY 14627
(716) 275-2121
http://www.rochester.edu/

5212. **Bausch and Lomb Science Scholarships** 75 to 100 scholarships ranging from $1,000 to $10,000. Based on SAT/ACT; must have received best record in science during high school.

5213. **Urban League** Numerous scholarships of $2,000 to students meeting certain criteria.

5214. **Xerox Scholar Program** Scholarships of up to full tuition to entering freshmen. Based on financial need, academic achievement, leadership, and community service. Deadline: April 15.

Yeshiva University
500 West 185th Street
New York, NY 10033
(212) 960-5277
http://www.yu.ed
yuadmit@ymail.yu.edu

5215. **Dr. S. Belkin Undergraduate Scholarships** Varying numbers of scholarships ranging from $250 to $1,000 to students who have at least a 90 GPA and who scored at least 1100 on SAT. Renewable.

5216. **Jacob Burns Scholars Awards** Varying numbers of scholarships of varying amounts to students meeting certain academic criteria.

5217. **Max Stern Scholars Awards** Varying numbers of scholarships of $5,000 to students in the top 5 percent of their class, with at least a 95 GPA, and who scored at least 1300 on SAT. Renewable.

5218. **Tuition Waivers** Numerous partial- to full-tuition waivers to students who are employees or children of employees.

NORTH CAROLINA

Duke University
2138 Campus Drive
Durham, NC 27706
(919) 684-8111
http://www.duke.edu
askduke@admiss.duke.edu

5219. **AB Duke** 20 scholarships of tuition to students in the top 10 percent of their class, with at least a 3.7 GPA, and scoring at least 1300 on SAT or 32 on ACT. Renewable.

5220. **A. J. Fletcher Music Scholarships** 13 scholarships of varying amounts to students who are non-majors.

5221. **Alumni** 3 scholarships of $3,000 to students in the top 10 percent of their class, with at least a 3.7 GPA, and who scored at least 1300 on SAT or 32 on ACT. Renewable.

5222. **Benjamin N. Duke Leadership Awards** 15 scholarships of varying amounts to students who have demonstrated leadership abilities and who are residents of North or South Carolina.

5223. **Duke Sponsored National Achievement Scholarships** 4 scholarships of varying amounts to students who meet certain academic criteria.

5224. **Duke Sponsored National Merit Scholarships** 10 scholarships of varying amounts to students who are designated National Merit finalists or scholars.

5225. **North Carolina Math Contest Awards** 2 scholarships of varying amounts to winners of the NC Math Contest who are North Carolina residents.

5226. **Reggie Howard Awards** 7 scholarships of $1,000 to students who meet certain academic criteria. Renewable.

5227. **Tuition Waivers** Numerous partial- to full-tuition waivers to students who are employees or children of employees.

North Carolina State University
P.O. Box 7001
Raleigh, NC 27695-6103
(919) 737-2011
http://www.ncsu.edu
undergrad-admissions@ncsu.edu

5228. **Allied Chemical Scholarships** 2 scholarship grants of $2,000 to students who have at least a 3.2 GPA on a 4.0 scale, are in the upper 20 percent of their class, and are majoring in or planning to major in chemical engineering. Deadline: February 1.

5229. **Aluminum Company Scholarships** 4 scholarship grants of $1,000 to undergraduate students who have at least a 3.2 GPA on a 4.0 scale and are in the upper 20 percent of their class. Deadline: February 1.

5230. **Alumni Class Scholarship** 1 scholarship of varying amount to a student meeting certain academic criteria.

5231. **Brooks Frizzelle Scholarships** 4 scholarship grants ranging from $1,000 to $1,250 to students majoring in agriculture who have financial need. Must be residents of Greene County, North Carolina. Deadline: February 1.

5232. **Burlington Industries Scholarships** 4 scholarship grants of $1,000 to undergraduate juniors who meet certain criteria. Must be North

Carolina residents and U.S. citizens. Deadline: February 1.

5233. **Carolinas Gold Association Scholarships** 5 scholarship grants of $1,000 to undergraduate sophomores, juniors, or seniors majoring in turfgrass agronomy or turfgrass management who meet certain criteria. Deadline: February 1.

5234. **Dean's Minority Scholarships** 50 scholarships of varying amounts to minority students meeting certain academic criteria.

5235. **Engineering Merit Scholarships** 10 scholarship grants of $1,000 to entering freshmen who are in the upper 20 percent of their class, will be majoring in engineering, and have demonstrated high potential for success. Deadline: February 1.

5236. **First Union National Bank Merit Awards** Varying numbers of scholarships of varying amounts to students meeting certain academic criteria.

5237. **Foundation Freshmen** 6 scholarships of $4,000 to students in the top 5 percent of their class with at least a 3.7 GPA. Renewable with a 3.0 GPA.

5238. **Foundation Honors** 40 scholarships ranging from $1,000 to $2,000 to students in the top 5 percent of their class with at least a 3.7 GPA.

5239. **Foundation/Recognition** 6 scholarships of $1,000 to students in the top 5 percent of their class with at least a 3.7 GPA. Renewable with a 3.0 GPA.

5240. **John T. Caldwell** 30 scholarships ranging from $3,500 to $5,000 to students in the top 5 percent of their class, with at least a 3.7 GPA. Renewable with a 3.0 GPA.

5241. **Joseph D. Moore Scholarships** 2 scholarships of varying amounts to students meeting certain academic criteria.

5242. **Kincaid Merit Awards** Varying numbers of scholarships of varying amounts to students meeting certain academic criteria.

5243. **NCSU Foundation Scholars Awards** 3 scholarships of varying amounts to students meeting certain academic criteria.

5244. **Powers Scholarships** 4 scholarship grants of $1,000 to entering freshmen who are in the upper 20 percent of their class and majoring in engineering. One grant is specifically for an out-of-state student. Deadline: February 1.

5245. **Pulp and Paper Foundation** 25 scholarships ranging from $850 to $3,000 to students pursuing a career in the paper industry in the South. Based on academic record, extracurricular activities, and SAT/ACT. Contact: P.O. Box 7502, North Carolina State University, Raleigh, NC 27695-7502. Deadline: February 1.

5246. **School of Agricultural and Life Sciences Scholarships** 93 scholarships of varying amounts to students meeting certain academic criteria who are majoring in an agricultural or life science.

5247. **School of Design Merit Awards** 8 scholarships of varying amounts to students meeting certain academic criteria who are design majors.

5248. **School of Education Merit Awards** 20 scholarships of varying amounts to students meeting certain academic criteria who are majoring in education.

5249. **School of Engineering Merit Awards** 206 scholarships of varying amounts to students meeting certain academic criteria who are majoring in engineering.

5250. **School of Forest Resources Scholarships** 40 scholarships of varying amounts to students meeting certain academic criteria who are majoring in forest resources.

5251. **School of Humanities and Social Science Awards** 52 scholarships of varying amounts to students meeting certain academic criteria who are majoring in either humanities or a social science.

5252. **School of Physical and Mathematical Sciences Awards** 43 scholarships of varying amounts to students meeting certain academic criteria who are majoring in a physical or mathematical science.

5253. **School of Textiles Scholarships** 29 scholarships of varying amounts to students meeting certain academic criteria who are majoring in textile engineering.

5254. **Tuition Waivers** Numerous partial- to full-tuition waivers to students who are senior citizens.

5255. **Winslow Foundation Scholarships** 27 scholarships of $1,000 to students who are residents of North Carolina, Maryland, or Washington, D.C., and have financial need. Deadline: February 1.

University of North Carolina
South Building, CB #9100
Chapel Hill, NC 27599-2200
(919) 966-3621
http://www.unc.edu/

5256. Alexander Morisey Minority Scholarships 2 scholarships of $1,000 to entering minority freshmen who plan on majoring in journalism. Based on academic achievement, financial need, and demonstrated ability. Renewable with a B average. Deadline: February 1.

5257. A. W. Huckle Scholarship 1 scholarship of $500 to an undergraduate junior or senior who is a journalism major. Based on academic achievement, financial need, and demonstrated ability. Renewable with a B average. Deadline: February 1.

5258. Beatrice Cobb Scholarship 1 scholarship of $500 to an undergraduate junior or senior who is a journalism major. Based on academic achievement, financial need, and demonstrated ability. Renewable with a B average. Deadline: February 1.

5259. Bob Quincy Scholarship 1 scholarship of $3,500 to an undergraduate junior or senior who is a journalism major. Based on academic achievement, financial need, and demonstrated ability. Renewable with a B average. Deadline: February 1.

5260. Carl Council Scholarships 2 scholarships of $2,000 to undergraduate juniors or seniors who are journalism majors. Based on academic achievement, financial need, and demonstrated ability. Renewable with a B average. Preference given to Orange County residents. Deadline: February 1.

5261. Charles R. Price Scholarships 1 scholarship of $5,000 to an undergraduate junior or senior who is a journalism major. Based on academic achievement, financial need, and demonstrated ability. Renewable with a B average. Deadline: February 1.

5262. Cultural Diversity Scholarships 29 scholarships of varying amounts to minority students who meet certain criteria.

5263. David Julian Whichard Scholarships 2 scholarships of $1,000 to undergraduate juniors or seniors who are journalism majors. Based on academic achievement, financial need, and demonstrated ability. Renewable with a B average. Deadline: February 1.

5264. Deborah Sykes Scholarship 1 scholarship of $500 to an undergraduate junior or senior who is a journalism major. Based on academic achievement, financial need, and demonstrated ability. Renewable with a B average. Deadline: February 1.

5265. Edward Heywood Megson Scholarship 1 scholarship of $500 to an undergraduate junior or senior who is a journalism major. Based on academic achievement, financial need, and demonstrated ability. Renewable with a B average. Deadline: February 1.

5266. Elkin Tribune–Thomas Fleming Scholarship 1 scholarship of $500 to an undergraduate junior or senior who is a journalism major. Based on academic achievement, financial need, and demonstrated ability. Renewable with a B average. Deadline: February 1.

5267. Fine Arts Awards 2 scholarships of varying amounts to students who are fine arts majors. Based on talent.

5268. Freedom Newspapers Scholarship 1 scholarship of $1,000 to an undergraduate junior or senior who is a journalism major. Based on academic achievement, financial need, and demonstrated ability. Renewable with a B average. Deadline: February 1.

5269. Gerald Johnson Scholarship 1 scholarship of $500 to an undergraduate junior or senior who is a journalism major. Based on academic achievement, financial need, and demonstrated ability. Renewable with a B average. Deadline: February 1.

5270. Glenn Keever Scholarship 1 scholarship of $500 to an undergraduate junior or senior who is a journalism major. Based on academic achievement, financial need, and demonstrated ability. Renewable with a B average. Deadline: February 1.

5271. Harvey Laffoon Scholarship 1 scholarship of $500 to an undergraduate junior or senior who is a journalism major. Based on academic achievement, financial need, and demonstrated ability. Renewable with a B average. Deadline: February 1.

5272. Henry Dennis Scholarship 1 scholarship of $250 to an undergraduate junior or senior who is a journalism major. Based on academic achievement, financial need, and demonstrated ability. Renewable with a B average. Deadline: February 1.

5273. Henry Lockwood Phillips Scholarship 1 scholarship of $500 to an undergraduate junior or senior who is a journalism major. Based on academic achievement, financial need, and demonstrated ability. Renewable with a B average. Deadline: February 1.

5274. **Holt McPherson Scholarship** 1 scholarship of $500 to an undergraduate junior or senior who is a journalism major. Based on academic achievement, financial need, and demonstrated ability. Renewable with a B average. Deadline: February 1.

5275. **John W. Harden Scholarship** 1 scholarship of $500 to an undergraduate junior or senior who is a journalism major. Based on academic achievement, financial need, and demonstrated ability. Renewable with a B average. Deadline: February 1.

5276. **Johnston** 100 scholarships ranging from $500 to $5,000 to students in the top 10 percent of their class with at least a 3.5 GPA. Renewable with a 3.0 GPA.

5277. **Johnathan Daniels Scholarship** 1 scholarship of $500 to an undergraduate junior or senior who is a journalism major. Based on academic achievement, financial need, and demonstrated ability. Renewable with a B average. Deadline: February 1.

5278. **Julius Hubbard Scholarship** 1 scholarship of $500 to an undergraduate junior or senior who is a journalism major. Based on academic achievement, financial need, and demonstrated ability. Renewable with a B average. Deadline: February 1.

5279. **Knight Distinguished Scholarships** 4 scholarships of $1,000 to undergraduate juniors or seniors who are journalism majors. Based on academic achievement, financial need, and demonstrated ability. Renewable with a B average. Deadline: February 1.

5280. **Louis Graves Scholarship** 1 scholarship of $500 to an undergraduate junior or senior who is a journalism major. Based on academic achievement, financial need, and demonstrated ability. Renewable with a B average. Deadline: February 1.

5281. **Mark Ethridge Scholarship** 1 scholarship of $250 to an undergraduate junior or senior who is a journalism major. Based on academic achievement, financial need, and demonstrated ability. Renewable with a B average. Deadline: February 1.

5282. **Mildred Gifford Scholarship** 1 scholarship of $500 to an undergraduate junior or senior who is a journalism major. Based on academic

achievement, financial need, and demonstrated ability. Renewable with a B average. Deadline: February 1.

5283. **Milne Scholarships** 15 scholarships of varying amounts to students who meet certain academic criteria and are residents of Weld County.

5284. **Minnie S. Rubinstein Memorial Scholarship** 1 scholarship of $2,000 to a minority graduate student majoring in journalism. Based on academic achievement, financial need, and journalistic ability.

5285. **Morehead** 60 full-costs scholarships. Renewable.

5286. **Music Awards** 35 scholarships of varying amounts to students who are music majors, based on talent.

5287. **N.C. Press Women Scholarship** 1 scholarship of $500 to a female undergraduate junior or senior who is a journalism major. Based on academic achievement, financial need, and demonstrated ability. Renewable with a B average. Deadline: February 1.

5288. **North Carolina Sheriffs' Association Criminal Justice Scholarships** Up to 10 scholarships of $2,000 to undergraduate students majoring in criminal justice, criminology, law enforcement, police administration, social services, or other law enforcement–related fields. Must be residents of North Carolina. Preference is given to children of any NC law enforcement officer. Selection based on financial need and career goal. Contact financial aid office.

5289. **O. J. Coffin Scholarship** 1 scholarship of $500 to an undergraduate junior or senior who is a journalism major. Based on academic achievement, financial need, and demonstrated ability. Renewable with a B average. Deadline: February 1.

5290. **Pete Ivey Scholarship** 1 scholarship of $500 to an undergraduate junior or senior who is a journalism major. Based on academic achievement, financial need, and demonstrated ability. Renewable with a B average. Deadline: February 1.

5291. **Pete McKnight Scholarship** 1 scholarship of $3,500 to an undergraduate junior or senior who is a journalism major. Based on academic achievement, financial need, and demonstrated ability. Renewable with a B average. Deadline: February 1.

5292. **Pogue "Honors Program"** 7 scholarships of $3,300 to students in the top 10 percent of their class with at least a 3.0 GPA. Renewable.

5293. **President's Honor Scholarships** 95 scholarships of varying amounts to students who meet certain academic criteria and are North Carolina residents.

5294. **Provost Honor Freshman Awards** 340 scholarships of varying amounts to entering freshmen who meet certain academic criteria.

5295. **Quincy Sharpe Mills Scholarships** 2 scholarships of $1,250 to undergraduate juniors or seniors who are journalism students. Based on academic achievement, financial need, and demonstrated ability. Renewable with a B average. Deadline: February 1.

5296. **R. C. Rivers Scholarship** 1 scholarship of $250 to an undergraduate junior or senior who is a journalism major. Based on academic achievement, financial need, and demonstrated ability. Renewable with a B average. Deadline: February 1.

5297. **Reader's Digest Scholarship** 1 scholarship of $250 to an undergraduate junior or senior who is a journalism major. Based on academic achievement, financial need, and demonstrated ability. Renewable with a B average. Deadline: February 1.

5298. **Roy Rabon Scholarship** 1 scholarship of $250 to an undergraduate junior or senior who is a journalism major. Based on academic achievement, financial need, and demonstrated ability. Renewable with a B average. Deadline: February 1.

5299. **Roy Wilkins Minority Scholarship** 1 scholarship of $250 to a minority undergraduate junior or senior who is a journalism major. Based on academic achievement, financial need, and demonstrated ability. Renewable with a B average. Deadline: February 1.

5300. **Roy Wilkins Scholarship** 1 scholarship of $250 to an undergraduate junior or senior who is a journalism major. Based on academic achievement, financial need, and demonstrated ability. Renewable with a B average. Deadline: February 1.

5301. **Steed Rollins Scholarship** 1 scholarship of $500 to an undergraduate junior or senior who is a journalism major. Based on academic achievement, financial need, and demonstrated ability. Renewable with a B average. Deadline: February 1.

5302. **University Alumni Awards** 15 scholarships of varying amounts to students who meet certain criteria and are related to alumni.

5303. **Vivien Edmonds Scholarships** 2 scholarships of $1,000 to minority students who are undergraduate sophomores who plan to major in journalism. Based on academic achievement, financial need, and demonstrated ability. Renewable with a B average. Deadline: February 1.

5304. **Walter Spearman Scholarship** 1 scholarship of $500 to an undergraduate junior or senior who is a journalism major. Based on academic achievement, financial need, and demonstrated ability. Renewable with a B average. Deadline: February 1.

5305. **William Cochran Scholarship** 1 scholarship of $500 to an undergraduate junior or senior who is a journalism major. Based on academic achievement, financial need, and demonstrated ability. Renewable with a B average. Deadline: February 1.

NORTH DAKOTA

University of North Dakota
P.O. Box 8357
Grand Forks, ND 58202
(701) 777-2011
http://www.und.nodak.edu

5306. **Athletic (Men)** Baseball, basketball, football, ice hockey, track and field, and wrestling scholarships.

5307. **Athletic (Women)** Basketball, softball, swimming and diving, track and field, and volleyball scholarships.

5308. **Freshman Honors Program** Numerous 400 scholarships ranging from $250 to $2,000 to students in the upper 10 percent of their class. Renewable.

OHIO

Antioch University
795 Livermore
Yellow Springs, OH 45387
(800) 543-9436
http://www.antioch-college.edu/

5309. **Alfred Hampton Memorial Scholarship** 1 to 2 scholarships of up to $5,000 to minority students meeting certain academic criteria. Renewable.

5310. **A. Morgan Public Service Scholarship** 1 scholarship of up to $5,000 to a student meeting certain academic criteria. Renewable.

5311. **Antioch Regional Scholarships** 16 scholarships of up to $3,000 to students meeting certain academic criteria who are local area residents. Renewable.

5312. **Arthur Morgan Public Service Scholarship** 1 scholarship of $5,000 to a student meeting certain criteria who has participated in public service projects.

5313. **Beatrice Kotas Scholarship** 1 scholarship of $1,000 to a student meeting certain criteria.

5314. **Dean Philip Nash Scholarship** 1 scholarship of up to $1,250 to a student meeting certain academic criteria. Renewable.

5315. **Dean's Scholarships** Up to 5 scholarships of $3,000 to students meeting certain academic criteria.

5316. **Dorothy E. Mooney Scholarship** 1 scholarship of up to $2,500 to students meeting certain academic criteria.

5317. **Evan Spalt Scholarship for Science and Math** 1 scholarship of $2,000 to a student who meets certain academic criteria and is either a science or math major.

5318. **Foreign Exchange Scholarships** 6 scholarships of $3,000 to students who are living and working in a foreign exchange program.

5319. **Horace Mann Presidential Scholarships** Up to 2 scholarships of up to $5,000 to students meeting certain academic criteria. Renewable.

5320. **Hughes Science Scholarships** Up to 3 scholarships of approximately $2,600 to students meeting certain academic criteria who are science majors. Renewable.

5321. **International Student Scholarships** 3 scholarships of varying amounts to international students who meet certain criteria.

5322. **J. B. Tripp Humanities Scholarship** 1 scholarship of $1,250 to a student meeting certain academic criteria who is majoring in the humanities.

5323. **J. D. Dawson Science Scholarship** 1 scholarship of $5,000 to a student meeting certain criteria who is a science major.

5324. **Nelson Urban Scholarships** 1 to 2 scholarships ranging from $1,000 to $5,000 to students meeting certain criteria.

5325. **Paula Carlson Scholarships** Up to 13 scholarships of $2,000 to students meeting certain criteria.

5326. **Spalt Scholarship** 1 scholarship of $2,000 to a student meeting certain criteria.

5327. **Tuition Waivers** Numerous partial- to full-tuition waivers to students who are employees or children of employees.

5328. **Upward Bound Scholarships** 1 to 2 scholarships of up to $3,000 to economically disadvantaged students meeting certain criteria who are Upward Bound participants. Renewable.

Cleveland Institute of Art
11141 East Boulevard
Cleveland, OH 44106
(800) 223-4700
http://www.cia.edu

5329. **Honorary Scholarships** 21 partial-tuition scholarships to entering freshmen. Based on portfolio, academic record, talent, and character.

5330. **Portfolio** 10 to 15 scholarships of 50 percent tuition to students with at least a 3.0 GPA who scored at least 1000 on SAT or 21 on ACT.

Ohio State University
Columbus, OH 43210-1200
(614) 292-3980
http://www.acs.ohio-state.edu

5331. **Bill Zipf Memorial Scholarship** 1 scholarship of $1,400 to an undergraduate sophomore or above who is majoring in agricultural communications. Must be a member or former member of 4-H.

5332. **Charles F. High Foundation** Numerous grants of varying amounts, totaling $163,000, to male students. Contact: 1520 Melody Lane, Bacyrus, OH 44820, (419) 562–2074. Deadline: June 1.

5333. **Charles W. Durfey Memorial Scholarship Fund in Journalism** 1 scholarship of $1,100 to an undergraduate meeting certain academic criteria who is a journalism major and is showing promise in reporting.

5334. **Dance Awards** 3 scholarships of varying amounts to students who meet certain criteria and are dance majors.

5335. **Distinguished Scholarships** 77 scholarships of varying amounts to students who meet certain academic criteria.

5336. **Frank J. Tate Scholarship in Journalism** 1 or more scholarships of up to $1,100 to undergraduates in upper division meeting certain criteria who are majoring in magazine management or news magazine reporting.

5337. **Frank M. Heller Memorial Award** 1 scholarship of $1,300 to an outstanding undergraduate freshman or sophomore meeting certain academic criteria who is a journalism major.

5338. **General University** Numerous scholarships ranging from $300 to $2,000 to students in the upper 10 percent of their class who scored at least 26 on ACT. Renewable.

5339. **George J. Kienzle Memorial Scholarship** 1 or more scholarships of up to $1,500 to undergraduate or graduate students meeting certain academic criteria, who have financial need, are journalism majors, and have demonstrated professional ability and promise.

5340. **Hameroff–Milenthal–Spencer Award** 1 or more scholarships of $1,000 to undergraduate seniors who meet certain criteria and are a journalism majors.

5341. **Jacob Meckstroth Memorial Scholarship** 1 or more scholarships of at least $500 to undergraduates meeting certain criteria, who are journalism majors, and student SPJ members. Must be in a news sector. Offered by the Central Ohio Professional Chapter of the Society of the Professional Journalists. Contact the Advisor, Student Chapter SPJ at the university.

5342. **James E. Pollard Memorial Scholarship Fund in Journalism** 1 scholarship of $1,250 to a high school senior with high academic achievement who will be enrolling in the School of Journalism or to an undergraduate with high academic achievement.

5343. **James W. Faulkner Scholarship** 1 scholarship of $400 to an undergraduate sophomore or above based on academic achievement, professional promise, and financial need. Renewable. Apply after freshman year.

5344. **John D. Fullen Scholarships** 2 or more scholarships of up to $2,950 to undergraduates meeting certain academic criteria who are journalism majors.

5345. **Joseph Simmons Myers Award** 1 scholarship of $600 to a graduating undergraduate senior meeting certain academic criteria, who is a journalism major and who has demonstrated professional promise.

5346. **Judy Stewart Mesenburg Award** 1 or more scholarships of $800 to undergraduates meeting certain criteria who are journalism majors.

5347. **Lester C. Getzloe Scholarship** 1 scholarship of $900 to an undergraduate or graduate student meeting certain criteria who is a journalism major.

5348. **Medalist Scholarships** 40 scholarships of varying amounts to students who meet certain academic criteria.

5349. **Michael V. DiSalle Scholarships** 1 or more scholarships of $1,250 to undergraduates meeting certain criteria who are journalism majors.

5350. **Music Scholarships** 25 scholarships of varying amounts to students who meet certain criteria and are music majors.

5351. **Ohio Newspaper Award** 1 scholarship of $700 to an undergraduate meeting certain academic criteria who is a journalism major.

5352. **OSU Honors Program** Numerous scholarships ranging from $300 to $2,000 to students in the upper 3 percent of their class who scored at least 28 on ACT. Renewable.

5353. **OSU National Achievement Awards** 3 scholarships of varying amounts to students who meet certain academic criteria.

5354. **OSU National Merit Awards** 74 scholarships of varying amounts to students who have been designated as National Merit Finalists.

5355. **Paul N. Williams Memorial Scholarship** 1 scholarship of $600 to an undergraduate student who is a journalism major. Based on outstanding investigative reporting.

5356. **Presidential Scholarships** 10 scholarships of varying amounts to students who meet certain academic criteria.

5357. **Richard Piergallini Scholarship** 1 scholarship of $350 to an undergraduate meeting certain academic criteria who is a journalism major and has demonstrated professional promise and personality.

5358. **Robert E. Schaefer Scholarships** 2 scholarships of $1,800 to undergraduates meeting certain academic criteria, who are journalism majors with an interest in the print media. Preference given to students from Ross County, Ohio.

5359. **Robert K. Richards Memorial Award** 1 or more scholarships of $650 to undergraduates meeting certain criteria who are journalism majors.

5360. **School of Journalism Alumni Association Minority Scholarships** 1 or more scholarships of $730 to a minority undergraduate sophomore or above meeting certain criteria who are journalism majors.

5361. **School of Journalism Scholarships** 1 or more scholarships of $500 to undergraduates meeting certain criteria who are journalism majors.

5362. **Tom Wilson Sports Scholarship** 1 scholarship of $700 to an undergraduate sophomore or above who has an interest in and aptitude for sports writing. Based on articles submitted to *The Lantern*.

5363. **Tuition Waivers** Numerous partial- to full-tuition waivers to students who are employees, children of employees, or senior citizens.

5364. **William Drenten Memorial Scholarship** 1 or more scholarships of $1,000 to undergraduates meeting certain criteria who are a journalism majors.

5365. **William H. Newton Award** 1 scholarship award of $600 to an undergraduate or graduate student who is a reporter for *The Lantern*.

5366. **William Randolph Hearst Scholarship** 1 or more scholarships of up to $950 to undergardaute sophomores or juniors who have or indicate promise of achieving outstanding performances as reporters and writers.

5367. **Wolfe Journalism Honor Medal** 1 scholarship of $500 plus a medal to an undergraduate meeting certain academic criteria who is a journalism major.

University of Cincinnati
Institutional Planning
Mail Location 127
Cincinnati, OH 45221
(513) 556-6000
http://www.uc.edu

5368. **Architecture Scholarships** Varying numbers of scholarships of varying amounts to students meeting certain academic criteria who are majoring in architecture.

5369. **Art and Planning Scholarships** Varying numbers of scholarships of varying amounts to students meeting certain academic criteria.

5370. **Conservatory of Music Awards** Varying numbers of scholarships of varying amounts to students meeting certain criteria who are music majors. Based on talent.

5371. **Creative Arts/Performance Awards** Varying numbers of scholarships of varying amounts to students meeting certain criteria who are creative arts or performance arts majors.

5372. **Design Scholarships** Varying numbers of scholarships of varying amounts to students meeting certain criteria who are architecture majors. Based on talent.

5373. **Engineering Awards** Varying numbers of scholarships of varying amounts to students meeting certain academic criteria who are engineering majors.

5374. **General University Scholarships** 80 scholarships of $1,000 to students in the upper 5 percent of their class, with at least a 3.5 GPA, and who scored at least 1150 on SAT or 27 on ACT. Renewable.

5375. **James Awards** Varying numbers of scholarships of varying amounts to students who meet certain criteria who are Kentucky residents.

5376. **Minority Awards** Varying numbers of scholarships of varying amounts to minority students who meet certain criteria.

5377. **National Merit Awards** Varying numbers of scholarships of varying amounts to students receiving National Merit designation.

5378. **Presidential Scholarship** 1 scholarship providing tuition costs to students in the top 5 percent of their class who scored at least 1350 on SAT or 28 on ACT. Renewable with a 3.0 GPA.

5379. Tuition Waivers Numerous partial- to full-tuition waivers to students who are employees or children of employees.

5380. Voorheis Honor Scholarships 40 scholarships of tuition to students in the top 5 percent of their class who scored at least 1350 on SAT or 28 on ACT. Renewable.

Youngstown State University
Youngstown, OH 44555
(330) 742-2000
http://www.ysu.edu
nsrysu@ysub.ysu.edu

5381. Dean's 96 scholarships of $1,500 to students in the upper 10 percent of their class with at least a 3.5 GPA. Renewable.

5382. Esther Hamilton Scholarship Fund 2 grants of $1,500 to entering freshmen from Mahoning County, Ohio. Must be in the top 25 percent of class. Contact: c/o Dollar Savings and Trust Company, P.O. Box 450, Youngstown, OH 44501, (216) 744-9000. Deadline: June.

5383. YSU Foundation 2,200 scholarships ranging from $200 to $1,500 to students in the upper 25 percent of their class, with at least a 3.0 GPA, and scoring at least 1000 on SAT or 23 on ACT. Renewable.

OKLAHOMA

Oklahoma Baptist University
500 West University
Shawnee, OK 74801-1910
(405) 878-2033
http://www.okbu.edu

5384. Academic Unlimited scholarships ranging from $500 up to tuition costs to students who scored at least 980 on SAT or 24 on ACT. Renewable with a 3.3 GPA.

5385. Acteen Awards Varying numbers of scholarships of varying amounts to students who are members of Acteens and have demonstrated leadership abilities.

5386. Departmental Scholarships Varying numbers of scholarships of varying amounts to students majoring in religious or biblical studies or fine arts.

5387. Future Bison Scholarships Varying numbers of scholarships of varying amounts to students who are children of alumni.

5388. Leadership 60 scholarships ranging from $400 to $1,000 to students in the top 50 percent of their class, with at least a 2.5 GPA, and scoring at least 720 on SAT or 16 on ACT.

5389. Ministerial Careers Awards Varying numbers of scholarships of varying amounts to students who are pursuing ministerial careers.

5390. Miscellaneous Scholarships Varying numbers of scholarships of varying amounts to students meeting certain criteria.

5391. Music Numerous scholarships ranging from $200 to $600 to students majoring in music. Renewable.

5392. Partnership Awards Varying numbers of scholarships of varying amounts to students who are Baptist and meet certain criteria.

5393. Reciprocal Tuition Awards Varying numbers of scholarships of varying amounts to students who are participants in the exchange student program.

5394. Royal Ambassadors Scholarships Varying numbers of scholarships of varying amounts to students who are members of Royal Ambassadors and have demonstrated leadership abilities.

5395. Scholastic Competition Awards Varying numbers of scholarships of varying amounts to students selected in a scholastic competition.

5396. Southern Baptist Minister's Dependents Awards Varying numbers of scholarships of varying amounts to students who are dependents of Southern Baptist ministers.

5397. Transfer Unlimited $500 scholarships to transfer students with at least a 2.5 GPA. Renewable with a 3.5 GPA.

5398. Tuition Waivers Numerous partial to full tuition waivers to students who are alumni, employees, children of employees, or senior citizens.

5399. Valedictorian Awards Varying numbers of scholarships of varying amounts to students who are their class valedictorian.

Oral Roberts University
7777 South Lewis
Tulsa, OK 74170-0540
(918) 495-6510
http://www.oru.edu
admissions@oru.edu

5400. Academic Scholarships Unlimited scholarships of varying amounts to students in the upper 10 percent of their class, with at least a 3.45 GPA, and scoring at least 1000 on SAT or 25 on ACT. Renewable.

5401. Arts Scholarships Up to 226 scholarships of approximately $1,900 to students meeting certain criteria who are music majors. Based on talent.

5402. Christian Educator's Scholarship Scholarships of $1,000 to undergraduate students whose major source of family income comes from one or both parents being involved in full-time teaching/ administration. Applicants must be under twenty-five years of age.

5403. Dean's Scholarships Up to 84 scholarships of approximately $3,000 (40 percent of tuition) to students who scored at least 1200 on SAT or 29 on ACT and who meet certain other academic, extracurricular, and leadership criteria.

5404. Departmental Awards Awards of varying amounts to students demonstrating talent and/or service rendered in the area considered. Contact specific department for audition or application.

5405. Early Bird Scholarships Scholarships of $500 to students who are accepted for admission between their junior and senior year of high school. The student must be fully accepted to ORU by September 1 of their high school senior year.

5406. Fine Arts Scholarships 63 scholarships of approximately $1,100 to students meeting certain criteria who are art majors. Based on talent.

5407. Home–School Scholarships Awards of $1,500 to students who have graduated from a home-school program. One-time and nonrenewable.

5408. International Charismatic Bible Ministers Scholarships Up to 92 scholarships of approximately 10 percent tuition discount to students who are dependent children or grandchildren of members of the International Charismatic Bible Ministries Fellowships. Must be under twenty-five years of age.

5409. International Scholarships Varying numbers of scholarships ranging from $1,000 to $4,000 to international students based on financial need, TOEFL scores, and/or ORU GPA. Must complete the International Student Financial Aid Application.

5410. Ministers Scholarships Up to 223 scholarships of approximately $1,500 to students whose primary family income is from one or both parents being involved in a full-time ordained ministry. Renewable with 2.0 GPA.

5411. National Merit Awards 10 scholarships of approximately $1,000 to students receiving National Merit designation.

5412. Presidential Scholarships 39 scholarships of approximately $8,300 (100 percent of tuition) to students who scored at least 1380 on SAT or 35 on ACT and meet certain other academic, extracurricular, and leadership criteria.

5413. Provost's Scholarships Varying numbers of scholarships of approximately $5,124 (60 percent of tuition) to students who scored at least 1260 on SAT or 31 on ACT and meet certain other academic, extracurricular, and leadership criteria.

5414. Regents' Scholarships 58 scholarships of approximately $6,350 (80 percent of tuition) to students who scored at least 1310 on SAT or 33 on ACT and meet certain other academic, extracurricular, and leadership criteria.

5415. Talent Scholarships Unlimited scholarships of varying amounts to students based on portfolio, audition, or talent. Renewable.

5416. Transfer Scholarships Varying numbers of scholarships ranging from $2,200 to $3,200 to students who meet certain academic criteria (college GPA ranging from 3.45 to 4.0) and have at least fifteen credit hours.

5417. Tuition Waivers Numerous partial- to full-tuition waivers to students who are employees or children of employees.

University of Oklahoma
1000 Asp Avenue
Norman, OK 73019-0430
(405) 325-2151
http://www.ou.edu

5418. Alumni Scholar 50 scholarships of $500. Renewable.

5419. Athletic (Men) Baseball, basketball, cross-country, football, golf, gymnastics, tennis, and track and field scholarships.

5420. **Athletic (Women)** Basketball, cross–country, golf, gymnastics, softball, tennis, track and field, and volleyball scholarships.

5421. **Boyd R. Gunning** 10 scholarships of $1,500. Based on academic merit. Renewable.

5422. **College of Business** 46 scholarships of varying amounts to students majoring in business.

5423. **College of Engineering Scholarships** 293 scholarships of varying amounts to students majoring in engineering.

5424. **National Merit** 184 scholarships of varying amounts to students designated as National Merit Finalists.

5425. **Oklahoma Scholars** 144 scholarships of varying amounts. Based on academic merit.

5426. **President's Leadership** 60 scholarships of $600.

5427. **University/Achievement** 150 scholarships ranging from $500 to $750 to students in the top 10 percent of their class, with at least a 3.75 GPA, and scoring at least 1200 on SAT or 27 on ACT.

OREGON

Lewis and Clark College
0615 S.W. Palatine Hill Road
Portland, OR 97219
(800) 444-4111
(503) 768-7000
http://www.lclark.edu

5428. **Barbara Hirschi Neely and Trustee Scholarships** Awards ranging from $5,000 to full tuition to Lewis and Clark students interested in science, natural systems, intercultural issues, or international issues. Must have outstanding academic credentials. Awarded to freshman students, but renewable. Deadline: February 1.

5429. **Cheney Foundation Scholarships** Scholarships of $1,000 for currently enrolled freshmen to use in their sophomore year. Open to all majors. Must demonstrate academic excellence and community and college service. Renewable. Deadline: February 15.

5430. **Dean's Scholarships** 20 scholarships of $2,500 to students meeting certain academic criteria. Renewable with 3.0 GPA.

5431. **Forensics Scholarships** Varying numbers of scholarships ranging from $500 to $3,000 to students who have outstanding records of achievement in debate and forensics. Renewable with 3.0 GPA. Deadline: February 15.

5432. **Music Scholarships** Varying numbers of scholarships ranging from $500 to $3,000 to students meeting certain criteria who are music majors. Based on talent.

5433. **National Merit Scholarships** Varying numbers of scholarships ranging from $750 to $2,000 to students who are designated National Merit Finalists.

5434. **Neely Scholarships** 10 scholarships providing tuition to students meeting certain academic criteria. Renewable with 3.3 GPA.

5435. **Robert B. Pamplin, Jr., Society of Fellows** Awards covering tuition and fees to entering freshmen who have demonstrated academic achievement. Students named to the Society of Fellows are guaranteed full tuition and fees without the use of loan programs as well as a $500 stipend each year for books, computers, travel expenses, etc. Renewable. Deadline: February 15.

5436. **Sanders Scholarships** 3 scholarships of $2,500 to students meeting certain academic criteria. Renewable.

5437. **Trustee Scholarships** 20 scholarships of $5,000 to students meeting certain academic criteria. Renewable with a 3.3 GPA.

University of Oregon
1217 University of Oregon
Eugene, OR 97403
(800) 232-3825
(503) 348-3111
http://www.uoregon.edu

5438. **Alyce Rogers Long Scholarship** 1 scholarship of $300 to an undergraduate or graduate student with an interest in high school journalism.

5439. **Eugene Register–Guard Allen Scholarships** 2 scholarships of $500 to students who are pursuing careers in journalism. Based on academic achievement, ability in journalism, and financial need.

5440. **Eugene Register–Guard Olde Timers Club Scholarship** 1 scholarship of $300 to an undergraduate sophomore or junior who has demonstrated promise in journalism, whose home is in the *Register-Guard* circulation area, and who who has financial need.

5441. **General University Scholarships** Varying numbers of scholarships ranging from $600 to $1,000 to students meeting certain academic criteria.

5442. **Janet Beigal Smith Memorial Scholarship** 1 scholarship of $300 to a student with a career interest in school publications and high school journalism.

5443. **Journalism Scholarships** Varying amounts of scholarships ranging up to $2,000 to students who are journalism majors and meet other criteria.

5444. **Lucien P. Arant Memorial Scholarships** 50 or more scholarships ranging from $500 to $1,500 to undergraduate and graduate students based on academic and journalistic achievement.

5445. **Merle Chessman Scholarship (provided by the *Daily Astorian*)** 1 scholarship of full tuition to a student who is a resident of Clatsop, Columbia, Tillamook, Umatilla, Morrow, Gilliam, Wheeler, or Grant counties. Based on academic achievement, financial need, and interest in print journalism. Recipient must work at the *Daily Astorian*, the *East Oregonian*, or the *Blue Mt. Eagle*.

5446. **Presidential Scholarships** 50 scholarships ranging from $1,000 to $2,000 to students with at least a 3.75 GPA who scored at least 1100 on SAT. Renewable with 3.25 GPA.

5447. **Robert B. Frazier Memorial Scholarship** 1 scholarship of $500 to an undergraduate junior or senior based on academic achievement and demonstrated journalistic ability.

5448. **Robert W. and Nancy Chanler Presidential Scholarship** 1 scholarship of $1,200 to a high

school junior or senior pursuing a career in newspaper journalism based on an outstanding high school record.

5449. **Robert W. Sawyer Memorial Scholarship** 1 scholarship of $2,000 to graduate students who are journalism majors and meet certain criteria.

5450. **Tuition Waivers** Numerous partial- to full-tuition waivers to minority students who meet certain criteria.

5451. **University of Oregon** 100 scholarships ranging from $100 to $2,500 to students with at least a 3.5 GPA. Renewable.

University of Portland
5000 North Willamette Road
Portland, OR 97203-5798
(503) 283-7147
http://www.up.edu

5452. **Academic/Merit** 35 scholarships ranging from $1,000 to $1,500 to students with at least a 3.3 GPA. Renewable.

5453. **Activity** Numerous scholarships ranging from $100 up to tuition.

5454. **Honors** Numerous $1,000 scholarships to students scoring at least 1000 on SAT. Renewable with a 3.0 GPA.

5455. **Incentive** Numerous $800 scholarships to students scoring at least 970 on SAT. Renewable with a 2.7 GPA.

5456. **President's** Numerous $1,200 scholarships to students scoring at least 1200 on SAT. Renewable with a 4.0 GPA.

5457. **Regents** Numerous $1,400 scholarships to students scoring at least 1080 on SAT. Renewable with a 3.5 GPA.

PENNSYLVANIA

Allegheny College
520 North Main Street
Meadville, PA 16335-3902
(800) 521-5293
(814) 332-3100
http://www.alleg.edu/
admiss@admin.alleg.edu

5458. **Allegheny College National Merit Scholarships** 18 scholarships of varying amounts to students who have been designated as National Merit Finalists.

5459. **Allegheny Presidential Scholar Awards** Up to 347 scholarships ranging from $1,500 to $3,000 to students in the top 10 percent of their class who score at least 1200 on SAT or 28 on ACT. Renewable with 3.0 GPA.

5460. **Allegheny Provost's Merit Awards** Up to 273 scholarships of varying amounts to students meeting certain academic criteria.

5461. **Competitive Scholarships** 60 scholarships ranging from $500 to $3,000 to students who meet certain academic criteria. Renewable with 3.0 GPA.

5462. **Research/Minority Scholarships** Up to 8 scholarships of $5,000 to minority students meeting certain academic criteria. Renewable.

5463. **Sesquicentennial Scholarships** 25 scholarships ranging from $2,100 to $3,600 to students meeting certain academic criteria. Renewable with a 3.0 GPA.

5464. **Teacher in Education** 6 scholarships of $3,000 to students in the top 10 percent of their class, with at least a 3.0 GPA, who scored at least 1200 on SAT or 28 on ACT and will be majoring in education. Renewable with a 3.0 GPA.

5465. **Tuition Waivers** Numerous partial- to full-tuition waivers to students who are employees or children of employees.

Carnegie Mellon University
5000 Forbes Avenue
Pittsburgh, PA 15213-3890
(412) 268-2000
http://www.cmu.edu
admissions@andrew.cmu.edu

5466. **Andrew Carnegie Awards** 14 scholarships of varying amounts. Based on academic merit.

5467. **Art/Design** 20 scholarships ranging from $1,500 to $10,000. Renewable.

5468. **Carnegie Tradition Awards** 28 scholarships of varying amounts, based on leadership and commitment to the work ethic.

5469. **CMU Merit Awards** 86 scholarships of varying amounts. Based on academic merit.

5470. **Music** 35 scholarships ranging from $500 to $3,000 to students majoring in music. Renewable.

Duquesne University
600 Forbes Avenue
Pittsburgh, PA 15282
(800) 456-0590
(412) 434-6220
http://www.duq.edu

5471. **Competitive** 300 scholarships ranging from $800 to $1,500 to students in the top 20 percent of their class, with at least a 3.25 GPA, and scoring at least 1100 on their SAT. Renewable.

5472. **Education** 50 scholarships of $1,000 to students in the top 20 percent of their class, with at least a

3.0 GPA, and scoring at least 900 on their SAT. Renewable.

5473. **Music** 60 scholarships ranging from $250 to $2,000. Renewable.

5474. **Parish** 50 scholarships ranging from $200 to $1,000 to students in the top 20 percent of their class, with at least a 3.25 GPA, and scoring at least 1000 on SAT. Renewable with a 2.75 GPA.

5475. **Spiritan** 15 scholarships of $1,000 to students in the top 10 percent of their class, with at least a 3.25 GPA, and scoring at least 1000 on their SAT. Renewable with a 2.75 GPA.

5476. **Tamburitzans** 40 scholarships covering total costs. Renewable.

5477. **University** 150 scholarships of $2,000 to students in the top 10 percent of their class, with at least a 3.5 GPA, and scoring at least 1100 on their SAT. Renewable.

Juniata College
1700 Moore Street
Huntingdon, PA 16652
(800) 526-1970
http://www.juniata.edu/vcxbn

5478. **Baker Peace and Conflict Studies Merit Scholarship** Scholarships of $1,000 to entering freshmen majoring in international affairs who are in the upper 20 percent of their class, with above-average SAT scores. Renewable for up to three years with a 3.0 GPA.

5479. **Croner Scholarship in Economics and Business Administration** 1 scholarship of varying amount to a student meeting certain academic criteria who is majoring in either economics or business administration.

5480. **Dow Chemical Scholarship** 1 scholarship of varying amount to a student meeting certain academic criteria.

5481. **Geographic Diversity Scholarships** 10 scholarships of $2,000 to students meeting certain criteria who are out-of-state residents.

5482. **Leadership Merit Recognition Awards** Up to 75 scholarships of varying amounts, totaling $225,000, to students meeting certain criteria who have demonstrated leadership abilities.

5483. **Lefties** 4 small scholarships to left-handed students. Must have financial need.

5484. **Merit Recognition Scholarships** 5 scholarships of varying amounts to students meeting certain criteria who are music majors. Based on talent.

5485. **Presidential Essay Awards** 15 scholarships of varying amount to students. Based on an essay competition.

5486. **Quinter Scholarships** 62 scholarships of varying amounts to students meeting certain academic criteria.

5487. **Simpson Scholarship** 1 scholarship of varying amount to students meeting certain academic criteria.

Messiah College
Grantham, PA 17027
(717) 766-2511
http://www.messiah.edu

5488. **Dean's** 300 scholarships ranging from $500 to $1,500 to students in the top 15 percent of their class, with at least a 3.0 GPA, and scoring at least 1000 on SAT or 22 on ACT. Renewable with a 3.0 GPA.

5489. **Founders** 28 scholarships of $2,500 to students in the top 5 percent of their class, with at least a 3.5 GPA, and scoring at least 1100 on SAT or 26 on ACT. Renewable with a 3.0 GPA.

5490. **President's** 100 scholarships ranging from $250 to $1,000 to students in the top 25 percent of their class, with at least a 3.0 GPA, and scoring at least 900 on SAT or 20 on ACT. Renewable with a 2.5 GPA.

Pennsylvania State University
University Park, PA 16802
(814) 865-1104
http://www.psu.edu
admissions@psu.edu

5491. **A. W. (Dude McDowell Memorial) Scholarship Internship** 1 scholarship internship of $1,500 to an undergraduate print journalism student to work as a summer intern at the Sharon Herald Company, Sharon, PA. Apply mid-spring semester of junior year.

5492. **Charles M. Meredith Sr. Scholarship** 1 scholarship of $1,000 to an undergraduate junior, senior, or graduate student pursuing a career with a country weekly paper. Must have at least a 2.0 GPA.

5493. **David and Mary Lee Jones Journalism Scholarship** 1 scholarship of $500 to an undergraduate student with demonstrated potential for journalistic achievement. Preference given to students who have completed a school-approved internship.

5494. **Delta Chi Scholarships** Scholarships for disabled students.

5495. **Franklin Banner Journalism Scholarship** 1 scholarship of at least $1,000 to fourth-semester undergraduate students who are currently enrolled as journalism or public relations majors. Must have graduated from a Pennsylvania high school. Based on academic achievement and recommendations.

5496. **Gene and Fran Goodwin Journalism Scholarship** 1 scholarship of at least $1,000 to a minority undergraduate or graduate student enrolled in or planning to enroll as a journalism major. Based on financial need.

5497. **George E. Graff Memorial Award** 1 scholarship of $600 to an undergraduate freshman interested in majoring in journalism.

5498. **Howard J. Lamade Journalism Scholarship** 1 scholarship of $1,000 to an undergraduate freshman interested in majoring in journalism. Recipient continues to receive the $300 Lamco Award each year as long as student remains in good standing in journalism.

5499. **Jerome Weinstein Journalism Scholarship** 1 scholarship of $1,000 to an undergraduate junior or senior. Preference given to a student intern at the *Centre Daily Times* in State College who is a print major.

5500. **The Journalism Fund** 1 scholarship of $500 to a student pursuing a career in journalism who meets certain criteria.

5501. **Lawrence G. and Ellen M. Foster Scholarships** 1 to 2 scholarships of $2,000 to undergraduate freshmen and above who are pursuing careers as newspaper writers, reporters, or editors. Based on financial need. Renewable.

5502. **Louis H. Bell Memorial Scholarship** 1 scholarship of $1,000 to a journalism student meeting certain criteria.

5503. **Newlin Memorial Award** 1 scholarship of $400 to an undergraduate junior majoring in journalism with an interest in foreign language study.

5504. **Ostar-Hutchison Daily Collegian Scholarship** 1 scholarship of $800 to an undergraduate sophomore or junior working on *The Daily Collegian* news staff whose involvement is jeopardized because of financial need.

5505. **Phi Sigma Delta Scholarships** Scholarships for disabled students.

5506. **Reuben Jaffe Memorial Journalism Scholarship** 1 scholarship of $500 to a minority undergraduate or graduate student enrolled or planning to enroll as a print journalism major.

5507. **S. W. Calkins Memorial Awards** 2 scholarships of $1,000 to undergraduate juniors or seniors who are pursuing careers in journalism.

5508. **Tuition Waivers** Numerous partial- to full-tuition waivers to students who are employees, children of employees, or senior citizens.

University of Pennsylvania
34th and Spruce Street
Philadelphia, PA 19104
(215) 898-5000
http://www.upenn.edu

5509. **Need-based Assistance** Numerous need-based scholarships, loans, and work-study programs open to anyone accepted for admission who has financial need. Contact the financial aid office.

University of Pittsburgh
4200 Fifth Avenue
Pittsburgh, PA 15260
(412) 624-PITT
(412) 624-4141
http://www.pitt.edu/
oafa@pitt.edu/

5510. **Challenge Grant** Varying numbers of grants of up to $1,000 to African American incoming freshmen majoring in the humanities or liberal arts. Selection based on at least a 3.0 GPA, class ranking (top 40 percent of the class), SAT/ACT score, and financial need exceeding $1,000. Contact the financial aid office. Deadline: January 15.

5511. **Challenge Scholarship** 30 scholarships ranging from $1,000 to $4,000 to African American incoming freshmen majoring in the humanities or liberal arts. Selection based on at least a 3.0 GPA, class ranking (top 40 percent of the class), SAT/ACT score, and financial need. Contact the financial aid office. Deadline: January 15.

5512. **Connection Transfer Scholarships** Varying numbers of scholarships of up to $2,000 to transfer students with at least a 3.5 GPA. Must be residents of Harrisburg County and transferring from a community college. Contact the financial aid office. Deadline: May 1.

5513. **Valedictorian Scholarships** Varying numbers of scholarships of $500 to incoming freshmen who were their class valedictorian. Must be residents of Pennsylvania. Contact the financial aid office. Deadline: January 15.

University of Scranton
800 Linden Street
Scranton, PA 18510-4501
(888) 727-2686
(717) 941-7400
http://www.uofs.edu/

5514. **Healthcare Scholarships** 7 scholarships of varying amounts to students meeting certain criteria.

5515. **Ignatian Scholarships** 8 scholarships providing tuition costs to students who are in the upper 5 percent of their class and scored at least 1300 on SAT. Renewable with 3.0 GPA.

5516. **Irish National Scholarships** 2 scholarships of varying amounts to students who meet certain academic criteria and are of Irish descent.

5517. **Loyola "Honors Program" Scholarships** Varying numbers of scholarships ranging from $1,000 to $7,000 to students in the top 15 percent of their class who scored at least 1150 on SAT. Renewable with 3.0 GPA.

5518. **Presidential Scholarships** Varying numbers of scholarships ranging from $500 to tuition costs to students in the top 10 percent of their class who scored at least 1150 on SAT. Renewable with 3.0 GPA.

5519. **Tuition Remission/Exchange Scholarships** Varying numbers of scholarships providing tuition remission to students who are dependents of employees.

Villanova University
800 Lancaster Avenue
Villanova, PA 19085-1672
(800) 338-7927
(610) 645-4010
http://www.vill.edu

5520. **Commuter Scholars Awards** 30 scholarships of varying amounts to commuting students meeting certain academic criteria.

5521. **Minority Commuter Scholarships** 13 scholarships of varying amounts to commuting students meeting certain criteria.

5522. **Presidential Scholarships** 30 scholarships of varying amounts to students meeting certain academic criteria. 5 scholarships are specifically for African American students.

5523. **Tuition Exchange Awards** 12 scholarships of tuition to students who are dependents of faculty or staff exchange members.

5524. **Tuition Waivers** Numerous partial- to full-tuition waivers to students who are employees, children of employees, or senior citizens.

5525. **Villanova National Merit Awards** 5 scholarships of varying amounts to students designated as National Merit Scholars.

5526. **Villanova Scholars Awards** 152 scholarships of varying amounts to students meeting certain academic criteria.

RHODE ISLAND

Brown University
Providence, RI 02912
(401) 863-1000
http://www.brown.edu
admission_undergraduate@brown.edu

5527. **Need-Based Assistance** Numerous need-based scholarships, loans, and work-study programs open to anyone accepted for admission who has financial need. Contact the financial aid office.

5528. **Tuition Waivers** Numerous partial- to full-tuition waivers to students who are employees or children of employees.

Johnson and Wales College
8 Abbott Park Place
Providence, RI 02903
(800) 342-5598
http://www.jwu.edu
admissions@jwu.edu

5529. **Gaebe Eagle Scout Award** Scholarships of $500 to an Eagle Scout who received the religious award of his faith.

5530. **Junior Achievement Scholarship** 2 scholarships of up to full tuition each year and unlimited partial scholarships to entering freshmen majoring in business, culinary arts, hospitality, or professional technology fields. Must have been members of a Junior Achievement applied economics class. Deadline: May 1.

5531. **Merit Scholarships** Varying numbers of scholarships of varying amounts to students meeting certain criteria.

5532. **Tuition Waivers** Numerous partial- to full-tuition waivers to students who are children of alumni, employees, or children of employees.

Providence College
Providence, RI 02918
(401) 865-1000
http://www.providence.edu
pcadmiss@providence.edu

5533. **Achievement Scholarships** 50 scholarships ranging from $2,000 to $10,000 to students in the top 10 percent of their class, with at least a 3.25 GPA, who scored at least 1200 on SAT. Renewable with a 3.25 GPA.

5534. **Balfour Scholarships** 6 scholarships of approximately $12,000 to Hispanic students meeting certain academic criteria.

5535. **Martin Luther King Scholarships** 32 scholarships of tuition to African American students in the top 50 percent of their class, with at least a 2.0 GPA, and who scored at least 900 on SAT. Renewable with a 2.0 GPA.

5536. **RODDY Foundation Scholarships** 1 or 2 scholarships providing tuition and fees to students in the top 5 percent of their class, with at least a 3.25 GPA, who scored at least 1200 on SAT and are pre-medicine majors. Renewable with a 3.25 GPA.

5537. **Southeast Asian "Honors Program" Scholarships** 2 scholarships of $15,935 to Asian students meeting certain academic criteria. Renewable with a 2.0 GPA.

5538. **Textron Scholarships** 2 scholarships of $22,000 to female students who meet certain academic criteria and are business majors.

5539. **Tuition Waivers** Numerous partial- to full-tuition waivers to students who are employees or children of employees.

SOUTH CAROLINA

Columbia College
1301 Columbia College Drive
Columbia, SC 29203
(800) 277-1301
http://www.colacoll.edu
admissions@colacoll.edu

5540. Dance Scholarships Varying numbers of scholarships ranging from $500 to $2,000 to students meeting certain criteria who are dance majors. Based on talent. Renewable.

5541. Music Scholarships Varying numbers of scholarships ranging from $500 to $3,500 to students meeting certain criteria who are music majors. Based on talent. Renewable.

5542. Leadership Scholarships 10 to 15 scholarships of $1,800 to students in the top 15 percent of their class, with at least a 3.5 GPA, and who scored at least 950 on SAT. Renewable with a 3.0 GPA.

5543. Presidential Scholarships 10 scholarships of $3,750 to students in the top 10 percent of their class, with at least a 3.5 GPA, and who scored at least 1200 on SAT. Renewable with a 3.0 GPA.

5544. Trustee "Honors Program" Scholarships 25 scholarships ranging from $1,000 to $1,800 to students in the top 15 percent of their class, with at least a 3.0 GPA, and who scored at least 1000 on SAT. Renewable with a 3.0 GPA.

Furman University
3300 Poinsett Highway
Greenville, SC 29613
(864) 294-2034
http://www.furman.edu
admissions@furman.edu

5545. Academic Scholarships Varying numbers of scholarships ranging from $1,000 to $3,000 to students who are in the top 5 percent of their class, with at least a 3.2 GPA, and who scored at least 1250 on SAT or 28 on ACT. Renewable with a 3.0 GPA.

5546. Daniel Music Awards 4 scholarships of varying amounts to students meeting certain criteria who are music majors. Based on talent.

5547. Liberty Awards Varying numbers of scholarships of varying amounts to students meeting certain academic criteria.

5548. Relatives of Clergy Awards 14 scholarships of varying amounts to students meeting certain criteria who are relatives of clergy.

5549. Scholar Awards 100 scholarships of approximately $1,500 to entering freshmen who are in the top 50 percent of their class who meet other academic criteria.

5550. Tuition Waivers Numerous partial- to full-tuition waivers to students who are minority students, children of alumni, employees, or children of employees.

5551. Wylie Awards Varying numbers of scholarships of varying amounts to students meeting certain academic criteria who are math majors.

University of South Carolina
Columbia, SC 29208
(803) 777-8134
http://www.sc.edu
admissions-ugrad@sc.edu

5552. Albert T. and Lila W. Scroggins Scholarship 1 or more scholarships of $500 to undergraduate sophomore, junior, or senior journalism majors.

5553. Alumni Association Scholarships Numerous scholarships of varying amounts to students meeting certain academic criteria.

5554. Alumni Legacy Scholarships 60 scholarships of varying amounts to students meeting certain academic criteria who have a relative who is an alumnus.

5555. Beaufort Watts Ball Scholarship 1 scholarship of $500 to an undergraduate rising junior journalism major who meets certain criteria.

5556. Ben J. Grant Scholarships 1 or more scholarship of $600 to undergraduate students majoring in mass communication.

5557. Bernard Baruch Awards Numerous scholarships of varying amounts to students meeting certain academic criteria.

5558. Creative Arts/Performance Awards 15 scholarships of varying amounts to students meeting certain criteria. Based on talent in band.

5559. **Edmund A. Ramsaur Scholarships** 1 or more scholarships of $1,000 to undergraduate juniors or seniors pursuing careers in writing.

5560. **George A. Buchanan Scholarship** 1 scholarship of $600 to a student majoring in news-editorial sequence who meets other criteria.

5561. **Greenville News and Greenville Piedmont Scholarship** 1 scholarship of $1,000 to a journalism student based on academic achievement.

5562. **Harry Parone Scholarships** Numerous scholarships of varying amounts to students meeting certain academic and athletic criteria.

5563. **Jesse A. Rutledge Scholarship** 1 or more scholarships of $600 to students majoring in news-editorial who have financial need.

5564. **Jim McAllister Memorial Scholarship** 1 scholarship of $500 to an undergraduate freshman or above who is majoring in news-editorial. Must be a resident of Greenville County, South Carolina.

5565. **John H. Earle Awards** Numerous scholarships of varying amounts to students meeting certain academic criteria.

5566. **John K. Cauthen Scholarship** 1 scholarship of $1,000 to a journalism student who is a South Carolina resident.

5567. **J. Rion McKissick Scholarship** 1 scholarship of $1,500 to a student majoring in journalism who meets other criteria.

5568. **Louis-McAllister Memorial Scholarship** 1 scholarship of $500 to undergraduate sophomores and above who are majoring in news-editorial.

5569. **Mark Timothy Hedgecoth Memorial Scholarship** 1 scholarship of $600 to a student majoring in news-editorial sequence. Based on academic achievement and financial need.

5570. **Rick Temple Scholarship** 1 scholarship of $1,000 for an undergraduate sophomore or above who is a journalism major.

5571. **Samuel L. Latimer Sr. and Sallie Belle Witherspoon Latimer Scholarships** 3 scholarships of $1,000 to students who are residents of York or Richland County in South Carolina and are majoring in news-editorial sequence.

5572. **The State-Record Scholarships** 1 or more scholarships of $1,000 to undergraduate students majoring in newspaper journalism who meet certain criteria.

5573. **Trustees' Endowment Scholarships** Numerous scholarships of varying amounts to students meeting certain academic criteria.

5574. **Tuition Waivers** Numerous partial- to full-tuition waivers to students who are senior citizens.

5575. **University President's Scholarships** Numerous scholarships of varying amounts to students meeting certain academic criteria.

5576. **University Scholars Awards** Numerous scholarships of varying amounts to students meeting certain academic criteria.

5577. **University Trustee's Scholarships** Numerous scholarships of varying amounts to students meeting certain academic criteria.

5578. **USC General Scholarships** Numerous scholarships of varying amounts to students meeting certain academic criteria.

5579. **Valedictorian Scholarships** Numerous scholarships of varying amounts to students who were their class valedictorian.

5580. **Yaghijan Endowment in Art Awards** numerous scholarships of varying amounts to students meeting certain academic, talent, and athletic criteria.

SOUTH DAKOTA

Augustana College
2001 South Summit Avenue
Sioux Falls, SD 57197
(605) 335-4111
http://ww.augie.edu
info@inst.augie.edu

5581. **Academic Achievement Awards** Varying numbers of scholarships of varying amounts to students who meet certain academic criteria.

5582. **Children of Alumni Awards** Varying numbers of scholarships of varying amounts to students who meet certain criteria and are children of alumni.

5583. **Communications Awards** Varying numbers of scholarships of varying amounts to students who meet certain academic criteria and demonstrate leadership abilities.

5584. **Debate Awards** Varying numbers of scholarships of varying amounts to students who meet certain criteria and will be members of the debate team.

5585. **Drama Awards** Varying numbers of scholarships of varying amounts to students who meet certain criteria and will be majoring in drama. Based on talent.

5586. **English Scholarships** Varying numbers of scholarships of $1,000 to students who meet certain academic criteria and will be English majors. Renewable.

5587. **International Student Scholarships** Varying numbers of scholarships of varying amounts to international students who meet certain criteria.

5588. **Matching Church Grants** Varying numbers of scholarships of varying amounts to students who meet certain criteria and are Lutheran.

5589. **Multiple Family Members Awards** Varying numbers of scholarships of varying amounts to students who meet certain criteria and are relatives of current students.

5590. **Music Awards** Varying numbers of scholarships of varying amounts to students who meet certain criteria and will be majoring in music. Based on talent.

5591. **Regents Scholarships** 10 scholarships covering total costs to students in the top 5 percent of their class, with at least a 3.5 GPA, and who scored at least 28 on ACT. Renewable with a 3.3 GPA.

5592. **Scholar Awards** Unlimited scholarships ranging from $500 to $3,500 to students who meet certain academic criteria. Renewable with a 3.0 GPA.

5593. **Science Awards** Varying numbers of scholarships of varying amounts to students who meet certain academic criteria and will be majoring in a science.

5594. **Transfer Scholarships** 5 scholarships of $3,500 to students who meet certain academic criteria and transferred from a two-year institution. Renewable with a 3.2 GPA.

5595. **Tuition Waivers** Numerous partial- to full-tuition waivers to students who are employees, children of employees, adult students, or senior citizens.

Dakota State University
Heston Hall
Madison, SD 57042
(605) 256-5111
http://www.dsu.edu
dsuinfo@columbia.dsu.edu

5596. **General/Academic** 50 scholarships ranging from $100 to $1,000 to students with at least a 3.0 GPA.

5597. **Gill/NFS** 28 scholarships of $1,600 to students with at least a 3.5 GPA. Renewable with a 3.5 GPA.

5598. **Info Systems Honors Program** 6 scholarships of $1,400 to students with a 3.5 GPA. Renewable with a 3.5 GPA.

South Dakota State University
Box 2201
Brookings, SD 57007
(605) 256-5139
http://www.sdstate.edu
sduadms@adm.sdstate.edu

5599. **Butler, Amdahl, and Clarkson Scholarships** Numerous scholarships ranging from $100 to $750 to incoming freshmen who are academically gifted and/or talented.

5600. **Larson Manufacturing Scholarships** 5 scholarships of $1,000 to first-year students whose parents are employed in the building products industries as manufacturers, wholesalers, retail distributors, or merchants.

5601. **Leaders of Tomorrow Scholarships** Varying numbers of scholarships of at least $600 to entering freshmen to award their high school academic success. Awarded to students who do not receive other SDSU academic scholarships. Selection based on academic achievement, GPA, ACT score, and class ranking.

5602. **Music Scholarships** Scholarships of varying amounts to students meeting certain criteria who are music majors. Recipients must be active performers in a music group. Must submit a separate application and either a personal or taped audition. Contact the Music Department.

5603. **National Merit Scholarships** 5 scholarships of at least $3,500 to students who receive National Merit designation of at least Semi-Finalist. Must list SDSU as their first-choice school. Renewable for four years.

5604. **Native American Scholarships** Scholarships of varying amounts to Native American students. Based on academic achievement and potential for academic success. Applicants must indicate tribal membership on their application to be considered.

5605. **Nichols Scholarships** Scholarships of varying amounts to students who are members of the Yankton Sioux Tribe. Applicants must indicate tribal membership on their application to be considered.

5606. **ROTC Scholarships** Scholarships providing full tuition, fees, books, and an allowance of $100 each academic month. Renewable for four years of undergraduate study. Contact: Army ROTC, Professor of Military Science, or Air Force ROTC, Professor of Aerospace Studies. Deadline: December 1 of high school senior year.

5607. **Stephen F. Briggs Scholarships** 12 scholarships of $5,000 to undergraduate students

meeting certain academic and financial criteria. 6 of the scholarships are awarded to engineering majors, and 6 to non-engineering majors. An on-campus interview is required for final selection.

5608. **Thurgood Marshall Scholarships** scholarships of varying amounts to African American students who demonstrate academic achievement and potential for academic success.

5609. **Valedictorian Scholarships** Scholarships of at least $600 to students who were ranked first in their class and do not receive other SDSU academic scholarships.

5610. **Wintrode Challenge Awards** 5 scholarships of $500 to students who may not have outstanding academic records but who show promise of academic and career success. Renewable for four years. A separate application must be obtained from the financial aid office.

TENNESSEE

Austin Peay State University
601 College Street
Clarksville, TN 37044
(931) 648-7011
http://www.apsu.edu/
mccorklec@apu02.apsu.edu

5611. **Academic Honors Scholarships** Up to 110 scholarships of $2,000 to students who are in the upper 10 percent of their class, with at least a 3.0 GPA, and who scored at least 24 on ACT. Renewable with a 3.0 GPA.

5612. **Academic Scholarships** Varying numbers of scholarships ranging from $500 to $900 to students who are in the upper 25 percent of their class, with at least a 3.0 GPA, and who scored at least 20 on ACT. Renewable with a 3.0 GPA.

5613. **Band Scholarships** Varying numbers of scholarships of varying amounts to students who meet certain criteria and are or will be members of the band. Based on talent.

5614. **Center for Creative Arts Scholarships** 30 scholarships of $775 to students who meet certain criteria and are or will be majoring in an art. Based on talent.

5615. **Dean's Scholarships** Up to 13 scholarships to $2,000 to students who are in the upper 10 percent of their class, with at least a 3.0 GPA, and who scored at least 24 on ACT. Renewable with a 3.0 GPA.

5616. **Emerging Leaders Scholarships** Varying numbers of scholarships of varying amounts to students who meet certain criteria and who demonstrate leadership potential.

5617. **Foundation Honors Scholarships** Up to 25 scholarships of approximately $500 to students who meet certain academic criteria.

5618. **General Scholarships** Varying numbers of scholarships ranging from $300 to $1,500 to students who are in the upper 25 percent of their class, with at least a 3.0 GPA, and who scored at least 19 on ACT. Renewable.

5619. **Kimbrough Scholarships** Up to 51 scholarships ranging from $500 to $2,000 to students who are in the upper 10 percent of their class, with at least a 3.0 GPA, and who scored at least 26 on ACT. Renewable with a 3.0 GPA.

5620. **Leadership Scholarships** Up to 175 scholarships of $1,500 to students who are in the upper 25 percent of their class, with at least a 3.0 GPA, who scored at least 20 on ACT and demonstrate leadership abilities. Renewable with a 2.8 GPA.

5621. **Martin Luther King Scholarships** Up to 37 scholarships of $2,000 to students who are in the upper 25 percent of their class, with at least a 3.0 GPA, who scored at least 19 on ACT. Renewable with a 3.0 GPA.

5622. **Multi-cultural Scholarships** Varying numbers of scholarships of $2,000 to minority students who are in the upper 25 percent of their class, with at least a 3.0 GPA, who scored at least 19 on ACT. Renewable with a 3.0 GPA.

5623. **Music Scholarships** Varying numbers of scholarships of varying amounts to students who meet certain criteria and are or will be majoring in music. Based on talent.

5624. **Performance Scholarships** Varying numbers of scholarships ranging from $100 to $1,500 to students who meet certain criteria and are majoring in a performance art. Renewable.

5625. **Presidential Scholarships** Up to 150 scholarships providing tuition costs to students who are in the upper 25 percent of their class, with at least a 3.0 GPA, and who scored at least 21 on ACT. Renewable with a 3.0 GPA.

5626. **Speech Scholarships** Varying numbers of scholarships of varying amounts to students who meet certain criteria and are or will be majoring in speech. Based on talent.

Belmont University
1900 Belmont Boulevard
Nashville, TN 37212
(615) 385-6403
http://www.belmont.edu/

5627. **Academic Scholarships** 40 scholarships ranging from $1,000 to $1,250 to students in the upper 10 percent of their class who scored at least 1100 on SAT or 25 on ACT. Renewable with a 3.0 GPA.

5628. **Dean's Scholarships** Varying numbers of scholarships of varying amounts to students meeting certain academic criteria.

5629. **Departmental Scholarships** 10 scholarships of $1,500 to students in the upper 10 percent of their class who scored at least 1100 on SAT or 25 on ACT. Renewable with a 3.0 GPA.

5630. **Presidential Scholarships** 4 scholarships providing tuition to students in the top 5 percent of their class who scored at least 25 on ACT. Renewable with a 3.0 GPA.

5631. **Tuition Waivers** Numerous partial- to full-tuition waivers to students who are employees, children of employees, or senior citizens.

David Lipscomb University
3901-4001 Granny White Pike
Nashville, TN 37204-3951
(800) 333-4358
http://www.dlu.edu/
admissions@dlu.edu

5632. **Cheerleader Awards** 3 scholarships of varying amounts to students meeting certain criteria who are cheerleaders.

5633. **Creative Arts/Performance Awards** Varying numbers of scholarships of varying amounts to students meeting certain criteria and participating or majoring in music (15), art (6), speech (5), yearbook (2), or newspaper editing.

5634. **Education Awards** Varying numbers of scholarships of varying amounts to students meeting certain academic criteria and majoring in education.

5635. **Honor Scholarships** Unlimited number of scholarships ranging from $100 to total tuition to students in the top 10 percent of their class, with at least a 3.0 GPA, and who scored at least 910 on SAT or 22 on ACT. Renewable with a 3.0 GPA.

5636. **Leadership Awards** 15 scholarships of varying amounts to students meeting certain criteria and demonstrating leadership abilities.

5637. **Minority Awards** Varying numbers of scholarships of varying amounts to minority students meeting certain criteria.

5638. **Nursing Profession Awards** Varying numbers of scholarships of varying amounts to students meeting certain academic criteria and majoring in nursing.

5639. **Orphans Awards** Varying numbers of scholarships of varying amounts to students meeting certain criteria who are orphans.

5640. **Pre-medicine Awards** Varying numbers of scholarships of varying amounts to students meeting certain academic criteria and majoring in pre-medicine.

5641. **Religious Service Awards** Varying numbers of scholarships of varying amounts to students meeting certain criteria who have participated in religious events.

Lambuth College
Lambuth Boulevard
Jackson, TN 38301
(901) 425-2500
http://www.lambuth.edu

5642. **Dean's** Numerous scholarships ranging from $600 to $2,000 to students in the upper 30 percent of their class, with at least a 3.0 GPA, and scoring at least 24 on ACT. Renewable with a 3.0 GPA.

5643. **Honors Scholarship** $800 per year for four years to an Eagle Scout with a B average. Must have acceptable SAT or ACT scores.

5644. **Junior College** Numerous $1,000 scholarships to transfer students. Renewable with a 2.0 GPA.

5645. **Leadership** Numerous scholarships ranging from $600 to $2,000 to students with a 2.5 GPA who scored at least 18 on ACT. Renewable with a 2.5 GPA.

5646. **Presidential** 10 scholarships ranging from $1,000 to $4,000 to students in the top 10 percent of their class, with at least a 3.0 GPA, and scoring at least 24 on ACT.

Rhodes College
2000 North Parkway
Memphis, TN 38112-1690
(800) 231-2391
(901) 726-3000
http://www.rhodes.edu
adminfo@rhodes.edu

5647. **Art Achievement Scholarships** 9 scholarships of varying amounts (approximately $8,500), totaling $76,800, to students meeting certain criteria who are art majors. Based on talent. Renewable with a 2.0 GPA.

5648. **Cambridge Scholarships** 20 scholarships providing three-fourths of tuition to students in the top 3 percent of their class, with at least a 3.8 GPA, and who scored at least 1350 on SAT or 31 on ACT. Renewable with a 3.0 GPA.

5649. **J. R. Hyde Scholarships** 2 scholarships of up to $13,030 to students in the top 1 percent of their class, with at least a 3.9 GPA, and who scored at least 1350 on SAT or 31 on ACT. Renewable with a 3.0 GPA.

5650. **Morse Scholarships** 17 scholarships of tuition (approximately $17,500) to students in the top 1 percent of their class, with at least a 3.9 GPA, and who scored at least 1450 on SAT or 33 on ACT. Renewable with a 3.0 GPA.

5651. **University Scholarships** 60 scholarships of one-half tuition (approximately $875) to students in the top 5 percent of their class, with at least a 3.7 GPA, and who scored at least 1230 on SAT or 29 on ACT. Renewable with a 2.5 GPA.

5652. **Walter D. Bellingarth Scholarships** 4 scholarships of up to $13,030 to students in the top 1 percent of their class, with at least a 3.9 GPA, and who scored at least 1350 on SAT or 31 on ACT. Renewable with a 3.0 GPA.

University of Tennessee–Knoxville
Knoxville, TN 37996-0210
(800) 221-8657
(423) 474-2184
http://www.utk.edu/

5653. **Band Awards** Varying numbers of scholarships of varying amounts to students who meet certain academic criteria and are members of the band. Based on talent.

5654. **College Committee Scholarships** Varying numbers of scholarships of varying amounts to students who meet certain academic criteria.

5655. **General University Scholarships** Varying numbers of scholarships of varying amounts to students who meet certain academic criteria.

5656. **Minority Scholarships** Varying numbers of scholarships of varying amounts to minority students who meet certain academic criteria.

5657. **Music Awards** Varying numbers of scholarships of varying amounts to students who meet certain academic criteria and are music majors. Based on talent.

5658. **Neyland Scholarships** Varying numbers of scholarships of varying amounts to students who meet certain criteria and have demonstrated leadership abilities.

5659. **Piano Awards** Varying numbers of scholarships of varying amounts to students who meet certain academic criteria and are piano majors. Based on talent.

5660. **Theater Awards** Varying numbers of scholarships of varying amounts to students who meet certain academic criteria and are theater majors. Based on talent.

5661. **Tuition Waivers** Numerous partial- to full-tuition waivers to students who are employees, children of employees, or senior citizens.

5662. **Vocal Music Awards** Varying numbers of scholarships of varying amounts to students who meet certain academic criteria and are vocal music majors. Based on talent.

5663. **Winner of Science and Engineering Fair Awards** Varying numbers of scholarships of varying amounts to students who meet certain academic criteria and are winners of the science and engineering fair.

Vanderbilt University
2305 West End Avenue
Nashville, TN 37212
(615) 322-2561
http://www.vanderbilt.edu
admissions@vanderbilt.edu

5664. **Blair School of Music Honor Scholarships** 29 scholarships of varying amounts to students meeting certain academic criteria who are music majors.

5665. **Chancellor's Scholarships** 23 scholarships of varying amounts to students meeting certain criteria.

5666. **Dean's Select Scholarships** 72 scholarships of varying amounts to students meeting certain academic criteria who have a major in the arts or sciences.

5667. **Engineering School Honors Awards** 6 scholarships of varying amounts to students meeting certain academic criteria.

5668. **George Peabody Scholarships** 11 scholarships of varying amounts to students meeting certain academic criteria and majoring in education.

5669. **Grantland Rice** A $7,500 scholarship. Essay is required. Renewable with a 3.0 GPA.

5670. **G. Vanderbilt Honor** 5 scholarships of $1,000 to students in the top 10 percent of their class who scored at least 1150 on SAT or 26 on ACT. Renewable with a 2.5 GPA.

5671. **Honors** 60 scholarships ranging from $500 to full tuition to students in the top 5 percent of their class who scored at least 1300 on SAT or 30 on ACT. Also based on an essay, talent, leadership, and recommendations. Renewable with a 3.0 GPA.

5672. **James Steward Awards** 2 scholarships of varying amounts to students meeting certain academic criteria and majoring in engineering.

5673. **Jesse Willis Awards** Varying numbers of scholarships of varying amounts to students meeting certain academic criteria who have an arts or science major.

5674. **Maggie S. Craig Award** 1 scholarship of varying amount to a student who is a resident of Giles County, Tennessee.

5675. **Marvin P. Friedman Awards** Varying numbers of scholarships of varying amounts to students meeting certain criteria who are California residents.

5676. **Memphis–Vanderbilt Scholarship** 1 scholarship of varying amount to a student meeting certain academic criteria.

5677. **National Achievement Scholarships** 7 scholarships of varying amounts to African American students meeting certain academic criteria.

5678. **National Merit Scholarships** 50 scholarships of varying amounts to students designated as National Merit Finalists.

5679. **Paul Harrawood Scholarships** 3 scholarships of varying amounts to students meeting certain academic criteria and majoring in engineering.

TEXAS

Angelo State University
San Angelo, TX 76909
(915) 942-2246
http://www.angelo.edu
admissions@angelo.edu

5680. **Band Awards** 25 scholarships of approximately $290 to students who meet certain criteria and are members of the band. Based on talent.

5681. **Choir Awards** 6 scholarships of approximately $190 to students who meet certain criteria and are members of the choir. Based on talent.

5682. **Dean Chenoweth Scholarship** 1 scholarship of at least $200 to a student who is a journalism major, has at least a 2.5 GPA, and has financial need. Deadline: March 1.

5683. **Drama Awards** 10 scholarships of approximately $210 to students who meet certain criteria and are drama majors. Based on talent.

5684. **Drill Team Awards** 6 scholarships of approximately $145 to students who meet certain criteria and are members of the drill team. Based on talent.

5685. **Harrison Youngren Scholarships** 2 scholarships of $750 to undergraduate juniors or seniors. Based on excellence in journalism. Deadline: March 1.

5686. **James H. and Minnie M. Edmonds Memorial Scholarship** 20 scholarship grants of $1,000 to undergraduate and graduate students who demonstrate financial need. Deadline: May 30.

5687. **Millard Cope Scholarship Awards** 2 or more scholarships of $500 to journalism majors who are pursuing a career in newspaper work. Deadline: March 1.

5688. **Robert G. Carr and Nona K. Carr Academic Scholarships** 1,000 scholarships ranging from $1,000 to $4,000 to students in the top 10 percent of their class, with at least a 90 GPA, and scoring at least 950 on SAT or 23 on ACT. Renewable with a 3.0 GPA.

5689. **Tuition Waivers** Numerous partial- to full-tuition waivers to students who are employees or children of employees.

Austin College
900 North Grand Avenue
Sherman, TX 75091
(800) 442-5363
http://www.austinc.edu
admission@austinc.edu

5690. **Academic Scholarships** Scholarships ranging from $1,500 to $3,500 to students who have demonstrated outstanding academic achievement.

5691. **Achievement Honors** 50 scholarships of $500. Based on academic merit.

5692. **Art Department Scholarship** 1 scholarship ranging from $1,000 to $2,000 to a student who meets certain criteria and is majoring in art. Renewable with portfolio review. The student is required to complete an Art Award application (available from the Art Department) and submit an art portfolio to the Art Department.

5693. **Brackenridge Scholarships** 2 scholarships of $2,000 for the first year and $1,500 for remaining undergraduate years to graduating high school seniors who are in top 20 percent of their class, graduated from a public high school in Bexar County, Texas, and have financial need based on the FAFSA. Renewable with a 2.5 GPA.

5694. **Edwin B. and Louise C. Jordan Scholarships** 5 scholarships of $3,000 to students who have demonstrated outstanding academic achievement. Preference will be given to those students with demonstrated financial need. Renewable each undergraduate year, provided students maintain at least a 3.0 cumulative GPA.

5695. **George Foundation Scholarships** Varying numbers of scholarships ranging from $2,000 to $4,000 to high school seniors and undergraduate students who reside in Fort Bend County, Texas, and rank in the top quarter of their class. Renewable for each undergraduate year provided the students continue to reside in Fort Bend County and maintain at least a 2.5 GPA.

5696. **Music Department Scholarships** 2 scholarships ranging from $750 to $2,000 to students who meet certain criteria and are majoring in music. Renewable if students maintain major and other Music Department requirements. Students must complete a Music Award application (available from the department) and must audition with the Music Department.

5697. **National Merit Scholarships** Varying numbers of four-year scholarships ranging from $250 to $2,000 to those students named National Merit Finalists who designate Austin College as their first choice. Austin College will supplement this scholarship to a maximum of $5,000 for each National Merit finalist. The students receive this supplement in lieu of any other Austin College scholarships for which they might be eligible.

5698. **Presbyterian Ministers' Dependents Grants** 3 scholarship grants ranging from $1,000 to $3,000 to students who meet certain criteria and are dependents of Presbyterian Ministers. Renewable with a 2.5 GPA.

5699. **Presidential Scholarships** 7 scholarships providing full tuition (approximately $21,500) to students who are in the top 5 percent of their class, scored at least a 1200 on SAT or 30 on ACT, and have superior academic achievement and scholarly motivation. Finalists for these awards will be invited to the campus for interviews with the Scholarship Committee. The scholarship is renewable for the sophomore year, provided a 3.25 cumulative GPA is maintained. At least a 3.5 cumulative GPA is required for renewal the final two years.

5700. **Rupert Lowe Scholarship** 1 scholarship paying full tuition. Student must be in the top 10 percent of class and have scored at least 1300 on SAT.

5701. **Transfer Honor Scholarships** Varying numbers of scholarships ranging from $1,000 to $3,000 to undergraduate transfer students who have at least a 3.25 GPA from all previous colleges attended. The students' high school record and test scores also will be considered.

Renewable for each year of undergraduate work, provided the students maintain at least a 2.5 GPA.

5702. **Trustee's Scholarships** Unlimited number of scholarships from $1,000 to $2,500. Student must be in top 25 percent of class and have scored 1100 on SAT.

Baylor University
P.O. Box 97008
Waco, TX 76798-7008
(800) 229-5678
(817) 755-1011
http://www.baylor.edu/
admissions-office@baylor.edu

5703. **Academic Scholarships** Varying numbers of scholarships in varying amounts to students meeting certain academic criteria.

5704. **Baptist Standard Scholarship** 1 scholarship of $800 to a journalism student meeting certain criteria.

5705. **Carmage Walls Journalism Scholarship Fund** 40 scholarships of $1,000 to journalism students based on journalistic ability, interest in journalism, financial need, character or motivation, and journalistic promise.

5706. **Charles D. Johnson Journalism Scholarship** 1 scholarship of $900 to a student based on journalistic promise and financial need.

5707. **Creative Arts/Performance Awards** 54 scholarships of varying amounts are offered to music students.

5708. **David A. Cheavens Scholarship** 1 scholarship of $900 to a journalism student meeting certain criteria.

5709. **Donald W. Reynolds Foundation Scholarships** 2 scholarships of $2,500 for two years ($5,000 total) to students majoring in journalism or mass communications. Students must apply while sophomores and use the scholarship during their junior and senior years.

5710. **E. S. James Scholarship** 1 scholarship of $800 to a journalism student meeting certain criteria.

5711. **Fentress Scholarship** 1 scholarship of $500 to a student with demonstrated journalistic ability and promise. Deadline: March 15.

5712. **Harry Provence Scholarship** 1 scholarship of $2,000 to a senior based on academic achievement and journalistic potential.

5713. **National Merit Standing** Unlimited number of scholarships covering 50 percent of tuition. Renewable.

5714. **Presidential Scholarships** Varying numbers of scholarships of varying amounts to students meeting certain academic criteria.

Hardin-Simmons University
2200 Hickory, HSU Drawer M
Abilene, TX 79698
(915) 670-1000
http://www.hsutx.edu
enrollservices@hsutx.edu

5715. **Acteen Scholarships** Varying numbers of scholarships of varying amounts to students based on leadership and Southern Baptist affiliation.

5716. **Assured Scholarships** Numerous scholarships of varying amounts to students meeting certain criteria.

5717. **Attainment Scholarships** Numerous scholarships of varying amounts to students meeting certain criteria.

5718. **Business Scholarships** Varying numbers of scholarships of varying amounts to students majoring in business who meet certain criteria.

5719. **Creative Arts/Performance Awards** Varying numbers of scholarships of varying amounts to students majoring in a creative or performance art.

5720. **Education Scholarships** Varying numbers of scholarships of varying amounts to students pursuing careers in education and who meet certain criteria.

5721. **Entering Students** Unlimited $1,000 scholarships to students who scored at least 1000 on SAT or 24 on ACT. Renewable.

5722. **Geology Scholarships** Varying numbers of scholarships of varying amounts to students majoring in geology who meet certain criteria.

5723. **Honors** Unlimited number of $600 scholarships to students in top 10 percent of their class who scored at least 1090 on SAT or 27 on ACT. Renewable.

5724. **Ministerial Grants** Grants of varying amounts to Southern Baptist ministerial students.

McMurry University
14th and Sayles Boulevard
Abilene, TX 79697
(915) 691-6226
http://www.McM.edu
mstrang@mcm.edu

5725. **Activity Scholarship** Varying numbers of
awards ranging from $200 to $1,000 for full-time
students who have at least a 2.0 GPA. Must be
majoring in art, band, choir, communication, or
theater. Deadline: March 15.

5726. **Endowed Scholarship** Varying numbers of
awards of varying amounts for full-time students
with a GPA of 2.0 or better. Individual award
restrictions may apply. Check with the financial aid
office for more information. Deadline: March 15.

Midwestern State University
3410 Taft Boulevard
Wichita Falls, TX 76308-2099
(800) 842-1922
(940) 689-4321
http://www.mwsu.edu

5727. **Academic Scholarships** Varying numbers of
scholarships ranging from $200 to $500 to
undergraduate students with at least a 3.5 GPA
and who scored at least 1150 on SAT or 26 on
ACT. Renewable with 3.0 GPA.

5728. **Departmental** 150 scholarships ranging from
$250 to $1,000 to students in top 15 percent of
their class, with at least a 3.2 GPA, and scoring at
least 1050 on SAT or 25 on ACT. Renewable.

5729. **Honors** 60 scholarships of $600 to students in
top 5 percent of their class, with a 3.0 GPA, and
scoring at least 1150 on SAT or 26 on ACT.
Renewable.

5730. **Regents** Numerous scholarships of $500 to
students in top 25 percent of their class, with at
least a 2.8 GPA, and scoring at least 1000 on SAT
or 23 on ACT. Renewable.

Our Lady of the Lake University
411 S.W. 24th Street
San Antonio, TX 78207-4666
(210) 434-6711
http://www.ollusa.edu
homid@lake.ollusa.edu

5731. **Academic** 120 scholarships ranging from $600 to
$1,800 to students in top 25 percent of their class,
with a 3.25 GPA, and scoring at least 1100 on SAT
or 24 on ACT. Renewable.

5732. **Achievement Awards** The following
scholarships of varying amounts are available

based on academic achievement: Distinguished
Presidential, University, Alumni, G.W., and
Brackenridge.

5733. **Agribusiness Scholarships** Varying numbers
of scholarships of $1,000 to students majoring in
agribusiness-related course work who meet
certain criteria. Must be U.S. citizens or legal
residents. Must have been Bexar County residents
for at least six months before applying.

5734. **Creative Arts** Numerous music scholarships of
varying amounts to music majors.

5735. **Former Employees of Local Military Bases
Scholarships** Up to 50 scholarships of $1,000 to
students who are former employees of local
military bases. Renewable with satisfactory
academic progress.

5736. **Leadership Internships** 4 scholarships of
$1,000 to students who are serving leadership
internships. Based on demonstrated leadership
abilities.

5737. **Single Parent Scholarship Program** Up to 25
scholarships of $1,000 to students who are single
parents. Renewable with satisfactory academic
progress.

5738. **Student Leadership Scholarships** 2
scholarships of $1,000 to students who have
served as elected student government president
or vice-president.

5739. **Student Newspaper Editor Scholarship** 1
scholarship of $1,000 to the student who is editor
of the college newspaper.

Prairie View A&M University
P.O. Box 2610
Prairie View, TX 77446-2610
(409) 857-3311
http://www.pvamu.edu

5740. **Academic** Numerous scholarships ranging from
$1,100 to $5,000 to students in top 10 percent of
their class, with a 3.0 GPA, and scoring at least
1100 on SAT or 24 on ACT.

5741. **Ethnic Recruitment** Numerous scholarships
ranging from $600 to $1,200 to students with at
least a 2.5 GPA and scoring at least 700 on SAT or
15 on ACT. Renewable.

Rice University
P.O. Box 1892
Houston, TX 77251
(713) 527-8101
http://www.rice.edu
admission@rice.edu

5742. **Bonham** 3 scholarships ranging from $500 to $2,000. Renewable.

5743. **Jameson American Decorative Arts Fellowships** Fellowships of $8,300 to undergraduate and graduate students in American design. Deadline: February.

5744. **Shepherd Society Music Awards** 16 scholarships of varying amounts to students based on talent.

5745. **W. M. Rice** 10 scholarships of tuition to students in top 5 percent of class who scored at least 1300 on SAT. Renewable with a 3.2 GPA.

St. Mary's University
One Camino Santa Maria
San Antonio, TX 78288-8500
(210) 436-3011
http://www.stmary.tx.edu

5746. **Amy Shelton McNutt Trust** Numerous $2,000 scholarships to college sophomores, juniors, or seniors majoring in business who have at least a 3.5 GPA. Based on academic achievement and leadership characteristics.

5747. **Brother Thomas Threadaway Tuition Scholarship** 14 scholarships of $500.

5748. **Greiner Scholarship** 10 scholarships of $2,500 to students with at least 550 verbal SAT score and 600 math score or at least 26 ACT score. Participation in extracurricular activities, honors, awards, and work experience are considered. Must maintain a 3.0 GPA. Renewable.

5749. **Markey Scholarship** Recognizes students in campus activities field.

5750. **President's Scholarship** 30 awards of $2,500 are made to students with at least 26 ACT score or SAT verbal score of 550 and math score of 600. Also based on participation in extracurricular activities, honors, awards, work, and GPA. Renewable.

Sam Houston State University
Huntsville TX 77341
(409) 294-1111
http://www.shsu.edu
admissions@shsu.edu

5751. **Academic "Honors Program"** Numerous scholarships ranging from $200 to $2,000 to students in top 10 percent of class with at least a 3.0 GPA. Renewable.

5752. **Cheryl Parish Scholarship** 1 scholarship of $300 awarded at the end of freshman year to a student with outstanding academic achievement, interest, and personality.

5753. **Communications Workshop Scholarships** 2 to 3 scholarships of $500 to entering freshmen who were outstanding participants in the summer Communications Workshop for High School Journalists. Apply during workshop.

5754. **Don Reid Journalism Scholarship** 1 scholarship of $500 to a journalism student meeting certain criteria.

5755. **Ferot Robinson Scholarship** 1 scholarship of $200 to a second-semester freshman who is a journalism major.

5756. **Gibbs Award** 1 scholarship of $500 to a female undergraduate junior who is a journalism major with at least a 3.0 GPA.

5757. **Houston Gulf Coast News Photographers Scholarships** 1 to 2 scholarships ranging from $300 to $500 to undergraduate juniors based on academic achievement and potential as a news photographer. Deadline: March 1.

5758. **Jesse Jones Scholarships** 2 scholarships of $300 to students who are journalism majors. Based on academic achievement, financial need, interest in journalism, and ability. Renewable. Deadline: March 1.

5759. **John Elmore Scholarship** 1 scholarship of $500 to an undergraduate sophomore, junior, or senior journalism major. Based on character and high moral standards. Deadline: March 1.

5760. **President's Endowed** Numerous $2,000 scholarships to students who scored at least 1200 on SAT or 30 on ACT. Renewable.

5761. **Rodeo Scholarships** 8 scholarships, totaling $3,748, to students who meet certain criteria.

5762. **Roy G. Clark Scholarship** 1 scholarship of at least $200 to an undergraduate sophomore or above who has demonstrated outstanding potential as a journalist.

5763. **Speech and Drama Awards** 9 scholarships of varying amounts to students who are speech or drama majors and who meet certain criteria.

5764. **Sponberg Scholarship** 1 scholarship of $500 to a journalism major. Based on academic achievement, financial need, and letters of recommendation. Deadline: March 1.

Shreiner College
Kerrville, TX 78028
(800) 343-4919
http://www.schreiner.edu

5765. **Campus Ministry Scholarships** Scholarships of $400 to students who are willing to work with campus ministry and/or with the church.

5766. **Choral Ensemble Scholarships** Scholarships of $2,500 to students who are in the top half of their class and have demonstrated evidence of success in singing, preferably with an organized choir, chorus, and/or ensemble. Deadline: June 1.

5767. **Competitive Academic** 30 scholarships ranging from $2,623 to $5,265 to students in the top 25 percent of their class who scored at least 1100 on SAT or 24 on ACT. Renewable with a 3.25 GPA.

5768. **Competitive Academic** 4 scholarships ranging from $2,623 to $5,265 to students with at least a 3.25 GPA. Renewable with a 3.25 GPA.

5769. **Culinary Arts Program Scholarships** Scholarships of $1,000 to students who have been accepted into the program.

5770. **Drama Scholarships** Scholarships of $1,500 to students in the top half of their class who have theater experience. Deadline: June 1.

5771. **Hatton W. Sumners Foundation Scholarships** Scholarships ranging from $2,500 to $3,500 to students who have demonstrated leadership abilities and have at least a 3.0 GPA. Deadline: March 20.

5772. **Hill Country College Fund Vocational Nursing Program Scholarships** Scholarships of $875 to students accepted into the Vocational Nursing Program who meet other criteria.

5773. **Honors Program Scholarships** Scholarships of $9,000 to students in the top 10 percent of their class, with at least a 1240 on SAT or 27 on ACT, or to transfer students with at least a 3.6 GPA. Students should have demonstrated leadership abilities. Contact the Office of Admission. Deadline: March 15.

5774. **Journalism Scholarships** Scholarships of up to $1,000 to students in the top half of their class who have experience in journalism and/or 35mm camera experience. Deadline: August 1.

5775. **Leadership Scholarships** Scholarships of $1,000 to $2,000 to first-time students in the top half of their class, with at least a 920 SAT or 20 ACT and at least a 2.75 GPA ($1,000), or 1010 SAT/ 21 ACT and at least a 3.0 GPA ($2,000). Contact the financial aid office. Deadline: March 31.

5776. **Leadership Scholarships** Scholarships of $1,000 or $2,000 to students with at least a 2.65 GPA ($1,000) or 2.80 GPA ($2,000) who have demonstrated leadership abilities.

5777. **National Presbyterian College Scholarships** Scholarships of $1,400 to first-time students who are members of the Presbyterian Church (USA) and are either U.S. citizens or permanent residents. Deadline: December 1.

5778. **Presbyterian Grants-in-Aid** Grants of $300 to students who are members of the Presbyterian Church (USA).

5779. **Valedictorian/Salutatorian Scholarships** Scholarships of $500 (commuters) and $1,000 (residents) to students who are ranked either one or two in their class.

Southern Methodist University
Dallas, TX 75275
(800) 323-0672
(214) 692-2000
http://www.smu.edu
ugadmission@smu.edu

5780. **Allen Merriam Journalism Scholarship** 1 scholarship of $1,000 to a student. Based on academic achievement, journalistic ability, and financial need. Renewable. Deadline: March 1.

5781. **Alumni Scholarships** Numerous $750 scholarships. Renewable.

5782. **Henry C. Becker Endowed Journalism Scholarship** 1 scholarship of at least $1,000 to a student. Based on academic achievement, journalistic ability, and financial need. Renewable. Deadline: March 1.

5783. **President's Scholar** 25 scholarships of tuition to students in top 10 percent of class. Renewable with a 3.3 GPA.

5784. **Special Characteristics Awards** Numerous scholarships of varying amounts are available in the following areas: United Methodist ministers' children and minority student awards.

5785. **University** Numerous scholarships ranging from $200 to full tuition. Renewable with a 3.0 GPA.

Southwestern University
University at Maple
Georgetown, TX 78626
(800) 252-3166
(512) 863-6511
http://www.southwestern.edu

5786. **Academic** 50 scholarships ranging from $1,000 to $4,000 to students in the top 10 percent of their class, with at least a 3.5 GPA, and scoring at least 1150 on SAT or 27 on ACT. Renewable with a 3.0 GPA.

5787. **Brown Scholars** 4 scholarships of $7,800 to students in the top 10 percent of their class, with at least a 3.5 GPA, and scoring at least 1300 on SAT or 30 on ACT. Renewable with a 3.0 GPA.

5788. **Fine Arts** Numerous scholarships ranging from $500 to $3,500. Renewable.

5789. **National Merit "Honors Program"** 15 scholarships of $5,000 to students in the top 10 percent of their class with at least a 3.5 GPA. Renewable with a 3.0 GPA.

5790. **Presidential Scholar** 4 scholarships of $6,500 to students in the top 10 percent of their class with at least a 3.5 GPA. Renewable with a 3.0 GPA.

Southwest Texas State University
San Marcos, TX 78666-4607
(512) 245-2111
http://www.swt.edu
admissions@swt.edu

5791. **Fred Adams Memorial Scholarships** 4 scholarships of $300 to journalism students meeting certain criteria.

5792. **Galveston County Press Club Scholarships** 3 scholarships of $250 each to undergraduate junior or senior journalism majors who are residents of Galveston County or graduated from a Galveston County High School. Based on financial need, character, and desire to enter journalism profession.

5793. **Houston Press Club Scholarships** 1 or more scholarships of at least $200 to undergraduate junior or senior journalism majors who are graduates of a Harris County high school or residents of Harris County. Based on financial need. Contact: Chairperson, Scholarship Committee, Suite 601, 2016 Main, Houston, TX 77002. Deadline: March 15.

5794. **Journalism Scholarships** Varying numbers of scholarships ranging from $200 to $1,000 to media journalism majors who meet certain criteria.

5795. **LBJ Achievement "Honors Program"** 25 to 30 awards of $1,000 to students in upper 25 percent of class who scored at least 1000 on SAT or 24 on ACT.

5796. **Merrick** 20 scholarships ranging from $1,000 to $1,500 to students scoring at least 1000 on SAT or 24 on ACT.

5797. **State Scholarship** 20 scholarships of $1,000 awarded to students in top 33 percent of class who scored at least 800 on SAT or 18 on ACT.

5798. **University Scholars** 7 awards ranging from $1,000 to $1,2000 to students scoring at least 1000 on SAT or 24 on ACT.

Texas A&M University
College Station, TX 77843-0100
(409) 845-1031
http://www.tamu.edu

5799. **Academic/Need Honors Program** 300 scholarships of $500 to students with at least a 3.25 GPA. Renewable.

5800. **Audrey Cardenas Memorial Scholarships** 2 to 3 scholarships of $1,000 to students. Based on academic achievement, journalistic promise, and financial need.

5801. **Bill Robinson Memorial Scholarship** 1 scholarship of $650 to a student demonstrating ability and promise in print journalism.

5802. **Bryan–College Station Eagle Scholarships** 2 scholarships of $250 to students majoring in journalism, with preference given to students pursuing careers in newspaper.

5803. **Creative Arts/Performance Awards** 40 scholarships of $1,000 to students majoring in some area of creative arts or performance.

5804. **Engineering Awards** 252 scholarships of up to $1,000 to students pursuing careers in engineering who meet certain academic criteria.

5805. **Enrolled Student Scholar Awards** Varying numbers of scholarships ranging from $300 to $1,500 to undergraduate students. Based on academic excellence. Some graduate awards are available. Deadline: March 1.

5806. **Honors** 300 awards ranging from $2,000 to $4,500 to students in upper 15 percent of class who scored at least 1250 on SAT or 29 on ACT. Renewable with a 3.0 GPA.

5807. **Joe C. Monroe–George Carlin Scholarships** 2 scholarships of $500 to students.

Based on academic achievement and professional promise in journalism.

5808. **Journalism** 6 scholarships ranging from $250 to $6,000. Inquire with journalism department for specific requirements.

5809. **Lechner Fellowship** 200 scholarships of $2,000 awarded to students in top 15 percent of class who scored at least 1200 on SAT or 29 on ACT. Based on academic record, SAT/ACT scores, extracurricular activities, and leadership. Renewable with a 3.0 GPA.

5810. **McFadden Scholarships** 40 scholarships of $2,000 to students in the top 15 percent of class who scored at least 1200 on SAT or 29 on ACT. Must be nominated by high school counselor. Based on SAT/ACT scores, extracurricular activities, and leadership. Renewable with a 3.0 GPA.

5811. **Merit Plus Scholarships** Scholarships of varying amounts to students designated as National Merit Finalists. May be supplemented by other scholarships, including National Merit Scholarships. Non-Texas residents receive out-of-state tuition waiver. Awarded yearly.

5812. **Moorman Agricultural Scholarship** 4 scholarships of $1,000 to students in the School of Agriculture. Based on scholastic standing in high school, leadership qualities in school, community, church or youth groups, financial need, and interest in agriculture. Contact dean of College of Agriculture or secretary, Moorman Company Fund, 1000 North 30th Street, Quincy, IL 62301-3496.

5813. **National Merit Scholarship** 113 scholarships of $750 to National Merit Scholarship Finalists designating Texas A&M University their first-choice school. May be supplemented by other scholarships, including National Merit Scholarships. Non-Texas residents receive out-of-state tuition waiver. Awarded yearly.

5814. **National Society of Professional Engineers** 3 scholarships of $1,000 for four years to students from outside the state of Texas. Must rank in the top 25 percent of their high school class and have a minimum 3.0 GPA and a verbal SAT score of 500 and math score of 600 (English ACT score of 22 and math score of 29). Candidates should apply as early as possible in their senior year so that interviews can be conducted in November. Deadline: December 15.

5815. **Opportunity** 625 scholarships ranging from $500 to $2,400 to students in upper 25 percent of class, with a 3.9 GPA, and scoring at least 1100 on SAT.

5816. **President's Achievement Awards** 4 scholarships of at least $2,500 to African American and Hispanic American undergraduate students who meet certain academic criteria.

5817. **President's Endowed Scholarships** Up to 250 scholarships of $2,000 to students meeting certain academic criteria.

5818. **School of Agriculture Awards** Up to 280 scholarships of up to $1,000 to students meeting certain academic criteria and pursuing agriculture-related careers.

5819. **So Ross Awards** Varying numbers of scholarships of up to $1,000 to students meeting certain academic criteria.

Texas A&M University—Corpus Christi
6300 Ocean Drive
Corpus Christi, TX 78412
(512) 991-6810
http://www.tamucc.edu

5820. **Bateman Family Scholarship** 1 scholarship of $600 to an undergraduate junior meeting certain academic criteria who is a general business major.

5821. **Behmann Brothers Foundation Scholarships** Varying numbers of scholarships of $600 to undergraduate juniors meeting certain academic criteria who are education majors.

5822. **Canales & Simonson, P. C. Scholarship** 1 scholarship of $2,000 to an undergraduate junior meeting certain academic criteria who is a political science major.

5823. **CCHR Management Association Scholarships** Varying numbers of scholarships of $600 to undergraduate students meeting certain academic criteria who are education majors. Must have an interest or internship in human resources.

5824. **Central Power & Light Scholarship** 1 scholarship of $1,000 to an undergraduate student majoring in business, computer science, or environmental science. Must reside in Central Power & Light territory.

5825. **C. J. Davidson Endowment Scholarships** Varying numbers of scholarships of $600 to single undergraduates who meet certain academic criteria and have financial need.

5826. **C. J. Watson Memorial Scholarships** Varying numbers of scholarships of $600 to undergraduate students meeting certain academic criteria who are education majors with emphasis in business.

5827. **Douglas Foundation Scholarships** Varying numbers of scholarships of $500 per semester to undergraduate students meeting certain academic criteria who are business majors.

5828. **Elaine Barbiere Foundation Scholarships** Varying numbers of scholarships of $500 to students meeting certain academic criteria who are nursing majors.

5829. **Fine Arts** Numerous scholarships to students in the fine arts who have at least a 2.5 GPA. Renewable with a 2.5 GPA.

5830 **Honors** Numerous scholarships ranging from $600 to $2,000 to students with at least a 3.0 GPA. Renewable with a 3.0 GPA.

5831. **Hubert McNally Scholarship** 1 scholarship of $600 to a full- or part-time student meeting certain criteria and who is a theater major.

5832. **James R. Dinn Scholarship** 1 scholarship of $300 per semester to an undergraduate student meeting certain academic criteria who is a business major with an interest in insurance.

5833. **John Stevenson Award** 1 scholarship of $1,000 to an undergraduate or graduate student meeting certain academic criteria and majoring in accounting. Recipient is selected by accounting faculty.

5834. **President's Scholarships** Numerous scholarships of $6,000 to students, in the top 10 percent of their class, with at least a 3.0 GPA, and who scored at least 1250 on SAT or 27 on ACT. Renewable with a 3.0 GPA.

5835. **University Honors Scholarships** Numerous scholarships of $2,000 to students, in the top 25 percent of their class, with at least a 3.0 GPA, and who scored at least 1150 on SAT or 23 on ACT. Renewable with a 3.0 GPA.

Texas A&M University—Kingsville
Campus Box 105
Kingsville, TX 78363
(512) 595-2111
http://www.tamuk.edu

5836. **Agriculture and Home Economics** 17 scholarships ranging from $200 to $5,000 to students meeting certain criteria who are agriculture or home economics majors.

5837. **Alcoa Foundation Scholarships** 2 scholarships ranging from $1,000 to $1,500 to students majoring in chemical or natural gas engineering, who scored at least 1010 on SAT (510 math) or 22 on ACT (25 math) and have at least a 2.7 GPA.

Contact the New School Relations or Enrolled Students Department. Deadline: March 31; November 15.

5838. **Alfred F. Gross Fund Scholarships** 2 scholarships of $500 to entering freshmen or undergraduate students majoring in industrial technology engineering who scored at least 850 on SAT (math 510) or 21 on ACT (math 25) and have at least a 3.0 GPA. Contact the New School Relations or Enrolled Students Department. Deadline: March 31; November 15.

5839. **Alumni Awards** 25 scholarships of $750 to students in the top 25 percent of their class who scored at least 850 on SAT or 21 on ACT. Renewable with a 2.5 GPA.

5840. **Alumni Honors Awards** Varying numbers of scholarships of up to $5,000 per year to entering freshmen who are in the top 10 percent of their class and scored at least 1280 on SAT or 29 on ACT, with at least a 3.0 GPA. Renewable with 3.5 GPA. Contact School Relations. Deadline: March 3.

5841. **Alumni Merit Awards** 8 scholarships of $1,000 to entering freshmen who are in the top 25 percent of their class, with at least 21 on ACT or 970 on SAT. Contact School Relations. Deadline: March 3.

5842. **Arts and Sciences Department Awards** 43 scholarships ranging from $200 to $5,000 to students who meet certain criteria and have a major in the Arts and Sciences.

5843. **Barnes & Noble Book Company Scholarship** 2 scholarships of $1,000 to entering freshmen in the top 25 percent of their class, who scored at least 1090 on SAT or 24 on ACT. Contact School Relations. Deadline: March 3.

5844. **Behmann Brothers Merit Awards** Varying numbers of scholarships of up to $5,000 awarded to students in the top 25 percent of their class who scored at least 1090 on SAT or 24 on ACT. Contact School Relations. Deadline: March 3.

5845. **Business Administration Awards** 14 scholarships ranging from $200 to $5,000 to students meeting certain criteria who are business administration majors.

5846. **Civil Engineering Fund Scholarships** 6 scholarships of $300 to entering freshmen or undergraduate students who scored at least 970 on SAT or 21 on ACT. Contact the New School Relations or Enrolled Students Department. Deadline: March 31; November 1.

5847. **Education Department Awards** 8 scholarships ranging from $200 to $5,000 to students who meet certain criteria and are education majors.

5848. **Engineering Department Awards** 39 scholarships ranging from $200 to $5,000 to students who meet certain criteria and are engineering majors.

5849. **Exxon Mechanical Scholarship** 3 scholarships of $600 to high school seniors or current undergraduate students majoring in mechanical engineering who scored at least 850 on SAT or 21 on ACT. Renewable. Contact the New School Relations or Enrolled Students Department. Deadline: March 31; November 15.

5850. **Freshman Housing Scholarships** Varying numbers of scholarships providing up to full room and board costs (approximately $5,300) to entering freshmen who are in the top 25 percent of their class and scored at least 970 on SAT or 21 on ACT. Renewable with a 2.75 GPA. Contact School Relations. Deadline: March 3.

5851. **General Scholarships** 33 scholarships ranging from $200 to $5,000 to students who meet certain criteria.

5852. **HBCU/MI Environmental Consortium Scholarships** 10 scholarships ranging from $500 to $1,800 to undergraduate students majoring in environmental engineering or physical science. Must have completed sixty credit hours. Contact the Enrolled Students Department. Deadline: April 15; November 15.

5853. **Hoeschst Celanese Corporation Scholarships** 2 scholarships ranging from $1,000 to $1,500 to high school seniors or undergraduate students majoring in chemical or natural gas engineering, with at least a 2.7 GPA, and who scored at least 1010 on SAT or 22 on ACT. Renewable with 2.7 GPA. Contact: New School Relations or Enrolled Students Department. Deadline: March 31; November 15.

5854. **Houston Chapter of API Scholarships** 3 scholarships ranging from $1,000 to $1,500 to entering freshmen or current undergraduates majoring in natural gas engineering. Must have scored at least 1000 SAT (510 math) or 25 ACT (25 math) and have at least a 3.0 GPA. Contact the New School Relations or Enrolled Student Department. Deadline: March 31; November 15.

5855. **Kleberg First National Bank Honors Scholars** 1 scholarship of up to $5,000 to an entering freshman who is in the top 10 percent of class, with at least a 29 on ACT or 1280 on SAT and at least a 3.0 GPA. Must be graduating from Kingsville, Kauger, or Bishop High School.

Renewable with 3.5 GPA. Contact School Relations. Deadline: March 3.

5856. **Presidential** 35 scholarships of up to $5,000 awarded to students in the top 25 percent of their class who scored at least 850 on SAT or 20 on ACT. Renewable with a 2.0 GPA.

5857. **Russel Honors Scholars** Varying numbers of scholarships of up to $5,000 to entering freshmen who are in the top 25 percent of their class, with at least a 1280 on SAT or 29 on ACT and at least a 3.0 GPA. Renewable with a 3.0 GPA. Contact School Relations. Deadline: March 3.

5858. **3M Foundation Scholarships** Varying numbers of scholarships of $1,000 to minority high school seniors and current undergraduate engineering majors who scored at least 950 on SAT or 23 on ACT, with at least a 2.8 GPA. Renewable with a 3.0 GPA. Contact the New School Relations or Enrolled Student Department. Deadline: March 31.

5859. **University** 10 scholarships of $1,000 awarded to students in the top 25 percent of their class who scored at least an 1100 on SAT or 25 on ACT. Award is renewable if student maintains a 3.0 GPA.

5860. **Yvonne Duffy Fund** Varying numbers of scholarships of $2,000 to entering freshmen and current undergraduate students who are or will be majoring in English. Entering freshmen must have been in the top 25 percent of their class and scored at least 970 on SAT or 21 on ACT. Undergraduate students must have at least a 2.8 GPA. Applicants should demonstrate financial need. Contact the New School Relations or Enrolled Department. Deadline: March 17; July 15.

Texas Christian University
2800 South University Drive
Forth Worth, TX 76129
(800) 828-3764
http://www.tcu.edu

5861. **Band Awards** 22 scholarships of at least $1,000 to students who meet certain criteria and are members of the band. Based on talent.

5862. **Chancellor's Scholarships** 20 scholarships providing tuition (approximately $11,000) to students in the top 5 percent of their class who scored at least 1300 on SAT or 30 on ACT. Renewable with 3.25 GPA.

5863. **Choir Awards** 10 scholarships of $1,000 to students meeting certain criteria who are members of the choir. Based on talent.

5864. **CYF Regional Executive Assistant Awards** 16 scholarships of approximately $4,188 to students who have demonstrated religious leadership and involvement.

5865. **Dean's Scholarship by Transfers** 24 scholarships of $2,000 to students transferring to TCU from other schools. Renewable if recipient maintains a satisfactory academic average.

5866. **M. E. Sadler Merit Scholarships** 20 awards ranging from $750 to $2,000 to National Merit Finalists who list Texas Christian University as their first choice. The amount of the award depends on financial need and may be matched with institutional funds to provide full tuition. Renewable with satisfactory academic average.

5867. **Ministers' Dependents Grants** 16 scholarships of approximately $4,188 to students meeting certain criteria who are dependents of Disciples of Christ ministers.

5868. **Music Scholarships** 12 scholarships ranging from $650 to $2,000 to students meeting certain criteria who are music majors. Based on talent.

5869. **National Hispanic Scholars Awards** 2 scholarships of approximately $8,000 to Hispanic students meeting certain academic criteria.

5870. **Nordan Awards** 8 scholarships of approximately $1,000 to students meeting certain academic criteria who are fine arts majors.

5871. **Orchestra Award** 13 scholarships of $1,000 to students meeting certain criteria who are members of the orchestra. Based on talent.

5872. **Theater Awards** 3 scholarships of $1,000 to students meeting certain criteria who are theater majors. Based on talent.

5873. **Valedictorian Awards** 6 scholarships ranging from $2,000 to $3,000 to students who were their class valedictorians.

5874. **Walsh Awards** 2 scholarships of $625 each to students meeting certain criteria who are creative or performance arts majors. Based on talent.

Texas Lutheran University
1000 West Court
Seguin, TX 78155
(210) 312-8000
http://www.lutheran.edu

5875. **Academic Excellence** Scholarships ranging from $1,500 to $2,000 to students in the top 5 percent of their class who scored at least 1150 on SAT.

5876. **Pacesetter Awards (PACE)** 30 to 37 scholarships of $3,000 to students in the top 5 percent of their class at the end of their junior year or who have composite ACT score of 27 or combined SAT score of 1150. Renewable with a 3.25 GPA.

Texas Tech University
Admissions Office
Lubbock, TX 79409
(806) 742-2011
http://www.ttu.edu

5877. **Joe H. and Mary Lee Bryant Scholarship** 1 scholarship of $1,000 to an undergraduate sophomore or higher. Based on academic achievement and financial need.

5878. **Marvin Jones–Dean's** Numerous $200 scholarships to students with a 3.0 GPA and scoring at least 1100 on SAT or 26 on ACT. Renewable if student maintains a 3.0 GPA.

5879. **Moorman Agricultural Scholarship** 4 scholarships of $1,000 to students in the School of Agriculture. Based on scholastic standing in high school; leadership qualities in school, community, church, or youth groups; financial need, and interest in agriculture. Contact: Dean of College of Agriculture or Secretary, Moorman Company Fund, 1000 North 30th Street, Quincy, IL 62301-3496.

5880. **Presidential** Numerous scholarships of $2,000 to students who score at least a 1350 on SAT or 31 on ACT. Renewable.

5881. **TTU** 140 scholarships of $500 to students with at least a 3.8 GPA who score at least a 1200 on SAT or 27 on ACT. Renewable with a 3.8 GPA.

5882. **University Scholar** 25 scholarships of $1,500 to students with a B+ average who score at least a 1350 on SAT or 31 on ACT. Renewable with a 3.5 GPA.

Texas Women's University
P.O. Box 425589
Denton, TX 76204
(940) 898-2000
http://www.twu.edu
admissions@twu.edu

5883. **Ethnic Recruitment "Honors Program"** 15 scholarships from $750 to $1,000 for minority students in the top 33 percent of their class who scored at least 800 on SAT or 18 on ACT.

5884. **Regents** Numerous scholarships of $3,500 to students who scored at least 1200 on SAT or 28 on ACT. Based on leadership, community service, and recommendation letters. Renewable with a 3.0 GPA.

5885. **TW General** 200 scholarships ranging from $400 to $500 for students with at least a 3.75 GPA in high school.

Trinity University
715 Stadium Drive
San Antonio, TX 78212
(210) 736-7011
http://www.trinity.edu
admissions@trinity.edu

5886. **Ellis Shapiro** Scholarships of $800 to a junior or senior in public relations or journalism.

5887. **Hearst Endowment** 2 scholarships of $1,000 to juniors or seniors majoring in communications with at least a 3.25 GPA.

5888. **President's Scholarship** 200 to 300 scholarships ranging from $1,000 to $4,500 to entering freshmen. Must have at least 1250 on SAT or 29 on ACT. A minimum 3.25 GPA must be maintained. Award is for tuition only. Renewable.

5889. **Trustees' Scholarship** 100 scholarships ranging from $1,200 to $6,000. Must be National Merit Finalists who list Trinity University as first choice. A minimum 3.25 GPA must be maintained. Deadline: February 1.

University of Houston
129 Ezekiel West Cullen Building
Houston, TX 77204-2161
(713) 749-1201
http://www.uh.edu
admissions@uh.edu

5890. **Academic Excellence "Honors Program"** 250 scholarships ranging from $500 to $1,500 to students in top 25 percent of their class who scored at least 900 on SAT or 21 on ACT.

5891. **Academic Recognition** 189 scholarships ranging from $500 to $1,500 to students with at least a 3.5 GPA and scoring at least 1100 on SAT or 26 on ACT. Renewable with a 3.0 GPA.

5892. **Alumni** 313 scholarships ranging from $1,000 to $1,500 to students in top 25 percent of their class and scoring at least 1200 on SAT or 28 on ACT. Renewable with a 3.0 GPA.

5893. **Cullen Leadership** 162 scholarships of $2,000 to students in top 25 percent of their class who scored at least 1250 on SAT and 30 on ACT. Renewable with a 3.0 GPA.

University of Texas at Austin
Austin, TX 78712-1157
(512) 471-3434
http://www.utexas.edu

5894. **Achievement** 500 scholarships of $2,000. Renewable with a 2.0 GPA.

5895. **Achievement Honors** 125 scholarships of $4,000. Renewable with a 2.0 GPA.

5896. **Blanche Projean Endowed Presidential Scholarships** Scholarships of $2,000 to students who are or will be enrolled in the College of Communications, based on academic achievement and financial need. Deadline: February 15.

5897. **Creative Arts/Performance Awards** Numerous scholarships of varying amounts to students majoring in art, drama, or music. Based on talent, portfolio, or audition.

5898. **Dedman Distinguished Scholars Awards** 6 scholarships ranging from $1,000 to $7,000 to students who are in the top 5 percent of their class and who will be pursuing a liberal arts major.

5899. **Departmental** 6,000 scholarships ranging from $200 to $5,000.

5900. **DeWitt C. Reddick Journalism Scholarships** 2 or more scholarships of $600 to upper-division journalism students in either news-editorial or magazine journalism.

5901. **Donald W. Reynolds Foundation Scholarship** 1 scholarship of $2,500 per year for two years to a student in print journalism. Must apply in sophomore year. Awarded in junior year, and renewable for senior year.

5902. **Earl Campbell Endowed Presidential Scholarship in Communication** 1 scholarship of $2,000 to a minority student who is or will be enrolled in the College of Communications. Based on journalistic ability and promise, with financial need considered in final selection. Deadline: February 15.

5903. **Engineering Scholarships** 3 scholarships of up to $2,500 to incoming freshman with at least a 3.0 GPA who are engineering majors. Must be U.S. citizens.

5904. **Frank Morrow Endowed Presidential Scholarships in Business Journalism** 2 scholarships of $2,000 to outstanding students pursuing careers in business reporting. Awarded after sophomore year. Students must have completed nine to twelve hours of business courses.

5905. **Freshman Scholarships** 70 scholarships ranging from $500 to $750 to students in the top 25 percent of their class who scored at least 1200 on SAT or 27 on ACT. Renewable with 3.5 GPA.

5906. **Headliners Club of Austin Scholarships in Journalism** 3 scholarships of $1,000 to journalism students. Based on financial need, academic achievement, and involvement in extracurricular activities.

5907. **Jesse H. Jones Endowed Centennial Scholarships** 8 scholarships of $750 to undergraduate and graduate students who are or will be enrolled in the College of Communications (including advertising and journalism). Based on journalistic ability and promise, with financial need considered in final selection. Deadline: February 15.

5908. **Jesse H. Jones Endowed Centennial Scholarships** 1 or more scholarships of $2,000 to undergraduate students who are or will be enrolled in the College of Communications (including advertising and journalism). Based on journalistic ability and promise, with financial need considered in final selection. Deadline: February 15.

5909. **John T. Jones Jr. Endowed Presidential Scholarship** 1 or more scholarships of $2,000 to students who are or will be enrolled in the College of Communications. Based on journalistic ability and promise, with financial need considered in final selection. Deadline: February 15.

5910. **Journalism** 27 scholarships ranging from $200 to $6,000. Inquire with Journalism Department for specific requirements.

5911. **Larry Temple Scholarships** 7 scholarships of $6,000 to undergraduate students who are majoring in liberal arts, fine arts, or social work. Preference given to Texas residents.

5912. **Lyde and Charles Devall Endowed Presidential Scholarships** 1 or more scholarships of $2,000 to students in journalism or mass media. Based on ability and promise, with financial need considered in final selection. Deadline: February 15.

5913. **Minorities Engineering** 35 scholarships ranging from $500 to $1,000 to students who scored at least 1000 on SAT or 24 on ACT. Renewable with a 2.0 GPA.

5914. **Minorities Engineering "Honors Program"** 125 scholarships ranging from $250 to $1,500 to students who scored at least 1000 on SAT or 24 on ACT. Renewable with a 2.5 GPA.

5915. **Terry Foundation Scholarships** 20 scholarships ranging from $1,000 to $7,000 to undergraduate students who are Texas residents, have demonstrated leadership abilities, have a high SAT score, and have financial need.

5916. **Texas Excellence Awards** 10 to 36 scholarships ranging from $1,000 to $7,000 to high school seniors in the top 5 percent of their class. Renewable with satisfactory academic progress.

5917. **Thomas Thompson Journalism Scholarships** 5 scholarships of $200 to undergraduate and graduate students in a print area of journalism.

5918. **Times–Mirror Minority Scholarships** 3 scholarships of $2,000 to undergraduate minority students who are or will be enrolled in the College of Communications. Based on journalistic ability and promise, with financial need considered in final selection. Deadline: February 15.

5919. **Transfer Scholarships** 25 scholarships ranging from $200 to $500 to students with at least a 3.5 GPA.

University of Texas at El Paso
500 West University Avenue
El Paso, TX 79968
(915) 747-5000
http://www.utep.edu

5920. **General and Departmental** Numerous scholarships ranging from $200 to $1,500 to students from various departments. Minimum 3.0 GPA required.

5921. **General Scholar** 75 scholarships ranging from $200 to $700 to students with at least a 3.0 GPA and scoring at least 1000 on SAT or 23 on ACT. Renewable with a 3.0 GPA.

5922. **National Action Council for Minorities in Engineering Scholarships** 15 scholarships ranging from $500 to $1,500 to incoming freshmen majoring in Civil, Electrical, Mechanical Engineering, or Engineering. Must have a minimum 3.0 GPA and financial need. Renewable with a 2.5 GPA. Deadline: April 1.

5923. **Presidential** 160 scholarships ranging from $1,000 to $2,000 are available to students. For the $1,500–$2,000 award: students must have at least a 3.7 GPA, be in the top 3 percent of their class, and have scored at least 1100 on SAT or 26 on

ACT. For the $1,000 award: students must have at least a 3.5 GPA, be in the top 5 percent of their class, and have scored at least 1000 on SAT or 24 on ACT.

5924. **Stevens and Clardy Fox** 50 scholarships of $1,000 to students with at least a 3.5 GPA and scoring at least 1000 on SAT or 24 on ACT. Renewable with a 3.2 GPA.

5925. **University Achievement "Honors Program"** 40 scholarships from $200 to $800 for students with at least a 3.0 GPA. Renewable with a 3.0 GPA.

5926. **University Endowed** 40 scholarships of $750 to students with at least a 3.3 GPA. Renewable with a 3.0 GPA.

University of Texas at San Antonio
San Antonio, TX 78285-0616
(800) 669-9019
http://www.utsa.edu

5927. **Academic/Bexar County** Numerous $1,200 scholarships to students in the top 25 percent of class with a 3.0 GPA. Renewable if a 3.0 GPA is maintained.

5928. **Academic/Minority "Honors Program"** 2 awards of $2,000 to students with a 3.0 GPA. Renewable with a 3.0 GPA.

5929. **Alumni Association Scholarships** Up to 10 scholarships ranging from $300 to $1,600 to entering freshmen who were in the top 25 percent of their high school class, and who have scored at least 700 on SAT or 18 on ACT. Deadline: April 1.

5930. **Andrew Gurwitz Endowed Scholarship** 1 scholarship of up to $2,000 to a student carrying at least fifteen hours per semester, who has at least a 3.0 GPA, is enrolled in both applied music lessons and an assigned music ensemble each semester, and is majoring in any area of music. Vocalists must audition for Madrigal Singers each fall semester and Opera Workshop each spring semester. Audition required. Deadline: April 1.

5931. **Barry M. Goldwater Scholarship** Varying numbers of scholarships of $7,000 to an undergraduate sophomore or junior interested in pursuing a career in mathematics, computer sciences, medical research, or engineering. Must be in the top 25 percent of their class, with at least a 3.0 GPA. Must be U.S. citizens or permanent residents. Contact the College of Sciences and Engineering. Deadline: November.

5932. **College of Business Undergraduate Scholarships** 10 scholarships of $1,000 to full-time undergraduate sophomores, juniors, and seniors majoring in a business-related field. Must have at least a 2.75 GPA and have completed forty-five credit hours. Based on academic merit, extracurricular involvement, financial need, and goals.

5933. **College of Fine Arts and Humanities Scholarships** Up to 12 scholarships of $1,000 to full-time undergraduates who have completed at least thirty college credit hours, are pursuing degrees in the College of Fine Arts and Humanities, have at least a 3.0 GPA, and have not received other merit-based scholarship support. Contact the College of Fine Arts and Humanities. Deadline: February 15 (fall); November 15 (spring).

5934. **George Muller Scholarships** 6 scholarships totaling $500 per year to students who are graduates of Blanco, Boerne, or Comfort high schools. Must be U.S. citizens and Texas residents. Contact the Scholarship Office. Deadline: March 31.

5935. **Indo-American Entrepreneurs Associate Scholarship** 1 scholarship of $3,200 to a full-time undergraduate or graduate student pursuing a degree in the College of Fine Arts and Humanities. Incoming freshmen must have graduated in the top 50 percent of their class and have at least 850 on SAT or 18 on ACT. Undergraduate and graduate students must be in good academic standing. Must be a U.S. citizen, resident alien, or international student with ancestry in the Indian subcontinent. Contact the College of Fine Arts and Humanities. Deadline: August 15 (fall); December 15 (spring).

5936. **Kelly Field National Bank Scholarship** 1 scholarship of $2,500 to a full-time undergraduate junior or senior pursuing a degree in finance. Must have at least a 3.0 GPA or better and financial need.

5937. **Marjory Powell Zachry Endowed Scholarships** Up to 4 scholarships of $1,500 and possibly other awards of varying amounts to students carrying at least fifteen hours per semester who have at least a 3.0 GPA, are enrolled in both applied music lessons and an assigned music ensemble each semester, and are majoring in piano, organ, or harpsichord performance (or one of these must be their principal instrument). Must make an exemplary contribution to the Division of Music through music performance and studies and make satisfactory progress toward completion of the degree. Audition required. Deadline: April 1.

5938. **Minority Access to Research Careers (MARC) Program** 5 scholarships of $5,460 to undergraduate freshmen and sophomores and 10 scholarships of $7,656 to undergraduate juniors or seniors. Recipients also awarded tuition and fees, and an $800 travel allowance is given to students majoring in a program in the College or Sciences and Engineering who have at least a 3.0 GPA. Must be committed to attending graduate school and pursuing a career in biomedical research. Preference is given to socioeconomically disadvantaged students. Contact the Minority Biomedical Research Support/MARC Office. Deadline: rolling.

5939. **Minority Biomedical Research Support (MBRS) Program** Scholarships providing $6,200 for undergraduates and $7,800 plus tuition and fees for graduate students, and a $700 travel allowance. Must be majoring in a program in the College of Sciences and Engineering and be interested in pursuing a biomedical research career. Undergraduates must have at least a 2.7 GPA and graduates must have at least a 3.0 GPA. Must be U.S. citizens or permanent residents. Graduate students must have been unconditionally admitted to UTSA. Preference given to socioeconomically disadvantaged students. Contact the Minority Biomedical Research Support/MARC Office. Deadline: rolling.

5940. **Music Performance Scholarships** 44 scholarships ranging from $200 to $2,000 to students carrying at least fifteen hours per semester, who have at least a 3.0 GPA, are enrolled in both applied music lessons and an assigned music ensemble each semester, and are music majors. Must make an exemplary contribution to the Division of Music through music performance and studies and make satisfactory progress toward completion of the degree. Vocalists must audition for Madrigal Singers each fall semester and Opera Workshop each spring semester. Audition required. Deadline: April 1.

5941. **NASA Undergraduate Scholar Awards for Research** Varying numbers of scholarships of $8,000 to incoming freshmen or undergraduates who haven't completed more than thirty-eight hours of college-level work, are either socially and economically disadvantaged or disabled, and demonstrate financial need. Must demonstrate an interest in science, mathematics, computer science, or engineering. Must have at least a 3.2 high school GPA and at least 1000 on SAT. Undergraduates must have at least a 3.0 GPA on all college-level work. Must be U.S. citizens. Contact the Associate Dean's Office.

5942. **Pfizer/UTSA Scholarship Program** 6 scholarships of $6,000 to undergraduate sophomores, juniors, or seniors majoring in biology or chemistry and with at least a 2.75 GPA. Must be U.S. citizens. Contact the Minority Biomedical Research Support/MARC Office. Deadline: rolling.

5943. **Presidential Honors Scholarships** up to 20 scholarships of $1,500 to entering students who were in the top 10 percent of their high school class and scored at least 1100 on SAT or 24 on ACT. Must also be applying for entrance to the UTSA Honors Program. Contact the University Honors Program Office. Deadline: February 1.

5944. **San Antonio Livestock Exposition, Inc. Scholarship** 10 scholarships of $10,000 ($1,250 per semester) to undergraduate students in the College of Sciences and Engineering or the College of Business that lead to a career in agriculture or agribusiness. Must demonstrate participation and leadership in extracurricular activities and demonstrate financial need. Contact the Scholarship Office. Deadline: March 31.

5945. **South Texas Geological Society Scholarships** 2 grants of $1,500 to undergraduate or graduate students majoring in geology to attend a summer field camp. Contact the Division of Earth and Physical Sciences. Deadline: January 15.

5946. **Southwest Gem and Mineral Society Scholarships** 3 awards of $700 to undergraduate juniors or seniors who are majoring in geology and have at least a 3.0 GPA. Contact the Division of Earth and Physical Sciences. Deadline: April 1.

5947. **Union Pacific Resources Scholarships** 2 scholarships of $1,000 to upper-division undergraduates or graduate students who are accounting majors who have distinguished themselves in the classroom and have participated in extracurricular activities. Contact the Division of Accounting and Information Systems.

5948. **UTSA Downtown Campus Scholarships** Scholarships of $2,000 to incoming freshmen who were in the top 40 percent of their high school class, with at least an 860 on SAT or 18 on ACT. Must enroll in at least three courses a semester at UTSA Downtown. Contact the Scholarship Office. Deadline: March 31.

5949. **UT System Alliance for Minority Participation (AMP)** 1 scholarship of $6,000 to an undergraduate student who has completed at least sixty undergraduate hours, has at least a 2.5 GPA, and is from an underserved population. Must be a U.S. citizen or permanent resident. Contact the Office of Minority Affairs and International Students.

University of the Incarnate Word
4301 Broadway
San Antonio, TX 78209
(210) 828-1261
http://www.uiw.edu

5950. **Academic Scholarships** 85 scholarships from $1,400 to $2,200. Students who have (1) minimum 3.0 GPA and a combined ACT score of 28 or 29, or a combined SAT score of 1050 to 1150, receive $2,200 per year; (2) minimum 3.0 GPA, 24 or 25 ACT score, or 980 to 1050 SAT score, receive $1,800 per year; (3) minimum 3.2 GPA with 22 or 23 ACT composite score or 880 to 970 combined

SAT receive $1,600 per year; (4) minimum 3.5 GPA with 20 or 21 ACT or 840 to 870 SAT receive $1,400 per year. A minimum 3.25 GPA must be maintained by all for renewal.

5951. **Transfer Scholarships** Numerous scholarships of $1,400 for students transferring with twenty-four credit hours who have at least a 2.35 to 3.2 GPA. Renewable with 3.2 GPA.

5952. **Transfer Scholarships** Numerous scholarships of $1,800 to students transferring with twenty-four credit hours and a 3.6 to 4.0 GPA. Renewable with 3.25 GPA.

UTAH

Brigham Young University
ASB A-153
Provo, UT 84602
(801) 378-4104
http://www.byu.edu
admissions@byu.edu

5953. **Academic Awards** 1,600 scholarships ranging from $200 to $1,950 to students who meet certain academic criteria.

5954. **Art Talent Award** 1 award providing up to half of tuition costs to a student who meets certain academic criteria, is an art major, and submits a slide portfolio for review.

5955. **Creative Arts/Performance Awards** 130 scholarships ranging from $100 to $1,550 to students in drama, dance, art, music, communication, or design technology who meet certain criteria. Based on talent.

5956. **Donald W. Reynolds Foundation Scholarship** 1 scholarship of $2,500 per year for two years to a journalism or mass communications major. Apply during undergraduate sophomore year. Renewable for senior year.

5957. **Ezra Taft Benson Scholarships** 24 scholarships ranging from $2,320 to $3,320 to students who have at least a 3.85 GPA, who scored at least a 3.85 GPA, who scored at least 31 on ACT, and are graduates of a Latter-Day Saints High School. Renewable.

5958. **Saul Haas Scholarships** (sponsored by Bonneville International Corporation) 3 scholarships of $250, $500, and $1,000 to an outstanding communications student based on ability, interest and intent, character, and

extracurricular activities. Before graduation, student must work an eight-week internship at one of Bonneville's properties. Contact the Department of Communications. Deadline: March 1.

University of Utah
200 South University Street
Salt Lake City, UT 84112
(801) 581-7281
http://www.utah.edu

5959. **American Handicapped Workers Foundation Scholarships** 2 scholarships of at least $2,000 to undergraduate or graduate students with a diagnosed disability. Deadline: March 1.

5960. **Congressional Teacher Scholarships** 8 scholarships of at least $5,000 to incoming freshmen who were in the top 10 percent of their high school graduating class and are interested in majoring in education. Preference is given to students pursuing teaching careers in math, science, or special education. Deadline: May 15.

5961. **Entrance Honors** 250 full-tuition scholarships to students with at least a 3.5 GPA and scoring at least 26 on ACT. Renewable with a 3.7 GPA.

5962. **Non-Resident** Numerous scholarships of up to full tuition to students with at least a 3.5 GPA.

5963. **President's** 35 scholarships of $7,000 to students with at least a 3.7 GPA who scored at least 28 on ACT. Renewable with a 3.5 GPA.

5964. **Special Characteristics Awards** 6 scholarships of varying amounts, totaling $8,860, to students meeting certain special criteria.

VERMONT

Southern Vermont College
Monument Avenue Extension
Bennington, VT 05201
(800) 378-2782
http://www.svc.edu

5965. **Commuter–Tutor Scholarships** 2 scholarships
of $500 to students with at least a 3.0 GPA who
meet other academic criteria. Renewable.

5966. **SAT Scholarships** Unlimited numbers of
scholarships of $500 to students who scored at
least 900 on SAT. Renewable.

5967. **Tuition Waivers** Numerous partial- to full-
tuition waivers to students who are employees or
children of employees.

University of Vermont
South Prospect Street
Burlington, VT 05401
(802) 656-3480
http://www.uvm.edu
admissions@uvm.edu

5968. **Tuition Waivers** Numerous partial to full
tuition waivers to students who are employees or
children of employees.

5969. **Vermont Scholar Awards** 15 scholarships
providing tuition and fees to students in the top
10 percent of their class who score at least 1200
on SAT. Renewable with 3.0 GPA.

VIRGINIA

College of William and Mary
Williamsburg, VA 23185
(757) 221-4000
http://www.wm.edu

5970. **James Monroe Scholarship** 8 scholarships
ranging from $3,000 to $8,000 to incoming
freshmen meeting certain academic criteria.

5971. **National Merit** 20 scholarships of varying
amounts are available to students selected as
National Merit Finalists.

5972. **Newcomb** 4 scholarships of $500 to students
meeting certain academic requirements.
Renewable with a 2.5 GPA.

5973. **Watson** 2 scholarships of $400 to students
meeting certain academic requirements.
Renewable with a 2.5 GPA.

5974. **William and Mary** 20 scholarships of varying
amounts to students who meet certain academic
requirements.

George Mason University
4400 University Drive
Fairfax, VA 22030-4444
(703) 993-1000
(703) 993-2400
http://www.gmu.edu/

5975. **Mason Scholars Scholarships** 10 scholarships
providing tuition and fees to students in the top
10 percent of their class, with at least a 3.6 GPA,
and who scored at least 1200 on SAT or 26 on
ACT. Renewable with 3.0 GPA.

5976. **Presidential Merit Scholarships** 10
scholarships providing tuition to students in the
top 10 percent of their class who have at least a
3.2 GPA. Renewable with 3.0 GPA.

5977. **Tuition Waivers** Numerous partial- to full-
tuition waivers (approximately $4,200) to students
who are employees or children of employees.

5978. **University Scholars Honors Program** 11
scholarships covering all costs (approximately
$9,200) to students with at least a 3.5 GPA who
scored at least 1200 on SAT or 25 on ACT.
Renewable with 3.0 GPA.

Hampden–Sydney College
P.O. Box 667
Hampden-Sydney, VA 23943
(804) 223-4388
http://www.hsc.edu

5979. **Allan** 6 scholarships of $2,500 to students in the
top 10 percent of their class who scored at least
1300 on SAT. Based on academic record,
community service, leadership, and interview.
Renewable with a 3.4 GPA.

5980. **Leadership** 6 scholarships of $750 to students in
the top 40 percent of their class who scored at
least 1050 on SAT. Based on community service,
leadership, and interview. Renewable with a 2.8
GPA.

5981. **Madison** 1 full scholarship to a student in the
top 5 percent of his or her class who scored at
least 1350 on SAT. Based on academic record,
community service, leadership, and interview.
Renewable with a 3.4 GPA.

5982. **Merit "Honors Program"** Numerous scholarships ranging from $750 to $12,460 to students in the top 25 percent of their class, with at least a 3.0 GPA and scoring at least 1000 on SAT. Based on exam, academic record, community service, leadership, and interview.

5983. **Patrick Henry** 6 scholarships of $1,250 to students in the top 20 percent of their class who scored at least 1150 on SAT. Based on academic record, community service, leadership, and interview. Renewable with a 3.0 GPA.

5984. **Venable** 6 scholarships of $1,750 to students in the top 10 percent of their class who scored at least 1200 on SAT. Based on academic record, community service, leadership, and interview. Renewable with a 3.2 GPA.

Longwood College
Farmville, VA 23901
(804) 395-2060
http://www.lwc.edu

5985. **Arts and Sciences** 5 scholarships of $1,000 to students meeting certain requirements. Renewable.

5986. **English** 2 scholarships of $2,000 to English majors who are in the top 10 percent of their class, with at least a 3.0 GPA, or scoring at least 1050 on SAT. Renewable with a 3.25 GPA.

5987. **Honors** 5 scholarships of $1,000 to students who scored at least 1100 on SAT and who meet other requirements. Renewable with a 3.25 GPA.

5988. **Longwood** 5 scholarships of $1,000 to students in the top 10 percent of their class, with at least a 3.35 GPA, and scoring at least 1050 on SAT. Renewable with a 3.35 GPA.

5989. **Minority** Numerous scholarships ranging from $750 to $1,000 to students in the top 30 percent of their class. Renewable.

5990. **Nance/Academic** 13 scholarships ranging from $500 to $1,200 to students in the top 30 percent of their class. Renewable.

5991. **Performance** Numerous scholarships ranging from $200 to $2,600 to students meeting certain requirements. Renewable.

5992. **Scott** 7 scholarships ranging from $750 to $1,000 to students in the top 30 percent of their class who meet certain requirements. Renewable.

5993. **Valedictorian "Honors Program"** Numerous scholarships of up to $1,000 to valedictorians. Renewable.

Old Dominion University
5115 Hampton Boulevard
121 Old Administration Building
Norfolk, VA 23529-0051
(800) 548-7638
http://www.odu.edu

5994. **Alumni Scholarships** 25 tuition scholarships providing tuition costs (approximately $4,000) for students in the upper 10 percent of their class, with at least a 3.25 GPA, and scoring at least 1100 on SAT.

5995. **Dominion Scholar Awards** 4 to 5 scholarships covering up to $4,000 for students in the top 10 percent of their class, with at least a 3.25 GPA, and scoring at least 1200 on SAT, who have demonstrated leadership abilities. Renewable with 3.25 GPA.

5996. **Monarch Honors Program Scholarships** 45 scholarships of $2,500 to students with at least a 3.25 GPA who scored at least 1100 on SAT.

5997. **Presidential Scholarships** Unlimited numbers of scholarships providing all costs (approximately $9,200) to students with at least a 3.25 GPA, who are National Merit Finalists, and who list ODU as their first-choice school. Renewable with a 3.25 GPA.

5998. **Regional Scholars Program** 33 scholarships of approximately $1,500 to students meeting certain academic criteria who are Tidewater area residents.

Randolph Macon College
Ashland, VA 23005
(800) 888-1762
(804) 798-8372
http://www.rmc.edu/

5999. **Campbell Scholarships** Up to 4 scholarships of $5,000 to students in the top 20 percent of their class who scored at least 1200 on SAT. Renewable.

6000. **Centennial Honors Program Scholarships** Varying numbers of scholarships of $2,000 to students in the top 15 percent of their class who scored at least 1100 on SAT. Renewable.

6001. **Chesney Scholarships** Up to 4 scholarships of $5,000 to students in the top 20 percent of their class who scored at least 1200 on SAT. Renewable.

6002. **Distinguished Scholars Program** 20 scholarships of $2,500 to female students who meet certain academic criteria.

6003. **Family Grants** 25 scholarships of varying amounts, totaling $120,215, to students meeting certain criteria.

6004. **Founders' Scholarships** Varying numbers of scholarships of $3,500 to students in the top 20 percent of their class who scored at least 1200 on SAT. Renewable.

6005. **Ira Lechner Honors Program Scholarships** Varying numbers of scholarships covering tuition costs (approximately $16,000) to students in the top 10 percent of their class, with at least a 3.5 GPA, and who scored at least 1200 on SAT. Renewable with 3.0 GPA.

6006. **Leadership Scholarships** 12 scholarships ranging from $500 to $1,500 to students who have demonstrated leadership abilities.

6007. **Minority Scholarships** 2 scholarships ranging from $4,000 to tuition costs to minority students in the upper 10 percent of their class, with at least a 3.5 GPA, and who scored at least 900 on SAT. Renewable.

6008. **One–Time Scholarships** 19 scholarships of $1,000 to students meeting certain academic criteria.

6009. **R–M Scholars** 8 to 20 scholarships ranging from $1,000 to $6,000 to students in the upper 10 percent of their class, with at least a 3.5 GPA, and who scored at least 1200 on SAT. Renewable.

University of Virginia
Charlottesville, VA 22906
(804) 924-0311
http://www.virginia.edu

6010. **Achievement Award** 50 scholarships of $2,700 or more to entering freshmen who are African American and residents of Virginia. Contact: Assistant Dean of Admissions, Office of Admissions, Miller Hall, Charlottesville, VA 22903, (804) 924–7751. Deadline: January 2.

6011. **Engineering Scholarships** Varying numbers of scholarships ranging from $250 to $2,500 to minority students majoring in engineering, chemical engineering, civil engineering, electrical engineering, or mechanical engineering, who meet certain academic criteria and demonstrate financial need. Contact the financial aid office. Deadline: February 1.

6012. **Jefferson "Honors Program, Honors College"** 19 scholarships ranging from $6,000 to $9,000. Based on nomination, recommendation, and interview. Campus visit required. Renewable.

6013. **Jerome H. Holland Scholarships** 5 scholarship grants of $5,000 to incoming African American freshmen who are not Virginia residents. Must be U.S. citizens. Renewable. Contact the financial aid office. Deadline: January 15.

6014. **University Achievement Awards** 54 scholarships of $2,700 to African American students meeting certain academic criteria who are Virginia residents. Contact the Assistant Dean of Admissions. Deadline: January 2.

Virginia Polytechnic Institute and State University
7201 Burress Hall
Blacksburg, VA 24601-0202
(540) 231-6267
http://www.vt.edu/
vtadmiss@vt.edu

6015. **Alumni Scholarships** 4 scholarships of $3,000 to students in the upper 5 percent of their class who score at least 1300 on SAT. Renewable.

6016. **Amoco Foundation Scholarships** 2 scholarships of $2,000 to undergraduate juniors and seniors who are majoring in geophysics. Renewable. Contact the Department Chairperson.

6017. **Competition Scholarships** 15 scholarships ranging from $2,000 to $3,000 to students in the upper 5 percent of their class who scored at least 1300 on SAT. Renewable.

6018. **Distinguished University Scholar Awards** 12 scholarships of $3,000 to students in the top 5 percent of their class who scored at least 1300 on SAT. Renewable.

6019. **Eleanor M. Crosby Scholarship** 1 scholarship of $2,500 to an undergraduate freshman or sophomore majoring in horticulture.

6020. **Marshall Hahn Scholarships** 200 scholarships ranging from $500 to $2,000 to students in the upper 5 percent of their class who scored at least 1300 on SAT. Renewable.

6021. **University Scholarships** 275 scholarships ranging from $500 to $3,000 to students in the upper 10 percent of their class, with at least a 3.5 GPA, and who scored at least 1100 on SAT.

WASHINGTON

Saint Martin's College
Lacey, WA 98503
(800) 368-8803
http://www.stmartin.edu
admissions@stmartin.edu

6022. **Chancellor's Scholarships** 7 scholarships providing half of tuition (approximately $6,500) costs to students meeting certain academic criteria. Renewable with 3.3 GPA.

6023. **Frost and Margaret Snyder Scholarships** 10 scholarships of $2,000 to undergraduate, graduate, and doctoral students who are or were Catholic high school graduates and who demonstrate financial need. Deadline: March 1.

6024. **President's Scholarships** 7 scholarships providing one-third of tuition (approximately $4,000) costs to students meeting certain academic criteria. Renewable with 3.3 GPA.

6025. **Valedictorian Scholarships** 6 scholarships of full tuition (approximately $13,000) to students who are ranked first in their graduating high school class. Renewable with a 3.5 GPA.

University of Washington at Seattle
Seattle, WA 98195
(206) 543-2100
http://www.washington.edu

6026. **Alumnae Board Scholarships** 15 scholarships of $2,907 to students meeting certain academic criteria. Renewable.

6027. **Mortar Board Scholarships** 10 scholarships ranging from $750 to $1,500 to students meeting certain academic criteria. Renewable.

6028. **Pulp and Paper Foundation Scholarships** 40 scholarships ranging from $1,800 to $5,000 to entering freshmen, transfer students, and undergraduates interested in a career in the pulp and paper industry. Renewable for up to four years with satisfactory progress. Based on academic record, SAT, career goals, and potential. Deadline: March 1.

6029. **NASA Space Grant "Honors" Program Awards** 10 scholarships ranging from $500 to $6,400 to students meeting certain academic criteria who have certain majors. Renewable with a 3.2 GPA.

6030. **National Merit Awards** 26 scholarships of at least $500 to students receiving National Merit designation who meet other criteria. Renewable.

6031. **President's Scholars Awards** 2 to 4 scholarships of $3,615 to students in the upper 5 percent of their class who meet other academic criteria. Renewable.

6032. **Undergraduate Scholars Awards** 100 scholarships of $1,400 to students in the upper 10 percent of their class who meet other academic criteria. Renewable.

Whitman College
345 Boyer Avenue
Walla Walla, WA 99362
(509) 527-5111
http://www.whitman.edu

6033. **Campbell Music** Numerous scholarships of varying amounts to students majoring in music. Renewable.

6034. **Garrett Awards** 3 scholarships ranging from $500 to $10,000 to students who have demonstrated leadership abilities.

6035. **President's** Numerous scholarships ranging from $500 to $10,000. Based on academic merit. Renewable.

6036. **Sherwood/Garrett** Numerous scholarships ranging from $500 to $10,000. Based on academic merit. Renewable.

WEST VIRGINIA

Bluefield State College
219 Rock Street
Bluefield, WV 24701
(304) 327-4000
http://www.bluefield.wvnet.edu

6037. **Academic** Numerous scholarships ranging from $1,060 to $4,180 to students with a 3.0 GPA.

6038. **Fine Arts Honors Program** $1,060 scholarships to students in the fine arts. Based on audition, portfolio, and talent.

West Virginia University
P.O. Box 6009
Morgantown, WV 26506-6001
(800) 344-9881
http://www.wvu.ed

6039. **Academic** Numerous scholarships ranging from $700 to $2,550 to students in the top 10 percent of their class and scoring at least 27 on ACT. Renewable.

6040. **Freshman Awards** Up to 253 scholarships of $500 to entering freshmen students who meet certain criteria.

6041. **Leadership Awards** 401 scholarships of approximately $500 to students who are state residents and have demonstrated leadership abilities.

6042. **Minority Awards** 59 scholarships of approximately $4,700 to minority undergraduate students who meet certain criteria.

WISCONSIN

Beloit College
700 College Avenue
Beloit, WI 53511
(608) 363-2000
http://www.beloit.edu

6043. **AFS** 5 scholarships ranging from $1,000 to $2,000 to students in the top 10 percent of their class who have at least a 3.5 GPA. Renewable with a 2.5 GPA.

6044. **C. Winterwood** Numerous $2,500 scholarships to students in the top 33 percent of their class with at least a 3.0 GPA. Based on essay, recommendations, community involvement, and interview. Renewable with a 2.0 GPA.

6045. **Joseph Coilie** 10 scholarships of $2,500 to students in the top 10 percent of their class, with at least a 3.5 GPA, and scoring at least 1100 on SAT or 25 on ACT. Renewable with a 3.0 GPA.

6046. **Leff** Numerous scholarships of $1,000.

6047. **Presidential** 25 scholarships of $3,000 to students in the top 10 percent of their class, with at least a 3.5 GPA, and scoring at least 1100 on SAT or 25 on ACT. Renewable with a 3.0 GPA.

6048. **Trustee** Numerous scholarships of $1,000. Renewable.

6049. **Upton** Numerous scholarships of $1,000 to students in the top 25 percent of their class with at least a 3.0 GPA. Renewable.

Carroll College
100 North East Avenue
Waukesha, WI 53186
(414) 547-1211
http://www.cc.edu
cc.info@ccadmin.cc.edu

6050. **Coulson Scholarships** Varying numbers of scholarships of tuition and fees to students meeting certain academic criteria. Renewable.

6051. **Presidential Scholarships** Unlimited scholarships ranging from $500 to $4,000 to students in the upper 10 percent of their class, who scored at least 1100 on SAT or 25 on ACT. Renewable with 3.0 GPA on a 4.0 scale.

Concordia University
Mequon, WI 53092-7699
(414) 243-5700
http://www.cuw.edu

6052. **Church Vocation Scholarships** 50 scholarships of varying amounts, totaling $32,789, to students who are members of a Lutheran church and meet certain criteria.

6053. **Creative Arts/Performance Awards** 4 scholarships of $1,000 to students in music or performing arts. Based on talent.

6054. **Dallman Organ Scholarships** 8 scholarships of $1,000 to students meeting certain criteria. Renewable with a 2.5 GPA.

6055. **Presidential Scholarships** 43 scholarships ranging from $500 to $6,000 to students with at least a 3.5 GPA. Renewable.

6056. **Regents Scholarships** 18 scholarships of varying amounts, totaling $38,725, to students meeting certain criteria.

Lawrence University
P.O. Box 599
Appleton, WI 54912
(800) 227-0982
http://www.lawrence.edu
excel@lawrence.edu

6057. **Conservatory Performance Scholarships** Varying numbers of scholarships ranging from $500 to $1,000 to students meeting certain criteria who are majoring in a performance art. Based on talent. Renewable.

6058. **Conservatory Trustee Scholarships** Varying numbers of scholarships of varying amounts to students meeting certain criteria who are majoring in a performance art. Based on talent.

6059. **Dow Chemical Scholarships** 2 scholarships of $2,500 to students meeting certain academic criteria. Renewable.

6060. **Henry Merritt Wriston Scholarships** 3 scholarship grants of at least $3,600 to incoming freshmen meeting certain academic criteria. Must submit writing samples. Renewable.

6061. **Heritage Scholarships** Varying numbers of scholarships of varying amounts to students meeting certain criteria.

6062. **Kimberly–Clark Honor Scholarships** 8 scholarships of $2,500 to students meeting certain academic criteria. Renewable.

6063. **Lawrence University International Students Scholarships** Varying numbers of scholarships of varying amounts to international students meeting certain criteria.

6064. **Lawrence University Scholarships** Unlimited numbers of scholarships of $2,500 to students meeting certain academic criteria. Renewable.

6065. **NASA/Wisconsin Space Grant Consortium Awards** Varying numbers of scholarships of varying amounts to students meeting certain academic criteria who are majoring in a science.

6066. **Scidmore Scholarships** Varying numbers of scholarships of varying amounts to graduating high school seniors from Rock County, Wisconsin, who meet certain other criteria.

6067. **Sweetman Scholarships** 2 scholarships ranging from $1,550 to $2,500 to students meeting certain academic criteria. Renewable.

6068. **Trustee Scholarships** 35 scholarships of varying amounts to students meeting certain academic criteria.

6069. **Tuition Waivers** Numerous partial- to full-tuition waivers to students who are employees or children of employees.

Marquette University
Milwaukee, WI 53233-9981
(800) 222-6544
http://www.mu.edu
go2marquette@vms.csd.mu.edu

6070. **Advanced Standing Scholarships** Unlimited numbers of scholarships ranging from $1,000 to $3,500 to students with at least a 3.0 GPA who meet other criteria. Renewable with a 3.0 GPA.

6071. **Anne Powers Schwartz Award** 1 scholarship of $500 to a journalism student with demonstrated superior writing skills.

6072. **Bradley Distinguished Scholar Awards** 10 scholarships providing half of tuition to students in the top 5 percent of their class, with at least a 3.5 GPA, and who scored at least 1300 on SAT or 29 on ACT. Renewable with a 3.0 GPA.

6073. **Clifford L. Helbert Scholarship Fund** Emergency funds of up to $500 to assist in paying for tuition or other needs to journalism majors who are unable to obtain financial assistance from other sources.

6074. **Communication Scholarships** Varying numbers of scholarships ranging from $1,000 to $2,000 to high school seniors who participate in an on–campus essay–writing competition each February. Based on grammar, style, content, and expression. Renewable for up to three years if majoring in communications or journalism and maintaining a B average.

6075. **Dean's Fund for Minority Students** Scholarship of up to $750 to minority students. Contact the Dean of the College of Communication, Journalism, and Performing Arts.

6076. **Departmental Awards** 16 scholarships of varying amounts to students meeting certain criteria.

6077. **Diom Henderson Memorial Award** 1 scholarship of $500 to a journalism student with superior writing skills.

6078. **Eugene J. Schumack Memorial Journalism Fund** 1 scholarship of $500 to a graduate student pursuing a journalism degree. Based on academic achievement.

6079. **Greater Milwaukee Scholarships** 20 scholarships of $1,000 to students in the top 25 percent of their class who are from the Milwaukee area. Renewable with a 3.0 GPA.

6080. **John and Leocadia Shiners Award** 1 scholarship of $600 to a journalism major pursuing a career in journalism.

6081. **Journalism Alumni Association Grants** 3 grants ranging from $600 to $800 to students (1 undergraduate junior and 2 undergraduate seniors) who are on the Dean's List, have demonstrated academic achievement, with professional competence, and have participated on school publications or internships in the media.

6082. **Milwaukee Press Club Ray Kenny Memorial Scholarship** 1 scholarship of $500 to a student with high academic achievement and professional competence as demonstrated by an internship in a press media or participation on a school publication.

6083. **Milwaukee Professional Chapter of the Society of Professional Journalists Scholarship** A scholarship of $500 to journalism majors who will be entering their undergraduate senior year. Contact the Journalism Department. Deadline: March 1.

6084. **MU Academic Scholarships** Unlimited numbers of scholarships to students in the top 10 percent of their class who scored at least 1100 on SAT or 24 on ACT. Renewable with a 3.0 GPA.

6085. **MU Honor Scholarships** Unlimited numbers of scholarships of $500 to students in the top 25 percent of their class who scored at least 1000 on SAT or 22 on ACT. Renewable.

6086. **Publication Scholarships** Varying numbers of full or partial scholarships to top staff members of *The Marquette Tribune*, *The Marquette Journal*, or *the Marquette Hilltop*.

6087. **Tuition Waivers** Numerous partial– to full– tuition waivers to students who are employees, children of employees, or senior citizens.

6088. **Wisconsin Newspaper Association Foundation Scholarships** 2 scholarships of $1,000 to journalism undergraduate juniors. Based on academic achievement and professional qualifications. Preference given to students with demonstrated professional ability in weekly or daily newspapers. Contact the Journalism Department during the fall semester.

Ripon College
P.O. Box 248
Ripon, WI 54971
(920) 748-8118
http://www.ripon.edu

6089. **Alumni Grant** 14 scholarships of $1,000 to children of alumni. Renewable.

6090. **Army ROTC Honors** Unlimited scholarships ranging from $500 to $1,500. Renewable.

6091. **Badger Boy** Numerous $1,500 scholarships to male students who were Badger Boys with at least a 3.0 GPA. Renewable with a 2.7 GPA.

6092. **Badger Girl** Numerous $1,500 scholarships to female students who were Badger Girls with at least a 3.0 GPA. Renewable with a 2.7 GPA.

6093. **Dawes** 1 scholarship of $7,500 to a student in the upper 10 percent of class, with a 3.0 GPA and scoring at least 1330 on SAT or 31 on ACT. Renewable with a 3.2 GPA.

6094. **Debate/Forensics** Numerous scholarships ranging from $500 to $1,500. Renewable.

6095. **Distinguished Honors** Numerous scholarships ranging from $500 to $2,500 to students in the upper 10 percent of their class with a 3.0 GPA and scoring at least 1190 on SAT or 25 on ACT. Renewable with a 2.7 GPA.

6096. **Music Honors** Numerous scholarships ranging from $500 to $1,250. Renewable.

6097. **Pickard Scholarships** 7 scholarships of varying amounts. Based on academic merit.

University of Wisconsin at Green Bay
2420 Nicolet Drive
Green Bay, WI 65311-7001
(920) 465-2000
http://www.uwgb.edu

6098. **Jazz/Choir** 14 scholarships of $400 to music students in jazz and choir. Renewable.

6099. **Leadership/Academic** 30 scholarships ranging from $500 to $800 to students in the top 25 percent of their class with at least a 3.0 GPA.

6100. **Talent** 12 scholarships of $300 to students in the top 25 percent of their class with a 3.0 GPA.

University of Wisconsin at Madison
A. W. Peterson Office Building
750 University Avenue
Madison, WI 53706
(608) 262-1234
http://www.wisc.edu

6101. **Guy Stanton Ford Educational Foundation, Inc.** 16 grants ranging from $37 to $491 to students who are members of Sigma Deuteron Charge of Theta Delta Chi fraternity. Contact: Treasurer, 119 Martin Luther King, Jr. Boulevard, Madison, WI 53703, (608) 257–4812.

WYOMING

University of Wyoming
Laramie, WY 82071
(307) 766-1121
http://www.uwyo.edu

6102. **COE Fine Arts Scholarship** (in Honor of James M. Boyle) 1 scholarship of $500 to a student meeting certain academic criteria who is currently enrolled in a studio art major.

6103. **Conrad Schwiering Western Fine Arts Scholarship** 1 scholarship of varying amount to a student meeting certain criteria. Preference given to students who reside in Wyoming and have interest in traditional Western landscape art.

6104. **Daniel and Nelie Beck** 16 scholarships of $500 to students with a 3.3 GPA and scoring 1100 on SAT or 25 on ACT. Renewable with a 3.0 GPA.

6105. **Donald Wiest Fine Arts Scholarship** 1 scholarship of $1,000 to an undergraduate junior, senior, or graduate student who meets certain criteria and is a studio art major. Award based on review of recent art work.

6106. **Fell–Oskins Fine Arts Scholarships** Several awards of varying amounts to undergraduate or graduate students currently enrolled as studio art majors. Award based on academic achievement and review of recent art work. Special preference is given to students whose residence is in Park County or the Big Horn Basin of Wyoming.

6107. **Hilma & John Delaplaine Scholarship/Art Education** 1 scholarship of varying amount to any currently enrolled undergraduate junior or senior in art education. Award based on review of recent art work and progress.

6108. **J. W. Van Dyke** Numerous scholarships ranging from $500 to $1,500 to students with a 3.0 GPA and scoring at least 1150 on SAT or 26 on ACT. Renewable with a 3.0 GPA.

6109. **Lucille Wright Fine Arts Scholarship** 1 scholarship of varying amount to an undergraduate or graduate student meeting certain criteria who is a fine arts major.

6110. **Robert D. Coe Fine Arts Scholarships** Several awards of varying amounts to incoming freshmen, transfer, undergraduate, or graduate students who meet certain criteria. Must be studio art majors studying painting, drawing, or printmaking.

ALPHABETICAL LISTING OF ALL SCHOLARSHIP SOURCES*

*Listings are by entry number, not page number.

Bellevue College (Bellevue, NE) 5024–5029

Belmont University (Nashville, TN) 5627–5631

Beloit College (Beloit, WI) 6043–6049

Bement Educational Grants Committee 754

Bend Foundation 755

Benjamin and Fedora Wolf Foundation 756

Berkeley Minor and Susan Fontaine Minor Foundation 757

Berkeley Repertory Theater 758

Bermuda Biological Station for Research 759

Bernard Daly Educational Fund 760

Bernice A. B. Keyes Trust 761

Berstein-Rein Internship Program 762

Bertelsmann Music Group 763

Beryl Buck Institute for Education 764

Beta Sigma Phi 765

Beta Theta Pi Fraternity 766–767

Bethany Bible College (Santa Cruz, CA) 3189

Bethune-Cookman College (Daytona Beach, FL) 3878–3880

Beverly Hills Theatre Guild 768

B. F. and Rose H. Perkins Foundation 769

Biola University (La Mirada, CA) 3190–3192

Birmingham-Southern College (Birmingham, AL) 2827–2849

Black American Cinema Society 770

Black & Veatch 771

Blackburn College (Carlinville, IL) 4227–4229

Blackfeet Tribal Education Grant 772

Black Student Fund 773

Blackwelder Foundation 774

Blaine House Scholars Program 775

Blanche and Thomas Hope Fund 776

Blinded Veterans Association 777

Blind Service Association Scholarship Awards 778

Bloomfield College (Bloomfield, NJ) 5060–5066

Bluefield State College (Bluefield, WV) 6037–6038

Blue Mountain Area Foundation 779

Blues Heaven Foundation 780

B. M. Woltman Foundation 781

Bodenwein Fellowships 782

Boeing 783

Boettcher Foundation 784

Borrego Springs Educational Scholarship Committee 785

Boston College (Chestnut Hill, MA) 4640–4645

Boston University (Boston, MA) 4646–4661

Bour Memorial Scholarship Trust 786

Bowerman Foundation 787

Bowfin Memorial Scholarship 788–789

Bowie State University (Bowie, MD) 4581–4584

Bowler & Associates 790

Boyle Scholarship Trust 791

Boynton Gillespie Memorial Fund 792

Boys and Girls Clubs of Chicago 793–794

Boys and Girls Clubs of San Diego 795

Boy Scouts of America 796–815

Boy Scouts of America National Office 816

Bozell Worldwide Public Relations 817

BP America Scholarship 818

Brigham Young University (Provo, UT) 5923–5958

Brigham Young University—Hawaii Campus (Laie Oahu, HI) 4183–4184

Broadcast Education Association 819–824

Broadcast Music, Inc. 825

Broadcast News Networks 826

Brookfield Zoo 827

Brookhaven Women In Science 828

The Brookings Institute 829

Brown University (Providence, RI) 5527–5528

Bruce L. Cary Foundation, Inc. 830

Bryan International String Competition 831

Buena Vista College (Storm Lake, IA) 4408–4410

Buffalo Foundation 832

Bureau of Indian Affairs Higher Education Grant Programs 833

Burger King Company 834

Burlington Educational Loan Fund 835

Burlington Northern Scholarship Program 836

Burson-Marsteller 837

Burt Snyder Educational Foundation 838

Business and Professional Women's Foundation 839–845

Butterfield & Butterfield 846

California Baptist College (Riverside, CA) 3195–3199

California Chicano News Media Association 847

California College of Arts & Crafts (San Francisco, CA) 3200–3202

California Community Colleges 848

California Congress of Parents and Teachers, Inc. 849–850

California Department of Education 851

California Department of Veterans Affairs 852–853

California Farm Bureau Scholarships 854

California Governor's Committee for Employment of Disabled Persons 855

California-Hawaii Elks Major Project, Inc. 856

California Institute of Technology (Pasadena, CA) 3203–3209

California Lutheran University (Thousand Oaks, CA) 3210–3213

California Masonic Foundation 857–858

California Newspaper Carrier Foundation 859

California Polytechnic State University (San Luis Obispo, CA) 3214–3238

California Society of Professional Engineers 860

California Society of Professional Journalists 861–862

California State Department of Rehabilitation 863

California State Polytechnic University (Pomona, CA) 3239–3241

California State PTA Student Loan Fund 864

California State University (Bakersfield, CA) 3242–3244

California State University (Chico, CA) 3245

California State University (Dominguez Hills, CA) 3246–3256

California State University (Fresno, CA) 3257–3259

California State University (Fullerton, CA) 3260 –3269

California State University (Long Beach, CA) 3270–3278

California State University (Los Angeles, CA) 3279–3291

California State University (Northridge, CA) 3292–3295

California State University (Sacramento, CA) 3296–3309

California State University (Stanislaus, CA) 3310–3311

California State University System 865

California Student Aid Commission 866–872

California Teachers Association (CTA) 873

The Callahan Group 874

Canaan Public Relations 875

Canadian Association of Broadcasters 876–877

Canadian Aviation Historical Society 878

Canadian Nurses Foundation 879

Cargill Scholarship for Rural America 880

Carl and Florence King Foundation 881

Carle C. Conway Scholarship Foundation, Inc. 882

Carleton College (Northfield, MN) 4733–4734

Carnegie Mellon University (Pittsburgh, PA) 5466–5470

Carolina Telephone Scholarship 883

Connecticut League for Nursing Scholarships 996

Connecticut Library Association (CLA) 997

Connecticut Society of Professional Engineers 998

Conrail Women's Aid Scholarships 999

Consortium of College and University Media Centers 1000

Consulting Engineers Council of Metropolitan Washington Scholarship 1001

Consulting Engineers Council of Metropolitan Washington-Virginia Scholarships 1002

Consulting Engineers Council of New Jersey 1003

Continental Grain Company-Wayne Feed Division 1004

Continental Grain Foundation 1005

Cook Scholarship Fund 1006

The Cooking Contest Chronicle 1007

Cooking Contest Newsletter 1008

Cooper Union (New York, NY) 5163

Coor's Brewing Company 1009

Cora W. Wood Scholarship Fund 1010

Corcoran School of Art (Washington, DC) 3836–3837

Cordelia Lunceford Beatty Trust 1011

Cornell University (Ithaca, NY) 5164–5170

Cornell University Summer College 1012

Corti Family Agricultural Fund 1013

Council of Energy Resource Tribes (CERT) 1014

Court Theatre-University of Chicago 1015

Covenant College (Lookout Mountain, GA) 4086–4092

Cox Newspapers 1016

Creede Repertory Theater 1017

Creighton University (Omaha, NE) 5030–5034

C. Reiss Coal Company Scholarships 1018

Creole Ethnic Association, Inc. 1019

Croatian Fraternal Union Scholarship 1020

Crosset Charitable Trust 1021

Crow Canyon Archeological Center 1022

Crown Princess Sonja International Piano Competition 1023

Crystal Foundation 1024

CSX Scholarship Program 1025

Culinary Institute of America (Hyde Park, NY) 5171–5172

Cummins Engine Foundation 1026

Curry Summer Internships 1027

D. A. Biglane Foundation 1028

D. D. Hachar Foundation 1029

Dairy Shrine Scholarships 1030

Dakota State University (Madison, SD) 5596–5598

Dallas-Fort Worth Association of Black Communicators 1031

Dane G. Hansen Foundation 1032

D'Angelo Young Artist Competition 1033

Daniel Ashley & Irene Houston Jewell Memorial Foundation 1034

Daniel Foundation of South Carolina 1035

Danish Brotherhood in America Scholarships 1036

Danish Sisterhood in America Scholarships 1037

Datapoint Corporation Merit Scholarship Program 1038

Daughters of Penelope 1039–1040

Daughters of Penelope National Scholarships 1041–1042

Daughters of the Cincinnati 1043

Dave Cameron Educational Foundation 1044

David and Eula Winterman Foundation 1045

David James Ellis Memorial Award 1046

David Laine Memorial Scholarships 1047

David Lipscomb University (Nashville, TN) 5632–5641

David S. Blount Educational Foundation 1048

David Wasserman Scholarship Fund, Inc. 1049

Davis-Hays and Co. 1050

Davis-Roberts Scholarship Fund, Inc. 1051

DCAT Scholarship Awards 1052

Deke Foundation 1053

Delaware Engineering Society, Inc. 1054

Delaware Higher Education Commission 1055–1060

Delius Association of North Florida, Inc. 1061

Delta Gamma Foundation 1062

Delta Kappa Gamma 1063

Delta Omicron International Music Fraternity 1064

Delta Sigma Theta Sorority 1065–1069

Delta Tau Delta Educational Fund 1070

DeMolay Foundation 1071

Dental Laboratory Technology Scholarships 1072

Denver Area Labor Federation, AFL-CIO 1073

Deo B. Colburn Educational Foundation 1074

Department of the Navy 1075

DePaul University (Chicago, IL) 4237–4241

DePauw University (Greencastle, IN) 4333–4341

Descendants of the Signers of the Declaration of Independence, Inc. 1076

Detroit District Metropolitan Opera Auditions 1077–1079

Detroit Free Press 1080

Devry, Inc., Scholarship Program 1081

Diet Center National Scholarship 1082

Digital Equipment Corporation 1083

Disciples of Christ Homeland Ministries 1084

Discover Card Tribute Awards 1085

Distributive Education Clubs of America (DECA) 1086

District of Columbia Natural Gas 1087

District of Columbia Office of Postsecondary Education, Research and Assistance 1088

District of Columbia Public Schools—Carvers Administration Services 1089

District of Columbia Society of Professional Engineers 1090

Dog Writer's Educational Trust Scholarships 1091

Dolphin Scholarship Program 1092

Dominican College of San Rafael (San Rafael, CA) 3336–3339

Donald & Evelyn Peters Foundation 1093

Donald W. Reynolds Foundation, Inc. 1094

Dougherty Foundation, Inc. 1095

Dow Jones Newspaper Fund 1096–1098

Drury College (Springfield, MO) 4781–4786

Duke University (Durham, NC) 5219–5227

Dupage Medical Society Foundation 1099

Duquesne University (Pittsburgh, PA) 5471–5477

Duxbury Yacht Club Charitable Foundation 1100

The Eagle Art Gallery 1101

Eagles Memorial Foundation, Inc. 1102

Eagleton War Memorial Scholarship Fund, Inc. 1103

The EAR Foundation 1104

Earthwatch Career Training Scholarship Program 1105

Eastern Connecticut State University (Willimantic, CT) 3746–3747

Easter Seal Society of Iowa 1106

East Texas Historical Association 1107

East-West Center 1108

Eaton Literary Agency 1109

Ebell of Los Angeles Scholarship Endowment Fund and the Mrs. Charles N. Flint Scholarship Endowment Fund 1110

Eckerd College (St. Petersburg, FL) 3882–3888

Foundation for European Language and Educational Centers 1243
Foundation for Exceptional Children 1244
Foundation for the Carolinas 1245
Foundation of the National Student Nurse's Association 1246
Foundation of the Wall & Ceiling Industry 1247
Fourteenth Air Force Association, Inc. 1248
Fourth Infantry Division Scholarships 1249
Fourth Marine Division Association 1250
Fox Educational Foundation 1251
Fox, Inc. 1252
Francis Nathaniel and Katheryn Padgett Kennedy Foundation 1253
Francis Ouimet Scholarship Fund 1254
Francis S. Viele Scholarship Fund 1255
Frank and Bea Wood Foundation 1256
Frank and Lydia Bergen Foundation 1257
Frank Family Memorial Scholarship Fund 1258
Frank F. Bentley Trust 1259
Frank Gannett Newspaper Carrier Scholarships 1260
Franklin College (Franklin, IN) 4342–4345
Frank P. And Clara R. Williams Scholarship 1261
Frank Roswell Fuller Scholarship 1262
Fraternal Order UDT/SEAL Educational Grant 1263
Fred Forsythe Educational Trust Fund 1264
Fred W. Wells Trust Fund 1265
The Freedom Forum 1266
Freedom from Religion Foundation 1267
Freedom's Foundation National Awards Program for Youth 1268
Free Sons of Israel 1269
Fresno Pacific College (Fresno, CA) 3340–3343
Fresno Philharmonic 1270
Friendship Fund, Inc. 1271
Friends of the National Zoo 1272–1273
Frito Lay, Inc. 1274
Frontier Nursing Service 1275
Frostburg State University (Frostburg, MD) 4585–4590
Frozen Food Association of New England 1276
Fukunaga Scholarship Foundation 1277
Fuller E. Calaway Foundation 1278
Fund for American Studies 1279

Furman University (Greenville, SC) 5545–5551
Furnas Foundation, Inc. 1280
Future Homemakers of America (FHA) 1281–1289
Future Teachers Scholarships 1290
Gadsden State Junior College (Gadsden, AL) 2856–2858
Gallaudet University (Washington, DC) 3838–3839
Gamma Iota Sigma Scholarships 1291
Gannett Foundation 1292
Garden Club of America 1293
Gardener Foundation 1294
Garland County Community College (Hot Springs, AR) 3126–3127
Gemco Charitable and Scholarship Fund 1295
GEM National Center for Graduate Education for Minorities, Inc. 1296
Gemological Institute of America (GIA) 1297
Genentech 1298
General Educational Fund, Inc. 1299
General Electric Foundation 1300
Gensler and Associates/Architects 1301
George Abrahamian Foundation 1302
George E. Stifel Scholarship Fund 1303
George Grotefend Scholarship Fund 1304
George J. Record School Foundation 1305
George Lurcy Charitable and Scholarship Fund 1306
George Mason University (Fairfax, VA) 5975–5978
George M. Pullman Educational Foundation 1307
Georgetown University (Washington, DC) 3840–3844
George T. Welch Testamentary Trust 1308
George Washington University (Washington, DC) 3845–3857
Georgia Institute of Technology (Atlanta, GA) 4112–4116
Georgia Society of Professional Engineers 1309
Georgia State University (Atlanta, GA) 4117–4120
Georgia Student Finance Commission 1310–1314
German Academic Exchange Service (DAAD) 1315–1319
Gertrude D. Curran Trust FBO Curran Music School 1320
Gilman Paper Company Foundation, Inc. 1321
Gina Bacháuer International Piano Competition Award 1322
Glass Bottle Blowers Association 1323
Gleaner Life Insurance Society Scholarship Awards 1324

Glenn Miller Birthplace Society 1325
Glimmer Train Press 1326
GMI Engineering and Management Institute (Flint, MI) 4695–4708
Golden Gate Restaurant Association 1327
Golden Gate University (San Francisco, CA) 3344–3345
Golden State Minority Foundation 1328
Goldey-Beacom College (Wilmington, DE) 3788–3798
Golstein Scottish Rite Trust 1329
Golf Course Superintendents Association of America 1330–1334
Good Samaritan Association 1335
Gould Farm 1336
Grace Margaret Watterson Trust 1337
Graham-Fancher Scholarship Fund 1338
Graham Memorial Fund 1339
Grand Army of the Republic Living Memorial Scholarship 1340
Grand Canyon University (Phoenix, AZ) 3054–3071
Grand Rapids Foundation 1341
Greater Kanawha Valley Foundation 1342
Great Projects Film Company 1343
Greenville College (Greenville, IL) 4242–4245
Gregg-Graniteville Foundation, Inc. 1344
Grey Forest Utilities 1345
Groves Fund 1346
Guam Society of Professional Engineers 1347
Guideposts Youth Writing Contest 1348
G. William Klemstine Foundation 1349
Hackney Literary Awards 1350
Hallmark Cards 1351
Hallmark-CRWEB 1352
Hampden-Sydney College (Hampden-Sydney, VA) 5979–5984
Harding University (Searcy, AR) 3128–3131
Hardin-Simmons University (Abilene, TX) 5715–5724
Harness Horseman International (HHI) 1353
Harness Horse Youth Foundation 1354–1357
Harness Tracks of America (HTA) 1358
Harold and Sara Wetherbee Foundation 1359
Harry S. Truman Memorial Scholarship Program 1360
Harry S. Truman Scholarship Program 1361
Harvard University (Cambridge, MA) 4665–4668

Lloyd D. Sweet Scholarship Foundation 1619

Longwood College (Farmville, VA) 5985–5993

Loren L. Zachary Society for the Performing Arts 1620

Los Angeles Times 1621

Louisiana Department of Veterans Affairs 1622

Louisiana Literature Prize for Poetry 1623

Louisiana State University (Shreveport, LA) 4523–4525

Louisiana State University and A&M College (Baton Rouge) 4526–4532

Louisiana Student Financial Assistance Commission 1624–1628

Louisiana Vocational Rehabilitation 1629

Loyola Marymount University (Los Angeles, CA) 3351–3362

Loyola University (New Orleans, LA) 4533–4535

Loyola University of Chicago (Chicago, IL) 4250–4258

Luby's Cafeterias 1630

LucasFilm 1631

Lupus Foundation of America 1632–1633

Lurleen Wallace State Junior College 2883–2884

Lutheran Brotherhood Member Scholarships 1634

Lutheran Brotherhood Senior College Scholarships 1635

Lutheran Campus Scholarship Program 1636

Lutheran Church of America 1637

Luso-American Education Foundation 1638

Lynn University (Boca Raton, FL) 3947–3956

Lyon College (Batesville, AR) 3145–3151

Macalester College (St. Paul, MN) 4740–4741

MacCurdy-Salisbury Educational Foundation, Inc. 1639

MacNeil/Lehrer Productions 1640

Madison Scholarship Committee 1641

Maine Bureau of Veterans Services 1642–1644

Maine Division of Educational Services 1645–1646

(Maine) Finance Authority of Maine (FAME) 1647

Maine Vocational-Technical Institutes 1648

Makarios Scholarship Fund, Inc. 1649

Manchester College (North Manchester, IN) 4349–4353

Maple Creek Willie Indian Scholarship Fund for California Indian Students 1650

Marcus and Theresa Levie Educational Fund 1651

Margaret and Irvin Lesher Foundation Scholarships 1652

Marie-Louise D'Esternaux Student Poetry Contest 1653

Marina Maher Communications 1654

Marine Corps Historical Center 1655

Marine Corps Scholarship Foundation 1656

Marin Educational Foundation 1657–1659

Marion and Ed Peeples Memorial Foundation Scholarship 1660

Marquette University (Milwaukee, WI) 6070–6088

Marvel Comics 1661

Maryland Higher Education Commission 1662–1667

Maryland State Scholarship Administration 1668–1674

Maryland Veterans Grants 1675

Massachusetts Institute of Technology (Cambridge, MA) 4669–4671

Massachusetts Office of Student Financial Assistance 1676–1682

Massachusetts State Federation of Women's Clubs 1683

The Master's College (Newhall, CA) 3363–3366

Materials Handling Education Foundation 1684

Mathcounts National Competition 1685

Matred Carlton Olliff Foundation 1686

The Matt Garcia Foundation Scholarships 1687

Maud Glover Folsom Foundation 1688

Maxwell House Coffee 1689

Maxwell Macmillan Scholarship Program 1690

McDonald's HACER Foundation 1691

McDonald's 1692

McDonnell Douglas Scholarship Foundation 1693

The McFarland Charitable Foundation 1694

McLean Hospital 1695

McMannis Educational Trust Fund 1696

McMurry University (Abilene, TX) 5725–5726

Memphis State University 1697

Merit Shop Foundation 1698

Mesa State College (Grand Junction, CO) 3659–3664

Messiah College (Grantham, PA) 5488–5490

Metro-Goldwyn/United Artists 1699

Metropolitan Business League (MBL) 1700

Metropolitan Museum of Art 1701

Metropolitan Opera 1702

Metropolitan State College (Denver, CO) 3665–3668

Michigan Department of Higher Education 1703–1710

Michigan State University (East Lansing, MI) 4709–4715

Michigan United Conservation Clubs 1711

Michigan Veterans' Affairs 1712

Microsoft 1713–1714

Midwestern State University (Wichita Falls, TX) 5727–5730

Migrant Dropout Reconnection Program 1715

Military Order of the Purple Heart 1716

Mills College (Oakland, CA) 3367–3370

Minerals, Metals & Materials Society 1717

Minnesota Chippewa Tribe Scholarship Fund 1718

Minnesota Foundation 1719

Minnesota Higher Education Services Office 1720–1734

Minority Scholarship Program 1735

Miss America Pageant 1736

Mississippi Office of State Student Financial Aid 1737–1747

Missouri League for Nursing, Inc. 1748

Missouri Review Editor's Prize 1749

Missouri Student Assistance Resource Services 1750–1759

Missouri Valley College (Marshall, MO) 4787–4790

Miss Teenage America Awards 1760

Mitchell Field Thrift Shop Scholarship 1761

Modern Woodmen of America Scholarship Program 1762–1763

Montana Commission of Higher Education 1764–1768

Montana Department of Social and Rehabilitation Services 1769

Montana State University (Bozeman, MI) 4989–4992

Montgomery G.I. Bill—Active Duty 1770

Moody Foundation Scholarships 1771

Moorman Agriculture Scholarships 1772

Morehouse College (Atlanta, GA) 4127–4129

Mote Marine Laboratory 1773

Mother Joseph Rogan Marymount Foundation 1774

Mount St. Mary's College (Los Angeles, CA) 3371–3373

MTV: Music Television 1775

Music Assistance Fund 1776

Nancy Jo Abels Scholarship Fund 1777

NAPA Valley Symphony Association 1778

National Academy for Nuclear Training Scholarship Program 1779

National Achievement Program for Outstanding Negro Students & National Merit Scholarship Program 1780

National Action Council for Minorities in Engineering (NACME), Inc. 1781

National Aeronautics and Space Administration (NASA) 1782–1783

National Air Transport Association 1784

National Amateur Baseball Federation 1785

National and Community Service 1786

National Art Materials Trade Association 1787

National Association for Campus Activities Educational Foundation 1788–1790

National Association for Sickle Cell Disease 1791

National Association for the Advancement of Colored People (NAACP) 1792–1794

National Association of American Business Clubs 1795

National Association of Black Accountants (NABA) 1796

National Association of Black Journalists 1797

National Association of Broadcasters 1798

National Association of College Broadcasters 1799

National Association of Colored Women's Clubs 1800

National Association of Educational Office Personnel 1801

National Association of Hispanic Journalists (NAHJ) 1802

National Association of Letter Carriers 1803–1804

National Association of Plumbing-Heating-Cooling Contractors 1805

National Association of Real Estate Editors 1806

National Association of Realtors 1807

National Association of Returning Students (NARS) 1808

National Association of Secondary School Principals (NASSP) 1809–1811

National Association of Social Workers 1812

National Association of Teachers of Singing Foundation 1813–1814

National Association of Water Companies—New Jersey Chapter 1815

National Association of Women in Construction 1816

National Athletic Trainer's Association 1817

National Audobon Society 1818–1819

National Baptist Convention, U.S.A., Inc. 1820

National Basketball Association 1821

National Black Nurses' Association 1822

National Black Police Association Scholarship 1823

National Business Aircraft Association 1824

National Campers and Hikers Association 1825

National Center for Indian Education 1826

National Collegiate Athletic Association (NCAA) 1827

National Commercial Finance Association 1828

National Council of Jewish Women (NCJW) 1829

National Council of State Garden Clubs, Inc. 1830

National Electronic Distributor Association (NEDA) Education Foundation 1831

National Executive Housekeepers Educational Foundation 1832

National Federation of Music Clubs 1833–1841

National Federation of Press Women 1842–1843

National Federation of State Poetry Societies, Inc. 1844

National Federation of the Blind (NFB) Scholarships 1845–1857

National Foster Parent Association 1858

National 4-H Awards 1859

National Frozen Food Association 1860

National Future Farmers of America (FFA) Center 1861–1932

National Geographic Society 1933–1934

National Guild of Community Schools of the Arts 1935

National Hispanic Scholarship Fund 1936

National Institute for Architectural Education Competition 1937–1939

National Institute for Music Theater 1940

National Institute of Neurological and Communicative Disorders and Stroke 1941

National Italian American Foundation (NIAF) 1942–1973

National Junior Classical League 1974

National Junior Horticulture Association (NJHA) 1975

National Merit Corporation Scholarship Program 1976–1978

National Music Camp Scholarships 1979

National Newspapers Publishers Association (NNPA) 1980

National Office Products Association (NOPA) 1981

National Press Foundation 1982

National Press Photographers Foundation 1983–1988

National PTA 1989

National Public Radio (NPR) 1990

National Radio Astronomy Observatory Summer Research Assistantships 1991

National Rifle Association (NRA) 1992

National Roofing Foundation 1993

National Scholarship Trust Fund 1994

National Science Teachers Association 1995–1998

National Security Agency (NSA) 1999–2000

National Society of Professional Engineers Educational Foundation 2001–2002

National Society of Public Accountants 2003

National Society of the Colonial Dames of America 2004

National Society of the Daughters of the American Revolution 2005–2013

National Society of the Sons of the American Revolution 2014

National Space Club 2015

National Speakers Association 2016

National Strength & Conditioning Association 2017

National Student Nurses Association 2018

National Student Nurses Association Foundation 2019

National Tropical Botanical Garden 2020

National Union of Hospital and Health Care Employees 2021

National University (San Diego, CA) 3374–3378

National Urban League, Inc. 2022

National Women's Health Network 2023

National Zoological Park 2024–2032

Native Daughters of the Golden West 2033–2037

Native Sons of the Golden West 2038

Natural Sciences and Engineering Research Council of Canada 2039

The Nature Conservancy (TNC) 2040

Naval Reserve Officers Training Corps 2041

Navy-Marine Corps Relief Society 2042–2049

Navy Relief Society 2050

Navy Supply Corps Foundation Scholarships 2051

Orphan Foundation of America Scholarship Program 2214

Otis/Parsons School of Art and Design (Los Angeles, CA) 3393–3394

Ouachita Baptist University (Arkadelphia, AR) 3152–3157

Our Lady of the Lake University (San Antonio, TX) 5731–5739

Our World-Underwater Scholarship 2215

Outdoor Writers Association of America 2216

Pacific Christian College (Fullerton, CA) 3395

Pacific Union College (Angwin, CA) 3396–3397

Palm Beach Atlantic College (West Palm Beach, FL) 3971–3975

Panama Canal Society of Professional Engineers 2217

Parapsychology Foundation 2218

Parents Without Partners 2219

Parkinson's Disease Foundation 2220

Paul and Mary Haas Foundation 2221

Pemco Foundation 2222

Pennsylvania AFL-CIO Scholarships 2223

Pennsylvania Department of Military Affairs 2224–2225

Pennsylvania Higher Education Assistance Agency (PHEAA) 2226–2229

Pennsylvania Society of Professional Engineers 2230

Pennsylvania State University (University Park, PA) 5491–5508

Pensacola Christian College (Pensacola, FL) 3976–3983

Pepperdine University (Malibu, CA) 3398–3409

Percy B. Ferebee Endowment 2231

Petro-Canada, Inc. 2232

PFLAG/New Orleans Chapter 2233

PGA Tour 2234

Phi Delta Kappa, Inc. 2235

Phi Eta Sigma Founders Fund Scholarships 2236

Phi Gamma Nu National Fraternity 2237–2238

Phi Kappa Theta National Foundation 2239

Phillips Petroleum Company Scholarships 2240

Phi Sigma Iota Scholarships Contest 2241

Phi Theta Kappa International Honor Society 2242–2245

Phi Upsilon Omicron National Office 2246

Phoenix College (Phoenix, AZ) 3075–3076

Photographic Art & Science Foundation 2247

Photographic Society of America Scholarship 2248

Photography Contest 2249

Physical Therapy Awards 2250

Physical Therapy Education Awards 2251

Physician Assistant Foundation of the American Academy of Physician Assistants 2252

Pilot International Foundation (PIF) 2253–2254

Pima Community College (Tucson, AZ) 3077–3079

Pipe Line Contractors Association of Canada 2255

Pitney Bowes, Inc. 2256

Pittsburgh New Music Ensemble 2257

Pitzer College (Claremont, CA) 3410–3411

Playwright's Center 2258

Poetry Society of America 2259–2260

Poets and Patrons of Chicago 2261

Point Loma Nazarene College (San Diego, CA) 3412–3416

Pomona College (Claremont, CA) 3417–3419

Portuguese Continental Union Scholarships 2262

The Poynter Fund 2263

Prairie Schooner 2264–2267

Prairie View A&M University (Prairie View, TX) 5740–5741

Presbyterian Church (USA) 2268–2273

Prescott College (Prescott, AZ) 3080–3082

President's Committee on Employment of People with Disabilities 2274–2276

Press Club of Houston 2277

Princeton University (Princeton, NJ) 5076–5078

Pro Bono Advocates 2278

Proctor & Gamble Co. 2279

Professional Aviation Maintenance Association 2280

Professional Horsemen's Association of America, Inc. 2281

Professional Secretaries International 2282–2283

Providence College (Providence, PA) 5533–5539

Public Employees Roundtable 2284

Public Housing Authorities Directors Association 2285

Puerto Rico Home Economics Program 2286

Puerto Rico Public Employees Scholarship Program 2287

Purdue University (West Lafayette, IN) 4354–4362

Quaker Chemical Foundation 2288

Queen Marie Jose Musical Prize Contest 2289

Quill & Scroll Foundation 2290

Quincy Writer's Guild Annual Creative Writing Contest 2291

Quinnipiac College (Hamden, CT) 3751–3754

Quota International Fund Fellowships 2292

Racine Environment Committee Educational Fund 2293

Radio and Television News Directors Foundation 2294

Radio Free Europe / Radio Liberty 2295–2296

Radio Technical Commission for Aeronautics 2297

Ralph McGill Scholarship Fund 2298

Randolph Macon College (Ashland, VA) 5999–6009

Random House, Inc. 2299

Raychem 2300

Real Estate Educators Association 2301

Rebekah Assembly of Texas 2302

Recording for the Blind 2303

Record-Journal Publishing Co. 2304

Red River Valley Fighter Pilots Association 2305

Reebok 2306

Regis University (Denver, CO) 3669–3676

Renew America 2307

Reserve Officers Association of the United States 2308–2309

Retired Officers Association 2310–2311

Rhode Island Commission on State Government 2312

Rhode Island Higher Education Assistance Authority 2313–2314

Rhode Island Society of Professional Engineers 2315

Rhode Island Vocational Rehabilitation Training Grants 2316

Rhodes College (Memphis, TN) 5647–5652

Rice University (Houston, TX) 5742–5745

Richard Eberhart Prize in Poetry 2317

Ripon College (Ripon, WI) 6089–6097

Robert Mondavi Winery 2318

Roberts Writing Awards 2319

Rochester Institute of Technology (Rochester, NY) 5187–5202

Rolling Stone Internships 2320

Rollins College (Winter Park, FL) 3984–3987

Rosalie Tilles Nonsectarian Charity Fund 2321

Rose-Hulman Institute of Technology (Terre Haute, IN) 4363–4365

Rosenbluth International 2322

Rotary Club (Downtown) of San Antonio 2323

Rotary Foundation Scholarships for International Understanding 2324–2327

University of the Ozarks (Clarksville, AR) 3183

University of the Pacific (Stockton, CA) 3583–3585

University of Utah (Salt Lake City, UT) 5959–5964

University of Vermont (Burlington, VT) 5968–5969

University of Virginia (Charlottesville, VA) 6010–6014

University of Washington (Seattle, WA) 6026–6028

University of Wisconsin (Madison, WI) 6101

University of Wyoming (Laramie, WY) 6102–6110

Urann Foundation 2637

USAA Dependent Scholarship Program 2638–2639

USAA National Merit Scholarship Program 2640

U.S. Bank of Oregon Foundation Team 2641–2645

Utah State Office of Education 2646–2650

Valparaiso University (Valparaiso, IN) 4388–4403

Van Buren Foundation, Inc. 2651

Vanderbilt University (Nashville, TN) 5664–5670

Vermont Department of Education 2652–2654

Vermont Society of Professional Engineers 2655

Vertical Flight Foundation 2656

VFW Ladies Auxiliary National Patriotic Creative Art Competition 2657

VFW Voice of Democracy Scholarship Program 2658

Vikki Carr Scholarship Foundation 2659–2660

Villanova University (Villanova, PA) 5520–5524

Virginia Airport Operators Council Aviation (VAOC) Scholarships 2661

Virginia Baptist General Board 2662

Virginia Commonwealth Department of Veterans' Affairs 2663

Virginia Council of Higher Education 2664–2669

Virginia Department of Health—Public Health Nursing 2670–2671

Virginia Forestry Association 2672

Virginia Museum of Fine Arts 2673

Virginia Polytechnic Institute and State University (Blacksburg, VA) 6015–6021

Virginia Society of Professional Engineers 2674

Virginia State Assistance for Physically Disabled Students 2675

Virginia State Assistance to Children of Veterans 2676

Virgin Islands Board of Education 2677–2678

Volkswagen of America, Inc. 2679

Von Trotha Educational Trust 2680

Wall Street Journal 2681

Wal-Mart Foundation 2682

Walt Disney Studios 2683

WAMSCO Young Artist Competition 2684

Washington Center for Internships and Academic Seminars 2685

Washington Congress of Parents and Teachers 2686

Washington International Competition 2687

Washington Internships for Students of Engineering 2688

Washington Post 2689–2690

Washington Press Association 2691

Washington Society of Professional Engineers 2692

Washington Society of Professional Journalists/Western WA Chapter 2693

Washington State Higher Education Coordinating Board 2694–2698

Washington University (St. Louis, MO) 4981–4988

Water Environment Federation 2699

Waverly Community House, Inc. 2700

Welsh Society of Philadelphia 2701

Wesleyan University (Middletown, CT) 3783–3785

Western Interstate Commission for Higher Education 2702

Western Maryland College (Westminister, MD) 4634–4636

Western State College of Colorado (Gunnison, CO) 3724–3729

Westinghouse Electric Corporation 2703

Westinghouse Science Talent Search Scholarships 2704

Westin Hotels & Resorts 2705

Westmont College (Santa Barbara, CA) 3586–3588

West Virginia Department of Veterans' Affairs 2706

West Virginia Department of Education 2707–2709

West Virginia Society of Professional Engineers 2710

West Virginia University (Morgantown, WV) 6039–6042

Weyerhaeuser 2711–2712

Whirly-Girls Memorial Scholarship 2713

White House Fellowships 2714

Whitman College (Walla Walla, WA) 6033–6036

Whitney Museum of American Art 2715

Whittier College (Whittier, CA) 3589–3592

Wichita Eagle 2716

Wichita State University Playwriting Contest 2717

The Widmeyer Group, Inc. 2718

Wildlife Habitat Council 2719

The Wildlife Society 2720

Wildwood Prize in Poetry 2721

William M. Grupe Foundation, Inc. 2722

William Randolph Hearst Foundation 2723–2726

Wilson Ornithological Society Research Grants 2727–2728

Wisconsin Congress Parents and Teachers, Inc. 2729

Wisconsin Department of Public Instruction 2730–2738

Wisconsin Department of Veterans' Affairs 2739

Wisconsin League for Nursing, Inc. 2740

Wisconsin Society of Professional Engineers 2741

Wisconsin State Vocational Rehabilitation 2742

WJBK-TV 2743

WMAL Radio 2744

WNBC-TV 2745

WNET-TV 2746

WNYC-TV 2747

WNYW-FOX Television 2748

Wolf Trap Foundation for the Performing Arts 2749

Woman's Auxiliary of the American Institute of Mining, Metallurgical & Petroleum Engineers, Inc. 2750–2751

Women and Foundations/Corporate Philanthropy (WAF/CP) 2752

Women Athletes' Voice of Encouragement (WAVE) 2753

Women Band Directors National Association 2754–2755

Women Grocers of America 2756

Women in Communications, Inc. 2757–2775

Women Marines Association 2776

Women of the Evangelical Lutheran Church in America 2777

Women Seamen's Friends Society of Connecticut 2778

Women's Equity Action League (WEAL) 2779

Women's Sports Foundation 2780

Women's Transportation Seminar (WTS) 2781

Women's Western Golf Foundation Scholarships 2782

Woods Hole Oceanographic Institution 2783

Worcester County Horticultural Society 2784

APPENDICES

A. Timetables
Middle School
High School
Undergraduate

B. College Resource Materials Scholarship
List Form

C. College & Scholarship Applications
Tracking Chart

D. Financial Aid Worksheets & Tables
Financial Assistance Analysis Chart
School Expenses
Parents' Expected Family
Contribution
Student's Expected Contribution
Total Family Contribution
Student's Needs
Financial Aid Awards
Tables

E. Résumés for High School and College Students

F. Athletic Recruitment Profiles
Males
Females

G. Request Letters
High School
Home-Schooled
College
Nontraditional

H. Request Postcards
   High School
   Undergraduate
   Nontraditional
   Return Receipt Postcard

I. Recommendation Letters
   Sample Form
   High School
   Undergraduate
   Nontraditional

Timetables

MIDDLE SCHOOL TIMETABLE

WHEN	WHAT TO DO
<u>SIXTH GRADE</u>	• Start asking questions about careers. • Ask your counselor if your school will be holding a Career Day. • Start thinking about colleges. • Make a Wish List of about 100 colleges you might like to attend. • Check at school library, public library, or Internet for college addresses. • Request catalogs from all the colleges on your list. The catalogs will list majors they offer and admission requirements. • Discuss and design your proposed high school course load with your parents and counselor. • Enter scholarship and writing competitions. • Update activities résumé you started in fifth grade.
<u>SEVENTH GRADE</u>	• If possible, take Algebra I. Be sure to try your best, because the grade might be on your high school transcript. • Update your high school course load plan and discuss changes with your parents and counselor. • Sign up and take a practice SAT. • Update your College Wish List, add new schools, and remove any that don't fit your needs. Cut list down to eighty colleges. • Attend or initiate a Career Day activity. • Enter scholarship and writing competitions. • Update activities résumé.
<u>EIGHTH GRADE</u>	• Update your high school course load plan and discuss changes with your parents and counselor. • Possibly take Algebra I or Geometry. • Take first year of a foreign language. • Sign up and take a practice SAT. • Update your College Wish List, add new schools, and remove any that don't fit your needs. Cut list down to sixty colleges. • Attend or initiate a Career Day activity. Ask your counselor or principal if your school can create a Career Day, or even Days. • Volunteer to help plan the event and ask local people to come talk about their careers. • Enter scholarship and writing competitions. • Start looking for a volunteer position to work in during the school year and summer. • Consider participating in a summer program that can help you learn to set goals and leadership skills. • Create an organizational system you will use in high school. • Update activities résumé.

HIGH SCHOOL TIMETABLE

WHEN	WHAT TO DO
FRESHMAN YEAR	☛ You, your parents, and your counselor should discuss and design the high school courses you will need to take to prepare you for college entrance and success.
	☛ Start looking for and applying to scholarship opportunities.
	☛ Work in a volunteer position in your community.
	☛ Start keeping a résumé of all the activities in which you participate both in and out of school.
	☛ Write for college information.
	☛ Take a practice SAT and/or ACT.
SOPHOMORE YEAR	☛ Update your course plan; take as many honors or advance placement courses as possible.
	☛ If you have not already done so, you might want to take a trial-run PSAT and SAT and/or ACT, to get used to taking standardized tests. Don't worry about your score.
	☛ Take the PLAN, a skills, career, and college assessment test.
	☛ Apply to any scholarships for which you qualify.
	☛ Update your résumé.
	☛ Narrow down your list of possible colleges.
	☛ Sign up for Honors, Advance Placement, and/or dual-credit courses for next year's schedule.
SUMMER JUNIOR YEAR	☛ Begin writing essays on your goals, role model, and life-affecting experience.
September	☛ Review and update your high school course plan.
	☛ Select at least five people to write needed recommendation letters.
	☛ Request scholarship applications.
	☛ Sign up for PSAT (top scores qualify for National Merit designation and scholarships).
	☛ Update your résumé.
October	☛ Take the PSAT.
	☛ Line up volunteer work or internship.
November	☛ Check school and public library and Internet for college addresses.
	☛ Send for college brochures and financial aid information.
December	☛ Evaluate PSAT score and GPA.
	☛ Narrow down your list of colleges to at least ten.
Spring	☛ Visit college campuses, if possible, and talk to financial aid counselors, professors, and students at colleges.
	☛ Sign up for Honors, Advance Placement, and/or dual-credit courses for next year's schedule.
April & May	☛ Take Advance Placement Tests and possibly SAT and/or ACT.
June	☛ Take SAT/ACT and any Achievement Tests required for college admission.
Summer	☛ Write and edit essays on your goals, role model, and life-affecting experience.
SENIOR YEAR	
September	☛ Request scholarship applications.
	☛ Sign up for SAT and/or ACT, if you haven't taken them yet.
	☛ Narrow down list of colleges to ten or fewer and write to colleges requesting admission applications and financial aid forms.
	☛ Update your résumé.
October	☛ Take SAT and/or ACT.
Through December	☛ Send in applications for college admission.
January	☛ Send in Free Application for Federal Student Aid (FAFSA) and any other required forms.
	☛ Send in financial aid applications as soon after January 1 as possible.

March & April	☛ Colleges send out acceptances.
	☛ College and processing agencies need to have received financial aid forms.
	☛ Sign up for Advance Placement Tests.
April & May	☛ Take Advance Placement Tests.
June 30	☛ Should have heard from most scholarships.
	☛ Financial aid office at your college must have received your application and Student Aid Report (SAR).
	☛ Send copies of outside-scholarship award letters you receive to the financial aid office of the college/university you will be attending.
Summer	☛ Update résumé.
	☛ Revise or write new goals, role model, and life-affecting experience essays for use in the coming year.

UNDERGRADUATE TIMETABLE

WHEN	WHAT TO DO
FRESHMAN & **SOPHOMORE**	★ Take any College Level Examination Program (CLEP) Tests to get credit for courses without having to take the course. ★ Design your proposed college course plan with your advisor. ★ If you're unsure about a major, take one or two courses each semester in areas of interest to you. ★ Continue applying to scholarship and writing competitions. ★ Inquire about clubs in your areas of interest and about service clubs you might join. This is a great way to make new friends who share your interests. ★ Look into and begin doing a volunteer activity within your community. ★ Begin your college activities résumé. ★ Create and use an organizational system to keep information on our activities, courses, and career interests. ★ In December of each year, go to your financial aid office (FAO) and request a copy of the Free Application for Federal Student Aid (FAFSA) and any other required financial aid forms. ★ Start inquiring about summer internship programs in your areas of interest. This is a great way to learn about careers, as well as earn money. ★ Apply to summer internship programs.
JUNIOR	★ Update and evaluate your college course plan with your advisor. ★ Declare your major. ★ Apply to scholarship and writing competitions. ★ Update your college activities résumé. ★ File required financial aid forms at the FAO. ★ Apply to summer internship programs. ★ Request information about graduate or professional school programs. ★ Determine if there are any courses that you must take for admission to graduate/professional school. ★ Sign up and take required admissions tests. ★ Apply to scholarships and writing competitions. ★ Start preparing your personal statement concerning your educational and professional goals.
SENIOR	★ Update your course plan to make sure you will have completed courses required for graduation. ★ Retake admissions tests, if necessary. ★ Request graduate/professional school applications. ★ Select three to five people to write recommendation letters. ★ Apply to scholarship and writing competitions. ★ Update your résumé. ★ Begin applying to graduate and professional schools, or for jobs. ★ Submit FAFSA and other required forms to FAO. ★ By March and April, receive acceptance letters to graduate or professional schools. ★ Schools send out financial aid packages. ★ Begin receiving scholarship award notifications.

APPENDIX B
College Resource Materials Scholarship List Form

Scholarship / Grant / Loan and Addresses	Date Info. Requested	Date Info. Received	Date Applied	Comments

APPENDIX C: College & Scholarship Applications Tracking Chart

Name & Address of College Application or Scholarship Application	Application Sent	Financial Aid Information Sent	Reference Letter Written by:	Date Reference Letter Requested	Receipt Acknowledged	Date Secondary School Report Given to Counselor	Receipt Acknowledged	Should Hear Results by:	Possible Award Amount	Result

APPENDIX D: Financial Aid Worksheets & Tables

Financial Assistance Analysis Chart

NAME OF SCHOOL									
Estimated Costs:									
Tuition & Fees									
Room & Board									
Books & Supplies									
Personal Expenses & Travel									
1. Total Budget									
Parents' Contribution									
Student's Contribution									
Student's Assets									
2. Total Personal Resources									
Types of Assistance:									
College Grants									
College Scholarship									
State Grants									
Federal Grants (Pell, SEOG)									
Outside Scholarship/Grant Aid									
3. Total Scholarship/Grant Aid									
4. Self-Help Work Study									
5. Total Free Aid Package (No Loans – Add 3+4)									
Perkins Loan									
Subsidized Stafford									
Unsubsidized Stafford									
6. Total Loan Package									
7. Total Financial Aid Package (Add 5+6)									

Note: If after reviewing your financial aid package you realize that you cannot afford what has been determined to be your contribution, contact your college/university financial aid office to see if additional funds can be found. Circumstances change and so can financial aid packages.

Financial Aid Worksheets

Part A. School Expenses

	College A	College B	College C
1. Tuition & fees	$	$	$
2. Books and supplies			
3. Dormitory/apartment costs			
4. Board/meals			
5. Personal expenses (laundry, entertainment, etc.)			
6. Transportation (2 round trips per year)			
7. Miscellaneous (child care, disability costs)			
Total (add 1–7)	$	$	$

Part B: Parents' Expected Family Contribution (EFC—Federal Methodology)

Based on Previous Year's Income

8. Father's wages, salaries, tips, and other expenses	$
9. Mother's wages, salaries, tips, and other expenses	$
10. Other parental income (child support, dividends, interest, Social Security, pension, welfare, etc.—include 401(k), 403(b), IRA/Keogh payments)	$
11. IRS allowable adjustments to income (alimony paid, business expenses, interest penalties, etc.—don't include IRA/Keogh payments)	$
a. Total Income (8 + 9 + 10 − 11)	$
Expenses	
12. U.S. income tax parents paid on previous year's income (not amount withheld from paychecks)	$
13. Social Security (FICA) tax (see Table 1)	$
14. State and other taxes (8% of **a**)	$
15. Employment allowance (a. 2-parent family with both parents working: allow 35% of lower salary to a maximum of $2,600; b. 1-parent family, allow 35% of salary to a maximum of $2,600; c. no allowance for a 2-parent family with only one parent employed.)	$
16. Income Protection Allowance (See Table 2)	$
b. Total allowances against income (12 + 13 + 14 + 15 + 16)	$
c. Available income (subtract, **a** − **b**)	$
Assets	
17. Other real estate equity (value − unpaid balance on mortgage)	$
18. Business or farm (total value − indebtedness × % from Table 3) If family is part owner of the farm or business, only include family's share of net value.	$
19. Cash, savings, and checking accounts	$
20. Other investments (current net value)	$
d. Total assets	$

Part B (continued)

Deductions	
e. Asset protection allowance (Table 4)	$
f. Remaining assets (subtract, **d** − **e** = remaining assets)	$
g. Income supplement from assets (multiply, **f** × 12%; if answer is a negative value, enter 0)	$
h. Adjusted available income (add, **c** + **g**)	$
i. Parent's EFC (multiply, **h** × taxation rate amount in Table 5)	$
j. Parent's EFC if more than one family member in college (divide, **i** by # of members in college at least half-time)	$

Part C: Student's Expected Contribution
Previous Year's Income

21. Yearly wages, salaries, tips, and other compensation	$
22. Spouse's yearly wages, salaries, tips, and other compensation	$
23. All other income of student (dividends, interest, untaxed income, and benefits)	$
k. Total income (add, 21 + 22 + 23)	$
Allowances	
24. U.S. Income tax student (and spouse) paid on previous year (not amount withheld from paychecks)	$
25. State and other taxes (enter 4% of **k**)	$
26. Social Security (FICA) tax (see Table 1)	$
27. Dependent student offset	$
l. Total allowances against student's income (add, 24 + 25 + 26 + 27)	$
m. Available income (subtract **k** − **l**)	$
Resources	
28. Contribution from income (line **m** × 50%. Cannot be less than $0)	$
29. Contribution from assets (multiply the total savings and other assets, such as stocks and bonds, but not home equity, by 35%)	$
30. Other gifts and scholarships already received	$
n. Total student resources (add, 28 + 29 + 30)	$

Part D: Total Family Contribution

o. Parents' expected contribution (Use **j** instead of **i** if more than one family member in college)	$
p. Student's expected contribution from resources (line **n**)	$
q. Total family contribution (add, **o** + **p**)	$

Part E: Student's Needs

r. Total college expense budget	$
s. Total family contribution	$
t. Student need (subtract, **r** − **s**)	$

Part F: Financial Aid Awards

	College A	College B	College C
u. Total student budget	$	$	$
v. Total family contribution			
w. Demonstrted financial need			
31. Federal Pell Grant			
32. State scholarships			
33. Institutional grants			
34. Federal Work-Study			
35. Federal Perkins Loans			
36. Federal SEOG			
37. Federal Stafford Loan			
38. Private Scholarships			
x. Total resources for college	$	$	$

Part G: TABLES

Table 1. Social Security (FICA) Tax Allowance	
Individual's yearly wage total equals	**Allowance per wage earner for Social Security (FICA) tax**
$ 1 to $62,700	7.65% of income earned by each wage earner (maximum $4,796.55/person)
$ 62,701 or more	$4,796.55 + 1.45% of income earned above $62,700 by each wage earner

Table 2. Income Protection Allowance					
Family size ☜ (including student)	**Number individuals in college ☜☜**				
	1	**2**	**3**	**4**	**5**
2	$11,750	$ 9,740			
3	14,630	12,630	$10,620		
4	18,070	16,060	14,060	$12,050	
5	21,320	19,310	17,310	15,300	$13,300
6	24,940	22,930	20,930	18,920	16,920

☜   For each additional family member, add $2,810.

☜☜ For each additional college student, subtract $2,000.

Table 3. Business or Farm Adjustments	
Net worth (nw)	**Adjusted net worth**
less than $ 1	$ 0
$ 1 to $ 85,000	$ 0 + 40% of nw
$ 85,001 to $250,000	$ 34,000 + 50% of nw over $ 85,000
$250,001 to $420,000	$116,500 + 60% of nw over $250,000
$420,001 or more	$218,500 + 100% of nw over $420,000

Table 4. Asset Protection Allowance		
Older Parent's Age	Two-Parent Family	One-Parent Family
25 or younger	$ 0	$ 0
26	2,400	1,700
27	4,700	3,300
28	7,100	5,000
29	9,500	6,600
30	11,800	8,300
31	14,200	10,000
32	16,600	11,600
33	18,900	13,300
34	21,300	14,900
35	23,700	16,600
36	26,000	18,300
37	28,400	19,900
38	30,800	21,600
39	33,100	23,200
40	35,500	24,900
41	36,400	25,400
42	37,300	26,000
43	38,300	26,500
44	39,300	27,100
45	40,300	27,800
46	41,300	28,300
47	42,400	29,000
48	43,400	29,700
49	44,500	30,400
50	45,900	31,200
51	47,100	31,900
52	48,300	32,700
53	49,800	33,500
54	51,300	34,300
55	52,600	35,100
56	54,200	36,100
57	55,900	36,900
58	57,600	38,000
59	59,600	39,100
60	61,400	40,000
61	63,200	41,100
62	65,400	42,300
63	67,700	43,500
64	70,000	44,900
65 or more	72,400	46,100

Table 5. Parents' Expected Family Contribution (EFC)	
Adjusted Available Income (AAI)	**Total parents' contribution**
less than $ 3,409	$−750
$ 3,409 to $10,500	+ 22% of AAI
$10,501 to $13,200	$2,310 + 25% of AAI over $10,500
$13,201 to $15,900	$2,985 + 29% of AAI over $13,200
$15,901 to $18,500	$3,768 + 34% of AAI over $15,900
$18,501 to $21,200	$4,652 + 40% of AAI over $18,500
$21,201 or more	$5,732 + 47% of AAI over $21,200

Résumés for High School and College Students

SAMPLE HIGH SCHOOL STUDENT'S RÉSUMÉ

Jane Doe

Student's Address City State Zip Code (area code) phone number SS#	Name of school attending now School address City State Zip Code (area code) phone number

LEADERSHIP POSITIONS AND OFFICES HELD

Activity	Office	Grade	Hours/Month
Freshman Dance Committee	Chair	9	20 hrs/1 month
HOSA National Convention	Welcome Comm. Chair	9	15 hrs/4 months
Church Youth Organization	Social Representative	9	4 hrs/month
Class Officer	Historian	9	2 hrs/month
School Newspaper	Editor	10	20 hrs/month
Math Club	Parliamentarian	10	3 hrs/month
Bowling Club	Founder/President	11	2 hrs/month
Students Against Drunk Drivers	Photographer	11	1 hr/month
Student Council	Representative	9	3 hrs/month
	Representative	10	3 hrs/month
	Treasurer	11	5 hrs/month
	President	12	10 hrs/month

MEMBERSHIPS AND OTHER ACTIVITIES

Club/Activity	Grade	Hours/Month
Clubs		
Community Service Club	11, 12	2 hrs/month
Drama Club	9, 10, 11, 12	1 hr/month
Spanish Club	9, 10, 11, 12	1 hr/month
Community Service		
Nursing Home Volunteer	9, 10, 11, 12	4 hrs/month
Parks & Recreation Sports Instructor	11, 12	20 hrs/wk/3 months
Sports		
Softball Team	9	24 hrs/month/3 months
Soccer Team	9, 10, 11, 12	20 hrs/month/3 months
Summer Activity		
UTHSC Medical School Intership Program	10, 11, 12	40 hrs/wk/6 weeks
Work Experience		
Baby-sitting	9, 10, 11, 12	8–10 hrs/month
Sunday School Teacher	9, 10, 11, 12	4 hrs/month
Taco Bell Server	12	40 hrs/month

HONORS AND AWARDS

Award	Place	Division	Grade
Academic Octathlon Team	member	A Division	9
District UIL Competition	4th	Biology	9
Regional Science Fair	3rd	Zoology	9
Regional Jr. Academy of Science	6th	Med & Health	9
Academic Octathlon Team	member	A Division	10
District UIL Competition	member	Science	10
Regional 4-H Competition	2nd	Hereford	10
Regional History Fair Essay Contest	2nd		10
Regional Science Fair	5th	Med & Health	10
Regional Jr. Academy of Science	1st	Med & Health	10
State Jr. Academy of Science	3rd	Med & Health	10
Who's Who Among American HS Students		Listed	11
Academic Decathlon Team	member	A Division	11
District UIL Competition	member	Science	11
Mu Alpha Theta (Math)		Inducted	11
National Honor Society		Inducted	11
Regional Science Fair	1st	Med & Health	11
Regional Jr. Academy of Science	2nd	Med & Health	11
Academic Decathlon Team	member	A Division	12
District UIL Competition	member	Science	12
Regional Science Fair	2nd	Med & Health	12
Regional Jr. Academy of Science	2nd	Med & Health	12
State Jr. Academy of Science	2nd	Med & Health	12
National Merit Finalist			12

SAMPLE HOME–SCHOOLED STUDENT'S RÉSUMÉ

Nicole Johnson
246 Bent Tree Court
Casper, WY 88801
(307) 555-1928
SS# 790-31-1111

LEADERSHIP POSITIONS

Activity	Office	Year	Hours/month
Home-Schoolers Association	Student Representative	9	2 hrs/month
Home-Schoolers Association	Student Representative	10	2 hrs/month
Home-Schoolers Association	Creative Writing Teacher	11	4 hrs/month
State Home-Schoolers Association	State Delegate	11	2 hrs/month
Home-Schoolers Association	Creative Writing Teacher	12	4 hrs/month
HSA Science Club	Founder/President	12	5 hrs/month

MEMBERSHIPS

Club/Activity	Year	Hours/month
Church Baseball Team	11	4 hrs/month
Church Youth Club	11, 12	3 hrs/month
Defensive Karate	12	4 hrs/month
4-H Club	9, 10, 11, 12	12 hrs/month
Home-Schoolers Service Club	10	2 hrs/month
HSA Bowling League	9	4 hrs/month
HSA Soccer Team	10	12 hrs/month
Casper Library Volunteer	11, 12	4 hrs/month
Nursing Home Volunteer	9, 10, 11, 12	4 hrs/month
Baby-sitting	11, 12	20 hrs/month

HONORS AND AWARDS

Award	Place	Division	Grade
4-H Club	2nd	Sewing	9
HSA Bowling League	2nd	District	9
HSA Scholastic Competition	3rd	Math	9
HSA Top Student Award	1st	Overall	10
HSA Soccer Team	1st		10
Amelia Student Awards	2nd	Short Stories	10
4-H Club	1st	Sewing	10
Church Baseball League	MVP		10
4-H Club	1st	Computers	10
HSA Scholastic Competition	1st	Writing	11
HSA Science Fair	3rd	Botany	11
4-H Club	1st	Computers	12
HSA Science Fair	2nd	Zoology	12
HSA Beta Club		Inducted	12

SAMPLE COLLEGE STUDENT'S RÉSUMÉ

John Smith

Attending: Trinity University
Classification: Sophomore

Major: Biology
Age: 19

Mailing Addresses

Permanent Address	**School**	**School's Address**
1234 Indian Valley	P.O. Box 5678	Trinity University
Portsmouth, VA 23702	Trinity Station	715 Stadium Drive
(804) 555-1111	San Antonio, TX 78284	San Antonio, TX 78212
SS#	(210) 555-9876	(210) 736-7011

LEADERSHIP POSITIONS AND OFFICES HELD

Activity	Office	Classification	Hours/Month
University Medical Center Hospital	Volunteer Coordinator	Freshman	5 hrs/month
Biology Club	Parliamentarian	Sophomore	4 hrs/month
Student Newspaper	Photographer	Sophomore	10 hrs/month

MEMBERSHIPS AND OTHER ACTIVITIES

Club/Activity	Classification	Hours/Month
Peer Counseling Committee	Freshman	3 hrs/month
Langley Tutoring Program (Science)	Freshman & Sophomore	4 hrs/month
Volunteer at Local Library	Sophomore	3 hrs/month

WORK/STUDY EMPLOYMENT

Employment	Classification	Hours/Month
Campus Tour Guide	Freshman	10 hrs/week
Typing Clerk	Sophomore	10 hrs/week

HONORS AND AWARDS

Award	Type	Year
Memorial Scholarship ($1,000)	Academic	Freshman
National Merit Scholarship		Freshman
National Writing Award	Essay	Freshman
Faraday Memorial Scholarship ($5,000)	Academic Achievement	Sophomore

SAMPLE NONTRADITIONAL STUDENT'S RÉSUMÉ

Erika Washington

Attending: Oakland City College
Classification: Junior

Major: Education
(Optional) Age: 34

Mailing Addresses

Permanent
905 Meadow Lane
Oakland City, IN 47660
(812) 555-3579
SS#

School's Address
Lucretia Street
Oakland City, IN 47660
(812) 749-4781

LEADERSHIP POSITIONS AND OFFICES HELD

Activity	Office	Classification	Hours/Month
Oakland First Baptist Church	Sunday School Teacher	Sophomore	4 hrs/month
PeeWee League Baseball	Transportation Coordinator	Junior	12 hrs/month
Stoffer Elementary School	Recreation Coordinator	Freshman	1 hr/month

MEMBERSHIPS AND OTHER ACTIVITIES

Activity	Classification	Hours/Month
Adult Literacy	Junior	4 hrs/month
Habitat for Humanity	Freshman	8 hrs/6 days
Volunteer at Battered Women's Shelter	Sophomore	3 hrs/month

WORK/STUDY EMPLOYMENT

Employment	Classification	Hours/Month
Baby-sitting Coop	Freshman, Sophomore, Junior	20 hrs/month
Clerk Typist	Sophomore	10 hrs/month
Library Clerk	Junior	10 hrs/month
Substitute Teacher	Junior	20 hrs/month

HONORS AND AWARDS

Honor	Division	Classification
National Writing Award	Essay	Freshman
Stoffer Elementary School Volunteer of the Year		Freshman
Children's Story Hour Contest Winner	Short Story	Sophomore
Soroptimist Club Scholarship Recipient	Academic	Sophomore
City-wide Writer's Contest Winner	Essay	Junior
Orville Redenbacher's 2nd Start Scholarship	Recipient	Junior

Athletic Recruitment Profiles

Sample 1: Males
JOE SMITH

1234 Oak Lane
Middleton, TX 77777
(512) 555-0987
SS# 678-32-5690

Washington High School
One Bear Claw Path
Middleton, TX 77717
(512) 555-BEAR/555-2327

Player Statistics

Height: 6' 5"
Weight: 195 lbs.
Age: 16 (01/14/82)

Approx. GPA: 3.51 on a 4.0 scale
Class Rank: 35/600
SAT or ACT score: 450 m 460 v
Expected Graduation: May 2000

Sport: Basketball
Conference: 5A

Position: Shooting Guard 2 & 3/Small Forward
Student Number: 54

Statistics

18 Average Points/Game
 7 Rebounds/Game

4 Assists/Game
3 Steals/Game

Average Playing Time: Generally plays the entire game unless team is up by 20 points

Honors	Division	Grade
Blessed Sacrament Academy League	Most Valuable Player	9
Eastside YMCA	All Division Team	9
Eastside YMCA	Division Champions	9
Roundball Ruckus	2nd Place	9
All Tourney Team	Member	10
American High School Athletic Award	Recipient	10
Basketball Team	District Champion	10
Basketball Team State Championship	Finalist	10
Eastside YMCA	All Division Team	10
Roundball Ruckus	Championship	10
Southside Recreation	All Star Game	10
Texas Christian Interschool League (TCIL)	All District	10
TCIL	All State	10
All City Team	Honorable Mention	11
All Tourney Team	Most Valuable Player	11
American High School Athletic Award	Recipient	11
Eastside YMCA	Division Champions	11
Hoop It Up (Austin, TX)	Champions	11
Hot Shots Tournament	Champions	11
Joe Ward Recreation	All Star Game	11
Roundball Ruckus Tournament	Champions	11
State Tourney Team	Member	11
TCIL	All District	11

Sample 2: Females
MARY DIAZ

Athletic Profile

13 Admiral Court
Portsmouth, VA 23222
(757) 234-9876
222-53-2431

Cradock High School
5913 Washington Highway
Portsmouth, VA 23222
(787) ADMIRAL/236-4725

Player Statistics

Height: 5' 11"
Weight: 130 lbs.
Age: 15 (01/14/82)

Approx. GPA: 4.74 on a 5.0 scale
Class Rank: 54/364
SAT or ACT score: 510 m 490 v
Expected Graduation: May 2001

Cradock High School Varsity Softball Team

Conference: Tidewater Scholastic League
Positions: Pitcher
Throws: Left
Arm: Exceptional

Sport: Softball
Speed: Mid 60s
Control: Excellent
Pitches: F.B., curve

Starter: Freshman
Stats: Freshman Year

W	L	ERA	IP	Comp G.	Shut O.	BB	H	K	2B	3B	HR	RS	ER
10	0	0.95	43	2	1	20	15	40	5	1	0	10	7

Honors:
Rookie of the Year
Most Valuable Player
Tidewater All District Champions
YWCA Women's Summer League

Starter: Sophomore
Stats: Sophomore Year

W	L	ERA	IP	Comp G.	Shut O.	BB	H	K	2B	3B	HR	RS	ER
5	0	0.92	40	2	1	15	12	35	3	1	1	7	6

Honors:
Virginia Women's Softball All-State Team
Tidewater All District Champions
YWCA Women's Summer League

Other Sports: Junior Varsity Tennis, Varsity Basketball, Volleyball

Request Letters for Use by High School, Home–Schooled, College, or Nontraditional Students

Sample Request Letter #1

Your Name
Street Address
City   State   Zip Code

Date

College/Foundation/Company Name
Street Address
City   State   Zip Code

Dear Committee Member:

   I am a (state year) graduating senior at _____ High School in ____(city, state)____.
I am interested in attending _____ College/University. I would like to major in _____
(or say that you are undecided). I am an (A, B, or C) student. I scored a _____ on the PSAT and a __
on the SAT. (It isn't necessary to give your scores if you don't want to.)

   I would like to request a scholarship application/a college catalog and financial aid information. Thank
you for your assistance.

Sincerely,

(Signature)

Name

Sample Request Letter #2

Your Name
Street Address
City   State   Zip Code

Date

College/Foundation/Company Name
Street Address
City   State   Zip Code

Dear Committee Member:

I am a __(state year)__ graduating home-schooled student. I have been home-schooled since I was in ____ grade. I am interested in attending _____ College/University. I would like to major in _____ (or say that you're undecided). I am an __(A, B, or C)__ student following a _____ curriculum. I scored a _____ on the SAT/ACT. (It isn't necessary to give your scores if you don't want to.)

I have also taken several college courses at _____, and maintained a ____ GPA on a ____ scale.

I would like to request a scholarship application/a college catalog and financial aid information. Thank you for your assistance.

Sincerely,

(Signature)

Name

Sample Request Letter #3

Your Name
Street Address
City   State   Zip Code

Date

College/Foundation/Company Name
Street Address
City   State   Zip Code

Dear Committee Member:

   (If stating your age, sex, or ethnicity is required, tell them.) I am in my ___(state year)___ in college. I attend _____ College/University. I am majoring in _____ and would like to (state your career goals as simply as possible). I am an (A, B+, B, C, etc.) student in my major and my GPA is _____.

   I would like to request an application and more information about the scholarships you offer. Thank you for your assistance.

Sincerely,

(Signature)

Name

Sample Request Letter #4

Your Name
Street Address
City   State   Zip Code

Date

College/Foundation/Company Name
Street Address
City   State   Zip Code

Dear Committee Member:

   I have been out of college for <u>(state amount of time).</u> I am planning on attending _____ College/University. I will be majoring in _____ and would like to <u>(state your career or educational goals as simply as possible)</u>.

   (If you've been doing work in your area of career interest, say so. For example: (1) I've worked as a legal secretary for five years and now want to attend college and law school. (2) I've worked in hotels in various capacities and would now like to study hotel management.)

   I would like to request a scholarship application/a college catalog and financial aid information. Thank you for your assistance.

Sincerely,

(Signature)

Name

Request Postcards for Use by High School, Undergraduate, or Nontraditional Students
and
_____ Return Receipt Postcard _____

Dear Sir or Madam:

I'm in high school and will be graduating in _____.
I am interested in receiving the following information:

____ **College Brochure**
____ **College Application**
____ **Financial Aid Information**
____ **Financial Aid Application**
____ **Internship Information**
____ **Internship Application**
____ **Scholarship Information**
____ **Scholarship Application**

Thank you for your assistance.

Sincerely,

Dear Sir or Madam:

I'm in high school and will be graduating in _____.
I am interested in receiving the following information:

____ **College Brochure**
____ **College Application**
____ **Financial Aid Information**
____ **Financial Aid Application**
____ **Internship Information**
____ **Internship Application**
____ **Scholarship Information**
____ **Scholarship Application**

Thank you for your assistance.

Sincerely,

Dear Sir or Madam:

I'm in high school and will be graduating in _____.
I am interested in receiving the following information:

____ **College Brochure**
____ **College Application**
____ **Financial Aid Information**
____ **Financial Aid Application**
____ **Internship Information**
____ **Internship Application**
____ **Scholarship Information**
____ **Scholarship Application**

Thank you for your assistance.

Sincerely,

Dear Sir or Madam:

I'm in high school and will be graduating in _____.
I am interested in receiving the following information:

____ **College Brochure**
____ **College Application**
____ **Financial Aid Information**
____ **Financial Aid Application**
____ **Internship Information**
____ **Internship Application**
____ **Scholarship Information**
____ **Scholarship Application**

Thank you for your assistance.

Sincerely,

Dear Sir or Madam:

I am currently an undergraduate _____.

I am interested in receiving the following information:

_____ **College Brochure**
_____ **College Application**
_____ **Financial Aid Information**
_____ **Financial Aid Application**
_____ **Internship Information**
_____ **Internship Application**
_____ **Scholarship Information**
_____ **Scholarship Application**

Thank you for your assistance.

Sincerely,

Dear Sir or Madam:

I am currently an undergraduate _____.

I am interested in receiving the following information:

_____ **College Brochure**
_____ **College Application**
_____ **Financial Aid Information**
_____ **Financial Aid Application**
_____ **Internship Information**
_____ **Internship Application**
_____ **Scholarship Information**
_____ **Scholarship Application**

Thank you for your assistance.

Sincerely,

Dear Sir or Madam:

I am currently an undergraduate _____.

I am interested in receiving the following information:

_____ **College Brochure**
_____ **College Application**
_____ **Financial Aid Information**
_____ **Financial Aid Application**
_____ **Internship Information**
_____ **Internship Application**
_____ **Scholarship Information**
_____ **Scholarship Application**

Thank you for your assistance.

Sincerely,

Dear Sir or Madam:

I am currently an undergraduate _____.

I am interested in receiving the following information:

_____ **College Brochure**
_____ **College Application**
_____ **Financial Aid Information**
_____ **Financial Aid Application**
_____ **Internship Information**
_____ **Internship Application**
_____ **Scholarship Information**
_____ **Scholarship Application**

Thank you for your assistance.

Sincerely,

Dear Sir or Madam:

I'm not currently in college, but would like to attend in the
_____. Please send me the following information:

___ College Brochure
___ College Application
___ Financial Aid Information
___ Financial Aid Application
___ Internship Information
___ Internship Application
___ Scholarship Information
___ Scholarship Application

Thank you for your assistance.

Sincerely,

Dear Sir or Madam:

I'm not currently in college, but would like to attend in the
_____. Please send me the following information:

___ College Brochure
___ College Application
___ Financial Aid Information
___ Financial Aid Application
___ Internship Information
___ Internship Application
___ Scholarship Information
___ Scholarship Application

Thank you for your assistance.

Sincerely,

Dear Sir or Madam:

I'm not currently in college, but would like to attend in the
_____. Please send me the following information:

___ College Brochure
___ College Application
___ Financial Aid Information
___ Financial Aid Application
___ Internship Information
___ Internship Application
___ Scholarship Information
___ Scholarship Application

Thank you for your assistance.

Sincerely,

Dear Sir or Madam:

I'm not currently in college, but would like to attend in the
_____. Please send me the following information:

___ College Brochure
___ College Application
___ Financial Aid Information
___ Financial Aid Application
___ Internship Information
___ Internship Application
___ Scholarship Information
___ Scholarship Application

Thank you for your assistance.

Sincerely,

Dear Sir or Madam:

    I am a nontraditional student interested in returning to college. Please send me the following information:

    _____ **College Brochure**
    _____ **College Application**
    _____ **Financial Aid Information**
    _____ **Financial Aid Application**
    _____ **Scholarship Information**
    _____ **Scholarship Application**

Thank you for your assistance.

Sincerely,

Dear Sir or Madam:

    I am a nontraditional student interested in returning to college. Please send me the following information:

    _____ **College Brochure**
    _____ **College Application**
    _____ **Financial Aid Information**
    _____ **Financial Aid Application**
    _____ **Scholarship Information**
    _____ **Scholarship Application**

Thank you for your assistance.

Sincerely,

Dear Sir or Madam:

    I am a nontraditional student interested in returning to college. Please send me the following information:

    _____ **College Brochure**
    _____ **College Application**
    _____ **Financial Aid Information**
    _____ **Financial Aid Application**
    _____ **Scholarship Information**
    _____ **Scholarship Application**

Thank you for your assistance.

Sincerely,

Dear Sir or Madam:

    I am a nontraditional student interested in returning to college. Please send me the following information:

    _____ **College Brochure**
    _____ **College Application**
    _____ **Financial Aid Information**
    _____ **Financial Aid Application**
    _____ **Scholarship Information**
    _____ **Scholarship Application**

Thank you for your assistance.

Sincerely,

The material you submitted:

_____ **Scholarship/Internship Application**
_____ **College Application**
_____ **Secondary School Report**
_____ **Personal Data Form**
_____ **Financial Aid Information**
_____ **Recommendation Letter**

from _____

arrived safely in our office on _____.

Sincerely,

The material you submitted:

_____ **Scholarship/Internship Application**
_____ **College Application**
_____ **Secondary School Report**
_____ **Personal Data Form**
_____ **Financial Aid Information**
_____ **Recommendation Letter**

from _____

arrived safely in our office on _____.

Sincerely,

The material you submitted:

_____ **Scholarship/Internship Application**
_____ **College Application**
_____ **Secondary School Report**
_____ **Personal Data Form**
_____ **Financial Aid Information**
_____ **Recommendation Letter**

from _____

arrived safely in our office on _____.

Sincerely,

The material you submitted:

_____ **Scholarship/Internship Application**
_____ **College Application**
_____ **Secondary School Report**
_____ **Personal Data Form**
_____ **Financial Aid Information**
_____ **Recommendation Letter**

from _____

arrived safely in our office on _____.

Sincerely,

Letter of Recommendation
Sample Form
and
Sample Letter of Recommendation for High School, Undergraduate, and Nontraditional Students

Letter of Recommendation Form

Name of applicant _____

(last)   (first)   (middle)

Home address _____

_____

School now attending _____

School address _____

How long have you known the applicant? _____

In what capacity have you known the applicant? _____

> Please comment on the following characteristics: motivation, responsibility, integrity, honesty, diligence, perseverance, cooperation, leadership, emotional stability, common sense, judgment, appearance, and academic ability. Specific examples are most helpful. Use only one side of each page.

Name: _____

Address: _____

_____

_____

Signature: _____ Date: _____

Sample Letter of Recommendation
<u>SAMPLE ONLY – DO NOT USE</u>

Name of applicant <u>Doe</u>   <u>Jane</u>   <u>S.</u>
                   (last)   (first)   (middle)

Home address   <u>1234 Indian Valley</u>
             (City,   State   Zip Code)

School now attending   <u>Langley High School</u>
School address   (City,   State   Zip Code)

Please comment on the following characteristics: motivation, responsibility, integrity, honesty, diligence, perseverance, cooperation, leadership, emotional stability, common sense, judgment, appearance, and academic ability. Specific examples are most helpful. Use only one side of each page.

Dear Committee Members:

I am honored to nominate **Jane Doe** for college admission.

I have worked with **Jane** for the last three years in an assortment of science activities and competitions. I have sponsored **Jane** in District UIL meets, Regional Science Fair, Junior Academy of Science, and many school co-curricular programs. **Jane** is one of the finest students I have ever taught.

Promptness is one way in which I evaluate my students for competitive programs. **Jane** is never late and never needs to be prompted to get items in on time. This year, as in the past, she was the first student to turn in her long-term science project. She is first in line on field trips, and she is first to seek out evaluation of her work.

Academically, **Jane** is in the top 1 percent of her class. To maintain such high grades while participating in many, many extra and co-curricular activities is exemplary. To date, **Jane** has participated in every Academic Decathlon team, every Regional Science Fair, every Junior Academy of Science, many practice UIL meets, and every District UIL meet since her admission to our school. **Jane** is not just active in the sciences. She has participated in and been a winner in our History Fair, and she is a keen government-economics student. She is a member of both Student Council and National Honor Society.

Integrity is of utmost importance to me as a 20-year teacher. **Jane** displays honesty and concern for her peers and her teacher. She concentrates on positive experiences and lends help to others when needed. An example of her sharing is her attention to other students during academic competition. I have seen her offer help to other students. She is kind to them. She offers them compliments. She is constructive with her suggestions.

Jane is very interested in the biological sciences. She has had some unique experiences in pure research already. She aspires to be a doctor. I hope you will give **Jane** your closest consideration. She is a fine young woman and an excellent student.

Name: _____

Address: _____

_____

Signature: _____ Date: _____

Sample Letter of Recommendation
SAMPLE ONLY – DO NOT USE

Name of applicant   Garcia   John   M.
                     (last)   (first)   (middle)

Home address   5869 Marble Falls
                     (City,   State   Zip Code)

School now attending   (College or university name)

School address   (City,   State   Zip Code)

Please comment on the following characteristics: motivation, responsibility, integrity, honesty, diligence, perseverance, cooperation, leadership, emotional stability, common sense, judgment, appearance, and academic ability. Specific examples are most helpful. Use only one side of each page.

Dear Selection Committee:

I am writing to enthusiastically support **John Garcia's** application to your scholarship program. I have come to know **John** well this year through the various activities in which the students participate, activities which for the most part I supervise. I find him to be personable, mature, bright, and full of energy. I believe **John** has lots of leadership potential and would benefit immeasurably from your support.

John is eager and doesn't have one ounce of introversion. He seems to get along with all kinds of people, working well with adults and peers. He is honest to a fault and possesses a strong sense of integrity and moral balance.

John recently returned to his native (city), during spring break to recruit qualified minority students for the university. He officially represented the school's Admissions Office in this capacity and did a fine job. He scheduled and organized the visits to numerous junior high and high schools in the (city) area and talked about his experiences at (college). His interpersonal skills enabled him to work effectively with all the various individuals involved in this demanding process.

All in all, **John Garcia** is an outstanding individual. His organizational and analytical skills are excellent. His interpersonal skills are highly developed and his ability to conduct himself in difficult situations is admirable. I sincerely hope you will assist in his development and training by helping him with a scholarship. He will repay you many times over with his contributions to the community.

Name: _____

Address: _____

_____

Signature: _____   Date: _____

Sample Letter of Recommendation
SAMPLE ONLY – DO NOT USE

Name of applicant   Jones-Smith   Linda   R.

                         (last)   (first)   (middle)

Home address   1928 Cherry Court

               Anywhere, CA 98765

School now attending   Santa Rosa Junior College

School address   1501 Mendocino Avenue   Santa Rosa, CA 95401   (800) 564-7752

Student's SS #:   530 - 65 - 1839   How long have you known the applicant?   5 years

In what capacity have you known the applicant?   Neighbor

> Please comment on the following characteristics: motivation, responsibility, integrity, honesty, diligence, perseverance, cooperation, leadership, emotional stability, common sense, judgment, appearance, and/or academic ability. Specific examples are most helpful. Please use only one side of each page. Additional pages may be added.

To whom it may concern:

I am writing on behalf of **Linda Jones–Smith**, who is applying for your scholarship, which she will use for educational purposes. **Linda** has been my neighbor for approximately five years.

To my knowledge, **Linda** has been a single mother for the last five years and has been caring for her two small children with very little assistance for all of those five years. She works during the year by cleaning homes. In order to have time for her classes and work, she has formed a baby-sitting co-op with three other single parents. In this way, all four nontraditional students are sure their children are getting caring attention and their parents are able to save money.

Linda has been working very hard at her classes and has been getting good grades for her efforts. I believe her hope is to further her education toward a degree so that she might earn more money to support her children. She doesn't receive any help from the children's father.

The **Smith** household is well maintained. The yard is always relatively neat, and the house has been very clean and tidy every time I visit her home. I'm sure **Linda** is trying to instill these habits in her children, because they help around the house and have excellent manners.

Her daughter, Nicole, has been involved in extracurricular activities, such as gymnastics classes and the Girl's Soccer Team. It is apparent that **Linda** is working hard to be a good parent, while also trying to better their situation by working toward her degree. It must be difficult for her to work, go to school, and still have time to be a loving and conscientious parent and maintain the home she rents.

I hope you will consider **Linda** for this scholarship. I know that she will accomplish her goals and go on to serve as a role model for her children.

Name: Mrs. Nellie Bates

Address: 1930 Cherry Court

               Anywhere, CA 98765

Signature: Date:

INDEX TO PART I

Cash for College™ Resource Store

In addition to our book *Cash for College™*, we have developed several products to assist in your quest for scholarship monies. The Resource Kit, Cash for College™ Organizer System, Audio/Video Tape Series, and the soon-to-be-released Cash for College™ CD-ROM companion to our book are all available so that you can utilize your time more wisely by concentrating on scholarship applications, not developing your own system. These products were developed to provide more detailed information on specific topics than could be provided in a book of this length. *Special Note*: Volume discounts available to libraries, school districts, and corporate clients.

College Resource Materials Products

The Resource Kit ($16.95)

Starter Pack
1   Timetable
1   Scholarship List Form
1   Scholarship and College
1   Application Tracking Chart
1   Financial Assistance Analysis Chart
1   Recommendation Letter Master
40 Information Request Postcards
40 Return Receipt Postcards

Résumé Guide
This 18-page booklet answers all of your questions and provides you with sample résumés.

Recommendation Letter Advisor
Contains 12 pages of advice, choosing who to write letters, and sample letters.

FAQ's Booklet
The Frequently Asked Questions Booklet answers questions, and contains checklists for middle, high school, and college students.

Cash for College™ Academic Year Calendar   ($9.95)
Academic year calendar, with essential information, major scholarship due dates, important test dates, hints, and other notes of interest.

Cash for College™ Organizer ($69.95)

1   Portable File with carrying handle
12 Files labeled by month for applications
1   File labeled for Awards & Certificates
1   File labeled for Recommendation Letters & Résumé
1   File labeled for Tracking Charts & Forms
1   File labeled for Financial Aid Forms
1   File labeled for Essays
1   File labeled Miscellaneous
1   Cash for College™ Academic Year Calendar
1   Resource Kit & 6 Highlighter Markers

Cash for College™ Audio/Visual Series

		Audio/Video
(1)	The Application Process Made Easy	$9.95/$19.95
(2)	Résumés That Work!	$9.95/$19.95
(3)	Letters (Query & recommendation)	$9.95/$19.95
(4)	Write It Right (Student or Parent)	$16.95/$26.95
(5)	The In's and Out's of Fin. Aid Pkgs.	$9.95/$19.95
(6)	Planning Ahead from A to Z	$9.95/$19.95
(7)	Choosing a College	$9.95/$19.95
(8)	Creative Nagging 101	$9.95/$19.95
(9)	Advice for Home-Schoolers	$9.95/$19.95
(10)	Nontraditional Students	$9.95/$19.95
Tape set (1 thru 8)		$79.95/$155.95

◆◆ Special Bonus Offer ◆◆
Buy five or more tapes—receive a free 60-minute motivational tape. Just Do It! Why students should never give up!

To order an item, use the Complete Order Form on the last page.
Be sure to include shipping and handling charges. Texas residents add sales tax.

Cash for College™ Resource Store

Order Form

◆ Please circle products you wish to order ◆

The Resource Kit	$ 16.95
Academic Year Calendar	$ 9.95
Organizer System	$ 69.95
Scholarship Search (Coupon Special)	$349.95

Shipping and Handling Charges

The Resource Kit	$ 3.25
Academic Year Calendar	$ 2.00
Organizer System	$ 12.00
Audio Tapes	$ 2.50 1st tape, 50¢ ea. add. tape
Video Tapes	$ 3.50 1st tape, 75¢ ea. add. tape
Scholarship Search (Coupon Special)	$ 8.00

Name: _____

Address: _____

City/State: _____

Zip: _____ Phone: ( ) _____

FAX: ( ) _____ E-mail: _____

Grade Level in School: _____

School District/College: _____

Make money order or check payable to:
College Resource Materials
1633 Babcock Rd., PMB 425
San Antonio, TX 78229-4725

Subtotal _____

TX residents add sales tax _____

Shipping & Handling _____

Total Amount Due _____

Phone: (210) 614-5919 FAX: (210) 614-5937
E-mail: mckee@cashforcollege.com   Website: http://www.cashforcollege.com
Please retain a copy of the completed order form for your records.

 # Special Coupon Offer

Personalized Scholarship Computer Search

with Resource Kit
with unlimited updates, and critiquing of résumés and essays

Regularly $399.95

Extra Special Bonus

Absolutely Free

1. Résumés That Work! Audio Tape $ 9.95
2. Choosing a College Audio Tape $ 9.95
3. Current Academic Year Calendar $ 9.95
4. Write It Right: How to Write a Winning Essay $16.95
   Audio Tape & Study Guide

Total Value $446.75

With This Coupon

Only $349.95

You Save $50.00

Add $8.00 Shipping & Handling

(210) 614-5919   (210) 614-5937 FAX   mckee@cashforcollege.com

The gift that keeps on giving!

Original coupon (copies not accepted) must be redeemed within 60 days of purchase and must be accompanied by the receipt of the book purchase. To utilize the Special Coupon Offer, send this coupon, the sales receipt, and check or money order to: College Resource Materials, 1633 Babcock Road, PMB 425, San Antonio, TX 78229. Coupon limit, one per customer. To order individual or additional items, use the Complete Order Form on the previous page. Be sure to include shipping and handling charges. Texas residents add sales tax.